Adobe® Flash® CS4 Professional Bible

00166624

CITY OF BRISTOL COLLEGE

Adobe® Flash® CS4 Professional Bible

Robert Reinhardt and Snow Dowd

WILEY

Wiley Publishing, Inc.

Adobe® Flash® CS4 Professional Bible

Published by
Wiley Publishing, Inc.
111 River St.
Hoboken, NJ 07030-5774

www.wiley.com

Copyright © 2009 by Wiley Publishing, Inc., Indianapolis, Indiana

ISBN: 978-0-470-37918-9

Manufactured in the United States of America

10 9 8 7 6 5 4 3 2 1

Published by Wiley Publishing, Inc., Indianapolis, Indiana
Published simultaneously in Canada

CITY OF BRISTOL COLLEGE

001666 24

006.786 — 29·6·10

REI — £33·99

9780470379189 — COL

No part of this publication may be reproduced, stored in a retrieval system or transmitted in any form or by any means, electronic, mechanical, photocopying, recording, scanning or otherwise, except as permitted under Sections 107 or 108 of the 1976 United States Copyright Act, without either the prior written permission of the Publisher, or authorization through payment of the appropriate per-copy fee to the Copyright Clearance Center, 222 Rosewood Drive, Danvers, MA 01923, (978) 750-8400, fax (978) 646-8600. Requests to the Publisher for permission should be addressed to the Permissions Department, John Wiley & Sons, Inc., 111 River Street, Hoboken, NJ 07030, (201) 748-6011, fax (201) 748-6008, or online at http://www.wiley.com/go/permissions.

LIMIT OF LIABILITY/DISCLAIMER OF WARRANTY: THE PUBLISHER AND THE AUTHOR MAKE NO REPRESENTATIONS OR WARRANTIES WITH RESPECT TO THE ACCURACY OR COMPLETENESS OF THE CONTENTS OF THIS WORK AND SPECIFICALLY DISCLAIM ALL WARRANTIES, INCLUDING WITHOUT LIMITATION WARRANTIES OF FITNESS FOR A PARTICULAR PURPOSE. NO WARRANTY MAY BE CREATED OR EXTENDED BY SALES OR PROMOTIONAL MATERIALS. THE ADVICE AND STRATEGIES CONTAINED HEREIN MAY NOT BE SUITABLE FOR EVERY SITUATION. THIS WORK IS SOLD WITH THE UNDERSTANDING THAT THE PUBLISHER IS NOT ENGAGED IN RENDERING LEGAL, ACCOUNTING, OR OTHER PROFESSIONAL SERVICES. IF PROFESSIONAL ASSISTANCE IS REQUIRED, THE SERVICES OF A COMPETENT PROFESSIONAL PERSON SHOULD BE SOUGHT. NEITHER THE PUBLISHER NOR THE AUTHOR SHALL BE LIABLE FOR DAMAGES ARISING HEREFROM. THE FACT THAT AN ORGANIZATION OR WEBSITE IS REFERRED TO IN THIS WORK AS A CITATION AND/OR A POTENTIAL SOURCE OF FURTHER INFORMATION DOES NOT MEAN THAT THE AUTHOR OR THE PUBLISHER ENDORSES THE INFORMATION THE ORGANIZATION OR WEBSITE MAY PROVIDE OR RECOMMENDATIONS IT MAY MAKE. FURTHER, READERS SHOULD BE AWARE THAT INTERNET WEBSITES LISTED IN THIS WORK MAY HAVE CHANGED OR DISAPPEARED BETWEEN WHEN THIS WORK WAS WRITTEN AND WHEN IT IS READ.

For general information on our other products and services or to obtain technical support, please contact our Customer Care Department within the U.S. at 877-762-2974, outside the U.S. at 317-572-3993 or fax 317-572-4002.

Wiley also publishes its books in a variety of electronic formats. Some content that appears in print may not be available in electronic books.

Library of Congress Cataloging-in-Publication Data: 2008942706

Trademarks: Wiley, the Wiley logo, and related trade dress are trademarks or registered trademarks of John Wiley & Sons, Inc. and/or its affiliates, in the United States and other countries, and may not be used without written permission. Adobe and Flash are registered trademarks of Adobe Systems Incorporated in the United States and/or other countries. All other trademarks are property of their respective owners. Wiley Publishing, Inc. is not associated with any product or vendor mentioned in this book.

About the Authors

After discovering Flash while working on an art project, Robert soon realized that there was a need for more comprehensive documentation of its capabilities. In 1998 not many people had even heard of Flash and publishers were wary of the limited market, but IDG Books Worldwide, Inc. (now Wiley Publishing, Inc.) committed to doing the *Flash 4 Bible*. The rest, as they say, is history. After studying and working together in Toronto for five years, Robert Reinhardt and Snow Dowd established a multimedia consulting and design company in Los Angeles in 1999 called [the MAKERS]. Five years in the Hollywood Hills saw them through the dotcom boom and bust and gave them the chance to work on a wide range of projects — without ever having to wear wool socks. Now based in Portland, Oregon, [the MAKERS] continue to do work for entertainment companies, educational institutions, entrepreneurs, independent artists, and nonprofit organizations — and enjoy wearing stylish rain boots. Snow and Robert have expanded their services by working with DesignProVideo.com to produce Flash training videos.

Robert Reinhardt — With a degree in photographic arts, Robert takes a holistic approach to the creation of compelling multimedia. For five years, Robert oversaw the growth of the Multimedia Platforms Group at Schematic, a worldwide interactive agency. There, he led various assignments including multimedia data analysis applications for Nielsen's Media and Entertainment division and created interactive applications for The Weather Channel's WeatherClassroom.com, DC Comics, and Microsoft Windows XP Media Center Edition spotlights for major cable networks. Robert now consults and trains a wide range of clients, from Adobe Systems to the Walt Disney Internet Group to UCLA's Center for International Emergency Medicine.

When he isn't building or consulting on Flash projects, Robert loves to teach and write about Flash and rich media technologies. In addition to this book, he is the coauthor of *Flash MX 2004 ActionScript Bible* (Wiley, 2004). He has developed and taught Flash workshops for Lynda.com, Art Center College of Design, and Portland State University, as well as conducted on-site training and seminars for clients in the United States and Canada such as LodgeNet, Wieden+Kennedy, and Scripps Networks. Robert has been a regular featured speaker at the Flashforward, FITC, Flashbelt, and SIGGRAPH conferences. Robert is also a writing partner for CommunityMX.com.

Snow Dowd — Snow initially collaborated with Robert Reinhardt on multimedia, film, and photography-based installation projects while earning a BFA in Image Arts and New Media at Ryerson University. During this time, she was also the production manager for Design Archive, one of Canada's preeminent architectural photography studios. Working with renowned photographers and an exacting international client base of architects and designers helped her gain a deeper appreciation for images, architecture, and industrial design.

Fully immersed in digital production since 1998, Snow is able to synthesize her background in visual arts and communication theory with an ever-evolving software toolkit. Focusing on content architecture and interface design, Snow strives to create print and Web projects that are beautiful, functional, and memorable. Snow was honored to be featured in the June 2005 spotlight on FlashGoddess.com — a great place to go if you've been wondering where all the women are in the Flash world.

About the Technical Editor

Jeremy Petty — Jeremy is a design engineer based in Portland, Oregon. His work has ranged from developing electro-mechanical systems used in a miniature TOF-mass spectrometer to designing tools sets for the sports apparel industry. For fun, he enjoys bicycling around the Portland area, searching for the prefect surface to longboard on, and spending time with his family.

Credits

Acquisitions Editors
Laura Sinise
Aaron Black

Project Editor
Katharine Dvorak

Technical Editor
Jeremy Petty

Copy Editor
Scott Tullis

Editorial Manager
Robyn Siesky

Business Manager
Amy Knies

Senior Marketing Manager
Sandy Smith

Vice President and Executive Group Publisher
Richard Swadley

Vice President and Executive Publisher
Barry Pruett

Project Coordinator
Patrick Redmond

Graphics and Production Specialists
Stacie Brooks
Andrea Hornberger
Jennifer Mayberry
Sarah Philippart

Quality Control Technician
Amanda Graham

Proofreader
Bonnie Mikkelson

Indexer
Christine Spina Karpeles

Media Development Project Manager
Laura Moss

Media Development Assistant Project Manager
Jenny Swisher

Media Development Associate Producer
Kit Malone

In 1997, Macromedia acquired a small Web graphics program, FutureSplash, from a company named FutureWave. FutureSplash was a quirky little program with the astounding capability to generate compact, vector-based graphics and animations for delivery over the Web. With Macromedia's embrace, Flash blossomed. In 2005, Adobe Systems, Inc. acquired Macromedia and, in three short years, has successfully integrated Flash into their family of powerhouse graphics, video, and design software. Not only has the Flash platform obtained ubiquity, but Flash content is now more easily created across a wide range of professional software applications. The Flash Player plug-in ships with most major browsers and operating systems. Flash graphics appear not only all over the Web, but also on television and movie screens, on phones, on kiosks, and even in art galleries.

As the Web-surfing public and the development community have continued to demand more of Flash, Adobe has delivered. After Creative Suite 3 was released, Adobe went out into the world and sat with people using its programs to see what they used, what they needed, and how the next generation of Creative Suite tools could support daily workflow and specialize tasks more effectively. The result is a release that promotes expressiveness and enhances efficiency while encouraging best practices in development — a functional and an inspiring combination that has earned rave reviews from visual designers and code-oriented developers at all levels.

The Flash CS4 Professional interface is consistent with other Creative Suite 4 (CS4) products; it has tool options and other editing features contained in streamlined panels and lots of important changes to the authoring environment. The Mac interface is nearly 100 percent identical to the Windows interface, with support for docked panels, tabbed panels, and enhancements to the coding environments in Flash CS4 and Dreamweaver CS4.

Flash movies can communicate directly with server-side scripts and programs, using standard URL-encoded variables, XML-formatted structures, Web services, or powerhouse data transfers from Flash Remoting–enabled servers. Sounds can be imported and exported as MP3 audio for high-quality music on the Web at the smallest file sizes. Flash Player 10 supports nearly every Web file format you'll ever come across. Loading of JPEG, PNG, GIF, MP3, FLV, AAC, and H.264 video content streamlines production and maintenance of dynamic high-volume media sites. The updated FLVPlayback component and the addition of custom tools, custom effects, and behaviors offer Flash users of all skill levels some exciting possibilities. Evidence of the dominance of the Flash format can be found in the wide range of third-party developers creating applications that output to the Flash movie format (.swf files). Flash has fulfilled its promise of becoming the central application for generating interactive content for delivery on the Web; the potential only seems to expand as more developers tap into the data-handling power of Flash and its increasingly sophisticated graphics capabilities as it continues to grow beyond the computer screen.

Is there any other Flash book for you?

Adobe Flash CS4 Professional Bible is the most comprehensive and exhaustive reference on Flash. It helps you get started on your first day with the program and will still be a valuable resource when you've attained mastery of the program. When you're looking for clues on how to integrate Flash with other programs so that you can deliver unique and compelling content in the Flash format, you'll know where to turn. We've put significant effort into this edition, updating all ActionScript content to use ActionScript 3.0, the most recent version of the ActionScript language available in Flash Player 9 or higher.

Flash is not just a single tool. You can think of Flash as a multitasking application. It's an illustration program, an image/sound/video editor, an animation machine, and a scripting engine, all rolled into one. In this book, we look at each of these uses of Flash and explain how all the features work together.

To address advanced scripting topics and more server-side development issues, Robert coauthored the *Flash ActionScript Bible* series with Joey Lott (Wiley), which has been updated and expanded with the past three releases of Flash. Roger Braunstein, Mims Wright, Josh Noble, and Joey have written the new *ActionScript 3 Bible* (Wiley, 2007) to fully address advanced use of the ActionScript 3.0 scripting language. If you're already adept at creating animation and basic interactive interfaces in Flash and you want to expand your knowledge of more complex coding techniques, you may want to compare the table of contents in this book with that of *ActionScript Bible* to determine which book covers the topics you're most interested in.

How to Get the Most out of This Book

Here are some things to know so you can get the most out of this book:

First, to indicate that you need to select a command from a menu, the menu and command are separated by an arrow symbol. For example, if we tell you to select the default workspace layout from the Flash application menu, the instructions will say to choose Window ⇨ Workspace ⇨ Essentials.

Parts I and II of the book are entirely dedicated to project planning and getting familiar with the Flash interface. Parts III and IV explain how to generate animation and integrate other media files into your Flash movies. Parts V through VIII gradually introduce you to the power of ActionScript and show you how to take advantage of Flash components to quickly create dynamic applications that support live data. Although this book was written to take a beginner by the hand, starting from page one, you can also use it as a reference. Use the index and the table of contents to find what you're looking for, and just go there, or jump in anywhere. If you already know Flash and want to get some details on sound, for example, just go to any of the chapters in Part IV, "Integrating Media Files with Flash."

This is a real-world production book: We've worked hard to ensure that our lessons, examples, and explanations are based on professional conventions. We've also continued the use of expert tutorials to bring you tips and techniques from talented people in the Flash industry, so that you can benefit from their specialized expertise. Tutorials that do not relate to Flash CS4 but still offer some valuable information on specific topics have been archived online: you can find them at www.flashsupport.com/archive.

The CD-ROM that accompanies this book contains many of the source Flash project files (.fla), with original artwork and ActionScript for the examples and lessons in the book. You can also find sample video files to encode with Flash video!

In order to create a forum for the delivery of updates, notes, and additional sample files, we have established an integrated Web site specifically for the *Flash Bible* series: www.flashsupport.com. At the Web site, you'll find new material and corrections that may be added after the book goes to print, and moderated forums where readers can share information or ask questions. We invite you to contribute your comments and suggestions for this edition so that we can continue to improve the material.

We have created a chapter-based evaluation system that makes it easy for you to let us know what parts of this book were most (or least) useful to you. Visit www.flashsupport.com/feedback and let us know what you think of the content as you progress through the book.

Icons: What Do They Mean?

Although the icons are pretty standard and self-explanatory (they have their names written on them!), here's a brief explanation of what they are and what they mean.

Tips offer you extra information that further explains a given topic or technique, often suggesting alternatives or workarounds to a listed procedure.

Notes provide supplementary information to the text, shedding light on background processes or miscellaneous options that aren't crucial to the basic understanding of the material.

CAUTION When you see the Caution icon, make sure you're following along closely to the tips and techniques being discussed. Some external applications may not work exactly the same with Flash on different operating systems and some workflows have inherent risks or drawbacks.

CROSS-REF If you want to find related information to a given topic in another chapter, look for the Cross-Reference icons.

NEW FEATURE The New Feature icons point out differences between Flash 8 and previous versions of Flash.

WEB RESOURCE For related information, resources, or software available online, look for the Web Resource icons.

ON the CD-ROM This icon indicates that the CD-ROM contains a related file and points you to the folder location.

How This Book Is Organized

This book has been written in a format that gives you access to need-to-know information very easily in every section (or part) of the book. If you are completely new to Flash, then you'll want to read Parts I through VI. After you have developed a familiarity with the Flash interface and the new drawing and effects tools, you can proceed to Parts VII and VIII. We've included step-by-step descriptions of real Flash projects to help you "leap" from the intro topics to the advanced topics. These sections of the book guide you through the production process, helping you apply ActionScript and production techniques that may be new to you.

If you've already used Flash, then you may want to review the changes to the Flash CS4 interface in Part I, and then jump right into other specific parts to learn more about character animation, ActionScript, creating artwork and content in other applications, and integrating Flash with HTML. There are many new features and workflow enhancements for new and experienced users alike in every section of the book, so even if you've done a lot of work in Flash, it's worth scanning each part for an introduction to new tools and techniques.

Part I: An Introduction to Flash Web Production

The first part of this book explores the Flash file format and how Flash CS4 fits into the evolution of the program (Chapter 1), explains the context in which Flash movies interact on the Web (Chapter 2), and gives an overview of multimedia planning and some specific techniques and suggestions that will make your Flash project development less painful and more productive (Chapter 3).

Part II: Mastering the Flash Environment

This part gives you all the information you need to feel comfortable in the Flash CS4 authoring environment. Get an introduction to, and some tips for, customizing the Flash UI (Chapter 4). Learn where to find your drawing tools and how to use them efficiently (Chapter 5), and then discover all the ways that Flash helps you to organize and optimize project assets (Chapter 6). Learn key color concepts relevant to multimedia production and find out why Flash has the best color tools yet (Chapter 7). Jump into using text-editing tools and see how to get the best-looking type and the smallest file sizes in your Flash projects (Chapter 8). Finally, learn how to modify text and graphics to get the most out of your Flash artwork (Chapter 9).

Part III: Creating Animation and Effects

After you've learned how to find your way around the Flash interface and how to create static graphics, you can get some perspective on animation strategies (Chapter 10). Learn to make things move and how to work with different symbol types to optimize your animation workflow (Chapter 11). Add polish and pizzazz with Flash filter effects and blend modes (Chapter 12). Finally, get special production tips for professional character animation and broadcast-quality graphics (Chapter 13).

Part IV: Integrating Media Files with Flash

Now that you're fluent in the Flash workspace, take your projects to the next level by adding sound, special graphics, and video assets. In Chapter 14, you learn the basics of digital sound, and how to import, optimize, and export high-quality sound for different types of projects. Chapter 15 gives you an overview of how to bring vector or raster artwork from other programs into Flash and how to protect image quality while optimizing your Flash movies. Chapter 16 introduces the exciting new video features of Flash CS4 and the new Adobe Media Encoder CS4 application, including the use of the high-quality AVC/H.264 video codec.

Part V: Adding Basic Interactivity to Flash Movies

Learn how to start using Flash actions to create interactive and responsive presentations. Get oriented in the Flash CS4 Actions panel and fundamental ActionScript in your movies (Chapter 17). Use ActionScript in Flash movies to control internal elements on multiple timelines, such as nested Movie Clips (Chapter 18). Use Flash CS4 components to create fast, clean interfaces for multipart presentations that also include some of the Accessibility options (Chapter 19).

Part VI: Distributing Flash Movies

You need to learn how to export (or publish) your Flash presentations to the .swf file format for use in an HTML document, or within presentations in other formats. Chapter 20 details options in the Flash CS4 Publish settings, and provides tips for optimizing your Flash movies in order to achieve smaller file sizes for faster download performance. If you prefer to hand-code your HTML, read Chapter 21, which describes how to use the <embed> and <object> tags and how to create plug-in detection systems for your Flash movies using the SWFObject JavaScript library. If you want to find out how to create a Flash stand-alone projector, or use the Flash stand-alone player, check out Chapter 22.

Part VII: Approaching ActionScript

Learn the basic elements of ActionScript syntax (Chapter 23), and how to use ActionScript to control properties and methods of MovieClip objects (Chapter 24). Learn about making functions and arrays (Chapter 25), detecting Movie Clip collisions, and using the ColorTransform, Sound, and PrintJob classes for dynamic control of movie elements (Chapter 26).

Part VIII: Applying ActionScript

Learn how to use ActionScript to animate elements in a Flash movie (Chapter 27). Get an introduction to runtime MP3, JPEG/PNG/GIF, and FLV loading features as well as how to share and load assets in multiple .swf files (Chapter 28). Start creating Flash movies that send data with the LoadVars object and learn to integrate XML data with Flash movies (Chapter 29). Take control of text fields using updated HTML tags, the TextFormat class, CSS (Cascading Style Sheets), and high-quality anti-aliasing options (Chapter 30). Part VIII includes a detailed chapter dedicated to building a Flash game from the ground up (Chapter 31). Find out how to use the many User Interface components that ship with Flash CS4 to enhance your Flash projects (Chapter 32). Finally, build a Gallery component from scratch that works with dynamic PHP scripts to load image thumbnails and display full-size downloadable JPEG images (Chapter 33).

Part IX: Appendixes

In the appendixes, you'll find directions for using the CD-ROM (Appendix A), and a listing of contact information for the guest experts is also available (Appendix B). You can also find information on digital sound basics that explains sound sampling rates and bit-depths (Appendix C), and information on digital video basics (Appendix D).

Getting in Touch with Us

You can find additional information, resources, and feedback from the authors and other readers at www.flashsupport.com. We want to know what you think of individual chapters in this book. Visit www.flashsupport.com/feedback to send us your comments.

If you have a great tip or idea that you want to share with us, we'd like to hear from you. You can also send comments about the book to info@theMakers.com.

Also, check Appendix B to learn more about this book's various contributors and guest experts, including URLs of their work and contact information for people who don't mind being contacted directly by our readers.

For quality concerns or issues with the CD-ROM, you can call the Wiley Customer Care phone number: (800) 762-2974. Outside the United States, call 1 (317) 572-3994, or contact Wiley Customer Service by e-mail at techsupdum@wiley.com. Wiley Publishing, Inc. will provide technical support only for CD-ROM installation and other general quality-control items; for technical support on the applications themselves, consult the program's vendor.

Adobe Wants to Help You

Adobe has created a Feature Request and Bug Report form to make it easier to process suggestions and requests from Flash users. If you have an idea or feature request for the next version or you find a bug that prevents you from doing your work, let the folks at Adobe know. You can find the online form at www.adobe.com/support/email/wishform.

The simple fact is this: If more users request a specific feature or improvement, it's more likely that Adobe will implement it.

Regardless of your geographic location, you always have access to the global Flash community for support and the latest information through the Adobe online forums at www.adobe.com/cfusion/webforums/forum/index.cfm?forumid=15.

For inspiration and motivation check out the Site of the Day, weekly features, and case studies at www.adobe.com/showcase.

Acknowledgments

This book would not have been possible without the dedication and talent of many people. Although much of the content in this edition has changed to reflect changes in the tools, there is also a good deal of content from dedicated contributors that has been carried over from the previous edition. We are always grateful for the added breadth and depth the tutorials from our guest experts bring to the content. First and foremost, we would like to thank the Flash development community. In our combined experiences in research and multimedia production, we haven't seen another community that has been so open, friendly, and willing to share advanced tips and techniques. It has been gratifying to be involved as the community keeps expanding and to see the innovators in the first wave of Flash development become mentors to a whole new generation. Thank you all for continuing to inspire and challenge audiences and each other with the possibilities for Flash.

We would like to thank everyone at Wiley Publishing who supported us as we researched and revised, week after week. Katharine Dvorak, our project editor, was friendly, professional, and compassionate with our writing schedule — we knew she was working just as hard as we were when we received near-instant replies late at night. A *Flash Bible* production team can't steer itself — our gratitude goes to Laura Sinise and Aaron Black, our acquisitions editors, and Scott Tullis, our copy editor. Jeremy Petty, our technical editor and dear friend, was instrumental in helping us keep our material honest and effective.

Many of the scripts provided in this book would not be complete without the "instant messenger" help provided by Joey Lott, Paul Newman, Danny Patterson, Bruce Hyslop, Roger Braunstein, Geoff Stearns, and Phillip Kerman. We'd also like to thank Richard Blakely and Jerry Chabolla at Influxis.com for providing the ongoing Flash Media Server hosting for this book's streaming video examples.

Of course, this book about Flash wouldn't even exist without the hard work of the people at Adobe who make it all possible. Many thanks to the developers, engineers, and support staff at Adobe, especially Jen Taylor, Richard Galvan, Mike Downey, Mike Chambers, Erica Norton, Nivesh Rajbhandari, Peter deHaan, and Jen deHaan. We're also indebted, as always, to all our intrepid fellow developers and authors, who helped us to get our bearings in early versions of Flash CS4.

Tutorials at a Glance

Contents at a Glance

Contents

Preface VII

Part I: An Introduction to Flash Web Production 1

Chapter 1: Understanding the Adobe Flash CS4 Blueprint 3

Contents

Contents

Part III: Creating Animation and Effects   309

Chapter 10: Animation Strategies 311

xxvii

Contents

Part IV: Integrating Media Files with Flash 471

Chapter 14: Adding Sound 473

Contents

Part V: Adding Basic Interactivity to Flash Movies   599

Chapter 17: Understanding Actions and Event Handlers 601

Chapter 18: Building Timelines and Interactions 627

Chapter 19: Making Your First Flash CS4 Project 641

Contents

Part VIII: Applying ActionScript   873

Chapter 27: Animating with ActionScript 875

Chapter 28: Sharing and Loading Assets 887

Chapter 29: Sending Data In and Out of Flash 929

Contents

Contents

Part I

An Introduction to Flash Web Production

If you're new to Flash or to multimedia production, this section gets you started on the right foot. If you are a veteran Flash user, this section gives you some perspective on the evolution of Flash and the workflow options available in Adobe Flash CS4.

Chapter 1 provides a comprehensive overview of the strengths and weaknesses of the Flash format and some background on where Flash came from and how it has evolved. Chapter 2 explores the various ways that Flash movies interact with other Web formats and introduces some of the issues that need to be considered when planning for specific audiences. Chapter 3 has expanded coverage of strategies for multimedia project planning, including descriptions of how to create flowcharts, site maps, and functional specification documents.

Chapter 1

Understanding the Adobe Flash CS4 Blueprint

IN THIS CHAPTER

Exploring the uses of Flash CS4

Identifying Flash file types

Introducing the structure of Flash documents

Since its humble beginnings as FutureSplash in 1997, the Flash authoring tool and the Flash platform have matured into a powerful tool for deploying a wide range of media content. With every new version released, the possibilities have increased for imaginative and dynamic content creation — for the Web and beyond. After Adobe acquired Macromedia in 2005, Adobe has expanded Flash capabilities in several Creative Suite products, as well as development tools such as Adobe Flex Builder. The Adobe user interface is consistent across powerhouse applications such as Adobe Photoshop, Adobe Flash, and Adobe Illustrator.

In this chapter, we introduce Flash CS4 and explore the many possibilities available for your productions. We also discuss how Flash compares to or enhances other programs that you may be familiar with.

Flash content can be viewed in a few different ways. The most common method is from within a Web browser, either as an asset within an HTML page or as a Web site completely comprised of a master Flash movie using several smaller Flash movies as loaded SWF assets. The Flash Player is also available as a stand-alone application (known as a *projector*), which can be used to view movies without needing a Web browser or the plug-in. This method is commonly used for deployment of Flash movies on CD-ROMs, floppy disks, or other offline media formats.

CROSS-REF You can learn more about projectors and stand-alones in Chapter 22, "Using the Flash Player and Projector."

The Key Is Integration

Flash has seen significant development over its 12 years in both capability and design. Consistently with each new release, designers and developers push the technology into new territory. In its current iteration, Flash CS4 enables you to create content that's compatible with Adobe Flash Player 10, one of the largest updates to the Flash Player. There are two sides of the integration coin: designing the user interface and high-end programming with ActionScript 3.0. Flash CS4 continues to satisfy both designers and programmers — all the new authortime visual effects in Flash CS4 and Flash Player 10 are fully programmable with ActionScript, the programming language of Flash.

Flash CS4 Professional, also referred to simply as Flash CS4, adds several enhancements to previous editions:

- **One version:** You don't have to worry about which version of the Flash authoring tool to purchase — there's only one version! If you haven't upgraded from Flash 8 or earlier, you might be using one of two editions of the Flash authoring tool. If you have Flash CS4, you have access to any feature we discuss in this book (and more!).

- **CS4 interface:** Flash CS4 sports a completely revised user interface layout, with tools and panels that match the look and feel of other Adobe Creative Suite applications such as a Photoshop and Illustrator. The panels can be docked or stacked, and panels can be reduced to icon-only or icon-and-text views.

- **Adobe document import:** Because Adobe oversees the development of Photoshop, Illustrator, and Flash, it's much easier to coordinate file format interoperability between the applications. You have more options than ever to faithfully bring Photoshop, Illustrator, and After Effects content into Flash documents. Many of the CS4 tools can now export XFL packages that enable a smooth workflow from tools such as Illustrator and After Effects into Flash.

- **Adobe Device Central CS4:** Flash CS4 ships with an updated version of Adobe Device Central. This program enables you to set up a Flash, Photoshop, Illustrator, or After Effects document prepped with the proper screen size and attributes for deployment to a wide range of mobile devices. Presets for manufacturers such as Nokia, Samsung, and Motorola determine the frame size, frame rate, FlashLite (or Flash Player) version, and ActionScript version compatible for each device.

- **Improved animation and drawing features:** It's easier than ever to apply motion tweens to your Flash artwork with the new Motion Editor panel and the Motion Presets panel. Every aspect of your motion tween can be accessed and updated in the Motion Editor panel, sporting a look and feel very similar to the Timeline panel of Adobe After Effects. Flash CS4 also includes a new Deco tool that can draw intricate patterned fills within your artwork.

- **Improved font menus:** If you've used other Adobe graphics software such as Photoshop and Illustrator, you likely miss the font family lists in past versions of Flash. In Flash CS4, you'll find a consistent font menu across the CS4 product line.

- **3D transformations:** You can now control a third dimension, or the Z axis, on two dimensional (2D) artwork created or imported into your Flash document, including video! You can animate the X, Y, *and* Z axis of objects in the new Motion Editor!

- **Inverse kinematics (IK):** Adobe added two new tools, the Bone tool and the Bind tool, to create linked segments that respond as a contiguous element. For example, if you want to create an animated frog, you can create the independent pieces of the frog's shape, connect them with the Bone tool, and then animate the entire frog! If you move one connected element in the chain of elements, the whole framework responds.

- **Adobe Flash Media Encoder:** Adobe did an excellent job retooling the compression settings and options for the Flash Video CS3 Encoder, which is now called the Adobe Media Encoder. Now you can export AVC/H.264 video content compatible with Flash Player 9 Update 3 or later.

- **Flash Player detection update:** Flash CS4 improves the Flash Player detection capabilities in the Publish Settings' HTML tab. Flash CS4 can create one HTML page that detects a target version of the Flash Player and displays the appropriate content. Geoff Stearns' SWFObject, which we covered in *Flash CS3 Professional Bible* (Wiley, 2007), is now the standard for Flash Player detection in Flash CS4.

- **Authoring for Adobe AIR:** You can now directly publish your Flash documents to the new Adobe AIR platform. AIR enables you to run Flash, HTML, and PDF content directly from the desktop, without a Web browser!

- **Updated Project panel:** The new Project panel in Flash CS4 requires much less work for you to get a set of folders and files ready for easy access in the authoring environment. You no longer need to manually create folder structures and link files to a project file.

- **Adobe Soundbooth sample sound library:** Flash CS4 ships with over 150 sound-effect audio files from Adobe Soundbooth. You can use these sound effects with your Flash content royalty free.

- **Improved Library panel:** The Library panel in Flash CS4 is now searchable, and you can now create new symbols in specific folders in the Library panel.

Many enhancements are not directly seen in the authoring environment, though. Flash Player 10 adds the following enhancements, among others:

- **Enhanced creative effects:** In addition to the 3D treatment of 2D objects mentioned earlier in this chapter, Flash Player 10 features a new custom filter-creation tool, the Adobe Pixel Bender toolkit. This new filter-creation tool, based on the scripting language called Hydra, enables you to build your own filter effects! There's also a completely revamped text layout engine, which can support right-to-left (RTL) languages such as Hebrew and Arabic, vertical text layout, and typographic elements like ligatures.

- **Visual performance improvements:** Flash Player 10 can offload more heavy graphics processing directly to the video graphics card. This hardware acceleration enables faster compositing of graphics and video content in your Flash files.

- **Audio/video enhancements:** You can use new transport protocols for real-time streaming video and peer-to-peer connections. Adobe has a new audio codec, Speex, added to Flash Player 10 for better real-time voice communications.

- **Enhanced local file access:** Previous releases of the Flash Player could only access file bytes but not display or manipulate them back to the local system without using a remote server to communicate and download updated content. Flash Player 10 now enables a user to load a local file and save new content back to the desktop without any server interaction.

TIP If you're targeting a Flash Player 6 audience, you might want to consider targeting Flash Player 10 as well. Why? Flash Player 6 is capable of running Express Install scripts, which enable a Flash movie to automatically update the installed version of the Flash Player. Also, users with Flash Player 7 or later can receive automatic player updates. By default, Flash Player 7 checks Adobe's site every 30 days for new player updates. This process occurs silently in the background and doesn't require the user to upgrade his or her player installation manually. Theoretically, then, within 30 days of the release of any new Flash Player, including Flash Player 10, most browsers that had Flash Player 7, 8, or 9 will then have Flash Player 10.

For a complete list of features in Flash CS4, open the new browser-based help system by choosing Help ➪ Flash Help, and then selecting Using Flash ➪ Using Flash CS4 Professional ➪ Resources ➪ What's New ➪ New Features.

Adobe also released new versions of Dreamweaver and Fireworks, as part of the CS4 Web Suite software bundle. The user interfaces for Flash, Dreamweaver, and Fireworks are very similar, each touting a Property inspector, dockable panel sets, and specialized tools to integrate the products with one another.

Although the broad array of Flash work created by Web designers and developers already speaks for itself, the sleek interface and the powerful new features of Flash CS4 surely inspire more challenging, functional, entertaining, informative, bizarre, humorous, beautiful, and fascinating experiments and innovations.

There are more ways to use Flash than there are adjectives to describe them, but here are just a few examples:

- Forms for collecting user information and dynamically loading custom content based on this interaction
- Real-time interaction with multiple users on a forum or support site, including live audio/video feeds of connected parties
- Complex online games with rich graphics and interaction, including multiplayer games
- A video portfolio using Flash Video capabilities and dynamic loading of content
- Animated ID spots and loading screens with built-in download detection
- A practical Web utility, such as a mortgage calculator or a search tool
- Robust chat rooms based on XML and server-socket technology
- An audio interface dynamically pulling in requested songs, using native Flash 8 support for MP3 loading
- Interactive conceptual art experimentations involving several users, 3-D, or recording and play-back of user interaction
- Shopping and e-commerce solutions built entirely by using Flash and server-side technology
- Interfaces for kiosks at museums, banks, and shopping centers
- Alternative content or movie attributes based on system capability testing (if a device or desktop doesn't support audio streaming, then a text equivalent of the audio transcript is presented to the user)
- Projectors used for creating slide show presentations in the style of PowerPoint, either on CD-ROM or an alternative storage device
- Broadcast-quality cartoons, advertising, or titling
- Optimized animations for the Web, and for mobile devices such as cellphones or PDAs
- An interface that addresses accessibility issues by modifying certain elements when a screen reader is active
- Flash movies specifically exported for use in digital video projects requiring special effects and compositing

This list is obviously far from complete and is ever expanding with each new release of the program. As you can probably tell from this list, if you can imagine a use for Flash, it can probably be accomplished.

The topography of Flash CS4

Before you attempt to construct interactive projects in Flash, you should be familiar with the structure of the authoring environment. Even if you already know a previous version of Flash, learning this is advisable. That's because with the release of Flash CS4, Adobe has reorganized existing features to the interface and has either moved or improved other features and functionalities. So, to get a firm footing in the new inter-face, we strongly suggest that you work your way through this book — from the beginning.

CROSS-REF Chapter 4, "Interface Fundamentals," introduces the updated Flash CS4 interface and gives you tips for customizing your workspace and optimizing your workflow.

Moreover, you need to proactively plan your interactive projects before you attempt to author them in Flash. An ounce of preplanning goes a long way during the production process. Don't fool yourself — the better your plan looks on paper, the better it performs when it comes to the final execution.

CROSS-REF We detail the foundation for planning interactive Flash projects in Chapter 3, "Planning Flash Projects," and you will find these concepts reiterated and expanded in chapters that discuss specific project workflows. Chapter 19, "Making Your First Flash CS4 Project," is a great place to start applying these planning strategies.

We consolidated the overview of interactive planning in the early chapters of the book. In later chapters, we included step-by-step descriptions of real-world projects that allow you to see how all the theory and planning suggestions apply to the development of specific projects.

CROSS-REF Chapter 31, "Creating a Game in Flash," walks you through the logic required to design and script a functional and engaging game. Chapter 33, "Building an Image Gallery Component," describes the process of creating an entire component from the ground up, utilizing many of the visual effects available in ActionScript.

There are two primary files that you create during Flash development: Flash document files (.fla) and Flash movie files (.swf). We discuss both of these formats next.

File types in Flash CS4

Flash document files (.fla) are architected to provide an efficient authoring environment for projects of all sizes. Within this environment, content can be organized into scenes, and the ordering of scenes can be rearranged throughout the production cycle. Layers provide easy separation of graphics within each scene, and, as Guide or Mask layers, they can also aid drawing or even provide special effects. The Timeline shows keyframes, motion and shape tweens, labels, and comments. The Library (which can be shared amongst movies at authortime or at runtime) stores all the symbols in your project, such as graphics, fonts, animated elements, sounds or video, and components.

Flash documents

 Throughout this book, you will see us refer to Flash documents (or Flash files), which are the .fla files created by Flash CS4 when you choose File ➪ New and choose one of the Flash File options from the General category tab. Unlike some graphics applications, such as Adobe Illustrator, the file icon or file extension for Flash documents does not reflect the version of the authoring tool. For example, all previous versions of Flash and now CS4 save Flash documents as .fla files. You cannot open later version documents in previous versions of the authoring tool. You do not use Flash documents with the Flash Player, nor do you need to upload these files to your Web server. Always keep a version (and a backup!) of your Flash document.

TIP Flash CS4 allows you to resave your Flash CS4 document file (.fla) as a Flash CS3 document file. Choose File ➪ Save As and select Flash CS3 Document in the Save as type menu. If you save the document in this manner, you can open the Flash document file in the Flash CS3 authoring application. If the Flash CS4 document used features unavailable in Flash CS3, you receive a warning as you save the document in the Flash CS3 format.

In Flash CS4, you have the option to create four different types of Flash files: Flash File (ActionScript 3.0), Flash File (ActionScript 2.0), Flash File (Adobe AIR), or Flash File (Mobile). If you are targeting Flash Player 8 or earlier, you should always choose ActionScript 2.0. If you are targeting Flash Player 9 or later, and you want to use the advanced coding style of ActionScript 3.0, you should choose Flash file

(ActionScript 3.0). You can change your target version of ActionScript and the Flash Player at any time by clicking the Flash tab in the File ⇨ Publish Settings dialog box. If you want to deploy a desktop application, choose Flash File (Adobe AIR). AIR applications require ActionScript 3.0. If you want to deploy content to mobile devices, use the Flash File (Mobile) option. This option automatically launches Device Central CS4, prompting you to choose a device profile to target with your Flash content.

NOTE Choosing Flash File (ActionScript 3.0) and Flash File (ActionScript 2.0) targets Flash Player 10 by default in the new document's publish settings. Be sure to change the targeted Flash Player version in the Flash tab of the Publish Settings dialog box (File ⇨ Publish Settings) to create Flash content targeted to the appropriate Flash Player version.

CROSS-REF Adobe Device Central CS4 is discussed in more detail in Chapter 20, "Publishing Flash Movies."

Figure 1.1 shows how Flash documents are composed of individual scenes that contain keyframes to describe changes on the Stage. What you can't see in this figure is the efficiency of sharing libraries among several Flash documents, loading other external assets (image, sound, video, or other Flash files) into a parent, or "master," Flash movie by using ActionScript, or creating interactive elements with scripting methods.

Flash movies

When you publish or test a Flash document, Flash CS4 creates a Flash movie file with the .swf file extension. This file format is an optimized version of the Flash document, retaining only the elements from the project file that are actually used. Flash movies are uploaded to your Web server where they are usually integrated into HTML documents for other Web users to view. You can protect your finished Flash movies from being easily imported or edited in the authoring environment by other users.

CAUTION The Protect from import option in the Publish Settings dialog box does not prevent third-party utilities from stripping artwork, symbols, sounds, and ActionScript code from your Flash movies. For more information, read Chapter 20, "Publishing Flash Movies."

Much of the information contained originally within a Flash document file (.fla) is discarded in the attempt to make the smallest file possible when exporting a Flash movie file (.swf). When your movie is exported, all original elements remain, but layers are essentially flattened and run on one timeline, in the order that was established in the Flash document. Practically all information originally in the file will be optimized somehow, and any unused Library elements are not exported with the Flash movie. Library assets are loaded into and stored in the first frame they are used in. For optimization, reused assets are saved to the file only once and are referenced throughout the movie from this one area. Bitmap images and sounds can be compressed with a variety of quality settings as well.

TIP Flash Player 6 and later movies can be optimized with a specialized Compress Movie option that is available in the Flash tab of the Publish Settings dialog box (File ⇨ Publish Settings). When you apply this option, you see drastic file-size savings with movies that use a significant amount of ActionScript code. By default, Flash Player 10 movies automatically have this compression feature enabled.

See Figure 1.2 for a graphic explanation of the characteristics of the Flash movie file (.swf) format.

CROSS-REF We discuss Flash Player detection in detail in Chapter 21, "Integrating Flash Content with Web Pages."

FIGURE 1.1

Elements of a Flash document (.fla) in the authoring environment

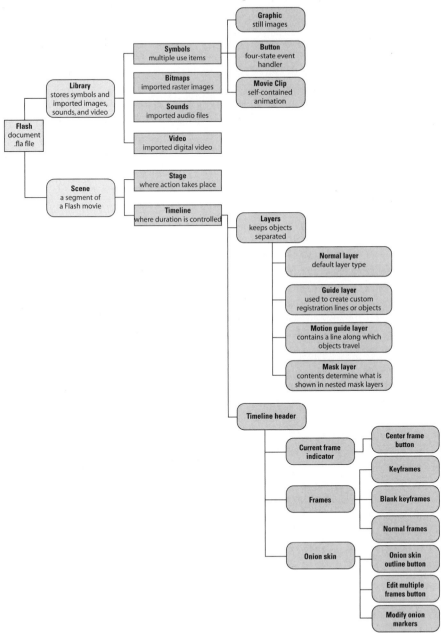

There are several other ways in which Flash movies, or their parts, can be played back or displayed. Since Flash 4, the Publish feature has offered provisions for the export of movies or sections of movies to either the QuickTime digital video format, the QuickTime Flash layer vector format, or the Animated GIF format. Parts of movies can also be exported as a series of individual bitmaps or as vector files. Single frames can also be exported to these formats.

Flash ActionScript files

ActionScript is the programming language used within Flash CS4 documents to create interactive functionality within the movie. You can store ActionScript code in external text files with the .as file extension. You can open .as files directly in Flash CS4 or your preferred code editing application, such as Adobe Flex Builder. ActionScript files can be compiled into a Flash movie by using the `#include` directive or the `import` keyword.

FIGURE 1.2

Overview of the Flash movie (.swf) format

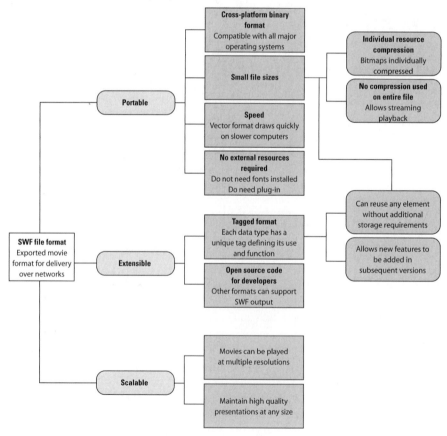

Using Flash Player Terminology

The difference between the naming conventions of the Flash Player plug-in and the Flash authoring software is potentially confusing. Adobe refers to its latest release of the player as Flash Player 10, tagging the version number at the end of the name rather than following the naming convention of some of its predecessors (that is, "Flash 5 Player"). One probable reason the Flash Player is numbered, rather than dubbed "CS" like the authoring software, is because a standard sequential number is required for plug-in detection.

When you publish Flash content to a Web site, don't be tempted to instruct visitors to download and install the "Flash CS4 Player." In versions past, you might have seen sites that required the "Flash MX Player." This terminology is confusing and misleading because there is no "Flash CS4 Player" for users to download. Always refer to the version number of the Flash Player, not the authoring tool.

Flash video files

The Flash Video file format (.flv file extension) and AVC/H.264 video files (.f4v file extension) are used for any video content played within the Flash Player. This file extension is used by any tool that creates Flash Video content, such as Adobe Media Encoder, Sorenson Squeeze, or On2 Flix. You cannot open .flv files in the Flash CS4 authoring tool, but you can import them into a Flash document file (.fla) or you can load them at runtime into Flash Player 7 or later movies. Flash Video files can also be uploaded to an Adobe Flash Media Server application and streamed in real time to Flash Player 6 or later movies.

 You can download the new Adobe Media Player from www.adobe.com **to play FLV, F4V, and compatible M4V, MP4, or MOV files.**

Flash Component files

The Flash Component file format (.swc file extension) is used for compiled clips included with Flash CS4 or that you purchase from third-party vendors or download from Adobe Exchange (www.adobe.com/exchange). You can't directly open a .swc file in the Flash CS4 authoring environment, but you can copy .swc files to your local settings for Flash CS4 so that the components show up in the Components panel. On Windows, you can copy .swc files to the following location (note that ⊃ denotes a continuation of the directory path):

```
C:\Documents and Settings\[Your User Name]\Local Settings\Application ⊃
Data\Adobe\Flash 8\en\Configuration\Components
```

On the Mac, you can copy to this location:

```
[Startup disk]\Users\[Your User Name]\Library\Application Support\ ⊃
Adobe\Flash CS4\en\Configuration\Components
```

These locations are only used to store additional components; the default components for Flash CS4 are stored in the Flash CS4 application folder.

NEW FEATURE **In Flash CS4, you can also use SWC files that class packages, and specify them in your classpath for ActionScript 3.0 documents.**

NOTE **The Flash Project file format (.flp file extension) is no longer used in Flash CS4. If you have FLP files from previous versions of Flash, you need to build a new project in the updated Project panel in Flash CS4 and link to your old project's files. For more information, read Chapter 3, "Planning Flash Projects."**

The Many Worlds of Flash CS4

Flash is a hybrid application that is like no other application. On the immediate surface, it may seem (to some) to be a simple hybrid between a Web-oriented bitmap handler and a vector-drawing program, such as Adobe Illustrator. But although Flash is indeed such a hybrid, it's also capable of much, much more. It's also an interactive multimedia-authoring program and a sophisticated animation program suitable for creating a range of animations — from simple Web ornaments to broadcast-quality cartoons. As if that weren't enough, it's also the host of a powerful and adaptable scripting language.

Over the past decade, ActionScript has evolved from a limited drag-and-drop method of enabling animation to a full-fledged object-oriented programming language very similar to JavaScript. Flash ActionScript can work in conjunction with XML (eXtensible Markup Language), HTML, and many other applications and parts of the Web. Flash content can be integrated with server-side technologies, including but not limited to Web services, remoting services (AMF, or Action Message Format), and Adobe Flash Media Server. The Flash Player offers built-in support for dynamically loading images, MP3s, video, and other data. Flash can work seamlessly with just about any Web application service, including Adobe ColdFusion, PHP, Microsoft .NET services, and XML socket servers, to deliver streamlined dynamic interactive experiences.

So, what's this evolving hybrid we call Flash really capable of? That's a question that remains to be answered by content creators such as you. In fact, we're hoping that you will master this application and show us a thing or two. That's why we've written this book: to put the tool in your hands and get you started on the road to your own innovations.

Because Flash is a hybrid application capable of just about anything, a good place to start working with this powerhouse is to inquire "What are the components of this hybrid? And if they were separated out, how might their capabilities be described?" Those are the questions that we answer in this chapter.

Bitmap handler

In truth, Flash has limited capabilities as an image-editing program. It is more accurate to describe this part of the Flash application as a bitmap *handler*. Bitmap images are composed of dots on a grid of individual pixels. The location (and color) of each dot must be stored in memory, which makes this a memory-intensive format and leads to larger file sizes. Another characteristic of bitmap images is that they cannot be scaled without compromising quality (clarity and sharpness). The adverse effects of scaling an image up are more pronounced than when scaling down. Because of these two drawbacks — file sizes and scaling limitations — overuse or overdependence of bitmap images may reduce the speed at which your Web site loads into a user's browser. However, for photographic-quality images, bitmap formats are indispensable and often produce better image quality and lower file sizes than vector images of equivalent complexity.

Vector-based drawing program

The heart of the Flash application is a vector-based drawing program, with capabilities similar to Adobe Illustrator. A vector-based drawing program doesn't rely upon individual pixels to compose an image. Instead, it draws shapes by defining points that are described by coordinates. Lines that connect these points are called paths, and vectors at each point describe the curvature of the path. Because this scheme is mathematical, there are two distinct advantages: Vector content is significantly more compact, and it's thoroughly scalable without image degradation. These advantages are especially significant for Web use.

Vector-based animator

The vector animation component of the Flash application is unlike any other program that preceded it. Although Flash is capable of handling bitmaps, its native file format is vector-based. So, unlike many other animation and media programs, Flash relies on the slim and trim vector format for transmission of your final work. Instead of storing megabytes of pixel information for each frame, Flash stores compact vector descriptions of each frame. Whereas a bitmap-based animation file format struggles to display each bitmap in rapid succession, the Flash Player quickly renders the vector descriptions as needed and with far less strain on either the bandwidth or the recipient's machine. This is a huge advantage when transmitting animations and other graphic content over the Web.

Video engine

The Flash Player plug-in can be considered one of the world's smallest video plug-ins. Flash Player 10 amazingly includes three primary video codecs for rendering video files: Sorenson Spark (Flash Player 6 or later), On2 VP6-E (Flash Player 8 or later), On2 VP6-S (Flash Player 9 Update 3 or later), and AVC/H.264 (Flash Player 9 Update 3 and later). Each generation of video codec increases the compression and image quality possibilities for your video content. You can import source video files directly into Flash CS4 document files (.fla), or create separate video files (.flv, .f4v, .mp4) that load into your Flash movies. Users do not need to have Apple QuickTime, Real Network's RealPlayer, or Microsoft Windows Media Player installed in order to view video in a Flash movie. The Flash Player provides a seamless solution.

CROSS-REF To learn more about this exciting aspect of Flash authoring, refer to Chapter 16, "Displaying Video." We also discuss the new Adobe Media Encoder CS4, an application designed to create the high-quality video content.

Audio player

Since Flash Player 6, Flash movie files (.swf) have had the capability to load MP3 files during runtime. You can also import other audio file formats into a Flash document file (.fla) during authortime. Sounds can be attached to keyframes or buttons, for background tracks or sound effects. A sound file's bytes can be distributed evenly across a timeline so that the .swf file can be progressively downloaded into the Flash Player, enabling a movie to start playing before the entire sound file has been downloaded.

NOTE A runtime file is one that loads when the Flash Player is running in its host environment, such as a Web browser or the test movie window of Flash CS4. An authortime file is one that is imported into your Flash document while you're using Flash CS4.

Multimedia authoring program

If the heart of Flash is a vector-based drawing program, then the body of Flash is a multimedia-authoring program (or authoring *environment*). Flash document files (.fla) can contain multiple media assets, including sound, still graphics, animation, and video. Moreover, Flash is a powerful tool for creating truly interactive content because it enables you to add ActionScript commands to dynamically control movie file (.swf) playback. Whether you are designing simple menu systems or customized and intuitive experimental interfaces, Flash content can be authored to recognize and respond to user input.

Animation sequencer

Most multimedia-authoring programs have a component for sequencing content as animation, and Flash is no exception. But in Flash, the animation sequencer is the core of the authortime application. The Timeline window controls the display of all content — static or animated — within your Flash project. Within the Timeline window, there are two areas that enable you to organize content in visual space and in linear time.

Layers and layer folders enable you to keep track of content that has been placed into your Flash document. The visibility of each layer can be controlled independently, making it easier to isolate specific elements as you are authoring. Layers are viewed from front to back within each frame of the Timeline — items on upper layers overlay other items on lower layers. Any number of items can be placed on a single layer, but you have less control over the stacking order within a layer. Within the same layer, ungrouped vector lines and shapes will always be on the bottom level, whereas bitmaps, text, grouped items, and symbol instances will be on the upper level.

TIP   Flash CS4 documents can use Layer folders. This is invaluable for organizing projects that involve many separate elements.

CROSS-REF   For a detailed tour of the Flash CS4 environment, refer to Chapter 4, "Interface Fundamentals." We discuss the process of making artwork and managing groups and symbols in Chapter 5, "Drawing in Flash," and in Chapter 6, "Symbols, Instances, and the Library," respectively.

The structure that creates the illusion of movement in a Flash movie is a series of frames. Each frame represents a still moment in time. By controlling how the playhead moves through these frames, you can control the speed, duration, and order of an animated sequence.

By changing the content in your layers on each frame, you can manually create frame-by-frame animation. However, one of the things that makes Flash such a popular animation machine is its ability to auto-interpolate or *tween* animation. By defining the content on a beginning and an end keyframe and applying a motion tween or a shape tween, you can quickly create or modify animated shape transformations and the movement of elements on the Stage.

CROSS-REF   We discuss the many ways of creating Flash animation in Part III: "Creating Animation and Effects."

Within one Flash document, you can also set up a series of separate scenes; each scene is a continuation of the same Main Timeline, but scenes can be named and reordered at any time. Scenes play through from first to last without interruption unless Flash's interactive commands ("actions") dictate otherwise.

CROSS-REF   We introduce the steps for using ActionScript for simple control of movie playback in Part V: "Adding Basic Interactivity to Flash Movies."

Programming and database front end

The past few versions of Flash brought a vast expansion of the possibilities for integrating Flash interfaces with server-side technology and dynamic loading of content by using XML and server technologies such as Adobe ColdFusion, PHP, Microsoft .NET, JSP, Flash Remoting, and Adobe Flash Media Server. These improvements largely came out of the development and maturity of ActionScript as a viable programming language. Flash has developed into an alternative front end for large databases, which means it can serve as an online store, MP3 player, or multiuser game and chat room — an amazing feat for an "animation program!"

With Flash CS4 there are virtually infinite possibilities at your fingertips. Using the components that ship with Flash CS4, you can tap advanced data structures and display them in a Flash movie. You can load JPEGs, GIFs, PNGs, MP3s, and Flash Video files into Flash at runtime (or "on-the-fly"), without having to use a special server technology. You can use a wide range of data formats, from XML to Web Services (SOAP) to Flash Remoting.

There are many other enhancements to the programming environment and functionality of Flash that experienced users will appreciate and new users will come to value. ActionScript 3.0 continues the evolution of Flash's scripting language to a mature format, more closely adhering to ECMAScript 4. These changes support ActionScript's move toward acceptance as a standard, object-oriented programming (OOP) language on its own.

> **TIP** If you consider yourself a computer programmer (especially one who learned how to program in another programming language), you will likely want to try out Adobe Flex Builder 3. Flex Builder is the premiere authoring tool for enterprise-level Web applications running on the Flash platform.

Desktop application authoring program

You can now create your Flash content as an Adobe AIR package for deployment as a desktop application. What is AIR? AIR stands for *Adobe Integrated Runtime*, and it's a framework that enables your Flash content to run as an installed application, just like any other application on your desktop such as Microsoft Word! After a user has downloaded the AIR installer from Adobe's Web site (around 15MB), the user can install AIR applications from any Web site. AIR applications can utilize Flash content (SWF, and all of its supported runtime formats such as MP3, JPEG, PNG, and so on), HTML content (AIR has its own Web rendering engine), and PDF files.

Summary

- Flash CS4 combines many of the key tools for multimedia authoring into one nimble program. The integration it facilitates with other programs and languages promotes better Web content and more advanced applications.
- Flash content is not only found on the Web. For example, it is also used for CD/DVD-ROM authoring, broadcast graphics, offline interfaces, and business presentations.
- Flash CS4 is a multifaceted application that can create a wide range of interactive products for the ever-growing variety of Web-enabled devices that surfers use to access the Internet.
- Careful planning of Flash development will undoubtedly save you time and effort in the long run.

Chapter 2

Exploring Web Technologies

O ver the years, many technologies have been developed to work in conjunction with Adobe Flash. Understanding the process of integrating these technologies will no doubt enable you to create more interactive and complex productions. If you're new to Flash, or you're looking for new ways to enhance or broaden the vision or scope of your Flash productions, you'll benefit from reading this chapter. It explores the placement of Flash within an ever-growing toolset for universal and "standards-based" Web development in use today.

Contextualizing Flash in the Internet Evolution

If you follow the development of "bleeding-edge" technology, you may have noticed how often software is created, updated, and made obsolete. At times, this cycle seems to happen almost on a daily basis. But exactly how many practical — and affordable — options exist for Web development? How can production teams develop consistent frameworks with a variety of server technologies to efficiently build Flash presentations and applications? In this section, we discuss how Flash CS4 continues to push the direction and limits of the Internet.

High expectations for Web experiences

Despite the devastation to Web production brought about by the "dotbomb" era (that is, the economic recession that occurred after many dotcom companies went out of business around the year 2000), the Internet economy has rebounded tremendously. People visiting your Web sites or using your Web-based applications expect to experience engaging interfaces with amazing graphics and sound. Clients who hire you expect that you can produce this type of material. Clients may also believe that everyone will be able to visit the site and download material instantaneously (regardless of connection speed limitations), and that every visitor will have the same experience. Before you consider whether Flash is the best tool to meet your clients' goals, let's step back for a moment and consider Flash's history.

With every release of a new version of the Flash Player, Web developers have access to bigger and better capabilities. We've seen a vast evolution from the early days in 1997 of mere vector animations, which were vastly smaller in file size compared to standard GIF animations. In 1998, Flash Player 3 made a marked improvement by introducing more control over these animations. At that time, Web sites with small games started to arrive on the development scene. That was also the year when Macromedia Generator was introduced, enabling dynamic graphics and data for Flash movies. Many companies were apprehensive about investing in Flash development because Flash was relatively new, although it was gaining ground as an accepted form of Web delivery.

In 1999, when Flash Player 4 was introduced, this attitude changed a great deal. The new version was much more powerful, and could accomplish many of the tasks that Generator provided in the past. Database interaction and dynamic content were suddenly possible in real time. However, Flash 4 was still a difficult application for developers to use; the programming interface for ActionScript code was limited by drag-and-drop functionality (which was avoidable only by using third-party software). This problem no longer existed in the 2000 release of Flash 5. Flash Player 5 could load XML data at runtime, and ActionScript "grew up" to come a bit closer to an object-oriented programming (OOP) language that strongly resembled JavaScript.

In 2002, Web designers and developers were handed the sixth version of Flash, dubbed "MX." Flash MX marked Macromedia's success at integrating all of their software products into a universal framework, where ColdFusion, Dreamweaver, Fireworks, Director, and FreeHand could all be used together to produce a new breed of Web experiences, including Rich Internet Applications. With the new software and player, XML data was processed remarkably faster, movies were made accessible to those with physical challenges, and Macromedia Generator was no longer necessary to incorporate dynamic graphics. Flash Player 6 could load JPEG and MP3 files at runtime. Developers could create reusable components that greatly decreased development time. Also, Flash Player 6 introduced support for video playback. Flash movies also became more browser friendly with named anchors that enabled specific sections of Flash movies to be bookmarked. ActionScript continued its development into more of a "real" programming language, as more objects and event handling were exposed in application programming interfaces (APIs). Perhaps most important, Flash Player 6 could integrate with new data transfer methods made available by Flash Remoting MX, which enabled serialized data to move more efficiently from application servers (such as ColdFusion MX) to Flash movies. Flash Communication Server MX 1.0 and 1.5, released shortly after Flash MX, enabled Flash movies to synchronize live data among several connected users simultaneously — developers could create live chat rooms, multiplayer games, and shared whiteboards, just to name a few applications. Flash Communication Server also added the capability to stream live or prerecorded audio/video streams to Flash Player 6.

NOTE   **Flash Communication Server is now split into two different products: Adobe Flash Media Server and Adobe Flash Media Interactive Server.**

Flash Player 7 was overwhelmingly optimized for speed. Everything from video playback to text rendering to ActionScript performance was vastly improved over Flash Player 6. This feature alone encouraged business clients and Web surfers alike to adopt the new player version; everyone loves faster performance. Of course, there was a whole lot more to Flash Player 7. It enabled you to customize the contextual menu (that is, the right-click menu) that Flash movies running in the player display, and, by default, HTML hyperlinks within Flash text supported Open in New Window and Copy Link options in the contextual menu. On the Windows platform, mouse wheel scrolling was now supported for internal Flash elements. Small text sizes could be rendered more cleanly (or crisply). JPEG or SWF content could be loaded and displayed inline with Flash text. Style sheets and CSS files added new formatting options to Flash text, enabling you to share styles from DHTML documents with your Flash content. Video lovers were enticed by the capability to load Flash Video files (.flv) directly into Flash movies, without the use of Flash Communication Server MX. Printing control was far superior in Flash Player 7 and ActionScript with the `PrintJob` API. Flash MX's UI components had been completely revamped and released as V2 components, and Flash MX Pro 2004 Pro could use Data and Streaming Media components.

A seismic shift for the Flash platform occurred with the release of Flash Player 8. This player further improved text rendering capabilities with the new FlashType engine. Now you could pull off 8-point type without resorting to a limited range of pixel-based fonts. The new filter and blend modes revolutionized the visual expressiveness of Flash user interfaces and animated content. The amazing On2 VP6 video codec pushed more and more Windows Media, QuickTime, and RealOne media producers over to Flash Video. Sites like ABC.com and MTV.com migrated nearly all of their Web video offerings over to Flash Video. The expanded image file support for runtime loading in ActionScript left no excuses for building your own image management utilities in Flash — with Flash Player 8 you could load PNG, JPEG, progressive JPEG, and GIF images into the Flash movie.

When Flash Player 9 was released in 2006, Adobe, fresh after the acquisition of Macromedia, built Adobe Flex Builder 2, which opened the Flash platform to many programmers who didn't want to learn a designer-centric tool like Flash. Flash Player 9 offered a brand-new ActionScript Virtual Machine, or AVM, to process more complex ActionScript code. This new code base was dubbed ActionScript 3.0. Flash Player 9 had two AVM's, one for earlier ActionScript (1.0 and 2.0) and one for the brand-new ActionScript language (3.0). Shortly after Flex Builder 2 was released, Adobe's teams developed consistent user interfaces (UIs) for the flagship products. Adobe also continued Macromedia's commitment to pushing the Web to a new definition of excellence by offering Flash developers a wide range of tools to build incredibly powerful applications. Both Flex Builder 2 and Flash CS3 could use the strength of ActionScript 3.0 to build high-end Web applications. At Schematic, where Robert works, ActionScript 3.0 was utilized in several new sites, including flip.com, a site that allows members to upload photos, videos, and audio and share the content with other members. Flash Player 9 also enabled Flash content to go full screen, and be viewed out of the browser window. Want to make that Flash Video clip go full screen? No problem! Flash Player 9 Update 3 extended video support by adding the popular AVC/H.264 video codec as well as its companion AAC audio codec for incredible video and audio quality that's compatible with other major video plug-ins such as Apple QuickTime Player. This update also provided cacheable runtime shared libraries for Flex 3 projects, enabling fast loading and initialization of rich Internet applications (RIAs) built in Flex Builder 3.

Between Flash Player 9 and the release of Flash Player 10, Adobe released a new desktop platform based on Flash, HTML, and PDF technologies called Adobe AIR, or Adobe Integrated Runtime. This new platform enabled Flex developers to build Flash content that ran natively on the desktop computer, outside of a Web browser. AIR applications behave just like other installed applications, having access to system resources and local storage. You can do things like drag and drop files from the desktop to interactive elements within your AIR application!

Now, Adobe has created the tenth major release of the Flash Player: Flash Player 10. As discussed in Chapter 1, Flash Player 10 extends three-dimensional (3D) support to all 2D objects you can create with Flash drawing tools. Real-time streaming protocols for audio and video have been updated to improve quality of service during playback. Hardware acceleration available in newer computer and video card processors can be leveraged in Flash Player 10 to increase the speed at which graphics are composited on the screen, especially with full-screen video. Hydra, a scripting language for custom filter effects, has been added to Flash Player 10, enabling you to build your own filters that work not only in Flash movies, but also in After Effects projects as well!

In the span of 12 years, we have seen an incredible evolution of Flash's predecessor FutureSplash to the most widely installed Web-based plug-in technology today: Flash Player 10. When Flash 5 was released, Flash was undoubtedly the key for Web branding, and it seemed as though every company wanted Flash content on its Web site. Flash has continued to enjoy this popularity, despite opponents calling the technology "unusable" or not compliant with Web standards. You could almost compare the introduction of Flash to that of the color television. It's difficult to return to largely static HTML pages after seeing the interactivity, animation, eye candy, and innovation that Flash sites offer to Web surfers — even those on slow connections or portable devices. Because of Adobe's efforts to keep the file size of the Flash Player smaller than most browser plug-ins, and the fact that it has been preinstalled on most systems for some time now, Flash remains a widely accessible and acceptable technology for Web deployment.

To Flash or not to Flash?

One of the crucial tasks of a Web designer or developer's job is to decide if Flash is the most appropriate tool to achieve the goals of a given project. Consider why you want — or need — to employ Flash in your work, because there are occasions when it may *not* be the best choice. It may not be wise to use this technology merely because it is "the thing to do" or is "cool." If you're pitching Flash projects to clients, it's a good idea to be prepared with reasons why Flash is the best tool to use to get the job done. Later in this chapter, we consider the benefits of other technologies, but for now consider what Flash can (and cannot) offer your projects.

An effective use of Flash

With the Flash CS4 authoring tool, you can create a wide range of presentation material or develop fully functional applications that run in a Web browser or on handheld devices:

- **Flash can generate very small file sizes while producing high-quality animation with optimal sound reproduction.** Even companies making world-renowned cartoons, such as Disney, use Flash for some of their work. Because of their small file sizes, Flash movies (such as cards or announcements) can even be sent via e-mail.

- **Nearly any multimedia file format can be integrated into Flash.** Vector images (such as EPS, FreeHand, Illustrator, and PDF files), bitmaps (GIF, PCT, TIFF, PNG, and JPEG), sound files (such as WAV, AIF, or MP3), and video (such as AVI and MOV) are all importable into your movies. Plug-in technology or third-party software is not required (although it does exist) to accomplish these imports. Nor is it required to play back your movies in Flash Player 10. Significant editing advantages sometimes exist when using imported files, such as symbol and layer formatting from FreeHand and Fireworks files. These features can be beneficial if you will be working with a client's raw resources.

- **Precise layouts with embedded fonts are possible with Flash.** Formatting is usually inconsistent when you use HTML to describe page layouts, and formatting can easily vary from one browser to the next. You can be confident your movies will be formatted and displayed consistently when viewed with the Flash Player.

TIP   Flash Player 8 and later add support for crisp-looking text at small point sizes. In previous versions of Flash, most embedded fonts did not display legibly at these sizes. You have precise control over how fonts render at small point sizes.

■ **Text, movies, images, and sound files can be displayed in your movie from a remote data source.** You can incorporate dynamic content into your movie as long as the data source (such as a database or XML file) can be accessed from your host Web server or application server. Flash Player 7 or later can consume Web services directly, allowing you to build B2B (business to business) applications that take advantage of public or private data sources, such as weather reports and stock information.

■ **Just as you can receive information from a database in your movie, you can send data from your movie to the database.** Flash movies can accept user input and send the data to a server. Built-in components make it easier and faster than ever before to build interactive elements that do not require an advanced knowledge of ActionScript. Your forms have the potential to be much more engaging with animation or sound additions. You can also use this technology to track user progression throughout your site and send the information to a database.

■ **With the proper server-side software, you can produce multiuser interactivity.** Since Flash Player 5, you have been able to use XML sockets for transmission of data between a socket server and one or more connected Flash movies. XML operates much faster when using Flash Player 6 and later. Also, with the release of Flash Communication Server MX (now Adobe Flash Media Interactive Server), developers now have a consistent API to create multiuser applications. Remote Shared Objects, one of the mechanisms employed by Adobe Flash Media Interactive Server, use an efficient and optimized binary protocol, Real-Time Messaging Protocol (RTMP), to broadcast data updates.

■ **A wide range of external runtime assets can be loaded into a Flash movie.** You can create a master Flash movie and then load external files into it for each individual area of the interface or presentation. Using this method of asset management enables you to delegate tasks in a team production environment, where several designers and developers can work simultaneously. This workflow also enables you to create byte-optimized large Web sites and applications, in which assets are downloaded on an "as needed" basis while the user interacts with the Flash movie. External assets include all image formats supported by today's Web browsers, including standard and progressive JPEG files, GIF files, and PNG files. You can load MP3 and AAC audio files, as well as FLV or H.264-encoded video content. While image assets are always progressively downloaded, audio and video assets can be streamed in real time.

NOTE A *progressive download* is any file type that can be used before the Flash Player actually receives the entire file. Progressive downloads are usually cached by the Web browser. You can stream MP3 files with the use of Adobe Flash Media Server or Adobe Flash Media Interactive Server. This server uses true streaming of all audio and video content, where nothing is cached by the Flash Player or the Web browser.

■ **Creating components in Flash CS4 enables developers to form reusable template interfaces or assets for Flash movies.** The components that ship with Flash CS4 greatly reduce the development time of interfaces that require common UI elements such as text input areas and radio buttons. Components can be easily customized in the Properties panel, and many settings can be changed without the use of ActionScript.

NOTE Many of the components that ship with Flash CS4 use the .swc file format in Flash documents. Components can be precompiled, which means that you cannot edit their internal elements or code unless you have access to the original source .fla file used to create them.

- **The Flash Player is available on many different platforms and devices, including Windows, Macintosh, Solaris, Linux, OS/2, SGI IRIX, Pocket PC, and many mobile devices.** Refer to www.adobe.com/shockwave/download/alternates for the latest version available for these and other alternative platforms. Just about any Web user can view Flash content by downloading and installing the latest version of the Flash Player.

- **Movies can be developed to run outside of the browser environment.** Projectors are Flash movies running from an embedded player, so you do not need a browser to view or use them. They can be burned onto DVDs or CD-ROMs, or saved to any other media-storage device. You can also use the new Adobe AIR framework to deploy Flash content as an installed application on the user's computer.

- **Like HTML pages, content from Flash movies can be sent to a printer.** The PrintJob API in Flash Player 7 or later ActionScript language offers you the capability to precisely control the layout of the printed page. The quality of the printed artwork and text from Flash movies is remarkable. You can send multiple pages to the printer at once and create content on-the-fly for the printed output.

These are only some of the things that Flash movies can do. Regardless of the intent of your production, verifying the use of this software is usually a good idea during preproduction. In the following subsection, we consider situations in which you may not want to use Flash to develop your content.

WEB RESOURCE We'd like to hear how you've come to use Flash technology in your projects. Post your comments at www.flashsupport.com/howdoyouflash.

When not to use Flash

If you're enthusiastic about Flash and have used Flash for previous Web projects, you can easily develop a bias in favor of Flash. It may even be hard to consider that other options could be better for development. Knowing which technology is best for each solution will assist you in offering the best-quality products to your clients.

- **Flash movies play in a Web browser, using a plug-in.** Despite the near ubiquity of the Flash Player, there are still some users who may need to download it. If you're using Flash CS4 to create Flash Player 10 movies, many visitors trying to view your site may need to update their players. It is also important to keep in mind that some workplaces or institutions (such as schools) will not allow their workers or students to install applications that include plug-ins and ActiveX controls on the systems.

- **The type and version of a Web browser can affect the functionality of a Flash movie.** Although internal ActionScript code should largely remain unaffected by browser brand and version, some scripting and interactivity with HTML documents (using JavaScript or VBScript) may be browser dependent.

TIP Later releases of Flash Player 6 and all subsequent releases of the Flash Player now support the WMODE (Window Mode) parameter of Flash content across most browsers — previously, this parameter was supported only by Internet Explorer on Windows. If you've ever seen transparent-background Flash ads that whiz across the browser window, then you're already familiar with the use of the WMODE parameter. For more information on this parameter, read Chapter 38, "Working with Dreamweaver 8" from *Flash 8 Bible* (Wiley, 2006), which is included as a PDF file on this book's Web site at www.flashsupport.com/archive.

■ **Web browsers do not automatically redirect to alternative content if the Flash Player is not installed.** You, as a developer, are required to create detection mechanisms for the Flash Player.

NEW FEATURE Flash CS4 has an updated detect-version option in the Publish Settings. You can learn more about this feature in Chapter 20, "Publishing Flash Movies." To learn how to use this detection feature and other custom detection methods for the Flash Player, refer to Chapter 21, "Integrating Flash Content with Web Pages."

■ **3D file formats cannot be directly imported or displayed in Flash movies.** To achieve 3D-style effects, frame-by-frame animation or ActionScript is required. Adobe Director, however, has built-in features for importing, creating, and manipulating 3D content.

TIP You can use the Papervision 3D framework to load and display 3D objects in a Flash movie. For more information, visit the Papervision 3D Web site at www.papervision3d. org. Also, in Chapter 16, "Displaying Video," you learn how a video of a 3D model can be used for 3D-like effects in a Flash Video.

■ **Typical search engines (or spiders) have a difficult time indexing the content of Flash movies.** When you make Flash-based sites, you should create some alternative HTML content that can be indexed by search engines. If you simply place Flash movies in an otherwise empty HTML document, your Web site will not likely be indexed.

TIP Flash CS4 enables you to add extended metadata to your Flash movie files (.swf). This metadata is added in the Document Properties (Modify ➪ Document) of the Flash document, and can be published with all Flash Player versions of the document. Search engines can index this metadata to provide better placement of your Flash content within search results. Flash CS4 can also add XMP (eXtensible Metadata Platform) data to SWF files. Go to the Publish Settings dialog box (File ➪ Publish Settings), click the Flash tab, and then click the File Info button to add the extended metadata to your content.

■ **Flash sites were never meant to completely replace text-based HTML sites.** For sites largely based on textual information with basic or simple graphics, there may be little point to using Flash. Selecting and printing text content from Flash movies is not always as intuitive as that of standard HTML sites. At this time, the Accessibility features of Flash Player 6 and later are supported only by Internet Explorer for Windows when used in conjunction with a select number of screen readers. A greater number of assistive technologies, however, support HTML pages.

TIP You can add right-click menu support to HTML-styled text containing URL links. For example, this feature of Flash Player 7 and later movies enables a user to open a link in a new browser window.

■ **In many circumstances, HTML is quicker, easier, and cheaper to develop than Flash content.** There are many established applications supporting HTML development, and clients can tap an ever-increasing designer and developer base for cheaper and competitive pricing.

Of course, there are always exceptions to any rule, and these suggestions should be considered as guidelines or cautions to be examined before you embark on any Flash development. In the following subsection, we examine other tools used to create multimedia content.

Alternative methods of multimedia authoring

Now let's focus on Flash's competition in the multimedia authoring arena. This section is not intended to give you a comprehensive background on these technologies. Rather, we seek simply to give you some context of Flash as it exists in the rest of the multimedia world.

Dynamic HTML

Dynamic HTML (DHTML) is a specialized set of markup tags that tap into an extended document object model (DOM) that version 4 browsers or later can use. Using `<layer>` or `<div>` tags, you can create animations and interactive effects with Web-authoring tools ranging from Notepad or TextEdit to Adobe Dreamweaver. You can actually combine Flash content with DHTML to create Flash layers on top of other HTML content. One problem with DHTML is that Mozilla-based browsers and Internet Explorer on Windows do not use it in the same way, but this problem is becoming more marginal as new versions of these browsers are released. Usually, you need to make sure that you have a specialized set of code (or minor modifications) for each browser type.

> **TIP** Flash Player 7 and later movies support the use of cascading style sheets (CSS) to share formatting specifications from DHTML pages with Flash text fields. Refer to Chapter 29, "Sending Data In and Out of Flash," for an introduction to this feature.

XML and XSL

XML stands for eXtensible Markup Language. XML looks like HTML, but it's really a language that can manage structured or related data, such as pricing information, contact information, or anything else that you would store in a database. XSL stands for eXtensible Stylesheet Language. XSL documents apply formatting rules to XML documents. Together, XML and XSL documents can create interactive data-driven Web sites. Although most browsers in use today can read and display XML and XSL documents, some older browsers do not support these formats. The Flash Player can be installed on just about every graphical Web browser available, regardless of the browser's version. As such, you can potentially reach more users with Flash content than you can with XML and XSL content. As you see later in this chapter, XML can also be used to supply data to Flash.

> **NOTE** The rise of AJAX, or Asynchronous JavaScript and XML, is enabling non-Flash technologies in the Web browser to provide more seamless Rich Internet Application–like functionality. For more information on AJAX, see the AJAX section at `www.flashsupport.com/links`.

Adobe Director

Originally, Macromedia's flagship product, Director, was *the* multimedia powerhouse authoring solution. Since its inception in the 1980s, Director has had the benefit of many years to establish its mature interface and development environment. Director can integrate and control many media types, including video, audio, and entire Flash movies. Director also has an Xtra plug-in architecture, which enables third-party developers to expand or enhance Director's capabilities. For example, you can use an Xtra plug-in to tap hardware-specific input and output, such as a motion detector or pressure-sensitive plate connected to the computer's serial port. Director 8.5 and later have added true 3D modeling support. You can create Shockwave games with textured models and lighting effects! However, there are two major drawbacks to Shockwave Director: It requires a larger download for the full player installation, and the player is available only for Windows and Macintosh platforms. Director remains a popular authoring tool for CD-ROM and DVD-ROM development.

Macromedia Authorware

Authorware, like Flash, was originally a technology developed by another company and then bought by Macromedia (and now Adobe) to add to its software lineup. Since the initial acquisition, Macromedia has significantly developed the features and capabilities of Authorware. It is an authoring application and a companion plug-in technology, with similar audio/video integration capabilities as Adobe Director. However, Authorware was developed with e-learning in mind. You can use it to structure training solutions and monitor student learning. We mention Authorware as a potential competitor to Flash because many Flash developers use Flash to create Web-training modules that interact with server-side databases.

Scalable Vector Graphics

The Scalable Vector Graphics (SVG) format is widely supported by some of the largest names in the industry, such as Microsoft and Adobe. This format has even been approved as a graphics standard for the Web by the World Wide Web Consortium (W3C), whose purpose is to form universal protocols regarding Web standards. SVG is much more than a graphics format; it is also an XML-based development language. Some Adobe tools, including Adobe Illustrator, can create files based on this technology. Adobe also creates the plug-in for using this file format on the Web, but the W3C is pushing for all browsers to provide built-in support for the format so that a third-party download is unnecessary. This may be necessary if SVG is ever to become a viable content format because Web surfers have been quite slow to adopt the SVG plug-in. For more information on this topic, you can refer to www.w3c.org/Graphics/SVG and www.adobe.com/svg.

Microsoft Silverlight

In 2007, Microsoft launched the first version of the Microsoft Silverlight plug-in, which closely matches the capabilities of the Flash Player plug-in. Silverlight 1.0 relies largely on a JavaScript-based scripting language to create interactive content with a tool such as Microsoft Expression Blend 2. Silverlight can play video content with the addition of the Windows Media Player plug-in for your Web browser. While Silverlight technology has yet to take hold with most Web sites, it is quickly gaining mind share with Web developers looking to add advanced data-driven capabilities to their online projects.

Microsoft PowerPoint

PowerPoint is usually considered a tool for making offline presentations to show in business meetings, conferences, and seminars. What is perhaps not as well known is how PowerPoint is sometimes used online for presenting such content. A PowerPoint viewer plug-in enables your browser to handle these files, and PowerPoint can export HTML versions of slide shows. Although PowerPoint enables anyone from a designer to a programmer to easily create slide-show presentations, Flash can be considered a more robust tool for creating dynamic, high-impact presentations.

 More and more designers who use Apple Mac OS X are choosing to create PowerPoint-like presentations in Apple Keynote, a product available in Apple's iWork bundle.

SMIL, Real Systems RealPlayer, and Apple QuickTime

SMIL (Synchronized Multimedia Integration Language) also looks a lot like HTML markup tags. SMIL enables you to layer several media components in SMIL-compatible players such as the Real Networks RealPlayer and the Apple QuickTime Player. You probably have seen SMIL at work when you load RealPlayer and see the snazzy graphics that compose the welcome screen interface. With SMIL, you can layer interactive buttons and dynamic text on top of streaming video or audio content. You may not even think of SMIL as a competing technology, but rather a complementary one — Flash can be one of the multimedia tracks employed by SMIL!

You can even use Flash as a track type in QuickTime, without the use of SMIL. When Flash 4 was released, Macromedia and Apple announced QuickTime Flash movies, which enabled you to create Flash interfaces that layer on top of audio-video content. The RealOne Player also plays "tuned" Flash files directly, without the use of SMIL. A tuned Flash file is weighted evenly from frame to frame to ensure synchronized playback. Note, however, that tuned files usually need to be strict linear animations without any interactive functionality.

NOTE Several multimedia companies are developing proprietary plug-in-based authoring tools for multimedia use on the Web and Internet-connected devices. To participate in a discussion of multimedia formats, check out the forum at www.flashsupport.com/mediaformats/.

Exploring Companion Technologies

Now that you have a better understanding of how Flash fits into the current World Wide Web, we can begin to discuss the technologies that contribute to Flash's well-being. In today's world of the Web developer, you not only need to know how to create your Flash movies, but also how to implement Flash into existing environments, such as a Web browser or your business client's Web-ready (or not-so-Web-ready) application servers and related data sources.

HTML is here to stay

HTML is not going anywhere, regardless of the prolific nature of Flash on the Web. Using HTML to your advantage is very important because it is undeniably the best solution for certain forms of Web deployment. In addition, sites constructed entirely in Flash often require HTML to function properly. Here's how HTML works with Flash:

- **Displaying and formatting the movie on a Web page requires HTML.** It isn't always easy to hand-code HTML to work with ActiveX for Internet Explorer and the plug-in for Mozilla-compatible browsers at the same time.

- **Placing some content within a Flash movie is not possible, so you sometimes need to link it from your movie to an HTML page.** For example, some PDF files cannot be imported into a Flash CS4 document and will need to be linked from the Flash movie to be viewed separately with Adobe Reader. Or, you may need to access video files created for the RealOne Player or Windows Media Player. You can place links to these source files, or link to an HTML document that embeds the source file.

TIP If you want to integrate PDF documents with Flash movies, you might want to explore Macromedia FlashPaper. FlashPaper is a Flash movie file (.swf) that contains a document viewer and the document itself, enabling you to embed large print-ready documents on the Web or even within your own Flash movies. For more information on FlashPaper, see the FlashPaper section at www.flashsupport.com/links.

- **If your end user is not willing or able to view your Flash content, HTML enables you to provide an alternative version of your Web site.** Despite the addition of accessibility options into Flash Player 6 and later, which enable screen-reader interaction, not all screen readers are currently able to access this feature. An HTML version of your content is sure to reach most of this potential audience.

Many people find learning, and perhaps even using, HTML to be painful and tedious. Accommodating the differences among browsers can sometimes be time consuming and dry work. However, knowing some HTML is highly recommended and well worth the effort. HTML should be understood by any Web professional. If you are uncomfortable with the code, using Macromedia Dreamweaver will help your transition into the HTML world.

Client-side scripting using JavaScript

ActionScript and JavaScript are similar beasts, especially since ActionScript developed into a full-blown language in ActionScript 2.0. By learning one language, you will be able to translate this knowledge with relative ease. Already knowing some JavaScript when entering the Flash realm definitely puts you at a strong advantage. However, JavaScript itself is frequently used in conjunction with Flash, as follows:

- With JavaScript, you can create customized browser popup windows that open from Flash movies. By "customized," we mean browser windows that don't have any scroll bars, button bars, or menu items across the top of the browser window.

- JavaScript can pass data into the Flash movie when the Web page containing the movie loads. Some browsers enable you to continually pass data back and forth between Flash and JavaScript. Also, you are able to dynamically pass variables from JavaScript right into the Flash movie.

- JavaScript can be used to detect the presence or absence of the Flash Player plug-in in the user's Web browser. Likewise, you can use VBScript on Internet Explorer for Windows to detect the Flash Player ActiveX control. JavaScript (or VBScript) can redirect the Web browser to alternative content if the player is not installed.

- Flash movie properties such as width and height can be written on-the-fly by using JavaScript. You can also detect various system properties (which is also possible by using ActionScript) in JavaScript code, and pass this information into Flash.

TIP Flash Player 8 introduced the `ExternalInterface` **API, which enables you to more easily pass parameters between a Flash movie and JavaScript. For more information on this functionality, read Chapter 21, "Integrating Flash Content with Web Pages."**

The world of Web services

By using Flash CS4, you can tap an ever-expanding world of data transfer directly to your Flash movies. If you've stayed in the loop of Web technologies, you've likely heard of *Web services*, which is a generic term to describe a standardized approach to transfer data from one Web application to another. Web services use a format known as Web Services Description Language (WSDL), which uses a type of XML formatting called Simple Object Access Protocol (SOAP). It's not really important to know these acronyms as much as it is to understand what they do. WSDLs (pronounced "whiz-duhls") enable you to share complex data structures in a uniform, standardized manner. As long as a technology such as the Flash Player or ColdFusion can interpret a Web service, it can utilize its data. And because all WSDLs use the same formatting, your Flash movie can easily access data from public services offered by various companies on the Web. Some of these services are free, such as those found at `www.capescience.com`. Others are more restricted, such as Amazon.com's Web Service program, which is available only to registered associates. You can create your own Web services with application servers such as Adobe ColdFusion as well. Web services simply provide a gateway from which your Flash movie can access data over the Internet.

WEB RESOURCE Just about anyone can become an Amazon.com associate. See `http://associates.` `amazon.com` **for more details about enrolling in Amazon's developer program for Web services. You don't have to use Amazon.com's Web Service, but it's a fun source of information to keep you engaged while you're learning how to use Web services with your Flash content.**

NOTE Don't forget Flash Remoting! Flash Player can send and receive data by using Flash Remoting gateways, which can be installed on a variety of application servers. Flash Remoting is built into Adobe ColdFusion and provides a faster and more efficient means of transferring data between a Flash movie and an application server than Web services can accomplish.

Adobe server technologies

Nowadays, it's always helpful to have more than just client-side Flash development skills. With Adobe Flash Media Interactive Server, Flash Remoting, and Adobe LiveCycle Data Services, more and more business clients are looking for experienced Flash designers and developers to add real-time interactivity to their company's Web sites or Internet-aware applications. Applications created for Flash Media Interactive Server use server-side ActionScript (ASC files) to describe and control the interactivity between a Flash movie and the server's resources, including real-time streaming audio/video media and synchronized data updates between multiple Flash clients and the application.

Recognizing Project Potential

In this section, we provide an overview of the categories of Flash projects that you can produce. This is just a starting point to prime your creative juices and break through any self-imposed limiting perceptions that you may have about Flash media. The categories we have devised here are by no means industry-standard terms — they're broad, generalized groups into which most Flash development falls.

Linear presentations

In the early days of Internet growth, Flash shorts (cartoons) were the media buzz. These cartoons generally played from start to finish in a very linear fashion. Generally speaking, these movies load and then play — and count on catching the user's attention through the story and animation. These movies sometimes contain advanced ActionScript for animation, including randomized movement or content.

NOTE Linear Flash presentations do not necessarily have to be displayed within a Web browser — or even online. Several film-production and advertising companies use Flash to create high-quality animation for use in broadcast TV and feature films.

Interactive presentations

Interactive presentations represent the next step up from linear presentations. They provide the user control over the way information is presented, the flow, or the experience altogether. Usually, Web sites of any construct will be considered an interactive presentation. If you have information or content in a section somewhere in a movie or Web site, then you probably have an interactive presentation. An interactive presentation enables end users to choose the content they see by enabling them to navigate throughout a site, bypassing some content while accessing other content. A Flash movie in this category may have all the content viewed stored in a container movie, or across several Flash files linked to a main site.

Data-driven presentations

The data-driven presentations category of Flash development represents any movies that load external data (either dynamic or static) to deliver the presentation to the user. For example, a weather site that uses Flash may download dynamic Flash graphics of precipitation maps to display to the site's visitors. These graphics may be customized for each user of the site, depending on where he or she lives. *Data-driven* may even simply mean that text information within the Flash movie changes from time to time. Simply put, anytime information is separated from the actual Flash movie, you can say it is data-driven.

Data-driven applications (or Rich Internet Applications)

The data-driven applications category is somewhat loosely defined as those Flash movies that enable the user to accomplish some sort of task or enable a transaction from the Flash movie to use an external remote data source. For example, an online Flash ATM (that is, bank machine) could allow a bank customer to log in to the bank's secure server, and transfer funds from one account to another or pay a bill. All these tasks would require a transaction from the Flash movie to the bank's server. Another example could be an online Flash shopping cart, in which visitors add products to their virtual carts, and check out with their final order. Again, these tasks would require the Flash movie to send and receive data. The term Rich Internet Application, or RIA, was coined during the Macromedia MX product line launch, and implies the use of integrated data and rich media within a graphical user interface (GUI), in or out of a Web browser. Typically, RIAs combine Flash movies with one or more server-side technology, such as Flash Remoting and Adobe Flash Media Interactive Server.

WEB RESOURCE **We'd like to know what you think about this chapter. Visit** www.flashsupport.com/ feedback **to send us your comments.**

Summary

- Expectations of Web sites produced by Flash developers and designers grow with every new version of Flash. With an ever-increasing list of features and capabilities included with each version of the Flash Player, sites not facilitating new technology (such as new forms of interaction or media content) can easily become overlooked or considered uninteresting.

- Flash CS4 has many features that make it a vital piece of authoring software for Web sites and applications. Some of the main reasons to use it include small movie file sizes and the capability to integrate rich media content.

- There are several multimedia file formats available on the Web today. Although most users have many of the popular plug-ins installed, some users have restricted bandwidth and computer system environments. Flash has the capability to produce small movie files that can play identically across several platforms and devices.

- In order to develop advanced Flash projects, you should know the necessary HTML, JavaScript, and data-formatting standards (which now include Web services) that enable Flash to interact with other environments and data sources. These languages broaden the capabilities for interactivity and access to large amounts of data.

Chapter 3

Planning Flash Projects

O ne of the most important steps — if not the most important step — to producing great Flash content is knowing what steps you'll have to take to move from the concept or idea of the Flash movie to the finished product. This chapter explores the basics of Flash production and how to use the Project panel in Flash CS4 to organize your files. Whether you're a freelance Web consultant (or designer) or a member of a large creative or programming department, knowing how to manage the Flash content production will save you plenty of headaches, time, and money.

IN THIS CHAPTER

Knowing your workflow

Managing Flash content production

Creating a functional specification document

Using the Project panel in Flash CS4

Workflow Basics

No matter what the size or scope, every project in which you choose to participate should follow some type of planned workflow. Whether it's for print, film, video, or Web delivery (or all four!), you should establish a process to guide the production of your presentation.

Before we can explore the way in which Flash fits into a Web production workflow, we need to define a holistic approach to Web production in general. Figure 3.1 shows a typical example of the Web production process within an Internet production company.

NOTE Web production processes have been generally derived from traditional software development processes. The methodologies for production discussed in this chapter all fit into a category known as the "waterfall model." In short, the waterfall model dictates that each phase of production is completed before the next phase is entered. One of the problems with the waterfall model is that the business client (usually) only sees the project working at the end of the production cycle.

In contrast, an "agile model" for production mandates a full production cycle on a smaller scale to be completed within one to four weeks, presenting a functional aspect of the project to the business client at the end of the iteration. It's beyond the scope of this book to discuss all the differences between a waterfall and agile approach, but you should make yourself familiar with these terms because they're becoming more widely used with Web production processes.

FIGURE 3.1

Two of the most common phases when generating Web content are preproduction and the actual production phase.

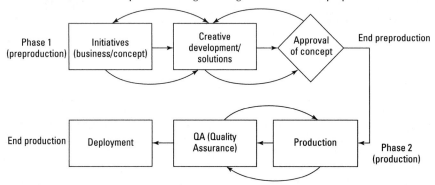

NOTE The phases of production have been coined differently by various project managers and companies. Some interactive agencies refer to preproduction as an "architecture phase" or a "planning phase." Preproduction may also involve a "discovery phase" which is a span of time before the architecture phase wherein the requirements for a project are determined.

Phase I: Establishing the concept and goals

As a Web developer or member of a creative team, companies (or representatives for other departments) will approach you to help solve problems with projects. A problem may or may not be well defined by the parties coming to you. The goal of Phase I is to thoroughly define the problem, offer solutions for the problem, and approve one or more solutions for final production.

The next-to-last question points to a bigger picture, one in which the client may already have several emotive keywords that define their brand. Try to define the emotional heart and feeling of their message — get them to be descriptive. Don't leave the meeting with the words *edgy* or *sexy* as the only descriptive terms for the message.

TIP Never go into a meeting or a planning session without a white board or a big pad of paper. Documenting everyone's ideas and letting the group see the discussion in a visual format is always a good idea. If all participants are willing, it's often useful to record the meeting with a digital voice recorder or video camera so that it can be reviewed outside of the meeting. There are also products on the market that enable you to record every detail of a meeting, such as Adobe Acrobat Connect, which enables you to conduct live meetings, as well as record them, over the Internet. Robert often uses his Tablet PC with Microsoft OneNote to record live audio that's synchronized with his notes from the meeting. You can find more information about Adobe Acrobat Connect at www.adobe.com/acrobatconnect.

You can also start to ask the following technical questions at this point:

- What type of browser support do you want to have?
- Do you have an idea of a Web technology (Shockwave; Flash; Dynamic HyperText Markup Language, or DHTML; Scalable Vector Graphics, or SVG) that you want to use?
- Does the message need to be delivered in a Web browser? Can it be in a downloadable application such as a stand-alone player? A CD-ROM? A DVD?
- What type of computer processing speed should be supported? What other types of hardware concerns might exist (for example, hi-fi audio)?

Of course, many clients and company reps look to *you* for the technical answers. If this is the case, the most important questions are

- Who's your audience?
- Who do you *want* to be your audience?

Your audience determines, in many ways, what type of technology to choose for the presentation. If the client says that Ma and Pa from a country farm should be able to view the Web site with no hassle, you may need to consider using an older version of the Flash Player (such as Flash Player 8) or building a non-Flash presentation (such as HTML and CSS). If the client wants the text on the Web site well indexed by search engines, you may also need to consider building a non-Flash version of the content. However, if they say that their ideal audience is someone who has a 56K modem and likes to watch cartoons, then you're getting closer to a Flash-based presentation. If the client has any demographic information for their user base, ask for it upfront. Putting on a show for a crowd is difficult if you don't know who's *in* the crowd.

Determining the project's goals

The client or company reps come to you for a reason — they want to walk away with a completed and *successful* project. As you initially discuss the message and audience for the presentation, you also need to get a clear picture of what the client expects to get from you.

- Will you be producing just one piece of a larger production?
- Do they need you to host the Web site? Or do they already have a Web server and a staff to support it?
- Do they need you to maintain the Web site after handoff?
- Do they expect you to market the presentation? If not, what resources are in place to advertise the message?
- When does the client expect you to deliver proposals, concepts, and the finished piece? These important dates are often referred to as *milestones*. The payment schedule for a project is often linked to production milestones.
- Will they expect to receive copies of all the files you produce, including your source .fla files?
- What are the costs associated with developing a proposal? Will you do work on speculation of a potential project? Or will you be paid for your time to develop a concept pitch? (You should determine this *before* you walk into your initial meeting with the client.) Of course, if you're working with a production team in a company, you're already being paid a salary to provide a role within the company.

Information Architects and User Experience

You may have already been bombarded with the idea of *information architecture*. Information architecture is the method by which sought data is represented and structured. Good information architecture is usually equivalent to intuitive user interface design — visitors to a well-organized Web site won't spend much time searching for what they want. More recently, the term "user experience design" is also bandied about, to refer to intuitive and user-centric interface design, organizing menus, buttons, navigation controls, and so on around the practical use of a product.

We mention information architecture because the steps in Phase I are similar to the steps that traditional architects take to build a comprehensive design and production strategy *before* they start to build any structure. Although this may seem obvious enough, the sad fact remains that many Internet sites (or projects) are planned as they're constructed. Indeed, we're told that production must move at Internet speed; thus, directives may be given without thorough research into other solutions for a given problem.

At this point, you'll want to plan the next meeting with your client or company reps. Give them a realistic timeframe for coming back to them with your ideas. This amount of time will vary from project to project and will depend on your level of expertise with the materials involved with the presentation.

Creative exploration: Producing a solution

After you leave the meeting, you'll go back to your design studio and start cranking out materials, right? Yes and no. Give yourself plenty of time to work with the client's materials (what you gathered from the initial meeting). If your client sells shoes, read up on the shoe business. See what the client's competitors are doing to promote their message — visit their Web sites, go to stores and compare the products, and read any consumer reports that you can find about your client's products or services. You should have a clear understanding of your client's market and a clear picture of how your client distinguishes their company or their product from their competitors'.

After you (and other members of your creative team) have completed a round of research, sit down and discuss the findings. Start defining the project in terms of mood, response, and time. Is this a serious message? Do you want the viewer to laugh? How quickly should this presentation happen? Sketch out any ideas you and any other member of the team may have. Create a chart that lists the emotional keywords for your presentation.

At a certain point, you need to start developing some visual material that articulates the message to the audience. Of course, your initial audience will be the client. You are preparing materials for them, not the consumer audience. We assume here that you are creating a Flash-based Web site for your client. For any interactive presentation, you need to prepare the following:

- An organizational flowchart for the site
- A process flowchart for the experience
- A functional specification for the interface
- A prototype or a series of comps

TIP You can use tools such as Microsoft Visio (http://office.microsoft.com/) or Omni Group's OmniGraffle for Mac (www.omnigroup.com/applications/omnigraffle). For more information on *Visio 2007 Bible,* published by Wiley, go to www.flashsupport.com/books/visio.

An *organizational flowchart* is a simple document that describes the scope of a site or presentation. Other names for this type of chart are *site chart, navigation flowchart,* and *layout flowchart.* It includes the major sections of the presentation. For example, if you're creating a Flash movie for a portfolio site, you might have a main menu and four content areas: About, Portfolio, Resumé, and Contact. In an organizational flowchart, this would look like Figure 3.2.

FIGURE 3.2

A sample organizational chart for a portfolio site

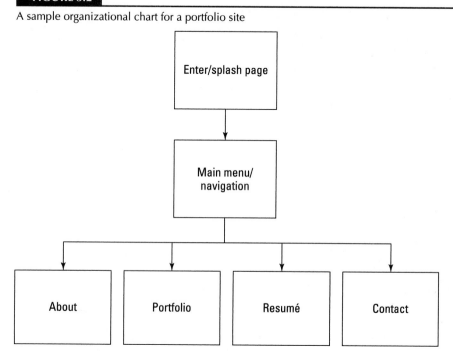

A *process flowchart* constructs the interactive experience of the presentation and shows the decision-making process involved for each area of the site. There are a few types of process charts. A basic process flowchart displays the decisions an end user will make. For example, what type of options does a user have on any given page of the site? Another type of flowchart shows the programming logic involved for the end-user process chart. For example, will certain conditions need to exist before a user can enter a certain area of the site? Does he or she have to pass a test, finish a section of a game, or enter a username and password? See Figure 3.3 for a preliminary flowchart for a section of our portfolio Web site. We discuss the actual symbols of the flowchart later in this chapter.

A *functional specification* (see Figure 3.4) is a document that breaks down the elements for each step in the organizational and/or process flowchart. This is by far the most important piece of documentation that you can create for yourself and your team.

FIGURE 3.3

The user watches an intro animation and is led through several short subsequent animations detailing each area of the portfolio. The user can then go to an area of his or her choice after this animation is complete.

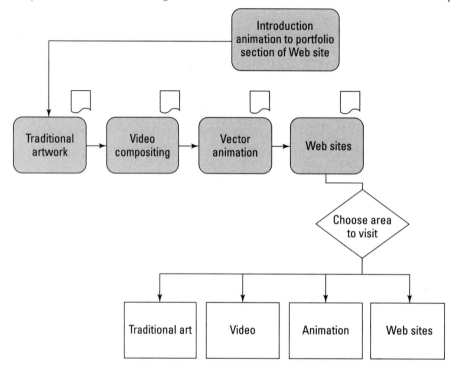

Each page of a functional specification (functional spec, for short) lists all the assets used on a page (or Flash keyframe, Movie Clip) and indicates the following information for each asset:

■ **Item ID:** This is part of the naming convention for your files and assets. It should be part of the filename, or Flash symbol and instance name. It should also be used in organizational and process flowcharts.

■ **Type:** This part of the spec defines the name you're assigning to the asset, in more natural language, such as Home Button.

■ **Purpose:** You should be able to clearly explain why this element is part of the presentation. If you can't, then you should consider omitting it from the project.

■ **Format:** This column indicates what technology (or what component of the technology) will be utilized to accomplish the needs of the asset. In an all-Flash presentation, list the symbol type or timeline element (frames, scene, nested Movie Clips) necessary to accomplish the goals of the asset.

NOTE   Functional specs come in all shapes and sizes. Each company usually has their own template or approach to constructing a functional spec. The client should always approve the functional spec so that you and your client have an agreement about the scope of the project.

FIGURE 3.4

This functional spec displays the six components of a Flash-based navigation bar, which will appear on the main menu of our portfolio content site.

Project:	Flash interface v2.0	Section:	1 of 5 (Main Menu)	
No.	Type	Purpose	Content	Format
1.A	Navigation bar	Provides easier access to site content.		A menu bar that is fixed at the top edge of the browser window.
1.A.1	Directory buttons	Provides a means of accessing any of the portfolio sections.	Names each content area. For example: audio, video, graphics, etc.	Horizontal menu list or ComboBox component (skinned).
1.A.2	Home button	Allows user to always get back to the opening page.	The text: "home"	Button component (skinned).
1.A.3	Search field	Provides a means of entering a specific word or phrase to search site contents.	A white text search field with the word "search".	Flash dynamic text field.
1.A.4	Sign up	Captures the users e-mail address for a site mailing list.	Text field(s) to enter name and e-mail address.	Button component generating a pop-up. Sign up using ColdFusion.
1.A.5	Back button	Allows the user to see the last page viewed without losing menu items.	The text "back".	Button component (skinned).
1.A.6	Logo or ID	Provides a means of personal branding.	A spider web, with text of the Web site name in Arial Narrow.	Graphics in Freehand and Flash.

Finally, after you have a plan for your project, you'll want to start creating some graphics to provide an atmosphere for the client presentation. Gather placement graphics (company logos, typefaces, photographs) or appropriate "temporary" resources for purposes of illustration. Construct one composition, or *comp*, that represents each major section or theme of the site. In our portfolio content site example, you might create a comp for the main page and a comp for one of the portfolio work sections, such as Animation. Don't create a comp for each page of the portfolio section. You simply want to establish the feel for the content you will create for the client. We recommend that you use the tool(s) with which you feel most comfortable creating content. If you're better at using Illustrator or Photoshop to create layouts, then use that application. If you're comfortable with Flash for assembling content, then use it.

CAUTION Do not use copyrighted material for final production use, unless you have secured the appropriate rights to use the material. However, while you're exploring creative concepts, use whatever materials you feel best illustrate your ideas. When you get approval for your concept, improve upon the materials that inspired you.

Then you want to determine the time and human resources required for the entire project or concept. What role will you play in the production? Will you need to hire outside contractors to work on the presentation (for example, character animators, programmers, and so on)? Make sure that you provide ample time to produce and thoroughly test the presentation. When you've determined the time and resources necessary, you'll determine the costs involved. If this is an internal project for your company, you won't be concerned about cost so much as the time involved — your company reps will want to know what it will cost the company to produce the piece. For large client projects, your client will probably expect a project rate — not an hourly or weekly rate. Outline a time schedule with milestone dates, at which point you'll present the client with updates on the progress of the project.

Exploring the details of the workflow process any further is beyond the scope of this book. However, there are many excellent resources for project planning. One of the best books available for learning the process of planning interactive presentations is Nicholas Iuppa's *Designing Interactive Digital Media* (Butterworth-Heinemann, 1998). We strongly recommend that you consult the *Graphic Artists Guild Handbook of Pricing & Ethical Guidelines* (Graphic Artists Guild, 2003) and the *AIGA Professional Practices in Graphic Design: American Institute of Graphic Arts* (Allworth Press, 1998), edited by Tad Crawford, for information on professional rates for design services.

Approving a final concept and budget

After you have prepared your design documents for the client, it's time to have another meeting with the client or company rep. Display your visual materials (color laser prints, inkjet mockups, and so on), and walk through the charts you've produced. In some situations, you may want to prepare more than one design concept. Always reinforce how the presentation addresses the client's message and audience.

When all is said and done, discuss the options that you've presented with the client. Gather feedback. Hopefully, the client prefers one concept (and its budget) and gives you the approval to proceed. It's important that you leave this meeting knowing one of two things:

- The client has signed off on the entire project or presentation.
- The client wants to see more exploration before committing to a final piece.

In either case, you shouldn't walk away not knowing how you'll proceed. If the client wants more time or more material before a commitment, negotiate the terms of your fees that are associated with further conceptual development.

Designing for Usability, by Scott Brown

As the authors of this book mention earlier in this chapter, the first step in developing a Flash site, or any other type of site, is to define the information architecture. In this tutorial, I show you how to define the goals and mission of the site.

Defining the goals and mission of the site

When you define the mission and goals for your project, you lay the foundation upon which to build it. To create a solid project foundation, you must begin by questioning everything, especially the company's business model. Start with these questions:

- What is the mission or purpose of the organization?
- Why does this organization want a Web site?

- Will the Web site support the mission of the organization?

- What are the short- and long-term goals of the Web site?

- Who is the intended audience?

- Why will people come to the site?

- Is the organization trying to sell a product?

- What is the product or products?

- Do we have a unique service?

- What makes the service different?

- Why will people come to the site for the first time?

- Will they ever come back?

- Why would they come back?

The list of questions can go on forever. After you've gathered a list of questions, you need to get the answers. Ask around the organization, ask your friends, ask strangers, ask anyone. After you've collected the answers, filter through them to create a list of goals based on the responses. From this list of goals, you must further define the answer to the question, "Who is the audience?"

Defining the audience

The audience can be defined as the potential users of the site and their intentions or tasks when they come to your site. Are they kids or adults? Are they Generation X, Y, or Z? Are they into rave music or country music?

So, who is your audience? It's not an easy question because there are so many possibilities. Start with a list of all the possible audiences that the organization would like to reach, and then rearrange the list in a ranking order of most important audience to least important audience. From the audience-ranking list, create a list of the possible goals and needs each audience has.

Creating character scenarios

With the list of possible goals, take the process one step farther by creating scenarios for the users. Think of it as writing a screenplay for your Web site. Create multiple characters who represent the majority of the visitors, giving them hobbies, likes, dislikes, and, most important, a task to complete on the site. The object of the scenario game is to get into the characters' heads to learn why and how they would use your site. Approaching the design from their viewpoints makes it easier for you to create a list of the needs and wants of the characters, a wish list if you will.

After you write the scenarios, the next step in the process is to gather the team together and analyze the Web sites of the competition.

Note from the authors: Character scenarios are often referred to as *use case scenarios*.

Analyzing the competition

Studying the competition gives you the chance to generate a list of the kinds of features they are offering and to determine whether your feature list, the one that you created from the scenarios, is missing anything. If your wish list lacks anything in comparison to your competition, now is a good time to expand the user's functionality requirements and to return to the scenarios to determine whether the competition's functionality matches your characters' needs. If it does, you should try to elaborate on the competition's functions and create new functions of your own — the classic case of outdoing your competition.

Reaching a consensus on what good design is

At this time in the process, have the team come together to develop a definition of what is "good site design." This step is most beneficial for any contract designer trying to gain an understanding of the client's design viewpoint. To create this "good design" definition, the team should observe a good number of sites and document everybody's likes and dislikes for each one. This way, everyone on the team will have a better understanding of what to strive for and what to avoid.

Structuring the content

Now you should have several documents to refer to — the project mission statement, the user functionality needs (wish list), and the organization's definition of good design. With these three documents in hand, the next step is to blend them into one master menu of content inventory. Think of each item on this list as a building block. You now have all the blocks needed to construct the site. The only problem is that these blocks are in a big pile and lack organization (structure). Naturally, the next step is to begin creating layouts of the site, providing structure. But before you can begin the page layout process, you need to educate yourself on some Web site usability issues.

Identifying factors of usability

Usability is a much-debated concept, but generally it means creating a site/project/interface that is functional and that your audience understands. A useable site aims to be a natural extension of a user's expectations and needs. A user-friendly site tries to mirror its structure to that of the user's experience and goals. Just to make the task at hand a little more complex, keep in mind that user expectations learned in other areas of life affect how the user will think your site works. So, how can you design a site to meet your user's expectations? Well, if you did your homework on your audience and wrote the character scenarios, you should have a pretty good idea of the target audience's expectations. Given that you know the general background of the user, you could include *metaphors* in the structure of the site. Using metaphors is a great way to help users draw upon knowledge they already have, thereby making the site easier to use. Matching the site structure to the user's experience minimizes the amount of time it takes for the user to learn how to operate or navigate the site. The shorter the learning curve for the site, the better. If you come to a site when you have a specific goal in mind, and it takes you ten minutes to figure out how to achieve your goal, would you call that a positive experience? Most likely not!

Your goal as the designer is to create an attractive site without distracting users from their goals. Forcing users to spend a noticeable amount of time trying to learn how to achieve their goals is very taxing on their patience, and it is a good way to create a negative experience. If you're trying to sell something, chances are you want customers to be happy, not annoyed. One way to make your customers' experience more enjoyable is to make it as easy as possible. So, how do you create a positive experience? Let's start with the most basic of user needs: the ability to navigate.

Users need to know at all times where they are in the site, where they have been, and where they can go. When developing a navigation system, be sure to keep the navigation visually consistent. Inconsistency in the navigation can confuse and frustrate the user. A great concept for a navigational aid is the use of a breadcrumb trail. The breadcrumb system is a visual way to show users the path they took to get to their current position in the site. This navigational convention is used on many resource sites and even in the Flash authoring environment itself — as you click to edit grouped shapes or symbols, the steps you take appear as text labels on the bar above the Stage. Beyond displaying the path of the user, this system gives the user the ability to backtrack to any page displayed in the path. However, remember that navigation is not the goal of the user, only an aid. The user is there to find or buy something; the user is there for the content. So, make the content the first read on all of your pages. Navigational elements are there to support the content, not eclipse it.

Of course, navigation isn't the only factor to consider when designing for usability. Other variables, such as the length of text on a page, can affect the usability of a site tremendously. It's a fact that reading text on a monitor is far more taxing on the eyes than reading text on paper. Therefore, people are less inclined to read large amounts of text on the Web. As designers, we must accommodate these changes in reading patterns. Keep these simple guidelines in mind when writing text for the Web. Try to make the text scannable, because readers skim Web content. Bold the important ideas or put key information in bulleted lists. But most of all, keep the text short.

In addition to the treatment of text, there are several other tips to help improve the usability of a site. The concept of redundant links is an excellent method to support users with different backgrounds and goals. With redundant links, a user has more than one way to get to the desired content. The user may have the option to click a text link, a graphic link, or even a text link that is worded differently. Each redundant link should be designed to accommodate a wide range of users. So, where on the page should all these usability elements go?

I can't tell you where you should place your navigation system or your redundant links. However, I can provide you with some information from eye-tracking studies that will help you make an educated decision. Yes, it is true that usability researchers are able to actually monitor and record what you're looking at when you're viewing a Web site. Researchers have found that when a Web page loads, our eyes are looking at the center of the page, and then move over to the left, and then sometimes to the right. Of course, these findings are dependent on the user's cultural background. Nevertheless, the scary finding is that the users rarely look to the right! This is most likely because most sites use the right side of the page as a place to add sidebar elements, items of lesser importance. This is also a good example of how a user's experience can affect his or her future experiences. So, how does Flash fit into Web site usability considerations?

Flash is a great design tool to create amazing interfaces. Flash gives the designer the freedom to create almost anything he or she desires. But the flexibility Flash gives to the designer is also the tool's greatest weakness from a usability perspective. Flash is great for creating animation; however, inexperienced Web designers can easily go overboard. Just because you can animate an object doesn't mean that you should. The eye is very sensitive to the smallest amount of animation or movement in its peripheral view, pulling the viewers' attention away from the site's main content. On the plus side, animation used as a transitional element is very beneficial for the user. Animated transitions enable the user to follow the navigation process, and gain a better understanding of how the site might work.

Similar to the problem of animation abuse, Flash enables the designers to create their own graphical user interface (GUI) elements. This is great for the designers, but users are often left out in the cold with all this newfound freedom. This design freedom forces the user to learn, almost from scratch, how to operate a scroll bar or a navigation bar. If you recall, I mention earlier the importance of a short learning curve for the users. The extreme creative versions of standardized GUI elements might rank high on the "cool" scale, but they really throw a monkey wrench into the user's goal and expectations. GUI standards are developed to help create a consistent experience across all platforms, thereby eliminating any unpleasant surprises. Again, these usability problems can be avoided in Flash if you understand the issues at hand and are able to find solutions based on the set standards.

Other usability issues with Flash arise from the actual plug-in nature of Flash. Unfortunately, because Flash requires a plug-in to work in Web browsers, Flash movies are unable to take advantage of some of the browser's built-in capabilities, such as the Back button and the tool's capability to display history for the links by changing the color of the links that have been clicked. The problem with the browser's Back button is that when a user clicks the button, the browser takes the user back to the previous HTML page, not to the previous state in the Flash movie. It's not a nice surprise for unsuspecting users. One solution to this problem is to pop up the Flash movie in a new browser window (via JavaScript) with all the browser's navigation elements removed (in other words, no toolbar, no location bar, no menus, and so on). No Back button on the browser, no problem right?

Building mockups of the site

You are now ready to begin mocking up the site structure by using index cards, sticky notes, and other common office supplies. Creating these paper mockups saves the development team a large amount of time. The beauty of the paper mockups is that you can quickly create a navigational system and find the major flaws without spending long hours developing a beautiful rendering of a structure that may be flawed. There is nothing worse than spending months developing a product with a faulty structure only to discover the mistake just before launch!

Testing the site on real users

Testing the site is the most important step in creating a useable site. The key to testing the site is *not* to test it on people in the organization, but to test it on people in the target audience. Test the site on the real users. It's usually easier to test the site by using people who are familiar with the project. The problem with that practice is that the people are familiar with the project. You want to test fresh eyes and minds in order to get optimum feedback. For testing purposes, create a list of several tasks to complete on the site. The tasks should be pulled from the list of possible users' goals defined in the early steps of the project. As the test subjects navigate through your project, pay close attention to how long it takes them. How many times did they have to click to find what they were looking for? How many had to resort to using a search feature (or wished that they could)? What elements seemed to cause confusion or delay? What elements attracted or held the users' attention? After each test subject has completed a task, or tried, give him or her a post-task questionnaire with questions such as:

"How would you rate the quality of the content on this site?"

Unacceptable –3 –2 –1 0 1 2 3 Excellent

Also, leave some room for the test subject to elaborate on the questions. After the testing is finished, review your findings and determine what needs to be fixed. After the problems are fixed, test the site again, but on new users. Repeat the process until you have a product that meets the defined goals of the organization and the users. Keep asking yourself this question: Is the interface helping the users accomplish their goals? When all else fails, you can always depend on the greatest guideline of the century: Keep it simple. Oh, how true.

Phase II: Producing, testing, and staging the presentation

When your client or company executives have signed off on a presentation concept, it's time to rock and roll! You're ready to gather your materials, assemble the crew, and meet an insane production schedule. This section provides a brief overview of the steps you need to take to produce material that's ready to go live on your Web site.

Assembling assets

The first step is to gather (or start production of) the individual assets required for the Flash presentation. Depending on the resources you included in your functional spec and budget, you may need to hire a photographer, illustrator, animator, or music composer (or all four!) to start work on the production. Or, if you perform any of these roles, then you should start creating rough drafts for the elements within the production. At this stage, you can also gather high-quality images from the client for their logos, proprietary material, and so on.

Making the Flash architecture

Of course, we're assuming that you're creating a Flash-based production. All the resources that you've gathered (or are working to create) in Phase 1 will be assembled into the Flash movie(s) for the production. For large presentations or sites, you'll likely make one master Flash movie that provides a skeleton architecture for the presentation, and use ActionScript to bring in material for the appropriate sections of the site.

Before you begin Flash movie production, you should determine two important factors: frame size and frame rate. You don't want to change either of these settings midway through your project. Any reductions in frame size will crop elements that weren't located near the top-left portion of the Stage — you'll need to recompose most of the elements on the Stage if you used the entire Stage. Any changes in your frame rate change the timing of any linear animation and/or sound synchronization that you've already produced.

Staging a local test environment

As soon as you start to author the Flash movies, you create a local version of the presentation (or entire site) on your computer, or a networked drive that everyone on your team can access. The file and folder structure (including the naming conventions) will be consistent with the structure of the files and folders on the Web server. As you build each component of the site, you should begin to test the presentation with the target browsers (and Flash Player plug-in versions) for your audience.

HTML page production

Even if you're creating an all-Flash Web site, you need a few basic HTML documents, including:

- **Plug-in detection with JavaScript** that directs visitors without the Flash Player plug-in to the Adobe site to download the plug-in.
- **HTML page(s) to display any non-Flash material** in the site within the browser.

You should construct basic HTML documents to hold the main Flash movie as you develop the Flash architecture of the site.

Staging a server test environment

Before you can make your Flash content public, you need to set up a Web server that is publicly accessible (preferably with login and password protection) so that you can test the site functionality over a non-LAN connection. This also enables your client to preview the site remotely. After quality assurance (QA) testing is complete (the next step that follows), you move the files from the staging server to the live Web server.

We've noticed problems with larger .swf files that weren't detected until we tested them from a staging server. Why? When you test your files locally, they're loaded instantly into the browser. When you test your files from a server — even over a fast DSL (digital subscriber line) or cable modem connection, you have to wait for the .swf files to load over slower network conditions. Especially with preloaders or loading sequences, timing glitches may be revealed during tests on the staging server that were not apparent when you tested locally.

> **TIP** You should use the Simulate Download feature of the Bandwidth Profiler in the Test Movie environment of Flash CS4 to estimate how your Flash movies will load over a real Internet connection. See Chapter 20, "Publishing Flash Movies," for more discussion of this feature.

Quality assurance testing

In larger corporate environments, you'll find a team of individuals whose sole responsibility is to thoroughly test the quality of a nearly finished production (or product). If you're responsible for QA, then you should have an intimate knowledge of the process chart for the site. That way, you know how the site should function. If a feature or function fails in the production, QA reports it to the creative and/or programming teams. QA teams test the production with the same hardware and conditions as the target audience, accounting for variations in:

- Computer type (Windows versus Mac)
- Computer speed (top-of-the-line processing speed versus minimal supported speeds, as determined by the target audience)
- Internet connection speeds (as determined by the target audience)
- Flash Player plug-in versions (and any other plug-ins required by the production)
- Browser application and version (as determined by the target audience)

> **WEB RESOURCE** It's worthwhile to use an online reporting tool to post bugs during QA. Many companies use the open source (freeware) tool called Mantis, a PHP/MySQL solution. You can find more information about Mantis at www.mantisbt.org/. Another popular bug reporting tool is Bugzilla (www.bugzilla.org).

After QA has finished rugged testing of the production, pending approval by the client (or company executives), the material is ready to go live on the site.

Maintenance and updates

After you've celebrated the finished production, your job isn't over yet. If you were contracted to build the site or presentation for a third party, you may be expected to maintain and address usability issues provided by follow-ups with the client and any support staff they might have. Be sure to account for periodic maintenance and updates for the project in your initial budget proposal. If you don't want to be responsible for updates, make sure that you advise your clients ahead of time to avoid any potential conflicts after the production has finished.

You should have a thorough staging and testing environment for any updates you make to an all-Flash site, especially if you're changing major assets or master architecture files. Repeat the same process of staging and testing with the QA team that you employed during original production.

> **WEB RESOURCE** You can find an online archived PDF version of Eric Jordan's tutorial, "Interface Design," on the book's Web site at www.flashsupport.com/archive. This tutorial was featured in *Flash MX Bible* (Wiley, 2002).

Using the Project Panel in Flash CS4

In this final section of the chapter, we show you how to use the Project panel in Flash CS4 by using some sample files we provide on this book's CD-ROM. You jump right into the Project panel, so you may want to review some of the content in the Help pages of Flash CS4 before proceeding. The Using Flash ⇨ Using Flash CS4 Professional ⇨ Managing documents ⇨ Working with projects section in the Help pages (Help ⇨ Flash Help) contains useful information about the Project panel.

NEW FEATURE The Project panel in Flash CS4 is completely different than the Project panel featured in the last three versions of the Flash authoring tool. The new Project panel is much easier to use than its predecessor, and you can set up project files with much less hassle.

Before you start using the Project panel, consider a scenario in which you would *want* to use the feature. The Project panel lets you access files related to a Flash production. You can include any file type you want in your project, and this is reflected in the Project panel. The panel essentially works as a modified file explorer, similar to Windows Explorer or the Finder (Mac), especially geared to Flash content. After you've created a Flash project, you can quickly open any document directly in Flash CS4 or another application. The project name is added as a new item in the drop-down menu at the top of the Project panel.

One important factor to keep in mind when you use the Project panel is that you should only open a local copy of the project's files on your computer. In this way, everyone working on the project has his or her own copy of the files. One member of the team can be editing, implementing, and testing changes while other members are doing the same with their copies. When a member is done editing a file, he or she can check the file back into the server.

CAUTION Unless you're implementing a version control system with your project files, you need to make sure that two or more members of the team do not attempt to make edits to the same file simultaneously or make edits to a copy of a file. Version control systems can merge changes to the same document. For example, if two people edit the same ActionScript document (.as file), the version control system merges the changes into one file and even flags potential conflicts during the process. Also, it's important to note that version control software cannot merge changes in two Flash documents (.fla files) because such files are binary, not ASCII (or Unicode). Usually, version control systems can merge only text documents.

Here's a quick review of the procedures you follow:

1. **Establish a new project structure with files and folders on your local system.**

2. **Create a new project in Flash CS4.** The primary setting for a new project is the location of your Flash files, where you'll store your local copy of the project files.

3. **Edit panel and project preferences to suit the needs of your project (optional).**

4. **Open and edit a file in the project.**

5. **Publish an entire project.**

The headings that follow elaborate on these five steps, and include the step numbers for easy reference.

1. Establishing a project structure

Before you can start making or editing documents in Flash CS4 for a project, you need to define a folder structure that the Project panel can use. In this section, you learn how to define a site and establish a local mirror copy of your site's files on your machine.

1. **On your computer, choose a location that you can use to store all the files with a project.** For example, if you're on Windows, you can create a folder named `sites` at the root of your C drive. If you're on a Mac, you can create a folder named `sites` at the root of your startup drive, such as Macintosh HD.

2. **Inside of the `sites` folder, copy the `robertreinhardt.com` folder from the `ch03` folder located on this book's CD-ROM.** As shown in Figure 3.5, the `robertreinhardt.com` folder has two subfolders, `src` and `deploy`.

> **TIP**　In Mac OS X, you can turn on Personal Web Sharing in the Sharing preferences (Apple menu ⇨ System Preferences). When this service is started, Mac OS X automatically creates a `Sites` folder in your user folder on the startup disk. You can use this `Sites` folder to test content from a Web browser, using the path `http://localhost/~your_user_name`. For example, if your user name is joann, your local path to the `Sites` folder is `http://localhost/~joann/`.

The `src` folder, short for *source*, will contain any source files, specifications, planning documents, raw assets (images, video, and sound), and so on. The `fla` folder inside of the `src` folder holds all Flash documents (.fla files) for the project.

The `deploy` folder, short for *deployment*, will contain any and all files that will be part of the final application, as a publicly accessible Web site or application. The `deploy` folder holds the files that will be uploaded to the public root folder of your Web server. These files are also called *runtime* files because they run in the Flash Player and Web browser from the live Web site. All the Flash movies (.swf files), runtime assets (JPEGs, MP3s, FLVs, and so on), and HTML documents will be kept here. The copy of `deploy` from the CD-ROM includes several subfolders to store external assets necessary for the Flash movie (.swf file) at runtime.

FIGURE 3.5

The layout of folders for a site named robertreinhardt.com

2. Creating the project in Flash CS4

After you create the file and folder structure, you're ready to create a new Flash project in Flash CS4.

1. **Open Flash Professional CS4.** Choose Window ⇨ Other Panels ⇨ Project (Shift+F8).

2. In the top drop-down menu, select New Project (shown in Figure 3.6).

FIGURE 3.6

The Project panel

3. **In the Create New Project dialog box, type a name for your project in the Project name field, such as** robertreinhardt.com. Click the folder icon to the right of the Root folder field, and browse to the robertreinhardt.com folder on your computer. In the ActionScript Version menu, choose the version of ActionScript that you will use with your Flash project. For this example, ActionScript 3.0 (AS3) is used, so the ActionScript 3.0 option is selected. Review the example settings shown in Figure 3.7. Click the Create Project button to build a new project setting in Flash CS4.

4. **After the project is created, you can expand the folder nodes to see the documents that reside in the project.** The Project panel automatically filters the file types shown in the folder nodes to include only those files commonly used in Flash production, such as .fla, .swf, and .as. When all the folder nodes are expanded (as shown in Figure 3.8), some files are not visible such as image, XML, HTML, and CSS files. In the next section, you learn how to modify preferences to add file extensions to the project's file filter.

It's highly likely that you'll have more than one Flash document (.fla file) in a project. As such, you should define the default document for the project. This file should be the master file, the one "most in charge" per se. This could be the Flash document that controls the loading of other runtime assets or the document that contains the most code. The published SWF file of the default document is the movie that is loaded into the Test Movie environment when you test a project. In the src/fla folder of the Project panel, right-click (or Control+click on the Mac) the Bio.fla document and choose Make Default Document in the context menu, as shown in Figure 3.9. The icon of the document should now include a gold star to indicate that it is the default document.

FIGURE 3.7

The Create New Project dialog box

FIGURE 3.8

The structure of the site within the Project panel, with default file extensions visible

FIGURE 3.9

The Make Default Document option in the context menu for a .fla file

 TIP The check box to the right of a .fla file in the Project panel determines if the document is published when you click the Test Project button. All .fla files are unchecked by default.

3. Changing project and panel preferences

After you have created a new project with existing files on your system, you can alter the Project panel's display of files and folders. In this section, you learn how to set up project properties and alter the panel preferences to show the additional runtime files (images, HTML, CSS, and so on) in the panel.

1. To create a shortcut to your ActionScript class files in the Project panel (and more important, to instruct the panel where to create new class files), click the options combo box at the top right corner of the panel (marked with a gear icon), and choose Project Properties, as shown in Figure 3.10.

2. In the Classes tab of the Project Properties dialog box, click the browse folder icon for the Save classes in field, as shown in Figure 3.11. Browse to the `classes` folder in the `src/actionscript` folder of the sample project files. Click OK to close the dialog box. The Project panel now displays the `classes` folder as a separate folder node (Figure 3.12). Note that a new folder was *not* created in the actual folder structure — you simply have a quicker way to find and access the class files for a project.

FIGURE 3.10

The options menu of the Project panel

FIGURE 3.11

The Classes tab of the Project Properties dialog box

3. **To change the file and folder filter preferences, choose Panel Preferences from the same options menu you used in step 1.** Click the Settings tab in the Panel Preferences dialog box, and enter the file extensions for the file types you want to see displayed in your Flash projects, as shown in Figure 3.13. For this example, you can enter the following extensions: png, css, html, and js. Click OK when you've finished adding your preferred extensions. When you expand the folder nodes in the Project panel, you should now see all the files for the example project (Figure 3.14).

FIGURE 3.12

The new classes node in the Project panel

FIGURE 3.13

The Settings tab of the Panel Preferences dialog box

 You may want to uncheck the Show hidden files option, which is enabled by default. Version control files, such as .svn and .git files, will be visible unless this option is unchecked.

FIGURE 3.14

The updated file view in the Project panel

4. Opening and editing files in the project

After you create a project and set up your preferences, you can open and edit documents from the Project panel.

1. **Double-click the master document, Bio.fla, to edit it in the Flash authoring environment.**

2. **With Bio.fla open, take a look at how the bio.swf file (located in the wwwroot folder) is published.** Choose File ⇨ Publish Settings. In the Formats tab, notice that a relative path is declared for the bio.swf file (see Figure 3.15) in the Flash field. The ../../deploy/ prefix tells Flash CS4 to publish this file two folders above the fla folder, inside of the deploy folder. Click Cancel to close the dialog box.

3. **You can also edit some text files, such as HTML and XML files, directly in the Flash CS4 authoring environment.** If you want to open a non-Flash-specific file in its associated application, you can right-click that file in the Project panel and choose Open File With Associated Application (Figure 3.16). If you have Adobe Dreamweaver associated with CSS files, you can right-click the styles.css file, choose this option, and edit the CSS file directly in Dreamweaver.

FIGURE 3.15

You can publish files with relative paths in the Formats tab.

5. Publishing the entire project

In this final section, you learn how to test an entire project and view the master document's movie in the Test Movie environment.

1. **Click the Test Project button in the lower left corner of the Project panel**. Flash CS4 publishes all the Flash documents (.fla files) set to publish in the project file. In our example, there's only one .fla file, `Bio.fla`. The newly published `bio.swf` file, located in the `deploy` folder, then opens in the Test Movie environment.

2. **When you finish testing the file, close the Test Movie window**. Remember, when you close and reopen Flash CS4, you can reopen all the project files for this example by choosing the site name in the Project panel's main drop-down menu.

 You can find the site files in the `ch03` folder on this book's CD-ROM.

FIGURE 3.16

The contextual menu of a file in the Project panel

WEB RESOURCE **We'd like to know what you think about this chapter. Visit** www.flashsupport.com/ feedback **to send us your comments.**

Summary

- Your clients rely on you to understand and guide the production process involved with Flash content creation.

- Careful planning helps you to create Flash solutions that best meet the goals of your project. The technical issues, such as usability, target audience, and delivery platform, should be balanced with the aesthetic aspects of experience design.

- To structure the development of Flash projects, many Web developers use a two-phase production model that involves six milestones: Business Initiative, Creative Solutions, Approval, Production, QA, and Delivery.

- During the production period, it is helpful to keep six key concepts in mind: asset assembly, a master Flash architecture, a local test environment, HTML page layout, a server staging environment, and proper QA testing. After production is finished, you also need to devise a strategy for systematic maintenance.

- You can use the Project panel in Flash CS4 to manage all the Flash documents for a site or application.

Part II

Mastering the Flash Environment

When you're ready to jump in and get started on the road to efficient and painless production, this section will give you all the information you need to feel comfortable in the Flash authoring environment. Chapter 4 introduces you to the updated Flash workspace and gives you tips for customizing the UI. You will learn where all your tools are stored and how to organize them to suit your workflow. Chapter 5 is where you'll find coverage of all the Flash drawing and selection tools, including an introduction to the new Spray Brush and Deco tools that enable you to create patterns with symbol instances. You'll also learn how to control snapping behavior and how to create and edit groups. In Chapter 6, you'll find out what makes Flash so much more powerful than simple vector graphics programs. Symbols and symbol instances are the basis for all optimized Flash projects, and the Library gives you all the options you need to keep your project assets organized.

Chapter 7 includes coverage of color issues specific to Web production and explains how to use the Swatches and Color panels to enhance your projects with custom colors, gradients, bitmap fills, and more. Chapter 8 guides you through the various options for creating and editing text in Flash, including dynamic and input text and vertical text and the anti-alias settings. You will also learn how to control font display and how to create and use font symbols. Finally, in Chapter 9, you will be introduced to the more advanced tools for editing graphics and text in Flash, including the Free Transform and Gradient Transform tools. Last but not least, you will discover the cool new 3D tools and learn how to use the z-axis to add the illusion of depth to your Flash graphics.

Chapter 4

Interface Fundamentals

This chapter gives you a tour of the Flash workspace and the various methods for organizing and navigating your documents. We define fundamental features of the authoring environment, but in some cases, defer detailed explanation of functionality to later chapters. This chapter orients new users to the program and introduces experienced users to some of the new Flash CS4 features.

Getting Started

When you walk into a studio, the first thing you need to know is where to find your tools. Although you might have an idea of where to start looking based on experience, nothing improves your workflow more than being able to reach for something without hesitation. This kind of familiarity and comfort in a workspace is a prerequisite for the mastery of any craft.

Fortunately, many of the features of the Flash CS4 interface will look familiar to you if you've worked in other graphics applications. However, there are some unique features that you need to understand before you can tackle your Flash projects with the ease of an expert. We begin by introducing the Flash interface and pointing out the tools available for managing and customizing your Flash "studio."

You'll soon notice that there is often more than one way to access an option. As we describe the steps for carrying out a task, we include shortcut keys or menu paths in parentheses. You should feel comfortable and ready to get to work in no time.

Welcome to Flash CS4

Flash CS4 presents the most polished and agile implementation, so far, of the flexible panel-based interface that has gradually evolved over the last few versions of Flash. Panels in Flash CS4 can now be resized more freely and docked or grouped easily with other panels or to the application window. Adobe has made a concerted effort with this release to streamline menus and smooth out workflow inconsistencies with various tools. Some small but significant modifications have also been made to the look and function of common tools, menus, and panels. We cover them as we discuss workflows for specific tasks throughout the book.

The changes in Flash CS4 are hinted at in the interface, but we give you a peek under the hood in this chapter. If you have been using Flash for a while, this version should speed up your workflow and boost your inspiration. If this is the first time you've tried Flash, you've picked a great time to start: Flash CS4 includes more ways to jump in and get started than ever before.

Start Page

The Start Page (shown in Figure 4.1) gives you quick access to tutorials and other help features and provides a handy way to choose the file you want to open or create.

FIGURE 4.1

The Start Page provides quick access to file lists, templates, and resource links.

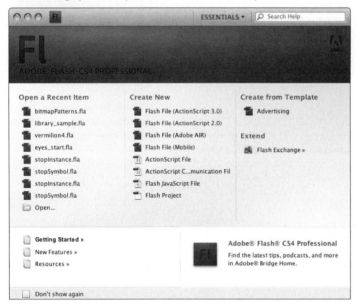

Flash content for mobile phones and other devices is increasingly popular, and Adobe supports developers through Adobe Device Central with templates designed specifically for commonly used handheld devices in different markets.

By default, the Start Page should appear when you first launch Flash and any time you close all Document windows while the program is running. After you have opened or created a new file, the Start Page automatically closes to make room on your desktop. If you prefer not to use the Start Page, select the Don't show again check box at the bottom of the panel, or change the settings for On launch in General Flash Preferences (Edit ➪ Preferences or Flash ➪ Preferences). This leaves you with the more limited, but familiar, option of using the application File menu (or shortcut keys) to create and open files.

The links at the bottom of the Start Page connect you to online content available through the Adobe Web site. These links are worth investigating if you want to get a quick introduction to Flash and a peek at the vast range of online resources available.

WEB RESOURCE If you want to introduce other friends or co-workers to the new features of Flash CS4, you can direct them to the information online at www.adobe.com/products/flash/features.

One of the most useful links in the Start Page is to Flash Exchange (under the Extend title). If you are connected to the Internet this link connects you to the Adobe Exchange page which includes a list of product-specific links. You can browse to the Flash Exchange for helpful tools and add-ons that Flash developers have made available through Adobe's site.

TIP You do need to be connected to the Internet to access Adobe's Help Resource Center: www.adobe.com/support/documentation/(language)/flash, but when you get there you have the option of downloading most of the reference manuals in PDF format for future reference (or browsing for the most current LiveDocs).

The first four options listed under the Create New title in the Start Page each target a different version of ActionScript — or rather they create a new Flash document with Publish settings auto-set to target a specific version of the Flash Player, using one of the various flavors of ActionScript:

- **Flash File (ActionScript 3.0):** ActionScript 3.0 can only be used with Flash Player 9 or later and should be specified if you plan to use advanced code that requires AS 3.0 capabilities or if you want to access the new tools that rely on AS 3.0 and Flash Player 10.

- **Flash File (ActionScript 2.0):** ActionScript 2.0 files created in Flash CS4 target Flash Player 10 by default, but these files can also be published to be backward-compatible with older versions of the Flash Player (as far back as Flash Player 6).

- **Flash File (Adobe AIR):** Create Flash files that target the Adobe AIR runtime framework. Adobe AIR enables you to use your HTML/Ajax, Flex, or Flash development skills to build and deploy cross-platform, rich Internet applications to the desktop.

- **Flash File (Mobile):** This option launches Adobe Device Central, which is a specialized authoring environment designed to support the development of Flash content for mobile devices. These files target the Flash Lite Player instead of the full Flash Player and are limited to a more simplified set of ActionScript (1.0 or 2.0, depending on the version of Flash Lite that is running on the target device).

CROSS-REF To learn more about Adobe Device Central and authoring content for Flash Lite, refer to Chapter 20, "Publishing Flash Movies."

The last four options in the Create New column of the Start Page enable you to launch a file for authoring or editing code in Flash without first creating a .fla:

- **ActionScript File:** Opens a file for authoring or editing ActionScript. File is saved with the .as extension.

- **ActionScript Communication File:** Opens a file for authoring or editing ActionScript for Flash Communication server. File is saved with the .ascs extension.

- **JavaScript File:** Opens a file for authoring or editing JavaScript for Flash. The file is saved with the .jsfl extension.

- **Flash Project:** Opens the new Flash Project panel to enable you to manage your Flash project files.

If you select the Advertising option listed under Create from Template in the Start Page (or use the application menu to select File ➪ New), you will see a secondary (New Document or New from Template) dialog box that has two different views: General and Templates. If you want to access some of the Flash document styles from Flash 8 that are no longer listed in the main Start Page, simply choose the General view and you can see an extended list of possible file types.

TIP The file Type list available in the General section of the New Document or New From Template dialog box is also a good way to browse the various file types because a preview and a description of each are available before you actually create and load a specific file.

Help menu options

The Flash CS3 Help panel has been replaced in CS4 with a quick-access menu of guided entry points to a vast array of online resources. The Flash Exchange is an online resource created to support use and development of Flash extensions. It is a great place to look for new tools, components, and effects that you can download and add to your Flash toolkit. The Flash Support Center is Adobe's primary vehicle for the distribution of up-to-date information about Flash and Flash-related topics. It is a searchable area with current (and archived) articles on many Flash topics. You can also find links to downloads, documentation, forums, and many other invaluable Flash-related resources and updates. Use Help ➪ Manage Extensions to load the control panel for managing installed Adobe extensions for Flash as well as other applications in the Creative suite.

The Flash CS4 interface on Macintosh and Windows

Before discussing the various Flash menu items, panels, and miscellaneous dialog boxes that you can use to control and customize your workspace, we begin with a look at the interface with its array of toolbars and panels as they appear on Macintosh and Windows with the Essentials workspace loaded. Use the Workspace menu at the top of the Document window to choose Essentials or the application menu to select Window ➪ Workspace ➪ Essentials if you want to load or reload this workspace.

The Flash authoring environment has been polished into a flexible system of panels that can be resized from any edge and docked individually or easily arranged into tabbed groups that can be expanded or collapsed as needed. The implementation of panels is consistent across products in the CS4 suite for both Mac and Windows. Throughout the book, we discuss each panel in context with the tools and tasks where it is used. As you'll quickly find, there are many ways to arrange these panels for a customized workflow. Your preferred panel layouts for different tasks can be saved as custom workspace layouts and recalled from the Workspace menu. To give you an idea of how workspaces support different workflows, Adobe has included a menu of ready-made workspaces arranged to suit specific types of production.

Figure 4.2 shows how the Essentials workspace (Window ➪ Workspace ➪ Essentials) looks on the Mac.

NOTE The Essentials workspace includes two tabbed panel groups that support commonly used features and reduce clutter: The timeline and the new Motion Editor are in a tabbed group that sits below the Document window, and a new vertical Properties panel with contextual sections for Position and Size, Properties, and Filters is grouped with the Library panel. The expanded Library panel also includes a pull-down menu for loading library content from different documents without having to manage multiple floating panels.

In addition to the Essentials, Developer, Designer, and Debug workspace layouts, Flash CS4 ships with a Classic preset that loads several of the panels as a group collapsed to icon view and docked with the new vertical Properties panel, as shown in Figure 4.3.

NOTE Although there are some minor differences between Macintosh and Windows interfaces for Flash CS4, these are due to differences in the operating systems that are apparent in any application. For the most part, however, we use Macintosh OS X and Windows XP illustrations interchangeably, pointing out differences only when they directly affect workflow.

NEW FEATURE The Tools panel can now be resized horizontally or vertically and it docks to any edge of the screen or with other panels.

TIP To prevent docking while you are moving panels, press the Control key while dragging.

For clarity, we have capitalized terms that refer to specific Flash interface features such as Document window, Stage, Timeline, Tools panel, and Options area. You may see these words lowercase in other parts of the text, where they are used as general terms rather than as labels for specific parts of the Flash interface.

FIGURE 4.2

The Essentials workspace for Flash CS4 as it appears on Macintosh OS X

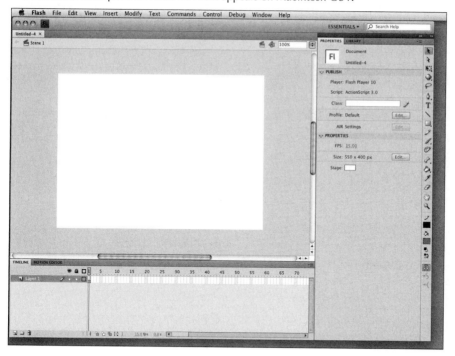

FIGURE 4.3

The icon view panel group that loads when you select Window ⇨ Workspace ⇨ Classic

We describe the actual uses and options for most of these various interface elements in the context of where the elements are applied. To get started with Flash, we introduce the Properties panel, Tools panel, Document window, Scene panel, Timeline, and Controller, along with the related menu items. We discuss the remainder of the panels and windows, and how they are used, in chapters on drawing, animation, interactivity, and other specific production topics.

> **NOTE** The Main toolbar is an optional feature available only on the Windows version of Flash. This toolbar gives you quick access to commonly used tool and panel options and it should not be confused with the Tools panel. The Controller and the Edit bar options found in the Window ⇨ Toolbars menu have the same function on Windows and Mac versions. The Controller is used to control the position of the playhead in the Timeline, and the Edit bar (which docks to the top of the Document window) includes controls for navigating scenes, editing symbols, and changing view settings.

> **CROSS-REF** We cover the use of the History panel in Chapter 9, "Modifying Graphics." We describe the Project panel in Chapter 3, "Planning Flash Projects."

What to expect from the Properties panel

The Properties panel is a centralized place to access most common options for various authoring items. The Properties panel in Flash CS4 has a new vertical orientation, and as you activate tools or select items in the Document window, relevant properties load into organized, collapsible sections within the panel. You can select or modify most options directly in the Properties panel, but for some items, buttons appear that you can use to launch additional menus or dialog boxes.

Depending on what is currently selected, the Properties panel displays relevant attributes for a document, frame, symbol instance, component instance, shape, or text box. Popup menus and editable value fields make it quick and easy to make changes without hunting through panel sets or the application menu. As shown in Figure 4.4, when an element is selected that can have code attached to it, a gray arrow appears on the right edge of the Properties panel. Clicking this icon launches the Actions panel for editing code on individual frames or symbol instances.

Generally, you will only need to access other panels for a few specialized editing tasks. Figure 4.4 shows how the Properties panel changes to display options relevant to the currently selected item.

The top figure shows the Properties panel, as it appears when the PolyStar tool is active (selected in the Tools panel) — displaying Stroke and Fill colors and options, buttons for launching Settings dialog boxes for line styles, and tool Options. The bottom figure shows the Properties panel (with collapsed sections) as it appears when a Button symbol instance is selected on the Stage — displaying instance properties and options.

Notice the Filters section (collapsed) at the bottom of the Properties panel when a symbol instance is selected. We explain the application of filters in later chapters. For now, all you need to know is that you can use the Filters section of the Properties panel to add and sort live filter effects.

FIGURE 4.4

The Properties panel, as it appears when the PolyStar tool is active (top), and when a Button symbol instance is selected (bottom)

Current tool icon and name

Panel group tabs

Collapse/Expand toggle
Panel options menu

Current tool (Polystar) properties and options

Current instance icon and name

Panel group tabs

Collapse/Expand toggle
Panel options menu
Launch Actions panel
Current symbol types

Current item (Button instance) properties and options

Because the Properties panel and the Tools panel provide access to all tool options (with the exception of some drawing and text attributes that are adjusted in the Preferences window), there are only four panels that you might need to open separately for additional options while drawing and editing graphics on the Stage. They are Color, for adding alpha, gradients, and custom colors; Align, for accurately arranging elements in relation to each other or to the Stage; Transform, for quickly making percentage-based scaling or rotation adjustments; and History, for tracking or changing your edits. You can optimize this simple setup even further by sorting panels into custom stacked or tabbed groups, as described in the next section.

Managing Windows and Panels

Most interface elements have built-in display controls (see Figure 4.5 for the tabbed panel controls that you will see on both Mac and Windows versions), but you can also manage what appears in your workspace with the main application menu. Rather than go through a laundry list of all the application menu options, we note the various features that apply to individual windows and panels as we describe their uses.

FIGURE 4.5

The controls we note here on the tabbed Mac Color and Swatches panel group are consistent with the control icons you will see on other panels for both Mac and Windows.

Gripper for docking/undocking
(and moving) panel group

Close button

Panel tabs

Expand/Collapse toggle

Drop-down options menu

Submenu for selecting
additional settings

Pop-up sliders
for setting values

Text field for displaying
and entering values

> **TIP** Double-click the topmost (dark gray) bar to collapse the panel group to icon view (or use the Expand/Collapse arrow toggle). Double-click the panel tabs to collapse the panel to a narrow tabbed text view.

Contextual menus

As in many other programs, you will find Flash contextual menus pop up in response to a right-click on a selected item in the Timeline, Library panel, or on the Stage. (Control+click for the Mac if you don't have a two-button mouse.) Contextual menus duplicate most functions and commands that are accessible either through the application menu or through the various panels and dialog boxes, which we discuss in this chapter. Because contextual menus show you only those options relevant to the element you have selected, they provide a handy authoring shortcut that can also help you get familiar with Flash.

Floating and docking panels

You can drag and drop individual panels to create vertical stacks or horizontal tabbed groups that maximize your workspace while keeping options handy. Figure 4.6 shows a tabbed panel group, a panel stack, and a free-floating panel.

FIGURE 4.6

Tabbed panel groups (left) are more space efficient than stacked (center) or individual floating panels (right).

Grouping panels for tabbed access is more space-efficient than just docking panels to the sides of your workspace or stacking panels vertically, but you will probably still want to stack some panels or panel groups to keep your workspace orderly. To group, dock, or stack panels, follow these steps:

1. **Grab the panel (or panel group) by clicking on the top gray bar of the panel.**

CAUTION Do not release the mouse until the panel is ready to dock!

2. **Drag the panel until it overlaps another open panel or panel group or until it is close to a side or to the bottom of your screen.** When Flash recognizes the panel overlap, a blue docking highlight appears at the top, bottom, or side of the panel that you want to dock to or along the side of your screen. Dragging your panel on top of another panel adds it as a tabbed group, and dragging your panel toward the bottom or top of another panel stacks it vertically. Dragging a panel to the side or bottom of your screen makes it "stick" there, so you'll have fewer floating panels cluttering your work space.

3. **Release the mouse, and the panel should remain docked or stacked.**

Unstacking or undocking panels is easy: Just click the top gray area (or tab) and drag to pull any panel away from the other panels in a stack or group and make it free floating.

Focus: Making panels or windows active

Prior to Flash 4, only one area of the application required users to pay attention to focus — when they were selecting colors for either the stroke or fill — because it was easy to confuse the two. As the interface has grown to include more panels and windows that can be active at different times within the Flash environment, focus has become an important aspect of the program. What is focus? *Focus* is a term used to describe which part of the application is active, or has priority, at a given time. For example, all panels, such as the Actions panel, do not automatically "have focus" — this means that you have to click within the panel to begin working there. Similarly, to return to the Document window or Stage to edit an element, you must click there to return focus to that aspect of the application. The Properties panel can actually remind you what area or element is active because it displays the attributes of the currently active item. Otherwise, if a panel or dialog box doesn't seem to respond, just remember to *focus* on what you're doing.

Creating custom workspace layouts

Whether you have chosen a layout from the Window menu (Window ➪ Workspace) or have just opened Flash with the default display, one of the first things you'll want to learn is how to customize the Flash environment to suit your workflow. Whether you're working on an 800-x-600 laptop screen, a 1024-x-768 dual-monitor setup, or a 1920-x-1200 LCD, panels give you the flexibility to create a layout that fits your screen real estate and production needs.

To save your current panel layout as a custom set that can be accessed from the Workspace menu the next time you open Flash, follow these simple steps:

1. **Open and arrange (by grouping or stacking) any panels that you want to include in your custom layout.**

2. **Go to Window ➪ Workspace ➪ New Workspace, or choose New Workspace from the Workspace drop-down menu at the top of the Document window.** A dialog box prompts you to name your layout.

3. **Enter a name that will help you remember why you made that panel set, such as** animation **or** scripting. Your custom layout now appears in the list of available workspaces in the drop-down menu (and in the application menu: Window ➪ Workspace).

Deleting or renaming workspaces is easy. Choose Manage Workspaces from the drop-down menu or select Window ➪ Workspace ➪ Manage Workspaces from the application menu to open the dialog box for editing the list of saved layouts. As shown in Figure 4.7, you have the option of renaming or deleting any of the custom files that appear in the Workspace list.

Do you really love your custom layout? You can save workspace layouts just as you would project files in order to share them with other people or take them with you when you upgrade to a newer version of Flash (or move to another machine). When you want to add them to your current version of Flash, just place the files in the Workspace Layouts folder and they'll appear in the menu, ready for you to use. The only limitation is that workspace layout files cannot be shared between the Mac and Windows versions of Flash.

FIGURE 4.7

The dialog box for managing saved workspace layouts makes it easy to delete or rename your custom layouts.

Workspace layouts are stored in a folder on your hard drive. After you find the Workspace folder, you can either add or delete any of these .xml files and the Workspace menu in Flash will update to show only the files that you currently have saved there.

- The standard directory path on Windows is

  ```
  C:\Documents and Settings\(username)\Local Settings\Application Data\
      Adobe\Flash CS4\(language)\Configuration\Workspace
  ```

- The standard directory path on Mac is

  ```
  HD\Users: (username)\Library: Application Support\Adobe\Flash CS4\
      (language)\Configuration\Workspace
  ```

Keyboard shortcuts

Keyboard shortcuts enable you to work more quickly because you avoid the hassle of clicking through a menu to activate a feature with your mouse. This is a workflow trick that many people use even when working in text-editing applications. Instead of browsing to the Edit menu to find the Copy command, you can just press the key combination Ctrl+C/⌘+C. We have included the default keyboard shortcuts for most tools and features as they are introduced by listing them in parentheses after the tool or menu item name. When key options are different on Mac and Windows, we list both. Thus the convention for showing the keyboard shortcut for Copy in both Windows and Mac would be Ctrl+C or ⌘+C.

A default set of keyboard shortcuts is available without having to change any settings, and these shortcuts are listed after most commands in the various application menus. However, if you want to use different shortcut keys for certain tasks or add a new shortcut key for a custom panel group or tool, you can make changes to the default settings in the Keyboard Shortcuts dialog box shown in Figure 4.8 (Edit ⇨ Keyboard Shortcuts, or in OS X go to Flash ⇨ Keyboard Shortcuts).

TIP By default, Flash CS4 uses the Adobe Standard set of built-in keyboard shortcuts, which is designed to be consistent on most applications in the Creative Suite. You can also select a built-in keyboard shortcut set from legacy versions of popular applications, including Flash 5, Illustrator 10, and Photoshop 6. Instead of manually changing a duplicate of the Adobe Standard set to match your favorite program, simply switch the Current Set using the menu list.

FIGURE 4.8

The Keyboard Shortcuts dialog box as displayed on Mac OS X. The appearance is slightly different on Windows, but the options available are the same.

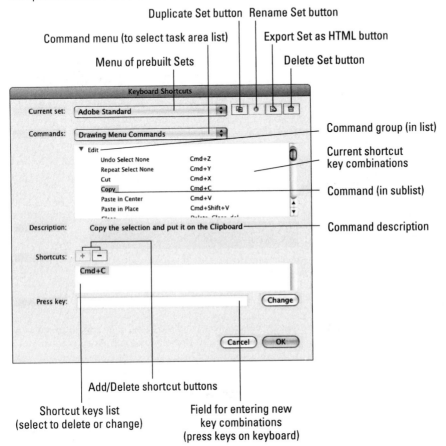

Duplicate Set button   Rename Set button

Command menu (to select task area list)   Export Set as HTML button

Menu of prebuilt Sets   Delete Set button

Command group (in list)

Current shortcut key combinations

Command (in sublist)

Command description

Add/Delete shortcut buttons

Shortcut keys list (select to delete or change)

Field for entering new key combinations (press keys on keyboard)

As shown in Figure 4.8, the Keyboard Shortcuts dialog box enables you to customize your Flash keyboard shortcuts to maintain consistency with other applications or to suit a personalized workflow. Not only can you choose keyboard shortcuts developed from other applications, but you can also save your modifications and custom settings. You can find the Keyboard Shortcuts dialog box in the application menu (Edit ⇨ Keyboard Shortcuts, or in OS X go to Flash ⇨ Keyboard Shortcuts). To create a new keyboard shortcut, you must first duplicate an existing set, from which you can then add or subtract existing shortcuts to form your custom set.

TIP The Export Set as HTML button in the Keyboard Shortcuts dialog box (shown in Figure 4.8) is a fantastic way to create a formatted table of shortcut keys that you can post near your desk or share with other people. This option enables you to name the file and choose a location to save it. Drag the saved HTML file into a browser window to see a nicely formatted reference table that you can read on-screen or print out.

NOTE Like workspace layout files, Keyboard Shortcut sets are stored on your hard drive. You can find them in the `Keyboard Shortcuts` folder in the same Configuration folder that we listed in the previous section for workspace layouts. You can navigate to this location on your hard drive and copy, back up, restore, delete, or otherwise manipulate any of these files from this folder. Keyboard shortcuts are transferable between machines, although we have had no success transferring them across platforms.

The Tools Panel

The vertical bar that appears docked on the right side of the interface in the Flash CS4 Essentials workspace is referred to as the Tools panel (see Figure 4.9). If you haven't just installed Flash, or if someone else has changed the defaults in Flash, you may not see the Tools panel on your screen. You can find it in the main Window menu (Window ➪ Tools) or open it with shortcut keys (Ctrl+F2/⌘+F2).

FIGURE 4.9

The Mac Tools panel is shown here in long view with the keyboard shortcuts for each tool. Aside from system display characteristics and docking behavior, the Tools panel is identical on both Mac and Windows.

Tite bar (drag to move Tools panel) — Display mode toggle
— Select arrow [V]
Subselection [A] —
Free transform [Q]/
3D Rotation [W]/ Gradient Transform [F]
3D Translation [G] —
Lasso (select) [L]
Pen [P] —
Text [T]
Line [N] —
Rectangle [R]/
Pencil [Y] — Oval [O]/Polystar
Brush/Spray Brush [B]
Deco tool [U] —
Paint Bucket [K]/ Bone tool [X]/Bind tool [Z]
Ink Bottle [S] —
Eyedropper (select) [I]
Eraser [E] —
Hand (grabber) [H]
Zoom (magnifier) [M] —
— Current Stroke Color chip
Current Fill Color chip —
Black and white — Swap Color (reverse
Options: Fill and Stroke)
modifiers available
for selected tool

Controlling the Tools panel

The Tools panel can now be scaled and collapsed just like any other panel in Flash CS4. As you scale the panel, the tool icons reflow to fit in one long column or in a horizontal row or a combination of the two. It can also be hidden (and unhidden) along with other panels by choosing Window ➪ Hide Panels or by pressing the F4 key, or it can be opened and closed independently by choosing Window ➪ Tools (Ctrl+F2/⌘+F2).

NOTE If you're using a Windows machine, don't confuse Tools with the menu item for Toolbars, which refers to a set of optional menus we describe in the section "The Flash CS4 interface on Macintosh and Windows" earlier in this chapter.

TIP To drag the Tools panel to the edge of the program window, yet prevent it from docking, press the Ctrl key while dragging.

If you would rather not see the tooltips that appear when pointing to tool icons in the Tools panel, you can turn them off in your General Preferences. (In OS X, go to Flash ➪ Preferences ➪ General; in Windows, go to Edit ➪ Preferences ➪ General, and under Selection options, uncheck Show tooltips.)

Reading the Tools panel

The Tools panel contains all 23 Flash tools, including 6 new Flash CS4 tools (see Figure 4.10 in the next section for tool icons and shortcut keys), as follows from left to right and top to bottom: Selection (arrow), Subselection, Free Transform (with Gradient Transform in the submenu), 3D Rotation (with 3D Translation in the submenu), Lasso, Pen, Text, Line, Rectangle (with other shape tools in the submenu), Pencil, Brush (with Spray Brush in submenu), Paint Bucket (with Ink Bottle in submenu), Eyedropper, and Eraser. The Flash View tools: The Hand and Zoom are below the drawing tools. Beneath the View tools is the Color area, with swatches for assigning Stroke color and Fill color, and buttons for Black and White and Swap Color (to reverse stroke and fill colors). The last section of the Tools panel is the Options area, where some of the available tool modifiers appear for any active tool.

CROSS-REF We explain the application of individual tools and options in the Tools panel in the chapters related to specific production topics that make up the remainder of Part II, "Mastering the Flash Environment."

Using Tool options

Depending on the tool selected, the Options area may display some of the options, or properties, that control the functionality of that particular tool, whereas other controls may appear in the Properties panel or in a panel that launches separately. Of the options located in the Options area, some appear as submenus with multiple options, while others are simple buttons that toggle a property on or off. (For example, if the Lasso tool is selected, the Magic Wand option can be turned on or off by clicking a toggle button in the Options area.) If an option has more than two settings, these are generally available in a submenu.

Many of the options that appear within the Options area of the Tools panel can also be accessed from the Properties panel, from the application menu, or with keyboard shortcuts.

Customizing the Tools panel

Because the Tools panel is the most convenient place to store and access drawing tools, Adobe has provided a user-friendly interface that makes it possible to add, delete, or rearrange the tools (and icons) that appear in the Tools panel. Open the dialog box shown in Figure 4.10 by choosing Edit ➪ Customize Tools Panel (or Flash ➪ Customize Tools Panel on a Mac) from the application menu. A preview of the Tools panel (in short view) on the left side of the dialog box makes it easy to select any of the squares to add or delete the tools that are stored in each section of the panel. The interface is very flexible, making it possible to put all your tools in one square if you want to, or even add the same tool to multiple squares — unless you enjoy changing things just for the sake of changing them, the main reason to use this option is really to add new tools.

FIGURE 4.10

Use the Customize Tools Panel dialog box to add or rearrange the tools available in the Tools panel.

Any tool square that has more than one tool stored in it displays a small black arrow below the currently active tool to indicate that a drop-down menu is available. By default, the tool icons appear in the drop-down list in the order that they are added to the Current selection list in the Customize Tools Panel dialog box. The first tool added to the list shows up in its assigned square in the Tools panel unless one of the other tools in the same square is selected from the drop-down menu. The most recently selected tool in any square is visible until Flash is restarted or another tool is selected from the same square.

All assigned tool shortcut keys remain mapped to individual tools and can be used to activate a specific tool regardless of which square the tool is stored in. If all the tools are removed from a square, that space on the Tools panel is left blank. Thanks to the Restore Default button in the Customize Tools Panel dialog box, you can have fun moving, grouping, or even deleting tools from different tool squares with the knowledge that you can always go back to the original layout. To illustrate the steps for adding a new Flash tool and storing it in the Tools panel, we have included a brief tutorial on a custom Grid tool developed by Joey Lott.

Adding New Tools to Flash, by Joey Lott

Authors' Note: Although it is beyond the scope of this book to describe the steps involved in actually scripting your own custom tools for Flash, we can tell you how to use custom tools that other developers have made. Joey Lott has generously agreed to let us include the code for one of his Flash tools on the CD-ROM. This brief tutorial is adapted from Joey's notes on how to install and use his "Grid" tool. We hope you will be able to follow these same steps to use other custom tools available from Adobe or from generous developers in the Flash community.

The first step to using a custom tool is to find the files that Flash needs to make the tool work in the authoring environment and the icon that will be visible in the Tools panel. Unless you happen to know some brainy coders, the best place to

look for new custom tools is in the Flash Exchange area of Adobe's site (www.
adobe.com/exchange).

The three files you will want to find and download are as follows:

- An XML file that describes the functionality of the tool and controls any
  "settings" that can be used to modify the final result

- A JavaScript-Flash file (.jsfl) that implements required methods for manipulating the Flash authoring tool based on parameters specified by the XML file

- A .png file that will appear in the Tools panel as the icon for the custom tool

 We have included `Grid.xml`, `Grid.jsfl`, and `Grid.png` on the CD-ROM in the
CustomTool subfolder of the `ch04` **folder.**

You have to save these files in your Flash CS4 Tools folder so that the tool can
be applied in the authoring environment.

- The standard directory path on Windows is

```
C:\Documents and Settings\(username)\Local Settings\Application Data\
    Adobe\Flash CS4\(language)\Configuration\Tools
```

- The standard directory path on Mac is

```
HD\Users: (username)\Library\Application Support\Adobe\Flash CS4\
    (language)\Configuration\Tools
```

After the three files for the Grid tool are saved to the Tools folder, the Grid tool
is added to the list of available tools in the Customize Tools Panel dialog box.

The steps for adding the Grid tool icon to a square on the Tools panel are the
same as those used to assign any other tool to a specific location in the panel:

1. Open the Customize Tools Panel dialog box (Edit ⇨ Customize Tools
Panel or Flash ⇨ Customize Tools Panel).

2. Select a location square on the Tools panel preview on the left side of the
dialog box, select the Grid Tool from the list of Available tools, and click
the Add button. (As shown in Figure 4.11, we chose to add the Grid Tool
to the Line Tool square.)

3. Click OK to apply your changes and close the dialog box.

Now that the Grid tool icon has been added to the Tools panel, you will be able
to select it from the square that you chose to store it in. As with the PolyStar tool,
you will notice that when the Grid tool is active, an Options button appears in
the Properties panel. Use this button to launch the Tool Settings dialog box
(shown in Figure 4.12) where it is possible to control the number of rows and
columns that you want to draw with the Grid tool.

FIGURE 4.11

Any tool added to the Tools folder — by saving the relevant .xml, .jsfl, and .png files there — appears in the Available tools list in the Customize Tools Panel dialog box.

After you choose settings for the grid and click OK to close the dialog box, you can draw a grid as easily as you would draw a rectangle with the Rectangle tool: Click the Stage and drag horizontally to create width and vertically to create height; the live preview lets you see how the grid looks before you release the mouse. You can select individual lines in the final vector grid, modify them with other drawing tools, group the lines, or convert them into a reusable symbol. This is a simple tool, but it creates perfect grids every time and saves you time and mouse miles, too!

Let's hope there will be many more useful and creative tools available that will open new possibilities for your Flash designs. You can continue to save other custom tool files to your Tools folder, and they will be added to the Available tools list in the Customize Tools Panel dialog box.

FIGURE 4.12

After they have been added to the Tools panel, custom tools and options can be used as easily as other standard Flash tools.

CAUTION Obviously, it would be a big mistake to save a custom tool file to your Tools folder if it had the same name as an existing tool. Unless you want to overwrite existing Flash tools, make sure you're using unique names for any custom tools that you add. If you'd rather not change the name of a tool, simply add a unique number to the tool name to avoid overwriting other files with the same name.

You can remove tool icons from the Tools panel at any time without actually deleting the files stored in the Tools folder, but if you decide you don't need a tool anymore, or if your Available tools list gets too cluttered, simply remove the relevant .xml, .jsfl, and .png files from the Tools folder (save them somewhere else if you liked the tool, trash them if you didn't).

The Document Window

The Document window is the worktable of your Flash project. This window tells you what document (.fla) is currently active and shows you where you are working in the project. When you open or create a new Flash file, a new Document window appears on the screen. You can have multiple files open simultaneously — click to move from one Document window to another. You have the option of choosing a document type from the Start Page (discussed earlier in this chapter; shown in Figure 4.1) or from the New Document dialog box invoked by the New File command: File ➪ New (Ctrl+N/⌘+N).

TIP If you prefer to bypass the New Document dialog box, you can create and open a basic Flash document in one step (by default this will be set to use ActionScript 3.0), by using the shortcut command Alt+Ctrl+N/Option+⌘+N).

Figure 4.13 shows the New Document dialog box for Flash CS4. The dialog box includes a General tab for opening Flash documents and a Templates tab for opening Flash documents that match common Web ad sizes.

FIGURE 4.13

Use the New Document dialog box in Flash CS4 to create new documents or open template files.

In addition to the basic Flash File (.fla) types targeting different versions of the Flash Player, the General tab includes several specialized file types which give developers more options for application development and script editing.

CROSS-REF Advanced authoring with Flash JavaScript and Flash form applications is beyond the scope of this book, but if you want to take your Flash development to the next level, there are books available on this topic.

Controlling the Document window

Even when you choose to hide all panels (F4), the Document window remains visible; closing the window closes your Flash project. On Mac, the Document window is always free-floating and can be moved anywhere on-screen by grabbing the top of the panel with your mouse, or scaled by dragging any side of the panel. By default, on Windows, the Document window is maximized to fill the workspace and it cannot be scaled or moved independently, unless you first click the document Restore Down button (between the Minimize button and the Close button) in the top right corner of the window (below the larger buttons that control the application). This "frees" the Document window from other panels in the program window so that you can move it around and scale it.

Flash CS4 optimizes screen real estate and makes it easier to work with multiple documents by automatically grouping open Document windows into the same tabbed format used for panels. As you create new documents or open existing documents during a session in Flash, they are added as sequential tabs along the top of the Document window. Click any tab to switch to a specific document, click and drag a tab to move it to a new position in the tab order, and click the small "x" icon to close a document.

TIP If you need to see two tabbed Document windows side by side (to facilitate dragging items from one file to another or to compare two files), use the `Duplicate Window` command (Window ➪ Duplicate Window) to make a clone of an original document. Any changes made in the cloned window also apply to the original file that is still available in the tabbed main Document window. Duplicate Document windows are indicated by a colon after the name followed by a number (a duplicate of `myFile` would be labeled `myFile:2`, then `myFile:3`, and so on), but these numbers do not affect the saved file name. To make things less confusing, you can close the tabbed version of the document and keep the free-floating clone as your working version. Take note of the shortcut keys for this command if you use it often: Alt+Ctrl+K/Option+⌘+K.

The main reason you may want to alter the default placement of the Document window is to organize your panel layouts to suit a dual-monitor workstation. Although you can drastically change the size and location of the Document window, generally you will want it centered in your workspace and scaled to allow you to comfortably work with objects on the Stage. Figure 4.14 shows the Document window on Mac as it appears with default settings and with the Document Properties dialog box open.

NEW FEATURE The Metadata fields that were in the Document Properties dialog box in Flash CS3 have been replaced with a new, more comprehensive metadata dialog box in Flash CS4. Available in Publish Settings — select the Flash category and then click the File Info button in the SWF Settings section. Title and description information entered in Publish Settings will be embedded in the published .swf file as metadata that will help search engines to find and catalog your Flash content. Unfortunately, this information is not automatically carried over to the .html file published from Flash.

The default document settings of Flash automatically create new documents with a size of 550 x 400 pixels, a white background color, and a frame rate of 24. All these attributes are displayed in the Properties panel and can be changed at any time. Clicking the Edit button in the Properties section of the Properties panel launches the Document Properties dialog box where you can enter a custom size or use the Match options to automatically create a document that fits your current printer page settings (Printer), include all the elements you have placed into your document (Contents), or restore the default size setting (Default).

> **TIP**
>
> If you want to change the default settings for all new documents, open the Document Properties panel by clicking the Edit button on the Properties panel or choosing Modify ➪ Document (Ctrl+J/⌘+J) from the application menu. After you have chosen the attributes you would like to assign to new documents, click the Make Default button at the bottom of the panel.

FIGURE 4.14

The Document window as it appears with the Document Properties dialog box open

Reading the Document window

The white Stage area is the central part of the Document window that becomes the visible area or "screen" of a published Flash movie (.swf). As we noted earlier, you can change the color and size of this "background" at any time, but it is best to establish these settings before you begin creating other elements.

The light gray work area (also called the *Pasteboard*) that frames the Stage enables you to place elements into your project while keeping them out of the visible area. This feature is useful if you want to show only part of an element or animate it as it moves onto the Stage. A good example of the utility of the Pasteboard feature can be seen in some cartoons in which very large background artwork hangs off the Stage (or View area) until it's called upon or tweened through to create the effect of a camera pan. The Stage and the Pasteboard are always available in the Document window (unless you toggle the Pasteboard off in the View menu). The Essentials panel layout also includes the Timeline docked below the Pasteboard because this is generally the most convenient place to use it, along with the new Motion Editor.

TIP   You can strip the Timeline panel out of the Document window and leave it free-floating, or you can redock it to the top or bottom of the Pasteboard. You can also dock the Timeline to either side of the Pasteboard, but this is usually an awkward view.

The narrow bar located above the Stage and Pasteboard is referred to as the Edit bar (shown earlier in context in Figure 4.14). This bar contains icons and a value box that help you navigate within a document.

Stage view control

Although the scale value box is at the end of the bar, we discuss it first because it can be useful even when you first begin putting artwork on the Stage. This value box, called the Stage View control, shows you the current scale of the Stage area and enables you to type new percentages or select a preset value from a submenu.

NOTE   The view percentages are based on the pixel dimensions of your project, as defined in Document properties, and your screen resolution. For example, if your project size is 500 x 400 pixels and your screen resolution is 1024 x 768, then the Stage area would occupy almost 50 percent of your screen if view scale was set to 100 percent (Ctrl+1/⌘+1).

The first three settings in the View submenu list are Fit in Window, Show Frame (Ctrl+2/ ⌘+2), and Show All (Ctrl+3/⌘+3); these settings automatically scale your Stage view to fit your current Document window size in various ways:

- Fit in Window scales the Stage view to fill the current Document window without cropping the visible area.
- Show Frame scales the Stage view to fill the current Document window with a narrow border of Pasteboard visible on all sides.
- Show All sets the Stage view to a scale that includes any elements you have placed on the Pasteboard outside the Stage. You can find these same view options from the application menu (View ⇨ Magnification).

There are two additional tools available in the Tools panel (see Figure 4.9 earlier in the chapter), which also control your view of the Stage and Pasteboard within the Document window:

The Hand tool (H) allows you to move the Stage area within the Document window by "grabbing" it (clicking and dragging). Double-clicking the Hand icon in the Tools panel quickly gives you the same Stage view as choosing the menu item Show Frame.

TIP   To toggle the Hand tool on while using any other tool, without interrupting your selection, hold down the spacebar.

The Zoom tool, or magnifier (M), does just what the name implies: It adjusts the scale of your Stage view. The available magnification range is between 8 percent and 2,000 percent. However, you can apply this handy tool in a few ways. With the Zoom tool active, clicking consecutively on the Stage pulls in closer to artwork with the *Enlarge* option (Ctrl+[+]/⌘+[+]), or moves farther away with the *Reduce* option (Ctrl+[−]/⌘+[−] key). Each click adjusts the Stage view magnification by half. Pressing the Option or Alt key as you click toggles the Zoom tool between Enlarge and Reduce. Double-clicking the Zoom tool icon in the Tools panel always scales the Stage view to 100 percent (Ctrl+1/⌘+1). One last way of applying the Zoom tool while it is active in the Tools panel is to drag a selection box around the area that you want to fill the Document window. Flash scales the Stage view to the highest magnification (up to 2,000 percent), which fills the Document window with the selected area.

Edit options

Now back to the other icons on the Edit bar. The location label on the top left edge of the window shows you the current scene and what part of the project you are editing. The sequence of labels that appear in this area are sometimes referred to as *breadcrumbs* because these labels show the steps, or the path, leading back to the Main Timeline from the location you're editing. When in Edit mode, you can use these sequential labels to step your way back to the Main Timeline of the current scene, or click the arrow in front of the labels to return to the Main Timeline of the first scene in your project. To the right is the Edit Scene icon, and at the far right is the Edit Symbols icon. Click these icons to access menus of scenes or symbols in the current document that can be opened and edited within the Document window.

Using scenes

The Scene panel (Shift+F2 or Window ➪ Other panels ➪ Scene) enables you to add, name, and sequence scenes. By default, when your Flash movie (.swf) is published, the scenes play in the order in which they are listed, as shown in Figure 4.15. Scenes can help to organize a Flash project into logical, manageable parts. However, with the increasingly robust power of ActionScript, there's been a trend among many developers to move away from scene-based architecture. Using individual Flash movies instead of scenes to organize sections of a project results in files that download more efficiently and that are easier to edit due to their modular organization. It's like the difference between one huge ball of all-purpose twine that's the size of a house, and a large drawer filled with manageable spools, sorted neatly according to color and weight.

Dividing logical project parts into separate documents also facilitates efficiency in team environments, where developers can be working on different pieces of a project simultaneously. Scenes can still be useful for organizing certain types of projects, such as simple presentations without a lot of graphics, or for animators who prefer to organize a cartoon in one file before handing it off for integration into a larger site structure.

Adding named anchor keyframes is another useful option for linear Flash presentations. These enable Forward and Back buttons in a Web browser to jump from frame to frame or scene to scene to navigate a Flash movie.

 You turn the option of making the first keyframe in a new scene a named anchor keyframe on or off in the Timeline section of the General Preferences panel (Ctrl+U/⌘+U).

CAUTION   Named anchors work well on Windows browsers but almost always fail on Mac browsers, so this is not a reliable option for Web navigation within a Flash movie if you expect some visitors to your site to be using Mac systems.

FIGURE 4.15

The Scene panel showing document scenes in the order they will play back by default

Scene list (default
playback order will be
from top to bottom)

Selection show current scene

Delete Scene button

Duplicate Scene button

Add Scence button

To navigate and modify scenes from within the Document window:

■ Click the Edit Scene button on the Edit bar and then choose the desired scene from the submenu.

■ Navigate to a specific scene from the application menu with the View ⇨ Go To command.

■ To add a new scene, either use the Scene panel's Add button — indicated by the page icon — or, from the Insert menu, use Insert ⇨ Scene. New scenes continue in the same auto-numbering sequence started with Scene 1. Thus, even if you delete Scene 2, the next added scene will be named Scene 3.

■ Use the Duplicate button on the Scene panel to make a copy of a scene, including all content on the scene's Timeline.

■ To delete a scene, use the Scene panel's Delete button — indicated by the trash can icon. (To bypass the alert asking if you want to delete the scene, use Ctrl+click/ ⌘+click.)

■ To rename a scene, simply double-click the scene name within the Scene panel and type a new name. Using numbers in scene names does not affect playback order; the scenes play from the top to the bottom of the list.

■ To rearrange scene order, simply click and drag a scene to alter its position in the Scene panel list. You can use actions to direct the movie to access scenes outside the default linear order. For more about actions, refer to Chapter 17, "Understanding Actions and Event Handlers."

CAUTION Although scenes give you the visual impression of having a whole new timeline to work on, they are really continuations of the Main Timeline that begins in the first scene of your document. If you're using any actions to control your movie playback, it's important to avoid duplicate naming on frame labels or named anchors. Thus, even if it seems logical, it isn't a good idea to label the beginning of each new scene "intro" because you won't be able to differentiate these labels as easily for targeting with ActionScript.

Using Document window menu options

There are several options available from the application menu that control display or editing in the Document window. These can be helpful when you're creating or placing elements on the Stage. All of these can be accessed from View on the application menu (notice the shortcut key combinations listed after most commands). The basic functions of these various commands are as follows:

- **Goto:** Leads to a submenu of scenes in the current movie, including four handy shortcuts to the First, Previous, Next, and Last scenes. This menu is also available from the Edit scene icon on the Edit bar in the Document window.

- **Zoom In:** Increases the scale of the Stage view by 50 percent.

- **Zoom Out:** Decreases the scale of the Stage view by 50 percent.

- **Magnification:** Leads to the same view options that are available in the Stage View Control on the top right of the Document window. Note that three of these options also have corresponding keyboard shortcuts.

- **Preview Mode:** Leads to a menu of various settings for rendering and displaying content in the authoring environment:

  - **Outlines:** Simplifies the view of elements on the Stage by showing all shapes as outlines, and all lines as thin lines. This option is helpful when reshaping graphic elements. It also speeds up the display of complex scenes and can assist in getting the general timing and sense of a movie. It is a global equivalent of the outline options available in the Timeline window for layers and frames.

  - **Fast:** Turns off both anti-aliasing and dithering to speed up the display. The default is *off*, to create the most accurate screen image, and it is only recommended that you turn this option *on* if you need to reduce demand on your processor.

  - **Antialias:** Dithers the edges of shapes and lines so that they look smoother on-screen. It can also slow the display, but this is only an issue with older video cards. This is actually a toggle in opposition with the Fast command: Turn this On and Fast goes Off.

  - **Antialias Text:** As with Antialias, this is also a toggle in opposition to the Fast command. It smoothes the edges of text *only* and is most noticeable on large font sizes. You can have only one Antialias option on at a time, so you can make a choice between smoothing text or smoothing shapes, depending on what content you're working with.

  - **Full:** Use this option for the most "finished" or high-definition preview. If you are working on intensive animation, it may slow down rendering of the display in the authoring environment.

- **Pasteboard:** Makes the light gray area that surrounds the Stage available for use. When the Pasteboard is visible, your Stage area appears centered in the Document window when you apply Show Frame or Show All. If the Pasteboard has been turned off in the View menu, then the Stage aligns to the top left of the Document window.

CAUTION Items that are selected and offstage when View ⇨ Pasteboard is toggled off can still be deleted, even if they are not visible. So it's best if you don't have anything selected when you choose to hide the Pasteboard.

- **Rulers:** Toggles the reference Rulers (which appear at the top and left edges of the work area) on or off — use Modify ⇨ Document (Ctrl+J/⌘+J) to change units of measurement. Rulers are a helpful reference for placing guides to align elements in a layout.

- **Grid:** Toggles visibility of the background Stage grid on or off. This grid does not export with the final Flash movie (.swf), but it does serve as an authoring reference. You can control the appearance of the Grid and the precision of grid snapping by adjusting the settings in the dialog box invoked with the Edit Grid command. When the Snap to grid option is active, it works even if the Grid is not visible. Edited Grid settings can be saved as the default by clicking the Save Default button, which enables you to have these settings as presets for all subsequent Flash movies.

NOTE The default Grid size of 18 pixels is equal to 0.25 inch. Grid units can be changed by entering the appropriate abbreviation for other units of measurement (for example: 25 pt, 0.5", 0.5 in, 2 cm, and so on) in the Grid Spacing entry boxes. Although the specified units *will* be applied to the grid, they will be translated into the current unit of measurement for the Ruler. Thus, if the Ruler is set to pixels, and the Grid units are changed to 0.5 in, then, on reopening the Grid dialog box, the Grid units will be displayed as 36 pix (because pixels are allocated at 72 pix = 1"). Changing Ruler units via Modify ⇨ Document also changes Grid units.

- **Guides:** When rulers are turned on, you can drag horizontal or vertical guides onto the Stage from respective rulers. These four commands control the parameters of these guides:

  - **Show Guides:** This is a simple toggle to either show or hide guides that you have dragged out from the rulers.

  - **Lock Guides:** This is a toggle that either locks or unlocks all current guides. This is useful to prevent guides from accidentally being moved after you have placed them.

  - **Edit Guides:** This command opens the Guides dialog box, where guide color and guide-specific snap accuracy can be adjusted. Also included are check boxes for the other three guide commands: Show Guides, Snap to Guides, and Lock Guides. This enables you to establish guide settings and then click the Save Default button to have these settings as presets for all subsequent Flash movies. To delete all guides from the Stage, press the Clear All button.

  - **Clear All:** The Clear All command gets rid of all visible guides in the current document. It does the same thing as the Clear All button in the Edit Guides dialog box.

- **Snapping:** Leads to a menu of various options for controlling snapping behavior in the authoring environment.

NOTE When Snap to Pixels is turned on, a 1-pixel grid appears when the Stage view is magnified to 400 percent or higher. This grid is independent of the Show Grid command.

- **Hide Edges:** Hides selection patterns so that you can edit items without the visual noise of the selection pixel "highlight." This applies only to currently selected items and allows a clean view without having to lose your selection. Most useful for seeing colors or fine lines that may appear visually distorted by the selection pattern.

- **Show Shape Hints:** This toggles shape hints to make them visible or invisible. It does not disable shape hinting. Shape hints are used when tweening shapes.

CROSS-REF For more about Shape tweens (or shape morphing) refer to Chapter 11, "Timeline Animation and the Motion Editor."

■ **Show Tab Order:** This is a toggle to turn on or off numbers that will mark the tab order set in the Accessibility panel for elements in the authoring environment.

Working with Flash templates

The library of predefined Flash documents available in the Templates tab of the New Document dialog box (or in the Create from Template list of the Start Page) has been modified since Flash CS3. The templates now consist of only a series of Flash documents sized to match common Web ad aspect ratios. The more comprehensive list of templates available in Flash CS3 has not been carried over to CS4.

To work with a Flash template, open it as you would any other Flash document. You can then add your own content to the Stage or modify the Timeline and save the finished document with a new name.

You can also create your own reusable template from any Flash document by choosing File ➪ Save As Template. Before the template is saved, you are given options for naming and assigning a category and description, making it easy to manage a whole library of custom templates. The preview visible for each template is actually just the content on the first frame of the template document. In some cases, this does not provide much visual information for how the template might be used. If you use templates often or if you create your own templates, you may find it helpful to modify the default previews to make them more informative.

TIP Although each template type has a different file structure and may contain different content, the preview for any template will include only the visible content in the Stage area on the first frame of the template file. Changing the content in the first frame of a template file also changes the preview for that template.

TIP The standard directory path for the Templates folder on Windows is

```
C:\Program Files\Adobe\Flash CS4\(language)\Configuration\
   Templates
```

The standard directory path on Mac is

```
HD/Applications/Adobe Flash CS4/(language)/Configuration/
   Templates
```

 WEB RESOURCE If you are interested in creating custom template previews, visit www.flashsupport. com/archive **to find Bill Perry's tutorial and example files from** *Flash MX 2004 Bible* **(Wiley, 2004).**

The Timeline Window

The Timeline is like nothing you will find in your analog studio, unless you have a time machine that enables you to move forward and backward in time and up and down between dimensions. This may seem like a rather far-fetched analogy, but understanding the behavior and purpose of a timeline is often the most foreign new concept to grasp if you have not worked in other time-based applications (such as Macromedia Director). A clear understanding of timelines is critical to production in Flash. Even if you know how to use all of your other tools, not knowing the Timeline makes working in Flash like trying to work in a studio with no light.

NOTE Flash MX Professional 2004 introduced an alternative to the Timeline authoring structure with form-based templates for application authoring. For more information on this feature, search Flash Help for "Slide screens and form screens."

The Timeline window is really composed of two parts: the Layer section, where content is "stacked" in depth; and the Timeline/Frames section, where content is planned out in frames along the duration of your movie, like on a strip of motion picture film. In the Layer section, you can label or organize your "stacks" of frame rows. You can also lock or hide individual layers or just convert their display to colored outlines on the Stage while you are editing. In the Timeline section you can control where and for how long content is visible and how it changes over time to animate when the movie plays back. You can also add actions to control how the playhead moves through the Timeline, making it start and stop or jump to a specific frame.

CROSS-REF You can find more on controlling the timeline for specific animation techniques in Chapter 11, "Timeline Animation and the Motion Editor." Actions are introduced in Part V, "Adding Basic Interactivity to Flash Movies."

Controlling the Timeline window

On both Mac and Windows, the most common position for the Timeline in Flash CS4 is docked below the Document window. If you don't see the Timeline when you open Flash, go to Window ⇨ Timeline (Ctrl+Alt+T/⌘+Option+T) to open it on-screen.

TIP Double-clicking the Timeline tab expands or collapses it faster than using the application menu to open and close it completely. This feature also makes it easy to collapse the Timeline window so that it doesn't take up screen space, while still leaving it available to expand again when you need it.

You can always adjust the position, size, and shape of the Timeline to suit your workflow. You can dock the Timeline to any edge of the Document window, or group it with other panels. You can also move it anywhere as a floating window, even exile it to a second monitor — leaving the Document window all for the Stage and Pasteboard.

- Move the Timeline by clicking and dragging the title bar at the top of the window. If the Timeline is docked, click the Timeline name tab and drag to undock the Timeline and reposition it.

- If it's undocked, resize the Timeline by dragging any edge. If it's docked, drag the bar at the top of the Timeline that separates the layers from the Stage area, either up or down.

- To resize the layer area for name and icon controls (to accommodate longer layer names or to apportion more of the view to frames), click and drag the bar that separates the layer name and icon controls from the Timeline frame area.

Using the Timeline Controller toolbar

The Controller (Window ⇨ Toolbars ⇨ Controller) is a small bar of buttons that provides basic control of the playhead. Access to the Controller can be helpful if you need to pan back and forth along an extended section of the Timeline. You can keep it on-screen as a floating bar, or dock it anywhere along the top or bottom of the Document window. Some developers prefer using the Controller to using shortcut keys for moving the playhead. Along with the commands available on the Controller bar, the application Control menu also lists some more advanced options, which we discuss in following chapters as they relate to animation and actions.

CAUTION   **Playback speed within the document (.fla) is not as accurate as it is in the movie file (.swf), so the Controller is not intended as a replacement for the Test Movie command (Control ⇨ Test Movie or Ctrl+Enter/⌘+Return).**

As you can see in Figure 4.16, the buttons on the Controller will be familiar to anyone who has used a remote control. The only special function to note is that the Play button toggles to start and stop; you don't have to use the Stop button.

TIP   **Using shortcut keys is often the preferred way to move along the Timeline. On both Windows and Mac, pressing Enter/Return works as a toggle to start and stop the playhead. If you prefer to move along the Timeline frame by frame, pressing the period key (.) moves forward one frame and pressing the comma (,) moves back one frame. A more intuitive way to remember these keys is to look for the less than (<) and greater than (>) symbols and to think of them as arrows that move forward and backward.**

FIGURE 4.16

The Controller showing callouts for the buttons as they are used to control movement of the playhead

Reading the Timeline

The Timeline graphically orders Flash content across two dimensions — time and depth — and provides you with some options for how this content is displayed on the Stage and within frames on the Timeline.

Visual display of time

The order of time is displayed by the sequence of frames arranged horizontally, from left to right, as they appear within the duration of your project. Thus, if your movie is set to 20 frames per second, frame 40 occurs at the 2-second point of your animation.

NOTE   **Although they say that time and space are without limits, the Flash authoring environment supports about 32,000 frames, and the .swf format officially supports only around 16,000, which is actually so long that you might never find your way from one end of the Timeline to the other. Organizing your work with scenes and Movie clips, or even in multiple documents, should save you from ever having to use a Timeline even a tenth of this length.**

WEB RESOURCE   **For more details on the limits of Flash, refer to the Adobe Tech Note Index:** www.adobe.com/cfusion/knowledgebase/index.cfm?id=tn_14437

You can insert, delete, copy, paste, and reorder frames as well as convert them to various specific frame types that control how elements animate. Current frame settings display in the Properties panel when a frame is selected, and you can also add/change a frame name or tween type here. The main controls for editing frames are found in the contextual menu (right-click on Windows or Control+click on Mac) or from the Timeline submenus under Edit, Insert, and Modify in the application menu.

As you work with frames, you'll find shortcut keys invaluable. These shortcut keys are listed in the application menu following most commands.

Visual display of depth

The Timeline layers enable you to separate content onto individual "transparent" work surfaces within the Document window. This enables you to animate or edit elements individually even if they occupy the same Timeline (or frame) space as other elements in the document. These layers are arranged vertically, holding content that stacks in the Document window from bottom to top. They enable you to organize content, actions, comments, labels, and sounds so that you can quickly find the parts of the project that you want to edit.

TIP Layer folders are a huge help to organizing multilayered documents. With layers moved inside a folder, they can be opened up for editing or hidden away (collapsed) to reduce the number of layers you have to navigate.

You can insert, delete, move, or rename layers and folders, as well as adjust how content is displayed in the editing environment. Items placed on layers higher in the layer stack can visually obscure other items in layers beneath them, without otherwise affecting each other. With the layer control icons shown at the top of the layer stack, you can set layer visibility (the Eye icon), editability (the Lock icon), and the display mode (the Square icon) to regular or outline only. Note, however, that these settings are visible within the editing environment only and do not affect the appearance of the final movie (.swf).

Timeline window features

Figure 4.17 shows the Timeline window, as it appears when it is undocked or floating. The various controls of the window interface are labeled here, but we defer detailed explanations of some of these controls to the drawing and animation chapters where we show you how they are applied.

FIGURE 4.17

The floating Timeline window with callouts showing the principal features and control elements

As shown in Figure 4.17, the principal features and controls of the Timeline are

Window features

- **Timeline (panel tab):** More than one Timeline can be opened and displayed in the Timeline panel at the same time. Individual Timeline tabs can be closed by clicking the "x" icon on the tabs, or the entire Timeline window can be minimized or closed by using the controls on the top right corner of the Timeline panel.

- **Timeline header:** The Timeline header is the ruler that shows frame numbers and measures the time of the Timeline — each tick is one frame.

- **Playhead or Current frame indicator:** The red rectangle with a line extending down through all layers is the playhead. The playhead indicates the current frame. Drag it left or right along the Timeline to move from one area of the Timeline to another. Push it beyond the visible area to force-scroll the Timeline. You can also drag the playhead at a consistent rate for a preview of your animation; this is called *scrubbing* the Timeline.

TIP On Windows, if you have a mouse with a scroll wheel, you can scroll up and down through the layers; or by holding down the Shift key while you scroll, you can move the playhead forward and backward along the Timeline. If all of your layers (or layer folders) are already visible in the Timeline window, then the scroll wheel just scrolls you forward and backward along the Timeline without moving the playhead.

Layer controls

- **Active layer icon:** To make a layer active, either click the layer's name, or select a frame or group of frames. The pencil icon appears, indicating that the layer is now active. That's in addition to this more obvious clue: The layer bar of the active layer is shaded darker than the inactive layer bars. Although you can select multiple layers or content on multiple layers, only one layer will be marked as active at a time. For more about frame selection and editing behaviors, see the section "Editing frames and layers," which follows this one.

- **Show/Hide layer toggle:** Click the dot beneath the eye icon to hide the contents of a layer from view on the Stage. When the layer is hidden, a red X appears over the dot. To return the layer to visibility, click the X. To hide or show all layers at once, simply click on the eye icon directly.

CAUTION Hidden layers do export, and any content on the Stage within a hidden layer becomes visible upon export. Even if the content is offstage and not visible, it may add considerably to the file size when a Flash movie (.swf) is published, so you should save your document (.fla) and then delete these layers or convert them to guide layers before your final export.

- **Lock/Unlock layer toggle:** This toggle locks or unlocks the layer to either prevent or enable further editing. When the layer is locked, a padlock icon appears over the dot. To lock/unlock all layers at once, click directly on the lock icon.

- **Outline Layer toggle:** This toggles the colored layer outlines on or off. When on, the filled square icon changes into an outline, and all elements in that layer appear as colored outlines in the Document window. The outline color for the layer can be changed with the Outline Color control of the Layer Properties dialog box, which can be accessed by double-clicking the square Outline color icons in the layer stack or by choosing Modify ➪ Timeline ➪ Layer Properties from the application menu.

■ **Frame View options:** This button, at the far right end of the Timeline, accesses the Frame View options menu, which affords many options for the manner in which both the Timeline header and the frames are displayed.

■ **Add layer:** Simply click this button to add a new layer above the currently active layer. By default, layers are given sequential numeric names. Double-click the layer name in the Layer bar to change the name. Click and drag any part of the Layer bar to move it to a new position in the stack, or drag it on top of a folder layer to place it inside the folder.

■ **Add Layer folder:** This button enables you to create folders for storing groups of layers. New folders are automatically placed above the currently selected layer and labeled in the same number sequence as layers. They can be renamed or moved in the same way as other layers.

■ **Delete layer:** This button deletes the currently active layer, regardless of whether it is locked. Flash always retains one layer in the Timeline, so if you have only one layer in your document, you can't delete it unless you add another layer to the Timeline.

TIP Because using the Delete key on your keyboard does not remove an active layer or folder, but rather removes all the content from those frames, it can be helpful to get in the habit of right-clicking (Windows) or Control+clicking (Mac) a layer that you want to remove, and choosing Delete from the contextual menu. You can always click the trash icon to dump a selected layer or folder, but this adds a few more mouse miles.

Frame controls

■ **Center frame:** Click this button to shift the Timeline so that the current frame is centered in the visible area of the Timeline.

■ **Onion skin:** This enables you to see several frames of animation simultaneously.

■ **Onion Skin outlines:** This enables you to see the outlines of several frames of animation simultaneously.

■ **Edit Multiple frames:** In general, onion skinning permits you to edit the current frame only. Click this button to make each frame between the onion skin markers editable.

■ **Modify Onion markers:** Click this button to open the Modify Onion Markers popup. In addition to making manual adjustments, you can use the options to control the behavior and range of onion skinning.

CROSS-REF Onion skinning is further described in Chapter 11, "Timeline Animation and the Motion Editor."

Timeline Status displays

■ **Current frame:** This indicates the number of the current frame.

■ **Current rate:** This indicates the frame rate of the movie, measured in frames, or frames per second (fps). The program default of 12 fps is usually a good starting point. Ideally, you should do some testing in the final playback environment before deciding on an optimal frame rate. You can double-click the Frame Rate Indicator to invoke the Document Properties dialog box (Modify ➪ Document or Ctrl+J/⌘+J), or set the frame rate directly in the Properties panel.

NOTE   The fps setting is not a constant or absolute; it really means "maximum frame rate." The actual frame rate is dependent upon a number of variables, including download speed, processor speed, and machine resources; these are variables over which you have no control. However, another factor, over which you do have control, is the intensity of the animation: Complex movement with multiple elements or many layers of transparency is more processor intensive than simple movement. Previewing real-world playback speed at different frame rates — on various machines — early on in your development process is *very* important.

■ **Elapsed time:** This indicates the total movie time, measured in seconds (or tenths of a second), which will elapse from frame 1 to the current frame — provided that the movie is played back at the optimal speed.

Editing frames and layers

After you learn to recognize the visual conventions of the Timeline and how it displays different types of frames, you will be able to learn a lot about what is happening in an animation just by reading the Timeline. Figure 4.18 illustrates the Flash conventions for frame and layer display.

FIGURE 4.18

Flash Timeline conventions for naming and display of various frame and layer types

Layers stored in folder   Waveform (sound layer)

Layer   Playhead   Frame label   Motion tween

Folder (collapsed)   Shape tween

Folder (open)   Broken tween

Frame view options

Frame action

Comment

Property keyframe

Endframe (blank)

Masked layer   Keyframe   Blank keyframe   Endframe (filled)

Mask layer   Guide layer | Frame span (filled frames) Frame span (blank frames)

Motion tween layer   Frame-by-frame (animation)

The Timeline features noted in Figure 4.18 are defined as follows:

- **Keyframe:** A keyframe is any frame in which the contents of the frame may differ from the contents of either the previous or subsequent frames. Filled (black) circles on the Timeline mark keyframes with content.

- **Blank keyframe:** A keyframe that does not contain any content has the same behavior as any keyframe, but it is marked by an empty (white) circle on the Timeline.

- **Property keyframe:** Property keyframes are unique to motion tween layers. They mark frames within a tween span where a property change is made. Property keyframes are auto-inserted when you make modifications to a target object in a motion tween. Property keyframes are represented by filled (black) diamonds on the Timeline.

- **Frame span:** Frame spans are the sections from a keyframe to an endframe (up to, but not including, the next keyframe to the right). Note that these spans can be selected by double-clicking, and dragged as a whole to a different location.
    - **Filled frame(s):** The intermediate frames in a span, following to the right of a keyframe (with content), are shaded gray.
    - **Empty frame(s):** The intermediate frames in a span, following to the right of a blank keyframe, are white. A black line also outlines the entire span.
    - **Endframe:** The final frame of a span, marked with a small white rectangle and a vertical line to the right of the rectangle.

- **Frame-by-Frame animation:** Frame-by-frame animation is animation composed entirely of keyframes. In a frame-by-frame animation, the content on every frame is changed manually (rather than tweened).

- **Tweened animation:** Tweened animation is movement or change in an element that Flash interpolates over a range of frames that extends from an initial keyframe. An arrow stretching across a colored frame span designates a shape tween or a classic motion tween. There are three types of tweens in Flash:
    - **Object-based motion tweens:** Motion tweens are indicated by a blue tint (without a black arrow) and can be applied only to symbols. Object-based motion tweens do not require an end keyframe.
    - **Classic motion tweens:** Motion tweens are indicated by a blue tint (with a black arrow) and can be applied only to symbols. Classic motion tweens require an end keyframe.
    - **Shape tweens:** Shape tweens are indicated by a green tint (with a black arrow) and can be applied only to primitive (nongrouped) shapes. Shape tweens require an end keyframe.

NOTE A dashed line replaces the normal tween arrow for classic motion tweens and shape tweens if a tween is broken or missing an element required for the tween to render properly. The best fix for this is to remove the tween, check the contents of the beginning and ending keyframe to ensure that they are ready to tween, and then reapply the tween to the beginning keyframe.

CROSS-REF For more coverage on making frame-by-frame animation and using tweens and motion presets refer to Chapter 11, "Timeline Animation and the Motion Editor."

- **Layer folder:** These folders are used to organize other layers, and they can be named and repositioned in the layer stack the same way as layers can. Layer folders do not have individual frame settings and thus show up in the Timeline display as a continuous gray bar. To expand (open) or collapse (close) folders, click the arrow toggle at the left of the folder name or use the contextual menu. Note that dragging a folder inside another folder creates subfolders.

- **Mask layer:** A mask layer is a layer that is used to selectively obscure the masked layers beneath it.

- **Guide layer:** A guide layer serves to hold content for reference only. Any elements on a guide layer are visible in the authoring environment but are not included with the final published .swf file.

CROSS-REF For more about mask layers and guide layers, refer to Chapter 12, "Applying Filters, Blends, Guides, and Masks."

- **Frame Label:** Labels are used to give frames meaningful names, instead of using frame numbers. The advantage of this is that named keyframes can be moved without breaking ActionScript calls assigned to them. Upon export, labels are included as part of the .swf. Use the field in the Properties panel to add a label to a selected frame. Press Enter/Return after typing a frame label or comment to ensure that the label takes.

- **Comment:** Comments are special labels, preceded by a double-slash (//). Comments do not export, so you can be as descriptive as you need to be without adding to the .swf size. However, you won't be able to read long comments unless you leave a lot of space between keyframes. Add comments in the Properties panel the same way as you add labels; just be sure that your text is preceded by two forward-slash characters.

NOTE The Properties panel includes a menu for selecting a frame text type. After you type into the Frame text field, you can select from three options in the Type menu: Name, Comment, or Anchor. Note: A frame "name" is generally referred to as a label.

- **Waveform:** This squiggly blue line in the sound layer is the waveform of a placed sound. This visual reference for your sound makes it easier to synchronize animated elements to a soundtrack.

- **Frame actions:** The small *a*s in frames 10, 20, and 58 of the actions layer designate the presence of frame actions.

ON the CD-ROM If you want to see how the various layer and frame types look in the authoring environment and what happens when you publish the file, open `framesAndLayers.fla` (the Timeline shown in Figure 4.18) from the `ch04` folder on the CD-ROM.

Frame specifics

The Timeline might look a bit chaotic or confusing at first, but there are a lot of cues to help you keep track of the content of your file. Empty keyframes are marked with an empty circle (white dot), the last frame of a span is marked with the empty bar icon, and keyframes with content are marked with a filled circle (black dot).

Flash MX 2004 introduced the option of using either Flash 4 or Flash 5 frame-selection behavior. In Flash 4, individual frames could be selected just by clicking them, even if they were part of a *span* (a series of frames following a keyframe). With Flash 5, span-based selection was introduced as the default behavior — all the frames in a span would be selected just by clicking one frame. Since Flash MX, the default has gone back to Flash 4 selection style, but double-clicking a frame selects a span. For the option of going back to the Flash 5 selection style, go to Edit ➪ Preferences (or Flash ➪ Preferences on OS X) and in the General section, under Timeline Options, select the Span-based selection check box.

TIP Although double-clicking a frame in the default selection style selects a span of frames, if the span is moved, it automatically extends along the Timeline until it meets another keyframe. This can be helpful or annoying depending on what you are trying to accomplish. With Span-based selection behavior enabled, when you relocate a span, it does not auto-extend and the original span length is preserved.

So that you can better understand the various frame-editing options available, we have listed them here with notes on the ways you can accomplish your intended result. Some of the methods differ, depending on whether you have enabled Span-based selection as described previously. For users of previous versions of Flash, this may take a little getting used to. For new users, deciding on a preference will be a matter of testing out both selection-style options. The default methods are listed here first, followed by the methods that differ when Span-based selection is turned on.

The default Flash CS4 selection methods are as follows:

- **Selecting frames:** The methods for selecting single frames and spans of frames have not changed since Flash 8.
  - **Frame spans:** To select a span of frames extending between two keyframes, double-click anywhere between the keyframes.
  - **Single frames:** To select a single frame within a span, or a keyframe outside of a span, simply click to select it.

NEW FEATURE Motion tween layers behave differently than standard layers for shape tweens or classic motion tween spans. To select individual frames within a span on a motion tween layer, you must Ctrl+click/⌘+click. Single-clicking a frame anywhere in the span selects the whole span as a single object.

  - **Multiple frames or spans:** To select multiple frames along the Timeline (within a span or independent of a span), click and drag in any direction until you have selected all the frames you want to include in the selection. You can also use Shift+click to add to a selection of frames.

NOTE The difference between selecting a frame by dragging over it, and moving a frame by selecting it and then dragging can be hard to differentiate. At first, you may find yourself moving frames that you only wanted to select. The trick is to be sure that you don't release the mouse after you click a frame before you drag to select other frames. Conversely, if your intention is to move a frame or a series of frames, you have to click and release the mouse to select them first and then click again and drag to move them.

- **Moving frames:** Select the frame(s) that need to be moved and then drag them to the new location.
- **Extending the duration of a span on a normal layer:** There are two ways to change the duration of a span, which is the same result as inserting frames (F5) or removing frames (Shift+F5) after a keyframe. To change where a span begins, select the keyframe and then drag the keyframe to the position where you want the span to begin. To change where a span ends, Ctrl+click/⌘+click the endframe and drag it to where you want the span to end, or select a blank frame beyond the endframe where you want the span to end and insert a frame (F5). This automatically extends the span and moves the endframe to the frame you have selected.
- **Extending the duration of a span on a motion tween layer:** To extend the animation and shift the property keyframes, simply click and drag the end of the tween span. To extend the tween without moving the existing property keyframes, hold down the Shift key while dragging the end of the tween span.

NOTE If you click and drag any frame or endframe in a standard layer without pressing the Ctrl key (or the ⌘ key on Mac), the frame is automatically converted into a keyframe as it is dragged to the new location.

- **Copying frames:** Select the frame(s) that you want to copy. Choose Edit ⇨ Timeline ⇨ Copy Frames from the main menu and then Paste Frames into a new location, or press the Alt or Option key while clicking and dragging to copy selected frames to another location in the Timeline.

- **Pasting frames:** Select the frame where you want the copied or cut frames to be inserted (Flash automatically adds frames or layers below and to the right of the selected frame to accommodate the pasted content), and choose Edit ⇨ Timeline ⇨ Paste Frames from the menu.

CAUTION Edit ⇨ Copy (Ctrl/⌘+C) is not the same as Edit ⇨ Timeline ⇨ Copy Frames (Alt+Ctrl+C/ Option+⌘+C). Using Copy only "remembers" and copies the content from a single keyframe, whereas Copy Frames "remembers" and copies content from multiple keyframes and even from multiple layers. To insert this content correctly in a new location, you have to remember to use the corresponding Paste commands: Paste (Ctrl+V/⌘+V), or Paste Frames (Alt+Ctrl+V/Option+⌘+V). You may notice that the contextual menu offers only the plural options (Copy Frames or Paste Frames). This is because the plural command safely works to move content from a single frame or from multiple frames. The singular command is just a simpler shortcut key to use if you know that you want only the content from one keyframe.

- **Inserting frames:** Select the point at which you want to insert a new frame, and select Insert Frame (F5) from the contextual menu or from the application menu (Insert ⇨ Frame). The visual "clue" that frames have been inserted is that the endframe of a span is moved to the right — this also pushes any following keyframes farther along the Timeline.

- **Inserting keyframes:** Select the point at which you want to insert a new keyframe, and select Insert Keyframe (F6) from the contextual menu or from the application menu (Insert ⇨ Timeline ⇨ Keyframe). Note that keyframes can be inserted within a span without extending the span (or pushing the endframe to the right). Thus, inserting a keyframe actually converts an existing frame into a keyframe. So, unlike frames, keyframes can be inserted without pushing other frames farther down the Timeline.

- **Inserting blank keyframes:** Select the point at which you want to insert a new blank keyframe, and select Insert Blank Keyframe (F7) from the contextual menu or from the application menu (Insert ⇨ Timeline ⇨ Blank Keyframe). Inserting a blank keyframe within a span clears all content along the Timeline until another keyframe is encountered.

NOTE If you already have content in the current layer and you insert a keyframe, a new keyframe is created that duplicates the content of the endframe immediately prior. But if you insert a blank keyframe, the content of the prior endframe ceases and the blank keyframe will, as its name implies, be void of content.

ON the CD-ROM For a hands-on example of frame-based Timeline editing, refer to the file `frames_ example.fla` in the `ch04` folder of the CD-ROM that accompanies this book.

- **Removing frames (to shorten a span):** Select the frame(s) that you want to remove, and then choose Remove Frames (Shift+F5) from the contextual menu or from the application menu (Edit ⇨ Timeline ⇨ Remove Frames). This does not work for removing keyframes; instead, it removes a frame from the span to the right of the keyframe, causing all the following frames to move back toward frame 1.

■ **Clearing a keyframe:** To remove a keyframe and its contents, select the keyframe and choose Clear Keyframe (Shift+F6) from the contextual menu or from the application menu (Modify ⇨ Timeline ⇨ Clear Keyframe). When a keyframe is cleared, the span of the previous keyframe is extended to fill all frames until the next keyframe on the Timeline. The same thing happens if you insert a keyframe in a span and then Undo it (Ctrl+Z/⌘+Z). Apply Undo (Edit ⇨ Undo) twice — the first Undo deselects the keyframe, and the second Undo clears it.

■ **Cutting frames (leaves blank frames or keyframes):** To replace selected frames in a span with blank frames, while keeping content in the remainder of the span intact, select the frame(s) you want to "blank" and then choose Cut Frames (Alt+Ctrl+X on Windows or Option+⌘+X on Mac) from the contextual menu or from the application menu (Edit ⇨ Timeline ⇨ Cut Frames). This "pulls" the content out of only the selected frames, without interrupting content in surrounding frames or shifting any keyframes on the Timeline. The content that you cut can be pasted into another position on the Timeline (as described previously).

CAUTION Selecting a frame or keyframe and pressing Delete removes the content from the entire span, but does not remove the keyframe itself, or change the length of the span. You can delete content from multiple layers this way, but it leaves all the empty frames and keyframes on the Timeline.

TIP Flash MX 2004 introduced a command called Clear Frames (Alt+Delete/Option+Delete). This is a flexible command that eliminates the content on a selected frame, keyframe, or span of frames without changing the number of frames in a span. If you select a keyframe and apply Clear Frames, the keyframe clears and the content of the keyframe is removed. If you select a normal frame and apply Clear Frames, the selected frame is converted into a blank keyframe to eliminate the content in that frame while preserving the content in other frames within the same span. This command is also listed in the contextual menu and in the application menu under Edit ⇨ Timeline ⇨ Clear Frames.

■ **Editing the contents of a keyframe:** Select the keyframe where you want to edit content. This moves the playhead to the selected frame so that its content is visible in the Document window, where it can be edited. Note that if you edit content on a keyframe or frame within a span, the changes apply to the current frame and the span it is part of.

CROSS-REF We detail numerous techniques for editing content in later chapters of this book that address specific types of content. For the most relevant information, look for chapters that describe the types of content you are working with — vector art, bitmaps, sound, video, and so on.

The span-based selection methods are as follows:

■ **Frame spans:** To select a span of frames extending between two keyframes, simply click anywhere between the keyframes.

■ **Single frames within a span:** To select a single frame within a span on a normal layer, press the Ctrl key (on Windows) or the ⌘ key (on Mac) and click a frame. Keyframes or endframes can usually be selected with a simple click.

■ **Single frames not within a span:** To select a single frame that is not part of a span, simply click to select it.

■ **Multiple frames or spans:** To select multiple frames along the Timeline (within a span or independent of a span), Shift+click to add to a selection of the frames.

Figure 4.19 shows a Timeline that illustrates some editing points. The top layer shows the Original layer, with content starting on a keyframe on frame 1, followed by a span of 19 frames, putting the endframe on frame 20. This layer was copied into all three lower layers, with the result that the initial content of all four layers was the same. When a frame was inserted at frame 10 of the Insert frame layer, the content was extended, pushing the endframe of the span to frame 21. When a keyframe was inserted at frame 10 of the Insert keyframe layer, the content was maintained in the new keyframe, but the span was not extended, as indicated by the gray filled frames in the span from frame 10 to frame 20. When a blank keyframe was inserted at frame 10 of the Insert blank keyframe layer, the content was cleared following the new blank keyframe, as indicated by the white frames extending from frame 10 to frame 20.

CROSS-REF For more information about how frames are used to author and control animation, refer to Chapter 11, "Timeline Animation and the Motion Editor."

FIGURE 4.19

Editing frames and keyframes on the Timeline

Layer specifics

Knowing how to work with layers makes all the difference between a well-ordered project and a chaotic mess of elements that you may never be able to sort out if you have to come back to edit later on. The necessity of a logical folder structure and consistent naming conventions is even more crucial in a team environment, where someone else may have to try to find her way around in your document. Like most good production habits, this may seem like extra work at first, but over time it pays off. As your projects get more complex and your archive of Flash documents grows, the few additional steps you take early on will be invaluable down the road.

Being organized doesn't mean you have to always put every layer into a folder, but rather that you just try to find the most efficient way of keeping track of where you've placed different elements. To make it easier to remember what content is on different layers, it's a good habit to give your layers meaningful names. It can also be helpful to use consistent abbreviations that help you to recognize what type of content is described by the name (such as "MC" for Movie Clip or "Anim" for animation). To edit a layer name, simply double-click the layer's name on the Layer bar and type into the text field.

TIP With all Flash projects in our studio, we begin the layer structure by creating three layers titled "actions," "labels," and "functions" — these are always kept at the top of the layer stack. On projects that we want to document very carefully, we also add a "comments" layer where the type of action or function added on the other layers can be noted. Although these layers don't hold content that is visible on the Stage, they make it easy to quickly find any actions placed on the Timeline and to see labels and comments that give an indication of how the movie is structured.

CROSS-REF For detailed methods and suggestions on organizing Flash documents, see Chapter 3, "Planning Flash Projects"; Chapter 19, "Making Your First Flash CS4 Project"; and Chapter 33, "Building an Image Gallery Component."

By default, new layers are stacked on top of the currently active layer. To rearrange layers, click in the area between the layer name and the layer toggle icons, and drag the layer bar to the desired position in the layer stack and release. To move layers into a folder, click and drag the layer bar onto any layer with a folder icon. To move a layer back out of a folder, drag it to a position above the folder name bar or below all the other layers contained in the folder.

The Layers contextual menu

Because many of the controls for layer options are built into the Timeline window, layer properties are one of the few attributes that are not displayed in the Properties panel (frame properties are visible when any layer is selected). The contextual menu (right-click on Windows or Control+click on Mac) provides convenient access to most of the commands you will need when editing layers, including commands otherwise found in the Layer Properties dialog box or in the application menu:

- **Show All:** Shows all layers. If some layers have had their visibility turned off, this makes them all visible.
- **Lock Others:** Unlocks the active layer and locks all other layers.
- **Hide Others:** Makes the currently active layer visible if it is not visible, and hides all others.
- **Insert Layer:** Inserts a new layer above the currently active layer with an auto-numbered name that continues the number sequence of existing layers and folders.
- **Delete Layer:** Deletes the active layer and all content stored on that layer.
- **Guide:** Transforms the current layer into a guide layer — a reference layer that is visible only in the authoring environment (.fla).
- **Add Classic Motion Guide:** Inserts a new motion guide layer directly above the current layer and automatically converts the current layer into a guided layer.

NOTE A guide layer differs from a motion guide layer. A motion guide layer is linked to a guided layer, which usually contains a (classic motion) tweened animation that follows a path drawn on the motion guide layer. A guide layer is not linked to a guided layer and is most often used for placing a bitmap design composition, or other items used for design reference that should not be visible in the final movie (.swf). Neither guide layers nor motion guide layers export with the project when the file is tested or published.

NEW FEATURE Motion tween layers (created when an object-based motion tween is applied) contain motion guides, so a separate motion guide layer is no longer needed unless you are working with classic motion tweens.

- **Mask:** Transforms the current layer into a mask layer.

- **Show Masking:** Use this command on either the mask or the masked layer to activate the masking effect. Essentially, this command locks both layers simultaneously, which makes the masking effect visible.

- **Insert Folder:** Inserts a new folder above the currently active layer or folder with an auto-numbered name that continues the number sequence of existing layers and folders.

- **Delete Folder:** Deletes the currently active folder, along with all the layers stored in that folder.

- **Expand Folder:** Opens the current folder to make any layers stored inside visible in the layer stack and on the Timeline.

- **Collapse Folder:** Closes the current folder to hide any layers stored in the folder. The elements existing on these stored layers are still visible in the Document window and in the movie (.swf), but the keyframe rows do not show up along the Timeline.

- **Expand All Folders:** Opens all folders to show any stored layers visible in the layer stack and on the Timeline.

- **Collapse All Folders:** Closes all folders to hide any layers that have been placed in folders. The elements existing on these stored layers are still visible in the Document window and in the movie (.swf), but the keyframe rows do not show up along the Timeline.

- **Properties:** Invokes the Layer Properties dialog box for the currently active layer. The Layer Properties dialog box can also be invoked directly by double-clicking the "page" icon or the colored square icon on any layer, and is always available in the application menu (Modify ⇨ Timeline ⇨ Layer Properties).

CROSS-REF For more in-depth coverage of using layer types, refer to Chapter 12, "Applying Filters, Blends, Guides, and Masks."

Using Frame View options

The main place to find options for controlling the appearance of the Timeline within the window is in the submenu available from the Frame View options button, as shown earlier in Figure 4.19.

As noted previously, the Frame View options menu is used to customize the size, color, and style of frames displayed within the Timeline. These features can prove very helpful when you're working with cartoon animation and want to see each frame previewed. Or, if you're working on an extremely long project with a huge Timeline, it can be helpful to tweak the size of the individual frames so that you can see more of the Timeline in the Timeline window.

When you use the Frame View option in conjunction with the Layer Height option of the Layer Properties dialog box, you can customize your Timeline display in several ways to better suit your particular project. Your options include:

- **Tiny, Small, Normal, Medium, Large:** These options afford a range of sizes for the width of individual frames. When working on extremely long animations, narrower frames facilitate some operations. Wider frames can make it easier to select individual frames and to read frame labels or comments.

- **Short:** This option makes the frames shorter in height, permitting more layers to be visible in the same amount of space. When working with many layers or folders, short layers help speed the process of scrolling through the stack.

- **Tinted Frames:** This option toggles tinted frames on or off. With Tinted Frames on, the tints are as follows:

    - **White:** Empty or unused frames (for any layer). This is the default. The white color of empty or unused frames is unaffected regardless of whether Tinted Frames is on or off.

    - **Gray:** There are two kinds of gray frames: (a) The evenly spaced gray stripes in the default (empty) Timeline are a quick visual reference that indicates every fifth frame, like the tick marks on a ruler. These stripes appear regardless of whether Tinted Frames are enabled. (b) The solid gray color with a black outline, which appears when Tinted Frames is enabled, indicates that a frame contains content, even if it isn't visible on the Stage.

    - **Blue:** Indicates a motion tween span.

    - **Green:** Indicates a shape tween span.

> **NOTE** Regardless of whether Tinted Frames is enabled, Flash displays tween arrows (and keyframe dots) across shape tween or classic motion tween spans. However, with Tinted Frames disabled, tweened spans are indicated by colored arrows, rather than colored fills, that show the type of tween.

> **NEW FEATURE** Object-based motion tweens on motion tween layers are always indicated by a blue fill. Their appearance does not change when the Tinted Frames setting is toggled on or off.

    - **A red arrow:** Indicates a classic motion tween, when Tinted Frames are off.

    - **A green arrow:** Indicates a shape tween, when Tinted Frames are off.

- **Preview:** As shown in Figure 4.20, the preview option displays tiny thumbnails that maximize the element in each frame. Thus, the scale of elements is not consistent from frame to frame.

- **Preview in Context:** As shown in Figure 4.20, when previewed in context, the same animation is seen with accurate scale from frame to frame (because elements are not maximized for each frame).

NOTE   The preview in frames option only shows content in keyframes. Thus, if you use this option to view a tweened animation, you see images displayed on the Timeline only for the first and last frames of the animation.

FIGURE 4.20

The Timeline displayed with the two preview options — Preview (left) and Preview in Context (right) — for the same frame-by-frame animation sequence

Printing

Although Flash is primarily a Web and animation program, it fully supports printed output. The functionality and specific dialog boxes vary slightly from the Mac to the PC, whereas other variations are subject to which printers and printer drivers are installed on your machine. The File ⇨ Page Setup dialog box is the most standard aspect of the program and the choices for paper size, margins, center positioning, and orientation are pretty intuitive.

The options available in the Layout area of the Page Setup dialog box on Windows or in the Print Margins dialog box on Mac (File ⇨ Print Margins) deserve a little more attention. The options here are

■ **Print Margins** (Mac only): Note the Disable PostScript check box. When you're printing single large areas of color surrounded by complex borders, problems may occur on PostScript printers. If you encounter such problems, try using the Disable PostScript check box in the Mac Print Margins dialog box (Edit ⇨ Print Margins) or in the Windows Preferences dialog box (Edit ⇨ Preferences ⇨ General ⇨ Printing Options). Otherwise, divide the complex area into several simpler areas and use the Modify commands (Modify ⇨ Shape ⇨ Smooth/Straighten/Optimize) to reduce the complexity of these areas (which may, however, drastically alter your artwork — so save first!).

- **Frames:** Use this drop-down menu to choose to print either All Frames of the animation or the ecological default, which is to print the First Frame Only.
- **Layout:** There are three basic options:
    - **Actual Size:** This prints the frame at full size, subject to the accompanying Scale setting: At what scale do you want to print your frames? You enter a percentage.
    - **Fit on One Page:** This automatically reduces or enlarges the frame so that it fills the maximum printable area, without distortion.
    - **Storyboard:** This enables you to print several thumbnails per page in the following arrangements: Boxes, Grid, or Blank. There are accompanying settings for Frames Across, Frame Margin, and Label Frames. This is a great tool for circulating comps and promotional materials.

 When printing Storyboard layouts, use File ⇨ Print Preview on Windows (or File ⇨ Print ⇨ Preview on Mac) to ensure optimal results.

The remaining options in the main menu differ on Mac and Windows machines, but the key tasks and locations are as follows:

- **Print:** Just print it! (The Mac option for Preview is found in the dialog box that opens from this command.)
- **Print Preview:** On Windows, use the Print Preview command to see an on-screen preview of how the printed output looks, based upon the options you've chosen in the Page Setup dialog box. On Mac, the Preview button is found in the Print dialog box (File ⇨ Print) and generates a PDF to give a preview of how the final page looks, based upon the options you've chosen in the Print Margins dialog box.
- **Send** (PC only): This command invokes the default e-mail client so that you can readily send the Flash file as an attachment.

It is important to note that the Document background color (or Stage color) is not included on printed output. If you want the background color to appear in your printed output, you must create a filled rectangle of the color that you want in the background and place it on a layer behind the other elements. The printer then recognizes this as artwork and includes it in the output.

WEB RESOURCE We'd like to know what you think about this chapter. Visit www.flashsupport.com/feedback to fill out an online survey with your comments.

Summary

- Flash CS4 offers some great new tools and workspace options in a flexible interface that is consistent cross-platform and with other applications in the Adobe Creative Suite.
- The new Motion tween layer type supports object-based motion tweens which are easier to create and edit than classic motion tweens. Motion tween layers can support a motion path with no need for a separate motion guide layer.
- The new Motion Editor enables you to work with individual tween curves for all the tweenable properties applied to a target object.
- The Start Page and robust Help features get you started quickly, whereas the options for saving custom workspace layouts and custom keyboard shortcut sets make it easy to optimize your workspace for specific production needs.

- The guided file setup workflow supported by Adobe Device Central gives developers a jump-start on Flash projects that target specific mobile environments.

- Tabbed panels, the new vertical Properties panel, and the new scalable Tools panel make it easy to optimize screen space and customize the editing environment to suit your monitor configuration and work style.

- Layer folders and frame-editing options make it easy to organize and navigate your document structure.

- Although Flash is mainly used to produce Web content, it fully supports printed output.

- If you need a quick reminder on any of the fundamental interface elements, this chapter will be your reference.

Chapter 5

Drawing in Flash

This chapter introduces the primary tools for creating and manipulating vector graphics in Flash, as well as some features of the Flash environment that affect how elements behave. The primary drawing tools have self-explanatory names: the Line, Oval, Rectangle, PolyStar, Pencil, Brush, and Eraser. However, these tools have a variety of options and modifiers that make them more sophisticated than they may at first appear. In this chapter, you learn to apply the primary options of these tools to create shapes and line art.

The selection tools — Selection (arrow), Lasso, and Subselection — are found in the top section of the Tools panel, and these work as your "hands" within the drawing space of Flash, enabling you to select elements or grab and adjust specific parts of a shape or line.

The Pen is a powerful tool that draws lines by laying down editable points. You use both the Pen and Subselection tools to manipulate the points; you can also use them to select and edit all lines and shapes to manually optimize artwork.

> **TIP** Like the Pen tool in Illustrator, the Pen tool in Flash has a series of different modes that you can select from the same tool space in the Tools panel by clicking and holding the Pen tool icon.

The built-in shape-creation tools of Flash and the adjustable shape-recognition settings make it easy even for people who "can't draw a straight line" to create useable elements for Flash interfaces.

> **TIP** Tools for creating dynamically editable shapes based on an Oval Primitive or Rectangle Primitive can be selected from the same tool space as the basic Oval, Rectangle, and PolyStar tools. The shape primitives can be adjusted with controls in the Properties panel even after they are drawn to create a variety of useful polygons — including rounded or beveled rectangles and open circles or curves.

In addition to drawing, in this chapter you also learn to apply some of the terrific tools Flash provides to help you organize and align elements as you create layouts.

IN THIS CHAPTER

Using shape and drawing tools

Working with Drawing Objects and Shape Primitive tools

Setting Brush tool and Eraser tool modes

Creating optimized lines and curves

Choosing fill and stroke styles

Using selection tools and options

Controlling snapping behavior

Aligning, scaling, and rotating artwork

Knowing the Edit menu commands

Creating symbol patterns with the Spray Brush tool and the Deco tool

CROSS-REF If you're comfortable using the core Flash drawing tools and design panels, you can skip to Chapter 9, "Modifying Graphics," for a deeper look into the options available for editing artwork, including the Free Transform tool, the Envelope modifier, new 3D tools, and the Commands feature, which you can use to record and repeat authoring steps.

The primary drawing tools can be divided into two groups: geometric shapes and freehand lines and strokes. Line, Oval, Rectangle, and PolyStar fall into the first category; Pencil, Brush, and Eraser fall into the second.

NOTE The default fill and stroke settings that Flash launches with are sufficient to get started with any of the drawing tools, but we introduce many more inspiring choices in "Using Fill and Stroke Controls," later in this chapter.

TIP The Object Drawing option in the Tools panel provides a workaround to the standard overlap and merge behavior of raw graphics. If you prefer shapes or lines on the same layer to behave more like groups and not interfere with each other as you are drawing, you can enable the Object Drawing mode and work with any of the standard drawing and shape tools to create well-behaved, autonomous drawing objects.

You will find two new tools in Flash CS4 that enable you to create patterns by using symbols. If you have worked with Illustrator, the Deco tool and the Spray Brush tool workflow will be familiar: You select a symbol to use as your "ink" and then set the parameters for your "brush," and with a click on the Stage, Flash creates a cool pattern for you that consists of many instances of your base symbol(s). This can save you hours of time, and the symbol instances can still be selected and edited individually after they have been placed on the Stage as part of a pattern. These symbol-based drawing tools are discussed in more detail toward the end of this chapter.

Using Geometric Shape Tools

As shown in Figure 5.1, the prebuilt geometric shapes available for creating graphics in Flash are easy to access from the Tools panel. The basic Line, Oval, and Rectangle tools are straightforward but infinitely useful. The Oval Primitive and Rectangle Primitive tools make it easier to create more complex shapes without having to manually move points or merge multiple shapes. Instead, you can use settings in the Properties panel to control the corner radius of your rectangles or the inner radius and fill areas of your ovals. The PolyStar tool creates a wide variety of geometric shapes defined by a separate Tool Settings dialog box — available from the Options button in the Tool Settings section of the Properties panel. You can use custom stroke styles and the various fill options (described later in this chapter) with any of these shapes to create nearly any graphic you may need. Geometric shapes are more optimized than freehand drawings, and you can combine or modify them in multiple ways to create your graphics.

NOTE The Rectangle Primitive and Oval Primitive tools are really not primitive at all — they create dynamic shapes that can be adjusted with controls on the Properties panel. However, if you choose to edit these shapes manually in the Document window, you are given an option to convert them to simple drawing objects. After shape primitives are converted to drawing objects, they can be edited directly in Edit mode but they no longer have the same options available in the Properties panel for modifying corner radius or fill angle settings.

The Oval tool

Drawing with the Oval tool (O) creates a perfectly smooth oval. You draw ovals by clicking and then dragging diagonally from one "corner" of the oval to the other — dragging more vertically creates a taller oval, whereas dragging more horizontally creates a wider oval.

FIGURE 5.1

The shape tools are all nested together in the Flash CS4 Tools panel.

Rectangle Tool (R)
Oval Tool (O)
Rectangle Primitive Tool (R)
Oval Primitive Tool (O)
PolyStar Tool

TIP To constrain the shape to a perfect circle, hold down the Shift key before releasing the mouse.

The Oval tool has no unique options, but it can be filled with any of the fill colors available in the Swatches panel (described in the "Choosing colors" section, later in this chapter) as well as "outlined" with any of the stroke styles or colors. Figure 5.2 shows some of the huge variety of shapes you can create by using the Oval tool with different stroke and fill settings.

FIGURE 5.2

Shapes created with the Oval tool, using different stroke and fill settings

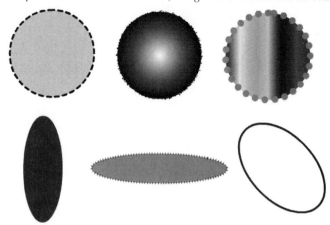

The Oval Primitive tool

If you need more complex shapes based on an oval, the Oval Primitive tool (available in the same drop-down Tools menu as the Oval tool) can save you a lot of time. With the Oval Primitive tool you can draw a basic oval and then modify angle and radius settings in the Properties panel (in the Oval Options section), to create donut or pie shapes, or open curves. Figure 5.3 includes just a few of the shapes that you can draw, along with the settings that were used to create them.

FIGURE 5.3

Shapes created with the Oval Primitive tool, using different angle and radius settings

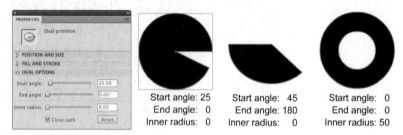

Start angle: 25	Start angle: 45	Start angle: 0
End angle: 0	End angle: 180	End angle: 0
Inner radius: 0	Inner radius: 0	Inner radius: 50

Don't overlook the Close path check box available in the Properties panel for oval primitives. By default, this check box is selected to create filled shapes, but if you prefer to create outlined shapes or curves, simply deselect the Close path check box. Figure 5.4 shows the same shapes as Figure 5.3, with the difference in effect created by deselecting the Close path check box.

FIGURE 5.4

Shapes created with the Oval Primitive tool, with the Close path check box deselected

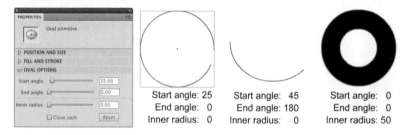

Start angle: 25	Start angle: 45	Start angle: 0
End angle: 0	End angle: 180	End angle: 0
Inner radius: 0	Inner radius: 0	Inner radius: 50

The Oval tool and Oval Primitive tool both have a "hidden" Settings dialog box that you can use to set the width and height of an oval before you draw it. To access this feature, select the Oval or Oval Primitive tool in the Tools panel (O), and then hold down the Alt (or Option) key as you click in the Document window where you want the shape to be drawn. The dialog box shown in Figure 5.5 pops up and you can set the width and height (in pixels). By default, the Draw from center check box is selected; if you prefer the shape to be drawn from the top left corner (originating where you clicked), deselect the check box. After you have entered the settings and clicked OK, the shape is drawn for you to the correct dimensions.

FIGURE 5.5

The Oval Settings dialog box can be used to generate shapes with precise width and height settings, instead of estimating size as you draw them manually.

> **TIP** The Oval tool and the Oval Primitive tool have the same shortcut key (O), but you can toggle between the two by holding down the Shift key as you press the shortcut key.

The Rectangle tool and Rectangle Primitive tool

The Rectangle tool (R) creates perfect rectangles, which means that all four sides are parallel, regardless of the length or width of the shape. Draw rectangles by clicking to place a starting corner and then dragging toward the opposite corner of your shape until you have the size and shape that you want.

> **TIP** To constrain the rectangle to a perfect square, hold down the Shift key before releasing the mouse.

Aside from choosing the stroke and fill to apply to a shape drawn with the Rectangle tool, there are also value boxes in the Properties panel under Rectangle Options for setting the radius for corners on the rectangle. The radius is set to 0 pt by default, to create rectangles with square or 90-degree corners. The range for radius settings is 100 pt to –100 pt, but unless the dimensions of the rectangle are equal to double the radius setting that you use, you will not see any additional effect by pushing the value farther. For example, the highest (or lowest) setting that would have a visible effect on a rectangle that was 30 x 30 pixels square would be 15 or –15. Choosing a more moderate radius setting creates rounded rectangles or squares with softened corners, and choosing negative values creates rectangles with indented corners (see Figure 5.6). By default, all rectangle corners are locked to have the same value, but if you want to create more interesting polygons you can click the lock icon in the Properties panel to "unlock" the corner values and enter different radius settings for each corner.

> **CAUTION** You'll want to choose the radius setting before you create a shape with the basic Rectangle tool because the radius cannot be reapplied or easily modified after the shape is drawn.

> **TIP** Like the Oval tool, the Rectangle tool and Rectangle Primitive tool also have a Settings dialog box that you can use to set the width, height, and corner radius to have Flash draw the shape for you. To access this feature, select the Rectangle tool in the Tools panel (R), and then hold down the Alt (or Option) key as you click in the Document window where you want the shape to be drawn.

Radius settings for rectangles made with the basic Rectangle tool cannot be adjusted after they are drawn, but shapes drawn with the Rectangle Primitive tool can be modified, using the options in the Properties panel, as long as they are not converted to drawing objects or broken apart into basic shapes.

FIGURE 5.6

Rectangles drawn with different radius settings create different degrees of roundness or inversion on the corners. Radius settings for rectangle primitives remain editable after they are drawn, and settings for basic rectangles "stick" and are not editable (from the Properties panel) after the shape is created.

Corner radius: 0   Corner radius: 10   Corner radius: -10

CAUTION The Corner Radius values do not reset automatically, so if you change the radius settings, you have to use the Reset button to return to drawing standard rectangles. Any radius setting entered in the Rectangle Settings dialog box accessed by Alt (or Option)+clicking in the Document window while the Rectangle tool is selected in the Tools panel is also transferred to the radius settings in the Properties panel.

Join and Miter settings

As shown in Figure 5.7, the Join menu includes three settings — Miter, Round, and Bevel — that you can apply to create three different join styles on any of your drawings or shapes with intersecting lines.

FIGURE 5.7

The three join styles available in the Join drop-down menu in the Properties panel create corners or angles with different types of line intersection.

When you select the Miter join style, you can further adjust the angle of the join by entering a setting between 1 and 60 in the Miter field. This field is a hot text value in Flash CS4, which means it can also be modified by clicking and dragging left or right to update the Miter angle. As shown in Figure 5.8, the visual difference between these different Miter angles is very subtle, and for most graphics you will probably be happy with the default setting of 3.

FIGURE 5.8

The sharpness of Miter joins can be adjusted by entering a setting between 1 and 60 in the Miter field.

The PolyStar tool

The PolyStar tool is so named because it is a multipurpose tool that can make a whole variety of different polygons and stars. If you're using the default Tools set in Flash, you'll find the PolyStar tool at the bottom of the shape tools submenu in the Tools panel. There is no shortcut key for the PolyStar tool.

When the PolyStar tool is active, an Options button appears in the Properties panel to open a Tool Settings dialog box that enables you to control the type of shape you want to draw. The composite in Figure 5.9 includes the Properties panel as it appears when the PolyStar tool is active, as well as the Tool Settings dialog box with the two shape styles available: polygon or star. You can set the number of sides for either shape by entering a value between 3 and 32 in the Number of Sides field. As shown at the top of Figure 5.9, a standard five-sided star is as easy to create as a triangle — that is, a polygon with three sides.

NOTE If you are a little confused by the inconsistent workflow for accessing settings dialog boxes for the different drawing tools, don't worry, we were too! Hopefully, these glitches will be smoothed out in future releases of Flash. For now, we just have to live with the fact that there isn't an Options button in the Properties panel for launching the Settings dialog box for the Oval or Rectangle tool, and the Settings dialog box for the PolyStar tool doesn't show up when you Alt (or Option)+click in the Document window.

FIGURE 5.9

A composite figure showing the Options button in the Properties panel (left) that launches the Tool Settings dialog box, used to create different shape styles (right)

The fields in the Tool Settings dialog box look the same whether you select polygon or star in the Style menu, but Star point size does not affect polygon shapes. If you are drawing a star, enter any number between 0 and 1 to control the depth of the star points. This might not look like much of a range, but you can enter decimal numbers, so you actually have 99 possible settings! As shown in Figure 5.10, numbers closer to 0 create sharper stars and numbers closer to 1 create blockier shapes.

FIGURE 5.10

Star point size decimal settings between 0 and 1 create various star shapes.

Star point size: 0.00   Star point size: 0.50   Star point size: 1.00

The Line tool

Drawing with the Line tool (N) enables you to create a perfectly straight line that extends from a starting point to an endpoint, simply by clicking a start position and dragging to the end position before releasing the mouse. Just select the Line tool in the Tools panel and start drawing in the Document window. You can select various line styles and stroke heights from the Properties panel, as well as set the color with the popup Swatches panel accessible from the Stroke color chip on either the Properties panel or the Tools panel. We describe the various options for line styles and colors later in this chapter. Snapping settings and guides can be used to help control where a line is placed and how precisely it connects to other lines. The Line tool conforms to the snapping settings we describe later in this chapter, in the "Simplifying snapping settings" section.

To restrict the line to 45-degree-angle increments, hold down the Shift key as you drag out the line.

Figure 5.11 shows how a line previews as you drag and how it appears when the mouse is released and the current line style and stroke height settings are applied.

FIGURE 5.11

Line tool preview (top) and the final line (bottom), displayed when the mouse button is released and line style is rendered

With the Cap option menu in the Properties panel, you can quickly switch a stroke from a rounded end to a square end to a flat or no cap end. Figure 5.12 illustrates how these cap styles render on a 10 pt line.

FIGURE 5.12

A 10 pt line rendered with different cap styles. These styles can be applied to any line using the Cap style menu in the Properties panel: None (top), Round (center), Square (bottom).

Using Drawing Tools

The tools for drawing freehand lines and strokes in Flash come with options for applying different combinations of line processing and shape recognition. So, what does that mean exactly? These are general terms for a class of options that you can set to assist accurate drawing and manipulation of basic shapes. These options can be applied dynamically as you draw with the Pencil or Brush tool, or applied cumulatively to an item selected with the Selection tool to clean up a shape or line that you've already drawn. These are some of the Flash assistants that can help even a drafting-challenged designer create sharp-looking graphics with ease.

NOTE The biggest challenge when drawing in Flash is finding a happy medium between the degree of line variation and complexity required to get the graphic look you want, and the optimization and file size that you need to keep your artwork Web friendly.

The Pencil tool

You use the Pencil tool to draw lines and shapes. At first glance, it operates much like a real pencil. You can use the Pencil tool with different line styles as you draw a freeform shape. But a deeper examination reveals that, unlike a real pencil, you can set the Flash Pencil tool to straighten lines and smooth curves as you draw. You can also set it to recognize or correct basic geometric shapes. For example, a crude lumpy oval can be automatically recognized and processed into a true, or *perfect*, oval. You can further modify these shapes and lines after you've drawn them by using the Selection and Subselect tools.

When the Pencil tool is active, one option besides the Object Drawing toggle appears at the bottom of the Tools panel. This is actually a button for the Pencil Mode popup menu, which sets the Pencil tool's current drawing mode. The three modes, or drawing styles, for the Pencil are Straighten, Smooth, and Ink. These settings control the way that line processing occurs as you draw.

Figure 5.13 shows the same freehand drawing done with the different Pencil modes. The drawing on the left was done with the Straighten mode, the drawing in the middle was done with Smooth mode, and the drawing on the right was done with Ink mode. As you can see, each mode is more effective for certain types of lines and shapes.

FIGURE 5.13

Similar sketches made by using the three different Pencil modes to show how line processing affects various shapes: Straighten (left), Smooth (center), and Ink (right).

Straighten   Smooth   Ink

To create a pleasing finished result, you'll most likely use different Pencil modes when working on individual elements of your drawing. Here are some notes on the characteristics of the three Pencil drawing modes that you can select in the Tools panel:

- **Straighten:** Drawing with the Straighten option processes your drawings while taking into account both line and shape recognition. This means that nearly straight lines are straightened, and wobbly curves are smoothed. Approximate geometric shapes, such as ovals, rectangles, and triangles, are recognized and automatically adjusted.

- **Smooth:** Drawing with the Smooth option reduces the zeal with which Flash automatically processes your drawings. With the Smooth option, line straightening and shape recognition are not applied, but curved lines are smoothed. Additionally, a line that ends near another line is joined automatically, if the Connect Lines tolerance is set to Can be Distant.

- **Ink:** Drawing with the Ink option turns off all line processing. Lines remain as you've drawn them. Your lines are *not* smoothed, straightened, or joined. There will always be a slight difference between the line preview and the final, rendered line, but this setting is as close to raw sketching as you can get in the Flash drawing environment.

The Brush tool

You use the Brush tool to create smooth or tapered marks and to fill enclosed areas. Unlike the Pencil tool, which creates marks with a single row of anchor points, the Brush tool actually creates marks by using filled shapes. The fills can be solid colors, gradients, or fills derived from bitmaps. Because the Brush paints only with a fill, the Stroke color chip does not apply to the marks drawn with the brush. The Brush tool is especially well suited for artwork created using a drawing tablet. A number of settings and options are available when the Brush tool is active, giving you precise control over the type of marks that it makes.

Adjusting Drawing Settings

You may adjust the degree to which shape recognition processes your Pencil drawings with the Drawing settings found in Edit ⇨ Preferences ⇨ Drawing (or Flash ⇨ Preferences ⇨ Drawing). By default, all the Drawing settings are Normal. You can adjust each option to make it more specific or more general. The optimal setting combinations depend on the style of drawing that you're trying to achieve, but in general, you really only need to adjust the default Normal settings for these controls if you find that you aren't getting the look you want by using the Straighten, Smooth, or Ink modes with the Pencil tool.

You can also choose to further simplify lines and shapes that you have drawn with the Pencil in Ink mode by using the Selection tool to select what you've drawn and then using either the Smooth or Straighten command by clicking the Smooth or Straighten button at the bottom of the Tools panel. Or, for maximum control, manually edit extraneous points with either the Pen or the Subselect tool (as we describe in the Pen and Subselect sections later in this chapter). Here are the various Drawing settings and options available in Preferences:

- **Connect Lines:** The Connect Lines setting adjusts how close lines or points have to be to each other before Flash automatically connects them into a continuous line or shape. This setting also controls how close to horizontal or vertical a line has to be for Flash to set it at an exact angle. The options are Must be Close, Normal, and Can be Distant. This setting also controls how close elements need to be to snap together when Snap to Objects is turned on.

- **Smooth Curves:** Smooth Curves simplifies the number of points used to draw a curve when the Pencil is in Straighten or Smooth mode. Smoother curves are easier to reshape and are more optimized, whereas rougher curves more closely resemble the original lines drawn. The options are Off, Rough, Normal, and Smooth.

- **Recognize Lines:** The Recognize Lines setting controls how precise a line has to be for Flash to recognize it as a straight line and automatically align it. The options are Off, Strict, Normal, and Tolerant.

- **Recognize Shapes:** The Recognize Shapes setting controls how accurately you have to draw basic geometric shapes and 90-degree or 180-degree arcs for Flash to recognize and correct them. The options are Off, Strict, Normal, and Tolerant.

- **Click Accuracy:** Click Accuracy determines how close to an element the cursor has to be for Flash to recognize it. The settings are Strict, Normal, and Tolerant.

These drawing settings do not modify the Straighten and Smooth options for the Selection tool, which reduce point complexity (or smooth angles) based on the settings you enter in the respective dialog boxes before you apply the command to a shape or line that has already been drawn.

The Brush mode menu

The Brush tool includes options for controlling exactly where the fill is applied. The Brush mode option menu reveals five painting modes that are amazingly useful for a wide range of effects when applying the Brush tool: Paint Normal, Paint Fills, Paint Behind, Paint Selection, and Paint Inside, as shown in Figure 5.14.

NOTE The Pressure toggle and the Tilt toggle are visible in the Options area only if you have a drawing tablet installed on your system.

FIGURE 5.14

The Brush tool and options (left); the Brush mode settings menu (right)

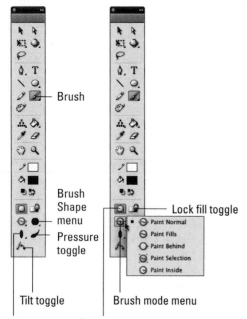

WEB RESOURCE **To learn more about tablets and read some fun tutorials, visit** www.wacom.com.

Figure 5.15 depicts the various ways in which the Brush modes interact with drawn and painted elements. The base image is a solid white rectangle drawn with a black outline. The boat outline is drawn with the Pencil tool in dark gray on top of the rectangle:

- A: **Paint Normal mode:** Applies brush strokes over the top of any lines or fills.
- B: **Paint Fills mode:** Applies brush strokes to replace any fills, but leaves lines untouched.
- C: **Paint Behind mode:** Applies brush strokes only to blank areas and leaves all fills, lines, or other items untouched. In Figure 5.15 (C), the only areas the brush mark covers are those in the background, outside the frame of the picture. Effectively, the brush has gone behind the entire shape. If the stroke had originated within the frame, it would have covered the white fill and gone behind the drawn gray lines and the black outline.
- D: **Paint Selection mode:** Applies brush strokes only to selected fills. In Figure 5.15 (D), a selection was made by Shift+clicking both the white fill inside the boat and inside the sail. The same gray brush marks drawn on the previous figure are now visible only inside the selected fills.
- E: **Paint Inside mode:** Applies brush strokes only to the singular fill area where the brush stroke was first initiated. As the name implies, Paint Inside never paints over lines. If you initiate painting from an empty area, the brush strokes won't affect any existing fills or lines, which approximates the same effect as the Paint Behind setting.

FIGURE 5.15

The result of painting with the Brush tool varies depending on the Brush mode. Paint Normal (A), Paint Fills (B), Paint Behind (C), Paint Selection (D), Paint Inside (E).

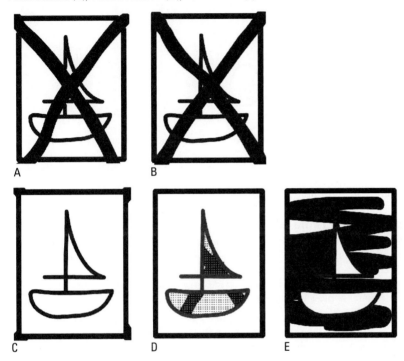

CAUTION Painting with the background color (such as white) is not the same as erasing. Although painting with a background color may appear to accomplish something similar to erasing, you are, in fact, creating a filled item that can be selected, moved, edited, deleted, and erased. Even if you can't see it, it adds to your file size. Only erasing erases!

Brush size and shape options

Although similar to Stroke height and style, the Brush size and Brush shape settings are unique to the Brush tool.

CROSS-REF The Lock Fill option is common to both the Brush tool and the Paint Bucket tool. For coverage of using the Lock Fill option with the Brush tool and the Paint Bucket tool, refer to Chapter 9, "Modifying Graphics."

In Flash, the size of applied brush marks is always related to the Zoom setting. Therefore, using the same brush diameter creates different-sized brush marks depending on what Zoom setting you work with in the Document window (see Figure 5.16). You can paint over your whole stage in one stroke, even with a small brush diameter, if your Zoom is at a low setting such as 8 percent; or you can use a large brush diameter to make detailed lines if your Zoom is at a high setting such as 1,500 percent.

FIGURE 5.16

Marks made by using the same brush size applied with the Document View at different percentages of Zoom

The Brush Shape option is a drop-down menu with nine possible brush shapes that are based on the circle, ellipse, square, rectangle, and line shapes. (Refer to Figure 5.14.) The oval, rectangle, and line shapes are available in various angles. You can combine these stock brush shapes with the range of brush sizes available in the Brush Size menu to generate a wide variety of brush tips. When using shapes other than circles, note that the diameter sizes chosen in the Brush Size menu apply to the broadest area of any brush shape.

Additional Brush options for drawing tablets

If you use a pressure-sensitive tablet for drawing, two extra options appear in the Tools panel when the Brush tool is active. (The Pressure and Tilt toggles are shown at the bottom of the Tools panel in Figure 5.14.) The Pressure toggle enables you to use pen pressure on a tablet to vary the thickness of brush marks as you draw. Working on a tablet with this option, you can create organic-looking strokes that taper or vary in width as you change the amount of pressure applied to the tablet surface.

> **TIP** To achieve pressure-sensitive eraser marks, use the eraser on the tablet pen while the Brush tool is active rather than the Eraser tool in the Tools panel.

Figure 5.17 shows a series of tapered marks created with a pressure-sensitive tablet, using a single Brush size and a consistent Zoom setting.

If you're drawing on a tablet that supports this feature, activating the Tilt toggle enables you to control the thickness and direction of strokes with the movement of your wrist. The degree of tilt is determined by the angle between the top of your stylus (or pen) and the top edge of the drawing tablet. This is a very subtle control that you'll most likely notice if you're using a large, tapered (or "flat") brush style — and if you spend hours drawing on a tablet! We didn't include a figure to illustrate this feature because it is hard to tell from finished artwork how it affects your drawings, but experienced artists will appreciate the "feel" that this option adds to the drawing environment.

> **NOTE** Support for the Tilt feature varies on different drawing tablets. If you have a Wacom tablet, you can get current drivers and feature documentation from www.wacom.com. It is beyond the scope of this book to describe different types and features of drawing tablets, but the drawing options available in Flash have been tested on a wide range of tablets, so the chances are good that they will work for you.

FIGURE 5.17

Drawing with the Brush tool on a pressure-sensitive tablet (with the Pressure option turned on in the Tools panel) creates tapered, calligraphic marks.

The Eraser tool

The Eraser tool (E) is used in concert with the shape and drawing tools to obtain final, useable art. As the name implies, the Eraser tool is primarily used for rubbing out mistakes. When the Eraser tool is active, three options appear on the Tools panel, as shown in Figure 5.18. Eraser mode and Eraser Shape are both drop-down menus with multiple options. For Eraser Shape, you can select rectangular or oval erasers in various sizes. Eraser modes are similar to the Brush modes we described previously.

You use the Eraser tool's one unique option, the Faucet toggle, to clear enclosed areas of fill. Using the Faucet is the equivalent of selecting a line or a fill and then deleting it, but the Faucet accomplishes this in one easy step. Select the Eraser tool, choose the Faucet option, and then click any line or fill to instantly erase it. Clicking any part of a selection with the Faucet deletes all elements in the selection.

The interaction of Eraser modes and artwork is consistent with the Brush modes available for the Brush tool. The only difference is that instead of adding a mark to a specified part of a drawing, the Eraser removes marks in a specified part of a drawing. Aside from Erase Normal, Erase Fills, Erase Selected Fills, and Erase Inside, which you will recognize from the previous descriptions of Brush modes, there is also an Erase Lines mode that enables you to remove any lines without disrupting fills.

FIGURE 5.18

The Eraser tool has three basic options: Eraser mode, Eraser shape, and Faucet.

Eraser tool

Faucet toggle

Eraser shape menu

Eraser mode menu

NOTE The Eraser tool erases only lines and fills that are in the current frame of the scene. It won't erase groups, symbols, or text. When you need to erase a part of a group, you have two options: Select the group and choose Edit ➪ Edit Selected from the application menu (or double-click the group), or select the group and choose Modify ➪ Ungroup from the application menu (Ctrl+Shift+G or ⌘+Shift+G).

TIP Drawing Objects have some of the same characteristics as grouped shapes, but they can be treated like raw shapes when you're using the Eraser tool — no need to break them apart.

The only alternative to using the Eraser tool to remove graphic elements or areas of drawings is to select them with the Selection, Subselect, or Lasso tool, and then delete them by pressing Delete (or Backspace).

TIP To quickly erase everything in the current keyframe (even from multiple layers), double-click the Eraser tool in the Tools panel. Don't double-click on the Stage with the Eraser selected; just double-click the Eraser button on the Tools panel. And — poof! — everything in the keyframe is gone.

Creating Precise Lines and Bezier Curves with the Pen Tool

You use the Pen tool (P) to draw precision paths that define straight lines and smooth curves. These paths define adjustable line segments, which may be straight or curved — the angle and length of straight segments is completely adjustable, as is the slope and length of curved segments. To draw a series of straight-line segments with the Pen tool, simply move the cursor and click successively: Each subsequent click defines the endpoint of the line. To draw curved line segments with the Pen tool, simply click and drag: the length and direction of the drag determines the depth and shape of the current segment. Both straight- and curved-line segments can be modified and edited by adjusting their anchor points and tangent handles. In addition, any lines or shapes that have been created by other Flash drawing tools can also be displayed as paths (points on lines) and edited with either the Pen tool or the Subselect tool (described in the section "Putting Selection Tools to Work").

> **TIP** If you're working on a background color that is too similar to your Layer Outline Color, the points on your line will be difficult to see and adjust. Remember that you can always change the Layer Outline Color to contrast with the background.

Creating shapes with the Pen tool takes a little practice, but it produces the most controlled optimization of artwork. Because no points are auto-created, every line and curve is defined only with the points that you place. This saves having to delete points from an overly complex path that may result from drawing with the Pencil or the Brush tool. To make drawing a little less mysterious, there is a submenu for the Pen tool that makes it easier to access some of its secondary capabilities. As shown in Figure 5.19, you can change the Pen tool from its default behavior of placing points (for drawing lines) to add, delete, or convert anchor points on a line that you've already drawn.

The Preferences for the Pen tool are located in the Pen tool section of the Drawing Preferences dialog box. (Choose Edit ➪ Preferences ➪ Drawing, or on OS X, Flash ➪ Preferences ➪ Drawing.) There are three optional settings to control preview, point display, and cursor style:

- **Show pen preview:** When you select this option, Flash displays a preview of the next line segment, as you move the pointer, before you click to make the next endpoint and complete the line.

- **Show solid points:** Select this option to invert the default display behavior for points along a selected line. The default is to show selected points as solid (filled circles) and unselected points as hollow (empty squares). When turned on, this option shows selected points as hollow (empty circles) and unselected anchor points as solid (filled squares).

- **Show precise cursors:** This option toggles the Pen tool cursor between the default Pen tool icon and a precision crosshair cursor. This can make selecting points much easier and is recommended if you're doing detailed adjustments on a line.

> **TIP** You can also use a keyboard shortcut to toggle between the two Pen cursor displays: Caps Lock toggles between the precise crosshair icon and the Pen icon when the Pen tool is active.

FIGURE 5.19

The submenu for the Pen tool in the Tools panel makes it easy to change modes as you create or modify lines and curves.

As you work with the Pen tool, you will notice that it displays a number of different icons to the lower right of the cursor. These Pen *states* tell you at any given time what action the Pen can perform on a line.

The Pen states and actions are as follows:

- The Pen displays a small (x) when it's over an empty area of the Stage and ready to place the first point in a line. Click to place the first point in a new line.

- When the Pen hovers over an endpoint that can be connected to close a path, it displays a small link icon (a square with a line through it). Click this point to close the path.

- When the Pen hovers over an endpoint that will not connect to close a path, it displays a slash (/). Click this point to select it as a starting point for a continuation of the path or as the first point for closing a path.

- When the Pen hovers over a curve point, it displays a carat (^) to indicate that clicking that point turns it into a corner point.

- When the Pen hovers over a corner point, it displays a minus (–) sign to indicate that clicking this corner point deletes it.

- When the Pen is over a path (a line between two points), it displays a plus (+) sign to indicate that clicking there adds a point to the path.

- With the Ctrl (or ⌘) key pressed, the Pen behaves like the Subselection tool, so it switches to the hollow arrow icon with a filled black box over lines, or a hollow white box over points.

- When adjusting a path with either the Pen tool or the Subselection tool, the default for selected points is a filled circle, whereas unselected points appear as hollow squares. Note that unselected points display a single tangent handle, bound toward the selected point, which displays two tangent handles.

TIP Dragging with the Subselection tool around the area of a line that you want to adjust by using points and tangent handles makes these controls visible (as shown in Figure 5.20), so you don't have to try and find them by trolling around with your cursor and watching the Pen state icon.

Figure 5.20 shows a line made with only straight-line segments and corner points, a line made with both straight segments and corner points and curved segments with curve points, and a line made of only curved segments and curve points. You can see that curved segments are controlled by tangent handles extended from the curve points, while straight segments just have corner points without tangent handles.

FIGURE 5.20

Lines made with the Pen tool can consist of straight segments and corner points (top), both straight segments with corner points and curved segments with curve points (middle), or only curved segments with curve points (bottom).

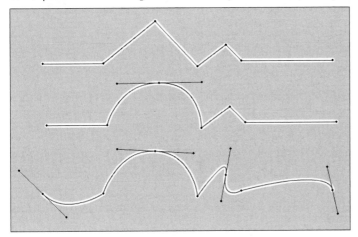

Now that you've toured the various Pen tool icons, Pen states, and line types, it's time to start drawing and see how these actually apply as you work. To draw and adjust a straight-line segment with the Pen tool, follow these steps:

1. **With the Pen tool active in the Tools panel, click to place the first point of your line on the Stage (wherever you want the line to start).**

2. **Choose the next position for a point and continue to click to create subsequent points and define individual line segments.**

   Each subsequent click creates a corner point on the line that determines the length of individual line segments.

NOTE Each click is a point along a continuous line. To end one line and begin a new line, double-click to place the final point in a line. This "breaks" the line so that the next click places a starting point for a new line rather than a continuation of the same line. A line should be ended or completed — by double-clicking or by closing your shape — before using the editing keys described in Step 3.

3. **To adjust straight segments, either switch to the Subselection tool in the Tools panel or press the Ctrl (or ⌘) key to temporarily toggle from the Pen tool to the Subselection tool, and then click a point to select it.** Continue pressing the Ctrl (⌘) key as you drag and move the point to change the angle or length of the segment.

 When you're creating straight lines with the Pen tool, press the Shift key to constrain lines to either 45-degree or 90-degree angles.

To draw and adjust a curved line segment with the Pen tool, follow these steps:

1. **Click to create the first anchor point.**

2. **Move to the position on the Stage for the next anchor point, click to place it, and without releasing the mouse, drag the Pen tool in the direction you want the curve to go.**

3. **When the preview of the line matches the curve that you want in the final line, release the mouse and move to click and place the next point in the segment.** Repeat this process to create subsequent curve points for curved segments, or simply click elsewhere without dragging to place a point and make the subsequent segment a straight line with a corner point.

4. **As when adjusting straight segments, switch or toggle to the Subselection tool and then click a point to select it.** Then drag and move the point to change the angle or length of the segment, or, after selecting a curve point with the Subselect tool, click and drag the tangent handles of the point to adjust the depth and shape of the curve.

Although both corner points and curve points may be adjusted, they behave differently:

■ Corner points and endpoints can be moved with the Subselection tool but they do not display tangent handles.

■ Because a curve point defines a curve, moving the tangent handle of a curve point modifies the curves on both sides of the point.

■ To convert a corner point into a curve point, simply select the point with the Subselection tool, and while pressing Alt (Option), drag the point slightly. A curve point with two tangent handles appears, replacing the original corner point.

■ To adjust one tangent handle of a curve point independent of the other handle, hold down Alt (Option) while dragging the tangent handle that you want to move.

■ To convert a curve point into a corner point, select the Convert Anchor point tool from the Pen submenu in the Tools panel and click any curve point once.

■ Endpoints cannot be converted into curve points unless the line is continued or joined with another line. To join two endpoints, simply click one endpoint with the Pen tool and then move to the point you want to connect it with and click again. A new line segment is created that joins the two points.

■ You can also use the arrow keys, located on your keyboard, to nudge selected corner and curve points into position. Press Shift to augment the arrow keys and to make them nudge 10 pixels with each click.

 You can also reshape any lines or shapes created with the Pen, Pencil, Brush, Line, Oval, Rectangle, or PolyStar tools, as described in "Putting Selection Tools to Work," later in this chapter.

WEB RESOURCE If you are finding it difficult to make sense of all the different Pen modes and options for editing Bezier curves, you might find it helpful to refer to Adobe's online help. You will find detailed descriptions of each element involved in working with Bezier drawing tools in the section for Using Flash CS4 Professional ➪ Creating and Editing Artwork ➪ Drawing ➪ Drawing with the Pen tool.

Using Fill and Stroke Controls

Now that you know where to find and use the drawing tools, it's time to get more creative with color and line styles. In the following sections, we introduce you to the controls for setting the fill and stroke applied to artwork drawn in Flash.

NEW FEATURE When the Pen, Pencil, or Line tool is activated in the Tools panel, you will notice a new Hinting check box in the Properties panel. When selected, this option constrains all points to whole pixel values to ensure that the lines or strokes are not blurry (which is sometimes the case if control points land in between whole pixel values).

Choosing colors

The stroke and fill colors that are applied with any of the drawing tools are determined by the current settings of the color chips located in the Flash Tools panel and in the Properties panel. You can set the fill and stroke colors before you draw something, or select an element on the Stage and adjust it by choosing a new color from the stroke or fill swatches. The Oval, Rectangle, PolyStar, Brush, and Paint Bucket tools all use the current fill settings — you can select colors before you draw a new shape or select an existing shape and modify it by changing the fill and stroke colors.

The color chips in the Tools panel display the most recently selected colors and are always visible regardless of what tool you're using. The Properties panel shows the color chip of the currently active item and displays the chips only if they can be applied with the tool you have active or to the item you have selected. Thus, if you select the Line tool, both Stroke and Fill color chips are visible on the Tools panel, but the Properties panel displays only a Stroke color chip (the Fill color chip displays a strikethrough icon). Although these chips indicate the current color, they're really also buttons: click any color chip to select a new color from the popup Swatches menu. The Swatches menu is shown in Figure 5.21 as it pops up from the Tools panel or from the Properties panel.

The popup swatches display the same color options as the main Swatches panel shown in Figure 5.22. Use shortcut keys (Ctrl+F9 or ⌘+F9) or select Window ➪ Swatches from the application menu to launch the Swatches panel. The Swatches popup includes an Alpha value box as well as a Hexadecimal color value box, another iteration of the No Color button (when it applies), and a button that launches the Color Picker. The Swatches menu opened with the Fill color chip includes the same solid colors available for Stroke, as well as a range of gradient fill styles along the bottom of the panel.

CROSS-REF We discuss the custom palette options available in the Swatches panel in detail, along with the Mixer panel and other colorful issues, in Chapter 7, "Applying Color."

FIGURE 5.21

The current Swatches popup is opened by clicking the Stroke or Fill color chip in the Tools panel (left), or by clicking a color chip on the Properties panel (top right).

Stroke color chip
Fill color chip
Hex value field
No color button
Launch Color Picker
Alpha value (not text)
Stroke Color chip
Fill Color chip
Dropper (cursor picks color)

Fill color chip
Swatch menu pop-up (with default Web 216 colors)

Choosing line styles

In Flash, for all tools that draw or display a line or outline, you control the thickness of the line — or stroke — either by dragging the Stroke Height slider or by entering a value in the Stroke Height numeric entry box. Both of these controls are available in the Properties panel, as shown in Figure 5.23. The stroke options are visible only when they can be applied — if a drawing tool that creates lines is active in the Tools panel or if you have selected an element with a stroke.

NOTE   Generally, in Flash, lines that are independent or not attached to any fill are referred to as *lines,* whereas lines or outlines on a filled shape are referred to as *strokes.* You use the same tools to create and edit lines and strokes.

FIGURE 5.22

Grouping the Swatches panel with the Color panel enables tabbed access to either panel.

Color panel tab

Swatches panel tab   Swatch panel options menu

Gradient fill swatches

Changes to stroke color and style apply to lines or curves drawn with the Pen, Line, Pencil, Oval, Rectangle, and PolyStar tools. For shapes, the changes apply only to the outline, not to the fill. As with fill color settings, you can select a stroke color and style before you create any artwork (as long as the tool you're going to use is active in the Tools panel), or you can select a line in the Document window with the Selection tool and change its appearance with the settings in the Properties panel.

TIP
You can set stroke heights up to 200. In our experience, any stroke with a height setting of more than about 25 becomes rather unwieldy. If you need a mark that big, instead of a giant stroke, you are probably better off using one of the shape tools to create a filled area.

NOTE
Depending upon the level of zoom, the height difference of some lines may not be visible on-screen, even though zooming in closer enables you to see that the stroke height is correct. Lines set to a height of 1 pixel or lower appear to be the same thickness unless the Stage view is zoomed to 200 percent or closer. However, all line heights still print correctly on a high-resolution printer and are visible in your final Flash movie (.swf) to anyone who zooms in close enough.

The Stroke Style drop-down menu (see Figure 5.24) offers the choice of Hairline or six standard, variable-width strokes. Hairline strokes always have the same 1-pixel thickness, even if the mark or shape that they outline is scaled larger after the stroke is applied. You can select and combine the other six line styles with any stroke height. If these styles do not deliver the line look you need, the Custom button (to the right of the Style menu) opens a Stroke Style dialog box (see Figure 5.24), which you can use to generate custom line styles by selecting from a range of properties for each preset line. Basic properties include stroke Thickness and Sharp corners. Other settings vary depending on what style of stroke you choose.

TIP
The Scale menu for strokes in the Properties panel enables you to control how lines scale when symbols are scaled in the authoring environment or the Flash movie is scaled in the Flash Player.

FIGURE 5.23

The Properties panel gives you all the controls you need to select the stroke height, color, and style, as well as an option to control how strokes scale in the Flash Player and a new Hinting option to constrain points to whole pixel values.

NOTE Points are the default unit of measurement for determining the spacing and thickness of line segments in the Stroke Style dialog box.

To closely examine a custom line before you begin drawing with it, select the Zoom 4x check box beneath the preview area of the Line Style dialog box. Note the Sharp corners check box, which toggles this Line Style feature on or off — select the check box to turn Sharp corners on.

FIGURE 5.24

The Stroke Style dialog box is opened with the Custom button on the Properties panel. The properties that appear vary depending on the style of line you select for adjustment.

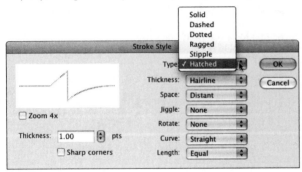

TIP Although there is no way to save custom line styles within the Stroke Style dialog box, you can create a separate document (.fla) and save samples of your favorite lines there. This eases your workflow if you want to reuse custom line styles extensively. You can apply these styles quite easily to other lines by opening the document and using the Eyedropper tool in conjunction with the Ink Bottle tool. For more information, see the sections on the Eyedropper and the Ink Bottle tools in Chapter 9, "Modifying Graphics."

Of course, the best way to get an idea of the variety of possible strokes is to experiment with settings and sizes for each style, but there are a few things to keep in mind as you work with stroke styles in Flash:

- The Hairline line style provides a consistent line thickness that doesn't visually vary at different zoom levels. This is the best line style to choose if you're creating artwork that you want to scale without losing the original line width. Regardless of whether an object with this stroke is enlarged or reduced in size, the Hairline stroke always displays as 1 point wide (as shown in Figure 5.25).

FIGURE 5.25

Hairline strokes always display at 1 point, even if they are scaled in the authoring environment or in the Player.

- The Solid line style draws a smooth, unbroken line. The customization variables for this style are limited to Thickness and Sharp corners. These two variables can also be adjusted on all line styles. The Solid line style is the optimal style for Web viewing because it requires fewer points to describe it and is consequently less file intensive. The smaller file sizes theoretically translate into faster download times when the artwork is transmitted over the Web. This really only becomes an issue if you're making extensive use of complex line styles.

- The Hatched line style thickness settings are different from the point size thickness settings that are available for all lines. The default thickness setting (measured in points) defines the thickness or height of the overall hatched line, whereas the hatch thickness setting defines the width of the individual vertical strokes that create the density of the hatched line texture.

Controlling Stroke Scale behavior

The Scale option is available only for solid lines, but it is very helpful for ensuring the consistency of scaled UI elements with outlines such as buttons. The various scaling behaviors you can set by using the Scale menu work only if you convert the raw stroke into a symbol. To make this easier to understand, here are the steps for applying the Scale option:

1. Select a Solid line style.
2. Set the stroke height to any height between 0.1 and 200.
3. Select the Scale behavior that works best for the specific element:

■ **None:** This produces a stroke that does not scale. A Solid stroke with Scale set to None has the same consistency as a Hairline but you are able to use any stroke height — instead of being restricted to the 1-point height for Hairline strokes. Figure 5.26 shows how a sample graphic with a 3-point stroke and a Scale setting of None appears when transformed with different amounts of scaling.

FIGURE 5.26

Strokes with Scale set to None always appear with the original stroke height.

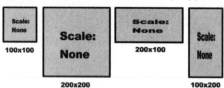

■ **Horizontal:** This produces a stroke that scales to match the horizontal transformation of an item. Vertical transformations have no effect on the scale of the stroke. Figure 5.27 shows how a sample graphic with a 3-point stroke and a Scale setting of Horizontal appears when transformed with different amounts of scaling.

FIGURE 5.27

Strokes with Scale set to Horizontal scale only in proportion to horizontal transformations.

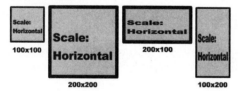

■ **Vertical:** This produces a stroke that scales to match the vertical transformation of an item. Horizontal transformations have no effect on the scale of the stroke. Figure 5.28 shows how a sample graphic with a 3-point stroke and a Scale setting of Vertical appears when transformed with different amounts of scaling.

FIGURE 5.28

Strokes with Scale set to Vertical scale only in proportion to vertical transformations.

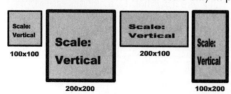

■ **Normal:** This produces a stroke that scales proportionally when it is scaled in any direction. This is generally the best setting to use if you want lines to maintain the same relative size as other scaled elements. However, if you want lines to have a fixed size no matter how big or small other elements are scaled, it is best to use the None setting. Figure 5.29 shows how a sample graphic with a 3-point stroke and a Scale setting of Normal appears when transformed with different amounts of scaling.

FIGURE 5.29

Strokes with Scale set to Normal scale in proportion with the greatest transformation in any direction.

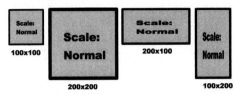

4. **Convert the graphic that contains the stroke into a symbol (Movie clip, Graphic, or Button).**

5. **Scale instances of the symbol in the authoring environment or in the Player and you will notice how the stroke scaling is constrained based on the Scale setting that you applied to the original stroke (in step 3).**

If you have ever tried to reuse a graphic that needed to be scaled while maintaining a specific size ratio to other elements — either relative or fixed — you will appreciate the level of control the Scale menu affords. The most common use for this option is constraining the scale behavior of a custom button that has to be adjusted to fit text of varying lengths. Generally, you want the stroke on the button to remain consistent while the button is stretched to accommodate the text. If you apply the Vertical Scale behavior, you will have a button with a stroke that stays the same no matter how long you stretch it horizontally to fit your text. But if you decide the buttons need to be a bit bigger overall, you can apply a vertical transformation and the stroke grows proportionally. What more could we ask for?

Optimizing Drawings

Aside from making a drawing more geometric, the main advantage of simplifying a shape or line is that it reduces the number of points that Flash has to remember and, thus, reduces the final file size. This is especially important for projects such as cartoons or animations that include a large number of hand-drawn shapes.

The most powerful tool for optimizing artwork precisely is found in the Optimize Curves dialog box opened by choosing Modify ⇨ Shape ⇨ Optimize. This feature gives you the option to control the level of optimization from 0 to 100. The new Preview check box enables you to see how different levels of optimization affect your artwork before deciding on a final setting and applying the command. If you select the Show totals message check box, you will see a dialog box appear to inform you how many points have been removed and what percentage reduction has been achieved after the optimization has been applied to your graphic each time you apply the modification.

NEW FEATURE The controls in the Optimize Curves dialog box have been updated. In Flash CS3 you could set a Smoothing value with a slider between None and Maximum and use a separate check box to apply multiple passes to achieve the greatest reduction in points. In Flash CS4, you can control the level of Optimization/Smoothing more precisely by using numeric values (this makes it easier to apply consistent levels of smoothing to different elements). The Use multiple passes check box is gone because multi-pass optimization is now done automatically, but there is a new Preview check box that makes it much easier to test optimization strength (and view the results) before applying the final command to your artwork.

Figure 5.30 shows a sketch drawn with the Brush tool with default smoothing before and after Optimize Curves was applied. The reduction in points appears in the dialog box. For illustration purposes, we made a drastic adjustment by applying Optimization strength at 100. For practical purposes, you should find a balance between optimization and drawing complexity by testing a range of settings.

FIGURE 5.30

Before (left) and after (right) Optimize Curves is used to reduce the complexity of a drawing made with the Brush tool with default smoothing. The reduction in points translates directly into a smaller file size.

NEW FEATURE You can apply the Optimize Curves command to the same artwork multiple times to achieve maximum reduction of points, but keep an eye on the totals message because when your artwork reaches a threshold of smoothing, continuing to apply the command starts to add points. If you see a negative value in the percentage of reduction, use the Undo command to step back to the artwork with the fewest points.

Putting Selection Tools to Work

Selection tools enable you to choose items that you want to edit in the Document window, as well as move or reshape specific elements. The three main selection tools — Selection, Subselection, and Lasso — provide different selection styles you can use for different editing tasks. The Subselection tool is used primarily as a companion to the Pen tool.

> **TIP** When you are busy with another tool, you can temporarily toggle to the Selection tool by pressing Ctrl (or ⌘).

The Selection tool

The Selection (arrow) tool (V) is used most commonly to select and move items — or multiple items — on the Stage. It is also used to reshape lines and shapes, in a way that is familiar to users who have worked in other vector graphics applications. The Selection tool's neighbor, which is differentiated with a white, rather than a black, arrowhead, is the Subselect tool (A). The Subselect tool is most useful for moving and editing anchor points created with the Pen tool and adjusting tangents on Bezier curves.

You can use the Selection tool to reshape a line or shape by pulling on the line (or shape) itself, or on its endpoints, curves, or corners. You can also use the Selection tool to select, move, and edit other Flash graphic elements, including groups, symbols, buttons, and text. When you click a raw stroke or fill, a mesh pattern appears to indicate that it has been selected. If the item you click is a symbol, a group, or a drawing object, a thin, colored line (called a *highlight*) indicates the selection status. You may set the highlight color in the General Preferences dialog box found under Edit ➪ Preferences (or in OS X, under Flash ➪ Preferences).

> **TIP** To temporarily turn off the selection mesh while editing an element, use View ➪ Hide Edges (Ctrl+H or ⌘+Shift+E). To toggle it back on, enter the same keyboard shortcut again. Even if you have toggled the selection off on one element, it is visible on the next element that you select.

Figure 5.31 shows a shape, a drawing object, a shape primitive, a group, and a Graphic symbol as they look when unselected (top) and as they appear when selected with the Selection tool. The first oval (a primitive shape) displays a mesh pattern when selected (left). The second oval (drawn with the Object Drawing option turned on), the third oval (drawn with the Oval Primitive tool), and the fourth oval (with the stroke and fill combined in a group) all display a thin, rectangular border when selected — the subtle differences being the color of the selection outline and the small, filled dot that designates the center point of the oval primitive. The final oval (which was converted into a Graphic symbol) displays a thin, rectangular border with a small crosshair icon in the top left corner and a white transformation point in the center when selected (right). You can move groups and symbols but not edit them directly on the Stage with the Selection tool unless you go into Edit mode.

> **NOTE** Drawing objects show a similar selection highlight as grouped shapes, but are actually a hybrid graphic style, which shares selected characteristics with raw shapes, grouped shapes, and Graphic symbols. Like raw shapes, you can modify drawing objects directly on the Stage with the Selection tool and any of the tools related to fills and strokes. Like grouped shapes, drawing objects do not erase or merge with other shapes if they overlap on the same layer (unless special commands are applied).

> **NEW FEATURE** Shape primitives have similar behavior to grouped shapes, but they have special editing options in the Properties panel that make them easy to modify. However, in order to edit a shape primitive with any of the selection tools, it must be converted into a drawing object or broken apart into a basic shape. The dynamic edit options in the Properties panel will no longer be available.

> **CROSS-REF** We explain the various ways of using grouped shapes in graphics in Chapter 9, "Modifying Graphics," and we discuss using and editing symbols in Chapter 6, "Symbols, Instances, and the Library."

In addition to clicking a line or shape to select it, you can select one or more items by dragging a marquee around them when the Selection tool is active. This operation is called *drag-select*. You can add additional items to a current selection by pressing Shift and clicking the items in sequence. When you drag-select to make a selection, previously selected items are deselected and excluded from the selection. In order to include previously selected items, press Shift as you drag-select. When a group is selected and you drag to move it on the Stage, holding down Shift constrains the movement range of the elements to 45 degrees. This is helpful if you need to move an element up or down while keeping it on the same axis or baseline.

FIGURE 5.31

Top row shows items unselected; bottom row shows Selection tool highlights (L-R) for a shape, a drawing object, a shape primitive, a group, and a Graphic symbol

Deselect one or more items by using any of the following methods:

- Pressing Esc
- Choosing Edit ➪ Deselect All
- Using the keyboard shortcut Ctrl+Shift+A (or ⌘+Shift+A)
- Clicking anywhere outside all the selected items

You can also use the Selection tool for duplicating items. Simply select an item (or line segment) with the Selection tool and press Alt (Option) while dragging the item to a new location. The original item remains in place, and a new item is deposited at the end of your drag stroke.

> **CAUTION**   Selecting a line with the Selection tool and then holding down Alt (Option) while dragging it to a new location duplicates it. Holding down Alt (Option) before dragging a line segment (that has not been selected) with the Selection tool adds a new corner point.

Moving multiple elements with the Selection tool

Text boxes, drawing objects, and groups are selected as single elements and move as a single unit. After you create text in a text box (we discuss text features in Chapter 8, "Working with Text"), Flash treats the text as one block, or group, meaning that all the individual letters move together when the box is selected. Similarly, a group of graphic elements — such as lines, outlines, fills, or shapes — can be grouped and moved or manipulated as a single element. However, when you move an item that is not grouped, only the selected part is moved. This situation can be tricky when you have ungrouped fills and outlines because selecting one without the other could unintentionally break up your shape. To group elements, select them all and apply the Modify ➪ Group command (Ctrl+G or ⌘+G). If necessary, you can ungroup them later by using Modify ➪ Ungroup (Ctrl+Shift+G or ⌘+Shift+G). We discuss grouping further in Chapter 9, "Modifying Graphics."

TIP Double-clicking the fill of a shape that has an outline stroke and a fill selects both. You can also use this strategy on lines with multiple sections. Double-clicking one section selects all the connected parts of a line, rather than just the closest segment.

The Drawing Object mode and the Shape Primitive tools make it easier to keep strokes and fills together. Drawing objects and shape primitives behave like grouped shapes: When you click anywhere on the shape, the stroke and fill are both selected so they move together. If you have drawn basic shapes with the Object Drawing toggle turned off, you can use the Modify ➪ Group command (Ctrl+G or ⌘+G) to group the lines and fills or use the Modify ➪ Combine Objects ➪ Union command to convert the raw lines and fills into a drawing object.

Modifying Selection preferences

In most cases, the default behavior for selection tools will support your workflow, but there are two preferences that you can modify to adjust selection behavior:

- **Turn off Shift select:** Prior to Flash 4, additional elements were added to a selection simply by clicking them. To use this older selection style, go to Edit (or on Mac Flash) ➪ Preferences, and under General ➪ Selection Options, clear the Shift select check box.

- **Turn on Contact-sensitive selection:** The standard selection behavior in Flash requires that a lasso or selection marquee completely enclose a group, drawing object, or symbol in order to select it. If you prefer to have these items included in a selection when the marquee touches any visible part, go to Edit ➪ Preferences and under General ➪ Selection options, select the Contact-sensitive selection and Lasso tools check box. Figure 5.32 illustrates the different selection results that you get when a marquee partially encloses a group, drawing object, or symbol when Contact-sensitive selection is left off (top) and when it is turned on (below).

FIGURE 5.32

To change the default nonselection result of partial selections in Flash (top), you can turn on Contact-sensitive selection behavior to select even partially enclosed items (below).

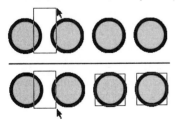

Using Selection tool arrow states to adjust or move drawings

In addition to the actions accomplished by selecting a line (or line section) and clicking an option, three arrow states — Move Selected Element, Reshape Curve or Line, and Reshape Endpoint or Corner — enable you to reshape and move parts of your drawings. It works like this: As you move the Selection tool over the Flash Stage, the arrow cursor changes state to indicate what tasks it can perform in context with various items (the line or fill) closest to the Selection tool's current position.

TIP When reshaping brush strokes or other filled items with the Selection tool, make sure that you don't select both the stroke and fill before trying to reshape the outline. If you do, you'll be able to move only the entire brush stroke — you won't be able to reshape it.

Figure 5.33 shows a series of (magnified) images that demonstrate the various arrow states as they appear and are applied. On the left, the original shape is shown with the arrow states displayed as the cursor is moved over the center of the shape, over a corner (B), and over a line (C). The center image shows the preview as the Move Corner arrow is used to extend the corner of the square and the Reshape Curve arrow is used to stretch the curve. The final image on the right shows the resulting changes to the original square.

FIGURE 5.33

Selection tool arrow states used to reshape and reposition an element: Move Selected Item arrow, Reshape Corner arrow (B), and Reshape Curve arrow (C)

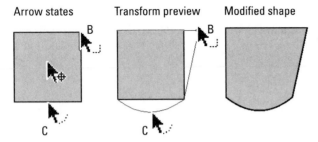

Figure 5.34 shows the various Selection tool arrow states used to modify a line. The lower images show the arrow state cursors, the center images show the preview as the mouse is dragged, and the top images show the resulting changes to the line when the mouse is released. You will notice that lines have to be selected in order to be moved without changing their shape with the Selection tool. If the line is not selected, the arrow displays only Move Corner or Reshape Curve states. If you want to add an angle to a line rather than add a curve, switch from Reshape Curve to Add Corner Point by holding down Alt (or Option) before clicking and dragging a line segment.

CAUTION   The icon visible next to the Selection tool arrow does not update when you switch from Reshape Curve to Add Corner Point by holding down Alt (or Option), but the behavior changes. After you click and move the line, the icon updates to match the behavior.

FIGURE 5.34

Using Selection tool arrow states to reshape and reposition a line (L-R: Move Selected Item, Reshape Corner, Reshape Curve)

> **TIP** Some brush strokes are easier to reshape if you view them as outlines (as described in Chapter 4, "Interface Fundamentals").

Knowing your Selection tool options

Figure 5.35 shows the three options that appear at the bottom section of the Tools panel when the Selection tool is active: Magnet (or snap to objects), Smooth, and Straighten. Because the various snap controls can be confusing at first, we compare the Magnet tool with the other snap settings available in Flash in the "Simplifying snapping settings" section, later in this chapter.

FIGURE 5.35

The Selection tool options available on the Tools panel

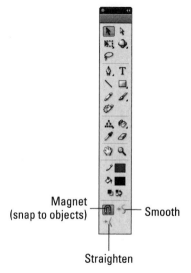

Magnet (snap to objects)

Smooth

Straighten

The Smooth and Straighten options available with the Selection tool (when a raw shape or drawing object is selected) are best used to clean up drawings by smoothing irregular curves or straightening crooked lines. Smoothing or Straightening reduces the number of bumps and variations (or points of transition) in a complex shape or line by reducing the number of points. The simplest curve or line is described by only one point at each end.

To simplify a shape or line, click the Selection tool and select the item you just sketched. Then click the Straighten or Smooth button in the Tools panel to get incremental adjustment. If you want more control over the way these commands are applied to your artwork, use Modify ⇨ Shape ⇨ Advanced Straighten or Modify ⇨ Shape ⇨ Advanced Smooth to open the new Advanced Straighten or Smooth dialog boxes. For hard-edged items such as a polygon, continue to click the Straighten button in the Tools panel or adjust the Straighten strength in the Advanced Straighten dialog box (with Preview turned on) until your rough sketch reaches the level of angularity that you like. For smooth-edged items that approximate an oval or an arc, continue to click the Smooth button in the Tools panel or adjust the Smoothing strength and the target angle range in the Advanced Smooth dialog box until your rough sketch has the amount of desired roundness.

TIP The controls in the Advanced Smooth dialog box can be a little confusing, but if you look at your drawing and consider if there are any angles that you do want to preserve and then use the angle menus to set a value range that excludes the angle you do want to keep (and not smooth), then it makes a little more sense. For example, if you have a 90-degree angle in your artwork (a clean corner) and you don't want that rounded off but you do want wider curves to be smoothed and narrower curves to be smoothed, you would set the first angle setting to Smooth angles below 89 degrees and the second setting to Smooth angles above 91 degrees. This would leave your 90-degree angle unsmoothed while applying smoothing to all the other angles in your drawing. If you have a hard time telling the difference between one result and another, don't be dismayed: This is a very subtle adjustment.

As shown in Figure 5.36, the simplified shape usually needs some further adjustment to get the result that you want after some of the points have been removed. The tools used for adjusting individual curves and points are the Pen tool and the Subselect tool.

You can apply the Smooth and Straighten options with the Selection tool to any selected shape or line to reduce the number of points and modify the form. The specific effect that these options have on your graphics is dependent on the Drawing settings that were used to create the original lines and the level of straightening or smoothing that you choose. By minimizing complexity in freehand drawings or shapes, Smooth and Straighten gradually reduce an erratic graphic into the most simplified form that can be described with the fewest points possible, while making curved lines straighter (when you apply Straighten) or sharp angles more rounded (when you apply Smooth).

NOTE In the example shown in Figure 5.36, we achieved maximum smoothing on all angles in the drawing by using only the Smooth angle above setting in the Smooth dialog box. With this set to 0 and the Smooth angle below check box deselected, you are allowing the smoothing algorithm to be applied to all angles in the drawing (from 0 degrees to 180 degrees). The same effect could be achieved by setting the Smooth angle below value to 180 and deselecting the Smooth angle above check box.

Although these assistants nudge a sketch or line style in the direction that you want, they don't add information; so don't be surprised if your drawing doesn't really look "better" or it takes a few tries to get the right balance between rough drawing and shape recognition.

The Lasso tool

The Lasso (L) is a flexible tool, somewhat resembling the selection equivalent of the Pen tool crossed with the Pencil tool. You use the Lasso primarily to make freeform selections and to group-select odd or irregular-shaped areas of your drawing. After areas are selected, they can be moved, scaled, rotated, or reshaped as a single unit. You can also use the Lasso tool to split shapes or select portions of a line or a shape. As shown in Figure 5.37, it has three options in the Tools panel: the Polygon mode button, the Magic Wand, and the Magic Wand properties.

The Lasso tool works best if you drag a loop around the area you want to select. (Hence, the tool name Lasso!) But if you slip or if you don't end the loop near where you started, Flash closes the loop with a straight line between your starting point and the endpoint. Because you can use the Lasso tool to define an area of any shape — limited only by your ability to draw and use the multiple selection capabilities of Flash — the Lasso tool gives you more control over selections than the Selection tool.

TIP To add to a previously selected area, hold down Shift before initiating additional selections.

FIGURE 5.36

Lines drawn with the Pencil tool (top left), can be selected with the Selection tool and simplified with the Advanced Smooth (center) or Advanced Straighten (right) options. A geometric shape (bottom) can be smoothed to have more curved lines (center) or straightened to have more angular lines (right).

FIGURE 5.37

The Lasso tool and options

Polygon mode

Polygon mode affords greater precision when making straight-edged selections, or in mixed mode, selections that combine freeform areas with straight edges. To describe a simple polygon selection, with the Lasso tool active, click the Polygon mode button to toggle on Polygon selection mode. In Polygon mode, you create selection points with a mouse-click, causing a straight selection line to extend between mouse-clicks. To complete the selection, double-click.

Mixed mode usage, which includes Polygon functionality, is available when the Lasso tool is in Freeform mode. To work in Freeform mode, the Polygon option must be in the off position. While drawing with the Freeform Lasso, press Alt (Option) to temporarily invoke Polygon mode. (Polygon mode continues only as long as Alt (Option) is pressed.) As long as Alt (Option) is pressed, a straight selection line extends between mouse clicks. To return to Freeform mode, simply release the Alt (or Option) key. Release the mouse to close the selection.

> **NOTE** Sometimes aberrant selections — selections that seem inside out, or that have a weird, unwanted straight line bisecting the intended selection — result from Lasso selections. That's usually because the point of origination of a Lasso selection is the point to which the Lasso snaps when the selection is closed. It takes a little practice to learn how to plan the point of origin so that the desired selection is obtained when the selection is closed.

The Magic Wand option and Magic Wand properties

The Magic Wand option of the Lasso tool is used to select ranges of a similar color in a bitmap that has been broken apart. After you select areas of the bitmap, you can change their fill color or delete them. Breaking apart a bitmap means that Flash subsequently sees the bitmap image as a collection of individual areas of color. (This is not the same as tracing a bitmap, which reduces the vast number of colors in a continuous-tone bitmap to areas of solid color.) After an image is broken apart, you can select individual areas of the image with any of the selection tools, including the Magic Wand option of the Lasso tool.

The Magic Wand option has two modifiable settings: Threshold and Smoothing. To set them, click the Magic Wand settings button to launch the Magic Wand Settings dialog box (shown in Figure 5.38) while the Lasso tool is active.

FIGURE 5.38

Use the Magic Wand Settings dialog box to adjust the selection range and level of smoothing.

The Threshold setting defines the breadth of adjacent color values that the Magic Wand option includes in a selection. Values for the Threshold setting range from 0 to 200: the higher the setting, the broader the selection of adjacent colors. Conversely, a smaller number results in the Magic Wand making a narrower selection of adjacent colors. A value of zero results in a selection of contiguous pixels that are all the same color as the target pixel.

The Smoothing setting of the Magic Wand option determines to what degree the edge of the selection should be smoothed. This is similar to anti-aliasing. (Anti-aliasing dithers the edges of shapes and lines so that they look smoother on-screen.) The options are Smooth, Pixels, Rough, and Normal.

The Subselection tool

The Subselection (arrow) tool (A) is the companion for the Pen and is found in the Tools panel to the right of the Selection tool. The Subselection tool has two purposes:

- To either move or edit individual anchor points and tangents on lines and outlines
- To move individual objects

When you position the Subselection tool over a line or point, the hollow arrow cursor displays one of two states:

- When over a line, it displays a small, filled square next to it, indicating that the whole selected shape or line can be moved.
- When over a point, it displays a small, hollow square, indicating that the point will be moved to change the shape of the line.

TIP If you use the Subselection tool to drag a selection rectangle around two items, you'll find that clicking and dragging from any line of an item enables you to move only that item, but clicking any point on an item enables you to move all items in the selection.

Figure 5.39 shows the use of the Subselection tool to move a path (A), to move a single point (B), to select a tangent handle (C), and to modify a curve by adjusting its tangent handle (D). Note that a preview is shown before releasing the handle.

The Subselection tool is most useful for modifying and adjusting paths. To display anchor points on a line or shape outline created with the Pencil, Brush, Line, Oval, or Rectangle tools, simply click the line or shape outline with the Subselection tool. This reveals the points that define the line or shape. Click any point to cause its tangent handles to appear. If you have a shape that is all fill, without any stroke, you'll need to position the cursor precisely at the edge of the shape in order to select or move it with the Subselection tool.

To convert a corner point into a curve point, follow these steps:

1. **Click to select the point with the Subselection tool.**
2. **While pressing Alt (Option), click and drag the point.** A curve point with tangent handles appears, replacing the original corner point.

NOTE By holding down Ctrl (or ⌘), the Pen tool can be used to mimic the function of the Subselection tool for moving lines or points but not for converting a curve point into a corner point.

FIGURE 5.39

Using the Subselection tool to modify lines and curves

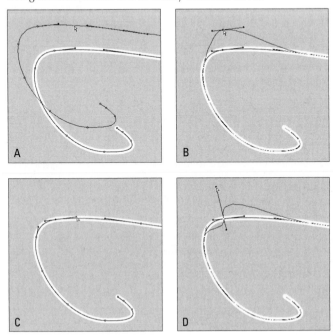

An important use of the Pen tool/Subselection tool combo is editing lines for optimal file size. The simpler your shapes, the smaller your file size and the faster your movie downloads. Most often, this involves deleting extraneous points. There are a few ways to delete points:

- Select the line or outline with the Subselection tool, which causes the individual points to appear as hollow circles along the line. Select the point that you want to remove. Press Delete.

- Select a line or outline with the Pen tool, and then position the cursor over the point that you want to remove. The cursor updates and displays a small inverted v (^) to the lower right, which is the Corner Point cursor. Click the point with the Corner Point cursor, and continue to hover over the point. After clicking with the Corner Point cursor, the cursor updates and displays a small minus sign (–) to the lower right, which is the Delete Point cursor. Click the point with the Delete Point cursor to delete it.

- When deleting more than one point from a closed shape, such as an oval or polygon, use the Subselection tool to drag and select any number of points. Press Delete to eliminate the selected points. The path heals itself, closing the shape with a smooth arc or line.

TIP If you use the Subselection tool to select a path and then Shift+select several points on it, those points can be moved in unison by dragging or by tapping the arrow keys.

TIP The submenu available in the Tools panel for the Pen tool makes it easier to set the Pen mode to remove or convert points without having to keep such a close eye on the contextual cues. Simply choose the Pen mode that you want to work within the Tools panel, click the line you want to edit to make the points visible, and begin adding, subtracting, or converting points, depending on the setting you've chosen.

Designing and Aligning Elements

After you've drawn some lines or shapes, you'll want to organize them in your layout. Flash provides some useful tools to help with moving or modifying elements that are familiar if you've worked in other graphics programs. Aside from using the Flash grid and manually placed guides with various snap settings to control your layout, you can quickly access the Align panel or the Info panel to dynamically change the placement of elements on the Stage. The Transform panel is the most accurate way to modify the size, aspect ratio, rotation, and even the vertical or horizontal "slant" of an element.

The precise alignment possible with panels and snapping controls is especially helpful if you're working with detailed artwork or multiple shapes that need to be arranged in exact relation to each other.

Simplifying snapping settings

There are five independent snapping settings in Flash. Snapping is a feature that gives you guidance when moving elements on the Stage and helps to align elements accurately in relation to each other, to the drawing grid, to guides, or to whole pixel axis points. The five different snapping controls can be turned on and off in the View ➪ Snapping submenu or in the Edit Snapping dialog box (shown in Figure 5.40), launched by choosing View ➪ Snapping ➪ Edit Snapping (Ctrl+/ or ⌘+/).

FIGURE 5.40

You can control Snapping settings in the Edit Snapping dialog box by using the Basic view, which shows only the top five check boxes, or the Advanced view, which expands the dialog box to include more Snap align settings, as shown here.

You can tell that an item is snapping by the appearance of dotted guide lines, as shown in the Snap Align example (see Figure 5.41), or by the appearance of a small circle beside the Selection tool arrow cursor, as shown in the Snap to Object and Snap to Grid examples (see Figure 5.42 and Figure 5.43). For best control of snapping position, click and drag from the center point or from an outside edge of an element.

The five main snapping modes are adjusted and applied as follows:

Snap Align

This feature gives you relative visual alignment guides as you move elements on the Stage. You'll either love or hate this option because it's the most "interactive" of all the snapping settings. The controls for Snap Align are in the Advanced settings of the Edit Snapping dialog box (shown in Figure 5.40). By default, Snap Align is set to display visual guides to alert you when an element is within 0 pixels of the movie border (aka the Stage edge), or within 0 pixels of another element in your layout.

As you move an element around on the Stage, you see dotted lines (see Figure 5.41) that alert you when the edge of the element is exactly 0 pixels from the edge of the Stage, or 0 pixels from the next closest fixed element. The dotted guide lets you know when the edges of the two elements are touching (or perfectly aligned), either vertically or horizontally. Modify the Movie border settings to change the alert or alignment distance between elements and the edge of the Stage. Modify the Horizontal or Vertical Snap tolerance settings to change the alert distance between elements. If you also want to see guides when elements are aligned to the center point of other elements, select the Horizontal or Vertical Center alignment check boxes.

TIP If you change the Horizontal or Vertical Snap Align settings to show a dotted line when an item is a specific distance from another item (such as 10 pixels — this was the default setting in Flash MX 2004), you still see the dotted line show up when the items are touching or within 0 pixels of each other. The fixed-distance Snap Align cue can be very helpful if you are trying to arrange items but you need them to be more than 0 pixels apart.

Snap to Objects

The Snap to Objects setting is a toggle that causes items being drawn or moved on-screen to snap to or align with other items on the Stage. Click the magnet icon in the Tools panel to turn snapping on or off (Shift+Ctrl+/ or Shift+⌘+/), or choose View ⇨ Snapping ⇨ Snap to Objects (a check mark appears next to the command if it's on). To control the tolerance of the magnet or the "stickiness" of the snap, use the Connect Lines setting found in Edit ⇨ Preferences ⇨ Drawing (or in OS X, Flash ⇨ Preferences ⇨ Drawing). By default, the Connect Lines tolerance is set at Normal. To make the magnet stronger, change the tolerance to Can be distant; to make it less strong, use Must be close. The Connect Lines control helps you to connect lines cleanly when drawing shapes or outlines.

As shown in Figure 5.42, object snapping is indicated by the "o" icon near the center point as an item is moved from its original position (left). When the item is dragged close enough to another item to snap to it, the "o" icon gets slightly larger, which indicates to you to release the mouse (right). This same visual cue works if you drag an item by a corner point rather than from a center point. Ovals can be aligned to the center point or to any point along their outer edge.

Snap to Grid

Snap to Grid (Ctrl+Shift+' [apostrophe] or ⌘+Shift+' [apostrophe]) is an option available under View ⇨ Snapping ⇨ Snap to Grid, which helps to align elements to guides or to the background grid. If Snap to Grid is turned on, elements show the snap icon by the Arrow cursor when you drag them close to a line in your grid, whether the grid is visible or not.

FIGURE 5.41

Snap Align guides give visual feedback for various alignment settings.

FIGURE 5.42

Snap to Objects indicated by a change in the size of the center point (or corner point) "o" icon as an item is moved to overlap with another item

To control the tolerance of this snapping feature, use the settings found under View ⇨ Grid ⇨ Edit Grid (Ctrl+Alt+G or ⌘+Option+G). The Grid Settings dialog box also includes check boxes for Snap to Grid and View Grid — these just give you another way to turn these tools on or off. Adjust the default horizontal and vertical spacing of the grid lines by entering new pixel values in the text fields. The first three settings in the Snap Accuracy menu are the same as those for Snap to Object, but there is an additional setting, Always Snap, which constrains elements to the grid no matter where you drag them. Figure 5.43 shows the default 18-pixel gray grid as it appears when it's made visible (View ⇨ Grid ⇨ Show Grid) with the Stage view zoom at 200 percent.

FIGURE 5.43

The snap icon as it appears when an element is dragged onto a grid line with Snap to Grid turned on (snapping works regardless of whether the grid is visible or not)

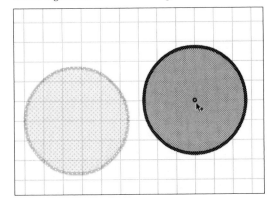

Snap to Guides

As we described in the previous chapter, guides are vertical or horizontal visual alignment tools that can be dragged onto the pasteboard or Stage *when rulers are visible*: Choose View ⇨ Rulers (Ctrl+Alt+Shift+R or ⌘+Option+Shift+R). If Snap to Grid is turned on when you drag guides out, they are constrained to the grid; otherwise, you can place guides anywhere. After guides are set, they are visible even if you turn rulers off; to toggle guide visibility use View ⇨ Guides ⇨ Show Guides (Ctrl+; [semicolon] or ⌘+; [semicolon]). As shown in Figure 5.44, Snap to Guides enables you to align an element to a guide, even if it is not aligned with the grid.

 Snap to Guides is independent of Snap to Grid, but guides can be placed only outside the grid when Snap to Grid is turned off.

 Rulers have to be visible to drag a guide onto the Stage, but after guides are placed, rulers can be turned off and guides will still be visible.

FIGURE 5.44

FIGURE 5.44

The snap icon as it appears when an element is dragged onto a guide with Snap to Guides turned on

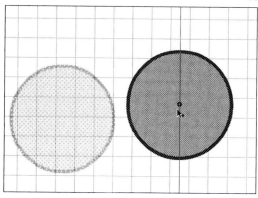

Snap to Pixels

Snap to Pixels is the only "global" setting that causes all elements to align with a 1-pixel grid that is visible only when the View scale is set to 400 percent or greater. This setting does not necessarily help you to align elements with each other, but it does help to keep elements from being placed "between pixels" by constraining movement of elements on the X and Y axes to whole pixels, rather than allowing decimals. There is no shortcut key for turning Snap to Pixels on, but you can always toggle it on and off from the View menu by checking or unchecking View ⇨ Snapping ⇨ Snap to Pixel. Figure 5.45 shows how the pixel grid appears when the View scale is at 400 percent. Items are constrained to whole pixel axis points if they are dragged from the center or from an outside edge.

FIGURE 5.45

The pixel grid visible when View scale is at 400 percent or higher with Snap to Pixels turned on

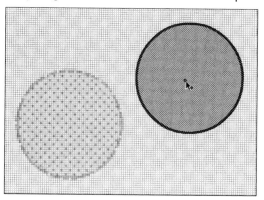

CAUTION If an item is positioned between pixels — for example if the X, Y position is 125.5, 200.5 — the Snap to Pixel feature does not *correct* the position to a whole pixel value. Snap to Pixels constrains only the movement of items to whole pixel values. Thus, the item example given here could be dragged to a new location only by *moving* in whole pixel values; so it might end up at a new location such as 130.5, 225.5. If you want to keep items aligned to whole pixel values, use the input fields in the Properties panel to manually enter a starting location with whole pixel X, Y values, and then use the Snap to Pixel option to *keep* items aligned with the 1-pixel grid.

TIP When you are working with an oval or other nonsquare polygon, you will notice that the X, Y values in the Properties panel may still show decimal pixel values even when Snap to Pixels is turned on. If you use the Info panel to change the shape's registration point from the default top-left setting to the center (click the center square in the Registration grid), you will have more success positioning and tracking the shape with whole pixel values.

Design panels

When you are drawing in Flash, the design panels — Align, Info, and Transform — can be your best friends. Use the Align panel to align, *regularize* (match the sizes of), or distribute several items on Stage, either relative to each other or to the Stage area. Use the Info panel to modify the coordinates, dimensions, and transformation points for items on the Stage. Use the Transform panel to scale, rotate, and skew an item.

NEW FEATURE You can also access width and height and x, y location values directly in the Position and Size section of the new vertical Properties panel.

The Align panel (Ctrl+K or ⌘+K), the Info panel (Ctrl+I or ⌘+I), and the Transform panel (Ctrl+T or ⌘+T) are available individually from the Windows menu, or they can be grouped into a tabbed panel that launches when you select any of the individual panels from the Window menu. Having these panels in a floating tabbed group is handy, but if you find that you use one more than the others, you might want to dock your favorite panels with the Properties panel for quick access.

The Align panel

The Align panel (Ctrl+K or ⌘+K), shown in Figure 5.46, is one of many features for which you'll be grateful every time you use it. It enables you, with pixel-perfect precision, to align or distribute items relative to each other or to the Stage.

FIGURE 5.46

Use the Align panel to both size and arrange items with ease.

The Align panel has five controls. The icons on the buttons show visually how selected items can be arranged:

- **To stage:** On the far right, you will notice a To stage button. When this button is selected, all adjustments are made in relation to the full Stage. To stage is actually a toggle you can turn on or off at any time — it retains the last chosen state even if the panel is closed and reopened.

- **Align:** There are six buttons in this first control. The first group of three buttons is for horizontal alignment, and the second group of three is for vertical alignment. These buttons align two or more items (or one or more items with the Stage) horizontally (top, middle, bottom) or vertically (left, middle, right).

- **Distribute:** This control also has six buttons: three for horizontal distribution and three for vertical distribution. These buttons are most useful when you have three or more items that you want to space evenly (such as a row of menu items). These buttons distribute items equally, again vertically or horizontally. The different options enable you to distribute from edge to edge, or from item centers.

- **Match size:** This control enables you to force two or more items of different sizes to become equal in size, and match items horizontally, vertically, or both.

- **Space:** This option enables you to space items evenly, again, vertically or horizontally. You may wonder how this differs from Distribute. Both are similar in concept, and if your items are all the same size, these options have the same effect. The difference becomes more apparent when the items are of different sizes:

    - Distribute evenly distributes the items according to a common reference (top, center, or bottom). For example, if one item is larger than the others, it may be separated from the other items by less space, but the distance between its top edge and the next item's top edge will be consistent with all the selected items.

    - Space ensures that the spacing between items is the same; for example, each item might have exactly 36 pixels between it and the next.

To align an item to the exact center of the Stage, do the following:

1. Click to select the item you want to center.
2. Click the To stage toggle in the Align panel.
3. Click the Align horizontal center button.
4. Click the Align vertical center button.

The Info panel

Use the Info panel (Ctrl+I or ⌘+I), shown in Figure 5.47, to give precise coordinates and dimensions to your items. Type the values in the fields provided, and by default, your item is transformed relative to its top left corner. The only limitation to this panel is that your selected item must be a drawing object, a group, a shape primitive, or a symbol — anything but a raw shape. For raw shapes, the values in the Info panel are read-only. The universal workaround is to use the Size and Position settings in the new vertical Properties panel.

CAUTION The registration point set in the Registration/Transformation point grid is actually a global setting that "sticks" even after you close the panel and change tools. After you change the registration point from top left to center, any new shapes or symbols that you create automatically have a center registration point. In most cases, it is best to stick with the default top left registration point because this is the standard for items that are loaded or positioned with ActionScript. Changing the registration point on one item back to top left does not have any effect on other items that were created with a center registration point.

FIGURE 5.47

Use the Info panel options to change the location and appearance of an item.

Width and Height (size)

Edit X, Y coordinates (location)

X, Y values for current mouse location

Registration grid (transformation point)

Color and Alpha values for current mouse location

The Info panel has these controls:

■ **Width:** Use this numeric entry field to alter the width of a selected item.

■ **Height:** Use this numeric entry field to alter the height of a selected item.

TIP Units for both Width and Height are measured in the units (pixels, inches, points, and so on) set in the Ruler Units option of the Document Properties dialog box found under Modify ⇨ Document (Ctrl+J or ⌘+J). Note, however, that upon changing the unit of measurement, the item must be deselected and then reselected in order for these readouts to refresh and appear in the current units.

■ **Registration grid:** The Registration grid is located just to the left of the numeric entry fields that are used for adjusting the X and Y location of any selected item. This grid consists of four small squares. Together, these squares represent the top corner of an invisible bounding box that encloses the selected item. Every shape created in Flash, even circles, resides within an imaginary rectangular bounding box that includes the extremities of the shape. The Registration grid enables you to toggle the selected item's registration point from the upper left corner to the center of its bounding box. The T icon on the top left square represents registration relative to the top left corner of the item, and the O icon on the bottom right square represents registration relative to the center of the item.

NOTE The X (horizontal) and Y (vertical) coordinates are measured from the upper left corner of the Flash Stage, which is the origin with coordinates 0,0.

- **X:** Use this numeric entry field to either read the X coordinate of the item or to reposition the item numerically, relative to the center point on the X (or horizontal) axis.

- **Y:** Use this numeric entry field to either read the Y coordinate of the item or to reposition the item numerically, relative to the center point on the Y (or vertical) axis.

- **RGBA:** This sector of the Info panel gives the Red, Green, Blue, and Alpha values for graphic items and groups at the point immediately beneath the cursor. Values for symbols, the background, or interface elements do not register.

- **+ X: / + Y:** This sector of the Info panel gives the X and Y coordinates for the point immediately beneath the cursor — including offstage or pasteboard values. A negative X value is to the left of the Stage, whereas a negative Y is located above the Stage.

To scale or reposition an item, select the item and then open the Info panel with shortcut keys or by choosing Window ➪ Info:

- Choose to scale or reposition the item relative to either the center or the upper left corner. (The icon toggles from the T icon on the top left to the O icon on the lower right to indicate the current setting.)

- To scale the item numerically, enter new values in the Width and Height fields, and then click elsewhere or press Enter to apply the change.

- To reposition the item numerically, enter new values in the X and Y fields (located in the *upper* half of the panel), and then either press Enter or click outside the panel to apply the change.

The Transform panel

The Transform panel (Ctrl+T or ⌘+T) gives you precise control over scaling, rotating, and skewing an item. With this panel, instead of making adjustments "by eye" — that may be imprecise — you enter numeric values in the appropriate fields and apply them directly to the selected item. As shown in Figure 5.48, the value fields in the Transform panel make it easy to modify the size and position of an element. However, after transformations are applied to an ungrouped basic shape or line, these numbers reset when the shape is deselected.

TIP If you're using the Properties panel to resize an item by pixel values, don't overlook the constrain option. When an item is selected on the Stage, a small lock icon appears beside the Width and Height fields. Click the lock to preserve the aspect ratio of an element as you enter a new value for width or height.

Some other powerful transform options are available from the Tools panel and from the Transform submenu of the Modify menu. We explain these more-complex editing tools in Chapter 9, "Modifying Graphics." However, the best place to start with transform options is the Transform panel, and these options are applied as follows:

- **Scale:** Use this to size the selected item by percentage. Enter a new number in the Scale field and press Enter. The shape scales to the specified percentage of its original size. To constrain the shape to its current proportions, click the Constrain check box. After a line or shape is deselected, the values in the Transform panel reset. The quickest way to get back to the original settings is to immediately use Edit ➪ Undo (Ctrl+Z or ⌘+Z) until it is reset. You can also get back to the original size mathematically by applying a new percentage that compensates for the changes you made before deselecting the item.

FIGURE 5.48

Use the Transform panel to scale, rotate, and skew items.

TIP

When you are using the Transform panel with groups, drawing objects, shape primitives, and symbol instances, you can reference or reset the original settings, even after the item has been deselected. We explain making and using symbols in Chapter 6, "Symbols, Instances, and the Library."

- **Rotate:** Click the radio button and then specify a rotation for the selected item by entering a number in the Rotate field. Press Return or Enter to apply the change to the selected item. The item rotates clockwise around its center point. To rotate an item counterclockwise, enter a negative number in the Rotate field.

- **Skew:** Items can be *skewed* (slanted in the horizontal or vertical direction) by selecting the Skew radio button, and then entering values for the horizontal and vertical angles. Pressing Return or Enter skews the item to the values entered.

- **Duplicate Selection and Transform:** Press this button and Flash makes a copy of the selected item (including shapes and lines) with all transform settings that have been applied to it. The duplicate is pasted in the same location as the original; select it with the Selection tool and move it to a new position to separate it from the original. Your original is left unchanged.

- **Remove Transform:** This button, at the bottom right corner of the panel, removes all transformation settings for a selected object. You can always use the Remove Transform (or "Reset") button for instances, groups, or type blocks to get back to 100-percent scale with no rotation or skew. However, after a shape or line is deselected, this button does not work. For shapes, this is really more like an "Undo All" button.

CROSS-REF

We discuss the 3D rotation and 3D center point options as they relate to working with 3D symbols in Flash in Chapter 9, "Modifying Graphics."

The Edit menu

We discuss many of the commands in the Edit menu in Chapter 4, but some of these commands can be helpful for creating or modifying graphics and are worth mentioning again here:

- **Undo:** When you make a mistake, before you do anything else, apply this command to get back to where you started. The default number for combined Undos that Flash remembers is 100; the maximum number is 300. Because Undo "memory" occupies system memory, you can set this level much lower if you find you don't rely on it. This setting is controlled in the General tab of the Flash Preferences dialog box.

NOTE It is possible to switch the Undo behavior from Document-level (the default behavior) to Object-level (legacy Flash-style). Document-level Undo stores a combined history stack for all items in the current document, while Object-level Undo stores individual history stacks for each item stored in the library. The benefit of using Document-level Undo (the default setting for Flash CS4) is that more commands or editing steps can be undone. For a complete list of steps that cannot be undone if you opt to use Object-style Undo (including most Create and Delete commands in the Library panel), refer to the section on Using the Undo, Redo, and Repeat menu commands in the Using Flash booklet in the Help panel. The Undo behavior and the number of undo steps that you want to buffer are controlled in the General section of the Preferences dialog box: File ➪ Preferences or Flash ➪ Preferences.

NOTE Undo does not transcend focus: You cannot Undo work on the Stage from the ActionScript panel: you must first return focus to the Stage to exercise Undo.

- **Redo:** The anti-Undo, this redoes what you just undid.
- **Repeat:** If you have not just used Undo, you will see this as an option that enables you to "double" whatever edit you may have made, or to apply it to another item.

CROSS-REF The History panel provides a flexible, nonlinear option for backtracking or repeating steps as you create and edit graphics. You can also use the History panel in conjunction with the Commands menu to track and save authoring steps that you can archive and reuse. We discuss these features in Chapter 9, "Modifying Graphics."

- **Cut:** This removes any selected item(s) from the Document window and places it on the Clipboard.
- **Copy:** This copies any selected item(s) and places it on the Clipboard, without removing it from the Document window.
- **Paste in Center:** Disabled if nothing has been copied or cut, this command pastes items from the Clipboard into the currently active frame on the currently active layer. You can also paste text into panel value fields.

NOTE The Paste in Center command places items in the center of the *currently visible* area in the Document window, not in the center of the Stage. Double-click the Hand icon in the Tools panel to center the Stage in the Document window before using Paste in Center if you want the pasted item to be placed in the center of the Stage.

- **Paste in Place:** This is like Paste, except that it pastes the object precisely in the same area of the Stage (or Work area) from which it was copied (but it can be on a new layer or keyframe).

- **Paste Special (PC only):** This is a Windows-only menu that enables some specialized copying of content into Flash. This is not recommended when working in a cross-platform environment because it is platform specific and limits how the document can be edited on other platforms.

- **Clear:** This removes a selected item(s) from the Stage *without* copying it to the Clipboard.

- **Duplicate:** This command duplicates a selected item or items, without burdening the Clipboard. The duplicated item appears adjacent to the original.

- **Select All:** This selects all items in the Document window in the currently active keyframe of the project.

- **Deselect All:** This deselects all currently selected items.

- **Find and Replace:** This command launches a powerful option that enables you to specify elements in a current Flash document or scene and modify them with settings you choose in the Find and Replace dialog box. For more detailed information on using the Find and Replace command, refer to Chapter 9, "Modifying Graphics."

- **Find Next:** This is a shortcut that searches through a Flash document or scene and finds the next item that matches the criteria set in the Find and Replace dialog box.

- **Timeline:** This submenu provides access to the most common commands used to modify frames in the timeline: Cut Frames, Copy Frames, Paste Frames, Clear Frames, Remove Frames, and Select All Frames. These commands are also available in the contextual menu on any frame in the timeline. This submenu also includes the commands for converting timeline animation into reusable script-based motion elements that can be copied, pasted or saved to share or use in other Flash files.

- **Edit Symbols:** Select an instance of a symbol and choose this command to modify the content of the symbol in Edit mode, an edit space that is independent from the Stage. For more about symbols and editing symbols, refer to Chapter 6, "Symbols, Instances, and the Library."

- **Edit Selected:** This command is enabled only if a group or symbol is selected on the Stage. It makes a selected group or symbol available in Edit mode. This same kind of edit space is invoked for symbols by choosing Edit Symbol.

- **Edit in Place:** This command opens a selected group or symbol in a separate tab of the Document window (shown in the location label area of the Document window), and enables you to edit this group or symbol while still seeing the other elements on the Stage, dimmed in the background for reference.

 Double-clicking a group or symbol on the Stage with the Selection tool has the same result as choosing the Edit in Place command.

- **Edit All:** From Edit mode, Edit All is used to go back to editing the main Flash scene. You can also do this by clicking the Scene location label of the Document window.

Creating Patterns with Symbols Using the Spray Brush Tool and the Deco Tool

Although the Deco tool and the Spray Brush tool are stored in the Tools panel along with all the other drawing and selection tools, we discuss them here in their own section because they are fundamentally different than the tools covered so far in this chapter. Instead of helping you to make lines or shapes manually, these tools auto-create patterns based on settings that you enter before you use them. And instead of using a fill or stroke color to create patterns, these tools use symbols (either the default symbol or a Movie clip or Graphic symbol that you create and then select from the library). The Spray Brush tool is great at making random patterns with variations in size, rotation, and distribution of symbol instances that make up the "spray." The Deco tool gives you powerful WYSIWYG tools for imposing order and geometric precision to the layout of multiple symbol instances, and the power to grow your own (easy to animate) vine patterns with just a click of your mouse.

These tools may require a little more work upfront (with setup and/or custom symbol creation), but they have the power to save you hours of time: Instead of tediously placing and positioning individual elements on the Stage to create a complex pattern or fill effect, you can simply click your mouse and Flash distributes instances of your selected symbol across the Stage, arranged exactly as you have specified. Magic! These tools are so fun and easy to use that we expect to see complex geometric patterns and funky random fills in many more Flash movies.

CROSS-REF For information on how to create your own symbols, skip ahead to Chapter 6, "Symbols, Instances, and the Library."

Applying random "ink" with the Spray Brush tool

The Spray Brush tool shares space in the Tools panel with the old-fashioned Brush tool. To toggle between the two, click and hold the Tool space until the popup shows both tools, and then select the one you want to work with. The icon for the Spray Brush gives you a good clue for how this tool works: like a can of spray paint. When you select the Spray Brush, you won't see options in the Tools panel as you do for the standard Brush tool, but instead you see controls in the Properties panel for selecting the symbol you want to work with and setting the size and angle of the Brush (which for this tool is actually the spray area covered when you click without moving your cursor). Figure 5.49 includes the Tools panel with the Spray Brush selected and the Properties panel with the Symbol and Brush settings used to create the pattern of dots shown on the far left. The special beauty of the Spray Brush tool is that the distribution of dots is somewhat random. If you have ever tried to create a "random" pattern by placing individual elements on the Stage, you will truly appreciate how much time and effort this tool can save.

FIGURE 5.49

With the default settings in the Properties panel, the Spray Brush creates a random pattern of dots as you click and drag on the Stage.

You can use the Spray Brush without creating any custom symbols by simply leaving the Symbol setting for Spray on no symbol (the Default shape check box will be selected). With this workflow you can choose a color for your spray and you can choose the area that the "ink" (or small dot/particles) scatter in with each click, but you can't alter the shape or size of the particles in the spray. The maximum settings allowed for width and height of the Brush area match the size of your current Stage size, but you can spray as large an area as you want by holding down the mouse and dragging to spray. Each time you click and release the mouse with the Spray Brush, you create a group of symbol instances. These groups can be selected and edited individually after they have been sprayed onto the Stage.

> **TIP**   To make editing easier, you might consider using the Select All (⌘+A) command and then ungrouping the spray groups so that you can handle the particles individually without having to click-in to a group to edit in place.

As shown in Figure 5.50, the Spray Brush gets a lot more interesting when you have some symbols in your library to work with.

FIGURE 5.50

Select a custom symbol as the spray, and then adjust the settings to create patterns by using multiple instances of your symbol with each click of the Spray Brush.

To specify a custom symbol spray pattern, do the following:

1. **Select the Spray Brush tool in the Tools panel.**

2. **Click the Edit button in the Symbol section of the Properties panel.** The Swap symbol dialog box appears, which shows a list of all the symbols in your current library. Select the symbol you want to use as your spray particle.

3. **Choose scale settings for the symbol.** In most cases, you get a more interesting result if you set the scale to less than 100 percent. You can use really large particles, but the Spray Brush is designed to work best with smaller particles (less than 100 pixels in width or height).

4. **Use the random settings to make the spray more interesting and organic:**

   - Random scaling adjusts the size of the particles so that there are varying sizes in each spray. The specific sizing is random and unpredictable, but the particles can vary from 1 x 1 pixel to the size set by your scale setting in step 3.

   - Rotate symbol adjusts the alignment of the spray so that your symbol instance is not always in its original position. It varies from 0 to 360 degree rotation, but the rotation of particles in each group is consistent.

   - Random rotation adjusts the alignment of the particles in each spray so that your symbol instance is in varying positions within each group. This option creates a nice random texture if you are working with an irregularly shaped particle.

5. **Set the size of the spray area by using the Brush width and height settings.** Choose a value between 0 and the width or height of your current document. Experiment with this setting to get the result you like best, but we found that an area equal to half the current document size worked well for controlling the brush while not restricting the distribution of symbols too much.

6. **Set rotation for the spray area (if you like), using the Brush angle setting.** Choose a value between 0 and 360. This setting has a visible result only if you have unequal values for the width and height of your spray area (set in step 5). Using a rotation of 90 has the same final result as swapping your Brush width and height settings.

7. **Click and drag to spray a symbol pattern onto the Stage.** Move the mouse to cover more area, or keep the mouse in one area to create a layered effect with a buildup of spray (or stacked symbol instances).

Symbol instances are sprayed and grouped each time you click the mouse. As shown in Figure 5.51, you may end up with a lot of groups if you click and spray multiple times.

FIGURE 5.51

Use Select all to see the symbol instance groups that make up a layered pattern created by the Spray Brush applied with multiple mouse clicks.

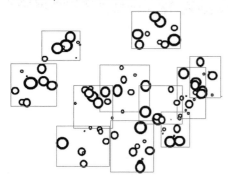

Creating order and pattern with the Deco tool

The Deco tool (U) is more like three tools in one. It's represented by one icon in the Tools panel but as shown in Figure 5.52, when you select it, you see a drop-down menu in the Property inspector that enables you to choose from three different drawing effects:

- **Vine Fill:** Auto-draws a vine pattern with leaf and flower symbols arranged on simple stems. The pattern originates where you click your mouse but continues to grow until it fills the shape that you have selected to place it in or you stop the effect (by hitting Esc or selecting another tool in the Tools panel). You can use the default symbols to create the vine (a simple leaf shape and a basic flower), assigning each a color if you want, or you can select your own symbol from the library for one or both of the leaf and flower elements.

- **Grid Fill:** Arranges symbol instances in rows and columns based on the spacing and scale you set in the Property inspector (Advanced Options). The pattern originates where you click your mouse and continues tiling outward until it fills a shape or you stop the effect. You can tile the default symbol (a black square) or choose any Movie clip or Graphic symbol in your library.

- **Symmetry Brush:** Provides control handles that enable you to direct the placement of multiple symbol instances in geometric patterns:

  - Reflect Across Line
  - Reflect Across Point
  - Rotate Around Point
  - Grid Translation

FIGURE 5.52

The Deco tool in the Tools panel has three different drawing effect options in the Property inspector that produce distinctly different results: (far left, top to bottom) Vine Fill, Grid Fill, Symmetry Brush. They all work by auto-arranging symbol instances on the Stage, but each has its own settings and controls for modifying the layout.

Growing patterns with the Vine Fill drawing effect

The Vine fill creates a simple pattern with the default symbols (as shown in Figure 5.52), but you can use it as a base for much more detailed designs. Keep in mind that the symbols you choose for the Leaf and Flower don't actually have to be leaves or flowers — they can be any symbol you choose. In Advanced Options you can choose a color and angle for the vine stem and also set a scale for the overall pattern and a length for the vine segments. As with any symbol instance, you have the option of editing your leaf and flower symbols after they have been drawn as part of the vine pattern. Figure 5.53 compares a Vine fill drawn with custom leaf and flower symbols with the same vine after the leaf and flower symbols have been edited.

You'll notice that the Vine fill "grows" in a kind of organic way after you click to start the fill. You can capture this fill pattern as frame-by-frame animation by selecting the Animate Pattern check box at the bottom of the Property inspector Advanced Options for the Deco tool Vine Fill drawing effect. The Frame step setting controls how often a new frame is added as the pattern grows: The range from 1 to 100 represents the percentage of the total pattern that is included in each frame. A setting of 100 puts only one keyframe on the timeline with the finished pattern in it, showing 100 percent of the drawing in just one step. A setting of 1 adds as many keyframes as there are elements in your vine pattern, showing the drawing in incremental steps with a keyframe for each step. For most purposes, a setting somewhere in the middle works just fine.

FIGURE 5.53

A Vine fill created with custom leaf and flower symbols (left) can be edited after it is drawn to have a very different look (right).

CAUTION The Vine fill works best if the symbols you choose for the leaf and flower nodes are small in size: generally under 25 pixels in any direction. If the symbols are too large, the vine has no room for both leaves and flowers unless you make the segments really long — which makes the pattern look less like a vine and more like a series of long lines. If you are working with large symbols, you can either edit the graphics to scale them down, or you can set the Pattern scale to a lower value to make the symbol instances small enough to fill the vine with a decent density of leaves and flowers.

TIP If you like the look of larger leaves and flowers, it works better to create the fill pattern with small graphics and then edit the source symbols to scale the graphics larger; the symbol instances for the leaves and flowers update but the vine pattern is not disrupted. This was the workflow for the vines shown in Figure 5.53.

Tiling patterns with the Grid Fill drawing effect

The Grid Fill does just as its name implies: it fills an area with a grid-based pattern of symbol instances. The default graphic is a black square (as shown in Figure 5.52), but you can specify any Movie clip or Graphic symbol in your library. As shown in Figure 5.54, the options for Grid Fill (available after you activate the Deco tool in the Tools panel and select Grid Fill from the drop-down menu in the Property inspector) enable you to choose a Fill symbol and set the horizontal and vertical spacing and scale for the symbol instances. The pattern starts wherever you click your mouse on the Stage, and it continues to tile outward until you stop the effect (by hitting Esc or choosing another tool in the Tools panel) or until it hits the inside edges of whatever shape you have chosen to fill. The tile is symmetrical in all directions, so you might find that there are empty spaces left in a filled graphic because the fill hit an area that it could not tile evenly. Figure 5.54 shows just three examples of tiled fills created with the Deco tool and the Grid Fill drawing effect.

FIGURE 5.54

Grid Fill creates a tiled pattern of symbol instances with the spacing and scale you choose. Here are just a few options: you can make the default shape small and dense (top), use a bitmap in a Graphic symbol as a fill for another shape (middle), or even apply the effect more than once to get layered geometric patterns (bottom).

As with all the Deco tool artwork, the symbol instances for Grid fills are grouped each time you click to start a fill, and the source symbols and symbol instances can be edited after the fill pattern is created.

Creating reflected patterns with the Symmetry Brush drawing effect

The Symmetry Brush has four different modes, and each mode has a different guide that appears on the Stage, enabling you to control the placement of symbol instances in a geometric pattern. Although the guides are unique for each mode, the principle is the same — use the guide to set up placement of symbol instances, and then click to place them on the Stage while the drawing effect builds a reflected pattern each time you click. Figure 5.55 shows the guides and the pattern created by each with the default graphic (a black square).

FIGURE 5.55

The four Symmetry Brush modes enable you to use draggable guides to dynamically control the placement and spacing of symbol instances: Reflect Across Line (A), Reflect Across Point (B), Rotate Around Point (C), and Grid Translation (D).

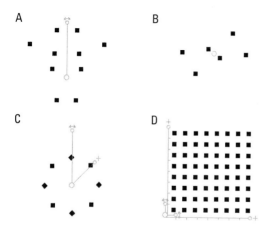

These guides are tricky to describe and are best explored in a tactile way, but here is some explanation for each one:

- **Reflect Across Line:** Click and drag the guide center point to position the guide in the area of the Stage where you want the pattern to originate. Click and drag the direction point — marked with a double arrow — anywhere within a 360-degree arc to orient the line that creates the reflection axis. Click on either side of the line to place symbol instances and expect to see an exact reflection on the other side of the line, mirroring placement on the Stage and distance from the axis.

- **Reflect Across Point:** Click and drag the guide center point to position the guide in the area of the Stage where you want the pattern to originate. Click on any side of the center point to place symbol instances and expect to see an exact reflection on the other side of the point, mirroring placement on the Stage and distance from the axis.

■ **Rotate Around Point (aka the clock-face effect):** Click and drag the guide center point to position the guide in the area of the Stage where you want the pattern to originate. Click and drag the direction point — marked with a double arrow — to anywhere within a 360-degree arc to orient the starting position for the first symbol instance in the circular pattern. Click and drag the spacing point — marked with an x — to anywhere within a 180-degree arc to set the angle of reflection.

Click anywhere around the two lines and expect to see reflections oriented around the center point and repeated as many times as there is room for in the reflection area. If you drag the spacing point closer to the direction point, you increase the reflection area and more symbol instances fill the space. If you drag the spacing point farther away from the direction point, you decrease the reflection area and fewer symbol instances fill the space.

NOTE If the spacing point is 180 degrees from the direction point (forming a straight line), you see only one reflection for each symbol instance you place, but the effect is different than the Reflect Across Line pattern because the reflected instances are at the opposite end of the axis line rather than directly across.

■ **Grid Translation:** Click and drag the guide center point to position the guide in the area of the Stage where you want the pattern to originate. Click and drag the spacing points — marked with plus signs (+) — to set the endpoints for the fill pattern on the x and y axis. Click and drag the position guides — marked with double arrows — to adjust the rotation angle for the grid. One pointer changes the rotation of individual symbol instances in relation to each other, creating a skew effect, and the other pointer changes the rotation of the whole group of symbol instances in relation to the center point. Click to place a symbol instance in the grid area and expect to see a grid fill the space between the two spacing points.

TIP It is easier to judge the effect of skew angles if you click to create a grid before you move the position guides from their default positions.

One quick way to get a feel for the varied powers of these different Symmetry Brush modes is to create a pattern in one mode and then change the mode in the Property inspector without modifying the artwork on the Stage. This enables you to see how different the patterns made by each guide can be even with the same source symbol instances and placement.

WEB RESOURCE We'd like to know what you think about this chapter. Visit www.flashsupport.com/feedback to fill out an online survey with your comments.

Summary

■ The geometric shapes available from the Tools panel are a quick, accurate way of creating basic elements that you can customize with various fill and stroke styles.

■ The Primitive Shape tools for creating dynamic ovals and rectangles make it much easier to draw and modify shapes without having to start from scratch or make permanent manual changes to the original shape to create rounded rectangles, open circles, and other useful graphics.

■ Settings dialog boxes for the Oval tool and the Rectangle tool make it possible for you to set the width and height of these shapes *before* they are drawn.

■ The Pencil, Brush, and Pen tools enable you to draw freeform or Bezier lines that you can edit by using the Pen submenu, Selection tool arrow options, or the Subselection tool.

- The Object Drawing option can be turned on while creating graphics with any of the drawing or shape tools. Drawing objects are hybrid graphics that share selective characteristics with shapes, grouped shapes, and Graphic symbols.

- Enhanced Smoothing controls, a Tilt toggle, and a Pressure toggle give artists who use tablets lots of options to customize the Flash drawing environment.

- The Scale control in the Properties panel gives you more precise control over strokes that will be scaled in the authoring environment (as symbol instances) or in the Flash Player (as final published content).

- Optimizing artwork manually by editing points with the Subselection tool, or automatically by using the Optimize Curves option, can greatly reduce file size by simplifying lines and curves.

- The Smooth and Straighten modifiers in the Tools panel are now augmented by dialog boxes that give you more control over the level of optimization — and in the case of Smoothing, the exact angles that you want to target. To access these more advanced smoothing controls, select Modify ⇨ Shape ⇨ Advanced Smooth or Advanced Straighten from the application menu.

- By adjusting and applying the various snapping modifiers, you can control how "auto" alignment behavior affects elements as you work. The Edit Snapping dialog box enables you to set or modify snapping behaviors quickly.

- In Flash CS4 you have the option of using Document-level Undo or going back to the legacy-style Undo (Object-level). There are advantages to using Document-level Undo (which is the default), but the legacy option has been maintained in response to users who wanted to go back to the Undo style that they were familiar with from older versions of Flash.

- New pattern tools enable you to use symbol instances as the basis for geometric or random fill patterns. The Spray Brush works like a spray can to scatter symbol instances as particles on the Stage. The Deco tool offers a range of different modes and guides for creating more organized patterns based on reflection and grids, plus a fun Vine Fill mode that lets you design your own organic fill with leaf and flower nodes.

Chapter 6

Symbols, Instances, and the Library

Symbols are the key to file-size efficiency and interactive power in Flash. A symbol is a reusable element that resides in the current movie's document Library, which you access with Window ➪ Library (Ô/Ctrl+L). After you convert an item in your Flash movie into a symbol, each time you use that item on your Main Timeline or within a Movie Clip Timeline, you're working with an instance of the original symbol. Unlike using individual graphic elements, you can use many instances of a symbol, with little or no addition to the file size.

Using symbols helps reduce the file size of your finished movie because Flash needs to save the symbol only once. Each time a given symbol is used in the project, Flash refers to its original profile. To support the variations of an instance, Flash needs to save information about the *differences* only — such as size, position, proportions, and color effects. If a separate graphic was used for each change, Flash would have to store a complete profile of all the information about that graphic — not just the changes, but also all of the points that specify what the original graphic looks like.

Furthermore, symbols can save you a lot of time and trouble, particularly when it comes to editing your movie. That's because changes made to a symbol are reflected in each instance of that symbol throughout the movie. Let's say that your logo changes halfway through production. Without symbols, you would have to find and change each copy of the logo. However, if you've used symbol instances, you need only edit the original symbol — the instances are automatically updated throughout the movie.

NEW FEATURE The new pattern drawing tools in Flash CS4 — Spray Brush and Deco — are an excellent use of symbols. Using multiple instances of a symbol to create a pattern enables you to quickly change the look of even complex patterns by editing the original symbol.

In this chapter, you learn to create and edit basic symbol types stored in your Document Library. You also learn to use symbol instances, both within the Main Timeline and within other symbols, and to modify individual instances of a symbol.

CROSS-REF Components are briefly mentioned in this chapter because they are stored in the Library, but we cover using and modifying components in Chapter 32, "Using Components."

Understanding the Document Library

The Library (⌘/Ctrl+L) is the storehouse for reusable elements, known as *symbols*, which can then be placed as symbol *instances* within a Flash movie. Imported sounds and bitmaps are automatically placed in the Library. Upon creation, Graphic symbols, Button symbols, and Movie Clip symbols are also stored in the Library. It's a good practice to convert main items within a Flash document into symbols, and to then develop your project from instances derived from these original symbols.

The main document Library panel, shown in Figure 6.1, is used to access stored assets for any files that are currently available in the tabbed Document window. Each file has its own unique Library list that displays all symbol assets used in the file as well as any assets that were imported or added to the Library to be saved with the file.

TIP The Flash Library panel includes a drop-down menu that provides quick access to the Library list of any project files (.fla) loaded into the Document window. Changing the view within the main Library panel is faster and more space efficient than opening and managing multiple Library panels.

NEW FEATURE All Library panels can be scaled vertically and horizontally by clicking and dragging the sides or the bottom of the panel. Panels can be docked to any other Library panel or to the Properties panel or the Document window — wherever you find it most convenient to keep your source symbols handy.

FIGURE 6.1

The main document Library panel provides access to assets for open .fla files (top left). Common Libraries (bottom) and other saved .fla files (top right) can be opened as External Libraries and used as asset source files.

Working with Common Libraries and External Libraries

External Libraries are panels that open separately from the main Library panel to provide access to stored assets for files that are not currently open in the Document window. You can open any saved Flash file as an External Library by choosing File ➪ Import ➪ Open External Library and browsing to the file that you want to load. All the stored symbols from your selected file will be visible in a floating External Library panel, but the document will not be visible in the Document window, and you cannot edit the symbols in the External Library unless you copy them to the main Library panel or to the Stage of a file that is open in the Document window.

Flash ships with three External Libraries called Common Libraries. These panels hold ready-made elements that you can drag into any document Library (or onto the Stage or Pasteboard in an open Document Window) to use in your own projects. Common Libraries behave exactly like any other External Library. Choose Window ➪ Common Libraries to open the submenu of Common Libraries that ship with Flash. The Buttons Library contains a selection of prebuilt Flash elements that you can reuse in any Flash project. The Classes Library contains compiled scripts that are used with the AS2 components that also ship with Flash. The Learning Interactions found in CS3 are no longer included as a Common Library, but the new CS4 Sound Library is an amazing resource with over 180 optimized sound files ready to drag and drop into your Flash movies. Many of the sounds are also built to loop seamlessly, so you can create background sounds without bloating your file size.

 Preview sounds by selecting them in the Library list and then clicking the play button in the preview window.

You can open and use the Common Library panels and any other External Library panels as free-floating panels (as shown in Figure 6.1) or you can stack or group them for tabbed access (as shown in Figure 6.2). After you copy assets to one of the document asset lists in the main Library panel (or into any of your project files in the Document window), you can close the External Library and work with the copied symbols without changing the original symbol source.

FIGURE 6.2

You can organize Common Libraries and External Libraries into panel stacks (left) or tabbed groups (right).

A helpful feature in all Flash CS4 Library panels is a new search field (as shown in Figures 6.1 and 6.2). You will find it right above the asset list marked by a small binocular icon. You can type the name of a specific element or just the first letter of the elements you want to find and sort in the asset list; as you type,

Flash shows you all elements that match the information you are entering. For example if you type in **b**, you might see "flowerButton," "symbol2," "BeamScan," and so on — anything with the letter *b* in the name. If you typed the full word **bu** you would see only "flowerButton" in the asset list. This feature can save a lot of time if you are sorting through a complex file with many elements stored in the Library. The search even looks in folders and shows you any matching items.

> **TIP**   **To add your own buttons, symbols, or even complete libraries for specific projects, first save them in a Flash document (.fla) with a descriptive name; then place that Flash file in the Libraries folder within the Configuration folder for Flash CS4 on your hard drive.**

The source files for the External Libraries that show up in the Common Libraries menu are stored in the Libraries folder of the Configuration folder for Flash CS4.

- The standard directory path on Windows is:
  ```
  C:\Program Files\Adobe\FlashCS4\ (language)\Configuration\Libraries
  ```
- The standard directory path to the application config folder on Mac is:
  ```
  HD\Applications\Adobe Flash CS4\(language)\Configuration\Libraries
  ```

Working with multiple Document Libraries

The Flash Library panel, shown in Figure 6.3, includes a drop-down project menu that lists all currently open files. This is a great space saver that makes it much easier to switch between different document Libraries without having to manage separate floating panels. By default, the Library panel switches views as you tab from one document to another in the Document window, but changing the Library view does not change the Document view — in other words, the Library panel is connected to the Document panel but not the other way around. This makes it easy to access a different Library while maintaining the view of your current file/ in the Document window.

If you want to keep a Library asset list for one project visible in the Library panel while tabbing to a different project file in the Document window, you can use the handy Pin toggle in the Library panel. Click the tack or pushpin icon to pin or "stick" the current asset list so it won't change when you tab to a new project in the Document window. Don't forget to click the Pin toggle again to turn it off when you want to unstick the Library asset list.

There are times when you may want to see the contents of more than one Library at a time — to compare files or to drag items from one Library to another. Click the New Library Panel button to create a duplicate floating Library panel at any time. You can then use the drop-down menu to switch the project view in one of the Library panels to compare items or to drag the contents of one Library to another. Like External Libraries or other floating panels, Document Library panels can be grouped (for tabbed access), stacked, or floated as individual panels.

You can access elements stored in the Library of any other Flash document (without opening the actual .fla file in the Document window) by choosing File ⇨ Import ⇨ Open External Library from the application menu and browsing to a .fla file. The Library opens next to the Document window of your current project as a floating panel that can be handled exactly like any of the Common Libraries. External Libraries (Library panels for files that are not open in the Document window) do not show up in the drop-down menu of the main Document Library panel, but they can be grouped or stacked with the main Document Library if you need to keep them handy without eating up screen space.

FIGURE 6.3

The Flash document Library panel includes a project menu, Pin toggle, and New Library button. As shown, you can use the New Library Panel button to launch a clone panel (right) for the current project view in the main Document Library (left).

You can copy assets from an External or Common Library to a current Document Library by dragging items from the source Library onto the current document Stage, or directly into the Library panel. This also works if you have two documents open, and you want to move assets between the two Libraries. It is also then possible to drag or copy and paste elements directly from one document Stage onto another, or drag an item from a source document Stage into a current document's Library.

NOTE Open documents are loaded into the tabbed Document window. If you want to view more than one Document Stage at a time, use the Window ⇨ Duplicate Window command to create a clone of one of the tabbed documents. You can then use the tabbed UI in the main Document window to switch views to any other open document while keeping a view of the cloned document in the duplicate Document window.

The shared Library feature makes it possible to link assets between project files (.fla) during production by using *authortime* sharing, or to link multiple published movie files (.swf) on the server with *runtime* sharing. Shared libraries create a more optimized workflow than saving individual copies of assets in multiple documents. You can learn more about linking symbols in your project files in "Using Authortime Shared Libraries" later in this chapter.

Reading the Library panel

Every Flash document has its own Library panel, which is used to store and organize symbols, sounds, bitmaps, and other assets such as video files. As shown in Figure 6.4, the item highlighted — or selected — in the Sort window is previewed in the Preview window. Each item in the Library has an icon to the left of the name to indicate the asset type. Click any heading to sort the window by Name, Kind (type), Use Count, or Linkage (all headings shown in Figure 6.1).

FIGURE 6.4

The Document Library (scaled to a narrow view)

If the item selected in the Library is a Button symbol, a Movie Clip, or a sound file with more than one frame on its timeline, a controller appears in the upper right corner of the Preview window. This Preview Stop/Play controller pops up to facilitate previewing these items. It's equivalent to the Play command in the options menu. As shown in Figure 6.5, the library options popup menu lists a number of features, functions, and controls for organizing and working with items in the Library.

FIGURE 6.5

The Library panel and the options popup menu

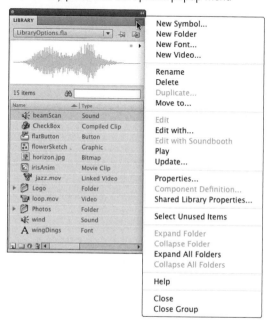

The following commands, found in the Library options menu, enable you to add or modify content stored in your document Library.

- **New Symbol:** Choose this command to launch the Create New Symbol dialog box where you can name and choose properties for a symbol, and then click OK to open Edit mode and place or create graphics on the symbol timeline. When a new symbol is created, it is stored at the root of the Library Sort window. You can drag it inside of any existing Library folders.

- **New Folder:** Items in the Library can be organized in folders. The New Folder command simply creates a new folder within the Sort window. New folders are "untitled" by default; double-click the folder text to type a custom folder name. This menu command is equivalent to the New Folder button at the bottom of the Library panel.

- **New Font:** Use this command to open the Font Symbol Properties dialog box, which is the first step in creating a font symbol for use within a Shared Library.

- **New Video:** Creates a new empty `Video` object in the Library.

- **Rename:** Use the Rename command to rename the currently selected item in the Sort window. Double-click any item title in the list to achieve the same thing.

- **Delete; Duplicate:** Select Duplicate to create a copy of an item and Delete to delete an item in the Sort window.

- **Move to:** Use the Move to option to open the Move to dialog box. You can move the currently selected element to an existing folder in your Library list or create a new folder (which will appear in your main Library list) to move it to.

NOTE You can also move Library items to folders by dragging them onto any folder icon.

- **Edit:** Choose Edit to access the selected symbol in Edit mode.

TIP Double-clicking a symbol on the Stage takes you into Edit in Place mode, a variant of Edit mode that enables you to see other elements on the Stage dimmed in the background for layout reference as you modify the symbol.

- **Edit with:** Provided that you have appropriate external applications installed, most imported assets (such as sounds, bitmaps, and vectors) have this command available to jump to the external editing environment of your choice.

- **Properties:** This command opens the related Properties dialog box for the particular symbol type — Sound, Bitmap, Symbol, Component, or Video Properties. The Properties dialog box is a central control that enables you to rename an element, access Edit mode, or access the Linkages dialog box from one location. This is also where you can define or edit the Source for any element.

- **Play (or Stop, if currently playing):** If the selected asset has a timeline or is otherwise playable (such as a sound), click this to preview the asset in the Library Preview window. If the asset is currently playing, this option is updated to Stop — in which case, click to stop playing.

- **Update:** Use this option if you've edited items subsequent to importing them into Flash. Items update without the bother of re-importing. You can also use this option to swap in a new element of the same kind to replace an item already used in your project.

- **Properties:** Use this command to open the Properties dialog box for the currently selected item (Symbol Properties, Sound Properties, Bitmap Properties, Font Symbol Properties, Video Properties, or (Component) Linkage Properties).

- **Component Definition:** This library option opens the Component Definition dialog box, which you use to assign parameters to Movie Clips to create your own components or modify parameters for compiled components. (Components are Movie Clips with customizable behavior that can be reused in projects.)

TIP You can also use the Component Inspector panel to set component parameters.

- **Shared Library Properties:** Use this command to open the Shared Properties dialog box, which is another aspect of runtime Shared Libraries.

- **Select Unused Items:** Select Unused Items to find any items stored in the Library that have not been used in the current project.

TIP Unused items are not included in your published movie file (.swf), but they add weight to your project file (.fla). The Select Unused Items command is a handy way to find these files so you can delete them to streamline your project file. Use Save and Compact or Save As to save your .fla file minus the extra weight of the unused items that you have deleted from the Library.

- **Expand Folder/Collapse Folder:** Use this command to toggle the currently selected folder in the asset window open or closed.

- **Expand All Folders/Collapse All Folders:** Use this command to toggle all folders and subfolders in the asset window open or closed.

- **Help:** Launches a Web browser to access Adobe help with info on Managing Assets in Flash or the local Flash help documents (if you are not connected to the Internet).

Selecting New Symbol, Duplicate, or Properties from the options menu while you have a symbol (Graphic symbol, Button symbol or Movie Clip) selected in the Library list launches the Symbol Properties dialog box, as shown in Figure 6.6. Use this dialog box to change the symbol's name and/or behavior (as a symbol type — Graphic, Button, or Movie Clip).

NOTE   If you choose the Properties option with other asset types selected, such as sound, video, or bitmaps, the Properties dialog box relevant to each item type launches rather than the Symbol Properties dialog box.

FIGURE 6.6

The Symbol Properties dialog box. Note the button for Advanced options — this expands the dialog box to include Linkage and Source information for the selected element.

Assign symbol behavior   Launch Symbol Edit mode

Expand options (to include Linkage, Sharing, and Source info)

Organizing Library panels

When your movies start to become complex, you'll find that the Library gets crowded, and it can be hard to find symbols. When this happens, you'll appreciate the capability to create and name folders for your symbols. You can organize your Library folders however you like, but here are a few suggestions for greater productivity:

- Create a separate folder for each scene.
- Create folders for symbol types, such as buttons, sounds, or bitmap imports.
- Store all symbols or graphics that relate to a specific element (such as a logo or an animated element) together in one folder.

NEW FEATURE   The new Search field included in all the CS4 Library panels is a wonderful tool for finding and organizing assets and should save beleaguered developers a bit of time and frustration.

When you build complex layered structures in your movie — a Movie Clip symbol on the first frame of a Button symbol, with a text symbol on the layer above it, and a sound on the layer above that — the Library doesn't visually track this hierarchy. But you can indicate this: Just put all the associated symbols in a folder with a name that describes the final element. You can also nest folders within other folders. Working with folders in the Library is almost exactly the same as working with folders in the Layers area of the Timeline window, as follows:

■ To create a folder, click the folder icon at the bottom left corner of the Library.

■ To move a file or folder into another folder, simply drag it over the target folder icon.

■ To move a folder that's been nested within another folder back to the top level of the Library, drag the folder until it is just above the Library list and over the word Name and release.

NOTE Putting symbols in different folders does not affect the links between them and their instances (as opposed to the way moving a graphic file into a new folder breaks an existing link on a Web page). Flash tracks and updates all references to Library items whenever you rename or move them into separate folders (within the same Library).

The Movie Explorer is a great way of getting a visual overview of the nested relationship of symbols, Movie Clips, and other items within your document. Refer to the end of this chapter for more on the Movie Explorer.

CAUTION If you change the Undo behavior in your Flash Preferences from Document-level to Object-level, you'll lose the option to undo some authoring steps. For example, any item that is deleted from the Library is gone forever, including all instances throughout the current document (.fla). If you decide that you shouldn't have deleted an item, the only cure is to close the file without saving any changes. When you reopen the file, the Library should be intact as it was the last time the file was saved.

TIP Flash offers an option to Import to Library that is especially useful when you want to bring in a series of items. Instead of having all the items dumped onto the Stage in your Document window, you can load them directly into the project Library. Select File ➪ Import ➪ Import to Library.

Defining Content Types

Understanding the behavior of various media types and learning to streamline asset management unlocks the true potential of Flash for combining compelling content with small file sizes. The basic structures for storing, reusing, and modifying content within a Flash project are not complicated, but the reason for using various symbol types does deserve explanation.

Resolving Conflicts between Library Assets

Importing or copying an asset into your current project Library occasionally opens a Resolve Library Conflict alert box asking if you want to Replace Existing Items and Instances. This alert box appears when you are trying to add a new asset to your Library with the same name as an asset already present in your current document. If you choose not to replace the existing item, the newly added items have the word *copy* added to their filenames. For example, if you have an item named *photo* in your current Library and attempt to add another item to the Library with the same name, the new item is given the name *photo copy* in the Library. To rename the added item, simply double-click the item name in the Library list and type a new name.

If you choose to replace the existing item in your Library, all instances are replaced with the content of the newly added item. If you choose to cancel the import or copy operation, the selected items are not added to your current document and the existing items stored in the Library are preserved.

Raw data

When you create graphics directly in Flash, using the shape tools, text tool, or any of the other drawing tools, you produce raw data or *primitive shapes*. You can copy and paste these elements into any keyframe on the timeline, but they do not appear in the project Library. Each time the element appears, Flash has to read and render all the points, curves, and color information from scratch because the information is not stored in the Library. Even if the shape looks exactly the same on keyframe 10 as it did on keyframe 1, Flash has to do all the work to re-create the shape every time it appears. This quickly bloats the size of the .swf file. Also, because each element is completely independent, if you decide to make any changes, you have to find and edit each appearance of an element manually. This is a daunting task if your project involves animation or nested symbols.

TIP The Find and Replace feature (Option/Alt+F) makes it easier to accomplish mundane editing tasks on multiple items within your Flash project file. We introduce the myriad uses for Find and Replace in Chapter 9, "Modifying Graphics."

TIP If you want to convert a raw graphic into a drawing object after it has been created, select the graphic on the Stage and apply the Modify ➪ Combine Objects ➪ Union command from the main menu. The raw graphic then behaves exactly like any other drawing object. To revert a drawing object to a raw graphic, use the Modify ➪ Break Apart command.

Drawing objects and shape primitives

You create drawing objects by turning the Object Drawing option toggle on in the Tools panel while using any of the drawing or shape tools. (This option is on by default, so if you haven't touched the toggle in the Tools panel, you will find yourself creating drawing objects when you use any of the drawing tools to make graphics.) Drawing objects have some of the characteristics of raw shapes and groups. They can be modified directly on the Stage (without having to click in to Edit mode) but they are self-contained and do not merge with or cut into other graphics on the same layer — unless you apply one of the Combine Objects commands. They can't be motion-tweened and they are not stored in the Library unless they are converted into one of the symbol types. The hybrid characteristics of drawing objects suit some workflows very well, but some graphic artists prefer to work in normal or Non-Object Drawing mode. Drawing objects can be combined seamlessly with raw graphics and symbols, and turning the Object Drawing option on or off does not have any effect on graphics you have already created.

The new Oval Primitive and Rectangle Primitive tools provide another way of making basic shapes with the advantage of using controls in the Properties panel that can be changed or reset even after the shapes are drawn. Like drawing objects, shape primitives do not merge with or erase other shapes, but they are not stored in the Library.

CAUTION Shapes or lines made with the Drawing Object toggle turned on and shapes made with the new Shape Primitive tools have some special behaviors in the authoring environment, but like basic shapes and groups, drawing objects and shape primitives are not stored in the Library unless they are converted into symbols. Symbols are the only method of storing artwork that reduces the file size impact of graphics that occur on more than one frame of a Flash movie.

Groups

One step toward making raw data more manageable is to use groups. By grouping a filled shape with its outline stroke, for example, it becomes easier to select both parts of the shape to move around in your layout. If you added a text element that you also wanted to keep aligned with your artwork, you could add this to the group as well. Groups can be inclusive or cumulative so that you can select multiple elements and create one group (⌘/Ctrl+G) that can be accessed on the same edit level by double-clicking the whole group once. If you add another element (even another group) to the first group, you will find that you have to click in to a deeper level to edit individual elements. In this way, groups can grow more and more complicated, which is helpful if you're trying to keep multiple elements in order.

The important thing to remember about groups, however, is that they are *not* symbols. Although groups have a similar selection highlight to symbols, you will notice that they don't have a crosshair icon in the center, and that the group information won't appear in your project Library. No matter how careful you are about reusing the same raw data and grouping elements to keep them organized, when it comes to publishing your movie (.swf) or trying to update any single element, you will be no better off than if you had just placed raw elements wildly into your project. Flash still treats each shape and line as a unique element, and the file size grows exponentially each time you add another keyframe containing any of your raw data, even if it is grouped. The best way to use groups in your project is for managing symbols, or to organize elements that you plan to keep together and convert into one symbol.

> **CAUTION** Using groups helps organize raw shapes or other elements in your .fla files, but it does not help to optimize the final .swf file. Using a lot of groups in your project file can actually *add* weight to the final published .swf.

Native symbols

Imported sound, video, bitmap, or font symbols are stored automatically in the Library to define *instances* of the asset when it is used in the project. In addition, three basic *container* symbol types can be created in the Flash authoring environment: Movie Clip symbols, Graphic symbols, and Button symbols, which all have timelines that can hold images, sounds, text, or even other symbols. Although it is possible to make the behavior of a symbol instance different from the behavior of the original symbol, it is generally best to decide how you plan to use a certain element and then assign it the symbol type that is appropriate to both its content and expected use in the project.

> **TIP** Dragging a primitive shape or group into the Library panel from the Stage automatically opens the Convert to Symbol dialog box so that you can name and assign a symbol type to the element before it is added to your Library.

To make a decision on what type of symbol to use, it helps to have a clear understanding of the benefits and limitations of each of the symbol types available in Flash. Each symbol type has specific features that are suited to particular kinds of content. Each symbol type is marked with a unique icon in the Library, but what all symbols have in common is that they can be reused within a project as symbol instances, all defined by the original symbol. A Flash project Library may contain any or all of the symbol types in the following sections, all created directly in Flash.

Graphic symbols

Graphic symbols are used mainly for static images that are reused in a project. Flash ignores any sounds or actions inside a Graphic symbol. Graphic symbols do not play independently of the Main Timeline and thus require an allocated frame on the Main Timeline for each frame that you want to be visible within the symbol. If you want a Graphic symbol to loop or repeat as the Main Timeline moves along, you have to include another whole series of frames on the Main Timeline to match the length of the Graphic symbol timeline for each loop.

A drop-down Options menu in the Properties panel enables you to control Graphic symbol playback. Select a Graphic symbol instance in your document and open the Looping section of the Properties panel to access the three settings in the Options menu:

■ **Loop:** This is the default setting for Graphic symbols. If the Graphic symbol extends along a time-line beyond its original length, the symbol restarts from the beginning. Graphic symbol looping does not play independently of the Main Timeline like Movie Clip looping — you still have to match the number of frames on the Main Timeline with the number of frames that you want to play in the Graphic symbol timeline.

■ **Play Once:** This setting eliminates looping by allowing the Graphic symbol timeline to play, and then holding on its last frame if it extends along a timeline beyond its original length.

■ **Single Frame:** This setting holds the Graphic symbol on one frame so that it behaves like a static graphic. You can select a specific frame within the Graphic symbol timeline to display as the static graphic. The appearance of the Graphic symbol is the same regardless of how far it extends along a timeline.

Movie Clip symbols

Movie Clips are actually movies within a movie. They're good for animations that run independently of the movie's Main Timeline. They can contain actions, other symbols, and sounds. You can also place Movie Clips inside of other symbols, and they are indispensable for creating interactive interface elements such as animated buttons.

Movie Clips can continue to play even if the Main Timeline is stopped. Thus, they need only one frame on the Main Timeline to play back any number of frames on their own timeline. By default, Movie Clips are set to loop. So, as long as there is an instance of the Movie Clip visible on the Main Timeline, it can loop or play back the content on its own timeline as many times as you want it to, without needing a matching number of frames on the Main Timeline. Movie Clip playback can be controlled with ActionScript from any timeline or even from an external code (.as) file.

Button symbols

Button symbols are used for creating interactive buttons. Button symbols have a timeline limited to four frames, which are referred to as *states*. These states are related directly to user interaction and are labeled Up, Over, Down, and Hit. Each of these button states can be defined with graphics, symbols, and sounds. After you create a Button symbol, you can assign independent actions to various instances in the main movie or inside other Movie Clips. As with Movie Clips, Button symbols require only one frame on any other timeline to be able to play back the three visible states (frames) of their own timeline.

Components

Components are prebuilt Movie Clips for interactive Flash elements that can be reused and customized. Each component has its own unique set of ActionScript methods that enable you to set options at runtime.

CROSS-REF Components are a great way to add interactive elements to your Flash projects, but it takes a little work to understand how to integrate and customize them to suit your needs. For more information on how to make the most of components, refer to Chapter 32, "Using Components."

Imported media elements

A Flash project Library also stores certain types of imported assets to define instances of the asset when instances are used in the movie. You can place these imported assets into native Flash symbol structures by converting a bitmap into a Graphic symbol or placing a sound inside a Button symbol, for example.

Bitmaps

Bitmaps are handled like symbols: The original image is stored in the Library and any time the image is used in the project it is actually a copy, or an *instance,* of the original. To use a bitmap asset, drag an instance out of the Library and onto the Stage. You manage Export settings for individual bitmaps from within the Library by choosing Properties from either the contextual menu or the Library options menu. However, you cannot apply color or alpha effects or any Flash filters to the bitmap instance unless you convert it into a native Flash symbol type (Graphic, Button, or Movie Clip).

NOTE   Bitmaps can be targeted with ActionScript to change their appearance dynamically at runtime. Although this takes some time to learn, the end result is usually a more optimized file that runs faster and is easier to modify or update. If you feel ready to move on from manual tweens and authortime effects to dynamic code-driven animation and effects, a good place to start is *ActionScript 3.0 Bible* (Wiley, 2008).

Vector graphics

Vector graphics, upon import from other applications, arrive on the Flash Stage as a group, and unlike bitmaps, may be edited or manipulated just like a normal group drawn in Flash. These elements are not stored in the Library until they have been converted to a native symbol type.

CAUTION   In previous versions of Flash, vector graphics consisting of drawing objects or shape primitives could be motion-tweened without being converted into symbols, but the new tweening workflow in Flash CS4 requires symbols for motion tweening. If you try to apply a motion tween to an element that is not already a symbol, you will be prompted by a dialog box to convert it or cancel the tween. Although drawing objects and shape primitives have benefits in the authoring environment, they do not get stored in the Library and have the same impact on file size as other raw vector graphics.

Sounds

The Library also handles sounds like symbols. However, they can be assigned different playback behavior after they are placed on a timeline. Flash can import (and export) sounds in a range of sound formats. Upon import, these sound files reside in the Library. To use a sound, drag an instance of the sound out of the Library and onto the Stage. You manage export settings for sound files within the Library by choosing Properties from either the contextual menu or the Library options menu. You can define playback behavior and effects with the Properties panel after placing a sound on a timeline.

CROSS-REF   Importing and using sounds effectively is a critical topic we cover in Chapter 14, "Adding Sound."

Video assets

Video assets, as with font symbols, can be embedded or linked. Embedded video assets, like bitmaps, can have color, alpha, and filter effects applied if they are first converted to a native Flash symbol type.

CROSS-REF   Flash supports alpha channels in video files. This opens up a whole range of exciting options for integrating video with other Flash content. For comprehensive coverage of working with video in Flash CS4, refer to Chapter 16, "Displaying Video."

Font symbols

Font symbols are symbols created from font files to make them available for use in dynamic text fields. Font symbols can also be defined as shared fonts to make them available to multiple movie files (.swf) without the file size burden of embedding the font into each file individually.

Graphic Symbols versus Movie Clip Symbols

Graphic symbols are a quick and tidy way of placing static information into a timeline, whereas Movie Clip symbols animate independently on their own timeline. Graphic symbols should be used to hold single frames of raw data, or multiple frames when it is important to preview your work while designing it, as with linear animation. You must use Movie Clips when ActionScript is involved, or when an animation must run regardless of what is happening around it. However, using one type of symbol instead of the other may not always involve clear-cut choices, because, often, either works. Consequently, to use symbols effectively, it's important to know the pluses, minuses, and absolutes of both Graphic symbols and Movie Clips. Here are some tips to keep in mind:

■ Instance properties of Graphic symbols (height, color, rotation, and so on) are frozen at design time, whereas Movie Clips can have their instance properties set on-the-fly with ActionScript. This makes Movie Clips essential for programmed content such as games.

■ Scrubbing the Main Timeline (previewing while working) is not possible with Movie Clips, although it is possible with Graphic symbols. This makes Graphic symbols essential for animating cartoons. Eyes open, eyes closed — it's that big of a difference.

■ Movie Clips can't (easily) be exported to video or other linear mediums. This is only significant if you plan to convert your .swf files to another time-based format.

■ A Graphic symbol's instance properties are controlled (modified) at design time, with the options available in the Properties panel. One advantage is that this is simple and sure because you have an instant preview of what's happening. In addition, this information is embedded right in that particular instance of the Graphic symbol — meaning that, if it is either moved or copied, all this information comes with it.

■ You can control a Movie Clip's instance properties at design time or set them with ActionScript. One advantage is that the actions do not need to be directly linked to the Movie Clip, which has the concurrent disadvantage that you must take care when moving Movie Clips that have visual qualities defined with ActionScript.

■ Graphic symbols that are animated (have more than one frame), and are nested with other animated Graphic symbols, may have problems with synchronization. For example, if you have a pair of eyes that blink at the end of a ten-frame Graphic symbol, and you put the Graphic symbol containing those eyes within a five-frame Graphic symbol of a head, the eyes will never blink. The head Graphic symbol will run from frame 1 to frame 5, and then return to frame 1, only displaying the first five frames of the eyes Graphic symbol. Or, if you nest the eyes Graphic symbol into a 15-frame head Graphic symbol, they will blink on frame 10, and then every 15 frames. That's ten frames, and then blink, and then they loop back to frame 1; however, when reaching frame 5 this time, the movie they are in loops back to frame 1 (it's a 15-frame movie), and, thus, resets the eyes to frame 1.

■ Movie Clips do not have the problem/feature described in the preceding bullet point. They offer consistent, independent timeline playback.

Authors' note: This comparison was contributed by Robin and Sandy Debreuil for the *Flash 5 Bible* (Wiley, 2001), and we still like how they articulate the important distinction between Graphic symbols and Movie Clip symbols.

Editing Symbols

Because every instance of a symbol is linked to the original, *any* edit applied to that original is applied to every instance. There are several ways to edit a symbol, which we cover in the following sections.

Modifying a symbol in Edit mode

Edit mode opens the Stage and timeline of the selected symbol in the Document window, replacing the view of the current keyframe in the Main Timeline with a view of the first keyframe in the symbol's time-line. To open a symbol in Edit mode, do one of the following:

- Select an instance on the Stage and choose Edit ⇨ Edit Symbols, or Edit Selected from the application menu.
- Select an instance on the Stage and right-click (Command/Ctrl+click), and then choose Edit from the contextual menu.
- Select an instance on the Stage and use the shortcut key (⌘/Ctrl+E).
- Double-click a symbol in the Document Library. (Double-clicking bitmaps, sound, video, and other nonnative symbol types launches the Properties dialog box instead of opening Edit mode.)

Editing a symbol in a new window

This method is useful if you're working on two monitors and want to quickly open a new window to edit in while keeping a view of the Main Timeline open and available. On Mac, these two windows are always sep-arate, but you can click either window to switch back and forth. On Windows, you can switch between these windows by choosing from the Window menu.

To edit a symbol in a new window, select an instance on the Stage and right-click (⌘/Ctrl+click), and then select Edit In New Window from the contextual menu.

Editing a symbol in place

The advantage of Edit in Place is that, instead of opening the symbol in a separate edit space, you can edit your symbol in context with the surrounding movie. Other elements present on the current keyframe are visible but dimmed slightly and protected from any edits you make on the selected symbol. To edit a sym-bol in place, do one of the following:

- Select an instance on the Stage and choose Edit ⇨ Edit in Place from the application menu.
- Select an instance on the Stage and right-click (⌘/Ctrl+click), and then select Edit in Place from the contextual menu.
- Double-click the instance on the Stage.

Editing symbols from the Library

You might not have an instance of your symbol available to select for editing in the Document window, but you can still edit it. Just edit it from the Library. Open your movie's Library with Window ⇨ Library from the application menu (⌘/Ctrl+L). Select the symbol in the Library that you want to edit and do one of the following:

- Double-click the symbol's icon (not its name), in the Library list.
- Right-click (⌘/Ctrl+click) and then select Edit from the contextual popup menu.
- If you have opened the Symbol Properties dialog box (see Figure 6.6), you can move to Edit mode by clicking the Edit button.

Returning to the Main Timeline or scene

After you edit your symbol, you'll want to go back to the scene in the Main Timeline to make sure that your changes work properly. Just do one of the following:

- Choose Edit ➪ Edit Movie from the application menu or use the shortcut keys — ⌘/Ctrl+E.
- Double-click in any empty area of the Edit Stage.
- Click the Return arrow at the left edge of the Edit bar to step back through any nested timelines until you reach the Main Timeline.
- Select the scene name in the left corner above the Stage view in the Document window, as shown in Figure 6.7.

FIGURE 6.7

The location label in the Document window Edit bar is used to identify the current edit space and to return to the Main Timeline of the current scene.

Return to Button ("basic Button") Timeline

Return to Main Timeline of current scene ("Scene 1")

Return to Movie Clip ("overAnim") Timeline

Return arrow steps back through nested elements to return to Main Timeline

Currently editing graphic symbol ("outline") timeline

Symbol edit space for Graphic symbol seen in Edit in Place mode

Movie Clip (dimmed)

Button symbol (dimmed)

Scene 1 Stage (dimmed)

Graphic symbol (selected)

Staying Oriented in Edit Space

Graphics editing in Flash occurs in one of two places: in the Main Timeline and on the Stage; or within a symbol, which has its own edit space and timeline. But how do you know when you are on the Scene Stage or when you are in Edit mode? Here's one clue: At the top of the Document window is the Edit bar. If you're working on the Scene Stage, you'll see a single tab with the name of the scene. Unless you name your scenes, this tab should simply say, Scene 1 (or Scene 2). However, in Edit mode, a second tab appears to the right of the scene name: This tab displays the name and icon of the current group or symbol (Movie Clip, Graphic symbol, or Button symbol). If you're editing a nested symbol, more tabs may appear. In this manner, you have convenient access to the hierarchy of your assets, no matter how deeply they are nested.

Edit mode is much like working on the regular Stage. You can draw with any of the drawing tools, add text, place symbols, import graphics and sound, and use ActionScript. When you're done working with a symbol, you have an encapsulated element, whether it is a static Graphic, a Movie Clip, or a Button. You can place this element as many times as needed on your Stage or within other symbols. Each time you place it, the symbol's entire contents and timeline (if it is a Button or a Movie Clip) are placed as well, identical to the original symbol stored in the Library. Remember that even if you access Edit mode from an instance on the Stage, all changes that you make propagate to every other instance derived from the original symbol in the Library. The only color changes that you can make to one instance at a time without affecting the other instances of the same symbol are those you apply by using the Color menu on the Properties panel, or by applying filters and blend modes to instances as we explain in the section, "Modifying Instance Properties."

The Stage (if it is not zoomed to fill the screen) is surrounded by a gray area. This is the work area or pasteboard, and it indicates the visible edges of the final movie as defined in the Document properties. The dimensions of any symbol, however, are not limited to the size of the Stage. If you make your symbols too large, when you place them on the Stage, portions that fall outside of the Stage are not visible in the final movie (.swf), but they still export and add to the file size. Remember that it is always possible to scale a symbol instance to make it smaller than the original symbol if necessary.

Modifying Instance Properties

Every instance of a symbol has graphic variables that you can modify. These properties apply only to the specific instance, not to the original symbol. Display properties such as brightness, tint, and alpha (transparency) can all be modified without creating a new symbol. An instance can also be scaled, rotated, and skewed. Filters and blend modes enable a range of cool visual effects that you can apply to symbol instances. With the Type menu in the Properties panel, you can also change the symbol type behavior of an instance without changing the original symbol. As we previously discuss, any changes you make to the original symbol in Edit mode are updated in each instance. This still holds true even if some of the instances also have properties that are modified individually.

NEW FEATURE   Scaling, rotating, and skewing in 2D space is kinda fun but the new 3D tools in Flash CS4 enable you to move or rotate a symbol in 3D space. Use the 3D Rotation or 3D Translation tools to modify symbol instances along the x, y, or z axis to create the illusion of depth on your Flash Stage. 3D tools are discussed in more detail in Chapter 9, "Modifying Graphics."

Applying basic color effects to symbol instances

Each instance of a symbol can have a variety of color effects applied to it. The basic effects are changes of brightness, tint, and *alpha* (transparency). Tint and alpha changes can also be combined for special effects. To apply color effects to a symbol instance by using the Properties panel:

1. **Select the instance in the Document window that you want to modify.**

2. **Select one of the options from the Style drop-down menu in the Color Effect section of the Properties panel.** Figure 6.8 shows the basic color effect options that can be applied to any symbol type.

FIGURE 6.8

The color effect Style menu has basic options to choose from (left). After a color effect is selected, the settings for that effect are available in the Properties panel (right).

The options available from the color effect Style menu are as follows:

■ **None:** No effect is applied.

■ **Brightness:** Adjusts the relative brightness or darkness of the instance. It ranges from 100 percent (white) to −100 percent (black); the default setting is 0 percent (no visible change to instance appearance). Use the slider to change the value or just type a numeric value into the entry field.

■ **Tint:** Enables you to shift the color of an instance. Either select a hue with the color picker or enter the RGB values directly, and then select the percentage of saturation (Tint Amount) by using the slider or by entering the percentage in the entry field. This number ranges from 0 percent (no saturation) to 100 percent (completely saturated).

■ **Alpha:** Enables you to modify the transparency of an instance. Select a percentage by using the slider or by entering a number directly. The Alpha percentage (or visibility setting) ranges from 0 percent (completely transparent) to 100 percent (no transparency).

■ **Advanced:** When you select the Advanced option from the Style menu, numeric values appear in two columns that enable you to adjust both the tint and alpha settings of an instance. The controls on the left reduce the tint and alpha values by a specified percentage, whereas the controls on the right either reduce or increase the tint and alpha values by a constant value. The current values are multiplied by the numbers on the left, and then added to the values on the right.

CROSS-REF The Advanced option includes a range with negative alpha values. Potential uses for this capability, together with more information about using color effects and other methods of transforming symbol instances, are detailed in Chapter 9, "Modifying Graphics."

Changing the symbol type of an instance

You don't need to limit yourself to the native behavior of a symbol. For example, there may be times when you want a Movie Clip to have the behavior of a Graphic symbol so that you can preview animation by scrubbing the Timeline. You don't have to go through the extra effort of creating a new symbol — just use the following steps to change the type of the instance as needed:

1. **Select the instance in the Document window you want to modify.**
2. **From the symbol Type drop-down list at the top of the Properties panel, select the desired behavior.** As shown in Figure 6.9, you can assign Graphic, Button, or Movie Clip behavior.

FIGURE 6.9

You can change the behavior of any selected symbol instance with the drop-down symbol Type menu in the Properties panel.

CROSS-REF The more-complex uses of symbol instances are covered in Parts V, "Adding Basic Interactivity to Flash Movies," and VII, "Approaching ActionScript."

Swapping symbols

There may be times when you need to replace an instance of one symbol with an instance of another symbol stored in your project Library. Luckily, you don't have to go through and re-create your entire animation to do this — just use the Swap Symbol feature, illustrated in Figure 6.10. This feature only switches the instance of the symbol for an instance of another symbol; all other modifications previously applied to the instance remain the same. Here's how to swap symbols:

1. **Select the instance that you want to replace.**
2. **Click the Swap symbol button in the Properties panel, choose Modify ⇨ Symbol ⇨ Swap Symbol from the application menu, or right-click (⌘/Ctrl+click) and choose Swap Symbol from the contextual menu.**
3. **Select the symbol that you want to put into the place of your current instance from the list of available symbols in your project Library.**
4. **Click OK to swap the symbols.**

FIGURE 6.10

Use the Swap Symbol dialog box to choose a replacement for a symbol instance without losing any transformations that have already been applied.

Selected instance on stage (original)

Preview of selected symbol (to replace original instance)

Swap Symbol dialog box

Swap symbol button in Properties panel

Duplicate symbol button

List of symbols stored in current Library

Building Nested Symbol Structures

Understanding the various symbol types individually is the first step, but the next step is integrating these building blocks to create organized, optimized Flash projects that are extensible, easy to edit, and fast to build. Although we cover the workflow for different types of Flash projects in other parts of this book, we can synthesize the overview of different symbol types by walking through the steps of creating a Button symbol with some nested animation and Graphic symbols.

To demonstrate building an animated Flash movie from various symbol types, we made a Button symbol called `basicButton` that uses some raw shapes, some Graphic symbols, and some Movie Clips, all nested inside a Button symbol timeline.

ON the CD-ROM The completed source file (`sampleButton.fla`) for this series of demonstrations is on the CD-ROM that accompanies this book in the `ch06` folder.

Converting a raw shape into a Graphic symbol

The best way to begin creating any graphic element is to first consider the final shape that you need and to try to find the most basic primitive shapes that you can use to build that element. Keep in mind that instances can be scaled, skewed, and adjusted with color effects. Instead of drawing three circles to make a snowman, you would make just one circle and convert that into a symbol so that you could build your snowman from scaled instances of just one symbol stored in the Library. A resourceful animator we know built a Christmas tree by reusing instances of a symbol he had made for a dog's tail in the same animation — a wagging tail and a tree all built from just one Graphic symbol stored in the Library! Raw graphics can be converted into Graphic symbols after they have been drawn, or you can first create a new Graphic symbol and then draw the raw shapes directly inside the Graphic symbol in Edit mode — either way, the end result is a contained visual element that is stored in the Library to define any instances that you need to place in your movie.

To build the simple graphics used in `basicButton`, you can begin by converting a raw shape into a Graphic symbol:

1. **Select the Oval tool and set the fill color to green and the stroke color to black with a stroke height of 3.**

2. **Click on the Stage and hold down the Shift key while dragging out the shape to create a perfect circle.** Double-click the fill with the Selection tool to select both the stroke and the fill, and then use the Properties panel to set the width to 75 and the height to 75. (If the Constrain check box is selected in the Properties panel, you only need to enter **75** in one of the value fields and the circle will scale evenly.)

> **TIP**
> An alternative workflow supported in Flash for creating an oval (after completing step 1), is to Option/Alt+click in the Document window to open the Oval Settings dialog box. Enter 75 for the width and height of the circle and click OK. Flash renders a circle in the Document window, centered on the point you clicked.

> **NOTE**
> If you open the Library panel — Window ⇨ Library (⌘/Ctrl+L) — you will notice that the shape you've drawn is not visible in the asset list because raw data is not stored in the Library.

3. **While the stroke and the fill are both still selected, press F8 or choose Modify ⇨ Convert to Symbol from the application menu.**

4. **In the Convert to Symbol dialog box, choose Graphic for the symbol type and give the symbol the name** plainCircle. Click OK. You should now see the plainCircle symbol with the Graphic symbol icon next to it in the Library panel.

> **TIP**
> You always have the choice of creating artwork on the Main Timeline and then converting it into a symbol *or* first inserting a new symbol and then creating artwork in the symbol drawing space. Either workflow achieves the same end result. In the plainCircle example, start by selecting Insert ⇨ New Symbol (⌘/Ctrl+F8). Enter the settings noted in Step 4, and then complete Steps 1 and 2 to draw the circle on the Graphic symbol timeline rather than on the Main Timeline. When you go back to the Main Timeline, you won't see an instance of plainCircle on the Stage, but the Graphic symbol should now be in the Library, and you can drag an instance into the Document window whenever you need it.

You can now reuse instances of this Graphic symbol in your document in as many places as you need it just by dragging an instance onto the Stage from the Library panel.

> **NOTE**
> For the basicButton example, you will need an instance of plainCircle inside of a new Button symbol rather than on the main Stage, so you can delete any instances of plain Circle from the Main Timeline before continuing with additional steps.

Using Graphic symbols in a button

Button symbols are similar to Movie Clips that have a special timeline structure linked to mouse states. For a button to take you to a new point on the Main Timeline or to load any other elements, ActionScript must be added to the button instance.

CROSS-REF We discuss adding actions to buttons for more advanced interactivity in Chapter 17, "Understanding Actions and Event Handlers."

In this example, the button simply works as a structure for an animation that reacts to the mouse. Begin by inserting a new Button symbol:

1. **Click the New Symbol button in the Library panel or choose Insert ⇨ New Symbol from the application menu or use the shortcut keys (⌘/Ctrl+F8).**

2. **In the Create New Symbol dialog box, choose Button as the symbol type, and for this example, give the symbol the name** basicButton. Click OK. This Button symbol is now stored in the Library and automatically opens in Edit mode in the Document window, so you can add some content to the button.

   You will notice that the Button Timeline shows four keyframes with labels that define the button state by mouse behavior: Up, Over, Down, and Hit. These various keyframes can have multiple layers and contain any visual element or sound that you want. The button states function as follows:

   - **Up:** Any elements placed in the Up keyframe are associated with the button as it appears on the Stage when the button is present but not activated by any mouse interaction.

   - **Over:** Any elements placed in the Over keyframe are associated with the button when the mouse rolls over it on the Stage, but as soon as the mouse rolls off the button it reverts to its Up state.

   - **Down:** Any elements placed in the Down keyframe are associated with the button only when the mouse is over it and clicked and held down. As soon as the mouse is released, the button reverts to its Over state.

   - **Hit:** The Hit keyframe is actually never visible on Stage, but this instead defines the area of the button that is "sensitive" to the mouse. Whatever shape is present on this frame is considered part of the button's *hit area*. It is important to note that it is better not to have holes or gaps in the hit area unless it is intended. For example, if you have text as a button, it is best to use a solid rectangle that matches the width and height of the total text area. Using the actual text would result in an irregular button hit area — whenever the mouse rolls into the space between letters, the button would revert to its Up state and could not be clicked.

TIP If you ever need an "invisible" button in your project, you can create one by adding artwork to the Hit keyframe only of a Button symbol. The button is visible in the authoring environment as a bright blue preview shape (defined by the graphics in the Hit state), but when the .swf file is published, the only indication that a button is on the Stage is the change in the mouse cursor when it enters the Hit area. You can add ActionScript to an invisible button to trigger events in your animation or to control the behavior of other elements in your movie. We discuss invisible buttons in more detail in Chapter 17, "Understanding Actions and Event Handlers."

For this example, you create animation to be placed into the various visible states, but the main shape of the button will always be consistent, so you can begin by creating a layer to define the main shape of the button.

3. Rename Layer 1 of the Button symbol timeline as buttonOutline **and insert two frames (F5) after the first keyframe to create a span of three frames (visible for Up, Over, and Down).**

4. **With the playhead set on the first keyframe, drag an instance of plainCircle onto the button Stage and make sure that it is now visible in the Up, Over, and Down states of the button, but not on the Hit state.**

5. **Center the instance on the button Stage by using the Align panel (⌘/Ctrl+K).**

6. **Select the instance of plainCircle and copy it to the Clipboard (⌘/Ctrl+C).**

7. **Create a new layer and name it** hitArea.

8. **Insert a blank keyframe (F7) on frame 4 (Hit).** To paste the copy of plainCircle into the center of the blank Hit keyframe, use Paste in Place (⌘/Ctrl+Shift+V). If you have done a straightforward paste instead, make sure that the instance of plainCircle is centered to the button Stage.

The timeline of your Button symbol should now look like Figure 6.11.

FIGURE 6.11

The Edit mode view of the basic Button symbol timeline, with Up, Over, Down, and Hit states defined with instances of the plainCircle Graphic symbol

9. Return to the Main Timeline by clicking the Scene 1 label in the Edit bar or by double-clicking an empty area of the Stage.

10. If you don't see an instance of your basicButton on the Stage of the Main Timeline, drag an instance out of the Library and place it on the first frame of the Main Timeline.

Animating Graphic symbols in a Movie Clip

After you have created some Graphic symbols to define your basicButton, you can now start building some animation to add to it. You can build animation by placing artwork in keyframes on the Main Timeline, but this limits how you can use the animation, and can make it difficult to add more elements to your project without disturbing the keyframe structure of the animation. If you need animated elements that can be reused, and quickly moved to different parts of the Main Timeline or placed into a Button symbol timeline, it is best to begin by creating a Movie Clip.

1. Click the New Symbol button in the Library panel or choose Insert ⇨ New Symbol from the application menu, or use shortcut keys (⌘/Control+F8).

2. In the Symbol Properties dialog box, choose Movie Clip as the symbol type and give this symbol the name overAnim.

3. Create a new circle on the first frame of the Movie Clip Timeline with a black stroke (with a height of 3) and no fill. Select the outline with the Selection tool and use the Properties panel to set its width and height to 25. Then use the Align panel to center it on the Stage.

4. Convert this raw shape into a Graphic symbol (Modify ⇨ Convert to symbol or F8) with the name outline.

5. Insert nine frames (F5) on the Movie Clip Timeline so that you have a span of frames from frame 1 to frame 10 with the outline Graphic symbol visible.

6. Select the instance of outline on the Stage in frame 1 and right-click/Ctrl+click and select Create Motion Tween from the contextual menu. (Or use the Application menu to select Insert ⇨ Motion tween.)

7. Now select the instance of the outline in frame 10 and use the Properties panel to change the width and height of the outline to 50 pixels high and 50 pixels wide. The graphic should stay centered on the Stage, but you can use the Align panel to make sure.

   You should now be able to drag the playhead from frame 1 to frame 10 in the timeline and see an animation of the outline growing in size. Figure 6.12 shows the view of the outline instance on frame 10 with a tween from frame 1 to frame 10.

FIGURE 6.12

The symbol timeline of the Movie Clip "overAnim" showing a motion tween of the Graphic symbol "outline," from frame 1 to frame 10

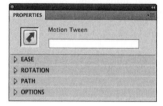

Adding a Movie Clip to a Button symbol

The final step in our example is to add the overAnim Movie Clip to the basicButton symbol. This is the secret to animated Button symbol: By nesting multiframe Movie Clip animations into the single frames assigned to the Up, Over, and Down states of the Button symbol timeline, you can create different animated "reactions" as the mouse rolls over or clicks the button.

1. **To go back inside your button and add animation in Edit mode, double-click the instance of basicButton on the Stage or the symbol in the Library.**

2. Create a new layer in the Button symbol timeline and name it outlineAnim. Make sure that this new layer is above the original buttonOutline layer.

3. On the outlineAnim layer, insert a new keyframe (F6) on frame 2 (Over).

4. Drag an instance of overAnim from the Library onto the button Stage in the keyframe you just created, and use the Align panel to center it.

5. To ensure that the animation is visible only on the Over state of the button, make sure that the content on the overAnim layer occupies only one frame on the Button symbol timeline. If the overAnim symbol extends into frame 3, either insert a blank keyframe (F7), or remove a frame (Shift+F5) to keep it contained on frame 2.

Your Button symbol timeline should now look like Figure 6.13.

FIGURE 6.13

The timeline of the Button symbol basicButton with the Movie Clip overAnim placed on the Over keyframe of the outlineAnim layer

You can test your Button symbol with this animation added to see how it is working, by pressing ⌘+Return/Ctrl+Enter on the keyboard to view the movie (.swf) in the Test Movie environment. Now when you roll over the green button with your mouse, you should see the outline circles animate. Remember that you still have only one keyframe on your Main Timeline, so this demonstrates how both a Button symbol and a Movie Clip symbol plays back their own timelines even if they are placed into a single frame on another timeline. You still need to add some animation for the Down state of the basicButton, so close the Test Movie (.swf) window to go back to the Button symbol timeline in the Document window.

Modifying a MovieClip instance

Instead of creating an entirely new animation to display on the Over state of our basicButton, you can reuse the overAnim Movie Clip and change its appearance by adding a color effect to the instance.

1. **Double-click the basicButton symbol instance to enter Edit mode.**
2. **Add a new layer to the Button symbol timeline and name it** outlineAnimTint.
3. **Insert a blank keyframe on frame 3 (Down).**
4. **Drag an instance of the overAnim Movie Clip from the Library, or just copy the Over frame on the outlineAnim layer and paste it into the blank keyframe you just created.**
5. **Select the instance of the overAnim Movie Clip that you placed on the Down keyframe and, in the Color Effect section of the Properties panel, choose Tint from the Style menu.**
6. **Choose white as the tint color from the Swatches that pop up from the color chip, and then enter a tint value of 100 percent by using the slider or by typing into the value box.**

   Your Button symbol timeline should now look like Figure 6.14.

Test your animated button again (Ctrl+Enter/⌘+Return) and you will see that the animation now appears when you click the button. But instead of the original black that appears on the Over state, the animation for the Down (click) state is white. The three visible states of your button should now resemble Figure 6.15.

You have seen how symbols are created, nested, and modified, and you are probably realizing that this basic animated Button symbol is only the beginning.

ON the CD-ROM If you want to deconstruct another layered symbol structure, we have included a silly, but slightly more complex, animated button on this book's CD-ROM. You will find the source file, surpriseButton.fla, in the ch06 folder. Figure 6.16 shows the three visible button states and diagrams the basic symbol nesting.

As your symbol structures get more layered and complex, it can be helpful to have some guidance when you are trying to navigate to a specific item in your project, or just trying to remember exactly how you organized things as you were building. Although careful use of layer names, frame labels, and symbol names is indispensable, the Movie Explorer (introduced later in this chapter) is a great assistant for finding your way through the structure of any Flash document.

FIGURE 6.14

The basicButton Timeline with an instance of the overAnim Movie Clip placed on the Down keyframe and modified with a color tint

FIGURE 6.15

The finished animated button as it appears in the Up, Over, and Down states

Up state

Over state

Down state

FIGURE 6.16

The animation as it appears in the three visible button states, Up, Over, and Down (left), with a diagram of the basic nested elements visible in each state (right)

A | | | | | | | Main Timeline: frame 1
B | | (X) | surprise (Button): frame 1 "Up"
C | eyeOutline (Graphic Symbol instance 2)
D | sleepingEyes (Movie Clip): frame 2
E | sleepingMouth (Movie Clip): frame 2

button Up

A | | | | | | | Main Timeline: frame 1
B | | (X) | surprise (Button): frame 2 "Over"
C | eyeOutline (Graphic Symbol instance 2)
F1 | | | eyesLook (Movie Clip instance 1): frame 4
G | mouthGrimace (shape)

button Over

A | | | | | | | Main Timeline: frame 1
B | (X) | surprise (Button): frame 3 "Down"
C | eyeOutline (Graphic Symbol instance 2)
F2 | eyesLook (Movie Clip instance 2): frame 8
H | mouthSurprise (shape)

button Down

Note: (X) = Hit frame of Button symbol

9-Slice Scaling for Movie Clip Backgrounds

Have you ever tried to resize the same background graphic to fit different content and found that the aspect ratio or corner angles were no longer consistent? This can be frustrating, and the workarounds in older versions of Flash — creating unique graphics for each use or manually splitting up scalable and nonscalable areas of a background or border — were time consuming and sometimes ineffective. The good news is that Flash includes a feature designed to solve this problem. The 9-slice, or Scale 9, option helps you selectively define the scaleable area of a Movie Clip to make it easier to transform and reuse.

To truly appreciate this feature you have to try it. Here's how:

1. Create a new symbol in your Flash document (Insert ⇨ New Symbol).
2. Enter a name for your symbol and select Movie Clip as the symbol type.
3. Select the check box to Enable guides for 9-slice scaling (shown in Figure 6.17).

FIGURE 6.17

Enable guides for 9-slice scaling is an option in Advanced symbol properties.

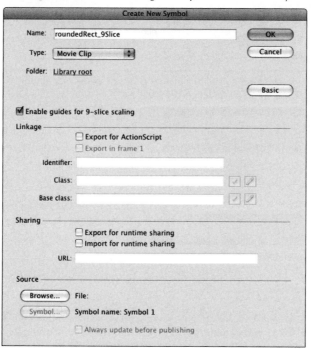

TIP Expand the Symbol Properties dialog box by clicking the Advanced button if you don't see the check box for 9-slice scaling.

4. **Click OK and enter the edit space for the new symbol; you'll notice a grid of dotted guide-lines on the Stage.** These four guides are used to split shapes into nine different regions (or slices) to control how the graphic is interpolated if the MovieClip instance is scaled.

   Don't worry about the guides just yet. Create your artwork on the Stage with any of the shape or drawing tools.

NOTE The most common use for Scale 9 is to preserve the corners on rounded rectangles used as button icons. For our example, we created a rounded rectangle by setting Fill and Stroke in the Properties panel, activating the Rectangle Primitive tool in the Tools panel, and then holding down Option (or Alt) and clicking on the Stage to open the Rectangle Settings dialog box. This makes quick work of creating a button icon — simply enter a width, height, and corner radius and click OK. The rectangle is drawn on the Stage for you.

5. **Make sure that your graphic is positioned in the center of the Stage.** Select all elements and use the center horizontal and center vertical buttons in the Align panel with the To stage toggle turned on.

6. **When you have your graphic sized and aligned as you want it, click and drag the guides to position them so that the curved areas of your graphic are not distorted when the scaled instance is rendered.** This is difficult to describe with text, but Figure 6.18 shows a centered rectangle with guides positioned to protect the rounded corners of the rectangle while allowing the center area of the graphic to be stretched when the symbol instance is scaled.

FIGURE 6.18

You can drag the four slice guides to isolate the outside edges of a graphic that should be protected when the center area is stretched to scale.

7. **To test the results of 9-slice scaling on your symbol, return to the Main Timeline and drag an instance of your symbol onto the Stage.** Use the Transform tools or the Transform panel to change the size or aspect ratio of the symbol instance. We scaled the rounded rectangle symbol instance in our example horizontally to 150 percent.

 A symbol with 9-slice scaling enabled appears with the dotted grids in the preview pane of the Library panel. The grids are not visible when the symbol is placed on the Stage.

 The effect of 9-slice scaling is visible in the authoring environment, so you don't have to test your movie to see the results of using this feature on a scaled Movie Clip.

The difference between 9-slice scaling and normal scaling is visible in the .fla and in the published .swf. As shown in Figure 6.19, the symbol without 9-slice scaling (left) is distorted when it's scaled larger, and the symbol with 9-slice scaling enabled (right) scales gracefully and preserves the original shape of the rounded corners.

ON the CD-ROM The example file shown in this section is also saved on the CD-ROM. Open 9Slice_ symbolScaling.fla or .swf from the ch06 folder.

How does this magic happen? If the final symbol is scaled horizontally, the three center sections (from left to right) stretch while the corners and the top and bottom edges are constrained. If the final symbol is scaled vertically, the three sections (from top to bottom) stretch while the corners and the left and right edges are constrained. If the symbol is scaled in both directions, the t-shaped center section stretches to fit, while the corners remain protected. It might take a few tries to get the hang of using 9-slice scaling, but it saves you a lot of time if you need to design consistent scalable graphics.

FIGURE 6.19

The symbol with 9-slice scaling enabled is rendered consistently in the .swf without any distortion. The rounded corners at the original size (top right) match the rounded corners at the scaled size (lower right).

You can enable 9-slice scaling when you create a new symbol, or you can enable it in the Symbol Properties dialog box for existing Movie Clip symbols — select the symbol in the Library list and choose Properties from the contextual menu or the panel Options menu.

TIP If you create a Movie Clip with artwork first and then enable 9-slice scaling by accessing the Symbol Properties dialog box from the Library, the slice guides automatically align to the outside edges of your artwork. You may still need to adjust the guides to get the exact result that you want, but the starting point will be much closer than if you enable the 9-slice scaling guides *before* you create the artwork.

Using the Movie Explorer

The Movie Explorer panel is a powerful tool for deciphering movies and finding items within them. You can open it from the application menu by choosing Window ⇨ Movie Explorer (Option/Alt+F3).

NOTE The Find and Replace command is a much more efficient choice if your goal is to dig up specific elements such as fonts or colors that you want to replace in your project file. We discuss the many uses of the Find and Replace feature in Chapter 9, "Modifying Graphics." We include coverage of the Movie Explorer here because it is still the best tool for discovering the structure of a file.

The Movie Explorer is an especially useful tool for getting an overview and for analyzing the structure of a Flash movie. This means that you can see every element in its relationship to all other elements, and you can see this all in one place. However, it's also useful for troubleshooting a movie, for finding occurrences of a particular font, and for locating places where you refer to a certain variable name in any script throughout a movie. As an editing tool, you can use it as a shortcut to edit any symbol, for changing the properties of an instance, or even for doing multiple selections and then changing the attributes of the selected items. Furthermore, the Find function is an incredible time-saver when working on complex project files.

Figure 6.20 shows the Movie Explorer as well as the Movie Explorer Settings dialog box, which you can open by clicking the Customize Which Items to Show button in the Movie Explorer (Customize is the far right icon in the row of filter buttons.).

FIGURE 6.20

The Movie Explorer displaying the file structure for the button example created in the previous section

Filtering buttons

As shown in Figure 6.20, there are several icon buttons across the top of the Movie Explorer panel. These are called filter buttons, and they have icons representative of their function. Click any button to toggle the display of those elements in your file. Note, however, that the Movie Explorer's display becomes more crowded as you select more buttons, and that it performs more slowly because it has to sift more data. From left to right, the buttons filter the display of the following kinds of content:

- Text
- Button symbols, Movie Clips, and Graphic symbols (placed instances)
- ActionScript
- Video, sounds, and bitmaps (placed instances)
- Frames and layers
- The Movie Explorer Settings dialog box

Also note the Find field. It enables you to search through all items that currently appear in the Movie Explorer to find specific elements by typing in the name of the symbol, instance, font name, ActionScript string, or frame number.

The display list

Below the icons is a window with the display list. Much like Windows Explorer, or the Mac Finder, the Movie Explorer displays items hierarchically, either by individual scene or for all scenes. These listings are expandable, so if you have selected the Text button, an arrow (or on Windows, a plus [+] sign) appears beside the name of any scene that includes text. Clicking the arrow (or plus sign) displays all the selected items included in that scene. This type of visual data display is also referred to as a "tree structure." Clicking a plus sign (or arrow) expands a "branch" of the tree. At the bottom of the display list, a status bar displays the full path for the currently selected item.

In Figure 6.21, the Text filter button has been selected. As shown, clicking the arrow sign beside the Text icon in the display list shows the complete text, including basic font information.

FIGURE 6.21

FIGURE 6.21

The Movie Explorer for the surpriseButton example included on the CD-ROM, with the Text filter button chosen to view text and font information inside the file

The Movie Explorer Options menu

The Options menu is accessed by clicking the options triangle in the upper right corner of the Movie Explorer panel. These commands enable you to control how much detail is shown in the display list and also to perform edits or revisions after you've found the specific items that you want to modify:

- **Go to Location:** For a selected item, this transports you to the relevant layer, scene, or frame.

- **Go to Symbol Definition:** This jumps to the symbol definition for the symbol that's selected in the Movie Elements area. (For this to work, both Show Movie Elements and Show Symbol Definitions must be toggled on.)

- **Select Symbol Instances:** This jumps to the scene containing instances of the symbol selected in the Symbol Definitions area. (For this to work, both Show Movie Elements and Show Symbol Definitions must be toggled on.)

- **Show in Library:** If the Library window is not open, this opens the Library and highlights the selected item. Otherwise, it simply highlights the item in the Library.

- **Rename:** This enables you to easily rename selected items.

- **Edit in Place:** Use this to edit the selected symbol in context on the Stage.

- **Edit in New Window:** Use this to edit the selected symbol in Edit mode in a separate window from the main Document window.

- **Show Movie Elements:** One of two broad categories for how filtered items are viewed in the display list, Show Movie Elements displays all elements in the movie, organized by scene.

- **Show Symbol Definitions:** This is the other category of the display List, which shows all the items that are related to each symbol. Both Show Movie Elements and Show Symbol Definitions may be displayed simultaneously.

- **Show All Scenes:** This toggles the display of Show Movie Elements between selected scenes and all scenes.

- **Copy All Text to Clipboard:** Use this command to copy text to the Clipboard. Text may then be pasted into a word processor or into another editing application.

CROSS-REF   We discuss text-related features in more detail in Chapter 8, "Working with Text."

CAUTION   Unfortunately, getting text back into Flash is not as easy as copying it to the Clipboard. If you copy a large amount of text to another application, you have to manually update individual text blocks in your Flash document to integrate any changes that were made to the text outside of Flash.

- **Cut:** Use this command to cut selected text.

- **Copy:** Use this command to copy selected text.

- **Paste:** Use this command to paste text that has been copied from Flash or another application.

- **Clear:** Use this command to clear selected text.

- **Expand Branch:** This expands the hierarchical tree at the selected location; it's the menu equivalent of clicking the tiny plus (+) sign or right-facing arrow.

- **Collapse Branch:** This collapses the hierarchical tree at the selected location; it's the menu equivalent of clicking the tiny minus (–) sign or down-facing arrow.

- **Collapse Others:** This collapses the hierarchical tree everywhere except at the selected location.

- **Print:** The Movie Explorer prints out, with all the content expanded, displaying all types of content selected.

You can also access the commands found in the Movie Explorer options menu via the contextual menu.

The contextual menu

Select an item in the Movie Explorer and right-click (/⌘/Ctrl+click) to open the contextual menu related to that particular item. Nonapplicable commands are grayed out.

Figure 6.22 shows the contextual menu of the Movie Explorer. Among the most useful commands is the Goto Location option at the top. When you can't find an item (because it's on a masked layer or is invisible), this command can be a lifesaver.

When you are planning or looking for ways to improve a project, the Movie Explorer can provide an excellent map to the structure and function of what you've already accomplished. Whenever it's relevant, print out the Movie Explorer; this can function as project documentation for finished work, providing a reference of all scripting and Movie Clip placement. As such, it can make returning to a project months later much easier. It can also facilitate collaboration among developers, whether they share the same studio or need to communicate long distance. Finally, for all the reasons we listed in this chapter, you can also use the Movie Explorer as a tool for both learning and teaching.

Now that you have a handle on working with symbols in one project file, let's go to the next step and see how you can work with symbols in multiple Flash files.

FIGURE 6.22

The Movie Explorer's contextual menu

Using Authortime Shared Libraries

Flash gives you two options for working with shared assets: authortime and runtime shared Libraries. Authortime sharing enables a development team to maintain consistency during production on multiple versions of a file or on various project files that use the same symbols by using a centralized internal source .fla file for fonts or other assets. Runtime sharing reduces file sizes and makes it easier to dynamically update content in projects that involve multiple .swfs without having to republish all the files. In runtime sharing, a Library of assets is created and published as a source movie (.swf) that is uploaded to the server to be shared with multiple linked movies (.swfs). Source assets in shared libraries can include any element that is normally created in a Flash movie, as well as assets such as bitmaps, fonts, sounds, or video that are imported and usually embedded in individual project files (.fla).

Runtime sharing involves URLs and linkage info, but authortime sharing is relatively simple and can be accomplished without even publishing any .swf files. You can update or replace a symbol in your current project (.fla) with any other symbol accessible on your local network. Any transformations or effects applied to instances of the symbol in your project file are preserved, but the contents of the symbol stored in the project Library are replaced with the contents of the new (or modified) source symbol that you choose to link to.

NOTE For clarity, we will refer to the currently open .fla file as a *project file*, and the .fla that contains symbols that you want to link to as the *source file*. In real-world production, you can give the files any name you want. However, adding a special identifier such as "Library" or "Source" to the .fla filenames that you plan to use for sharing can help you (and your team) minimize confusion.

ON the CD-ROM We have included two sample files with some basic symbols that you can use to try out the symbol-linking feature. Both `shapeProject.fla` and `shapeSource.fla` are in the `ch06` folder on this book's CD-ROM.

To link a symbol from one project Library to another, you need a source file and a project file. Open the project file and follow these steps.

1. In the current project (or `shapeProject.fla`) Library panel, select the symbol (Graphic symbol, Button, or Movie Clip) that you want to link to a source symbol.

2. Choose Properties from the contextual menu or from the Library options menu, and under Source in the Symbol Properties dialog box, click the Browse button to find the .fla file that contains the symbol you want to use as a source. After you find the .fla that will be your source, select it in the file list and click Open (as shown in Figure 6.23).

    The Select Source Symbol dialog box (shown in Figure 6.24) opens automatically to enable you to choose the specific symbol in the source library that you want to link to the symbol in your current project file.

TIP You can also click the Advanced button in the Create New Symbol dialog box to access Source options and set linkage when you first create a symbol in your project.

3. Select a symbol in the source Library file list and click OK to close the Select Source Symbol dialog box.

FIGURE 6.23

Browsing for a source file in the Symbol Properties dialog box

FIGURE 6.24

The Select Source Symbol dialog box, where you specify a linked symbol

Before you close the Symbol Properties dialog box, notice that the path to the source file is now listed and that you can select a check box for Always update before publishing (as shown in Figure 6.25). Select this check box if you want Flash to check for changes in the source file and automatically update all linked symbols each time you publish a .swf from the project file.

FIGURE 6.25

The source path shown in the Symbol Properties dialog box with the Always update before publishing check box selected

4. **Click OK to close the Symbol Properties dialog box.** The symbol name in your project Library remains the same, but the content of the symbol in all instances used in your project file should now contain the updated content that will match the content of the symbol you chose in the source file.

5. **Save your project file to preserve the linkage information for your symbol.**

Should any changes be made to the content of the symbol in the source .fla, you can either publish a .swf from the project file to see Flash automatically check for changes and update all linked symbols (with the Always update before publishing check box selected in the Symbol Properties dialog box), or you can use the Update command to manually get the most recent version of the symbol into your project file before you publish a .swf. To see how this works, follow these steps:

1. **Open the source .fla and make some changes to the symbol (using Edit mode) that you originally linked to and then save and close the file.** You can change the appearance of the symbol, but don't change the symbol name.

2. **Open a project file that contains the symbol you want to update, and either ensure that the Always update before publishing check box is selected in Symbol Properties before publishing an .swf to force Flash to check for changes to the source symbol and automatically update your project Library, or go to Step 3.**

3. **Select the symbol in the Library and use the options menu or the contextual menu to select the Update command.**

4. **In the Update Library Items dialog box (shown in Figure 6.26), select the symbol that you edited in the source Library and click Update.** You now see the content of the symbol in your project Library updated to reflect the changes made in the source file.

FIGURE 6.26

Use the Update Library Items dialog box to manually update the content of symbols in your project file.

It probably seems like more hassle than it's worth to keep content current in one or two files, but you will find it very helpful should you need to update symbols in multiple project files consistently.

WEB RESOURCE We'd like to know what you think about this chapter. Visit www.flashsupport.com/feedback to fill out an online survey with your comments.

Summary

- You can organize the Library with folders and symbols, and rearrange assets without breaking their linkage to instances deployed within the project.

- The Flash Library panel streamlines the controls for working with multiple documents. Instead of having to manage a separate Library panel for each open document, you can view different Library lists within a single panel.

- The Flash CS4 Library can be docked and scaled like any other panel. The new search field at the top of the panel makes it easier to find items in complex project files.

- Symbols are the building blocks of Flash. They save you time, reduce your file size, and add flexibility to your movies. When you use ActionScript to control symbol behavior or display, symbols are considered as objects within an object-oriented authoring environment.

- Flash handles imported sounds, bitmaps, and video assets as symbols. They reside in the Library, and instances of these assets are deployed within a Flash project.

- In addition to imported assets, there are three other kinds of symbols that can be created within Flash: Graphic symbols, Movie Clips, and Button symbols.

- Movie Clip symbols and Button symbols have timelines that play independently from the Main Timeline. Although Graphic symbols also have their own timelines, they are still tied to the Main Timeline and require a frame for every frame of their own timeline that is visible.

- Using symbol instances within a project is as easy as dragging an asset or symbol from the Library and onto the Stage, although it's usually best to have a new layer ready and to have the appropriate keyframe selected.

- You can edit symbols a number of ways. Any edits to a symbol in Edit mode are reflected by all instances of that symbol throughout the project.

- 9-slice scaling solves the problem of distorted graphics due to inconsistent scaling on multiple symbol instances. You can reuse and resize a rounded rectangle or pill button without worrying about mismatched stroke widths and stretched corners.

- The Properties panel offers a central control for modifying individual symbol instances. You can modify the color and transparency of instances of a symbol via the Color Effect controls. Furthermore, you can reassign symbol types by using the Type drop-down menu, and can even replace specific instances with other symbol instances by using the Swap symbol button.

- The Movie Explorer is a powerful tool for navigating movies and finding specific items within them.

- Shared Libraries streamline your workflow if a project involves multiple files that use assets that may need to be updated. Shared libraries are also useful for keeping files current and consistent in a team production environment.

Chapter 7

Applying Color

efore we get into the specifics of applying color with Flash, we want to discuss some of the fundamental theory behind working with color that's destined to appear on the Web. Limited color displays are not as common as they were in the early days of Web graphics, but it is useful to have a basic understanding of the various contexts and limitations of digital color. This chapter introduces some resources that may be helpful to you for Flash work and as references for color issues that may come up in other productions. Whether you're designing corporate graphics or creating a photo album to share online, consistent and accurate color is a key factor in the quality of your projects. We explore the options available in Flash for choosing and modifying your color palette by using the Color panel and discuss how colors can be accessed from the Tools panel. We also show you how to work with the Properties panel menus, Swatches panel, and Color panel to select, change, mix, and apply solid colors, gradients, and even bitmap fills.

CROSS-REF Flash symbol instances can be tweened so that they change color over time. Although this involves color, the selection of colors for the original symbol used in the tween is merely a rudimentary application of fill and line color, as we describe in this chapter. We discuss applying the Color Effect controls (available in the Properties panel) to symbol instances in Chapter 9, "Modifying Graphics." We cover methods for controlling color with ActionScript and the Flash Color object in Chapter 24, "Controlling Movie Clips."

CROSS-REF We cover filters and blend modes in Chapter 12, "Applying Filters, Blends, Guides, and Masks." You can use these features to modify the color and appearance of symbols, but they do not replace the basic color tools (described in this chapter) used to modify text, shapes, and Graphic symbols.

IN THIS CHAPTER

Introducing color basics

Working with Flash color

Organizing the Swatches panel

Creating and importing custom color sets

Using the Color panel to modify colors

Adding transparency to strokes and fills

Making and applying gradient fills

Selecting bitmap fills

205

Introducing Color Basics

Computer monitors display color by using a method called *RGB color*. A monitor screen is a tightly packed array of pixels arranged in a grid, where each pixel has an address. For example, a pixel that's located 16 rows down from the top and 70 columns over from the left might have an address of 70,16. The computer uses these addresses to send a specific color to each pixel. Because each pixel is composed of a single red, green, and blue dot, the colors that the monitor displays can be "mixed" at each pixel by varying the individual intensities of the red, green, and blue color dots. Each individual dot can vary in intensity over a range of 256 values, starting with 0 (which is *off*) to a maximum value of 255 (which is *on*). Thus, if red is *half-on* (a value of 127), while green is *off* (a value of 0), and blue is fully *on* (a value of 255), the pixel appears reddish blue or purple.

The preceding paragraph describes unlimited, full color, which is sometimes referred to as *24-bit color*. Most computers now use 24-bit color to deliver cleanly rendered graphics without a hitch. In the early days of Web graphics, computer systems were incapable of displaying full color; these limited color displays were either 8-bit or 16-bit. Although a full discussion of bit depth is beyond the scope of this book, it is important to note several points:

- Using 24-bit color is required to accurately reproduce photographic images and smooth color transitions in gradients.

- Because 8-bit and 16-bit systems are color challenged, they can display only a limited number of colors, and they must dither-down anything that exceeds their *gamut,* which is their expanse of possible colors. *Dithering* means that, in order to approximate colors that are missing from the palette, the closest colors available are placed in proximity to each other to fool the eye into seeing a blended intermediate color. This can result in unwanted pixel patterns.

- Some image formats, such as GIF, use a color palette that limits them to 256 colors. This is called *indexed color.* Indexed color is ideally suited for reproducing vector graphics that have solid fills and strokes, but often creates noticeable *banding* (uneven color) when applied to photographic images.

- Bitmap (or photographic) images do not accurately translate an indexed color palette, so matching color between GIF images and JPEG images can be unpredictable, because the JPEG expands the original indexed palette of a GIF file to include colors that may not be within the Web-safe color palette.

- Calibration of your monitor is essential for accurate color work. For more information, check out the Datacolor learning page at http://spyder.datacolor.com/learn_whyandwhen.php.

Discussing Web-safe color issues

By default, the Swatches panel (Ctrl+F9 or ⌘+F9) loads with Web 216 colors, and if the swatches are modified, this swatch palette can always be reloaded from the Options menu at the upper right of the panel. Web 216 restricts the color palette to Web-safe colors. However, *intermediate colors* (meaning any process or effect that generates new colors from two Web-safe colors) — such as gradients, color tweens, filters, transparent overlays, and alpha transitions — are not constrained to Web-safe colors.

NOTE The Mac and Windows platforms handle their color palettes differently, so browsers don't always have the same colors available to them across platforms. For designers, these differences led to inconsistent, unreliable color — unless they were careful to choose colors from the Web-safe palette. The Web-safe palette is a selection of 216 colors that's consistent on both the Mac and Windows platforms for Netscape, Explorer, and Mosaic browsers. The Web-safe palette contains only 216 of 256 possible indexed colors, because 40 colors can vary between Mac and Windows displays.

When there are more than 16 million possible colors, why would you settle for a mere 216? Consider your audience. Choose a color strategy that enables the majority of your viewers to see your designs as you intend them to appear. Web-safe color is not a concern for most people these days, but there may be a few exceptions. For example, if you're designing an e-commerce site for a very broad audience on a mix of platforms with the potential for some users to be on very old monitors, then you might consider limiting your work to the Web-safe palette. On the other hand, if you're designing an interface for a stock photography firm whose clients are most likely using newer computers, then color limitations are probably not an issue. In either case, keep in mind that no one will see the exact same colors that you see. The variables of hardware, calibration, ambient light, and environmental influences are unavoidable. If you do settle for 216 colors, remember that the value of color in Web design (or any design or art for that matter) has to do with color perception and design issues, and numbers have little to do with that.

Using hexadecimal values

Any RGB color can be described in hexadecimal (hex) notation. This notation is called *hexadecimal* because it describes color in base-16 values, rather than in base-10 values like standard RGB color. This color value notation is used because it describes colors in an efficient manner that HTML and scripting languages can digest. Hex notation is limited to defining *flat color,* which is a continuous area of undifferentiated color. In HTML, hexadecimal notation is used to specify colored text, lines, backgrounds, image borders, frame cells, and frame borders.

A hexadecimal color number has six places. It allocates two places for each of the three color channels: R, G, and B. So, in the hexadecimal example 00FFCC, 00 signifies the red channel, FF signifies the green channel, and CC signifies the blue channel. The corresponding values between hexadecimal and customary integer values are as follows:

16 integer values:	0	1	2	3	4	5	6	8	9	10	11	12	13	14	15
16 hex values:	0	1	2	3	4	5	6	8	9	A	B	C	D	E	F

The Web-safe values in hexadecimal notation are limited to those colors that can be described by using combinations of the pairs 00, 33, 66, 99, and FF. White is described by the combination FFFFFF, or all colors *on* 100 percent. At the other end of the spectrum, black is described by the combination 000000, all colors on 0 percent, or *off.* A medium gray would be described by the combination 666666, or all colors on 40 percent.

Using color effectively

According to some designers, the issue of color on the Web has been seriously confused by the misperception that people can set numbers to give them Web-safe colors, and that, if they do this, they will have *good* color. When designers get caught up in the excitement of layered patterns and multicolored text, they sometimes overlook the fact that the end result isn't very legible or "easy on the eyes." A little restraint can go a long way toward making your designs both appealing and legible. Although we all want to be creative and unique, certain color rules can actually be more liberating than restricting.

Although unconventional design choices can add an element of surprise, a touch of humor, or just a visual punch that helps your layout stand out from the rest, it is vital that you don't compromise your end goal. When you get noticed, you want to deliver your message successfully — whether that message is "Buy this product" or just "Hey, this is a cool site." If you start to carefully deconstruct the layouts that grab your attention, you will probably find that there are consistencies to the choices that were made in the design, regardless of the content. You'll begin to notice that even the most bizarre or cutting-edge designs share certain features that make them eye catching and memorable.

Much of the underlying strategy in a design may be transparent, or not *consciously* perceived by the viewer. But don't make the mistake of thinking that individual preference is completely unpredictable. The secret to successful design is leveraging the unconscious visual language that your audience is physically and culturally conditioned to respond to. Individual viewers may have specific preferences for certain colors or styles, but they all recognize and understand many of the same visual conventions.

Although learning to apply all these conventions and to integrate them into your own design style can take years of study and practice, there are some fundamental "truths" that will serve you well, no matter how long you've been designing:

- **Color is relative:** Humans perceive color relative to the context of other colors in which the color is set. Most art schools offer at least one course about color. They often start with color experiments that are conducted with pieces of colored paper. An early assignment is to make three colors look like more than three colors — by placing small scraps of the same color on larger pieces of different colors. Students are always amazed to learn how much a person's perception of a single color is influenced when it's placed on different-colored backgrounds. Figure 7.1 shows how the same shade of gray can appear lighter or darker depending on the background color. The lesson is that color is *not* an absolute — it never was before computers, and it never will be to the human eye.

FIGURE 7.1

The same gray circle displayed on different background values appears to be darker or lighter by comparison.

- **Contrast is king:** Only one thing is more important than color: contrast. *Contrast* is the relative difference in lightness or darkness of items in a composition. Here's a good test: Take a colorful design that you admire and reduce it to grayscale. Does it still work? Contrast is a major factor in good color composition. Figure 7.2 shows different amounts of contrast created by relative differences in value.

FIGURE 7.2

Varying levels of color contrast determine legibility and emphasis.

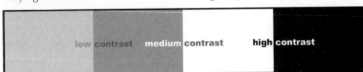

low contrast   medium contrast   high contrast

To ensure a strong design, it can be helpful to work on your initial layouts in grayscale. When you have contrast working for you, you can start to add color with the confidence that the design will not be visually *muddy* — or hard to read — because of poor contrast. Often, the same color scheme can be a disaster or a huge success, all depending on the contrast you create in the design. The concept of contrast also applies to other characteristics of your design — size, texture, even mood. Try to use contrast wherever you want to create emphasis or add drama. But remember: If you make everything huge and flashing red, or extra-small and pale gray, you will no longer have any contrast. The strength of contrast is in variety. Figure 7.3 shows how contrast can be achieved by varying the size and style of your text — even if the font stays the same. Create even more contrast by mixing fonts with different visual character: A sans-serif with thick strokes contrasts nicely with a script font with calligraphy-style strokes.

FIGURE 7.3

Variety in the size and shape of elements also adds visual contrast.

low **MEDIUM** **HIGH**
contrast contrast c o n t r a s t

- **Less is more:** Keep in mind that the power of contrast should always be used in moderation. White text on black backgrounds can be great for headlines, but after more than a few paragraphs, it makes the reader feel as though his or her retina is actually being burned by the text on the screen — one of the best ways to keep someone from actually reading your copy. Also, don't be afraid of empty space; the impact of individual elements is often dependent on having a little room to breathe. One element in a striking color is much more effective than a whole page filled with competing colors.

- **Start at the beginning:** Visual hierarchy is the best secret weapon in any designer's arsenal. Although you may not be sure what the most important element is in your design, if you don't give readers a place to start, chances are you'll lose their attention. By deciding on the order of importance for elements in your design and then using contrast, size, and color to guide readers through your layout, you'll create motivation for them to actually stick around long enough to absorb your message. Think of your content as the elements of a good story: In order to make the narrative compelling, you have to have a catchy intro, a juicy middle, and a rewarding ending or payoff. You might argue that you want to let readers make their own choice about where to start (like starting at the back of a novel), but if you don't create a visual structure, readers won't feel empowered to make any choices. Presented with a big muddle of uncertain order, they will most likely move on to a design where they can find the beginning, middle, and end at a glance, before deciding what they want to read first. Figure 7.4 shows a layout with poorly defined visual hierarchy compared to an example with stronger contrast and clearer hierarchy. The page with the more clearly defined hierarchy gives the reader more clues about the order of importance of each element on the page. Of course, these examples don't even use color, but as we mention earlier, it can be best to plan the structure of your layout before adding color to support it.

FIGURE 7.4

Adding contrast to a weak design (left) makes for a stronger visual hierarchy (right) and orients readers in your layout.

 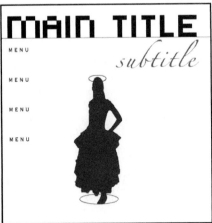

Weak contrast = muddy visual hierarchy   Strong contrast = clear visual hierarchy

Here's the bottom line: Color can help a good design look *great,* and when used with strategy, it can help engage the viewer and sell your message. But no amount of color can save a poorly planned design, so consider the underlying structure, contrast, and visual hierarchy of your layout before adding color.

Innumerable books on color theory and many different software solutions that can provide inspiration and take the guesswork out of choosing color schemes are out there. These are just three sources that can help you create harmonious color families for your designs:

- **Kuler from Adobe Labs:** This color-focused site offers ready-made themes submitted by designers, a color forum, and a Flash-based Web tool that you can use to create your own color themes. Themes are available for download if you are signed in to the Adobe site and can be used with any of your Adobe CS applications. Explore themes or contribute your own at http://kuler. adobe.com.

NEW FEATURE You can access the Kuler application directly from Flash by selecting Window ⇨ Extensions ⇨ Kuler. This makes it easier to quickly search for themes or create your own while working in Flash. The best part is an option to load themes into the Flash Swatches panel with just one click!

- **Color Schemer:** A handy utility that generates a palette of harmonious colors for any key color that you want to start with. The full version of the software is available in a Windows version and an OS X version. The online version is helpful regardless of what platform you use. Try it out at www.colorschemer.com/online.html.

  You can generate lists of RGB or hexadecimal colors from the Web-safe palette and choose to darken or lighten all colors in the palette until you find the exact color set you like. Color Schemer also offers a basic color tutorial that will help you understand how to generate harmonious palettes. You can find it at www.colorschemer.com/tutorial.html.

■ *Pantone Guide to Communicating with Color*: A wonderful reference book by color guru Leatrice Eiseman (published by North Light Books in 2000). This colorful book includes a wealth of information about the science and psychology of color, as well as a guide to a whole range of color families, grouped according to mood. Get inspired to add meaningful color to your projects.

> **TIP** The Pantone system for specifying ink color is the industry standard for communication between designers and printers. Pantone swatch books are indispensable and well worth the investment if you do any print work. Visit www.pantone.com to learn more. Pantone has also developed systems to help designers and retailers who need to specify and display color consistently in a digital environment. Visit www.therightcolor.com to learn more if you are developing online catalogs or other projects that require precise color matching. Pantone also offers swatch books with both CMYK and hex color values printed on them to make color matching between screen graphics and printed graphics easier. If you are a designer who "thinks in Pantone," you might find it worthwhile to invest in Pantone's Colorist software. Available for Windows and for Mac, Colorist makes Pantone swatches available from programs that do not have built-in Pantone color libraries (including Flash and Fireworks).

Working in the Swatches Panel

The Swatches panel (Ctrl+F9 or ⌘+F9) is the most commonly used source for selecting colors as you work in Flash. Although the controls for loading or modifying specific palettes are available only on the main Swatches panel, both the Tools panel and the Properties panel give you quick pop-up menus to access whatever colors are currently loaded. If the main Swatches panel isn't visible, you can always find it in the application menu under Window ⇨ Swatches. Figure 7.5 shows the Fill Swatches for the default Web 216 colors as they appear in the popup menu in the Tools panel (A), on the main Swatches panel (B), and in the Properties panel popup (C). The Swatches panel is shown with the Options menu that is invoked by clicking the top right corner of the panel.

> **TIP** For a quick way to change the transparency of a selected color, go to the Swatches popup menu and try out the handy Alpha field. You can also adjust Alpha levels on fill colors by using the Color panel.

Tools that create fields of color, or fills, include the Brush, the Paint Bucket, and the various Shape tools. Each of these tools is accompanied by the Fill color button, which appears in the Tools panel and in the Properties panel. Although the Fill Swatches popup menu is similar to the Stroke popup menu, it has one significant difference: It includes another row of swatches at the bottom, which are gradient swatches — click one to fill with a prebuilt gradient style.

Tools that create lines, or strokes, include the Line, Pencil, Ink Bottle, Pen, and — because they create outlines around fills — any of the Shape tools. These tools rely on the Stroke color button, which appears in both the Tools panel and the Properties panel.

For all drawing tools, basic color selection is accomplished by clicking either the Stroke or Fill color buttons, and then choosing a color from the Swatches popup. This popup displays the same swatch set that is currently loaded in the Swatches panel. It also includes a hexadecimal color-entry box — which facilitates keyboard entry, as well as cut-and-paste of hex values. Depending upon the tool you select, the Swatch menu available from the Tools panel may display a No Color button above the solid swatches as well as a button that launches the Color Picker.

> **TIP**   You can remove a fill or stroke from a selected shape or Drawing Object by using the None (or No Color) button in any of the Swatches menus. If the line or stroke shows the selection grid, you can also use Edit ⇨ Clear or press the Backspace (Delete) key to remove a line or stroke. Shapes can be selected directly; Drawing Objects must be in Edit mode.

> **TIP**   If you decide after you invoke the Swatches popup that you don't want to change your selected color after all, hit the Escape key or make sure that your mouse is over the original color swatch when you click to close the popup.

The color chips appearing on the Tools panel always display the most recently selected Stroke and Fill colors, and the Properties panel displays the color chips relevant to the active tool or the currently selected item.

FIGURE 7.5

The default color palette as it appears in the Tools panel popup (A), the Swatches panel (B), and the Properties panel popup (C)

Available swatches

B. Color Swatches panel with options

Duplicate Swatch
Delete Swatch

Add Colors...
Replace Colors...
Load Default Colors

Save Colors...
Save as Default

Clear Colors

Web 216

Sort by Color

Help

Close
Close Group

Available Gradient fills

Hexadecimal value field

Launch Color Picker

No color button

Alpha value field

Alpha: 100 %

A. Tools panel Swatches pop-up

C. Properties panel Swatches pop-up

NOTE Drawing Objects behave like grouped shapes, but the fill and stroke colors applied to Drawing Objects can be modified without opening them in Edit mode. When a Drawing Object is selected (by single-clicking) with the Selection tool, the selection grid isn't visible (as it would be on a raw shape), but you can apply a new fill or stroke color by using any of the Swatches menus. To open a Drawing Object in Edit mode, double-click with the Selection tool.

If the color you want is not available in the current Swatches menu, you may opt to invoke the Color Picker by clicking the Color Picker button. Alternatively, you may also open the Color panel to create a new color and add it to the currently loaded selection of swatches. The Swatches panel enables you to load, add, delete, and modify various color sets for individual documents. Whatever changes are made to the Swatches panel are saved with the document (.fla) that is currently active.

TIP With any of the Swatch popups active, your cursor icon turns into an Eyedropper. If you roll over colors outside of the swatches area while continuing to hold down the mouse, you will notice that you can "sample" colors from anywhere on your desktop. When you find a color you like, release your mouse and the color loads into Flash as your currently selected color. Don't forget to add the color to the Swatches panel if you want to save it in the color library of your current file. We describe the steps for adding and saving swatches later in this chapter.

Swatches panel options

Think of the Swatches panel (see Figure 7.6) as a paint box or a way to organize your existing swatches and to manipulate the display of colors that are available in the other panels. Use the Swatches panel to save color sets, import color sets, and reorder or change selected colors. The options menu of the Swatches panel provides the controls used to sort or modify individual swatches as well as various color sets:

- **Duplicate Swatch:** Use this to duplicate a selected swatch. It can be useful when you want to make a range of related color swatches by duplicating and then editing a series of swatches with the Color panel.

TIP You can duplicate a selected swatch with just two clicks. First, select a swatch with the Selection tool or use the Dropper tool to pick a color from any item on the Stage. As you move the cursor into the space below the current solid swatches set (above the gradient swatches), the cursor icon changes from a dropper into a paint bucket. Just click, and a new swatch is added to the color set. Changed your mind? Hold down Ctrl or ⌘ and click the added swatch with the scissors that replace your mouse cursor, and the swatch disappears.

- **Delete Swatch:** Botched a swatch? Select and delete it here.
- **Add Colors:** Opens the Import Color Swatch menu, which is a simple dialog box used to locate, select, and import color sets. Add Colors retains the current color set and appends the imported color set at the bottom of the panel.

CAUTION Be careful about creating huge color sets! In some cases, the Swatch color popups may extend beyond the visible screen and you'll have to use the Swatches panel to scroll to choose colors that are hidden off-screen. This can happen if you add colors from a complex GIF image to the default Web 216 set.

- **Replace Colors:** Also opens the Import Color Swatch menu. However, Replace Colors replaces the current color set when it loads the selected color set. With the exception of the gradient swatches, if the current set has not been saved, it will be lost.
- **Load Default Colors:** Clears the current color set and replaces it with the default Web 216 swatch palette. Again, if the current set has not been saved, it will be lost. Flash allows you to change the specification for your default color palette if you prefer not to use Web 216. (See Save as Default.)

- **Save Colors:** Opens the Export Color Swatch menu, which is used to name and save color sets to a specific location on your hard drive. Color sets may be saved in either the Flash Color Set (.clr) or Color Table (.act) format, which can be used with Fireworks and Photoshop. Gradients can only be imported and exported from Flash by using the .clr format.

- **Save as Default:** Saves the current swatch set as the default set to be loaded in the Swatches panel for all new Flash documents.

- **Clear Colors:** Removes all colors currently loaded in the Swatches panel, leaving only the black-and-white swatches and a grayscale gradient.

- **Web 216:** Loads the Web-safe palette. This option makes it safe to mess with the swatches in Flash because no matter what you do, you can always just reload this original default color set.

> **TIP** You can override the default Web 216 color set by switching the Color panel to either the RGB or HSB (hue, saturation, brightness) color spaces. You can then mix your own fresh colors, add them to the Swatches panel, and save that palette as the default. Another alternative is to locate the Photoshop Color Tables on your hard drive (or download a specialty color table from the Web) and replace the default set with a broader gamut.

- **Sort by Color:** This organizes the swatches by hue instead of by mathematical number and can visually be a more logical way to find colors in your current set. Note, however, that after you apply this sort, you have no way to toggle back to your original swatch order (other than reloading the default Web 216 swatch set). So it is best to save any custom palette first before sorting so that you have the option of going back to the other display if you prefer it. Figure 7.6 shows the Web 216 palette as it appears by default sorted numerically (left) and as it appears sorted by color (right).

FIGURE 7.6

The Web 216 palette as it appears by default sorted by number (left), and how it appears after being sorted by hue with the Sort by Color option (right)

Importing custom palettes

The option of loading custom swatches is helpful if you're developing a Flash project that you want to match with a predefined palette — whether this is out of necessity or just for inspiration. For example, you can match your Flash elements to a corporate logo or to the range of hues in a photo that you love. In addition to loading the colors in a specific GIF file, Flash allows you to load RGB color palettes from other graphics applications that have been saved as Color Tables (in the .act or .clr format.)

Loading a custom color theme from the Kuler panel

Flash CS4 includes a panel to access Kuler, a fun color tool from Adobe that organizes color into a series of five selected swatches called a *theme*. This Web-based extension includes a ratings system and live comments on themes created and uploaded by a growing community of Kuler users. You can browse themes to use as is or modify, or create your own theme from scratch by using an interactive color wheel and a menu of color modes. Figure 7.7 shows the browse mode (left) and the create mode (right) of the simplified Kuler application included with Flash CS4 (Window ➪ Extensions ➪ Kuler).

FIGURE 7.7

The Kuler panel in Flash CS4 can be used to browse color themes made by other people (left) or to create your own custom theme with Adobe's user-friendly color tool (right).

After you've chosen or created a theme (series of swatches) in Kuler, you can use the handy one-click Add to Swatches button at the bottom of the Kuler panel (see Figure 7.7) to automatically add the swatches in your selected theme to the main Flash Swatches panel. If you create a Kuler account, you can also use the online MyKuler page to save and sort your favorite themes.

TIP If you would prefer to have *only* the swatches that you are moving from Kuler show up in the Swatches panel, use the Clear Colors command in the Swatches panel Options menu *before* you add the theme from the Kuler panel. By default, a black swatch and a white swatch remain in the Swatches panel even after you apply the Clear Colors command, but otherwise, you will have a clean slate for your Kuler theme swatches.

Five colors may be all you need to create a perfect design, but if you need more, don't hesitate to add a few more themes to your Swatches panel or modify the colors in the Color panel to create additional variations.

TIP Don't forget to upload the themes you are especially proud of to the Kuler site to share with other people too. Choose a descriptive name and check back to see what people have to say about your color savvy!

Loading a custom GIF color palette

To simplify your Flash Swatches to match the colors in a company logo or other GIF image, follow these steps:

1. Choose Replace Colors from the Swatches panel options menu and, in the Import Color Swatch dialog box, specify a GIF file to define the imported color set.

2. After Flash loads the colors from the GIF image into the Swatches panel, save the document (.fla) to keep these colors as the loaded set.

3. To organize the loaded color set in the Swatches panel by hue, choose the Sort by Color option. You can always add or delete swatches from this new set.

4. If you want to use your custom color set in other files, use the Save Colors command in the Swatches panel options menu to save a Color Table (.act) or Flash Color Set (.clr).

A sample source GIF image and the resulting imported Swatches palette are shown in Figure 7.8.

FIGURE 7.8

The simple logo GIF (left) that we specified as the source for the Replace Colors command. The resulting colors loaded in the Swatches panel (right) match the colors in the logo.

TIP The color settings defined in the original authoring environment (such as Adobe Illustrator or Photoshop) for saved GIF files affects the colors available for loading to the Flash Swatches panel. For the widest range of colors, use 256 colors and an adaptive palette. To get only the exact colors used in a graphic, manually restrict the number of colors that can be included by typing a number that matches the number of colors in the original graphic. For example, if a logo that you plan to use as a source file for your swatches is red, blue, yellow, black, and white, restrict the GIF to five colors when you export it from the original authoring application.

Creating and loading a custom color table

If you want to save a color palette that matches the hues in a photograph that is not already in GIF format, you can also generate a color table in Photoshop.

To create a color table in Photoshop (or Illustrator), follow these steps:

1. Open a source bitmap image (.jpeg, .tif, .psd or .png).

2. Use the Save for Web and Devices command to access the settings that allow you to choose the file type and color space that you want to export. To create a color table, set the file type to GIF, choose Adaptive (or Restrictive if you want your swatches to be Web safe) color, and set the number of colors you want to include in the color table. Although you can include anywhere from 2 to 256 colors in your color table, you will not likely need more than 16. Preview the swatches in the Color Table (on the right side of the Save for Web dialog box).

NOTE Although Photoshop includes a menu option for creating a color table (Image ⇨ Mode ⇨ Color Table), this option is available only if the source image is first converted to Indexed color. Also, the Color Table dialog box offers only limited control of the swatches that are exported, so we prefer to use the Save for Web workflow.

3. **When you have a set of swatches that you are happy with, choose Save Color Table from the Color Palette menu** (accessed from the icon in the top right corner of the Color Table preview). The settings used for the sample file are shown in Figure 7.9.

4. **Give the color table a name that you will remember (such as tulip_field) and save the .act file to a folder where you can find it again.** Creating a Custom Palettes folder on your system, where you can store and organize any of the color tables or source GIFs that you may want to use again, is a good idea.

5. **Open a Flash document (.fla), and from the Swatches panel options menu choose Add Colors if you want new colors added to the currently loaded set (or Replace Colors if you want to use only your new colors).**

6. **From the Import Color Swatch dialog box, browse to your color table (.act) file and select it.** Flash loads the new colors into the Swatches panel, and you can then sort and save this set with your document.

FIGURE 7.9

Use the Save for Web command and the Color Table settings in Adobe Photoshop to create a custom color palette from a photograph.

The sample source bitmap image and the resulting color table loaded into the Swatches panel are shown in Figure 7.10.

FIGURE 7.10

A photo (in GIF format) used to generate a color table (.act), and the resulting color set loaded into the Flash Swatches panel

 In the previous example, we created a color table from an image of a tulip field. You can find the source bitmap (tulip_bitmap.tif) and the color table (tulip_field.act) files, along with a Flash document (tulipColors_loaded.fla) that has a GIF imported and the color palette loaded, in the colorTable folder in the ch07 folder on the CD-ROM.

Using the Color Panel

Think of the Color panel as the "boss" of the Swatches panel. The Swatches panel handles the color inventory and serves up the available colors, but the Color panel has the power to modify those colors and add variations to the current set. The Color style menu available on the Color panel allows you to choose the type of color pattern that you want to work with — including solid colors, linear and radial gradients, and bitmap fills.

TIP Gradient styles can be used with strokes as well as with fills. This option has potential for creating custom line styles for borders and other decorative lines.

As shown in Figure 7.11 and Figure 7.12, the Color panel enables you to create new colors, with settings in any of three color spaces — RGB, HSB, or hex — using either manually entered values or the "rainbow" color picker field. All colors are handled with four channels, which are RGBA (red, green, blue, alpha); these values can be individually adjusted by using the Color value fields and slider controls. The Tint slider control enables you to dynamically shift your current color darker or lighter. A Fill or Stroke color selected in any of the Swatch menus appears in the Color panel where it can be modified.

As shown in Figure 7.12, colors modified in the Color panel can be added to the palette loaded in the Swatches panel — just select Add Swatch from the Color panel options menu and the color is added below the colors currently loaded in the Swatches panel.

Any color swatch selected in the Swatches panel is loaded into the Color panel as a starting point only — modifications made in the Color panel do not change the original color in the Swatches panel. The new color or gradient that you create by using the controls in the Color panel (shown in Figure 7.13) are added as a new swatch only when you select Add Swatch from the options menu. You can always edit your custom color by selecting the new (saved) swatch, but the modified version is treated as a new color and also has to be added to the Swatches panel separately.

FIGURE 7.11

The Flash Color panel

Swap color button
(reverses fill and stroke color)

No color button
(clears stroke or fill)

Black and white color
button (resets to
black stroke,
white fill)

Color selection field

Current color marker

Fill Type menu

Options menu

Alpha value field

Color (Red, Green, Blue)
value fields

Preview swatch

Hex value field

Tint slider

FIGURE 7.12

Colors modified in the Color panel can be added to the Swatches panel.

Grid behind color indicates Alpha

Modified color added to the Swatches panel

TIP Unlike swatches selected from the Swatches panel, a fill or stroke selected in the Document window can be edited "live" in the Color panel. You can see the changes you make applied to the original fill or stroke if it remains selected.

CAUTION The colors you create and add to the Swatches panel are saved with the document (.fla) as long as you do not reload the default set or overwrite the loaded swatch set. If you want to save your custom mixed colors, remember to save the Flash color set (.clr) to a folder by using the Save Colors command in the Swatches panel before you reload the default Web 216 color set or Replace Colors with a new palette.

When you select a color from the Swatches popup palette, the cursor converts to a Dropper tool that enables you to sample color from anywhere in the interface just by clicking the color you want to pick up. You can pluck colors from icons in the Flash application, from any element that you have in the Document window, and even from elements on your desktop or in other application windows that are currently open.

FIGURE 7.13

The Color panel preview swatch splits to compare colors as you use the Color Picker or the Tint slider to make adjustments.

Current color marker

Last chosen color marker

Current color

Last chosen color

TIP The same Dropper feature is available from any of the Swatches popups, but the colors you select this way are not stored in the Swatches panel unless you use the Color panel's Add Swatch option.

NOTE The mouse cursor does not always display as a Dropper but if you have a popup Swatches palette active, you will notice that the color chip at the top of the palette will update to match the color that your cursor is over and if you click to select it, the color loads into the currently active color chip (fill or stroke).

Adjusting fill and stroke transparency

The Alpha control in the Color panel (and in the Swatches popups) is used to adjust the transparency of stroke and fill colors, either to modify a selected graphic (shape or Drawing Object) or to create a new color that can be added to the Swatches panel.

There are two ways to change the alpha value for a selected color: Either drag the Alpha slider until the preview display looks right, or enter a numeric value directly in the Alpha value box. Numeric entry is useful when you already know what level of transparency is required, and the slider is useful for tweaking the transparency by eye to get it just right — as indicated in either the stroke or fill color chip or the color preview in the Color panel. In Figure 7.14, a stroke color and a fill color have both been adjusted to 50 percent alpha and then added to the Swatches panel. While the Alpha slider is being dragged to a new setting, the preview displays the original 75 percent alpha value (at the bottom) as well as the current 50 percent alpha value (at the top). The rectangle below the panels shows the 50 percent alpha stroke and fill applied to a shape. The Flash grid has been turned on (View ⇨ Grid ⇨ Show Grid) so that the alpha is easier to see — on a flat white background, the color just looks lighter rather than transparent.

FIGURE 7.14

New levels of alpha can be applied to fills and strokes, and the modified swatches can be added to the Swatches panel for reuse.

Most recently set Stroke color

Most recently set Fill color

Alpha value field

50% Alpha
(last selected setting)

50% Alpha Stroke and Fill applied

Alpha slider control   Modified colors added to the Swatches panel

75% Alpha (preview of current setting)

CAUTION Alpha transparency results in more of a performance hit than a color tint, especially if there are a lot of overlapping animated transparencies. If you can achieve the effect that you want by using a *tint* instead (fading to a solid color), then save the alpha effect for graphics that you need to layer on top of other elements or textured backgrounds.

CROSS-REF You can apply blend modes to symbols to create different types of layered effects. We describe this feature in Chapter 9, "Modifying Graphics."

Working with gradient fills

Gradients are composed by blending two or more colors together in bands across a plane (*a linear gradient*) or from the center to the edge of an object in concentric circles (*a radial gradient*). You can modify these two basic styles of gradient fill to create virtually unlimited variations.

Figure 7.15 shows the gradient-editing controls in the Color panel, with the preview display for a linear gradient on the top, and for a radial gradient on the bottom. When working with linear gradients, the position of the color pointers on the Edit bar correspond to control points on the blend from left to right. When used in conjunction with radial gradients, the Gradient Edit bar corresponds to the *radius,* or a slice from the center out to the edge, of the circular gradient. Color pointers at the left end of the Gradient Edit bar represent the center — or inside — of the radial gradient, and color pointers at the right end represent the outside border. The active color pointer is identified by a black fill in the pointer, and unselected color pointers have a white fill in the pointer.

FIGURE 7.15

The Color panel displaying edit controls and preview for a linear gradient (on the left) and for a radial gradient (on the right)

The main Swatches panel and any of the fill Swatches popups display the prebuilt linear and radial gradients that are included in the default palette. To edit an existing gradient swatch, just select it from the any of the fill Swatches popups or select it from the main Swatches panel, and it loads into the Color panel where the relevant controls appear automatically. The other option is to start by choosing a gradient style from the central fill Type menu on the Color panel to load a basic linear or radial gradient. After you create a custom gradient in a document, your settings appear when you go back to the Color panel menu. To start with an unmodified default gradient, just select one from the fill Swatches palette. Figure 7.16 shows the two methods of selecting a gradient style to work with.

FIGURE 7.16

You can select default gradient styles (and saved custom gradients) from any of the fill Swatches popups, or set one of the basic grayscale gradient styles with the fill Type menu in the Color panel.

Color panel

Fill Type menu   Swatches panel

Gradient swatch area
default gradients and
saved custom gradients

Controlling gradient fill colors

The colors in a gradient and the distribution of blending are adjusted by sliding the color pointers along the Gradient Edit bar in the Color panel. These pointers are the access points to the key colors that define the gradient. After you click a pointer to make it active, you can assign the color that will be blended in its range, either by double-clicking to invoke the Swatches popups or by picking a color in the color selection field. You can also use the value fields and the color slider controls to modify an assigned color in a gradient the same way as any solid color. Although you may never need more than two or three points to create your gradients, Flash CS4 supports up to 15 control points in a single gradient.

CAUTION   When you are editing a gradient fill, selecting a solid color swatch from the Swatches panel does not have the same effect as selecting a solid color swatch from the Swatches popup for each color pointer in the Color panel. Clicking a solid color swatch in the Swatches panel replaces your entire gradient in the Color panel with a solid fill style. Clicking a swatch from a Swatches popup on one of the gradient color pointers replaces only the color on the currently selected pointer — leaving the rest of your gradient intact.

You can adjust the pattern of the blend by clicking and dragging any of the color pointers to slide them to new positions along the Gradient Edit bar. You can add additional color pointers to the gradient range by clicking anywhere along the Gradient Edit bar. These additional pointers create new control points in the gradient that can be dragged to new positions or assigned new colors to define the gradient pattern. To remove color pointers, simply drag them downward away from the Gradient Edit bar; they detach and disappear, taking their assigned color and control point with them. Figure 7.17 shows a basic radial gradient modified with the addition of a new control point and changes to the control point colors. To save a custom gradient to your Swatches panel, choose Add Swatch from the Color panel options menu.

FIGURE 7.17

A two-point radial gradient from white to black (on the left), modified by setting the left pointer to gray and adding a central color pointer set to white (on the right)

Two-point radial gradient   Three-point radial gradient

By selecting an element on the Stage, you can also apply or modify an existing gradient fill or stroke by using the Color panel. When an item is selected in the Document window, you see the current fill and stroke displayed in the Color panel. Any changes you make in the Color panel while the item is selected updates on the item dynamically. Remember to select Add Swatch from the options menu if you want to store the new gradient in the Swatches panel.

 NOTE   The current fill (and/or stroke) of an item selected in the Document window is automatically loaded in the Color panel.

 TIP   To make it easier to see how a gradient looks in a selected shape, you can toggle off the display of the selection mesh by using Shift+Ctrl+E (Shift+⌘+E).

If you need some new ideas for gradient styles, Illustrator or Fireworks would be a great addition to your toolkit. Flash supports the import of Fireworks PNG files, and most filters and gradient styles added in Fireworks are preserved and editable when the file is imported to Flash. Fireworks ships with a huge library of ready-made gradient styles, including simple but handy Rectangle and Contour styles and fancier ones such as Satin, Starburst, and Ripple. Some of these gradient styles are too complex for the Flash authoring environment to support, but you can import them as bitmaps and jump out to Fireworks to edit them if you need to. You can add Fireworks or Illustrator gradient styles that Flash supports to your Swatches panel and reuse or modify them. Now those same old shaded buttons you have to keep making might just be more fun!

Using alpha settings with gradients

As we mention previously, all the normal Color sliders and value fields apply to control points on a gradient. You may have noticed already that this means you can add alpha to the blend range of any gradient. To create a soft transition between a bitmap or a patterned background and a solid color, you can create a gradient from a 0 percent alpha to a 100 percent alpha of the same solid color. To demonstrate just one application of this feature, we will walk through the steps of adding the appearance of a vignette (or softened edge) to a photograph imported into Flash:

1. **Import a bitmap into Flash and place it on the Stage; then lock the bitmap layer.**

2. **Create a new layer above the bitmap layer and name it** gradient (see Figure 7.18).

FIGURE 7.18

An imported bitmap placed on the Stage with a new layer above it for the gradient

---

3. **Open the Color panel and set the fill Type to radial, or select the default grayscale radial gradient from the fill Swatches panel.** Leave the Overflow menu on the default (Extend) setting.

CROSS-REF The Overflow style menu for gradient and bitmap fills in the Color panel provides more control over fill rendering. Three Overflow settings determine how the edges of a gradient or bitmap image is rendered if they need to extend beyond the bounding box of the original applied fill. We include more detailed coverage of these settings in Chapter 9, "Modifying Graphics."

4. **Select the Rectangle tool and use the Properties panel to set the stroke color to black, with a stroke height of 2.**

5. **Select the gradient layer and then use the Rectangle tool to drag out a rectangle on the Stage that is the same size as the photograph on the layer below (see Figure 7.19).**

FIGURE 7.19

Finished rectangle with a radial gradient fill and a black stroke of 2. The rectangle is dragged out to match the size of the photograph on the layer below.

6. **Select the fill of the rectangle and then select the left (white) color pointer on the Gradient Edit bar and assign it a color of black (see Figure 7.20).** Set the Alpha value on the left color pointer to 0 percent.

FIGURE 7.20

Both color pointers are assigned a color of black for the selected gradient fill and the left pointer is assigned Alpha 0 percent.

7. Press Shift+Ctrl+E (Shift+⌘+E) to hide the selection mesh and adjust the position of the color pointers by sliding them along the Gradient Edit bar, until you like the way the blend looks on top of the photo (see Figure 7.21).

FIGURE 7.21

You can preview the final gradient as you move the color pointer to adjust the edges of the alpha blend.

> **TIP** If you applied the Drawing Object option when you drew the original gradient rectangle, you won't have to worry about turning off the selection mesh. The thin, blue outline that shows up on a selected Drawing Object doesn't interfere with the live gradient preview like the dotted mesh that appears on a selected raw shape does.

> **CROSS-REF** Select any gradient item (fill or stroke) with the Gradient Transform tool (nested in the Tools panel with the Free Transform tool) and you see the edit handles that you can use to modify the center point, scale, and rotation of your gradient within the selected item. We describe the Gradient Transform tool in more detail in Chapter 9, "Modifying Graphics."

> **TIP** As you read through the steps in this example, you might have wondered why we assigned the same color to both color pointers; because one of the pointers is set to an alpha value of 0 percent, perhaps it doesn't matter which color is used? The answer is that you *can* create a "fade" effect with a radial gradient made from two different colors, but the blend is not clean unless you use only one color. Although the endpoint of the gradient assigned an alpha value of 0 percent is "clear," the interstitial bands of the gradient are tinted by whatever color you have assigned to the color pointer before changing the alpha value.

Selecting bitmap fills

Another handy feature available in the Color panel is the Bitmap fill option. This option enables you to choose any bitmap, in the Library or elsewhere on your system, to use as a fill for shapes drawn in Flash. When the image loads into a selected shape, it tiles to fill the shape.

To apply a bitmap fill directly to an existing shape, perform the following steps:

1. **Select the fill of a shape (or select a Drawing Object) with the Selection tool.**
2. **Open the Color panel and choose Bitmap from the fill Type menu.**
3. **If you have bitmaps stored in your current document Library, they will be available from the Bitmap Preview area of the Color panel.** Simply click the thumbnail of the bitmap that you want to apply and it automatically fills the selected shape.
4. **If you do not have any bitmaps available in the current document, selecting Bitmap from the fill Type menu in the Color panel launches the Import to Library dialog box, where you can browse your system and specify a bitmap to be imported and applied as a fill.**

Figure 7.22 shows a selected shape with a bitmap fill applied from the available thumbnails in the Color panel Preview area.

FIGURE 7.22

A bitmap fill applied to a selected shape. The bitmap is chosen from images stored in the Library, which appear as thumbnails in the Color panel Preview area.

Preview of active Bitmap fill

Bitmap fill applied to currently selected Drawing object

Thumbnail previews for available Bitmap fills

Bitmaps stored in Library

CROSS-REF The appearance of a Bitmap fill varies depending on how it is loaded (or assigned) to a specific item. We cover the various ways of loading Bitmap fills and the results you can expect in more detail in Chapter 9, "Modifying Graphics."

Working with Droppers, Paint Buckets, and Ink Bottles

We've introduced the various ways of controlling your palette and setting stroke and fill colors on items selected with the Selection tool. There is one other set of tools used for applying colors and fills that makes modifying existing artwork even easier. You have already seen the Dropper tool in action when you select a color from the Swatches popups — the mouse pointer automatically converts to a dropper and allows you to pick up a color from any visible element to be loaded into the active fill or stroke color chip.

This same tool can be summoned at any time by clicking the Eyedropper tool (I) icon in the Tools panel. Notice that when the Eyedropper tool is used to pick up a fill color or bitmap, it immediately converts into the Paint Bucket tool (K) if you roll outside the area of the item you've sampled. The Paint Bucket enables you to dump the selected fill into any other shape just by clicking inside its fill area. If you have a fill or stroke selected when you invoke the Eyedropper tool, any other fill or stroke (color or style) that you pick up with the Dropper tool is applied instantly to the selected item.

When you sample a stroke with the Eyedropper tool, it converts into an Ink Bottle tool (S), which you can use to apply the stroke to any other item. If the item already has a stroke, it will be modified, and if the item did not previously have a stroke, the Ink Bottle tool adds one.

WEB RESOURCE We'd like to know what you think about this chapter. Visit www.flashsupport.com/ feedback **to fill out an online survey with your comments.**

Summary

- The science of color on the computer is far from accurate. Many variables are involved in the presentation of color over the Web.

- Web-safe color does not ensure "good color" — many strategies go into applying color skillfully, but contrast can be the defining factor that makes or breaks your design.

- Although Flash doesn't directly support color scheme plug-ins, colors can be loaded into the Swatches panel from source GIF files or custom color table (.act) files, or they can be sampled with the Dropper tool to load them into the active color chip.

- Adobe's online color theme tool, Kuler, is now built into Flash in a handy panel that includes a one-click button for loading themes into the Swatches panel.

- The Swatches popup available from any of the color previews or color pointers in the Color panel gives immediate, intuitive access to the currently loaded swatches and all custom colors that have been added to the main Swatches panel. It also permits direct insertion of hexadecimal values.

- The Color panel is used to create and modify gradients and select bitmaps to be used as fills, in addition to adjusting the alpha and tint of new or existing colors. Custom colors added to the current swatches are available in any of the Swatches popups.

- Flash supports 15-point gradients and many editable gradients imported from Fireworks, Illustrator, or Photoshop.

- The Eyedropper, Paint Bucket, and Ink Bottle tools work together to select and apply fill and stroke colors. We discuss the options for these tools, along with the Gradient Transform and Free Transform tools, in Chapter 9, "Modifying Graphics."

- Advanced color capabilities of Flash include color tweening, blend modes, scriptable color, and negative alpha. We discuss these topics in more detail in subsequent chapters.

Chapter 8

Working with Text

For designers who love fonts, Flash is a dream come true. Even if you never plan to animate anything, you may want to use Flash simply to see your fonts displayed how you want them, wherever and whenever you need them on the Web. Of course, there are a few exceptions to this unequivocal freedom, but Flash has options that give you text styles to meet nearly any project criteria.

NEW FEATURE Flash CS4 has finally caught up with other design applications by implementing Adobe CoolType font menus that separate font selection into Family and Style menus so that you can more easily specify the exact font that you want to use. This change is visible in all areas of the program where font settings are controlled.

Because Flash is a vector program, it enables you to integrate most fonts within the movie without any fuss. For standard text content, this means that fonts don't have to be rendered into bitmap elements — the .swf files that Flash publishes (or exports) include all the necessary information for the font to appear properly on every browser as long as the Flash Player is installed.

NEW FEATURE Flash CS4 enables developers to embed alternative character sets (aka variant glyphs) when publishing Flash movies for Flash Player 10. This feature is discussed in more detail later in this chapter.

In this chapter, we introduce the various text types available in Flash and explain how and why they are used. This chapter also covers some basic font management issues and offers strategies for handling fonts in your project files (.fla) as well as in your published movies (.swf).

Flash includes some nifty Static Text options for handling vertical and right-to-left-reading text. We show you these options, along with the other character and paragraph controls and the live filters available in the Properties panel. In this chapter we also touch on some features for optimizing text and working with international character sets in Flash.

IN THIS CHAPTER

Finding resources to help you learn more about typography

Understanding Flash text field types

Creating text boxes and choosing text types

Using the Properties panel to specify styles and alignment

Controlling font export and display

Using font symbols and shared libraries

Troubleshooting font management

Reshaping and manipulating text characters

Applying live filters to static text

Considering Typography

Typography is the formal term for the design and use of text. Although Flash has the capability to deliver finely designed typography to your audience, this is no guarantee that Flash solves all type design challenges. Unfortunately, no matter how well Flash renders text, it can't disguise bad design or make up for a designer's lack of knowledge about working with type. As with color, sound, animation, or any other specialized area of production, the amount you can learn about typography is really only limited by your interest.

Although many people can get by without ever studying typography formally, they are missing the chance to leverage one of the most powerful and complex tools of graphic design. Computers have changed the way that final designs are created, but they have not changed the fundamental principles and uses of typography. The best part about studying typography is that your knowledge will be equally useful no matter what medium or digital tool you are working with.

Because type is such an important and long-standing aspect of design, there are innumerable resources available to guide and inspire you. Just wander through the graphic design section of any bookstore or do a search online for *typography,* and you will find something that can introduce you to the basics or help develop the skills you already have.

This chapter includes some common typography terms that are familiar to most people who have designed with text. Although a more detailed explanation of the source and meaning of these terms is beyond the scope of this book, you can follow visually how things like *tracking* and *leading* apply to text in Flash.

Text Field Types in Flash

Flash allows you to include text in your projects in a variety of ways. Often one Flash project will contain several different text types, each suited to a specific kind of content. We describe the steps for creating text boxes and editing type later in this chapter, but begin here with an overview of the three main text types used in Flash:

- **Static:** Static text boxes are used for display type or text content created at authortime (in the .fla) that won't change at runtime (in the .swf).
- **Dynamic:** Dynamic text fields are used to hold text content that is generated at runtime from a live data source, or text that updates dynamically, such as weather information or sports scores.

CROSS-REF   Even if your text content is not auto-updated, there are benefits to storing and editing text in a format such as XML that can be loaded into Flash without having to open or republish the FLA file. This workflow is described in Chapter 29, "Sending Data In and Out of Flash."

- **Input:** Input text fields are exactly what they sound like, fields created for text that users enter at runtime. You use input text fields whenever you need users to do things such as enter passwords or answer questions.

NOTE   For the purpose of brevity, we often refer to both dynamic and input text fields as *editable text fields* because both text field types can be modified at runtime (unlike static text boxes, which can be modified only at authortime).

ON the CD-ROM   You will find examples of text field styles in the `textSamples.fla` file in the `ch08` folder on the CD-ROM.

The Text tool is used to create text boxes and to enter and modify type. When you first create a text box in Flash, the default text type is Static, but you can assign it a different text type in the Properties panel at any time. Subsequent text boxes are automatically assigned the type style you have selected most recently. This makes it quicker to create a series of text boxes of the same type, but it means you should double-check the settings if you need text boxes of different types.

Figure 8.1 shows the new layout of Text controls in the Flash CS4 vertical Properties panel. Basic options are not as exposed as they were in the old horizontal Property inspector, but the good news is that text controls (along with live filters), are now organized into a series of drop-down sections in one panel rather than a mish-mash of menus and popup panels as in previous versions of Flash.

FIGURE 8.1

The new streamlined vertical Properties panel includes all the text controls organized into a series of drop-down sections. These controls are available when the Text tool is active or a static text box is selected on the Stage.

CROSS-REF If you convert a text box into a Movie Clip and apply a motion tween, additional options become available in the Properties panel, including color effects, blend modes, and even 3D position and view controls. These more advanced options are discussed in Part III, "Creating Animation and Effects."

Static text boxes

Although the term *static text* sounds limiting, this type of text box actually offers the most design options at authortime. Static text boxes can be scaled, rotated, flipped, or skewed, assigned alpha levels, and modified with filters while preserving editable text characters. Static text can also be animated or layered like any other graphic element in Flash. By default, Flash embeds the outlines for any fonts used in static text for display on other machines, but you may also specify a generic device font to reduce the size of your final movie or to eliminate *anti-aliasing* (or *smoothing*) on small text.

TIP The various options for anti-aliasing in Flash should enable you to find a setting that renders smooth, legible text, even at small point sizes. If it turns out that you still prefer aliased text, simply choose the Bitmap text (no anti-alias) setting from the drop-down menu to preserve the original pixel font outlines.

TIP The Options section of the Properties panel exposes the Link entry field. This helpful feature allows you to select sections of static or dynamic (horizontal) text and enter a URL to create a text link to a Web page or to an e-mail address in your Flash movie without any additional coding.

By default, static text boxes are horizontal, and they can be either *expanding* boxes, which allow you to keep typing along one line as it extends to fit the type, or *fixed-width* boxes, which constrain your text box to a set width and auto-wrap the text to fit. These two types of text fields look the same when you select them by clicking once with the Selection tool, but when you double-click, you can see the text box handle icon that indicates the current behavior of the box. Figure 8.2 shows the respective icons for expanding, or *label,* text and for fixed-width, or *block,* horizontal static text.

FIGURE 8.2

The handle icons for expanding (left) and fixed-width (right) horizontal static text boxes

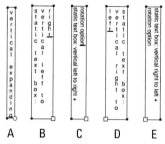

TIP All text boxes and text fields in Flash have handles that make it possible to resize the text area just by clicking once with the Selection tool and then dragging one of the handles. Scaling the text area does not change the size of the type as it does in some other applications.

Static text boxes in Flash include the option for left-to-right-reading or right-to-left-reading vertical text boxes. Have you ever wanted a line of text characters to stack vertically, but found it tedious to use a hard return between each letter? Thanks to vertical text, you can easily switch your type alignment from horizontal to vertical, with characters that are either stacked or rotated. This eliminates the headache of trying to read sideways while editing type — with a simple menu choice you can switch from vertical to horizontal and back again with no hard returns or freehand rotations required. Figure 8.3 illustrates how the vertical text and rotate text options change the orientation of static text.

FIGURE 8.3

Vertical text box orientations: (A) vertical expanding, (B) vertical fixed-height left to right, (C) vertical fixed-height left to right with rotate option, (D) vertical fixed-height right to left, and (E) vertical fixed-height with rotate option

A   B   C   D   E

Aside from giving designers authoring in English more options for cool layouts, this feature makes Flash much friendlier for designers authoring in language sets that require vertical or right-to-left character flow. You can modify the alignment of vertical text to anchor it to the top, center, or bottom of the text box.

Although the default orientation for text in Flash is horizontal and left to right, you can easily modify existing text boxes by using the Orientation menu options in the Paragraph section of the Properties panel. These settings are "sticky" so that new text boxes have the same orientation unless you choose another option from the menu. The default settings can also be modified in the Vertical text settings in the Text category of the Flash Preferences dialog box, as shown in Figure 8.4 (File ➪ Preferences or, in OS X, Flash ➪ Preferences).

To make all new static text boxes automatically orient vertically, select the Default text orientation check box. To change the default text flow, select the Right to left text flow check box. You also have the option of disabling kerning on vertical text by selecting the No kerning check box.

FIGURE 8.4

Changing the default Vertical text settings in the Flash Preferences dialog box

NEW FEATURE You can control the size of the new font previews in your Font menu by choosing a setting from the last drop-down menu in the Text category of Flash Preferences (see Figure 8.4). If you prefer to keep things simple and just browse font names without previews, deselect the check box for Show font preview and you revert to a Flash CS3–style Font menu.

Editable text fields: Dynamic and input

Editable text, like static text, begins as a *block,* but when it's converted to dynamic or input behavior, these editable text boxes are referred to as *text fields.* Think of an editable text field as an empty window with a name attached to it. When text or data is sent to the Flash movie (.swf), it is sent to a specific named text instance, which ensures that it appears in the proper window or editable text field. Dynamic text fields can display information supplied from a database, read from a server-side application, or loaded from another Flash movie (or another part of the same Flash movie).

Because dynamic text fields are generated or edited on-the-fly (at runtime), there are limitations on how much you can control the appearance of the text at authortime. You cannot apply special formatting or shape modifications (such as *skewing* or *kerning*) directly to dynamic text fields. However, Flash recognizes dynamic text field instances the same way it recognizes Movie Clip instances, so you can assign a name to a dynamic text field instance and use ActionScript to control its appearance.

> **NOTE**   All editable text fields are recognized as nameable instances of the `Text Field` object.
> You should use variable names to identify editable text fields only for backwards
> compatibility with legacy versions of the Flash Player (Flash Player 5 or earlier), and the variable name
> or `var` attribute of a text field should not be the same as its instance name.

You can author dynamic text horizontally in expanding or fixed-width fields, but you cannot rotate or
modify it with the Vertical text option. Figure 8.5 shows how a dynamic or input text field appears when
it's unselected (A) and how the field type is indicated by the handle icons when the text is double-clicked. If
you plan to work with multiline text fields, but you have limited space for the text, you can set the text field
behavior to *scrollable* in the Text menu (Text ➪ Scrollable); this enables the text to extend outside the
visible area of the text box.

FIGURE 8.5

An unselected dynamic or input text field is indicated in the authoring environment by a dashed outline (A); when
selected, you can adjust the size of the field by dragging any of the handles on the blue outline (B); when double-
clicked for editing, the field displays either an expanding handle icon (C), or a fixed-width handle icon (D); and if
the text field is set to be scrollable, the square handle changes from white/empty to black/filled (E).

A   Dynamic or Input text box: unselected

B   Dynamic or Input text box: selected

C   Dynamic or Input text box: expanding

D   Dynamic or Input text box:
     fixed width

E   Dynamic or Input text box: multiline width with
     more text than will fit and Text>Scrollable

When the Render text as HTML button in the Character section of the Properties panel is toggled on, Flash
recognizes rich text formatting, such as links and font styles indicated in dynamic text with HTML tags, and
applies them when the text is rendered in the Flash movie (.swf).

> **TIP**   If you change the size of an expanding text field by dragging one of the selection handles,
> the field automatically converts into a fixed-width text field. To change a fixed-width text
> field into an expanding text field, double-click the square fixed-width handle icon.

The Text Tool and the Properties Panel

Although Flash is neither a design program, like Illustrator, nor a traditional page-layout program, like
InDesign, its text-handling capabilities are robust and easy to use. Although you can create nearly any style
of text directly in Flash, you can also import text created in other applications as vector artwork. With
compatible applications such as Illustrator and Photoshop, you can even preserve your type in editable text
boxes when it is imported to Flash.

Working with the Text tool

The Text tool, shown in Figure 8.6, delivers a broad range of control for generating, positioning, and modifying text. Although the Text tool is located in the Flash Tools panel, when the tool is active, the controls for working with text are in the Properties panel.

FIGURE 8.6

The Text tool is used to create text boxes and text fields in Flash.

Creating static text boxes

To create text in your current Flash document, click the Text tool in the Tools panel (or press T on your keyboard) to activate it. You may choose to create new text in your Document window with either of two methods:

- **Label text:** To enter text on one extending line, click the Document Stage and begin typing. To control the width of a line of label text, you can either enter hard returns with the Enter or Return key as you type, or you can convert the label text into block text by dragging any of the handles to a specific width or height — the round label text icon changes to a square block text icon to indicate that the box is now constrained.

TIP   If your text continues beyond the viewable area of the Document window, you can add some line breaks, click and drag to move the label text box, or choose View ↵ Pasteboard and use the scroll controls on the Document window to shift your view of the text as needed.

- **Block text:** To define the area that will constrain your type by auto-wrapping as you enter more characters, click the Document Stage and drag the text area to the width that you want. You can change the width of your block text at any time by dragging the handles that appear when the text area is selected or in Edit mode. Refer to Figure 8.2 (right image) for an example of the square box text icon.

TIP   Convert a text block into label text by double-clicking the square corner icon (visible in Edit mode), which changes to a round icon to indicate that the box is now extending instead of constrained.

> **NOTE** You can use the blue handles that appear when you select a text box with the Selection
> tool to change the size of your text boxes or text fields without double-clicking or using
> the Text tool to enter Edit mode. However, the icons that indicate whether a text box is extending (label
> text) or constrained (block text) are visible only in Edit mode.

One characteristic of the Flash Text tool that might surprise you is that static text boxes that do not contain any text are cleared from the Stage. As long as a static text box contains even one character, it remains on the Stage until you delete or move it manually. Adobe Illustrator has adopted this same behavior because it eliminates the hassle of a project cluttered by empty invisible text boxes. Editable text fields *will* remain visible even if you have not entered any text characters at authortime.

Modifying or deleting text

Flash handles text as a group, which allows you to use the Text tool to edit the individual letters or words inside a text area at any time by clicking the text box and then typing or drag-selecting specific characters. To select the whole block or group of text, you can click once anywhere on the text with the Selection tool.

To delete individual characters, click and drag to select them with the Text tool or use the Backspace key (the Delete key on a Mac). To delete a whole group of text, select it with the Selection tool and then use the Backspace key (or Delete key).

> **TIP** Double-clicking a text block with the Selection tool invokes Edit mode and activates the
> Text tool — this enables you to modify the individual characters or change the text box
> style, without having to switch to the Text tool first. Holding down the Shift key as you use the arrow
> keys to move left or right in a text field selects the text as the cursor moves across it.

You can use most common text-editing/word-processing commands in Flash. Cut, Copy, and Paste move selected text within Flash and also between Flash and other applications that handle type. Flash provides a built-in Check Spelling command and a handy Search and Replace command.

The Check Spelling settings are quite sophisticated, and you can customize them by using the Spelling Setup dialog box available from the application menu (Text ➪ Spelling Setup) or launched with the Setup button in the Check Spelling dialog box. As shown in Figure 8.7, these options enable you to work with language-specific features and control what areas of your Flash document to include when Check Spelling is applied.

After you choose your settings, you can choose Text ➪ Check Spelling from the application menu, and Flash opens the Check Spelling dialog box (shown in Figure 8.8). You can then go through various text elements in your Flash document and modify or replace errors (with the help of suggestions), as you would in any other program with a spell-check feature.

The Movie Explorer panel makes it easy to find and modify text if you are working with a complex document. To access this feature if it is not already open, use the application menu (Window ➪ Movie Explorer) or the Alt+F3/Option+F3 shortcut keys to invoke the Movie Explorer panel, and modify text in any of the following ways:

- **To see all the text used in your current document:** Set the Movie Explorer to Show Text with the option button at the top of the panel. The contents of each text box is listed along with the font and point size that is used.

- **To search for a specific item:** Enter the font name, instance name, frame number, or ActionScript string in the Find field of the Movie Explorer panel.

- **To edit the contents of individual text boxes:** Double-click any listing in the Movie Explorer panel, and type in the field as you would if you were editing a filename in any other list.

- **To specify a new font or font size:** Select any text item listing that you want to change in the Movie Explorer and then simply change the font settings in the Properties panel. Use Shift+select to select multiple items in the Movie Explorer if you want to apply a change to more than one text box at a time.

■ **To copy text:** Use the Copy command in the Movie Explorer options menu to copy a currently selected line of text to the Clipboard, or to copy all the text in your current document to the Clipboard without having to select items individually in the Movie Explorer, use the Copy All Text to the Clipboard command in the Movie Explorer options menu.

FIGURE 8.7

The Spelling Setup dialog box gives you a range of settings to control how the Check Spelling command is applied to your documents.

FIGURE 8.8

Check spelling with ease in Flash

Setting text attributes in the Properties panel

The Text tool does not include options in the Tools panel because the extensive text controls are centrally located in the Properties panel. You create all Flash text in text blocks or boxes with the same Text tool, but when you create text, you can assign it specific appearance settings and behavior with the Properties panel.

Although you can always access font selection, size, and style menus from the application menu (Text ➪ Font, Text ➪ Size, and Text ➪ Style), the options for controlling text are not visible in the Properties panel unless the Text tool is active or you select a text box with the Selection tool. The options available in the Properties panel vary slightly, depending on the kind of text you select.

Static text options

When working with static text, you can modify the following text attributes in the Properties panel. As shown in Figure 8.9, these settings are organized into named sections of the Properties panel:

- **T**
  - **(Text type):** The text type drop-down at the top of the panel enables you to specify Static Text, Input Text, or Dynamic Text for your text box type. Set this behavior first to invoke the relevant options in the Properties panel.

- **POSITION AND SIZE** (This section appears in the Properties panel only if you select a text box in the Document window.)
  - **X and Y:** Values are auto-filled relative to the top left corner when you place a text box on the Stage, but you can use these fields to change the position at any time. It can be especially helpful if you want to ensure that your text box is aligned precisely in a specific location or to a whole pixel value position.
  - **W**(idth) and **H**(eight): These values are auto-filled when you create a text box in the Document window. Only Width can be manually adjusted on static text fields because Height is auto-set determined by the content of the text box. On dynamic text fields, you can modify both Width and Height to control the appearance of scrolling text boxes (by showing a set number of lines at a time).

- **CHARACTER**
  - **Family:** When the Text tool is active, this field displays the name of the current font. Click the arrow button to open a scrolling menu of available fonts. Choose a font from this scrolling menu to set the font for the next text element that you create. Or, to change the font of existing text in the Document window, first select individual characters with the Text tool or the whole group with the Selection tool, and then choose a different font from the scrolling menu. When you select a font from the Properties panel menu, you'll see a preview of the highlighted font in the style or typeface that will appear.
  - **Style:** This new drop-down menu replaces the faux Bold and faux Italic toggle buttons that were available in the Flash CS3 Property inspector. If the font you have chosen in the Family menu (above) includes designed styles and you have them installed, they show up in this menu. For example, if you have selected *Verdana* in the Family menu, you might see *Bold Italic* show up in the Style menu. If designed styles are not available, then you can apply faux Bold and/or faux Italic style to the text by using this menu.

> **NOTE**   **Many computer programs (including Flash) that handle type permit you to approximate a bold and/or italic version of a font, even if this style is not available in the original installed font; this has led to some confusion about font styles. If a font was originally designed to include a bold or italic version, it will be available in the Style menu after you have chosen the font family. With many fonts, the faux Bold or faux Italic style may appear very similarly to the designed Bold or Italic style, but**

with well-designed fonts, the shapes and proportions of individual characters are designed separately for each style. Theoretically, the original designed letter shapes for each style should look better than a normal letter shape thickened with an outline to create a faux Bold style, or slanted to create a faux Italic style. Type designers will sleep better at night if you use the faux style options only as a last resort.

- **Size:** When the Text tool is active, it displays the current font size in the Size entry field. You can change the font size by holding your mouse down over the text area and sliding it left or right to decrease or increase the value, respectively, or by clicking and typing a specific point size number in the field.

- **Letter spacing:** You use this value field to change the space or tracking between individual letters. The default setting of 0 applies the built-in tracking and kerning of the font; any setting between +1 and +60 adds space between characters; any setting between −1 and −60 decreases space between characters (extreme settings cause the letters to overlap).

 With a section of text selected, you can use Ctrl+Alt+arrow keys/⌘+Option+arrow keys to increase or decrease spacing between characters. The higher the Zoom setting, the smaller the spacing increments will be.

- **Type Color chip:** Click this button to open the Swatches popup menu, which in addition to offering current and temporary swatches, also enables you to acquire a color from anywhere within the interface by sampling with the dropper arrow.

- **Auto kern check box:** If the font includes built-in kerning information, which evens out the spaces between letterforms, select this to activate automatic kerning. On vertical text, this setting can be overridden by the Vertical text settings in the Flash Preferences dialog box (refer to Figure 8.4). When No Kerning is selected in Preferences, the Auto kern check box in the Properties panel applies only to horizontal text.

- **Anti-alias option menu:** Use this menu to select the level of anti-aliasing (or smoothing) to apply when the Flash Player renders your type. If you do not want to include font outlines in your file, select Use device fonts to render text by using a font that is available on each user's computer.

- **Selectable:** Use this toggle button to make selected text, or text that's entered subsequently, selectable when it appears on users' machines. This allows users to copy and paste your text into other text-editing applications or browser windows. Note: The next two toggle buttons (for HMTL text and Text border) are available only for dynamic text fields.

- **Superscript/Subscript:** These two toggle buttons modify the baseline alignment of your text. Superscript shifts horizontal text above the baseline and vertical text to the right of the baseline. Subscript sets horizontal text below the baseline and vertical text to the left of the baseline. Note: If you set a text field to be selectable or dynamic, you cannot use the Superscript or Subscript toggles.

- **PARAGRAPH**
  - **Format:** These four buttons modify the alignment of text for Left, Center, Right, or Full Justification. When you're editing, the alignment you choose affects only those paragraph(s) you've selected. When entering text, use these options to predetermine the alignment before text entry, and all subsequent text will be aligned accordingly. On vertical text, these buttons modify alignment to Top, Middle, Bottom, or Full Justification.
  - **Spacing:** Set the values for indenting and line spacing. On vertical text these values modify the top margin and column spacing, respectively (which makes the indent setting redundant with the left or top margin setting on vertical text).
  - **Margins:** Set the values for left and right text margins. On vertical text, these values modify top and bottom margins, respectively.

NOTE The default unit of measurement for margin settings is determined by the ruler units defined on the file. You can change ruler units in the Document Properties dialog box, which you access from the application menu with Modify ⇨ Document or from the keyboard by pressing Ctrl+J/⌘+J).

- ▣ **Orientation:** This popup menu enables you to select the flow direction for your text. The default is Horizontal, which orients text from Left to Right in rows along a horizontal baseline. The vertical text options are Vertical Left to Right, and Vertical Right to Left — these options automatically orient the text in columns that progress from left to right or from right to left, respectively.

- ▣ **Paragraph Rotate toggle:** This very handy button (which appears to the right of the Orientation menu when you choose a Vertical setting) flips the characters in your Vertical text box so that the type is turned sideways — or is actually resting on the vertical baseline. This is an effective alternative to creating horizontal text and then using Free Transform to rotate the text box 90 degrees.

- ■ OPTIONS

  - ▣ **Link entry:** This option is available only for horizontal static or dynamic text fields. By selecting a text box or an individual word in the Document window, and then entering a URL in this Link entry field, you can add a hyperlink to selected text. The text link is identified in the authoring environment with a dotted underline — the underline is not visible in the published .swf file, but the mouse pointer changes to indicate a link when it is positioned over the text.

  - ▣ **Target menu:** This menu is accessible after you enter a URL in the Link field, and it allows you to select a destination for the loaded URL. The options will be familiar to anyone who has worked with HTML page structures. For more information, refer to the description of the getURL() action in Chapter 17, "Understanding Actions and Event Handlers."

- ■ **Filters:** This area of the Properties panel can be used to apply and manage live filters that enable you to add visual effects to your text.

CROSS-REF Filters are described in the "Modifying Text" section later in this chapter and in more detail in Chapter 12, "Applying Filters, Blends, Guides, and Masks."

Editable text options

The options available for dynamic and input text are predominantly the same, but there are a few important options that are unique for these two editable text types. Figure 8.10 shows the Properties panel as it appears when you specify dynamic behavior for your text. We label only the additional options not shown in Figure 8.9 here.

The following options can be applied to either dynamic or input text:

- ■ **Text field instance name:** As described previously, this identifier allows the Flash Player to put your dynamic data in the correct field.

- ■ **HTML text:** When this toggle is turned on, Flash preserves rich text styles when displaying dynamic text. This includes font, font style, hyperlink, paragraph, and other formatting consistent with permissible HTML tags. You can also enable HTML so that the entry field accepts formatting that has been assigned to it in the Actions panel. For more information, refer to Chapter 30, "Applying HTML and Text Field Formatting."

- ■ **Text border:** Use this toggle to draw the text field with a border and a white background that will be visible in your published movie (.swf).

■ **Character Embedding:** When preparing a file for export, you can control how much font information is included with the .swf. The Character Embedding dialog box (see Figure 8.11), opened from the Character Embedding button in the Properties panel, is explained in the next section.

■ **Behavior:** Use this drop-down menu to choose how your text is organized in the text field. Choose between Single Line, Multiline (with line breaks), and Multiline with no text wrap.

FIGURE 8.9

The main options available for static text in the (expanded) Properties panel

Type (fill) Color chip

Font (point) Size menu

- Text type menu
- Position fields (X and Y within document window)
- Size fields (width and height for selected text box)
- Font Family menu
- Font Style menu
- Letter spacing menu
- Auto kern checkbox
- Anti-alias settings menu
- Subscript toggle
- Superscript toggle
- Text align options
- Indent/Line spacing settings
- Left/Right margin settings
- Text orientation menu
- Web address or mail to link
- Link Target menu

Selectable text toggle

FIGURE 8.10

The additional options available in the Properties panel when Dynamic Text behavior is selected

— Text field Instance name

— HTML text toggle

— Text border toggle
— Character Embedding settings

— Text Behavior
(for breaks and wraps)

— Variable field
(AS 2.0 or 1.0 only)

The Link and Target value fields are not available in the Properties panel when Input Text behavior is selected because you cannot add links to text that users enter. The only additional control available in the Properties panel for input text fields is the Maximum Characters value field. Use the Maximum Characters value field to specify the maximum number of characters that a user can enter in this particular text field. The number of characters can be limited to any number between 0 and 65,535. This feature is generally used for controlled content, such as passwords.

Character Embedding

By default, Flash embeds the characters you enter in a static text field so that they appear properly on any computer. Things get a little more complicated for dynamic or input text fields because there is the possibility for content to be added *after* the file is published. Instead of just auto-embedding every possible character, Flash enables you to control your file size by choosing the characters that are available at runtime. The Character Embedding dialog box (shown in Figure 8.11) is there to help you define the most relevant character set to embed with your specific text field.

You can specify that no characters are embedded by clicking the Don't Embed button, or you can pick from a long list of character or *glyph* sets to be embedded. You can also enter a more selective range of characters by typing them directly into the field at the bottom of the dialog box (under "Include these characters:"). The Auto Fill button automatically loads all the unique glyphs or characters in the currently selected text box into the Include field to be embedded with the final .swf. The counter for total number of glyphs (at the bottom of the dialog box) updates based on your settings, to show the total number of unique glyphs that are embedded with the final exported file.

> **NOTE** The Character Embedding options include international language sets and specialized sets such as music symbols. These glyph sets can be very large, but this is a useful feature if you are creating dynamic text fields that need to display specialized characters or alternative glyphs.

FIGURE 8.11

The Character Embedding dialog box for specifying embedded font information to be exported with your final .swf

Application menu commands

Some of the text settings in the Properties panel are also available from the application Text menu:

- Under Text ➪ Font, you can select from the same available fonts listed in the Properties panel's Family menu, but the list is slightly larger so it is easier to read.
- Under Text ➪ Size, you can select a specific font point size from a list, instead of using the Font size slider in the Properties panel.
- Under Text ➪ Style, the commands include:
  - **Bold:** Ctrl+Shift+B/⌘+Shift+B
  - **Italic:** Ctrl+Shift+I/⌘+Shift+I
  - **Faux Bold** (for fonts that don't have a built-in bold style)
  - **Faux Italic** (for fonts that don't have a built-in italic style)
  - **Subscript**
  - **Superscript**
- Under Text ➪ Align, the commands include:
  - **Align Left:** Ctrl+Shift+L/⌘+Shift+L
  - **Align Center:** Ctrl+Shift+C/⌘+Shift+C

- **Align Right:** Ctrl+Shift+R/⌘+Shift+R
- **Justify:** Ctrl+Shift+J/⌘+Shift+J
- Under Text ⇨ Letter Spacing, you will find a list of options that offers an alternative way to adjust the space between characters. If you have the Properties panel open as you apply these commands manually, you see the letter spacing or tracking value field update. Manual tracking has the advantage that you can apply it either to selected (highlighted) text characters or to the pair of text characters on either side of the cursor:
  - **Increase:** To increase text character spacing by one-half pixel, press Ctrl+Alt+→/ ⌘+Option+→. To increase text character spacing by two pixels, press Shift+Ctrl+Alt+→/ Shift+⌘+Option+→.
  - **Decrease:** To decrease text character spacing by one-half pixel, press Ctrl+Alt+←/ (⌘+Option+←. To decrease text character spacing by two pixels, press Shift+Ctrl+Alt+←/ Shift+⌘+Option+←.
  - **Reset:** To reset text character spacing to normal, press Ctrl+Alt+↑ /⌘+Option+↑.
- **Scrollable:** This option is available only when an editable text box is selected. When applied to a dynamic text field, this option makes it possible to enter and scroll through text that extends beyond the frame of the text box. Apply this option by choosing Text ⇨ Scrollable from the application menu or from the contextual menu when a dynamic text box is selected, or by pressing Shift and double-clicking the handle of a dynamic text box.
- **Check Spelling:** Opens the Check Spelling dialog box (shown in Figure 8.8).
- **Spelling Setup:** Opens the Spelling Setup dialog box (shown in Figure 8.7).

Font Export and Display

By default, Flash embeds all fonts used in static text boxes in order to deliver WYSIWYG (what-you-see-is-what-you-get) display in the published movie (.swf). As long as font outlines are available for the text you use in your Flash document (.fla), the published movie (.swf) appears consistently, regardless of what fonts the user has installed on his or her machine.

In order to edit a Flash project (.fla), you need to have the original fonts available, unless you are willing to view the document with a substitute font in the authoring environment. If you select a text box that appears with a substitute font, you should still see the name of the original font listed in the Properties panel, although it will be marked by parentheses. As long as the font formatting is not modified, Flash preserves all the original font information so that when the document (.fla) is opened again on a machine that has the original font, any edits that were made by using the default font are rendered correctly. Although you can make text edits while working with a default font, you need to have the original font installed in order to publish the final movie (.swf) with the design intact.

Smoothing text with anti-alias settings

The consistent text display of embedded fonts is what endears Flash to type-obsessed designers, but a small price must be paid: Every embedded font adds to the final file size, and anti-aliasing (smoothing) can sometimes make fonts too blurry. The good news is that for most projects, the additional weight is not an issue, and the anti-aliasing controls in Flash make it easy to customize the level of anti-aliasing as needed. If file size is a critical issue, you may choose to use device fonts or a runtime shared library. If you prefer the look of bitmap (aliased) fonts, that setting is still available in the Font rendering menu (see Figure 8.12).

FIGURE 8.12

The Font rendering menu makes it easy to choose a setting that suits your design style and file size requirements.

Figure 8.13 compares aliased with anti-aliased text in two published .swfs: one with Anti-alias for readability applied (left) and one with Anti-alias for animation applied (right).

FIGURE 8.13

The two default settings for anti-aliasing in Flash (readability and animation) render more smoothly than Bitmap (aliased) text.

ON the CD-ROM For a truer (on-screen) comparison between these different text options, refer to the files in the `textSmoothing` folder inside the `ch08` folder on the CD-ROM.

The Anti-alias for readability setting does an amazing job of rendering smooth, legible type, even at small sizes. This setting has only two drawbacks: It contributes to larger file sizes and it can only be rendered with Flash Player 8 or later. The Anti-alias for animation setting smoothes text almost as well as the Anti-alias for readability setting, but it ignores kerning information in order to create slightly smaller files and to render animated text more quickly. This is the only anti-aliasing option that renders on older versions of the Flash Player.

CAUTION Advanced Flash anti-alias settings (Anti-alias for readability and Custom anti-alias) do not render if text is skewed or flipped, but work fine if text is rotated or scaled. The advanced anti-alias settings do not carry over to files that are exported in .png format or printed. If the more advanced anti-alias settings "break," the text is auto-rendered with the more simplified Anti-alias for animation setting.

If you feel the need to polish your text further, use the Custom anti-alias controls (shown in Figure 8.14) to adjust the thickness and sharpness of the rendered text. With a little trial and error, you should find the exact level of anti-aliasing that suits the size and style of the font you are using.

The settings ranges for thickness and for sharpness are different, but for both, "normal" is 0. Select a higher number to increase the level of the effect, and choose a lower number to decrease or reverse the effect. Figure 8.15 illustrates "high," "normal," and "negative" combined settings, but these settings are really only meaningful if you adjust them individually and observe the results on your own specific font sample.

FIGURE 8.14

Custom anti-alias controls enable you to find a setting that smoothes text just how you like it.

FIGURE 8.15

The combination of thickness and sharpness set in the Custom Anti-Aliasing dialog box determines the look of your rendered anti-aliased text.

Custom Antialiased
thickness: 200 / sharpness: 400

Custom Antialiased
thickness: 0 / sharpness: 0

Custom Antialiased
thickness: -200 / sharpness: -400

CAUTION   Anti-alias for readability and Custom anti-aliasing settings work only on files published for Flash Player 8 and later. To make your files compatible with older versions of the Flash Player, you must use Anti-alias for animation, bitmap (aliased) text, or device fonts. For very large text (larger than 48 point), the more simplified Anti-alias for animation setting is recommended over the advanced Flash settings. It is best to apply advanced anti-aliasing options to improve the legibility of very small text or unusual text styles on projects that do not need to be backwards compatible.

    If you are working on OS X, you may not notice much difference between aliased and anti-aliased text because the system applies automatic smoothing on any screen text, even on application menu lists. Although this feature cannot be turned off completely, the text smoothing controls in your System preferences panel (in the Appearance category) allow you to specify between the lowest setting (only smoothes text larger than 12 points) and the highest setting (only smoothes text larger than 4 point). The default setting smoothes any text larger than 8 points.

Rendering outlines with the Bitmap text setting

The Bitmap text option makes it possible to quickly convert any selected text from anti-aliased to a prerendered aliased outline that is embedded with the final .swf. The aliased outline adds less to your file size than the anti-aliased font information, if the font is at a size below about 24 point. Another advantage of using the Bitmap text option is that you can create a "custom" aliased outline from any font on your machine, which gives you many more creative options than the three basic device fonts. Unlike device fonts, text converted to aliased outlines in Flash can also be rotated or scaled — although it doesn't always look that great, at least it does appear in the published .swf.

Despite the benefits of using bitmap text, we can't say it's a *great* option because it doesn't always give you the crisp, clean results you might hope for. In fact, this feature is only really useful when it's applied to fonts in the mid-size range. When it's applied to fonts between 12 and 24 point, the Bitmap text feature renders a fairly crisp outline and eliminates the "blur" associated with anti-aliased text smoothing. Unfortunately, when it's applied to smaller text (between 6 and 11 point), most fonts completely fall apart and became illegible blocky pixel shapes. On text larger than 24 point, the Bitmap text feature usually makes the text look rough and can bloat the file size more than when including standard font outlines.

Understanding device fonts

Device fonts are three basic font style designators identified by a preceding underscore in your font menu. These fonts will be familiar to anyone who has worked with HTML text. Although they are not as exciting as some custom fonts, entire design styles are based on these "generic" fonts — think minimal and unpretentious. You will find the three device font designations, _sans, _serif, and _typewriter, in either the Properties panel font menu or in the application menu under Text ➪ Font. These device font labels tell the Flash Player to use any equivalent font available on a viewer's system. The formatting that you have applied to the text in your Flash document (.fla), such as bold or italic style and point size, is preserved and applied to the font the Flash Player selects from the viewer's system to render the text in your movie (.swf).

To give you an idea of how device fonts relate to installed fonts, _sans usually becomes Arial or Helvetica, _serif usually becomes Times or Times New Roman, and _typewriter becomes Courier. Because these settings utilize the default fonts on the user's machine, Flash doesn't have to include their outlines in the exported .swf, and the final movie file size is reduced.

Device fonts are always available and always take little time to render, but they cannot be rotated or skewed and occasionally they vary slightly in their metrics from player to player and across platforms. Another important difference between standard embedded fonts and device fonts is that Flash anti-aliases or smoothes embedded fonts, while device fonts remain unsmoothed or aliased.

Working with the Use Device Fonts setting

You will notice that even if you have not used one of the device fonts from your font menu, you can still select the Use Device Fonts setting in the Anti-alias menu. This is a terrific "compromise" option if you strive for more specific control over the Flash Player's font choices, but still want to take advantage of the file size savings device fonts offer. When the Use Device Fonts setting is applied, the font is not embedded — only the Font name, Font family/style (serif/sans serif/monospace), and other information are added to specify the font, which adds no more than 10 or 15 bytes to the final .swf file. This information is used so that the Flash Player on the user's system knows if the font is installed or not. If the original font is available, it appears exactly as you designed it. If the original font is not present, then the Flash Player still knows whether the substitute font should be serif or sans serif.

The Use Device Fonts option also works as a toggle to turn off anti-aliasing. This means that even if the user has all the fonts used in your Flash movie installed, Use Device Fonts changes how the type appears:

- **When Use Device Fonts is selected:** No anti-aliasing or smoothing is applied to the device font, whether it is available on your system or not.
- **When Use Device Fonts is *not* selected:** The font outline is embedded and all characters are smoothed (even if the font is available). Smoothed text can sometimes be too blurry at small point sizes.

To accurately preview the Use Device Fonts setting on your machine, if you have a font manager (as most Web designers do), you need to make sure that you're careful about your font activation settings. Make sure that activation is turned *off* for the fonts that you want to test so that the Flash player does not find them when it renders the movie (.swf) — this enables you to see what might happen to your design when your system auto-substitutes other fonts.

For best results with this specific Use Device Fonts option, we suggest that you limit your font selection to those fonts that most of your audience is likely to have (all those common fonts that come installed with their machines), or those that translate into one of the default device fonts without wreaking havoc on your design. It is better to be conservative and design your layout with Times, Arial, and Courier than to go wild with custom fonts that will most likely be substituted very differently when the movie is viewed on someone else's machine. Otherwise, for unusual fonts, we suggest that you either embed the full font outline information (and apply one of the anti-alias settings) or, for limited areas of text (such as headlines), that you use the Bitmap text option to generate a custom aliased outline or break the text apart to manually create vector shapes, as we describe later in this chapter.

Troubleshooting font display

Although Flash does an amazing job of displaying fonts consistently and cleanly, even on different platforms, the success of your font export depends entirely on the quality and completeness of the font information available when the Flash document is created (.fla). Because Flash can access font information on your system while you are working in the authoring environment, many of the font display problems that can come up during production are visible only when the Flash movie (.swf) is published.

To display fonts in the published movie (.swf), the Flash Player relies on the font information embedded in the movie, or on the fonts installed on the user's system. If there are discrepancies between the information available to the Flash Player and the font information that was available to the Flash authoring application when the document was created, you will run into font display problems.

When you encounter problems with fonts (as you almost always do at some point), a good guide to font management is indispensable. We can't describe everything that can go wrong when working with fonts here, and solutions often vary depending on how you are storing and managing your fonts. Ideally, you should find resources that are specific to the platform and programs you are using.

TrueType, Type 1 PostScript, OpenType, and bitmap fonts (Mac only) can all be used in Flash. Although Flash exports the system information about the fonts that are used, a damaged or incomplete font may still appear correctly in the authoring environment (.fla). However, the exported movie (.swf) will appear incorrectly on other systems if the end user doesn't have the font installed. This is due to the fact that Flash can display the font within the editor by using the screen font; it does not recognize that particular font's outline and can't export information needed to display the text in the .swf. You can avoid font display problems by using the universal device fonts (_sans, _serif, or _typewriter fonts).

Controlling font substitution

If Flash cannot find font information on your machine to match what is specified in a file (.fla) when you open it in the authoring environment, you are notified by the Font Mapping dialog box (shown in Figure 8.16) and prompted to select fonts installed on your system to substitute for display.

NOTE If you publish or export a document without viewing any of the scenes containing missing fonts, the dialog box appears only when Flash attempts to publish or export the .swf.

The first time that a scene with missing font information appears in the authoring environment, you are prompted by the Font Mapping dialog box to choose one of the following options:

- **Choose Substitute fonts:** The Font Mapping dialog box enables you to specify individual substitutions from the fonts available on your system for each missing font. The Missing Fonts column in the dialog box lists all fonts specified in the document that Flash can't find on your system. To choose a substitute font for a missing font, select the font name in the Missing Fonts list and then use the Substitute font menus at the bottom of the dialog box to specify a font family and style. Click OK to apply the settings and close the dialog box.

- **Apply System Default:** This button substitutes missing fonts with the Flash system default font. You can always change the Font Mapping default settings in the Text category of Flash preferences when you have the document open (Edit ➪ Preferences ➪ Text, or on OS X, Flash ➪ Preferences ➪ Text).

FIGURE 8.16

The Font Mapping dialog box is used to view missing fonts and to modify mapping of substitute fonts.

Even though the text appears in a substitute font, Flash includes the name of the missing font in the Properties panel font menu (see Figure 8.17). Flash preserves the original font specification when the file is saved so that the text appears correctly when the document (.fla) is opened on a system with the missing fonts installed. You can even apply the missing font to new text by selecting it from the font menu in the Properties panel.

FIGURE 8.17

The missing font name appears in the font menu, even when text appears in a substitute font in the authoring environment.

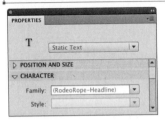

Because appearance attributes such as size, leading, and kerning may render differently with a substitute font, you may have to adjust any modifications you make while viewing text in a substitute font when the document is opened on a machine with the original font available.

To view all the missing fonts in the currently active document or to reselect font mappings, choose Edit ➪ Font Mapping (or in OS X, Flash ➪ Font Mapping) from the application menu and repeat the same steps described previously to choose new substitute fonts. To view all the font mapping settings saved on your system or to delete font mappings, close all Flash documents before opening the Font Mapping dialog box or making changes to the listed mapping.

Font Symbols and Shared Font Libraries

Using font symbols and shared libraries in your Flash authoring workflow offers several benefits that can make it worth the little time it takes to set them up. Although you can nest a static text box inside any other symbol type if you want to reuse a specific text element in your movie, this does not change how the text is published in the Flash document. Using instances of a symbol to place repeated text elements, such as logos or taglines, offers the same benefits as converting artwork into symbols — you can make changes to the symbol stored in the library and the change is propagated to every instance in your document, and you can also modify the appearance of individual instances without changing the original symbol.

The difference between text nested in another symbol type and a real font symbol is that font symbols can actually be used to store the display information for an entire font. When placed into a runtime shared library, font symbols can be used to link text in one movie to the font display information in a source movie; this allows you to use custom fonts without having to embed the font information in every Flash movie (.swf) individually. This workflow is especially effective on projects that involve multiple .swf files using the same custom fonts. The bonus is that if your client suddenly decides that they prefer "Leonardo script" to "Chickenscratch bold" (or whatever font switcheroo they might come up with), you can make the change in your source font symbol without even opening any of the other files (as long as the new font is given the same name and it still fits in your layouts).

This all sounds great so far, right? Now for the reality check: Because you are storing font information in a separate file from your layouts, there is one more factor that you have to manage. The source font library (.swf) can be in the same directory as your other movie (.swf) files, or it can be stored on a completely different server. It is very important to decide on the storage location of your source font files (.fla and .swf) before you begin linking text in your other Flash documents (.fla) to shared font symbols because the URL that defines the relative or absolute path is stored in each .fla file, and your font links will be broken if you later change the source movie's location.

NOTE Runtime shared assets do not need to be available on your local network when you are editing .fla documents that rely on linked assets, but the shared asset .swf must be available at your specified URL in order for the published movies (.swf) to display the linked assets at runtime.

As you can imagine, having your font links fail is a major disaster; therefore, many developers believe that relying on an external font source isn't worth the risk. On the other hand, there is always an element of uncertainty with Web delivery, so it might not be fair to eliminate what is otherwise an excellent way to optimize font management in your Flash layouts. As with any Web production, just be sure to test early and often as you develop a Flash project that uses shared fonts.

You can use shared libraries to store other symbol types, but it is best to organize different kinds of assets in separate .fla files. For now, we focus on making font symbols and creating a source file for a shared font library.

Creating a font symbol

Font symbols can be integrated in your workflow in two ways. If you plan to use font symbols within a Flash document (.fla) simply as a way to make edits faster in that one document, and you don't mind exporting the font information with every .swf, you can create a font symbol directly in the main library of your current document and rely on authortime sharing to update instances of the font. However, if you want to save file size by linking to the font symbol information for runtime sharing, you should open a new Flash document before creating your font symbols. In either case, the initial steps for creating a Flash font symbol are the same:

1. **Open the Library panel where you want to store the font symbol.**
2. **From the library options panel, choose New Font (see Figure 8.18).**
3. **In the Font Symbol Properties dialog box that appears, enter a name for your font symbol and select the font you want to embed in the file (see Figure 8.19).** The name that you enter shouldn't be the same as the original font name but rather should indicate how the font is being used in your project. For example, if you are using an Impact font for your titles, instead of naming the font symbol "Impact," you could name it "titleFont" or some other name that informs you (and the rest of your team) how the font is being used.
4. **If you also want the option to use faux Bold or Italic style on text linked to your font symbol, select the Style check boxes for Bold and/or Italic to include these characters with the embedded font.** Select the Bitmap text check box to create aliased outlines of your font symbol. If you choose to render an aliased outline of a font, you also need to enter the font size that you want to use by typing it in the Size field. This increases the size of your source movie only — the additional size is not passed on to other .swf files that link to the font symbol for runtime sharing.

CAUTION If you create a font symbol without the Bold or Italic options selected in the Font Symbol Properties dialog box, and then try to apply the options in the Properties panel to create faux Bold or Italic style on text that is linked to the symbol, you will encounter one of two problems. If the text you are modifying is in a static text box, then the applied styles will appear, but the additional font information for the modified characters will be exported with your published file, thus increasing the size of the .swf. If the text you are modifying is in a dynamic or input text field, the text will not display in the published .swf file because the Flash Player will not find the font information needed to render the bold or italic type on-the-fly. These same rules apply to aliased outlines rendered at a specific font size.

FIGURE 8.18

Choosing to insert a new font symbol from the Library panel options menu

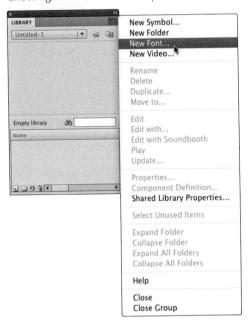

FIGURE 8.19

Selecting a font to store in the new font symbol and giving it a reference name

5.   **Now when you browse the font menu available in the Properties panel or from the application menu (Text ⇨ Font) you will see your new font listed with the other fonts installed on your system.** Font symbols are also differentiated from regular fonts in the menu with an asterisk (*) following the name it has been given (see Figure 8.20).

The next step required to use the font symbol in your project depends on how you choose to integrate font symbols into your workflow. As we mention earlier in this chapter, using symbols for authortime asset sharing can make propagating changes throughout a document easier, but any assets used in your document will still be embedded in each movie (.swf) that you publish. Creating a separate library for storing symbols and linking these as runtime shared assets in multiple movies takes a little more work, but it gives you the benefit of both streamlined updates and smaller file sizes. The most appropriate workflow depends on the scope and content of your particular project and on how willing you are to manage the risks involved with using runtime shared assets.

FIGURE 8.20

Font symbol names are followed by an asterisk in the Properties panel's font family menu (or in the application Text menu). Font symbols are also added to the Library list.

Updating font symbols at authortime

If you intend to use a font symbol as an authortime shared asset only, you can simply leave it in your current library so that the font is available in the font menu whenever you want to use it in your project. You can modify any of the text boxes that use your font symbol in the same way as any other text. There is no limit on the number of colors or sizes that you can use or on what you can type into each text box.

The main reason that this is a more flexible workflow than simply nesting text inside other symbols for reuse is that you can actually change the *content* used in individual text boxes that reference a font symbol, whereas you can only modify the *appearance* of text that is nested in a symbol instance.

The process for updating instances of a font symbol used within one Flash document (.fla) is much the same as updating any other symbol type or imported asset stored in the library:

1. Open the current document library and select the font symbol that you want to modify.
2. Choose Properties from the library options menu or from the contextual menu.
3. In the Font Symbol Properties dialog box, simply select a new font from the font menu, but don't change the font name that you had previously chosen. (Now it makes sense why naming your font symbol with the same name shown in the font menu isn't a good idea, right?)

   You will find that all text that was in your old font is updated to the new font that you have chosen, while maintaining all other formatting and style attributes.

> **TIP** If you don't see your text boxes update to the new font immediately after you change it in the Font Symbol Properties dialog box, you may need to click one of the text boxes with the Selection tool — this usually prompts Flash to refresh the display.

Using font symbols in runtime shared libraries

In order to make your font symbol available for use in other Flash movies without having to embed the font information in each file, you need to create links from individual *destination* files to your *source* file or shared library. This workflow optimizes file sizes by eliminating the storage of redundant font information between linked movies. As with HTML files, you have to specify a path in order for the Flash Player to locate font information in one movie (.swf) for text display in another. Because the font information is retrieved from a .swf file by the Flash Player and supplied to another .swf for text display, it is referred to as *runtime* asset sharing.

If you have already followed the steps to create a font symbol in an otherwise empty Flash document (.fla), the next part of the process is to enter an identifier and a location (path) that will "lead" the Flash Player to your shared library. As we mentioned previously, you need to know where the published source movie (.swf) will be stored before you can create font links to other documents. The location (or path) can be relative or absolute.

> **TIP** To keep your linkage intact while preserving source file version numbers as you develop your project, you might want to use the Publish Settings dialog box to give your published source .swf a generic name (such as `titleFontSource.swf`) while using a more specific naming convention for your source .fla files (such as `titleFontSource101.fla`). This eliminates the hassle of going back to your destination movies and changing the linkage information if you decide you need to move to a new version name to keep track of modifications to your source file (.fla).

To help clarify how runtime shared fonts are stored and accessed, we walk through the three possible scenarios for font symbol use and show you how each appears in the authoring environment (.fla) and in the published movie (.swf).

> **ON the CD-ROM** The Flash files illustrated in this section are included in the `ch08` folder on the CD-ROM. You will find both the `fontSource` files (shared library file) and the `fontLink` files (destination document) in the `fontSymbols_complete` folder with final linkage properties. As long as the files are kept together in the same storage location, the font linkage should remain intact. If you want to use unfinished files to complete the steps in this section, open the files in the `fontSymbols_start` folder. We have also included a `fontEmbed` example file with the same text entered on the Stage, but with embedded font information (including uppercase, lowercase, and punctuation for Impact), rather than linked font information to demonstrate the difference in file size.

The first file you will be working with is a source document, or the Flash document that contains the font symbols that you want to use as runtime shared assets.

> **CAUTION** If you are using the files from the CD-ROM to follow this example, you may need to modify the font symbol in `fontSource.fla` to match a font that you have on your system (instead of "Impact") before you can use Test Movie to publish the .swf file (Step 5).

1. **Open your source document and select your font symbol in the library.** If you are looking at the files on the CD-ROM, open `fontSource.fla` from the `fontSymbol_start` folder and select the font symbol called NewFont in the library.

2. **Choose Properties from the library options menu or from the contextual menu.** From the Font Symbol Properties dialog box (see Figure 8.21), access Linkage properties by clicking the Advanced button.

3. **Change the original font symbol name (in our example `NewFont`) to something that helps you to remember what this font symbol is used for in your project (such as `titleFont`).** This identifier appears after the font symbol name in the library.

FIGURE 8.21

Setting up Linkage properties for a font symbol in the Flash source document (.fla)

4. **Select the Export for runtime sharing check box.** Notice that Export in frame 1 is automatically selected as well — leave that check box selected for now. The font name that you updated in Step 3 should auto-fill in the Identifier field in the Linkage properties section of the dialog box.

CAUTION Don't close the Font Symbol Properties dialog box until you have completed the next step.

5. **In the URL field (at the bottom of the dialog box), enter the path to the storage location for the source movie (.swf) that you will publish after you have finished choosing settings in the source document (.fla.)** The link can be relative or absolute depending on how you will be storing your project .swfs:

   ■ If you are planning to keep the source movie (.swf) in the same folder as your individual destination movies (.swf), all you need to enter in the URL field is the name of your source .swf file — in our example, `fontSource.swf`.

   ■ If the source .swf file will be stored in a different folder or even on a separate server than the destination (linked) .swf files, you must enter an absolute path (Web address) in the URL field to specify the exact storage location of your source .swf file, such as `http://your server.com/projectdirectory/sourceName.swf`.

6. **Save your source .fla file to the final storage location by using File ⇨ Save (Ctrl+S/⌘+S) and test your source .swf by using Control ⇨ Test Movie (Ctrl+Enter/⌘+Return).** Although nothing appears in the published .swf, if you turn on the Bandwidth Profiler (from the application menu: View ⇨ Bandwidth Profiler, or with shortcut keys (Ctrl+B/⌘+B), you see the size of the font information for all the embedded characters included in your font symbol. Our sample font symbol source file was 17K (see Figure 8.22).

FIGURE 8.22

The published source movie (.swf) with embedded font information for the font symbol to be used in other destination movies as a runtime shared asset

You have successfully created and saved a runtime shared asset. Now you can create another Flash document that references the font information stored in `fontSource.swf` so that you can use your custom font without having to embed the font information:

1. **Create a new Flash document or open the `fontLink.fla` file from the CD-ROM, and make sure that you have the Library panel for the current document open.**

2. **Link another document to the font information in your shared library in one of two ways:**

   - If you have already created a document that uses font symbols as described in the section on authortime sharing and decide to link to a runtime shared asset instead, you can enter the identifier and the URL of the shared library movie (.swf) in the Linkage properties for any font symbol in your library. Enter the identifier and the URL exactly as they appear in your font source file, but use Import for runtime sharing instead of Export for runtime sharing (as shown in Figure 8.23). You should now find that all instances of the font symbol in your current document are updated with the font information stored in the shared asset movie (.swf) — as long as it is available on your server when you publish the movie for your current document.

NOTE   **To enter linkage information manually, you need to have a font symbol in the document Library selected so that you can access the Font Symbol Properties dialog box from the options menu or from the contextual menu.**

   - If you are authoring a document (.fla) that does not yet contain any font symbols and you want to link to your runtime shared asset, you can simply drag the font symbol from the source library into the current document library. With your destination document and Library panel open, choose File ➪ Open or File ➪ Import ➪ Open External Library and navigate to the Flash document (.fla) for your shared asset. You can then drag your source font symbol from the shared asset library and drop it into your destination document library. If you access Properties for the font symbol that you dragged into your library, you will see that Flash automatically inserts the identifier and URL for the shared asset. You can now use the font in your new document and it is linked to the font information stored in the runtime shared asset movie (.swf).

3. **When a font symbol in your library has the identifier and URL entered in its Linkage properties, you can use the linked font in your document by selecting it from your font menu and using the Text tool as you normally would.** When you publish your movie (.swf), you will notice that your file size is much smaller than it would be with embedded font information. For an example of this, compare the file size listed in the Bandwidth Profiler shown in Figure 8.24 (linked = 143 B) with Figure 8.25 (embedded = 4754 B).

FIGURE 8.23

Linkage settings for a font symbol in a destination movie refer to the font information stored in the runtime shared library.

FIGURE 8.24

The published .swf file from a document using linked font information from a runtime shared asset

4. **If you decide that you want to disable runtime sharing for a font symbol in a destination document, you can clear the Import for runtime sharing check box in the Properties dialog box.** The font information for the characters used in your file are now embedded with the .swf file, so the file size is larger, but the Flash Player no longer requires access to the shared asset.

CAUTION Text rendered with advanced anti-alias settings (Anti-alias for readability or Custom anti-aliasing) must be embedded. For text using linked font information, use the Anti-alias for animation setting.

FIGURE 8.25

The published .swf file from a document using embedded font information

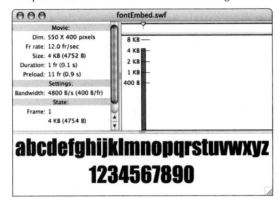

Modifying Text

In addition to all the text-handling capabilities we discuss earlier in this chapter, there are some fun ways that you can modify the appearance of text to create custom effects. Static text fields can be scaled, skewed, or flipped, and the color or alpha can be changed while keeping the text editable. In early versions of Flash, if you wanted to create a drop shadow or special fill effect, it was necessary to break the text apart to create individual shapes. Luckily, live filters were introduced with Flash 8 that could be applied to text or graphics to create special effects that can easily be added, combined, or removed while preserving the original, editable object.

NEW FEATURE In Flash CS4, filters are now available in the Properties panel.

ON the CD-ROM We have included the Flash files for the modified text shown in this section on the CD-ROM. If you want to look at these in the Flash authoring environment, you can open the file modifyText_manual.fla or modifyText_filters.fla in the ch08 folder.

Editing text manually

Figure 8.26 illustrates some of the ways that text can be modified without using filters. Any of these styles of manually modified text are compatible with older versions of the Flash Player.

TIP If you plan to animate individual text characters, you can quickly move each letter onto its own layer by first applying the Break apart command (Ctrl+B/⌘+B) to a text box and then using the Distribute to Layers command (Shift+Ctrl+D/Shift+⌘+D).

Custom text information adds to your file size, so it is best to reserve these treatments for special text such as titles or graphics. If you are working with longer sections of text (such as an article or a story), it is better to use common fonts or device fonts to help keep your files smaller and to make the text easier to read.

FIGURE 8.26

Text boxes can be modified with Free Transform options (top). To create individual characters, apply Break apart once (middle), and apply it again to create graphic text (bottom). Graphic text can be modified like any other shape in Flash.

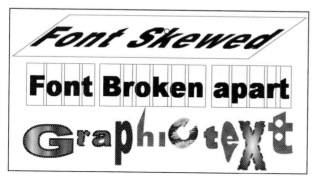

> **TIP**   With long sections of text, you may need to add scrolling, and this is much easier to do if you use dynamic text or live filters. If you use modified static text or graphic text, you can still add scrolling behavior by creating animation and controls manually, but this is more time consuming and requires your final .swf to have more information embedded in it.

Scaling text

By selecting a text box with the Free Transform tool, you can scale your text by dragging the transform handles, but this is not recommended as a way to increase the size of text unless it has been broken into vector shapes. Flash has to interpolate the normal font outlines to scale text this way, which can result in jagged edges when the movie is published. When sizing text, it is much better to simply modify the font size setting (by selecting or entering a new point size) to ensure a clean outline when the text is exported.

Sampling and sharing text attributes

If you want to use the same font attributes on a variety of text boxes, it is often best to modify one text box so that it has all the qualities you want — including color, size, font, style, and line or character spacing. You then have two options for transferring these attributes to other text boxes by using the Eyedropper tool:

- **To modify existing text boxes:** You can select other text boxes with the Selection tool and then activate the Eyedropper tool in the Tools panel and click your modified text to sample its attributes and transfer them to all the other selected text boxes simultaneously. This is much more efficient and consistent than trying to remember what settings you used and changing them manually on different text boxes.

- **To set attributes for new text boxes:** You can load the visual attributes of any manually modified text into the Properties panel by activating the Eyedropper tool and clicking the text to acquire its appearance. The Text tool is automatically activated after text is sampled, so you can immediately begin creating new text with the settings now loaded in the Properties panel.

Converting text into vector shapes

The Break apart command (Ctrl+B/⌘+B) is used to reduce symbols to grouped shapes, and it can also be used to modify static text. Applying Break apart once to a text box breaks a line of text into individual characters; applying the command again converts the characters into *graphic text* (vector lines and fills).

Individual text characters can be grouped or changed to symbols. To make it easier to use individual characters in tweened animation, you can apply the Distribute to Layers command (Modify ➪ Timeline ➪ Distribute to Layers) to automatically place each character on its own layer.

Graphic text can be modified by using any of the drawing tools, reshaped with the Selection and Subselect tools, or distorted with any of the Free Transform options. You can also select special fills, such as bitmaps or gradients, to create patterned text, or use the Eraser tool to delete pieces of the letter shapes (see Figure 8.27).

FIGURE 8.27

Using the Eraser tool to delete parts of a graphic letter shape

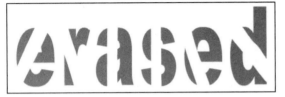

However, after text characters have been converted to lines and fills, they can no longer be edited as text. Even if you regroup the text characters and/or convert the text into a symbol, you can no longer apply font, tracking, or paragraph options. To streamline your workflow, consider how you can combine graphic text with normal text for some effects — instead of converting all text into graphic shapes.

There are a few tips and guidelines to remember when converting text to shapes in Flash:

- To convert text characters to component lines and fills, you must first select or highlight the text characters that you want to convert, and then choose Modify ➪ Break apart from the application menu. To undo, choose Edit ➪ Undo (Ctrl+Z/⌘+Z) from the application menu.
- Rotation and Break apart can be applied only to fonts with available outline information, such as TrueType fonts.
- On Macs, PostScript fonts can be broken apart only if a type manager is installed that handles PostScript fonts.
- Bitmap fonts disappear from the screen if you attempt to break them apart.
- Breaking apart a text field that has filters applied to it removes the filters before the text is converted into shapes.

As you experiment with graphic text, you may want to refer to some of the other chapters that cover working with shapes.

Moving beyond the box with live filter effects

Flash filters open up the possibilities of creative text treatments even if you aren't all that "creative." With one handy little section at the bottom of the Properties panel (Filters), you can modify your text without breaking it apart. Filters can even be applied to dynamic text because the filters are rendered at runtime; they're "live." Filters are easy to add and combine and you can edit the content of your text field at any time without breaking the effect. Figure 8.28 shows just a few simple examples of how you can modify text fields by using Flash filters.

FIGURE 8.28

A few of the effects that can be added to text by using filters while preserving the editability of the text field

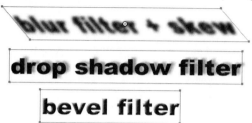

Filters can be found in the Properties panel in the Filters section. To apply filters to a text field, select the text field, and then use the controls in the Properties panel to add or adjust filters (see Figure 8.29). Filters can be combined and layered to create a wide range of visual effects.

CROSS-REF You can animate filters by creating a tween span and then using the Motion Editor to adjust these settings over time. There is also a new library of motion presets built into Flash CS4 (Window ⇨ Motion Presets), which can be applied to text fields or to graphics to create animated effects and transitions. But, animation involves getting to know the Motion Editor, and we will save that discussion for Part III, "Creating Animation and Effects."

FIGURE 8.29

Adding and combining filters in text fields is easy with the Filter controls in the Properties panel.

WEB RESOURCE   **We'd like to know what you thought of this chapter. Visit** www.flashsupport.com/
feedback **to fill out an online survey with your comments.**

Summary

- Flash CS4 makes working with text easier and more precise than ever by centralizing text controls in the new vertical Properties panel and offering separate menus for specifying font family and style.

- Flash offers robust and well-organized text-editing controls, but you can make the most of these tools only if you are familiar with, at least, the basic principles of typography.

- Studying the history of type in visual communications is one of the most practical and inspiring things you can do to improve your design skills.

- The option for converting any font into an aliased outline that can be embedded with the final movie (.swf) overrides the default smoothing or anti-aliasing that can make some text look slightly blurry.

- Complete font information must be available on your system in order for Flash to render and export the text properly to the final movie (.swf). If you need to open a Flash file (.fla) that includes fonts not available on your system, you can choose temporary substitute fonts without damaging the original font information stored in the file.

- Creating font symbols and storing them in shared libraries for either authortime updates or runtime linkage can help you manage large projects by centralizing font sources and making updates faster and easier.

- Linkage properties for font symbols are now accessed via the Advanced button in the Font Symbol Properties dialog box, rather than the separate Linkage Properties dialog box.

- You can add visual interest to your text with filters while still keeping options open for editing the content of the text field. Because filters are rendered dynamically, they can be applied to dynamic text even if the content changes at runtime.

Chapter 9

Modifying Graphics

After becoming familiar with the Flash authoring environment and learning to use the Drawing tools, you are now ready to move on to the fun part: messing with the basic shapes and text elements you have made to achieve custom results.

In this chapter, we revisit some of the core tools to show you new ways to apply them. We also introduce some specialized tools that exist only to transform your artwork. Following a look at how the Eyedropper, Paint Bucket, and Ink Bottle work together to modify strokes and fills, we show you how to use the Gradient Transform tool to create custom fills.

The Modify Shape submenu offers some special commands you can apply to alter lines and fills, whereas the Modify Transform submenu includes various options for skewing, stretching, rotating, flipping, and rotating shapes.

Before explaining the Flash stacking order and how to create compound shapes, we introduce the powerful Free Transform tool and the Envelope modifier that enables you to warp and distort multiple shapes simultaneously. Other features worth exploring include the stepped Break apart command on text and the indispensable Distribute to Layers command — these two features combined make animating text infinitely easier than it was in early versions of Flash.

CROSS-REF For coverage of advanced color effects and filters, refer to Chapter 12, "Applying Filters, Blends, Guides, and Masks."

Last but not least, we cover the Find and Replace command and the History panel. We introduce the options for these flexible features and demonstrate some ways you can use them to modify your graphics, without even using any tools!

As we introduce various techniques and tools, we show you how to apply them for modifying artwork and adding the illusion of depth and texture to your 2D graphics.

IN THIS CHAPTER

Sampling and swapping fills and line styles

Applying the Gradient Transform tool to control gradient and bitmap fills

Using Modify Shape options

Working with the Free Transform tool and the Transform panel: Skewing and rotating

Working with 3D tools: Perspective, Translation, and Rotation

Stacking, grouping, and arranging item types

Combining drawing objects

Using Break apart and Trace bitmap

Creating and managing compound shapes

Autopilot editing with Find and Replace

Sampling and Switching Fills and Strokes

You can always use the Selection tool to select a stroke or fill so that you can modify it by using any of the Swatches popups or the Stroke Style menu on the Properties panel. But, what do you do if you want to add a stroke or fill to a shape that was drawn without one or the other? The answer to this dilemma is found in a trio of tools that work nimbly together to provide one of the most unique graphics-editing solutions found in Flash. You use the Eyedropper tool to acquire fill and stroke styles or colors, and use the Paint Bucket and Ink Bottle tools to transfer these characteristics to other shapes.

NOTE These tools only apply changes directly to shapes, shape primitives, or drawing objects, so to modify an element that has been grouped or converted into a symbol, you must first access the element in Edit mode.

The Eyedropper tool

As we introduced in Chapter 7, "Applying Color," the dropper icon that appears when you use the Selection tool to select colors from any of the popup Swatches menus is similar to the Eyedropper tool available in the Tools panel. However, when pulled out of the Tools panel directly, the Eyedropper tool (I) has slightly different behavior. Although you cannot use the Eyedropper tool to sample colors from elements outside the Document window, you can use it to sample line and fill styles or to simultaneously change the stroke and the fill color chips to the same sampled color.

CROSS-REF For more information about this feat, refer to Chapter 7, "Applying Color."

NOTE When used to acquire colors, the Swatches panel Eyedropper tool is limited to picking colors from swatches within the panel. However, the droppers that you access from the Swatches popup menus in the Color panel or Tools panel can acquire colors from other visible areas, such as the system background, items on the desktop, or items open in other applications. The functionality of this feature is not totally consistent so here are some tips to making it work:

When picking colors by using the dropper from the Color panel swatches popup, press and hold the mouse as you roll over color chips in the popup or colors anywhere on your desktop and release the mouse only when you are hovering over the color that you want to sample. The preview in the swatches popup changes as you roll over different colors, and the color chip changes when you release the mouse to load the color that you have selected.

If you are using the dropper from the Tools panel color chip swatches popup, the behavior is a bit different: Click once on the color chip to open the swatches popup, and then move the dropper to roll over any color in the popup or on your desktop and click again to pick the color and load it into the current color chip. The droppers available from the swatches popups for any of the color chips in the Properties panel work the same way as the droppers in the Tools panel swatches pop-up but they are limited to picking colors from within the Flash application (or the currently loaded swatches).

The Eyedropper tool doesn't have any options in the Tools panel because they are all built in. As you hover over an item, the Eyedropper tool displays a small icon to indicate whether it is over a line or a fill that can be sampled by clicking. When a line is sampled, the Eyedropper tool automatically converts to the Ink Bottle tool, and when a fill is sampled, the Eyedropper tool converts to the Paint Bucket tool.

The composite image shown in Figure 9.1 shows the icons that appear when you use the Eyedropper tool to sample a fill (A) and apply it to another shape with the Paint Bucket tool (B), and sample a stroke (C) and apply it to another shape with the Ink Bottle tool (D).

FIGURE 9.1

The Eyedropper tool used to sample a fill and apply it with the Paint Bucket tool (A, B) and to sample a stroke and apply it with the Ink Bottle tool (C, D)

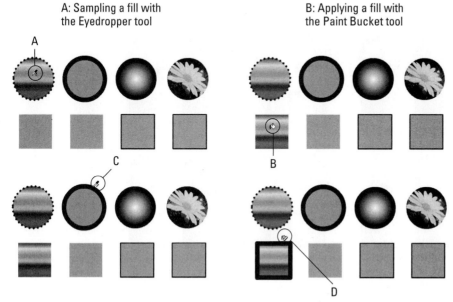

A: Sampling a fill with the Eyedropper tool

B: Applying a fill with the Paint Bucket tool

C: Sampling a stroke with the Eyedropper tool

D: Applying a stroke with the Ink Bottle tool

Any items already selected when the Eyedropper tool samples a stroke or fill immediately acquire the applicable stroke or fill style. This is the quickest way to transfer the fill or line styles of one element to a whole group of elements. Figure 9.2 shows the Eyedropper tool used to sample a fill with one (A) or more (B) elements already selected.

> **TIP** When you press and hold the Shift key while clicking a line or stroke color with the Eyedropper tool, the Fill and the Stroke color chips both convert simultaneously to the newly selected color so that it can be applied with any of the other drawing tools.

The Ink Bottle tool

You use the Ink Bottle tool (S) — refer to Figure 9.1 (D) — to change the color, style, and thickness of existing outlines. It is most often used in conjunction with the Eyedropper tool. When the Ink Bottle tool is in use, pay attention to the following three options:

- The current Stroke Color option on the Tools panel or the Properties panel
- The Stroke weight (or thickness) setting in the Properties panel
- The Stroke Style setting in the Properties panel

The Ink Bottle applies the current stroke color and line style, either sampled with the Eyedropper tool or chosen from the popup in the Tools panel or the controls in the Properties panel.

FIGURE 9.2

The Eyedropper tool also instantly converts selected elements to the sampled fill or stroke style.

A: One item selected while
fill is sampled with Eyedropper

Result: One item converted
to new fill style

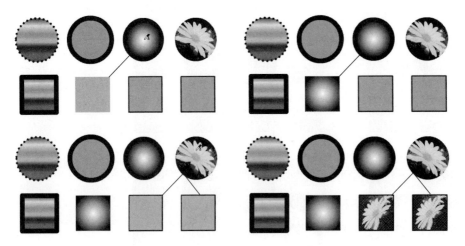

B: Two items selected while
fill is sampled with Eyedropper

Result: Two items converted
to new fill style

CAUTION When you click to sample a line with the Ink Bottle tool, all other currently *selected* lines are changed simultaneously.

The Ink Bottle tool is especially useful for applying custom line styles to multiple lines. You can build a collection of custom line styles either off Stage or in a special custom line palette saved as a single-frame Flash movie. You can then acquire these line styles whenever you want to reuse them.

TIP You can add Flash files with graphics libraries that you plan to reuse to the application's Libraries folder so that they can be easily accessed from the Window ➪ Common Libraries menu.

NOTE Depending on the level of zoom, some lines may not appear accurately on the screen — though they print correctly on a high-resolution printer. You may adjust Stroke weight in the Fill and Stroke section of the Properties panel.

The Paint Bucket tool

You use the Paint Bucket tool to fill enclosed areas with color, gradients, or bitmap fills. Although the Paint Bucket tool is a more robust tool than the Ink Bottle tool, and it can be used independently, it's most often used in conjunction with the Eyedropper tool. As discussed earlier in this chapter, when the Eyedropper tool picks up a fill, it first acquires the attributes of that fill and then automatically changes itself to the Paint Bucket tool. When the Paint Bucket tool is active, shown in Figure 9.3, two options are available from the Tools panel: Lock Fill and Gap size. The Gap size drop-down menu offers four settings to control how Flash handles gaps or open spaces in lines when filling with the Paint Bucket tool.

FIGURE 9.3

The Paint Bucket tool and Gap size options

When you use the Eyedropper tool to acquire a bitmap fill, the Eyedropper tool is automatically swapped for the Paint Bucket tool and a thumbnail of the bitmap image appears in place of the fill color chip. This procedure also automatically engages the Paint Bucket Lock Fill option.

NOTE The scale of the bitmap fill is consistent, no matter how it is selected and applied. As described later in this chapter, you can use the Gradient Transform tool to modify the scale of a bitmap fill as needed.

CAUTION Using the Paint Bucket to fill with white (or the background color) is not the same as erasing. Painting with white (or the background color) may appear to accomplish something similar to erasing. However, you are, in fact, creating a filled item that can be selected, moved, deleted, or reshaped. Only erasing erases!

Another helpful behavior of the Paint Bucket tool is that the exact location where you click to apply the Paint Bucket tool defines the highlight point for the fill. This has no visible effect when filling with solid colors or bitmap fills, but when filling with gradients it affects how the fill is rendered within the boundaries of the shape. Figure 9.4 illustrates how the highlight of a gradient fill varies based on where it was "dumped" with the Paint Bucket.

TIP You can also adjust the highlight and the center point of the rendered gradient with the Gradient Transform tool after a shape is filled.

FIGURE 9.4

The highlight location of gradient fills can be defined by the position of the Paint Bucket tool when the fill is applied to a shape.

As with the Ink Bottle tool, the Paint Bucket tool can be especially useful for applying custom fill styles to multiple items. You can build a collection of custom fill styles either off-screen (on the Pasteboard) or in a special, saved, custom-fills-palette, single-frame Flash movie. You can then acquire these fills whenever necessary.

CAUTION If you click with the Paint Bucket tool on one of several selected fills, *all* the selected fills simultaneously change to the new fill.

Using the Paint Bucket Gap size option

As shown in Figure 9.3, the Gap size option dropdown offers four settings that control how the Paint Bucket treats gaps when filling. These settings are Don't Close Gaps, Close Small Gaps, Close Medium Gaps, and Close Large Gaps. These tolerance settings enable Flash to fill an outline if the endpoints of the outline aren't completely joined, leaving an open shape. If the gaps are too large, you may have to close them manually with another drawing tool. Figure 9.5 illustrates how the Gap size option settings affect the Paint Bucket fill behavior.

TIP The level of zoom changes the apparent size of gaps. Although the actual size of gaps is unaffected by zoom, the Paint Bucket's interpretation of the gap is dependent upon the current Zoom setting. When zoomed in very close, the Paint Bucket tool finds it harder to close gaps; when zoomed out, the Paint Bucket tool finds it easier to close gaps.

FIGURE 9.5

Paint Bucket fill applied with various Gap size settings: (A) original oval outline with decreasing gap sizes, left to right, with no fill; (B) gray fill applied with Don't Close Gaps; (C) gray fill applied with Close Small Gaps; (D) gray fill applied with Close Medium Gaps; (E) gray fill applied with Close Large Gaps

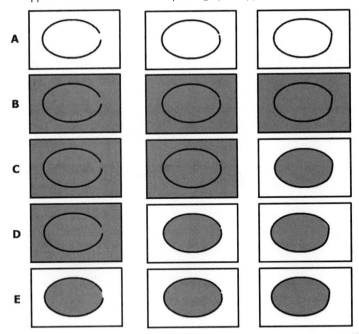

Using the Paint Bucket Lock Fill option

The Paint Bucket's Lock Fill option is the same as the Brush Lock Fill option — it controls how Flash handles areas filled with gradient color or bitmaps. When this button is turned on, all areas (or shapes) painted with the same gradient or bitmap appear to be part of a single, continuous, filled shape. The Lock Fill option locks the angle, size, and point of origin of the current fill to remain constant throughout any number of selected shapes. Modifications made to the fill in one of the shapes are applied to the other shapes filled by using the same Lock Fill option.

CROSS-REF Working with gradient colors is discussed in Chapter 7, "Applying Color."

To demonstrate the distinction between fills applied with or without the Lock Fill option, we created five shapes and filled them with a bitmap with Lock Fill off. As shown in Figure 9.6, on the left, the image was rendered individually from one shape to the next. On the right, those same shapes were filled with the same bitmap, but with Lock Fill on. Note how the image is now continuous from one shape to the next. Bitmap fills are automatically tiled to fill a shape, so the bitmap fill on the right was also scaled with the Gradient Transform tool to make it easier to see the continuation of the image between the various shapes.

FIGURE 9.6

Fill applied with Lock Fill turned off (left), compared with fill applied with Lock Fill turned on and then scaled by using the Gradient Transform tool (right)

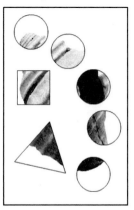

NOTE When you use the Eyedropper tool to pick up a fill or gradient from the scene, the Lock Fill button is automatically toggled on.

CAUTION If the shapes you are filling with the Paint Bucket tool were created with the Object Drawing option turned on or drawn with one of the Shape Primitive tools, you can use the Lock Fill option to get a fill that continues from one shape to the next, but when you try to adjust the fill with the Gradient Transform tool, you will find that the fills are transformed individually instead of as a group. The workaround for this glitch is to use raw shapes when you apply a locked fill that you plan to transform. If you started with drawing objects or shape primitives, use the Break Apart command before you try to use the Gradient Transform tool to adjust a continuous fill on multiple shapes.

Transforming Gradients and Bitmap Fills

You will find the Gradient Transform tool (F) in a dropdown within the same tile on the toolbar as the Free Transform tool (Q). Gradient Transform is used only to modify bitmap or gradient fills and does not apply to simple color fills. The Gradient Transform tool does many of the same things the Free Transform tool does, but it modifies only the *fill* of a shape without changing the stroke or outline appearance at all. This is a lot like shifting, rotating, or scaling a larger piece of material behind a frame so that a different portion is visible.

The Gradient Transform tool has only one option in the Tools panel, but, as with the Eyedropper tool, it does apply differently depending on the type of fill selected. To use the Gradient Transform tool, select it in the Tools panel, and then simply click an existing gradient or bitmap fill. A set of three or four adjustment handles appears, depending on the type of fill. The following three transformations can be performed on a gradient or bitmap fill: adjusting the fill's center point, rotating the fill, and scaling the fill. The extra set of adjustment handles appearing on bitmap fills enables them to be skewed. The Magnet option in the Tools panel toggles on Snapping behavior, making it easier to constrain transformations to even adjustment increments. Figure 9.7 illustrates the various adjustment handles on three types of fills.

FIGURE 9.7

The Gradient Transform tool applied to a radial gradient (A), a linear gradient (B), a tiled bitmap fill (C), and a scaled bitmap fill (D). Each handle type has an icon to indicate its function.

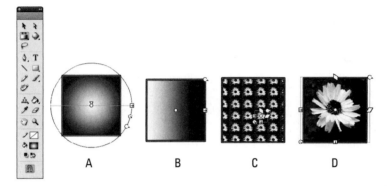

The position of these handles may shift if a fill (or bitmap fill) has been variously copied, rotated, or pasted in any number of ways. The fundamental rules are as follows:

- The round center handle moves the center point.
- The extra center pointer on radial gradients moves the highlight.
- The round corner handle with the short arrow rotates.
- The square edge handles scale either vertically or horizontally.
- The round corner handle with a long arrow scales symmetrically.
- The diamond-shaped edge handles on bitmap fills skew either vertically or horizontally.

TIP   To see all the handles when transforming a large element or working with an item close to the edge of the Stage, choose View ➪ Pasteboard from the application menu or use the shortcut keys Shift+Ctrl+W/Shift+⌘+W.

Adjusting the center point with the Gradient Transform tool

If the fill is not aligned in the shape as you would like it to be, you can easily move the center point to adjust how the shape outline frames the fill. To adjust the center point, follow these steps:

1. **Deselect the fill if it has been previously selected.**
2. **Choose the Gradient Transform tool from the Tools panel.**

3. Click the fill.

4. Bring the cursor to the small circular handle at the center of the fill until it changes to a four-arrow cursor, pointing left, right, up, and down, like a compass, indicating that this handle can now be used to move the center point in any direction.

5. Drag the center circular handle in any direction you want to move the center of the fill.

Figure 9.8 shows a radial gradient (left) repositioned with the Gradient Transform tool (right).

FIGURE 9.8

Adjusting the center point of a gradient fill with the Gradient Transform tool

The Gradient Transform option enables you to adjust the highlight of a radial gradient without moving the center point of the fill. As shown in Figure 9.9, you can drag the extra pointer above the center point circle to move the highlight of the gradient along the horizontal axis. If you want to move the highlight along a vertical axis, use the rotate handle to change the orientation of the fill.

FIGURE 9.9

The Gradient Transform handle enables you to adjust the highlight of a radial gradient without moving the center point of the fill.

TIP The Paint Bucket tool is also a handy way to set the highlight point of a gradient fill. Select the gradient that you want to apply, and then click inside the shape where you want the highlight to be. You can keep clicking in different areas of the shape with the Paint Bucket to move the highlight around until you like it.

Rotating a fill with the Gradient Transform tool

To rotate a gradient or bitmap fill, find the small circular handle that's at the corner of the fill. (In a radial gradient, choose the lower circular handle.) This circular handle is used for rotating a fill around the center point. Simply click the circular handle with the Rotate cursor and drag clockwise or counterclockwise to rotate the fill. Figure 9.10 shows a bitmap fill (left) as it appears when rotated clockwise (right).

TIP Activate the Snap to Objects toggle in the Tools panel if you want to use snapping behaviors to help guide rotating or scaling of a fill. (Turn behaviors on or off in the application menu under View ➪ Snapping.)

FIGURE 9.10

Rotating a bitmap fill with the Gradient Transform tool

Adjusting scale with the Gradient Transform tool

To resize a bitmap fill symmetrically (to maintain the aspect ratio), find the round corner handle with an arrow icon, which is usually located at the lower left corner of the fill. On rollover, the diagonal arrow icon appears, indicating the direction(s) in which the handle resizes the fill. Click and drag to scale the fill symmetrically. On radial gradients, you use the round-corner handle with the longer arrow icon to scale with the gradient aspect ratio constrained. Linear gradients have only one handle for scaling, and this handle always scales in the direction of the gradient banding.

To resize a fill asymmetrically, find a small square handle on either a vertical or a horizontal edge, depending on whether you want to affect the width or height of the fill. On rollover, arrows appear perpendicular to the edge of the shape, indicating the direction in which this handle resizes the fill. Click and drag a handle to reshape the fill.

Figure 9.11 shows the three fill types with their respective scale options. Linear gradient fills (left) can be scaled only in the direction of the gradient banding, but they can be rotated to scale vertically (lower) rather than horizontally (upper). Radial gradient fills (center) can be expanded symmetrically (upper) with the circular handle, or asymmetrically (lower) with the square handle. As with linear gradients, they can be rotated to scale vertically rather than horizontally. Bitmap fills (right) can be scaled by the corner handle to maintain the aspect ratio (upper), or dragged from any side handle to scale asymmetrically (lower).

CAUTION Adjusting bitmap fills with the Gradient Transform tool can be tricky business. On tiled fills, the transform handles are often so small and bunched together that they are difficult to see. On full-size bitmaps, the handles are sometimes outside the Stage, and it can be hard to find the handle that you need. It can also be unpredictable where the handles appear when you select a bitmap fill with the Gradient Transform tool — often they are outside the shape where the fill is visible. Our advice is to use this workflow only when you have no other choice. In general, it is a much better idea to decide on the size for a bitmap and create a Web-ready image that you can use without scaling before you import it to Flash.

NOTE The right column of Figure 9.11 is a good example of how changes applied to one tile in a bitmap fill are passed to all the other tiles within the shape.

FIGURE 9.11

Scaling fills symmetrically (top) and asymmetrically (bottom)

Setting gradient fill overflow styles

As you work with scaled gradient fills, you will quickly notice that your shape is always filled from edge to edge but that the fill area may not appear quite how you'd like it to. In early versions of Flash, you were stuck with the solid color fill around the edges when a gradient was scaled smaller inside of a shape. This default behavior is now part of the Overflow menu in the Color panel that gives you some other options for how a gradient renders when it is scaled down. As shown in Figure 9.12, there are three different overflow styles:

- **Extend:** Extends the colors on the outside edge of the gradient to create a solid fill beyond the edge of the rendered gradient
- **Reflect:** Alternates flipped (reflected) versions of the original gradient until the shape is filled from edge to edge
- **Repeat:** Renders the color pattern of the original gradient repeatedly until the shape is filled from edge to edge

Skewing a bitmap fill with the Gradient Transform tool

To skew a bitmap fill horizontally, click the diamond-shaped handle at the top of the image; arrows appear, parallel to the edge of the fill, indicating the directions in which this handle skews the fill. Drag to skew the image in either direction. Figure 9.13 shows a bitmap skewed horizontally (left) and vertically (right). Note that the skew procedure is still active after it has been applied, meaning that the skew may be further modified — this behavior is common to all functions of the Gradient Transform tool.

FIGURE 9.12

Different overflow styles applied to a linear gradient (top right) and a radial gradient (bottom right) using the Overflow menu in the Color panel (left). Overflow styles applied to the fills from left to right: Extend, Reflect, Repeat.

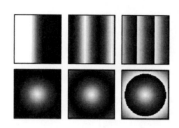

FIGURE 9.13

Skewing a bitmap fill with the Gradient Transform tool

 Gradient fills cannot be skewed; they can be scaled only on the horizontal or vertical axis.

 If you get carried away with the Gradient Transform tool and you want to get back to the original fill position and size, double-click the center icon of the shape to reset all transformations.

Gradient Transform Used for Lighting Effects

You apply the Gradient Transform tool most often to get a patterned fill or a gradient aligned and sized within its outline shape. A simple way of adding more depth to shapes is to modify gradient fills so that they appear to reflect light from one consistent source. You can choose to emulate a soft light for a more even illumination, or to emulate a hard, focused light that emphasizes dramatic shadows. As you create a composition on the Stage, you can use the Gradient Transform tool to modify individual elements so that they appear to share a common light source. Figure 9.14 illustrates how a default radial gradient (left) can be modified to emulate a soft (center) or hard (right) illumination.

FIGURE 9.14

Applying Gradient Transform to create different illumination effects

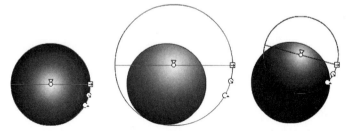

To show how these lighting effects can be applied to create the illusion of 3D, we created a little scene by using only radial fills that were modified with the Gradient Transform tool. Figure 9.15 shows the radial gradients as they appeared when we drew them with the default settings (left) and how the scene appeared after we modified the gradients with Gradient Transform and some basic shape scaling as we describe later in this chapter.

ON the CD-ROM If you want to deconstruct this example, we have included the file on the CD-ROM with both the unmodified and the final transformed shapes. You will find the file named SphereLighting.fla in the ch09 folder of the CD-ROM.

FIGURE 9.15

The Fill Transform tool used to modify default radial gradient fills (left) to create the illusion of 3D lighting effects (right)

Applying Modify Shape Menu Commands

Three specialized commands found in the application menu (under Modify ➪ Shape) provide modification options that you cannot achieve with any other tools in Flash.

CROSS-REF We discuss the Selection tool, Subselection tool, and the Smooth, Straighten, and Optimize commands (also found in the Modify Shape menu), in Chapter 5, "Drawing in Flash."

Convert Lines to Fills

Lines to Fills does exactly what its name implies: It converts lines defined by single points into shapes defined by an outline of editable points. To apply the Lines to Fills command, simply select any lines that you want to convert before choosing Modify ➪ Shape ➪ Convert Lines to Fills. After a line has been converted in this way, you can edit it like any other filled shape, including adding bitmap or gradient fills or applying the Selection or Subselection tools to adjust the corners and curves of the outlined shape.

 You can render strokes and lines by using gradients without converting them into fills.

Creating scalable artwork

The Lines to Fills command is especially important because it provides the one solution for maintaining line-to-fill ratios when scaling raw graphics that would require lines to appear at smaller than 1 point size. Fills do not have the same display limitation as lines, and they maintain visual consistency as they are scaled larger or smaller. In Figure 9.16, the image on the left was drawn with the Pencil tool to make lines around the eyes and on the whiskers of the cat cartoon. When it was scaled, the lines were not visually consistent with the fills. The image on the right was modified by using the Lines to Fills command before scaling it down to 25 percent size. In this case, the ratio between the outlines around the eyes and the whiskers was consistent with the other filled shapes in the cartoon.

 If you convert your raw graphic into a symbol before you scale it, the ratio of lines to fills also stays consistent.

CROSS-REF The stroke scale settings in the Properties panel are discussed in Chapter 5, "Drawing in Flash." These settings are helpful for maintaining a specific stroke weight on graphics that will be scaled horizontally or vertically, but they do not solve the display issue discussed here (and shown in Figure 9.16), when scaled lines need to appear at less than 1 point.

FIGURE 9.16

Use the Lines to Fills command to ensure consistency when scaling raw graphics.

100% scaled lines   100% scaled fills

25% scaled lines   25% scaled fills

NOTE Remember that in Flash, the smallest line size that can be displayed is 1 point. Lines with a height of less than 1 point all appear to be the same size on-screen when viewed at 100 percent scale. The difference in size is visible only when the view is scaled larger (zoomed in). However, the lines print correctly on a high-resolution printer and are visible in the published .swf if the content is zoomed.

Expand Fill

The Expand Fill command has two options you can use to size fills up or down evenly on all sides of a shape. To apply the command, select the fill(s) that you want to modify, and then choose Modify ⇨ Shape ⇨ Expand Fill. The Expand Fills dialog box appears, where you can choose to expand or inset (shrink) the fill by a specific pixel value. Keep in mind that this command applies differently than a normal scale modification. The fill expands or shrinks from all sides evenly, so an extreme modification can cause a shape to bloat to the extent that unfilled areas are obscured, or conversely it can cause a shape to shrink to the point that some of the areas are no longer visible. When applied moderately, the Expand Fill command can be very helpful for adjusting multiple filled shapes consistently, without scaling lines in the same area of the artwork.

CAUTION **You cannot apply the Expand Fill command to drawing objects with strokes unless you first break them apart or open them in Edit mode so that you can select the fill without also selecting the stroke.**

Figure 9.17 includes a rectangle, a cartoon cat, and a sketch of some grapes. The original shapes are shown on the left, the expanded fills in the center, and the inset fills on the right. As you can see, expanding fills often obscures the strokes surrounding a shape, whereas choosing to inset a fill leaves space between the fill and any surrounding stroke.

FIGURE 9.17

Modifying an original shape (A) with the Expand Fill command, using the Expand option (B) or the Inset option (C) respectively bloats or shrinks a fill by a specified pixel amount.

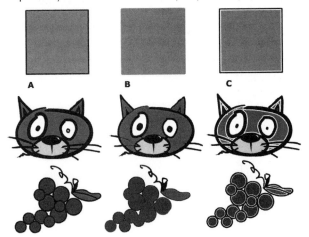

NOTE **Each of the fills in the graphics shown in Figure 9.17 were added by clicking or Shift+clicking (rather than dragging out a selection marquee) to avoid including any strokes in the final selection that was modified with the Expand Fill command.**

You can also use the Expand Fill command to create custom text forms. Figure 9.18 shows how the original text shape (left) can be modified by using either the Expand or Inset option. To create bloated balloon-like text (center), or shrunken, eroded text (right), you first have to apply the Modify ⇨ Break Apart command (Ctrl+B/⌘+B) twice to reduce the text to simple filled shapes. By selecting all the letter shapes before applying the Expand Fill command, you can modify the whole word at the same time.

FIGURE 9.18

Text broken apart into letter shapes (A) can be expanded (B) or inset (C) to create custom text effects.

Expand **Expand** Expand
A   B   C

Soften Fill Edges

The Soften Fill Edges command was the closest thing to a static blur available before Flash 8. Fortunately, Flash 8 and newer versions support a much more sophisticated Blur filter that renders smoother softened edges and enables you to change the color of the item even after the blur is applied. The only advantages that the Soften Fill Edges command has over the Blur filter are that you can use it to modify raw shapes or drawing objects and choose whether to render it inside or outside the item's original fill boundary. This command, as with the Expand Fill command, can be applied only to fills and gives you the option to expand or inset the shape by a specific number of pixels.

CAUTION Flash enables you to select a line and choose the Soften Edges command from the Modify ⇨ Shape menu. After you apply the command, however, the line just disappears from the Stage — surprise! If you make this mistake, you can recover your line by immediately choosing Edit ⇨ Undo (Ctrl+Z/⌘+Z).

The blurry effect of Soften Fill Edges is created by a series of banded fills around the original fill that decrease in opacity toward the outermost band. You can control the number and width of these bands by entering values in the Soften Fill Edges dialog box (shown in Figure 9.19) to create a variety of effects, from a very subtle blurred effect to a dramatic stepped appearance around the edges of the fill.

FIGURE 9.19

The Soften Fill Edges dialog box with settings for controlling the edge effect

The Soften Fill Edges dialog box controls the following features of the fill modification:

- **Distance:** Defines the number of pixels the original shape expands or shrinks
- **Number of steps:** Sets the number of bands that appear around the outside edge of the fill
- **Expand or Inset:** Controls whether the bands are added to the outside edge of the fill (expand) or stacked on the inside edge of the shape (inset)

Figure 9.20 shows how the original fill (left) appears after Soften Fill Edges is applied with the Expand option (center), or with the Inset option (right).

FIGURE 9.20

Applying Soften Fill Edges with the Expand option and with the Inset option

The width of the individual bands equals the total number of pixels set in Distance divided by the Number of steps. When the edge of the shape is magnified, the individual bands can clearly be seen. Figure 9.21 compares a series of eight bands, each 1 pixel wide, created by using a Distance setting of 8 and a Number of steps setting of 8, compared with the smooth softened edge that results from applying a Blur filter with an X and Y setting of 8.

FIGURE 9.21

A magnified view of the banded edge of a fill created by applying Soften Fill Edges (left) compared to the smooth softened edge created by applying the Flash Blur filter (right)

As with the Expand Fill command, Soften Fill Edges can create interesting text effects when applied to broken-apart letter shapes. Figure 9.22 shows an effect created by combining the original white text with a "shadow" made by applying the Soften Fill Edges command to a broken-apart copy of the text that was filled with dark gray.

FIGURE 9.22

A glow effect created by layering the original text over a copy that was broken apart, filled with dark gray, and modified by using Soften Fill Edges

You can achieve an effect similar to the shadow shown in Figure 9.22 by applying the Glow filter to an editable text field and selecting the knockout option. We cover the various Flash filters in Chapter 12, "Applying Filters, Blends, Guides, and Masks."

Free Transform Commands and Options

The commands we have looked at so far in this chapter are generally used for localized modification of lines or fills. In this section, we introduce some commands that are applied to create more dramatic change of whole items or even groups of items.

You can apply the basic transform commands to any element in the Flash authoring environment, but it is important to know that any transformations applied to symbols, groups, drawing objects, or text blocks are saved in the Info panel even if they are deselected and then reselected later. This enables you to easily revert these items to their original appearance. The transform settings for primitive shapes, on the other hand, are reset to the default values in the Info panel as soon as they are deselected. This means that while a primitive shape is actively being modified, you can revert to the original appearance, but as soon as you apply a change and deselect the shape, its modified appearance will be considered original the next time you select it. As shown in Figure 9.23, there are various ways to access the transform commands available in Flash.

FIGURE 9.23

The various ways to access transform commands in Flash — the Transform panel (left), the Modify Transform submenu (center), and the Free Transform tool (right)

The Transform panel

The Transform panel (Ctrl+T/⌘+T) includes value fields for horizontal and vertical scale percentages, degrees of rotation, and degrees of vertical and horizontal skew. You can use these fields for visual reference or as a way to enter precise transform values. The Transform panel also includes two important buttons:

- The Copy and Apply Transform button is used to duplicate the selected item with all transformations included. When you select this button, you may not notice that anything has happened to your selected item — this is because Flash places the duplicate exactly on top of the original. To see both the original and the duplicate, drag the duplicate to a new position in the Document window.

- The Reset button reverts a transformed symbol, group, or text field to its original appearance and returns all values in the Transform panel to the default settings. You can also achieve this by choosing Modify ⇨ Transform ⇨ Remove Transform. If you want to remove only the most recently applied modification, use Edit ⇨ Undo (Ctrl+Z /⌘+Z).

The Modify Transform menu

The commands found in the application menu under Modify ⇨ Transform enable you to choose specific combinations of transform options as well as a couple of "shortcuts" for commonly needed modifications. Special note should be taken of the two commands that are unique to the application menu:

- **Rotate 90 degrees CW or Rotate 90 degrees CCW:** Used to rotate any selected items by a half-turn in the chosen direction (clockwise or counterclockwise) around the central axis point of the selection.

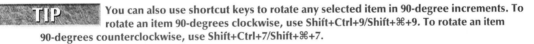 You can also use shortcut keys to rotate any selected item in 90-degree increments. To rotate an item 90-degrees clockwise, use Shift+Ctrl+9/Shift+⌘+9. To rotate an item 90-degrees counterclockwise, use Shift+Ctrl+7/Shift+⌘+7.

- **Flip Vertical or Flip Horizontal:** Used to place the item in a mirrored position either on the vertical axis (calendar flip) or the horizontal axis (book flip).

The Free Transform tool

The Free Transform tool (Q), available directly from the Tools panel, enables you to apply transform commands dynamically with various arrow icons. These icons appear as you position the pointer over the control points or handles of the selected item. You can also invoke various transform states from the contextual menu. Although the position of these arrow icons can vary with the position of the pointer, they provide a consistent indication of what transformation will be applied from the closest available handle. To finish any transformation, simply deselect the item by clicking outside of the current selection area.

- **Move arrow:** This familiar arrow indicates that all currently selected items can be dragged together to a new location in the Document window.

- **Axis point or transformation point:** By default, this circle marks the center of shapes as the axis for most transformations or animation. By dragging the point to a different location, you can define a new axis or transformation point for modifications applied to the item. To return the axis point to its default location, double-click the axis point icon.

- **Skew arrow:** This arrow is generally available on any side of an item between transformation points. By clicking and dragging the outline, you can skew the shape in either direction indicated by the arrows.

- **Rotate arrow:** This arrow is generally available near any corner of an item. By clicking and dragging, you can rotate the item clockwise or counterclockwise around the transform axis. Note that if you position the arrow directly over the closest corner handle, the Rotate arrow is usually replaced with the Scale Corner arrow. To rotate around the opposite corner point without moving the axis point, press the Alt (Option) key while dragging. To constrain rotation to 45-degree increments, press Shift while dragging.

- **Scale Side arrow:** This arrow is available from any handle on the side of an item. Clicking and dragging scales the item larger or smaller, in one direction only, relative to the transform axis.

- **Scale Corner arrow:** This arrow appears only on the corner handles of an item and is used to evenly scale the item larger or smaller, in all directions from the transform axis. To constrain the aspect ratio of the shape, press Shift while dragging.

Transforming shapes, symbols, text, and groups

Figure 9.24 shows how a symbol (or drawing object) and a shape appear differently after they have been modified, deselected, and then reselected with the Free Transform tool. The symbol (left) displays transform handles that are aligned with the originally modified item, and the values of the transformation settings are preserved in the Transform panel. The shape (right), however, displays transform handles aligned to default values unrelated to the original modifications, and the values in the Transform panel are reset to their defaults.

FIGURE 9.24

The Free Transform handles and Transform panel settings that appear for a symbol or drawing object (left) and for a simple shape (right) that have been reselected after an initial modification

Free Transform limit options

The first two options in the Tools panel for the Free Transform tool (shown in Figure 9.23) are toggles to limit the modifications that can be applied to a selected item. It can sometimes be easier to use the Free Transform tool with more specific behavior. When the Rotate and Skew button or the Scale button is toggled on, all other modifications are excluded.

The Rotate and Skew toggle protects the selected item from being scaled accidentally while you're rotating or skewing it. This Tools panel option is equivalent to choosing Modify ➪ Transform ➪ Rotate and Skew from the application menu.

The Scale toggle protects the selected item from all other transformations while it is being sized larger or smaller. This Tools panel option is equivalent to choosing Modify ➪ Transform ➪ Scale from the application menu.

Free Transform special shape options

The last two options in the Tools panel for the Free Transform tool — Distort and Envelope — are not available for symbols, groups, or text fields. However, when you're transforming drawing objects or primitive shapes, you can use these two options to create complex modifications not easily achieved with other Flash tools.

NOTE Remember that you can access the raw shapes in a group or symbol by entering Edit mode. You can also convert text fields into shapes by applying the Break Apart command (twice).

Distort works by widening or narrowing the sides of the item, or stretching out the corners. This transform option does not bend or warp the shape; it allows sides of the shape to be scaled individually. To apply Distort, first select a shape with the Free Transform tool in the Tools panel, and turn on the Distort toggle in the Options area of the Tools panel. You can then click and drag handles on the sides or corners of the item to stretch or compress individual sides. This is equivalent to selecting a shape with the Selection tool and choosing Modify ➪ Transform ➪ Distort from the application menu or selecting Distort from the contextual menu.

TIP You can also apply the Distort option to a shape that has been selected with the Free Transform tool by pressing Control (⌘) while dragging a side or corner handle. To taper a shape or move two adjoining corner points an equal distance simultaneously, press Shift while dragging any corner handle with the Free Transform tool.

Figure 9.25 shows an original shape being modified with the Distort option (left), and the final shape with distort handles, as they appear when the shape is reselected (right).

FIGURE 9.25

Free Transform applied to a shape, using the Distort option

The Envelope option enables you to work with control points and handles much the same way you would when editing lines or shapes with the Subselection tool. The powerful difference is that the Envelope can wrap around the outside of multiple items so that the control points and handles curve, scale, stretch, or warp all the lines and shapes contained within the Envelope selection.

To apply the Envelope, first select a shape or multiple shapes with the Free Transform tool and then toggle on the Envelope option in the Tools panel. The Envelope offers a series of control points and tangent handles. The square points are used to scale and skew the shape(s), whereas the round points are actually handles used to control the curve and warp of the shape(s). You can also access the Envelope option by selecting the shapes you want to transform and choosing Modify ➪ Transform ➪ Envelope from the application menu, or by selecting Envelope from the contextual menu.

Figure 9.26 shows an original shape being modified with the Envelope option (left), and the final shape with Envelope handles, as they appear when the shape is reselected (right).

FIGURE 9.26

Free Transform applied to a shape, using the Envelope option

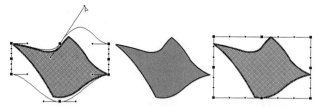

Manipulating Symbols in 3D Space

You can create faux-3D effects by skewing and scaling graphics with the Free Transform tool (as described in the previous section); however, this task has been made a whole lot easier by the new 3D tools available in Flash CS4. Instead of using your math and geometry skills to approximate perspective, you can simply click and drag intuitive handles and Flash applies distortion to your graphics to give them the appearance of existing in 3D space.

The 3D Rotation tool and the 3D Translation tool are both found in the Tools panel just below the Free Transform tool. Settings for these tools can be accessed in the Transform panel when the 3D tools are active or a 3D symbol is selected in your Document window. If you haven't worked with 3D tools before, the various options can be a little disorienting at first, but with a little trial and error you will soon get your bearings.

NOTE To use the 3D tools in Flash, the Publish settings of your FLA file must be set to Flash Player 10 and ActionScript 3.0. All elements must be converted into Movie Clip instances to apply 3D Rotation or Translation.

To help you get started, we have included definitions for some of the terms you will come across when working with Flash symbols in 3D space:

- **x-axis:** Sets the position of the symbol in relation to the Stage, tracked from left to right. Rotating (transforming) a symbol around the x-axis is like flipping a Rolodex. Moving (translating) an object along the x-axis makes it appear closer to the left or right side of the Stage.

- **y-axis:** Sets the position of the symbol in relation to the Stage, tracked from top to bottom. Rotating a symbol around the y-axis is like turning a revolving door. Moving an object along the y-axis makes it appear closer to the top or bottom of the Stage.

- **z-axis:** Sets the position of the symbol in relation to the depth of the space. This is the third axis that was added to Flash CS4 to support transformation and rotation of symbols for (faux) 3D. Rotating an object around the z-axis is like spinning a bicycle tire or moving the hands of a clock, although the center point can be adjusted so it is not always in the middle of the symbol. Moving an object along the z-axis makes it appear larger (closer) or smaller (farther away).

- **3D Translation:** Changing the location of a symbol in 3D space is called a translation. The 3D Translation tool provides handles for moving a symbol along the x, y, and z-axis individually.

- **3D Transformation:** Rotating an object in 3D space is called a transformation. The 3D Rotation tool provides handles for rotating a symbol along the x, y, and z-axis individually or along the x and y-axis at the same time — for "free rotation."

- **3D Center point:** By default, the 3D center point is usually the center point of the symbol, but by moving the 3D center point you can change the way 3D transformations (rotations) affect the symbol, in the same way that changing the center point for scaling or rotating an object in 2D space modifies the outcome of any changes.

- **Global 3D space:** This is the default setting for the 3D tools and means that any changes to location or rotation of a symbol are made in relation to the main Stage drawing area.

- **Local 3D space:** This is an alternative setting for the 3D tools (a toggle button at the bottom of the Tools panel appears when 3D tools are active), and it restricts changes to location or rotation of nested symbols to the drawing space of the container symbol.

CROSS-REF   **3D rotations and translations can be animated to create cool effects, but we defer discussion of tweened 3D to Chapter 11, "Timeline Animation and the Motion Editor."**

Controlling the camera view: Perspective and vanishing point

There is only one camera view in the authoring environment for your Flash movie. The camera view consists of a perspective angle and a vanishing point: These global settings are available in the 3D Position and View section of the Properties panel when a symbol with 3D translation or rotation is selected on the Stage. Changing the settings affects all 3D symbols in your Flash movie, but does not affect other elements.

NOTE   **If you are controlling 3D Movie Clips with ActionScript rather than using the 3D tools in the authoring environment, you can create multiple vanishing points and unique camera views for each Movie Clip.**

The perspective angle sets the viewing "lens" for all of your 3D elements. The range of settings for perspective angle is from 1 degree to 180 degrees. The default perspective angle is 55 degrees to approximate a standard camera lens view. Think of the perspective angle setting as the zoom factor of your viewing lens. Smaller numbers move the view farther away and make 3D transformations less dramatic — they flatten the view. Larger numbers move the view closer and make 3D transformations more extreme — they emphasize any changes in the angle or rotation of an element. Figure 9.27 shows the same 3D Movie Clip (a rectangle with a 45-degree y-axis rotation), viewed with three different perspective angle settings.

Another way to understand this feature is to compare it to our normal perception of objects in real space. If we are looking at a sculpture from a distance of 30 feet and we walk 10 steps to the left or right, our view does not change very much — we still see more or less the same side of the sculpture. However, if we are standing closer to a sculpture, say 3 feet away, and we walk the same 10 steps to the right or left, our view changes dramatically.

TIP   **If you change the Stage size of your Flash document, the perspective angle changes automatically to preserve the appearance of existing 3D symbols. You can turn this behavior off in the Document Properties dialog box.**

The Vanishing point setting determines the end point of the z-axis and controls the direction that 3D symbols travel if they are moved along their z-axis. Imagine it as an invisible anchor point in deep space which has a magnetic pull that makes all of your 3D translations extend in its direction. In real space, the vanishing point is that place in your field of vision where parallel lines seem to come together. If you were looking down a road on a perfectly flat plain, it would be the spot where the road appeared narrower and narrower until finally it ended in a dot on the horizon — that dot is the location of the vanishing point.

FIGURE 9.27

Increasing the perspective angle setting "zooms" the view closer, making 3D transformations look more extreme. The same Movie Clip viewed with three different perspective angle settings (from L-R): 10 degrees, 50 degrees (the default setting), 120 degrees.

By default, the vanishing point is set in the center of the Stage, but you can modify the setting at any time to a different x, y location — on or off the Stage. To view or set the vanishing point in the Properties panel, a 3D symbol must be selected on the Stage. Figure 9.28 illustrates the result of a 45-degree x-axis rotation with vanishing points in different locations. Figure 9.29 illustrates how the vanishing point affects the direction that a 3D symbol travels as it moves along the z-axis.

FIGURE 9.28

The location of the vanishing point determines the end point for the z-axis and the direction that objects recede into space. The same Movie Clip with a 3D rotation viewed with three different vanishing point locations (from L-R): top left corner of the Stage, center of the Stage (the default setting), and bottom right corner of the Stage.

Transforming symbols with the 3D Rotation tool

The 3D Rotation tool enables you to spin objects around the x, y, or z-axis and creates the illusion of depth by skewing and scaling your graphics based on the degree of rotation and the vanishing point and perspective angle settings. Figure 9.30 shows a simple rectangle with a drop shadow added (top) and the result of a 45-degree rotation applied along the x, y, and z-axis, respectively.

FIGURE 9.29

The location of the vanishing point determines the direction that 3D objects travel when they move along the z-axis. The original symbol (top left) looks smaller but remains centered when a 200-pixel translation along the z-axis is applied with the vanishing point in the middle of the Stage (top right). The same translation along the z-axis has a different result when the vanishing point is located in the top left corner of the Stage (bottom left) or in the bottom right corner of the Stage (bottom right).

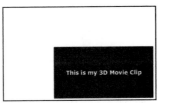

To apply the 3D Rotation tool (W), activate it in the Tools panel, then select a symbol on the Stage. When you select a symbol with the 3D Rotation tool, a target overlay (shown in Figure 9.30) appears, guiding you in moving the symbol in 3D space. The red vertical crosshair enables x-axis rotation, the green horizontal crosshair enables y-axis rotation, the inner blue circle enables z-axis transformation, and the outer orange circle enables free transformation (around the x and z-axis at the same time). To rotate an object, click and drag from the guide that represents the axis you want to use — dragging clockwise adds a positive transformation, and dragging counterclockwise adds a negative transformation. An object can be rotated around any axis from 0 degrees to 360 degrees in a positive or negative direction. When you release the mouse, you will notice that the 3D Position in the Properties panel updates, and if you have the Transform panel open (Window ➪ Transform), you can see the exact degree of rotation in the 3D Position and View section of the panel.

NOTE If you rotate an object more than 180 degrees, Flash automatically updates the values in the Transform panel to the smallest equivalent value. For example, applying a positive transformation to rotate an object 190 degrees around the x-axis has the same end result as applying a negative transformation to rotate it –170 degrees, so after you release the mouse and apply the transformation, Flash updates the value in the x-axis field of the Transform panel to be –170 degrees rather than 190 degrees.

FIGURE 9.30

The same degree of rotation (here 45 degrees) has different visual results when applied to the three different axes of a 3D Movie Clip (x, y, z). You can rotate an object around just one axis or you can combine two (or even all three), to position a symbol exactly where you want it in the faux 3D space of the Flash Stage.

Original rectangle
(symbol) with drop shadow

Transform panel
(showing 3D rotation)

3D Rotation on x axis

Result: rectangle with 45 degree x rotation

3D Rotation on y axis

Result: rectangle with 45 degree y rotation

3D Rotation on z axis

Result: rectangle with 45 degree z rotation

The final result of 3D rotation is affected by the location of the 3D center point. The 3D center point is indicated by the white dot at the center of the 3D target overlay when the 3D Rotation tool is active and a 3D symbol is selected. The default location for the 3D center point is at the center of the selected symbol. Click and drag to reposition the center point (or transformation center point) to another location on your current symbol or even outside of the symbol. Moving the 3D center point away from the center of the symbol increases the arc of any 3D rotations — this can be helpful for specific effects but it can also make it more likely that your symbol will move dramatically and end up outside the viewable Stage area. Double-click the 3D center point dot to reset it to the center of the symbol. If you prefer to set rotation values in the Transform panel, select the symbol you want to modify and use the hot text fields for x, y, and z-axis in the 3D Rotation section of the panel. You can also modify the location of the 3D center point by using the hot text fields for x, y, and z-axis in the 3D Center point section of the Transform panel. Figure 9.31 shows the difference in result when the same rectangle is rotated around the y-axis with three different 3D center point locations.

FIGURE 9.31

The 3D center point determines the origin point for 3D transformations. Here you can see how a y-axis rotation applies differently when the 3D center point is located in the center of the symbol (A), compared to the top left corner of the symbol (B) or the bottom right corner (C).

The **Remove Transform** button at the bottom right corner of the Transform panel returns your symbol to its unmodified state with just one click. The **Duplicate Selection and Transform** button beside the **Remove Transform** button makes an exact copy of your current selection — but be warned that you won't notice until you move the copy because it will be stacked on top of your original.

Symbols can be rotated in global space (relative to the main Stage drawing area), or if they are nested Movie Clips, they can be rotated in local space (relative to the container Movie Clip's drawing area). The toggle for global or local rotation is at the bottom of the Tools panel when the 3D Rotation tool is selected — the default setting is for global rotation.

You can temporarily toggle the 3D Rotation tool from global mode to local mode while dragging to move a symbol along any axis by pressing the **D** key.

To rotate multiple objects simultaneously, activate the 3D Rotation tool (W) in the Tools panel, and then select multiple symbols on the Stage (Shift+click or drag a selection field around multiple items). The Rotation guides/target will be centered on the most recently selected item. All the selected symbols rotate around the 3D center point, which appears in the center of the guide. To change the position of the 3D center point, you can do any of the following while you have a selection active on the Stage:

1. Drag the center point to a new location.
2. Shift+double-click any of the current symbols to move the center point to that symbol.

3. Double-click the 3D center point to auto-position it at the center of the current group of selected symbols.

4. Change the values for the x, y, z location of the 3D center point in the Transform panel.

Moving symbols with the 3D Translation tool

The 3D Translation tool enables you to move objects forward and backward in space along the z-axis, left and right in space along the x-axis, and/or up and down in space along the y-axis. For nested Movie Clips, 3D Translations can be global (relative to the main Stage) or local (relative to the parent Movie Clip's drawing area). To apply the 3D Translation tool (G), activate it in the Tools panel, then select a Movie Clip on the Stage. As shown in Figure 9.32, the 3D Translation tool consists of two arrow guides for moving along the x and y-axis and a center blue dot for moving along the z-axis. Click the head of the red horizontal arrow and drag your object left or right along the x-axis. Click the head of the green vertical arrow and drag your object up or down along the y-axis. Click the blue dot and drag your object forward or back along the z-axis. To reposition the guides for the 3D Translation tool, press and hold Alt/Option and then click and drag the blue dot to a new location. Double-clicking the center blue dot auto-positions the guides back at the center of your symbol.

Changes to the location of your 3D symbol updates the x, y, and z values in the Position and View section of the Properties panel. These values are also hot text fields, so you can position your 3D symbol by changing the values directly in the Properties panel. Moving an object along the z-axis changes its apparent size relative to the Stage. The apparent width and height also appear in the 3D Position and View section of the Properties panel, but these are read-only values, unlike the original width and height values in the Position and Size section of the Properties panel, which are editable hot text fields. You can also move multiple items simultaneously with the 3D Translation tool; Refer to the instructions for the 3D Rotation tool in the previous section.

FIGURE 9.32

The 3D Translation tool provides controls for moving symbols along the x, y, and z-axis.

Y = axis control arrow

Z = axis control dot ●——→ X = axis control arrow

This is my 3D Movie Clip

Modifying Item Types

In previous chapters, we have focused on the features of the timeline and how your Flash projects are ordered in time from left to right. Now we are going to look at the arrangement of items from the front to the back of the Stage, or the stacking order of elements in Flash. In this section, we explain how multiple items can be moved together, and how the Union, Break apart, and Trace bitmap commands are applied to change item types.

Stacking order

Within a single layer, Flash stacks items of the same type in the same order they are placed or created, with the most recent item on top, subject to the *kind* of item. The rules that control the stacking order of various kinds of items are simple:

- Within a layer, ungrouped raw shapes or lines are always at the *bottom* level, with the most recently drawn shape or line at the top of that layer's stack. Furthermore, unless you take precautions, drawn items either compound with, or cut into, the drawing beneath them.

- Groups, drawing objects, and symbols (including bitmaps) stack above lines and shapes in the *overlay* level. To change the stacking order of several items, it's often advisable to group them first, as we describe in the next section of this chapter.

To change the stacking order within a layer, first select the item that you want to move. Then, do one of the following:

- **To move the item to the top of the stacking order,** choose Modify ➪ Arrange ➪ Bring to Front (Alt+Shift+↑/Option+Shift+↑).

- **To move an item to the bottom of the stacking order,** choose Modify ➪ Arrange ➪ Send to Back (Alt+Shift+↓/Option+Shift+↓).

- **To move the item up one position in the stacking order,** choose Modify ➪ Arrange ➪ Bring Forward (Ctrl+↑/⌘+↑).

- **To move the item down one position in the stacking order,** choose Modify ➪ Arrange ➪ Send Backward (Ctrl+↓/⌘+↓).

Remember the stacking-order rules: You won't be able to bring an ungrouped drawing above a group or symbol. If you need that drawing on top, group it and then move it, or place it on a separate layer.

CROSS-REF We detail the Align panel (Ctrl+K/⌘+K) used to distribute items in a layout in relation to each other or to the Stage in Chapter 5, "Drawing in Flash."

To stack an item in a lower layer above an item in a higher layer, you simply change the order of the layer among the other layers: First, activate the layer, and then drag the Layer bar to the desired position in the layer stack of the timeline.

TIP Regardless of the number of layers in a Flash project (.fla), neither the file size nor the performance of the final .swf file is adversely affected because Flash flattens layers upon export.

Grouping

As discussed in Chapter 5, grouping shapes or lines makes them easier to handle. Instead of manipulating a single item, group several items to work with them as a single unit. Grouping also prevents shapes from being merged with or cropped by other shapes. In addition, it's easier to control the stacking order of groups than it is to control ungrouped drawings. Here's how to create groups:

1. **Use Shift+click to select multiple items or drag a selection box around everything that you want to group.** This can include any combination of items: shapes, lines, and symbols — even other groups.

2. **Choose Modify ➪ Group (Ctrl+G/⌘+G).** The selected elements are now grouped.

3. **To ungroup everything, select the group and then use Modify ➪ Ungroup (Ctrl+Shift+G/ ⌘+Shift+G).** Ungrouping only separates grouped items; it does not break apart bitmaps, symbol instances, or text as the Break apart command does.

Be careful when ungrouping. Your newly ungrouped drawings may alter or eliminate drawings below in the same layer.

To edit a group:

1. **Select the group and then choose Edit ⇨ Edit Selected, or double-click the group.** Everything on the Stage — except for items in the group — is dimmed, indicating that only the group is editable.

2. **Make changes in the same way you would edit individual primitive shapes or symbols.** If there are other groups or symbols included in a larger group, you'll have to click in deeper to edit those items. You can keep double-clicking on compound groups to gradually move inside to the deepest level or primitive shape available for editing. You can use the location labels to move back out level by level (or double-click an empty area of the Stage), or go to Step 3 to return to the Main Timeline.

3. **To stop editing the group, choose Edit ⇨ Edit All, or use the location labels to return to the main scene.** Other items on Stage return to normal color.

Applying Break apart

The Modify ⇨ Break apart command (Ctrl+B/⌘+B) is rather like an Undo command for groups, drawing objects, and symbols as well as a deconstruction tool for text and bitmaps. To use Break apart, simply select an item and then apply the command. Occasionally you must apply the Break apart command more than once to reduce a compound group to its core shapes. When applied to a symbol instance, Break apart reduces the instance to raw shapes that no longer are linked to the original symbol stored in the library.

Breaking apart text

Text reduced to shapes by using Break apart can be filled with gradients and bitmaps and also modified with the shape Transform options. We show specific examples of using the Break apart command in Chapter 8, "Working with Text," and in Chapter 15, "Importing Artwork." Figure 9.33 illustrates how text is broken apart in two stages so that the original block (left) is first separated into individual letters (center), and then when broken apart a second time, it is reduced to shapes (right).

FIGURE 9.33

A text field (left) broken apart once (center) and then once again (right)

 Breaking apart complex symbols or large text blocks can add to the file size of your final movie.

Creating Metallic Type

To demonstrate how text characters can be modified after they've been converted to shapes, we have applied some gradient fills to create the illusion of shiny metal letters. The file for this effect is titled `metalType.fla` and is included in the `ch09` folder of the CD-ROM. Start with a document that has a dark gray background.

1. First type a word or words on the Stage to create a text block. This effect works best if applied to a bold, sans serif font at a fairly large point size. We used Verdana bold set at 50 pt.

2. Select the text block and apply the Break apart command (Ctrl+B/ ⌘+B) once to break the text block into individual letters, and then a second time to convert the letters into shapes.

3. With the letter shapes still selected, load a default grayscale linear gradient into the Color panel and then adjust it so the gradient is dark at each end with a highlight in the center. Set the left and far right Color pointers to black (#000000) and then add a new Color pointer in the center of the Edit bar and set it to white (#FFFFFF), as shown in Figure 9.34.

FIGURE 9.34

Text shapes selected and filled with a custom linear gradient created in the Mixer panel

4. Use the Gradient Transform tool to rotate the gradient fill clockwise to a 45-degree angle in each letter shape. You may also scale each fill slightly or adjust individual center points to align the highlight on each letter, as shown in Figure 9.35.

FIGURE 9.35

Linear gradients aligned in each letter shape with the Gradient Transform tool

5. To create a more three-dimensional look, make a copy of all the letter shapes in a new layer below the current layer. Use the Copy (Ctrl+C / ⌘+C) and Paste (Ctrl+V/⌘+V) commands. Turn the visibility of the original layer off (click the Eye icon) for now so you can see only the copied letter shapes.

6. Select all the copied letter shapes, and using the Color panel, reverse the gradient fill colors. Set the center Color pointer to black and both end Color pointers to white, as shown in Figure 9.36.

FIGURE 9.36

Copied letter shapes on a new layer with reversed gradient fill applied

7. Use the Modify ⇨ Shape ⇨ Expand Fill command to expand the fill in all the selected letters by 2 pixels.

8. If you turn the visibility of both layers back on, you should see that you now have two opposing gradient fills, and the copied letter shapes are slightly larger than the original letter shapes. Figure 9.37 compares the letters with the original gradient and the letters with the modified gradient.

FIGURE 9.37

Original letter shapes with gradient fill (top) and copied letter shapes with reversed and expanded gradient fill (bottom)

9. Lock the original layer, and then select all the copied letter shapes on the lower layer and drag them behind the original letter shapes so that they're aligned just slightly above and to the right of the original shapes. This creates the illusion of a metallic beveled edge on the original letter shapes, as shown in Figure 9.38.

FIGURE 9.38

Copied letter shapes aligned behind the original letter shapes to create the illusion of a beveled metallic edge

Breaking apart bitmaps

When applied to bitmaps placed in the Document window, Break apart enables you to select the bitmap image with the Eyedropper tool to apply as a fill to other shapes. This is not the same as tracing a bitmap, which reduces the vast number of colors in a bitmap to areas of solid color and converts it to vector format, as described in the section that follows. Figure 9.39 shows an imported bitmap placed on the Stage and sampled with the Eyedropper tool to create a colored fill in the rectangle below (left) compared to the same bitmap broken apart and sampled with the Eyedropper tool to create an image fill in the rectangle below (right).

FIGURE 9.39

A bitmap and the fill that results from sampling it with the Eyedropper tool when it is intact (left) and when it has been broken apart (right)

It isn't necessary to break apart bitmaps to use as fills because they can be specified with the Mixer panel, as described in Chapter 7, "Applying Color." But breaking apart bitmaps enables you to selectively edit them and modify the visible area of the bitmap with the shape Transform options.

CAUTION Although you can apply the Distort and Envelope modifiers of the Free Transform tool to a bitmap after it has been broken apart, they may not give you the result you expect. Instead of distorting or warping the actual bitmap image, you'll find that these modifiers reveal how Flash "sees" bitmap fills. The visible area of the bitmap is not really treated as a shape but rather as a mask, or shaped window, that enables a certain part of the bitmap to be visible. You can distort or warp the viewable area, but the bitmap itself is not modified, as it is when you apply the Rotate or Skew modifiers.

Figure 9.40 illustrates a bitmap that has been broken apart (left) so that colored areas in the background of the image can be selected with the Magic Wand option of the Lasso tool (center) and then deleted to leave the flower floating on the white Stage (right). You can clean up any stray areas of unwanted color by using the Lasso tool or the Eraser tool.

FIGURE 9.40

A bitmap broken apart and selectively deleted, using the Magic Wand option of the Lasso tool

About the Magic Wand option

You use the Magic Wand option of the Lasso tool (shown at the bottom of the Tools panel in Figure 9.40) to select ranges of a similar color in either a bitmap fill or a bitmap that's been broken apart. After you select areas of the bitmap, you can change their fill color or delete them, without affecting the Bitmap Swatch in the Color panel. You can adjust what pixels the Magic Wand picks up by modifying the Threshold and Smoothing settings in the dialog box opened by clicking the Magic Wand settings button in the Options area of the Tools panel.

Magic Wand Threshold setting

The Threshold setting defines the breadth of adjacent color values that the Magic Wand includes in a selection. Values for the Threshold setting range from 0 to 200 — the higher the setting, the broader the selection of adjacent colors. Conversely, a smaller number results in the Magic Wand making a narrower selection of adjacent colors.

A value of zero results in a selection of contiguous pixels that are all the same color as the target pixel. With a value of 20, clicking a red target pixel with a value of 55 selects all contiguous pixels in a range of values extending from red 35 to red 75. (If you're comparing selection behavior with Photoshop, you'll notice a slight difference because in Photoshop a Tolerance setting of 20 selects all contiguous pixels in a tighter range of values extending from red 45 to red 65.)

Magic Wand Smoothing setting

The Smoothing setting of the Magic Wand option determines to what degree the edge of the selection should be smoothed. This is similar to anti-aliasing. (Anti-aliasing dithers the edges of shapes and lines so that they look smoother on-screen.) The options are Pixels, Rough, Normal, and Smooth. Assuming that the Threshold setting remains constant, the Smoothing settings differ as follows:

- **Pixels:** Clings to the rectangular edges of each pixel bordering similar colors.
- **Rough:** With this setting, the edges of the selection are even more angular than with Pixels.
- **Normal:** Results in a selection that's somewhere between Rough and Smooth.
- **Smooth:** Delivers a selection with more rounded edges.

Tracing bitmaps

You use the Trace bitmap command to convert an imported image from a bitmap to a native Flash vector graphic with discrete, editable areas of color. This unlinks the image from the original symbol in the library (and also from the Bitmap Swatch in the Color panel). You can create interesting bitmap-based art with this command. However, if your intention is to preserve the look of the original bitmap with maximum fidelity, you must work with the settings — and you will most likely find that the original bitmap is actually smaller in file size than the traced vector image. Figure 9.41 includes a selected bitmap image on the left and the final vector image that resulted from the settings shown in the Trace Bitmap dialog box on the right.

FIGURE 9.41

Select a bitmap (left) and choose settings in the Trace Bitmap dialog box to define the final vector image (right).

TIP The Trace Bitmap dialog box includes a handy Preview button that enables you to test settings before you apply them. The preview is rendered more quickly than the final trace conversion, and using this option saves you from having to use the Undo command and then reopen the Trace Bitmap dialog box each time you want to try a different setting.

To trace a bitmap, follow these steps:

1. **Use the Selection tool to select the bitmap that you want to trace.** It can be in Edit mode or directly on the Stage.
2. **Choose Modify ➪ Bitmap ➪ Trace Bitmap to open the Trace Bitmap dialog box and set the options according to your needs:**
   - **Color threshold:** This option controls the number of colors in your traced bitmap. It limits the number of colors by averaging the colors based on the criteria chosen in Color threshold

and Minimum area. Color threshold compares RGB color values of adjacent pixels to the value entered. If the difference is lower than the value entered, adjacent pixels are considered the same color. By making this computation for each pixel within the bitmap, Flash averages the colors. A lower Color threshold delivers more colors in the final vector graphic derived from the traced bitmap. The range is between 0 and 500, with a default setting of 100.

- **Minimum area:** This value is the radius, measured in pixels, which Color threshold uses to describe adjacent pixels when comparing pixels to determine what color to assign to the center pixel. The range is between 1 and 1,000, with the default setting being 8.

- **Curve fit:** This value determines how smoothly outlines are drawn. Select Very Tight if the shapes in the bitmap are complex and angular. If the curves are smooth, select Very Smooth.

- **Corner threshold:** This setting determines how sharp edges are handled; choose Many Corners to retain edges and Few Corners to smooth the edges.

3. **Click OK.** Flash traces the bitmap, and the original pixel information is converted to vector shapes. If the bitmap is complex, this may take a while. Depending on the settings you have chosen, the final look of the traced graphic can vary between being very close to the original or very abstracted.

TIP   If your objective is for your traced bitmap to closely resemble the original bitmap, set a low Color threshold and a low Minimum area. You'll also want to set the Curve fit to Pixels and the Corner threshold to Many Corners. Be aware that using these settings may drastically slow the tracing process for complex bitmaps and result in larger file sizes. If animated, such bitmaps may also retard the frame rate dramatically.

As shown in Figure 9.42, the traced bitmap can vary in how closely it resembles the original bitmap. The image in the center was traced with lower settings to achieve a more detailed image: Color threshold of 25, Minimum area of 2 pixels, Curve fit of Pixels, and Corner threshold of Many Corners. The image on the right was traced with higher settings to create a more abstract graphic image: Color threshold of 300, Minimum area of 25 pixels, Curve fit of Very Smooth, and Corner threshold of Few Corners.

FIGURE 9.42

Bitmap images can be traced to create different styles of vector graphics by using low settings (center) or high settings (right).

CAUTION   If you drag a bitmap from the Library panel onto the Stage and then attempt to acquire the bitmap fill by first tracing the bitmap and then clicking with the Eyedropper tool, be careful of how selection affects the results. If the traced bitmap is still selected, clicking with the Eyedropper tool acquires the nearest color and replaces the entire traced bitmap with a solid fill of the acquired color. If the traced bitmap is not selected, the Eyedropper tool simply acquires the nearest solid color and loads it into the fill color chip.

Working with Drawing Objects and Combine Object Commands

Drawing objects were introduced with Flash 8 to make the drawing environment a little more user friendly. In older versions of Flash, you had to take special care to avoid unexpected results when shapes overlapped on the same layer (as described in the section on working with compound shapes). There are times when compound shapes can be helpful, but most people will find it easier to work with drawing objects. If you turn the Object Drawing toggle on (in the Options area of the Tools panel) at any time, it remains on until you turn it back off. This makes it easy to draw in the mode that suits you best without having to remember to turn the toggle on or off all the time.

> **TIP** If you draw a shape with the Object Drawing toggle turned off and decide that you would prefer to work with a drawing object rather than a raw shape, simply select the shape and use the Modify ⇨ Combine Objects ⇨ Union command to convert the shape into a drawing object. Conversely, drawing objects can be reverted to raw shapes by using the Modify ⇨ Ungroup or the Modify ⇨ Break Apart command.

In the simplest terms, drawing objects are containers for raw shapes. They cannot hold animation (like symbols can) or even other drawing objects. If you try to add a drawing object to the Stage when you have another drawing object open in Edit mode, you see a warning dialog box when you return to the Main Timeline. As shown in Figure 9.43, Flash automatically converts the original drawing object into a group so that the new drawing object can be nested inside it.

FIGURE 9.43

Drawing objects cannot contain animation, symbols, or other drawing objects — they are intended as holders for raw shapes only.

If you have worked in Flash before, you may be wondering why you would even bother to use a drawing object instead of just using a simple group to manage raw shapes. Like groups, drawing objects do not show up in the document library and they cannot have filters applied to them. However, unlike groups, you can modify drawing objects without having to open them in Edit mode, and you can animate them by using Classic motion tweens without first converting them into symbols. Another key reason to use drawing objects is to take advantage of the Combine Objects commands (as shown in Figure 9.44). These commands will be familiar to anyone who has used the Pathfinder panel in Illustrator:

- **Union:** Merges the selected objects into one combined object.
- **Intersect:** Deletes everything except the area of the topmost object where it overlaps the lower objects.
- **Punch:** Deletes the topmost object and punches out the area where it overlaps other objects.
- **Crop:** Deletes everything except the areas of the lower objects where the upper object overlaps.

FIGURE 9.44

Two drawing objects (far left) combined, using various Combine Objects commands to get different final results (from left to right): Union, Intersect, Punch, Crop

There are only a few other things to keep in mind when working with drawing objects:

- You can modify drawing objects with the Selection and Transformation tools in the same way as raw shapes, but you cannot select the fill and stroke inside a drawing object individually unless you open it in Edit mode.

- You can change the appearance of the fill and stroke separately just by selecting the object and using any of the swatches menus, but if you try to apply the Expand Fill command to a drawing object that contains a stroke, you see the stroke disappear unless you have ungrouped or broken apart (into raw shapes) the drawing object or opened it in Edit mode.

- The selection highlight for drawing objects and groups selected on the Stage look exactly alike, but you can tell what type of item you are working with by checking the item description in the Properties panel. Groups and drawing objects share some characteristics, but they are *not* the same thing.

- The Lock Fill option doesn't work with drawing objects in the same way that it works with other filled shapes. Although you can use the Lock Fill command to create a fill that visually continues from one object to another, you will find when you try to apply the Gradient Transform tool that you have to adjust the fills individually for each object.

CROSS-REF As described in Chapter 5, "Drawing in Flash," you also have the option of creating shape primitives by using the Oval Primitive and Rectangle Primitive tools. Shape primitives have many of the same advantages as drawing objects, but they can be modified by using settings in the Properties panel — including handy controls for rounded corners and precise curves.

CAUTION If you try to open a shape primitive in Edit mode, you see a warning dialog box with the option of converting the shape primitive into a drawing object (if you say OK, you lose access to the special settings in the Properties panel).

Working with Compound Shapes

If you have been drawing and modifying artwork in Flash with the Object Drawing option turned off, you've probably noticed that Flash has a unique way of handling lines and fills that reside on the same layer of your document. Items of the same color merge, whereas items of a different color replace or cut out other items where they overlap. Flash treats lines or strokes as separate items than fills, so these can be selected and moved or modified independently of each other, even if they are the same color. Figure 9.45 shows how Flash allows lines and fills to be selected individually, even if they are the same color.

TIP By double-clicking an element, you can select all the related segments. This works for selecting the stroke and fill of a shape or for selecting connected sections of a segmented line (such as the four sides of a rectangle).

FIGURE 9.45

A gray oval fill with a gray stroke may not appear to have a discrete outline, but Flash allows these two elements to be selected separately.

Both lines and fills are divided into segments at points of intersection. Figure 9.46 shows a fill split into two independent shapes by drawing a line on top of it (top) or modified by merging with a fill of the same color and being cut out by a fill of a different color (bottom).

FIGURE 9.46

A fill split by an overlapping line drawn on the same layer (top). Two fills of the same color merge into a compound shape when they intersect on the same layer (bottom).

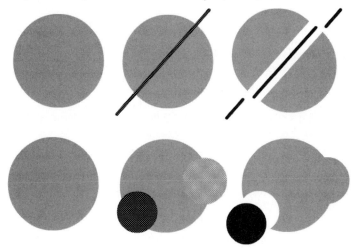

These behaviors can be destructive or helpful to your artwork, depending on how you manage individual elements. The key point to remember is that primitive shapes cannot be overlapped on the same layer while deselected without affecting each other. If items are grouped or converted into drawing objects or symbols, they remain independent and are not compounded or deleted by intersection with other items. Items on layers are also autonomous and do not merge with or erase items that exist on other layers.

You can move lines or fills over other primitive shapes without affecting them, as long as they remain selected. As soon as they are deselected, they intersect or merge with adjacent primitive shapes on the same layer. Figure 9.47 illustrates the process of moving a selected shape over and then off of another shape while keeping the two shapes independent (top), and the result if the shape is deselected while it is overlapping another shape, before being reselected and moved, to create a compound shape (bottom).

FIGURE 9.47

A shape moved across another shape while being continuously selected (top) compared to a shape that is deselected while on top of another shape, and then reselected and moved (bottom)

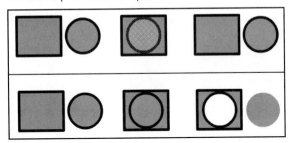

Editing with Find and Replace

Although you can use the Movie Explorer to search for some elements in a project file so that they can be modified, it doesn't automate updates in the same speedy way that the Find and Replace panel, shown in Figure 9.48, does.

NOTE   **Find and Replace is opened from the Edit window rather than from the Window menu, but it does open a real panel and not just a dialog box. Although the Find and Replace panel takes up a lot of room on your desktop, you could dock it with other panels for quick access if you prefer that to using the menu or shortcut keys.**

If you have used the Find and Replace feature in any other application (even in a basic text-editing program), you will be familiar with the main buttons in the Find and Replace panel (Find Next, Find All, Replace, and Replace All). Open the Find and Replace panel by choosing Edit ➪ Find and Replace in the application menu (Ctrl+F/⌘+F).

The real benefits of using this panel become clearer when you look at the items you can select to search for; these include:

- **Text:** Search for words, partial words, or whole paragraphs in text fields, frames, layers, parameters, strings, or in ActionScript in your current project or current scene.

- **Font:** Search for fonts by name, style, and even size, within your current project or scene.

- **Color:** Pick a color from the popup swatches (or enter a hexadecimal value in the field) to search for fills, strokes, or text where a specific color is used in the current project or scene.

- **Symbol/Sound/Video/Bitmap:** Use the handy drop-down list that lists all symbols (or sounds, or video, or bitmaps) used in your current project to pick a symbol to search for and a symbol to use as a replacement.

As you select each item in the For: drop-down list, options relevant to that item become available in the panel. These options give you very precise control over the type of edits that you want to make. Now that replacing a color or font, or even a specific word in your entire project file, is as easy as making a few quick selections in the Find and Replace panel, those dreaded last-minute revisions might almost seem fun.

FIGURE 9.48

The Find and Replace panel makes revisions so easy, they're almost fun.

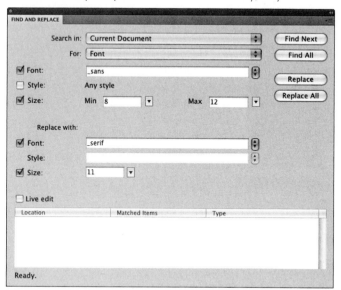

> **CAUTION**   Although any effects or transformations that you have applied to a symbol instance (and any formatting you have applied to text) should be preserved if you change it by using the Find and Replace panel, you have to verify that the newly inserted content appears as you expect it to. If a font is much larger, it might not fit into your layout, or if a replacement bitmap is much larger or smaller than the original, you may have to make some manual adjustments to get everything polished. These are the same kinds of adjustments you would expect to make if you used the Swap symbol feature.

Using the History Panel

The History panel found in the Other Panels list (Ctrl+F10/⌘+F10) enables you to escape the linear limitations of Undo/Redo. As you work in your project file, the History panel records your editing steps in a sequential list (see Figure 9.49). The History panel stores steps taken in the active project file during the current editing session only. It does not store steps from the last time you had a project file open or from other files edited during the same session. You *can* save and move steps from one file or session to another, but it requires you to use some of the special features of the History panel, described later in this section.

> **NOTE**   Flash gives you the option of using Document-level Undo (which creates one History/ Undo stack for all the items in a current session) or the legacy-style Object-level Undo (which creates a unique History/Undo stack for key editing areas of the Flash authoring environment: Stage, Movie Clip timelines, and the ActionScript panel). The default is set to Document-level Undo, but if you find it helpful to be able to step back through Movie Clip edits individually, you can change this setting in the General section of Flash Preferences. To access the object-level Undo stack, you must open a Movie Clip (not an instance) in Edit mode.

FIGURE 9.49

The History panel lists steps taken as a file is authored or edited.

Non-sequential step selections

Undo/Redo slider | History options menu

Editing Text

Replay steps button

Save steps (as a command) button

Undone steps (greyed out)

Elements in current worksession   Copy steps (to clipboard) button

CAUTION Making changes to your Undo style or number of saved steps in Flash Preferences clears the History panel, deleting all the Undo steps for your current session.

You can use the History panel as a reminder of the steps taken to create a special graphic effect, or you can use it as a nonlinear authoring control. Should you need to get back to a specific step in your authoring session, you can use Undo (Ctrl+Z/⌘+Z) over and over and over, or you can simply open the History panel and drag the edit pointer on the left side of the panel upward to go back in time until you reach the point at which you want to jump back into authoring. As long as you don't make any edits at an earlier point in the History list, you can easily scroll forward again if you need to redo your steps — without wearing out the Ctrl+Y/⌘+Y keys! However, if you undo a step (or a series of steps) and then make changes to your project file, you can no longer redo the steps in the History panel. This is where the History panel does behave a little like a time machine — as long as you don't change anything, you can jump backward and forward in time, but as soon as you change something, you lose the option of going "back to the future."

TIP Click to the left of a step in the History panel to jump to that point without scrolling. All steps listed after the point that you click will be undone and grayed out until you scroll forward again (or click to the left of an item closer to the bottom of the list).

The options menu and the buttons along the bottom of the History panel are the keys to the more advanced editing tasks that you can accomplish when you take your steps a step farther. (Refer to Figure 9.49 for callouts on the location of History panel controls.)

Replay Steps

The Replay Steps control repeat or reapply a series of sequential or nonsequential steps in your current History list.

1. **Select sequential items by dragging or by Shift+clicking the text labels in the list.** Select nonsequential items by Ctrl+clicking/⌘+clicking.

2. With a step (or series of steps) selected, you can apply the step(s) to a new item — by selecting the item with the Selection tool and clicking the Replay button or choosing Replay Steps from the options menu.

All currently selected steps are applied (in order) to the item, and a new step labeled "Replay Steps" is listed in the History panel. You can use the Replay Steps item in the History list to apply the same steps again without having to select the original steps individually.

Copy Steps

This command enables you to move steps from one document to another. Here's how it works:

1. Select steps from your History panel list (as described in the previous section).
2. Choose Copy Steps from the options menu.
3. In the Flash document where you want to reuse the steps, select an item to which you want to apply the steps.
4. Choose Edit ➪ Paste in Center (Ctrl+V/⌘+V).

The editing steps copied from your original file are applied to the item in your current file and a new item is added to the History panel, labeled Paste Steps.

Clear History

This is a helpful command to use if you want to start from a clean slate before performing a series of editing steps that you plan to save. Clear History deletes all the listings in the History panel of your current document. You can't undo this choice, but you will see a Warning dialog box that gives you the chance to change your mind before it's too late. (Closing a Flash document also clears the History list.) The number of steps listed in the History panel can be limited by the *Undo levels* set in the General Flash Preferences dialog box. The default setting is 100, but it can be set as high as 300 or as low as 2. Every item recorded in the History panel eats up some memory and disk space, so choose the lowest setting that suits your authoring style.

History View

You should leave this setting on Default unless you plan to use the History panel as a tool for helping you write new JavaScript commands. This is a very exciting potential use of the History panel, but it is beyond the scope of this book. If you are familiar with JavaScript, you can try different View settings to get more information that helps you deconstruct the steps in an editing workflow.

Save As Command

If you're not quite ready to start writing your own JavaScript from scratch, this is a terrific shortcut that makes it easy to save and reuse custom editing workflows.

1. Select the step(s) from the History panel that you want to save and reuse.
2. Choose Save As Command from the options menu (or click the small disk icon at the bottom right of the History panel).
3. In the Save as Command dialog box, give the command a meaningful name. You might call the steps used to create a fancy custom-type treatment "Headline style."

   By the magic of Flash, your custom command now appears in the Command menu list.

4. **You can apply your specific editing steps in any document by selecting an item and choosing Commands ➪ Headline style (or whatever commands you have created and named).**

The options at the top of the application Command menu give you some controls for managing your custom commands and for using commands from other sources. The Get More Commands menu item loads a link to the online Flash Exchange, where you can find new commands contributed by other Flash developers (look for JavaScript Flash or .jsfl files). If you download a custom command script, you can use the Run Command menu option to browse to the .jsfl file and apply it to an item in your current project. The possibilities are wide open.

WEB RESOURCE **We'd like to know what you think about this chapter. Visit** www.flashsupport.com/feedback **to fill out an online form with your comments.**

Summary

- After you've mastered the basic drawing tools in Flash, there are innumerable methods for modifying artwork to create custom effects.

- You can use the Eyedropper, Ink Bottle, and Paint Bucket tools together to select and apply fill and stroke styles to multiple items or to swap styles between items.

- You can use the Gradient Transform tool to modify gradient fills and bitmap fills for precise alignment and appearance inside individual shapes.

- The new 3D tools (3D Rotation and 3D Translation) make it easier to simulate 3D space by providing intuitive controls for rotating and shifting Movie Clip symbols along the x, y, and z-axis (available only in Flash CS4 targeting Flash Player 10 or later).

- The Perspective angle and Vanishing point settings (available in the Properties panel when a 3D symbol is selected) control the view or camera lens for your entire Flash movie (but only have an effect on 3D symbols).

- Drawing objects share some characteristics with raw shapes, groups, and symbols, but they have a unique role in Flash authoring.

- Shape primitives must be converted into drawing objects if you want to open them in Edit mode, but this workflow removes access to the settings available in the Properties panel that make it easy to modify Oval or Rectangle primitives.

- Drawing objects and shape primitives, like groups and symbols, do not interact when they overlap on the same layer. If you want to merge or crop drawing objects, the Combine Objects commands provide some options that will be familiar to people who have used pathfinder options in other vector drawing programs.

- The Free Transform tool has two powerful options that you can apply to shapes or drawing objects only, as well as two options that restrict the Free Transform behavior to make it easier to achieve specific tasks.

- Flash organizes artwork with specific parameters, and you can use the Modify ➪ Arrange commands to help define the stacking order when you're working with similar items on the same layer.

- You can use the Break Apart command to convert bitmaps and text so you can edit them like shapes to create special effects.

- You use the Trace bitmap command to convert imported bitmaps into vector graphics with varying degrees of detail.

Part III

Creating Animation and Effects

Now that you're comfortable with the Flash tools and making static graphic symbols and groups, it's time to move on to creating animated elements and dynamic effects. Chapter 10 introduces some of the fundamental production and planning issues that you need to consider when designing animated elements. Chapter 11 gives you all the information you need to start working with time-based content. Learn to create frame-by-frame and tweened animation (including the new Flash CS4 object-based motion tweens), and how to use Movie Clips to control display of content on multiple timelines. Meet the new Motion Editor and learn how to use it to edit property keyframes and custom easing curves. Chapter 12 is dedicated to introducing the creative possibilities of the filters and blend modes available in Flash CS4, as well as coverage of how to create mask and guide layers when you need them. If you are interested in character animation, Chapter 13 provides comprehensive coverage of character animation and the tricks that professional animators use to create engaging and optimized cartoons that can go beyond the Web. You will also get an introduction to the amazing new IK tools in Flash CS4 that bring the power of inverse kinematics to the Flash authoring environment for the first time!

Chapter 10

Animation Strategies

Have you ever wondered what makes some animation so compelling and other animation so dull? Regardless of the content of a site, or even the style of the site's graphics, some animation is engaging, whereas other animation is annoying or even pathetic — we've all seen it, limping or flashing across our screens at one time or another.

Of course, your response to animation is partly determined by what you're expecting from an interface (sometimes you want diversion, and other times you want to find information — fast!). Most designers are aware of the issues of usability and relevance they should consider when adding animation to an interface (whether they decide to ignore them or not). But, what happens after you've done all your audience research and content planning and you decide that animation would be appropriate for your project?

The next step should be fun, right? Unfortunately, unless you have the privilege of working with a skilled animator, you're actually entering one of the most complex and challenging areas of visual design. Although most people recognize "good" animation when they see it, the leap from *appreciating* motion to *designing* motion is difficult, even for people who have natural aptitude.

The good news is that you possess an innate understanding of physics, even if you've never taken a science class in your life — you know what to expect when you bounce a ball. But can you interpret the ball's motion and re-create it frame by frame in an animation? The challenge of designing motion is translating daily experiences into a time-based, 2D environment. Your eyes and brain tell you if something isn't right, but how do you know what can be done to correct it? The ability to analyze perceptions that we normally take for granted is the true skill of animation and motion graphics design.

With experience, animators can intuitively finesse the many visual factors that effectively communicate motion — even bending the rules to suit their personal animation styles or to convey specific atmospheres and characters. But, the first step toward making better animation is to become familiar with some of the fundamental concepts and laws that govern matter in the real world.

Establishing Ground Rules

No matter what the style or purpose your animation ultimately has, you'll need to establish guidelines for yourself if you want to create an engaging and convincing experience for the user. This may feel limiting at first, but these self-imposed ground rules make content more meaningful to your audience. The most commonly recognized example of structured, shared expression is music. Even the wildest music is based on an underlying structure of notes and timing (or else it isn't exactly music).

Structure is also one of the key characteristics that shape great books or even movies. Consider the difference between a private journal and a well-crafted story, or the difference between a home movie and an engrossing film. This doesn't mean that you're stuck repeating the same old narrative over and over again or that you have to follow someone else's rules. But if you have free license to create any experience for your audience, it's even more important to decide on the rules that will guide your designs so that all the elements and animations support your idea.

Artists who prefer not to follow the most commonly used conventions must work even harder to establish their own signature style — or to create content defined by the consistent choices they make. As in music, the possible choices for the basic aspects of animation are practically infinite — a little faster, a little slower, spinning or bouncing or wiggling or jumping or fading or . . . you get the idea. The guidelines that you establish for each project help you make the right decisions. There isn't an exact formula for "good animation" (the variables are too broad), but after you create some rules for yourself, you'll be able to make the choices that best support your goals for a specific animation.

Defining Variables

To establish guidelines that support your design process, you first have to analyze the choices that are relevant to the content. Is the tone of the project peaceful, quiet, fast, slick, funny, scary? Try to be as specific as you can about the approach that best suits your content, and then try to make consistent choices that support that description. Some of the questions that may help you to frame the basic elements of your project include:

What kind of motion suits the style of the project or personality of a character?

How does color communicate your theme or idea?

How does sound support the atmosphere or character?

If you try to make a design that is "all of the above," it will end up being too vague and confusing to keep anyone interested. One of the hardest things to learn as a designer (and to communicate to clients) is that if you try to make a site (or story) that is a little bit of everything, in an attempt to suit all audiences, you only weaken your message and your branding, and/or dilute the experience for everyone. The very best designs are consistent enough that they allow anyone to understand them (or at least get what they're about), and specific enough in style that they have a memorable personality and attitude.

Of course, there are some things that do appeal to many people — humor or surprise, well-executed visual complexity, engaging and functional navigation. But even these elements can be too generic; they need to be added to your design with a specific (and hopefully original) style. After you decide what style is appropriate for the project, you can begin to plan the elements that will create the experience for the audience.

Considering these factors for every project may seem like over thinking, but try to see how often you can apply at least some of the questions we outline in this section to really focus your design strategy. After a few tries, it should be much easier, and you'll be on your way to establishing a personal style that you can adapt to different projects.

The environment

What planet are you on? As you begin planning and building a virtual environment, even in a 2D space, thinking of it as a real place is helpful. Decide what kind of place you want it to be and what characteristics will help the audience to understand where they are.

Is this a soft, fuzzy world where everything floats gently as it moves, or is this a hard, metallic world where things are heavy and make fast, abrupt movements, or maybe it is even a liquid world where things are very smooth and quiet, with organic movement? These are extreme examples; obviously, the possibilities are endless. Try to include all the factors that define an environment as you experience it visually:

How light or dark is it?

Is everything very distinct or blurred and layered?

How crowded or open is the space?

How quickly can things move?

How much does gravity affect objects?

Is space (depth) limited or endless?

The main thing to keep in mind is that all the elements and movement that you add to the design should help the audience locate themselves in the world you create. Aside from natural environmental analogies, try to consider historical and cultural context, too. Is the environment meant to have a retro feel or a postmodern feel? Is it influenced by multicultural elements, or defined only by a very specific subculture?

If you find yourself thinking, "Well, all I really want is to make a cool site that the audience will like," then remember the point we made previously: The more specific you can be about the kind of environment you want to create, the better chance you have of making a design that the audience will be interested in. Most of us are pretty jaded viewers by now, and something that looks trendy or resembles a jumble of many other things we've seen before is not likely to hold our attention very long.

The materials

As you consider the overall environment that you want to create, you also have to decide on the smaller details that will be consistent with your idea. Even if you're working purely with Flash strokes and fills, trying to imagine the kinds of materials that would be most appropriate for your graphic elements can be helpful. Do you want elements to be jagged and hard or fuzzy or squishy? How much volume do shapes or graphic elements have? Are any of the items transparent? Considering these questions can help you make decisions about line styles and perhaps even colors, but most important, these decisions can help you design motion that is convincing and appropriate for each item.

If your materials are soft, motion will include a lot of stretching and squashing and maybe even jiggling. If you want materials to seem hard, motion will probably be smoother, with sharper, cleaner transitions. If objects are heavy, they will have a lot more inertia. If objects are very light, they need to move in a way that conveys weightlessness. Some of these types of motion are hard to describe, but if you can visualize them clearly (or even better, find examples in real life), you'll have an easier time planning and making your animation.

Even if you decide that your "materials" are actually best kept very flat and graphic (such as construction paper or felt cutouts), then you can focus on that kind of look and avoid throwing in gradient fills or shiny highlights. The most important thing is to simply have a clear concept in mind that enables you to make (and explain) the design choices that best support your content.

The motion

Choosing to add animation to an item can be a quick decision, but finding the right kind of motion to add can take a lot more time. If you've made some of the decisions we suggested so far in this chapter, you'll have a much easier time narrowing down the style of motion that you want to add.

Flash provides some great options for controlling the speed and pattern of motion, but until you have a clear "flight path" mapped out, you won't be able to use these tools effectively. There are few things worse than spending a lot of time creating an animation, only to realize that the motion lacks personality or seems meaningless. Most ineffective animation is the result of poor planning. This is one area of design where endless options can work against you. It can be fun, and helpful for learning, to play with different kinds of movement in Flash, but this isn't the best way to develop a project, unless you're already an experienced animator. "Designing" animation by simply throwing together some random tweens and timeline effects is the visual equivalent of whistling tunelessly or absentmindedly strumming a guitar — entertaining for the person doing it, very annoying for everyone else!

Although experienced animators develop an intuitive sense of timing and rhythm, designers who are just starting to experiment with motion will have a better chance of success if they have a very specific example to refer to. References for animation (or styles of movement) can be found almost anywhere in the real world — you just have to observe carefully, and, if possible, document the motion with video or a sequence of stills. Often, the documentation will surprise you. It wasn't until cameras were used to photograph sequences of horses running that artists realized there were moments during their trot cycles that all four hooves were off the ground.

These are some resources that we have found inspiring as motion references:

- **Eadweard Muybridge:** Eadweard Muybridge is a photographer who did some of the first "stop-motion" images ever made. His classic photographic sequences can be found in books published in the Dover Pictorial Archive Series (Dover Publications). The National Museum of American History provides some background for and examples of Muybridge's work on its Web site at `http://americanhistory.si.edu/muybridge/index.htm`.

- **Lawrence Jordan:** Lawrence Jordan created strange and wonderful animated films by using cutout graphics and stop-frame animation. In his 40-year career, he produced a body of work that has been influential for many artists working in new media. You can learn more about him in an essay in the *Bright Lights Film Journal* at `www.brightlightsfilm.com/30/lawrencejordan.html`.

- **Bruce Conner:** Bruce Conner is a visionary and groundbreaking artist who works in a variety of mediums. He was honored with an exhibit at the Walker Art Center in 1999–2000, and they have produced the most comprehensive Catalog on his work to date. You can find out more about Bruce Conner on the Walker Art Center Web site at `www.walkerart.org/programs/vaexhibconner.html`.

- **Rose Pietrovito:** This quiet Canadian designer creates fresh, deceptively simple Flash animation through her company Dzinenmotion. She has won numerous awards and has been featured in publications internationally. For a hit of inspiration and some wonderful examples of how effective clean design, clever motion, and relevant sound can be, explore Rose's portfolio at `www.dzinenmotion.com`.

- **Erik Natzke:** An early Flash pioneer who has continued to push the envelope and innovate new ways of creating motion graphics and abstract digital "paintings" with ActionScript. You might find Natzke at a Flash conference near you, but you can check in on his creative endeavors at `http://jot.eriknatzke.com`.

WEB RESOURCE If you are interested in seeing work by Bruce Conner and other influential experimental filmmakers on DVD, a good source is Canyon Cinema: `http://canyoncinema.com`.

Of course, you probably also have examples in mind of animation that you've seen and admired. Looking at other animators' work can be a great way to analyze "how it's done," but you should always aspire to develop a unique style rather than copy someone else's directly. The history of animation is rich and full of many examples of diverse styles that have been effective. By looking back at the work done by great animators and filmmakers, you're likely to find something that inspires you and offers new possibilities for the ways that you can render images and motion on a 2D screen.

Adding Personality

As many great animations have shown, any object can be given its own personality. No medium is really quite as effective as animation for enabling you to give life to the characters that would otherwise stay in your imagination. Even if you don't aspire to be a character animator in the strictest sense, any element that is animated within your Flash projects should have some recognizable personality. You don't have to add eyes and a mouth to an object in order for it to be expressive. In fact, the main expression of any animated element should be conveyed by the way it moves, even more strongly than by the exact composition of the graphic.

You can add personality to a line or a letter as easily as you can add personality to a cartoon character. A common exercise done in art schools to help students realize the expressive power of abstract lines and shapes is to give the students a list of atmospheres or emotions that they have to interpret and communicate with purely abstract lines and forms. The most surprising thing about this exercise is how similar most people's drawings turn out to be. Although the drawings do not include any concrete symbols or signs, students realize how concise their shared visual language really is (even if they aren't always conscious of it).

As an animator, you can draw on the common visual vocabulary to communicate a great deal to your audience without having to spell it out. Most people would probably recognize angry movement or joyous movement if they saw it. Certainly, some personal and cultural variations in interpretation exist, but the basic recognition is usually very consistent. As with some of the other topics we've described so far in this chapter, this is an aspect of motion design that may not seem relevant to every project at first. However, if you take the time to consider how you want to connect with your audience, you'll probably be able to pin down a fairly specific emotional tone or personality that you want your animation to have.

CROSS-REF Flash animator Felix Stumpf describes his process for planning and creating atmospheric Flash animation in his tutorial in Chapter 13, "Character Animation Techniques." One of his tools for testing concepts is to create a moodboard with rough animation and sample music that he can then use as a stylistic guide for the final project.

The next step is to observe and experiment to find the kinds of motion that best represent the personality or tone that you want the audience to recognize. Some of the factors that you can consider when designing expressive motion include the following:

■ **Speed:** How fast or how slowly does an object move? Does it accelerate or decelerate?

- **Timing and rhythm:** How does the object's movement loop or change over time? Finding music to help with the timing and pace of an animation is often helpful.

- **Consistency or irregularity:** How much variety is there in an object's movement? Does it follow a repeated pattern, or a random path of motion?

- **Anticipation or surprise:** Does the object give some visual foreshadowing as it moves, or does it make sudden, unexpected movements?

- **Freedom or constraint:** How large or small are the movements that the object can make? Does it move all around your composition or stay in a very restricted area? How much of the object moves at any one time?

The "meaning" of these various kinds of movement can be debated as much as the "meaning" of various colors. However, it is safe to assume that, overall, enough consistency among viewers exists on the meaning of certain kinds of motion for it to be an effective way of communicating the character of an object. If you're not sure how your audience will read a certain motion, just test it out on a few people — show them what you're working on, and then ask them what emotion or personality *they* think the object has. If enough people recognize the mood that you want your animation to have, you succeeded! If most people are confused or have very different responses, you probably need to simplify your animation and clarify what you're trying to communicate. It's not likely that most people would be able to read that an object has slightly low self-esteem but is feeling optimistic. However, most people recognize movement consistent with extreme shyness or joy (or any other simple and exaggerated emotion).

Exaggeration is the foundation of the art of animation. Define the kind of movement that may communicate a particular emotion to your audience, and then see how far you can push it. In some cases, you may want very overt movements, and in other cases, you may want more conservative or subtle movements; by pushing the boundaries, you can assess your options and find the right balance for a particular character or object.

Keeping Ideas Fresh

Some of the greatest modern works of art and music are based on the concept of *permutation* — the process of exploring all the possibilities within a specific, usually limited, group of elements. Permutation of a limited set of options can yield more surprising or unique results than unlimited options because it forces you to work within defined boundaries that enable the content of your work to influence the final result in ways that you may not have previously considered.

For example, if you allow yourself to choose any colors from a full palette, this may seem very liberating. But the truth is, you'll probably choose colors (or at least color combinations) that are familiar or comfortable for you, without even giving some new options a real chance. You can achieve much more inventive uses of color by forcing yourself to work with a truly random selection of colors (or to create an effective design with a more limited palette). You might be surprised by how well pink and brown go together, or by how much you can do with just a few colors. At the very least, experimenting with randomness or intentional limitation in a design can help open up new possibilities and keep your work from getting stale.

Manipulating Perception and Illusion

As you spend time analyzing motion in the real world and motion in more stylized animations, you will become more aware of some of the tricks that your eyes can play on you. Animators, like magicians, know how to take advantage of people's often-unreliable perception to create illusions. By understanding how the audience's eyes and minds put visual information together to "see" things, clever performers and designers are able to convince the audience that they're seeing something that may not actually be happening.

Another interesting phenomenon that makes an animator's job a little easier is referred to as *suspension of disbelief*. This is something you participate in whenever you really *want to believe* you're seeing something — children are often the best at this. When you push doubt aside, your eyes can be very forgiving as your brain works even harder to compensate for any gaps that may spoil the illusion or the spectacle that you want to believe in.

Some visual tricks in animation have been used so consistently that people now expect them as conventions, instead of seeing them as poorly rendered versions of a real-life motion. Most people recognize that a swirling cyclone of lines, with hands and feet or other objects occasionally popping out of it, is usually a fight. The oval blur or circular scribble at the bottom of a character's legs is not a cloud, but, in fact, their feet spinning extra fast. Lines radiating from an object don't mean that it is spiky; instead, they can mean that it is shiny or hot or even smelly. (One old standby cartoon convention is a light bulb appearing over a character's head when he or she suddenly gets an idea.) Figure 10.1 shows a sequence by animator Richard Bazley that uses the simple but effective technique of blurred lines to simulate motion that is faster than the eye can see. This classic device can be modified to show rockets blasting off or wind rushing by or any object moving so quickly that it becomes a blur.

FIGURE 10.1

Blurred lines in an animation effectively communicate the idea of wind or fast-moving elements rushing by.

© 2002 Richard Bazley

ON the CD-ROM We have included .swf files for most of the examples we discuss in this chapter on the CD-ROM. Because the figures show only a few frames from an animation, you can get a better idea of how a motion plays by reviewing the files in the `ch10` folder of the CD-ROM. We thank animators Richard Bazley, Tom Winkler, and Sandro Corsaro for kindly sharing some of their examples with us.

There are innumerable examples of cartoon tricks, but the main thing to keep in mind is that you don't have to draw every detail of a movement to make it convincing. Instead, it's better to find ways that you can exaggerate the motion to make it more expressive. A well-executed illusion saves you time drawing and also makes your animation more fun to watch.

Viewpoint, framing, and depth

By thinking of the Flash stage area as a camera viewfinder rather than as a sketch pad, you can start crafting the various scenes in your animation to have some of the same expressive qualities as shots from a well-edited film. The ability to manipulate the viewpoint is one of the strongest storytelling devices available to filmmakers and animators alike. Audiences have come to accept (and expect) seeing things from new angles and perspectives. Screen images have evolved from the basic wide-angle, theater-audience perspective of early film to the spinning, time-defying, 360-degree *Matrix* views of action — don't be afraid to push your "camera" beyond the limits of normal human perception. Choosing how to frame animation can have as much of an effect on your audience as the actual content in each scene. The traditional bird's-eye or mouse's-eye reconsideration of viewpoint is as effective in a digital design as it is in sketches or drawings. Try to use your content to inspire a framing strategy that adds both interest and meaning to your designs.

Depth is another key element to consider when composing a scene and choosing a viewpoint. Traditional animators are cautious to avoid awkward line intersections caused by overlapping elements. When the lines from two different elements bump into each other unintentionally, it can make a drawing look flat — this is known as a *tangent*. Tangents interrupt the illusion of depth created by scaling and layering elements in a composition. The main thing to avoid is an overly busy layout that may confuse the viewer's understanding of the picture plane. Try to keep elements that are meant to be behind or in front of other elements from looking as though they are joined or existing uncomfortably in the same space. Add a little more separation between elements to maintain visual clarity.

With careful planning, overlapping elements add depth to your designs. Notice in Figure 10.2 that overlapping the larger figure on the right with the border helps it jump into the foreground, whereas overlapping the smaller figure on the left makes it hard to tell which element is supposed to be in front.

Another common device used to add depth to a scene is to choose a viewpoint that enables you to add a natural frame or border around the image. By giving viewers a reference point for where they are located in the plane of the image, you can exaggerate the feeling of depth. In drawing or painting, windows are often used to frame a view in the distance, but in animation, you can find more original frames by choosing unique viewpoints. In a scene from Richard Bazley's animated film *The Journal of Edwin Carp*, he uses the view from the back of a police van to add depth to a simple composition of two characters talking. Imagine how much flatter and less interesting the scene shown in Figure 10.3 would be if the characters were not framed by the outline of the van.

FIGURE 10.2

Overlapping should be planned (as shown in the example on the right) to avoid tangents that may flatten out the depth of the composition (as shown on the left).

In another scene, Bazley uses the convention of a character running into the camera to enhance the feeling of panic as Edwin Carp's mother runs down a hallway. As shown in Figure 10.4, by using an extreme viewpoint, Bazley makes a simple scene more humorous and dramatic while still being very efficient with his artwork.

FIGURE 10.3

By using a clever but logical framing device, Richard Bazley has added a great deal of depth to this animated scene.

© 2002 Richard Bazley

FIGURE 10.4

By using an extreme viewpoint, an otherwise simple motion tween can add drama and humor to a scene.

© 2002 Richard Bazley

Anticipation

Anticipation is one of the primary techniques used to give animation personality and life. If you haven't spent much time studying animation, it's easy to overlook, but animation without anticipation appears robotic. Anticipation communicates the organic tension that exists in real-life motion. Visualize a baseball pitcher winding up before he throws a fastball. If the ball just flew out of his hand without his body first coiling back to gather force, you wouldn't have the visual information to understand that the force was transferred from the pitcher's body to the ball. It would appear that the ball just suddenly had the capability to fly on its own. Figure 10.5 shows a classic example of anticipation as a character gathers force before launching into a run.

The principle of anticipation can be used to add extra life to almost any motion. Picture how an element would gather force before jumping into the main movement, and then add a drawing or two to exaggerate that movement in your animation. Generally, anticipation can be communicated by reversing the main motion for a few frames before and after a tween (or frame-by-frame sequence). For example, if an item is going to move to the left, have it back up a little to the right first, and then after it stops moving to the left, have it stagger back a little to the right before reaching its final resting point. If an item is going to suddenly get larger, have it shrink just a little first before popping up to the larger size, and then allow the item to grow just a little beyond the final size so that it can appear to settle into the final size at the end of the animation. These inverted motions at the beginning and ending of an animated sequence are also referred to as *bounces* because they can be compared to the motion of a ball bouncing. Depending on the effect you're trying to achieve, bounces can be very small and subtle or extremely exaggerated. Figure 10.6 illustrates how a small bounce can be added to give anticipation and follow-through to an animated head turn. This same kind of bounce works equally well on eye blinks and on almost any other small movement that needs a little extra life.

FIGURE 10.5

By winding up before taking off in a run, a character communicates the urgency and force behind his movement.

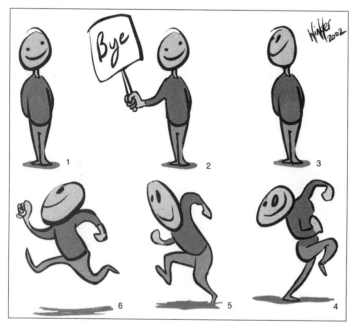

FIGURE 10.6

Subtle bounces add anticipation and follow-through to head turns and other movements.

character designs © www.sandrocorsaro.com

Although you may not at first be conscious of these extra movements when you watch a cartoon, it is one of the conventions that an audience associates with polished, professional animation. If you start to watch carefully for anticipation and follow-through motions, you'll see them on nearly every movement in well-crafted animations.

Secondary motion

Of course, some items don't need to bounce like a ball, but instead, should flap or float as they move. Though it's helpful to keep the pattern of a bounce in mind, the modified patterns that you apply to items to visually show the forces of acceleration or gravity in motion are called *overlapping action*. A single object or character can have multiple overlapping actions — overlapping action added to smaller details of an item is also called *secondary motion*. After you've planned the basic motion pattern of your main element, consider how you can add life and detail to your animation with overlapping action and secondary motion.

Figure 10.7 shows an example of an animation with overlapping action added to a character's belly as he runs. Secondary motion has been added by also animating the character's hat with overlapping action. The combination of these smaller motion patterns with the pattern of the basic run cycle makes the animation dynamic and gives the character personality.

FIGURE 10.7

Overlapping action and secondary motion add life and personality to animation.

WEB RESOURCE Expert animator Richard Bazley provided suggestions for efficient and engaging animation in a tutorial he contributed to *Macromedia Flash MX 2004 Bible* (Wiley, 2004). This tutorial is archived online for readers who want to learn more about specialized animation techniques. Go to `www.flashsupport.com/archive`. One of the things you will notice about Bazley's work is that he often adds frame-by-frame secondary motion to make simple tweened animation more dynamic and lifelike.

Understanding the Laws of Nature

Depending on your learning style, you may find it easier to simply observe and copy patterns of movement or to analyze the underlying principles of force that cause these patterns. Either approach can be effective. Even if you're more of a visual person than a theory-oriented person (as many animators are), an overview of some of the basic principles of physics can help to give you a framework for understanding the limitless variations of animated motion. The stylized interpretations of movement found in motion graphics and cartoons often defy the laws of nature — that's what makes them so entertaining. However, if you don't know the basic physics that dictate motion in reality, it can be more difficult to extrapolate convincing motion to fantastic lengths.

Advanced interactive motion can be designed by using physics formulas to define the behavior of objects controlled with ActionScript. Although the math may look a little bit intimidating at first, it's often easier to understand when you can get visual feedback on how the numbers directly affect motion patterns. In fact, more than a few top designers claim to be math impaired, but the beauty of motion controlled by numbers has given them the incentive to learn (or relearn) some of those scary calculus and physics equations. Spending a little time polishing up your math skills can enable you to efficiently script realistic, organic motion that would be insanely time consuming, or even impossible, to render manually. Even if you never intend to use ActionScript to define the patterns of motion in your animations, a basic understanding of how physics and math can be used to calculate motion makes it much easier to plot movement and plan your drawings. Math and physics, as with color and type, are a powerful part of the vocabulary of motion graphics. Regardless of how you choose to apply them, these principles can be helpful for planning and modifying animation.

Almost all animated motion can be analyzed or designed by using Newton's Laws. If you sat through a science class in high school, these scientific descriptions of how objects interact with force will sound familiar. Of course, in animation you aren't required to obey these laws. In fact, you'll probably create more interesting animations by pushing these laws to the limits or even by inverting them to create objects with unexpected behavior.

Law #1: Inertia

Objects that are at rest will stay at rest, and objects in motion will stay in motion unless acted upon by an unbalanced force. In animation terms, objects should show a change in force if they're going to have a change in motion. This is communicated visually with anticipation and with overlapping actions, as we describe earlier in this chapter. Most animation seems much more lifelike with forgiving transitions. Enable objects to ease in and out of motion and to settle into new positions in your composition. Unless you want them to appear robotic, objects don't just change behavior suddenly without showing some anticipation and delayed secondary animation. You can add an element of surprise to an object's movement by intentionally disregarding inertia. For example, if an object stops cold without any visual indication of a change in force, it appears jarring and hard, or if a very small object takes a long time to accelerate, it seems hesitant.

Law #2: Acceleration

The acceleration of an object as produced by a net force is directly proportional to the magnitude of the net force, in the same direction as the net force, and inversely proportional to the mass of the object. In animation terms, speed is dependent on a combination of mass and force; increasing force increases speed, whereas increasing mass decreases speed. An important related concept is *terminal velocity*. Although most people have heard this term, not everyone can explain what it means. Basically, when an item is falling fast enough for air resistance to be strong enough to prevent gravity from increasing the speed, then it has reached terminal velocity or the maximum speed of its fall. Objects with greater mass take longer to reach terminal velocity, and so they accelerate for longer, generally hitting the ground while still accelerating. An object with less mass quickly reaches terminal velocity and appears to float to the ground because it doesn't gain any more speed. Figure 10.8 shows an animation of the classic acceleration test — two objects dropped from the same height.

By modifying the principles of acceleration, you can create whimsical environments where cannonballs might float and feathers crash to the ground (or any other variation you can think of).

FIGURE 10.8

Acceleration is determined by mass, and objects with more mass take longer to reach terminal velocity.

Law #3: Action/reaction force pairs

This is the most commonly quoted of Newton's Laws: "For every action there is an equal and opposite reaction." Although this law is often used as a metaphor for human behavior, it was originally intended to explain how forces interact and affect objects. This is the law that explains how far backward a character may fall when pulling on a rope that breaks. The force is directed along the rope and acts equally on objects at either end of the rope — the end result is that a character literally pushes himself backward by pulling on the rope, as shown in Figure 10.9.

This is also the law that explains why a ball bounces back into the air when it strikes the ground. If there weren't any gravity or friction acting on the ball, it would bounce back to the exact height that it originally fell from. The actual result is that the ball reaches only a percentage of its original height with each bounce; this percentage depends on how hard the surface is and how heavy and/or bouncy the ball is. You can plan a realistic series of bounces by using a consistent percentage to calculate the descending height of each bounce. The bounce shown in Figure 10.10 was calculated by using a multiple of 0.5 (or ½) for the distance traveled in each bounce.

ON the CD-ROM This bounce will be much improved by adding some easing to make the acceleration more realistic. To see the final result animated, open the `bounce50percent.swf` file in the `ch10` folder of this book's CD-ROM. Ideally, a convincing bounce also includes some stretch'n squash — one of the most common animation tricks used to make motion look more realistic. We discuss this in more detail in Chapter 13, "Character Animation Techniques."

FIGURE 10.9

The force of pulling on a rope causes the character to fly backward when the rope breaks.

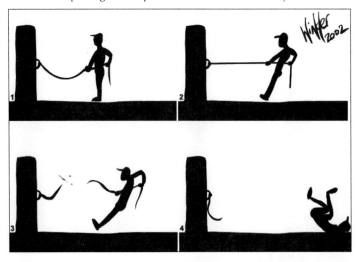

FIGURE 10.10

A starting pattern for a bounce can be plotted by using a consistent multiple to calculate the height of each bounce.

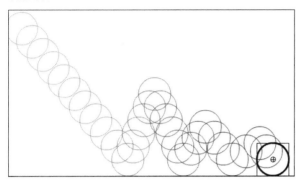

If you're interested in exploring the formulas for more advanced motion patterns, any basic physics textbook can help you get started. Some useful sources that we recommend for motion designers are

- Processing, an open source tool that is being developed to support artists and educators who are interested in learning to work with code structures to create graphics and interactive projects. Although the code is not identical to ActionScript, you will find the examples inspiring and helpful as a beginning step toward using math to describe motion. Visit `www.processing.org` to learn more. The Learning section of the site includes a growing library of examples with graphics and commented code.

- Jack's Page, a Web site created by physics teacher Jack Orb to provide information on basic physics and optics for computer-rendered graphics (with sample JavaScript): `www.kw.igs.net/~jackord/j6.html#p1`.

WEB RESOURCE We'd like to know what you think about this chapter. Visit `www.flashsupport.com/feedback` to send us your comments.

Summary

- To engage an audience, it's important for motion to have meaning. Meaning is derived when an animation includes visual cues that are part of our common vocabulary.

- Motion should support the underlying concept and content of your project. If motion is simply added as decoration without having some connection to the ideas in the content, it distracts, rather than enhances, your design.

■ Motion can communicate mood, emotion, and personality as effectively as text or color. Although the meaning of certain styles of motion can have a different personal or cultural impact, the way that core emotions are linked to styles of motion is remarkably similar for most people.

■ Careful observation and documentation of motion in daily life will help you build a reference library to draw from when creating animation. Exaggeration and interpretation are crucial for developing a personal style. However, your animation will not be convincing unless you can build on a core understanding of motion in the real world.

■ There are many useful tricks or conventions that you can learn to give your animation a more professional look. Overlapping action and secondary motion add life and personality to basic animated movements. Anticipation and follow-through also help make an animation more convincing and entertaining to watch. Without these finishing touches, animation appears flat and lifeless, no matter how many tweens you use.

■ Physics equations can be invaluable for designing advanced motion patterns. Even if you don't have a propensity for numbers, spending some time exploring how basic equations explain force makes it easier to analyze and re-create organic motion. A little math and science combined with your graphics can help to create magic.

Chapter 11

Timeline Animation and the Motion Editor

In this chapter, we discuss the basic methods and tools used to create animations in the Flash authoring environment. Animation is the process of creating the illusion of movement or change over time. Animation can be the movement of an item from one place to another, or it can be a change of color over a period of time. The change can also be a morph, or transformation, from one shape to another. Any change of either position or appearance that occurs over time is animation. In Flash, changing the contents of successive frames (over a period of time) creates animation. This can include any or all of the changes we have mentioned, in any combination.

> **NOTE** Animation *is* possible without extending Flash content beyond one frame, but this requires you to apply transformations to graphics by using ActionScript commands and/or mathematical equations that are executed by code rather than triggered by the Flash timeline. We suggest you use *ActionScript 3.0 Bible* (Wiley, 2008) as a companion to this book when you are ready to go to the next level with your Flash projects.

Basic Methods of Flash Animation

Flash supports three basic methods of animation:

- **Frame-by-frame animation** is achieved by manually changing the individual contents of each of any number of successive keyframes.

- **Keyframe-based tweened animation** is achieved by defining the contents of the start and endpoints of an animation (with keyframes) and allowing Flash to interpolate the contents of the frames in between. Flash CS4 has two kinds of keyframe-based tweening:

- Shape tweening

- Classic (motion) tweening

- **Object-based motion tweening** is an amazing evolution of keyframe-based (or Classic) motion tweening. In Flash CS4, you can now apply a tween to a target object on the Stage, and by simply moving or transforming the object, property keyframes (and a motion path, if needed) are auto-created to track and animate the changes. The many benefits of the new tween method and the new Motion Editor are explained in more detail in "Using Tweens for Animation" later in this chapter.

Advanced Flash developers tend to animate almost exclusively by controlling Movie clips with ActionScript. Although this might seem intimidating to illustrators or animators who are more comfortable using analog tools, this programmatic approach to creating motion (and even artwork) dynamically makes sense. After all, computer animation is the art of orchestrating items according to various properties over time — and in the digital realm numbers describe all properties, even color.

NEW FEATURE Timeline Effects have been removed from Flash CS4, but there is a new Motion Presets panel that enables users to create or import, save, reuse, and share custom tween patterns. These XML-based tween files work more seamlessly than Timeline Effects ever did.

CROSS-REF If you are authoring content for ActionScript 3.0, you can make use of the Copy Motion as ActionScript 3.0 menu command to convert timeline-based animation into ActionScript 3.0 code. The methods for using the Copy Motion as ActionScript 3.0 command are described in Chapter 28, "Sharing and Loading Assets."

Flash components, the Motion Presets panel, and the Copy Motion as ActionScript 3.0 command make it easier than ever for beginning programmers to integrate ActionScripted elements into Flash projects. But, before you jump into scripted animation, it helps to know how to animate in the Flash authoring environment by using layers, frames, and symbols.

Frame-by-Frame Animation

The most basic form of animation is frame-by-frame animation. Because frame-by-frame animation employs unique drawings in each frame, it's ideal for complex animations that require subtle changes — for example, facial expressions. However, frame-by-frame animation also has its drawbacks. It can be very tedious and time consuming to draw unique art for each frame of the animation. Moreover, all those unique drawings contribute to a large file size. In Flash, a frame with unique art is called a *keyframe*. As shown in Figure 11.1, frame-by-frame animation requires a unique drawing for every movement or change, which makes nearly every frame a keyframe.

FIGURE 11.1

When you use keyframes to gradually add to the artwork, the text appears to be written out letter by letter in the final animation.

The example shown in Figure 11.1 (`keyframe.swf`) was created by inserting a series of blank keyframes (F7) and then working backward from the artwork in the final frame to paste the text and erase letters in (reverse) sequential keyframes. In the final effect, the text appears letter by letter until the whole word is written out in keyframe 10. This process of modifying your original artwork in each frame to create a sequence is one use of frame-by-frame animation. Another approach is to create completely unique artwork in each blank keyframe (F7).

As shown in Figure 11.2, the changes in the lines from frame to frame can add a lot more motion to the final animation. If you are a skilled illustrator, you will be able to keep enough consistency from keyframe to keyframe that the animation will seem to be the same shape or figure moving to a new position. If you are an aspiring illustrator, you may end up with a lot more variation among your drawings! As long as you are not trying to get a very precise sequence, this variation can actually be a lot of fun to watch — every line dances and moves in your final animation. Keep in mind that you are not restricted to just one series of frames; you can keep adding elements with their own keyframe sequences on separate layers.

ON the CD-ROM **The source files for the examples in this section are included on the CD-ROM — they're in the `Keyframe` folder of the `ch11` folder.**

The images shown in Figure 11.2 are from the file `faceFramebyFrame.fla`. This sequence of drawings was originally done on top of a short video clip of a real person. If you're learning to draw motion, video can be a good starting point — place it in a guide layer so it won't add to the file size of your final movie. If you work in a loose style, the roughness of the individual traced drawings can add more life to the final animation.

CROSS-REF Felix Stumpf creates very engaging animation by using video as a reference for life-like motion. His fluid drawing style adds a unique flair to his finished Flash portfolio presentation at www.felixstumpf.de. Learn more about Felix's techniques in his tutorial for Chapter 13, "Character Animation Techniques."

FIGURE 11.2

A loosely sketched sequence can be paced by adding more "repeater" frames between the unique keyframe images.

Adding keyframes

To add a keyframe to the Timeline, select the frame that you want to convert into a keyframe, and then do one of the following:

- Convert a frame into a keyframe:
  - Right-click (or Control+click on Mac) the frame and select Insert Keyframe from the contextual menu.
  - Choose Insert ⇨ Timeline ⇨ Keyframe from the application menu.
  - Press F6 on the keyboard.
- Convert a frame into a *blank* keyframe:
  - Right-click (or Control+click on Mac) the frame and select Insert Blank Keyframe from the contextual menu.
  - Choose Insert ⇨ Timeline ⇨ Blank Keyframe from the application menu.
  - Press F7 on the keyboard.

NOTE If you select a frame in a span, the selected frame converts to a keyframe without adding to the length of the span. If you insert a keyframe at the end of a span, the keyframe adds to the length of the sequence. If you convert a frame in a span to a blank keyframe, all content clears from the keyframe and the following frames of the span.

TIP If you need to make a sequence of keyframes, but you would rather not have to press F6 or F7 repeatedly to create individual keyframes, you can select a range of frames and use the Modify ⇨ Timeline ⇨ Convert to Keyframes (F6) or Modify ⇨ Timeline ⇨ Convert to Blank Keyframes (F7) command to quickly convert all selected frames to keyframes or blank keyframes.

Creating frame-by-frame animation

The basic steps for creating a frame-by-frame animation are as follows:

1. **Select the frame in which you want your frame-by-frame animation to begin.** If it's not already a keyframe, use Insert ⇨ Timeline ⇨ Keyframe (F6) to convert it.

2. **Either draw or import the first image for your sequence into this keyframe.** Wherever possible, use symbols and flip, rotate, or otherwise manipulate them for reuse to economize on file size.

3. **Select the next frame and either carry the artwork from the previous keyframe forward for modification by adding a keyframe (F6), or, if you want to create a completely new image from scratch or place a different imported image, make the next keyframe a blank keyframe (F7).**

4. **Continue to add keyframes and change the contents of each keyframe until you complete the animation.**

5. **Play back your animation by returning to the first keyframe and then selecting Control ⇨ Play from the application menu (Enter or Return key).** Or, preview the animation in the test movie environment by choosing Control ⇨ Test Movie (Ctrl+Enter/ ⌘+Return).

Modifying Multiframe Sequences

To control the pacing of your animation, you can add more frames (F5) between the keyframes (creating a *span*), or add more keyframed (F6) images to the sequence to extend its length. Adding more frames between keyframes "holds" or pauses the animation until the playhead hits the next keyframe with changed content. In the example shown in Figure 11.2, the face holds on some frames while the butterfly continues to move in keyframed drawings on its own layer. To speed up (or shorten) animation, you can remove frames (Shift+F5) or keyframes (Shift+F6) to shorten the sequence. You can make changes in the length of a span by selecting a frame in the span that you want to modify and using the application menu commands (or shortcut keys), or you can simply drag the endframe of the span to change its position on the Timeline.

TIP If you drag the endframe of a span to a new position, Flash automatically inserts a new keyframe to mark the new position. If you want to change the length of a span without adding more keyframes, hold down the Ctrl/⌘ key while clicking and dragging the endframe to a new position.

Inserting more frames does work to slow down an animated sequence, but generally if you insert more than two frames between keyframes, the movement is interrupted and the animation starts to look too choppy. Try adding more keyframes to the sequence with very subtle change to the content in each keyframe if you want to create a slower, smoother animation.

NEW FEATURE The default frame rate in Flash CS4 is 24 fps, twice what it has been in all previous versions of Flash. This change reflects the fact that most people viewing Flash Player 10 content have enough processor speed and bandwidth to handle smooth playback of high fidelity animation. Many animators (especially those using Flash to create motion graphics) have been pushing the frame rate up for years, and Adobe finally decided to just reset the default for the rest of us.

By default, Flash loops the content on your timeline, so if you want a sequence to be repeated, you don't need to draw it over and over again. If you notice that your animation disappears before it loops to play again, check to make sure that there are no extra empty frames at the end of the sequence, or that the endframe of one of your sequences is not farther down the Timeline than the endframe of the element that disappears. Although you won't see anything on the Stage in these frames, Flash still plays those frames if they exist on the Timeline. Obviously, blank frames can be used in an animation whenever you want to empty the Stage — either as a pause between sequences or to create the illusion that your artwork has disappeared.

To illustrate how blank frames play back in an animation, we've created a silly example with a face and a rectangle that persist in every frame and some text that exists only on some frames (see Figure 11.3).

FIGURE 11.3

You can insert blank keyframes to clear artwork from the Stage. Remember that the playhead continues along the Timeline if there are frames on any one of the layers, even if the artwork on other layers is no longer present.

Frame Rate and Animation Timing

An underlying factor that affects the playback of all animation is the project frame rate. The frame rate appears in the Document Properties dialog box (Modify ➪ Document) or in the Properties panel if you click in the Document window of an open file without selecting any items on the Stage. The allowable frame rate range is between 0.01 and 120 frames per second (fps) — the default setting in Flash CS4 is 24 fps. The most commonly used range is somewhere between 12 fps (for most Web sites and for low-bandwidth animation) and 24 fps (for faster animation and complex effects intended for broadcast).

It might seem like a good idea to push the frame rate higher to get smoother-looking animation, but the reality of Web delivery is that you can't be sure that your audience will have the bandwidth or the processor speed to play back the animation as you intended. There is nothing worse than seeing your gorgeous animation stuttering and dropping frames. In most cases, 12 fps provides all the momentum you need to drive your animation and effects — you can create quick cuts, smooth fades, or anything in between just by adjusting your artwork and pacing your frames appropriately.

Although you can always change the frame rate after you've authored a file, it makes sense to decide on a final frame rate *before* you start designing and testing complex animation sequences. Re-timing animation by inserting or removing frames and changing the duration of tweens is always an option, but it is painful to go back and try to match the original pacing of a file that was created by using a different frame rate.

Onion skinning

Traditional animators worked on layers of transparent cels using a light table. This made it possible for them to create consistent drawings and to plan the pacing of movement in a sequence of cels. As you move from keyframe to keyframe in Flash, you might feel that you are working blind because you can see the artwork only on the current frame. If you are creating artwork for a sequence of related keyframes, it is crucial to have some visual indication or "map" of the changes from frame to frame. Fortunately, Flash has an effective digital version of the traditional light table — this handy feature is called *onion skinning*. In Flash, onion skinning enables you to see several frames of your artwork displayed at one time. The onion skin markers on the timeline determine the number of frames that are visible. You can turn onion skinning on or off whenever you need to by using the toggle buttons at the bottom of the Timeline window. As shown in Figure 11.4, there are actually two options for onion skinning: Onion Skin or Onion Skin Outlines.

TIP Layers that are locked will not be onion skinned, even if there is artwork on multiple frames within the onion skin markers — this is helpful if you need to keep the view from getting too cluttered with multiple overlays. Generally, onion skinning works best if all layers are locked except the layer that you plan to edit.

The current frame (indicated by the position of the playhead) is displayed at 100 percent opacity, while the other frames in the sequence are displayed at a slightly reduced opacity or as outlines, depending on the Onion Skin button you have selected.

TIP If you don't like the color of the outlines that appear when you turn on Onion Skin Outlines, you can change the setting for Outline color in the Layer Properties dialog box. (Double-click the layer icon or choose Properties from the contextual menu.)

The number of frames that are included in the onion skin display can be controlled either by choosing a setting from the Modify Onion Markers menu (shown in Figure 11.5), or by selecting the round marker handles with the Selection tool and sliding them to a new position on the Timeline. The number of frames that you select from the Modify menu is shown before and after the current frame — so in our example with Onion 2 selected, the onion markers actually span five frames (the current frame, plus two frames on each side).

FIGURE 11.4

Onion Skin shows grayed-out or ghosted artwork on multiple frames, and Onion Skin Outlines shows colored outlines of the artwork on multiple frames. It's hard to see the "color" here, but notice that the lines are thinner with Onion Skin Outlines (right).

Onion Skin | Onion Skin Outlines

Editing multiple frames

One of the drawbacks of manually creating unique artwork on every frame is that changes can be very time consuming. If you decide to change the color or size of an element or perhaps edit out a feature of your artwork, repeating this edit on every frame of a sequence is tedious and labor intensive.

FIGURE 11.5

You can control the number of frames visible when onion skinning is turned on with the Modify Onion Markers menu, or by dragging the onion skin markers to a new position on the Timeline.

The Find and Replace panel (Edit ⇨ Find and Replace) makes it easier to replace colors and text in a Flash document, but erasing or moving an element that appears in a multiframe sequence can still be time consuming.

Fortunately, Flash provides a Timeline option that can make repeated edits on multiple frames much more efficient. Edit Multiple Frames enables you to see and select items on multiple frames for simultaneous modification. As shown in Figure 11.6, the Edit Multiple Frames option is turned on with the toggle button below the Timeline. When this feature is active, you can use any of the selection methods (Selection tool, Lasso, application menu, or shortcut keys) to select the parts of your artwork that you want to move, modify, or delete. This feature is especially helpful for edits that need to be consistent from frame to frame, such as moving all of your artwork to a new position in your layout.

Using the Lock feature to protect layers that you don't want to edit makes it much easier to select and edit multiple elements on specific layers. Using the Lasso tool or the Selection tool to drag-select items on the Stage includes only items on unlocked layers in your selection. The Select All command (Edit ⇨ Select All) makes quick work of ensuring that all unlocked elements within the Edit handles are selected before you apply a change.

FIGURE 11.6

With Edit Multiple Frames toggled on, you can select elements on individual keyframes in a sequence (left) to be modified simultaneously (right).

The frames visible and available for selection are marked by a gray span on the timeline with start and end handles. You can adjust the number of frames included in the span with the Selection tool by clicking and dragging the round handles on the timeline to a new position.

Using Tweens for Animation

Tweening is one of the most powerful capabilities of Flash. Whether you are creating character animation or motion graphics, or even the most basic button effect, you will find tweening indispensable. After you have planned your animation and created the initial artwork, you can use Flash tweening to generate the transitional images between one keyframe and another. This is the tool that makes it possible for artists to quickly generate smooth, precise animation — without spending half their lives manually filling in unique graphics on every frame. Instead, you can establish a beginning point and an endpoint, and make drawings, or key art, only for each of those points. Then you let Flash interpolate and render, or *tween*, the changes between the keyframes. Tweening can be used to render changes in size, shape, color, position, and rotation.

Tweening also minimizes file size because you don't have to include unique information on each frame in the animation. Because you define the contents of the frames at the beginning and endpoint (keyframes), Flash has to save only those graphics, plus the values needed to make the *changes* on the frames in between. Basically, Flash has to store only the difference between the beginning frame and the endframe so that the images on the frames in between can be calculated and rendered.

The other significant benefit of using tweens to generate an animated sequence is that if you want to make a change, you only need to modify the beginning or endpoint and Flash instantly updates the images in between.

Three kinds of tweens can be created in Flash — shape tweens, motion tweens, and Classic (motion) tweens — each applied for specific purposes. The type of tween that you want to apply is selected from the frame or object contextual menu or from the application Insert menu. Tween types are represented on the Timeline by a colored fill. Motion tweens are represented by a blue fill without an arrow, and shape tweens and classic tweens are represented by a fill with a continuous arrow on the span between the start keyframe and the end keyframe of the animation — a green fill for shape tweens and purple fill for classic tweens.

NOTE There is one other type of tween layer that Flash auto-creates to hold IK armatures: Pose layers are marked by a small running figure and like motion tween layers, they save changes made to the contents of the layer in property keyframes to enable animation. Pose layers cannot be inserted or created manually, they are only added to your layer stack when you use the Bone tool to link symbol instances or create an armature inside of a shape. This workflow is described in Chapter 13, "Character Animation Techniques."

NOTE If a shape tween or classic tween is incomplete, either because the wrong tween type has been applied or because information on one of the defining keyframes is missing, the continuous arrow is replaced with a dashed line.

CROSS-REF Because the new object-based motion tween model introduced with Flash CS4 is the preferred workflow, we do not discuss classic tweening in detail in this edition of the book. For more information on classic tweening, refer to the archived "Timeline Animation" chapter from *Flash CS3 Professional Bible* (Wiley, 2007) on `www.flash support.com/archive` or search the Flash Help files for "classic tween."

Shape tweening

Shape tweening is useful for morphing basic shapes — for example, turning a square into a circle, or animating the drawing of a line by tweening from a dot to a finished line. Flash can shape tween only raw *shapes* or drawing objects, so don't even try to shape tween a group, symbol, or editable text — it won't work. You can tween multiple shapes on one layer, but for the sake of organization and animation control, it's best to put each shape on its own layer. This enables you to adjust the speed and length of shape tweens individually and also makes it much easier to figure out what's going on if you need to edit the file later.

TIP The Object Drawing (J) toggle in the options area of the Tools panel makes your production process more streamlined if you are drawing items to animate. Drawing objects are a more flexible art type but they can still be shape tweened like raw shapes. You can make objects with any of the normal drawing tools as long as you select the Object Drawing toggle. If you want to convert a raw shape into an object after it is drawn, select the shape, and then choose Modify ⇨ Combine Objects ⇨ Union from the application menu.

ON the CD-ROM The `smileTween.fla` example file is located on the CD-ROM in the `shapeTween` subfolder of the `ch11` folder.

Figure 11.7 shows an animated "smile" created by interpolating the graphics between a dot and a curved stroke with a shape tween. Flash nimbly handles this simple transition, rendering a gradually extending line on the frames between the dot of the pursed mouth and the final curve of the smile.

FIGURE 11.7

After a dot is drawn on keyframe 1 and an arc is drawn on keyframe 5, a shape tween is applied to render the shapes on the frames in the span between, creating an animation.

Here are the steps for creating a shape tween:

1. **Select the frame in which you want to start the animation.** If it's not already a keyframe, convert it to one (F6).

2. **Draw your starting image on the Stage (see Figure 11.8).** Always remember that shape tweening works only with *shapes* or drawing objects — not groups, symbols, or editable text. To shape tween these items, you first need to break them into shapes (Modify ➪ Break Apart). It also helps to keep your animated graphics on a separate layer from the rest of your artwork.

FIGURE 11.8

The contents of the first keyframe in your span define the starting point for the shape tween.

3. **Insert a keyframe (F6) on the Timeline where you want the animation to end, and modify the artwork to define the endpoint of the animation (see Figure 11.9).** If you want to create the artwork in the final frame from scratch, insert a blank keyframe (F7) instead of a keyframe that includes the artwork from the first keyframe.

4. **Select the keyframe at the beginning of the span that you want to interpolate with a shape tween.** Remember that results are easiest to control and modify if you tween only one shape per layer.

5. **Choose Shape Tween from the application Insert menu or choose Create Shape Tween from the contextual menu (opened by right-clicking or Control+clicking the keyframe where you want to start the animation).** The span between the start keyframe and the end keyframe of your animation appears with a green fill and an arrow to indicate that a shape tween has been applied, as shown in Figure 11.10.

FIGURE 11.9

The contents of the final keyframe after your span define the ending point for the shape tween.

When the applied tween is selected in the Timeline, the Properties panel updates to present two options in the Tweening section (shown in Figure 11.11):

■ Set the Ease value if you want to vary the rate or speed of the animation. This is useful if you want to create the effect of acceleration or deceleration. If you want your animation to start slowly and progressively speed up, push the value down (by clicking and dragging left) to add an Ease In. This causes "in" to display adjacent to the slider and updates the value field with a negative number (between –1 and –100). For an animation that starts fast and progressively slows, push the value up (by clicking and dragging right) to add an Ease Out. The word "out" appears and a positive number (between 1 and 100) displays in the value field. If you want the rate of your animation to stay constant, leave the value in the middle (0). You can also click (and release) the hot text value field to type any number between –100 and 100 directly into the field.

NOTE
We added an Ease In (–100) to the `smileTween` sample file to make the animation look a little more realistic.

■ Select a Blend type from the drop-down menu. Distributive blending creates smoother interpolated shapes, whereas Angular blending creates interpolated shapes that preserve corners and straight lines. If your endpoints contain shapes with corners and lines, select Angular blending. Otherwise, use the default Distributive blending.

FIGURE 11.10

On the first keyframe, specify Shape as the tween type with the contextual menu (or choose Create Shape Tween from the application Insert menu).

6. Preview the animation by choosing Control ⇨ Play (Enter) from the application menu, or use Control ⇨ Test Movie (Ctrl+Enter/⌘+Return) to publish a .swf.

FIGURE 11.11

Easing values and animation Blend style can be selected in the Tweening section of the Properties panel.

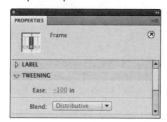

TIP

If the overall speed of the tween seems too fast or too slow, you can extend or reduce the length of the span. The fastest way to increase the span on all visible layers is to move the playhead to the center of the span, make sure that none of the frames are selected on any of the layers and that the layers are all unlocked, and then use the F5 key to add more frames. We added five frames to the overall span of the smileTween sample to slow the animation down.

NOTE

If you delete the artwork on the start or the end keyframes, you will notice that the arrow icon on the Timeline is replaced with a dashed line. This indicates that the tween is broken or incomplete. To restore the tween, it is usually best to select the first keyframe and choose Remove Tween from the application Insert menu (or from the frame contextual menu). Then check your timeline and your artwork to make sure that you have shapes on both a beginning and an end keyframe for Flash to interpolate. When you think all the elements are in place, select the first keyframe and reapply the shape tween by using the Insert menu (or the contextual menu).

Adding shape hints

Because Flash calculates the simplest way to interpolate from one shape to another, you occasionally get unexpected results if the shapes are complex or extremely different from one another. Shape tweening becomes less reliable the more points there are to be calculated between the defined keyframes. In our example, we have added a keyframe at the end of the span with the eyes of the character changed from circles to stars. We want the animation to be a smooth transition from the rough circle to the star shape in each eye. As shown in Figure 11.12, a basic shape tween results in some odd in-between shapes.

FIGURE 11.12

When a shape tween is added to create an animation from one keyframe to another, the transition artwork that Flash generates may not look how you expect it to.

One way of making the in-between artwork more precise is to insert keyframes in the middle of the shape tween so that you can manually adjust the shapes that Flash has generated. Another option that enables you to control a tween without modifying any artwork is to add *shape hints* for Flash to follow when rendering the in-between shapes. Shape hints enable you to specify points on a starting shape that should match with specified points on the final shape. This helps Flash to "understand" how the shapes are related and how the transitional images should be rendered. Compare Figure 11.12 with Figure 11.13 to see the improvement that shape hints can make in the precision of in-between shapes.

ON the CD-ROM To compare the difference made by adding shape hints to the animation, open eyeTween.fla (or .swf) and eyeTweenHints.fla (or .swf) from the shape Hints subfolder in the ch11 folder on the CD-ROM.

FIGURE 11.13

Placing shapes on individual layers and adding shape hints to control the way that Flash renders in-between shapes improves the precision of shape tweens.

CAUTION When you are copying and pasting a span of frames into a new timeline — such as from the Main Timeline to a Movie clip timeline — Flash disconnects the shape hints from the shape. When pasting is confined to a single timeline, hints stay as you placed them.

Shape hints can be added only to artwork on keyframes that define the beginning and ending points of a shape tween. To add shape hints to the artwork in a shape tween, follow these steps after you have created a basic shape tween:

1. **Select a shape on the starting keyframe and choose Modify ⇨ Shape ⇨ Add Shape Hint from the application menu (Shift+Ctrl+H/Shift+⌘+H).** Flash places a small red circle, labeled with a letter *a*, onto the Stage — this is your first shape hint. Additional hints can be added, and they will also be identified alphabetically.

2. **To specify a point on your starting shape, use the Selection tool to select and move the first hint (a) — position it on an area of the shape (for example, a corner or a curve) that you want to match up with an area on the final shape, as shown in Figure 11.14.**

FIGURE 11.14

Shape hints positioned on a shape in the starting keyframe for a shape tween

When you move the playhead to the final keyframe of your shape tween, you will see a lettered hint that matches the one that was placed on the starting keyframe.

3. **Position this hint with the Selection tool so that it marks the area of the final shape that should match up with the area specified on the starting shape.** Flash recognizes the hint only if it attaches correctly to the artwork. You will know that your hints are positioned properly when their fill color changes from red to green on the final keyframe (see Figure 11.15) and from red to yellow on the starting keyframe.

4. **Preview the new in-between shapes by** *scrubbing* **the Timeline (dragging the play-head with the Selection tool to review frames in the tweened sequence).**

5. **Continue to add or reposition hints until Flash renders the in-between shapes correctly.**

6. **To remove an individual hint, drag it off the Stage with the Selection tool.** To remove all hints from an active keyframe, choose Modify ➪ Shape ➪ Remove All Hints from the application menu. A shortcut is to right-click (Control+click on Mac) any of the hints to open the contextual menu, shown in Figure 11.16, for these and other options as you are working.

FIGURE 11.15

Shape hints aligned to points on a shape in the ending keyframe of the tween

TIP If the shape hints are not visible after you have placed them, make sure that the Show All Hints option in the contextual menu is toggled on, or use the application menu to choose View ➪ Show Shape Hints (Alt+Ctrl+H/Option+⌘+H). This option is available only if the layer and keyframe that contain the hints are currently active.

FIGURE 11.16

The contextual menu offers some options for working with shape hints.

Motion tweening

Motion tweening is useful for animating Movie clips, Graphic symbols, and editable text; however, it cannot be used to animate groups, drawing objects, or raw shapes (unless these are first converted into Movie clip or Graphic symbols). As the name suggests, motion tweening is applied to move an item (or target object), from one place to another, but it's capable of much more. Motion tweening can also be used to animate the scale, skew, rotation, color, or transparency of a symbol. Flash filters and the new 3D properties available in Flash CS4 can also be animated with motion tweens, as described later in this chapter.

 Motion tweening can only be applied to one target object per layer — use multiple layers to motion tween multiple targets in the same span of the Timeline.

NEW FEATURE The concept of controlling motion tween properties with custom easing curves that was introduced with Flash CS3 has been expanded with the new Motion Editor in Flash CS4. As we explain later in this chapter, the Motion Editor enables you to control easing and other properties of a tween with curved interpolation paths that can have multiple control points (also known as property keyframes) for adjusting animated elements. You can apply a single curve to all properties of the tween, or create unique curves to adjust the progression of various properties individually within the same tween span. The Motion Editor may look complex at first, but it is user friendly and has many similarities to the After Effects UI.

Object-Based Tweens Versus Classic Tweens

Flash CS4 introduces a new object-based model for motion tweens. Motion tweens can now be created more easily and are harder to "break" because they exist on special tween layers that limit editing options. The workflow used to create motion tweens in older versions of Flash required the same keyframe setup as shape tweens, and the resulting tween on a normal layer could easily be disrupted by accidentally adding new artwork or deleting content on one of the keyframes. These keyframe-based motion tweens are now referred to as classic tweens. There are special cases when classic tweens are required, but for most workflows the new motion tween model gets the job done more easily and effectively.

Here are the limitations you may encounter with the new motion tween model that could prompt you to use classic tweening as a workaround:

- Drawing tools cannot be used on a tween layer.
- Frame scripts are not allowed in a motion tween span.
- Object scripts for a tween target cannot be changed in a motion tween span.
- Eases apply for the duration of a tween span. To achieve easing on specific frames within a tween span, custom ease curves are required.
- Motion tweens can animate only one color effect per tween span.
- You cannot swap symbols or set a specific frame of a graphic symbol to appear in a property keyframe within a tween span.

Here is a summary list of the benefits of the new motion tween model that will hopefully convince even those who don't like change to leave classic tweening in the past:

- Motion tweens require only an initial keyframe. All subsequent property keyframes required to track changes made to the target object are auto-created as you make edits to the target object on the motion tween layer.

- Target objects that change position during a tween span automatically have an editable motion path assigned to them. This Bezier motion path can be easily modified or moved without having to relink the object to the path.

- Motion tweens are required to animate 3D objects. Classic tweens cannot be applied.

- Motion tweens consider text a tweenable object type.

- Motion tween spans are treated as a single object on the timeline and can be resized, moved, or extended without the hassle of selecting multiple keyframes.

- A target object can be swapped out or deleted and replaced with another tweenable object without losing any of the tween properties. The properties are applied to any new target object pasted into the tween layer without disrupting the animation.

The new tweening method introduces a new property keyframe concept that is slightly different than the traditional keyframes used in classic tweens. Property keyframes are represented on the Timeline by black diamond-shaped markers rather than the filled circle marker associated with a standard keyframe. Keyframes are used to place an element on the Stage while property keyframes are used to modify or move an element within an object-based tween span. Keyframes can be added manually to the Timeline on any layer type, but property keyframes are auto-added to tween layers only when you make a change to a selected element in a tween span either on the Stage or by using the Properties panel or Motion Editor. Multiple property keyframes can be stored within a single frame or keyframe on the Timeline, and you can view them independently in the Motion Editor or by modifying the View Keyframes setting in the tween layer contextual menu.

Like a shape tween, a motion tween is more efficient than frame-by-frame animation because it doesn't require unique content for each frame of animation. Yet it is *not* appropriate for all effects — sometimes you'll need to use either frame-by-frame animation or shape tweening to create the kind of inbetweens you want in a sequence.

ON the CD-ROM Create your own file from scratch, or open `motionTween_start.fla` from the `motionTween` subfolder of the `ch11` folder on the CD-ROM. To view the final animation, open `motionTween_final.fla` (or .swf) from the same location.

Here's how to create a motion tween:

1. **Select the frame in which you want to start your animation.** If it's not already a keyframe, make it one by choosing Insert ➪ Timeline ➪ Keyframe (F6).

2. **Draw or import the image that you want to tween.** Remember that you can motion tween only symbols and text (editable text blocks).

- If you already have the element as a symbol in your current Library, you can just drag an instance from the Library onto the Stage. Place each symbol that you want to animate on a separate layer, as shown in Figure 11.17.

- If you are using a raw shape, group, drawing object, or bitmap, you have the option of converting it into a named Movie clip or Graphic symbol before applying the tween or applying the tween and saying "yes" to the dialog box prompt, allowing Flash to convert the target object into an auto-named Movie clip for you.

FIGURE 11.17

The artwork on the first keyframe of the span you want to motion tween should be a symbol or a text box on its own layer, unless you want to let Flash do the dirty work for you and worry about renaming the symbols it adds to your Library later.

3. **Apply a motion tween.** There are two ways to do this:

   - Select the target object on the Stage and apply the Insert ⇨ Motion tween command from the application menu, or right-click (Control+click on Mac) and select Create Motion Tween from the contextual menu.

   - Select any frame following the initial keyframe containing the target object and apply a motion tween by using either the contextual menu or the application menu.

   The tween span appears in the Timeline as a blue fill. If the tween has a target object, the initial keyframe is a black (filled) dot; if the tween does not have a target object the initial keyframe is a white (empty) dot.

4. Scrub the Timeline to any frame within the tween span where you want to modify the target object.

5. **Select the target object and edit it as you would any symbol in your Flash movie — using tools in the Tools panel or settings in the Properties panel.** Remember that you can move tweened elements, as well as scale, skew, rotate, or add filters to them. In our example, we wanted the character to glance up and to the side, so we scrubbed to the last frame in the tween span and moved the eye symbol to the final position we wanted the tween to land on and scaled it up to 125 percent (as shown in Figure 11.18). Finally, to give the animation a little more character, we modified the straight motion path by clicking and dragging with the Selection tool to create a slight curve.

6. **After you have a tweened animation working for the first eye and a motion tween span set up for the second eye, select the first eye and use the Copy Motion and Paste Motion commands in the contextual menu to apply the same scale and motion path properties to the second eye tween.**

FIGURE 11.18

Modify the features of the symbol that you want to interpolate with a motion tween at any point in the tween span — Flash auto-inserts property keyframes to keep track of the changes.

Read This Before Using Create Motion Tween

If you have not converted your artwork into a symbol before using the Create Motion Tween command, Flash automatically converts any item in the selected keyframe into a Movie clip symbol with the generic name of Symbol followed by a number (Symbol1, Symbol2). Although this might seem like a handy shortcut, it actually creates a mess that you will need to clean up later.

Because the symbols are auto-created and named, you do not have the same control over how your Library is organized and how your artwork is optimized. It is much better to analyze the most efficient way to convert your artwork into symbols and to reuse those symbols as much as possible than to allow Flash to make generic symbols that may be redundant. As with all elements in your Flash project, it is also much more useful to assign meaningful names to your symbols that will help you navigate the project when you need to make edits.

Manually creating and naming your own symbols before assigning a tween to specific keyframes or target objects helps avoid redundant or confusing items being added to your document (.fla) Library. The new warning dialog box for motion tweens always reminds you if you haven't converted the target object into a symbol — instead of choosing OK and letting Flash do the work for you, choose Cancel and convert your target object into a named symbol before reapplying the tween.

Modifying motion tween properties

In addition to the changes that you can make to an animated target object on the Stage by using the Selection tool and the Transform panel, there are some specialized options available in the Properties panel when you select a motion tween span (blue shaded frames on a tween layer). These settings can be used to add finesse to an animation after you have your basic motion tween working:

- **Ease:** As described previously in the Shape tweening section, Ease settings control the interpolation pattern of a tween. A default setting of 0 interpolates the changes in the motion tween at a consistent rate from beginning to end. Increasing the Ease value (within a range of 1 to 100) makes the change start more quickly and then gradually slow down — creating an *ease out*. Decreasing the Ease value (within a range of –1 to –100) makes the change start more slowly and gradually speed up — creating an *ease in*. Easing in works well to build anticipation, and easing out works well to make items settle more naturally at the end of a motion.

TIP   As you try different Ease values, you may realize that you want your tween to ease in and ease out, but still move quickly in the middle. Luckily, the Motion Editor enables custom easing control by using a visual curve to map the rate of interpolation in a tween. Using curves to adjust easing anywhere along a tween rather than applying a fixed value on the initial keyframe opens up a whole range of creative possibilities and makes the process a lot more fun. The Motion Editor is discussed later in this chapter.

■ **Rotation:** You can rotate tweened items with this option. You can set the number of rotations or the degree of rotation. One rotation is equal to 360 degrees — Flash automatically calculates the number of whole rotations when you enter a rotation of more than 360 in the degree field. If you want your target object to do only a partial rotation, enter a value less than 360 degrees. Select a rotation direction from the drop-down menu: None rotates your item in the direction that requires the least amount of motion, while Clockwise and Counterclockwise rotate your item in the indicated direction. In both cases, the rotation is completed as many times as you specify in the Rotate value field or as many times as Flash calculates from the value you enter in the degree field. If you type 0 in the Rotate field, or select None from the drop-down menu, no rotation occurs (other than rotation that has been applied to the symbol with the Transform panel). As shown in Figure 11.19, we applied an Ease out value of 100 to the sample file from the previous section, motionTween, to make the eye motion look more natural.

NEW FEATURE The new 3D Rotation and 3D Translation tools can be applied to a Movie clip in a tween span to convert it into a 3D symbol. Settings for 3D symbols can then be modified on the Stage or in the Properties panel.

CAUTION Alpha effects and intensive filters in motion tweens slow most fps (frames per second) settings. The only way to make sure that the fps is honored, no matter how intensive the animation might be, is to use a stream sync sound that loops over the course of any critical fps playback. For more on the relationship between streaming sounds and fps rate, see Chapter 14, "Adding Sound."

FIGURE 11.19

Basic options for motion tweens are available in the Properties panel when a tween span is selected in the Timeline.

- **Orient to path:** When your item follows a path (or motion guide), turning this selection on forces the item to orient its movement to that path. We describe this feature in more detail in the section later in this chapter on editing motion paths.

- **Sync Graphic symbols:** When this setting is activated on a tween, you can replace the symbol in the first keyframe and it automatically updates in the remaining frames and in any other synchronized keyframes that follow. This setting is also important if your animation is contained within a Graphic symbol. Flash recalculates the number of frames in a tween on a Graphic symbol's Timeline so that it matches the number of frames available on the Main Timeline. Sync ensures that your animation loops properly when the animated symbol is placed in the Main Timeline, even if the frame sequence in the Graphic symbol is not an even multiple of the number of frames assigned to the symbol in the Main Timeline.

 You can tell if a tweened sequence is synchronized by observing that the vertical lines separating the keyframes from the span are not visible when this setting is applied.

Working with motion tween spans and layers

When you apply a motion tween to a target object, the tween span is rendered on a special tween layer — you'll notice that the standard layer icon changes from a simple page to something that looks like a square in motion. If the target object is the only element on the original layer when you apply a motion tween, the layer *converts* from a standard layer into a tween layer. However, if there are other elements on the original layer, the target object moves to a new auto-inserted tween layer *created* by Flash. In either case, the tween span occupies the same number of frames in the tween layer as the target object occupied on the original layer. The exception to this rule occurs when the target object occupies only one frame in the original layer, in which case, Flash adds enough frames to the tween span to create one second of animation. That is, if the frame rate of your Flash movie is 24 fps, the default length for auto-created tween spans will be 24 frames.

Other elements can be motion tweened on the same span of the Timeline, as long as they are on separate layers (see Figure 11.20). You can interpolate different features on each tween and also apply any control settings (property keyframes or keyframes) that you want — Flash reads and renders the motion on each tween layer independently.

Tween layers restrict some authoring options to protect the tween span:

- **Adding graphics:** You cannot add additional elements to a tween layer with the drawing tools or the Text tool. If you attempt these actions, a dialog box reminds you that tween layers do not support drawing.

- **Adding symbols:** If you paste a symbol or drag a symbol from the Library onto the Stage while a tween layer (with a target object) is active, a dialog box gives you the option of replacing the original target object with the new symbol you are trying to place. Choose OK only if you want to swap the symbols for the duration of the tween.

FIGURE 11.20

Multiple items can be animated simultaneously by creating tweens on individual layers.

■ **Pasting graphics:** If you try to paste a raw shape (including shape primitives or drawing objects) onto the Stage while a tween layer is active, Flash tries to interpret the shape as a motion path. If the shape is anything but a simple stroke with a beginning and end point, a dialog box reminds you that the shape is not a valid motion path and cannot be pasted into a tween layer.

■ **Adding keyframes:** You can add keyframes (F6) and empty keyframes (F7) to a tween layer but only before or after a tween span. Using the Insert Keyframe command from the application menu or the F6 shortcut on a frame within a tween span (the blue shaded frames on a tween layer) actually inserts a *property* keyframe (marked by a black diamond), locking all properties for the target object to their current value on that frame. This is not a recommended workflow unless you have a special reason for locking all properties on that frame. It's best to rely on Flash to create individual property keyframes as needed when you modify the target object or use the tween layer contextual menu to specify the property you want to keyframe (Insert Keyframe ➪ Position, Scale, Skew, and so on). Using the Insert ➪ Timeline ➪ Blank Keyframe command from the application menu or the F7 shortcut within a tween span has no result.

As you work with content on tween layers, there are some special workflows that will help you manipulate motion tween spans:

- **Extending animation:** A motion tween span can be as short as one frame. Dragging the end of a tween span to the right extends the animation farther along the Timeline, shifting all the property keyframes as needed to keep the flow of the animation consistent. The longer a tween span is, the longer the animation takes to complete, so any motion or change in properties will be slower. Conversely, dragging the end of a tween span to the left shortens the duration of a tween and makes any changes happen more quickly. Keep in mind that the speed of the overall animation is also constrained by the frame rate setting for your Flash movie.

- **Extending a tween span:** Holding down the Shift key as you drag the end of a tween span lengthens the tween span without moving any of the property keyframes. This means that the pacing for changes in position or property that you have already established in your animation do not change, but the final state of the target object is visible on the Stage as long as the blue tween span is extended along the Timeline. You can, of course, make additional changes to the target object at any point in the tween, regardless of which method you use to extend the span.

- **Moving a tween span:** You can move a tween span by selecting it as a single object and dragging it to a new location on the Timeline — either on the same layer or on a different layer. If you drag a tween span onto a normal layer, it converts into a tween layer. Any existing content in the frames where you place the tween span are cleared and replaced with the animation in the tween span.

- **Replacing a target object:** As described earlier, you can drag or paste a new symbol into a tween layer and Flash gives you the option of replacing the current target object. You can also select the current target object and use the Swap Symbol command to choose a new target object from your Library. You can even delete the original target object and then drag or paste a symbol into the tween layer to automatically become the new target object without any fear of "breaking" the tween — another benefit of the new motion tween model over the old classic motion tween.

- **Viewing property keyframes:** As you make changes to a target object in a motion tween span, you will see diamond-shaped markers added to the timeline to mark each property keyframe. If you want to control which property keyframes are visible in the span, use the tween layer contextual menu (right-click or Control+click on Mac) to access the View Keyframes submenu. By default, all properties are set to visible. Click any property in the list to toggle it off or back on or use the global settings of All or None.

Editing motion paths

One of the most elegant aspects of the new object-based motion tween model is that motion paths are auto-created on the same layer as the target object. Points along the path correspond to frames in the tween span, and the position or shape of the path can be changed at any point in the tween.

NOTE This workflow is miles ahead of the classic tween model in previous versions of Flash that required a separate layer for a manually created motion guide, and necessitated careful alignment and snapping to keep the tweened object attached to the path.

To create and edit a motion path in a motion tween span, follow these steps:

1. **After setting up a motion tween (as described in the previous section), scrub the Timeline to any frame in the tween span (besides the starting keyframe).** If you want the motion to happen over the duration of the tween span, scrub to the final frame in the span. In our example, we moved the playhead to frame 20 and then selected the target object. Select the target object on the Stage and move it to a new X, Y location — use the Selection tool to click and drag or enter new X and/or Y values in the Position and Size section of the Properties panel.

   As shown in Figure 11.21, after you move a target object, a blue line appears, marking the shortest distance between the original location of the target object and the new location of the target object. The dots along this motion path represent the individual frames in the span between the original keyframe and the frame where you moved the target object. The frame where you moved the target object to a new location becomes a position property keyframe.

FIGURE 11.21

The initial keyframe in the motion tween sets the starting position for the target object (left); moving the target object to a new position in any other frame of the tween span creates a motion path and inserts a position property keyframe (right).

CAUTION   If you move the target object at a frame in the middle of the span and then decide you want to move it again in a frame farther along the span (or farther back), just keep in mind that any frames where you move the target object become position property keyframes. These are visible in the Timeline and on the motion path as diamond-shaped markers. If you prefer to enable Flash to interpolate the motion evenly from beginning to end within a tween span, remove any interstitial position property keyframes and work with the motion guide or the easing curves to create the motion pattern you want between the initial keyframe and the final frame in the tween span. If you leave in a series of random position property keyframes, you may find that your animated motion lags or speeds up unexpectedly in different sections of the motion path.

2. **Scrub the timeline to preview the motion as the object follows the path.** If you are happy with the motion, you're finished! If you like to change the route that the target object takes, the motion path can be modified with the Selection tool or the Subselection tool. In our example, we clicked and dragged the motion path to add a large curve for the target object to follow. As shown in Figure 11.22, this new path is longer but there is still the same number of frame markers (round dots) along the path — equal to the number of frames between the first keyframe and the final position property keyframe in the tween span.

FIGURE 11.22

The motion path can be modified with the Selection tool (left) to change the route that the target object takes between keyframes within the tween span (right).

CROSS-REF You might notice that the motion path is actually a Bezier path, and you can use the Subselection tool and the Pen tool to modify control points and handles to adjust the curves and angles in the motion path just as you would any other stroke. The white squares that mark position property keyframe changes along the motion guide when the line is selected with the Pen or Subselection tool are cubic Bezier anchor points; these can be used for controlling the shape of the line. The smaller round dots along the line mark all the "normal" frames in the span and cannot be used as control points for changing the shape of the line unless you convert a frame into a property keyframe (by manually changing the position of the target object on that frame). Refer to Chapter 5, "Drawing in Flash," if you need information about working with Bezier controls.

3. If you want to move the whole path (and the target object) to a different location on the Stage, click (and release) to select the path and then click and drag it to a new location. This is different than clicking (and not releasing) the mouse to drag the path in order to change its shape.

   You can delete the path at any time and the position property keyframes are deleted along with the motion path. You can also copy and paste the path if you want to reuse it or have multiple items follow the same path on different tween layers.

Adding control to animation along a motion path

Even after you have succeeded in modifying a motion path in a tween span, you may find that the movement of the animated element is not exactly as you would like. Fortunately, you can modify how a target object follows a motion path in a few different ways.

Using Orient to path

The first control to consider is found in the Properties panel when the first keyframe of your motion tween is selected. The Orient to path check box (shown in Figure 11.23) creates property keyframes on every frame of the tween to track changes in rotation (z-axis), helping the target object stay oriented as it follows a curved path and keeping it headed along the path. When Orient to path is not active, an animated item maintains the same orientation throughout the tween, with no relation to the curves or loops in the path.

FIGURE 11.23

By default, a tweened item maintains the same orientation as it moves along a curved path (left). Selecting Orient to path keeps an animated item headed along the curves or loops in a motion path (right).

Registration and center point alignment

The second important factor that determines how an animated element moves along a motion path is where the registration point of the symbol is located. By default, the registration point is generally at the center of the symbol, but this may not be the point of the item that you want to snap to the path. To modify the alignment of a target object, you can modify the registration point of the symbol (see Figure 11.24).

To modify the registration point of a tweened symbol on a motion path, follow these steps:

1. **Select the symbol on the first keyframe of the tween.**

2. **Activate the Free Transform tool in the toolbox, and drag the registration point (small white circle icon) to a new location.** You'll see the motion path move to snap-align to the new registration point on the target object. You may have to select the motion path and move it back into position in relation to the Stage or artwork on other layers, but the target object also moves and the new registration point remains locked to the path.

FIGURE 11.24

When Free Transform is active, you can modify the registration point that defines how a target object tracks along a motion path without changing the alignment of the artwork in relation to the symbol center point.

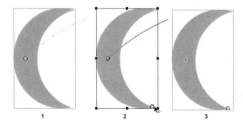

Working with motion presets

As many of us had to learn the hard way, animation is not as easy as it looks. Something as simple as a bounce or a dimensional zoom requires attention to timing and scale — and if the animation is going to have any dimension or character, physical properties of weight and density need to be conveyed as the object moves or reacts to other elements in the scene. Although experienced animators can create believable motion without breaking a sweat, this can be a tall order for even the most skilled graphic designer or programmer. In an attempt to make the learning curve a little less steep, Adobe has included a collection of starter animation presets. These ready-made object-based motion tweens can be previewed and applied from the Motion Presets panel (Window ➪ Motion Presets). Only one preset can be applied to a target object; applying a second preset replaces the first one.

To apply a Motion preset, follow these steps:

1. **Open the Motion Presets panel (shown in Figure 11.25).** Preview animation by selecting any presets listed in the Default Presets folder (or any other folder if you have loaded or saved custom presets of your own).

2. **Select a tweenable target object on the Stage (on its own layer) and click the Apply button in the Motion Presets panel.** If the object you have selected is not a Movie clip or a Graphic symbol or a text field, a dialog box reminds you that the object must be one of these element types before the motion preset can be applied.

   The motion preset creates a tween by using your selected object as the target. You can scrub the Timeline to preview the result (or use the Test Movie command). The tween span, property keyframes, or motion path applied to your target object by the motion preset may not align as you expect with your Stage size or elements on other layers — that's why these are considered animation starter files.

CAUTION If you apply a motion preset and then decide to remove it, using the Remove tween command removes the tween span from the Timeline, but property changes applied to the target object may still "stick." You can use the Properties panel to remove filters or color effects or other changes made to your target object by the motion preset, but this can be a little tricky to dig through. Another option is to use the Undo command rather than the Remove tween command to get rid of any changes the motion preset made.

FIGURE 11.25

The Motion Presets panel

You can modify the animation created by a motion preset in the same way you would modify any other motion tween. If you end up with a customized result that you want to save and use again, simply select the tween span or the target object and use the contextual menu to choose Save as Motion Preset. You can also click the page icon at the bottom of the Motion Presets panel to save your selected tween as a preset. Motion presets are stored as XML files in the following directory locations:

- **Windows:** `HD\Documents and Settings\<user>\Local Settings\ Application Data\Adobe\Flash CS4\<language>\Configuration\Motion Presets\`

- **Macintosh:** `HD/Users/<user>/Library/Application Support/Adobe/Flash CS4/<language>/Configuration/Motion Presets/`

Motion preset XML files can also be exported or imported, using the Motion Presets panel.

WEB RESOURCE   For more detailed information about working with custom motion presets, including how to create a preview for a custom XML file, refer to Adobe Help: Using Flash CS4 Professional ➪ Timelines and Animation ➪ Motion tweens ➪ Applying motion presets.

NOTE   If you are working with classic tweens, the Copy Motion and Paste Motion commands can be a helpful shortcut for reusing animation patterns. These commands can be found in the contextual menu when a tween span is selected, or in the Application menu under Edit ➪ Timeline. For more information about using the Copy Motion and Paste Motion commands with classic tweens, refer to the archived content from *Flash CS3 Professional Bible* (Wiley, 2007): "Chapter 11: Timeline Animation" at `http://www.flashsupport.com/archive`.

Adjusting Easing and Tween Properties with the Motion Editor

The concept of custom easing curves introduced with Flash CS3 has been expanded, and editing controls for tweened property curves can now be accessed from a new Motion Editor panel in Flash CS4. The panel is docked for tabbed access with the Timeline panel when you load the Essentials Workspace, or you can add it to any Workspace layout by choosing Window ➪ Motion Editor. As shown in Figure 11.26, the Motion Editor panel enables you to see individual tween properties separated out into discrete layers. The values on each keyframe of a specific property can be viewed and modified by using numeric hot text controls and/or visual tweening curves that graph property changes (vertically) over time (horizontally, left to right).

This panel may be a little intimidating when you first open it, but keep in mind that you don't really *need* to use this panel unless you want to fine-tune the animation you've already created with other Flash tools. You can think of the Motion Editor as the engine room: If everything is going smoothly up on deck and you are happy with the way the animation is running, there's really no need to go down below and get your hands dirty. On the other hand, if you like to see how things work, the Motion Editor does a great job of laying out all the changes that happen in a tween span so that you can analyze it in frame-by-frame and property-by-property detail.

FIGURE 11.26

The Motion Editor panel displays the property values for property keyframes in a selected motion tween span. Individual values can be modified, using hot text controls or tweening curves.

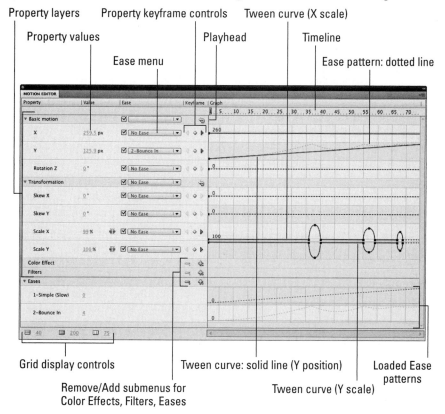

You can modify the individual curves of any of these properties should you want them to be rendered at a different pace to create a custom tween effect:

- **Basic motion:** This section groups together the X, Y, and Z (rotation) values for the target object. Because these properties are always related (a target object always has an X, Y, and Z value to locate it on the Stage), their property keyframes have to match up and they have some special editing rules that other properties don't have:

  - You can add or remove control points on the tween curves for these properties, but you cannot modify them with Bezier controls.

  - To toggle interstitial keyframes in a tween span for these properties from roving to non-roving, use the contextual menu or drag a roving keyframe to a vertical frame divider to make it non-roving.

■ It is best to edit the basic motion of a target object by working directly with the motion path on the Stage. The Motion Editor can be helpful for moving property values to new frames in the tween span or for setting exact pixel values for the target location in some property keyframes.

NOTE Roving keyframes enable Flash to render motion more smoothly by shifting keyframes as needed over the span of a tween. Non-roving keyframes lock specific X, Y, and Z values (or target object positions) to specific frames within a tween span.

■ **Transformation:** This section groups together the Skew and Scale properties for both the x and y axis of the target object. Any differences in size or skew between the target object in the initial keyframe and the last property keyframe of a tween span can be interpolated at different rates.

■ **Color Effect:** You can control any color changes from one property keyframe to the next in a tween by editing the tween curve. You can add color effects to a target symbol by using the submenu in the Motion Editor or by using the settings in the Properties panel.

■ **Filters:** If filters have been applied to create changes in an item's appearance in the span of a tween, the pattern of change can be adjusted with custom easing. Filters can be added to a target symbol from the submenu in the Motion Editor or from the Properties panel.

TIP To link X and Y value pairs so that they always match when changes are made to either property, click the Link X and Y Property Values button (to the left of the Ease menu) for either property.

In most cases, you only need to create custom tween curves for one or two properties to achieve a very polished final result. The possibilities can be a little overwhelming at first and the flexibility of custom easing curves might work against you: As you modify the curves in myriad ways, it can be difficult to keep track of which curves work best for specific effects. Fortunately, a few tricks can help as you experiment:

■ Use the Properties panel controls first because these are a little less complicated. The settings you apply with the Properties panel are translated into curves that you can use as a starting point when you shift over to the Motion Editor.

■ Copy and paste patterns from one property to another if you have created a tween curve that you like and you want another property to progress in the same pattern. Right-click (or ⌘+click on Mac) in the graph area of a tween pattern that you want to copy and choose Copy from the contextual menu. Select the graph area of a property layer that you want to change and use the contextual menu to choose Paste to instantly shift the curve to match your custom settings. This technique also works to copy custom easing patterns and to apply a custom easing pattern to a property tween curve.

■ To reverse the direction of a property tween, select the graph area and choose Reverse Keyframes from the contextual menu.

■ If an individual curve gets too complicated or you change your mind, just use the contextual menu in the graph area to choose Reset Property.

■ Use the Reset Values button for the category to reset all the curves for a section of properties in the Motion Editor to non-tweened values.

364

Controlling property views in the Motion Editor

As in the Properties panel, you can control what property values are visible in the Motion Editor by expanding and collapsing sections of the panel with the property layer controls. When a property layer arrow is twirled down, the property name, value setting (for current position in the tween span), Ease setting (if any), and visual tween curve (plotted across the frames of the current tween span) are all visible. To facilitate editing in the tween curve area of the panel, you can click any expanded layer a second time to expand the layer view even farther. The number of frames visible in the tween curve area and the height of expanded and collapsed layers can be modified with the Grid display controls (bottom left corner of Figure 11.26) to suit your screen size (or eyesight):

- **Graph size:** Sets the minimum height of the layers in the graph for collapsed layers. Can be set in a range between 20 pixels and 20 pixels less than the current setting for Expanded Graph size.

- **Expanded Graph size:** Sets the maximum height for expanded layers in the graph. Can be set in a range between 20 pixels more than the current (collapsed) Graph size and 500 pixels. We found 200 to be a good working size.

- **Viewable frames:** Zooms in and out of the current tween span to show a set number of frames in the curves area of the panel. The range is from 1 frame to the total number of frames in the currently selected tween span.

CAUTION Patterns in your tween curves and eases can be hard to see in the Motion Editor if you are zoomed in too close to the tween span. It helps to zoom out and get oriented by pushing the number of viewable frames up to show your complete tween span before zooming in again, if needed, to focus on a more limited number of specific frames. The timeline only shows numbers every fifth frame, so it becomes more useful as a navigation aid when you look at ten or more frames at a time.

Editing tween curves and property key frames

The tween curves in the Motion Editor track changes in object properties over the life of your tween span. Most properties can be modified independently from frame to frame (changes can be locked in by using a property keyframe or they can be interpolated in a curve from one control point to the next). Tween curves can be edited in a similar way to strokes (or motion paths), using the Selection tool or the Pen tool:

- Drag control points left or right to set a property value at a specific frame in the tween span. Dragging a control point left sets the value sooner in the tween, and dragging it right sets it later in the tween.

CAUTION Dragging a control point past other control points on the same property curve clears those points.

- Increase a property value by dragging a curve or control point toward the top of the grid. Decrease a property value by dragging a curve or control point toward the bottom of the grid.

- Add or Remove control points by moving the playhead to the frame you want to edit and using the Add or Remove Keyframe button in the Motion Editor (yellow diamond icon between next and last keyframe buttons).

 You can also use the contextual menu to add or remove control points as well as using shortcut keys with the Selection tool: Ctrl+click/Option+click on an empty area of the curve to add a point, or on an existing point to remove it.

- Curves with smooth points can be adjusted with Bezier handles. To toggle a control point between corner and smooth modes, Alt+click/⌘+click the point. Tween curves pass through smooth points as rounded curves with incremental value changes, and corner points enable more abrupt changes in value with an angled transition.

TIP **To adjust a specific curve point, you can also use the contextual menu to choose Smooth Point, Smooth Right, Smooth Left, or Corner Point.**

Eases and custom eases

Although tween curves and eases appear on the same grid, they are edited differently. Tween curves are generated when you make any changes to a tweened property and enable you to edit the curve directly to adjust the rate of change for a specific property at any time. Eases are preset interpolation patterns that enable you to control the percentage of change that happens in each section of a tween span; you can also think of this as the pattern of the change. Easing is applied only if you want the *rate of interpolation* for a specific property (or all tweened properties) to change over the span of a tween. If you want the interpolation to be spread evenly on all frames that come between one property keyframe and the next, you don't have to add any easing.

Eases are managed in the Eases section at the bottom of the Motion Editor and applied by using the Ease menu for each property layer (shown in Figure 11.26). As discussed in the Animation Strategies chapter of this book, animation relies heavily on physics and the laws of the natural world. For this reason, Adobe was able to anticipate some of the ease patterns that you might find most useful and include them in the Eases submenu (available when you click the plus icon (+) at the top of the Eases section of the Properties panel). Any eases that you add to the Eases section of the Motion Editor are available in the Ease menu for each property in the layers above. For Figure 11.26, we added just two of the ready-made eases that ship with Flash CS4 to the Eases section of the panel to give you an idea of how different these patterns can be. We also applied the Bounce pattern to the tween for the Y value of the Basic motion property so that you can see how the dotted ease pattern overlays the original tween curve.

It takes some practice to get the feel for using easing curves to control tweens, but we're sure you can already see how many more options for different styles of motion you'll have if you use easing:

- **Diagonal lines continue in an even motion.** The more closely the percentage of change matches the progression in frames, the more even the transformation will be. (Try any of the Simple eases.)
- **Gradual curves can add smooth acceleration or deceleration.** A reverse curve that creates gradual slopes at the beginning and end as well as a steeper pitch in the middle creates an Ease In/Ease Out effect. (Try the Stop and Start ease or the Sine Wave ease.)

- **Bumps in a curve can add a stuttering motion.** For example, if an anchor point at the frame 10 marker is set at the 50% change line and you add an anchor point at the frame 15 marker that is set to pull the curve back down to the 25% tween line, you cause the tween to progress and then reverse and then progress again at a quicker rate to reach 100% transformation by the last frame of the tween. (Try the Bounce ease or Sawtooth Wave ease.)

- **Flat (horizontal) lines add pauses.** The frames continue, but the percentage of change is forced to plateau or hold at a specific point of transformation. (Try the Square Wave ease or Random ease.)

- **Vertical lines create quick jumps.** The percentage of change has to increase, but it doesn't have any frames to gradually make the change. (Try the Square Wave ease or the Random ease.)

CAUTION You can add or delete eases at any time, but keep in mind that removing an ease from the Eases section of the Motion Editor also removes it from any property layer that you've applied it to.

After you add an ease to a tween property, you can still edit the tween curve (either in the Motion Editor or by making changes to the target object on Stage or in the Timeline), and the ease curve responds, but it keeps its basic shape. Ease curves can be modified in the Eases section of the Motion Editor by changing the hot text values within the allowable range for each ease pattern:Patterns with one long curve enable you to push the pattern from one end of the tween to the other and flip the pattern by changing the value from negative to positive (making it an ease in or an ease out), while repeating patterns with discrete sections joined by corner points enable you to set the number of repeating sections in the pattern.

TIP If you set easing for a tween span in the main Properties panel, the value of Ease In or Ease Out that you apply renders in the Motion Editor as a Simple(Slow) curve, and the value applies to all tweened properties. This is a good way to get an idea of how the visual curve relates to the standard easing values.

If you need to go beyond the ease patterns that ship with Flash CS4, you can select the Custom option at the bottom of the Add Ease menu in the Motion Editor. This adds a Custom layer in the Eases section with an editable (solid rather than dotted) line loaded in the graph area. You can use the Selection or Pen tool to modify this line with Bezier handles or by adding additional curve or corner points. Custom patterns are available in the Ease menus for any of the property layers, and changes that you make to your patterns update on any layers that you've added them to.

TIP You can add as many custom ease patterns to the Motion Editor as you need to — they will all have the same name, but they will also be numbered in the order that you added them so you can tell them apart. Custom eases are saved with your Flash project file but do not carry over from one file to the next (unless you do some copying and pasting from file to file or use motion presets to save your animation along with any custom eases).

As with anything else, it pays to start simple. Experiment with changing the ease curve of one property and if you get something you like, copy it to a new custom ease layer before you move on with another modification. If a curve works great to create an interesting effect on one property, try applying it to something else. Before long, you will have a library of files with cool tween patterns that you can copy and paste from instead of having to re-create a curve from scratch each time.

Animating 3D properties

We describe the process for working with 3D symbol properties in Chapter 9, "Modifying Graphics," but you can take this new feature a step farther and animate the changes you make to 3D position or rotation. If you have already created a 3D symbol on the Stage (by applying the 3D Rotation (W) or 3D Translation tool (G) to a Movie clip, you can use the 3D symbol as a target object for a motion tween. Changes made to the target object on the Stage by using the 3D settings or tools create property keyframes that are interpolated in the tween span and displayed in the Motion Editor along with other properties.

A great way to get started with 3D animation is to try one of the motion presets that tween 3D properties. After you apply a motion preset (as described earlier in this chapter), you can modify any of the settings or curves in the Motion Editor. We used the motion preset for 3D Rotation ("spiral-3D" from the Default Presets folder in the Motion Presets panel) as a starting point in our example file. This motion preset animates the target object around the z-axis, but the final result is that the object ends up looking backward in the end frame of the tween, as shown in Figure 11.27.

FIGURE 11.27

The spiral-3D motion preset tweens the Rotation Y property for the target object from 0 degrees to 180 degrees over a span of 50 frames. In the final frame of the tween, our target object is backwards. When the tween loops, the object "jumps" back to its proper orientation when the playhead returns to the initial keyframe in the tween.

To create a more seamless looping animation, we used two different approaches:

- In the `3D_rotationReverse.fla` file, we made the animation look as though the graphic is rotating 180 degrees to face backward and then rotating the opposite direction to face forward again. We did this by inserting a control point on the Rotation Y tween curve, setting the value on the new property keyframe to 180 degrees, and then changing the value in the final property keyframe to 0 degrees. As shown in Figure 11.28, the resulting tween interpolates the rotation from 0 degrees to 180 degrees and then back from 180 degrees to 0 degrees. The animation is faster because the graphic rotates forward and then backward through the 180-degree arc within the same number of frames, but you can always extend the tween farther along the Main Timeline to give the animation more time.

FIGURE 11.28

Creating a repeating pattern in a tween curve with matching values in the final property keyframe and the initial tween keyframe creates a smooth transition for looping animation.

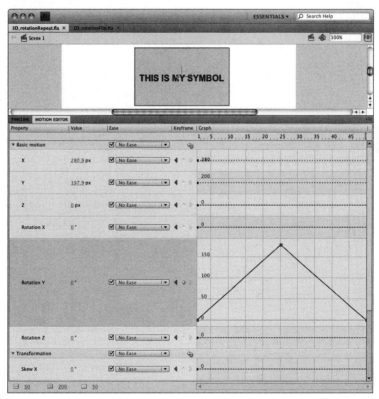

TIP

The same effect we created by modifying the curve for the Rotation Y property can be achieved on animation with multiple property changes, or even on frame-by-frame animation sequences by editing the Main Timeline. Copy the whole tween span and place the copy farther down the Timeline on the same layer to follow seamlessly after the first tween. A shortcut for creating a copy of a tween span is to hold down the Alt (Option) key while dragging the span to a new location, and then use the contextual menu to choose Reverse Keyframes on the copied span. Repeating and reversing a tween span is almost always a good way to get a seamless looping animation and to avoid a "blip" at the end of your sequence when the position in the final frame of a tween jumps back to the starting position at the beginning of the span. Having a tween run forward and then run backward before returning to the beginning of the span creates a seamless transition.

■ In the 3D_rotationFlip.fla file, we inserted a property keyframe halfway through the tween (when the target object was approximately 90 degrees along the z-axis or "sideways" to the viewer) and applied a vertical flip to the graphic (Modify ⇨ Transform ⇨ Flip Vertical) so when the graphic finished the second half of the tween it would not appear backwards. This is equivalent to setting the Scale X property for the graphic to –100. Because any changes made to a tweened target object on the Stage are interpolated in all the frames between property keyframes, the flip we applied was being eased in during the first half of the tween span and this interfered with the smooth rotation animation. Figure 11.29 shows the original tween curves after we applied the flip in frame 26 of the tween span.

The solution is to force the flip to happen in just one frame instead of tweening it over all the frames in the first half of the span. This is accomplished by using two property keyframes side by side in the Timeline with an X-scale of 100 in the first keyframe (or no flip) and an X-scale of –100 in the second keyframe (or full flip). You can either make these changes directly to the target object on the Stage by using the Transform panel to modify the X-scale value on two frames somewhere around the center of the tween span, or you can open the Motion Editor and modify the tween curve for the Scale X property in the Transformation section of the panel. Insert a new control point just before the control point that flips the graphic, and then move the new control point up to keep the curve flat (no transformation) for the first half of the tween span, with a sharp drop from +100 to –100 over just one frame, as shown in Figure 11.30.

FIGURE 11.29

Flipping the target object on the Stage resulted in a tweened curve interpolating the change in the Scale X property from 100 to –100 over the first half of the tween span.

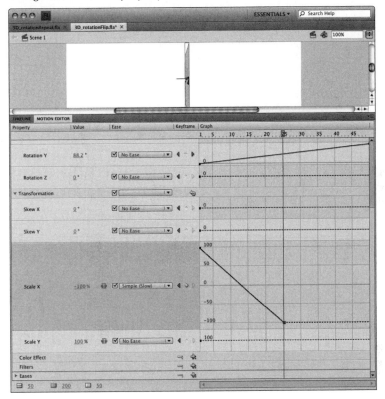

FIGURE 11.30

Inserting a new control point on the curve enables us to force the change in Scale X value to happen over just one frame instead of interpolating it over the first half of the tween span. Adding and shifting the control point on the curve is equivalent to adding a property keyframe and forcing the Scale X value to its original value in the frame just before the frame that changes it to –100.

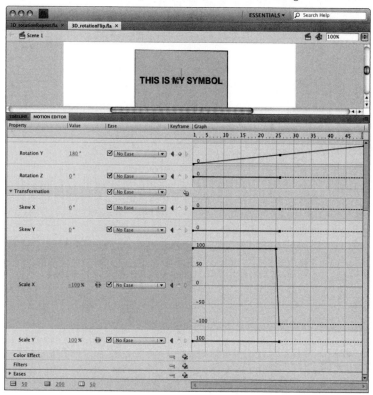

To see the original animation created by applying the motion preset for 3D Rotation, open `3D_rotationPreset.fla` from the 3DAnim subfolder in the ch11 folder on the CD. Compare the original with the modified files, `3D_rotationRepeat.fla` and `3D_rotationFlip.fla`, found in the same folder.

Although describing these changes takes up a lot of page space, it really is just a couple of quick editing steps and you can see how much time is saved by using motion presets and the Motion Editor rather than creating animation from scratch. The key to success when working with animation (2D or 3D) is to first understand the individual properties and how changes in their value modify the appearance of your target object. Testing property changes first by using a non-animated target object enables you to plan the key positions in your animation. If you then work with the Motion Editor, you will have a better idea of which curves you need to modify and the values to enter on property keyframes to get the animated result you are hoping for. If you know where you want to start and how you want to end, Flash does a pretty great job of figuring out all the steps in between to render smooth animation.

Integrating Multiple Animation Sequences

So far in this chapter, we've looked at creating different types of animation on the Main Timeline. Adding multiple tweens to the Main Timeline can soon result in a jumble of colored spans and keyframes that might be hard to navigate when you need to make edits. Authoring all animation sequences on the Main Timeline also puts you at risk of unintentionally displacing multiple sequences as you make edits.

The best solution for keeping your project (.fla) files manageable as you continue to add animation is to move animation sequences off the Main Timeline and organize them instead on individual symbol timelines. This makes it much easier to move or reuse animation and also ensures that any edits you make to individual animation sequences do not disrupt sequences on other symbol timelines. Graphic symbols and Movie clip symbols can both be used to hold multiple layers of animation, but they have different uses.

As we discuss in Chapter 6, all symbols have their own timelines, so you could just as easily store an animation in a Graphic symbol as in a Movie clip. However, there are some important differences to keep in mind:

- A Graphic symbol timeline must still be tied to frames on the Main Timeline, while a Movie clip timeline plays back independently, regardless of how many frames it is assigned on the Main Timeline.

- The benefit of using a Graphic symbol to store an animated sequence is that it can be previewed frame by frame directly in the authoring environment, even if it is nested. You *can* preview animation on a Movie clip timeline in Edit mode, but you cannot see how the animation on the Movie clip timeline syncs with animation on other symbol timelines or with the Main Timeline until you publish the movie or use the Test Movie command.

- Another significant limitation of Graphic symbols is that they cannot be targeted with ActionScript. Movie clip symbols can be targeted with ActionScript to control the playback of each symbol instance independently, as opposed to having all animation tied to frame sequences on the same (main) timeline.

The extent to which you separate and nest animated elements depends on the complexity of the project and also on how you intend to reuse animation. In general, any elements that will always be linked together on playback can be stored in the same symbol. If you want to have the option of altering playback speed or placement of certain elements independently, then these should be stored in discrete symbols. For example, if you have an animated logo that may be used in a project separately from an animated title, then these two elements should be in individual symbols. On the other hand, if the logo always appears in the same way with the title, then these two elements can be stored in a single symbol (on separate layers, if necessary).

TIP It is always possible to use the Properties panel to change the behavior (or symbol type) of a symbol instance on the Stage. If you are working with multiple Movie clips and you need to sync some parts of the animation, it can be helpful to temporarily assign a Movie clip instance Graphic symbol behavior so that you can see the animation on its timeline in the main authoring environment. Don't forget to switch the instance back to Movie Clip behavior before you publish your movie.

Moving tweens onto symbol timelines

Certainly, it is more efficient to plan your project structure before you begin adding animation so that you can nest animation in symbols as you create the project, but Flash is flexible enough to enable you to optimize the organization of your animation sequences even after you have strewn them around on the Main Timeline.

To illustrate how tweens are moved from the Main Timeline to symbol timelines, we will modify a file called tweensTimeline.fla, which includes layers with shape tweens, motion tweens, and classic motion tweens keyframed on the Main Timeline.

ON the CD-ROM We have included two files in the Integrate subfolder of the ch11 folder on the CD-ROM for you to refer to: the original tweensTimeline.fla with tweens on the Main Timeline, and the modified tweensNested.fla with tweens moved onto symbol timelines.

To reorganize a file (.fla) that has animation built on the Main Timeline, follow these steps:

1. **Analyze the Main Timeline carefully to see how the various animated sequences need to relate to each other in the final .swf file.** Decide which frame spans and layers you need to keep tied together and which should be independent.

2. **Pay close attention to how the transitions between different animated sequences are handled on the Main Timeline.** If two different phases of a tween share a common keyframe (for example, if you have scaled an element in one tween and then rotated the same element in a span that continues from the final keyframe of the first tween), you must keep these tweens together or else insert an additional keyframe before you separate them in order to keep both tweens intact.

NEW FEATURE Object-based tween spans that follow each other on the same tween layer can simply be selected and dragged to move apart from each other; Flash automatically inserts a blank keyframe to hold the space between the two tween spans on the Timeline.

TIP To be certain that linked sequential tweens can be separated without getting messed up, it can be helpful to add two manually inserted "divider keyframes" at the point that you want to split the tween: You can remove the tween from the first divider keyframe, leaving the second divider keyframe (F6) to maintain the beginning of the tween that follows. This ensures that there is no interpolation between the end keyframe of the first tween and the start keyframe of the second tween.

3. **Select the span or Shift+select the beginning and end keyframes of the sequence that you want to move off the Main Timeline.** Clicking the layer icon also selects all frames and tween spans on a layer.

4. **With all frames in the sequence selected, choose Copy Frames from the contextual menu (see Figure 11.31) or Edit ⇨ Timeline ⇨ Copy Frames from the application menu (Alt+Ctrl+C/Option+⌘+C).**

FIGURE 11.31

You can select frame spans on multiple layers to move at one time. Be sure to use Copy Frames rather than simply Copy to move all the frames to the Clipboard.

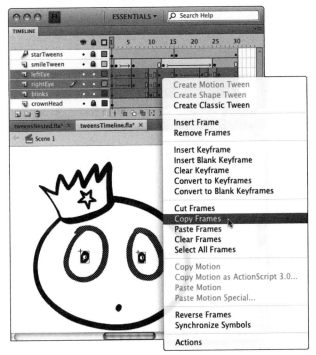

5. **Create a new symbol by choosing Insert ➪ New Symbol from the application menu (Ctrl+F8/⌘+F8).** Set the symbol type to Movie Clip or Graphic and give it a name that will be useful for identifying the animation, as shown in Figure 11.32.

   After you click OK to close the Create New Symbol dialog box, the symbol automatically opens in Edit mode — you will see the symbol timeline rather than the Main Timeline in the Timeline window.

6. **Select the first frame of the symbol timeline and choose Paste Frames from the contextual menu, as shown in Figure 11.33.** Or choose Edit ➪ Timeline ➪ Paste Frames from the application menu (Alt+Ctrl+V/Option+⌘+V).

   Flash automatically inserts enough layers and frames to accommodate the content you paste into the symbol timeline (see Figure 11.34). Your animation sequence is now stored inside the symbol, and you can easily access it from the Library for reuse or editing.

FIGURE 11.32

In the Create New Symbol dialog box, select a symbol type and enter a meaningful name for your new symbol.

Create as many new symbols as you need to hold all the individual animation sequences that you want to work within your project. When you are finished, you should have a set of easily identifiable named symbols in your Library containing animated elements that are now efficient to edit or reuse.

NOTE You may notice that there are two consecutive motion tween spans on the tween layer for the starAnim sequence. Although these could have been integrated into one tween span by working with property keyframes and curves in the Motion Editor, we opted to leave them separate so that we could reuse the Movie clip that contained the animation of the star spinning without the animation of it falling.

Organizing symbol instances on the Main Timeline

In the previous section we suggested *copying* your animation sequences from the Main Timeline to be pasted into individual symbol timelines — even though this results in redundant content. The rationale for leaving the original sequences on the Main Timeline rather than cutting them as you move content into separate symbols, is that they provide a useful reference for where the symbol instances should be placed on the Stage and how they should be arranged on the Main Timeline. The simplest way to "rebuild" your animation, using the nested symbols you have created, is to insert a new layer for each symbol on the Main Timeline directly above the original sequence that was copied. As you drag each symbol instance onto the Stage, you can align the artwork with the original sequence on the Stage and also determine how many frames the symbol should occupy on the Main Timeline.

FIGURE 11.33

Select the first frame in your new symbol timeline and use Paste Frames to insert the frames and layers from the Clipboard.

FIGURE 11.34

When you use Paste Frames to place the content from the Clipboard into your symbol, layers and keyframes are preserved.

Using the example from the previous section, we show you how to replace the tweened sequences on the Main Timeline with nested symbol instances.

1. Insert a new layer on the Main Timeline directly above the original tweened sequence by selecting the original layer and using the New Layer button in the Timeline window or choosing Insert ⇨ Timeline ⇨ Layer from the application menu (or the contextual menu).

CAUTION Check the labels above the Timeline to be sure that you are editing the Main Timeline (Scene 1) and not one of the named symbol timelines. If there are any names listed in the crumb menu to the right of Scene 1, click the back arrow or the Scene 1 label to return to the Main Timeline before you start placing symbol instances on the Stage.

2. Drag an instance of your nested animation symbol from the Library onto the Stage in the new layer and align it with the content on the other layers (see Figure 11.35).

TIP Use the Lock Others command to protect content on your original layers while you drag and position the symbol instance on your new layer. Your keyboard arrow keys can be helpful for "nudging" an item into final alignment if dragging is not precise enough.

FIGURE 11.35

The original animation layers can help you to sequence and visually align the new symbol instances as you rebuild your project.

After you finish placing the new symbol instance in the Main Timeline, you can delete the layers containing the original tweened sequences (which are now redundant). You will quickly see how much cleaner and easier to modify the Timeline becomes when the tweened and frame-by-frame sequences are replaced with nested symbol instances, as shown in Figure 11.36.

FIGURE 11.36

The Main Timeline becomes easier to manage as you replace the tweened and frame-by-frame sequences with nested symbol instances.

In the previous example, we moved the timeline animation sequences to Graphic symbol timelines to make it easier to preview the animation on the Main Timeline. However, in most production contexts, it is best to use Movie clip symbols to hold animation because instances of Movie clips can be targeted with ActionScript. Also, Movie clip timelines loop independently of the Main Timeline, so you can repeat an animation sequence as many times as you want, either by holding on a single frame of the Main Timeline or by extending the span of the Movie clip so that it remains visible as the Main Timeline continues to play. In the next section, we work with Movie clip symbol instances to demonstrate how to reuse animated symbols and how to add some variation to the instances.

Reusing and Modifying Tweened Symbol Instances

Cleaning up the Main Timeline is one good reason to move animation onto symbol timelines. An even better reason is to make it easier to reuse and modify instances of the animated symbols after you have them stored in your Flash Library.

In the our example file, we have placed multiple instances of a Movie clip on a layer in the Main Timeline to create some animated background elements (see Figure 11.37).

FIGURE 11.37

Movie clips make it easy to use multiple instances of an animated element.

As discussed in previous chapters, you can modify the appearance of symbol instances without having to edit the contents of the original symbol. This can be helpful when you are working with static elements, but it really becomes indispensable when you are working with animated elements. Imagine the time it would take to copy and paste a series of tweens or a frame-by-frame sequence on the Main Timeline and then to edit the artwork on each keyframe just to change the scale or the color of your animated element each time you want to use it. Now be very happy that the little extra time spent moving your animated sequences off the Main Timeline and into symbols makes it possible to drag and drop your animated elements and then to scale, rotate, or apply filters or color effects to get endless variations without ever having to edit the original keyframe artwork.

ON the CD-ROM We have included the original and the modified version of our example file so that you can see how the symbol instances were changed — compare tweensModify_start.fla and tweensModify_final.fla in the Modify subfolder in the ch11 folder of the CD-ROM.

In our example (see Figure 11.38), we have modified the appearance of some of the animated stars by transforming instances of the original starSpin Movie clip.

The beauty of symbols is that you always have the option of modifying the appearance of individual symbol instances or making global changes by modifying the artwork in your original symbol. If you decide that an element should be changed every place that it appears, editing the original symbol is much quicker than modifying all the symbol instances individually.

FIGURE 11.38

By transforming symbol instances, you can add almost endless variation to the appearance of your animated sequences without having to modify any keyframe artwork.

> **TIP** If you decide that you want to keep the static shape, but not the animation or the link to the original symbol in the Library for some of the symbol instances you have placed on the Main Timeline, you can use Modify ⇨ Break Apart (Ctrl+B/⌘+B) to "break" the link to the animated symbol. The original artwork (or static shape) remains on the Stage, but any changes made to the original symbol in the Library are not carried over to the now unlinked shape.

Controlling symbol instances with ActionScript

You can use ActionScript to control the playback of each element independently of the Main Timeline. For example, instead of stopping everything on the Main Timeline, you can place a `stop()` action on the starSpin symbol timeline to hold the animation of the stars while the other elements continue to play (as shown in Figure 11.39, top). Any ActionScript placed directly on the symbol timeline applies to all instances of the symbol. If you are working with Movie clip symbols, you have the additional option of naming individual symbol instances and *targeting* them with ActionScript placed on a keyframe in the Main Timeline (as shown in Figure 11.39, bottom). This method enables you to stop the animation on some stars, while letting others continue to spin as the animation on the Main Timeline plays.

> **ON the CD-ROM** To see the difference between adding ActionScript directly to a symbol timeline to stop all instances and targeting a specific named symbol instance with ActionScript on the Main Timeline, compare `stopSymbol.fla` (or .swf) with `stopInstance.fla` (or .swf).

FIGURE 11.39

ActionScript can be added to symbol timelines (top) or used to target symbol instances (bottom) to control the playback of animated elements, independent of the Main Timeline.

CROSS-REF   For more information about controlling symbol timelines and symbol instances with ActionScript, refer to Part V, "Adding Basic Interactivity to Flash Movies."

Make Flash work for you

We could fill an entire book with illustrations of the various ways that you can move, edit, and recombine your animated timeline sequences, but the basic principles are always the same. Use symbols to keep your files optimized and your options open. Nest symbols to keep your project organized. Try to keep your Main Timeline uncluttered and easy to modify by putting frame-by-frame animation and tweens on symbol timelines. Use Movie clip symbols if you plan to target instances of the symbol with ActionScript. Let Flash do as much work for you as possible, but don't be afraid to manually tweak animated sequences by applying custom tween curves, inserting property keyframes, or modifying artwork. Use layers to keep elements organized and when you need to animate multiple items on the same span of the Timeline. Plan and design your animation in logical sections rather than in complex groups — you can add complexity by nesting multiple symbols. Avoid redundant work and keep your files small and easy to manage by reusing artwork and animation whenever possible.

WEB RESOURCE We'd like to know what you think about this chapter. Visit `www.flashsupport.com/feedback` to fill out an online survey with your comments.

Summary

- The Flash authoring environment includes several features that have been adapted from tools that are used for creating traditional animation. Onion skinning, keyframes, and tweens are the digital equivalents of layered transparent cels, keyart, and manual inbetweens.

- There are three basic ways to create animation: frame-by-frame animation, two types of keyframed animation (shape and classic motion tweens), and a new object-based motion tween that uses property keyframes rather than standard keyframes. Most projects require a combination of all three types of animation.

- The new motion tween model is object based, which makes it possible to delete the target object without "breaking" the tween and transfer the animation properties easily to a new target object. Object-based tweens do not require keyframes but instead track changes made to the target object on auto-inserted property keyframes. Property keyframes can be modified (along with animation curves and easing curves), using the new Motion Editor panel.

- Tween spans for object-based motion tweens exist on tween layers (a new layer type) that limit editing options in order to protect the tween.

- You can use shape tweens only to interpolate raw shapes (including broken-apart text), and you can use motion tweens only to interpolate editable text or symbols.

- Tweens add less to file size than frame-by-frame animation because Flash calculates the difference between the keyframes instead of having to store unique artwork for every frame in a sequence. However, tweens can be very processor intensive if complex transitions or alpha layers need to be interpolated and rendered.

- You can modify the pace of tweened animation by extending or shortening the span of the tween and also by adjusting the Easing settings to create acceleration or deceleration in a sequence.

- The new Motion Editor opens a whole range of possibilities for controlling the interpolation of properties in a tween. Properties can be set to progress along a single curve, or their individual curves can be modified to create more sophisticated tween effects.

- Timeline Effects have been replaced by a new Motion Presets panel that gives you a list of ready-made animation patterns that can be applied to Movie clip symbols and modified by using the Motion Editor panel.

- Saving your own motion presets (or importing XML files for other custom motion presets) enables you to reuse animation patterns without having to use ActionScript or repeat tween steps for timeline animation that you want to use on more than one item.

Chapter 12

Applying Filters, Blends, Guides, and Masks

This chapter introduces you to some of the key tools in the Flash authoring environment that support expressiveness — another term for creative options for designers. If you've worked with other graphics programs, you'll appreciate the creative potential of filters and the Blends menu built into the Properties panel. If you've never used a filter or heard of a blend mode, you'll be relieved to discover how easy it is to apply these features and amazed at how much they can do to enhance your projects.

We also explain how layers can do more than just hold the content of your Flash movie, and show you how to turn normal layers into guides or masks.

Applying Filters in Flash

Filters offer shortcuts for adding visual polish to your Flash designs. Instead of manually editing shapes to create drop shadows or adjusting gradient fills to create bevels, you can simply apply a live filter and use the built-in settings to adjust the final effect. Filters are rendered on-the-fly and although they change the appearance of your symbol instances, they do not result in any additional symbols being generated and added to the library. In addition, filters do not interfere with the "editability" of your content — you can always modify the original text or symbol instance without "breaking" the filter effect. Filters can be layered in any order, and you can make modifications to the individual filter settings at any time. You can also add or control filters at runtime with ActionScript, but for now we'll focus on applying filters in the authoring environment — which doesn't require any code! Filters are rendered as you add or adjust them so you can always see just what you'll get when the final movie is published.

IN THIS CHAPTER

Applying Flash filters

Animating filter effects with motion tweens

Understanding differences between color properties and color filters

Working with blends

Working with layers as guides

Adding masks

Setting up elements for animation with Distribute to Layers

385

NEW FEATURE Filters are now found in a section of the vertical Properties panel rather than in their own panel. Filters applied to animated symbol instances can be adjusted with custom curves in the new Motion Editor panel.

Adding and adjusting filters

As shown in Figure 12.1, filters are now in their own section of the CS4 vertical Properties panel. To apply a filter, follow these steps:

1. **Select an item on the Stage that is compatible with filters — a Movie clip instance, Button symbol instance, or text field.**

2. **Open the Properties panel, and scroll down or resize the panel until you can see the Filters section (click the arrow on the left to twirl the Filters live list open if it isn't open already).**

3. **Click the small Add Filter page icon (shown in Figure 12.2) on the far left side of the row of control buttons at the bottom of the Filters section.** This opens the Filters menu (shown in Figure 12.1).

After a filter is selected from the drop-down menu, it appears in the live list in the Filters panel and you see the filter effect (with default settings) applied to your selected item.

FIGURE 12.1

The Filters section of the Properties panel makes it easy to add live effects.

As shown in Figure 12.2, the settings for each applied filter are accessible in twirl-down sections of the live Filters list. You can keep all the twirl-down sections open so filter settings are visible (by scrolling or expanding the Properties panel), but it's easier to manage the list if you collapse the filter settings and only open them one at a time when you need to modify a setting. The settings vary for each filter, but after you become familiar with the options, you'll find it easy to adjust individual filters. To remove a filter at any time, simply select the name of the filter in the live list and click the trash can (–) icon at the bottom of the panel section.

 All blue numeric values for filter properties are hot text fields that can be adjusted by clicking and dragging or by double-clicking and then typing new values.

TIP Applied filters can be temporarily toggled off (and back on) to preview different filter combinations by clicking the eye icon at the bottom of the panel section.

Some filter effects have unique controls, but most are created with different combinations of a series of basic settings. The default filter settings are a good starting point, and in some cases they might even give you the result you want, although most likely you'll need to modify the settings to achieve a satisfactory final effect.

It would be an overwhelming task to document every combination of settings on every filter, but an overview of the main settings will provide you with enough guidance for experimentation:

FIGURE 12.2

Individual settings for applied filters can be adjusted at any time by selecting a filter in the live list. Controls for filters have been improved in CS4 and they are easily accessible in the Properties panel.

Open live filter(twirled down)

Collapsed live filter(twirled up)

Filter properties

Selected text field with filters applied

Add Filter   Remove filter   Live Filter list

Presets   Reset filter properties

(Copy to) Clipboard   Disable/Enable toggle

- **Blur X, Blur Y:** Sets the distance that the edge of a shape extends horizontally (X) and vertically (Y) to create a graduated or softened edge for shadow, blur, bevel, and glow effects. This has the same effect as the distance setting in the Soften Fill Edges dialog box for shapes. The default blur distance is 5 and the range is from 0 to 100. By default, the lock icon is turned on to constrain the X and Y settings to the same value, creating a symmetrical, graduated effect. If you prefer to make the X and Y settings independent of each other, toggle the constrain option off by clicking the lock icon.

- **Strength:** Sets the opacity of the rendered effect. The default setting is 100. The range is from 0 to 1,000. However, for all practical purposes, the effective range for most filters is from 0 (invisible) to 100 (solid center area with normal falloff in graduated area). Increasing the strength of a filter beyond 100 percent adds opacity to the stepped (or softened) areas of the shape. The opacity is increased incrementally from the most solid area to the least solid area of the stepped edge.

CAUTION At the maximum Strength setting of 1,000 percent, all the steps within the blur distance of a filter are rendered at 100 percent opacity, which usually counteracts the visual impact of the filter. The result is an expanded solid shape with a slightly jagged edge, rather than a nice-looking shadow or bevel.

- **Quality:** Sets the fidelity or smoothness of the rendered effect. This setting has a major impact on the performance of the published movie. By default, Quality is set to Low. As the quality is increased to Medium or High, gradients are rendered more smoothly and the steps in blurs are softened, but the performance of the final movie is reduced. Your Flash movies perform better if you can achieve the visual effect you need by making adjustments to the Color and/or Blur settings rather than increasing the Quality setting.

TIP To make a Glow or Drop Shadow look less harsh, adjust the color to be a closer match to the background color rather than reduce strength or increase quality. Color settings have the least impact on the performance of the final movie.

- **Angle:** Sets the direction of offset to be applied with the Distance setting. If Distance is set to 0, changing the Angle (or degree of offset) has no visible effect. The default is a 45-degree angle and the range is 0 to 360 degrees. The higher the Distance setting, the more obvious the offset direction or angle will be.

- **Distance:** Sets the pixel value for the distance between the center point of the original item and the center point of the rendered filter (gradient). The default setting is 5 and the range is from −32 to 32 pixels. If the distance setting is 0, the rendered gradient and the original item are center aligned.

CAUTION If the Distance setting is 0 and the Blur setting is less than 5, it can be hard to see a filter effect if it is rendered outside (or behind) the original item.

- **Color:** Click color chips to access currently loaded swatches and set colors used to render Drop Shadow or Glow effects. The default solid color for Drop Shadow is Black (#000000); the default solid color for Glow is Red (#FF0000). The solid color that is set with the color chip automatically fades from solid to transparent to create a soft glow or shadow effect. The Bevel filter requires both a Shadow and a Highlight color — by default, these are set to black (#000000) and white (#FFFFFF), respectively. The Gradient Bevel and Gradient Glow filters make it possible to add multiple colors to rendered gradient effects. Click the color anchors on the gradient strip to access currently loaded swatches and set control points in the gradient.

NOTE The opacity of the center color anchor for gradient bevels and the left (outer) color anchor for gradient glows are fixed in position and set to 0 percent alpha. The color of these pointers can be changed, but the alpha level and anchor position can be changed only on the other anchors (or new anchors added to the gradient strip).

In addition to the adjustable settings, there are some check box options that expand the visual possibilities for filters:

- **Knockout:** Converts the original shape into a transparent area, while leaving the rendered effect visible in any area that was not cut out by the original shape.

- **Filter types:** For Blur and Drop Shadow filters, this is a check box to switch the rendered gradient from outside to inside the boundary of the original shape. For the multicolor gradient filters (Bevel, Gradient Glow, and Gradient Bevel), the options are listed in a drop-down menu that enables the filter to be set to render inside (Inner), outside (Outer), or inside *and* outside (Full) the boundaries of the original item.

CAUTION The Bevel filter works best when left at the default Inside setting. Outside and Full bevels require some adjustment to create a realistic, dimensional result rather than a messy, doubled-up drop-shadow effect.

TIP Inner Gradient Glow effects are easier to create with a custom gradient fill instead of applying the Gradient Glow filter with the Inner setting. A gradient fill is also less demanding at runtime than a Gradient Glow filter.

- **Hide object:** This option is the secret to creating sophisticated drop shadows (as we describe later in this chapter). When Hide object is enabled, the original object disappears, but the drop shadow is preserved.

NOTE Although Hide object and Knockout both convert the original shape into a transparent area, they do not have exactly the same result. The Hide object option preserves the entire gradient area rendered by a filter effect, and the Knockout option creates a "cutout" effect when combined with filters that are not set to render inside the boundaries of the original shape. Although Hide object can be selected when the Knockout option is also selected, there is no visible difference to the rendered graphic. If you decide to use the Knockout option, it is best to uncheck the Hide object option to avoid rendering redundant filters at runtime.

The filter settings described thus far relate to the various gradient-based filters. You will notice that the Adjust Color filter settings are unique. The values available with the Adjust Color filter settings for adjusting various color qualities will be familiar to anyone who has worked in image-editing programs like Photoshop or Fireworks. Flash updates the selected item on the Stage as you make color adjustments, so it is easy to experiment with the filter settings. However, it is important to know when to apply the Adjust Color filter and when to use the color controls available from the Properties panel.

CROSS-REF We discuss the differences between the Adjust Color filter and the Color Effect settings in the Properties panel in "Controlling Color: Properties versus Filters" later in this chapter.

Creating dimensional shadows

One limitation of the Drop Shadow filter is that it does not have a built-in skew setting. The workaround for creating a drop shadow with more depth illustrates how you can use the Hide object option and the Transform panel to enhance shadows created with the Drop Shadow filter. Here are the steps:

1. Place a text field, Movie clip, or Button instance on the Stage.

2. Create a new layer below the original content layer. Click the Insert Layer icon in the Timeline (or choose Insert ⇨ Timeline ⇨ Layer from the application menu). Drag the new layer to reorder it below the original layer in the layer stack.

3. **Copy the item from Step 1 to the new layer.** To do this, select the keyframe where the item exists and hold the Option key while dragging the keyframe content to the new layer, or select the item and use the copy command (Ctrl+C/⌘+C/), and then activate the new layer and use the Paste in Place command (Shift+Ctrl+V/Shift+⌘+V).

4. Lock the original content layer.

5. **Select the duplicate item on the lower layer and use the Transform panel to apply a stretch and skew.** As shown in Figure 12.3, we set the vertical scale to 130 percent and the horizontal skew to –45 degrees.

6. Open the Filters panel or activate the Filters tab in the Properties panel.

7. **Click the plus symbol and select Drop Shadow from the Filters list.** In the Drop Shadow settings, select the Hide object check box. Otherwise, the default settings are a good place to start.

   As shown in Figure 12.4, the default settings can be modified to create a softer shadow. In our example, the shadow Color was changed to medium gray (#666666), the Strength was set to 50 percent, and the Quality was set to Medium.

ON the CD-ROM We've included the finished file shown in Figure 12.4 on the CD-ROM so you can see how the shadow animates along with the original character. `CharacterAnim_Shadow.fla` and `CharacterAnim_shadow.swf` are both in the `DropShadow` subfolder of the `ch12` folder on the CD-ROM.

FIGURE 12.3

Use the Transform panel to modify the duplicate symbol instance so it creates a more realistic offset shadow.

FIGURE 12.4

A Drop Shadow filter applied to the skewed symbol instance with the Hide object option enabled, and a few adjustments to the default settings, results in a more realistic, dimensional shadow.

Combining filters and saving custom presets

Multiple filters added to one item are rendered in the order they appear in the live list, from top to bottom. Changing the order of filters by dragging a filter name up or down in the live list changes the final result of the combined effect, but the settings for each filter are preserved and editable.

If you have created a special combination of filters or found a custom filter setting that you want to reuse, the Presets option makes it easy to save and access your own list of filter effects.

To save a filter setting or filter combo to the Presets menu, follow these steps:

1. **Select the item that has the filters and settings applied that you want to save.**

NOTE   All filters in the live list for the selected item will be saved with the preset, including any filters that are toggled off. When the custom filter is applied from the Presets menu to another item, the settings will be identical.

2. **In the Filters section of the Properties panel, click the multi-page icon to open the filter Presets menu (as shown in Figure 12.5).** From the Presets menu, select Save As.

FIGURE 12.5

The Presets menu in the Filters section of the Properties panel enables you to manage and apply any custom filter settings or filter combinations that you want to save for reuse.

3. **Type a name for your custom filter settings or filter combo (as shown in Figure 12.6) and click OK.**

   The named preset is added to the bottom of the Presets menu, along with any other saved Presets (in alphabetical order), shown in Figure 12.7, and can be applied to other items.

FIGURE 12.6

You can name and save custom settings for a specific filter or a combination of filters in the Presets menu for reuse.

FIGURE 12.7

Saved filter presets appear alphabetically in the Presets menu — the presets are saved on an application level for reuse in any active document.

CAUTION When a preset is applied to an item, any other filters that have been applied to that item are cleared and replaced with the filters (and settings) that were saved with the preset. To see the live filter list for the applied preset, you may have to deselect and then reselect the item to which it was applied — forcing the panel to update.

After a preset is applied to an item, the settings can be modified on that item without corrupting the saved preset. Unfortunately, the Presets list doesn't have a centralized edit option, but you can select the Rename or Delete option from the Preset menu to load your list of currently saved presets into dialog boxes that enable you to rename an item or remove an item from the list. If you want to share your filter presets with other people, all you have to do is provide them with the XML file that is saved for each preset in the Flash Configuration folder. The standard file paths for saved filter presets are as follows:

Windows:

```
C:\Documents and Settings\username\Local Settings\Application
    Data\Adobe\Flash CS4\language\Configuration\Effects\filtername.
    xml
```

Macintosh:

```
Macintosh HD/Users/username/Library/Application Support/Adobe/
    Flash CS4/language/Configuration/Effects/filtername.xml
```

After the XML files are copied into the same location on other people's computers, the presets appear in their Presets menu when they start Flash CS4. Filter swapping is an easy way to share creative resources and to keep effects consistent for projects that rely on filters for a specific look.

Although you may occasionally find it helpful to combine filters, it is best to try and achieve the result you want by first adjusting the settings of a single filter and/or modifying the symbol instance by using the Color Effect settings in the Properties panel or the Transform tools. As with any intensive effect rendered at runtime, multiple filters have a negative impact on the performance of the published Flash movie.

Animating filters with motion tweens

The Flash engineers have done a great deal of work to make it as easy as possible to combine filters with motion tweens for animated effects. The result is a very intuitive system that works behind the scenes to support tweens while preserving editable filter settings.

NOTE Filters are not necessarily incompatible with shape tweens, but because filters can only be applied to symbols or text fields and shape tweens can only be applied to primitive shapes, filters and shape tweens never get a chance to work together. The only work-around for this rule is to create a shape tween inside of a Movie clip and then apply a filter to the Movie clip. In this case, the final visual result is a combination of a shape tween and a filter, but they remain on separate timelines.

You can apply a filter to an item and then tween it, or you can select an item that has been tweened and add a filter to enhance the motion — in most cases, you'll get exactly the animated effect you were hoping for. The only time you'll need to know what is going on behind the scenes is when you don't get the result you want on the first try.

Here are some notes that should help you troubleshoot if things go wrong when you try to combine filters and motion tweens:

■ Filters "stick" to symbol instances, so if you insert a keyframe (with the same content as the initial keyframe) and set up a motion tween, the settings and the stacking order in the live list automatically match in the first keyframe and the last keyframe of the tween.

■ If you add a filter to a symbol in one keyframe of a tween, Flash automatically adds a matching filter with all the settings adjusted to create "no effect" to the symbol in the other keyframe. This is also called a "dummy filter" because it has no visible effect on the symbol, but it is required to support the tween.

■ If you remove a filter from a symbol in one keyframe of a tween, Flash automatically clears the matching filter from the other keyframe.

■ If you apply different filters (or different combinations of filters) on two different keyframes and then apply a tween, Flash analyzes the symbol with the most filters and applies dummy filters to the symbol in the other keyframe to support the tween. The visual difference between the two symbols is interpolated in the span of the tween.

■ You can modify filter settings to create a visual change from the first keyframe to the last keyframe in a motion tween. The differences are tweened evenly across the span unless you use the Motion Editor to adjust the interpolation.

■ The knockout and type of gradient (such as inner, outer, or full) filter settings do not interpolate properly as part of a tween if they are set differently on the beginning and end keyframes. If the filter options in the first keyframe and the end keyframe of a tween are inconsistent and cannot be interpolated properly, Flash applies the options set in the first keyframe to the frames in the span of the tween.

Using the Motion Editor to control filter interpolation

By default, the interpolation of any differences in filter settings from the first keyframe to the last frame match the interpolation of the motion tween — that is, the filters change at the same rate as any other characteristics of the item that have been modified to create animation in the tween. The default Simple (Slow) easing setting applies equally to all changes in the characteristics of an item. As described in Chapter 11, if you need more precise control over the interpolation of different aspects of a tween, you can use the Motion Editor to add easing for tweened characteristics including Motion, Transformation, Color Effect, and/or Filters. As shown in Figure 12.8, the Motion Editor enables you to create a unique interpolation curve for each of the various properties that can be animated in a tween. You can set a unique curve to apply to all properties, or set unique curves for selected properties, leaving the default curve for others.

To access easing settings for filter properties in a tween:

1. Select a motion tween in the Timeline or select a tweened item on the Stage.

2. Click the Motion Editor tab (to the right of the Timeline tab in the Essentials CS4 workspace layout).

3. Scroll down until you see the filter properties that you want to modify or adjust in the tween. Note that each property in an applied filter has its own easing setting. The options available for easing depend on the eases you have loaded into the Easing section of the Motion Editor. By default, Simple (Slow) is loaded and available as a setting for all properties.

4. To add additional easing options, click the plus (+) icon in the Eases section of the Motion Editor. Select a preset easing curve from the drop-down menu (shown in Figure 12.9), or add your own custom curve — if you can think of any that aren't already in the list!

TIP If you want a larger view of a specific easing curve, double-click any row to expand it. Double-click again to return it to normal height.

FIGURE 12.8

The interpolation of filters in a tween can be controlled separately from the interpolation of other characteristics by adding and/or adjusting a custom easing curve.

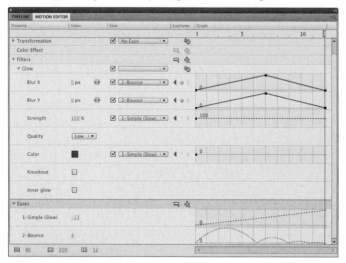

FIGURE 12.9

Add as many of the preset easing curves as you want in the Easing section of the Motion Editor, or create your own custom easing curve.

Controlling Color: Properties versus Filters

The Adjust Color filter loads a set of controls for making color adjustment to Movie clips, Button symbols, and text fields. The best way to explain these controls is to compare them to other Flash color settings. Some of these controls are unique and some replicate settings available in the Color panel (for raw shapes, shape primitives and drawing objects) and/or in the Properties panel Color menu. These three different color control areas are shown in Figure 12.10, with an additional diagram (A1) to call out the features of the Color panel that overlap with slider settings for the Adjust Color filter.

The controls shown in Figure 12.10 enable various workflows for setting and adjusting color in the Flash authoring environment. In most cases, you start with the Color panel (or Swatches panel) to choose and/or modify fill and stroke colors for initial primitive shapes or drawing objects. After the raw graphics are converted into reusable symbols, the Color Effect settings available in the Properties panel and/or the Adjust Color filter can be applied to modify symbol instances without changing the original fill and stroke colors. The sliders and hot text values for adjusting color with either of these options are easy to use, and you will most likely achieve the result you want with just a little experimentation. However, there are important differences between the Color Effect properties and the Adjust Color filter settings, and the interaction of the different settings can become quite complex. To clarify the functions (and the advantages or limitations) of the various settings available with these two options, we have included a brief section for each.

WEB RESOURCE If you want to learn more about various color models and the differences between HSV/HSB (hue, saturation, value; or hue, saturation, brightness) and HSL (hue, saturation, lightness) color spaces, a good place to start is Wikipedia: `http://en.wikipedia.org/wiki/HSB_color_space`.

Adjust Color filter

Figure 12.11 shows a sample of the range of color transformations that can be achieved with the hot text controls that load into the Filters section of the Properties panel when you apply the Adjust Color filter to Movie clip instances, Button instances, or text fields.

CROSS-REF The grayscale version of the sample color transformations shown in Figure 12.11 gives you a hint of what is possible with the Adjust Color filter, but the color version of this figure included in the color insert in this book is much more informative.

ON the CD-ROM We have included the source file with the various transformed Movie clip instances shown in Figure 12.11 on the CD-ROM. Open `AdjustColorFilter.fla` from the `ColorEffectsvsFilters` folder in the `ch12` folder on the CD-ROM to see the samples in the Flash authoring environment. To see these same transformations applied to a sample bitmap, open `AdjustColorFilter_bitmaps.fla` from the same location.

FIGURE 12.10

The options for adjusting color in Flash include the Color panel (A), the Color Effect menu (B), and the Adjust Color filter (C) — which enables instance-level color transformations similar to the raw color edits supported in the Color panel.

Finally, you can make subtle adjustments (on an instance level) to Movie clips, Button symbols, and text fields, without having to go back to the Color panel and change the stroke and fill colors of the original symbol. Unlike the Color Effect options in the Properties panel, the Adjust Color filter makes it easy to combine different types of color transformation without manually adjusting individual RGB values. By default, all settings are loaded as "neutral" — values are set to 0 so that no color transformation is visible on the selected item when the filter is first applied. Color transformations are applied for instant visual feedback as the values are adjusted. Filters apply on an instance level, and settings can be modified at any time by selecting an instance and choosing Adjust Color from the live filter list in the Properties panel. The following values can be applied individually or in combination to Movie clips, Button symbols, and text fields:

FIGURE 12.11

The Adjust Color filter enables subtle color transformations of symbol instances and text fields.

- **Brightness:** Alters the RGB values for the original color to make it appear lighter or darker without changing the hue. The range for filter Brightness is –100 to +100. The default or no change value is 0. The numeric value that appears in the Brightness field is added to the RGB values of the original color to create a new shade, within the minimum and maximum values of 0 and 255, respectively. For example, a red fill (255, 0, 0) set to +50 brightness transforms into light red (255, 50, 50). The same red fill (255, 0, 0) set to –50 brightness transforms into dark red (205, 0, 0). As shown in Figure 12.12, the results of changing Brightness with the Adjust Color filter are different than the results of changing Brightness with the Color Effect settings.

NOTE Although the range for the Brightness filter and the Brightness Color Effect might seem the same at first glance, the significantly different results that these two options achieve are due to one being a relative (or percentage-based) setting and the other being an absolute (or decimal-based) setting. The Brightness filter is applied as an absolute numeric value, and the Color Effect Brightness property is applied as a relative percentage-based value. Regardless of the original color, setting Color Effect Brightness to 100% shifts the RGB values to white (255, 255, 255) and –100% Brightness shifts the RGB values to black (0,0,0). Any other Brightness setting is calculated as the percentage between these two extremes, and the RGB values are transformed accordingly.

- **Contrast:** At the minimum contrast setting of –100, all RGB values are forced to 64, 64, 64, making everything medium gray. The RGB values at the maximum contrast setting of 100 vary depending on the original colors, but they are forced closer to 0 or 255. The default or no change value is 0. The greater the numeric difference between RGB values, the greater the amount of contrast. In visual terms, light colors get lighter and dark colors get darker as contrast is *increased*, whereas all colors are brought closer to medium gray as contrast is *decreased*.

FIGURE 12.12

Numeric settings applied with the Adjust Color filter Brightness result in less extreme value changes than Percentage settings applied with the Color Effect Brightness.

- **Saturation:** Saturation can also be thought of as the intensity or purity of color. At the minimum saturation setting of –100, the image is rendered in grayscale with no color intensity, similar to the hues found closer to the *bottom* of the color selection field in the Color panel. At the maximum saturation setting of 100, the colors are as intense or as close to pure color as possible, similar to the hues found closer to the *top* of the color selection field in the Color panel.

- **Hue:** The Hue slider has a different range than the other Adjust Color filter sliders. To span the full range of the 360-degree color wheel, the slider values are from –180 to 180. The default or no change value is 0. If you were looking at a real color wheel, reducing the hue value would be equivalent to moving counterclockwise around the wheel, and increasing the hue value would be equivalent to moving clockwise around the wheel. At either extreme (–180 or 180), the resulting color would be directly opposite the original color on the color wheel. The relationship of colors directly opposite on the color wheel is known as *complementary*.

WEB RESOURCE There are many books and online resources dedicated to color theory, and there are many different versions of the color wheel. A good explanation and an illustration of an RGB color wheel can be found at www.color-wheel-pro.com/color-theory-basics.html. Color Wheel Pro is one of many software programs available to help designers create successful color schemes by using color wheel relationships as a guideline.

CAUTION Flash Filters (including the Adjust Color settings) are compatible only with Flash Player 8 and later. If you plan to publish content for earlier versions of the Flash Player, you are limited to using the Color Effect settings in the Properties panel to make adjustments to the appearance of symbol instances, or using the Color panel to modify the original stroke and fill colors in primitive shapes.

Color properties

As we introduced in Chapter 6, "Symbols, Instances, and the Library," the Color Effect settings in the Properties panel provide some options for modifying the appearance of symbol instances without changing the original symbol stored in the library. After a Color Effect style is selected from the Color drop-down menu, the controls needed to apply the color adjustment appear in the Properties panel. By default, "neutral" settings (0 percent change) are loaded as a starting point. After the values for a property are modified, they are stored and loaded as the default when you select another instance. The Color Effect settings loaded in the Properties panel are simple and intuitive and enable you to make basic color adjustments by using familiar controls:

- **Brightness:** The Brightness Color property has the same range as the Brightness setting in the Adjust Color filter (–100 to 100); however, as described previously, the Brightness property creates more drastic color transformations because it is applied as a relative or percentage-based value. At the minimum Brightness setting (–100), all RGB values are forced to black (0,0,0), and at the maximum Brightness setting (100), all RGB values are forced to white (255,255,255).

- **Tint:** The color theory definition of a tint is a color produced by adding white to a pure color. The Tint property in Flash enables you to select any color (not just white) to "mix" with the original color. You can also select how much of the new color you want to mix with your original colors — from the lowest setting of 0 percent to the maximum setting of 100 percent. At the minimum setting, the original colors are unchanged. At the maximum setting, the new tint color completely replaces all the original colors. At the default setting of 50 percent, the rendered color values are an even mix of the original colors and the selected tint color.

- **Alpha:** This setting controls how opaque the selected instance will be. The values that control alpha are counterintuitive (as they are in the Color panel). At the minimum alpha level of 0 percent, the item is transparent. At the maximum alpha level of 100 percent, the item is fully opaque or "solid."

Using advanced color effects: Understanding relative and absolute color settings

The Advanced effect option shown in Figure 12.13 includes two columns of settings for Red, Green, and Blue color channels, plus the setting for Alpha. These settings are accessible when a symbol instance is selected on the Stage and the Advanced option is chosen from the Style drop-down menu in the Color Effect section of the Properties panel. Although these columns may seem redundant at first, they actually provide very different options for controlling the appearance of instance color. The important difference between these two types of controls is that the first column creates *relative* changes by applying percentage-based adjustments, and the second column creates *absolute* change by adding or subtracting integer values.

FIGURE 12.13

The default Advanced effect settings shown with the symbol instance `testStar`, with no effect applied

TIP The most recent transformation that was applied to an item by using any of the other Color Effect styles is preserved if you decide to switch to the Advanced color effect style. The equivalent values are transferred to the RGB or Alpha values for the Advanced color effect. This is a helpful way to get started with more complex transformations instead of starting from scratch. For example, you could select a Tint setting and then switch to the Advanced color option to add an alpha setting that would be combined with the RGB values carried over from the original tint.

Other than playing with these settings, the easiest way to understand what some of the possible combinations produce is to dig out your calculator and find a chart of RGB color swatches (with decimal values rather than hex values). By taking the RGB values in your original instance, multiplying them by the percentage entered in the relative value field, and adding the value shown in the absolute color field, you arrive at the new RGB value that appears in the symbol instance when the effect is applied. If this sounds confusing, read on.

ON the CD-ROM Because color examples are not very helpful illustrated in black and white, we have included the relevant graphics in a Flash file that you can open for reference. Compare the Advanced Color Effect (relative) layer with the Advanced Color Effect (absolute) layer in `colorEdits.fla` in the `ColorEffectsVsFilters` folder in the `ch12` folder on the CD-ROM.

Relative color control

The first column of values adjusts the color of the instance relative to the percentages of color (or alpha) present in the original with a range of –100 percent to 100 percent. The default, or "no effect," setting is 100 percent. With these controls, 100 percent red does not change everything to pure red or 255 red, but rather it displays 100 percent of the current percentage of red in the existing colors. For example, yellow (255, 255, 0) cannot be made more orange by increasing the amount of red because 255 x 100 percent is still 255 — the maximum amount of red. However, if you reduce the percentage of green to 45 percent of the original value, the ratio of red is increased, making the visible color shift to orange (255, [255 x 45 percent], 0 or 255, 102, 0).

This process of reducing the amount of the opposite (or complementary) color to alter the ratio of colors is called *subtractive* color adjustment, and it can be helpful to remember some basic color theory to predict how it will alter the appearance of your symbol instance. Because the color value changes that you make are applied to all the colors in your symbol, the overall effect can be more complex than just shifting one color in your palette. You will find, for example, that *reducing* the percentage of red and green to 0 for the testStar symbol instance (see the `colorEdits.fla` file on the CD-ROM) causes the gray and white areas to shift to blue, whereas the red and green areas shift to black, and the originally black areas remain unaltered.

Because the maximum value for relative Alpha is also 100 percent, this control cannot be used to increase the alpha setting of an instance. For example, a symbol that has an alpha fill of 50 percent cannot be made to appear more solid because 100 percent of 50 percent is still only 50 percent alpha.

Absolute color control

The settings in the right column are referred to as *absolute* color controls because they add or subtract color in concrete amounts regardless of the color values in the symbol instance. The scale of absolute color is from −255 to 255, and the default or "no effect" setting is 0. When absolute color is applied to a symbol instance, it is possible to make more drastic global color changes than you can make with relative color adjustments.

The effect of absolute color value changes made with the Advanced color effect is similar to the effect of using the Tint color effect. What makes these controls more advanced is that not only can you add a tint by increasing the value of certain colors, but you can also add an *inverse* tint by using negative values. So, for example, you could add a red tint to all the colors present in the testStar symbol instance, with the exception of white and pure red (which already contain 255 red), by entering a value of 255 Red, or you could add a yellow tint to all colors containing blue by entering a value of −255 Blue; this makes pure blue (0, 0, 255) turn to black (0, 0, 0), and white (255, 255, 255) turn to pure yellow (255, 255, 0).

ON the CD-ROM You can see the original `testStar` symbol instance and several modified examples, including those described in this section, in the Advanced Color Effect (absolute) layer of `colorEdit.fla` in the `ColorEffectsVsFilters` folder in the `ch12` folder on the CD-ROM.

Perhaps one of the most unique feats that absolute values can perform is to make a symbol instance that contains alpha fills or strokes appear less transparent. Because the alpha settings are absolute, it is possible to shift an item with an original alpha setting of less than 100 percent to any opacity level between invisible (−255) and completely solid (255).

If you've entered negative values in the relative alpha setting, you can even make an area with an alpha fill visible while solid areas are made invisible. Consider a shape that has an area of solid fill (100 percent or 255 alpha) and an area of transparent color (40 percent or 102 alpha). If this shape is converted into a symbol and then modified by using the Advanced color effect options, you could enter a relative alpha value of −100 percent and an absolute alpha value of 255. When these effect settings are applied, the solid fill in the symbol instance would be invisible with 0 percent alpha (255 x −100 percent + 255 = 0), whereas the originally transparent fill would be visible with 60 percent alpha (102 x −100 percent + 255 = 153). Compare the modified `testStar` instance shown in Figure 12.14 with the original instance shown in Figure 12.13.

FIGURE 12.14

Using a combination of relative and absolute alpha values, the transparency levels in the original `testStar` instance can be inverted.

The confusion that these settings sometimes cause has created debate about whether negative alpha settings can really be applied. As long as you can remember that outside of the absolute settings for the Advanced color effect, 0 percent alpha is invisible, whereas with the Advanced color effect settings, a 0 alpha setting is equal to no effect, you will be able to prove as we just did, that negative alpha effects can be used to invert alpha values, similar to the way that negative color effects can be used to invert color values.

Layering Graphics with Blend Modes

If you use Photoshop or other image-editing applications, you may be familiar with using blend modes, although for many people this remains a somewhat mysterious tool. Blends are rendering tools that analyze the pixel values of overlapping images (the blend image and the underlying base images) to create a rendered image that is a mix of the two. The type of blend applied determines the formula used to generate the pixel values in the combined image. Blend modes can be applied to Movie clip and Button symbol instances in the authoring environment by using the Blending menu in the Properties panel (shown in Figure 12.15). The blend image interacts with any underlying images that it overlaps, even if they are not on the same layer.

TIP   The dotted line breaks that separate the blend modes in the Blending menu may seem arbitrary, but they actually differentiate the blend modes into groups based on the type of effect they have on images. Keep this in mind while you read the descriptions of each blend mode in the next section; you will start to notice similarities in the modes that are grouped.

FIGURE 12.15

The Blending menu is available in the Display section of the Properties panel when you select a Movie clip or Button instance.

Understanding blend modes

Predicting the exact outcome of various blend modes is tricky because blends use different formulas on a pixel-by-pixel basis to mix the blended image with underlying images, and the result depends on the pixel values of both the underlying images (or *base color*) and the overlapping image (or *blend color*). The most common advice for working with blends is to experiment until you get a result that you like — we encourage you to do exactly that! However, it is helpful to have some idea of how each blend works and what visual problems they can solve. Compare Figure 12.16, which shows two source bitmaps (left and center), overlapped with blending set to Layer or Normal (right), to Figure 12.17, which shows the results of Flash blend modes applied to mix the images in various ways.

NOTE You'll notice that we didn't include an image in Figure 12.17 to illustrate the Layer blend mode applied by itself. That is because the Layer blend mode has no effect, unless it is combined with a nested Erase or Alpha blend mode.

FIGURE 12.16

A base image (left) and a blend image (center) overlapped with blend mode set to Normal or Layer create a standard layered graphic with no mixing of pixel values (right).

 + =

Base image   Blend image   Layer (or Normal)

FIGURE 12.17

The 12 different effects that can be created by applying blending to layered images. The results vary depending on the images that are combined, but the formula used for each blend type is consistent. Unlike other blend modes, the Alpha and Erase blend modes require a nested structure with a Layer blend applied to the parent symbol instance.

Darken   Multiply   Lighten   Screen   Overlay   Hard Light

Add   Subtract   Difference   Invert   *Alpha   *Erase

*Nested in an MC with Layer blend mode applied

The blend modes available in Flash include the following:

- **Normal:** The default blend mode for new symbol instances. No interpolation is applied and pixel values are left unchanged.

- **Layer:** Creates no visual effect on its own, but is required for Alpha and Erase blend modes to work.

- **Darken:** Compares the brightness of the pixels in the base image with the pixels in the blend image. Pixels in the base image that are lighter than the blend image are replaced with pixels from the blend image. Pixels in the base image that are darker than the blend image are left unchanged.

- **Multiply:** Multiplies the RGB values of the pixels in the base image with the pixels in the blend image. The resulting pixels are a darkened combination of both the base image and the blend image. Multiplying any color with black results in solid black; multiplying any color with white leaves the pixels unchanged.

- **Lighten:** Compares the brightness of the pixels in the base image with the pixels in the blend image. Pixels in the base image that are darker than the blend image are replaced with pixels from the blend image. Pixels in the base image that are lighter than the blend image are left unchanged. The blend image always disappears when it's layered over white.

- **Screen:** Analyzes the color values and multiplies the inverse of the blend and base colors. The resulting pixels are a lightened combination of both the base image and the blend image. Screening with black leaves the base image unchanged. Screening with white produces solid white. The blend image always disappears when it's layered over white.

- **Overlay:** Pixels are screened or multiplied depending on the pixel values in the base image. If the base color is lighter than mid-gray, the image is lightened (screened), and if the base color is darker than mid-gray, the image is darkened (multiplied). The blend image overlays the base image while preserving the highlights and shadows of the base image. The resulting image is an even blend of the base image and the blend image, usually with increased contrast in both images. Overlaying black results in a shaded version of the base image. Overlaying white results in a bleached version of the base image. The blend image disappears when it's layered over any pure color (black, white, pure red, pure green, and so on).

- **Hard light:** Pixels are screened or multiplied, depending on the pixel values in the blend image. If the blend color is lighter than mid-gray, the image is lightened (screened). If the blend color is darker than mid-gray, the image is darkened (multiplied). The base image is mixed with the blend while preserving the highlights and shadows of the blend image. Overlaying pure black or pure white results in solid black or solid white, respectively.

- **Add:** Adds the color values of the blend image to the color values of the base image. The result is a bleached-out combination of the two images. Adding pure white results in a solid white image; adding pure black has no effect on the base image.

- **Subtract:** Subtracts the blend color value from the base color value. The result is a darkened combination of the two images. Subtracting pure white from any color results in a solid black image. Subtracting pure black has no effect on the base image.

- **Difference:** Analyzes the color values in the base and the blend and subtracts the brighter values from the darker values. The result is a reversal of color values. Black blended with any color has no effect. White blended with any color inverts the color. The resulting image looks like a film negative of the combined images.

- **Invert:** Inverts the base image in any areas overlapped by the blend image. The contents of the blend image have no bearing on the transformation of the base color values; the blend image acts merely as an "active area" for the inversion effect.

- **Alpha:** Alpha blend mode can be used to apply the contents of a nested Movie clip with alpha areas as a mask for an image in a parent Movie clip with Layer blend mode applied.

- **Erase:** Erase blend mode can be used to apply the contents of a nested Movie clip as an eraser to cut out an area of an image in a parent Movie clip with Layer blend mode applied.

TIP Using a solid fill with Alpha set to 0% in an Alpha blend has the same effect as using a solid fill in an Erase blend.

Applying basic blends

That's a lot of visual calculation to try and imagine without actually using blends. The steps for applying the "basic blends" (all but Alpha and Erase) are straightforward:

1. **Select a Movie clip or Button symbol instance that you want to use as a blend image to layer with underlying base images.**

TIP   Images on layers above the layer with the blend symbol instance are not transformed by the blend mode. Don't forget that you can use the Modify ➪ Arrange commands if you need to modify the stacking order of images on the same layer.

2. **Open the Display section in the Properties panel, and from the Blending menu, select a blend type.**

That's it! You can see how the blend image interacts with different base images by dragging it to overlap other images in your Flash authoring environment. Color effects and filters can be used in combination with blend modes to get different hybrid results. All these effect tools interact to transform graphics rendered in the authoring environment, but they remain editable and each can be adjusted independently on an instance level. You can apply multiple blend modes on the same layer, but only one blend mode to any single symbol instance. The only compound blend modes are Alpha and Erase, which must be applied on a symbol timeline and combined with a Layer blend mode on the parent symbol instance, as described in the next section.

CAUTION   The background color of your Flash movie interacts with blend modes too. This is helpful to remember if the blend image is larger than the base image and you start getting unexpected results in the overhang areas. Applying a Layer mask to the blend image so that it is trimmed to match the base image removes any unwanted overhang areas that are mixing with the background color.

Applying compound blend modes: Alpha and Erase

Alpha and Erase blends are a great complement to Flash's standard masking tools, which can be counterintuitive at times. If you want to create a cutout in a shape by using a traditional mask, you actually have to create a shape on a mask layer that covers all the areas *except* the area you want to cut out. If you have been working in Flash for a while, this workflow is probably second nature, but when it comes to more subtle mask effects, like gradients or irregular shapes, it can be a headache to have to reverse-engineer a mask graphic. With Alpha blends, what you see is what you get — or rather, what you *don't* see is what you *won't* get! The steps for creating a compound blend are as follows:

1. **Create a Movie clip with content that will function as the base image (or convert an existing graphic that you want to mask into a Movie clip).**

2. **Open the Movie clip in Edit mode to access the Movie clip timeline.** To do this, double-click an instance on the Stage or the symbol name in the Library list.

3. **Create a new layer on the Movie clip timeline above the existing content that will be the base image for the Alpha or Erase blend.** To protect the base image(s), you may want to lock all layers but the new layer.

NOTE The base image or color can be any graphic type — shape primitive, drawing object, bitmap, or symbol instance — as long as it is nested inside of a Movie clip or Button symbol. The blend image has to be a Movie clip or Button symbol instance.

4. **In the new layer, create a graphic that will act as a mask.** Blend masks are the opposite of normal Flash layer masks in that the content in the Alpha or Erase blend symbol instance defines an area to make *invisible* in the base image rather than an area to make *visible*.

CAUTION Any content in a symbol instance with an Erase blend mode applied defines the area to be punched out of (or erased from) the underlying base image. The content of a symbol instance with an Alpha blend mode applied has no effect unless it contains areas with transparency; the amount of information erased from the base images will match the level of Alpha transparency in the blend symbol instance. A symbol instance with content set to 0 percent Alpha and applied as an Alpha blend has the same effect as an Erase blend.

5. **Convert the content on the blend layer into a Movie clip or Button symbol.**

6. **Select the symbol instance and position it on the Stage (still on the base image Movie clip timeline) to overlap the base image so that it defines the area you want to Erase or Alpha out.** Next, use the Blending menu in the Properties panel to apply an Alpha or Erase blend mode. The content of the blend image disappears, but don't panic — continue to the next step to complete the compound blend.

7. **Return to the Main Timeline.** (Double-click an empty area of the Stage or use the Scene button at the top of the Document window.)

8. **Select the parent symbol instance (that contains your base image and the currently invisible blend image), and use the Blending menu to apply a Layer blend.** If you opened the base symbol from the Library in Step 2, make sure that you have an instance dragged onto the Stage on the Main Timeline so you can apply the Layer blend mode to the instance.

Voila! You should see the content of your blend image punched out (Erase blend) or rubbed out (Alpha blend) of the base image; either the background color of the Flash movie or any underlying images on the Stage will be visible through the empty areas created in the base image.

ON the CD-ROM Open `Erase_blend.fla` from the `Blending` folder in the `ch12` folder on the CD-ROM if you want to analyze an example of the nested symbol structure required to render Erase and Alpha blend modes successfully.

In addition to supporting a more intuitive workflow for creating masks and enabling Alpha-based masks, compound blends can be used to create animated transition effects. Continue to the next section if you want to try using an Alpha blend to create an animated color fade effect.

Creating an animated Alpha blend

The following example uses an animated Alpha blend to selectively fade out a black-and-white image to reveal a color image. The trick for this effect is to use two instances of the same color image, with the Adjust Color filter applied to make one instance a grayscale version. There are a lot of steps, but the final file structure is straightforward and the effect is pretty cool, so let's get started:

1. Open a new Flash document.

2. **Import a color bitmap and convert it to a Movie clip (or place an existing Movie clip instance on the Stage, preferably one with bright colors).**

3. **Place two instances of the Movie clip on the Stage so that they are layered and aligned — select both instances and use the Vertical Center and Horizontal Center align commands.**

4. **Select the topmost Movie clip instance and use the Adjust Color filter (in the Filters section of the Properties panel) to set the Saturation of the image to –100.** This drains the color out so that it looks grayscale.

5. **With the grayscale Movie clip instance still selected, use the Blending menu (in the Display section of the Properties panel) to apply Layer blend mode.** You won't see any visible change yet.

6. **Double-click the grayscale Movie clip instance to access the Movie clip timeline in Edit mode.**

7. **Create a new layer at the top of the layer stack in the Movie clip timeline.** Lock the other layer(s) with the bitmap or graphics you plan to use as a base image.

8. **Select the Oval tool (O) in the Tools panel and set the Fill color to use a default radial gradient.** Use the Color panel to apply 0 percent Alpha to the right color anchor. This should create a circular gradient fill that has a transparent center that fades out to black. Set the stroke color to None.

9. **Click and drag on the Stage to create a circle that covers only a small area in the center of the original image.** In our file, the circle image was 100 x 100 pixels.

10. **Select the new circle and convert it into a Movie clip named** `alpha circle`.

11. **Use the Blending menu to apply an Alpha blend mode to the** `alpha circle` **Movie clip instance.** The circle Movie clip disappears, but don't panic. As you can see by the filled keyframe on the layer, the content is still there and you can select it to see the selection outline for the invisible instance.

12. **Double-click the** `alpha circle` **instance to access the Movie clip timeline and insert frames (F5) to extend the span of the circle graphic to frame 20.** Convert frame 20 into a keyframe (F6).

13. **Select the circle graphic in keyframe 20 and use the Transform panel or the Position and Size section of the Properties panel to increase the size of the circle so that it is larger than the bitmap base image.** We scaled the circle up to 400 x 400 pixels.

14. **Select keyframe 1 (still in the alpha circle timeline) and apply a shape tween.** You should now be able to scrub the Movie clip timeline to see the small circle in frame 1 scaling up to the size of the larger circle in frame 20.

15. **In order to see the Alpha blend applied as a mask, you have to return to the Main Timeline (click the Scene button).** The grayscale bitmap image should now have an area in the center that is "erased" in a soft, gradient circle that allows some of the color image to show through.

16. **The animated effect is visible only in the published .swf file or the Test Movie environment.** Press Ctrl+Return/⌘+Return to test the file and preview the animation.

> **ON the CD-ROM** To see the final result of our example file, open `anim_Alpha_blend.swf` from the `Blending` folder in the `ch12` folder on the CD-ROM. To analyze the file structure, open `anim_Alpha_blend.fla` from the same location.

You can always go back inside the nested symbols to modify the level of alpha in the blend image or change the style of fill from a radial gradient to a linear gradient or even a solid fill (with alpha set to less than 100 percent). The level of masking matches the level of alpha in the contents of the Alpha blend symbol instance. Alpha blends can be used to mask any type of image — even bitmaps or shape primitives. The only requirement is that the Alpha blend must be applied to a symbol instance and that symbol instance must be nested inside a Movie clip with a Layer blend applied. This is just one way of using a blend mode to create an interesting visual effect. There are many other possibilities, and when you understand the workflow for applying basic and compound blends, the rest is just a matter of experimentation!

Working with Special Layer Types: Guides and Masks

Besides storing and organizing the contents of your Flash project, layers offer some special features that help you create more advanced animation. Standard layers can be locked, hidden, or displayed as outlines, but they can also be converted into guide layers or mask layers. You can use each of these layer types to accomplish specific authoring tasks.

Flash gives you the flexibility to quickly change the behavior of layers at any time in the authoring environment so that you can take advantage of the special characteristics of each of these layer types as needed.

With the layer buttons at the lower left corner of the Timeline window, you have the option of creating standard layers and folder layers. If you have already created a standard layer, you can convert it into a guide, mask, or folder layer by using the contextual menu (opened by right-clicking or Ctrl+clicking the layer bar), or by changing settings in the Layer Properties dialog box (opened by double-clicking the layer icon or by choosing Modify ➪ Timeline ➪ Layer Properties from the application menu).

Flash automatically converts layers if you drag them into specific positions in the stacking order with other layer types. Although this sounds a bit cryptic, it will make sense as you read about each layer type and how it affects other layers. Each layer type has a unique icon, as shown in Figure 12.18.

FIGURE 12.18

A unique icon in the layer stack identifies each of the layer types. You can quickly assign or change the behavior of a layer by using the contextual menu.

> **NOTE**   Motion guide layers (shown in Figure 12.18) are now considered a "classic" feature because motion guides are created automatically on the same layer as your tweened item when you use the new tweening workflow in Flash CS4. This is a wonderful improvement to Flash and in most cases, motion guide layers are not missed. If you want to learn more about classic motion guides and how to apply them, refer to the archived content from *Flash CS3 Professional Bible* (Wiley, 2007): "Chapter 13: Applying Layer Types." You can find it online at www.flashsupport.com/archive.

Using guide layers

Guide layers are the only layer types (aside from classic motion guide layers) that are not exported with your final Flash movie (.swf). Guide layers are used primarily when you need to use an element as a reference in the authoring environment (.fla), but you don't want it to be part of the finished movie (.swf). To convert an existing layer into a guide layer, you can use the contextual menu and select Guide. Alternatively, you can open the Layer Properties dialog box (shown in Figure 12.19) by double-clicking the layer icon (or choosing Modify ➪ Timeline ➪ Layer Properties from the application menu) and then selecting the Guide check box.

> **TIP** As you are developing a project, it can be helpful to "turn off" certain layers while you're testing content on other layers. For example, by temporarily turning a layer that contains a large background graphic into a guide layer, the movie (.swf) renders more quickly for preview in the Test Movie environment. Remember to turn all layers that you want exported back into normal layers before publishing your final movie (.swf), either by unchecking Guide in the contextual menu or by selecting the Normal check box in the Layer Properties dialog box.

FIGURE 12.19

Use the Layer Properties dialog box to convert a standard layer into a guide layer, mask layer, or even a layer folder.

You can place bitmaps and video sequences in guide layers if you want to use them as references for drawings or animated sequences that are drawn in Flash; think of it as working with tracing paper to redraw images. The content on a guide layer adds to the file size of the Flash document (.fla), but it won't be included with or add to the file size of the exported movie (.swf). Guide layers are also useful when organizing layouts in Flash that require special alignment, such as a circular or diagonal arrangement of multiple elements.

To create a guide layer that serves as a reference for aligning a custom layout, follow these steps:

1. **Add a new layer to your Flash document (.fla) and make it a guide layer.** Use the contextual menu or the Layer properties dialog box to convert a standard layer into a guide layer.

2. **Place an imported image on the guide layer for reference, or use the Flash drawing tools to create any guide image needed (such as a circle or a freeform line).**

3. **Drag the guide layer below your art layers in the stacking order, or add a new layer above the guide layer if you need a fresh layer for arranging artwork.**

4. **Make sure that Snap to Objects is active by toggling on the Magnet option in the Tools panel or choosing View ⇨ Snapping ⇨ Snap to Objects in the application menu.**

NOTE   The guide layer workflow is especially helpful if you are trying to match a layout or design comp that might have been given to you in another format. Unfortunately, the Snap to Objects feature works only if the content of your guide layer is in a vector format. If you are working with a .pdf or a bitmap in the guide layer, the Snap to Objects feature won't be any help for aligning items on other layers with the content of the guide layer: In this case, you will find standard workspace guides (dragged onto the Stage with rulers toggled on in the View menu) more helpful.

5. Use the Arrow tool to drag elements on the art layers into alignment with the reference on the guide layer (see Figure 12.20).

FIGURE 12.20

Use snapping to align the center point of elements on your art layers with a reference shape or line on your guide layer (in vector format).

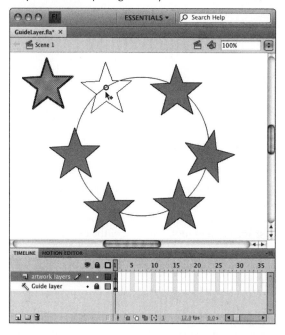

When you test your movie (Ctrl+Enter/⌘+Return), you won't see the content of the guide layer appear in the .swf (see Figure 12.21).

6. Add to or modify the reference content on the original guide layer or add additional guide layers if needed.

FIGURE 12.21

The content of the guide layer is not visible when the movie is published or viewed in the Test Movie environment.

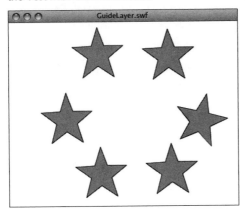

Adding masks

In the real world, a mask is used to selectively obscure items beneath it. In Flash, a mask layer is used to define the *visible* area of layers nested beneath it. Multiple layers can be nested as *masked* layers beneath a single mask layer. As with guide layers, the content on mask layers is not visible in the final .swf because it is intended only to modify how content in nested masked layers is rendered.

ON the CD-ROM The various examples discussed in this section can be found in the `MaskLayers` subfolder of the `ch12` folder. You may find it helpful to examine the structure of these files to understand the many ways that mask layers can be applied.

Almost any symbol or filled shape (excluding strokes) may be used to create a mask. However, Flash ignores bitmaps, gradients, transparency, colors, and line styles in a mask layer. Masks may be animated or static. The only other limitations are that you cannot apply a mask to content in another mask layer, and mask layers cannot be placed within Button symbol timelines.

CROSS-REF You can also use ActionScript to guide or control animation and to apply dynamic masking. For an introduction to these more advanced alternatives to mask layers, refer to Chapter 26, "Interacting with Movie Clips."

CAUTION Although groups, text boxes, and Movie clips or Graphic symbols can all be used to define a mask, only one such item is recognized on a single mask layer. You can use multiple primitive shapes to define a mask, but they override all other items existing on the same mask layer.

Masking with a filled shape

Here's how to create the simplest form of mask:

1. **Make sure that the content that will be visible through the mask is in place on its own layer, with visibility turned on.** This becomes the masked layer.

2. **Create a new layer stacked above the masked layer.** This becomes the Mask layer.

3. **In the Mask layer, create the "aperture" through which the contents of the masked layer are viewed.** This aperture can be any filled item, text, or placed instance of a symbol that includes a filled item. (Of course, lines can be used as masks if they are first converted to fills with the Modify ➪ Shapes ➪ Convert Lines to Fills command.)

4. **Position your mask content over the content on the masked layer (see Figure 12.22) so that it covers the area that you want to be visible through the mask.**

5. **Right-click (or Ctrl+click) the layer bar of the mask layer to open the contextual menu (see Figure 12.23), and choose Mask from the menu (or use the Layer Properties dialog box to change the layer behavior from Normal to Mask).**

FIGURE 12.22

Position the content on the upper layer to cover the area that you want visible in the lower layer(s) when the mask is applied.

FIGURE 12.23

Convert the upper layer into a mask layer by selecting Mask from the contextual menu.

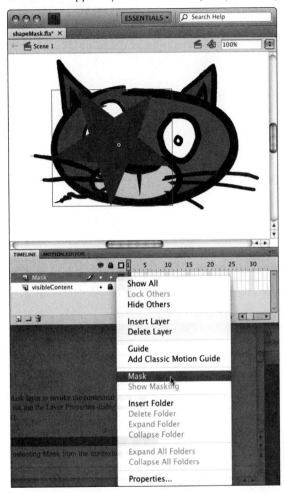

The layer icons change to indicate that the masked layer is now subordinate to the Mask layer and both layers are automatically locked to activate the mask. The contents of the masked layer are now visible only through the filled portion(s) of the mask layer, as shown in Figure 12.24.

6. **To reposition, or otherwise modify, the mask layer, temporarily unlock it (see Figure 12.25).**

FIGURE 12.24

When the mask is active, the content on the mask layer is no longer visible, but it defines the visible area of the content on the masked layer underneath.

7. **To reactivate masking, lock the mask layer again (and confirm that the masked layer is also locked).** The contextual menu for mask layers and masked layers includes Show Masking. This handy command locks the mask layer and all nested masked layers for you.

CAUTION When you first start working with mask layers, it is easy to forget to lock both the mask layer and the masked layer to make the mask effect visible. If you are ever having trouble editing or viewing your masked effect, just remember that when the layers are unlocked, the mask art is visible and editable, and when the layers are locked, the final masked effect is "turned on."

Masking with a group

Multiple filled shapes can also be grouped and used as a mask, as long as the mask layer doesn't also contain primitive ungrouped shapes. Grouped shapes on the same layer as ungrouped shapes are ignored when the mask is applied. If a mask is composed of multiple items, using a group makes it easier to position the mask, as shown in Figure 12.26.

FIGURE 12.25

FIGURE 12.25

With the mask layer unlocked, the contents are visible and editable.

FIGURE 12.26

Grouped filled shapes make it easier to position multipart masks.

Masking with a symbol instance

As you are reminded in nearly every chapter of this book, working with symbols is working smart because doing so helps to reduce file size. Because symbols composed of filled shapes can be used as masks, there's no reason not to use a symbol from your Library to make a mask. (If you've already made a shape on your mask layer, go ahead and convert it into a symbol so that you can use it again without adding to the final file size.) Reusing symbol instances to define masks is especially logical if you are making multiple masks that all have the same basic shape. For example, if you need a rectangular or oval mask, you will often find a symbol in your Library that was created to define the active area of a button or some other basic element. It is smarter to modify an instance of an existing symbol so that it works as a mask rather than to add redundant elements that increase your file size.

> **NOTE**   Although in theory you can use a Button symbol instance as mask artwork, note that a Button symbol instance placed into a mask layer no longer functions as a button. The result of this workflow is similar to selecting a Button symbol instance and assigning it Graphic symbol behavior in the Properties panel.

To illustrate the way that symbols can be reused as both graphic content and as mask elements, we have used instances of a symbol as static content on a masked layer and then motion tweened another instance of the same symbol on a mask layer to create an animated oval reveal. Figure 12.27 shows the symbol instance used on the Mask layer (on the left), the symbol instances used on the art layer (in the center), and the final mask effect visible when both layers are locked (on the right).

FIGURE 12.27

Instances of one oval symbol combined to create a graphic and a mask effect

> **ON the CD-ROM**   Open the `symbolMask.fla` example from the `MaskLayers` folder inside the `ch12` folder on this book's CD-ROM to see the animated effect.

Masking text

Not only can text be masked, but it can also be used to mask other graphics. To mask text, simply set up your mask and art layers, as described in the preceding section, with the text to be masked on the lower layer, and the filled item that you'll use for your aperture on the mask layer, as shown in Figure 12.28.

To use text as a mask, the layers should be set up as described previously. In this situation, the text (which goes on the mask layer) looks as though it was filled by whatever is placed on the lower layer. For this to be effective, a larger point size and fuller, bold letterforms are best, as shown in Figure 12.29.

FIGURE 12.28

Masking a text block with a tweened shape (shown on top) and the final reveal effect (shown on the bottom)

| CAUTION | Although you can type as much text as you want in a single text box to apply as a mask, you can have only one text box per mask layer. To use multiple text boxes as mask elements, add separate mask layers for each text box. |

FIGURE 12.29

A bitmap pattern (left) placed on the art layer and masked with text (right)

Because the edges of mask letterforms may be hard to discern if the image underneath is not a solid color, it can be helpful to add a drop shadow to make the mask letters more legible. However, a drop shadow or an outline added to the text on the mask layer would not be visible, so you must copy the text onto a normal layer stacked above the mask layer as follows:

1. **To keep the text copy aligned with the text mask, use Copy (Ctrl+C/⌘+C) and Paste in Place (Shift+Ctrl+V/Shift+⌘+V) to place a copy of the text into the normal layer exactly on top of the mask text.**

2. **After you have copied the text in the mask layer, lock both the mask layer and the masked layer to protect them while you are working on the normal layer.** The solid copied text completely obscures the masked image below, but you can apply a filter and use the Knockout option to drop out the fill of the text characters so that the masked content on the other layers is visible.

3. **Select the copied text, and then use the Filters section in the Properties panel to add a Drop Shadow filter.** The settings that we applied to our example, including the Knockout option, are shown in Figure 12.30. You can adjust the intensity and color of the shadow and the position of the copied (knocked-out) text until you like the end result.

FIGURE 12.30

Apply a Drop Shadow filter with the Knockout option to the copy of your text to add more visual definition to the letter shapes.

  The Glow Filter works to define the text too, as long as you apply the Knockout option.

Of course, you can also animate content on masked layers separately from the content on mask layers. But the endless possibilities for layering masks and masked content starts to get confusing when the additional variable of animation is thrown in. To make the best use of these features, take the extra time to carefully consider the most efficient way to achieve the final effect that you want. First consider what you want to see on the Stage, and then plan any animation of visible elements.

The next step should be adding a mask if needed, and finally adding animation to the mask itself. Try to create your effects with the fewest possible animated elements: You will waste less production time and end up with a more optimized file.

> **TIP** When working on multiple nested layers, it can be visually confusing to work on animation while all layers are displayed. Click the dot in the Eye toggle column to hide or show specific layers in the Timeline so that you can concentrate on only the elements that you are currently editing. Also, to avoid changing the wrong items, lock all layers that you are not currently modifying.

Keeping some basic principles in mind as you are working with multiple masks and animated elements will help you to follow the logic of masking in Flash:

- The mask always goes above the item that it reveals.

- Filled items on mask layers function as windows that reveal content on the masked layers nested beneath them.

- The content on mask layers is visible in the authoring environment only if the mask layer is unlocked. For the applied mask to preview properly in the authoring environment, both the mask layer and the masked layer(s) must be locked.

- Mask layers apply only to layers that are nested below them as masked layers. Normal layers or guide layers that may be lower in the layer stack (but not nested with the mask layer) are not affected by the mask.

- Multiple layers can be nested below a single mask layer, but masks cannot be applied to other mask layers, and each mask layer can contain only one masking item (with the exception of multiple primitive shapes or drawing objects).

- Content on mask layers is not visible in the final movie (.swf).

Using Distribute to Layers

The Distribute to Layers command (Shift+Ctrl+D/Shift+⌘+D) is a great time-saver if you're managing multiple elements that you need to move to animate on individual layers. If you've imported several items to the Document window, or you've created a complex graphic that you decide needs to be split up on different layers, you can use this command to do most of the work for you. Instead of having to manually create new layers and copy and paste items one by one, you can select a number of individual items in the Document window and apply Distribute to Layers to have Flash automatically create a layer for each selected item.

To apply Distribute to Layers:

1. **Select the items that you want to have moved to discrete layers.** These items can be symbols, groups, shapes, text blocks, and even bitmaps or video objects.

2. **Choose Modify ⇨ Timeline ⇨ Distribute to Layers from the application menu, or choose Distribute from the contextual menu.** Strokes and fills for an individual shape are kept together on the same layer, as are items in a group or a multipart symbol. The

items you select can be on different source layers, but they must all be on the same frame of the timeline.

3. **When items have been distributed to new layers, you can delete any old layers that have been left empty and rename any new layers that Flash gave awkward names to.**

The auto-created layers are stacked from top to bottom below the currently selected layer in the order that the selected items were created. So the most recently created item should be placed on a layer at the bottom of the stack, just above the layer that was formerly below the selected layer, and the item that was created before the others in the selection is placed at the top of the stack, just below the currently selected layer. If you are completely disoriented by now, have a look at Figure 12.31 to see a file with the layer order before applying Distribute to Layers to the selected items, and look at Figure 12.32 to see how the new layers are stacked and named.

FIGURE 12.31

A Flash document with the original layer structure for some bitmaps, symbols, shapes, and a broken-apart text block to be distributed to layers

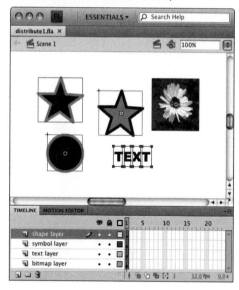

Characters from a broken-apart text block are stacked in layers in the same order that the text block was created (from left to right, right to left, or top to bottom). Flash names auto-created layers with the following conventions:

- A new layer made for any asset stored in the library (a symbol, bitmap, or video clip) is given the same name as the asset.

- A new layer made for a character from a broken-apart text block is named with the text character or letter.

CAUTION When you apply Distribute to Layers to text blocks that have not been broken apart, new layers are named with the entire text string. It is best to rename these layers because they usually are difficult to read and may even exceed the 64-character limit for layer names.

- A new layer made for a shape (which is not stored in the library) is named in the same numeric sequence as other layers in the current document (Layer 1, Layer 2, and so on).

- A new layer made for a named symbol instance is given the instance name rather than the stored symbol name.

Any layer can always be renamed after it has been created.

WEB RESOURCE We want to know what you think about this chapter. Visit `www.flashsupport.com/feedback` to send us your comments.

FIGURE 12.32

The same Flash document after Distribute to Layers has been applied. All selected items have been moved to newly created, auto-named layers, leaving the original layers empty.

Summary

- Filter options in the Properties panel include layering filters and saving presets, without any scripting or special timeline structures required.

- The built-in filters are somewhat limited on their own. The good news is that filters can be combined with blend modes, properties, Transform tools, and tweens to expand their potential well beyond the default settings.

- The options to copy and paste filters from one item to another or save filter settings as presets are time-savers if you want to reuse specific filter effects on multiple elements in your movie.

- Filter properties are included in the new Motion Editor for animated elements, making it easier to create or modify custom easing curves to adjust the progression of various properties individually in the same tween.

- Understanding the unique powers of the Adjust Color filter and the Color Effect styles available in the Properties panel gives you many options for controlling the appearance of symbol instances, including the option of using negative values to invert the color or alpha of an element.

- The Blend mode menu in the Properties panel brings some of the power of Photoshop into the Flash authoring environment: Graphics can be blended in subtle and interesting ways.

- The three layer types available in the Flash authoring environment are Normal, Mask, and Guide. A unique layer icon identifies each layer type. Classic motion guides are also still available in Flash CS4, but in most cases you can use the auto-created motion guides created with the newly optimized CS4 motion tween workflow.

- You can assign or modify layer types in the Layer Properties dialog box, which you open by double-clicking any layer icon.

- When you select multiple items on the same layer and use the Distribute to Layers command, they can automatically be moved to new, auto-created layers.

- You use guide layers to hold content that is needed only for reference in the authoring environment, or to speed up movie testing as you develop a project — by temporarily keeping the content on specific layers from being exported with the .swf.

- You can mask any content that you create in a Flash document with a static or animated mask layer.

- You can use filled shapes, text, and symbol instances to define the mask area (or window) on a mask layer, but this content is not visible in the final movie (.swf).

Chapter 13

Character Animation Techniques

lash is a powerful tool that continues to grow in popularity as a professional production option for creating high-quality cartoons and animated broadcast graphics. The best thing about Flash cartoons is that you don't always know they were created in Flash when you see them. Flash allows artists to create characters in nearly any style they can dream up. Although Flash makes it especially easy to produce clean, geometric designs, it can also be used for sketchy hand-drawn styles, or even for collage animation that uses source material from photos or video. This is the result of Flash's unique drawing tools, media-friendly authoring environment, and scalability. By "scalability," we mean that a Flash cartoon can be scaled down for delivery on the Web or scaled up to the size and resolution needed for video or film presentation. Creating broadcast cartoons can be extremely complex — specialized techniques are covered in many books and classes — so in this chapter we focus on some basics to get you started.

Although Flash includes some special techniques, most of the basic principles of animation apply regardless of the authoring environment or production process you choose. You can often learn more about animation principles by watching classic animated films than by looking at 'toons online — at least at those examples created by "animators" who know how to motion-tween but have not spent any time learning techniques for effective character animation.

A growing number of artists with traditional animation skills are making the transition to working directly in Flash, and there are even a few Flash experts who have taken the time to study animation. Individuals able to combine knowledge of classic animation principles with technical aptitude in Flash have the best chance of finding success in this challenging field.

Working with Large File Sizes

Because Flash output is usually intended for the Web, Flash file size is often a dominant concern. But when creating cartoons for broadcast output, this concern is thrown to the wind. In cartoon land, you create for digital video output via QuickTime or Windows AVI, and these file sizes can be huge. It's common for such projects to expand into the gigabytes, so it's important to have the equipment to handle this kind of work. This means the more RAM and hard drive space you have, the happier you will be. If you try to build a full-length animation masterpiece in one Flash file, you'll be setting yourself up for a rocky and inefficient production process. As you continue to add artwork and animation to your Flash file, it takes longer to render a .swf for preview, and it takes even longer to render a sequence for raster output. You can use several strategies to make your animation more manageable. As we describe in this section, start with a good storyboard and follow through with a series of separate Flash files organized into scenes.

You'll spend many hours working on your animation, so back it up as often as you can! The project file is precious. Make a habit of keeping incremental backups on various hard drive volumes or archived CDs or DVDs so that you won't lose everything when disaster strikes (it will). A good plan is to make a new copy on a different hard drive volume or disc after each major change, rotating through two or three different storage locations. This way, if Flash eats your project file or a disc or drive fails, you can always go back to the version you saved an hour ago (which should be on a different disc) without losing much time. The same versioning logic used in other documents can be applied to your Flash animation files: Start with `myFile_100`, go to `myFile_101`, `myFile_102`, and so on as you make small adjustments and revisions. When you get to a significant change or a semifinished version of your file, save it as `myFile_200`, and so on. This makes it easy to find your way back to a specific phase of the project at any time.

Storyboarding scenes and shots

Let's assume that you already have characters and a story and you want to build a cartoon based on that inspired beginning. Although it's okay to experiment and develop characters, never start a serious cartoon project without a storyboard. The storyboard is your road map, your plan, your menu of things needed, and your best friend when your project gets complicated. The storyboard can be loose and roughly sketched out, but it should help you start to see the flow of your story and to make decisions about how best to communicate it visually.

ON the CD-ROM   You'll find a storyboard template on the CD-ROM, in the `ch13` folder. It's an .eps (`storyboardMAC.eps` or `storybPC.eps`) template form that includes all the essentials of a basic storyboard. Print it out as is, or import it into Illustrator, or Flash, and modify it to suit your needs.

As you sketch the overall story, you can break up the narrative into workable cartoon scenes. Long before Flash, cartoonists used the term "scene" to describe something quite different than a Flash scene. By cartoon scenes, we mean phases in a narrative, similar to movie or TV scenes. Remember that cartoons are fast-paced adventures; most cartoon scenes last less than 30 seconds. Generally, a cartoon scene can stand alone, but it needs other scenes to complete the story. Fast-paced as it is, 30 seconds of animation still require between 360 and 720 frames in the Flash timeline. It becomes unruly if you rely solely upon Flash's Scene feature — you'd do a lot of scrubbing, just trying to cover one scene.

After your cartoon scenes are in order, you can start to establish the camera angles or "shots" for key moments. A *shot* is a break or change in the camera framing or viewpoint. For example, in a soap opera dialogue scene, the camera cuts back and forth between characters to show each person talking — one scene includes many shots. Although the art of cinematography is beyond the scope of this book, the same tricks used to add drama to live action are involved when deciding shots in a cartoon scene. Always try to introduce variety in the viewpoint; think of ways to add interest with close-ups or extreme angles. If you're looking at a series of shots with characters all in the same basic position within the frame, keeping the same distance from the viewer, you're looking at a scene that will turn out to be pretty dull. If you can cut some visual contrast into the scene while still pushing your narrative forward, you'll have a better chance of keeping your viewers hooked in long enough to connect with your characters and to appreciate your story.

Flash scenes and project files

Never create an entire cartoon in one Flash project file (.fla)! Even trying to load the huge files can cause problems for Flash. Instead, create a separate Flash project file for each storyboard scene and use Flash's Scene function to organize shots within a cartoon scene. (This may seem confusing at first, but the utility of this method will become clear as you work on your masterpiece.) In other words: The Flash project file is a storyboard scene, and the shots, or Flash scenes, are nested within the project file.

TIP   The Scene panel (Shift+F2), found in the Window ⇨ Other Panels submenu, is used to add, delete, or rename scenes. It's also where you navigate your scene list. Keep in mind that each scene has its own timeline, which you will see in the Timeline panel when you load a scene to work on.

Voices, sound effects, and ambient sound

The single most important work you'll do in your cartoon is not the drawing, but the voices of your characters; the voices give the characters heart and depth. In fact, some animators prefer to record the voices first and then use the performance of the voice actors as inspiration for the animated characters' movements and expressions. Obtaining a voice can be as simple as speaking into a microphone in front of your computer or as complex as having a highly paid professional speaking into a microphone in a studio. The key here is not the type of voice, but the emotion put into it. If you capture a unique voice with the right emotion, it can be taken into an editing program, such as Adobe Soundbooth, Sound Forge, or Acid Pro, and tweaked with effects to render the exact cartoon sound that you're looking for. Audio effects, including adjustments to pitch and timing, can always be added digitally; human emotion cannot. Here are just two of the many voice resources available online:

- www.voicecasting.com
- www.world-voices.com

Another important part of cartoons is the use of *sound effects*. Adobe has generously included a slew of high-quality sound effects in the new CS4 Sounds library (Window ➪ Common Libraries ➪ Sounds): You might even find just the right one for your next project. If you need to look farther, a link at the top of the Sounds library list prompts you to take advantage of the additional built-in sounds available with Adobe Soundbooth.

NEW FEATURE   **The Sounds library was not available in Flash CS3, but it's back in CS4 with more and better sounds ready for use in any Flash project. These sounds can be a great way to prototype or to give a client an idea of what's possible in Flash before you commit to recording or buying more custom sounds.**

Many collections are available on CD-ROM and online. You can even find sound effects CDs in bargain bins at your local music store. A couple of the collections that we keep on hand are *The Ultimate Digital Sound Effects Library* from the Sound Effects Company, and *Crashes, Collisions & Catastrophes* from Madacy Records. We also recommend any of the *Loops for Acid* CDs from Sonic Foundry — the company that produced these loops is now called Peace Love Productions. The sounds included in these collections can be imported into any sound-editing program to be mixed into your own original soundscapes. If you've never worked with someone who specializes in custom sound creation, you might be amazed at the magic he or she can add to even simple animation.

WEB RESOURCE   **One source that offers an exhaustive library of effects, backgrounds, and ambient sounds at affordable prices (with MP3 links that allow you to preview them online), is www.sounddogs.com. A site that offers a range of royalty-free sound effects along with a good selection of free sound effects is www.partnersinrhyme.com. A popular site for thousands of royalty-free sounds is www.platinumloops.com.**

WEB RESOURCE   **For more artistic ambient sounds or custom sound for branded sites, it's best to find a creative professional who can work with you. It might seem expensive at first, but it will save you money and time in the long run and will add value to your animation. One of our favorite sound designers is also the organizer of an excellent annual Flash conference in Minneapolis. Dave Schroeder works his magic at www.pilotvibe.com.**

Sometimes, you just can't find the sound you need. Fortunately, it's not difficult to set up your own little *Foley stage* or sound effects recording area. A good shotgun microphone (highly directional for aiming at sound) and DAT recorder are ideal, although you can get by with less.

The capture device (audiotape, DAT, miniDV, MD, and so on) should be portable, not only in order to get it away from the whirring sound of hard drives and fans, but also to enable you to take it on location when needed. Another advantage of a battery-powered portable device is that static from power line voltage won't be a problem. After you get started and begin playing around, you'll be surprised at the sounds that you can create with ordinary objects. Squeeze your dish soap bottle, and you might notice that when amplified, it makes a nice whoosh. Great for the fast limb movement of that character doing a karate chop. Crumpled paper can sound like fire — when you get started, you never know what you might put to use around the house. Be creative — innovate!

The voices and the sound effects in a cartoon grab your attention and punctuate action, but listen more closely when you watch an engaging animated piece (or any film), and you will gain appreciation for the subtle art of *ambient* sounds. These background noises add tone and atmosphere, making a scene rich and believable. Ambient sound should almost be "felt" more than heard so it doesn't distract from your main narrative. Because it is layered behind the more dominant sounds, you can often get away with looping a short sample of ambient sound. Think of wind or water sounds or distant city noises: They have some variation but they also tend to have a repetitive rhythm. And of course, don't overdo it. Well-timed silence can be a powerful narrative device, too!

WEB RESOURCE Adobe has recognized the need for a sound tool that is user friendly for creative people who work in Flash and After Effects. The new application is called Soundbooth and it comes bundled with several of the Adobe Creative suites. For more information and trial versions, visit `http://labs.adobe.com/technologies/soundboothcs4`.

Some Cartoon Animation Basics

In the world of film, movies are shot at 24 frames per second (fps); in video and 3D animation, 30 fps is the norm. But for cartoons, 12 to 15 fps is usually all that's needed. The cartoon language of motion that we've all learned since childhood has taught our minds to expect this slightly jumpy quality of motion in a cartoon. As an animator, this is good for you, because 15 fps means half the amount of hand-drawing work that 30 fps requires. It also means that you can get your cartoon done within your lifetime and maybe take a day off here and there. Actually, there are a lot of scenes in which as few as three drawings per second will suffice — depending on how well you can express motion with your art or drawing. The rule of motion here is that things that move quickly require fewer frames (drawings), and things that move slowly require more frames. This is the main reason you rarely see slow-motion sequences in cartoons. Broadcast cartoons have lots of fast-paced motion. Fewer drawings are produced more quickly, making the production less costly. These are very significant factors when battling tight budgets and scary deadlines.

NEW FEATURE The default frame rate in older versions of Flash was 12 fps. In Flash CS4 it has been boosted to 24 fps. A faster frame rate ensures that menu transitions and other animated elements (especially tweens) that don't require a redraw of the entire screen play more smoothly. More people are looking at your Flash work on faster machines, so you can push the performance to a new level. Keep in mind that if you are doing hand-drawn or frame-by-frame animation, you will still find it best to work at a lower frame rate for most projects.

Expressing motion and emotion

The hardest part of animation is expressing motion and emotion. Learning to do this well saves time and makes your work more effective. One of the best exercises you can do in this respect is to simply watch the world around you. Videotaping or downloading cartoons and advancing through them at single-frame speed can give you insight on different ways that the "real world" is translated to cartoonland. Another good learning trick is to import raster video to your Flash timeline so that you can use a live action sequence as your guide and practice drawing on top of it. Although this can help you get a feel for the mechanics of motion, it's really just a start. Cartoons are engaging *because* they so often deviate from, or even defy, the predictable motion we see every day.

Exaggerate everything! After all, this is what makes it a cartoon.

CROSS-REF We have included a tutorial in this chapter by Felix Stumpf, who uses video as a reference for his simple but wonderfully engaging hand-drawn animations. To see an archived version of his original award-winning portfolio site, visit `www.felixstumpf.de/ illustration/portfolio/html_kunstkatalog/index.html`.

WEB RESOURCE Tex Avery was a pioneering animator who created cartoons with overblown and hilarious motion, which revolutionized animation. You can read about him at `www. brightlightsfilm.com/22/texavery.html`.

Anticipation

Anticipation is a technique used to indicate that characters are about to do something, such as take off running. Before lunging into the sprint, characters slowly back up, loading all their motion into their feet until their motion reverses and sends them blasting off in the other direction. In a more subtle form, this is shown in Figure 13.1, when Weber the pelican crouches before he takes flight from his perch on the pier.

FIGURE 13.1

Anticipation is used to accentuate Weber's takeoff.

Weight

Keep the weight of objects in mind. This helps to make your cartoon believable. A feather falls more slowly than an anvil. The feather also eases out (slows down) before landing gently on the ground, while the anvil slams into the ground with such force as to make a gashing dent in it. Humor can play a role here by giving extreme weight to things that do not have it (or vice versa), thereby causing a surprise in the viewer's preconceived notion of what should happen — surprise is the seed of humor.

Overlapping actions

Visualize a jogging Santa Claus, his belly bouncing up and down with each step. Because of its weight, his belly is still on a downward motion when the rest of his body is being pushed upward by the thrust of his leg. This opposing motion is known as *overlapping actions*. Overlapping action does not only happen in an up-and-down motion; it can happen in any direction. An example of side-to-side overlapping actions is shown in Figure 13.2. Note that, as the bully thrusts forward, Weber's body reacts in the opposite direction . . . only to catch up just in time for the thrust to reverse and go the other way.

FIGURE 13.2

Overlapping actions can accentuate movement in any direction.

Blurring to simulate motion

Blurring is a technique or device that animators use to signify a motion that's moving faster than the frame rate can physically show. In film, this manifests itself as a blurred out-of-focus subject (due to the subject moving faster than the camera's shutter can capture). You may have already employed this effect in Photoshop, with the Motion Blur filter. In cartoon animation, blurring is often (and easily) described with blur lines. Blur lines are an approximation of the moving subject using line or brush strokes that trail off in the direction that the subject is coming from. When used properly, this great device can save hours of tedious drawing. An example of animated motion blur used to indicate a spinning motion is shown in Figure 13.3, which is a sequence in which the *word* "Weber" turns into Weber the pelican.

FIGURE 13.3

Blur lines simulate the effect of motion that is "faster than the eye can see."

ON the CD-ROM To see animated examples of the blurred line effect, look in the `R_Bazley` folder inside the `ch13` folder on the CD-ROM. Richard Bazley has used blurred lines effectively to create a collapsing ceiling and a rush of wind.

Using Video As a Basis for Fluid, Hand-Drawn Animation, by Felix Stumpf

There are as many different styles of hand-drawn animation as there are animators. But, if you want to create vivid animation with a realistic look, using video as a visual reference is a great shortcut. Combining fluid, hand-drawn lines with the movement style of live video results in an engaging hybrid that allows room for individual drawing techniques while maintaining lifelike, cinematic scale and motion. Very skilled animators can achieve this type of fluid animation by drawing freehand, but even then, it can be tricky to capture the mannerisms and personality of a real person.

A simple way of capturing these subtle elements, even with very few lines, is to create a series of video stills to use as a template for ink drawings that can be sequenced in Flash and combined with other graphics or sound to complete the scene.

The line animation that I used to introduce myself on my portfolio site (`www.felixstumpf.de/illustration/portfolio/html_kunstkatalog/index.html`) was created by importing a still sequence from a video clip shot on a plain background into Photoshop, and then printing the frames out to use under tracing paper as a reference for pen and ink drawings. I find that six drawings per second are usually sufficient to translate the main flow of motion from the video clip to the traced animation.

NOTE Shooting on a plain background with lighting that separates the figure from the background makes it much easier to trace the outline of the figure. Most video-editing programs (such as Final Cut or Premiere) export a series of stills in a format compatible with Photoshop and Flash. I generally use pict files (.pct), but any compatible lossless format will do.

The decision to draw on tracing paper or to import the video stills into Flash or Photoshop and use digital drawing or painting tools to trace over the video image is mostly a stylistic one. With practice, you can create artwork with the same speed and accuracy with analog or digital tools, but you may find that you prefer the look or feel of one over the other for certain projects. I use both methods, and the choice is usually dependent on the mood I'm going for in the final piece. Whether I create the line drawings on paper, in Photoshop, or directly in Flash, I use the original video clip (not the still frames) as a guide for positioning and pacing the final image sequence. This is one of the secrets to maintaining lifelike motion in the animated version.

ON the CD-ROM The evolution of the intro to Felix's portfolio site is shown through the clips included in the `fstumpf` subfolder of the `ch13` folder on the CD-ROM. Open `video.swf` to see the original video footage and open `animation.swf` to see how the line drawings are lined up with the video. To view `finalversion.swf` to see how the polished animation looks with text elements added in Flash, drag the protected .swf into a browser window.

Figure 13.4 shows a screenshot from the video clip (down-sampled to 8 frames/ sec), used as a reference for my drawings. Turning and walking quickly toward the camera while crossing the frame from left to right sets up a dramatic change in scale and position that gives the animated outline more impact.

FIGURE 13.4

Shooting on a plain background makes it easier to isolate the movement of the figure in the animation.

Figure 13.5 shows one of my scanned drawings overlaid with the video in Flash to match up with the pacing and position of the original live action. By following the main lines of action but letting some parts of the outline drop out and shift as the figure moves, I am able to add an organic, fluid character to the outline, which makes the interpretation more artistic.

FIGURE 13.5

Although the pacing and key outlines are sequenced to follow the video template exactly, the sketched lines introduce some looseness.

Figure 13.6 shows a series of stills from the finished animation. The video layer has been removed and the line art translates the original flow nicely.

TIP The more images you use, the more fluid your animations will look. I've found that a good rule of thumb is to use 6 images (frames) per second for Web and 25 images (frames) per second for film.

FIGURE 13.6

Working with line art gives you the freedom to add other graphic elements or text that interacts with the animated figure seamlessly.

Frame 8   Frame 21   Frame 36

Regardless of which drawing environment you prefer, the key to success is to pay careful attention to the proportions and flow of the still sequence and to be as precise as possible in following the main outlines of the figure. If you choose to draw in Flash, you may find it easier to create one traced outline and then modify that outline in each subsequent frame instead of starting the outline from scratch for each frame. Even small distortions have a big impact on the final impression of the piece and may throw off the unique characteristics of motion that make the character identifiable. On the other hand, once you get the main action translated smoothly, it can be fun to throw in some variation and take a bit of artistic license to make the visuals more realistic or more fanciful — depending on the final look you're going for.

I tend to draw a lot of elements from memory (such as the music player and the rolling paper that the figure interacts with on my portfolio site). This frees me up to invent an environment for the figure and saves a lot of money on props! Combining fluid video-style motion with freehand drawings gives you the benefit of starting with realistic proportions and lifelike movements but still leaves room for invention and imagination expressed in your own unique drawing style.

TIP As with any other Flash project, it helps to keep elements organized on individual layers: Keep the video on a guide layer, import or draw the main image sequence on another layer, and place any additional drawn elements on their own layers.

After I have some traced animation sequences completed, I put them together with sketches of other content and use sample music to rough out my ideas for the flow of the complete site. I call these rough files *moodboards,* and I use them to test my ideas and page designs before I move on to optimizing and integrating final elements in an interactive Flash structure. It takes much less time to prototype a series of screens as a linear animation than it does to build an interactive model, so I can test different versions of my ideas before investing resources on the final project.

ON the CD-ROM One version of my concept for the animation flow with other elements on my portfolio site is illustrated in the `moodboard.swf` file included in the `fstumpf` subfolder in the `ch13` folder on the CD-ROM. If you compare the moodboard with the final version of my live site, you will notice that the layout is not exactly the same, but the atmosphere is very similar.

WEB RESOURCE Check out the final results of Felix's traced video sketches with other line art elements in his inventive portfolio presentation at `www.felixstumpf.de/illus tration/portfolio/html_kunstkatalog/index.html`.

Animator's Keys and Inbetweening

In Chapter 11, "Timeline Animation and the Motion Editor," you learned about two Flash animation methods: frame-by-frame and tweening. This section focuses on traditional cartoonist frame-by-frame techniques, together with traditional cartoonist's keys and inbetween methods, to accomplish frame-by-frame animation. Despite the similarity of terminology, this topic heading does not refer to a menu item in Flash. Instead, it should be noted that animation programs such as Flash have derived some program terminology (and methods) from the vintage world of hand-drawn cel animation. Vintage animators used the methods of *keys* and *inbetweening* to determine the action a character takes in a given shot. It's akin to sketching, but with motion in mind. In this sense, keys are the high points, or ultimate positions, in a given sequence of motion. Thus, in vintage animation:

- Keys are the pivotal drawings or highlights that determine how the motion plays out.
- Inbetweens are the fill-in drawings that smooth out the motion.

In Flash, the usual workflow is to set keyframes for a symbol and then to tween the intervening frames, which harnesses the power of the computer to fill the inbetweens. Although this is fine for many things, it is inadequate for many others. For example, a walk sequence is too subtle and complex to be created simply by shape- or motion-tweening the same figure — each key pose in the walk requires a unique drawing. So, let's take a look at the traditional use of keys and inbetweens for generating a simple walk sequence that starts and ends according to a natural pace, yet also generates a walk loop.

Walk cycles (or walk loops)

Humans are incredibly difficult to animate convincingly. Why? Because human movement is delightfully sloppy — and we are keenly aware of this quality of human movement, both on a conscious and a subconscious level. (Another term for this is *body language*.) Experienced animators create walk cycles with life not by using perfectly repeating patterns, but rather by using the dynamic quality of hand-drawn lines to add just the right amount of variation to basic movements.

The most difficult aspect of creating a walk cycle is giving the final walk distinctive qualities that support the role that the character plays. This again is something that only gets easier with practice. There is no substitute for drawing skill and time spent studying human movement, but to get started it can be helpful to study a basic walk pattern.

ON the CD-ROM We've included the three walk cycle examples we show in this section on the CD-ROM for you to open and analyze. You will find the files in the `walk_cycles` folder inside the `ch13` folder of the CD-ROM.

Many 3D programs have prebuilt walk cycles that you can modify. We begin with a basic walk made in Poser (a popular 3D character rendering and animation program from Smith Micro) and output it as an image sequence that was then imported and traced in Flash. As you can see in Figure 13.7, this walk cycle was composed of ten different poses, but the final result is fairly generic and robotic.

FIGURE 13.7

A traced sequence from a basic walk cycle that was created in Poser

Notice that the main pivot points of the figure create a balanced pattern that can be used as a basis for many other kinds of figures. Also notice that as the figure moves through the cycle, there is a slight up-and-down movement that creates a gentle wave pattern along the line of the shoulder. This wave motion is what keeps your figure from looking too mechanical. It is important to remember that the final pose in the cycle is not identical to the first pose in the cycle — this is crucial for creating a smooth loop. Although it might seem logical to create a full cycle of two strides and then loop them, you will get a stutter in the walk if the first and last frames are the same. Whatever pose you *begin* the cycle with should be the next logical "step" after the final pose in your cycle so that the pattern loops seamlessly.

Although the figures are shown here with the poses spaced horizontally, you actually draw your poses on individual frames (best done on a Movie clip timeline), but align the drawings on top of each other so that the figure "walks in place" as if on a treadmill. After you have established your walk cycle, you add the horizontal movement by tweening the walk cycle Movie clip. As shown in Figure 13.8, by using a motion tween to scale the walk cycle Movie clip and moving it from one corner of the Stage to another, you can create the illusion that the figure is walking toward the viewer.

FIGURE 13.8

A series of angled poses in a walk cycle work well to create the illusion that the figure is walking toward the viewer if the final Movie clip is scaled as it is motion-tweened from the far corner to the near corner of the Stage.

The speed of the motion tween has to match the speed of the walk cycle. If the tween is too slow (too little distance or too many frames), the figure will seem to be walking in place. If the tween is too fast (too much distance or too few frames), the figure will seem to be sliding over the ground. Play with the ratio of your motion tween, and if the figure needs to walk faster or slower, make adjustments to the walk cycle itself instead of just "pushing" or "dragging" the figure with your motion tween. Also keep in mind that a figure should seem to walk more quickly as it gets closer to the viewer. In the skeleton walk example, the motion tween is eased in so that as the figure gets closer (larger), the walk appears to cover ground more quickly.

Achieving realistic human walk cycles can take hours of work and require very complex walk cycles (often 30 or more poses). Fortunately, many cartoons actually have more personality if they use a simplified or stylized walk cycle that suits the way they are drawn. Figure 13.9 shows a walk cycle that required only three drawings to create a serious but childlike stride for an outlined character.

FIGURE 13.9

A stylized walk cycle created by flipping and reusing the same three drawings for both legs of an outlined character

In the Flash file on the CD-ROM (`walkToon.fla`), you will notice that the legs, arms, torso, and head of the character are all animated on separate layers. This allows you to reuse the same drawings for both sides of the body — by simply offsetting the pattern so that the legs swing in opposition to each other, with the leg on the far side layered underneath the leg on the near side. This economy of effort is helpful not only because it is faster, but also because it makes it easier to maintain the symmetry of your character if you are trying to keep the motion simple and stylized.

Repeaters

If you open the source file (`walkToon.fla`), you will notice some spans of nonkeyed frames (repeaters) in the Movie clip timeline for the cartoon walk. We used these to economize drawing time and to slow the walk of the character. If a speedier walk was called for, we would simply shorten these spans to eliminate repeater frames. A good basic rule about repeaters is to add no more than one repeater frame between keys; adding more causes the smoothness of motion to fall apart. If the motion must proceed more slowly, you have to draw more inbetweens.

Fortunately, with Flash onion skinning (the capability to see before and after the current time in a dimmed graphic), which we discuss in Chapter 11, "Timeline Animation and the Motion Editor," the addition of a few more inbetweens is not an enormous task. In fact, onion skinning is indispensable for doing inbetweens, and even for setting keys. One pitfall of onion skinning is the tendency to trace what you're seeing. It takes practice to ignore the onion lines and use them only as a guide. You need to remember that the objective is to draw frames that have slight, but meaningful, differences between them. Although it can mean a lot more drawing, it's well worth it. Because you'll use your walk (and running) cycles over and over during the course of your cartoon, do them well.

> **TIP** One real time-saver in creating a walk cycle is to isolate the head and animate it separately via layers or grouping. This trick helps to prevent undesirable quivering facial movements that often result from imperfectly traced copies. Similarly, an accessory such as a hat or briefcase can be isolated on a separate layer. Finally, if the character will be talking while walking, make a copy of the symbol and eliminate the mouth. Later, you'll add the mouth back as a separate animation. We describe lip-syncing techniques later in this chapter.

Types of walks

So far, we've covered the mechanics of a walk cycle. But for animators, the great thing about walking — in all its forms — is what it can communicate about the character. We read this body language constantly every day without really thinking about it. We often make judgments about people's moods, missions, and characters based on the way that they carry themselves. Picture the young man, head held high, briskly striding with direction and purpose: He is in control of the situation and will accomplish the task set before him. But if we throw in a little wristwatch checking and awkward arm movements, then that same walk becomes a stressful "I'm late." Or, witness the poor soul — back hunched, arms dangling at his sides. He moves along, dragging his feet as if they each weigh a thousand pounds. That tells the sad story of a person down on his luck. Finally, what about a random pace, feet slipping from side to side, sometimes crisscrossing, other times colliding, while the body moves in a stop-and-start fashion as if it was just going along for the ride? Is that someone who couldn't figure out when to leave the bar? Of course, these are extreme examples. Walks are actually very subtle and there are limitless variations on the basic forms. But if you begin to observe and analyze these details as they occur in everyday life, you'll be able to instill a higher order in your animations. Simply take time to look. It's all there waiting for you to use in your next animation. Then remember that because it's a cartoon, *exaggerate!*

Coloring the Art

In traditional animation, characters were first inked in as outlines and then filled with color and shading. Coloring was the most tedious and time-consuming job of all: endless thousands of cels to be hand painted and dried. Most often, armies of low-paid workers in faraway lands did it. But with Flash it's a snap! That's because of Flash's wonderful (and sometimes mysterious) gap-jumping fill tool, the Paint Bucket. With Flash, you never run out of paint, and it dries instantly — a real time-saver to be sure!

The model sheet

Here's a coloring time-saver that you can use for yourself within Flash: Use a fully colored model of your character at the start of a cycle or scene. This will serve as a color model and will be discarded when the cycle or shot is finished. It's very important to keep a model sheet, which is an archive of color models — finished, fully colored characters — to maintain consistent color across the span of the project. (It's also quite useful at the start of future projects.)

Although Flash has the capability to save color sets, it's still difficult to remember which yellow was used on a certain area of the character, especially when there are ten different yellows in the palette. Making such a color mistake — even a slight shade off — causes unsightly flicker on playback. The Eyedropper tool makes no mistakes. So, to develop good animation habits, start a model sheet. When you begin a scene, copy the appropriate color model and paste it into the cycle, setting it off to the side of the active art in the first frame (if needed, ungroup it). Acquire the color that you need with the Eyedropper tool and then set about the business of filling.

When filling, we've found that the most efficient method is to go through the entire cycle with one color, filling all objects of that color. Then go back to the beginning and sweep through again, doing the next color. This method saves you the tedium of continually having to change the Paint Bucket's color, and also minimizes the possibility of mistakes. If some places fill while others don't, you'll probably need to adjust the Paint Bucket Gap size modifier.

TIP The Find and Replace feature in Flash makes it easy to do a global swap if you decide that orange would really be a better color than red (or whatever suits your fancy). With your project file open, choose Edit ⇨ Find and Replace (Ctrl+F/⌘+F), and then use the controls to search the entire document or individual scenes for a color and set the color you want to use instead. Flash does the rest!

Gap problems

There are times when the gaps in a line are not visible but the Paint Bucket tool just won't work. In this case, keep looking because the gaps are there. If it just doesn't work, no matter how much you zoom in and click with the Paint Bucket tool, you may need to zoom in and use the Selection tool to close the gap by adjusting a stroke. In a situation in which it's not aesthetically pleasing to do that, use the Brush tool (set to the same fill color and to paint fills only) to fill the gaps manually. Perhaps this would be the case on a head and neck that you don't want connected to the body (remember we discussed earlier the advantages of animating the head separately). You would use the Brush tool to paint a stroke of fill connecting the inked lines and then fill the larger areas with the Paint Bucket tool.

Speed coloring

A good way to speed up the coloring process is to allocate one of the mouse buttons (if you have a programmable mouse) to perform the keyboard shortcut for step-forward advancing (which is the > key). If you have a pressure-sensitive graphics tablet, you can allocate a button on the pen to do the same. With a setup like this, you can leave the cursor in pretty much the same place and click-fill, click-advance, click-fill, click-advance, and so on.

Temporary backgrounds

Another problem that's easily solved is the process of filling areas with white. If you're like most people, you probably work on the default background color of white, which makes it impossible to distinguish when filling white areas. In this case, it's helpful to create a very light color that you don't plan to use in the final art, something like a light pink. While coloring, temporarily change the background color in the Properties panel or in the Movie Properties dialog box (Modify ➪ Document) to the substitute color for the background of the entire movie. This makes it much easier to see what you're doing when using white as a fill color for objects such as eyeballs, teeth, and clouds. Then when you're done coloring, you can set the background color back to white.

Flash Character Design Strategies, by Sandro Corsaro

Flash offers a cheaper, faster, and more malleable approach to creating animation than anything in the history of animation. Although traditional animation production can be unforgiving, the Flash authoring environment offers animators a variety of starting points in fulfilling their visions. Many creative types who are experienced with Flash can delve into projects with simple thumbnail sketches or even with just concepts in their heads. Purists, and developers working with larger teams, generally prefer the traditional storyboard route. Whether it is intended for Web or broadcast, creating an efficient Flash animation begins and ends with the strategy of your initial design. That design can be on paper, in Flash, or even in your head. What is crucial is that on some level, there is a clear and concise plan in the design.

For the purposes of this tutorial, I will show you two simple examples involving design strategy.

By now you should be familiar with the concept of breaking elements into reusable parts or pieces. For Web purposes, this keeps the file small and saves the artist production time. This systemized approach to animation is the evolution of *limited animation* — the cut-out system that hasn't changed since it was first applied by Hanna-Barbera for television shows such as *The Flintstones* and *Scooby Doo*. When Fred would talk, his mouth would be on one layer, while his head and body would be on another. If Fred tilted his head during a rant, his mouth and head would tilt during the animation, while his upper body would be held. Why do you think all those great Hanna-Barbera characters always had some sort of accessory (like a tie or necklace) around their necks? This design strategy was effective even with a constrained budget because it allowed for maximum animation with minimal artwork.

Today, Flash has the potential to revolutionize the production process by building on the animation techniques used in the past. Just like the traditional cel method, inactive Flash layers can be "held" while action layers continue with additional frames of movement. The newest feature of this evolution is that symbols, unlike old-school painted cels, can be flipped, stretched, and squashed without having to redraw the artwork. A traditional painted animation cel of a left arm could not be reused for the right arm. On the simplest level, appendages can be flipped, rotated, and scaled to complete character designs. The model sheet I created in Flash of Da Boss (shown in Figure 13.10) is an example of effective reuse of artwork.

FIGURE 13.10

By designing the character in reusable pieces, you can simplify your workflow while increasing the options for how the character can be animated.

443

ON the CD-ROM To see the animated Flash version of the model sheet for Da Boss, drag `model Sheet.swf` from the `S_Corsaro` subfolder in the `ch13` folder on the CD-ROM into a browser window.

The script called for this character to be constantly pacing his office. When I designed the character, I broke him into three distinct parts, each with its own animation. The first part was the combed-over hair. I kept it as a separate piece from the head, so it could undulate up and down as he paced. This provides a nice secondary action to his walk. Although the hair is a small detail, without the initial planning, attempting to add it later in the animation process would have proven frustrating and time consuming. The second animation was the inertia of the heavy upper body. As Da Boss walked, his body needed to convey a sense of weight and power. Utilizing the animation principle of stretch and squash, the symbol of his upper body cycles through various shapes in conjunction with his walk.

The final and most dynamic component of the character's movement is the leg cycle taking place on the layer underneath his upper body. Only one leg has actually been drawn — the other is offset and placed on a lower layer to create a looped walk. As the legs move into each keyframe, the first two elements I described previously are adjusted to create the secondary animation. On the low points of the walk, his weight squashes down, while his hair holds (or pauses) for a momentary beat. A progression of movement follows in the next few keyframes to get to the inverse position of this low point.

Besides the basic model movement, a turnaround was also needed for the animators to work with this character. Obviously, some of the views can be flipped, but what about the front and back? Copy and paste your front view to create your back view. Build on your finished artwork to create the new artwork. Figure 13.11 illustrates how the front view of the Da Boss was modified to create the back view. Unlike the traditional animation process, which travels in distinct and separate stages from point A to B to C, think of Flash animation as a more integrated progression as point A *becomes* B, which *transforms* into C. Always try to build on your work, rather than start from scratch each time you need a new movement or character.

Perhaps the most convincing example of the benefits of strategizing your design can be understood by referring to Figure 13.12. These were three different characters intended to be used for broadcast purposes, but the actual animation only had to be created once.

ON the CD-ROM To see how the motion is actually reused in the example shown in Figure 13.12, drag `reuseWalk.swf` from the `S_Corsaro` subfolder in the `ch13` folder on the CD-ROM into a browser window.

FIGURE 13.11

With small modifications, the same artwork can be used for the front and back of the character.

FRONT SYMBOL   BREAK APART   MAKE CHANGES   BACK SYMBOL

sandrocorsaro.com

FIGURE 13.12

When a character is designed strategically, you can reuse your animation as well as your artwork to quickly create other characters.

How do we get from here to here in three minutes?

Answer: REUSE! REUSE! REUSE!

Because of the strategy involved in the original character design, I was able to transform him into the other two characters, reusing both his Graphic symbols and the actual animation. By tweaking the timing of one leg on the run cycle, and obviously making some other artistic changes, the skateboarder character was created from the same artwork as the character running to catch a bus.

Flash is a very sophisticated authoring environment for animation, but, nonetheless, there is no substitute for knowledge of motion. To create truly compelling and intriguing animation in any genre, you must understand the scientific fundamentals of this art. The best place to learn about the principles of animation is in the daily environment around you. Observe the way things move; then strategize how to translate that movement efficiently using the tools available in Flash.

Flash Tweening

You can use Flash tweening to help your cartooning. Now that you've created some symbols, such as the walk cycle, here's where you can save a great deal of time, making them slink and prance across the view without drawing every tedious frame. The hard manual drawing work is done; now you'll choreograph the character. After you've built a library of various walks, runs, turnarounds, and standstills (a piece of walk cycle that ends with the character just standing still), you can use computer power to help you tell a story. Remember that you can always create more symbols of the character as needed — you can even steal from other symbols to create new ones.

Panning

Use the techniques we discuss earlier in this chapter to get your walking symbol looping, stationary in the middle of the view. Then move the background elements to give the illusion of the camera following alongside the walking character, a sort of dolly. We describe the trick for creating extra long pans later in this chapter. It usually requires a little experimentation to get the motion of the background to match the stride of the step. If the timing isn't correct, you'll notice that the feet seem to skate across the ground. To fix this, adjust the speed of the background by either increasing or decreasing the number of frames in the tween of the background. Another trick is to set the walking symbol to start at one end of the view and to move to the other by tweening the symbol itself. What's really cool is to use a mixture of both. Again, to get it just right, experiment and look closely at other examples that have the effect you want.

Instance swapping

There comes a time when the star of your show must stop walking (or running, or whatever he's doing) and reach into his pocket to pull out a hot-rod car and make his getaway. This is where instance swapping comes in. The setup for instance swapping in the middle of an action sequence is slightly different for the new CS4 motion tween layer than it is for a classic tween span, but the steps for swapping a symbol are the same.

At the end of a classic tween span, create a keyframe on the next frame (the frame immediately following the last keyframe in the tween), and then turn off motion-tweening for that keyframe in the Properties panel. This causes the symbol to stop at whichever frame the cycle ended on in the timeline. With CS4 motion tweening, symbol swapping on any keyframe in a tween replaces the symbol throughout the entire tween span. There is no option to turn off motion tweening on a single frame in a tween span. The workaround is to use the Copy/⌘+C command to copy the animated symbol from the last frame of the tween span, then insert a blank keyframe (F7) on the next frame (the frame immediately following the last keyframe in the CS4 tween span) and use the Paste in Place command (Shift+⌘+V) to place the symbol in exactly the same place on the Stage in the static frame.

To swap the symbol, follow these steps:

1. **Click the symbol to select it on the Stage.**
2. **Open the Properties panel.**
3. **Click the Swap Symbol button.**
4. **In the Swap Symbol dialog box, select the symbol that you want to replace it with (in this case, the one where he reaches into his pocket).**
5. **Click OK.**

If you loop the play of the symbol, you can also choose the frame on which the symbol's cycle starts. Other choices limit the symbol to playing once and play just a single frame (still).

CAUTION When you swap a symbol instance on a classic motion tween, if the Synch check box is selected in the Properties panel, the old symbol instance will not be replaced with the new one, which is Swap Symbol failure. If you turn off tweening on the frame where you swap the symbol, synchronization is not an issue. Symbol swaps on CS4 motion tween layers work with or without the Synch graphic symbols check box selected.

Finally, unless you've drawn all your symbols to perfect scale with each other, this new symbol may not fit exactly. No problem! To fix this, simply enable onion skinning from the Main Timeline, and set it to show the previous frame (the frame the tween ended on). Now you can align and scale the new symbol to match the ghosted image. We can't begin to tell you how much you'll use this simple instance-swapping function when you create your cartoon. This is one of the unique functions that sets Flash apart from all other cel-type animation programs. After you have a modest library of predrawn actions, the possibilities for combining them are endless.

Motion guides

Although not terribly useful for tweening a walking character, the Flash Motion Guide feature is tops for moving inanimate objects. If your character needs to throw a brick, a straight tween between points and some blur lines will do fine. If he needs to lob that brick over a fence to clang a pesky neighbor, then motion guides are the ticket. Here's how:

1. **Turn the brick into a Graphic symbol if you haven't already.** This makes it easier to make changes to the brick later.

2. Create a motion tween with the brick moving from its starting point to its ending point on the other side of the fence (or on top of the neighbor's head).

3. **Use the Selection tool to modify the motion guide to create a nice rounded arc for the brick to follow as it sails up and over the fence.** If the brick bounces off the neighbor's head before hitting the ground, include a second arc from head to ground.

WEB RESOURCE If you are working with a classic tween, you would need to create a separate motion guide layer and draw your own motion guide for the brick to follow. Because motion guide layers are a deprecated feature in Flash CS4, we don't describe the classic workflow here. The new CS4 auto-created motion guides on motion tween layers are much easier to work with, but if you want to explore working with classic tweens and motion guide layers, this workflow is described in *Flash CS3 Professional Bible* (Wiley, 2007) and you can review the archived content online at www.flashsupport.com/archive.

Although your brick is flying smoothly, something's wrong. Again, the computer made things too darned smooth. You could insert a few keyframes in the tween and rotate slightly here and there to give it some wobble. But that's still not convincing. You want this brick to mean business! Here's what to do: Because the brick is already a symbol, go back to the brick symbol and edit it, adding a few more frames to the symbol timeline. Don't add more than three or four frames; doing so will slow it down. At each of these new frames, mess up the brick a little here and there; differ the perspectives a little from one frame to another. Then when you go back to your main timeline, the brick should be twitching with vengeance as it sails toward its target.

Lip-Syncing

Now here's the part we've all been waiting for: A word from our character. If you do it properly, lip-syncing is where a character can really spring to life. You accomplish this by drawing the various mouth positions that are formed for individual *phonemes,* which are the basic units of sound that make up a spoken word. Then these phonemes are melded together into *morphemes,* which are distinct units of a word, like a syllable. Morphemes are then strung together over the course of a sentence to present the illusion of a talking, animated character. Most languages, although populated with thousands of words, are really made up from around 30 to 60 distinct sounds, or phonemes. For cartooning, these phonemes can be reduced to about ten basic mouth positions. Some of these positions can be repeated for more than one sound because many sounds share roughly the same mouth positions. Although there are more subtleties in the real world, for cartoons, reliance upon transitions between mouth positions is convincing enough.

Earlier, we suggested that the face in an action (walk) cycle should be drawn without a mouth. That's because this method facilitates the use of layers (in the timeline) for the addition of lip-syncing. To do this, create a layer above the character so that you can freely draw in the mouth positions needed to add lip-syncing. It's also very helpful to put the voice track on another separate layer directly above the Mouth layer. This makes it easy to see the waveform of the sound while you draw, giving important clues to where and when the sound occurs visually.

To preview sound, you can scrub the timeline, that is, drag the playhead, or current frame indicator, and hear the sound as you drag. This functionality is limited to streaming sounds, which means that the sounds have their Sync option in the Properties panel set to Streaming. The capability to hear the sound and see the animation in real time is an important tool for lip-syncing. This real-time feedback is critical for getting the timing just right. There's nothing worse than being plagued with OGMS (Old Godzilla Movie Syndrome), in which the mouth doesn't match the sounds coming from it.

Shape morphing is not for lip-syncing

You may be asking, "What about using shape morphing to save time in lip-syncing?" Well, shape morphing is a wonderful tool, but for lip-syncing, it's more hassle than it's worth. Your mouth drawings will become very complicated because they consist of lips, tongue, teeth, and facial features. Furthermore, because shape morphing only seems to work predictably on the simplest of shapes out of the box, shape hinting is required. Thus, by the time you've set all hinting (and even hinting heavily still leaves you with a mess at times), you might have had an easier time and obtained a better result (with greater control) if you had drawn it by hand.

Expression and lip-syncing

In terms of control and expression, it's important to remember to use the full range of expression when drawing the talking mouths. Happy, sad, or confused — these give life to your character. Furthermore, always emphasize mouth movements on those syllables that correspond with spikes of emotion in the voice track. These sections usually have a spike in the waveform that's easily recognized in the voice track. This device helps to convince the viewer that proper sync is happening.

Lip-sync tricks

There are a few more tricks to help ease the load. When characters talk, they do not always have to be looking you square in the face. Try lip-syncing the first few words to establish that the character is speaking, and then obscure the character's mouth in some natural way. (See Figure 13.13.) The head and body of a character can move with the words being said, but the mouth can be hidden by changing the angle of the head, or with a prop such as a microphone, or even with a moustache — think about this when designing your character's features. A bit of design savvy can save time without detracting from a character's purpose in the story line.

FIGURE 13.13

Lip-syncing tricks include economy of effort, such as having a character begin to speak and then turn away naturally (left). Appropriate props and even moustaches can also be used to hide mouths (right).

Many animators use a mirror placed nearby and mouth (act out) the words they're trying to draw. This is extremely helpful when learning to do lip-sync. It is also of great help in mastering facial expressions. Just try not to get too wrapped up in drawing every nuance you see. Sometimes less is more. Another trick that you can use to ease the load is to reuse lip-sync. Do this by copying frames from previous stretches of mouth movements to new locations where the words are the same, and then tweak the copied parts to fit the new dialogue. Still, there is no magic lip-sync button. Even with all these tricks, effective lip-syncing is hard work. It's also one of the more tedious tasks in animation and takes practice to get it right.

Syncing with music and sound effects

Because our brain works to create connections between sound and visual input, it is relatively easy to make movement in your animation match up with audio elements in your soundtrack. If you've already succeeded with lip-syncing work, then this type of syncing is easy. All that's required is a bit of instance swapping set to the beat of the music. If you study your music waveform for visual clues and then scrub it for the sound, you're sure to find the exact section where the change in action (instance swap) needs to go. You don't have to make your sync tight to every note. To keep the shot engaging, sync to the highlights, or hard beats.

Adding sound effects is really the fun part. It's easy and highly effective. Either working from your storyboard, or as you're animating, you'll know where you want to insert a sound effect. For example, when the anvil hits the head, a CLANK is needed there. If the effect you need is on hand, great! Just make sure that it has the necessary duration, and then plug it in at the frame where it should start. For broadcast animation, you'll set the sound sync to Streaming for the soundtrack exclusively. In addition to using separate layers for each voice track, it's wise to confine your sound effects to a layer or two. This leads to less confusion; yet using two layers enables more than one sound effect to occur at a time.

ON the CD-ROM For the following Expert Tutorial, we've supplied a short track for your use, `lip_track.wav` or `lip_track.aif`, which you'll find in the `B_Turner` subfolder inside the `ch13` folder of the CD-ROM. These tracks include the major sounds used in the English language.

Lip-Syncing Cartoons, by Bill Turner

For animated characters to really come alive, you need to know how to do lip-sync. To get quality lip-sync effects, you either need to draw them yourself or hire someone else to do it for you. Although this tutorial can't possibly cover every circumstance known to human communication, it can get you started on the road to lip service. There are some prequalifications: First, you must be able to draw in Flash, which usually means drawing with a tablet, preferably a pressure-sensitive graphics tablet (such as a Wacom tablet); and second, you need to have a recorded voice track on its own layer in Flash.

Because lip-sync can't be described in a simple a, b, c routine tutorial, you'll be required to improvise — in your style of drawing. I can't tell you how to do that. Style comes from years of practice and experimentation. But if you do know how to draw and you do have a style, then the intention here is to provide a context in which you might discover the basic trick of lip-sync.

The major sounds, known as phonemes, are less numerous than you might think. It's how these sounds meld together to become words and sentences that add an aura of complexity. Although one might surmise, from the alphabet, that there are 26 sounds, there aren't nearly that many. That's because many letters have the same basic mouth shape, movement, and pronunciation. And because we're now in the land of cartoons, we can simplify even further — the really great cartoons are often the simple ones built of tireless simple reinterpretation.

In this tutorial, to keep it simple, you'll deal with the two dominant views of talking heads: *profile* and *face forward*. A face forward talking head is probably the easiest to animate in Flash because the mouth can be animated on a layer that's situated in the layer stack above a drawing of a mouthless head. A talking head in profile is more difficult because of the need to redraw the portion of the face that extends down from the nose, to and including the chin, for *every* frame. Of course, including nose-to-chin movements can also enhance the animation of a face-forward talker, and doing so would make for a more expressive animation. But I want to move quickly here.

In Figure 13.14, you see a mouthless head (provided on the CD-ROM in the B_Turner folder for both demonstration and practice) in both of the basic orientations: face forward and profile.

The spoken test line reads, "Zinkle Meyers is very talented on the bongo drums. Flip Flap beats his hands on the smooooth skins. Dig the rhythm. Excellent!" Creating lip-sync for this line requires a number of mouth positions. To demonstrate the concepts, the first sentence of this test line is supplied, already drawn to lip-sync. Your task is to draw the mouth positions for the remainder of the spoken text.

ON the CD-ROM To help get you started, Bill Turner supplied a fully functional .fla file for you to work on, with the base character already drawn (lipsync.fla). You can find the file in the ch13/B_Turner folder on the CD-ROM.

The Sync option

If you were setting this file up from scratch, you'd want to start by placing the voice soundtrack on its own layer in the timeline. You'd rename this layer with a meaningful name, such as "voice," and then, in the Properties panel, you'd set the Sync option to Stream.

Never use Event as the Sync option for any sound that must sync to the Flash timeline. Otherwise, the timing of the voice will not be locked to the frame rate, meaning that the mouth drawings may not appear simultaneously with their appropriate sounds, thus losing sync.

FIGURE 13.14

A mouthless head in both of the basic orientations: face forward and profile with sound and animation layers for adding lip-sync

Getting into sync

The best way to understand lip-sync is to have the sample file open. Note that there is a visible waveform (the little squiggly stuff) that shows where the peaks and valleys of the sound occur across the timeline. Note, too, that the voice is brought in as a separate asset. It's on its own layer, separate from background sounds or music. It would be impossible to see the voice within the waveform if it was premixed with other sounds before bringing it into Flash. If you're producing a cartoon show, it's best to have each character recorded separately, particularly in cases in which they may talk over each other simultaneously. This separation gives you more control when animating. In fact, the entire animation is broken into layers for ease of editing. There's at least one layer for each major element. You might also note that the bongo soundtrack is set to Event. This is useful while authoring because it mutes the track when scrubbing the timeline to listen for timings in the voice track. If both were set to streaming, it would be more difficult to concentrate on the voice alone. (You must remember to reset this option to Stream when syncing is completed, or you could just delete that layer until after you are done animating the mouth.)

The phonemes

Now for the phonemes, there are several standard mouth positions for most of the major sounds, as shown in Figure 13.15. Although this is not a rigid rule, it does provide a good basis from which to expand into greater mastery of lip-sync. First, you'll note that the word *Meyers* begins on frame 12 of the animation. The mmmm sound is best represented with the bottom lip tucked slightly under the top lip. Try saying mmmm to see for yourself. In the word *Meyers*, this mmmm sound lasts two frames and is then followed by the long *I* sound. Notice that we didn't sync the word as it is spelled, e-y-e, because that's more complicated than it needs to be. The word *Meyers* is usually pronounced M-I-ER-Z, with the *ER* being just an *ease-out* (mouth holds shape but gets slightly smaller as phoneme trails off) of the long *I* sound. The word ends with the Z phoneme, which is simply drawn with the mouth slightly open, and the tongue at the top of the mouth.

FIGURE 13.15

You can combine a few basic phonemes to create lip-synced speech.

In the next section of speech, the "very talented" part is a fast-moving set of syllables, so every available frame is needed to represent it. Here, you'll notice that most of the movement occurs when the tongue engages the roof of the mouth for both the *T* and *L* phoneme. Now, because the *T* and *L* are nearly the same mouth position, you can use the luxury of duplicating frames. Similarly, the *V* sound requires the same basic mouth formation as the *M* sound, so you could copy this one as well from the Meyers word. Although the *B* sound, in *bongos*, uses nearly the same mouth as M and V, we don't copy that one. Here, we draw a new mouth to add a bit of chaos because we don't want the mouth to look like a machine. The logic behind deciding which part to copy and which part to make new drawings for is a large part of the art of lip-sync. In short, it's all about balancing how much new artwork you really want to do, while avoiding obvious repetition.

Now that I've given you an insight into how this is done, I've left the rest of the phrase for you to complete. To accomplish this, you'll probably want to reuse many of the supplied mouth positions to sync the remaining voice. Remember that timing is the most crucial part. You can determine where a new mouth position is needed, or where the mouth needs work, by slowly scrubbing the timeline. Then, if you need new mouths, simply draw them in. I highly recommend doing this drawing yourself because this practice will start you on your way to becoming a master of lip-sync.

Backgrounds and Scenery

As discussed in previous chapters, in Flash you work in an area that is called the Stage area. For broadcast animation (or any other kind, for that matter), it is better to think of it as the viewfinder of a camera. The main difference between this camera and the traditional kind, or even those used in 3D animation, is this: *You can't move it.* So, to give the illusion of camera movement, everything within the view must move. This is not as hard as it might seem with Flash's capability to use animated graphic symbols. A good example is in Richard Bazley's animated short, *The Journal of Edwin Carp.*

In a scene where the view seems to pan up from Edwin's bed to show a crack in the ceiling, all the elements on the Stage have to move to create the illusion of a camera move. Here is a rundown of the steps for creating this effect, as shown in Figure 13.16.

1. A Graphic symbol of the entire scene of animation that was larger than the camera's view was made (so that white space wouldn't show at the edges).
2. The symbol was placed in the Main Timeline.
3. The symbol was scaled and placed on the first keyframe to frame the medium view of Edwin in his bed.
4. The symbol was then scaled and placed on a later keyframe to frame the view of the cracked ceiling.
5. By tweening between these two keyframed views, the illusion of a camera zoom out and pan up is created as the whole scene moves on the Stage.

ON the CD-ROM We include this scene and several others from *The Journal of Edwin Carp*, an animated feature film that was done entirely in Flash, on the CD-ROM in the `R_Bazley` folder inside the `ch13` folder.

NOTE If you are interested in getting the full-length animation on DVD, contact Richard Bazley by email at `richard@bazleyfilms.com`.

FIGURE 13.16

A few shots from the bedroom scene in *The Journal of Edwin Carp*

Runtime bitmap caching

We're all waiting for the day when intensive animation plays as smoothly on the Web as it does when output for offline viewing. That day is getting closer with every build of the Flash Player. Flash 8 introduced a feature to optimize playback of complex vector graphics in Movie clip or Button symbols by caching them as bitmaps, or *surfaces*, at runtime. The benefit of caching complex vectors as bitmaps is that the Flash Player does not have to tie up the CPU by constantly redrawing these background vectors as other elements are animating in front of them. Your animation will play back faster and smoother. You can apply this option with ActionScript or by selecting a Movie clip (or Button) instance in the Document window and selecting the check box in the Properties panel to Use runtime bitmap caching.

Runtime bitmap caching optimizes Web playback only for Flash movies with complex background images that are static or panned vertically or horizontally. The position, but not the content, of the cached symbol can change without requiring the Flash Player to redraw the vector information. Bitmap caching fails if the Movie clip (or Button symbol) is larger than 2880 pixels in any direction or if the Movie clip is rotated. You will not notice a significant improvement with bitmap caching on simple vector graphics. Before you publish your final Flash movie, it is always best to test with bitmap caching turned on and turned off to see which delivers the best performance for the specific graphics and animation in your file.

Bitmaps

As we mention previously, when you're designing with Flash for the Web, use raster (bitmap) images with a careful eye on their file size. But for broadcast output, there's no limit. Not only can you use as many images as you'd like (within system constraints), but also doing so makes a richer, far more attractive finished product. And, unlike the .swf format, when they're output as raster video, even animations built with a lot of bitmaps play at the proper frame rate. So move, animate, scale, and rotate them — even play sequences of them. The sky and RAM are the only limits.

QuickTime limitations

Beginning with Flash 4, Flash expanded its import capabilities to include raster video — QuickTime and AVI. When using video output for broadcast, you can export to these formats, too, and video that has been embedded in a Flash project file (.fla) shows up when output to .swf format. In the past, Flash did not recognize alpha channels embedded in the QuickTime 32-bit animation codec (which supports traveling mattes, or alphas). The workaround was to use mask layers on the video in Flash. One of the most impressive features introduced with Flash 8 (Professional edition only) was the capability to import video with an alpha channel. If you can set up a basic blue or green screen and create some nice alpha channels on your video, you can take advantage of all that work when you bring the video into Flash CS4 and start layering your video with other elements.

Remember that you also have the option to link the video file rather than save it within the Flash project file (thank goodness) — Flash makes a pointer to it instead. This keeps your file sizes much more manageable. The only drawback to linking video instead of embedding it is that it won't show up when output to the .swf format.

The option of combining video with vector animation has brought tremendous functionality to Flash because animations can be keyed, or composited, over (or behind) live video without having to recomposite in After Effects. To take advantage of this, keep your live video at the same frame rate as the Flash project. Note, however, that Flash exports only the audio from the video clip in some formats, so you may need to reapply sound in a video-editing application. An alternate solution is to bring the video and audio tracks into Flash separately and to synchronize them there before exporting to your chosen format.

WEB RESOURCE You can find an archived version of the "Exporting Animation" chapter from *Macromedia Flash MX 2004 Bible* (Wiley, 2004) at www.flashsupport.com/archive. The chapter includes more detailed information about the various options for exporting animation and audio.

Building layered backgrounds in Photoshop

The drawing and effect tools in Flash have become more robust with each release. Blend modes and gradient controls make it easier for artists to get the effects that were previously possible only in raster applications. Our suggestion is to try working directly in Flash first, but if you need to go back to Photoshop, you'll be happy to know that the two applications work well together. By using layers in Photoshop to create artwork, multiplane shots are easily accomplished in Flash. Using layers is very important to the organization of the animation. It is not uncommon for a single shot to require more than 20 layers to keep things where they need to be in the visual stacking order. When designing backgrounds (or *scenery*, to be more precise), remember that, at some point, background elements may need to be foreground elements. For example, the sky will always be in the background, so it is on a layer farthest down in the stack. Other background elements, however, may sometimes need to be in the foreground to facilitate movement of the character, either in front of or behind him. To allow flexibility in how your various elements interact, you should keep them on separate layers.

When creating layered backgrounds, using Photoshop and alpha channels delivers the most versatility. When using Photoshop for scenery elements, it's mandatory to work in layers and to save a master file with all layers intact. Elements can then be exported to individual files (with alpha channels) as needed. (Retaining the master layered Photoshop file gives you maximum options later, if edits or changes occur. It can also be used as a resource for subsequent animations, so don't flatten or discard your master layered Photoshop file. Instead, number and archive it!) Why the alpha channels? When translating the Photoshop elements into Flash vector scenery, they automatically mask themselves — so a little preplanning in Photoshop can save lots of time later.

Flash mask layers

Whoops! You got to a point where you didn't use layers and now you need a mask. Some situations may be either too complicated or else unforeseeable in the original design. Flash mask layers can come to the rescue. Here's the good news: You can mask (and animate the mask) interactively with the other elements while in Flash. The bad news is that it might be more difficult to create a precise mask in Flash than to export an alpha channel from the original Photoshop file. A classic example of masking used in character animation is the black circle that closes in on a scene at the end of an animated episode. This simple animated shape mask is easy to add in Flash. Masks also come in handy to create reveals or to make elements seem to grow or shrink as they are gradually unmasked or masked on the Stage.

Long pans

Long pans are a standard device of animated cartoons; an example is when Fred Flintstone runs through the house and furniture keeps zipping past (that must be one looooong living room). This can be done a couple of ways in Flash. For landscape backgrounds, it's usually best to first create a very wide graphic (bitmap or vector) of the landscape and then to motion-tween it horizontally, with keyframes for stopping and starting as needed within the tween. If something is either falling or ascending, use a tall graphic and motion-tween vertically. Another solid technique is to create art of the objects that will pan (such as clouds) and then loop them as the background layer, across the view. To get smooth results when using looping, don't use easing in or out with the tween setup. Also, to maintain constant speed, maintain the exact number of frames between the keyframes. Then, copy the tween by Alt (Option) dragging the selected tween frames to the desired area in the timeline. Repeat copying until you've covered the time needed.

CAUTION For Web animation, it is best to use Movie clips for looping animation, but if you are planning to output your animation to video, you have to lay out all animation in keyframes on the Main Timeline (or in Graphic symbols). When your Flash animation is exported to video, only the first frame of any Movie clips appear, unless you use After Effects or Macromedia Director to translate the .swf file before final output.

In the Weber cartoon scene of a chase along the beach, a camera pan was created by tweening a symbol of the whole beach scene horizontally. As shown in Figure 13.17, the "camera view" reveals only a small area of the larger background scene.

FIGURE 13.17

The chase scene from the Weber cartoon is created with a looping pan.

TIP The area around the visible Stage in Flash is called the "pasteboard," and it can be utilized to support workflows that require extra-long graphics that will be tweened across the Stage. This feature is also handy for developers who like to store extra elements off the Stage where they won't be visible in the final .swf. Think of it as the theatre wings of your Flash stage.

Multiplane pans

To provide 3D-motion depth during the pan, keep this rule in mind: An object that is farther away appears to move more slowly (than a nearer object) as it moves across the view. This takes some experimenting to get it right, but when mastered, this adds a professional touch to your animations. For example, in a 100-frame pan of a beach scene looking toward the water:

- The sky moves very slowly at 100 pixels total.
- The water moves more quickly at 125 pixels total.
- The character on the beach moves more quickly than the water at 150 pixels total.
- A parked car in the immediate foreground moves most rapidly at 250 pixels total.

Blurring to simulate depth

The multiplane camera was used in early Disney films to give a feeling of depth in the animation of flat artwork. There was physical space between the individual cels when photographed. By using a short-depth-of-field lens, the artwork that was farther away from the lens lost focus slightly. (You may have noticed this in still photography yourself.) A good example of this is the pier scene from the Weber cartoon, which is shown in Figure 13.18. Even if you set up your scenery by using bitmaps, you can re-create this effect.

In Photoshop, it's a simple case of using incrementally higher doses of Gaussian blur on the layers of your scenery that are farther way. The farther the object is, the more blur that is applied — just be sure that the blur is applied to the alpha channel that Flash will use in compositing. To get the same effect in Flash, gradually apply more intensive levels of blur by using the Blur filter. Photographers use this technique to bring attention to the element in the shot that is in focus. Using it in animation enhances the illusion of depth. However, using it in the foreground can also portray atmospheric elements, such as fog.

FIGURE 13.18

The opening pier scene from the Weber cartoon has a feeling of depth created by using increasing levels of blur on the background layers.

Creating IK Armatures with the Bone Tool and Bind Tool

Inverse Kinematics or *IK* is an animation technique that is new to Flash but familiar to anyone who has worked with more specialized character animation or modeling programs. Instead of animating the individual parts of an object as isolated elements, IK creates relationships or links between elements so that the movement of one element affects the movement of other related elements. The classic example of this is a hand moving while connected to a wrist, which is also connected to an elbow, and then to a shoulder. Each distinct part of the structure can initiate movement, but as one part moves, the other parts of the structure stay connected to it and move accordingly. This example is consistent with the behavior of IK bones in Flash because the bones do not bend, but the joints between the bones enable the shape to move in almost any direction, subject to the varying limitations in rotation and movement of each joint. For example, the shoulder joint can move quite freely in a circular motion but it can't easily change its position in space (unless the torso moves), while the elbow joint has a more limited range of rotation but a greater freedom of movement in space.

If you have spent time trying to animate characters or design elements in Flash with multiple parts that you wanted to move individually, while keeping them connected to each other, you will appreciate how much easier this type of animation is in Flash CS4. The new Bone tool enables you to apply IK in two ways: You can link individual symbol instances so that they can move as a chain or rotate in relation to one another or you can create a skeleton inside of a shape that can be used to control the movement of the shape for realistic animation.

The Bone tool gets its name from the fact that the links that make up an IK armature are similar to the bones in a skeleton: They do not bend but they rotate at joints and allow the symbol instances or shapes around them to bend and change size and position within a controllable range. Armatures can be linear or branched. You may want to experiment with linear structures to get a feel for the hierarchy of bones and the characteristics of joints before you move on to creating more complex branched structures.

 The IK tools are only available if your project file is targeting Flash Player 10 and using ActionScript 3.0.

To create a linear IK armature linking a series of symbol instances, follow these steps:

1. **Place a series of symbol instances on the Stage**. You can use multiple instances of the same shape or a variety of different symbol instances. Our starting file with seven scaled instances of the same circle symbol is shown in Figure 13.19.

FIGURE 13.19

A series of symbol instances arranged on a single layer in Flash are ready to be connected by the Bone tool into an IK armature.

2. Activate the Bone tool (X) and click on the symbol instance that you want to start your bone chain.

NOTE The initial symbol instance in the chain will have a fixed x, y position by default, while the connected instances can be moved on the Stage with the Selection tool. Think of the first symbol instance as the anchor point of your animation. If you wanted to have a blade of grass that could bend and move in the wind, you would start from the root of the grass and grow the chain upward instead of starting at the top of the grass and growing the chain down toward the root.

3. **Hold down the mouse and drag to see a preview of the bone that will connect the first symbol instance to the next one in your chain.** Release the mouse when the end of the bone is connected to the next symbol in the chain. The end point of the bone automatically snaps to the center point of the symbol instance as you drag over it.

4. **Click the second symbol in the chain and drag a new bone to connect to the third symbol in the chain.** Continue clicking and adding sequential bones to create a series of joined symbol instances. Figure 13.20 shows our sample file with the first half of a bone chain created to connect the symbol instances into an IK armature.

FIGURE 13.20

As you connect each symbol instance with a bone, the instance becomes part of your IK armature and is moved onto the auto-created pose layer.

Notice that each time you connect a symbol with a bone to add it to your bone chain or IK armature, Flash moves the symbol onto an auto-created pose layer (designated by a small running figure) in the Timeline. If you start with six symbol instances in a layer on the Stage and then connect them all with the Bone tool, you will see that the original layer is empty and all the symbols are on the pose layer when you are finished creating your bone chain. You can select symbol instances in the chain to access instance properties or select the individual bones in the armature to access IK controls in the Properties panel.

As shown in Figure 13.21, each bone has settings for the following properties:

■ **Speed:** This setting is used to slow down the movement of bones to simulate weight. The default setting of 100 percent is equal to free motion or no weight. The lowest setting of 0 percent is equal to no motion or dead weight. In most cases, you will get a nice feeling of organic weight by using values in the middle of this range.

■ **Joint Rotation:** By default this setting for movement around the bone joint is enabled and unconstrained. If you want to freeze a joint, deselect the Enable check box. If you want to limit the range of motion for the joint, select the Constrain check box and set a Minimum and/or a Maximum angle of rotation within the 360-degree range of the joint.

FIGURE 13.21

You can select each bone in an IK armature to access controls in the Properties panel and fine-tune the behavior of your chain.

TIP Positive and negative angles are calculated from the original position of the bone. A value range of –45 degrees to 45 degrees would allow the joint to move to both sides of its current position within a 90-degree arc. A value range of 0 to 90 degrees would also enable the joint to move in a 90-degree arc but only to one side (clockwise) from its current position.

- **Joint X Translation and Joint Y Translation:** By default, these settings for movement of a joint within the chain are disabled. This keeps the length of bones in a chain fixed and makes it a little easier to get predictable motion as you click and drag an IK armature to create poses. If you want more freedom to move individual symbol instances or bones within a chain and you don't mind dealing with bones growing or shrinking within your armature, you may choose to enable free movement along the x and/or y axis by selecting the Enable check box for the respective property. Values are in pixels and are calculated relative to the original position of a bone on the Stage. To limit how far joints can move from their original location, you can set Minimum and/or Maximum values for either axis.

TIP Although you can enable a joint to move within a range that takes it well outside the Stage area, you might find it easier to control your armature if you use conservative ranges for the X and Y Translation properties to keep the armature from drifting too far outside the Stage.

The pose layer that Flash creates to hold your IK chain is a special layer type that, like a motion tween layer, will capture changes that you make on the Stage and save them in property keyframes.

NOTE A pose layer can only contain one armature. If you are working with multiple armatures, you can animate each one on its own pose layer.

If you want to animate your IK armature, follow these steps:

1. **Extend the frame span by inserting additional frames on the pose layer.** Select the initial frame in the span and use the F5 key add one frame at a time or select the frame number that you want the span to extend to and then use the F5 key to auto-extend the span to that frame.

2. **Scrub the Timeline to a frame where you would like to add a new pose.**

3. **Use the Selection tool or the Properties panel to make changes to the position (or shape) of your armature.** As shown in Figure 13.22, a property keyframe will be added to the span of the pose layer to save the changes. If you scrub the Timeline, you will see an animation of the symbol instances in your IK chain moving from the original position to the new position (or series of poses) that you created in the pose layer.

FIGURE 13.22

You can change the position of your IK chain in a series of property keyframes to create poses that are animated on the pose layer.

Selecting any frame in the span of the pose layer loads settings for the IK animation into the Properties panel. As shown in Figure 13.22, you can apply easing to the animation as well as choose whether the IK armature is animated at authortime (enabling you to create a series of poses and a set animation sequence) or at runtime (enabling the viewer to click and drag the armature to interact with it "live"). You can also change the bone display Style from the default setting of Solid to Wire or Line to find the view that suits you best.

All the settings discussed so far are applicable to bones linking chains of symbol instances or bones used to create an armature inside of a shape. However, the way that bones interact with symbol instances is quite different from the way they control the movement of a shape. To create an IK armature inside of a shape, follow these steps:

1. **Use the Brush tool or any of the shape drawing tools to create a filled shape that you want to add an IK skeleton or armature to.** IK works best if you make a simple, solid shape without a stroke. Our starting shape is shown in Figure 13.23.

2. **Select the Bone tool in the Tools panel.**

3. **Click inside the shape and drag to create the first bone in the armature.** In most cases, you will want to start at one end of the shape and continue clicking and dragging to set up a series of bones that progress to the other end of the shape. The shorter you make the bones, the more joints you can include in the armature and the more "flexible" the shape will be.

FIGURE 13.23

A simple filled shape drawn in merge or object drawing mode can be transformed into an articulated shape by adding an IK armature with the Bone tool.

As with bones added to symbol instances, bones added to a shape will be saved on a new pose layer that can be used to animate the articulated IK armature. A preview of our example shape (with bones added) being moved into a new pose is shown in Figure 13.24.

One challenge of animating shapes with IK bones is that the outline of the shape will sometimes distort or fracture as you move the skeleton. The companion tool for the Bone tool, called the Bind tool (Z), helps you control how the shape relates to the bones in your armature. The way these two tools work together is similar to how the Subselection tool works with the Pencil or Pen tool. After you have created an armature inside of a shape with the Bone tool, you can use the Bind tool to select a bone and see the related control points along the edges of the shape highlighted (with a yellow outline). You can also use the Bind tool to select individual points along the edge of the shape and see the related bone or bones highlighted (with a yellow outline). These two different views of the armature-shape relationship are shown in Figure 13.25.

In this way, you can get a clearer idea of how the shape is tied or bound to the bones. More important, you can reassign points or bind them to different bones within the armature. To do this, simply click a point on the edge of the shape with the Bind tool and drag the yellow highlight to the bone that you want it to be tied to, or conversely, you can click a bone with the Bind tool and then drag highlights to specific points along the edge of the shape. Either way, you will be able to adjust the way that the shape reacts to changes in the position of the bones. Keep in mind that points can be bound to more than one bone. The Bind tool is most helpful for smoothing out distortion around joints that are very close together, where outline points may be connected to the wrong bone(s).

FIGURE 13.24

Moving one bone in the armature drags the other bones along in a continuous chain that controls the motion and form of the articulated shape. Changes to the shape will be saved as property keyframes on the pose layer to create an animation of the motion.

FIGURE 13.25

Bones can be selected with the Bind tool to show the points that are bound to them (left), or points can be selected with the Bind tool to show which bone(s) they are bound to (right).

Although the IK tools (the Bone tool and the Bind tool) make the task of animating related shapes infinitely easier, they do not eliminate the learning curve for creating this type of animation. It takes a lot of experience to make the most of IK and to anticipate exactly how an armature should be designed and tuned to support different shapes and poses.

WEB RESOURCE As you push your skills into new territory, it helps to find some animation role models who can lead you in defining your style and exploring the full potential of the tools. You can find some inspiring examples and some approachable tutorials online at www.coldhardflash.com, a site that features work from a range of independent Flash animators and Flash animation studios.

Finishing Up

When you have a shot done, it's often helpful to see it play at full speed. Unfortunately, Flash is unable keep up with all the sounds, bitmaps, and complicated vectors that go into broadcast-quality animation. Plus, it's impossible — even with the most macho of processors — to play the shot at full speed without hiding a bunch of elements. But, hey, you're the director of this masterpiece: It's time for dailies, and you need to see it all.

The best way to do this and to cut down on file size is to export a raster video at 320 x 240 pixels, using the standard QuickTime Video codec (Mac) or the Microsoft Video 1 codec. These codecs are for draft purposes only, so the video may have banding and artifacts from compression, but the point is to generate something that even a machine that's ill equipped for high-end video output can display easily at full frame-rate speed. This method is of great help in revealing those areas of the animation that still need further tweaking and work before going out to the final published version. The general movement and pace of the shot will make itself known. Look for errors such as unintended jumpiness in frames, and color shifts or inconsistencies between views. Furthermore, your lip-syncing efforts will either be a glory to behold or a disaster in need of medical attention. Other things, such as sound clipping (pops in high-volume sound) also become apparent here. To put it bluntly, if the preview makes you cringe, then it needs work. If not, you're on your way to final output.

NOTE Flash video has become the cross-platform format of choice for video on the Web. If your animation is going to be seen online or in the context of a Flash presentation (such as a kiosk or projection), you will be better off using Flash video than another video format such as QuickTime. With Flash video, your animation can be integrated seamlessly with other Flash elements and no other players will be needed to run the file.

Final output

Now, after checking endlessly, you're ready for the final video file of the shot to be rendered. Back it up one more time. Then, when you've safely archived your final project file, it's time to choose the codec that your playback equipment can use and render one out for the tube. When you have rendered all your shots at full screen, you can take them into Premiere or After Effects or Macromedia Director for more detailed editing and tweaking, using all the power that these applications offer. For example, you might want music to play gently in the background across all of your scenes. Although this would be a headache to piece together with separate Flash project files, it's a snap in Premiere. Again, the possibilities are endless.

Post production

You spend so much time working diligently to make your animation look great in Flash, and ironically, you might find after you output your animation, that it looks "too good" for broadcast. The solid color fields and clean edges of vector animation can be jarring when translated to the broadcast context. You might even find that some of your colors "bleed" on-screen, if they are out of the NTSC safe range.

If you want your Flash animation to have more of a classic animation look, you need to reduce the saturation of out-of-gamut colors and roughen the graphics up a bit by adding some organic visual texture. The easiest way to do this is to take advantage of the filters available in Adobe After Effects. The Broadcast Colors filter enables you to reduce luminance or saturation of colors that are not in the Color Safe range. When you have color sorted out, you can work on texture. By adding a subtle Gaussian blur and a touch of Film grain, you can give your perfect, cold Flash animation some of the warm fuzzy film feel. The trick is to use a very light hand with these filters: The end result shouldn't be so overt that it's distracting — unless that's something you really want the viewer to notice! Figure 13.26 shows an example of how slight the change can be to really make a difference for broadcast work.

ON the CD-ROM To see a "live" comparison of the before and after files shown in Figure 13.19, open `JibJab_Willy.swf` (original file) and `JibJab_Willy.mov` (filtered file) from the JibJab folder in the `ch13` folder on the CD-ROM.

NOTE If you want to take your production one step farther, you can find plug-ins for After Effects that offer even more filter options. DigiEffects is one great source for a whole range of plug-ins designed to simulate film and create organic effects like scratches, film flicker, hair, dust, and dirt. Find more information and free trial versions at `www.digieffects.com`.

WEB RESOURCE We'd like to know what you think about this chapter. Visit `www.flashsupport.com/feedback` to send us your comments.

FIGURE 13.26

Flash artwork that looks too "clean" for broadcast (top) can be modified with filters in After Effects to look more organic (below).

Summary

- Flash can be a powerful tool for creating broadcast-quality cartoons. In such cases, many of the usual file size concerns related to Flash development are set aside because the final output do not have to be Web-friendly.

- The task of a cartoon animator is to express motion and emotion. Anticipation and overlapping actions are basic tools cartoon animators use to add drama to a character's movement.

- Flash tweening, including instance swapping and motion guides, is one of the most useful Flash cartooning tools.

- Lip-syncing, which is critical to fine cartoon animation, is not a push-button task — even with Flash, an animator must understand the relationship between expression and lip-sync, and have a working knowledge of phonemes, as well as syncing with music and sound effects.

- The filters and blend modes in Flash make it easier to achieve sophisticated-looking animation without having to use other applications for special effects.

- The new Bone tool and Bind tool make it possible to create poseable chains of symbol instances or shapes with articulated skeletons. These articulated elements are referred to as armatures and enable you to leverage inverse kinematics (IK) to quickly animate related elements on auto-created pose layers.

- After a cartoon is created in Flash, final output may include using either Premiere or After Effects for the final polish that makes it look more like "real film."

- The key point of this entire chapter is this: Computers can save time, but only artists can animate!

Part IV

Integrating Media Files with Flash

You can create a wide range of graphic elements directly in Flash, but most projects also require imported assets. This section covers the three main media types that you can use to enhance your Flash projects. Chapter 14 introduces the process for importing and controlling sound in Flash. This chapter also covers various compression options and how to edit and export sound from Flash. Learn techniques that help you to get the most bang per byte in your final Flash movies. Chapter 15 addresses the specific workflow and optimization issues related to importing vector and bitmap artwork (and text) from other programs to the Flash authoring environment. Find out how to maintain color consistency and how to preserve layers and vector outlines when moving graphics from other programs, including Adobe Illustrator and Adobe Photoshop. Flash offers a whole range of possibilities for video content. Chapter 16 focuses on the process for optimizing and integrating video, including coverage of the new AVC/H.264 video codec, Adobe Media Encoder CS4, and the FLVPlayback component.

Chapter 14

Adding Sound

O ne of the more neglected — or perhaps understated — aspects of multimedia development is sound. Because many people who use Flash or create multimedia come from graphic arts backgrounds, it's no surprise that sound is often applied as the last effect to an otherwise visually stunning presentation — there may be little or no consideration for the soundtrack in early stages of development. Moreover, it's the one element that is usually taken from a stock source, instead of being the Flash designer's original work. (Exceptions exist, of course, as Flash designers have demonstrated time and time again.)

NOTE It goes without saying that as Web projects or applications grow in scope, production teams tend to include specific members responsible for unique tasks, from graphic design to user interface design to sound design.

You can use sound in Flash movies to enhance interactive design with navigation elements, such as buttons, to layer the visitor's experience with a background soundtrack, to add narration, or for more experimental uses. In this chapter, we focus on the fundamentals of importing and integrating sound files into your Flash project. We also discuss the intricacies of controlling audio output, with particular attention to MP3 bit rates. You'll learn how to use the Publish Settings dialog box and compare it with the enhanced control that is available for customizing compression from within the Sound Properties dialog box of the Library panel. This chapter guides you through using audio within a Flash document and suggests tips for getting the most bang per byte in the final Flash movie file (.swf).

CROSS-REF You can read more about sound in Appendix C, "Digital Audio Basics." To learn how to load external MP3 files into a Flash movie at runtime, read Chapter 28, "Sharing and Loading Assets." If you need to create ActionScript 2.0 code or use the Behaviors panel for legacy Flash projects, refer to our coverage in previous editions of the *Flash Bible*.

473

Identifying Sound File Import and Export Formats

Flash CS4 can work with a wide variety of sound file formats. In this section, you learn what sound file types you can bring into a Flash document file (.fla) and how Flash can compress audio in a variety of formats in the final Flash movie file (.swf).

Import formats

You can import most sound file formats in either the Windows or Mac version of Flash CS4. All major sound file types, such as MP3 and WAV, are compatible on both versions. After you import a sound file into a Flash document, you can edit the resulting .fla file on either platform.

Flash CS4 can import the following sound file formats:

- **MP3 (MPEG-1 Audio Layer 3):** Among the many advantages of MP3 sound files for Flash users, the most obvious is that they are cross-platform. Flash CS4 can import MP3 files with either Windows or Mac versions of the tool. This single advantage improves Flash workflow in cross-platform environments. Other advantages are the efficiency of MP3 compression, the increasing availability of MP3 files, as well as the ease of creating MP3 files with common players such as Windows Media Player or Apple iTunes. For more information about MP3s, see the "MP3s Demystified" sidebar at the end of the section.

- **WAV (Windows Wave):** Until the relatively recent support for MP3, WAV files reigned for nearly a decade as the standard for digital audio on Windows PCs. Still, the WAV format remains the primary acquisition sound format, the format in which you record sound from a microphone or other sound source on your computer. Flash can import WAV files created in sound applications and editors such as Sound Forge or ACID. The imported WAV files can be either stereo or mono and can support varying bit depths and frequency rates. You can import WAV files directly into Flash CS4 on a Mac.

- **AIFF or AIF (Audio Interchange File format):** Much like WAV on the PC, the AIFF format is one of the most commonly used digital audio formats for sound acquisition on the Mac. Flash can import AIFF sounds created in sound applications and editors such as Bias Peak or Adobe Soundbooth CS4. Like WAV, AIFF supports stereo and mono, in addition to variable bit depths and frequency rates. Unassisted, the Windows version of Flash CS4 cannot import this file format. But when QuickTime 4 or later is installed, you can import AIFF files into Flash CS4 on Windows. The Windows version of Flash CS4 recognizes, properly opens, and can edit Flash documents created on the Mac that contain AIFF sounds.

■ **Sun AU:** This sound format file (.au) was developed by Sun Microsystems and Next, and it is the native sound format on many Solaris and UNIX systems, just as WAV and AIFF are native to Windows and the Mac, respectively. The Sun AU format is frequently used with sound-enabled Java applets on Web pages.

■ **QuickTime:** You can import QuickTime audio files (.qta or .mov) directly into Flash CS4, provided that you have QuickTime 4 or later installed. After you import a QuickTime audio file into a Flash document, the sound file appears in the library just as any other sound would.

■ **Sound Designer II:** This proprietary audio file format created by Digidesign is used with its signature professional audio suite, Pro Tools. You can import sounds that you save in this file format into the Mac version of Flash CS4. If you need to use a Sound Designer II file (.sd2 file extension) with the Windows version of Flash CS4, you can import the file directly if you have QuickTime 4 or later installed.

NOTE With Flash CS4, you can link proxy sound files to Musical Instrument Digital Interface (MIDI) and Melody For i-mode (MFI) files that can be played back on mobile devices with Flash Lite.

TIP Don't rely upon the imported sound that's embedded in the Flash document file (.fla) as your master or backup sound file. Always retain your original master sound file as a backup or for reuse in other multimedia projects.

These sound file types are structural or "architecture" based, meaning that they simply indicate the wrapper used to encode digital audio. Each of them can use a variety of compression techniques or a variety of audio *codecs*. A codec is a *c*ompression and *dec*ompression module for digital media. Sound and video is encoded (compressed) with a specific technique by an application or device. After it is encoded, it can be played back (decompressed) by a media player that has access to the codec module. In order for a sound file to play on your computer, you must have the audio codec used in that file installed on your system. MP3 files, for example, can be compressed in a variety of bit rates and frequencies, as can WAV and AIF files. After Flash imports a sound file, the wrapper type (AIF, WAV, AU, and so on) is stripped. Flash simply stores the sound file as generic PCM (Pulse Code Modulation) digital audio. Moreover, Flash converts any imported 8-bit sound file into a 16-bit sound file. For this reason, it's best not to use any precompression or low bit depths on your sound files before you bring them into Flash CS4.

NOTE You can adjust individual MP3 sound files in the Flash document's Library panel to retain their original compression. This is the sole exception to the rule we just mentioned in the preceding paragraph. As you'll see later in this chapter, however, Flash CS4 may need to recompress all sound files in a Flash movie, depending on their use in the movie's timeline.

MP3s Demystified

MP3 is an amazing compression technology as well as a file format. It excels at the compression of a sound sequence — MP3-compressed files can be reduced to nearly a twelfth of their original size without destroying sound quality. MP3 was developed under the sponsorship of the Motion Picture Experts Group (MPEG), using the following logic: CD-quality sound is typically sampled at a bit depth of 16 (16-bit) at sample rate 44.1 kHz, which generates approximately 1.4 million bits of data for each second of sound — but that second of sound includes a lot of data for sounds that most humans cannot hear! By devising a compression algorithm that reduces the data linked to imperceptible sounds, MP3 developers made it possible to deliver high-quality audio over the Internet without excessive *latency* (the delay between loading a sound and playing it). Another way of describing this is to say that MP3 uses perceptual encoding techniques that reduce the amount of overlapping and redundant information that describes sound. As you'll learn later in this chapter, the Flash Player can actually buffer stream sounds (which you can create from any sound file imported into Flash); this means that the sound begins to play in the Flash movie before the sound file has been downloaded in its entirety. Shockwave Audio, the default audio compression scheme for Adobe Director–based Shockwave movies, is actually MP3 in disguise.

Export formats

You can decide which sound encoding to use for audio when publishing Flash document files to Flash movie files (.swf). Although the default publish settings in Flash CS4 is to export all audio with the MP3 format, you can export sound in several other audio formats. We note the benefits and drawbacks of each format in the list that follows.

NOTE Flash CS4 enables you to export device sounds in a Flash movie, for playback on mobile devices that use file formats such as MIDI and MFI. We provide an overview of this feature in this section.

Regardless of the format that you choose in your document's publish settings for exporting your sounds, you can individually specify a compression scheme for each sound in the Flash document's library. Furthermore, each format has specific options and settings that we examine later in this chapter.

- **ADPCM (Adaptive Differential Pulse-Code Modulation):** ADPCM is an audio compression scheme that converts sound into binary information. It is primarily used for voice technologies, such as fiber-optic telephone lines, because the audio signal is compressed, enabling it to carry textual information as well. ADPCM works well because it records only the difference between samples and adjusts the encoding accordingly, keeping file size low. ADPCM was the default setting for older versions of Flash, such as Flash 2 and 3. It isn't as efficient as MP3 encoding, but is the best choice for situations in which compatibility is required with *all* older Flash Players.

■ **MP3 (MPEG-1 Audio Layer 3):** Over the last three years, MP3 has become the standard for digital audio distributed on the Internet. Although MP3 compression delivers excellent audio quality with small files, it's much more processor intensive than other compressors. This means that slower computers — and we mean slow, as in Pentium I or pre-PowerMac G3 processors — may gasp when they encounter a high bit-rate MP3 audio while simultaneously processing complex animations. As always, it's wise to know your audience. When in doubt, test your Flash movie with MP3 audio on slower computers. Flash Players 4 and higher support MP3 playback.

NOTE Not all versions of the Flash Player support MP3 sound. With Flash Player 6 and higher, you can use ActionScript's `System.capabilities.hasMP3` (ActionScript 2.0) or `flash.system.Capabilities.hasMP3` (ActionScript 3.0) property to determine if the hosting player device supports MP3 audio. You can learn more about this use of ActionScript in the Help documentation that ships with Flash CS4.

■ **Raw (Raw PCM):** Flash can export sound to .swf files in a raw audio format. If you use this setting, Flash won't compress any audio. However, uncompressed sound makes very large files that would be useless for Internet-based distribution. As uncompressed sound, audio in the imported sound file retains its original fidelity. We recommend that you use the Raw format only for Flash movies that you intend to export as linear animation for output to video-editing applications.

■ **Speech (Nellymoser):** This audio codec introduced with Flash Player 6 is specifically designed for audio sources that contain mostly human speech, such as narration or instructional content. Macromedia (before Adobe acquired the company) licensed audio technology from Nellymoser, Inc., which specializes in the development of voice-only audio codecs. All sounds that use the Speech codec are converted to mono sounds. You can see the real power of this codec in live streaming audio delivered by Adobe Flash Media Server, because this codec is incredibly efficient and a fast encoder with a low server and client processor overhead. For example, if you want to use a `NetStream` object in ActionScript to stream live audio from a microphone, the Speech codec optimizes the audio information very efficiently. You must use Flash Player 6 or later to play sounds encoded with this format.

■ **Device sound:** With Flash CS4, you can link device sound files to imported sounds in your Flash movie. You use device sounds specifically for playback of Flash movies on mobile devices enabled with Flash Lite, a version of the Flash Player. Because the desktop Flash Player cannot play device sound file formats, you import regular sound files such as MP3s into your Flash document. These sounds are then used in a proxy fashion — you add the sound to event handlers (keyframes, buttons, and so on) just as you would any other sounds. Before you publish the Flash movie file (.swf), however, you change the settings of the sound file in the Library panel to point to a device sound. When the Flash movie is published, the device sound is embedded and used within the Flash movie, not the original imported sound.

CROSS-REF We examine the specific export options for each audio format later in this chapter. This section will help you determine which format you should use for your specific needs.

Table 14.1 shows the compatibility of Flash's audio export formats with various platforms.

TABLE 14.1

Audio Export Formats for Flash Players

Export format	Flash 3 or earlier	Flash 4 and 5	Flash 6 or higher	Comments
ADPCM	Yes	Yes	Yes	Good encoding scheme; compatible with all Flash players; works well for short sound effects such as button clicks
MP3	No	Yes	Yes	Best general-use encoding scheme; ideal for music tracks
Raw	Yes	Yes	Yes	No compression; lossless; large file sizes
Speech	No	No	Yes	Excellent compression for human speech; avoids "tinny" sounds for voices; ideally suited for real-time compression with Flash server-side applications
Device sound	No	No	No	Sound export feature available in Flash CS4; for use with MIDI and MFI files for playback on mobile devices with Flash Lite

Importing Sounds into Flash

In the preceding section, we discussed the various sound formats that Flash CS4 can import and export. In addition to covering the merits of the MP3 and Speech codecs, we also explained the uses of platform-specific AIF (Mac) and WAV (Windows) audio files. But we didn't delve into the process of importing sound into Flash CS4. So, let's get started.

NOTE When working with sound, you may encounter some interchangeable terminology. Generally, these terms — *sound file, sound clip,* and *audio file* — all refer to the same thing, a single digital file in one of several formats that contains a digitally encoded sound.

Unlike other imported assets, such as bitmaps or vector art, Flash won't automatically insert an imported sound file into the frames of the active layer on the Timeline. In fact, you don't have to select a specific layer or frame before you import a sound file. That's because all sounds are sent directly to the library immediately upon import, regardless of whether you use File ⇨ Import ⇨ Import to Stage or Import to Library. After import, the sound becomes part of the Flash document file (.fla), which may make the file size balloon significantly if the sound file is large. The sound does not become part of the Flash movie file (.swf), nor does it add to the size of the Flash movie *unless* it is assigned to a keyframe, as an instance of that sound, or it is set to export for use in ActionScript.

> **TIP** Flash Players 6 and later allow a Flash movie to load MP3 files directly. We show you how to load and attach sounds with ActionScript in Chapter 28, "Sharing and Loading Assets."

To import a sound file into the Flash CS4 authoring environment, follow these steps:

1. **Choose File ⇨ Import ⇨ Import to Library or Import to Stage (Ctrl+R or ⌘+R).** For sound assets, these commands work identically.

2. **From the Files of type list (Windows) or Enable list (Mac) in the Import dialog box, select All Sound Formats.**

> **CAUTION** On the Mac OS X version of Flash CS4, you may need to choose All Files in the Show menu in order to select an appropriate sound file.

3. **Browse to the sound file that you want to import.**

> **ON the CD-ROM** If you're looking for a sample audio file, you can import the `atmospheres_1.mp3` or the `atmospheres_1_short.mp3` file found in the `resources` folder of this book's CD-ROM.

4. **Click Open.** The sound file you select is imported into your Flash document file (.fla) and arrives in the document's library with its filename intact. If the Library panel is closed, you can open it by choosing Window ⇨ Library, or by using the keyboard shortcut (Ctrl+L or ⌘+L). With the Library panel open, locate the sound, and click it to highlight the name of the sound file where it appears in the Library list. The waveform appears in the Library preview pane, as shown in Figure 14.1. Click the Play button above the waveform to audition the sound.

> **CROSS-REF** Refer to "Fine-Tuning Sound Settings in the Library" later in this chapter for an explanation of how you can specify unique compression settings for each sound in a document's library. You may also load sounds from a shared library. Refer to Chapter 28, "Sharing and Loading Assets," to learn more about shared libraries. Chapter 29 also shows you how to preload an MP3 file into a Flash movie file (.swf). To learn how to assign a linkage identifier string to an asset, such as a sound file, refer to Chapter 26, "Interacting with Movie Clips."

FIGURE 14.1

This is a stereo sound in the Flash document's library.

You can also import sound files into a Flash document by dragging the sound file from the desktop to the Library panel. On the Mac, you can drag the sound file to the Stage as well. This method can be especially useful when you have searched for a sound file by using the operating system's search tool (Start ➪ Search in Windows, or Spotlight in the Mac OS) and want to quickly bring the sound file into Flash CS4.

How Sound Is Stored in a Flash Movie

Earlier in this chapter, we mentioned that when you import a sound file into a Flash document file (.fla), an entire copy of the sound file is stored within the document. However, when you place a sound on a timeline, a reference is made to the sound in the library. Just as symbol instances refer to a master or parent symbol in the Library panel, sound "instances" refer to the master sound resource in the Library panel.

Throughout this chapter, we use the term "instance" for sound assets with this understanding in mind. When the Flash document is published as a Flash movie, the master sound in the library is compressed and stored *once* in the final movie file (.swf), even though there may be several instances of that sound used through the movie (for example, in multiple frames on multiple timelines).

This type of efficient storage, however, applies to event sounds only. Whenever you use stream sounds, the sound file is stored in the Flash movie each time you refer to the sound in a timeline. For example, if you compressed a sound to export from Flash as a 3K sound asset in the final movie file (.swf), you could reuse that sound as an event sound several times without adding significant bytes to the file size. However, that same compressed sound (at 3K) would occupy 12K in the final movie if it was placed four times as a stream sound on keyframes within the movie. We discuss event and stream sounds later in this chapter, so you may want to refer to this sidebar at a later point.

It is also worth mentioning that Flash CS4 must have enough available RAM on the computer system to accommodate imported sound files. For example, if you import a 30MB WAV file into a Flash document, then you must have an additional 30MB of RAM available to the application. On Windows operating systems and Mac OS X, you will not likely experience problems with memory usage, where virtual memory exists alongside the physical RAM within the computer.

Assigning a Sound to a Button

The interactive experience can be enhanced by the addition of subtle effects. The addition of sounds to correspond with the various states of a button is perhaps the most obvious example. Although this effect can be abused, it's hard to overuse an effect that delivers such meaningful user feedback. Here, we show how different sounds can be added to both the Over (rollover) and the Down (press) states of a button.

CROSS-REF For more general information about creating the buttons themselves, see Chapter 6, "Symbols, Instances, and the Library," and see Chapter 17, "Understanding Actions and Event Handlers," to learn how to add code to buttons.

Because buttons are stored in the library, and because only instances of a Button symbol are deployed within the Flash movie, sounds that are assigned to a button work for all instances of that Button symbol. However, if different sounds are required for different buttons, a new Button symbol must be created (see the following Tip note for an exception to this "rule"). You can create a new Button symbol from the same Graphic symbols as the previous button (provided it was built out of symbols) or duplicate it in the Library panel by using the Duplicate command in the Library panel's options menu.

To add a sound to the Down state of a button symbol, follow these steps:

1. **Create a new button symbol (Insert ⇨ New Symbol) or choose a symbol from the Buttons Library (Window ⇨ Common Libraries ⇨ Buttons).**

2. **Drag an instance of the button from the Buttons Library panel (or the document's Library panel) to the Stage.**

3. **Edit the Button symbol by double-clicking it on the Stage or in the Library panel.** Both methods transfer the working environment into Edit mode.

4. **Add a new layer to the button's timeline, label the new layer "sound," and then add keyframes to this layer in the Over and Down columns.** Your timeline should look similar to Figure 14.2.

5. **Select the frame of the button state where you want to add a sound for interactive feedback (such as a clicking sound for the Down state), and then access the Properties panel by choosing Window ⇨ Properties (Ctrl+F3 or ⌘+F3).** An alternative method (with the frame selected) is to simply drag the sound from the Library panel onto the Stage. You should now have the Properties panel open, as shown in Figure 14.3.

FIGURE 14.2

The timeline for your button should resemble this one.

FIGURE 14.3

The Properties panel controls the options for sound usage on a given frame.

6. **Choose the sound clip that you want to use from the Sound section's Name menu.** This menu lists all the sounds that have been imported and that are available in the library of the current movie. In this example, we used the `click.wav` sound found in the `resources` folder of the book's CD-ROM.

7. **Use the Sync menu to choose *how* you want the sound to play.** For this lesson, simply use the default, which is the Event option. We'll defer our exploration of the other options in the Sync menu to a later section.

You have now added a sound to your button state. Remember that you're still in Edit mode, so to test the button, return to the Scene 1 timeline (that is, the Main Timeline) either by clicking the Scene 1 location label at the upper left corner of the Document window, or by pressing Ctrl+E (⌘+E), and then choose Control ⇨ Enable Simple Buttons, or Control ⇨ Test Movie.

To add a sound to the Over state of a Button symbol, simply retrace the preceding steps, referencing the Over state of the button wherever appropriate. Remember that different sounds can be assigned to the Up, Over, and Down states of a Button symbol. A sound that is added to the Up state plays whenever the mouse rolls out of a button's hit area.

ON the CD-ROM For a completed example of this button, refer to the Flash movie `button_sound.` `fla` located in the `ch14` folder on this book's CD-ROM. This movie has a button with sounds attached and was made with the same technique described in this section.

Adding Sound to the Timeline

In addition to the use of sounds to enhance the interactivity of buttons, another popular use for sound in Flash is to provide a background score. The simplest way to achieve this is to place the sound within its own layer in the Main Timeline (Scene 1), at the precise frame in which you want the sound to begin. To do this, you must first import the sound (as described earlier in this chapter) and create a new layer for it.

ON the CD-ROM If you don't have access to sounds, you can use the sample sound `atmospheres_1` to practice. This sound is in the `resources` folder on the CD-ROM. It is available in both WAV and AIF formats.

NEW FEATURE Adobe Flash CS4 now ships with over 180 sound effects in the Sounds library (Window ⇨ Common Libraries ⇨ Sounds). These sound files have been culled from Adobe Soundbooth CS4's libraries. You can open this library and drag the sounds into your own Flash document's library to use for examples in this chapter.

Adding sound files to a timeline is similar to assigning sound to a button. To add sounds to a timeline, follow these steps:

1. **Add a new layer in the Timeline window and label the layer with the name of the sound.** You can use a name such as "sound" or "background track."

2. **Create a keyframe on the sound layer at the frame where you want the sound to begin.**

3. **With that keyframe selected, open the Properties panel.** Make sure that you have expanded the view to show all the sound attributes.

4. **If you remembered to import the sound that you want to use, you can now choose that sound clip from the Sound section's Name menu.** If you find yourself stuck at this point, review the preceding steps and/or retrace your steps through the methodology for adding sound to a button.

5. **From the Effect menu, choose how Flash should handle the sound.** The Effect menu offers several preset fading and panning treatments, plus Custom, which invokes the Edit Envelope dialog box. For no special effect, choose None. For more about the Effect presets and the Edit Envelope dialog box, refer to the subsequent section "Editing Audio in Flash."

6. **From the Sync menu, choose one of four options — Event, Start, Stop, or Stream — to control how you want the sound to be synchronized.** See the next section, "Organizing Sounds on the Timeline," for a detailed explanation of Sync options.

7. **Specify how many times you want the sound to loop.** To loop the sound indefinitely (for example, as a background track), choose Loop in the second drop-down menu in the Sync parameters. If you want the sound to loop only for a specific number of times, choose Repeat in the menu and enter a number in the text field to the right of the menu. For specific information about looping stream sounds, refer to the next section.

8. **Perform any last-minute editing or finessing of the sound file (see "Editing Audio in Flash" later in this chapter).**

Your sound is now part of the timeline. Its waveform is visible on the layer to which it was added. Test your sound by pressing Enter on your keyboard, which plays the timeline; or, for sound with a Sync setting of Stream, manually "scrub" the sound by dragging the playhead across the timeline. To perform the most accurate test of the sound, use either Control ⇨ Test Scene or Control ⇨ Test Movie to see and hear it as a Flash movie file (.swf).

TIP   If you sync a sound to a timeline by using the Stream feature, you should test your Flash movie file (.swf) on various platforms and machines with different processor speeds, especially if the timeline is always playing animation. What looks and sounds good on a fast computer might be less impressive on an older legacy machine, like a first- or second-generation Pentium or PowerMac G3 computer.

Organizing Sounds on the Timeline

The Flash Player can play several sound layers at once within a Flash movie; each layer functions like a separate sound channel, and Flash mixes them on playback. This capability of Flash might be considered a built-in economy sound mixer. There is, however, a practical limit because each sound layer potentially increases the movie's file size, and the mix of multiple sounds may burden the computer it's being run on.

TIP   Flash Player 8 or later movies can play up to 32 simultaneous sound channels. In older versions of the Flash Player, you are limited to 8 simultaneous sound channels. A stereo sound consumes two channels, and a mono sound consumes one channel.

Enhanced viewing of sound layers

Because sound is different from other types of Flash content, some users find that increasing the layer height of the sound layers eases working with multiple sounds in a timeline. That's because a taller layer height provides a better visual cue due to the unique waveforms of each sound. To increase the layer height for individual layers, follow these steps:

1. **Right-click (or Control+click on the Mac) the layer in the Timeline window, and then choose Properties from the contextual menu.**

2. **At the bottom of the Layer Properties dialog box, change the layer height from the default 100 percent to either 200 or 300 percent.** Note that these percentages are relative to the settings chosen in the options menu (located at the top right corner) of the Timeline window.

CROSS-REF For more information on the Timeline window, see Chapter 4, "Interface Fundamentals." For an actual example of this enhanced viewing, open the file `enhanced_view.fla`, located in the `ch14` folder on the CD-ROM.

TIP Your movie's frame rate, as specified in the Document Properties dialog box (Modify ⇨ Document), affects the number of frames that a sound occupies on a timeline. For example, at Flash's default setting of 24 frames per second (fps), a 30-second sound clip extends across 720 frames of the timeline. At 30 fps, the same 30-second clip expands to 900 frames — but in either case, the time length of the sound is unchanged.

Organizing sound layers with a layer folder

Flash CS4 offers a great organization tool for layers in any timeline: layer folders. To nest sound layers in a layer folder, create a new layer folder and then drag each of the sound layers to the folder. Each layer you drop on the folder nests within the folder.

Synchronizing Audio to Animations

In film editors' lingo, to *synchronize*, or *sync*, sound means to precisely match picture to sound. In Flash, sound can be synchronized to the visual content of the Timeline. Flash sync affords several options for the manner in which the audio clip is related to graphics or animation on a timeline. Each of these sync options is appropriate for particular uses, which the following sections discuss.

The Sync options in the sound area of the Properties panel control the behavior of sound in Flash movies, relative to the timeline in which the sound is placed. The Sync option you choose depends on whether your sound is intended to add dimension to a complex multimedia presentation or to add interactivity in the form of button-triggered sound, or whether it is intended to be the closely timed soundtrack of an animated cartoon.

Event

Event is the default Sync option for all sounds in Flash, so unless you change this default to one of the other options, the sound automatically behaves as an event sound. Event sounds begin with the keyframe in which they occur and then play independently of the timeline. If an event sound's duration is longer than the remaining frames of its timeline, it continues to play even though playback on the timeline has stopped. If an event sound requires considerable time to load, the movie pauses at that keyframe until the sound has loaded completely. Event sounds are the easiest to implement and are useful for background soundscapes and other sounds that don't need to be synced. Again, Event is the default Sync setting in the Sound menu of the Properties panel.

CAUTION Event sounds can degrade into a disturbing inharmonious round of out-of-tune sound loops. If the timeline holding the event sound loops before the sound has completed, the sound begins again — over the top of the initial sound that has not finished playing. After several loops, the resulting effect can become intolerable. To avoid this effect, use the Start Sync option.

Start

The Start Sync option is similar to an Event option, but with one crucial difference: If any instance of that sound is already playing, then no other instance of that sound can play. In other words, the Start Sync option tells the sound to begin playing only if other instances have finished playing or if it's the first instance of that sound to play. This option is useful if you want to avoid the layering problem discussed in the preceding Caution note for event sounds.

> **NOTE** **Start sounds are actually a type of event sound. Later in this chapter, when we refer to Audio Stream and Audio Event settings in the Publish Settings dialog box, realize that Start sounds belong to the Audio Event category.**

Stop

The Stop Sync option is similar to the Start Sync option, except that any and all instances of the selected sound stop playing when the frame containing the Stop Sync option is played. This option comes in handy when you want to mute a specific sound in a crowd of others. For example, if you created a sound mixer with an arrangement of Button instances, you could assign the Stop Sync option to a mute button for each of the sounds in the mixer.

Stream

Stream sounds are similar to a traditional soundtrack in a video-editing application. A stream sound locks to the timeline and has priority over visual content. When you choose a stream sound, the Flash Player attempts to pace the animation in sync with the sound. However, when animations either get too complex or are run on slower machines, the Flash Player skips — or drops — the frames as needed to stay in sync with the stream sound. A stream sound stops when the playhead reaches the last frame that includes the waveform of the stream sound; likewise, a stream sound pauses if the timeline containing the stream sound is stopped. A stream sound can be *scrubbed*; by dragging the playhead along the layer's frames in the Timeline window, the stream sound plays in direct relationship to the content as it appears, frame by frame. This is especially useful for lip-sync and coordinating the perfect timing of sound effects with visual events.

To use sound effectively, it's important to understand how stream sounds work. When a Flash document is published as a Flash movie file (.swf) and the Sync option for a sound is set to Stream, Flash breaks the sound into chunks that are tied to a timeline. The bytes within the movie are arranged according to the linear order of the Main Timeline (that is, Scene 1). As such, if you have a stream sound that stretches from frames 1 to 100 of the Main Timeline and the movie contains a total of 200 frames, the stream sound's bytes is evenly distributed over the first 50 percent of the file's bytes.

> **TIP** **When adding sounds to a timeline, no matter how many times you tell a stream sound to loop, a stream sound stops playing wherever the visual waveform in the Timeline window ends. To extend a stream sound's duration, add as many frames as necessary to a stream sound's layer.**

Stopping Sounds

The default behavior of event sounds is to play through to the end, regardless of the length of the timeline on which they exist. However, you can stop any sound, including event sounds. Place another instance of the same sound at the keyframe where the sound should stop and assign this instance as a Stop sync option. This Stop setting can be on any layer, and it stops all instances of the specific sound. Let's give this a try.

Stopping an event sound

In this section, we show you how to stop an event sound by using two different methods. The first method uses a Stop sound on a keyframe in the Main Timeline (Scene 1). The second method uses a button instance with a stop sound on its Down state.

1. **Create a Flash ActionScript 3.0 document that has an event sound placed on the first keyframe and has enough frames on the timeline to display the entire wave-form of the sound.**

ON the CD-ROM You can use the `enhanced_view.fla` file from this book's CD-ROM as a practice file. If you use this file, change the Sync setting of the sound to Event in the Properties panel.

2. **Create a new layer in the Timeline window, and name this layer** stop sound.

3. **On the stop sound layer, pick a frame that's about five seconds into the sound shown on the original layer.**

4. **Create a keyframe on this frame in the stop sound layer.**

5. **With this keyframe selected, open the Properties panel.**

6. **In the Name menu of the Sound section, choose the same sound file that was used in the original sound layer.**

7. **In the Sync menu of the Properties panel, choose Stop.** As a stop sound, this setting tells the Flash Player to stop any and all instances of the sound specified in the Sound menu.

8. **Save your Flash document and test it (Control ⇨ Test Movie).** When the playhead reaches the keyframe with the stop sound, you should no longer hear the Event sound.

Now, we show you how to play and mute an event sound by clicking buttons. You'll place an event sound on one Button symbol instance, and then a stop sound on another Button symbol instance.

1. **In a new Flash ActionScript 3.0 document, create a copy of the Play and Stop buttons from the classic buttons ⇨ Circle Buttons folder in the Buttons Library (Window ⇨ Common Libraries ⇨ Buttons).** To do this, drag each of the buttons from the Buttons Library panel to your document's Stage. Close the Buttons Library when you are done. Rename Layer 1 to buttons. Your document's Stage should resemble Figure 14.4.

FIGURE 14.4

The Play and Stop buttons on the Stage

2. **Import a sound file to use as your event sound.** You can use the `atmospheres_1.mp3` sound file from the book's CD-ROM.

3. **In the document's Library panel, double-click the Play button to edit the symbol.**

4. **In the Timeline window, create a new layer and name it** sound.

5. **Insert a keyframe on the Down state of the sound layer.**

6. **Select the keyframe made in Step 5 and open the Properties panel.**

7. **Select the imported sound's name in the Name menu of the Sound section, and leave the Sync menu at the default Event setting.** When you are finished, your document should resemble Figure 14.5.

8. **Double-click the Stop button in the Library panel.**

9. **Repeat Steps 3–7. This time, however, choose Stop in the Sync menu for the atmospheres_1 sound.**

10. **Save your document and test it (Control ⇨ Test Movie).** In Test Movie mode, click the Play button. You should hear the imported sound begin to play. When you click the Stop button, the sound should stop playing.

You may have noticed that, if you click the Play button repeatedly, new instances of the sound begin to play, overlapping with the original playing sound instance. Regardless, the Stop Sync option stops all of them. If you want to prevent the Play button from enabling this type of overlap, go back to the sound keyframe on the Play button and change its Sync option to Start.

FIGURE 14.5

This sound plays when the Play button is clicked.

ON the CD-ROM You can find a completed example of the Play and Stop buttons exercise as stop_ sound.fla, located in the ch14 folder on the CD-ROM.

Stopping a single instance of a stream sound

You can also stop a single instance of a stream sound. To do this, simply place an empty keyframe in the sound layer at the point where the sound should stop.

1. Open the enhanced_view.fla file, located in the ch14 folder of the book's CD-ROM.

2. Switch the layer view of the atmospheres_1 layer back to 100% in the Layer Properties dialog box.

3. Select the first frame of the atmospheres_1 layer.

4. In the Properties panel, switch the Sync option to Stream.

5. Select frame 60 of the atmospheres_1 layer, and insert a blank keyframe (F7). This is the point where the stream sound will stop playing.

6. Save your Flash document and test it (Control ⇨ Test Movie). Notice that the sound stops playing at frame 60. You can open your Bandwidth Profiler (View ⇨ Bandwidth Profiler) in the Test Movie mode to see the playhead move as the movie plays.

The Bandwidth Profiler also reveals something we touched upon earlier: Stream sounds export only the actual portion of the sound that's used within frames of a layer in the Timeline window. In our example, 60 frames' worth of the atmospheres_1 sound was about 12K (at default MP3 compression, 16 kilobits per second, or Kbps).

Stopping all sounds

You can stop the sounds that are playing in all timelines (including Movie Clips) at any point by following these steps in a Flash ActionScript 3.0 document:

1. **If there isn't already an actions layer in the Timeline window, add a layer, label it** actions, **and select the frame that occurs at the point where you want all sounds to stop.** Make this frame into a keyframe.

2. **With the keyframe selected, open the Actions panel by pressing F9 (or Option+F9 on Mac), or by navigating to Window ⇨ Actions.** The title bar of the Actions panel should read Actions — Frame.

3. **Click the flash.media booklet in the left pane of the panel.** Then click the SoundMixer booklet, followed by the Methods booklet.

4. **Double-click the** stopAll **action.** The ActionScript code SoundMixer.stopAll(); appears in the Script pane of the Actions panel, as shown in Figure 14.6.

FIGURE 14.6

Any sound that's currently playing stops when the movie reaches a keyframe with a SoundMixer.stopAll () action.

NOTE We've updated all ActionScript code in this edition of the book to use ActionScript 3.0. If you need to create ActionScript 2.0 code for legacy projects, refer to previous editions.

5. **Save your Flash document and then test it with Control ⇨ Test Movie.** When the movie's playhead reaches the frame with the `SoundMixer.stopAll()` action, every sound currently playing stops.

The `SoundMixer.stopAll()` action stops only sounds that are playing at the time the action is executed. It does not permanently mute the sound for the duration of the movie. You can proceed to reinitialize any sounds any time after the `SoundMixer.stopAll()` action has executed. If you want to stop playback again, you must enable another `SoundMixer.stopAll()` action or use a stop sound.

Editing Audio in Flash

Although Flash was never intended to perform as a full-featured sound editor, it does a remarkable job with basic sound editing. If you plan to make extensive use of sound in Flash, we recommend that you consider investing in a more robust sound editor. You'll have fewer limitations and greater control over your work.

Sound-editing controls

Flash CS4 has basic sound-editing controls in the Edit Envelope dialog box, which is accessed by clicking the Edit button in the Sound section of the Properties panel. (As you may recall from previous sections, you must first select the keyframe containing the sound, and then view the settings in the Properties panel.) The Time In control and the Time Out control, or Control Bars, in Edit Envelope enable you to change the In (start) and Out (end) points of a sound. You use the envelope handles to create custom Fade-in and Fade-out effects. The Edit Envelope dialog box also enables you to edit each sound channel separately if you are working with a stereo (two-channel) sound.

NOTE The edits you apply to a sound file in the Edit Envelope dialog box affect only the specific instance you have assigned to a keyframe. The original file that resides in the Flash document's Library panel is neither changed nor resaved.

A sound's In point is where the sound starts playing, and a sound's Out point is where the sound finishes. The Time In control and the Time Out control are used for setting or changing a sound's In and Out points. Here's how to do this:

1. **Start by selecting the keyframe of the sound you want to edit, and then access the Properties panel.**

2. Click the Edit button in the sound attributes area of the Properties panel to open the Edit Envelope dialog box, as shown in Figure 14.7.

3. Drag the Time In control and Time Out control (located in the horizontal strip between the two channels) to define or restrict which section plays.

4. Use the envelope handles to edit the sound volume by adding handles and dragging them up or down to modulate the volume.

FIGURE 14.7

The sound-editing tools and options of the Edit Envelope dialog box, which is accessed from the Properties panel

Left channel

Time Out control bar

Properties panel

Time In control bar

Envelope handles

Click the Edit button to open the Edit Envelope dialog box

Play   Right channel

Zoom in

View by frames

Stop

Zoom out

View by seconds

5. Click the Play button to hear the sound as edited before returning to the authoring environment.

6. Rework the sound if necessary.

7. When you've finessed the points and are satisfied with the sound, click OK to return to the Properties panel.

8. Save your Flash document.

492

Applying effects from the Effect menu of the Properties panel

You can apply a handful of preset fades and other effects to a sound by selecting the effect from the Effect menu located in the sound attributes area of the Properties panel. For many uses, the Flash presets are more than sufficient, but if you find yourself feeling limited, remember that more subtle effects can be created in an external sound editor. We describe Flash's preset effects in detail here:

- **None:** No effect is applied to either of the sound channels.

- **Left Channel/Right Channel:** Plays only the right or left channel of a stereo sound.

- **Fade Left to Right/Fade Right to Left:** This effect lowers the sound level of one channel while raising the level of the other, creating a panning effect. The effect occurs over the entire length of the sound.

- **Fade In/Fade Out:** Fade In gradually raises the level of the beginning of a sound clip. Fade Out gradually lowers the level at the end of a sound. The default length for either effect is approximately 25 percent of the length of the clip. We've noticed that even if the size of the selection is edited with the control bars, the duration of the Fade In/Fade Out remains the same. (Thus, a 35-second sound clip with an original default Fade In time of 9 seconds still has a 9-second Fade In time even when the selection's length is reduced to, say, 12 seconds.) You can resolve this problem by creating a custom fade.

- **Custom:** Any time you manually alter the levels or audio handles within the Edit Envelope dialog box, Flash CS4 automatically resets the Effect menu to Custom.

Creating a custom Fade-In or Fade-Out

For maximum sound-editing control within Flash, use the envelope handles to create a custom fade or to lower the audio levels (or amplitude) of a sound. In addition to creating custom fades, you can lower the levels creatively to create subtle, low-volume background sounds. Here's how:

1. **Select the keyframe of the sound you want to edit.**
2. **Click the Edit button of the Properties panel to open the Edit Envelope dialog box.**
3. **Click the envelope lines at any point to create new envelope handles.**
4. **After handles have been created, you can drag them around to create your desired volume and fading effects.** The lines indicate the relative volume level of the sound. When you drag an envelope handle downward, the line slopes down, indicating a decrease in the volume level, while dragging an envelope handle upward has the opposite effect. The Edit Envelope control is limited to eight envelope handles per channel (eight for left and eight for right).

 You can remove envelope handles by dragging them outside the Edit Envelope dialog box.

Other controls in the Edit Envelope control

Other useful tools in the Edit Envelope dialog box warrant mention. Refer to Figure 14.7 for their locations.

- **Zoom In/Zoom Out:** These tools either enlarge or shrink the view of the waveform, and they are particularly helpful when you're altering the In or Out points or envelope handles.

- **Seconds/Frames:** The default for viewing sound files is to represent time in seconds. But viewing time in frames is advantageous for syncing stream sound. Toggle between viewing modes by clicking either the Seconds or Frames button at the lower right of the Edit Envelope dialog box.

The Repeat/Loop option

This option appears in the Properties panel, yet a measure of its functionality occurs in conjunction with the Edit Envelope dialog box. The Repeat/Loop drop-down menu and field is used to set the number of times that a sound file repeats (or loops indefinitely). You can use a small looping selection, such as a break beat or jazz riff, for a background soundtrack, or loop a short ambient noise for an interesting effect. To test the quality of a looping selection, click the Edit button, which takes you to the Edit Envelope dialog box, where you can click the Play button for a preview of your loop. If the loop isn't perfect or has hiccups, use the In and Out control bars and envelope handles to trim or taper off a blank or adversely repeating section.

> **TIP** Flash links looped sounds and handles them as one long sound file (although it's really one little sound file played repeatedly). Because this linkage is maintained within the editing environment, the entire expanse of a looped sound can be given a custom effect in the Edit Envelope dialog box. For example, a simple repeating two-measure loop can be diminished over 30 loops. This is a subtle effect that performs well, yet is economical in terms of file size. Note, however, that this applies only to event sounds.

Sound Optimization Overview

You need to be aware of several considerations when preparing Flash sound for export. For Web-based delivery, the primary concern is to find an acceptable middle ground between file size and audio quality. But the concept of acceptability is not absolute; it is always relative to the application. Consider, for example, a Flash site for a record company. In this example, sound quality is likely to be more important than file size because the audience for a record company expects quality sound. In any case, consideration of both your audience and your method of delivery helps you determine the export settings you choose. Luckily, Flash CS4 has capabilities that enhance the user's experience both by optimizing sounds more efficiently and by providing improved programming features to make download delays less problematic.

There are two ways to optimize your sound for export. The quickest, simplest way is to use the Publish Settings dialog box and apply a one-setting-optimizes-all approach. This can work well if all of your sound files are from the same source. For example, if all of your sound material is speech based, then you may be able to use global settings to encode all of your Flash sound. However, if you have a variety of sound sources in your movie, such as a combination of musical scores along with narrative tracks, then the Publish Settings dialog box may not deliver the highest possible level of optimization.

If you demand that your Flash movie has the smallest possible file size, or if your Flash project includes audio from disparate sources, or uses a combination of audio types — such as button sounds, background music, and speech — it's better to fine-tune the audio settings for each sound in the library. This method gives you much better control over output.

CROSS-REF This chapter discusses only the audio-centric Publish features of Flash CS4. We explain general Publish Settings features in greater detail in Chapter 20, "Publishing Flash Movies."

Publish Settings for Audio

To take a global approach to the control of audio output quality, choose File ➪ Publish Settings (Ctrl+Shift+F12 or Shift+Option+F12 on Mac) to access the Publish Settings dialog box. Then choose the Flash tab of the Publish Settings dialog box, as shown in Figure 14.8. This tab has three areas where the audio quality of an entire Flash movie can be controlled *globally*.

TIP You can also access the Flash tab of Publish Settings by using the Properties panel. Click the document's Stage or work area, and in the Properties panel, click the Settings button to the right of the Publish label.

The Flash tab of the Publish Settings dialog box has three options for controlling audio quality:

- **Audio Stream:** Controls the export quality of stream sounds. To customize, click Set. This gives you a number of options, which we describe in the section that follows. Flash supports MP3, which is the optimal streaming format.

- **Audio Event:** Controls the export quality of event sounds. To customize, click Set. This gives you the same number of options as the Set button for Audio Stream. We describe these options in the next section.

- **Override Sound Settings:** If this box is checked, Flash uses the publish settings instead of the individual audio settings that are fine-tuned in the Library panel for the current document. For more information, see "Fine-Tuning Sound Settings in the Library" later in this chapter.

FIGURE 14.8

The Flash tab of the Publish Settings dialog box has several options to control audio quality.

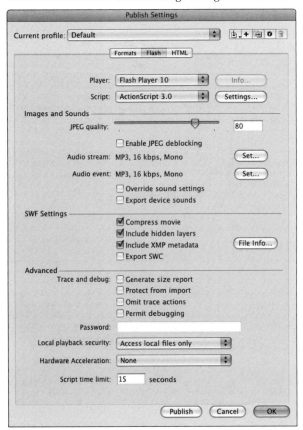

The Set options

Audio stream and Audio event have individual compression settings, which can be specified by their respective Set button options. If you click either Set button on the Flash tab, the same Sound Settings dialog box appears — it is identical for both Audio Stream and Audio Event, which means that the same options are offered for both types of sound. The Sound Settings dialog box, shown in various permutations in Figure 14.9, displays numerous settings related to the control of audio quality and audio file size. The type of compression you select governs the specific group of settings that appear.

NOTE The impact of individual sound settings may be overridden by another setting. For example, a Bit Rate setting of 160 Kbps may not result in high-quality sound if the Quality is set to Fast. Optimal results require attention to all the settings. It's like a set of interlinked teeter-totters: A little experimentation reveals the cumulative or acquired impact of each setting on the others. However, the need to experiment here is hobbled by the lack of a preview mechanism. By contrast, tuning a sound in the library is much more serviceable because there's a sound preview button adjacent to the settings controls. For more about this workflow, refer to "Fine-Tuning Sound Settings in the Library" later in this chapter.

FIGURE 14.9

The various options in the Sound Settings dialog box

A

B

C

D

The specific options that are available in the Sound Settings dialog boxes are always related to the compression, or audio-encoding scheme, selected in the Compression drop-down menu. That's because different compression technologies support different functionalities:

- **Disable:** This option turns off all sounds that have been assigned in the Properties panel to keyframes in any timeline. If this option is selected, only sound that has been linked and attached for use in ActionScript plays in the movie (see Chapter 26, "Interacting with Movie Clips," for more information on this use). All other sound sources assigned in the movie are omitted from the final movie file (.swf). No additional options accompany this setting.

- **ADPCM:** With ADPCM selected in the Compression menu, the following options are available:

  - **Convert Stereo to Mono:** Mixes the right and left channel of audio into one (mono) channel. In sound-engineer parlance, this is known as "bouncing down."

  - **Sample Rate:** Choose from sampling rates of 5, 11, 22, or 44 kHz. Increasing the sample rate of an audio file to something higher than the native sample rate of the imported file simply increases file size, not quality. For example, if you import 22 kHz sounds into the Flash movie, selecting 44 kHz does not improve the sound quality. For more information on sample rates, see Appendix C, "Digital Audio Basics."

  - **ADPCM Bits:** Set the number of bits that ADPCM uses for encoding. You can choose a rate between 2 and 5 bits. The higher the ADPCM bits, the better the audio quality. Flash's default setting is 4 bits.

- **MP3:** If you select MP3 in the Compression menu, you can set the following options:

  - **Convert Stereo to Mono:** Mixes the right and left channel of audio into one (mono) channel. This is disabled at rates below 20 Kbps because the lower bit rates don't allow stereo sound.

  - **Bit Rate:** MP3 measures compression in Kbps. The higher the bit rate, the better the audio quality. Because the MP3 audio compression scheme is very efficient, a high bit rate still results in a relatively small file size. Refer to Table 14.2 for a breakdown of specific bit rates and the resulting sound quality.

  - **Quality:** Choose Fast, Medium, or Best quality. These settings determine how well Flash CS4 analyzes the sound file during compression. Fast optimizes the audio file in the shortest amount of time, but usually with less quality. Medium analyzes the sound waveform better than the Fast setting but takes longer to compress. Best is the highest-quality setting, but it takes the longest time to compress the sound file. Note that the file size of the final compressed sound is not affected by any Quality setting — it simply instructs Flash how well it should analyze the sound during compression. The longer Flash takes to analyze a sound, the more likely the final compressed sound captures the high highs and the low lows. If you have a fast computer processor, we recommend that you use the Best setting during your final Flash movie publish. During development and testing, you may want to use Fast to avoid long waits.

- **Raw:** When Raw (also known as Raw PCM audio) is selected in the Compression menu, there are two options:

  - **Convert Stereo to Mono:** Mixes the right and left channels of audio into one (mono) channel.

  - **Sample Rate:** This option specifies the sampling rate for the Audio Stream or Audio Events sounds. For more information on sample rate, refer to Appendix C, "Digital Audio Basics," on this book's CD-ROM.

- **Speech:** When the Speech codec is selected in the Compression menu, only one option is available: Sample Rate. Any sound compressed with the Speech codec is converted to mono (one-channel) sound. Even though the Speech codec licensed from Nellymoser was designed for 8 kHz, Flash CS4 "upsamples" this codec to those frequencies the Flash Player supports. See Table 14.3 for an overview of these sampling rates and how they affect sound quality.

TABLE 14.2

MP3 Bit Rate Quality

Bit rate	Sound quality	Good for
8 Kbps	Very bad	Best for simulated moonwalk transmissions. Don't use this unless you want horribly unrecognizable sound.
16 Kbps	Barely acceptable	Extended audio files where quality isn't important, or simple button sounds.
20, 24, 32 Kbps	Acceptable	Speech or voice.
48, 56 Kbps	Acceptable	Large music files; complex button sounds.
64 Kbps	Good	Large music files where good audio quality is required.
112–128 Kbps	Excellent	Near-CD quality.
160 Kbps	Best	Near-CD quality.

TABLE 14.3

Speech Sampling Quality

Sample rate	Sound quality	Good for
5 kHz	Acceptable	Sound playback over extremely limited data connections, such as 19.2 Kbps wireless Internet modems used by mobile devices.
11 kHz	Good	Standard telephone-quality voice audio.

continued

TABLE 14.3	*(continued)*	
Sample rate	**Sound quality**	**Good for**
22 kHz	Excellent	Not recommended for general Internet use. Although this setting produces higher fidelity to the original sound, it consumes too much bandwidth. For comparable sound, we recommend using a midrange MP3 bit rate.
44 kHz	Best	See description for 22 kHz.

> **TIP** As a general rule, if you use the publish settings to control audio export globally, we recommend choosing MP3 at 20 or 24 Kbps. This results in moderate-to-good sound quality (suitable for most Flash projects), and the ratio of file size to quality gives reasonable performance. A range of 20 to 24 Kbps is an acceptable data rate for speech and short sound effects, while 96 to 128 Kbps is a better data rate for longer sounds and music.

Supporting audio and MP3 playback

Although this is becoming less of an issue with the desktop versions of the Flash Players, it may still be important to consider that MP3 or audio playback may not be supported by all Flash Players, especially device-based players. You can use ActionScript to check the capabilities of the Flash Player installed on a user's system. Using the `flash.system.Capabilities` class, you can check to see whether an MP3 decoder is installed. The specific property is

```
flash.system.Capabilities.hasMP3
```

> **TIP** In FlashLite 1.1 or later, you can use the `_capMP3` global property at runtime to determine if MP3 playback is supported on a particular device.

More important, though, you can script your movies to check whether the Flash Player has access to general audio output. Some devices with the Flash Player may not have any audio output. This property is

```
flash.system.Capabilities.hasAudio
```

> **CAUTION** These class paths of the ActionScript 3.0 language are available only in Flash Player 9 or higher. Earlier versions of the Flash Player simply use `System.Capabilities`, not `flash.system.Capabilities`.

Fine-Tuning Sound Settings in the Library

The Publish Settings dialog box is convenient because it permits you to tweak a minimal set of sound adjustments, whereupon Flash exports all of your "noncustomized" stream sounds or event sounds at the same rate and compression. However, if you have many sounds and you are seriously concerned about obtaining the ideal balance of both optimal sound quality and minimum file size, you must export them at different rates and compressions. Consequently, for the fullest level of control over the way in which Flash compresses sound for delivery, we recommend you optimize each sound, individually, in the Library panel. In fact, it would be impossible for us to overemphasize this bit of sound advice: *We recommend you optimize each sound, individually, in the library.*

> **TIP** As you become more advanced with Flash CS4, particularly with ActionScript, you will likely want to load MP3 files directly into Flash movies because they play in a browser. We discuss these features in Chapter 28, "Sharing and Loading Assets."

Settings for audio in the library

Audio settings in the Library panel are similar to those discussed previously for the Publish Settings dialog box. These settings appear in the Sound Properties dialog box, as shown in Figure 14.10. To access these settings, either double-click the icon of the sound in the library; select the sound as it appears in the library and click the Properties button or choose Properties from the Library panel's options menu; or right-click the sound symbol in the library and choose Properties.

> **TIP** Flash CS4 also enables you to access the compression settings alone for a sound file by right-clicking (or Control+clicking on the Mac) the sound file in the Library panel and choosing Export Settings from the contextual menu. The options in the Sound Settings dialog box are the same compression settings discussed in this section.

FIGURE 14.10

The Sound Properties dialog box enables you to control the compression settings and to precisely balance all other related settings for each individual sound in the library.

The top half of the Sound Properties dialog box displays status information about the sound file: To the far left is a window with the waveform of the selected audio; to the right of the waveform is an area that displays the name of the file together with its location, date, sample rate, channels, bit depth, duration, and file size.

NOTE   The file location indicates the full absolute path to the sound file (for example, `C:\` `Inetpub\wwwroot\mysound.mp3`) if you save your Flash document file (.fla) in a volume or hard drive that is different than the location of the sound file.

The lower half of the dialog box is titled Export Settings. The first setting is a menu used to select the compression scheme. The Compression options, and the subsequent compression-related options that appear in the other settings, are exactly the same as the sound options of the Publish Settings dialog box discussed earlier in this chapter.

NOTE   If you imported an MP3 file, the Sound Properties dialog box automatically appears and enables the Use imported MP3 quality check box. The data rate of the imported MP3 file is then used for any event sound compression. However, if you use the MP3 file for stream sounds, the MP3 file is recompressed according to the Stream sound settings in the Publish Settings dialog box.

Estimated results appear beneath the Export Settings. Here, the estimated final file size (after compression) of the clip is shown, together with the compression percentage. This is an extremely important tool that is easily overlooked.

CAUTION   The estimated final file size is just that, an estimate. In our tests, the file size reported in the Sound Properties dialog box was consistently different from the actual file size reported by the size report generated during publishing. You can generate a text file containing detailed information about your final movie by enabling Generate size report in the Flash tab of the Publish Settings dialog box. When enabled, you can view the size report in the Output window in Test Movie mode.

The buttons to the right of the Sound Properties dialog box offer the following options:

- **Update:** Click this button to have Flash check for an update of the audio file (if the original MP3, WAV, or AIFF file has been modified), and update it accordingly. Generally, this works only on the machine on which the audio file was originally imported. If you stored your files on a network server, all the members of your Flash production team should be able to use this feature.

- **Import:** This enables you to import another audio file into the Flash environment. The imported audio file overwrites the existing sound appearing in the Sound Properties dialog box, but retains the original sound's name. This feature is useful if you originally imported a placeholder or low-quality sound and need to specify a new file to be used in its place.

- **Test:** This excellent feature enables you to audition the export quality of the sound based on the options that you've selected from the Compression menu (and supporting options in the Export Settings).

- **Stop:** Click this button to stop (silence) the sound that has been auditioned by using the Test button.

Fine-tuning your audio in the Sound Properties dialog box of the Library panel has three benefits. Foremost of these benefits is the ability to set specific compressions and optimizations for each individual sound. Another benefit is the Test button. This is an excellent way to audition your audio file and to know what it will sound like when it is exported with different compression schemes and bit rates — hearing is believing. Finally, the estimated results, which display how each setting will affect the compressed file size, is a powerful tool that helps you obtain the desired balance of quality and file size. In contrast, optimizing sounds with the publish settings is more of a blind process — it is not only more global, it's also more of a painful trial-and-error method.

Combining methods for controlling sounds

One of the coolest things about Flash audio is that you can combine the two methods of controlling sounds, using both the publish settings and the Library panel's Sound Properties dialog box to streamline your workflow while still maintaining a relatively high degree of control over sound quality. (This method works best if you already have some experience with sound behavior in Flash.)

For example, let's assume that you have three different event sounds in your Flash project. Two of these are simple button sounds. You decide that you won't require specialized compression for the sound used with the buttons. So, based on your prior experience of sound behavior in Flash, you go directly to the publish settings and set event sounds to publish as MP3 at 48 Kbps with Best quality.

NOTE We assume that you have left the sounds used for the buttons untouched in the Library panel, leaving the Compression setting in the Sound Settings dialog box at Default. The Default option tells Flash to handle the compression for these sounds with the publish settings.

But the third sound is a loop of background jazz music that you want to be heard at near-CD quality. For this sound, you access the Sound Properties dialog box and try a number of combinations — and test each one — until you find a balance between file size and audio quality that pleases your ears. For example, you may decide to assign this sound to export as an MP3, stereo at 64 Kbps, with Quality set to Best.

Final Sound Advice and Pointers

Here are a few final notes about sound and some pointers to more complex sound-related topics that may help you work with sound files in Flash CS4.

VBR (Variable Bit Rate) MP3

Adobe has licensed the Fraunhofer MP3 codec, which supports streaming MP3 with a constant bit rate. However, neither Flash CS4 nor any Flash Player supports Variable Bit Rate (VBR), or VBR MP3, encoding for stream sounds. VBR MP3 is a variant of MP3 that uses specialized algorithms to vary the bit rate according to the kind of sound being compressed. For example, a soprano solo would be accorded a higher bit rate than a crashing drum sequence, resulting in a superior ratio of quality to file size. There are a number of sound applications, such as Apple iTunes and the MP3 creation packs available for Windows Media Player, that export VBR MP3. If you have access to a sound application that exports VBR MP3, you'll be happy to know that you can import your VBR MP3 sound files, which are (theoretically) optimized for file size and quality beyond the compression capabilities of Flash CS4, and that you can maintain the compression of such files by doing the following:

- In the Flash tab of the Publish Settings dialog box, leave the option to Override Sound Settings unchecked.

- In the Sound Properties (or Export Settings) dialog box for each sound in the Library panel, choose MP3 for the Compression option in Export Settings and select the Use imported MP3 quality check box.

- The Sync option (located in the Properties panel) for the sound *cannot* be set to Stream.

If you choose to use VBR MP3 files in your Flash documents, you may need to test the following options of VBR compression in your MP3 creation software:

- **Bit rate:** Test the minimum bit rate that VBR will use for the MP3 file. Regular MP3 files use CBR, or Constant Bit Rate, which keeps the sound's bit rate steady through the entire sound file. With VBR, the bit rate can vary in ranges that you specify. Some higher bit rates, such as 320 Kbps, may not import well into the Flash CS4 authoring tool.

- **Quality:** Most VBR-enabled MP3 software enables you to also pick an arbitrary quality setting for VBR MP3 files. Using terminology like Lowest, Medium Low, and High (and several in between), or percentages (1–100%), you can alter the quality of the bit rate. Note that this "quality" is not necessarily used in the same manner that Flash CS4 refers to quality for MP3 compression.

You may find that Flash CS4 gives you an import error for some VBR- (and CBR-) encoded MP3 files, although we haven't encountered this error with the last two releases of the Flash authoring tool. If a particular setting creates an MP3 file that can't be imported into Flash CS4, try another bit rate and/or quality combination. However, we have found that Flash has inconsistent behavior when it comes to importing MP3 files. For example, you may find that one VBR setting/combination does not work for a particular sound file, but that it works fine for others. Even more strangely, MP3 files that won't import into the Flash authoring environment load just fine into the Flash Player at runtime via ActionScript.

> **WEB RESOURCE** You can find more information about VBR encoding at www.fezguys.com/columns/057.shtml.

Robert Reinhardt also contributed a chapter to August de los Reyes et al's *Flash Design for Mobile Devices* (Wiley, 2002) covering a null sound technique that can kick a Flash movie into a stream sound playback mode by using smaller, more file-efficient event sounds.

Optimizing sounds for bandwidth usage

It goes without saying that every Internet content creator strives to make every file and data transaction as small and efficient as possible to accommodate the majority of slow network connections in use today. As a Flash designer or developer incorporating sound into your projects, you'll want to properly plan sound usage in an effort to avoid 1MB .swf file downloads.

Table 14.4 explores many of the available network bandwidths that are in use on the Internet. However, as you've likely experienced, it's highly unusual to actually get the full download (or upload) speed out of your network connection. Variables such as network congestion, server load, and phone line conditions affect the quality of your network speed. Using the same formula that Adobe uses to determine approximate download speeds in the Bandwidth Profiler (within Test Movie mode), we calculated estimated bandwidth speeds for the connection speeds shown in Table 14.4. Because Flash CS4 displays compressed sound information in Kbps units, we converted these connection speeds into Kbps bit rates. More important, though, we also provided a 50-percent portion of this bit rate, as you'll likely need to save room for other Flash material, such as vector artwork, bitmap graphics, and animations.

TABLE 14.4

Bit Rates for Flash Movies

Hardware support	Theoretical bandwidth	Estimated bandwidth	Percent of theoretical	100% bit rate	50% bit rate
14.4 Kbps	1.8 KB/s	1.2 KB/s	67	9.6 Kbps	4.8 Kbps
19.2 Kbps	2.4 KB/s	1.6 KB/s	67	12.8 Kbps	6.4 Kbps
28.8 Kbps	3.6 KB/s	2.3 KB/s	64	18.4 Kbps	9.2 Kbps
33.6 Kbps	4.2 KB/s	2.8 KB/s	67	22.5 Kbps	11.2 Kbps
56 Kbps	7 KB/s	4.7 KB/s	67	37.6 Kbps	18.8 Kbps
64 Kbps	8 KB/s	5.4 KB/s	67	43.2 Kbps	21.6 Kbps
128 Kbps	16 KB/s	10.7 KB/s	67	85.6 Kbps	42.8 Kbps
256 Kbps	32 KB/s	21 KB/s	67	168 Kbps	84 Kbps
384 Kbps	48 KB/s	32 KB/s	67	256 Kbps	128 Kbps
768 Kbps	96 KB/s	64 KB/s	67	512 Kbps	256 Kbps
1.5 Mbps	192 KB/s	129 KB/s	67	1,032 Kbps	516 Kbps
11 Mbps	1,408 KB/s	943 KB/s	67	7,544 Kbps	3,772 Kbps

Using Table 14.4 as a guide, try to plan your Flash project for your target audience. Actually, you may have more than one target audience. As such, you may need to develop several versions of your sound assets, with each version targeted to a specific connection speed.

After you've decided your target audience(s), you can determine the maximum Kbps that your sound files should use. Table 14.5 shows you the bit rates of Raw, Speech, and ADPCM mono sounds. We don't include MP3 bit rates here because they're already calculated (and available) in the Compression menu of the Sound Properties dialog box: 8, 16, 20, 24, 32, 48, 56, 64, 80, 112, 128, and 160 Kbps. In Table 14.5, we show bit rates that are suitable for analog modem connections (14.4, 28.8, 33.6, and 56 Kbps) in bold.

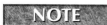 If you want to see the actual sample rate used by Flash CS4's MP3 compression options, see Table 14.7 later in this chapter.

TABLE 14.5

Mono Bit Rates for Streaming Sound

Sampling rate	Raw	Speech	ADPCM 2-bit	ADPCM 3-bit	ADPCM 4-bit	ADPCM 5-bit
5 kHz	80 Kbps	10 Kbps	10 Kbps	15 Kbps	20 Kbps	25 Kbps
11 kHz	176 Kbps	22 Kbps	22 Kbps	33 Kbps	44 Kbps	55 Kbps
22 kHz	352 Kbps	44 Kbps	44 Kbps	66 Kbps	88 Kbps	110 Kbps
44 kHz	704 Kbps	88 Kbps	88 Kbps	132 Kbps	176 Kbps	220 Kbps

In Tables 14.6 and 14.7, we calculate the file sizes that 1 second of mono (one-channel) sound occupies in a Flash movie file (.swf). Use the values in these tables as multipliers for your sound file's actual length. For example, if you know that you have a 30-second soundtrack file, the final Flash movie file size (containing just the audio) would be about 60K with ADPCM 3-bit, 5 kHz compression. Regardless of the actual content of the digital audio, these encodings produce consistent file sizes based on length and resolution.

TABLE 14.6

File Sizes in Bytes (KB) for One Second of Mono Audio

Sample rate	Raw	Speech	ADPCM 2-bit	ADPCM 3-bit	ADPCM 4-bit	ADPCM 5-bit
5 kHz	11,037 (10.8)	1,421 (1.4)	1,397 (1.4)	2,085 (2.0)	2,774 (2.7)	3,463 (3.4)
11 kHz	22,061 (21.5)	2,829 (2.8)	2,777 (2.7)	4,115 (4.0)	5,532 (5.4)	6,910 (6.8)
22 kHz	44,109 (43.1)	5,581 (5.5)	5,541 (5.5)	8,296 (8.1)	11,051 (10.8)	13,806 (13.5)
44 kHz	88,205 (86.1)	11,085 (10.8)	11,065 (10.8)	16,576 (16.2)	22,086 (21.6)	27,597 (27.0)

TABLE 14.7

File Sizes in Bytes (KB) for One Second of Mono MP3 Audio

Bit rate	Size	Output sample rate	Bit rate	Size	Output sample rate
8 Kbps	1,263 (1.2)	11 kHz	56 Kbps	5,605 (5.5)	22 kHz
16 Kbps	2,511 (2.5)	11 kHz	64 Kbps	8,543 (8.3)	44 kHz
20 Kbps	3,135 (3.1)	11 kHz	80 Kbps	10,716 (10.5)	44 kHz
24 Kbps	3,369 (3.3)	22 kHz	112 Kbps	14,980 (14.6)	44 kHz
32 Kbps	4,487 (4.4)	22 kHz	128 Kbps	17,112 (16.7)	44 kHz
48 Kbps	5,605 (5.5)	22 kHz	160 Kbps	17,112 (16.7)	44 kHz

NOTE You may notice that some bit rate settings in Table 14.7 create the same file size for the MP3 compression. This is a known bug of the Flash authoring tool. You may also find that the Convert Stereo to Mono option for MP3 compression does not affect the outcome of some settings.

Extracting a sound from a Flash document

Sometime you may be handed a Flash document file (.fla) that has sound embedded within it and be told that the original sounds have either been lost or are no longer available. Here's how to extract a sound from such a file:

1. **Back up the file.** If the original file is named `sound.fla`, you might resave it as `sound_extraction.fla`. If you want to start with an exercise file, save a copy of the `enhanced_view.fla` file, located on the book's CD-ROM. You can skip Steps 2–7 if you are using this file.

2. Add a new layer in the Timeline window, at the top of the layer stack.

3. **Label this layer** sound extraction.

4. With the first frame of this layer selected, open the Properties panel.

5. In the Sound section's Name menu, specify the sound file from the Library panel that you want to export.

6. **Add enough frames to the sound extraction layer so that you can see the entire waveform of the sound file.**

7. **Delete all other layers.**

8. **Open the Library panel and locate the sound that needs to be extracted from the file.** In the example file, the sound is named `atmospheres_1.wav`. Note that any other assets within this file are irrelevant to this process. That's because Flash uses only library items that have actually been used within the movie.

9. **Double-click the sound icon for `atmospheres_1.wav` in the Library panel to open the Sound Properties dialog box.**

10. **Set the Compression to Raw.** This ensures that the sound is exported as uncompressed audio.

11. **Select a sample rate that matches the one listed to the right of the waveform display, near the top of the Sound Properties dialog box.** If the sound is specified as a stereo sound, make sure that the Convert Stereo to Mono option is unchecked.

12. **Access the Flash tab of the Publish Settings dialog box, and make sure that the Override Sound Settings check box is *not* checked.** Now you're ready to extract the sound file from the Flash document file (.fla). You've created a movie that will ignore all other assets in the library except this sound, and you've told Flash to export the sound with the original sample rate of the sound, as uncompressed (Raw) audio.

13. **Choose File ➪ Export Movie, and specify a file location, name, and file type.** If you're using the Windows version of Flash CS4, choose WAV Audio as the file type. If you're on a Mac, choose QuickTime.

14. **For Windows users, the Export Windows WAV dialog box appears with those sound specifications.** In the Sound Format menu, make sure the audio specifications match those of your audio source in the Library panel; then click OK. For Mac users, the QuickTime Export Settings dialog box appears. Here, click the QuickTime settings button in the lower left corner. Ignore all the options except Sound Format. In this menu, select the sound setting that matches the specifications of the sound file. For this example, this setting should be 44 kHz 16 Bit Stereo. Click OK.

15. **For Windows users, the process is complete.** You now have a WAV copy of your Flash movie sound asset. For Mac users, you still have a couple of steps to complete:

    1. Open the exported QuickTime movie in the QuickTime Player Pro. You must have the Pro version installed.

    2. Choose File ➪ Export.

    3. Select Sound to AIFF in the Export menu.

    4. Click the Options button, and in the Sound Settings dialog box, set the Compressor to None and choose a sample rate, bit depth, and channel type that match the sound from the Flash document. For this example sound, this should be 44.1 kHz, 16 bit, and Stereo. Click OK.

If you're using Apple QuickTime Pro 7 or later, choose Linear PCM in the Format menu and the sampling settings that match your source audio in the Flash movie.

5. Finally, specify a filename and location for the exported file, and click Save.

CROSS-REF We defer several sound-related topics until after our discussion of Flash CS4's ActionScripting capabilities. Work your way to Chapter 26, "Interacting with Movie Clips," and Chapter 28, "Sharing and Loading Assets."

WEB RESOURCE We'd like to know what you think about this chapter. Visit www.flashsupport. com/feedback to send us your comments.

Summary

- Flash movie files (.swf) can use four types of audio compression: ADPCM, MP3, Raw, and Speech. ADPCM is compatible with all versions of the Flash Player. MP3 is compatible with most versions of Flash Player 4 and higher. The Speech codec is compatible with Flash Player 6 and higher.

- When sound is imported to a Flash document, it's added and displayed in the Library panel. You can assign sounds from the Library panel to a keyframe on a timeline. You can also use sounds with ActionScript.

- Sounds can be assigned to the Up, Over, and Down states of a Button symbol.

- The Sync options control how a sound plays in relation to the rest of a timeline.

- Use the Loop setting in the Properties panel to multiply the length of the original sound.

- Stream sounds force the Flash Player to keep playback of a timeline in pace with the sound.

- Use a `SoundMixer.stopAll()` action to stop all sounds currently playing in the movie.

- The Effect menu in the Properties panel contains useful presets for sound channel playback. You can perform custom edits with the Edit Envelope dialog box.

- Global audio compression is controlled in the Flash tab of the Publish Settings dialog box.

- Use the Sound Properties dialog box in the Library panel to customize the audio compression schemes of individual sounds.

- The Sound Properties dialog box enables you to test different compression settings and to hear the results. The Export Settings section of this dialog box also provides useful file size information.

- You can bring and export Variable Bit Rate (VBR) MP3 sound files into Flash without degrading the encoding; however, Flash itself cannot encode by using VBR.

Chapter 15

Importing Artwork

A lthough Flash gives you powerful options for creating and modifying a variety of graphics, you don't have to limit yourself to the Flash authoring environment. That's because Flash also has the capability of importing artwork from a wide range of sources. You can import both vector and raster graphics, and you can use both formats in a variety of ways.

In this chapter, we discuss the differences between vector graphics and raster or bitmap images. We also show you how to import external artwork so that you can use it in a Flash movie, as well as tell you about the Flash features that you can use to handle imported bitmap images and vector graphics.

We define all the formats that Flash supports and go over some of the issues to consider when preparing artwork for import from various programs. We also introduce some Flash features that are helpful for managing imported assets and give some insight into optimizing your final file size.

Defining Vectors and Bitmaps

In addition to various sound and video formats, Flash supports two types of image formats: vector and bitmap. *Vector* graphic files consist of an equation that describes the placement of points and the qualities of the lines between those points. Using this basic logic, vector graphics tell the computer how to display the lines and shapes, as well as what colors to use, where to put them on the Stage, and at what scale.

Flash is a vector program. Thus, anything that you create with the Flash drawing tools is described in vector format. Vector graphics have some important benefits: They're small in file size and they scale accurately without distortion. However, they also have a couple of drawbacks: Highly complex vector graphics may result in very large file sizes, and vectors aren't really suitable for creating ontinuous tones, photographs, or artistic brushwork.

Bitmap (also referred to as *raster*) files are described by an arrangement of individual pixels, which are mapped in a grid — like a piece of graph paper with tiny squares. Each square represents a single pixel, and each of these pixels has specific color values assigned to it. So, as the name implies, a bitmap image maps out the placement and color of each pixel on the screen. A line is "drawn" by filling each unique pixel, rather than simply using a mathematical formula to connect two points as is done with vectors.

NOTE Do not be confused by the name *bitmap*. You might already be familiar with the bitmap format used by Windows, which has the file extension .bmp. Although *bitmap* may refer to that particular image format, it's frequently applied to raster images in general, such as GIF, JPEG, PICT, and TIFF files, as well as many others.

Although bitmap images aren't created in Flash, they can be used within Flash projects. To do this, you need to use an external bitmap-editing application and then import the bitmaps into Flash. Figure 15.1 shows a vector image and a bitmap image of the same graphic, scaled at 100 percent.

FIGURE 15.1

A vector image drawn in Flash (left) and the same image imported as a bitmapped GIF graphic (right)

Although these vector and bitmap images are of similar quality at their original size, their differences become more apparent when the same images are scaled to a larger size. Unlike vector graphics, bitmap images become more pixilated as they are scaled larger because there is a finite amount of information in the image and Flash has to spread this information over more pixels. As we explain later in this chapter, Flash is able to interpolate the pixel information by using Smoothing to reduce the jagged appearance of the scaled pixel pattern, but this can also cause the image to look blurred. Figure 15.2 shows the difference between vector and bitmap graphics when scaled in Flash with Smoothing turned off.

FIGURE 15.2

The same vector (left) and bitmap (right) image scaled to 200 percent in Flash to illustrate the difference in image quality

Simple bitmap images are often larger in file size than simple vector graphics, but very complex bitmap images (for example, a photograph) can be smaller and display better quality than vector graphics of equal complexity. Figure 15.3 shows a bitmap image compared to a vector image of equal complexity (created by tracing the bitmap). The original bitmap is a smaller file and better suited for reproducing the photographic image.

FIGURE 15.3

File size comparison of an imported bitmap image (left) and a traced vector image of equivalent complexity (right)

Original bitmap 16 KB   Traced vector image 198 KB

The rule of thumb is to use scalable, bandwidth-efficient vector graphics as much as possible within Flash projects, except for situations in which photographs — or photographic-quality, continuous-tone images — are necessary for special content.

> **TIP** Most 8-bit raster images are GIFs, and they are most frequently used for images with large areas of solid color, such as logos and text. Rather than use this image type in Flash, consider re-creating or tracing this artwork with Flash drawing tools. The final Flash movie (.swf) will not only be smaller; it will also look cleaner and be scalable.

Knowing the File Formats for Import to Flash

You can import a variety of assets (in compatible formats) directly into your Flash project library, or you can import or copy and paste from another application into the Flash Document window. Assets can also be dragged from one Flash Document window or library to another. Files must be a minimum size of 2 pixels by 2 pixels for import into Flash.

> **CAUTION** Copying and pasting bitmap images into Flash from other applications does not always transfer transparency settings, so it may not be the best workflow for some assets. Using the Import dialog box and specifying that the artwork be imported as an editable object preserves transparency settings from Fireworks .png files.

The import menu (Ctrl+R or ⌘+R) gives you the option to limit imports to a specific format or to choose broad media categories. Unless you find it helpful to have some files grayed out when you dig through lists to find items to import, you will most likely be happy just using the most inclusive menu setting: All Files.

> **CROSS-REF** For a full discussion of importing and handling sound assets, refer to Chapter 14, "Adding Sound." Flash-compatible video formats are documented in Appendix D, "Digital Video Basics."

For now, let's focus on a brief summary of the image formats for Flash import, as shown in Table 15.1.

> **NOTE** The QuickTime warning dialog box that would pop up when bitmap images requiring QuickTime support were imported to older versions of Flash no longer appears. Although QuickTime support is still needed for some file types, the warning has been retired to make the process more seamless.

TABLE 15.1

Image Formats for Flash Import

File type	Extension	Description	Platform
Adobe Illustrator (CS4 files are most compatible)	.ai, .eps	Adobe Illustrator files are imported into Flash as vector graphics (unless they contain bitmap images). The importer plug-in is required to import files from Adobe Illustrator 8 and earlier. *To import PDF files to Flash CS3 or CS4, you must first open them in Illustrator and resave in AI (or EPS for Flash CS4) format.*	Windows Macintosh
AutoCAD DXF	.dxf	Drawing eXchange format is the original inter-program format for AutoCAD drafting software. Because this format does not support fills, it is mainly used for drafting plans or schematic drawings. This format is used by most CAD, 3D, and modeling programs for transferring drawings to other programs.	Windows Macintosh
(Windows) Bitmap	.bmp, .dib	Although Bitmap is a Windows format for bitmap images, don't be confused by the format name; not all bitmap images are Windows Bitmaps. Bitmap can be used with all Win and some Mac applications. It allows variable bit depths and compression settings with support of alpha channels and supports lossless compression. It is ideal for high-quality graphics work.	Windows Macintosh
Enhanced Metafile	.emf	Enhanced Metafile is a proprietary Windows format that supports vectors and bitmaps internally. This format is occasionally used to import vector graphics, but for most professional graphics work, this is not a recommended format.	Windows
Flash movie	.swf, .spl	Flash Player files are exported Flash movies. The movie is flattened into a single layer and scene, and all animation is converted to frame-by-frame animation.	Windows Macintosh
FreeHand	.fh	This is the vector-based format of FreeHand (v.7 or later).	Windows Macintosh
GIF image or animated GIF	.gif	Graphic Interchange Format (GIF) was developed by CompuServe as a bitmap image type that uses lossless compression. It is limited to a 256-color (or less) palette and is not recommended as a high-quality Flash export format, even for Web use.	Windows Macintosh

continued

TABLE 15.1		*(continued)*	
File type	**Extension**	**Description**	**Platform**
JPEG image	.jpg	Joint Photographic Experts Group (JPEG) is a bitmap type that uses lossy compression. Supports 24-bit RGB color. Recommended for Web-friendly compression of photographic images. Because of small file size, JPEG is often the native format for digital still cameras. No support for alpha channels.	Windows Macintosh
MacPaint image	.pntg	This is a legacy format for the old MacPaint program.	Windows Macintosh
PICT image	.pct, .pict	PICT image is compatible with many Win and all Mac applications. It enables variable bit depths and compression settings with support of alpha channels (when saved with no compression at 32 bits), supports lossless compression, and can contain vector or raster graphics. PICT image is ideal for high-quality graphics work.	Windows Macintosh
PNG image	.png	The Portable Network Graphic (PNG) format is another type of bitmap image that supports variable bit depth (PNG-8 and PNG-24) and compression settings with alpha channels. PNG files imported to Flash from Fireworks or Photoshop as editable objects (unflattened) preserve artwork in vector format. Lossless compression schemes make it ideal for high-quality graphics work. It is the recommended media type for imported images with alpha channels or filter effects.	Windows Macintosh
Photoshop image (2.5 or later)	.psd	This is the native layered format for most versions of Photoshop.	Windows Macintosh
QuickTime image	.qtif	This is the static raster image format created by QuickTime. It is not commonly used.	Windows Macintosh
Silicon Graphics image	.sgi	This is an image format specific to SGI machines.	Windows Macintosh
TGA image	.tga	The TGA, or Targa, format is a 32-bit format that includes an 8-bit alpha channel. It was developed to overlay computer graphics and live video.	Windows (with QT4) Macintosh

File type	Extension	Description	Platform
TIFF image	.tif or .tiff	TIFF is a lossless, cross-platform image type used widely for high-resolution photography and printing.	Windows Macintosh
Windows Metafile	.wmf	Windows Metafile is a proprietary Windows format that supports vectors and bitmaps internally. This format is generally used to import vector graphics.	Windows

TIP **Although you can export to the GIF format from Flash, this should be considered an option for raw-information transfer only, not as a means for creating final GIF art. For optimal quality and control, export a PNG sequence from Flash that can be brought into Fireworks for fine-tuning and final GIF output.**

Preparing Bitmaps

Flash is a vector-based application, but that shouldn't stop you from using bitmaps when you *need* them. There are many situations in which either the designs or the nature of the content require that photographic images be included in a Flash project. You can import a wide variety of bitmap image types, including JPEG, GIF, BMP, and PICT by using the methods described in the next section.

Considering that it's a vector-based program, Flash supports bitmap graphics extraordinarily well. However, because the most common use of Flash movies is for Web presentations, you always need to keep file size in mind. Here's what you can do to limit the impact of bitmap images on Flash playback performance:

- Limit the number of bitmaps used in any one frame of a Flash movie.
- Remember that, regardless of how many times the bitmap is placed on the Stage, the actual bitmap (or its compressed version in the .swf file) is downloaded before the first occurrence of the bitmap (or its symbol instance).
- Try spreading out bitmap usage, or hide a symbol instance of the bitmap in an earlier frame before it is actually visible, so that it loads when you need it.

TIP **If you need to include several high-resolution bitmap images in your Flash movie, consider using an ActionScript preloader or try breaking up the project into several linked Flash movies.**

When you want to bring raster images into Flash documents, you should know what portion of the Flash Stage the image will occupy. Let's assume that you're working with the default Flash document size of 550 x 400 pixels. If you want to use a bitmap as a background image, it won't need to be any larger than 550 x 400 (as long as your movie is not scalable). So, assuming that you're starting with a high-resolution image, you would downscale the image to the largest size at which it will appear in the Flash movie *before* you import it into Flash; for our example, that would be 550 x 400.

> **TIP**   Use an image-editing program such as Fireworks or Adobe Photoshop to downsize the pixel width and height of your source image if necessary.

If you mask bitmaps with a mask layer in the Flash timeline, the entire bitmap is still exported. Consequently, before import you should closely crop all images that will be masked in Flash. For example, if all you need to show is a face, crop the image so that it shows the face with as little extraneous background information as possible.

Be aware that Flash doesn't resize (or resample) an image to its viewed or placed size when the Flash movie (.swf) is created. To illustrate how the size of an imported bitmap can affect the size of a final Flash movie (.swf), we compared two different image resolutions used in identical layouts. Using the same source image, we sized the JPEG at two different pixel dimensions, and then placed it in two identical Flash documents (.fla). The first source version of the image had a 400-x-600-pixel dimension, and the second source version had a 200-x-300-pixel dimension — exactly half the size of the first. In both Flash documents, the final image was displayed at 200 x 300 pixels.

In the first Flash document (we'll call it Movie A), we imported the larger JPEG and resized it by 50 percent (using the Info panel) to match the smaller image. In the second Flash document (Movie B), we imported the smaller JPEG and placed it at its original size, occupying the same portion of the Flash Stage as the image in Movie A. Although both Flash movies exported a bitmap of the same display size on the Flash Stage, the resulting .swf files (using the same level of JPEG compression on export) had drastically different file sizes. Movie A was 44.1KB, whereas Movie B was 14.8KB! Movie A is nearly three times larger than Movie B. The difference in image resolution could be seen when a view magnification greater than 100 percent was used within the Flash Player; the larger JPEG in Movie A was much less pixilated than the smaller JPEG in Movie B.

Raster Images: Resolution, Dimensions, and Bit Depth

Resolution refers to the amount of information within a given unit of measurement. Greater resolutions mean better quality (or more image information). With respect to raster images, resolution is usually measured in pixels per inch (when viewed on a monitor) or dots per inch (when output on film or paper).

What is resolution?

The resolution of an original image changes whenever the scale of the image is changed, while the pixel dimensions remain fixed. Thus, if an original photograph is scanned at 300 pixels per inch (ppi) with dimensions of 2 x 2 inches, subsequently changing the dimensions to 4 x 4 inches results in a resolution of 150 ppi. Although a 4-x-4-inch image at 300 ppi could be interpolated from the original image, true resolution is *lost* as an image is scaled larger. When an image is digitally enlarged, the graphics application simply doubles existing pixel information, which can create a softened or blurred image. Reducing the scale of an image has few undesirable side effects — although a much smaller version of an original may lose some fine details.

Because all raster images consist of pixels, and because resolution simply describes how many pixels are arranged in a given area, the most accurate way of referencing raster images is by using the absolute pixel width and height of an image. For example, a 4,000-x-5,000-pixel image could be printed or displayed at any size with variable resolutions. This image could be 4 x 5 inches at 1,000 ppi, or it could be 8 x 10 inches at 500 ppi — without any loss of information. Remember that resolution simply describes how much information is shown per unit. When you reduce the pixel width and height of an image, the resolution is lowered accordingly, and after any pixels are thrown out, discarded, or interpolated, they're gone for good.

Raster images: Bit depth

Bit depth is an important factor that influences image quality and file size. *Bit depth* refers to the amount of information stored for each pixel of an image. The most common bit depths for images are 8-bit and 24-bit, although many others exist. An 8-bit image contains up to 256 colors, while a 24-bit image may contain 16.7 million color values. Depending on their file format, some images can also use an 8-bit alpha channel, which is a multilevel transparency layer. Each addition to an image's bit depth is reflected in a considerable file size increase: A 24-bit image contains three times the information per pixel as an 8-bit image. Mathematically, you can calculate the file size (in bytes) of an image with the following formula (all measurements are in pixels):

```
widthxheightx(bit depth ÷ 8) = file size
```

Note: You divide bit depth by 8 because there are 8 bits per byte.

When importing 8-bit images in formats such as GIF, BMP, and PICT, it is preferable to use the default Lossless (PNG/GIF) compression setting in Bitmap Properties to avoid adding Flash's default Publish Settings Quality 24-bit JPEG compression. 8-bit images that use Web-safe color palettes ensure greater display predictability for people viewing your Flash artwork on older systems with 8-bit video cards.

Preserving Bitmap Quality

When you choose to use bitmap images, remember that they do not scale as well as vector drawings in the authoring environment. Furthermore, bitmaps become degraded if the viewer scales your final movie so that the bitmap is displayed larger than its original size. Here are a few points to consider that will help you maintain the quality of your presentation when using bitmaps:

- Know your audience, and design for the largest screen (at the highest resolution) that your audience may have. Or, if you deviate from this, remember that audience members with optimal equipment will see a low-quality version of your work. If you're using ActionScript to load image assets, consider having low-res and high-res versions of the images available.

- Measure your largest hypothetical image dimensions in pixels. One way to determine these dimensions is to use the Flash Info panel to read the size of a placed image or a placeholder shape. Another way is to take a screen capture of your mock-up, and then measure the intended image area in Photoshop.

- Create or resize your bitmap image to the maximum hypothetical dimensions. If there are any rotations or skews required, you may have to do a test to see if the final result is cleaner when the transformation is done in your image-editing program or in the Flash authoring environment.

- Import images into Flash at the maximum required size, and then scale them down to fit into your layout.

The advantage of using this approach is that the movie can be scaled for larger monitors without causing the bitmap image to degrade. The disadvantage is that it requires sending the same large bitmap to all users. A more sophisticated solution is to use JavaScript to detect browser dimensions and then send the appropriately scaled bitmaps to each user. Other workaround solutions that may help preserve the quality of your final presentation without adding file size include the following:

- Restrict scaling capability of your published movie. You can do this by using HTML options in the Publish settings or using ActionScript.

- Set the bitmap's compression to Lossless (GIF/PNG) if it is already optimized in GIF format or if you want to preserve an alpha channel or editable filter effects in a .png or a .psd file.

- Trace the bitmap to convert it to a vector graphic (covered later in this chapter).

- Never apply double JPEG compression to your images. If you have compressed and saved images in JPEG format outside of Flash, be certain to select the Use imported JPEG data check box when importing the images to Flash.

Before sizing and importing bitmaps, you need to consider how you will set the dimensions for the Flash movie (.swf) in the HTML tab of the Publish Settings dialog box. You also need to know whether the bitmap is to be scaled in a motion tween. If the Flash movie scales beyond its original pixel width and height (or if the bitmap is scaled larger in a tween), bitmap images will appear at a lower resolution with a consequent degradation of image quality.

If you're uncertain of the final size that you need for a bitmap in Flash, it may be best to import a temporary low-resolution version of the image — being careful to store your original high-resolution version where you can find it later. Whenever you need to place the bitmap, drag an instance of the symbol onto the Flash Stage. Then during final production and testing, after you've determined the required pixel size for the maximum scale of the final bitmap, create and swap-in a higher-resolution image, as follows:

1. **Double-click the icon of the original low-resolution bitmap in the Flash library to access the bitmap's properties.**

2. **In the Bitmap Properties dialog box, click the Import button and select the new, higher-resolution version of the bitmap.** After import of the high-res image, all instances of the bitmap update automatically, with the scaling, animation, and placement of the image maintained.

Importing and Copying Bitmaps

Flash has the option to import bitmaps directly to the document library, in addition to the standard option of importing to the document Stage. When a bitmap file is imported to the Stage, it is added to the library as well. To import a bitmap into Flash, follow these steps:

1. **If you want to import an item to the Stage, make sure that there's an active, unlocked layer.** If no layer is available for placement of the imported item, the Import to Stage command is dimmed and you can use only the Import to Library option.

2. **Choose File ⇨ Import ⇨ Import to Stage (Ctrl+R or ⌘+R) or File ⇨ Import ⇨ Import to Library.** The Import (or the Import to Library) dialog box opens (shown in Figure 15.4).

3. **Navigate to the file that you'd like to import, select it, and click the Import or Import to Library button.**

The important difference between Import and Import to Library is that the latter option places the asset directly into the document library without placing an instance on the Stage.

Because Flash offers full support for the PNG image format (including lossless compression and multilevel transparency and some Fireworks filters), PNG is an ideal format for images that you intend to import into Flash. The PNG format has two types: PNG-8 and PNG-24. Generally, only PNG-24 images support 24-bit color and an alpha channel, but the file sizes can often be prohibitive. Fireworks makes it possible to create PNG-8 files with transparency for import to Flash.

FIGURE 15.4

The Import dialog box as it appears on Mac OS X. You can import multiple files in the same batch by selecting them from the file list before clicking Import.

CAUTION   When you are using bitmap images with transparent areas, display problems can occasionally occur with certain color settings and file types. For troubleshooting assistance, refer to the Adobe TechNote on "Transparency support in Flash" at `www.adobe.com/support/flash/ts/documents/transparent_bitmaps.htm`.

Importing sequences

When using the Import to Stage option, if you select an image from a series of images in the same storage location that include sequential numbers at the end of their filenames, Flash prompts you to import the files as a sequence. If that's what you want to do, click Yes in the dialog box (shown in Figure 15.5) to have Flash import all the files and place them in numeric sequence on successive keyframes of the current timeline. Otherwise, click No, and only the single file that you've selected is placed on the Stage.

FIGURE 15.5

You can import images in a numbered sequence and place them on successive keyframes automatically by using the Import to Stage option.

If you are importing a series of stills to be used sequentially to create animation (stills from a video sequence, for example), this feature can save a lot of the time you would spend placing and ordering images manually. The most efficient workflow is to create a Movie Clip symbol before importing the images so that the sequence can be placed directly on the Movie Clip Timeline. This method creates an animated element that can easily be placed anywhere in your Flash project. If you have already imported a sequence to the Main Timeline and decide that it would be more easily managed as a symbol, simply create a Movie Clip, and then cut the images from the Main Timeline and paste them into the Movie Clip Timeline.

WEB RESOURCE   For more coverage on how to create bitmap sequences from QuickTime video, go to the archived *Flash MX Bible* (Wiley, 2002) Chapter 41, available online at `www.flashsupport.com/archive`.

Although sequential import is not an option when using Import to Library, it is possible to manually select multiple images for import while using either of the Import dialog boxes. In order to bring more than one file into Flash in the same batch, Shift+click to select multiple items in sequence or use Ctrl+click (or ⌘+click) to select multiple nonsequential items in the file list of the Import dialog box.

Working with layered bitmap files

If you are working with graphic files that go beyond simple, single-layer bitmap images, finding the best way to translate those files to Flash may require some trial and error. Both Fireworks files (PNG) and Photoshop files (PSD) can contain bitmap and vector artwork, as well as text and masks or filters on multiple layers. Fireworks files may also contain frames and guides. You can always opt to flatten elements into a single bitmap file to preserve the exact appearance of the image, or you can choose to preserve editable paths and layers for more flexibility in the Flash authoring environment.

Each layered file imported from Photoshop or Fireworks with editable objects preserved is nested in a new folder in the Flash library that automatically has the same name as the imported file. You can change the default name of these folders and reorganize your Flash library as needed to keep the structure clean. You may find it helpful to create a folder for imported elements and nest all the folders that Flash creates for you so that your library does not get too cluttered.

TIP   Keep in mind that Movie Clip symbols Flash creates to preserve editable files imported from Photoshop or Fireworks are stored along with any bitmaps or other assets in the folders that Flash auto-creates for each file. If you are using a Movie Clip symbol more than once, you may want to rename and move it to a location that is easier to access — such as into the main file list in the Flash library — instead of leaving it in the nested folder.

NOTE   Flash can support some effects and blends created in Fireworks or Photoshop. If an effect is supported in Flash, it is preserved as an editable Flash filter. If an effect is too complex for Flash to preserve, the image can be rasterized to preserve the appearance of the image, but the effect will not be editable in the Flash authoring environment.

Importing Photoshop (PSD) files

Flash CS4 offers a detailed import dialog box for layered Photoshop files (shown in Figure 15.6) that makes it easy to control elements of the file to be flattened (as bitmaps) or imported as editable objects.

CAUTION   Although layered Photoshop files can be saved in TIFF or PNG format, these files are flattened on import to Flash, and you do not have the same control over the conversion of specific elements as you do with PSD files. PSD is the only Photoshop file format that can be brought into Flash with the option to keep layers and editable elements intact.

When importing images from Photoshop into Flash, you are prompted by the Photoshop Import Settings dialog box to select each layer in the file and make choices for the following import options:

- Import this image layer as:
  - **Bitmap image with editable layer styles:** This setting automatically creates a Flash Movie Clip and place the elements onto the Movie Clip Timeline while preserving the image, masks, and other effects (supported by Flash) as editable.

FIGURE 15.6

Use the import dialog box to choose conversion settings for Photoshop PSD files.

- **Flattened bitmap image:** This setting flattens the image into a single layer in the main Flash timeline and preserves the appearance of any masks or filters, but they will not be editable in Flash.

■ **Import this text layer as:**

- **Editable text:** Brings the text in as an editable Flash text box, and may require font substitution if you do not have the same font available in Flash. The text is placed on a layer in the Main Timeline or on a Movie Clip Timeline (depending on the other settings you choose).

- **Vector outlines:** Converts the text to individual letter outlines to preserve the appearance of the characters and the layout. You can modify the text by using Flash drawing tools, but you cannot edit with Flash text tools.

- **Flattened bitmap image:** Converts the text into a single image to preserve appearance but limits editing options to those that can be applied to bitmaps.

■ **Create Movie Clip for this layer:** If you have selected this option (or it has been auto-selected to preserve editable elements), you have the option of assigning an instance name and modifying the registration point.

- **Instance name:** You only need to assign an instance name if you plan to target the Movie Clip with ActionScript.

■ **Registration:** In most cases, you won't need to worry about changing the default registration point because the convention is to work with the top left corner as a reference for position and scale.

■ **Publish settings:** You have three options:

■ You may opt to import the image without any additional compression (**Lossless**).

■ You may set a custom compression setting for each layer or image as you import it (**Lossy: Custom**).

TIP Use the Calculate Bitmap Size button to preview the effect of different Custom compression settings before you decide on the final level to apply to your imported image.

■ Or, you may opt for the default setting, which applies the level of compression you have set globally for your Flash movie in Publish Settings (**Lossy: Use publish setting**).

■ **Convert layers to:**

■ **Flash Layers:** Puts the contents of each image layer onto a new layer in the selected Flash timeline (either on the Main Timeline or on a Movie Clip Timeline).

■ **Keyframes:** Puts the contents of each image layer into a new keyframe on a single layer in the selected Flash timeline (either on the Main Timeline or on a Movie Clip Timeline).

Along with the layer-specific settings listed above, there are two handy check boxes at the bottom of the dialog box that enable you to apply two additional (optional) settings for all layers in the file:

■ **Place layers at original position:** This setting ensures that the placement of the imported elements is consistent with the original file, relative to the top left corner of the Stage. If you do not select this check box, the imported elements are just placed in the center of the visible area of the Document window (including the pasteboard) — which usually turns out to be a somewhat random location unless you have been very precise with your zoom setting and your scroll bars to position the Stage within the viewable area of the Document window.

■ **Set stage size to same size as Photoshop canvas:** This is very helpful if you are importing an image to a new Flash file and you want to match the sizes, but it may disrupt your layout if you already have other elements placed in the Flash file you are importing to.

If all these options seem like more than you need, you can simplify things by leaving the default settings for each layer as is, or you can select some (or all) of the layers (using Shift+Select or Ctrl+Select) to apply a more limited set of options to all the layers at once.

TIP Although you have more than one layer selected in the Import dialog box, you may also choose to use the Merge button to flatten the layers into a single bitmap to streamline your file. This preserves the appearance of the layered image but limits your editing options in Flash to those available for simple non-layered bitmaps.

If you want to fine-tune your import settings without having to make selections each time you see the Photoshop Import dialog box, you can choose your own default settings in the Flash Preferences panel (File ⇨ Preferences ⇨ PSD File Importer, or on Mac Flash ⇨ Preferences ⇨ PSD File Importer). You can preset all the available settings for layered PSD files, as shown in Figure 15.7.

FIGURE 15.7

Flash Preferences enable you to preset defaults for all the options available with the PSD file importer.

Importing Fireworks (PNG) files

The import dialog box for Fireworks files has fewer options than the import dialog box for PSD files, but it still supports the import of layered, editable files (as shown in Figure 15.8).

CAUTION Although Photoshop files saved in PNG format show up in the file list when you browse for PNG files, they do not invoke an import dialog box with options but are flattened into a single-layer bitmap on import. Only PNG files saved from Fireworks enable you to preserve layers and editable shape or text elements on import to Flash.

FIGURE 15.8

Use this special import dialog box to choose conversion settings for Fireworks PNG files.

When importing PNG images from Fireworks into Flash, you are prompted by the Fireworks PNG Import Settings dialog box to make selections for the following import options:

- **Import as a single flattened bitmap:** Select this check box to import the PNG as one rasterized image to the current layer on the Main Timeline or to the library. When this option is selected, all other options are unavailable. If you choose this option, you may want to apply Flash JPEG compression to the bitmap image either in Bitmap Properties or in Publish Settings. To edit a flattened image, you can launch Fireworks from inside Flash and edit the original PNG file (including any vector data or text).

- To import more complex files, use these options to control the import structure:

  - **Import:** Page or Layer or Frames — select the option that best describes the location and structure of the Fireworks content you want to bring into Flash.

  - **Into:** Current frame as a Movie Clip to import the PNG file to a new Flash Movie Clip Timeline with all frames and layers intact, or New Layer to import the PNG file into a single new layer in the current Flash document at the top of the stacking order. All Fireworks layers are flattened, but not rasterized unless specified, and any frames in the Fireworks file are included on the new layer.

- Use these settings to control whether content is rasterized or kept editable:

  - **Objects:** Select either Import as bitmaps to maintain appearance to rasterize Fireworks fills, strokes, and effects in Flash as part of a flattened bitmap image, or select Keep all paths editable to preserve vector paths in Flash. Some Fireworks fills, strokes, and effects may be lost on import.

  - **Text:** You can select the same options as those listed for Objects.

As with most files created in external applications, you will find that rasterized and flattened Fireworks artwork and text imports more consistently to Flash, but you also lose all the benefits of having editable vector art and text fields. Although the option for launching Fireworks at any time to edit the original PNG file does make rasterized Fireworks images less limiting than other bitmaps, it is usually worth the little extra time you might need to spend simplifying your artwork to get it to import to Flash with vectors and editable text intact. Any special fills or textures that have been applied to your text in Fireworks are lost if you choose to preserve editable text on import to Flash.

NOTE Although gradients imported from FreeHand are converted to raw Flash shapes with gradient fills, gradients imported from Fireworks are converted to Movie Clip symbols that appear in the library in a folder labeled `Fireworks Objects`. It is still possible to edit the gradient fill just by opening the symbol in Edit mode (or double-clicking the symbol instance).

CAUTION If you import a Fireworks PNG file by cutting and pasting into Flash, all vector elements are rasterized into a flattened bitmap image.

Copying and pasting a bitmap into Flash

Here's how to use the Clipboard to import a bitmap into Flash:

1. **Copy the bitmap from your image-editing application to your Clipboard.** (Most programs support the Ctrl+C or ⌘+C shortcut key.)

2. **Return to Flash and make sure that you have an active, unlocked layer that you can paste the bitmap into; this can be on the Main Timeline or on any symbol timeline.**

3. **Paste the bitmap onto the Stage by choosing Edit ⇨ Paste in Center from the menu (Ctrl+V or ⌘+V).**

CAUTION When you are pasting a selected area from Photoshop, any transparency (alpha channel) is ignored or renders with unpredictable patterns that you'll have to mask out in Flash. The bitmap name is also replaced with a default numbered asset name. In most cases, results are much more consistent if you import the image file instead of copying and pasting it into Flash.

Applying color effects, alpha, and filters to bitmaps

A bitmap has some of the same advantages as the native Flash symbol types: It is automatically added to the library when you import it, and instances can be dragged onto the Stage and even used in motion tweens. However, filters and color (and alpha) effects are not available in the Properties panel when you select a bitmap instance. If you want to change the alpha settings or color tint of an imported image or apply any of the Flash filters, you must first convert the bitmap into a symbol.

Convert the bitmap into a Flash symbol type (F8) — use Movie Clip or Button symbol behavior if you want to use Flash filters. You can use the same name for the symbol instance as the original bitmap image. Filters and Color Effect settings are available in the Properties panel when you select the new (converted) symbol instance. Unfortunately, if you have placed other instances of the raw bitmap in your Flash file before nesting the bitmap in a symbol, not all the instances of the bitmap are automatically linked to the symbol you create, and you cannot use the Swap button to insert a Flash symbol instance in place of a bitmap instance.

TIP Library folders are very helpful for managing large sequences of images that need to be converted into symbols. We usually create a "Bitmap source" folder and an "Image symbol" folder to make it easy to keep track of where all the assets are. Keep in mind that edits to the bitmap are visible in the Flash symbol, but changes to the Flash symbol do not change the original bitmap.

Of course, using an external image-editing program is always an option, too. The features we describe in the next section can assist you if you plan to edit images outside of Flash.

Setting Bitmap Properties

The Bitmap Properties dialog box, shown in Figure 15.9, has several options that are used to control the quality of your imported bitmaps. Settings in the Bitmap Properties dialog box override the default JPEG compression setting for the document that is controlled in the Flash tab of the Publish Settings dialog box (File ⇨ Publish Settings).

FIGURE 15.9

The Bitmap Properties dialog box controls the compression settings applied to bitmaps imported into Flash.

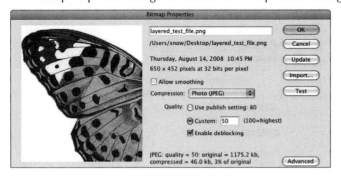

TIP The Advanced button expands the Bitmap Properties dialog box to show Linkage properties. In addition to importing or exporting for runtime sharing, bitmaps can be set to export for ActionScript. If you decide to enter or modify Linkage properties for a bitmap after it has been imported, you can access these same options by selecting the symbol in the library and choosing Linkage from the contextual menu or from the Options menu.

Follow these steps to use the Bitmap Properties dialog box:

1. Open the Library panel by choosing Window ➪ Library (Ctrl+L or ⌘+L) to access bitmaps in your current project (.fla).

2. Double-click one of the bitmap's icons, or use the contextual menu for a selected image to open the Bitmap Properties dialog box. You can also select Properties from the Library Options menu, or, with the bitmap highlighted, click the Properties button at the bottom of the Library panel.

3. Now, set the properties of your bitmap as needed:

   ■ **Preview window:** This displays the bitmap according to the current settings.

TIP Although the preview window in the Bitmap Properties dialog box may show only a small portion of your image, you can move the picture around within the preview window by clicking and dragging the image to view different areas.

   ■ **Name:** This is the name of the bitmap, as indicated in the library. To rename the bitmap, highlight the name and enter a new one.

   ■ **Image Path, Date, Dimensions:** Beneath the filename, Flash lists the local path, dimensions, and date information for the source of the imported image (not available if you pasted the image from the Clipboard).

   ■ **Update:** This feature enables you to re-import a bitmap if it's been altered outside of Flash. Flash tracks the original location of the imported bitmap and looks for the original file in that location when the Update button is clicked.

   ■ **Import:** This opens the Import Bitmap dialog box. When using this button, the new imported bitmap replaces the current bitmap (and all instances, if any), while retaining the original bitmap's name and all modifications that have been applied to the image in Flash.

   ■ **Test:** This button updates the file compression information, which appears at the bottom of the Bitmap Properties dialog box and the image in the preview window. Use this information to compare the compressed file size to the original file size after you have selected new settings.

   ■ **Allow smoothing:** Select this check box to enable Flash to anti-alias, or smooth, the edges of an image. Results may vary according to the image. Generally, this is not recommended for non-scaled graphics because it can soften the image. However, smoothing can be beneficial for reducing jagged edges on low-res images scaled in an animation. Figure 15.10 shows the effect of smoothing applied to a GIF image (top), and smoothing applied to a JPEG image (bottom).

FIGURE 15.10

Compare the images with Flash smoothing (right) to the images with no smoothing (left).

Scale 100

Scale 200

GIF no smoothing   GIF allow smoothing

Scale 100

Scale 200

JPEG no smoothing   JPEG allow smoothing

■ **Compression type drop-down:** The compression setting enables you to set the bit-map's compression to either Photo (JPEG) or Lossless (PNG/GIF). Photo is good for complex bitmap images (photographs for example); Lossless is better for graphic bit-map images with simple shapes and fewer colors. Play around with these settings to see which works best to give you a balance between file size and image fidelity for each particular image. Figure 15.11 shows a comparison of these two settings applied to an imported GIF image (top) and applied to an imported JPEG image (bottom).

FIGURE 15.11

Top: A GIF image imported to Flash by using PNG/GIF (Lossless) compression (left) and imported with forced JPEG (Lossy) compression (right). Bottom: A JPEG image imported to Flash by using JPEG (Lossy) compression (left) and imported with forced PNG/GIF (Lossless) compression (right).

■ **Use imported JPEG data/Use publish setting:** If the imported image is a JPEG, the first option appears — select this check box to avoid double JPEG compression. If the image is not a JPEG, the second option appears — select this check box to apply the global JPEG Quality setting defined in the Publish Settings dialog box for your current document. To apply a new compression setting for an image, click the Custom radio button and enter a value between 1 and 100. Click the Test button on the right to update the preview window. You will also see compression comparison info at the bottom of the panel. Custom settings are not recommended for imported JPEGs because they result in double JPEG compression. On uncompressed source files, higher quality settings produce more detailed images but also larger file sizes.

■ **Enable deblocking:** This new option for smoothing specifically designed to help reduce banding and JPEG artifacts is available when you apply Custom compression (but only if you are targeting Flash Player 10 in your Publish settings). It can almost make double JPEG compression work — but you always get better results if you find a way to avoid recompressing JPEG images.

Being prepared for common problems

Flash retains existing JPEG compression levels on any imported JPEG image, but, if a Custom setting is specified in the Bitmap Properties dialog box, it applies additional JPEG compression (set in the Quality field) when the movie is published or exported. Recompressing an image that has already been compressed usually leads to serious image degradation, due to the introduction of further compression artifacts. When importing JPEGs, you'll note that the Use imported JPEG data radio button is selected by default in the Bitmap Properties dialog box. This is the preferred setting because recompressing a JPEG is generally detrimental to image quality.

TIP If you import JPEG images, make sure that you either test the results of further JPEG compression or select the Use imported JPEG data radio button in the Bitmap Properties dialog box, which is accessible from the Flash library.

You can apply compression settings to each individual bitmap in the library with the Flash Bitmap Properties dialog box to determine the quality that you need before you use the general JPEG settings in the Export Movie or Publish Settings dialog box. Any Quality defined in the Bitmap Properties dialog box overrides the JPEG Quality in Publish Settings. To apply the Publish Settings compression to an image, you must select the Use document default radio button in the Bitmap Properties dialog box.

CROSS-REF We discuss JPEG export settings for Flash movies (.swf) in greater detail in Chapter 20, "Publishing Flash Movies."

Cross-browser consistency

We've received more than a few queries about image formats and Flash's capability to transcend issues of browser inconsistency, so here's the answer. Many image formats, such as PNG, are not supported across all browsers. When you import such an image format into Flash and publish or export to the SWF format, you have accomplished browser independence, because the Flash movie (.swf) is browser independent and the image has been encapsulated within the SWF format. (The image is not being sent to the browser in the imported format and then magically empowered to display.) Conversely, if you export any Flash document (.fla) to PNG or to any other format that's subject to cross-browser inconsistency, browser independence is lost.

Using the Bitmap Buttons in the Properties Panel

When a bitmap is selected in the Document window, the Properties panel displays the bitmap's name, symbol type, current size, and X, Y location. In addition to these basic bitmap properties, the Properties panel offers two useful options: the Swap button and the Edit button.

Swap

The Swap button opens the Swap Bitmap dialog box (shown in Figure 15.12), allowing you to specify a different bitmap from the current project library to replace the bitmap selected in the Document window. This can be considered a localized equivalent of the Import option of the Bitmap Properties dialog box. Instead of replacing the original bitmap symbol in the library and all instances of the image, the Swap button simply replaces the currently selected bitmap instance without altering the symbols in the library or any of the other instances of the bitmap that may occur in your project. (This feature is also available from the application menu under Modify ➪ Bitmap ➪ Swap bitmap.)

FIGURE 15.12

The Swap Bitmap dialog box lists all the bitmap symbols available in your current project library.

Edit

The Edit button in the Properties panel opens the selected bitmap for editing outside of Flash, either in your default image-editing application or the application that was used to save the bitmap file, if it is installed on your system. After you edit the image and choose Save, it automatically updates in the Flash document. If you prefer to select a specific application for editing a bitmap, select the bitmap in the library before choosing Edit With from the options menu or the contextual menu. The Edit With menu item launches the Select External Editor dialog box that enables you to browse or search for a specific application installed on your system (or network). When you have selected the application of your choice, it launches and the bitmap opens for editing.

NOTE Bitmaps imported from Fireworks (as .png) or Photoshop (as .psd) with individual layers specified as editable objects cannot be edited with an external image editor, so the Edit button is not visible in the Properties panel when these items are selected in the Flash authoring environment.

Making Sense of Bitmap Compression

Although we did some sample testing to try to show you all the possible image-compression combinations and the final results, the truth is that the optimal settings are entirely dependent on the quality of the original image and the final appearance needed in the context of your design. The main goal when testing various compression strategies should always be to find a balance between image quality and file size. The ideal balance will vary depending on the purpose the image serves in your presentation. For example, when using bitmap images in animation sequences, you may find that you can get away with using higher compression settings because the detail in the image may not be as important as it would be if you used the image in a catalog or some other presentation where the detail and color would be more critical.

The following compression workflows are intended to serve only as general guidelines. You will have to experiment with the specific value settings in each case to find the best results for your particular content and project needs.

24-bit or 32-bit lossless source files

If you have 24-bit (or 32-bit including an alpha channel), high-resolution source images saved without compression in PNG, PICT, PSD, or TIFF format, you have two workflow options:

- **Set JPEG compression in the Bitmap Properties dialog box:** If you want to control the compression applied to each imported image individually, set a Custom JPEG compression (Quality) setting that achieves the best balance of image quality and file size for each imported image in your library. This approach gives you the option of applying more compression to some images than to others.

- **Set JPEG compression in the Publish Settings dialog box:** If your source images have similar color and content, as well as consistent resolution, you may find it more efficient to use the compression settings in the Publish Settings dialog box to apply the same JPEG compression to all of your images. This makes it faster to test different compression settings on all the images in your project at once. If this is the workflow that you choose, make sure that the Use document default quality radio button is selected in the Bitmap Properties dialog box for each imported image. This ensures that the Quality settings in the Publish Settings dialog box are applied when the Flash movie (.swf) is published.

> **TIP** If you want to test and set different compression settings for individual layers in an imported Photoshop file, you can do this in the Publish settings section of the Import dialog box. Choose Lossy compression and select the Custom button, then enter a value between 0 and 100 in the Quality field. Use the Calculate bitmap size button to apply the compression and check the file size of the image (or layer). This feature enables you to apply different levels of compression to individual layers within a Photoshop image.

The main benefit to importing uncompressed source files is that you are not tied to a specific resolution and thus maintain the option of changing compression settings at any time in the development process. The main drawback is that your project files (.fla) are much larger, and each time you test your movie (.swf), you have to wait for Flash to apply JPEG compression on the images. This might not seem important at first, but the cumulative time loss over the course of developing a project does add up.

TIP As we mentioned previously, it can be helpful to work with lower resolution place-holder images as you develop a project. You can use the Import option in the Bitmap Properties dialog box to load your high-resolution images in the final stages of the project.

The image formats PNG-24, PSD, PICT, and TIFF also support alpha channels when they're saved with 32-bit color. Alpha channels enable the import of complex masks that might otherwise be difficult to create in Flash. You may be surprised to see that even after you apply Flash JPEG compression to an imported PNG, PSD, PICT, or TIFF image, the transparency is maintained.

CAUTION Although Fireworks files are saved with the .png file extension, the options for importing Fireworks PNG files are different from those for importing PNG files saved from Photoshop. For more information about importing Fireworks PNG files, see the section "Importing Vector Artwork," later in this chapter.

8-bit lossless source files

Source files in 8-bit formats are restricted to 256 (or fewer) colors and are optimized to a file size that is Web friendly. These files are usually saved in GIF or PNG-8 format and are best suited for graphics that have simple shapes and limited colors, such as logos or line drawings. PNG-8 and GIF files can still support an alpha channel, but unlike 24-bit images, you will not want to apply any JPEG compression to these files when they're brought into Flash.

CAUTION To avoid display problems, when exporting GIF files with transparency for use in Flash, the index color and the transparency color should be set to the same RGB values. If these settings are not correct, transparent areas in the imported GIF may display as solid colors in Flash. For more information on this issue, refer to the Adobe TechNote on Transparency support in Flash at www.adobe.com/support/flash/ts/documents/trans parent_bitmaps.htm.

Applying JPEG compression to 8-bit files generally results in larger files and degraded image quality (refer to Figure 15.7). To preserve the clean graphic quality of 8-bit images, follow these steps:

1. In the Import dialog box or in the Bitmap Properties dialog box, **make sure that Lossless (PNG/GIF) compression is selected.** This is the default for imported 8-bit images, but it never hurts to double-check to ensure that it hasn't been changed by mistake.

2. **Decide whether to leave the default setting for Allow smoothing in Bitmap Properties.** The image will have sharper edges if this option is unchecked, so it is best to make a decision on this setting depending on whether you prefer smoothed edges when the image is scaled larger.

Remember that the JPEG Quality specified in Publish Settings does not apply to imported images that have been set to Lossless compression in the Bitmap Properties dialog box.

Source files with lossy compression

Although JPEG is the native bitmap compression format in Flash, you may want to use an alternative application for optimal JPEG compression on images. In our experience, JPEG compression from Fireworks often produces smaller file sizes and more consistent image quality than JPEG compression applied in Flash. If you have created an optimized Web-ready JPEG by using your preferred lossy compression method or a client has delivered source files in JPEG format, you will want to avoid adding additional compression to these images when importing to Flash.

If you find that a JPEG file size is not reduced enough to fit the parameters of a particular project, it is better to go back to the uncompressed source file to redo the JPEG compression than it is to apply additional compression in Flash. As in all media production, double JPEGing images in Flash produces diminishing returns: By the time you get the file down to a size that you want, it has so many compression artifacts that it is generally unusable. By going back to the uncompressed source file and adjusting your compression settings to produce a new JPEG file, you end up with a cleaner image and a smaller file size than you would by compounding the JPEG compression in Flash.

For optimal results when importing JPEG images to Flash projects, the main settings to consider are the Use imported JPEG data and the Allow Smoothing check boxes in the Bitmap Properties dialog box.

■ To maintain the original JPEG compression of your imported image, simply select the check box to Use imported JPEG data from the Bitmap Properties dialog box. When this check box is selected, the original compression is preserved and the JPEG Quality specified in Publish Settings is not added to your imported JPEG image.

■ Smoothing is only advised if you will be scaling the JPEG image in Flash and you want to minimize the jagged edges with anti-aliasing. The compromise of Smoothing is that the image also appears slightly blurred — this may or may not be desirable, depending on the detail in the original image.

Although you can clear the Use imported JPEG data check box and choose a setting in the Quality field, remember that this compression is added to the compression on the original image and causes inferior results.

NEW FEATURE If you are targeting Flash Player 10, you can take advantage of a new smoothing option available in the Bitmap Properties dialog box when you choose to apply Custom compression to imported images. To see if it helps your image look better, select the Enable Deblocking check box and use the Test button to update the image in the preview window. You will notice the benefit of deblocking more clearly if you are using Quality settings below 50.

Converting Rasters to Vectors

Have you ever wanted to take a scan of a "real" pen-and-ink drawing that you made and turn it into a vector graphic? It's not hard to do, and the results are usually pretty close to the original (see Figure 15.13). You can also turn continuous-tone or photographic images into vector art, but unless the image is very high contrast, the converted version will not likely bear much resemblance to the original. However, this can be useful for aesthetic effects.

FIGURE 15.13

Compare the raster version (left) of the sketch to its traced vector version (right).

As described in Chapter 9, "Modifying Graphics," bitmap images can be traced in Flash to convert them to vector shapes. Earlier in this chapter, Figure 15.3 illustrated why this is not recommended for complex photographic images — the file size will be huge and the image quality will not be as satisfactory as the original bitmap. However, converting rasters to vectors allows you to create some unique visual effects in Flash. After an image has been traced, you can use any of the Flash tools available for shapes, including the Distort and Envelop options of the Free Transform tool. You can also select parts of the image individually to modify colors, or even add custom gradient or bitmap fills.

The Trace bitmap command is different from using the Break Apart command on a bitmap. When an image is broken apart, Flash perceives it as areas of color that can be modified or sampled for use as a fill in other shapes. Break Apart actually duplicates the automatic conversion handled by the Color panel to show bitmaps from the library in the bitmap fill menu. Although you can modify images that are broken apart with the drawing and painting tools, you cannot select shapes within the image with the Selection tool or apply the Optimization command, Smooth/Straighten options, or Distort and Envelop modifiers as you can with a traced vector image.

To apply Trace Bitmap, select a bitmap image (such as a scanned drawing) that has been imported to Flash (ideally with lossless compression and no Smoothing) and placed on the Stage; then choose Modify ⇨ Bitmap ⇨ Trace Bitmap from the application menu to open the Trace Bitmap dialog box, as shown in Figure 15.14.

FIGURE 15.14

Use the Trace Bitmap dialog box to select settings for converting a raster image into vector shapes.

We detail the settings for the Trace Bitmap command in Chapter 9, but the default settings can be a good place to start. Higher Color Threshold and Minimum Area values reduce the complexity of the resulting Flash artwork, which means smaller file sizes. This process is most effective when applied to simple images with strong contrast. In these cases, tracing a bitmap graphic can actually reduce the file size and improve the appearance of the scaled image. Traced vector images scale seamlessly without any loss of quality.

TIP   **The vector lines and fills created by tracing an imported bitmap are not always exact, but you can use the Smooth and Straighten modifiers or any of the other drawing tools to "touch up" the artwork.**

In order to get the best results from using Trace Bitmap, we advise reducing the number of colors in the original image before importing it to Flash. Figure 15.15 shows an imported image that was converted to indexed color and reduced to ten colors in Photoshop before saving as a GIF image for import to Flash. After the image is traced, you can simplify the shapes further by applying the Optimize command (Modify ⇨ Shape ⇨ Optimize), which simplifies the image and reduces the final file size. You can also use any of the drawing tools to further modify the image.

FIGURE 15.15

A reduced-color GIF image (left) can be traced and then cleaned up and simplified by using the Optimize command and Eraser tool in Flash (right).

Using External Vector Graphics

All artwork drawn in Flash is vector based; however, not all vector graphics created in other applications import seamlessly to Flash. As shown in Table 15.1, Flash is friendly to external vector formats, including FreeHand and Adobe Illustrator. Some vector graphics may be simple objects and fills, whereas others may include complex blending or paths that add significant weight to a Flash movie. Although most vector graphics are by nature much smaller than raster graphic equivalents, don't assume that they're optimized for Flash use.

Importing vector graphics from other applications is fairly simple and straightforward. However, because most vector graphics applications are geared for print production (for example, publishing documents intended for press), you need to keep some principles in mind when creating artwork for Flash in external graphics applications:

- **Limit or reduce the number of points describing complex paths.**

- **Limit the number of embedded typefaces (or fonts).** Multiple fonts add to the final movie's (.swf) file size. As described later in this chapter, converting fonts to outlines is one way to avoid adding extra fonts to your Flash file.

- **To ensure color consistency between applications, use only RGB colors (and color pickers) for artwork.** Flash can use only RGB color values and automatically converts any CMYK colors to RGB colors when artwork is imported. Color conversions can produce unwanted color shifts.

 When Flash imports a vector file with any placed grayscale images, the images is converted to RGB color, which also increases the file size.

- **Unless you're using FreeHand or Fireworks, you may need to replace externally created gradients with Flash gradients, or accept the file size addition to the Flash movie.** Gradients created in other drawing applications are not converted to editable Flash gradients when the file is imported; instead, they are rendered as complex banded graphics with clipping paths or as rasterized, bitmap images.

- **Preserve layers where possible to help keep imported artwork organized.** Some vector formats use layers, and Flash can recognize these layers if the graphic file format is correctly specified. Layers keep graphic elements separate from one another and can make it easier to organize items for use in animation.

- **If the artwork you are importing includes large areas of solid color, such as a plain background, consider excluding those parts of the graphic from import.** They can easily be replaced in Flash after the more complex parts of the artwork are brought in.

Importing Vector Artwork

The import dialog boxes for Adobe Illustrator files (in .ai or .eps format) and Photoshop files (in .psd format) enable fairly precise control of how these files are translated when brought into Flash — including unique settings for each layer, if needed. The other good news is that unlike Flash CS3, Flash CS4 also imports most EPS files. Sadly, PDF workflows that were supported before Flash CS3 are still not an option. Vector graphics from many other applications can be imported into Flash with relative ease by using the Import to Stage or Import to Library command. Browse for files by using the All Files setting or specify Adobe Illustrator, Photoshop, FreeHand, or PNG (Fireworks) file in the Import dialog box. Layered files and files with bitmap and vector elements open an Import Options dialog box with relevant settings. Use these settings to control how your file is handled in the Flash authoring environment. As long as you do *not* choose to import as bitmap, vector graphics are generally imported as editable groups either on the Main Timeline or in a Movie Clip Timeline.

NEW FEATURE Flash CS4 brings back support for the import of EPS files created with Adobe Illustrator. However, to import editable graphics from PDF files to Flash CS4, they must still be opened in Illustrator and resaved in AI or EPS format.

NOTE Simple bitmap files such as single-layer TIFF, GIF, or JPEG files do not require any custom settings and import directly (without opening an Options dialog box), after you browse for the file and choose Import.

Vector artwork is saved in the library on import only if it includes clipping paths or gradients that cannot be converted to editable Flash fills. In these cases, Flash automatically adds a folder of nested graphic symbols with masks or bitmap symbols to the library to preserve the appearance of elements that cannot be converted to drawing objects or simple grouped shapes.

You can also copy and paste or even drag and drop artwork from external applications, but this gives you less control over how the vector information is translated in Flash — for example, transparency or special fill types may be lost and any layers are flattened into the currently selected Flash layer.

Because generic numbered layer names, such as Layer 1, may be redundant with layers already present in your Flash document, it is helpful to give layers meaningful names in the original file before importing to Flash. To avoid unexpected color shifts, you should convert your color space to RGB in any external application before saving files that will be imported to Flash.

CAUTION You must specify Illustrator 7 or later in the Adobe Illustrator document options when saving AI files to ensure color consistency for artwork imported to Flash. If you choose Illustrator 6 or lower format, RGB values are not saved and color shifts may result.

To import a vector file to Flash, simply follow these steps:

1. To import a file to the Stage of your Flash document, make sure that you have an empty, unlocked layer selected, and choose File ⇨ Import ⇨ Import to Stage.

2. In the Import dialog box, choose a file format to browse by using the Files of Type (Win) or Show (Mac) menu.

3. Find the vector file that you want to import and select it from the file list.

4. **Choose Import.** If the application you are importing from includes options for how the artwork will be placed in Flash, you are prompted to make choices from an Import Options dialog box. Depending on your options, the artwork is imported to a single layer or to multiple layers or keyframes in your main Flash timeline or to a Movie Clip symbol timeline after you click OK.

NOTE If you choose to rasterize the vector artwork into a bitmap image when importing to Flash, remember to apply JPEG compression by using the Quality setting in the Bitmap Properties dialog box; or if the Use document default quality radio button is selected, set JPEG Quality in the Publish Settings dialog box before exporting your Flash movie (.swf).

5. To edit the imported graphic with Flash shape tools, ungroup the elements (Shift+Ctrl+G or Shift+⌘+G) or double-click parts of the group or drawing object until you are able to select strokes and fills in Edit in place mode.

TIP Double-clicking a grouped item or drawing object takes you into Edit in place mode, but if the item is in a compound group, you may have to continue double-clicking to dive into the nested elements until you are able to isolate the stroke and fill of one part of the group for modification.

6. To store elements in the library so that they are reusable, convert them to graphic symbols or Movie Clip symbols.

TIP If you have imported a layered sequence into multiple Flash keyframes on the Main Timeline, consider cutting and pasting the frames into a new Movie Clip symbol to keep the Main Timeline uncluttered.

Although you can scale, move, or rotate the grouped elements, to modify individual parts of the graphic you must either ungroup the elements or dive into Edit mode until you are able to select the strokes and fills of a particular element.

NOTE Where possible, imported graphics are interpolated as Flash drawing objects. This makes it easier to edit stroke and fill properties without having to ungroup or click into Edit mode.

Any small inconsistencies in fill style are easy to fix after the elements are ungrouped in Flash. Remember that you can delete fills, add strokes, scale, or otherwise modify the imported artwork with any of the Flash tools.

To make the artwork efficient to reuse and update, it is best to convert the whole graphic into a symbol. If you intend to animate parts of the graphic individually, convert these into discrete symbols and place them on separate layers.

CROSS-REF For more information on working with drawing objects and grouped artwork in Flash, refer to Chapter 9, "Modifying Graphics." For more information on using symbols, refer to Chapter 6, "Symbols, Instances, and the Library."

TIP If you use a program such as FreeHand, Illustrator, or InDesign that enables you to define Flash-compatible symbols and layers in your graphic files, you can save some time when the file is imported to Flash.

Copying and pasting a vector image into Flash

Here's how to use the Clipboard to import a vector image into Flash:

1. **Select all vector elements that you want to include.**

2. **Copy the selected items from your vector drawing application to the Clipboard.** Most programs support Ctrl+C or ⌘+C.

3. **Return to Flash and make sure that you have an active, unlocked layer that you can paste the vectors into.** This can be on the Main Timeline or on any symbol timeline.

4. **Paste the graphics onto the Stage by choosing Edit ⇨ Paste in Center from the menu (Ctrl+V or ⌘+V).** If you are pasting from Illustrator, you will see the Paste options dialog box (shown in Figure 15.16), which enables you to control how the copied vector artwork is converted when it pastes into Flash. If you are pasting from Fireworks, you see the normal Fireworks Import options dialog box (shown earlier in Figure 15.8) that enables you to select where the artwork is pasted and how it is interpreted in the Flash authoring environment.

FIGURE 15.16

The Paste options dialog box for Illustrator artwork enables you to select how graphics are converted when they are pasted into a Flash document.

5. **You may want to ungroup, regroup, or move parts of the pasted graphic onto new layers in your Flash document for better organization and for animation.**

Importing Adobe Illustrator files

Illustrator is one of the most commonly used applications for transferring vector artwork into Flash. When importing Illustrator files, you can preserve editable vector paths, text fields, and most gradient and pattern fills in addition to named layers and Illustrator symbols. Figure 15.17 shows the options available from the Illustrator Import dialog box, which is opened when importing files with the Illustrator extension (.ai or .eps) into Flash.

Although Illustrator can export a variety of file formats, including SWF, EPS, and PDF, the native AI format gives you the most editing options for files imported to Flash. As with the Photoshop importer, the default options for the Illustrator importer can be modified in Flash preferences (shown in Figure 15.18), and relevant settings can also be adjusted uniquely on-the-fly for each file that you import.

FIGURE 15.17

The Illustrator Import dialog box is used to specify how the graphics and file structure of an Illustrator (.ai or .eps) file are handled when brought into Flash.

FIGURE 15.18

Preferences for the Illustrator Import dialog box can be modified in Flash to establish default settings that best match your workflow.

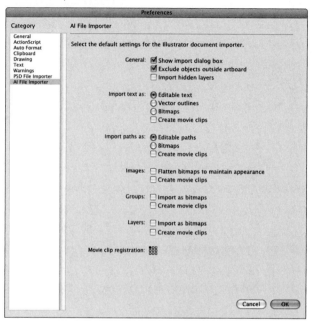

Remember to convert your Illustrator file to RGB color mode. If the file is in CMYK, you are warned with an incompatibility note in the import dialog box. If you proceed to import the file without changing the color settings in Illustrator, the file is converted automatically from CMYK to RGB on import to Flash, and this may cause unexpected color shifts. To ensure seamless translation of Illustrator elements imported into Flash, observe the following guidelines:

- Any placed grayscale elements in Illustrator are converted to RGB color when imported to Flash, which may increase file size.

- Be cautious with compound shapes: When importing overlapping elements that you want to keep intact in Flash, place them on separate layers in Illustrator and import the layers into Flash. If items on a single layer are overlapping when imported, they may be divided or merged at intersection points in the same way as ungrouped shapes created in Flash. Graphics on separate layers are converted into drawing objects on import to Flash and do not accidentally merge unless you break them apart into raw shapes.

- Flash supports up to 15 colors in an imported gradient fill. If a gradient created in Illustrator contains more than 15 colors or special styles (such as contour), Flash uses clipping paths to interpret the gradient. Clipping paths increase file size. To work around this issue, use gradients that contain 15 or fewer colors and use standard gradient styles in Illustrator or replace the imported gradient with a Flash gradient fill as described later in this chapter.

As shown in Figure 15.19, Flash recognizes text and simple gradient or pattern fills imported from Illustrator, making it easy to edit these elements directly in the Flash authoring environment. Effects supported in Flash are also imported and editable. Effects that are not yet available in the Flash authoring environment can either be imported as rasterized bitmaps to preserve their appearance, or they can be sacrificed to preserve the editable content in the file.

FIGURE 15.19

You can edit Illustrator files directly in Flash, but you still need to convert shapes and text elements into symbols to store in the library for reuse. Layer and symbol names from the Illustrator file can also be transferred to the Flash file on import.

NOTE   Imported Illustrator symbols are preserved as editable elements, and they are automatically stored in the library in a folder that Flash creates.

TIP   Remember that gradients created in Adobe Illustrator can be directly exported to SWF format as Flash gradients. However, if the gradient contains more than 16 colors or uses special alignment (such as contour gradients), Flash adds clipping paths when it is imported. Also, remember that Flash always interprets FreeHand blends as a series of paths, which can increase file size and sometimes add banding to the blend.

Optimizing Vectors

All vector graphics are made up of paths in one shape or another. A path can be as simple as a straight line with two points, a curved line with two points, or 500 or more points along an irregular shape or fill. For this reason, vector graphics are best suited for graphic images such as logos, architectural drawings, and clip art that do not include continuous tones. Fonts are also made up of paths. As you've seen with Flash-drawn graphics, you can scale them to any size without any loss of resolution, unlike raster (bitmap) artwork, which cannot scale larger than its original size without loss of resolution.

NOTE Vector graphics are eventually *rasterized,* so to speak. The vector formatting for drawn shapes and text is more of a simplified storage structure that contains a mathematical description (that is, smaller than a bit-for-bit description) of an object or set of objects. When the vector graphic is displayed, especially with anti-aliasing, the video card needs to render the edges in pixels. Likewise, the PostScript RIP (Raster Image Processor) of a laser printer needs to convert the vector information, or an EPS (Encapsulated PostScript) file, into printer "dots."

When you use imported vector graphics in Flash movies, you should minimize the number of points describing curved lines or intricate outlined graphics (for example, "traced" raster images). The problem with creating cool graphics in vector-based applications such as Illustrator, FreeHand, and 3D Studio Max is the large number of points used to describe lines. When these graphics are imported into Flash, animations are slower and harder to redraw (or refresh) on the computer screen. In addition, the file size of the Flash movie grows considerably. Most vector applications include features that enable you to optimize or simplify artwork before importing it to Flash.

There are also a number of ways that you can simplify artwork after it has been imported to Flash. We have discussed many of these Flash features in previous chapters, but we briefly summarize them here.

Interpreting complex vector artwork

Specialized graphics programs, such as Adobe AfterEffects and Autodesk 3ds Max, can create some astonishing vector-based graphics. However, when you import vector versions of those graphics into Flash, they either fall apart (display horribly) or add unrealistic byte chunks to your Flash movie. But this doesn't mean that you can't use these intricate graphics in your Flash movies. You can try several different procedures with intricate vector artwork, including smoothing, as described previously, to make complex graphics more Flash friendly.

Depending on the specific use of the artwork, you may also be able to output small raster equivalents that won't consume nearly as much space as highly detailed vector graphics. However, in some instances, the best solution is a bit more labor intensive. To get just the right "translation" of a complex vector graphic in your Flash movie, you may need to try redrawing the artwork in Flash. Sound crazy and time consuming? Well, it's a bit of both, but some Flash designers spend hour after hour getting incredibly small file sizes from "hand-tracing" vector designs in Flash.

Another approach is to loosen up and make stylized interpretations of complex graphics using fewer lines. For example, if you made a highly detailed technical drawing of a light bulb and wanted to bring it into Flash, you could import the original version of the drawing into Flash, place it on a locked guide layer, and use Flash drawing tools to re-create a stylized sketch version of the object (see Figure 15.20).

WEB RESOURCE Third-party Flash SWF tools can help to speed up the work of optimizing vector artwork — for example, Electric Rain's Swift 3D can simplify 3D models and output .swf files. Visit their site to learn more about software that can help you with your 3D Flash work: www.erain.com.

FIGURE 15.20

Compare the original imported vector artwork of the light bulb (left) with the stylized version hand drawn in Flash (right).

Converting text to outlines

Another aspect of vector graphics that you need to keep in mind — especially when working with other designers — is font linking and embedding. With most vector file formats, such as Illustrator, FreeHand, or EPS, you can link to fonts that are located on your system. However, if you give a design file to someone who doesn't have those fonts installed, he or she won't be able to see or use the fonts. Some formats enable you to embed fonts into the document file, which circumvents this problem. However, whether the fonts are linked or embedded, you may be unnecessarily bloating the size of the vector graphic.

You can break apart imported text in Flash by using the Modify ➪ Break Apart command (Ctrl+B or ⌘+B). You have to first break the text into letters and then break them apart a second time to get basic shapes.

You can also convert any text into outlines (or *paths*) in most drawing or illustration programs (see Figure 15.21). In FreeHand, select the text as a text block (with the Selection tool, not the Text tool) and choose Text ➪ Convert to Paths. In Adobe Illustrator, select the text as an object and choose Type ➪ Create Outlines.

FIGURE 15.21

Make sure that you have finished editing your text before converting it into outlines. The text at the top can be edited, whereas the text at the bottom can be modified only as individual shapes.

Editable text

Editable text

If you have a lot of body text in the graphic, you may want to copy the text directly into a Flash text box and use a _sans, _serif, or other device font. These fonts do not require additional file information (as embedded fonts do) when used in a Flash movie.

Optimizing curves

You can also reduce the complexity of paths within Flash by using the Modify ➪ Shape ➪ Optimize command. This has the same effect as the Simplify command in Illustrator or FreeHand, with a couple of extra options. When working with bitmaps or symbols, be sure to use the Modify ➪ Break Apart command, and if you are working with a group, ungroup it (Modify ➪ Ungroup) before you use the Optimize command (Alt+Shift+Ctrl+C or Option+Shift+⌘+C) — you can't optimize groups or symbols. Figure 15.22 shows the effect of maximum smoothing on a complex seashell graphic.

CROSS-REF For a more detailed description of the Optimize curves options, refer to Chapter 5, "Drawing in Flash."

FIGURE 15.22

A complex vector graphic simplified with maximum smoothing

Runtime bitmap caching

Flash 8 introduced *bitmap caching*, a feature designed to improve rendering performance of animation that uses complex vector graphics. The Cache as bitmap option appears as a small check box in the Display section of the Properties panel when a Movie Clip instance is selected in the Flash authoring environment (as shown in Figure 15.23). If bitmap caching is enabled, Flash converts the vector graphic into a bitmap image at runtime. The advantage of using this technique is evident only as you start to build more complex files that require Flash to redraw elements in an animation. If your vector artwork is optimized and uses very few points, converting from vector to bitmap does not offer any performance improvements. However, if you have created a highly detailed vector background that you will use to layer with other animated elements, Flash can dedicate more resources to rendering smooth animation if the background is converted into a cached bitmap. Because the bitmap graphic is rendered only once, the speed and smoothness of your animation is not hindered by Flash having to constantly redraw the points and lines that make up your vector background. These same principles apply if you are using a very complex vector graphic that is motionless but modified with filter effects. Bitmap caching makes it possible for Flash to convert the complex vectors into a simpler pixel surface while it dedicates resources to rendering the filter transformations.

ON the CD-ROM The file shown in Figure 15.23 is included on the CD so you can test the performance difference yourself, even with a simple tween. Open the `bitmapCaching.fla` file in the `ch15` folder and test the movie to preview the animation with Cache as bitmap enabled. Then select the Movie Clip, turn off Cache as bitmap, and test the movie again. You should notice that the graphics look cleaner (less screen redraw) and the animation plays more smoothly when Cache as bitmap is turned on.

FIGURE 15.23

Bitmap caching can be enabled in the Display section of the Properties panel when a Movie Clip or Button symbol is selected in the authoring environment.

There are a few limitations to bitmap caching that you should keep in mind:

■ Bitmap caching uses significantly more memory than rendering vectors. Use bitmap caching only when it will noticeably improve the performance (smoothness) of your animation.

■ If your animation requires a very close zoom on vector content, it may look pixilated if the cache as bitmap option is enabled for that item.

■ Bitmap caching will fail if it is applied to a symbol that is larger than 2,880 pixels tall or wide.

■ If the graphic with bitmap caching enabled is nested inside of another symbol that is rotated or scrolled, bitmap caching is ignored for the nested graphic.

■ If the Flash Player runs out of memory (producing an error), bitmap caching is canceled.

CROSS-REF Bitmap caching can also improve performance on applications with scrolling text fields or overlapping windows. For an example of using bitmap caching with a scrollable text field, refer to Chapter 30, "Applying HTML and Text Field Formatting."

Working with XFL: The Flash Format of the Future

Even though Flash has been around for many years, the .fla file format used to save Flash project information has not yet been opened up to third-party developers. This is why you won't find other applications that can save or publish in the .FLA format. There are some applications (from Adobe and from other companies) that publish .swf files, but the SWF format is mainly a display format and does not support development and editing like the FLA format does. In a radical move, Adobe is shipping some CS4 products with a new file format option built in. Figure 15.24 shows the options available for XFL files saved from InDesign CS4.

AfterEffects CS4 will also be able to export XFL files, and Flash will be able to open (not import) these files from Adobe applications and from third-party sources. XFL files, like FLA files, include all the assets used in a project along with the XML information that describes the structure of the file. XFL presents a brand new opportunity for developers and designers to share files and even create their own tools. The impact of this new file format may be gradual, but if it catches on, it will be the Flash format of the future. For now, most people just need to know that XFL files can be opened in Flash with similar results to opening any other Flash project file.

TIP XFL files are actually zipped files that include a folder of binary assets (sounds, images, and so on) used in the project and XML files that describe the internal database of the Flash document. To see these files without opening the XFL file in Flash, simply change the .xfl file extension to .zip, and then unzip the file.

WEB RESOURCE We'd like to know what you think about this chapter. Visit www.flashsupport. com/feedback to send us your comments.

FIGURE 15.24

The export options available for XFL files created in InDesign CS4 make it easy to set up content for transfer into Flash.

Summary

- Flash can use a variety of external media, which enables you to select the most effective format for various types of content.

- Bitmap smoothing has improved with newer versions of Flash. Even rotated or scaled bitmaps look less jagged on the edges than they did in early versions of Flash.

- Deblocking is a new type of smoothing designed to reduce compression artifacts on bitmap images imported to Flash files targeting Flash Player 10.

- Bitmaps are best suited for photographic images or images that contain detailed shading and/or complex color blends.

- Bitmaps can be converted to vector artwork in a variety of ways. This process works best on simplified bitmap images or when it is used to create special image effects.

- Vector graphics are most often used for logos, line drawings, and other artwork that does not include complex patterns and blends.

- Flash supports the import of layers, editable text, and gradients from some graphics applications, including Photoshop, Fireworks, and Adobe Illustrator. You will need to put some care into preparing files to get the best results, but being able to reuse your file structure and editable elements created in other applications can save you a lot of time.

- Flash CS4 includes preferences for the Illustrator and Photoshop importers that enable you to control how layered files from these applications are translated into Flash.

- Flash has fairly robust support for imported gradients and preserves many Fireworks effects as editable filters in the Flash authoring environment.

- The bitmap caching feature in Flash can greatly improve playback performance in movies that use complex vector graphics as background elements or scrolling content.

- Most graphics applications include their own options for reducing the complexity of vector art. However, using Flash's various tools for optimizing vector artwork can also be an effective way to reduce your final file size.

- XFL (.xfl) is a new open file format that may soon replace .fla as the preferred format for saving and sharing Flash documents. In Flash CS4, you can open XFL files (created in AfterEffects or InDesign) but not export or save back to that format.

Chapter 16

Displaying Video

One of the most exciting features introduced with Flash Player 6 was the power to add digital video footage to a Flash movie file (.swf)! Designers and developers alike had long awaited this feature. With Flash Player 6 or later, video encoded with Sorenson Spark codec can be played without relying upon additional browser or system plug-ins such as Apple QuickTime or RealNetworks RealPlayer. Flash Player 7 improved the capabilities and performance of video playback, enabling you to load .flv files directly into Flash movies at runtime from a standard Web server, without the aid of Adobe Flash Media Server. With Flash Player 8, you could take advantage of another video codec, the On2 VP6 codec, which yields better compression (that is, smaller file size) with superior image quality to the Sorenson Spark codec used in Flash Player 6 and 7. With Flash Player 9, the power of full-screen mode was added to present your Flash Video content larger than life! Now, with Flash Player 10, you can deploy video by using the AVC/H.264 video codec and the AAC audio codec — these codecs are among the highest quality codecs available today.

IN THIS CHAPTER

Compressing video in Flash CS4

Using the Video Import wizard

Unleashing the FLVPlayback component

Adding cue points to video clips

Playing alpha video .flv files

NOTE Adobe added the AVC/H.264 and AAC playback capabilities to Flash Player 9.0.115, also known as Flash Player 9 Update 3. That version was made available to the public between the Flash CS3 and CS4 release cycles.

Adobe has added more tools to make it easier for you to integrate video into your Flash movies. In this chapter, we show you how to perform a wide range of video procedures, from importing a source clip to playing the video clip within the FLVPlayback component.

Integrating Video: The Solutions

In Flash CS4, there are three ways in which you can deploy video content. The following sections provide a high-level overview of these methods.

> **NOTE**   You can also play Flash-compatible video content in Adobe AIR applications by using any of the methods discussed in the following sections.

Loading a Flash Video file at runtime

Starting with Flash Player 7–compatible movies, you can load Flash Video files (.flv) at runtime. When we say "runtime," we mean that you can create a separate Flash Video file (.flv), upload it to your Web server, and use ActionScript code or a component to load the video directly into your Flash movie (.swf) as it plays in the browser. You can create Flash Video files by:

- Importing a video file into a Flash document, and then exporting the Embedded Video symbol from the document's Library panel as a Flash Video file (.flv)

- Encoding a Flash Video file with the new Adobe Media Encoder CS4 application, which is part of Flash CS4

- Using a third-party video compression tool designed to export Flash Video files (.flv) such as Sorenson Squeeze, On2 Flix, Telestream Episode Pro, or Rhozet Carbon Coder

Real-time streaming a Flash Video file at runtime

In the previous section, you learned that it's possible to load a Flash Video file directly into a Flash movie file (.swf) as it plays in a browser. However, when you use this type of loading, the Flash Video file is loaded and cached as any other asset accessed at runtime. As such, if you have a large video file but only want to watch the last portion of the video, you'll have to wait until most of the video file has been downloaded.

One way you can offer your users the fastest access to Flash Video files (.flv) is to stream the video in real time with Adobe Flash Media Server (also known in previous editions as Macromedia Flash Communication Server) or a Flash Video Streaming Service provider. With this server technology, a Flash Video file is only temporarily cached on the playback computer. You can more easily protect copyrighted material, and users can seek to any point in the video with minimal wait times.

> **NOTE**   Adobe Flash Media Server is a specialty server product that works separately from a standard Web server. You can set up and install your own Flash Media Server, or you can purchase hosting from companies such as Influxis.com.

> **WEB RESOURCE**   For a list of Flash Video Streaming Service providers, see the Flash Video Hosting Providers section at `www.flashsupport.com/links`.

Embedding video into a Flash movie

The third method that you can use to view video is to embed the video file in the Flash document file (.fla), where it is then published directly inside the Flash movie file (.swf). This method is compatible with Flash Player 6 or later movies. Adobe Media Encoder CS4 can encode your video with the Sorenson Spark, On2 VP6, or the AVC/H.264 codec (discussed later in this chapter). It's important to understand that these codecs don't require additional plug-ins for playback — the Web user needs only to have Flash Player 6 or later (for Sorenson Spark), Flash Player 8 or later (for On2 VP6), or Flash Player 9.0.115 or later (for AVC/H.264) installed on the browser. Flash-compatible video codecs do not use any system-level video codecs; the codecs are built into the Flash Player plug-in.

When you import a video clip as an Embedded Video object, the video is stored in the library as a Flash Video file (.flv).

 You can only embed .flv files in a Flash document. AVC/H.264 video content cannot be embedded into a Flash document.

 You can also use a third-party application to create a Flash movie file (.swf) with embedded video.

Importing the Video

Digital video, as with other external media assets that Flash can import, is something that you need to create before working with it in a Flash document. In today's economic climate, you might not only be a Web designer or developer; you might also wear the part-time hat of a videographer. Be sure to read our coverage of video in Appendix D for a primer on shooting and producing better-looking video. The appendix also discusses the various video formats that you can import into Flash CS4.

After you have created a video file in the desired import format, you're ready to prepare the video for use in a Flash movie. This section introduces you to the AVC/H.264, On2 VP6, and Sorenson Spark codec options available for Flash-based video content. In the latter half of this section, we walk you through the process of importing one of the sample files on this book's CD-ROM.

An overview of codec options

Flash Player 9.0.115 and later can play MPEG-4 files that use the AVC/H.264 codec. This codec is one of the best video codecs available today, and is used for a number of video deployment applications, from Web-based video to Blu-ray HD content to high-quality consumer video camcorders. The AVC/H.264 codec has been licensed by Adobe from MPEG-LA (www.mpeg-la.com) for noncommercial playback in the Flash Player. Flash Player 8 and later movies have the capability to use another high-quality video codec, On2 VP6. This codec, created by On2 (www.on2.com), has been licensed by Adobe to be used with Flash Player distribution. Both the AVC/H.264 and On2 VP6 codecs feature superior compression and image quality compared to the Sorenson Spark codec introduced with Flash Player 6.

NOTE   As mentioned in the previous paragraph, Adobe has licensed only a noncommercial usage of the AVC/H.264 codec. MPEG-LA has a summary of licensing options for commercial content on their Web site at `www.mpegla.com/avc/AVC_TermsSummary.pdf`.

WEB RESOURCE   You can view side-by-side comparisons of equivalent bitrate Flash Video files with an example on this book's support site at `www.flashsupport.com/bonus/ codec_comparison`. You can compare the quality of an AVC/H.264, On2 VP6, and Sorenson Spark file.

The AVC/H.264 codec, however, doesn't come without a price. Playback of AVC/H.264 content requires Flash Player 9.0.115 or later. Adoption of Flash Player 9.0.115 is already past the 80 percent mark, as evidenced by recent surveys Adobe has conducted. Furthermore, AVC/H.264 files may require more CPU power and more RAM (memory) to play compared to older Flash-compatible video codecs. Slower machines, such as Apple Power Macintosh G3 computers and Pentium II computers, may have trouble playing back AVC/H.264 and On2 VP6-encoded files.

TIP   Make sure that you test your Flash Video file's playback on a variety of machines so that you accurately gauge your expectations for the target audience(s) of your Flash content. Larger video frame sizes (greater than 320 x 240) with newer video codecs might tax the CPU of any computer using less than an Intel Core 2 Duo processor.

If you're willing to sacrifice some visual quality of your Flash Video content and want the security of appealing to a larger audience (that is, people who have Flash Player 8 or later), you may want to encode your video content with the On2 VP6 codec. Flash Player 8 is available on over 98 percent of desktop computers in mature markets! You could also opt to use the Sorenson Spark codec, which has the greatest compatibility of all Flash-based video codecs. Sorenson Spark video requires more data rate (or bitrate) than AVC/H.264 or VP6 for equivalent quality. The Sorenson Spark codec is the least processor-intensive codec available in the Flash Player — if you need to target slow devices, you may find that the Sorenson Spark codec is the best codec to use. The quality of Sorenson Spark encoding is not necessarily poor compared to other Web video codecs; however, Adobe Media Encoder CS4 can only encode video in the Basic edition of the codec. You need to use a third-party video encoder to encode video with the higher-quality Pro edition of the Sorenson Spark codec.

NOTE   Flash Player 8 and later can decode only VP6 video content. If you're broadcasting live camera output from a Flash movie to a Flash Media Server application, Flash Player 6 and later uses the Sorenson Spark codec for all live streams. Adobe has released the Flash Live Media Encoder, a stand-alone application that can stream live AVC/H.264 or On2 VP6 video to a Flash Media Server. For more information on this product, go to:

`www.adobe.com/products/flashmediaserver/flashmediaencoder`

Video codecs can compress image data in two different ways — temporally and spatially. A temporal compression algorithm, or *interframe compressor*, compares the data between each frame and stores only the differences between the two. A spatial compression algorithm, also known as *intraframe compression*, compresses the data in each frame, just as the JPEG format compresses data in a still image. Most video codecs designed for Web playback, including AVC/H.264, On2 VP6, and Sorenson Spark, do not use a lossless compression technique. Rather, some color and detail information is thrown out in an effort to minimize the amount of data saved with each frame. For example, if the original video source recorded a sunset with 80 shades of orange, the compressed version of the sunset may include only 50 or fewer shades of orange. You may have noticed the extremes of lossy compression in Web videos where a person's face is hardly distinguishable, looking more blocky than human.

NOTE Historically speaking, most new codecs developed in the last few years rely upon the ever-increasing computer processor speeds to efficiently decompress each frame of video on playback. For this reason, you may want to test video playback on a number of machines and devices that support your targeted Flash Player version and video decoding.

All Flash-based video codecs use interframe (temporal) compression, but they also use intraframe compression when making keyframes. (You will see how tricky keyframes can be in just a moment.) A keyframe in video footage is similar to a keyframe in a Flash timeline. A keyframe defines a moment in time where a significant change occurs. For example, if a section of video has three hard cuts from one scene to another to another, the compressed version of that video should have a keyframe at the start of each scene. A keyframe then becomes the reference for subsequent frames in the video. When the following frame(s) are compared to the keyframe, only the differences are remembered (or stored) in the video file. As soon as the scene changes beyond a certain percentage, a new keyframe is made in the video. Video keyframes are created while the movie is being compressed.

CAUTION Video keyframes are the reason you should be careful with special effects or video filter usage in transitions from scene to scene in your video production software. The more frequently your video changes from frame to frame, the more keyframes your video file needs. Keyframes take up more file size than interframes between the keyframes, and if your video data rate can't accommodate the creation of those keyframes, the overall quality of your video degrades.

Compressing video with Adobe Media Encoder CS4

Flash CS4 ships with an exciting new stand-alone application called Adobe Media Encoders CS4. On Windows, you can find this application at Start Menu ➪ Programs ➪ Adobe Media Encoder CS4. On Mac, on your startup disk, look for the Adobe Media Encoder CS4 application in the `Applications/Adobe Media Encoder CS4` folder.

When you run the Flash CS4 Video Encoder application, you see the interface shown in Figure 16.1.

FIGURE 16.1

The Adobe Media Encoder CS4 application

The Adobe Media Encoder CS4 works as a batch processor for the same encoding engine that is used for other CS4 applications such as Adobe Premiere CS4 and Adobe After Effects CS4. You can specify all of your encoding settings in the Adobe Media Encoder CS4 application. Some benefits to using Adobe Media Encoder CS4 include:

- **Adding multiple source video files:** You can drag and drop (or browse to) one or more video source files on your computer or network into the application's queue.

- **Duplicating settings:** After you've specified the settings on one source clip, you can click the Duplicate button to add another entry in the queue with the same clip and its settings. You can then adjust the new duplicate's settings to a different data rate.

- **Saving the queue:** You can save the list of video clips in the queue to resume work in another session. However, you can't save the queue list as an external project file.

- **Deinterlacing capability:** If you have a source clip that is captured from an interlaced video source, such as NTSC footage from a miniDV or DVCAM camcorder, you can de-interlace the footage in Adobe Media Encoder CS4.

- **Cue point import/export:** Adobe Media Encoder CS4 enables you to save your cue point data to an external XML file and create cue point data in an XML file that can be imported directly into the Cue Points tab of the tool.

NOTE The encoding options available in Adobe Media Encoder CS4 depend on your installed Adobe CS4 applications. If you only have Flash CS4 installed, your encoding presets are limited to the FLV and F4V file formats.

You start the encoding process by dragging a video source file to the queue pane. You can also click the Add button to browse to a video source file on your system. After a source file is added to the queue, you determine how you want to compress the original source clip into the Flash-compatible video file. From the queue pane (shown in Figure 16.2), you can choose from 22 presets as a starting point for your preferred compression options.

FIGURE 16.2

The Preset menu in the queue pane

The encoding profiles are listed in two formats, FLV (Flash Player 8 or later) and F4V (Flash Player 9.0.115 or later). Each of these formats has three general preset groups:

- **Same as Source:** These presets create an output file whose dimensions and frame rate match that of the source file.

- **HD (High Definition) quality:** The presets labeled with 1080p and 720p create output files with frame rates that match the source file and dimensions that are quarter, half, or full resolution HD. You should only use HD source files with dimensions that match the preset name. For example, if you have a 1080i or 1080p (1920 x 1080, or anamorphic 1440 x 1080) HD source file, you should use the 1080p presets if you want HD quality encoded Flash video. If you have a 720p (1280 x 720) HD source file, you should use the 720p preset for HD quality. 1080p quarter resolution HD is actually a misnomer; if you choose an HD quarter resolution preset, the output size is 480 x 270, which is one sixteenth the resolution of 1920 x 1080. The 1080p half resolution HD preset is also a misnomer, and is the "real" quarter resolution preset, producing output at 960 x 540.

■ **Web quality:** These presets create various resolutions, frame rates, and data rates for deploying Flash-compatible video geared to Internet connection speeds.

After you have selected a preset, you can customize the encoding settings by clicking the name of the preset in the queue pane. In the following sections, we explore video and audio settings available within a preset. To follow along, add a source video clip to the queue pane, select a preset, and click the underlined preset name.

 If you edit a preset, the preset name changes to Custom. You can save an edited preset as a new preset to reuse within Adobe Media Encoder CS4.

General export settings

On the right-hand side of the Export Settings dialog box (shown in Figure 16.3), you can edit the video and audio compression settings. At the top of the Export Settings section, you can save a customized preset, load a preset, and delete a preset. You can also choose which tracks of the source clip you want to encode. By default, the Export Video and Export Audio boxes are selected.

FIGURE 16.3

The general export settings

Video tab

Expand the displayed settings by clicking the mode toggle button (the double down-arrow button), shown earlier in Figure 16.3. Click the Video tab (shown in Figure 16.4) to control how the video track of the source file is encoded to the Flash Video (.flv) or the H.264 for Flash (.f4v) format.

FIGURE 16.4

The Video tab of the Export Settings dialog box

The Basic Video Settings section of this tab has the following options:

- **Codec:** This menu selects the codec used for compression. Sorenson Spark is the codec compatible with Flash Player 6 and later, whereas On2 VP6 is available in Flash Player 8 and later. If you choose a F4V preset, the MainConcept H.264 Video codec is automatically selected.

- **Encode alpha channel (FLV only):** This option determines if an alpha channel in the source video file will be compressed and included with a .flv file using the On2 VP6 codec. We discuss the alpha channel encoding capability of the On2 VP6 codec later in this chapter.

- **Resize Video:** This option resizes the original dimensions of the source video clip. If selected, you can enter a new width and height for the encoded Flash Video clip. If you've captured high-resolution video footage from your DV camcorder (that is, source video with dimensions of 640 x 480 or larger), you may want to reduce the frame size to a more Web-friendly size, such as 320 x 240. You can create smaller video file sizes with a combination of smaller video dimensions and reduced data rates. If you're using DV footage (or any footage with a non-square pixel aspect ratio), be sure to use proper square pixel sizes, such as 160 x 120, 320 x 240, and so on. Unlock the constraints by clicking the chain link button to the right of the width and height fields.

- **Frame Rate:** This menu controls the encoded frame rate of the output video clip. The Same as source option encodes the video clip with the same rate as your original video clip. You can also choose fixed frame rates, from 10 frames per second (very choppy) to 30 frames per second (very smooth).

- **Field Order:** This option enables you to control interlaced output. For Flash-compatible video, you should only choose None (Progressive).

- **Profile and Level:** These options are available only for F4V and H.264 output. The Profile options include Baseline, Main, and High. If you're targeting playback on slower devices such as older Pentium or PowerMac computers, you may want to use the Baseline profile for H.264 because less processing power is required. If you're targeting modern computers, you should use the Main and High profiles. The High profile produces the best quality, but requires the most processing power for playback. The Level menu's options conform your video settings to predefined H.264 specifications. Levels are defined from 1.0 to 5.1 — the higher the level, the larger the video dimensions and faster the frame rate.

The Bitrate Settings of the Video tab contain the following options:

- **Bitrate Encoding:** This option, if available for your selected codec, enables you to control how the bitrate of the video track is encoded. CBR, or Constant Bit Rate, encoding is designed for real-time streaming deployment of video. If you plan to use an Adobe Flash Media Server (or equivalent RTMP hosting service) for your video deployment, use CBR encoding. VBR, or Variable Bit Rate, encoding is designed for local or HTTP playback. If you're planning to deploy your video content on a Web server, use VBR encoding.

- **Encoding Passes:** This option determines how well the video track is analyzed during the encoding process. If you choose One, the encoder reads the source file and writes the output file sequentially frame by frame. If you choose Two, the encoder analyzes the source video clip with the first pass, looking for optimization points along the way, and then encodes and outputs the video file on the second pass. You should opt to use a 2-pass encoding setting whenever possible. The only reason you would choose 1-pass encoding is to create your output file more quickly for a draft video.

- **Bitrate:** This slider controls the data rate used by the output video clip. This setting, more than any other, influences the file size and image quality of the encoded clip. The lower the bitrate, the lower overall quality you'll see in your output clip. If your codec selection enables only one bitrate slider, the value indicates the average bitrate for the entire clip. The H.264 codec enables you specify a Target (or average) Bitrate, as well as a Maximum Bitrate. The Maximum Bitrate is available only for VBR encoding. Generally speaking, you should use a bitrate between 300 and 800 Kbps for Web-based video content.

The Advanced Settings section of the Video tab contains the following option:

- **Set Key Frame Displacement:** This option determines how often keyframes within the Flash Video content are created. As discussed earlier in the chapter, keyframes are needed to store differences between frames in the video clip. If you use the default value (deselected), Flash CS4 determines how often a keyframe should be generated. If you enable this option, you can specify your own keyframe interval with the slider. The lower the value you specify, the more frequently the encoder creates keyframes within the output video clip. The higher the value, the less frequently the encoder creates keyframes. Be very careful with custom settings here: If your data rate isn't high enough to support the keyframe interval you specify, the overall image quality is sacrificed to maintain the keyframe interval.

Audio tab

The Audio tab, shown in Figure 16.5, controls the compression settings for the audio track of the source video clip.

FIGURE 16.5

The Audio tab of the Encoding screen

The Basic Audio Settings section of this tab has two options:

- **Codec:** This option controls the audio codec used for the output clip. If you are targeting a .flv file, you can use only the MPEG Layer 3 (MP3) codec. If you are targeting a .f4v file, you can choose variants of the AAC codec, which is the next-generation MP3 codec. AAC + Version 1 and AAC + Version 2 are more complex audio codecs that produce higher-quality audio for equivalent bitrates, at the expense of higher computer processor utilization.

- **Output Channels:** You can choose how the source video's audio track is output in the new compressed file. The Mono option mixes a stereo (dual channel) audio input into one channel. The Stereo option retains left and right channels from the source video clip. Unless your content demands stereo sound, we recommend using a single (mono) channel for audio output.

■ **Frequency and Audio Quality:** If you're using the AAC codec, you can choose a sampling rate and quality setting for the audio track. We recommend you use a sampling rate of 44.1 kHz or higher at High quality.

In the Bitrate Settings section of the Audio tab, you can set the following option:

■ **Bitrate:** You can modify the data rate of the audio channel, choosing a value between 16 to 256 Kbps (MP3) or 56 to 320 Kbps (AAC). Unless you're encoding high-quality musical scores, an audio data rate between 48 and 64 Kbps is usually adequate.

NOTE The audio data rate is separate from the video data rate. As such, you should mentally add both rates to get a clear picture of the total data rate required for the Flash Video clip. For example, if you specify a video data rate of 400 Kbps and an audio data rate of 96 Kbps, the total data rate for the clip is 496 Kbps.

Cue Points section

When you view the Export Settings in advanced mode, the cue points section appears at the lower left side of the dialog box. This section enables you to insert embedded markers within the final output video file. The details of this section are discussed later in this chapter.

Crop tool

The Crop tool is available in the Source tab located at the upper left corner of the Export Settings dialog box. The Crop tool enables you to change the borders (or cropping) and size of your original source clip before it is encoded.

TIP Cropping video clips might be necessary if your original footage is letterboxed (that is, black bands are above and below the actual picture area of the clip) or if you captured video with an analog video capture card that retains black borders on the video clip.

When you finish specifying the encoding parameters for the clip, you're ready to encode the clip. After you close the Export Settings dialog box, you can click the Start Queue button in the main window of Adobe Media Encoder CS4, and your clip will go start compressing. When the .flv or .f4v file finishes the encoding process, you can use the video file with a Flash file.

Using the Video Import wizard

In Flash CS4, you can import Flash-compatible video files by using the File ➪ Import ➪ Import Video command. First, we review the stages of video import. Later in this section, you can follow a step-by-step exercise that shows you how to compress a sample clip on this book's CD-ROM. You can follow along here to familiarize yourself with the process.

NOTE If you want to use Flash Video in your Flash document, you must be using Flash Player 6 or later as the targeted version in the Publish Settings dialog box (File ➪ Publish Settings). If you want to use the On2 VP6 codec, you must target Flash Player 8 or later. If you want to use the H.264 codec, you must target Flash Player 9.0.115 or later.

Choosing a target Flash Player version

Before you start using the Import Video option, you need to determine which Flash Player you want to target. The Import Video process is optimally geared to preparing output for the FLVPlayback component, available in two versions with Flash CS4. If you create or open a Flash file (ActionScript 2.0) targeting Flash Player 8 or later, the Import Video process can prepare the settings for the ActionScript 2.0 (AS2) version of the FLVPlayback component. If you create or open a Flash file (ActionScript 3.0) targeting Flash Player 9 or later, the Import Video process is enabled to set up the ActionScript 3.0 (AS3) version of the FLVPlayback component.

The options you can use during the video import vary based on the Flash Player version and ActionScript version you have selected in the Flash tab of the Publish Settings dialog box (File ➪ Publish Settings).

Choosing a source clip: The Select Video screen

When you first select the Import Video option from the File ➪ Import menu in Flash CS4, you see the Select Video screen of the Import Video dialog box, as shown in Figure 16.6. On the Select Video screen, you can browse to a Flash-compatible video file. To proceed to the next stage of import, click the Next button.

 On the Mac, all Next buttons within the Video Import wizard process are labeled as Continue buttons, as shown in Figure 16.6.

FIGURE 16.6

The Select Video screen

```
┌─────────────────────────────────────────────────────────────┐
│                         Import Video                          │
│ Select Video                                                  │
│                                                               │
│                                                               │
│   Where is your video file?                                   │
│   ⦿ On your computer:                                         │
│       File path:  ( Browse... )                               │
│       /Volumes/Storage HD/HomeGarden_416K_Cues.flv            │
│       ⦿ Load external video with playback component           │
│       ○ Embed FLV in SWF and play in timeline                 │
│       ○ Import as mobile device video bundled in SWF          │
│                                                               │
│   ○ Already deployed to a web server, Flash Video Streaming Service, or Flash Media Server: │
│       URL: [                                               ]   │
│       Examples:  http://mydomain.com/directory/video.flv      │
│                  rtmp://mydomain.com/directory/video.xml      │
│                                                               │
│                                                               │
│   Learn about Flash Media Server                              │
│                                                               │
│   Learn about Flash Video Streaming Service                   │
│                                                               │
│              ( Launch Adobe Media Encoder )                   │
│                       ( Go Back ) ( Continue ) ( Cancel )     │
└─────────────────────────────────────────────────────────────┘
```

ON the CD-ROM You can find several source clips in the `resource` folder of this book's CD-ROM.

After you select a source clip, you can choose how you want to include the video clip in your Flash movie. With Flash CS4, you have three options:

- **Load external video with playback component:** This option is the default selection, enabling the wizard to automatically configure parameters for the FLVPlayback component. If you are going to deploy your video content with a Web server, choose this option.

- **Embed video in SWF and play in timeline:** This option adds the encoded video clip to the current Flash document's Library panel. Because the audio track of the compressed video clip will be within the Flash movie, you should make sure that you match the encoder's frame rate to that of your Flash movie.

CAUTION Only proceed with the Embed video in SWF option if you need to insert short video clips directly into your Flash movie (.swf) file. If you're processing clips longer than a minute in duration, you should proceed with a progressive download or streaming option.

- **Import as mobile device video bundled in SWF:** This option inserts a source video file "as is" into the Flash file's library. If you intend to distribute mobile video formats, such as 3GP, with a Flash Lite 2.0 or later movie, you can use this option to create an embedded copy of a video file within the published Flash movie (.swf file). You should bundle only video formats that are supported by the mobile device you are targeting for deployment. (Note that the Flash Video format is not natively supported by current mobile devices running Flash Lite 2.0.)

NOTE The other deployment options featured on this screen can be used for video already uploaded to a Web server or Adobe Flash Media Server application.

Formatting the embedded video content: The Embedding screen

If, and only if, you selected the Embed FLV in SWF and play in timeline option in the Select Video screen, you determine how you want Flash CS4 to place the encoded video content into the current document. On the Embedding screen (shown in Figure 16.7), you can choose from the following options:

- **Symbol type:** This menu lets you choose how you want the video content to be nested within the Flash document.

  - **Embedded video:** This option simply places the Flash Video clip as an Embedded Video symbol in the Library panel.

  - **Movie clip:** This option places the Flash Video clip inside of a Movie Clip symbol in the Library panel. Note that you still have a separate Embedded Video symbol of the Flash Video clip; this option saves you the step of creating a new Movie Clip symbol and placing the Embedded Video symbol onto its timeline.

  - **Graphic:** This option behaves identically to the Movie clip option, except that the video content is nested within a graphic symbol in the Library panel.

- **Place instance on stage:** This option, if selected, places an instance of the video clip on the current timeline of the Flash document. The instance will be of the symbol type selected in the menu discussed previously.

- **Expand timeline if needed:** This option, if selected, adds more frames to the current timeline of the Flash document to accommodate the length of the video clip. For example, if the timeline had 10 frames and your clip is 100 frames long, 90 new frames would be added to the timeline.

- **Include audio:** This menu controls how the audio track (if it exists) of the video asset is handled. The selected value keeps the audio track bound inside of the embedded video symbol after import. When you use this option, you control the compression of the audio track via the audio stream settings in the Flash tab of the Publish Settings dialog box (File ➪ Publish Settings). If you deselect this option, the audio track is stripped from the video asset; the audio, then, is not imported into the Flash document.

If you click the Next button from the Embedding screen, the wizard goes to the Finish Video Import screen, discussed later in this section.

FIGURE 16.7

The Embedding screen

Controlling the video content: The Skinning screen

If you choose the Load external video with playback component option in the Select Video screen, the next screen in the wizard process is the Skinning screen. This screen enables you to pick a control bar for the FLVPlayback component. You learn more about the options on this screen in the step-by-step exercise that follows this section.

Reviewing your settings: The Finish Video Import screen

After you have taken the care to specify the encoding options you want for your Flash Video clip, you can quickly review some of the presets on the final screen, as shown in Figure 16.8. Click the Finish button to complete the video import process.

FIGURE 16.8

The Finish Video Import screen

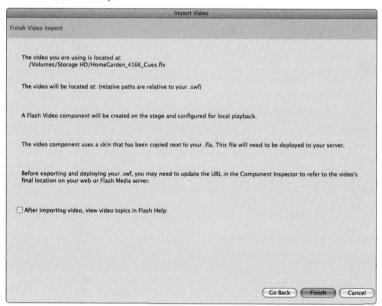

Deploying video files with Flash CS4

With Flash CS4, you have several more options for deploying and encoding video content. In this section, you learn about how to deploy an existing .flv or .f4v file that you have uploaded to your Web server. The Flash CS4 Video Import wizard automatically sets up the parameters for a new FLVPlayback component in your Flash document.

1. **Create a new Flash file.** If you want to use the updated AS3 version of the FLVPlayback component, create a new Flash file (ActionScript 3.0), which targets Flash Player 10. If you want to target Flash Player 8, create a new Flash file (ActionScript 2.0) and change the Flash Player version to 8 in the Publish Settings dialog box.

2. **Choose File ➪ Import ➪ Import Video.** The Select Video screen of the Import Video dialog box (see Figure 16.9) presents you with two options:

   - **On your computer:** This field and Browse button enable you to select a digital video source clip on your local computer or computer network.

   - **Already deployed to a web server, Flash Video Streaming Service, or Flash Media Server:** This option enables you to enter a fully qualified domain name pointing to an existing .flv file on a server.

3. **Choose the second radio button option in this screen, and enter the following URL:**
   `http://www.flashsupport.com/video/lizard_112k_vp6.flv`

4. **Click the Next button (or Continue button on Mac) to proceed to the Skinning screen.** After the Select Video screen, the Video Import wizard takes you to the Skinning screen (see Figure 16.10).

FIGURE 16.9

The Select Video screen

5. **Choose the playback control skin for your video clip.** This skin is used by the FLVPlayback component instance that the Video Import wizard places on to the current document's Stage at the end of the importing process. The skin options vary based on the ActionScript version and Flash Player version specified for the Flash file.

> **TIP** **Full-screen capability is supported in Flash Player 9 or later. The ActionScript 3.0 (AS3) version of the FLVPlayback component includes skin files featuring a full-screen toggle button. Also, the AS3 version of the FLVPlayback component enables you to choose a custom skin background color during the skin selection process.**

You can select one of several skins in the Skin menu. All these skins are separate .swf files included with the Flash CS4 installation. Whichever skin you choose is automatically copied to the location of the current Flash document you're importing the video file into. This .swf skin file must be uploaded along with your Flash document's .swf file to the Web server so that the FLVPlayback component can load the skin into the Flash movie. If you prefer to make your own video playback controls to use with the FLVPlayback component, you can choose None in the Skin menu. You can also choose Custom Skin URL and enter the path (relative or absolute) to the skin .swf file you created for the FLVPlayback component.

FIGURE 16.10

The Skinning screen

6. **After you pick a skin, click the Next button.** As shown in Figure 16.11, you are taken to the Finish Video Import screen (as described in the earlier coverage of the Video Import wizard). The Finish Video Import screen describes the steps you will need to take after you have finished the import process.

FIGURE 16.11

The Finish Video Import screen

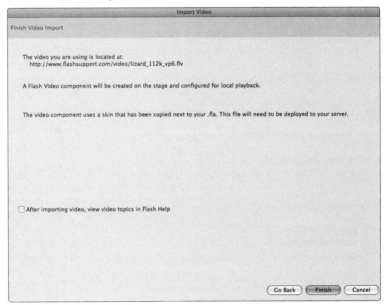

7. **Click the Finish button.** Flash CS4 loads the metadata from the .flv file you specified during the Import Video process. The width and height data from the .flv file are used to size the instance of the FLVPlayback component that Flash CS4 places in the center of your Stage area, as shown in Figure 16.12. Rename Layer 1 to **fp**, short for *FLVPlayback*. In the Properties panel, name the instance `fp` as well.

8. **Save the document as** `deploy_http_video.fla`. After you have saved the file, test the movie (Ctrl+Enter/⌘+Enter). When the movie loads, the lizard video clip plays in the FLVPlayback component instance (see Figure 16.13). The skin you selected earlier in this exercise also appears, enabling you to control the playback of the video clip.

 You can find the completed file, `deploy_http_video.fla`, in the `ch16` folder of this book's CD-ROM.

FIGURE 16.12

The FLVPlayback component

FIGURE 16.13

The remote video clip playing in the FLVPlayback component

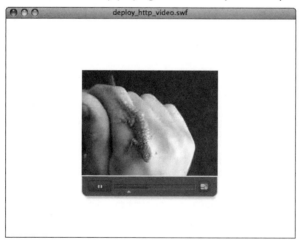

TIP If you want to try loading another .flv file into the FLVPlayback instance, you don't have to repeat the Import Video procedure. Instead, select the `fp` instance on the Stage and open the Component Inspector panel (Shift+F7). Select the Parameters tab, and change the `contentPath` value (AS2) or `source` value (AS3) to the new video filename (or location). You can also change the skin file in the Parameters tab.

Also, if you want to test the a skin featuring a full-screen toggle button (available only with the AS3 version of the FLVPlayback component), be sure to use the Flash Only - Allow Full Screen template in the HTML tab of the Publish Settings dialog box (File ➪ Publish Settings). Refer to Chapter 20 for more information on publishing Flash movies.

Using the FLVPlayback Component (AS3)

In the last section, you saw the FLVPlayback component at work in Flash CS4, as inserted into your Flash document with the Video Import wizard. In this segment of the chapter, you learn more "under the hood" usage of the FLVPlayback component. Remember, you can access two versions of the FLVPlayback component in Flash CS4, one for ActionScript 2.0 (Flash Player 8) and one for ActionScript 3.0 (Flash Player 9). In this section, you learn about the ActionScript 3.0 version of the component.

CROSS-REF This part of the chapter explores many ActionScript-based features of the FLVPlayback component and its event model. For an introduction to components, read Chapter 32, "Using Components." We also utilize more advanced ActionScript in many of these examples. To learn more about ActionScript, be sure to read Parts V, VII, and VIII of this book.

Working with the Component parameters

You don't have to use the Video Import wizard to add an FLVPlayback component instance to your movie. In fact, you can just drag and drop the component from the Components panel (Window ➪ Components) to the Stage of your Flash file. You can access the following parameters of an FLVPlayback (AS3) component instance from the Parameters tab of the Component Inspector panel (Window ➪ Component Inspector).

NOTE All these parameters can also be used in ActionScript, with the same spelling. For example, if you have an instance of the FLVPlayback component named `fp`, you can set the `autoPlay` parameter to `false` with code: `fp.autoPlay = false;`.

- `align`: This parameter determines how the borders of the video clip align to the display area of the FLVPlayback component. The available options are `center`, `top`, `left`, `bottom`, `right`, `topLeft`, `topRight`, `bottomLeft`, or `bottomRight`. The default value is `center`. Alignment values are apparent only if your FLVPlayback instance is sized larger than the native frame size of the video and `noScale` is the value for the `scaleMode` property.

■ autoPlay: This parameter determines if the video loaded into the component automatically plays (true) or loads in a paused state (false).

■ cuePoints: This property specifies the cue points that are linked to the playback of the FLV file. If you create embedded cue points (see our coverage later in this chapter), this property auto-fills within the Properties panel after you select a new .flv file with the source property. If you double-click the cuePoints field, the Cue Points dialog box opens (see Figure 16.14), where you can create new ActionScript-based cue points or view embedded cue points. Embedded cue points cannot be changed. We discuss cue points later in this chapter.

FIGURE 16.14

The Cue Points dialog box

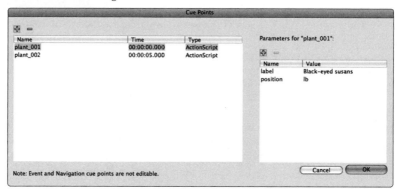

■ preview: This new parameter controls which frame of the Flash Video clip is displayed in the FLVPlayback component while authoring the Flash file. If you double-click this property's value in the Parameter tab, the Select Preview Frame (see Figure 16.15) dialog box opens. You can then watch the video clip and pause on a frame you want to use while authoring the Flash file. The preview image is displayed only in the authoring environment; when you publish the Flash movie (.swf file), the preview image is not displayed. The preview feature is useful when you need to layer other design elements around the FLVPlayback component and need a visual reference to content within the video clip.

TIP The Select Preview Frame dialog box also enables you to export a still image (as a PNG file) of the preview frame. You can use this PNG file for a thumbnail of the video, or load it at runtime in ActionScript to serve as a poster frame for the video.

■ scaleMode: This parameter controls how video content fits within the display area of the component. If the display area uses an aspect ratio different than that of the video content and this property is set to exactFit, the video stretches vertically and/or horizontally to fit the display area. If the property is set to maintainAspectRatio, the video content maintains its aspect ratio regardless of the display area's aspect ratio. If the property is set to `noScale`, the Flash Video clip displays at its native size, regardless of the dimensions of the FLVPlayback instance.

FIGURE 16.15

The Select Preview Frame dialog box

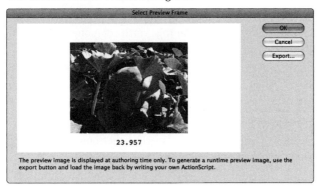

- `skin`: This property, when accessed in the Properties panel, opens a dialog box from which you can choose a skin .swf file for the component. The values in this menu match the skins available in the Skinning screen of the Video Import wizard.

- `skinAutoHide`: This property controls if the skin .swf used for the component hides itself if the user's mouse cursor is not over the video display area. If set to `false`, the skin is always visible. If set to `true`, the skin disappears when the user's mouse cursor rolls off the component.

- `skinBackgroundAlpha`: This new property controls the opacity of the skin background color. The range of values is between 0 and 1, where 1 represents full opacity (no transparency) and 0 represents full transparency (no opacity). You can specify decimal values for partial opacity, such as 0.5, which is 50% transparent.

- `skinBackgroundColor`: This new property controls the background color of the skin. You can use the color picker for this property's value in the Parameters tab to choose a custom color.

- `source`: This property determines which .flv file is loaded into the component. You can use a relative path (for example, `myVideo.flv`), an absolute path (for example, `/videos/myVideo.flv`), or a fully qualified domain (for example, `www.flash support.com/video/lizard_112k_vp6.flv`).

- `volume`: This updated property controls the loudness of the .flv file's audio channel, if one exists. You can use a value in the range of 0 to 1, with 0 being absolute silence and 1 being the maximum loudness of the audio channel. You can use decimal values as well to indicate partial loudness. For example, a value of 0.5 indicates half of the original loudness of the audio track.

Using FLVPlayback Custom UI components

With Flash CS4, you can also add custom UI components specifically designed to be used with the FLVPlayback component. In ActionScript, you can tell an FLVPlayback instance to use other components for playback control. The following properties represent component references used with the FLVPlayback component:

- `backButton`: This property specifies the component to seek to cue points prior to the current playhead time.

- `bufferingBar`: This property controls which component displays the buffering status of the video clip.

- `captionButton`: This property controls which component toggles the display of captions for the video.

- `forwardButton`: This property specifies the component to seek to cue points past the current playhead time.

- `fullScreenButton`: This property specifies the component to toggle full-screen mode with the video image area of the FLVPlayback component.

- `muteButton`: This property specifies the component that can toggle the muting of the video's audio track.

- `pauseButton`: This property controls which component can pause the video playback.

- `playButton`: This property controls which component can initiate playback of the video file.

- `playPauseButton`: This property specifies which component can toggle between play and stop states of the video stream.

- `seekBar`: This property specifies the component that displays the scrubbing area and playhead control for the video.

- `stopButton`: This property controls which component stops and resets the stream back to its starting position.

- `volumeBar`: This property specifies the component that controls the volume setting of the video clip.

We show you how to practice using a few custom UI components with an FLVPlayback instance. The following steps introduce you to the process of adding a play/pause button and a seek bar:

1. **In Flash CS4, create a new Flash file (ActionScript 3.0) and save it as** `flvplay back__as3_custom.fla`.

2. **Rename Layer 1 to** fp. On frame 1 of this layer, drag an instance of the FLVPlayback component from the Video nesting to the Stage.

3. **In the Properties panel, name the instance** `fp`.

4. **Open the Component Inspector panel and click the Parameters tab.** Double-click the value for the skin parameter. In the Select Skin dialog box, set the Skin type to None, as shown in Figure 16.16.

5. **Create a new layer named** custom UI **and place this layer above the fp layer.**

FIGURE 16.16

The Select Skin dialog box

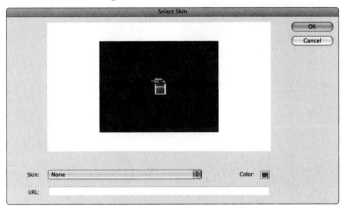

6. **Open the Components panel and expand the Video group.** With frame 1 of the custom UI layer selected, drag an instance of the PlayPauseButton component to the Stage. Place the new instance below the fp instance, near the left corner.

7. **In the Properties panel, name the new instance ppb, as shown in Figure 16.17.** Now, you need to link the ppb instance to the fp instance in ActionScript.

8. **Create a new layer named** actions, **and place it at the top of the layer stack.**

9. **Select frame 1 of the actions layers and open the Actions panel (F9/Option+F9).** In the Script pane, add the following actions:

```
//FLVPlayback fp;

fp.playPauseButton = ppb;
fp.source = "stella_raw.flv";
```

NOTE For this example, make sure that you have copied the stella_raw.flv file from the resources folder to the same location on your computer where you saved the .fla document in step 1.

FIGURE 16.17

The PlayPauseButton component

TIP A quick way to see the code hints for an authortime instance in the Actions panel is to use a code comment specifying the data type followed by the instance name. In this code example, the FLVPlayback code hints appear for the `fp` instance because of the `//FLVPlayback fp;` line of code.

10. **Save the Flash document and test it (Ctrl+Enter/⌘+Enter).** The `stella_raw.flv` file automatically plays in the `fp` instance. You can click the `ppb` instance to pause the video, and click it again to resume playback.

11. **Go back to the Flash document.** Let's add another custom UI component. Select frame 1 of the custom UI layer. From the Components panel, drag an instance of the SeekBar component to the Stage, to the right of the PlayPauseButton instance.

12. **Name the SeekBar instance skb in the Properties panel.** Optionally, use the Free Transform tool to stretch the width of the SeekBar instance to span the remaining width of the FLVPlayback instance.

13. **Select frame 1 of the actions layer and open the Actions panel.** Add the following bold code to the existing script:

```
//FLVPlayback fp;

fp.playPauseButton = ppb;
fp.seekBar = skb;
fp.source = "stella_raw.flv";
```

14. **Save the Flash document and test it (Ctrl+Enter/⌘+Enter).** You should see the playhead of the SeekBar instance move to the right as the video plays (see Figure 16.18).

You can continue adding other custom UI components from the Components panel and specifying the new instance names to the corresponding property of the `fp` instance in the frame 1 script of the actions layer.

> **TIP**
>
> You can also modify the graphics used by the custom UI components. Open the Library panel to view the skin symbols in the **FLV Playback Skins** folder.

FIGURE 16.18

The SeekBar component displaying the current position of the video

---

> **ON the CD-ROM**
>
> You can find the completed file, `flvplayback__as3_custom.fla`, in the ch16 folder of this book's CD-ROM. Note that this sample links to a relative path for the .flv file, located in the `resources` folder.

Working with Cue Points

In general terms, a *cue point* is a specific time within a video clip where something of significance occurs. For example, you might want a cue point at the start of each cut or scene within a video, or when something noteworthy is said within the audio track of a video clip. With Flash-compatible video, you can build systems that work with two types of cue points:

- **Embedded cue points:** Using Adobe Media Encoder CS4, which is included with Flash CS4, you can insert cue points within a video clip before the encoder compresses the clip. The resulting .flv file embeds each cue point on a keyframe in the video track. There are two types of embedded cue points:

- navigation: This type of cue point marks the video frame as a point that the user can seek to, using the forward and back buttons of the FLVPlayback component, or with ActionScript code.

- event: This type of cue point marks the video frame as a point that can be detected with an event handler in ActionScript code. You cannot seek to event cue points unless you modify the functionality of the FLVPlayback component code.

- **ActionScript cue points:** This type of cue point is one that is not embedded with the .flv file. An ActionScript cue point is added, as its name implies, via ActionScript code. For example, if your .flv file doesn't have cue points, you can create cue points with an XML file specifying the times and names of the cue points. You can load the XML file at runtime, and pass each cue point value to the FLVPlayback component. You can specify ActionScript cue points in the Parameters tab of the Component Inspector panel for an FLVPlayback instance, or use the `FLVPlayback.addASCuePoint()` method.

> **CAUTION** By default, ActionScript cue points cannot be used as navigation cue points. You need to modify methods of the FLVPlayback instance in order for ActionScript cue points to work with seek buttons.

In ActionScript code, you can detect which type of cue point is fired during playback. A cue point object in ActionScript has a `type` property, which is set to a String value of `"navigation"`, `"event"`, or `"actionscript"`. You can also use the `fl.video.CuePointType` class to retrieve constants for these String values.

In the following steps, you learn how to use Adobe Media Encoder CS4 to create cue points for video footage of garden plants. Each plant featured in the video will have a cue point, specifying its name and the location of the name on the screen. The cue points will be used to dynamically create text fields (with drop shadows!) on top of the video. You add both navigation and event cue point types to this footage. The navigation cue points work with the forward/back seek buttons of the FLVPlayback component, and they create the text labels for each plant type. The event cue points remove the text label before the next label fades and blurs onto the Stage.

> **TIP** You can import and export cue points from Adobe Media Encoder CS4 to an XML file. You can then reuse the cue points with other compression settings or clips, or share the data with other members of your Flash production team. If you don't want to type all the cue point data for this exercise, simply import the `HomeGarden_CuePoints.xml` file from the `resources` folder of this book's CD-ROM into the Cue Points section of Adobe Media Encoder CS4.

> **ON the CD-ROM** Make a copy of the `HomeGarden_Full-Res.avi` file from the `resources` folder of this book's CD-ROM.

1. **Open the Adobe Media Encoder CS4 application.** On Windows, you can find this application shortcut at Start ➪ Programs ➪ Adobe Media Encoder CS4. On the Mac, you can find this application here: `[Startup disk]: Applications: Adobe Media Encoder CS4`.

2. Click the Add button on the right-hand side of the application and browse to your copy of the `HomeGarden_Full-Res.avi` **file.** Add this file to the queue.

3. **In the Preset column for the new video clip, choose FLV – Web Large, NTSC Source (Flash Player 8 or later).**

4. **Click the preset name in the queue to access the Encoding Settings dialog box, as shown in Figure 16.19.** Make sure that the dialog box is toggled to advanced mode.

FIGURE 16.19

The Encoding Settings dialog box

5. **In the Cue Points section, located at the lower left of the dialog box, click the Add (+) button to add a cue point at the start of the video clip.** Change the name of the cue point to **plant_001**. Change the Type menu to Navigation. Under the parameters area of the dialog box, click the Add (+) button to add a new parameter named **label**. For the value, type **Black-eyed susans**. Add another parameter named **position** with a value of **rb**. This position value stands for "right bottom" and it will be used to properly position the `label` text for the cue point. See Figure 16.20 for these settings.

> **CAUTION** Watch your spelling for parameter names and values. You must consistently name your parameters in order for your custom ActionScript code to work.

6. **Now, scrub the video playhead below the preview area to the next scene.** The next cue point should be added at 4;17 seconds, as shown in Figure 16.21. Add a cue point by clicking the Add (+) button on the left, and name the cue point **exit_001**. Change the Type to Event. For this exercise, you won't need any parameters for event cue points.

You can click the playhead marker and nudge it with the Left and Right Arrow keys to finesse the playhead time.

7. **Now that you're familiar with the cue point addition process, add the cue points at the approximate times shown in Table 16.1.** (Feel free to choose your preferred values.) When you are finished, your cue point list should resemble Figure 16.22.

FIGURE 16.20

The new plant_001 cue point

 Double-check the label and position parameters for each cue point before you start the encoding process.

Also, if you don't want to type each cue point into the Cue Points tab, you can click the folder icon to import the complete set of cue points, HomeGarden_CuePoints.xml, from the resources folder of this book's CD-ROM.

8. **In the Export Settings area of the dialog box, click the Audio tab.** Change the Output Channels to Mono and the Bitrate to 16 Kbps. This particular video clip has an audio track that is silent (meaning, there is an audio track, but it just recorded silence).

 Even if you don't need an audio track, we advise you to include a silent audio track for the clip in your video-editing program. We have found that video playback for larger files is significantly closer to the clip's frame rate if there is an audio track to sync to.

FIGURE 16.21

The exit_001 cue point

FIGURE 16.22

The complete cue list

9. **Click OK to close the Export Settings dialog box.** Click the Output File value, and type **HomeGarden_1516K_Cues.flv**. This new filename indicates the total bit rate of the FLV file and the presence of cue points.

10. **Click OK to accept all the new encoding settings.** Back in the main application window, click the Start Queue button to begin the encoding process. The lower area of the application window displays the encoding progress, as shown in Figure 16.23.

11. **Before you close the Adobe Media Encoder CS4 application, choose File ⇨ Save Queue.** This option saves your clip's settings (and cue points!) so you can reedit and reencode if you made a mistake.

FIGURE 16.23

The encoding progress in the Adobe Media Encoder CS4 application

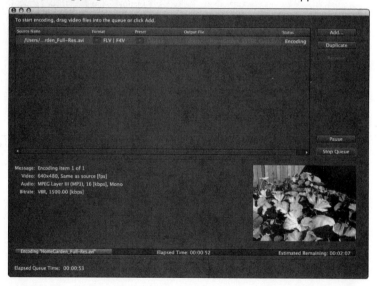

TIP   You can export cue point data to an XML file in the Cue Points section of the Export Settings dialog box. Click the disk icon in the cue points toolbar to specify an output filename. The cue points file for the sample footage is already saved and included in the resources folder of this book's CD-ROM.

Now you're ready to build the Flash document to play the .flv file.

12. **Open Flash CS4 and create a new Flash file (ActionScript 3.0).** Save the document as cuepoints_embedded_as3.fla, in the same location as the new .flv file compressed in Step 9.

The Flash CS4 interface with Essentials Workspace

Learn to customize your workspace in Chapter 4

Working with Color

Default Web 216 swatches

Web 216 Sort by Color

Custom gradient controls

Source GIF image and loaded
custom color swatches

Get to know the Flash CS4 Color and Swatches panels in Chapter 7

Use the Adjust Color filter to quickly modify graphics

Learn to use Flash filters in Chapter 12

Use blend modes for static and animated effects

Learn to apply blend modes and combine them with filters in Chapter 12

Make better drop shadows and other dynamic effects

Learn to create animated drop shadows in Chapter 12

Create artwork with Flash drawing and effects tools

Create and modify custom gradients for lighting effects in Chapter 9

Use new CS4 tools to make instance-based patterns

Make random patterns with the Spray Brush tool

Make decorative patterns with the Deco tool

Discover the Spray Brush tool and the Deco tool in Chapter 5

Anticipation

Overlapping action

character designs © **www.sandrocorsaro.com**

Bounces for head turns

Learn from examples by expert animators in Part III

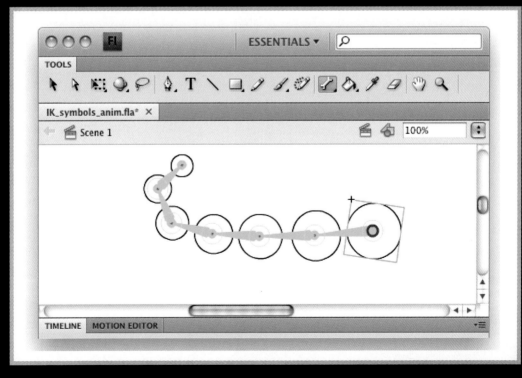

Find coverage of 3D tools in Chapter 11 and IK tools in Chapter 13

Use video as a basis for fluid hand-drawn animation

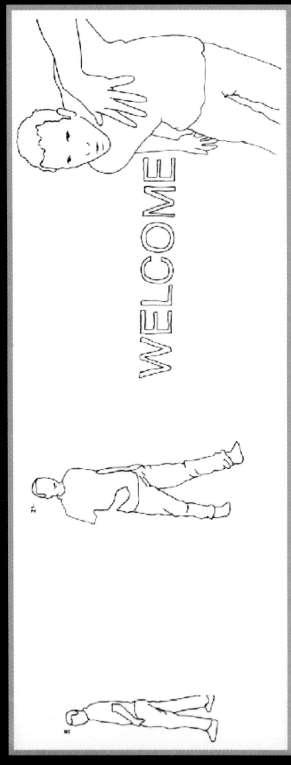

Animator Felix Stumpf explains his technique in Chapter 13

Learn the pros and cons of vector and bitmap graphics

Trace scanned artwork to create more scalable graphics

DIGITAL VIDEO PRODUCTION

■ INTRODUCTION   VIDEO EQUIPMENT   AUDIO EQUIPMENT   EDITING SOFTWARE

Welcome to the Digital Video Production primer. In this presentation, you will learn about the various pieces of equipment and editing tools you will need to create video on your computer.

Video Equipment outlines different classes of camcorders, as well as the basic accessories necessary for acquiring video footage.

Audio Equipment lists various sound recording devices that can enhance the quality of your audio tracks.

Editing Software describes specific applications that can be used to capture, edit and add effects to your

"Making Your First Flash CS4 Project" in Chapter 19

Hello   Hello   Hello

Animate objects in 3D with ActionScript in Chapter 25

Enable high-resolution printing from Flash in Chapter 24

"Using the FLVPlayback Component (AS3)" in Chapter 16

You can also use FLV files with embedded cue points with the ActionScript 2.0 version of the FLVPlayback component.

13. Change the dimensions of the Flash document to 800 x 600 in the Modify ⇨ Document dialog box.

14. **Rename Layer 1 to** fp. On frame 1 of this layer, drag an instance of the FLVPlayback component from the Components panel to the Stage. In the Properties panel, name the instance fp.

15. **In the Parameters tab of the Component Inspector panel, select a skin for the FLVPlayback instance.** For our example, we used the SkinUnderAllNoVolNo CaptionNoFull.swf skin. For the source parameter, browse to the HomeGarden_ 1516K_Cues.flv file created in Step 9.

16. **Create a new layer named** embedField. This layer will be used to hold an embedded font for the video labels. On frame 1 of the embedField layer, use the Text tool to create a dynamic text field offstage, above the Stage area. Type the text **Arial** in the field. In the Properties panel, make sure that the type is set to Dynamic, and name the instance embedField. In the font menu, choose the font face Arial. In the Character section of the Properties panel, click the Character Embedding button, and in the Character Embedding dialog box, select the Uppercase, Lowercase, and Punctuation ranges, as shown in Figure 16.24.

FIGURE 16.24

The Character Embedding dialog box

Next you learn how to use the document class feature for ActionScript 3.0 files in Flash CS4.

17. **Create a new ActionScript file by choosing File ⇨ New and selecting ActionScript File in the Type column of the New Document dialog box.** Save this file as `EmbeddedCues.as`. Instead of putting ActionScript code on the first frame of the `cuepoints_embedded_as3.fla` timeline, you can add ActionScript 3.0 code to a document class file. For this example, the `EmbeddedCues.as` file serves as the document class.

18. **In the `EmbeddedCues.as` file, add the code shown in Listing 16.1.** This script has the following functions:

    ■ `init`: This function is invoked as soon as the Flash movie starts. The `init()` function is called from the constructor function of the `EmbeddedCues` class. The `init()` function creates event listeners for the FLVPlayback instance, `fp`, and creates a new instance of the ActionScript 3.0 `Timer` class, which replaces the functionality provided by the ActionScript 2.0 `setInterval()` function. The `updateTimer` instance is utilized by the `onScrubStart()` and `onScrubFinish()` functions discussed later in this list.

    ■ `onVideoMarker`: This function is used as the listener for the `MetadataEvent.CUE_POINT` event broadcasted by the ActionScript 3.0 version of the FLVPlayback instance, `fp`. The event object (e) passed to this listener contains an `info` property, which represents the data of the embedded cue point (cue). The `label` and `position` values that you assigned to each cue point in the Flash CS4 Video Encoder are available in the `parameters` property of the cue point object (cue). If the cue point's `type` property is `"navigation"`, then the `showLabel()` function is invoked with the `label` and `position` values. If the cue point's `type` property is `"event"`, the `removeLabel()` function is invoked.

    ■ `showLabel`: This function creates a `TextField` object named `labelField`, which is positioned on the movie's Stage according to the `position` value passed by the cue point. A `DropShadow` filter is also created and passed to the `filters` property of the `labelField` instance. The `TextFormat` object, `tf`, specifies the Arial font that was embedded in step 16.

> **CROSS-REF** For more information on `TextFormat` objects, read Chapter 30, "Applying HTML and Text Field Formatting."

    ■ `removeLabel`: This function removes the `labelField` instance from the Stage. Whenever a cue point with a `type` of `"event"` is played, this function is invoked to remove the label from the movie.

    ■ `onScrubStart`: This function is used as a listener of the `VideoEvent.SCRUB_START` event broadcasted by the FLVPlayback instance, `fp`. When the video clip is scrubbed with the seek bar, the `onScrubStart()` function is invoked. Here, the `updateTimer` instance continuously invokes the `updateLabel()` function, discussed later in this list.

- onScrubFinish: This function is used as a listener of the VideoEvent.SCRUB_FINISH event broadcasted by the FLVPlayback instance, fp. When the user releases the mouse button from the seek bar, this function is invoked, stopping the update-Timer instance initiated by the onScrubStart() function.

- updateLabel: This function, invoked as a listener of the updateTimer instance in the init() and onScrubStart() functions, calls the showLabel() function, using label and position data retrieved by the FLVPlayback.findNearestCue Point() method. This method can use the playhead's current time (fp.playhead Time) to return the cue point that is closest to the scrubbing arrow of the seek bar.

19. **After you've added the code to the EmbeddedCues.as file, save the file.**

20. **Go back to the cuepoints_embedded_as3.fla file, and deselect any instances on the Stage.** (You can press the Esc key to deselect any selections.) Open the Properties panel to view the document's properties. In the Document Class field, type **EmbeddedCues**, as shown in Figure 16.25. This name indicates the class file to use for the Flash document. The filename of the ActionScript file is used, without the .as file extension.

21. **Save the Flash document and test it (Ctrl+Enter or ⌘+Enter).** The video clip should automatically play, displaying the plant names on top of the video display area (Figure 16.26). If you drag the playhead of the seek bar, you should still see the names of the plants appear on top of the video.

FIGURE 16.25

The document class field in the Properties panel

FIGURE 16.26

A dynamic text label on top of the video area

> **ON the CD-ROM** You can find the completed file, `cuepoints_embedded_as3.fla`, in the ch16 folder of this book's CD-ROM.

TABLE 16.1

Cue Points for the HomeGarden_Full-Res.avi File

Time	Name	Type	Label	Position
00;00;00;00	plant_001	Navigation	Black-eyed susans	rb
00;00;04;17	exit_001	Event	–	–
00;00;05;01	plant_002	Navigation	Echinacea	rb
00;00;09;24	exit_002	Event	–	–
00;00;10;07	plant_003	Navigation	Dinnerplate dahlia	rt
00;00;14;25	exit_003	Event	–	–
00;00;15;07	plant_004	Navigation	Pumpkin patch	rt
00;00;23;05	exit_004	Event	–	–
00;00;23;12	plant_005	Navigation	Giant pumpkin	lb
00;00;28;06	exit_005	Event	–	–
00;00;28;19	plant_006	Navigation	Huckleberry bush	lt

Time	Name	Type	Label	Position
00;00;33;06	exit_006	Event	–	–
00;00;33;13	plant_007	Navigation	Huckleberries	rt
00;00;38;07	exit_007	Event	–	–
00;00;39;08	plant_008	Navigation	Strawberries	rb
00;00;43;07	exit_008	Event	–	–
00;00;44;03	plant_009	Navigation	White roses	lb
00;00;48;21	exit_009	Event	–	–
00;00;49;03	plant_010	Navigation	Mallow	rb
00;00;56;00	exit_010	Event	–	–
00;00;56;13	plant_011	Navigation	Shrub rose	rt
00;01;01;02	exit_011	Event	–	–
00;01;01;15	plant_012	Navigation	Chocolate mint bush	rb
00;01;05;20	exit_012	Event	–	–

ON the CD-ROM If you don't want to type the code in Listing 16.1, you can find the completed code in the `Listing16.1.as` file or `EmbeddedCues.as` file located in the `ch16` folder of this book's CD-ROM.

LISTING 16.1

The EmbeddedCues Document Class

```
//FLVPlayback fp;

package {

    import flash.display.Sprite;
    import flash.text.TextField;
    import flash.text.TextFormat;
    import flash.text.TextFieldAutoSize;
    import flash.text.AntiAliasType;
    import fl.video.FLVPlayback;
    import fl.video.MetadataEvent;
    import fl.video.VideoEvent;
    import flash.utils.Timer;
    import flash.events.TimerEvent;
```

continued

LISTING 16.1   *(continued)*

```
import flash.filters.DropShadowFilter;

public class EmbeddedCues extends Sprite {

    private var labelField:TextField;
    private var isScrubbing:Boolean = false;
    private var updateTimer:Timer;

    function EmbeddedCues(){
        init();
    }

    private function init():void {
        fp.addEventListener(MetadataEvent.CUE_POINT, onVideoMarker);
        fp.addEventListener(VideoEvent.SCRUB_START, onScrubStart);
        fp.addEventListener(VideoEvent.SCRUB_FINISH, onScrubFinish);

        updateTimer = new Timer(30);
        updateTimer.addEventListener(TimerEvent.TIMER, updateLabel);

    }

    public function onVideoMarker(e:MetadataEvent):void {
        var cue:Object = e.info;
        if(cue.type == "navigation" && cue.parameters.label != null ){
            showLabel(cue.parameters.label, cue.parameters.position);
        } else if(cue.type == "event" && !isScrubbing){
            removeLabel();
        }
    }

    public function onScrubStart(e:VideoEvent):void {
        isScrubbing = true;
        updateTimer.start();
    }

    public function onScrubFinish(e:VideoEvent):void {
        isScrubbing = false;
        updateTimer.stop();
    }

    private function showLabel(label:String, pos:String):void {

        removeLabel();

        var tf:TextFormat = new TextFormat();
        tf.font = "Arial";
        tf.size = 24;
```

```
   tf.color = 0xFFFFFF;

   var ds:DropShadowFilter = new DropShadowFilter();
   ds.blurX = 0;
   ds.blurY = 0;
   ds.distance = 1;

   labelField = new TextField();
   with(labelField){
      width = 30;
      height = 30;
      autoSize = TextFieldAutoSize.LEFT;
      embedFonts = true;
      antiAliasType = AntiAliasType.ADVANCED;
      defaultTextFormat = tf;
      text = label;
      filters = [ds];
   }

   var horiz:String = pos.toLowerCase().substr(0,1);
   var vert:String = pos.toLowerCase().substr(1,1);
   var xPos:Number;
   var yPos:Number;
   if(horiz == "l"){
      xPos= fp.x + 20;
   } else if(horiz == "r"){
      xPos = fp.x + fp.width - 20 - labelField.width;
   }
   labelField.x = xPos;

   if(vert == "t"){
      yPos = fp.y + 10;
   } else if(vert == "b"){
      yPos = fp.y + fp.height - labelField.height - 10;
   }
   labelField.y = yPos;

   addChild(labelField);
}

private function removeLabel():void {
   if(labelField != null){
      removeChild(labelField);
      labelField = null;
   }
}

private function updateLabel(e:TimerEvent):void {
   var cue:Object = fp.findNearestCuePoint(fp.playheadTime);
```

continued

LISTING 16.1 *(continued)*

```
        if(cue.type == "navigation"){
            showLabel(cue.parameters.label, cue.parameters.position);
        }
    }
  }
}
```

Working with Video Alpha Channels

One of the most exciting features of the On2 VP6 codec is its capability to utilize alpha channels within video content. Flash CS4 on its own cannot create a true alpha channel for a video clip: You need to use a dedicated video effects application, such as Adobe After Effects or Adobe Premiere Pro to create a matte for the video track. The process of selecting areas of the video to mask for transparency is known as *keying*. Essentially, you use the video application to select a key color, which is used to create a mask for the video. The accuracy and sharpness of a mask depend on the quality of the keying plug-in. Adobe After Effects offers several keying plug-ins to help you professionally matte your video content.

For the purpose of our coverage in this book, we provide you with the QuickTime .mov files that already have masks created by Adobe After Effects. The general process for keying involves a series of steps:

1. **Acquire video footage.** To successfully mask a subject in the video, you should shoot the subject against an evenly lit green screen or blue screen. You may have seen special effects footage shot on such screens, for action thrillers such as *The Matrix*.

2. **Import the footage into a video effects application.** Using a program such as Adobe After Effects, you can add the footage to a composition. Within the composition, you can add key filters to select the green or blue areas of the content.

3. **Render the footage with an alpha channel.** After you have key filters in place, you can render the footage with an alpha channel. You need to use a video codec that supports alpha channels, such as the Animation codec. In After Effects, make sure you choose RGB + Alpha in the Channels menu of the Video Output settings.

4. **Encode the footage with the On2 VP6 codec.** After you have the rendered QuickTime file, you can process the file with Adobe Media Encoder CS4 or another Flash Video encoding tool. In the Flash Video encoding settings, make sure that you choose the Encode alpha channel check box.

Live action footage

In this section, you learn how to use footage of our dog Stella that was shot against a green screen. The footage already has an alpha channel that was created in Adobe After Effects. You superimpose the footage of Stella on a static .png image imported into a Flash document.

Make a copy of the `stella_alpha.mov` file found in the `resources` folder of this book's CD-ROM.

1. In Flash CS4, open the `live_action_starter.fla` from the `ch16/alpha_live_action` folder of this book's CD-ROM. This file is set to publish for Flash Player 10 compatibility, using ActionScript 3.0. Save the document as `live_action.fla`. This document already has a background .png image on the Stage, as well as a masked image of a branch near the trail.

2. **Make a copy of the `stella_alpha.flv` file from the `ch16/alpha_live_action` folder of this book's CD-ROM.** Move the copy to the same location as the `live_action.fla` file you saved in step 1.

3. **In the Flash document, create a layer named** vid, **and place it between the bg_mask and bg layers.**

4. **Open the Library panel (Ctrl+L or ⌘+L).** Click the options menu of the panel (in the top right corner) and choose New Video. In the Video Properties dialog box, choose Video (ActionScript-controlled) as the Type option (see Figure 16.27). Click OK.

FIGURE 16.27

The Video Properties dialog box

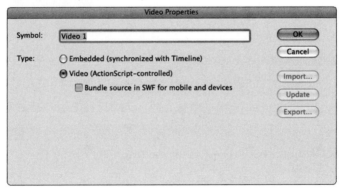

5. **Drag an instance of the new Video symbol from the Library panel on the Stage, at frame 1 of the vid layer.**

6. **Select the new Video instance, and in the Properties panel, name the instance** vid. Set the width to **152** and the height to **180**. Position the X value at **154** and the Y value at **180**. See Figure 16.28.

NOTE The dimension 152 x 180 uses the same aspect ratio as that of the source clip.

FIGURE 16.28

The vid instance

7. **Create a new layer named** actions **and place this layer at the top of the layer stack.**
   Select frame 1 of the actions layer, and open the Actions panel (F9/Option+F9). Add the
   following code. The code creates a new NetStream instance to play the stella_
   alpha.flv file, and attaches the stream to the vid instance.

```
var vid:Video;
var nc:NetConnection = new NetConnection();
nc.connect(null);
var ns:NetStream = new NetStream(nc);
ns.client = this;
ns.play("stella_alpha.flv");
vid.attachNetStream(ns);

function onMetaData(info:Object):void;
```

8. **Save the Flash document and test it (Ctrl+Enter/⌘+Enter).** The footage of Stella
   should be superimposed between the graphic of the branch and the forest background, as
   shown in Figure 16.29.

FIGURE 16.29

The alpha video footage playing on top of the forest background

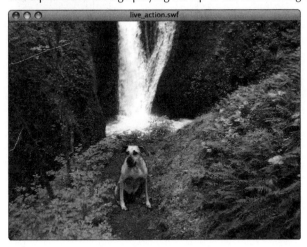

ON the CD-ROM You can find the completed files in the ch16/alpha_live_action folder of this book's CD-ROM. You can also find another alpha video example in the ch16/alpha_3D_model folder of this book's CD-ROM.

WEB RESOURCE We'd like to know what you think about this chapter. Visit www.flashsupport.com/feedback to send us your comments.

Summary

- Flash-compatible video can be deployed as .swf files, .flv, or .f4v files. You can load .flv files from a Web server or stream them from a Flash Media Server or Flash Video Streaming Service provider.

- You can compress source video files in Adobe Media Encoder CS4.

- Flash Player 9.0.115 or later is required for .f4v files using the new AVC/H.264 video codec. Flash Player 8 or later is required for .flv files using the On2 VP6 codec. You can use the Sorenson Spark codec with Flash Video content in Flash Player 6 or later.

- The H.264 and On2 VP6 codecs offer superior compression and image quality compared to Sorenson Spark. However, H.264 and VP6 require more computer processing power and memory.

- The Adobe Media Encoder CS4 application can add embedded cue points to an .flv file. These cue points can be detected in ActionScript.

- The ActionScript 3.0 version of the FLVPlayback component offers you a wide range of control skins and takes the guesswork out of implementing video content with your Flash movies.

- The On2 VP6 codec supports alpha channels within video content. You can create alpha channels in video applications such as Adobe After Effects.

Part V

Adding Basic Interactivity to Flash Movies

So far you've been learning how to make things — drawing shapes, creating symbols, and working with frames and adding special assets. In the next three chapters you learn how to integrate these various elements and how to make things happen. In this edition of the Flash Bible, you learn ActionScript 3.0 from the ground up! Chapter 17 introduces the concepts you need to understand when adding interactivity to presentations. Chapter 17 also gives you an orientation in the Flash CS4 Actions panel. Chapter 18 gives you the skills needed to control playback of multiple timelines. Find out how easy it is to use ActionScript to control the display of internal elements in your Flash movies, including nested Movie Clips. If you want to apply these concepts and techniques to real Flash production, Chapter 19 has just what you need — a step-by-step explanation of how to build a basic Flash presentation with a nonlinear interface. The project implements other important features such as components and accessibility options.

Chapter 17

Understanding Actions and Event Handlers

I nteractivity in a Flash movie can broadly be thought of as the elements that react and respond to a user's activity or input. A user has many ways to give input to a Flash movie, and Flash has even more ways to react. But how does interactivity actually work? It all starts with actions and event handlers.

Actions and Event Handlers

Even the most complex interactivity in Flash is fundamentally composed of two basic parts: the *behavior* (what happens), and the *cause* of the behavior (what makes it happen). Here's a simple example: Suppose you have a looping soundtrack in a movie and a button that, when clicked, turns the soundtrack off. The *behavior* is the sound turning off, and the *cause* of the behavior is the mouse clicking the button. Another example is stopping an animation when it reaches a certain frame on its timeline. When the last keyframe of the animation is played (the *cause*), an action on that keyframe stops the animation (the *behavior*). In Flash, the building blocks of behaviors are referred to as *actions*.

> **NOTE** Flash CS4 features an interactive authoring tool called the Behaviors panel. Our usage of the term *behaviors* in the preceding description should not be confused with this feature. The Behaviors panel can be used only for legacy Flash movies that require ActionScript 2.0. In this edition of the book, we discuss only ActionScript 3.0 code.

The first step in learning how to make interactive movies is becoming familiar with the list of possible actions. However, actions can't act without being told to act *by* something. That something is often the mouse pointer coming

IN THIS CHAPTER

Knowing events and event handlers

Adding interactivity with the Behaviors panel

Understanding Flash actions

Using the Actions panel with Script Assist

Learning your first Flash actions

Executing actions with event handlers

Using getURL

in contact with a button, but it can also be a keystroke, or simply a command issued from a key-frame. We refer to any occurrence that can cause an action to happen (such as the button click in the preceding example) as an *event*. The mechanism you use to tell Flash what action to perform when an event occurs is known as an *event handler*. This cause-and-effect relationship seems obvious, but it is an extremely important concept.

For the purposes of creating basic interactivity, the difference between an action and the cause of an action is merely a practical detail. As the set of Flash actions, collectively known as *ActionScript*, continues to grow with each release of the Flash authoring tool (and, therefore, the interactive capabilities that they provide), understanding the relationship between actions and the things that cause them can be the key to adding more sophisticated behavior to your movies with traditional programming techniques. Every interactive framework, whether it is Adobe Flash or Adobe Director or Apple DVD Studio Pro, has unique handlers for specific events. Table 17.1 relates interactive events with Flash handlers.

NOTE   Any ActionScript covered in this chapter refers to ActionScript 3.0. For any examples in this chapter, make sure you choose Flash File (ActionScript 3.0) from the splash screen when you create a new file.

TABLE 17.1

Events and Flash Handlers

Event	Type	Event Handler	Example
Playback	Time-based	Keyframes MovieClip instance NetStream instance	Timeline plays until it reaches a certain frame; a MovieClip instance monitors the amount of time that has passed in a movie; when a video stream stops playing, another stream begins playback.
Mouse	User input	SimpleButton instance MovieClip instance Sprite instance Mouse class	A visitor clicks a button; mouse movement is detected over a MovieClip instance.
Key press	User input	SimpleButton instance MovieClip instance Keyboard class	A user presses the Enter key to submit a form; an alert appears if the Caps Lock key is enabled.
Window resize	User input	Stage class	A user clicks the maximize button on a Flash projector or Web browser window and Flash elements respond accordingly.
Microphone or webcam activity	Audio/video input	Microphone class Camera class	When a user stops talking into a microphone, a graphic turns red; a stream starts to record audio and video when the movement is detected in front of a webcam.
Data	System-based	URLLoader instance XML instance	Search results appear in the Flash movie when the results have fully loaded.

Although the breadth and depth of ActionScript involved with the interactions described in Table 17.1 may seem overwhelming, don't worry — we're taking it one step at a time. First, you'll learn how to set up the Actions panel, and then we'll look at actions that control movie playback. Later, you'll also learn how to call these actions in various ways with three kinds of event handlers: button manipulation, keyframes, and keystrokes.

What is ActionScript?

Every interactive authoring system uses a language (or code) that enables elements within the system to communicate. Just as there are several languages that people use to speak to one another around the globe, there are hundreds of programming languages in use today. In an effort to make Flash more useable to computer programmers, Flash's scripting language, called ActionScript, strongly resembles JavaScript, a fundamental element for adding advanced interactivity to HTML pages. Right now, we focus on using the most basic Flash ActionScript.

NOTE Since Flash Player 9 and Flash CS3 have been released, you can use a completely revamped version of ActionScript called ActionScript 3.0, or AS3. The new version is more complex than previous versions, but is more maintainable and scalable for Flash projects. ActionScript 3.0 will feel more familiar to developers who have used other object-oriented programming languages such as C++ or Java.

CROSS-REF If you're interested in learning the fundamental building blocks of ActionScript programming, check out our advanced coverage of ActionScript in Chapters 23 – 35. The three chapters of Part V are intended to provide a starting point for Flash designers and developers who are new to Flash actions and interactive concepts. Some chapters in Part VII and IX of this book cover specific aspects of ActionScript 3.0. For more expanded coverage of ActionScript 3.0, refer to *ActionScript 3.0 Bible* (Wiley, 2008).

Navigating the Actions panel

Flash CS4 has a specific interface element that enables you to add interactive commands to Flash movies — the Actions panel. You don't use menus or wizards to add interactive functionality — you type the ActionScript code describing the interactivity in (or out of) the Actions panel. You can open the Actions panel in a number of ways:

- Go to Window ➪ Actions.
- Press the F9 key/Option+F9.
- Click the ActionScript icon button at the top right corner of the Properties panel.
- Alt+double-click/Option+double-click a keyframe in the Timeline window.

If you have a keyframe selected in the Timeline window, the Actions panel will be titled Actions – Frame (see Figure 17.1). If you have a Movie Clip symbol instance selected on the Stage, you'll see the name Actions – Movie Clip. If you have a button symbol instance selected on the Stage, the Actions panel will be titled Actions – Button. If you have a component selected, the Actions panel will read Actions – Component. Don't be confused — there is only one Actions panel. Flash CS4 simply lets you know the object to which you are assigning actions.

TIP   The Actions panel in Flash CS4 features a Script Assist mode. Script Assist enables you to code ActionScript by selecting actions and filling in parameters, instead of writing out all the code by hand. If you used Normal mode in Flash MX or earlier, you'll be happy to know that Normal mode is essentially reintegrated as Script Assist in Flash CS4.

As shown in Figure 17.1, the Actions panel in Flash CS4 has three distinct areas (counterclockwise from the left): the Actions toolbox, the Script navigator, and the Script pane. The Script Assist area is available within the Script pane. There are two auto-snap dividers, one dividing the Actions toolbox and Script navigator from the Script pane, and another subdividing the Actions toolbox and Script navigator. You may want to practice opening and closing these dividers, as well as dragging each to your preferred width and height, respectively. Figures 17.1 and 17.2 show a breakdown of the Actions panel in Flash CS4. The following list details the three areas:

FIGURE 17.1

The Actions panel enables you to instantly add, delete, or change Flash movie commands.

- The Actions toolbox contains several nested booklets of ActionScript commands. You can select actions to add to the Script pane. The booklets that appear default to the version of ActionScript that your Flash document specifies in the Flash tab of the Publish Settings dialog box (File ➪ Publish Settings).

TIP The Actions toolbox has a booklet selection drop-down menu. The default set of booklets appearing in the toolbox pertain to ActionScript 1.0, 2.0, and 3.0, but you can switch to other sets of booklets, including various versions of Flash Lite. Each Flash Lite booklet displays only actions compatible with the Flash Lite players that ship on mobile devices and phones.

- The Script navigator can jump to any script within your Flash document. When you select a keyframe or object in this pane, any code attached to the item appears in the Script pane.

TIP The Script navigator shows the actions for the entire document, not just for the current timeline.

- The Script pane displays the current code for an item selected on the Stage, a keyframe selected in the Timeline window, or an item selected in the Script navigator. You can type, copy, cut, and paste code into the Script pane, as long as you are not working in Script Assist mode. An options bar is located at the top of the Script pane as well. The options bar contains several buttons to modify, search, debug, or format your code in the Script pane. You can also find most of these options in the panel's options menu, located in the top right corner of the panel.

TIP You can click the pin icon at the bottom tab of the script in the Script pane. You can pin multiple scripts in the Script pane, and quickly tab between them.

- The Script Assist area within the Script pane enables you to visualize your code with contextual parameters, as fill-in text fields or drop-down menus, as shown in Figure 17.2. The Script Assist mode is most useful for beginners learning ActionScript for the first time. To enter Script Assist mode, click the Script Assist button on the options bar of the Script pane. Not all actions have the same ease of use within Script Assist; more complex ActionScript code is not well suited for Script Assist mode. When Script Assist mode is enabled, you cannot edit code manually within the Script pane, and you cannot switch the active booklet set.

You can add actions to the Script pane in one of three ways:

- Drag an action from the Actions toolbox to the Script pane.
- Select an action from the Actions menu, accessed by clicking the plus (+) icon.
- Double-click an action in the Actions pane.

FIGURE 17.2

The Script Assist mode displays a more user-friendly interface for controlling action parameters.

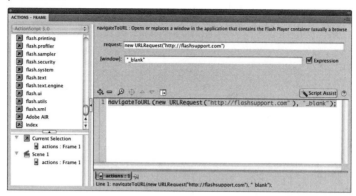

To delete actions, select the action line(s) in the Script pane, and press Delete or Backspace on the keyboard.

After you have added an action to the Script pane, you can specify parameters (or arguments) for the action. Depending on the action, you may or may not need to type such parameters. By default, Flash CS4 provides code hints as you type actions into the Script pane. The Show Code Hint button enables you to see the parameters for an action, as shown in the `navigateToURL` action in Figure 17.1.

More important, the Script Assist mode makes it much easier for you to add and adjust settings for basic actions, especially those you find in the Timeline Control booklet. You use the Script Assist mode throughout this chapter to learn the basic control actions.

NOTE The Script Assist mode is much more useful for legacy ActionScript 1.0 and 2.0 syntax. For ActionScript 3.0 syntax, most actions have limited options revealed in Script Assist mode.

You should get in the habit of clicking the Check Syntax button (the blue check mark) to make sure you didn't mistype an action. If you have an error, the Output panel displays some information related to the error, indicating the line number where the syntax error occurs.

CROSS-REF In Chapter 23, "Knowing the Nuts and Bolts of Code," you can also learn about referencing actions in the Help panel of Flash CS4.

A brief primer on code syntax

Some of the most difficult concepts for beginners to understand with code writing are white space, parentheses (( )), semicolons (;), and curly braces ({ }). In the following paragraphs, you learn how each of these affects your ActionScript code.

White space

White space is a collective term referring to any blank areas between lines of code. It includes spaces inserted by the spacebar, indentations inserted with the Tab key, and line returns inserted with the Enter or Return key. When Flash CS4 compiles your ActionScript code into the Flash movie, the white space between your lines of code usually does not generate any errors. For example, the following code works exactly the same:

```
navigateToURL(new URLRequest("http://flashsupport.com"));
```

or

```
navigateToURL(new URLRequest(
        "http://flashsupport.com"
        )
    );
```

or

```
navigateToURL(  new URLRequest(  "http://flashsupport.com"  )  );
```

However, white space is an issue when it separates the key terms in the action, such as:

```
navigate To URL(new URL Request("http://flashsupport.com"));
```

The spaces between `navigate`, `To`, and `URL` will cause an error when Flash CS4 tries to create the Flash movie.

 To check if your syntax is correct, click the Check Syntax button in the Actions panel. If you do have any white space errors, the Output panel displays information related to the error. Also, if your code has errors, you are prevented from entering the Script Assist mode.

Parentheses

Many, but not all, actions require parentheses after the action term, such as `SoundMixer.stopAll()`, `navigateToURL()`, or even `play()`. A general rule to remember is that if the action requires a parameter, such as `navigateToURL()`, then parentheses are required as well.

NOTE **Parameters are also referred to as arguments.**

However, many actions, such as `play()` and `stop()`, still require parentheses, even though they do not use any arguments. Another rule for parentheses is that any open parenthesis (( ) must eventually be followed by a closing parenthesis ( )). A habit we like to encourage is counting the number of opening parentheses in a script and then counting the number of closing parentheses. If the numbers don't match, you need to review your code to find the place where you forgot to include a parenthesis.

Deprecated and Incompatible Actions: What Are They?

As the ActionScript language of Flash continues to expand and encompass new functionality, older actions coexist with newer and better actions (or methods, properties, event handlers, and functions, which we discuss later). Although Flash Player 10 continues to support ActionScript 2.0 and earlier actions, it's better not to use older actions if the newest version of the Flash Player has a new way of accomplishing the same task. Older actions that have been replaced with a new action (or new way to perform the same task) are called *deprecated actions*. If you switch the Actions toolbox to ActionScript 1.0 & 2.0, the Actions panel in Flash CS4 houses all deprecated actions in the Deprecated booklet of the Actions pane. Why shouldn't you use these actions? As you'll see in more advanced scripting, ActionScript 2.0 and 3.0 have specific syntax to target Movie Clips and determine whether certain frames have loaded, among other features of the ActionScript "dot syntax" language.

Although you should avoid actions that are highlighted in the Deprecated booklet if possible, Flash Player 10 continues to support them if you're publishing with ActionScript 1.0 or 2.0.

Flash CS4 also lets you know if certain actions are not supported with the Player version that is selected in the Flash format tab of the Publish Settings dialog box (File ➪ Publish Settings). Note that you can also find the Player version setting in the Properties panel when you click an empty area of the Stage or the work area. If an action is not supported by the version you have selected, the action is highlighted in yellow. The following figure shows this type of highlighting in the Actions panel. Notice that the tooltip (or rollover description) indicates which version of the Flash Player supports the action.

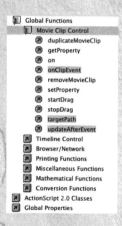

Flash Player 4 (or earlier) and Flash Lite 1.0/1.1 do not support the onClipEvent or update AfterEvent actions (among others) because these actions were introduced in Flash Player 5.

Semicolons and curly braces

You've probably already noticed that most actions include a semicolon (;) at the end of the code line. In practice, many coders forget to include semicolons. Usually, Flash is very forgiving if you omit semicolons, but by no means should you be encouraged to omit them. The general rule for semicolons and curly braces is mutually inclusive: If your action doesn't end with a closing curly brace (}), it should end with a semicolon. As with parentheses, all opening curly braces must eventually be followed by a closing curly brace (}). Curly braces are commonly used with `if` and `function` declarations.

CROSS-REF You'll learn more about `if` statements and functions in Part VII, "Approaching ActionScript."

Your First Five Actions

Now that you have a general picture of what actions do, let's look at five common actions in detail. At this point, we're describing only the functionality of each action, not how to add an action to your movie. We provide information on adding an action in the next section, "Making Actions Happen with Event Handlers."

CROSS-REF You will find coverage of further actions in later chapters.

Actions in the Flash interface appear alphabetically sorted from top to bottom. In the following sections, complementary actions are grouped together.

gotoAndPlay() and gotoAndStop()

These "go to" actions change the current frame of the movie to the target frame specified as the action's parameter. There are two variations:

- `gotoAndPlay()`: Changes the current frame to the frame specified, and then executes a `play()` action. `gotoAndPlay()` provides the capability to show animated sequences as preludes to individual content areas. `gotoAndPlay()` also gets frequent use in choose-your-own-adventure style animations, in which the user guides an animated character through different paths in a narrative.

NOTE If you use a `gotoAndPlay()` action to go to a frame that has a `stop()` action, the timeline stops at the new frame.

- `gotoAndStop()`: Changes the current frame to the frame specified and then halts playback on that frame. `gotoAndStop()` is often used to produce toolbar-style interfaces where the user clicks buttons to view different areas of content in a movie.

Both actions enable you to jump to certain areas of the Flash movie. The parameters of these actions start with the largest time unit, the scene, and end with the smallest one, the frame.

You can specify frames in other scenes as the target of goto actions with the scene parameter. As shown in the following code, you type the name of the scene first, with double quotes around the name, and then the frame number (without quotes) or frame label. In this example, "Scene 2" is the name of the scene and "animate_in" is the frame label in that scene to jump to.

```
gotoAndPlay("Scene 2", "animate_in");
```

However, if you specify only one parameter in a gotoAndPlay or gotoAndStop action, the parameter is interpreted as a frame label. For example, the following code tells the current timeline to jump to its "menu" frame label:

```
gotoAndStop("menu");
```

CAUTION   Scenes are largely a deprecated structure for Flash content. Although you may be tempted to create multiple scenes, we highly discourage the practice. Usually, if you're inclined to create a new scene, your document is getting too big. You should make a new Flash document whose Flash movie is loaded at runtime into your primary Flash movie. You learn how to load SWF files in Chapter 28, "Sharing and Loading Assets."

There are three methods of specifying the frame to which the movie should go when it receives a goto action. The methods for specifying the frame are

- **number:** Specifies the target frame as a number. Frame 1 is the beginning of the movie or scene. Frame numbers should not use surrounding quotes, as frame labels do. The following action tells the current timeline to jump to frame 10 and start playing:

```
gotoAndPlay(10);
```

- **label:** Individual keyframes can be given names via the Label section's Name field in the Properties panel. After a frame is labeled, a goto action can target it by name. To specify a label as the target of a goto action, type the name of the frame as the action's parameter. The following example tells the Flash movie to go to the frame labeled "products" and stop at that frame.

```
gotoAndStop("products");
```

- **ActionScript expression:** Specifies the target frame as an interpreted ActionScript code segment. You use expressions to dynamically assign targets of goto actions. Here's a quick example of a string variable being used as a frame label:

```
var targetLabel = "products";
gotoAndPlay(targetLabel);
```

Notice that the term targetLabel does not use quotes because it is not the actual frame label name. When the Flash Player interprets this action, it looks up the value of targetLabel, which is "products", and inserts that value into the gotoAndPlay action. With strict data typing in ActionScript 3.0, the same action looks like this:

```
var targetLabel:String = "products";
gotoAndPlay(targetLabel);
```

CROSS-REF   Expressions are covered in Chapter 23, "Knowing the Nuts and Bolts of Code."

CAUTION Using frame numbers to specify the targets of goto actions can lead to serious scalability problems in Flash movies. Adding frames at the beginning or in the middle of a movie's timeline causes the subsequent frames to be renumbered. When those frames are renumbered, all goto actions that use frame numbers must be revised to point to the correct new number of their target frames.

In the vast majority of cases, goto actions that use a frame label to specify target frames are preferable to goto actions that use a frame number to specify target frames. Unlike numbered frame targets, goto actions with labeled frame targets continue to function properly, even if the targeted frame changes position on the timeline.

nextFrame() and prevFrame()

The nextFrame() and prevFrame() actions act like a gotoAndStop() action, in that they both transport the timeline to a new position and stop.

- nextFrame(): This action tells the current timeline to move forward one frame and stop playback. nextFrame() can be used in conjunction with prevFrame to quickly set up a slideshow-style walk-through of content, where each of a series of contiguous keyframes contains the content of one "slide." This action does not use any parameters. The following code moves the timeline to the next frame:

  ```
  nextFrame();
  ```

- prevFrame(): This action moves the current timeline backward one frame and stops playback. For example, if the timeline is on frame 20, and the movie runs a prev Frame() action, the timeline moves to frame 19. As with the nextFrame() action, prevFrame() does not use any parameters:

  ```
  prevFrame();
  ```

nextScene() and prevScene()

These actions advance the Flash movie to a new scene. Here's how they work:

- nextScene(): This action tells the current timeline to move to the first frame of the next scene. You can use nextScene() for more elaborate slide shows or demonstration movies, where each scene contains animated content with a stop action on the last frame. The last frame of the scene then contains a button using the nextScene() action. This action does not use any parameters. The following code tells the movie to jump to the next scene:

  ```
  nextScene();
  ```

- prevScene(): This action jumps the movie to the previous scene. For example, if the playhead is in Scene 2, the timeline moves to the first frame of Scene 1. As with the nextScene() action, prevScene() does not use any parameters:

  ```
  prevFrame();
  ```

NOTE   The nextScene() and prevScene() actions do not automatically recycle the scenes when the last or first scene is reached, respectively. For example, if you have three scenes and use a nextScene() action while the movie is on the last scene, the movie does not jump back to the first scene.

CAUTION   As we mention earlier, you should avoid the use of multiple scenes in your Flash document. Although you may find it simpler to segment your Flash content across several scenes as you begin to learn Flash, most seasoned Flash designers and developers use only one scene, and separate content across several Movie Clip symbols placed on one or more frames of Scene 1. Scenes are not compatible with standard targeting syntax, as you'll learn in the next chapter.

play() and stop()

These simple actions are the true foundations of Flash timeline control. play() sets a movie or a Movie Clip instance in motion. When a play() action is executed, Flash starts the sequential display of each frame's contents along the current timeline.

The rate at which the frames appear is measured as frames per second, or fps. The fps rate can be set from 0.01 to 120 (meaning that the play action can cause the display of as little as 1 frame every 100 seconds to as many as 120 frames in 1 second, subject to the limitations of the computer's processing speed). In Flash CS4, the default fps is 24.

NEW FEATURE   Flash CS4 uses a default frame rate of 24 fps. Previous versions of the Flash authoring tool used 12 fps. 24 fps is much more commonly used for Flash and Flex projects in real-world application development. Some animated content may perform better at a slower frame rate such as 12 fps, especially for deployment to slower devices such as mobile phones.

After play() has started, frames continue to appear one after the other, until another action interrupts the flow, or the end of the movie or Movie Clip's timeline is reached. If the end of a movie's timeline is reached, the movie either loops (begins playing again at frame 1, Scene 1) or stops on the last frame.

After the end of the Movie Clip's timeline is reached, playback loops back to the beginning of the clip, and the clip continues playing. To prevent looping, add a stop() action to the last frame of your Movie Clip.

NOTE   A single play() action affects only a single timeline, whether that timeline is the main movie timeline or the timeline of a Movie Clip instance. For example, a play action executed inside a Movie Clip does not cause the Main Timeline to begin playing. Likewise, any goto action on the Main Timeline doesn't migrate to the Movie Clips that reside there. A timeline must be specifically targeted to control playback along that timeline. If there is no specified target, the action is referring to its own timeline. However, this is not the case for animations within graphic symbol instances. An animation in a graphic symbol is controlled by actions on the timeline in which the symbol instance is present — Flash ignores actions on a graphic symbol's timeline.

The `stop()` action, as you may have guessed, halts the progression of a movie or Movie Clip that is in a play state. `stop()` is often used with buttons for user-controlled playback of a movie, or on frames to end an animated sequence.

> **TIP** Movie Clip instances placed on any timeline begin to play automatically. Remember to add a `stop()` action on the first frame of a Movie Clip if you don't want it to play right away.

navigateToURL()

Want to link to a Web resource from a Flash movie? No problem. That's what `navigate-ToURL()` is for. For ActionScript 3.0, you can find the `navigateToURL()` action in the flash.net ⇨ Methods booklet of the Actions panel. `navigateToURL()` is simply Flash's method of making a conventional hypertext link. It's nearly the equivalent of an anchor tag in HTML (`<a href="...">`), except that Flash's `navigateToURL()` can also send variables for form submission. `navigateToURL()` can be used to link to a standard Web page, an FTP site, another Flash movie, an executable, a server-side script, or anything that exists on the Internet or on an accessible local file system.

> **CAUTION** The `navigateToURL()` action can be used only with ActionScript 3.0 content. If you need to publish legacy ActionScript 1.0 and 2.0 content, use the `getURL()` action.

`navigateToURL()` has two parameters that are familiar to Web designers and developers (the first one, `url`, is required for this action to work):

- `URLRequest`: This is the network address of the page, file, script, or resource to which you are linking, formatted within a `URLRequest` wrapper. Any value is permitted (including ActionScript expressions), but the linked item can be displayed only if the reference to it is correct. The `URLRequest` value is directly analogous to the `HREF` attribute of an HTML anchor tag. You can use a relative or absolute URL as well. Examples:

```
http://www.yoursite.com/
ftp://ftp.yoursite.com/pub/documents.zip
menu.html
/cgi-bin/processform.cgi
    /script/form.cfm
```

> **TIP** You can specify secure domain URLs by using the `https` protocol for SSL (Secure Sockets Layer) connections.

- `window`: This is the name of the frame or window in which you want to load the resource specified in the url setting. The `window` parameter is directly analogous to the `target` attribute of an HTML anchor tag. In addition to enabling the entry of custom frame and window names, the `window` parameter can use the following browser-standard target names:

- ■ "_self": Loads the URL into the same frame or window as the current movie. If you do not specify a window parameter in the getURL action, this behavior is the default.

- ■ "_blank": Creates a new browser window and loads the URL into it.

- ■ "_parent": Removes the current frameset and loads the URL in its place. Use this option if you have multiple nested framesets, and you want your linked URL to replace only the frameset in which your movie resides.

- ■ "_top": Loads the URL into the current browser and removes all framesets in the process. Use this option if your movie is in a frame, but you want your linked URL to be loaded normally into the browser, outside the confines of any frames.

NOTE   Frame windows and/or JavaScript windows can be assigned names. You can target these names by manually typing the name in the Window field. For example, if you had a frame defined as <frame name="main". . .>, you could load specific URLs into a frame named main from a Flash movie.

TIP   The navigateToURL() action works in the Test Movie environment. Both the Flash stand-alone player and the Test Movie command give you access to external and/or local URLs.

Here are some examples of how you can write a navigateToURL() action. The following code tells the browser to load the URL www.wiley.com into the current browser window:

```
navigateToURL(new URLRequest("http://www.wiley.com"));
```

Alternatively, you can specify a unique target for the loaded URL. The following example loads an HTML document named menu.html into a frame named menu_frame:

```
navigateToURL(new URLRequest("menu.html"), "menu_frame");
```

A more advanced usage of the navigateToURL() action sends variables from the Flash movie to a Web server's script, which is set up to receive the variables. The following code opens a Google. com search results page for the term "Flash Video":

```
var googleURL = new URLRequest("http://google.com/search");
    var searchData = new URLVariables();
    searchData.hl = "en";
    searchData.q = "Flash Video";
    googleURL.data = searchData;
    navigateToURL(googleURL, "_blank");
```

As we mention with the goto actions, you can also use expressions with navigateToURL() actions. Expressions can be used as parameters of any ActionScript action. The following example uses a string variable to specify the URL used by a navigateToURL() action:

```
var siteURL = new URLRequest("http://www.flashsupport.com");
navigateToURL(siteURL);
```

You should start familiarizing yourself with the ActionScript notation that Flash uses for each action (see Table 17.2). As you use Flash for more advanced interactivity, you'll need to have a firm grasp of code notation. Part VII, "Approaching ActionScript," teaches you how to start building more advanced code.

TABLE 17.2

Common Actions and ActionScript Notation

Action	ActionScript Notation	Arguments
gotoAndStop	gotoAndStop(arguments);	Scene name (frame Label, number, or expression)
gotoAndPlay	gotoAndPlay(arguments);	Scene name (frame label, number, or expression)
nextFrame	nextFrame();	None
prevFrame	prevFrame();	None
nextScene	nextScene();	None
prevScene	prevScene();	None
play	play();	None
stop	stop();	None
navigateToURL	navigateToURL(arguments);	URLRequest instance, target frame, or window

Making Actions Happen with Event Handlers

The ten common actions we discuss in the previous sections provide many of the behaviors that you need to make an interesting interactive Flash movie. But those actions can't make your movies interactive on their own. They need to be told when to happen. To tell a Flash movie when an action should occur, you need event handlers. Event handlers specify the condition(s) under which an action can be made to happen. For example, you might want to mouse-click a button to initiate a play() action, or you might want a movie to stop when a certain keyframe in the timeline is reached. Creating interactivity in your movies is simply a matter of deciding what event you want to detect (mouse-click, keystroke, and so on), adding the appropriate event handler to detect it, and specifying the action(s) that should be performed when it happens.

Before we describe each event handler in detail, in the next section we show you an example of exactly how an event handler merges with an action to form a functioning interactive button.

Combining an action with an event handler to make a functioning button

Imagine that you have a short, endlessly looping movie in which a wire-frame cube rotates. Now imagine that you want to add a button to your movie that, when clicked, stops the cube from rotating by stopping the playback of the looping movie. Here's what you need to do:

ON the CD-ROM For this exercise, you can use the `rotatingCube.fla` file located in the `ch17` folder on this book's CD-ROM. The finished file is named `rotatingCube_complete.fla`.

1. **Open the starter Flash document,** `rotatingCube.fla`. Save this document as `rotatingCube_complete.fla` on your local hard drive.

2. **Make a new layer called** button.

3. **Place a button on the button layer.** You can use Flash CS4's sample Stop button found in the classic buttons ⇨ Circle Buttons folder of the Buttons library (Window ⇨ Common Libraries ⇨ Buttons). See Figure 17.3 to see this button's placement on the Stage.

TIP Selecting buttons and editing button properties sometimes can be tricky if buttons are enabled in the Flash authoring environment. For easier button manipulation, disable buttons by unchecking Enable Simple Buttons under the Control menu.

FIGURE 17.3

The Stop button on the Stage

4. **Select the button instance, and open the Properties panel.** Name the instance **stop-Button**. Button symbol instances must be named to be accessible by ActionScript.

5. **With the** `stopButton` **instance selected, open the Actions panel (F9/Option+F9).** Add the following code to the Script pane. This code enables a function named `onButtonClick()` to respond when the stopButton instance is clicked. The `MouseEvent.CLICK` constant represents the word `"click"`. You learn about more `MouseEvent` constants later in this chapter.

```
stopButton.addEventListener(MouseEvent.CLICK, onButtonClick);

function onButtonClick(evt){
    stop();
}
```

NOTE In computer programming, a constant is a reserved word with a predefined value.

6. Now that you have a button in your Flash movie that stops the movie's playback when it is clicked, save your Flash document (.fla), and test the movie by choosing Control ⇨ **Test Movie.** When you click the button, the rotating cube animation should stop.

To make any interactivity in your movies, you simply have to apply the basic principles you used to make the stop button: Decide which action (or actions) you want to happen, and indicate when you want that action to happen with an event handler. Let's look now at more event handlers you can use to make those actions happen.

The Flash event handlers

Three primary event handlers exist in Flash: those that detect mouse activity on button symbol instances (button manipulation), those that recognize when a key is pressed on the keyboard (key presses), and those that respond to the progression of the timeline (keyframes).

Working with mouse events and buttons

Event handlers that occur based on the user's interaction with a button rely entirely on the location and movement of the mouse pointer. If the mouse pointer comes in contact with a button symbol's hit area, the pointer changes from an arrow icon to a finger pointer icon. At that time the mouse is described as "over" the button. If the mouse pointer is not over a button, it is said to be *out* or *outside* of the button. General movement of the mouse *without* the mouse button depressed is referred to as *rolling*. General movement of the mouse *with* the mouse button pressed is referred to as *dragging*.

CROSS-REF If you don't know how to make a button symbol and its various states, read Chapter 6, "Symbols, Instances, and the Library."

CAUTION Event handlers and actions for buttons can be placed only on button *instances*, not on the four frames in the timeline of the original button symbol. One of the features in Flash CS4 is that it does not enable you to place *any* actions in a button symbol timeline.

Here are the mouse-based events for Flash display objects that use the `addEventListener()` method. Each of these events is case-sensitive when typed in ActionScript 3.0 code.

MouseEvent.MOUSE_DOWN

A single mouse-click can actually be divided into two separate components: the downstroke (the *press*) and the upstroke (the *release*). A `MouseEvent.MOUSE_DOWN` event occurs when the mouse pointer is over the hit area of a button *and* the downstroke of a mouse-click is detected. This event is best used for control panel–style buttons, especially toggle switches.

> **CAUTION**   Typically, developers should program reversible decisions for primary navigation so that users can abort their clicks by rolling the cursor away from the hit area before releasing the mouse. For example, a user might click a button for more information and decide he or she would rather not get that information. We do not recommend using the `MouseEvent.MOUSE_DOWN` event for important user moves such as these because it does not give users an opportunity to abort their moves.

MouseEvent.MOUSE_UP and MouseEvent.CLICK

These events occur when the mouse pointer is over the hit area of a button *and* both the downstroke and the upstroke of a mouse-click are detected. The `MouseEvent.CLICK` event is the standard button-click event.

> **TIP**   If you use the Track as Menu Item behavior for a button instance in the Properties panel, a button responds to a `MouseEvent.MOUSE_UP` event over its Hit state even if the mouse was pressed outside of the button's hit area.

MouseEvent.ROLL_OVER

This event occurs when the mouse pointer moves onto the hit area of a button without the mouse button depressed.

> **NOTE**   To perform standard rollover button effects, such as graphic art changes or sound events, you can insert graphics and sound on to the Over state of the button symbol timeline. It's common practice, however, to create Movie Clip instances that use mouse event handlers for specialized rollover effects. You learn more about this advanced usage of Movie Clips in Chapter 24, "Controlling Movie Clips." You can also find a bonus file demonstrating Movie Clip–based rollovers at www.flashsupport.com/bonus/button_transition/ button_anim_as3.html.

MouseEvent.ROLL_OUT

This event occurs when the mouse pointer moves off of the hit area of a button without the mouse button depressed. This event is commonly used for switching an advanced button's graphic state back to its original state when the user rolls off the button.

Capturing time events with keyframes

The keyframe event handler depends on the playback of the movie itself, not on the user. Just about any action can be attached to any keyframe on the timeline. An action attached to a keyframe is executed when the playhead enters the keyframe, whether it enters naturally during the linear playback of the movie or as the result of a `goto` action. So, for example, you may place a `stop` action on a keyframe to pause the movie at the end of an animation sequence.

NOTE In ActionScript 3.0 code, button handlers can be defined in keyframes, but the code referenced by a button handler does not execute when the playhead enters the frame where that code exists.

In some multimedia applications, keyframe event handlers can differentiate between the playhead *entering* a keyframe and *exiting* a keyframe. Flash has only one kind of keyframe event handler (essentially, on enter). Hence, as a developer, you do not need to add keyframe event handlers explicitly — they are a presumed element of any action placed on a keyframe. As we mention in an earlier note, ActionScript 3.0 can employ a more advanced event model. You learn about different event models in Chapter 24, "Controlling Movie Clips."

TIP Complex movies can have dozens, or hundreds (or even thousands!), of actions attached to keyframes. To prevent conflicts between uses of keyframes for animation and uses of keyframes as action containers, it is highly advisable to create an entire layer solely for action keyframes. Name the layer actions and keep it on top of all your layers for easy access. Remember not to place any symbol instances, text, or artwork on your actions layer. You can also create a labels layer to hold — you guessed it — frame labels.

The process for adding an action to a keyframe is as follows:

1. **Create a keyframe on a timeline.** This keyframe can exist in the Main Timeline (that is, Scene 1) or a Movie Clip symbol timeline.

2. **Select the keyframe in the Timeline window, and open the Actions panel.** The Actions panel title should read Actions – Frame.

3. **Type your desired actions in the Script pane.**

In the next section, you get a little more hands-on experience adding actions to both buttons and keyframes.

Creating Invisible Buttons and Using getURL

In this section, you learn how to create an "invisible button" and practice the use of `navigate-ToURL()` actions. An invisible button is essentially a button symbol that has only a Hit state defined, with empty Up, Over, and Down states. After you create an invisible button, you can use it to convert any type of Flash element into a button. By dragging an instance of the invisible button on top of another piece of artwork or symbol instance on the Stage, you can add interactivity to that element.

ON the CD-ROM Make a copy of the `themakers_ad_starter.fla` file, located in the **ch17** folder of the book's CD-ROM. This file contains a sample layout of graphics and text for a mock Flash ad, sized for display on a Microsoft Windows Mobile 6 device screen.

With the starter Flash document (.fla) open in Flash CS4, quickly familiarize yourself with the existing content. There are four layers on the Main Timeline (Scene 1). The comments layer indicates what the Flash document is, the border layer contains a black outlined box with no fill, the graphics layer contains a graphic symbol of branding artwork, and the animText layer contains a Movie Clip instance featuring a tweened animation. Go ahead and test this movie (Control ➪ Test Movie) to see how these elements currently play. When the animation finishes, you should see the artwork shown in Figure 17.4.

FIGURE 17.4

The artwork of the Flash movie designed for a Windows Mobile screen

In this exercise, you're going to add two invisible buttons to this movie. One is an oval-shaped button that fits over the thumbprint graphic, and another is a rectangular-shaped button that fits over the company's name. The thumbprint button, when clicked, opens the e-mail client to send an e-mail to the company. When the user clicks the name button, a new browser window opens displaying the company's Web page.

1. **In the starter Flash document, create a new layer named** actions. Place this layer just underneath the comments layer.

2. **Save the starter document as** makers_ad.fla. Currently, there is more than one frame on the Main Timeline, and if you were to develop this Flash movie further, you wouldn't want the playhead going past the first frame without some input from the user.

3. **Select the first frame of this layer and open the Actions panel (F9,/Option+F9), and type the following code in the Script pane:**

```
stop();
```

4. **With this first frame of the actions layer still selected, open the Properties panel and in the Label section's Name field, type** //stop. This adds a frame comment of //stop to the layer in the Timeline window. This comment provides a quick visual cue about the behavior of this keyframe. Now you're going to make your first invisible button.

5. **Choose Insert ➪ New Symbol (Ctrl+F8/⌘+F8) and make a new button symbol named** invisibleButton_rect. This button will be the rectangular button that is placed over the company's name. Flash takes you right inside the symbol's workspace as soon as you click the OK button in the Create New Symbol dialog box.

6. **Rename Layer 1 to** hit area graphic. On this layer of the button symbol's timeline, create a keyframe for the Hit state. Move the playhead in the Timeline window to this new keyframe.

7. **Select the Rectangle tool, and draw a uniform square on the symbol's Stage.** The square can be any color, although we prefer red for invisible buttons. If you drew the shape with a stroke, delete the stroke. Select the square, and in the Properties panel, give the square a width and height of **50** pixels. Then using the Align panel, center the square on the Stage. Your button symbol and timeline should now resemble Figure 17.5.

FIGURE 17.5

The square acts as the active area of the button symbol.

8. **Now, go back to Scene 1 (the Main Timeline), and create a new layer.** Rename this layer **linkButton**, and place it above the graphics layer.

9. **Open the Library panel (Ctrl+L/⌘+L), and drag an instance of the** `invisibleButton_rect` **symbol to the Stage.** Place this instance over the company's name. In the Properties panel, name this instance **linkButton**.

10. **Using the Free Transform tool, size the instance to fit the size of the text, without overlapping other elements on the Stage, as shown in Figure 17.6.**

FIGURE 17.6

The linkButton instance resized over the company's name

11. **With the Selection tool, select frame 1 of the actions layer, and open the Actions panel (F9/Option+F9).** Your Action panel title bar should read Actions - Button. In the Script pane, add a button listener for the `MouseEvent.CLICK` event, directing the Web browser to a new Web page when the `linkButton` instance is clicked. Add the following code below the existing `stop();` action:

```
linkButton.addEventListener(MouseEvent.CLICK, onLinkClick);

function onLinkClick (evt) {
    var siteURL = new URLRequest("http://www.theMakers.com");
    navigateToURL(siteURL, "_blank");
}
```

For this example, we used the URL http://www.theMakers.com. When you're link-ing to domain names, make sure that you specify the transfer protocol (such as http://, ftp://, and so on). If you are linking to relative URLs, specify the name of the HTML document (or other resource) that you want to access. This onLinkClick() handler containing the navigateToURL() action directs a button click on this instance to [theMAKERS] Web site, in a new browser window.

12. **Save your Flash document, and test it by using Control ⇨ Test Movie (Ctrl+Enter/ ⌘+Enter).** In the Test Movie window, roll over the company's name in the Flash movie. Notice that this area is an active button. When you click the button, a new browser win-dow opens, displaying the company's Web page.

13. **Now, go back to the Flash document and add another invisible button.** You'll use a different procedure this time. On the Scene 1 timeline, create a new layer and name it **emailButton**. Place this layer above the linkButton layer.

14. **On the first frame of the emailButton layer, select the Oval tool, and draw a perfect circle anywhere on the Stage.** Again, you can use any fill color you want. If the circle has a stroke, delete the stroke. With this circle selected, open the Properties panel and give the circle a width and height of **50** pixels.

15. **With the circle selected, choose Modify ⇨ Convert to Symbol (F8).** In the Convert to Symbol dialog box, make a button symbol named **invisibleButton_oval** and click OK.

16. **Now, edit the new symbol, either by double-clicking the instance on the Stage, or by double-clicking its listing in the Library panel.** On this symbol's timeline, rename Layer 1 to **hit area graphic**. Now, select the keyframe for the Up state, and drag it to the Hit state. Note that you may need to click, and then click and drag the keyframe for this method to work properly. When you are finished, your circle shape should be on only the Hit area of the button's timeline.

17. **Go back to the Scene 1 timeline, and you'll notice that your circle button is now an invisible button, just as our rectangular one is.** Move the circular invisible button over the thumbprint graphic, and use the Free Transform tool to shape the circle as an oval that closely matches the shape of the thumbprint, as shown in Figure 17.7. Also, name the instance emailButton in the Properties panel.

18. **Select frame 1 of the actions layer, and open the Actions panel.** Repeat Step 11 of this exercise, referencing the new emailButton instance. This time, however, we'll use a mailto: URL, as in "mailto:info@theMakers.com". Type this value within a URLRequest wrapper. For this navigateToURL() action, however, you do not need to specify a window parameter. Add the following code below the existing lines of code:

```
emailButton.addEventListener(MouseEvent.CLICK, onEmailClick);

function onEmailClick (evt) {
   var mailURL = new URLRequest("mailto:info@theMakers.com");
   navigateToURL(mailURL);
}
```

FIGURE 17.7

The thumbprint graphic now has an invisible button on top of it.

You can specify subject lines and body text in `mailto:` URLs as well, just as you can with HTML documents. For example, the following code opens a new e-mail message window addressed to **info@theMakers.com**, with a subject line of "Web Feedback" and body text of "Here are my comments." The following code should be typed as one line of code. Do not type the ⤸ character, which indicates a continuation of the same line of code.

```
"mailto:info@theMakers.com? ⤸
    subject=Web%20Feedback&body=Here%20are%20my%20comments%3A");
```

19. **Save your Flash document once again, and test the movie.** When you click the active area over the thumbprint graphic, the default e-mail client on your system should open, displaying a new message window with the To: field predefined to the URL you typed in Step 18.

TIP You can also change the title and description metadata published with the .swf file by choosing Modify ➪ Document. This metadata can be included with older .swf formats, including Flash Player 6! If your Flash movie is on a publicly accessible Web page and crawled by a search engine, the metadata can be read by the engine and indexed.

Now you know how to make invisible buttons and add `navigateToURL()` actions to them. In your own work, you may come to realize the true benefit of invisible buttons: You can quickly drag several instances of either invisible button shape (oval or rectangle) to the Stage to create active areas. This offers two benefits: First, you don't have to make button symbols from regular graphics that don't need four button states, and second, you can make "hidden" areas in interactive puzzles or games.

> **TIP** As you become more agile with ActionScript, you can start to use Movie Clip instances as button handlers. You learn more about this usage of Movie Clips in Chapter 24, "Controlling Movie Clips."

> **WEB RESOURCE** We'd like to know what you think about this chapter. Visit `www.flashsupport.com/feedback` to send us your comments.

Summary

- ActionScript is Flash's interactive language. It is a set of actions that enables Flash to communicate with internal elements (timelines, symbols, sounds, and so on) and external Web pages and scripts.

- ActionScript 3.0, or AS3, is the newest version of the scripting language for the Flash Player. AS3 is available only in Flash Player 9 or later. You must use ActionScript 1.0 or 2.0 for legacy Flash content playable in Flash Player 8 or earlier.

- Flash CS4 includes a scripting mode called Script Assist, which enables you to see your code in a more user-friendly layout.

- Flash interactivity is based on a relatively simple structure: An event handler waits for something to happen (a playback point being reached or the user providing input), and when that something does happen, it executes one or more actions (which alter the movie's playback, behavior, or properties; load a file; or execute a script).

- All actions need an event handler to activate them. Event handlers include keyframes on a timeline, button clicks, mouse movements, and key presses. More advanced event handlers are discussed in later chapters.

- Invisible buttons enable you to create interactive areas on top of other Flash artwork or symbols.

Chapter 18

Building Timelines and Interactions

U nlike most multimedia authoring applications, Flash has the capability to use multiple simultaneous timelines in its movies. So far, most of the examples in this book have only one timeline. You've seen how to add basic actions to your movies to make them interactive. Now you begin exploring the world of multiple movie timelines by using the Movie Clip symbol.

A Brief History of Movie Clips: The Key to Self-Contained Playback

A powerful piece to the Flash movie format is the Movie Clip symbol, introduced in Flash Player 3. Movie Clips enable Flash developers to create complex behaviors by nesting self-contained sequences of animation or interactivity inside each other. These sequences can then be placed as discrete, self-playing modules on the Main Timeline (that is, Scene 1). Initially, the key to the power of Movie Clips was their capability to communicate with and control each other via the `tellTarget` action.

In Flash Player 4, the role of Movie Clips was expanded — they could be used with ActionScript. That capability put Movie Clips at the foundation of advanced interactivity in Flash. In Flash Player 5, when ActionScript matured into a full-blown scripting language that mirrored JavaScript, Movie Clips became the central object of programming. In Flash Player 6, Movie Clips could utilize more compiler directives, which enabled them to become full-blown user-interface components. In Flash Player 7, Movie Clips and components continued to evolve and play a vital role in the organization of a Flash movie's content and interactivity.

In Flash Player 8, Movie Clips gained new filter effects, blend modes, and bitmap-caching optimizations. With Flash CS4Player 9, Movie Clips received a new sibling, the Sprite class, which is available only in ActionScript 3.0. (A sprite instance is essentially a single-frame Movie Clip instance, and is discussed more in the note that follows). With the release of Flash Player 10, the role of Movie Clips remains unchanged. In this chapter, you look at several key features of the Movie Clip symbol.

NOTE   If you're planning on building projects written in ActionScript 3.0, the role of the `MovieClip` class has changed dramatically. `MovieClip` instances should be used only for multiple-frame timeline-based animations. In ActionScript 3.0, several new classes, including the `Sprite` class, have been introduced to take over most of the functionality that was previously assigned to the `MovieClip` class. Regardless of which version of ActionScript you plan to use, you should understand the fundamentals of the `MovieClip` instances discussed in this chapter and throughout the book. This edition of the *Flash Bible* includes more coverage of ActionScript 3.0 (AS3). For more comprehensive coverage of ActionScript 3.0, refer to *ActionScript 3.0 Bible* (Wiley, 2008).

How Movie Clips interact within a Flash movie

Previous chapters dealt with Flash movies as a single sequence of frames arranged along a single timeline. Whether the playback along that timeline was linear (traditional animation) or nonlinear (where the playhead jumps arbitrarily to any frame), our example movies have normally comprised only the frames of a single timeline. Ostensibly, a single timeline may seem to provide everything you'd need to create any Flash behavior, but as you get more inventive or ambitious, you'll soon find yourself conceiving ideas for animated and interactive segments that are thwarted by the limits of a single timeline.

Suppose that you want to create a looping animation of a dog with its tail wagging. You decide that the tail should wag every 5 seconds and the dog should bark every 15 seconds. On a single timeline, you'd need a loop of 360 frames to accommodate the timing of the bark (assuming a frame rate of 24 frames per second), and repeating keyframes for the wagging tail artwork every 120 frames. Although animating a dog in that manner would be a bit cumbersome, it wouldn't be impossible — until your dog had to move around the screen as an integrated whole. Making the bark and the wagging tail loop while the whole dog moved around complex paths for extended periods of time would quickly become impractical, especially if the dog was only one part of a larger environment.

Now imagine that you could make the dog by creating two whole separate movies, one for the tail and one for the barking mouth and sound. Could you then place those movies as self-contained, animated objects on the Main Timeline, just like a graphic or a button? Well, you can — that's what Movie Clips are all about. Movie Clips are independent sequences of frames (timelines) that can be defined outside the context of the Main Timeline and then placed onto it as objects on a single frame. You create Movie Clips the same way you create a Graphic symbol in Edit mode. Unlike a graphic symbol, a Movie Clip (as the name somewhat implies) acts in most cases just like a fully functional movie or .swf file, meaning, for example, that frame actions in Movie Clip time-lines are functional. After you have created a Movie Clip as a symbol, you drop instances of it into any keyframe of the Main Timeline or any other Movie Clip timeline. The following are some general Movie Clip principles:

- During playback as a Flash .swf file, a Movie Clip instance placed on a timeline begins to play as soon as the frame on which it occurs is reached, whether or not the Main Timeline (or the clip's parent timeline) is playing.

- A Movie Clip plays back autonomously, meaning that as long as it is present on the Stage it is not governed by the playing or stopping of the Main Timeline.

- Movie Clips can play when the Main Timeline is stopped, or stay halted when the Main Timeline plays.

- Like a Graphic or a Button symbol, Movie Clips can be manipulated on the Stage — you can size them, skew them, rotate them, place effects such as alpha blending on them, or tween them, all while the frames within them continue to play.

> **TIP** Movie Clip instances can use filter effects and blend modes. You create these effects in real time and set them in the Properties panel or with ActionScript code.

- All timelines play at the frame rate specified by the Document Properties dialog box (Modify ➪ Document) or the Properties panel (when the Document window is focused, and all items on the Stage are deselected). However, it is possible to modify playback behavior of a timeline with ActionScript routines.

In our dog wagging and barking example, the tail and head of the dog could be looping Movie Clips, and then those Movie Clips could be nested inside another Movie Clip symbol (representing the entire dog). This "whole" dog clip could then be tweened around the Stage on the Main Timeline to make the dog move. You could use the same principle to move a Movie Clip of a butterfly with flapping wings along a motion path.

One movie, several timelines

Because a Flash movie can have more than one timeline existing in the same space and time, there must be a way to organize Movie Clips within the Main Timeline (Scene 1) of your Flash document. Just as artwork can be placed inside any symbol, symbol instances can be nested within other symbols. If you change the contents of the nested symbol, the parent symbol (the symbol containing the other symbol) is updated as well. Although this may not seem special, it's of extreme importance to Movie Clips and Flash interactivity. Because the playback of each Movie Clip timeline is independent from any other timeline, you need to know how to tell Flash which Movie Clip you want to control.

The Flash movie diagram in Figure 18.1 illustrates multiple timelines. This Flash movie has two layers on the Main Timeline: Layer 1 and Layer 2. Layer 1 has a Movie Clip (instance "A") that exists for 19 frames on the Main Timeline. Layer 2 has a Movie Clip (instance "B") that exists for 10 frames on the Main Timeline, but it also contains a nested Movie Clip (instance "C").

FIGURE 18.1

This figure shows one method of diagramming Flash timelines.

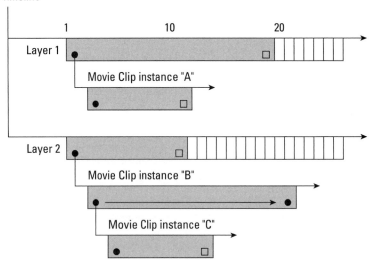

In Figure 18.1, if the Main Timeline has a `stop` action on the first frame, all three Movie Clips continue to play unless there are `stop` actions on their first frames or they are told to stop by actions targeted to them. If the Main Timeline plays to frame 20, instance "A" will no longer be on the Stage, regardless of how many frames it may have on its timeline. Figure 18.2 shows a more practical diagram of a timeline hierarchy.

FIGURE 18.2

Flash movies can be flow-charted in this fashion. This diagram is similar to the Movie Explorer's method of displaying Flash movie information.

In Figure 18.2, you can see three Movie Clips. Two of them, `ballAnim` and `dog`, occupy space on the Main Timeline. The other one, `dogTailAnim`, is nested within the `dog` Movie Clip. Each Movie Clip instance on any given timeline *must* have a unique name — you can't have two or more Movie Clip instances on the same timeline using the same instance name. The instance name is specified in the Properties panel, as shown in Figure 18.3. To see the settings for a particular instance, you must have the instance selected on the Stage before referencing the Properties panel.

FIGURE 18.3

Among other things, the Properties panel enables you to name each Movie Clip instance that appears on the Stage.

> **TIP** The suffix `Anim` is the naming convention we use to designate a symbol name (in the library) containing an animation. As you can see in Figure 18.3 we name the instance `dog`, without any naming convention for the data type. If you use ActionScript 2.0, you can derive your own naming convention as long as you type all `MovieClip` instance variables. You learn more about these concepts later in the chapter.

Now that you understand how multiple timelines can exist within a Flash movie, let's see how you can make Movie Clips communicate with one another.

Targets and Paths Explained

If you already studied Movie Clips in Chapter 6, "Symbols, Instances, and the Library," you probably know that they provide the solution to our animated dog problem. However, you might not have guessed that Movie Clips can also add logic to animation and Flash interfaces. Let's take our animated dog example a little farther: When dogs bark, their tails may stop wagging. Our hypothetical dog may look strange if it is barking and wagging at the same time. Suppose we wanted to stop the tail wagging during every bark. We'd have to have some way for the barking head Movie Clip to control the tail Movie Clip so that we could tell the tail to stop wagging when the dog barks, and then tell the tail to return to its wagging loop again when the bark is over.

Well, you have a few ways to control the tail Movie Clip from the barking head Movie Clip. In Flash Players 3 and 4, the `tellTarget` action was used to let actions on any timeline (including Movie Clip timelines and the Main Timeline) control what happens on any other timeline. How? `tellTarget` simply provided a mechanism for extending basic actions such as `play` and `stop`, enabling them to specify (or *target*) the timeline upon which they should be executed. Targets are any Movie Clip instances that are available at the current "state" of a Flash movie — you can't target a Movie Clip that isn't displayed (or existing) on the Stage. For example, suppose you had two Movie Clips, one on frame 1 and another on frame 10 of the Main Timeline. If the Main Timeline was stopped on frame 1, you couldn't target the Movie Clip on frame 10 because the instance is not on the current frame.

Since Flash Player 5, developers have been able to direct actions to specific timelines by attaching the same actions as *methods* to a `MovieClip` object (we define methods in the sidebar, "What Is Dot Syntax?"). As such, the `tellTarget` action is a deprecated action; it's still supported in current Flash Players, but it's been replaced with more versatile actions and syntax that makes its use outdated. For an overview of deprecated actions, see the sidebar on deprecated actions in Chapter 17. In this chapter, you work exclusively with the preferred ActionScript dot syntax to control Movie Clip instances. First, however, you need to understand how targeting works in Flash movies.

NOTE If you're new to scripting, read the "What Is Dot Syntax?" sidebar.

TIP If you're building Flash movies for mobile devices with Flash Lite 1.0/1.1, you need to use the `tellTarget` action to control Movie Clip instances. Flash Lite 1.0/1.1 is based on the Flash Player 4 specification.

Earlier in this chapter, you found out how multiple Movie Clip timelines appear on the Stage. It's entirely possible to nest several Movie Clip instances within another Movie Clip instances. To understand how Movie Clip instances communicate with one another by using actions, you need to have a firm grasp on Movie Clip paths. A path is simply that — the route to a destination, an address *per se*. If you have a Movie Clip instance named `tailAnim` inside a `dog` Movie Clip instance, how is Flash supposed to know? What if there was more than one `tailAnim` in the entire movie, with others nested in other Movie Clip instances besides the `dog` instance? You can specify a Movie Clip instance's path in an absolute or a relative mode.

Absolute paths

An *absolute path* is the full location information, or target, for a given Movie Clip instance from any other location (or target). Just like your postal address has a street name and number and a ZIP code so that people can find you on a map, all Movie Clip instances have a point of origin: the Main Timeline (that is, Scene 1). Flash CS4 only displays dot notation with absolute and relative paths.

NOTE Dot notation and dot syntax are synonymous terms and are used interchangeably throughout this book.

What Is Dot Syntax?

The Flash 5 authoring tool introduced a new method of writing all ActionScript called *dot syntax*. Earlier versions of Flash used a natural-language scripting environment that was menu-based, in which actions could be read and understood easily and accessed via popup menus and dialog boxes. Although most people prefer easy-to-use scripting environments, the production demands of complex interactive projects are often compromised by such menu-driven scripting environments. Computer programmers prefer to create, edit, and debug scripting with a language they can access and modify easily. Consequently, we see the best of both worlds with Flash CS4.

ActionScript adheres closely to the ECMA-262 specification, the same specification upon which JavaScript is based. JavaScript is the universal scripting language most browsers use for Dynamic HTML (DHTML) documents. Therefore, Flash ActionScript uses a dot syntax, also known as *dot notation*. What does that mean? It means that all actions are written within a standard formula that is common with object-oriented programming (OOP) languages:

```
Object.property = value;
```

or

```
Object.method();
```

The examples beg four things to be defined: objects, properties, methods, and values. An *object* is any element in a program (in this case, the Flash movie) that has changeable and accessible characteristics. Objects can be user-defined (in other words, you create and name them) or predefined by the programming language. Flash has several predefined objects, also called *classes*, meaning that they're already built into the ActionScript language. We look at object types in more detail in later chapters. An important object (and perhaps the easiest to conceptualize) is the MovieClip object. Any Movie Clip instance on the Stage is a MovieClip object, such as ballAnim or dogTailAnim. An object has characteristics, or *properties*, that can be updated or changed throughout the movie. An example of a MovieClip property is scale, which is referred to as scaleX and scaleY. We look at MovieClip properties in Chapter 24. Properties always have some data accompanying them. This data is called the property's *value*. Using the previous example, at full size, a MovieClip object's scaleX is 100 (the scale property uses percent as the unit of measure). For a MovieClip object named ballAnim, this would be represented in ActionScript syntax as:

```
ballAnim._scaleX = 100;
```

Finally, objects can be enacted upon by procedures that do something to or with the object. These procedures are called *methods*. One method for the MovieClip object is the gotoAndPlay() method, which was used as a basic action in Chapter 17. In Flash Player 5 or later movies, methods can be created for your own objects or predefined for existing Flash objects. Any goto action can be used as a method of any MovieClip object, as in:

```
ballAnim.gotoAndPlay("start");
```

The preceding example tells the ballAnim instance to direct its playback head to the frame label start on its timeline. This chapter helps you understand how to use the gotoAndPlay() method for Movie Clips.

Dot notation follows the ActionScript language conventions. With ActionScript 3.0 dot notation, the Main Timeline becomes

```
root
```

A Movie Clip instance named `dog` on the Main Timeline (or `root`) would have an absolute path of

```
root.dog
```

Notice that a period, or dot, separates the term `root` from `dog`. The dot denotes a parent-child relationship; the `dog` instance is a "child" of its parent, `root`. And, following suit, a Movie Clip instance named `tailAnim` that is nested within the `dog` Movie Clip would have the absolute path of

```
root.dog.tailAnim
```

Relative paths

A *relative path* is a contextual path to one timeline from another. From a conceptual point of view, think of a relative path as the relationship between the location of your pillow and the rest of your bed. Unless you have an odd sleeping habit, the pillow is located at the head of the bed. You may change the location of the bed within your room or the rooms of a house, but the relationship between the pillow and the bed remains the same. Another example that can illustrate the difference between absolute and relative references is the postal address example we used earlier. An absolute reference to your residence would use your full street address, city, state, and ZIP code. However, if you're giving directions to a friend of yours who lives nearby, you're more likely to tell your friend, "From your house, walk two blocks down A street, and turn right on B street. I'm five houses down on the left side of the street."

With Flash, relative Movie Clip paths are useful within Movie Clip instances that contain several nested Movie Clip instances. That way, you can move the container (or parent) Movie Clip from one timeline to another and expect the inner targeting of the nested Movie Clip instances to work. To refer to a timeline that is above the current timeline in dot notation, use

```
this.parent
```

Here, the term `this` refers to the current timeline from where the action is being called, and `_parent` refers to the current timeline's parent timeline. You can use relative dot notation to refer up and down the hierarchy at the same time. For example, if you have two nested Movie Clips, such as `tailAnim` and `barkingAnim`, within a larger Movie Clip named `dog`, you may want to target `tailAnim` from `barkingAnim`. The relative dot path for this task is

```
this.parent.tailAnim
```

This path tells Flash to go up one timeline from the current timeline, `barkingAnim`, to its parent timeline (the `dog` timeline), and then look for the instance named `tailAnim` from there.

You can also use successive `parent` references to travel up in the timeline hierarchy multiple times, such as

```
this.parent.parent
```

Using the dog instance example again, if you wanted to control the Main Timeline (which is the parent timeline of the dog instance) from the tailAnim instance, you could use parent.parent in the target path of an action executed from the tailAnim timeline.

> **NOTE** You can directly control the Main Timeline by using the reference root. The root keyword is specific to ActionScript 3.0. If you're planning to develop with ActionScript 1.0 or 2.0, use the legacy keyword _root. This edition of the *Flash Bible* exclusively covers ActionScript 3.0. For information about ActionScript 1.0 and 2.0, refer to past editions of the *Flash Bible* (Wiley).

As with absolute paths, we recommend that you become familiar with using the dot notation for relative paths.

Okay, that's enough theory. Now, you're going to practice nesting Movie Clips inside of other Movie Clips, as well as target actions at specific instances by using dot notation.

Targeting Movie Clips in Flash CS4

In this section, you see how to make Movie Clips interact with one another by using dot notation and ActionScript. Specifically, you're going to create the barking and wagging dog example we discuss at the beginning of this chapter. You begin this exercise with a starter Flash document file (.fla) located on the book's CD-ROM.

> **ON the CD-ROM** Open the stella_starter.fla file found in the ch18/stella folder of this book's CD-ROM.

With the starter file open in Flash CS4, test the movie by using Control ⇨ Test Movie. You'll see that our dog, Stella, is wagging her tail. At timed intervals, she barks. Right now, her tail keeps wagging as she barks. In this exercise, we show you how to stop her tail from wagging while she is barking. Close the Test Movie window and take a look at the Library panel. You'll find the following assets listed:

- **bark.wav:** This is the sound file used for Stella's bark. You will find this sound on the bark layer of the barkAnimClip timeline.
- **BarkAnim:** This Movie Clip symbol contains the animation for Stella's barking head. If you double-click this symbol in the Library panel, you'll see that the timeline has two layers, one for the sound and another for the head animation. This symbol is used in the stellaClip symbol.
- **BodyGraphic:** This graphic symbol is artwork of Stella's body and legs. There is no animation on its timeline. The BodyGraphic symbol is used in the Stella symbol.
- **HeadGraphic:** This Graphic symbol is artwork of Stella's head. You'll find a couple of instances of this symbol in the BarkAnim symbol.
- **Stella:** This Movie Clip timeline contains instances of the BarkAnim, BodyGraphic, and TailAnim symbols.

- **TailAnim:** This Movie Clip symbol contains two instances of the TailGraphic symbol. Each instance is rotated differently to create the wagging effect.

- **TailGraphic:** This Graphic symbol contains the artwork for Stella's tail.

Now, you're going to add some behaviors to the movie. First, you'll need to name the instances in the movie. ActionScript can find a Movie Clip instance only by its instance name. Using the Properties panel, you'll add instance names to all the Movie Clip instances.

After the instances are named, you can then target the instances with ActionScript. In this example, you'll target the `tailAnim` instance from the `barkAnim` instance. When the keyframe containing the barking mouth inside of `barkAnim` is reached, the movie tells `tailAnim` to go to and stop on a specific frame. When the barking is over, `tailAnim` is told to continue playing.

1. With `stella_starter.fla` open in Flash CS4, resave the document as `stella_absolute.fla`. In this tutorial, you use absolute paths with your targets.

2. **Select the instance of the Stella symbol on the Stage, on the Main Timeline.** Open the Properties panel, and name the instance `dog` in the instance name field, as shown in Figure 18.4.

FIGURE 18.4

You can name Movie Clip instances in the Properties panel.

3. **Double-click the `dog` instance on the Stage to edit the Stella symbol in the Library panel.** Select the `BarkAnim` symbol instance, and again, using the Properties panel, name this instance `barkAnim` in the instance name field.

4. **Select the `TailAnim` symbol instance located on the tailAnim layer.** Name the instance in the Properties panel, using the name `tailAnim`.

5. **With all the Movie Clip instances named, you can now target actions to specific timelines.** Your first goal is to stop the wagging tail while Stella barks. Double-click the `barkAnim` instance to edit the BarkAnim symbol's timeline.

6. **On the BarkAnim timeline, create a new layer and rename it `actions`.** Place this layer at the top of the layer stack. On frame 14 of this new layer, insert an empty keyframe (F7). Frame 14 is the frame just before the stream sound on the bark layer begins. On frame 14, you want to tell the `tailAnim` instance to stop playing, so give this keyframe a frame comment that indicates this behavior. With the keyframe selected, open the Properties panel and, in the frame label Name field of the Label section, type **stop wagging** and choose Comment in the Type menu, as shown in Figure 18.5.

    After you have assigned a comment on the frame, you're ready to write the ActionScript to perform the described behavior.

FIGURE 18.5

You can use frame comments to describe the actions on a keyframe.

7. **With frame 14 selected on the actions layer, open the Actions panel (F9/Option+F9)**
   Make sure that you are not working in Script Assist mode. Click the Target Path selector
   icon (see Figure 17.1 in Chapter 17 for its location). The Insert Target Path dialog box
   opens. Click the plus icon (+) on Windows or the twirl-down arrow on Mac next to the
   dog instance to reveal the nested instances, barkAnim and tailAnim, as shown in
   Figure 18.6. Select the tailAnim instance because it contains the wagging animation
   that you want to stop. Finally, make sure that the Absolute option is selected in the Mode
   setting. Click OK.

FIGURE 18.6

The Insert Target Path dialog box can help you build the path to a Movie Clip instance.

In the Script pane of the Actions panel, you now see the path to the instance root.dog.
tailAnim.

8. **After this name, type** .stop();. As described in the last chapter, the stop() action
   halts a playing timeline. When you are finished, the Script pane should contain the following code:

```
root.dog.tailAnim.stop();
```

TIP

You can see code hints if you use ActionScript 3.0 strong data typing with a variable
name, which we discuss in Chapter 23, "Knowing the Nuts and Bolts of code." To
try this technique, delete the line of code from Step 8, and type the following code:

```
var mc:MovieClip = root.dog.tailAnim;
```

After you've declared a variable and its data type, the Actions panel can display code hints for
that data type. On line 2, type:

```
mc.
```

As soon as you type the period (.) after the variable name mc, the Actions panel displays all the
properties and methods of the MovieClip class. You can click the entry you want to use, and
the Actions panel adds it to the existing line of code. If there are other parameters for the new
code, the Actions panel displays code hints for those parameters as well.

9. **Use this same technique to tell the `tailAnim` instance to start playing again after the bark has ended.** In the BarkAnim symbol timeline, create yet another actions layer. You can make more than one to prevent overlap of your frame comments. Place this new actions layer beneath the original actions layer. On frame 23 of this second actions layer, insert an empty keyframe (F7). Assign a frame comment of **//start wagging** in the Label section of the Properties panel for this keyframe.

10. **Repeat Steps 7 and 8 for the action on this keyframe.** This time, however, type a `.play();` action from the code hints menu in the Actions panel. When you are finished, the following code should be on frame 20 of the actions layer:

    ```
    root.dog.tailAnim.play();
    ```

11. **Test your movie.** Save the Flash document, and use Control ⇨ Test Movie to view your movie. When Stella barks, her tail should stop wagging. When the bark is over, the tail should resume wagging.

ON the CD-ROM This example has shown you how to target Movie Clip instances by using absolute paths built with the Insert Target Path dialog box in the Actions panel. However, you can also try using relative paths to target the instances. In the `ch18/stella` folder of the book's CD-ROM, open the `stella_relative.fla` file to see an example of relative path addressing. Note that this example also uses a `gotoAndStop(4)` action on the `//stop wagging` keyframe to make sure that Stella's tail is pointed down during the bark. You can also find a completed example file for the exercise you just completed, `stella_absolute.fla`.

WEB RESOURCE We'd like to know what you think about this chapter. Visit `www.flashsupport.com/feedback` to send us your comments.

Summary

- Movie Clips are a cornerstone of Flash interactivity for ActionScript projects. Each Movie Clip has its own independent timeline and playback.

- Each Movie Clip instance needs a unique name on any given timeline. You cannot reuse the same name on other Movie Clip instances on a timeline. You can, however, use the same instance name on different timelines.

- There are two types of target paths for Movie Clips: absolute and relative. Absolute paths start from the Main Timeline and end with the targeted instance name. Relative paths start from the timeline that's issuing the action(s) and end with the targeted instance name.

- The Insert Target Path dialog box can help you build the path to a Movie Clip instance to use with another action.

Chapter 19

Making Your First Flash CS4 Project

Now that you've learned the basic principles behind Flash actions, you probably want to start creating a presentation to put on a Web site. This chapter integrates several basic production principles and teaches you how to make a simple interactive Flash movie that has basic navigation and text functionality. After you have completed this chapter's lessons, you'll be more prepared for the nitty gritty of ActionScript in Part VII of the book.

> **NOTE**   In this edition of the *Flash Bible*, we've updated all examples with interactivity to use ActionScript 3.0, which is compatible with Flash Player 9 or later. If you need to create projects with legacy versions of ActionScript (1.0 or 2.0), refer to previous editions of the *Flash Bible* (Wiley).

The Main Timeline as the Site Layout

Before you can start creating a Flash project, you need to know what you're communicating — what is the basic concept of the experience? Is this an all-Flash Web site? Is this a Flash animation that introduces some other type of HTML-based content? For the purposes of this chapter, you create a Flash movie for a basic all-Flash presentation. In a sense, this project is the Flash equivalent of a Microsoft PowerPoint presentation. Let's look at the completed project (shown in Figure 19.1) that you will create in this chapter.

> **ON the CD-ROM**   In a Web browser, open the `main.html` document, located in the `ch19/deploy` folder of this book's CD-ROM. This movie contains two completed sections of the presentation.

FIGURE 19.1

The completed presentation

When you load the `main.html` file into a browser with the Flash Player 10 installed, you see the presentation's title, "Digital Video Production," along with four navigation buttons that take you to each section of the presentation. The opening section, Introduction, has scrolling text featuring the TextArea UI component. When you click the Video Equipment button in the navigation bar, a Movie Clip featuring five video items appears along with another instance of the TextArea component. The Next and Previous buttons enable you to browse the video items. Each video item uses a custom component that blurs and fades the item onto the stage.

If you have a screen reader installed and are using the Windows operating system, you will hear the screen reader describe each item in the Introduction section. A screen reader is an application that assists visually impaired computer users by speaking text aloud. The Flash Player 9 ActiveX control works only with screen readers that adhere to the MSAA (Microsoft Active Accessibility) specification built into Windows operating systems. As of this writing, only a handful of screen readers, such as the Window-Eyes screen reader by GW Micro and JAWS from Freedom Scientific, adhere to MSAA. In this chapter, you learn how to add accessibility information to elements in your Flash document.

Creating a plan

When you know what goals you want to achieve with your Flash content, you should map the ideas on paper (or with your preferred project planning or flowchart software). We create a basic presentation for digital video production that has four areas: introduction, video equipment, audio equipment, and editing software. Our organizational chart for this site has four discrete areas, as shown in Figure 19.2.

FIGURE 19.2

Our organizational chart helps us plan our Flash movie architecture.

In this chapter, you create the first two sections: introduction and video equipment. If you prefer, you can continue to develop the presentation with graphics provided on the CD-ROM.

Setting up a local folder structure

As described in Chapter 3, "Planning Flash Projects," an ideal production environment separates your authortime files, such as Flash documents (.fla), from your runtime files, such as Flash movies (.swf) and Web pages (.html). Before you begin creating content in Flash CS4, follow these steps to create suitable folders for your project's content:

1. **Pick a location on your local hard drive to store the files for this chapter.** Create a folder named `ch19` in this location.

2. **Inside of the `ch19` folder, create two folders: `deploy` and `src`.** The `deploy` folder will contain the runtime files, and the `src` folder will hold the authortime files.

3. **Inside of the `src` folder, create a folder named `actionscript`.** Inside of the `actionscript` folder, create a folder named `includes`. The `includes` folder will store ActionScript files (.as) that contain code referenced from the Flash documents (.fla) stored in the `src` folder.

Now you have the necessary folder structure to begin building the project in this chapter.

Determining Flash movie properties

After you've made your organizational chart, you'll want to determine the frame rate, size, and color of the Flash document. We've skipped much of the "real-life" planning involved with Flash-based Web sites, which are discussed in Chapter 3, "Planning Flash Projects." For this example, we have made a starter Flash document for you to use that contains all the elements necessary to complete the chapter. This document contains some of the basic graphic elements already positioned on the Stage.

ON the CD-ROM Make a copy of the `main_starter.fla` document, located in the `ch19/src` folder of this book's CD-ROM. Before you open this file, you should install the Miniml font files, available on the book's Web site at `www.flashsupport.com/bonus/fonts`.

Open the starter document in Flash CS4. This document uses a frame size of 640 x 480 (to maintain the aspect ratio of most computer monitors), a standard frame rate of 24 fps (frames per second), and a white background color. These are set in the Document Properties dialog box, shown in Figure 19.3, which is accessed by choosing Modify ⇨ Document (Ctrl+J/⌘+J).

FIGURE 19.3

The Flash document properties

Mapping presentation areas to keyframes

When the Flash document properties have been determined, you can create a Main Timeline structure for the presentation. Because there are four areas in the project (introduction, video equipment, audio equipment, and editing software), you'll have keyframes on the timeline that indicate those sections.

1. **Create a new layer and name it** labels. Place this layer at the top of the layer stack in the Timeline window.

2. **With the Selection tool, select frame 10 of the labels layer, and press the F7 key.** This creates a keyframe on frame 10.

TIP It's usually a good idea to leave some empty frame space in front of your "real" Flash content. You can later use these empty frames to add a preloader, as discussed in Chapter 28, "Sharing and Loading Assets."

3. **With the keyframe selected, open the Properties panel.** In the Name field of the Label section, type **intro**. After you have typed the text, press Tab (or Enter) to make the name "stick."

4. **Repeat Steps 2 and 3 with frames 20, 30, and 40, with the frame labels video, audio, and software, respectively.**

5. **Select frame 50 of the labels layer, and press F5.** This enables you to read the very last label, software. Your Timeline window should resemble Figure 19.4.

FIGURE 19.4

You use frame labels to differentiate each section of the site.

6. **Select frame 50 on all other layers in the Timeline window, and press F5 to extend the content on these layers across the entire timeline, as shown in Figure 19.5.**

FIGURE 19.5

The content in the heading, background, and frame layers will be present throughout the entire movie.

7. **Save your Flash document as** `main_100.fla` **in the** `src` **folder you created earlier in this chapter.**

8. **Make a new layer, and rename it** actions. Place this layer below the labels layer. Add a keyframe on frame 10 of the actions layer, and open the Actions panel (F9/Option+F9)). Type the following code into the Script pane:

```
stop();
```

9. **Close the Actions panel, and open the Properties panel.** Make sure that frame 10 of the actions layer is selected. In the <Frame Label> field, type **//stop**. The / / characters assign a frame comment rather than a frame label. Although this step isn't necessary for the functionality of the movie, frame comments can provide quick and easy access to the designer's or programmer's notes. Your Timeline window should now look like Figure 19.6.

10. **Save the Flash document again.**

FIGURE 19.6

Unlike labels, you cannot use frame comments in ActionScript. Comments can provide quick visual references for ActionScript code.

At this point, the Flash document has a skeleton architecture (a blueprint) for your interactive functionality. Now you'll add some content to each section of the movie.

ON the CD-ROM   You can find the `main_100.fla` document in the `ch19/src` folder of this book's CD-ROM.

Creating content for each area

In this section, you create navigation artwork for each area of the presentation. You also build some content for the video section.

1. **Resave the Flash file you modified in the last section as** `main_200.fla`. Save the file in the `src` folder.

2. **Create a new layer named** menu. Place this layer beneath the actions layer. Insert a keyframe on frame 10 of the menu layer.

3. **On frame 10 of the menu layer, use the Text tool to add a static text block with the text** Introduction. For this example, we use the Miniml font hooge 05_53 at 12 points with bold formatting. Use the Properties panel to set these options. Place the text near the left edge of the Stage below the heading, as shown in Figure 19.7.

ON the CD-ROM   If you don't have this font installed, install the Miniml font files available for download at `www.flashsupport.com/bonus/fonts`.

4. **Repeat Step 3 for the text** Video Equipment, Audio Equipment, **and** Editing Software. Space these text blocks across the Stage beneath the heading, as shown in Figure 19.8. Again, all these text blocks should be on frame 10 of the menu layer. Later, you will convert each of these text blocks to a button symbol.

   Now, you create a graphic that lets the user know which section is currently active. To do this, you add a black square that will appear next to the appropriate text block. When the presentation starts, the black square will be next to the Introduction text. When the user navigates to the Video Equipment section, the black square will appear next to the Video Equipment section. Open the Library panel, and expand the graphics folder. There, you will find a graphic symbol named marker. You will use this symbol in a moment.

FIGURE 19.7

Use the Text tool to add the Introduction text to the Stage.

FIGURE 19.8

Add text that describes each section of the presentation.

5. **Create a new layer on your Main Timeline (that is, Scene 1), and name it** marker. Place this layer underneath the menu layer.

6. **On frame 10 of the marker layer, insert a keyframe.** Drag the marker symbol from the Library panel to the Stage. Position the instance of the marker to the left of the Introduction text, as shown in Figure 19.9.

7. **Insert another keyframe (F6) on frame 20 of the marker layer — make sure you do not insert empty keyframes.** Move the instance of the marker at frame 20 to the left of the Video Equipment text, as shown in Figure 19.10.

8. **Repeat Step 7 from frames 30 and 40 of the marker layer, moving the marker instance to the left of the Audio Equipment and Editing Software text, respectively.** You now have the marker changing its position for all sections of the timeline.

FIGURE 19.9

This marker designates the active section.

FIGURE 19.10

When the user goes to the Video Equipment section, the marker appears next to the Video Equipment text.

Main Timeline versus Scene Structure

Arguably, you might be wondering why you are using keyframes to delineate each section, rather than new scenes. There are a few reasons to use one scene (in other words, one Main Timeline):

■ You can see the entire layout of the site very easily on one timeline.

■ You can blend interstitials (transitions between each area of the site) over two sections more easily. It's much easier to have one Movie Clip instance span the area between two section keyframes on the Main Timeline.

■ Scenes are not scriptable objects like Movie Clip instances are. You have greater flexibility with Movie Clips than you do with scenes.

Ultimately, the decision is yours. Make sure that you determine your Flash architecture well before you start production within the Flash CS4 authoring environment. It's not a simple task to re-architect the layout after production has begun.

Now you'll add a slide show of the video equipment that can be used for digital video production. This slide show will appear in the Video Equipment section of the presentation. For this, you create a Movie Clip symbol that has each product graphic on a separate keyframe.

1. **Create a new symbol by using Insert ⇨ New Symbol (Ctrl+F8/⌘+F8).** Make sure that the Type option is set to Movie clip, and give it a name of **videoEquip**.

2. **Flash CS4 automatically switches to Edit mode on the videoEquip timeline.** Rename Layer 1 to **items**.

3. **Add keyframes to frames 2, 3, 4, 5, and 6 of the items layer.** There are six items in the `videoItems` folder of the Library panel, and each item is put on its own keyframe.

4. **Move the playhead to frame 1 of the videoEquip timeline, and drag the dvTape Movie Clip symbol from the `videoItems` folder of the Library panel to the Stage.** When an instance of the symbol is on the Stage, name the instance `tape` in the `<Instance Name>` field of the Properties panel.

5. **Continue moving the playhead to the next frame, dragging another item to the Stage for each frame.** Place cameraLow on frame 2, cameraMid on frame 3, cameraHigh on frame 4, dvDeck on frame 5, and dvCable on frame 6. Make sure that you name each instance in the Properties panel, using the following names: `camLow`, `camMid`, `camHigh`, `deck`, and `cable`. When you're finished, press the < and > keys to review your frames. Check Figure 19.11 to compare your work. You may want to center each graphic on the Stage by using the Align panel (Ctrl+K/⌘+K). As you progress with this exercise, you can adjust the exact placement of each item. Before you proceed to the next step, check that each instance is named in the Properties panel.

6. **Now you need to insert an actions layer for this Movie Clip symbol.** Create a new layer, and rename it **actions**. Select frame 1 of the actions layer, and open the Actions panel. Add a `stop` action to make sure that the items don't automatically loop when the movie loads:

   `stop();`

7. **Return to the Main Timeline (Scene 1) by clicking the Scene 1 tab in the upper left corner of the document window.**

8. **Create a new layer, and rename it** content. Place this layer underneath the marker layer. Insert a new keyframe on frame 20 of the content layer.

9. **Open the Library panel, and drag the videoEquip symbol from the library to the Stage.** Place it just left of the center of the Stage, as shown in Figure 19.12. In the Properties panel, name this instance `equip`.

10. **Select frame 30 of the content layer, and press the F7 key.** This inserts a blank keyframe. Now, the `equip` instance will show only in the Video Equipment area of the timeline.

11. **Save your Flash document.**

FIGURE 19.11

You should have six filled keyframes on the item layers of the videoEquip timeline.

FIGURE 19.12

The equip instance will be present only in the video section of the timeline.

Now you have some content in the Flash document. In the next section, you add navigation controls to the presentation.

 You can find the `main_200.fla` document in the `ch19` folder of this book's CD-ROM.

Adding Navigation Elements to the Main Timeline

In the last section, you created a timeline for a digital video production presentation. You inserted content placeholders for the intro, video, audio, and software sections of the timeline, and you made a Movie Clip with video item graphics to place in the video section. However, the user has no way of actually getting to any section except the intro frame. In this section, you convert the text blocks in the menu to button instances, whose actions control the position of the playhead on the Main Timeline.

Creating text buttons for a menu

In this part of the exercise, you make menu buttons that enable the user to navigate to the different areas of the Flash movie.

1. Resave the `main_200.fla` file as `main_300.fla` in the `src` folder.

2. On the Main Timeline of the file, select frame 10 of the menu layer.

3. With the Selection tool, select the Introduction text block. Press F8 to convert this text into a symbol. In the Convert to Symbol dialog box, name the symbol **introButton**. Assign it a Button type. Click the top left corner of the Registration box, as shown in Figure 19.13.

FIGURE 19.13

The introButton symbol settings

4. **Select the button instance on the Stage, and at the top field of the Properties panel, type introBtn in the Instance name field.** You will target the button in ActionScript 3.0 code you create later in this chapter. Naming your instances is a good habit to get into.

   Now you need to add a Hit state to the introButton timeline. By default, Flash CS4 uses the last frame of a Button symbol timeline for the Hit state, unless content is added to the Hit state keyframe.

5. **Double-click the `introBtn` instance on the Stage to switch to Edit mode.**

6. **On the timeline of the introButton symbol, select the Hit frame of Layer 1.** Press the F7 key to insert an empty keyframe.

7. **Click the Onion Skin Outlines button in the Timeline window toolbar.** This enables you to view the previous frames of the introButton timeline, as shown in Figure 19.14.

8. **Select the Rectangle tool, and draw a filled rectangle that covers the same area of the Introduction text block.** You can use any fill color because the user never sees the Hit state. Make sure you turn off the stroke, or delete the stroke after the shape is drawn. Your button's timeline should resemble the one shown in Figure 19.15.

FIGURE 19.14

Onion skinning enables you to align the contents of several keyframes accurately.

FIGURE 19.15

The Hit state defines the "active" area of the button instance in the movie. When the user's mouse pointer enters this area, the Over frame of the button appears.

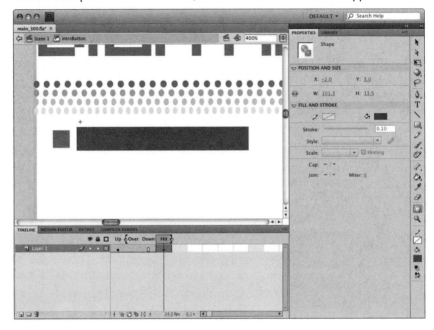

9. **Select the shape you drew in Step 8, and press F8 to convert it to a graphic symbol named** hitArea. As with the introButton symbol, make sure that the Registration icon is active in the top left corner. You will reuse this shape for the other buttons in this section.

   Next you add an Over state to the introButton so that the user has a visual indication that it's an active button.

10. **Select the Over frame of Layer 1, and press F6.** This copies the contents of the previous keyframe into the new one. Select the Introduction text block with the Selection tool, and change the fill color to a shade of blue such as #0099CC in the Tools panel or the Properties panel. You can also turn off Onion Skin Outlines at this point.

11. **Return to the Main Timeline (that is, Scene 1) of your document, and save your Flash document.** Choose Control ⇨ Test Movie to test the states of the introButton. You can also use Control ⇨ Enable Simple Buttons to preview the graphical states of a button instance directly on the Stage.

    Now you add ActionScript to the movie to enable interactivity with the introBtn instance. To aid the maintenance of ActionScript code for a project, you can create a separate ActionScript file (.as) to hold the code and use an include directive in the Flash document (.fla) to reference the external code.

12. **Choose File ⇨ New.** In the New Document dialog box that appears (Figure 19.16), select ActionScript File and then click OK.

FIGURE 19.16

The New Document dialog box

TIP One of the visual benefits to using an ActionScript file is that you have a much larger document window to write your ActionScript code. With an ActionScript file, you do not use the Actions panel to insert ActionScript code. You can also easily switch to an ActionScript file from another document that is open in Flash CS4.

13. **Choose File ➪ Save, and save the ActionScript file as** `main_menu.as` **in the** `src/actionscript/includes` **folder you created earlier in this chapter.**

14. **In the ActionScript file, type the following code.** (Do not type the ⮑ character, which indicates a continuation of the same line of code.)

```
//SimpleButton introBtn;

import flash.events.MouseEvent;
import flash.display.SimpleButton;

introBtn.addEventListener(MouseEvent.CLICK, onMenuClick);

function onMenuClick(evt:MouseEvent):void {
   var btn:SimpleButton = evt.currentTarget as SimpleButton;
   var frame:String = btn.name.substring(0, ⮑
      btn.name.indexOf("Btn"));
   this.gotoAndStop(frame);
}
```

The first line of code tells the Flash CS4 authoring environment to display the code hints of the `SimpleButton` class for the `introBtn` instance. In ActionScript 3.0, a button symbol belongs to the `SimpleButton` class.

The `import` statements tell the ActionScript compiler to reference the `MouseEvent` and `SimpleButton` classes that are part of the intrinsic Flash Player classes.

The `introBtn.addEventListener()` line of code tells the `introBtn` instance to trigger a function named `onMenuClick` whenever the user's mouse clicks the `introBtn` instance. The click event is designated by `MouseEvent.CLICK`.

The function named `onMenuClick` processes the mouse click event. The first line of code within the function retrieves a reference to the button broadcasting the event. Here, the reference named `btn` refers back to the `introBtn` instance. The second line of code determines which frame the Flash movie should now show by examining the button's name. The `introBtn` instance (`btn.name`) contains the name of the frame to which it belongs, `intro`. The variable named `frame` is then passed to a `gotoAndStop()` action which moves the playhead on the Main Timeline to the proper frame label.

CROSS-REF   You learn more about functions in Chapter 25, "Using Functions and Arrays."

15. Save the `main_menu.as` file, and switch back to the `main_200.fla` document.

16. On the Main Timeline, create a new layer named menu actions, and place this layer above the existing actions layer.

17. Insert an empty keyframe (F7) on frame 10 of the menu actions layer. Select this frame and open the Actions panel (F9,/Option+F9). In the Script pane, type the following line of code. The `include` directive tells the ActionScript compiler to grab the contents of the `main_menu.as` file whenever you test or publish the Flash movie (.swf):

```
include "actionscript/includes/main_menu.as";
```

To make sure that you've typed the path correctly, click the Check Syntax button (designated by a blue check mark) in the toolbar of the Actions panel. If the Output panel reports any errors, make sure that you saved `main_menu.as` in the location stated in Step 15.

If you test your movie at this point, your `introBtn` instance won't do anything — the playhead already stops on the `intro` frame label when the movie starts.

18. Add a button for each section on the site. Repeat Steps 3–10 for each section name in your movie. Note that you should reuse the hitArea graphic symbol from Step 9 for the remaining buttons — use the Free Transform tool to size each new instance of hitArea to match the size of the text block in the button symbol. You should end up with four named button instances on the Stage: `introBtn`, `videoBtn`, `audioBtn`, and `softwareBtn`.

   When you're finished making all the buttons, make a folder in the Library panel named `buttons`, and move the button symbols and the hitArea graphic into the new folder.

19. Go back to the `main_menu.as` file, and create additional listeners for the new button instances, as shown in the following code:

```
//SimpleButton introBtn;
//SimpleButton videoBtn;
```

```
//SimpleButton audioBtn;
//SimpleButton softwareBtn;

import flash.events.MouseEvent;
import flash.display.SimpleButton;

introBtn.addEventListener(MouseEvent.CLICK, onMenuClick);
videoBtn.addEventListener(MouseEvent.CLICK, onMenuClick);
audioBtn.addEventListener(MouseEvent.CLICK, onMenuClick);
softwareBtn.addEventListener(MouseEvent.CLICK, onMenuClick);

function onMenuClick(evt:MouseEvent):void {
    var btn:SimpleButton = evt.currentTarget as SimpleButton;
    var frame:String = btn.name.substring(0, ⤸
        btn.name.indexOf("Btn"));
    this.gotoAndStop(frame);
}
```

20. Save the `main_menu.as` file.

21. Save your Flash document (.fla file) as main_300.fla in the src folder and test it (Ctrl+Enter/⌘+Enter).

ON the CD-ROM You can find the `main_300.fla` document in the `ch19/src` folder of this book's CD-ROM. The completed `main_menu.as` file is located in the `ch19/src/actionscript/includes` folder.

When you test your Flash movie, you should be able to click each button to go to each area of the movie — you should see the square marker move to each category name when you click the name. If a button isn't functioning, double-check the code in the `menu_actions.as` file. Make sure that each button instance is named in the Properties panel. In the next section, you add buttons to the videoEquip Movie Clip symbol so that the user can browse the pictures of the video items.

Browsing the video items

In this section, you go inside the videoEquip symbol and add some navigation buttons for the video items.

1. Resave the main_300.fla file as `main_400.fla`.

2. From the Main Timeline, double-click the `equip` instance on frame 20 of the content layer. Flash CS4 switches to Edit mode.

3. Make a new layer on the videoEquip timeline, and rename the layer buttons. Place this layer below the actions layer.

4. Open the Buttons Library (Window ➪ Common Libraries ➪ Buttons). In the Buttons Library panel, double-click the classic buttons folder, and then double-click the

Circle Buttons folder. Drag the circle button — next instance symbol to the Stage. Place the button instance below and to the right of the `mcTape` instance. Name the new button instance `nextBtn` in the Properties panel.

5. **With the circle button — next instance selected, press Ctrl+D (⌘+D) to duplicate the instance on the Stage.** Name the duplicate instance `prevBtn` in the Properties panel. Move the duplicate instance to the left of the original arrow button. With the Free Transform tool selected, enable the Rotate modifier in the Tools panel. Rotate the duplicated button 180 degrees. Press Shift while rotating, to lock in 45-degree steps.

6. **Select both arrow buttons, and align them horizontally to each other by using the Align panel.** Insert some descriptive text next to the instances, as shown in Figure 19.17.

FIGURE 19.17

Add text to the buttons to describe their functionality.

As discussed in the last section, you can create an external ActionScript file (.as file) to contain code for your Flash document. Start by replacing the existing `stop()` action on frame 1 of the videoEquip timeline with an `include` directive pointing to an ActionScript file.

7. **Select frame 1 of the actions layers, and open the Actions panel (F9/Option+F9).** Delete the `stop();` action, and type the following line of code:

```
include "actionscript/includes/video_equipment.as"
```

You create this new ActionScript file in the next step.

8. **Create a new ActionScript file (File ⇨ New) and save the file as** `video_equipment.as` **in the** `src/actionscript/includes` **folder you created at the beginning of the chapter.**

9. **In the new script file, type the following code.** This code uses the same event, `MouseEvent.CLICK`, as the main menu buttons. Here, the `onPrevClick()` and `onNextClick()` functions act as listeners, sending the Movie Clip timeline to the previous or next frame, respectively.

```
//SimpleButton prevBtn;
//SimpleButton nextBtn;

import flash.events.MouseEvent;

prevBtn.addEventListener(MouseEvent.CLICK, onPrevClick);
nextBtn.addEventListener(MouseEvent.CLICK, onNextClick);

stop();

function onPrevClick(evt:MouseEvent):void {
    this.prevFrame();
}

function onNextClick(evt:MouseEvent):void {
    this.nextFrame();
}
```

10. **Save the** `video_equipment.as` **file, switch back to your Flash document (.fla file), and test it by choosing Control ⇨ Test Movie (Ctrl+Enter/⌘+Enter).** Click the Video Equipment button, and try the new navigation arrows for your video items catalog.

You can enhance your presentation by adding information in the videoEquip Movie Clip symbol. In the next section, you add a scrolling text window that displays descriptions of the video items.

ON the CD-ROM You can find the `main_400.fla` document in the `ch19/src` folder of this book's CD-ROM.

The topic of Flash usability has received a lot of press, particularly because many Flash interfaces are considered experimental or nonintuitive to the average Web user. Since December 2000, Adobe has maintained a special usability section in its Web site. You can read usability tips and view examples of interface design at `www.adobe.com/devnet/flash/testing_usability.html`.

Closely related to usability is accessibility: How easily can someone with a disability access the content within your Flash movie? We show you Flash movie accessibility options in the final section of this chapter.

Text Scrolling with the TextArea Component

Continuing from the previous Flash movie example with the digital video production presentation, you learn how to create basic scrolling text by using the TextArea component in Flash CS4. You can scroll text in Flash files (ActionScript 3.0) with either the UIScrollBar or the TextArea component. We demonstrate the use of the TextArea component for one item in the videoEquip symbol to get you started.

1. Resave the `main_400.fla` file as `main_500.fla`.

2. **In the Flash document you created from the previous section, double-click the `equip` instance on the Stage, at frame 20 of the content layer.** Flash CS4 switches to Edit mode.

3. **Add a new layer, and rename it** infoArea. Move this layer beneath the buttons layer, and select frame 1 of the infoArea layer. Now, open the Components panel (Ctrl+F7/ ⌘+F7). In the User Interface nesting, drag an instance of the TextArea component to the Stage, to the right of the `tape` instance.

4. **Use the Free Transform tool to stretch the component instance.** This instance should accommodate several lines of text19. The size of the instance should match the size of the text area you want to appear in the scrolling text window. In the Properties panel, name the TextArea instance `infoArea`.

5. **Open the Component Inspector panel (Shift+F7).** With the `infoArea` instance selected on the stage, change the `editable` setting to `false`; the user should not be able to change the contents of the text field at runtime. Your videoEquip timeline should resemble Figure 19.18.

   Now, you'll need to supply some text to the `infoArea` instance. You can specify text directly in the `text` or `htmlText` parameter of the instance in the Properties panel, but for this project you'll learn how to format HTML text that is assigned in ActionScript to the TextArea component. Open the `item_1.rtf` document in a text editor such as WordPad or TextEdit. This file is located in the `ch19/src/text` folder of this book's CD-ROM. Now, open the `item_1_formatted.txt` document on the CD-ROM, and compare it to the `item_1.rtf` version. (You may want to enable word wrapping in your text editor so that you can see all the text in the TXT file.) You'll notice that all the text in the TXT file is specified in one continuous nonbreaking line. Moreover, any carriage returns in `item_1.rtf` have been replaced with `<br/>` tags in the TXT version. Some characters, such as the double quotes around the word "data," have been escaped in the TXT file — that is, the character is preceded by a backslash (\ ). These special formatting characters ensure that ActionScript correctly displays the text.

6. **Select all the text in the `item_1_formatted.txt` file, and copy it.** Later in this exercise, you'll paste the text into your own ActionScript code.

FIGURE 19.18

This text field displays the text associated with the first video item.

7. **On the videoEquip timeline, create a new layer and rename it** actions - text. Place this layer below the existing actions layer.

8. **Select frame 1 of the actions - text layer, and open the Actions panel (F9/ Option+F9).** Here, you set a variable named `info` to the text to be displayed in the TextArea instance. In the Script pane, type the following code:

   ```
   info = "";
   ```

9. **Between the pair of double quotes you typed in Step 8, paste (Ctrl+V/⌘+V) the copied text into the Script pane.** Initially, the text should appear on one line, but you can choose Word Wrap in the options menu of the Actions panel to see all the text, as shown in Figure 19.19.

10. **After the semicolon (;) at the end of the code you created in Steps 8 and 9, press Enter to start a new line of code.** Type the following code:

    ```
    updateText(info);
    ```

    You define the `updateText()` function in the next step. This function processes the text stored in the `info` variable and displays it in the `infoArea` instance.

FIGURE 19.19

The Actions panel displaying the code to assign text to the TextArea component

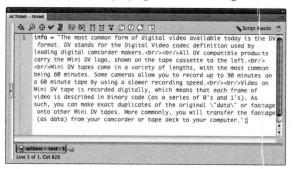

11. **Reopen (or switch back to) the** `video_equipment.as` **file you created in the last section.** Add the new code shown in bold in the following code block:

```
//SimpleButton prevBtn;
//SimpleButton nextBtn;
//TextArea infoArea;

import flash.events.MouseEvent;

prevBtn.addEventListener(MouseEvent.CLICK, onPrevClick);
nextBtn.addEventListener(MouseEvent.CLICK, onNextClick);

var info:String;

stop();

function onPrevClick(evt:MouseEvent):void {
   this.prevFrame();
}

function onNextClick(evt:MouseEvent):void {
   this.nextFrame();
}

function updateText(val:String):void {
   infoArea.htmlText = val;
   infoArea.verticalScrollPosition = 0;
}
```

This new code declares the `info` variable as a `String` variable, which can store text information. The `updateText()` function processes `String` data passed to it, setting the `htmlText` property of the `infoArea` instance to the new HTML text passed into the function. The vertical scrollbar's scroller is reset to the top of the scrollbar, if the amount of text requires a vertical scrollbar to appear.

12. Save the `video_equipment.as` file, and switch back to the Flash document (.fla file). Test the Flash document (Ctrl+Enter/⌘+Enter). Click the Video Equipment navigation button, and try the TextArea component. If the text is not appearing or scrolling, go back to the authoring environment and double-check the ActionScript code on frame 1 of the actions - text layer as well as the new code added to the `video_equipment.as` file. Do not proceed with any steps until the TextArea component is functioning properly.

    Now, you're ready to set up the text for the second item on the videoEquip timeline.

13. Select frame 2 of the actions - text layer, and press F7 to insert an empty keyframe. Add the same actions and text as shown in Steps 8 and 10, but this time, copy and paste the text from the `item_2_formatted.txt` file (located in the `ch19/src/text` folder of this book's CD-ROM).

14. Save your Flash document (.fla file) and test it (Ctrl+Enter/⌘+Enter). When you navigate to the Video Equipment section, you should be able to click the Next button to see the text for item 2.

15. Repeat Step 13 for frames 3, 4, 5, and 6 of the actions - text layer. When you are finished, you should have six separate action keyframes, one per item on the timeline.

16. Save your Flash document again, and test it (Ctrl+Enter/⌘+Enter). When you go to the Video Equipment section, you should be able to click the Next button to reach each video item's description field, and the field should be scrollable.

The next step in real production would be to finesse the artwork and to add transitional effects between each video item. The next section shows you how to add a custom Fade component that we created for your use in this exercise.

NOTE You already added the ActionScript code in Step 11 to reset the scroll bar's position for each new item.

The `verticalScrollPosition` property controls the vertical position of the scroller. Setting it to zero resets the position to the top. So, if the user scrolls to the bottom of one description and presses the Next button, the next item's description reads from the top.

ON the CD-ROM You can find the completed document, `main_500.fla`, in the `ch19/src` folder of this book's CD-ROM. You can also find the finished `video_equipment.as` file in the `ch19/src/actionscript/includes` folder.

Using the Custom BlurFader Component

So far, much of the material and artwork used in this presentation could have been accomplished with a traditional HTML page layout in Adobe Dreamweaver with GIF or JPEG graphics. In this section, you add a fade effect to each of the video items in the videoEquip symbol. We created a custom component that can be applied to any Movie Clip instance on the Stage. This component fades a Movie Clip instance in or out, based on settings in the Component Inspector panel. To see this fade effect in action, open the `main.swf` file from the `ch19/deploy` folder in Flash Player

10. When you go to the Video Equipment section, each item fades and blurs in. In other words, the alpha of each Movie Clip instance animates from 0 to 100 percent while the blur value gradually decreases.

The BlurFader component snaps to Movie Clip instances. Because we built the component for you, you won't find the BlurFader component in the Component panel along with the Flash CS4 components. The BlurFader component is located in the starter document's library and has been saved in each version of the `main_` document that you created in previous sections. Here's how to add the BlurFader component to the video items in the videoEquip symbol:

1. **Open your saved Flash document from the previous section, and resave the file as** `main_600.fla`.

2. **On frame 20 of the content layer, double-click the** `equip` **instance on the Stage to edit the symbol.**

3. **Select frame 1 of the items layer, and open the Library panel.** Drag the BlurFader component to the `tape` instance on the Stage. When you release the mouse button, the BlurFader component should snap to the top left corner of the `tape` instance, as shown in Figure 19.20. We made a custom icon for this BlurFader component: a little gradient box with the text BF. Select the BlurFader instance and name it `bf_1` in the Properties panel.

FIGURE 19.20

The BlurFader component snaps to the top left corner of the Movie Clip instance.

NOTE The BF icon does not show up in the actual Flash .swf file — it appears only in the authoring environment.

4. **You can view the default settings for the BlurFader component instance in the Component Inspector panel.** Select the component instance at the top left corner of the `tape` instance, and open the Component Inspector panel (Shift+F7). This component has three options, as shown in Figure 19.20: Direction (*in* to fade in the targeted instance, *out* to fade out the targeted instance), Duration (how long the transition should last, in seconds), and `Target Clip` (the Movie Clip instance that the BlurFader component instance has snapped to).

5. **Save the Flash document, and test it (Ctrl+Enter/⌘+Enter).** When you click the Video Equipment button, the first video item fades into the Stage.

6. **Repeat Step 3 for the other Movie Clip instances on frames 2, 3, 4, 5, and 6 of the items layer.** Make sure that you name each new instance of the BlurFader component, using the frame number as a suffix, such as `bf_2`, `bf_3`, and so on. Otherwise, the blur and fade effect does not execute on the new items.

7. **Save the Flash document again, and test it.** After you click the Video Equipment button, click the Next button. Each video item fades into the Stage.

If you want to use the BlurFader component in other Flash documents that use ActionScript 3.0, simply drag the BlurFader component from one library to another document's library. Alternatively, you can copy and paste the BlurFader component instance from one document to another. Try different Duration values for the BlurFader component (in the Component Inspector panel) to see how the fade animation is affected in the Flash movie.

NOTE The BlurFader component adds about 2KB to the file size of your Flash movie file (.swf).

 You can find the completed document, `main_600.fla`, in the `ch19/src` folder of this book's CD-ROM.

Making the Movie Accessible

In the final section of this chapter, we show you how to add accessibility information to your Flash presentation. As we mention earlier in this chapter, screen readers on the Windows operating system, working in concert with the Flash Player 6 or later ActiveX control, can read aloud the content inside of Flash movies. Window-Eyes from GW Micro was engineered to work with Flash Player 6 or later through the use of MSAA (Microsoft Active Accessibility) technology. As of this writing, Window-Eyes is one of a limited number of screen readers capable of accessing Flash content.

NOTE You can download a demo version of Window-Eyes for the Windows operating system at `www.gwmicro.com`. This version works only for 30-minute durations — you need to restart your computer to initiate a new session.

We recommend that you review the Accessibility information in the Flash CS4 Help panel. Choose the Help ⇨ Flash Help command in the Flash CS4 application. We provide a quick overview of the Accessibility features of Flash CS4 in this section.

> **NOTE**   Since Flash MX 2004, Adobe has added accessibility support to the authoring environment as well. This feature enables designers and developers with disabilities to more easily use Flash to author Flash movies. To find out more information about this feature, search with the term "accessibility" in the Help panel.

Screen readers access information within the Flash movie differently, depending on the features of the specific screen reader. Here we discuss accessibility options as they relate to Window-Eyes. You will add some content to the Introduction section of the presentation that Window-Eyes can read aloud.

1. Resave the last Flash document you created in the previous section as `main_700.fla`.

2. Insert an empty keyframe at frame 10 of the content layer on the Main Timeline (that is, Scene 1).

3. On frame 10 of the content layer, drag an instance of the TextArea component from the Components panel to the left side of the Stage. In the Component Inspector panel, name this instance `infoArea`. Change the `editable` setting to `false`.

4. Open the `introduction_formatted.txt` document in the `ch19/src/text` folder of this book's CD-ROM. Copy the text in this document. Select the `infoArea` instance in your Flash document, and paste the copied text into the `htmlText` setting of the Component Inspector panel, as shown in Figure 19.21.

5. With frame 10 of the content layer active, drag an instance of the cameraHigh Movie Clip symbol (located in the `videoItems` folder) from the Library panel to the Stage. In the Properties panel, change the alpha of this instance to 30 percent. Name the instance `camHigh` as well.

   Now you will use the Accessibility panel to add information to specific elements in the Introduction section of the presentation. You can open the Accessibility panel by choosing Window ⇨ Other Panels ⇨ Accessibility.

   You can add general information about your Flash movie by deselecting all elements on the Stage (you can press the Esc key to do this quickly) and opening the Accessibility panel.

   The Make Movie Accessible option enables the screen reader to see elements inside the Flash movie. If this option is cleared, the screen reader cannot read any elements of the Flash movie.

   The Make Child Objects Accessible option enables the screen reader to access elements other than the current Name and Description in the Accessibility panel.

Clear the Auto Label option. Auto Labeling tells Flash Player 6 or later to describe buttons and other elements by associating the closest text object to the element. For example, if you had some text underneath a Button instance, Auto Label would assign this text to the Button instance for the screen reader.

The Name field enables you to assign a title to the Flash movie, and the Description field enables you to add a quick summary about the Flash movie. Window-Eyes reads the Name contents, but not the Description contents. Let's add some general information to the current Flash document.

FIGURE 19.21

The TextArea component can display HTML formatted text in the authoring environment. The screen reader can read aloud this text field's contents.

6. **Deselect all the elements on the Stage, and open the Accessibility panel.** Select the Make movie accessible and Make child objects accessible options, and clear the Auto label option. In the Name field, type the presentation's title: **Digital Video Production**. In the Description field, type the following text: **A primer for digital video equipment and accessories.** (See Figure 19.22.)

FIGURE 19.22

The Accessibility panel controls options for the Flash movie and its elements.

7. **Now select the Introduction button on frame 10 of the menu layer.** In the Accessibility option, enter the options shown in Figure 19.23. Note that you do not assign a keyboard shortcut description for this example. The Name and Description for this button is read after the general information you added in the previous step. Window-Eyes says the word "button" before it reads the name. For this example, Window-Eyes says, "Button. Introduction. Access the introduction section of the presentation."

NOTE If you do want to have a keyboard shortcut read by the screen reader, then you should type the text for any modifier key or combination including the + character, such as Ctrl+E. You also must add ActionScript to the movie to enable the key press that you described in the Accessibility panel.

FIGURE 19.23

Window-Eyes can read the Name and Description contents for buttons.

8. Repeat Step 7 for each button instance in the menu layer.

9. Select the `infoArea` instance on frame 10 of the content layer, and make sure that the **Make movie accessible** and **Make child objects accessible** check boxes are selected in the **Accessibility** panel. It is not necessary to add a description to this text field — the text inside of the field is read automatically by the screen reader.

10. Select the `camHigh` instance on frame 10 of the content layer, and make sure that the **Make child objects accessible** and **Make object accessible** options are not selected in the **Accessibility** panel. Not all elements need to be read by the screen reader, and this graphic does not need to be revealed to visually impaired users.

11. **Save your Flash document, and preview it in Internet Explorer for Windows.** Make sure that the Window-Eyes application is active. As soon as the movie loads into the browser, Window-Eyes reads the information for the movie and then reads the name and descriptions of the buttons. Then it reads the text inside of the description text field. After Window-Eyes reads the last Flash element, it speaks the word "bottom," indicating that the end of the Web page has been reached. If you add body text to the HTML document, Window-Eyes reads that text as well.

ON the CD-ROM You can find the completed Flash presentation, `main_700.fla`, in the `ch19` folder of this book's CD-ROM. This document contains the first two sections of the presentations — on your own, try adding your content to the remaining sections by using techniques you learned in this chapter.

You can continue to add more accessibility information to other elements in the Flash document. You can even add information to elements within Movie Clip symbols. Try adding descriptions to the buttons inside of the videoEquip symbol.

NOTE Screen reader technology can interface only with Flash movies played by the Flash Player 6 or later ActiveX control. Screen readers cannot access Flash movies played by the stand-alone Flash Player 6 or later.

WEB RESOURCE We'd like to know what you think about this chapter. Visit `www.flashsupport.com/feedback` to send us your comments.

Summary

■ Before you can start to create an interface in Flash, you need to have a plan for your Flash movie timeline. Create an organizational chart outlining the sections of the presentation.

■ Determine your Flash movie properties (frame size, frame rate, and background color) before you undergo production in Flash.

■ If you don't have final art for a Flash production, you can still create a functional prototype of the presentation by using placeholder graphics. When the final artwork is ready, replace the placeholder graphics with the final artwork.

- You can create simple slide shows or product catalogs by using sequential keyframes and buttons with `nextFrame()` and `prevFrame()` actions.

- The Hit area of a text-based Button symbol should always be defined with a solid shape.

- You can achieve basic text scrolling by adding the TextArea component to your Flash movie.

- You can apply time-based alpha and blur effects to artwork with the custom BlurFader component.

- You can add accessibility information to Flash movies. Windows-based screen readers designed to work with Flash Player 6 or later, such as GW Micro's Window-Eyes, can read this information.

Part VI

Distributing Flash Movies

When you finally have your project assembled in the Flash authoring environment and you're ready to prepare it for final presentation, this section explains all the options available for delivering Flash content to your audience. Chapter 20 details just about every option and setting in the Publish Settings dialog box for Flash CS4 that controls your final file size and format. This chapter includes tips for optimizing your file sizes for faster downloads and better performance. Chapter 21 covers several HTML techniques relevant to integrating Flash content on Web pages. Learn how to create plug-in and version detection systems for your Flash movies. This chapter also introduces you to the ExternalInterface API for sending commands to JavaScript. If you are planning to distribute Flash content offline or you want to avoid plug-in problems, Chapter 22 walks you through the various methods for distributing your Flash movies as self-contained executable applications for CD/DVD-ROMs or other removable storage devices and using the Flash standalone player.

Chapter 20

Publishing Flash Movies

If you have read Parts I through V of the book, you're probably more than ready to get your Flash movies uploaded to your Web server to share with your visitors. This chapter shows you how to create Flash movies (.swf files) from Flash CS4 so that they can be played with the Adobe Flash Player plug-in or ActiveX Control for Web browsers. We show you how to test your Flash movies, prepare Flash movie options, and adjust other output formats from Flash CS4, such as HTML documents and image formats.

> **TIP** In this chapter, you also learn how to take advantage of Flash CS4's Flash Player detection option. This feature adds the necessary JavaScript code to your HTML document in order to check the Flash Player plug-in version installed in a user's browser.

Testing Flash Movies

You have four ways to test your Flash movies: in the authoring environment by using the Control ➪ Play command, in the authoring environment by using the Test Movie and Test Scene commands, in a browser by using the Publish Preview command, or in the stand-alone Flash Player by using Flash movie files (.swf) made with the Publish or Export Movie commands. You should test your Flash movie file (.swf) before you transfer Flash movies to your Web server or to the intended delivery medium for several reasons:

- Flash document files (.fla) have much larger file sizes than their Flash movie file (.swf) counterparts. To accurately foretell the network bandwidth that a Flash movie requires, you need to know how large the final Flash movie will be. If the download demand is too overwhelming for your desired Internet connection speed (for example, a 56K modem), you can go back and optimize your Flash document.

- The Control ➪ Play command in the Flash authoring environment does not provide any runtime information. When you use the Test Movie or Scene command, you can view the byte size of each frame and how long it will take to download the .swf file from the Web server.

- Movie Clip animations and actions targeting Movie Clip instances cannot be previewed by using the standard Control ➪ Play command (or the Play button on the Controller) in the Flash authoring environment.

TIP   You can temporarily preview Movie Clip symbol instances within the Flash authoring environment (for example, the Timeline window) by changing the symbol instance behavior to Graphic rather than Movie Clip. Do this by selecting the instance, opening the Properties panel, choosing Graphic in the behavior drop-down menu, and setting the Looping section's options menu to Play Once or Loop. However, if you switch the behavior back to Movie Clip, you will have lost the original instance name of the Movie Clip.

- Most scripting done with ActionScript cannot be previewed with the Play command. Enabling Simple Frame Actions or Simple Buttons in the Control menu has no effect with most ActionScript 3.0 syntax. You need to use Test Movie to try out most interactive functions in a Flash movie.

TIP   Any actions that require the use of remote server-side scripts, Flash Remoting, or Adobe Flash Media Server connections to load variables, movies, or XML data work in the Test Movie environment. You do not need to view your .swf files in a browser to test these actions, unless your server-side functionality has IP address restrictions that would prohibit playback from your local machine.

- Accurate frame rates cannot be previewed with the Play command (Control ➪ Play) in the authoring environment. Most complex animations appear jerky, pausing or skipping frames when the Play command is used.

Using the Test Scene or Test Movie command

You can test your Flash movies directly within the Flash CS4 interface by using the Control ➪ Test Movie or Test Scene command. When you choose one of these commands, Flash CS4 opens your Flash document in a new window as a Flash movie file (.swf). Even though you are "testing" a Flash movie, a new .swf file is actually created and stored in the same location as the Flash document file (.fla). For this reason, always saving your Flash document before you begin testing it is a good idea.

CAUTION   If your movie is currently titled Untitled-1, Untitled-2, and so on in the application title bar, it usually indicates that the document has not yet been saved. Make sure that you save your Flash movie with a distinct name before testing it.

TIP   Flash CS4 opens all tested movies in a separate nontabbed window. On the Windows version of Flash CS4, the Test Movie window hosts the playback and debugging commands. On the Mac version of Flash CS4, the application menu bar changes depending on which type of tab or window was focused (authoring document versus movie file).

Before you use the Test Scene or Test Movie command, you can specify the settings of the resulting Flash .swf file. The Test Scene or Movie command uses the specifications outlined in the Publish Settings dialog box to generate .swf files. We discuss the Publish Settings dialog box later in this chapter. For the time being, you can use the Flash CS4 default settings to explore the Test Scene and Movie commands.

Test Movie

When you choose Control ⇨ Test Movie (Ctrl+Enter/⌘+Enter), Flash generates an .swf file of the entire Flash document that is currently open. If you have more than one Flash movie open, Flash CS4 creates an .swf file for the one that is currently in the foreground and that has "focus."

> **TIP** You can publish multiple .fla files at the same time by using the Project panel. To learn more about the Project panel, read Chapter 3, "Planning Flash Projects."

Test Scene

If you are working on a lengthy Flash document with multiple scenes, you may want to test your scenes individually. You can do this by using Control ⇨ Test Scene (Ctrl+Alt+Enter/ ⌘+Option+Enter). The process of exporting large movies via Test Movie may require many minutes to complete, whereas exporting one scene requires a significantly smaller amount of time. Movies that require compression for several bitmaps and MP3 sounds usually take the most amount of time to test. As you'll see in the next section, you can analyze each tested scene (or movie) with the Bandwidth Profiler.

> **TIP** You can use the Test Scene command while in Edit mode to export an .swf file that contains the current symbol timeline. The movie won't contain anything else from your Flash document. Note that the symbol's center point becomes the top left corner of the playback stage.

> **NOTE** As we mention earlier in this book, we highly discourage the use of multiple scenes in a Flash document (.fla file). Scenes are a legacy structural unit for Flash content, and should be used only for long-form animation destined for broadcast use, such as video production for television or film.

Using the Bandwidth Profiler

Do you want to know how long it will take for a 56 kilobits per second (Kbps) modem to download your Flash movie or scene? How about a cable modem? The Bandwidth Profiler enables you to simulate any download speed.

> See the `ch20` folder of this book's CD-ROM for a Flash document named `bandwidth.fla`. We use that Flash document for this section.

To use the Bandwidth Profiler, you first need to create a movie or scene to test. When you create a Flash movie with the Control ⇨ Test Movie or Scene commands, Flash opens the .swf file in its own window.

One Reason to Use Imported MP3 Files

If you have imported raw audio files such as .wav or .aif files into your Flash document, you may notice lengthy wait times for the Test Movie or Publish commands to complete. Why? The default MP3 encoding process consumes much of the computer processor's power and time.

Flash CS4 has three MP3 compression qualities: Fast, Medium, or Best. Fast is the default MP3 quality setting — this is by far the fastest method of encoding MP3 sound. Because MP3 uses perceptual encoding, it compares a range of samples to determine how best to compress the sound. Fast compares a smaller range of samples than either Medium or Best. As you increase quality, the sampling range increases.

This process is similar to building 256-color palettes for video files; it's best to look at all the frames of the video (instead of just the first frame) when you're trying to build a palette that's representative of all the colors used in the video. Although MP3 doesn't quite work in this fashion, the analogy is appropriate. So, at Best quality, the MP3 encoding scans more of the waveform to look for similarities and differences. However, it's also more time intensive.

As strange as it may seem, the quality does not affect the final size of the Flash movie file (.swf). The bit rate of the MP3 sound is the same regardless of the quality setting. Again, we'll use an analogy — consider the file sizes generated by three different digital cameras that have the same number of pixels in the pictures. The best camera, which has the highest-quality lens and recording mechanism, produces better-looking pictures that capture detail *and* produces the same file size as the others. This is one of the few times where it's not about the amount of information stored in the compressed file — it's a matter of the accuracy and quality of the information within that quantity.

If you want to avoid the wait for Flash CS4 to publish Flash movies that use MP3 compression, we recommend that you compress your source audio files to the MP3 format (including support for VBR — Variable Bit Rate — compression) and import those MP3 files into Flash CS4. Unless the MP3 sound file is used for Stream Sync audio, Flash CS4 exports the audio in its original MP3 compressed format.

For more information on sound in Flash movies, read Chapter 14, "Adding Sound."

View menu

The Test Movie or Test Scene viewing environment opens your Flash movie in a dedicated window with its own View and Control menus.

 On the Mac, the View and Control menus appear in the application menu bar, not in the Test Movie window.

The first three commands in the View menu are the same as those of the Flash Player plug-in viewing controls, while the others are specific to the testing environment:

- **Zoom In:** Selecting this option enlarges the Flash movie. The shortcut key for this command is Ctrl+=/⌘+=.

- **Zoom Out:** Selecting this option shrinks the Flash movie. The shortcut key for this command is Ctrl+-/⌘+-.

- **Magnification:** This submenu enables you to change the zoom factor of the movie. The Flash movie appears at the original pixel size specified in the Modify ⇨ Document dialog box when 100 percent (Ctrl+1/⌘+1) is the setting. For example, if the movie size is 500 x 300 pixels, it takes up 500 x 300 pixels on your monitor. If you change the size of the viewing window, the movie may be cropped. The lower section of this submenu enables you to change the viewable area of the Flash movie.

NOTE In the Test Movie environment, only the 100% and Show All options are enabled in the View menu. The other magnification options are enabled in the authoring environment.

- **Bandwidth Profiler:** To view the Bandwidth Profiler in this new window, use View ⇨ Bandwidth Profiler (Ctrl+B/⌘+B). The viewing window expands to accommodate the Bandwidth Profiler. Here's a breakdown of each section of the profiler:

  - The left side of the profiler displays three sections: Movie, Settings, and State. Movie indicates the dimensions, frame rate, size (in KB and bytes), duration, and preload (in number of frames and seconds). The Settings area displays the current selected connection speed (which is set in the View ⇨ Download Settings menu). State shows you the current frame playing and its byte requirements. If you're using the Simulate Download feature (discussed later in this section), the State section displays the percent of the movie that has loaded.

  - The larger right section of the profiler shows the timeline header and graph. The lower red line beneath the timeline header indicates whether a given frame streams in real time with the current modem speed specified in the Control menu. For a 28.8 Kbps modem, any frame above 200 bytes may cause delays in streaming for a 12 frames per second (fps) movie. Note that the byte limit for each frame is dependent on frame rate. For example, a 24 fps movie has a limit of 120 bytes per frame for a 28.8 Kbps modem connection.

  - When the Bandwidth Profiler is enabled, two other commands are available in the View menu: Streaming Graph (Ctrl+G/⌘+G) and Frame By Frame Graph (Ctrl+F/ ⌘+F).

- **Streaming Graph:** By default, Flash opens the Bandwidth Profiler in Streaming Graph mode. This mode indicates how the Flash movie streams into a browser (see Figure 20.1). Alternating light and dark gray blocks represent each frame. The size of each block indicates its relative byte size. For our `bandwidth.swf` example, all the frames will have loaded by the time our playhead reaches frame 13 when the movie is played over a 56 Kbps connection. The shortcut key for Streaming Graph is Ctrl+G/⌘+G.

FIGURE 20.1

The Streaming Graph indicates how a movie will download over a given modem connection. Shown here is our `bandwidth.swf` as it would download over a 56 Kbps modem.

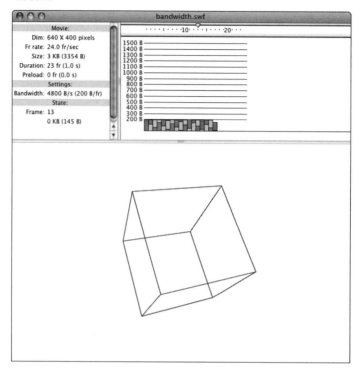

- **Frame By Frame Graph:** This second mode available to the Bandwidth Profiler lays each frame side by side under the timeline header (see Figure 20.2). Although the Streaming Graph enables you to see the real-time performance of a Flash movie, the Frame By Frame Graph enables you to more easily detect which frames are contributing to streaming delays. If any frame block goes beyond the red line of the graph (for a given connection speed), the Flash Player halts playback until the entire frame downloads. In the `bandwidth.swf` example, frame 1, weighing in at 420 bytes, is the only frame that may cause a very slight delay in streaming when the movie is played over a 28.8 Kbps connection. The remaining frames are right around 200 bytes each — right at the threshold of 200 bytes per frame for a 28.8 Kbps modem connection playing a 12 fps Flash movie. The shortcut key for Frame By Frame Graph is Ctrl+F/⌘+F.

NOTE If you use Flash CS4's new XMP metadata feature in the Publish Settings dialog box (discussed later in this chapter), you add bytes to the first frame of your Flash movie. Depending on the amount of information you specify, you shouldn't see much more than a few hundred bytes added to your overall .swf file size.

FIGURE 20.2

The Frame By Frame Graph shows you the byte demand of each frame in the Flash movie.

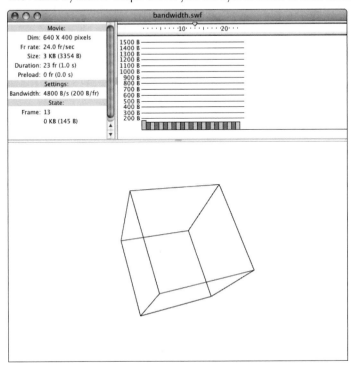

- **Simulate Download:** When the Simulate Download option is enabled, the Bandwidth Profiler emulates the chosen modem speed (in the View ⇨ Download Settings menu) when playing the Flash movie. The Bandwidth Profiler counts the bytes downloaded (displayed in the Loaded subsection of the State heading) and shows the download/play progress via a green bar in the timeline header.

> **TIP** The Simulate Download command also applies to loaded runtime assets, such as SWF, JPEG, and MP3 files. For example, when a `loadMovie()` action begins to load another file, the left side of the Bandwidth Profiler shows the progressive download at the simulated download speed. This feature applies only to assets that are loaded locally, from your system, and not over an Internet connection.

- **Download Settings:** The View menu also features a submenu of connection speeds, which work in tandem with the Streaming and Frame By Frame Graphs:

  - **14.4, 28.8, 56K, DSL, T1:** These settings determine what speed the Bandwidth Profiler uses to calculate estimated download times and frame byte limitations. Notice that these settings use more practical expectations of these modem speeds. For example, a 28.8 modem can theoretically download 3.5 kilobytes per second (denoted as KB/s in the Download Settings menu), but a more realistic download rate for this modem speed is 2.3 kilobytes per second.

   ■ **User Settings 6, 7, and 8:** These are user-definable speed settings. By default, they are all 2.3 KB/s.

   ■ **Customize:** To change the settings for any of the modem speeds listed previously, use the Customize command to input the new value(s).

■ **Quality:** The Quality submenu controls the visual appearance of graphics within the Flash movie. By default, all graphics are displayed at High quality. You can choose from Low, Medium, or High quality in this menu.

■ **Show Redraw Regions:** This option enables you to see which areas of the Flash movie are being updated on the screen. For example, if you have a Graphic symbol animation playing in the movie, a red outline frame appears around that portion of the Stage. Any and all redraw regions are bounded by such a red frame. You can use this feature to determine how much work the Flash Player is doing to redraw the Stage — many performance and playback issues are the direct result of too much screen redrawing.

Control menu

Use the Control menu to play (Enter key) or rewind (Ctrl+Alt+R/⌘+Option+R) the test movie. Rewinding pauses the `bandwidth.swf` movie on the first frame. Use the Step Forward (. or > key) and Step Backward (, or < key) commands to view the Flash movie frame by frame. If a Flash movie doesn't have a `stop()` action on the last frame, the Loop command forces the player to infinitely repeat the Flash movie.

You can use the Disable Keyboard Shortcuts command to turn off the shortcut keys for all the commands available in Test Movie mode. This is especially useful if you have enabled interactive key presses within ActionScript for your movie. For example, enabling the Return or Enter key for a button conflicts with the Play command (Control ⇨ Play). As such, when you press Enter while you test your movie, the movie plays to the next frame and the button actions are ignored.

A Word about the Export Movie Command

Even though Flash streamlines the process of creating Flash movies with the Publish commands (discussed in the next section), it is worth mentioning that the File ⇨ Export Movie command provides another route to creating an .swf file. Although the Publish command is the quickest way to create HTML-ready Flash movies, the Export Movie command can be used to create updated .swf files that have already been placed in HTML documents, or Flash movies that you intend to import into Adobe Director movies. You can find the "Working with Director" chapter from *Macromedia Flash MX 2004 Bible* (Wiley, 2003) archived at this book's Web site, www.flashsupport.com/archives. In practice, we find that we rarely use the Export Movie command. If you don't need HTML documents published with your Flash movie, simply clear the HTML option in the Formats tab of the Publish Settings dialog box.

Debug menu

The Debug menu contains List Objects and List Variables commands. List Objects can be used to show the names of Movie Clip instances or ActionScript objects in the Output window, and the List Variables command displays the names and values of any currently loaded variables, ActionScript objects, and XML data.

Using the size report

Flash also lets you view a text file summary of movie elements, frames, and fonts called a size report. In addition to viewing Frame By Frame Graphs of a Flash movie with the Bandwidth Profiler, you can inspect this size report for other "hidden" byte additions such as font character outlines. You can enable the size report to be created by accessing the Publish Settings dialog box (File ➪ Publish Settings), clicking the Flash tab, and checking the Generate size report option. When it is enabled, you can view the size report in two ways:

- After you publish, publish preview, or export a Flash movie, go to the folder where the .swf file was created. In that folder, you'll find a text file accompanying the Flash movie. This file is named after your Flash movie's name, followed by "Report" and the .txt file extension, as in `bandwidth Report.txt`.

- When you test your Flash movie by using the Control ➪ Test Movie command, the Output panel opens automatically in front of the Test Movie window. The report automatically loads into the Output panel.

 A sample size report, called `bandwidth Report.txt`, is included in the ch20 folder of this book's CD-ROM.

Publishing Your Flash Movies

After you've made a dazzling Flash movie complete with motion tweens, 3D simulations, and ActionScripted interactivity, you need to make the Flash movie useable for the intended delivery medium — the Web or a CD- or DVD-ROM, to name a couple. As mentioned in the introduction to this book, you need the Flash CS4 application to open .fla files. Because the Flash Player plug-in uses .swf files, you must export or publish your .fla file in a format that your audience can use. More important, Flash documents are authoring documents, while Flash movies are optimized for the shortest delivery times and maximum playback performance.

You can convert your Flash document files (.fla) to Flash movie files (.swf) by using either the File ➪ Export Movie, Control ➪ Test Movie, or File ➪ Publish/Publish Settings command. You can specify just about all file format properties in one step by using the File ➪ Publish Settings command. After you've entered the settings, the File ➪ Publish command exports any and all file formats with your specified parameters in one step — all from the Flash CS4 application.

Three commands are available with the Publish feature: Publish Settings, Publish Preview, and Publish. We discuss each of these commands in the following sections.

Publish Settings

The Publish Settings command (File ➪ Publish Settings) is used to determine which file formats are exported when the File ➪ Publish command is invoked. By default, new Flash documents created with Flash CS4 use Publish Settings that export a Flash movie file (.swf) and an HTML file with the proper markup tags to utilize the Flash Player 10 plug-in or ActiveX control. If you want to customize the settings of the exported file types, you should familiarize yourself with the publish settings before you attempt to use the Publish command.

> **TIP** The Publish Settings dialog box has many features that were introduced in Flash MX 2004 and Flash CS3, with some updates in Flash CS4. You should be aware that the default ActionScript language version is AS2 or AS3 for new Flash documents in Flash CS4.

Selecting formats

Choose File ➪ Publish Settings to access the Publish Settings dialog box, which is nearly identical for both the Windows and Mac versions of Flash CS4. The dialog box opens to the Formats tab, which has check boxes to select the formats in which your Flash document will be published (see Figure 20.3). For each Type that is checked, a tab appears in the Publish Settings dialog box (with the exception of the Windows and Mac projector options). Click each type's tab to specify settings to control the particulars of the movie or file that will be generated in that format.

If you click the Use Default Names button, all the File fields fill in with the name of your Flash document, followed by the file format's suffix. For example, if your movie is named `sample.fla` and you click the Use Default Names button, this is the base from which the names are generated in publishing. Thus, `sample.swf`, `sample.html`, `sample.gif`, and so on would result.

> **TIP** You can enter nonversion-specific filenames for Flash documents that you incrementally save as you work. For example, if you have a Flash document named `main_100.fla`, set the Flash movie filename to `main.swf`, and then every new Flash document version you save (for example, `main_101.fla`, `main_102.fla`, and so on) still produces a `main.swf` file. This way, you can consistently refer to one Flash movie file (.swf) in your HTML code and incrementally save your Flash documents. However, if you work on large Flash projects with a team of Flash designers and developers, you should consider using version control software, such as SVN (Subversion), CVS (Concurrent Versioning System), or Microsoft SourceSafe. With version control software, you don't need to resave files with new names; rather, you check in your changes to the version control system, which keeps track of each file version. We briefly discuss version control in Chapter 3, "Planning Flash Projects."

FIGURE 20.3

The Formats tab of the Publish Settings dialog box enables you to select the published file formats and use default or custom names for these published files.

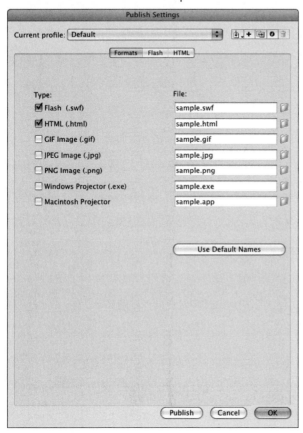

TIP   You can specify which folder a publish document is created and stored in. All the file formats have a folder icon to the right of the File field. If you click the folder icon, you can browse to a specific location where your published file will be created. You can use relative or absolute paths with the filenames in the Formats tab.

Using the Flash settings

The primary and default publishing format of Flash CS4 documents is the Flash movie .swf format. Only Flash movies retain full support for Flash actions and animations. To control the settings for the Flash movie, choose the Flash tab of the Publish Settings dialog box, as shown in Figure 20.4.

FIGURE 20.4

The Flash tab of the Publish Settings dialog box controls the settings for a movie published in the Flash format.

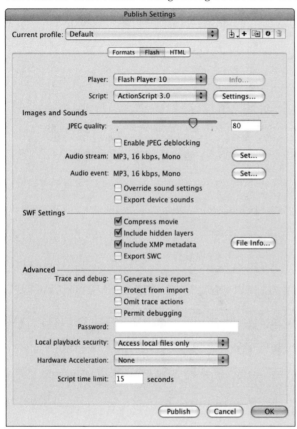

Here are your options in the Flash tab:

- **Player:** This drop-down menu provides the option to publish movies in any of the Flash movie formats. To ensure complete compatibility with all the new Flash CS4 features, select Flash Player 10. Each release of the Flash Player has added specific features and capabilities. If in doubt, you should test your choice of version in that version's Flash Player.

TIP   Flash CS4 has Flash Lite options in the Version menu. Flash Lite 1.0/1.1 is the most common Flash Player shipping with some mobile phones, such as DoCoMo phones in Japan. Newer phones may have Flash Lite 2.0, 2.1, or 3.0 installed. If one of these options is selected, make sure that you are using a Stage size that is compatible with the screen size of the

mobile handset on which the movie will be deployed. Several templates are available for devices in the Global Phones, Japanese Phones, and PDA categories of the Template tab of the File ⇨ New dialog box. The new Adobe Device Central application that ships with Flash CS4 can help you find the right Flash document settings for a wide range of mobile devices. For more information on Device Central, read Chapter 22, "Using the Flash Player and Projector."

■ **Script:** This option controls how ActionScript is compiled in a Flash movie file (.swf). You can choose ActionScript 1.0, ActionScript 2.0, or ActionScript 3.0. By default, ActionScript 2.0 is selected if you created your Flash document with the Flash file (ActionScript 2.0) option. ActionScript 3.0 is selected if you chose Flash file (ActionScript 3.0). Use ActionScript 2.0 or 3.0 only if you use the ActionScript 2.0 or 3.0 coding features, or if you use components that ship with Flash CS4, such as the FLVPlayback component or the UI components. If you code ActionScript the same way that you did in Flash MX or Flash 5, choose ActionScript 1.0.

TIP Flash CS4 can compile ActionScript 2.0 code so that it is compatible with Flash Player 6. If you choose ActionScript 2.0 and set the Version menu to Flash Player 6, Flash CS4 automatically compiles ActionScript 2.0 in a format that Flash Player 6 understands.

Also, keep in mind that ActionScript 1.0 or 2.0 code is case-sensitive *if* it is published for Flash Player 7 or later. In Flash Player 7 or later movies, variables, instance names, and other terms in ActionScript are case-sensitive. For example, if you accidentally refer to a variable named myName as myname, Flash Player 7–compiled movies are not as forgiving as Flash Player 6–compiled movies.

■ **JPEG quality:** This slider and text-field option specifies the level of Joint Photographic Experts Group (JPEG) compression applied to bitmapped artwork in the Flash movie. The value can be any value between (and including) 0 to 100. Higher values apply less compression and preserve more information of the original bitmap, whereas lower values apply more compression and keep less information. The value entered here applies to all bitmaps that enable the Use document default quality option, found in the Bitmap Properties dialog box for each bitmap in the document's Library panel. Unlike the audio settings discussed in a moment, no "override" option exists to disregard settings in the library.

■ **Enable JPEG deblocking:** This new feature reduces the visual artifacts that appear in JPEG images within your Flash movie (.swf file) when you use a low JPEG quality value. This feature is available only in Flash Player 10.

■ **Audio stream:** This option displays the current audio compression scheme for stream audio. By clicking the Set button (see Figure 20.4), you can control the compression applied to any sounds that use the Stream Sync setting in the Sound area of the Property inspector (when a sound keyframe has focus). Like the JPEG quality option discussed previously, this compression value is applied to any stream sounds that use the Default compression in the Export Settings section of each audio file's Sound Properties dialog box in the document's library. See Chapter 14, "Adding Sound," for more information on using stream sounds and audio compression schemes.

- **Audio event:** This setting behaves exactly the same as the Audio Stream option, except that this compression setting applies to Default compression-enabled event sounds. See Chapter 14, "Adding Sound," for more information on event sounds.

TIP Flash CS4 supports imported MP3 audio that uses Variable Bit Rate (VBR) compression. However, Flash cannot compress native sounds in VBR. If you use any imported MP3 audio for Stream Sync audio, Flash recompresses the MP3 audio on export.

- **Override sound settings:** If you want the settings for Audio stream and Audio event to apply to all stream and event sounds, respectively, and to disregard any unique compression schemes specified in the document's library, check this option. This is useful for creating multiple .swf file versions of the Flash movie (hi-fi, lo-fi, and so on) and enabling the Web visitor to decide which one to download.

- **Export device sounds:** In Flash CS4, you have the option of exporting device sounds with your Flash movie. You use this option only if you are using one of the Flash Lite options in the Version menu. To learn more about the use of this feature, use the search phrase "device sound" in the Help panel (Help ⇨ Flash Help) in Flash CS4.

- **Compress movie:** This option compresses Flash Player 6 or later movies only. When enabled, this compression feature greatly reduces the size of text- or ActionScript-heavy Flash movies. However, you may see little or no size difference on other Flash elements, such as artwork and sounds. Compression cannot be used on Flash Player 5 or earlier movies.

- **Include hidden layers:** This option enables you to control hidden layers with your SWF file. For example, if you hide a layer in a Movie Clip symbol, that layer does not export with the SWF file if this option is unchecked in the Flash tab. By default, hidden layers export with the SWF file.

- **Include XMP metadata:** This new feature in Flash CS4 allows you to employ Adobe's eXtensible Metadata Platform (XMP) to classify and describe your Flash content. XMP information can be added to just about any file format created by Adobe tools. This option is enabled by default with new Flash files created in Flash CS4, and automatically includes the file creator (Adobe Flash CS4 Professional) and creation date information with the published Flash movie (.swf file). Click the File Info button to modify the metadata included with your content. Note that you can view a SWF file's metadata in Adobe Bridge CS4, included with the default installation of Adobe Flash CS4.

- **Export SWC:** If you've built a document class file for your Flash document, you can export the class as a precompiled component, or SWC file. This option is available only if you use Flash Player 9 or later and ActionScript 3.0.

- **Generate size report:** As discussed earlier in this chapter, the size report for a Flash movie can be very useful in pinpointing problematic bandwidth-intensive elements, such as font characters. When this option is checked, the Publish command exports a text (.txt) file. You can view this document separately in a text-editor application such as Notepad or TextEdit.

- **Protect from import:** This option safeguards your Flash movies on the Internet. When enabled, the .swf file cannot be imported into the Flash CS4 authoring environment or altered.

CAUTION The Protect from import option does *not* prevent a Web browser from caching your .swf files. Also, Adobe Director can import and use protected Flash movies. Flash utilities such as SWF Decompiler from www.sothink.com can break into any .swf file and extract artwork, symbols, video clips, and sounds. There's even an application called ActionScript Viewer from www.buraks.com/asv that can extract ActionScript from your .swf files! For this reason, you should always use server-side scripts to verify sensitive data such as password entries in Flash movies, rather than internal ActionScripted password checking with if/else conditions. Don't store sensitive information such as passwords in your source files!

- **Omit trace actions:** If this option is selected, Flash CS4 removes any trace() actions used in your Flash document's ActionScript code. trace() actions open the Output panel in Test Movie mode for debugging purposes. In general, if you used trace() actions, you should omit them from the final Flash movie — they can't be viewed from the standard version of the Flash Player anyway. trace() actions add to the final Flash movie (.swf) file size. For final production and live deployment, you should enable the Omit trace actions option to reduce the overall file size.

- **Permit debugging:** If this option is selected, you can access the Debugger panel from within the Debug Movie environment, or from a Web browser that is using the Flash Debug Player plug-in or ActiveX control. To install the Flash Debug Player plug-in or ActiveX control, go to the Players folder in your Adobe Flash CS4 application folder. There, you find a Debug folder. With your browser applications closed, run one (or more) of the following files:

  - **Install Flash Player 9 ActiveX.msi** to install the ActiveX control for Internet Explorer on Windows 98/ME/2000/XP/Vista.

  - **Install Flash Player 9 Plugin.msi** to install the plug-in for Mozilla-compatible browsers such as Firefox or Netscape on Windows 95/98/ME/NT/2000/XP/Vista.

  - **Install Flash Player 9 UB** to install the plug-in for Mozilla-compatible browsers such as Apple Safari or Mozilla Firefox on Macs running OS X 10.1 or greater.

- **Password:** If you selected the Permit debugging option, you can enter a password to access the Debugger panel. Because you can debug movies over a live Internet connection, you should always enter a password here if you intend to debug a remote Flash movie. If you leave this field empty and check the Permit debugging option, Flash CS4 still prompts you for a password when you attempt to access the Debugger panel remotely. Simply press Enter when this prompt appears if you left this field blank.

- **Local playback security:** This feature enables you to control the access to local or networked assets from the published Flash movie. In older releases of the Flash Player, a Flash movie file (.swf) could potentially access local files, representing a security hole. A Flash movie, for example, had the capability to load text files on the local computer and transmit the contents of that file to a remote server. Now, local Flash files are able to accept data from both local and network sources. However, if you choose to send data to a network source, you are able to receive only from a network source, with no data available locally. For more information on this feature, search the Help panel in Flash CS4 with the term "local playback security." Note that a Flash projector can potentially read local files and transmit information to other networks.

- **Hardware Acceleration:** This new feature in Flash CS4 allows you to control whether the SWF file can take advantage of the user's hardware to enhance playback of the Flash content. You have three options in this menu:

  - **None:** This value disables the use of any direct communication from the Flash Player to graphics hardware on a user's computer. The Web browser (or host environment for the Flash Player runtime engine) handles all graphics processing. By default, this value is selected.

  - **Level 1 - Direct:** This value enables the Flash Player to directly draw graphics to the screen instead of delegating the responsibility to the host environment, such as a Web browser.

  - **Level 2 - GPU:** This value offloads all graphics drawing directly to the Graphics Processing Unit (GPU), better known as your computer's video graphics card. If you are targeting users with modern-day computers (Core 2 Duo) with fast video graphics capabilities, this option improves graphics rendering and video playback. The level of performance varies based on the power of the user's video graphics card.

  For most Flash content, the default value of None is acceptable. If animation and video playback within your Flash content seems to behave slower than expected on modern computer systems, try using the Level 1 or Level 2 options to improve performance.

- **Script time limit:** This option enables you to specify a timeout value for script execution. For example, if you create complex ActionScript code that temporarily bogs down the Flash Player, you can specify a longer time out value in this box. If a script executes longer than the time limit, the Flash Player presents a "script running slowly" dialog box to the user, enabling the user to abort the script.

When you are finished entering the settings for the Flash movie, you can proceed to other file type settings in the Publish Settings dialog box; or you can click OK to return to the authoring environment of Flash CS4 so that you can use the newly entered settings in the Test Movie or Scene environment. You can also export a Flash movie (and other file formats currently selected in Publish Settings) by clicking the Publish button in the Publish Settings dialog box.

Using the HTML settings

HTML is the language in which most Web pages are written. The HTML tab of the Publish Settings dialog box (see Figure 20.5) has a number of settings that control the way in which Flash CS4 publishes a movie into a Web page with HTML tags specifying the Flash Player.

FIGURE 20.5

The HTML tab controls flexible Flash movie options — you can change these options without altering the actual Flash movie (.swf file).

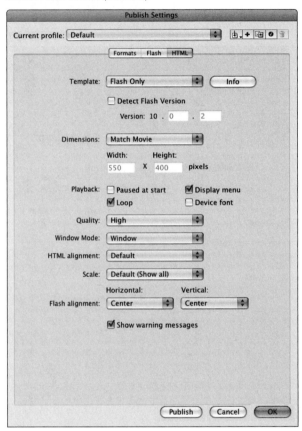

NEW FEATURE The Flash Player detection capabilities have been updated in the HTML publish settings to use a single HTML file with embedded JavaScript code. Flash no longer creates or uses the `AC_RunActiveContent.js` file included from past releases of the Flash authoring tool. Although Adobe has improved the Flash Player detection script utilized by Flash CS4's publish feature, we still recommend implementing the SWFObject JavaScript library, which is discussed in Chapter 21, "Integrating Flash Content with Web Pages."

The settings available in the HTML tab include:

- **Template:** Perhaps the most important (and versatile) feature of all publish settings, the Template setting enables you to select a predefined set of HTML tags to display your Flash movies. To view the description of each template, click the Info button to the right of the drop-down list (shown in Figure 20.5). All templates use the same options listed in the HTML tab — the template simply places the values of those settings into HTML tags scripted in the template. You can also create your own custom templates for your own unique implementation of Flash movies.

  You can view the "source" of each template in the HTML folder found inside the `en/FirstRun/HTML` folder (Windows or Mac) of the Flash CS4 application folder. These template files have .html extensions, and you can use Adobe Dreamweaver, Notepad (Windows), TextEdit (Mac), or any text editor to view and edit the files. All the preinstalled templates include HTML tags to create an entire Web page, complete with `<head>`, `<title>`, and `<body>` tags. The following templates are available in the HTML tab:

  - **Flash For Pocket PC 2003:** With this template, Flash creates an HTML document that can display the Flash movie within the Pocket IE application running on a Pocket PC. This template also creates the necessary tags to display the same Flash movie in the regular desktop versions of Internet Explorer and Netscape. At the time of this writing, Flash Player 7 was the latest public release available for the Pocket PC.

> **NOTE**   If you are designing Flash movies for the Pocket PC, be sure to check out the PDA document templates. Choose File ➪ New, click the Templates tab, and choose the PDA category. The Windows Mobile templates work with the screen dimensions of most Pocket PCs.

  - **Flash HTTPS:** This template looks nearly identical to the Flash Only template (discussed next). The only difference with this template is that the download locations for the ActiveX control and plug-in page use `https://` rather than `http://`. If you are loading your Flash movie file (.swf) from a secure URL and page, it's recommended that any and all URLs used within that document use secure URLs as well. A secure URL always starts with `https://`.

  - **Flash Only:** This default template inserts the `<object>` and `<embed>` tags for a Flash movie. It does not perform any browser or plug-in detection. If the user does not have the Flash Player plug-in or ActiveX control, the browser may produce an error message, a missing plug-in icon, or a prompt to download the latest plug-in or ActiveX control, depending on the browser configuration. The HTML this template produces may allow an earlier Flash Player (such as Flash Player 4) to attempt playback of your newer Flash movie. Keep in mind that any version of the Flash Player tries to render any Flash movie file. However, you may get unpredictable results when a newer-version Flash movie loads into an older player.

> **NOTE**   The Flash Only template includes JavaScript code to create the `<object>` and `<embed>` tags.

■ **Flash Only -- Allow Full Screen:** This template behaves like the Flash Only template but also inserts the necessary tag attributes to enable full-screen playback of Flash movies in Flash Player 9 r28 or later. This new feature allows Flash movies to "take over" the entire screen and play outside of the browser window.

■ **Flash with AICC Tracking:** Use this template if you are creating Flash movies that incorporate components from the Learning Interactions Library (Window ⇨ Other Panels ⇨ Common Libraries ⇨ Learning Interactions). Use it also if you want the components in the Flash movie to comply with the Aviation Industry CBT Committee (AICC) training guidelines. The template creates JavaScript/VBScript functions that can work with the ActionScript of the learning components. For more information on AICC guidelines, see www.aicc.org. Note that this template functions only in Web browsers that support the fscommand() action from Flash movies.

■ **Flash with FSCommand:** Use this template if you are using the fscommand() action in your Flash movies to communicate with JavaScript in the HTML page. The fscommand() is discussed in Chapter 21, "Integrating Flash Content with Web Pages." The necessary <object> and <embed> tags from the Flash Only (Default) template are also included.

■ **Flash with Named Anchors:** If you are using named anchors in the Main Timeline of your Flash document, you should use this template for your published HTML document. This template creates the necessary JavaScript to enable the Back button on your Web browser with named anchors within your Flash movie. Named anchors allow you to designate specific keyframes (and scenes) that register in the browser's history when played. This feature works in Internet Explorer for Windows, but not in Mozilla-based browsers such as Firefox or Safari.

■ **Flash with SCORM 1.2 Tracking:** This template creates the HTML and JavaScript/VBScript functions to enable communication between Flash movies that use the components from the Learning Interactions Library and the HTML page. SCORM, which stands for Shareable Content Object Reference Model, is a set of guidelines for learning systems created by the U.S. Department of Defense Advanced Distributed Learning (ADL) Initiative. Both SCORM and AICC guidelines aim to promote interoperability among learning and training systems. Note that this template functions only in Web browsers that support the fscommand() from Flash movies.

■ **Flash with SCORM 2004 Tracking:** This template has the same functionality as the last template, except that the codebase has been updated to support SCORM 2004 features.

■ **Image Map:** This template does not use or display any Flash movie. Instead, it uses a GIF, JPEG, or PNG image (as specified in the Publish Settings dialog box's Format tab) as a client-side image map, via an <img> tag with a USEMAP attribute. Use a frame label of #map in the Flash document file (.fla) to designate which frame is used as the map image. See the section, "Using the GIF settings," later in this chapter for more details.

- **Detect Flash Version:** This updated feature of Flash CS4 enables you to add version detection to your Flash content. For the most basic use, simply select this check box and leave the default versions. The version appearing in the HTML tab reflects the version of the Flash Player you selected in the Flash tab of the Publish Settings dialog box. For more advanced use, you can specify major and minor versions of the currently selected Flash Player version. The Detect Flash Version feature creates all the necessary JavaScript to detect the Flash Player on modern browsers. The options for this feature include two fields:

  - **Minor Revision:** This text field controls the minor version revision number you want to require. Note that, to date, there have been no minor revisions to any publicly released Flash Players — Adobe has released only incremental revisions.

  - **Incremental Revision:** This text field displays the incremental revision number of the Flash Player you want to require. You can edit this value directly in the dialog box. For example, if you want to require the Flash Player 6 r65 option in the Flash tab, you can enter the number **65** in this field. The detection script would then check for r65 or later.

> **TIP** The Detect Flash Version feature does not create an alternate HTML content page. With Flash CS4, the alternate content HTML is specified in the JavaScript. To include your own custom alternate content, you can edit the JavaScript in Adobe Dreamweaver or your preferred text editor. Also, we highly recommend using Geoff Stearn's SWFObject JavaScript library as a preferred Flash Player detection script. You learn more about SWFObject in Chapter 21.

- **Dimensions:** This setting controls the width and height values of the <object> and <embed> tags. The dimension settings here do not change the original Flash movie; they simply create the area through which your Flash movie is viewed on the Web page. The way that the Flash movie "fits" into this viewing area is determined with the Scale option (discussed later). Three input areas exist: a drop-down menu and two text fields for width and height. The options here are

  - **Match Movie:** If you want to keep the same width and height that you specified in the Document Properties dialog box (Modify ➪ Document), use this option in the drop-down menu.

  - **Pixels:** You can change the viewing size (in pixel units) of the Flash movie window by selecting this option and entering new values in the Width and Height text fields.

  - **Percent:** This option scales the movie to the size of the browser window — or a portion of it. Using a value of 100 on both Width and Height expands the Flash movie to fit the entire browser window. If Percent is used with the proper Scale setting (see the description of the Scale setting later in this chapter), the aspect ratio of your Flash movie is not distorted.

> **TIP** The ActionScript **Stage** class and its supporting methods enable you to disable or override automatic scaling of the Flash movie. For example, the following action added to frame 1 of your Flash movie disables scaling: **Stage.scaleMode = "noScale";**. If you want to center your Flash movie's Stage in a browser window, you can set the size to Percent in the HTML tab, and the Scale setting to No scale.

■ **Width and Height:** Enter the values for the Flash movie width and height here. If Match Movie is selected, you shouldn't be able to enter any values. The unit of measurement is determined by selecting either Pixels or Percent from the drop-down menu.

■ **Playback:** These options control how the Flash movie plays when it is downloaded to the browser. Each of these options has <object> and <embed> attributes if you want to control them outside of Publish Settings. Note that these attributes are not viewable within the Publish Settings dialog box — you need to load the published HTML document into a text editor to see the attributes.

■ **Paused at start:** This is equivalent to adding a stop() action on the first frame of the first scene in the Flash movie. By default, this option is off — movies play as soon as they stream into the player. A button with a play() action can start the movie, or the Play command can be executed from the Flash Player shortcut menu (by right-clicking or Control+clicking the movie). Attribute: play="true" or "false". If play="true", the movie plays as soon as it is loaded.

■ **Loop:** This option causes the Flash movie to repeat an infinite number of times. By default, this option is on. If it is not checked, the Flash movie stops on the last frame unless some other ActionScripted event is initiated on the last frame. Attribute: loop="true" or "false".

■ **Display menu:** This option controls whether the person viewing the Flash movie in the Flash Player environment can access the shortcut menu via a right-click (Windows) or Control+click (Mac) anywhere within the movie area. If this option is selected, the visitor can select Zoom In/Out, 100 percent, Show All, High Quality, Play, Loop, Rewind, Forward, and Back from the menu. If this option is not selected, the visitor can select only About Flash Player from the menu. Attribute: menu="true" or "false".

■ **Device font:** This option applies to Flash movies played only in the Windows version of the Flash Player. When enabled, this option replaces fonts that are not installed on the Player's system with anti-aliased system fonts. Attribute: devicefont="true" or "false".

■ **Quality:** This menu determines how the Flash artwork in a movie renders. Although it would be ideal to play all Flash movies at high quality, slower processors may not be able to redraw anti-aliased artwork and keep up with the frame rate. The options for this setting include the following:

■ **Low:** This setting forces the Flash Player to turn off anti-aliasing (smooth edges) completely. On slower processors, this may improve playback performance. Attribute: quality="low".

■ **Auto Low:** This setting starts in Low quality mode (no anti-aliasing) but switches to High quality if the computer's processor can handle the playback speed. Attribute: quality="autolow".

■ **Auto High:** This setting is the opposite of Auto Low. The Flash Player starts playing the movie in High quality mode, but if the processor cannot handle the playback demands, it switches to Low quality mode. For most Web sites, this is the optimal setting to use because it favors higher quality first. Attribute: quality="autohigh".

■ **Medium:** This quality produces anti-aliased vector graphics on a 2 x 2 grid (in other words, it smoothes edges over a 4-pixel square area), but it does not smooth bitmap images. Artwork appears slightly better than the Low quality, but not as smooth as the High setting. Attribute: `quality="medium"`. This quality setting works only with the Flash Player 5 or later.

■ **High:** When this setting is used, the Flash Player dedicates more of the computer's processor to rendering graphics (instead of playback). All vector artwork is anti-aliased on a 4 x 4 grid (16-pixel square area). Bitmaps are smoothed unless they are contained within an animation sequence such as a motion tween. By default, this setting is selected in the HTML tab of the Publish Settings dialog box. Attribute: `quality="high"`.

■ **Best:** This mode does everything that High quality does, with the addition of smoothing all bitmaps — regardless of whether they are in motion tweens. This mode is the most processor-intensive. Attribute: `quality="best"`.

● **Window Mode:** The Window Mode setting works only with any version of the Flash ActiveX control on Internet Explorer for Windows 95/98/ME/NT/2000/XP or with Flash Player 6 r65 and later for Mozilla-compatible browsers on Windows or Mac OS X. If you intend to deliver to one of these browsers and/or this version of the Flash Player, you can animate Flash content on top of DHTML content. One of the following values can be selected from this menu:

■ **Window:** This is the "standard" player interface, in which the Flash movie plays as it would normally, in its own rectangular window on a Web page. Attribute: `wmode="window"`.

■ **Opaque Windowless:** Use this option if you want the Flash movie to have an opaque (that is, nontransparent) background and have DHTML or HTML elements behind the Flash movie. Attribute: `wmode="opaque"`.

■ **Transparent Windowless:** This option "knocks out" the Flash background color so that other HTML and DHTML elements can show through. You have likely seen this type of Flash movie and effect used on several commercial Web sites, where Flash ads animate across the screen on top of the HTML document. Note that the Flash movie's frame rate and performance may suffer on slower machines when this mode is used because the Flash movie needs to composite itself over other non-Flash material. Attribute: `wmode="transparent"`.

● **HTML alignment:** This setting works much like the ALIGN attribute of <img> tags in HTML documents, but it's used with the ALIGN attribute of the <OBJECT> and <embed> tags for the Flash movie. Note that these settings may not have any effect when used within a table cell (<td> tag) or a DHTML layer (<div> or <layer> tag). The options for this setting include the following:

■ **Default:** This option left-justifies the Flash movie in the browser window. If the browser window is smaller than a Flash movie that uses a Pixel or Match Movie dimensions setting (see the Dimensions setting earlier in this section), the Flash movie is cropped.

■ **Left, Right, Top, and Bottom:** These options align the Flash movie along the left, right, top, or bottom edge of the browser window, respectively.

- **Scale:** This setting works in tandem with the Dimensions setting discussed earlier in this section, and it determines how the Flash movie appears on the HTML page. Just as big-screen movies must be cropped to fit the aspect ratio of a TV screen, Flash movies may need to be modified to fit the area prescribed by the Dimensions setting. The settings for the Scale option include the following:

  - **Default (Show all):** This option fits the entire Flash movie into the area defined by the Dimensions setting without distorting the original aspect ratio of the Flash movie. However, borders may appear on two sides of the Flash movie. For example, if a 300-x-300-pixel window is specified in Dimensions and the Flash movie has an aspect ratio of 1.33:1 (for example, 400 x 300 pixels), a border fills the remaining areas on top of and below the Flash movie. This is similar to the "letterbox" effect on wide-screen video rentals. Attribute: `scale="showall"`.

  - **No border:** This option forces the Flash movie to fill the area defined by the Dimensions setting without leaving borders. The Flash movie's aspect ratio is not distorted or stretched. However, this may crop two sides of the Flash movie. Using the same example from Show All, the left and right sides of the Flash movie are cropped when No Border is selected. Attribute: `scale="noborder"`.

  - **Exact fit:** This option stretches a Flash movie to fill the entire area defined by the Dimensions setting. Using the same example from Show All, the 400 x 300 Flash movie is scrunched to fit a 300 x 300 window. If the original movie showed a perfect circle, it now appears as an oval. Attribute: `scale="exactfit"`.

  - **No scale:** This option prevents the Flash movie from scaling beyond its original size as defined in the Document Properties dialog box (Modify ⮂ Document). The Flash Player window size (or the Web browser window size) has no effect on the size of the Flash movie. Attribute: `scale="noscale"`.

- **Flash alignment:** This setting adjusts the `salign` attribute of the `<object>` and `<embed>` tags for the Flash movie. In contrast to the HTML Alignment setting, Flash alignment works in conjunction with the Scale and Dimensions settings, and determines how a Flash movie is aligned within the Player window. This setting has the following options:

  - **Horizontal:** These options — Left, Center, and Right — determine whether the Flash movie is horizontally aligned to the left, center, or right of the Dimensions area, respectively. Using the same example from the Scale setting, a 400-x-300-pixel Flash movie (fit into a 300 x 300 Dimension window with `scale="noborder"`) with a Flash Horizontal Alignment setting of Left crops only the right side of the Flash movie.

  - **Vertical:** These options — Top, Center, and Bottom — determine whether the Flash movie is vertically aligned to the top, center, or bottom of the Dimensions area, respectively. If the preceding example used a Show All Scale setting and had a Flash Vertical Alignment setting of Top, the border would occur only below the bottom edge of the Flash movie.

- **Show warning messages:** This useful feature alerts you to errors during the actual Publish process. For example, if you selected the Image Map template and didn't specify a static GIF, JPEG, or PNG file in the Formats tab, Flash returns an error. By default, this option is enabled. If it is disabled, Flash suppresses any warnings during the Publish process.

Using the GIF settings

The Graphics Interchange File (GIF) format, developed by CompuServe, defined the first generation of Web graphics and is still quite popular today, despite its 256-color limitation. In the context of the publish settings of Flash CS4, the GIF format is used to export a static or animated image that can be used in place of the Flash movie if the Flash Player or plug-in is not installed. Although the Flash and HTML tabs are specific to Flash movie display and playback, the settings of the GIF tab (see Figure 20.6) control the characteristics of a GIF animation (or still image) that Flash CS4 publishes.

FIGURE 20.6

You can finesse every subtle aspect of a GIF animation or still image with these settings of the GIF tab of the Publish Settings dialog box.

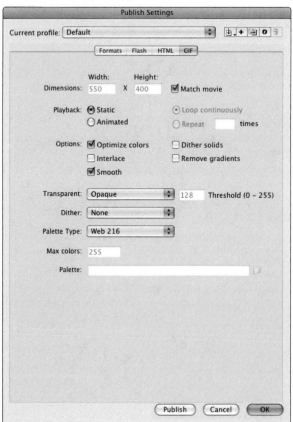

The settings in the GIF tab include the following:

- **Dimensions:** This setting has three options: Width, Height, and Match movie. As you might have guessed, Width and Height control the dimensions of the GIF image. These fields are enabled only when the Match movie check box is unchecked. With Match movie checked, the dimensions of the GIF match those of the Flash movie that is being published.

- **Playback:** These radio buttons control what type of GIF image is created and how it plays (if Animated is chosen):

  - **Static:** If this button is selected, Flash exports the first frame of the Flash movie as a single still image in the GIF format. If you want to use a frame other than the first frame, use a frame label of #Static on the desired frame. Alternatively, you could use the File ⇨ Export Image command to export a GIF image from whatever frame the Current Frame Indicator is positioned over.

  - **Animated:** If this button is selected, Flash exports the entire Flash movie as an animated GIF file (in the GIF89a format). If you don't want to export the entire movie as an animated GIF (indeed, a GIF file for a Flash movie with more than 100 frames would most likely be too large to download easily over the Web), you can designate a range of frames to export. Use a frame label of #First on the beginning frame of a given range of frames. Next, add a frame label of #Last to the ending frame of the desired sequence of frames. Flash actually is pretty good at optimizing animated GIFs by saving only areas that change over time in each frame rather than the entire frame.

  - **Loop continuously:** When the Animated radio button is selected, you can specify that the animated GIF repeats an infinite number of times by selecting the Loop continuously radio button.

  - **Repeat _ times:** This option can be used to set up an animated GIF that repeats a given number of times. If you don't want the animated GIF to repeat continuously, enter the number of repetitions here.

- **Options:** The options in the Options settings control the creation of the GIF's color table and how the browser displays the GIF:

  - **Optimize colors:** When you are using any palette type other than Adaptive, this option removes any colors preexisting in the Web 216 or custom palettes that the GIF image does not use. Enabling this option can only save you precious bytes used in file overhead — it has no effect on the actual quality of the image. Most images do not use all 216 colors of the Web palette. For example, a black-and-white picture can use only between 3 and 10 colors from the 216-color palette.

  - **Interlace:** This option makes the GIF image download in incrementing resolutions. As the image downloads, the image becomes sharper with each successive "scan." Using this option is typically a personal preference. Some people like to use it for image maps that can provide basic navigation information before the entire image downloads.

■ **Smooth:** This option anti-aliases the Flash artwork as it exports to the GIF image. Text may look better when it is anti-aliased, but you may want to test this option for your particular use. If you need to make a transparent GIF, smoothing may produce unsightly edges.

■ **Dither solids:** This option determines whether solid areas of color (such as fills) are dithered. In this context, this type of dithering would create a two-color pattern to mimic a solid color that doesn't occur in the GIF's color palette. See the discussion of dithering later in this section.

■ **Remove gradients:** Flash gradients do not translate or display very well in 256 or fewer colors. Use this option to convert all Flash gradients to solid colors. The solid color is determined by the first color prescribed in the gradient. Unless you developed your gradients with this effect in mind, this option may produce undesirable results.

■ **Transparent:** This setting controls the appearance of the Flash movie background, as well as any Flash artwork that uses alpha settings. Because GIF images support only one level of transparency (that is, the transparent area cannot be anti-aliased), exercise caution when using this setting. The Threshold option is available only if Alpha is selected. The options for this setting include the following:

■ **Opaque:** This option produces a GIF image with a solid background. The image has a rectangular shape.

■ **Transparent:** This option makes the Flash movie background appear transparent. If the Smooth option in the Options setting is enabled, Flash artwork may display halos over the background HTML color.

■ **Alpha and Threshold:** When the Alpha option is selected in the drop-down menu, you can control at what alpha level Flash artwork becomes transparent by entering a value in the Threshold text field. For example, if you enter 128, all alphas at 50 percent become completely transparent. If you are considering an animated GIF that has Flash artwork fading in or out, you probably should use the Opaque transparent option. If Alpha and Threshold were used, the fade effect would be lost.

■ **Dither:** *Dithering* is the process of emulating a color by juxtaposing two colors in a pattern arrangement. Because GIF images are limited to 256 colors (or fewer), dithering can often produce better-looking images for continuous-tone artwork such as gradients. However, Flash's dithering seems to work best with the Web 216 palette. Dithering can increase the file size of a GIF image.

■ **None:** This option does not apply any dithering to the GIF image.

■ **Ordered:** This option applies an intermediate level of dithering with minimal file size overhead.

■ **Diffusion:** This option applies the best level of dithering to the GIF image, but with larger file size overhead. Diffusion dithering has a noticeable effect only when the Web 216 palette is chosen in Palette Type.

- **Palette Type:** As we mention earlier in this section, GIF images are limited to 256 or fewer colors. However, this grouping of 256 is arbitrary: Any set of 256 (or fewer) colors can be used for a given GIF image. This setting enables you to select predefined sets of colors to use on the GIF image. See Chapter 7, "Applying Color," for more information on the Web color palette. The options for this setting include:

  - **Web 216:** When this option is selected, the GIF image uses colors only from the limited 216 Web color palette. For most Flash artwork, this should produce acceptable results. However, it may not render Flash gradients or photographic bitmaps very well.

  - **Adaptive:** With this option selected, Flash creates a unique set of 256 colors (or fewer, if specified in the Max colors setting) for the GIF image. However, these adapted colors fall outside of the Web safe color palette. File sizes for adaptive GIFs are larger than Web 216 GIFs, unless few colors are chosen in the Max colors setting. Adaptive GIFs look much better than Web 216 GIFs, but they may not display very well with 8-bit video cards and monitors.

  - **Web Snap Adaptive:** This option tries to give the GIF image the best of both worlds. Flash converts any colors close to the 216 Web palette to Web safe colors and uses adaptive colors for the rest. This palette produces better results than the Adaptive palette for older display systems that use 8-bit video cards.

  - **Custom:** When this option is selected, you can specify a palette that uses the ACT file format to be used as the GIF image's palette. Macromedia Fireworks and Adobe Photoshop can export color palettes (or color look-up tables) as ACT files.

- **Max colors:** With this setting, you can specify exactly how many colors are in the GIF's color table. This numeric entry field is enabled only when Adaptive or Web Snap Adaptive is selected in the Palette Type drop-down menu.

- **Palette:** This text field and the folder browse button are enabled only when Custom is selected in the Palette Type drop-down menu. When enabled, this dialog box is used to locate and load a palette file from the hard drive.

Using the JPEG settings

The Joint Photographic Experts Group (JPEG) format is just as popular as the GIF format on the Web. Unlike GIF images, however, JPEG images can use much more than 256 colors. In fact, JPEG files must be 24-bit color (or full-color RGB) images. Although GIF files use lossless compression (within the actual file itself), JPEG images use lossy compression, which means that color information is discarded in order to save file space. However, JPEG compression is very good. Even at its lowest-quality settings, JPEG images can preserve quite a bit of detail in photographic images.

Another significant difference between GIF and JPEG is that GIF images do not require nearly as much memory (for equivalent image dimensions) as JPEG images do. You need to remember that JPEG images "uncompress" when they are downloaded to your computer. Although the file sizes may be small initially, they still open as full-color images in the computer's memory. For example, even though you may get the file size of a 400-x-300-pixel JPEG image down to 10KB, it still requires nearly 352KB in memory when it is opened or displayed.

Flash publishes the first frame of the Flash movie as the JPEG image, unless a #Static frame label is given to another frame in the Flash movie. The limited settings of the JPEG tab of the Publish Settings dialog box (see Figure 20.7) control the few variables of this still photo-quality image format:

- **Dimensions:** This setting behaves the same as the GIF Dimensions setting. Width and Height control the dimensions of the movie. But these fields are enabled only when the Match movie check box is unchecked. With Match movie checked, the dimensions of the JPEG match those of the Flash movie.

- **Quality:** This slider and text field work exactly the same way as the JPEG Quality setting in the Flash tab of Publish Settings. Higher values apply less compression and result in better quality, but they create images with larger file sizes.

- **Progressive:** This option is similar to the Interlaced option for GIF images. When enabled, the JPEG image loads in successive scans, becoming sharper with each pass.

FIGURE 20.7

The settings of the JPEG tab are limited because JPEGs are still images with relatively few variables to address.

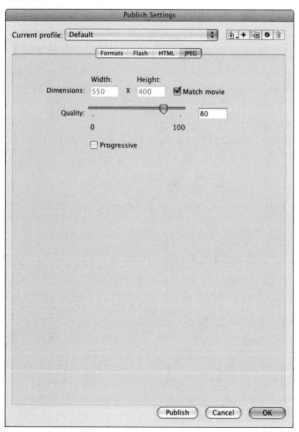

Using the PNG settings

The Portable Network Graphic (PNG) format is another still-image format. The PNG specification was developed in 1996 by the W3C (World Wide Web Consortium), and the format is an improvement over both the GIF and JPEG formats in several ways. Much like JPEG, it is excellent for transmission of photographic quality images. The primary advantages of PNG are variable bit depths (images can be 256 colors or millions of colors), multilevel transparency, and lossless compression. However, some browsers do not offer full support for all PNG options without some kind of additional plug-in. When in doubt, test your PNG images in your preferred browser.

The settings of the PNG tab (see Figure 20.8) control the characteristics of the PNG image that Flash publishes.

FIGURE 20.8

The settings found on the PNG tab closely resemble those on the GIF tab. The PNG was engineered to have many of the advantages of both the GIF and JPEG formats.

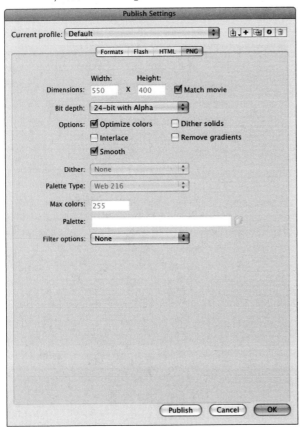

The PNG tab options are

- **Dimensions:** This setting works just like the GIF and JPEG equivalents. When Match movie is checked, you cannot alter the Width and Height of the PNG image.

- **Bit depth:** This setting controls how many colors are created in the PNG image:

  - **8-bit:** In this mode, the PNG image has a maximum color palette of 256 colors, similar to the palette function of GIF images. When this option is selected, the Options, Dither, Palette Type, Max Colors, and Palette settings can be altered.

  - **24-bit:** When this option is selected, the PNG image can display any of the 16.7 million RGB colors. This option produces larger files than 8-bit PNG images, but it renders the Flash artwork most faithfully.

  - **24-bit with Alpha:** This option adds another 8-bit channel to the 24-bit PNG image for multilevel transparency support. This means that Flash treats the Flash movie background as a transparent area so that information behind the PNG image (such as HTML background colors) shows through. Note that, with proper browser support, PNG can render anti-aliased edges on top of other elements, such as HTML background images!

NOTE Flash CS4's PNG export or publish settings do not reflect the full range of PNG options available. PNG can support transparency in both 8-bit and 24-bit flavors, but Flash enables transparency only in 24-bit with Alpha images.

- **Options:** These options behave the same as the equivalent GIF publish settings.

- **Dither, Palette Type, Max colors,** and **Palette:** These settings work the same as the equivalent GIF publish settings. Because PNG images can be either 8- or 24-bit, these options apply only to 8-bit PNG images. If anything other than 8-bit is selected in the Bit depth setting, these options are disabled. Refer to the previous section for more information.

- **Filter options:** This drop-down menu controls what type of compression sampling or algorithm the PNG image uses. Note that this does not apply an art or graphic "filter effect" as the filters in Adobe Photoshop do, nor does it throw away any image information — all filters are lossless. It simply enables you to be the judge of what kind of compression to use on the image. You need to experiment with each of these filters on your Flash movie image to find the best filter-to-file-size combination. Technically, the filters do not actually look at the pixel data. Rather, they look at the byte data of each pixel. Results vary depending on the image content, but here are some guidelines to keep in mind:

  - **None:** When this option is selected, no filtering is applied to the image. When no filter is applied, you usually have unnecessarily large file sizes.

  - **Sub:** This filter works best on images that have repeated information along the horizontal axis. For example, the stripes of a horizontal American flag filter nicely with the sub filter.

■ **Up:** The opposite of the sub filter, this filter works by looking for repeated information along the vertical axis. The stripes of a vertical American flag filter well with the up filter.

■ **Average:** Use this option when a mixture of vertical and horizontal information exists. When in doubt, try this filter first.

■ **Path:** This filter works like an advanced average filter. When in doubt, try this filter after you have experimented with the average filter.

■ **Adaptive:** This filter provides the most thorough analysis of the image's color and creates the most accurate color palette for the image. However, it usually provides the largest file sizes for the PNG format.

Creating Windows and Mac projectors

To export a Mac stand-alone projector, check the Macintosh Projector option in the Formats tab. To publish a Windows stand-alone projector, check the Windows Projector option in the Formats tab.

> **NOTE** The Mac Projector published by Flash CS4 is designed for playback on Mac OS X (10.1) and later. If you want to publish a projector compatible with Mac OS 9.x or earlier, you must use Flash MX 2004 or earlier.

Publish Preview and Publish Commands

After you have entered the file format types and specifications for each in the Publish Settings dialog box, you can proceed to preview and publish the file types you selected.

Using Publish Preview

The Publish Preview submenu (accessible from File ⇨ Publish Preview) lists all the file types currently enabled in the Publish Settings dialog box. By default, HTML is the first file type available for preview. In general, the first item enabled in the Formats tab of the Publish Settings dialog box is the first item in the submenu and can be executed by pressing Ctrl+F12/ ⌘+F12. Selecting a file type in the Publish Preview menu launches your default browser and inserts the selected file type(s) into the browser window.

Using Publish

When you want Flash to export the file type(s) selected in the Publish Settings dialog box, choose File ⇨ Publish (Shift+F12). Flash creates the new files wherever the Flash movie was last saved. If you have selected an HTML template in the HTML tab of the Publish Settings dialog box, you may receive a warning or error message if any other necessary files were not specified. That's it! After you've tested the files for the delivery browser and/or platforms of your choice, you can upload the files to your Web server.

Using Publish Profiles

Flash CS4 includes a profile feature in the Publish Settings dialog box. You can save the settings from all the enabled format tabs in Publish Settings to a custom profile. You can create as many profiles as you need. The profiles that you create are document-specific. They are saved with the Flash document file (.fla), and by design, you cannot access the profiles of one document directly from another. However, you can export a profile from a Flash document and import it into another.

To choose, create, modify, or delete profiles, open the Publish Settings dialog box (File ➪ Publish Settings). At the top of the dialog box, you will find the Profile features available in Flash CS4. See Figure 20.9 and the following description list.

- **Profile Name:** This drop-down menu displays the currently active profile. Every new Flash CS4 document has a Default profile. If you open a Flash document from an earlier version of Flash (such as Flash MX 2004 or Flash 8) in Flash CS4 and resave it as a Flash CS4 document, the original document publish settings are stored in a Flash MX, Flash MX 2004, Flash 8, or Flash CS3 Settings profile.

- **Import/Export Profile:** If you click this button, you can choose Import or Export from this option's menu. If you want to use one document's publish settings in another document, you need to first export the current profile. Profiles are exported as XML documents. In the other document, you can then import the XML profile document.

- **Create New Profile:** This button adds a new profile name to the Profile Name menu, using the current profile's settings as a starting point. If you click this button, the Create New Profile dialog box appears, prompting you to enter a new profile name.

- **Duplicate Profile:** This button makes a copy of the currently active profile. If you click this button, the Duplicate Profile dialog box appears, prompting you to enter a new profile name for the copy.

- **Profile Properties:** This button opens a dialog box wherein you can change the name of the currently active profile. No other properties are associated with a profile.

- **Delete Profile:** Clicking this button removes the currently active profile from the document.

Changes to profiles do not need to be saved. When you choose a profile from the Profile Name menu, any settings that you change, enable, and so on are automatically saved to the current profile as long as you click OK to close the Publish Settings dialog box. If you click the Cancel button, any changes you make are not saved to the current profile.

FIGURE 20.9

The Profile features in the Publish Settings dialog box

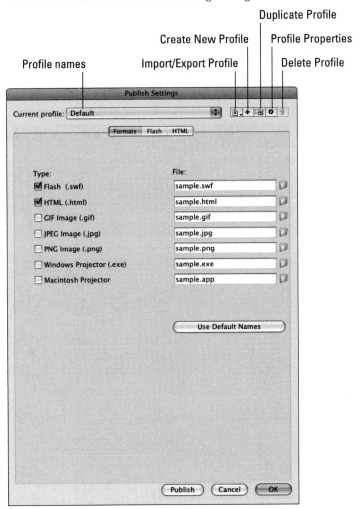

Duplicate Profile

Create New Profile | Profile Properties

Profile names | Import/Export Profile | Delete Profile

Summary

- To minimize your wait during publishing or testing Flash movies, you may want to use MP3 files for all of your Event Sync sounds.

- Test your Flash movies and scenes within the Flash authoring environment. The Bandwidth Profiler can provide vital information about frame byte requirements and can help you find problematic streaming areas of the Flash movie.

- The size report that can be generated from the Export Movie or Publish commands for Flash movies lists detailed information related to individual elements, such as audio, fonts, and frame byte size.

- The Publish Settings dialog box enables you to pick any number of file formats to export at one time. You can control just about every setting imaginable for each file type and use HTML templates to automate the insertion of Flash movies into your Web pages.

- Flash movies published from Flash CS4 can have specific local playback security options, preventing unscrupulous Flash content creators from accessing private information on another person's computer.

- Flash CS4 offers a Flash Player version detection feature in the Publish Settings dialog box. With this feature, you can create an HTML page that detects which version of the Flash Player a user has and direct him or her to appropriate content on your site.

- The profiles feature in Flash CS4 enables you to quickly load publish presets that you can apply to one or more Flash documents.

Chapter 21

Integrating Flash Content with Web Pages

If you're not one for automated HTML production by using templates, this chapter is for you. In this chapter, we teach you the ins and outs of the <object> and <embed> tags, as well as some tips on how to check for the Flash Player with Flash CS4's detection features or SWFObject. At the end of this chapter, we examine how Flash movies can interact with JavaScript and DHTML (Dynamic HTML) by using the new `ExternalInterface` actions from Flash.

NOTE **Many thanks to Geoff Stearns for his ongoing commitment to provide one of the best open source Flash Player detection scripts, SWFObject, to the Flash community. You can find more information about SWFObject later in this chapter.**

IN THIS CHAPTER

Defining HTML tags and attributes for the Flash Player

Detecting the Flash Player plug-in or ActiveX control with SWFObject

Sending commands with the `ExternalInterface` API to JavaScript

Writing Markup for Flash Movies

In Chapter 20, you learn how to use the Publish feature, which included automated HTML templates. These templates created the necessary HTML tags to display Flash movies on Web pages. In this section, we discuss the use of Flash movies in your handwritten HTML documents. You can also use this information to alter HTML documents created by the Publish feature.

NOTE **In the following code examples, we use an asterisk (*) when displaying optional parameters that are not in the default options that are enabled in the Flash Only HTML template. We also use the term *plug-in* to mean both the Mozilla-compatible plug-in and the ActiveX control for Flash Player 10.**

You can use two tags to place Flash movies on a Web page (such as an HTML document): <object> and <embed>. You need to include both of these plug-in tags in HTML documents, as each tag is specific to a browser: <object> for Internet Explorer (IE) on Windows and <embed> for Mozilla-compatible browsers on Windows and Mac. Each tag works similarly to the other, with some slight differences in attribute names and organization. Remember that if both sets of tags are included with the HTML, only one set of tags is actually read by the browser, depending on which browser is used to view the Web page. Without these tags, the browser cannot display Flash movies with other HTML elements such as images and text.

WEB RESOURCE You can, however, directly link to Flash movie files (.swf) as an alternative method for displaying Flash content. That method, however, precludes the use of parameters to control the look and playback of the Flash movie — it would be the same as loading the Flash movie straight into the stand-alone Flash Player. For more information on direct linking, see Colin Moock's tutorial, "Filling the Browser Windows Using the <frameset> Tag," found at the book's Web site, www.flashsupport.com/archive.

Using the <object> tag

Microsoft Internet Explorer for Windows and any browser that adheres to the HTML 4.01 specification from the World Wide Web Consortium (W3C) use this tag to enable the Flash Player ActiveX control (Internet Explorer for Windows) or plug-in. You can use the <object> tag to specify where in your HTML document layout you want a Flash movie (.swf file) to appear.

CAUTION The implementation of the <object> tag discussed in this section is oriented to Internet Explorer for Windows implementation. We strongly encourage you to use the SWFObject JavaScript library discussed later in this chapter for the best method of Flash content integration with HTML content.

NOTE Flash Player 6 introduced a Stage class that enables you to control or override many of the same properties that the Player HTML tags specify. For more details on the Stage class, refer to the *Flash ActionScript Bible* series (Wiley).

```
A.  <object
B.      classid="clsid: clsid:d27cdb6e-ae6d-11cf-96b8- ⊃
        444553540000"
C.      codebase="http://download.macromedia.com/pub/ ⊃
        shockwave/cabs/flash/swflash.cab#version=10,0,0,0"
D.      width="550" height="400"
E.      id="home"
F.      align="middle">
G.      <param name="allowScriptAccess" value="sameDomain" />
H.      <param name="allowFullScreen" value="false" />
I.      <param name="movie" value="home.swf" />
J.      <param name="play" value="false" />
K.      <param name="loop" value="false" />
L.      <param name="menu" value="false" />
M.      <param name="quality" value="high" />
N.      <param name="scale" value="noborder" />
```

```
O.        <param name="salign" value="LT" />
P.        <param name="wmode" value="transparent" />
Q.        <param name="devicefont value="true" />
R.        <param name="bgcolor" value="#FFFFFF" />
S.        <param name="flashvars" value="title=My%20Movie" />
T.        <param name="base" value="." />
U.  </object>
```

> **NOTE** Flash CS4's HTML templates use XHTML-compliant code. Notice that all the tags use lowercase, and that all `<param>` tags end with a `/>`.

A. `<object`: This is the opening tag containing the ID code and locations of the ActiveX control for the Flash Player. Note that this opening tag includes the attributes lettered B through F.

B. `classid`: This lengthy string is the unique ActiveX identification code. If you are inserting the `<object>` tag by hand in a text editor, make sure that you copy this ID string exactly.

C. `codebase`: Like the `codebase` attribute of a Java `<applet>` tag, this attribute of the `<object>` tag specifies the location of the ActiveX control installer file (.cab) as a URL. Notice that the `#version=10,0,0,0` portion of the URL indicates that the Flash Player version 10 should be used. You can also specify specific minor releases, such as `#version=6,0,65,0`, which would require Flash Player 6.0 r65 ActiveX control or later. If the visitor doesn't have the ActiveX control already installed, Internet Explorer automatically downloads the control from this URL.

> **TIP** If you want to make a secure Web page with Flash content, make sure that the `codebase` URL uses `https://` rather than `http://`.

D. `width` **and** `height`: These attributes control the actual width and height, respectively, of the Flash movie as it appears on the Web page. If no unit of measurement is specified, these values are in pixels. If the `%` character is added to the end of each value, the attribute adjusts the Flash movie to the corresponding percent of the browser window. For example, if 100 percent was the value for both `width` and `height`, the Flash movie fills the entire browser, except for the browser gutter. See Colin Moock's tutorial at the Web archive for this book to learn how to minimize this gutter thickness.

E. `id`: This attribute of the `<object>` tag assigns a JavaScript/VBScript identifier to the Flash movie so that it can be controlled by DHTML JavaScript/VBScript functions. By default, this attribute's value is the name of the actual .swf file, without the .swf extension. Each element on a DHTML page should have a unique `id` or `name` attribute. We discuss the `name` attribute in the next section.

F. `align`: This attribute of the `<object>` tag determines how the Flash movie aligns on the HTML document. The acceptable values for this attribute are `left`, `right`, `top`, `bottom`, or `middle`. As with `<img>` tags in HTML, the `align` attribute gives very loose layout control. It's likely that you'll want to rely on other HTML tags and cascading style sheets (CSS) to position a Flash movie with other HTML elements.

G. `<param name="allowScriptAccess" value="sameDomain" />`: This is the first set of `<param>` subtags within the `<object></object>` tags. Each parameter tag has a unique `name=` setting, not to be confused with JavaScript names or ids. `allowScriptAccess` controls how the Flash movie can access JavaScript or VBScript functions contained within the HTML document. A Flash movie can try to invoke a JavaScript or VBScript function by using an ActionScript `fscommand()` or `getURL()` line of code. There are three values supported: `always`, `never`, and `sameDomain`. The value `always` enables the Flash movie to access scripts on the page, and `never` prohibits the Flash movie from accessing scripts. The value `sameDomain`, which is the default value, enables a Flash movie to access scripts on the page *only* if the Flash movie resides on the same domain as the HTML page containing the movie. The `allowScriptAccess` attribute is supported by Flash Player 6 r40 and later.

H. `<param name="allowFullScreen" value="false" />`: This parameter specifies if the Flash movie can utilize full screen mode when playing in a Web browser window. If set to `false`, a Flash movie cannot play outside of the browser in full screen mode. If set to `true`, a Flash movie's stage can take over the entire desktop screen area and play outside of a Web browser window. You must script full screen capability within your Flash movie to use this feature. The ActionScript 3.0 version of the FLVPlayback component in Flash CS4, for example, includes a full screen feature. The `allowFullScreen` attribute is supported only by Flash Player 9 r28 or later.

I. `<param name="movie" value="home.swf" />`: This parameter determines which Flash movie file (.swf) is loaded into the document. The `value` attribute specifies the filename of the Flash movie, as a relative or absolute URL. Note that you can pass Flash variables to the movie directly by specifying them after the filename. For example, `home.swf?firstName=Jeremy` passes a variable named `firstName` with a string value of `Jeremy` to the `root` timeline (that is, `_level0`). You can use the newer `flashvars` (item S) HTML attribute to do this type of data transfer as well.

> **NOTE**   In ActionScript 3.0, variables declared with the `flashvars` attribute are accessed through the `parameters` property of the `LoaderInfo` class on the `root` instance.

J. `<param name="play" value="false" />`: This optional parameter tells the Flash Player whether it should start playing the Flash movie as it downloads. If `value` equals `false`, the Flash movie loads in a "paused" state, just as if a `stop()` action was placed on the first frame. If the `value` equals `true`, the Flash Player starts playing the movie as soon as it starts to stream into the browser. If this tag is omitted, the Flash Player behaves as if `play` equals `true`.

> **NOTE**   If you do have a `stop()` action on the first frame of your movie, setting `play` to `true` does not override the `stop()` action.

K. `<param name="loop" value="false" />`: This optional setting tells the Flash Player whether the Main Timeline should repeat when the playhead reaches the last frame. If `value` equals `false`, the playhead does not loop. If `value` equals `true`, the playhead loops. If this parameter tag is omitted, the Flash Player by default loops playback of the Main Timeline.

NOTE If you have a `stop()` action on the last frame of the Main Timeline, the Flash movie does not loop, regardless of the HTML loop value.

L. `<param name="menu" value="false" />`: This setting controls the display of the Flash Player contextual menu that can be invoked by right-clicking (Windows) or Control+clicking (Mac) the Flash movie in the Web browser. If you set this option to `false`, the menu displays the options shown in Figure 21.1. If you set this option to `true`, all the options are available to the end user, as shown in Figure 21.2. Also, the player's Settings option is available in both modes of the menu.

NOTE The default Play, Stop, and Rewind options that were available in Flash Player 6 and earlier are no longer available in Flash Player 7 or later.

NOTE If you have installed the Debugger version of Flash Player 10, the contextual menu displays a Debugger option in both modes of the `menu` attribute (`true` and `false`). Figure 21.2 shows the Debugger option. For more information on using the Debugger, read Adobe's DevNet article at `www.adobe.com/devnet/flash/articles/as3_debugger.html`.

FIGURE 21.1

The Flash Player menu with control options disabled

FIGURE 21.2

The Flash Player menu with control options enabled

NOTE Flash Player 7 and later supports additional items that you can script into the contextual menu, using the `ContextMenu` class. You learn how to use this class in Chapter 33, "Building an Image Gallery Component." For more detailed information on the usage of this class, refer to the Flash CS4 Help panel and the *Flash ActionScript Bible* series (Wiley).

M. `<param name="quality" value="high" />`: This parameter controls how the Flash movie's artwork renders within the browser window. `value` can be `low`, `autolow`, `autohigh`, `high`, or `best`. Most Flash movies on the Web use the `high` value because this setting forces the Flash Player to render the movie elements anti-aliased. For a full description of each of the `quality` settings, refer to Chapter 20, "Publishing Flash Movies."

N. `<param name="scale" value="noborder" />`: This optional parameter controls how the Flash movie scales in the window defined by the `width` and `height` attributes of the opening `<object>` tag. Its value can be `showall`, `noborder`, `exactfit`, or `noscale`. If this entire subtag is omitted, the Flash Player treats the movie as if the `showall` default setting was specified. The `showall` setting fits the Flash movie within the boundaries of the `width` and `height` dimensions without any distortion to the original aspect ratio of the Flash movie. Again, refer to Chapter 20 for a complete description of the `scale` settings and how they work within the dimensions of a Flash movie.

O. `<param name="salign" value="lt" />`: This parameter controls the alignment of the Flash movie within the space allocated to the viewing area of the movie in the browser window. For example, if you size your Flash movie to use 100 percent of the width and height of the browser window, a `value` of `lt` aligns the Flash movie to the left and top of the browser window. The acceptable values for this parameter are shown in the following list. For more information, refer to our coverage in Chapter 20, "Publishing Flash Movies."

- `l` : left edge, centered vertically
- `r` : right edge, centered vertically
- `t` : top edge, centered horizontally
- `b` : bottom edge, centered horizontally
- `lt` : left and top edges
- `rt` : right and top edges
- `lb` : left and bottom edges
- `rb` : right and bottom edges

P. `<param name="wmode" value="transparent" />`: This Player option works with all versions of the Flash Player if you are using Internet Explorer (version 3 or later) for Windows, or with Flash Player 6 r65 or later on Internet Explorer, Netscape, and most Mozilla-based browsers. If you are targeting an audience that uses these browsers, you can control how the Flash movie's background color appears on top of the HTML or DHTML elements on the Web page. There are three acceptable values:

- `window`: This value is the default appearance of movies playing in the Flash Player on Web pages. With this value, movies play within the area specified by the `width` and `height` attributes (discussed in item D), and the background color of the Flash movie's stage (as defined by Document Properties, or item Q, later in this section) appears.

- `opaque`: This value provides the same visual appearance of the movie's stage as `window` does. However, if you want to animate other DHTML objects in front of or behind a layer containing the Flash movie, it is recommended that you use the `opaque` value.

- `transparent`: This value enables the stage of the Flash movie to act like an alpha channel. When enabled, the Flash movie appears to float on the HTML page, without any background color to reveal the corners of the Flash movie's stage. Again, although this feature is somewhat extraordinary, it functions only with specific browsers and later versions of the Flash Player plug-in. Also, because the browser must anti-alias the Flash artwork on top of other HTML elements, playback of Flash animations may suffer.

Q. `<param name="devicefont" value="true" />`: This feature controls how Flash text appears in the browser window and works only on the Windows operating system. Like the device fonts with the Flash authoring environment (_sans, _serif, and _type-writer), this option can display any and all embedded text to system fonts such as Times and Arial. To do this, set `value` to `true`. To disable device font rendering in this fashion, set `value` to `false`. If this tag is omitted from the HTML, the `value` defaults to `false`. Finally, the rules of Flash device fonts apply to system device fonts as well. For example, device or system fonts cannot be masked, rotated, or manipulated with the Transform panel or the Property inspector.

NOTE This seldom-used setting does not work predictably from use to use. In our tests, we could not get `devicefont` to work consistently from movie to movie, nor could we propose any reasonable use for it. It's likely that this is a legacy setting, meaning that it was made available for machines that had slow video or computing performance when the Flash Player was first introduced to the market.

R. `<param name="bgcolor" value="#FFFFFF" />`: This parameter name, `bgcolor`, controls the background color of the Flash movie. If you published an HTML document via the Publish command, the `value` is automatically set to the background color specified by the Modify ⇨ Document command in Flash. However, you can override the Movie setting by entering a different value in this parameter tag. Note that this parameter, like all HTML tags and attributes concerning color, uses hexadecimal code to describe the color. For more information on color, see Chapter 7, "Applying Color."

S. `<param name="flashvars" value="title=My%20Flash%Movie" />`: This Flash Player 6 and later attribute enables you to declare variables within the Flash movie when it loads into the Web browser. `flashvars` stands for "Flash Variables." This feature enables you to circumvent the browser URL length limitation for declaring variables in the Flash movie's filename, as we discuss in item H of this list. For example, you can use client-side (for example, JavaScript) or server-side (for example, ColdFusion, ASP, PHP) scripting to dynamically write the `value` for this tag in your HTML, passing information from databases into the Flash movie at load time.

> **TIP** If you use Flash Remoting services with your Flash movie, be sure to declare the `gatewayUrl` variable in `flashvars`. The `gatewayUrl` variable specifies the location of the Flash Remoting gateway, such as `<param name="flashvars" value="gatewayUrl=http://mydomain.com/flashservices/gateway" />`.

T.   `<param name="base" value="." />`: This attribute tells the Flash movie how to interpret any relative paths used with ActionScript. The default value is `"."`, which means that Flash resolves any relative paths within ActionScript to the same directory that the Flash movie resides in. For example, if `base` is set to `"."`, the following action in ActionScript 3.0 looks for an HTML document named `form.html` in the same directory as the Flash movie file (.swf):

```
navigateToURL(new URLRequest("form.html"));
```

You can use dot notation with the `base` attribute, such as `"../"`, or specify a fully qualified domain name, such as `"http://www.myserver.com/section_1"`, to let the Flash movie know that all relative paths should be resolved from that starting point.

> **WEB RESOURCE** You can read Macromedia's tech notes about the `base` attribute by perusing the links in the "Flash and HTML Tags" category at `www.flashsupport.com/links`.

> **CAUTION** In our tests, we only saw the `base` attribute recognized by `getURL()` or `navigateToURL()` actions. Other actions that use URLs, such as `loadMovie()`, `LoadVars`, `XML`, and `NetStream`, did not use the `base` attribute to resolve relative URLs. If you keep your Flash movie files (.swf) in a separate folder from assets that need to be loaded into the Flash movies, you should pass the starting path into the Flash movie with `flashvars` (see item S in this list) and append that value to all of your relative paths in ActionScript.
>
> Also, if you use dot notation with the `base` attribute, such as `"../"`, the path is oddly interpreted relative to the *HTML* document, not the Flash movie.

U.   `</object>`: This is the closing tag for the starting `<object>` tag. As we show you later in this chapter, you can put other HTML tags between the last `<param>` tag and the closing `</object>` tag for non-ActiveX-enabled browsers, such as Netscape or Apple Safari. Because Internet Explorer for Windows is the primary browser that currently implements `<object>` tags, most browsers simply skip the `<object>` tag (as well as its `<param>` tags) and read only the tags between the last `<param>` and `</object>` tags.

> **TIP** We recommend that you consistently apply quotes around names and values, such as `<param name="bgcolor" value="#FFFFFF" />`. This syntax is especially important for the `flashvars` attribute.

Using the <embed> tag

Netscape, Mozilla-based browsers, and browsers on a Macintosh (including Internet Explorer for Mac) use the <embed> tag to display nonbrowser, native file formats that require a plug-in, such as Adobe Flash Player and Shockwave Director or Apple QuickTime. Following is a sample listing of attributes and values for the <embed> tag. Again, attributes with an asterisk are generally optional for most Flash movie playback.

NOTE The <object> tag can be used with most Mozilla-based browsers, but the implementation is somewhat different than that of Internet Explorer for Windows. You learn more about using the <object> tag for Mozilla-based browsers in our coverage of SWFObject later in this chapter.

```
A.  <embed
B.      src="home.swf"
C.      play="false"
D.      loop="false"
E.      quality="high"
F.      scale="noborder"
G.      salign="lt"
H.      wmode="transparent"
I.      devicefont="true"
J.      bgcolor="#FFFFFF"
K.      width="550" height="400"
L.      swLiveConnect="false"
M.      name="home"
N.      id="home"
O.      align="middle"
P.      allowScriptAccess="sameDomain"
Q.      allowFullScreen="false"
R.      flashvars="name=Lucian"
S.      type="application/x-shockwave-flash"
T.      base="."
U.      pluginspage="http://www.macromedia.com/go/ ⤶
            getflashplayer">
V.  </embed>
```

A. <embed: This is the opening <embed> tag. Note that lines B through T are attributes of the opening <embed> tag, which is why you don't see the > character at the end of line A.

B. src: This stands for *source,* and it indicates the filename of the Flash movie. This attribute of <embed> works exactly like the movie parameter of the <object> tag.

C. play: This attribute behaves in the same manner as the play parameter of the <object> tag. If you omit this attribute in your HTML, the Flash Player assumes that it should automatically play the Flash movie.

D. loop: This attribute controls the same behavior as the loop parameter of the <object> tag. If you omit this attribute in your HTML, the Flash Player automatically loops playback of the movie's Main Timeline.

E. `quality`: This attribute controls how the Flash movie's artwork appears in the browser window. Like the equivalent `quality` parameter of the `<object>` tag, its value can be `low`, `autolow`, `autohigh`, `high`, or `best`.

F. `scale`: This attribute of `<embed>` controls how the Flash movie fits within the browser window and/or the dimensions specified by `width` and `height` (item K). Its value can be `showall` (default if attribute is omitted), `noborder`, `exactfit`, or `noscale`.

G. `salign`: This attribute controls the internal alignment of the Flash movie within the viewing area of the movie's dimensions. See the description for the `salign` parameter of the `<object>` tag for more information.

H. `wmode`: This attribute controls the opacity of the Flash movie's background color and works only with specific browser and Flash Player version combinations. See the `wmode` parameter description in the `<object>` tag for more details.

I. `devicefont`: This attribute controls the appearance of any text within a Flash movie and functions correctly only on the Windows operating system. See the description for `devicefont` in the `<object>` tag section.

J. `bgcolor`: This setting controls the Flash movie's background color. Again, this attribute behaves identically to the equivalent `<param>` subtag of the `<object>` tag. See that tag's description in the preceding section.

K. `width` and `height`: These attributes control the dimensions of the Flash movie as it appears on the Web page. Refer to the `width` and `height` descriptions of the `<object>` tag for more information.

L. `swLiveConnect`: This is one attribute that you won't find in the `<object>` tag. This unique tag enables Netscape's LiveConnect feature, which enables plug-ins and Java applets to communicate with JavaScript. By default, this attribute is set to `false`. If it is enabled (the attribute is set to `true`), the Web page may experience a short delay during loading. The latest versions of Netscape don't start the Java engine during a browsing session until a Web page containing a Java applet (or a Java-enabled plug-in such as the Flash Player) is loaded. Unless you use `fscommand()` actions in your Flash movies, it's best to omit this attribute or set its value to `false`.

M. `name`: This attribute works in tandem with the `swLiveConnect` attribute, enabling the Flash movie to be identified in JavaScript. The value given to the `name` attribute is the Flash movie object name that can be used within your JavaScript programming.

N. `id`: This attribute is also used for JavaScript functionality. It's uncertain whether this value is necessary if the name attribute exists, but Flash MX 2004's Flash with FSCommand HTML template (in the Publish Settings dialog box) includes both the `name` and `id` attributes. The `id` attribute should use the same value as the `name` attribute.

O. `align`: This attribute behaves exactly the same as the `align` parameter for the `<object>`. See its description in the preceding section for more information.

P. `allowScriptAccess`: This attribute controls how the Flash movie can access JavaScript from `getURL()` and `fscommand()` actions. See the description of `allowScriptAccess` in the `<object>` tag coverage earlier in this chapter.

716

Q. `allowFullScreen`: This attribute determines the full screen capability of a Flash movie running in Flash Player 9 r28 or later. See the description of `allowFullScreen` in the `<object>` tag coverage earlier in this chapter.

R. `flashvars`: This attribute assigns variables to the Main Timeline of the Flash movie at runtime. See the description of `flashvars` in the `<object>` tag coverage earlier in this chapter.

S. `type="application/x-shockwave-flash"`: This attribute tells the browser what MIME (Multipurpose Internet Mail Extension) content-type the embedded file is. Each file type (TIF, JPEG, GIF, PDF, and so on) has a unique MIME content-type header, describing what its content is. For Flash movies, the content-type is `application/x-shockwave-flash`. Any program (or operating system) that uses files over the Internet handles MIME content-types according to a reference chart that links each MIME content-type to its appropriate parent application or plug-in. Without this attribute, the browser may not understand what type of file the Flash movie is. As a result, it may display the broken plug-in icon when the Flash movie downloads to the browser.

T. `base="."`: This attribute tells the Flash movie how to resolve relative paths used in the movie's ActionScript code. See the description of `base` in the `<object>` tag coverage earlier in this chapter.

U. `pluginspage`: Literally "plug-in's page," this attribute tells the browser where to go to find the appropriate plug-in installer if it doesn't have the Flash plug-in already installed. This is not equivalent to a JavaScript-enabled auto installer or detection page. It simply redirects the browser to the URL of the Web page where the appropriate software can be downloaded.

V. `</embed>`: This is the closing tag for the original `<embed>` tag in line A. Some older or text-based browsers such as Lynx are incapable of displaying `<embed>` tags. You can insert alternate HTML (such as a static or animated GIF image with the `<img>` tag) between the `<embed> </embed>` tags for these browsers. Some browsers may require that you insert these alternate tags between a `<noembed></noembed>` set of tags within or after the `<embed></embed>` tags.

CAUTION You may be surprised to learn that all versions of Internet Explorer (IE) for the Mac cannot read `<object>` tags. Rather, IE for Mac uses a Netscape plug-in emulator to read `<embed>` tags. However, this emulator does not interpret all `<embed>` tags with the same level of support as Netscape. As a result, the `swLiveConnect` attribute does not function on IE for Mac browsers. This means that the `fscommand()` action is not supported on these browsers.

Detecting the Flash Player

What good is an awesome Flash experience if no one can see your Flash movies? Because most Flash content is viewed with a Web browser, it's extremely important to make sure that your HTML pages check for the existence of the Flash Player plug-in before you start pushing Flash content to the browser. There are a variety of ways to check for the Flash Player, and this section provides an overview of the available methods.

NEW FEATURE As we mention in Chapter 20, "Publishing Flash Movies," Flash CS4 includes an updated Flash Player detection feature within the Publish Settings dialog box. You learn how to create a set of detection pages with this new feature later in this chapter.

Plug-in versus ActiveX: Forcing content without a check

The Flash Player is available for Web browsers in two forms: the Flash Player plug-in (as a Netscape-compatible, or Mozilla-compatible, plug-in) and the Flash Player ActiveX control (for use only with Microsoft Internet Explorer on Windows 98/ME/2000/XP/Vista).

If you directly insert a Flash movie into a Web page with the <embed> tag (for Mozilla browsers), one of two scenarios happen:

- The browser has the Flash Player plug-in and loads the Flash movie.
- The browser does not have the Flash Player plug-in and displays a broken plug-in icon.

If the second scenario occurs and the pluginspage attribute of the <embed> tag is defined, the user can click the broken plug-in icon and go to the Adobe site to download the Flash Player plug-in. If the pluginspage attribute is not specified, clicking the broken plug-in icon takes you to a generic plug-in page provided by the browser vendor.

If you insert a Flash movie into an HTML document with the <object> tag (for Internet Explorer on Windows only), one of two scenarios happen:

- The browser has the Flash Player ActiveX control and loads the Flash movie.
- The browser does not have the Flash Player ActiveX control and auto-downloads and installs the ActiveX control file from the Adobe site.

NOTE Newer versions of Windows XP (that is, with Service Pack 2 or SP2 installed) will likely get an additional warning represented as a strip across the top of the Web page attempting to initiate the installation of a new ActiveX control. The user must also click this strip and accept the download of the ActiveX control.

The ActiveX control auto-downloads and installs only if the classid and codebase attributes of the Flash movie's <object> tag are correctly specified. Depending on the user's security settings, the user needs to grant permission to a Security Warning dialog box to commence the download and install process.

Although using the <object> and <embed> tags by themselves is by far the simplest method for integrating Flash content into a Web page, it's not the most user-friendly method of ensuring that the majority of your Web visitors can view the Flash content. Flash CS4 uses an updated JavaScript detection mechanism, replacing the older JavaScript approach used in Flash CS3.

NOTE Since Flash Player 4 was released, many seasoned Flash developers have used small Flash movies known as *sniffers* to detect the presence of the Flash Player in a user's Web browser. Sniffers are virtually hidden from the visitor to a Web site, and they direct an entry HTML page to a new location (using a getURL( ) action) where the real Flash content (or site) exists. If the Player is not installed, the sniffer movie cannot play and directs the HTML page to a new location. If this happens, a special `<meta>` tag in the `<head>` of the HTML document directs the browser location to a screen that informs the visitor to download the plug-in or ActiveX control. However, page redirection mechanisms are not ideal for search engine optimization — we recommend using SWFObject as discussed later in this chapter.

Detecting the Flash Player with Flash CS4

In Flash CS4, Adobe has made the process of using a sniffer methodology incredibly simple. In the following steps, you learn how to use the Detect Flash Version feature to properly direct a user to Flash Player 6 r65 content.

NOTE You can check for Flash Player 4 or later with the Detect Flash Version feature. For demonstration purposes, we chose Flash Player 6 r65 because Flash MX 2004 introduced a new optimization feature for .swf files generated for this version (or later) of Flash Player 6.

CAUTION If you used the Detect Flash Version in older versions of Flash such as Flash MX 2004, be sure to review this section. The feature no longer uses three HTML pages for the detection process. Everything from the detection to the content display to the alternate content display occurs on one HTML page.

1. **Create a new Flash document by choosing File ⇨ New.** In the New Document dialog box, choose Flash File (ActionScript 3.0) and click OK. Alternatively, open an existing .fla file that you have created and skip to Step 4.

2. **Save the new Flash document as** `detection_test.fla`.

3. **Add some placeholder text to the Stage by using the Text tool.** Because this example is checking for Flash Player 9 r28, you can type **This is Flash Player 9 r28 content.**

4. **Choose File ⇨ Publish Settings.** By default, both the Flash and HTML formats are selected in the Formats tab of the Publish Settings dialog box. The filenames for these formats should reflect the current .fla filename, such as `detection_test.swf` and `detection_test.html`, respectively.

5. **To keep the new version settings in a separate profile, click the Create New Profile (+) button at the top of the Publish Settings dialog box.** Name the profile FP9 r28 Detection, as shown in Figure 21.3. Click OK to close the dialog box, but leave the Publish Settings dialog box open.

FIGURE 21.3

The Create New Profile dialog box, showing the new profile name

6. **Click the Flash tab.** In the Version menu, choose Flash Player 9. In the ActionScript version menu, choose ActionScript 3.0 if not already selected. See Figure 21.4 for a review of these settings.

7. **Click the HTML tab of the Publish Settings dialog box and select the Detect Flash Version check box.** The two editable text fields to the right of the Version label should now be enabled. The major version of the Flash Player is fixed to the Player version you chose in the Flash tab. The first of the two editable fields represents a Minor Revision value; to date, Adobe hasn't released any minor revisions of the Flash Player, but this feature is enabled just in case Adobe does release any minor revision during the life cycle of the Flash CS4 authoring tool. The second field represents the Incremental Revision value. Since Flash Player 4, Adobe has released several incremental revisions of the Flash Player for each player cycle.

FIGURE 21.4

The Flash Player 9 settings in the Flash tab

WEB RESOURCE To get a sense of how many incremental revisions of Flash Player 7 were released, see the "Flash Player Release Notes" category at www.flashsupport.com/links.

8. **Type 28 in the second field, as shown in Figure 21.5.** If you wanted to check for a different incremental version of Flash Player 9, you could enter that value instead. Click OK to close the dialog box, and go back to the HTML tab of the Publish Settings dialog box.

9. **In the Publish Settings dialog box, click the Publish button.** Flash CS4 generates all the necessary JavaScript within the published HTML document to properly detect the Flash Player version. Click OK to close the Publish Settings dialog box.

10. **On your desktop, navigate to the folder where you saved your original .fla file.** If you created the sample document in Step 1, you want to find the location of detection_test.fla. In this location, you will see the HTML file created for the detection process.

FIGURE 21.5

The Publish Settings dialog box

11. **In your own Web browser, load the** `detection_test.html` **page.** If your browser has Flash Player 9 r28 or later, the browser should display your `detection_test.swf` movie. This process works because the `detection_test.html` page uses JavaScript to check the installed Flash Player version, if one exists. If you open the HTML document in a text editor such as Adobe Dreamweaver CS4, you'll see that lines 286–291 declare the version numbers you entered in the HTML tab of the Publish Settings dialog box. The JavaScript code compares these values to the version of the Flash Player that loaded the movie. If the Flash Player matches (or exceeds) the version requirements, the Flash content tags (`<object>` and `<embed>`) are written to the HTML page with JavaScript. Otherwise, the alternate content specified on line 330 in the JavaScript code is loaded into the browser window.

NOTE   Adobe provides generic alternate content that you should replace with your own preferred HTML tags indicating what you want to the user to do if the version of the Flash Player required is not installed.

12. **To accurately test your pages over an Internet connection, upload all the files** (except the .fla file) to your Web server and load the `detection_test.html` document from the Web server URL to redo the test.

ON the CD-ROM   You can find all these files created for this detection example in the `ch21/ flashcs4_detection` folder of this book's CD-ROM. The JavaScript in the `detection_test_fcs4b.html` version of the document contains additional alternate content that is specified in an `alternate.js` file, also included on the CD-ROM. If you want to find the latest "Get Flash Player" graphics to use in your Web pages, go to `www.adobe.com/ macromedia/style_guide/buttons`.

If you want to test the detection mechanism with an older version of the Flash Player, we recommend that you use an older Flash Player installer with a Mozilla-compatible browser. The process of uninstalling an ActiveX control used by Internet Explorer is much more difficult to do.

WEB RESOURCE   You can find just about every past version of the Flash Player at `www.adobe.com/ cfusion/knowledgebase/index.cfm?id=tn_14266` for testing purposes. As mentioned previously, we recommend that you install the older versions with a Mozilla-compatible browser. If you are using Mac OS X, the first Flash Player released for Mac OS X was version 5.

You can set up your Mozilla-compatible browser's plug-ins folder to accommodate multiple versions of the Flash Player plug-in. When you installed Flash CS4, the latest release of Flash Player 9 should have automatically been installed to your Mozilla-based browser's `Plugins` (or `plugins`) folder. The plug-in file, named `NPSWF32.dll`, can be moved outside of the `Plugins` folder, into a new parent folder that you create. For the following example, we'll use Mozilla Firefox as our test browser.

WEB RESOURCE   Mozilla Firefox is a free Web browser that you can download at `www.mozilla.org/ products/firefox/`. Firefox has quickly become the preferred cross-platform browser of many Web developers.

We prefer to create a _Flash Players folder in the C:\Program Files\Mozilla FireFox folder, and put each Flash Player version plug-in file into its own folder, as shown in Figure 21.6.

CAUTION Regardless of the Flash Player version you install, all Flash Player plug-in files for Mozilla-compatible browsers have the same name on Windows: NPSWF32.dll. For this reason, you must isolate multiple installations of the Flash Player into their own folder.

FIGURE 21.6

A sample Flash Players folder structure for use with Mozilla Firefox on Windows

You can do the same procedure on Mac OS X, where all browsers share the same plug-in folders. That's right! Mozilla, Firefox, Internet Explorer, and Apple Safari all refer to the same plug-ins folder. On your boot disk, such as Macintosh HD, browse to the Library\Internet Plug-Ins\ folder. In this location, you find the Shockwave Flash NP-PPC plug-in file. As Figure 21.7 shows, you can create a Library\Internet Plug-Ins (DISABLED) folder to store other versions of this plug-in file.

CAUTION On Mac OS X, you may need to re-create the same plug-in structure with the Users\[Your User Name]\Library\Internet Plug-Ins\ folder. Or, you may just want to remove any Flash Player plug-in files within this folder. Mac OS X should then default to the main Library\Internet Plug-Ins\ folder.

FIGURE 21.7

A sample Flash Players folder structure for use with Mozilla Firefox or Apple Safari on Mac OS X

This process takes some time because you have to download and run each installer from the URL we mentioned in the earlier Web Resource note, and move the NPSWF32.dll file from the Plugins folder to its own folder in the Flash Players folder. When you're done, however, you'll have an efficient system for checking your content against older versions of the Flash Player. Simply move the current NPSWF32.dll file into its appropriate _Flash Players folder, and move the desired test version from its Flash Players folder into the Plugins folder.

> **TIP**   If you use Firefox 3.0, you're in luck. Alessandro Crugnola has built Flash Switcher, a free Flash Player plug-in utility that includes past versions of the Flash Player and swaps your installed version of the player with a convenient menu built right into the browser window! For more information, see www.sephiroth.it/firefox/flash_switcher/.

Detecting the Flash Player with SWFObject

Although the Adobe Flash CS4 detection features work wonderfully, you should know about a popular and widely used JavaScript library, SWFObject. This JavaScript code, created by Geoff Stearns, can be downloaded at code.google.com/p/swfobject/. We've included the latest version, 2.1, in the ch21/swfobject/swfobject_2-1 folder on this book's CD-ROM. In this section, you learn how to use SWFObject with Flash content.

> **NOTE** SWFObject 2.0 and later supports two methods of publishing Flash content: static and dynamic. In this walk-through, we use the static method, which is more Web standards@ndcompliant. For more information, visit `code.google.com/p/swfobject/wiki/documentation`.

Reviewing the content

We've included a Flash movie named `trafficLightGreen.swf` in the `ch21/swfobject` folder. This file displays a vector graphic of a flashing green traffic light, as shown in Figure 21.8. The SWFObject code displays this movie only if Flash Player 9 r28 is installed, which is required for full screen capability.

FIGURE 21.8

A sample Flash movie

An alternative non-Flash piece of content has also been provided in the `ch21/swfobject` folder: `trafficLightRed.gif`, as shown in Figure 21.9.

FIGURE 21.9

A sample alternate graphic

The HTML document displays this GIF file in the following cases:

- Flash Player 9 r28 or later is not installed.
- JavaScript has been disabled by the user in the Web browser's preferences.

Copy both the SWF and GIF files from the CD-ROM to a preferred location on your computer. Be sure to save the HTML file discussed in the next section to the same location.

Creating the HTML document

In this section, you learn how to build an HTML file that uses the SWFObject library to determine which piece of content, the Flash movie or the GIF graphic, to display in the Web browser.

CAUTION In the code samples shown in this section and throughout the book, do not type the ⤵ character, which indicates a continuation of the same line of code.

1. **In Adobe Dreamweaver CS4, create a new HTML file by choosing File ⇨ New.** In the New Document dialog box, choose Blank Page, and then HTML in the Page Type column, None in the Layout column, and XHTML 1.0 Strict in the Doc Type menu, as shown in Figure 21.10. Click OK to create the file, and assign a document title of **SWFObject Detection**. If you don't have Dreamweaver, create a new HTML file in your preferred HTML editor and insert the code shown in Listing 21.1. If you're using Dreamweaver, switch to code view.

FIGURE 21.10

The New Document dialog box in Adobe Dreamweaver CS4

2. **Save the HTML file as** `swfobject_sample.html`.
3. **Copy the** `swfobject.js` **and** `expressInstall.swf` **files from the** `ch21/` `swfobject/swfobject_2_1` **folder to the same location as your HTML file saved in Step 2.** The `swfobject.js` JavaScript file contains the Flash Player detection code,

and the `expressInstall.swf` file is a prebuilt Flash movie (.swf file) that automatically downloads the latest version of the Flash Player if the required Flash Player version is not available. Note that the `expressInstall.swf` file requires Flash Player 6 r65 or later to be installed to initiate the automated plug-in download-and-install process.

4. **After the closing `</title>` tag and before the closing `</head>` tag, insert the following code to load the SWFObject code into the HTML document:**

```
<script type="text/javascript" src="swfobject.js"></script>
```

5. **Between the `<body></body>` tags, add the code shown in Listing 21.2.** The `<div>` container specifies both the Flash movie (.swf file) that you want to appear on the page as well as the alternate content that you want to appear if the required version of the Flash Player is unavailable. The alternate content is also indexed by search engines.

6. **Go back up to the `<head>` section of your HTML document and add the following code.** This code creates a new SWFObject instance in JavaScript. If the required Flash Player version is installed (version 9 r28), the `<div>` content displays the Flash movie specified in the `<object>` tags. Review the code comments to see the parameters required for a new SWFObject instance.

```
<script type="text/javascript">
   swfobject.registerObject("flashContent", "9.0.28", ↵
   "expressInstall.swf");
</script>
```

7. **Save the HTML file and test the file in a Web browser.** If the browser has Flash Player 9 r28 installed, you should see the green traffic light animation. If the browser has an earlier version of the Flash Player or does not have any version of Flash Player installed, the red traffic light graphic appears.

LISTING 21.1

The HTML Starter Code

```
<!DOCTYPE html PUBLIC "-//W3C//DTD XHTML 1.0 Strict//EN" "http://www.w3.org/ ↵
   TR/xhtml1/DTD/xhtml1-transitional.dtd">
<html xmlns="http://www.w3.org/1999/xhtml">
<head>
<meta http-equiv="Content-Type" content="text/html; charset=utf-8" />
<title>SWFObject Detection</title>
</head>

<body>
</body>
</html>
```

LISTING 21.2

The Flash Movie and Alternate Content

```
<div>
    <object id="flashContent" classid="clsid:D27CDB6E-AE6D-11cf-⊃
    96B8-444553540000" width="105" height="185">
        <param name="movie" value="trafficLightGreen.swf" />
        <!--[if !IE]>-->
        <object type="application/x-shockwave-flash" ⊃
        data="trafficLightGreen.swf" width="105" height="185">
        <!--<![endif]-->
            <img src="trafficLightRed.gif" width="105" height="185" ⊃
            align="left"/>
            <p style="font-family:Verdana, Arial, Helvetica, ⊃
            sans-serif; position: relative; top: 50px; width: ⊃
            300px;">Please download the <a ⊃
            href="http://www.adobe.com/go/getflashplayer">latest ⊃
            Flash Player</a> for the best experience.</p>
        <!--[if !IE]>-->
        </object>
        <!--<![endif]-->
    </object>
</div>
```

ON the CD-ROM You can find the finished HTML code in the `ch21/swfobject` folder on this book's CD-ROM.

Using Flash Movies with JavaScript and DHTML

The ActionScripting features of Flash Player 8 or later have increased the range of interactive and dynamic possibilities for Flash movies on the Internet. Prior to Flash Player 4, Flash movies could interact with external HTML or scripts only through the `fscommand()` action. This meant mapping commands and variables to JavaScript, which, in turn, passed information to the document object model of DHTML, Java applets, or CGI (common gateway interface) scripts. Now that Flash movies can directly send and receive data to server-side scripts, just about anything can be done within the Flash movie. If you want to directly communicate with the Web browser or the HTML document, you need to use JavaScript with either `fscommand()` actions or the `ExternalInterface` API (application programming interface) introduced with Flash Player 8.

> **TIP** The `ExternalInterface` API is part of the `flash.external` package in ActionScript 2.0 and 3.0, and is available in Flash Player 8 or later (AS2) and Flash Player 9 and later (AS3). This new set of actions (collectively known as an API) enables you to communicate directly with the Flash movie's hosting environment. Unlike the older `fscommand()` action, the `ExternalInterface` API enables you to receive data from the hosting environment immediately, without setting up callback handlers.

A word of caution to Web developers

This section covers the `ExternalInterface` API actions, which, when used in Flash movies on Web pages, are supported by the following browsers:

- Internet Explorer 4.0 and later for Windows 98/ME/2000/XP
- Mozilla 1.7.5 and later
- Mozilla Firefox 1.0 and later
- Opera 9.0 and later
- Apple Safari 1.3 and later

Our coverage of the `ExternalInterface` API assumes that you have a working knowledge of JavaScript and Flash ActionScript. If you don't know how to add actions to frames or buttons, read Chapter 17, "Understanding Actions and Event Handlers." If you don't know JavaScript, you can still follow the steps to the tutorials and create a fully functional Flash-JavaScript movie. However, because this isn't a book on JavaScript, we don't explain how JavaScript syntax or functions work.

Understanding how Flash movies work with JavaScript

As we mention earlier, Flash Player has a class called `ExternalInterface`. This class has methods that can invoke commands (passing optional arguments, or parameters) from a Flash movie to its hosting environment, such as JavaScript in a Web browser. What does this mean for interactivity? The `ExternalInterface` API offers the capability to have any Flash event handler (button instance, frame actions, and so on) initiate an event handler in JavaScript. Although this may not sound too exciting, you can use `ExternalInterface` actions to trigger anything that you would have used JavaScript alone to do in the past, such as updating HTML form text fields, changing the visibility of HTML elements, or switching HTML background colors on the fly. We look at these effects in the next section.

Flash movie communication with JavaScript is not a one-way street. You can also monitor and control Flash movies with JavaScript. Just as JavaScript treats an HTML document as an object and its elements as properties of that object, JavaScript treats a Flash movie as it would any other element on a Web page. Therefore, you can use JavaScript functions and HTML hyperlinks (`<a href>` tags) to control Flash movie playback.

NOTE For JavaScript to receive Flash events, you need to make sure that the attribute `allowScriptAccess` for the `<object>` and `<embed>` tags is set to `"sameDomain"` or `"always"`. By default, most Flash CS4 HTML templates have this set to `"sameDomain"`. If you're testing your Flash movies and HTML documents locally, you should temporarily switch the value to `"always"`; otherwise, JavaScript does not receive the events from the Flash movie.

WEB RESOURCE This edition of the *Flash Bible* features coverage of the `ExternalInterface` API in ActionScript 3.0 available in Flash Player 9 or later. If you want to read more about the older `fscommand()` method of sending data to and from the Flash Player and JavaScript, refer to the archived document at www.flashsupport.com/archive.

Changing HTML attributes

In this section, we show you how to dynamically change the `bgcolor` attribute of the `<body>` tag with an `ExternalInterface` action from a Flash movie while it is playing in the browser window. In fact, the background color changes a few times. Then after that has been accomplished, you learn how to update the text field of a `<form>` tag to display what percent of the Flash movie has been loaded.

ON the CD-ROM Before you start this section, make a copy of the Flash document `countdown_starter.fla` located in the `ch21/ExternalInterface` folder of this book's CD-ROM. This is a starter document to which you will add ActionScript 3.0 code.

Adding ExternalInterface actions to a Flash movie

Open the `countdown_starter.fla` Flash document from this book's CD-ROM, and use Control ⇨ Test Movie to play the Flash .swf file. You should notice that the filmstrip countdown fades to white, and then to near black, and then back to its original gray color. This countdown continues to loop until the entire first scene has loaded into the Flash Player. When the first scene has loaded, playback skips to a video clip of a younger Robert swinging around and around. There's more to the Flash movie, but for now, that's all you need to deal with.

Our goal for this section of the tutorial is to add function calls to specific keyframes in the `countdown_starter.fla` document. When the Flash Player plays the frame with a function call, the Player sends a command and argument string to JavaScript. JavaScript then calls a function that changes the background color to the value specified in the argument string of the function. To be more exact, you'll create a function named `changeBgColor` in ActionScript. This function, when invoked (or "called"), invokes a corresponding function named `changeBgColor` in the JavaScript code created later in this section. You'll add code to invoke the `changeBgColor()` function to the frames where the color fades to white, black, and gray. When the Flash movie changes to these colors, JavaScript changes the HTML background colors.

Here's the process:

1. **Select frame 1 of the actions layer, and open the Actions panel (F9,/Option+F9).** In the Script pane, add the following code. Make sure that you are not in Script Assist mode. This code, written in ActionScript 3.0 syntax, imports the `ExternalInterface` class and creates a `changeBgColor()` function that accepts one argument named `color`.

This argument is passed to the `call()` method of the `ExternalInterface` class. The `call()` method takes one or more parameters. The first argument is always the name of the method (or function) to call in the hosting environment, and subsequent arguments are passed to the called method. In this example, you need to pass only one argument, `color`, to the JavaScript host environment.

```
import flash.external.ExternalInterface;

function changeBgColor(color:String):void {
    ExternalInterface.call("changeBgColor", color);
}
```

2. **On frame 16 of the Main Timeline, add a keyframe on the actions layer.** With the keyframe selected, open the Actions panel (F9/Option+F9). Type the following action into the Script pane:

```
changeBgColor("#FFFFFF");
```

This action invokes the `changeBgColor()` function you defined on frame 1 in the previous step. The argument string `#FFFFFF` is passed to that function. The Flash function named `changeBgColor()` passes that argument to the hosting environment's `changeBgColor()` function as well, changing the HTML background color to white.

3. **On frame 20, add another action to the corresponding keyframe on the actions layer.** With frame 20 selected, open the Actions panel and type the following code:

```
changeBgColor("#333333");
```

The argument `"#333333"` is used to change the HTML background color to a dark gray.

4. **On frame 21 of the actions layer, follow the same instructions as you did for Step 3, except use `"#9E9E9E"` for the argument string.** This changes the HTML background color to the same color as the Flash movie countdown graphic.

5. **On frame 66 of the actions layer, add another action invoking the `changeBgColor()` function.** (Add this action after the existing action on this frame.) This time, use an argument string of `"#000000"`, which changes the HTML background color to black.

6. **Now that you've added several actions, try them out in the browser.** Save the document as `countdown_100.fla`, and open the Publish Settings dialog box (for more information on publish settings, refer to Chapter 20, "Publishing Flash Movies"). In the Formats tab, make sure that only the Flash format check box is selected. Change the Flash filename to `countdown.swf`. Click OK to close the Publish Settings dialog box. Choose the File ➪ Publish command to export the Flash movie.

Next, you build the JavaScript code that is added to the HTML file Flash publishes.

Enabling JavaScript for Flash movies

In this section, you add the necessary JavaScript to make the `ExternalInterface.call()` action work in the browser. Remember, you added this action to the `changeBgColor()` function on frame 1 of the Flash movie. What follows in Listing 21.3 is the JavaScript code that defines the custom function `changeBgColor` that we have created for you.

Make a copy of the `countdown_swfobject_starter.html` file from the `ch21/ ExternalInterface` folder of this book's CD-ROM. Copy the file to the same location as the `countdown.swf` file published in the last section. Add the code in Listing 21.3 to the `countdown_swfobject_starter.html` file.

NOTE   **The line numbers reflect the actual line numbers in the HTML document. Also, remember that the ⊃ indicates a continuation of the same line of code. Do not insert this character into your HTML document.**

LISTING 21.3

The JavaScript Code to Enable the ExternalInterface Actions

```
10.    <script type="text/javascript" language="javascript">
11.    <!--
12.    function changeBgColor(hexColor){
13.        document.bgColor = hexColor;
14.    }
15.    //-->
16.    </script>
```

The following is a line-by-line explanation of the code:

10: This HTML tag initializes the JavaScript code.

11: This string of characters is standard HTML comment code. By adding this after the opening `<script>` tag, non-JavaScript browsers ignore the code. If this string wasn't included, text-based browsers such as Lynx might display JavaScript code as HTML text.

12: This is where the function `changeBgColor()` is defined. Remember that the `change BgColor()` function in the Flash ActionScript specifies `"changeBgColor"` in the `ExternalInterface.call()` method. There is one argument defined for the function: `hexColor`, representing the hexadecimal color value passed from the Flash movie.

13: This line of code passes the argument `hexColor` to the `document.bgColor` property, which controls the HTML background color.

14: This line of code ends the function defined in line 12.

15: This end comment closes the comment started in line 11.

16: The closing `</script>` tag ends this portion of JavaScript code.

That's it! We also added `<center>` tags around the `<div>` tag to center the Flash movie on the HTML page, and we added the `allowScriptAccess` parameter in the `<object>` tag, respectively, to `"always"`. After you've manually added the custom lines of JavaScript code, you can load the HTML document into either Internet Explorer or a Mozilla-compatible browser (see the caveats mentioned at the beginning of this section). When the Flash Player comes to the frames with `changeBgColor()` actions, the HTML background should change along with the Flash movie. Next, you add a `<form>` element that displays the percentage of the Flash movie that has loaded into the browser window.

ON the CD-ROM You can find this version of the `countdown_100.fla` document in the `ch21/` `ExternalInterface` folder on this book's CD-ROM. You will also find `countdown.` `swf` and a fully JavaScripted HTML document called `countdown_swfobject_100.html`.

Adding a percentLoaded() method

With Flash Player 8 or later and the `ExternalInterface` API, JavaScript can also communicate back to the Flash movie. In the Flash movie, you need to define callback handlers by using the `ExternalInterface.addCallback()` method. This method lets you set up custom functions that are exposed to the hosting environment.

In this section, you create a JavaScript `percentLoaded()` method to display the Flash movie's loading progress update as a text field of a `<form>` element. First, you add the necessary `ExternalInterface` action and custom function to the Flash movie, next you add HTML `<form>` elements, and then you add the appropriate JavaScript.

1. **Open the** `countdown_100.fla` **file that you modified in the previous section.** Select frame 1 of the actions layer, and open the Actions panel (F9/Option+F9). Add the code shown in Listing 21.4 after the first import statement but before the `changeBgColor` function declaration. (Do not type the ⤸ character because it denotes a continuation of the same line of code.)

   The `import flash.display.LoaderInfo;` statement makes ready the `LoaderInfo` class necessary for accessing the Flash movie's percent-loaded information. The `import flash.sysem.Security;` statement makes available the `Security` class that defines which Web domain can access content with the Flash movie (.swf file).

   The `Security.allowDomain("*");` action allows JavaScript to access the Flash movie's methods and properties. Use the "*" value only when testing the file locally. If you intend to upload a live example to your Web server, specify the Web server's domain name.

   The next block of code uses an `if` statement to check whether the `ExternalInterface` capabilities are available in the current host environment, such as a Web browser. If `ExternalInterface` is available, an ActionScript function named `getPercent` `Loaded` is exposed to JavaScript with the `ExternalInterface.addCallback()` method. This method takes two arguments: the name you want to use in JavaScript to call the Flash function (`"getPercentLoaded"`, although you could specify a different name here to use in JavaScript if you preferred), and the Flash function name that is invoked when JavaScript calls the function named as the first argument (`getPercent` `Loaded`). The `catch` statements are invoked only if an error is encountered when the Flash movie tries to access JavaScript with the `addCallBack()` method. The `throw` `new Error()` actions display an error dialog at runtime to alert the user to an error encountered during playback.

   The function `getPercentLoaded()` does not use any arguments. The purpose of the `getPercentLoaded()` function is to return the percent loaded of the Flash movie file (.swf).

2. Save your Flash document as `countdown_complete.fla`, and publish your Flash movie.

3. In a text editor such as Adobe Dreamweaver, Notepad, or TextEdit, open the `countdown_swfobject_100.html` document from the previous section. Immediately resave this document as `countdown_swfobject.html`.

4. Add the following HTML after the `<object>` and `<embed>` tags:

```
<form method="post" action="" name="flashPercent" ⏎
   style="display:show">
  <input type="text" name="labelField" size="5" ⏎
  style="display:show" />
</form>
```

The code in Step 4 uses two `name` attributes so that JavaScript can recognize them. Also, the DHTML `style` attribute assigns a `display:show` value to both the `<form>` and `<input>` tags.

5. Add the JavaScript code shown in Listing 21.5 to your HTML document after the `changeBgColor()` function. The following `percentLoaded` function tells the browser to update the `<form>` text field with the percent of the Flash movie currently loaded. When the value is greater than or equal to 100, then the text field reads 100 percent and disappears after two seconds. This code also declares a `thisMovie()` function, which returns a reference to the Flash object in the `<object>` tag. The `thisMovie()` function is used in the `percentLoaded()` function to call the Flash movie's `getPercentLoaded()` function you wrote in Step 1 of this section, to retrieve the loaded percent of the Flash movie. After the `percentLoaded()` function is declared in JavaScript, you use the `setInterval()` function in JavaScript to continuously invoke the `percentLoaded()` function, every 100 milliseconds. This interval is cleared when the Flash movie is fully loaded. (The ⏎ indicates a continuation to the same line of code. Do not type this character in your code.)

NOTE The `thisMovie()` function code is a slightly modified version of an example taken directly from Adobe's `ExternalInterface` API example code shown in the documentation that is accessed through the Help panel. Also, you might notice that JavaScript has some of the same function names that Flash ActionScript does. Both JavaScript and ActionScript have a `setInterval()` function to enable you to call a function continuously at a specific interval.

6. Save the HTML document and load it into a browser. If you run into errors, check your JavaScript syntax carefully. A misplaced `;` or `}` can set off the entire script. Also, the function names specified in the Flash ActionScript code and the JavaScript code are case-sensitive and must be exactly the same. If you continue to run into errors, compare your document to the `countdown_swfobject.html` document on this book's CD-ROM. We also recommend that you test the preloading functionality from a remote Web server. If you test the file locally, the Flash Player may throw a security error dialog box.

LISTING 21.4

The ActionScript Code for the percentLoaded() Function

```
import flash.external.ExternalInterface;
import flash.display.LoaderInfo;
import flash.system.Security;

Security.allowDomain("*");

if (ExternalInterface.available) {
    try {
        ExternalInterface.addCallback("getPercentLoaded", getPercentLoaded);
    }
    catch (error:SecurityError) {
        throw new Error(error.message);
    }
    catch (error:Error) {
        throw new Error(error.message);
    }
} else {
    throw new Error("ExternalInterface not available for this host ⤸
    environment.");
}

function getPercentLoaded():Number {
    var li:LoaderInfo = this.loaderInfo;
    var lb:Number = li.bytesLoaded;
    var tb:Number = li.bytesTotal;
    return Math.floor((lb/tb)*100);
}
```

LISTING 21.5

The JavaScript Code for the percentLoaded() Function

```
function thisMovie(movieName) {
    var isIE = navigator.appName.indexOf("Microsoft") != -1;
    return (isIE) ? window[movieName] : ⤸
    document.getElementById(movieName);
}

function percentLoaded(){
    try {

        var movie = thisMovie("countdown");
```

continued

735

LISTING 21.5 *(continued)*

```
     var pl = movie.getPercentLoaded();

 if(pl >= 100 ){

     document.flashPercent.labelField.value= "100 %";

     setTimeout("document.flashPercent.labelField.style.⊃
      display = 'none'", 2000);

     clearInterval(checkID);

    } else {

     document.flashPercent.labelField.value = pl + " %" ;

    }

  }

  catch(err){

    alert("Can't determine percent loaded... Aborting..");

    document.flashPercent.labelField.style.display = 'none';

    clearInterval(checkID);
  }
          }
 var checkID = setInterval(percentLoaded, 100);
```

CAUTION Remember that this type of interactivity won't work on all browsers, and it requires the use of Flash Player 8 or later.

Okay, that wasn't the easiest task in the world, and, admittedly, the effects might not have been as spectacular as you may have thought. Now that you know the basics of Flash and JavaScript inter-activity, however, you can take your Flash movie interactivity one step farther.

WEB RESOURCE We want to know what you think about this chapter. Visit www.flashsupport. com/feedback to send us your comments.

Summary

■ You can customize many Flash movie attributes by adjusting the attributes of the `<object>` and `<embed>` tags in an HTML document. Scaling, size, quality, and background color are just a few of the Flash movie properties that can be changed within HTML without altering the original .swf file.

■ Flash CS4 includes a Detect Flash Version feature in the publish settings. This feature automatically creates an HTML document with the appropriate JavaScript and HTML tags to check for a version of the Flash Player that you specify.

■ The SWFObject JavaScript library is a clean and concise method for adding Flash content to HTML pages, as well as detecting and requiring a specific version of the Flash Player.

■ Flash movies can interact with JavaScript and HTML elements on a Web page. This type of interactivity, however, is limited to the 4.0 or later versions of Internet Explorer (on 32-bit Windows versions) and more current versions of Mozilla-compatible browsers.

■ Flash Player 8 or later can receive events and data from JavaScript. For example, JavaScript can query a Flash movie to determine how much of it has downloaded to the browser.

Chapter 22

Using the Flash Player and Projector

This chapter, the last in Part VI, explores alternative means of distributing your Flash movies as self-contained executable applications for CD/DVD-ROMs or other removable storage devices. We also look at the broad support available for the Flash Player plug-in for Web browsers.

Using the Stand-Alone Flash Player and Projector

The stand-alone Flash Player and projector enable you to take your Flash right off the Web and onto the desktop without having to worry whether users have the plug-in. In fact, you don't even need to worry about them having browsers! Stand-alone players and projectors have similar properties and limitations, although they're slightly different.

- **Stand-alone player:** This is an executable player that comes with Flash CS4. You can open any .swf file in this player. The stand-alone player can be found in the `Adobe/Flash CS4/Players/Release` folder (Windows) or the `Adobe Flash CS4: Players:Release` folder (Mac) on the volume where you installed Flash CS4.

- **Projector:** A projector is an executable copy of your movie that doesn't need an additional player or plug-in to be viewed. It's essentially a movie contained within the stand-alone player. The projector is ideal for distribution of Flash applications on CD-ROMs or DVD-ROMs. Figure 22.1 shows a Flash movie played as a projector on Windows.

FIGURE 22.1

A movie playing as a projector

For the sake of simplicity, we refer to both projectors and movies played in the stand-alone Flash Player as *stand-alones* in this discussion. Because both the projector and stand-alone player have similar properties and limitations, you can apply everything discussed here to either one you choose to use.

NOTE Due to the differences in operating systems, Flash stand-alones on Mac have the application menu listed in the system bar at the top of the Mac desktop area. On Windows, the application menu bar is part of the stand-alone window, as shown in Figure 22.1.

Creating a projector

When you have finished producing a Flash movie, it's fairly simple to turn it into a projector. You have two ways to create a stand-alone projector. Turning your Flash movies into Flash Player 10 stand-alone projectors typically adds 4MB (Windows projectors) or 13MB (Mac projectors) to the final file size.

Method 1: Using the Publish command

The simplest way to make a Flash projector file is to use the Publish feature of Flash CS4. In three short steps, you can have a stand-alone Flash movie presentation.

1. **Choose File ⇨ Publish Settings from the application menu.**

2. **When the Publish Settings dialog box opens, select the Formats tab and check the projector formats.** Publish both Windows and Mac projectors by using this method. Figure 22.2 shows the Publish Settings dialog box with the appropriate formats selected. Be sure to select the Flash tab to control how your Flash movie is compiled (Flash Player version, ActionScript version, and so on).

FIGURE 22.2

Select the projector formats in the Publish Settings dialog box.

3. Click the Publish button in the Publish Settings dialog box, and your Flash movie will be published in all the formats (for example, .swf, .gif, .jpg, and projector formats) specified with Publish Settings.

Method 2: Using the stand-alone Flash Player

You can also create a Flash projector file by using the stand-alone Flash Player executable file that ships with Flash CS4. You can find the stand-alone Flash Player in the Players/Release folder of the Flash CS4 application folder.

NOTE If you use this method to create a projector, you can make a projector for the current platform only. Thus, if you are using the Windows version of the stand-alone Flash Player, you can create a Windows projector only.

1. **Export your Flash movie as an .swf file by using File ⇨ Export Movie.** Alternatively, you can use the Publish feature to create the .swf file.

2. **Open the exported Flash movie file (.swf) in the stand-alone Flash Player.**

3. **Choose File ⇨ Create Projector from the stand-alone player's application menu, as shown in Figure 22.3.**

4. **When the Save As dialog box opens, name the projector and save it.**

FIGURE 22.3

Choose File ⇨ Create Projector from the stand-alone player menu.

Distribution and licensing

Distribution of stand-alone projectors or the Flash Player is free; you don't have to buy a license to distribute either the stand-alone Flash Player or projector. However, according to Adobe, you need to follow specific guidelines for distributed Flash Players and projectors. You can download the run-time license agreement and Adobe logos from the Adobe Web site. For more information, check out www.adobe.com/products/players/fpsh_distribution1.html.

Distribution on CD-ROM or DVD-ROM

The Flash platform has become increasingly popular for use on multimedia CD-ROMs or DVD-ROMs, especially as embedded .swf files in larger Adobe Director projectors. Stand-alones can be used as front-ends for installations, splash screens for other programs, or even as complete applications. When you combine the good looks of a Flash interface with a few `fscommand` actions (see the next section for more information) and put them together on a CD-ROM (or DVD-ROM) that's programmed to start automatically on insertion, you have a first-class product.

CAUTION As a general rule, don't try to send projector files (.exe files) as attachments to e-mail messages. Most current e-mail clients, such as Microsoft Outlook, do not allow you to open an e-mail containing an executable file, protecting you against computer virus infections.

Stand-Alone Limitations and Solutions

When you create a stand-alone, the task may not be as simple as taking your Flash document and exporting it as a projector. This section briefly discusses issues that may affect the performance of your projector.

When you distribute your Flash movies as stand-alones, you may think that you won't have to worry about streaming and download. As a consequence, stand-alones are often made considerably larger than a typical Flash movie — which can be a mistake! Very large movies (5MB or more) may not play well on slower computers with Pentium III (or PowerMac G4) or older processors. Remember that Flash movies require the computer processor to compute all those vector calculations, especially for rich animation. When you try to give a slower computer a large Flash movie to load, it may not be able to handle it.

TIP One way to get around this limitation is to break your movies into several smaller movies. You can use the loadMovie/unloadMovie actions to open and close other movies within the original movie. You should use these actions in your stand-alones.

You should also test your movies on a variety of computers, especially if you plan to put a lot of development time and money into distributing them on CD-ROM. Some processors handle the movies better than others, and you often have to decide which processor you want to target as the lowest common denominator.

Using the Flash Player Plug-in for Web Browsers

Flash movies can be played only in Web browsers that have the Flash Player plug-in or ActiveX control installed. Macromedia has made huge strides in making the plug-in prepackaged with newer Web browsers and operating system installation programs, eliminating the need for users to manually download and install the plug-in themselves. Unfortunately, the Flash Player 9 version of the plug-in will likely only be included in future releases of Web browsers and operating systems. Remember that earlier versions of the plug-in can *try* to play Flash movies published for Flash Player 9; however, new features in Flash Player 9–based movies (such as ActionScript 3.0, full-screen movie sizes, and so on) will not be available.

NOTE For up-to-date information on the Flash Player plug-in, see Adobe's download page at www.adobe.com/shockwave/download/alternates.

The Flash Player on Mobile Devices

The development for the Flash Player is so demanding that Macromedia dedicates an entire department's worth of resources to the job. The Flash Player has been made available for Pocket PC devices using the Pocket PC 2002/2003 and Windows Mobile 5 and 6 operating systems from Microsoft. Computer hardware manufacturers such as Hewlett-Packard/Compaq and Casio currently manufacture a wide range of PDAs (personal digital assistants) that can use the Flash Player via the Pocket Internet Explorer Web browser or a stand-alone player. At the time of this writing, Flash Player 7 was available for most Pocket PCs and devices running Windows Mobile 5 and 6. As the computer processing power of Palm, Handspring, and Sony devices (that implement the Palm OS) increases, we see Flash Player support being extended to these devices.

Nokia and DoCoMo have released phones in Japan that can play full-color Flash animations as well! These phones use a version of the Flash Player called Flash Lite. With version 1.0/1.1 of this player, you can create Flash movies that use Flash 5 objects and Flash 4 ActionScript. For more information on Flash Lite, visit the following page on Adobe's site:

`www.adobe.com/products/flashlite/`

It's no surprise that the Flash Player is being adopted so widely by computer and device manufacturers. The .swf format allows rich media such as animation, sound, and video to be transmitted over incredibly slow (or congested) networks. Until high-speed wireless access becomes more available, we'll likely need to keep wireless connection speeds such as 19.2 Kbps (CDPD-based networks) or 25 to 60 Kbps (GPRS-based networks) in mind while developing Flash movies that a universal audience can access.

If you plan to deploy Flash content to Flash Lite, be sure to check out Adobe Device Central CS4, which is included with Adobe Flash CS4 Professional. This application enables you to create Flash content specifically sized and published for a wide variety of mobile devices.

Supported operating systems

Since Flash 3, Adobe has greatly expanded its platform support for the Flash Player plug-in. At the time of this writing, you can download Flash Players for Windows 95/98/ME/NT/2000/XP/Vista and for Power PC and Intel Macs. By the time this book is published, version 9 players should be available for Linux *x*86. At conferences worldwide, Adobe has demonstrated that Flash graphics can be ported to a variety of GUIs (graphical user interfaces) and operating systems. We've also seen Flash graphics showing up in add-on applications for entertainment consoles such as the Sony PlayStation and set-top boxes from Motorola.

Supported browsers

The Flash Player plug-in works best with Mozilla-compatible and Internet Explorer browsers. Any browser compliant with Netscape Navigator 2.0's plug-in specification or Internet Explorer's ActiveX technology can support the Flash Player plug-in or ActiveX control, respectively. Note that Mac versions of Internet Explorer or Apple Safari use a Netscape plug-in emulator to use the Flash Player plug-in rather than an ActiveX control.

For AOL subscribers, any version of AOL's 3.0 through 9.0 browsers (except for the earliest 3.0 release that used a non-Microsoft Internet Explorer shell) supports Adobe plug-ins.

For a comprehensive list of supported browsers (and Flash compatibility), see the Adobe tech note at `www.adobe.com/support/flash/ts/documents/browser_support_matrix.htm`.

Plug-in and Flash movie distribution on the Web

Anyone can download the Flash Player plug-in for free from the Adobe Web site. You can direct visitors of your Web sites to Adobe's Flash Player download page, `www.adobe.com/go/getflashplayer`. In fact, according to Adobe's licensing agreement, if you're publishing Flash movies on your Web site, you need to display the "Get Shockwave Player" logo or "Get Flash Player" logo on your Web site. This logo should link to Adobe's download page, which we just listed. However, you can't distribute the plug-in installer yourself — you need to license the right to distribute any plug-in installer from Adobe. For more details on licensing, see `www.adobe.com/licensing/`.

You can find the official Adobe button graphics at:

`www.adobe.com/macromedia/style_guide/buttons/`

Plug-in installation

In Chapter 20 we discuss the Publish feature of Flash CS4 and the use of preformatted HTML templates to deliver your Flash movies to your Web site. The template and/or handwritten HTML that you use for your Flash-enabled Web pages determines the degree of difficulty your visitors will have upon loading a Flash movie.

Adobe has also officially named the auto-update experience of the Flash Player plug-in as Express Install. This feature refers to the nearly pain-free process of upgrading from Flash Player 6 or later to the latest version of the Flash Player. Flash Player 7 was released with an auto-update feature, enabling new versions of the plug-in to download without the hassle of installing an updated ActiveX control or downloading a plug-in installer application.

WEB RESOURCE You can change the auto-update preferences of your Flash Player installation by visiting the following Adobe Web page:

`www.adobe.com/support/documentation/en/flashplayer/help/settings_manager05.html`

By default, the Flash Player checks for an updated version of the plug-in every 30 days. You can change the time interval to as little as 7 days.

Using the Settings in Flash Player 6 and Later

Flash Player 6 introduced the Settings option from the Flash Player's contextual menu, which can be accessed by right-clicking (or Control+clicking on Mac) a Flash movie. When you choose the Settings option, the Macromedia Flash Player Settings dialog box opens. This dialog box has four tabs, which are discussed in the following sections.

Privacy

This tab, shown in Figure 22.4, controls the access of the current Flash movie to your Webcam and microphone. Whenever a Flash movie tries to access your Webcam or microphone, the Flash Player opens this tab to ask you for permission. You can choose Allow, which gives the Flash movie access to your camera and microphone, or Deny, which stops the Flash movie from gaining access to these devices. You can also select the Remember check box so that the Flash Player remembers the choice you made, preventing the dialog box from opening during subsequent visits to the same Flash movie (or Web site hosting the Flash movie). If you click the Advanced button in the Privacy tab, a new Web browser opens and loads the help page for the Settings options on Macromedia's site.

 Flash movies can stream live audio and video to Flash Media Server applications by using the `Camera`, `Microphone`, and `NetStream` objects.

The Privacy option applies to any and all Flash movies hosted on the domain listed in the Privacy tab.

WEB RESOURCE For the most up-to-date information on the Privacy tab, refer to the following page on Macromedia's site:

`www.adobe.com/support/flashplayer/help/privacy/`

You can also access the Global Settings manager on Adobe's site, which enables you to control the privacy settings for all sites you have visited. Go to the following URL:

`www.adobe.com/support/flashplayer/help/settings/global_privacy.html`

FIGURE 22.4

The Privacy tab

Local Storage

As shown in Figure 22.5, the Local Storage tab controls how much information can be stored on your computer from the Flash Player. Since Flash Player 6, Flash movies can be engineered to store data on the user's machine, with the use of local Shared Objects. The SharedObject class in ActionScript enables you to store customized information on a user's machine, just like cookies can store information from a Web application.

FIGURE 22.5

The Local Storage tab

By default, a Web site and Flash movies hosted on that site can allocate as much as 100K of data on a user's machine. If a Flash movie hosted from a Web site requests more than this amount, the Flash Player automatically opens this tab asking for the user's permission to store more data. You can click the Never Ask Again option to prevent the Flash Player from automatically opening this tab when a site requests to store more data than its allotted amount.

WEB RESOURCE You can find the latest information about the Local Storage tab at:

www.macromedia.com/support/documentation/en/flashplayer/help/
help02.html.

CROSS-REF To learn more about using the SharedObject class, refer to Chapter 31, "Creating a Game in Flash." For more extended coverage, read the *Flash ActionScript Bible* series (Wiley).

Microphone

The Microphone tab, shown in Figure 22.6, controls the source of audio input to a Flash movie. Depending on your computer system, you may have several audio capture devices listed in this tab's menu. If you don't have an audio capture device on your system, then you may not see any options available in this panel. You can use this tab to control the sensitivity of the microphone (or capture device) by adjusting the slider position. The tab provides real-time audio monitoring with a bar graph. You can click the Reduce Echo check box to minimize the echo or feedback from a speaker that is located near your microphone.

FIGURE 22.6

The Microphone tab

WEB RESOURCE For more information on Microphone settings, see www.adobe.com/support/ flashplayer/help/microphone.

Camera

The Camera tab, shown in Figures 22.7 and 22.8, controls the camera source used by the Flash Player. If your computer does not have a camera (or digital video capture card, which includes FireWire, or IEEE 1394, cards), then you may not see a camera source listed in this tab. If you have multiple video capture sources, you can use this tab to control which source is used for live streams going out of the Flash movie into a Flash Media Server application.

FIGURE 22.7

The default view of the Camera tab

You can click the camera icon in the Camera tab to see live video from your chosen capture source, as shown in Figure 22.8. If you do not see any picture in this area after you click the camera icon, you may have a problem with your capture driver or the Flash Player may be incompatible with the driver.

FIGURE 22.8

An active preview of a camera's output in the Camera tab

 For more information on the Camera tab and its settings, see the following page on Macromedia's site: `www.adobe.com/support/flashplayer/help/camera`.

Player Utilities

You can also reformat and modify stand-alones for both Windows and Mac. A few software companies create applications specifically designed to modify Flash movies and stand-alones. Here is a list of Web site URLs for those companies:

- `www.flashjester.com`
- `www.multidmedia.com`
- `www.northcode.com`
- `www.screentime.com`
- `www.alienzone.com/screensaver_features.htm`
- `www.goldshell.com`

Some of these companies offer more than just one utility for Flash movie development, such as the JTools of FlashJester. For updates to this list, check out this book's Web site, listed in the preface of this book.

TIP You can find directories of Flash utilities at `www.flashmagazine.com` and `graphicssoft.about.com/cs/flashtools`.

One of our favorite utilities is Versiown, created by Goldshell Digital Media. This handy utility allows you to modify the properties of a Flash (or Director) projector file, specifically .exe versions for Windows. With Versiown, you can:

- Add or modify the version information that shows up in the Properties dialog box, accessible by right-clicking the .exe file and choosing Properties.
- Add a custom icon for the .exe file of the projector. Together with an icon utility such as IconBuilder from Iconfactory (which is a filter plug-in for Adobe Photoshop), you can make custom .ico files to be used as icons for your Flash projectors.

749

You can download trial versions of Versiown at www.goldshell.com/versiown. A trial of IconBuilder is available at www.iconfactory.com/ib_home.asp.

NOTE You can use the Get Info dialog box (Mac OS X) on Mac files to easily replace the icon image for Flash projector files on Mac. Open the .ico file made from IconBuilder in an image editor such as Adobe Photoshop, use Edit ⇨ Select All to select the entire image, copy it to the Clipboard (Edit ⇨ Copy), and paste it into the picture area of the Get Info dialog box.

WEB RESOURCE We'd like to know what you think about this chapter. Visit www.flashsupport. com/feedback to send us your comments.

Summary

- Flash movies can be viewed in Web pages with the Flash Player plug-in or ActiveX control. You can also play Flash movie files (.swf) with the stand-alone Flash Player included with the Flash CS4 application, or you can publish a Mac or Windows projector that packages the stand-alone Flash Player and .swf file into one executable file.

- You can freely distribute a Flash movie projector or stand-alone Flash Player as long as you adhere to the guidelines outlined at Adobe's Web site.

- Flash movies can be distributed with other multimedia presentations such as Macromedia Director projectors. Your Flash movies can be distributed on a CD-ROM or DVD-ROM.

- You can enhance your Flash movies with third-party tools such as FlashJester's JTools for Flash.

Part VII

Approaching ActionScript

Now that you're comfortable in the Flash authoring environment, it's time to see what you can do when you move beyond basic timelines and start architecting and controlling content with ActionScript. Chapter 23 introduces the basic syntax of ActionScript code so that you understand why all those brackets, dots, and quote marks are used. In Chapter 24 you learn how to control methods and properties of MovieClip objects. If you thought animating Movie Clips was fun, wait until you start to apply more sophisticated control to multiple elements with ActionScript! Chapter 25 covers using functions and arrays, two of the most crucial techniques for organizing and controlling dynamic data. Chapter 26 takes you to the next level of Movie Clip control with an overview of how to detect collisions, and how to use the ColorTransform, Sound, and PrintJob classes to control dynamic movie elements.

Chapter 23

Knowing the Nuts and Bolts of Code

IN THIS CHAPTER

Describing interactive problems

Speaking the ActionScript language

Understanding the value of variables

Working with conditionals

For many serious Web developers, Flash's enhanced programming capabilities are the most important new feature of each product release. Just when you think they've added it all, the Adobe Flash team manages to pull more rabbits out of the hat. Elements inside Flash movies can be dynamic, have properties calculated on-the-fly, and respond to user input. Movies can communicate with server-side applications and scripts by sending and receiving processed and raw data. What does this mean for your movies? It means that you have the capability to produce truly advanced movies (such as online secure banking applications, product configurators, hotel reservation systems, Flash asteroids, a multiplayer role-playing adventure game, or a navigational interface with a memory of the user's moves, just to name a few). It also means that Flash can be used to produce complex Web or desktop applications, such as database-driven e-commerce product catalogs, without the need for proprietary server-side applications.

NOTE For over three years, Adobe has had another tool, Flex Builder, that enables the creation of complex Flash applications and that outputs the same SWF file format that the Flash authoring tool does. Flex Builder 3 enables you to build Rich Internet Applications (RIAs) by using a markup language called MXML and a scripting layer written in ActionScript 3.0. The Flex framework is included with Flex Builder. This framework enables you to add common application elements (buttons, windows, data grids) and state management. More and more RIAs are being built with the Flex development environment rather than the Flash authoring tool.

Although you can still use any version of ActionScript for Flash content produced in Flash CS4, the structure of ActionScript programming has taken a tremendous leap forward with the ActionScript 3.0 version specification. ActionScript 3.0, or AS3, is a highly evolved form of programming compared to ActionScript 2.0 (or AS2) and older syntaxes used in Flash Players 5 and earlier. We feel that AS3 requires a fundamental understanding of basic programming, and as such, have updated our coverage in the *Flash Bible* series by using ActionScript 3.0 principles.

AS3 programming, introduced in Flash CS3, adheres closely to ECMAScript Edition 4–compliant standards. The Actions panel, now in its sixth version, only becomes more efficient at helping you code. Most of the advanced components in Flash CS4 continue to use the ActionScript 3.0 model, using complex event handling, and make it simpler for you to add interface elements and integrate data into your Flash projects. Flash CS4 continues to enable designers and developers alike to build the foundations for Rich Internet Applications, or RIAs, which bring a new world of real-time data and ease of use to the Web. These topics, however, are far beyond the scope of motion tweens and animations. In this chapter, we introduce you to the programming structure of ActionScript and explain how to start using code within your Flash movies.

CROSS-REF If you are new to scripting, we highly recommend that you review Part V, "Adding Basic Interactivity to Flash Movies," before you begin this chapter. As mentioned in previous chapters, all ActionScript coverage in this edition of the *Flash Bible* uses ActionScript 3.0 conventions.

WEB RESOURCE For more information about ECMAScript Edition 4, see the original proposal at `www.ecmascript.org`.

Breaking Down the Interactive Process

Before you can become an ActionScript code warrior, realize that this isn't just a weekend activity: If you want to excel at Flash ActionScripting, you must commit the time and energy necessary for the proper revelations to occur. You'll not likely understand programming simply by reading this chapter (or the whole book). You need to create some trials for yourself, testing your textbook knowledge and applying problem-solving techniques.

You might be thinking, "Oh no, you mean I have to revisit that torture of grade school math?" Not exactly, but programming, like math, requires strong reasoning and justification skills. You need to be able to understand how values (for example, the height of a `MovieClip` instance) are determined, what type of changes you can perform on those values, and how changes to one value might affect another value. If you're feeling overwhelmed, don't worry. We take this one step at a time.

Define your problems

Regardless of what interactive authoring tool you use (Adobe Dreamweaver, Adobe Flash, Adobe Director, and so on), you can't begin any production work until you have a clear idea of the product. What is it that you are setting out to do? At this point in the process, you should use natural language to describe your problems; that is, define your objective (or problem) in a way that you understand it. For example, let's say that you want to make a quiz. You'll have to run through a list of goals for that interactive product:

- Is it a true/false test?

- Or will it be multiple choice?

- Or how about fill-in-the-blank?

- Is it an essay test?

- How many questions will be on the quiz?

- Will there be a time limit for each question?

- Will you notify the person of wrong answers?

- How many chances does the person get to answer correctly?

Other questions, of course, could help define what your product will encompass. Don't try to start Flash production without setting some project parameters for yourself.

Clarify the solution

After you have defined the boundaries for the project, you can start to map the process by which your product will operate. This step involves the procedure of the experience (in other words, how the person will use the product you are creating). With the quiz example, you might clarify the solution as:

1. The user starts the movie and types his or her name.

2. After submitting the name, the user is told that he or she has 10 minutes to complete a 25-question quiz that's a combination of true/false and multiple-choice questions.

3. Upon acknowledging the instructions (by pressing a key or clicking a button), the timer starts and the user is presented with the first question.

4. The timer is visible to the user.

5. The first question is a true/false question, and the correct answer is false.

6. If the user enters a true response, a red light graphic appears and the sound of a buzzer plays. The user is asked to continue with the next question.

7. If the user enters a false response, a green light graphic appears and the sound of applause plays. The user is asked to continue with the next question.

8. This process repeats until the last question is answered, at which point the score is tallied and presented to the user.

The preceding eight steps are similar to a process flowchart, as we discuss in Chapter 3, "Planning Flash Projects." In real-life production, you would want to clarify Step 8 for each question in the same amount of detail as Steps 5–7 did. As you can see, when you start to map the interactive experience, you'll have a much better starting point for your scripting work. Notice that we're already using logic, with our `if` statements in Steps 6 and 7. We're also determining object properties such as `visible` in Step 4. Although you may not know all the ActionScript involved with starting a timer, you know that you have to learn how time can be measured in a Flash movie.

We use the terms *scripting, programming,* and *coding* interchangeably throughout this chapter and in other parts of the book.

Translate the solution into the interactive language

After you have created a process for the movie to follow, you can start to convert each step into a format that Flash can use. This step consumes much of your time as you look up concepts and keywords in this book, the *Flash ActionScript Bible* series (Wiley), or Adobe's updated Help system that ships with Flash CS4. It's likely that you won't be able to find a prebuilt Flash movie example to use as a guide, or if you do, that you'll need to customize it to suit the particular needs of your project. For the quiz example, we could start to translate the solution as:

1. Frame 1: Movie stops. User types name into a text field.

2a. Frame 1: User clicks a Submit button symbol instance to initiate the quiz. The instructions are located on frame 2. Therefore, an action uses a `gotoAndStop(2)` action to move the playhead to the next frame.

2b. Frame 2: Static text is shown, indicating the guidelines for the quiz.

3. Frame 2: User clicks a Start Quiz button symbol instance. An action delegated from the button instance starts a timer and moves the playhead to frame 3.

4. Frame 3: The current time of the timer appears in a text field, in the upper right corner of the Stage.

5. Frame 3: The first question is presented in the center of the Stage. A button with the text True and a button with the text False are located just beneath the question. The correct answer for the question is hidden in a variable name/value. The variable's name is `answer`, and its value is `false`. This variable declaration appears as a frame action on frame 3. A variable, called `score`, is also declared to keep track of the correct answer count. Its starting value is `0`.

6a. Frame 3: If the user clicks the True button, an `if/else` action checks whether answer's value is equal to `true`. If it is, an action sets the `visible` property of a `greenLight` `MovieClip` instance to `true`, and initiates and plays a new `Sound` object for the `applause.wav` file in your library. Also, the value of `score` increases by 1. If the value of `answer` is not `true`, an action sets the `visible` of a `redLight` instance to `true`, and initiates and plays a new `Sound` object for the `error.wav` file in your library. The value of score is left as is.

6b. Frame 3: A `Button` instance appears, and when it's clicked, it takes the user to frame 4.

7a. Frame 3: If the user clicks the False button, an `if/else` action checks whether answer's value is equal to `true`. If it is, an action sets the `visible` property of a `greenLight` instance to `true`, and initiates and plays a new `Sound` object for the `applause.wav` file in your library. Also, the value of `score` increases by 1. If the value of `answer` is not `true`, an action sets the `visible` of a `redLight` instance to `true` and initiates and plays a new `Sound` object for the `error.wav` file in your library. The value of `score` is left as is.

7b. Frame 3: A `Button` instance appears, and when it's clicked, it takes the user to frame 4.

Although there is more than one way we could have translated this into ActionScript-like syntax, you'll notice that a few key concepts are presented in the translation: where events occur (frames or buttons), and which elements (for example, Button symbols or `MovieClip` instances) are involved.

Most important, you'll notice that we used the same procedure for both the True and the False buttons. Even though we could hardwire the answer directly in the button actions, we would have to change our button actions for each question. By reusing the same logic for each Button instance, we have only to change the value of the answer variable from frame to frame (or from question to question).

Granted, this example was already translated for you, and 90 percent of your scripting woes will be in the translation process — before you even have a testable Flash movie. You need to learn the basic terminology and syntax of the ActionScript language before you can start to write the scripting necessary for Steps 1–7, and that's exactly what the rest of this chapter (and the rest of Part VII) begins to teach you.

CROSS-REF Because the vocabulary of the ActionScript language has become so immense, Robert Reinhardt and Joey Lott created a separate *Bible* series, on Flash ActionScript, to thoroughly address the syntax of ActionScript. However, if you are new to scripting and programming, we recommend that you start with our coverage of ActionScript here before reading the *ActionScript Bible* (Wiley).

The Basic Context for Programming in Flash

With the enhanced Actions panel (also known as the ActionScript editor) in Flash CS4, you can program interactivity by writing interactive commands directly into the Script pane of the Actions panel.

TIP Flash CS4's Actions panel can show you hidden characters, such as character spaces and line breaks, in your code. Choose Hidden Characters from the options menu of the Actions panel to see these characters. Due to the reactions of many Flash designers and beginner developers, the Actions panel also has a Script Assist feature, which replaces the "Normal mode" of Flash MX's Actions panel. For more information on Script Assist, see Chapter 17.

In the Actions panel, you can type your code from scratch, as well as insert your code with the help of Action booklets or the new Script Assist feature. Syntactically, ActionScript looks and feels very much like JavaScript. Adobe has gone to great lengths to make ActionScript compatible with ECMAScript 4 (the standard programming guidelines derived from JavaScript). And like other object-oriented languages, ActionScript is composed of many familiar building blocks: variables, operators, conditionals, loops, expressions, built-in properties, subroutines, and native functions.

Accessing ActionScript commands

All the ActionScript commands are found in the Flash interface in the Action booklets or plus (+) button menu of the Actions panel. However, assembling actions with one another is not something

Flash CS4 automatically performs. Although it is beyond the scope of this chapter to fully explain fundamental programming principles, we can give you a sense of the whole of ActionScript by providing an organized reference to each of its parts.

Actions list organization in the Actions panel

In the Actions panel, you can cut, copy, and paste code within the Script pane from one area of your movie to another by using Ctrl+X/⌘+X, Ctrl+C/⌘+C, and Ctrl+V/⌘+V, respectively. You are free to select partial or entire lines of code, and modify the code in any way you want. With Flash CS4, you can even edit your code in your preferred text editor! If you want to create your own programming macros in other programming applications, you can write your scripts outside of the Flash authoring environment and copy the final code into the Actions panel when you're done.

> **TIP** To make sure that you don't have any syntax errors after reorganizing code, click the Check Syntax button in the Actions panel toolbar. Flash alerts you if there are scripting errors by placing messages in the Output panel.
>
> Also, use the Script Navigator in the lower left corner of the Actions panel to quickly switch back and forth between keyframe or object code. For example, you can choose one frame in the Script Navigator, copy its code, and then switch to another frame to paste the code.
>
> If you decide to write ActionScript with another editor, you can use the `include` directive to load the contents of the external code file (.as) into the Flash movie at publish or export time. For more information on the `include` directive, read the sidebar, "Using the `include` Directive", later in this chapter. You can find an example of the include directive in Chapter 30, "Applying HTML and Text Field Formatting."

The Help documentation

Don't know what the methods of the `Sound` object are? Need to see if the `getVersion()` function works in a Flash Player 4–compatible movie? Flash CS4 has conveniently nested everything related to help documentation in the new CS4 Help system. Among other items, the Help system, which is loaded into your default Web browser, contains all the syntax of the ActionScript language. You can access the Help system in a few ways:

- Choose Help ➪ Flash Help, or press F1.
- Click the Reference icon in the Actions panel.
- Right-click/Control+click an action in the left-hand Script pane of the Actions panel and choose View Help in the contextual menu.

We'll quickly show you how to use the new Help panel in an actual Flash document:

1. **Open a new Flash file (ActionScript 3.0), using File ➪ New or the Flash CS4 splash page.**
2. **Select frame 1 of Layer 1, and open the Actions panel by pressing F9/Option+F9.**

3. **Add the following code, which creates a new Loader instance to load an external Flash movie (.swf file) or image file:**

```
var extMovie:Loader = new Loader();
```

4. **Select the text** `Loader` **that occurs after the equals (=) operator, making sure *not* to select the** `();` **portion of the action.** Click the Help icon (that is, the circle with the question mark) at the top right of the Actions panel. The Help page opens, displaying the definition for the `Loader` class, as shown in Figure 23.1. You can select other actions from the left pane of the Help panel and view their descriptions.

FIGURE 23.1

The Help page with the definition for `loadMovie`

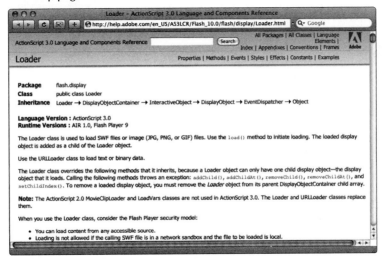

ActionScript 1.0 and 2.0

So why all the fuss about ActionScript now? Let's make one thing clear right away: For most Flash designers and developers, or rather for most of the work that's done in Flash, the graduation of ActionScript 1.0 and 2.0 to 3.0 may mean next to nothing at all. This isn't to say that ActionScript 3.0 should be ignored or is not a monumental leap forward for Flash programming. We simply want to calm or allay any fears you might have after reading about ActionScript 3.0 from other sources. If you've used ActionScript in Flash versions prior to MX 2004, then ActionScript 1.0 refers to the coding styles that those versions of the application used.

Using the `include` Directive

A ctionScript has a processing directive that enables you to insert external text files (with an .as file extension). You can write ActionScript in any text or script editor and save that text separately from the Flash document file (.fla). When you publish a Flash movie file (.swf) from the Flash document, Flash CS4 retrieves the .as file and inserts the actions to the action list where the `include` action was issued. For example, the following code can be written in a `contact.as` file, which, as the name implies, contains a person's contact information for the Flash movie:

```
var contactName:String = "Joseph Farnsworth";
var contactStreet:String = "675 Locust Street";
var contactCity:String = "Chicago";
var contactState:String = "IL";
var contactPhone:String = "312-555-1342";
var contactEmail:String = "jfarnsworth@mycompany.com";
```

Note that this code is written in the ActionScript 3.0 format, which we discuss in this chapter. In a Flash document, you could insert this code into a keyframe of the Main Timeline (or a Movie Clip timeline) by using the `include` action:

```
include "contact.as";
```

Why is the `include` action useful? For experienced programmers, the `include` command gives you the freedom to write ActionScript in any text editor. You can define entire code libraries of custom functions. You can then reuse the .as files from movie to movie. In ActionScript 3.0, custom classes *must* be defined in a separate .as file, but they do not use the `include` directive; rather, AS3 classes are brought into a Flash movie by using the `import` keyword.

Note that the `include` action is executed only upon publishing or testing the Flash movie. You should not upload .as files to your Web server. Include files cannot be inserted at runtime by the Flash Player. Anytime you change the .as file, you must republish your Flash movie file (.swf).

You can find more information on the `include` action in Chapter 30, "Applying HTML and Text Field Formatting." As we discuss in Chapter 3, "Planning Flash Projects," you can track all the .as files in the Project panel of Flash CS4 as well.

ActionScript 3.0 introduced a couple of major structural changes to the way in which you can code Flash ActionScript. To begin with, it uses strong data typing. You learn more about data typing in Chapter 25, "Using Functions and Arrays," but for now, know that ActionScript 3.0 imposes some rules on how you can assign values to variables, functions, and other objects in your code. Unless you're creating code that uses custom classes and object-oriented programming concepts such as inheritance and prototypes, you won't really need to worry about whether your code will work as ActionScript 3.0 code. Another big change with ActionScript 3.0, as with ActionScript 2.0, is case-sensitivity. Prior to Flash Player 7, most ActionScript terms were case-insensitive, meaning you could refer to object references or variables with varying cases, such as:

```
var firstName = "Robert";
var lastName = "Reinhardt";
var fullName = firstName + " " + lastName;
```

In ActionScript 1.0, you could have used the following code as the last line, without receiving an error:

```
var fullName = firstname + " " + lastname;
```

However, in ActionScript 2.0 and 3.0, that same line of code would be incorrect because `firstname` and `lastname` are not using the same case as the original variables.

Why should the distinction between ActionScript 1.0, 2.0, and 3.0 even be an issue? For starters, when you publish a Flash movie for Flash Player 9 or 10, you need to decide how Flash CS4 will compile the ActionScript code in your document. In the Publish Settings dialog box, you can choose which ActionScript version to publish in the Flash tab. Unless directed otherwise, you publish most of the Flash movies for Part VII of this book as ActionScript 3.0, even though it pretty much looks and feels like ActionScript used in previous versions of the Flash authoring tools.

One Part of the Sum: ActionScript Variables

In any scripting or programming language, you need some type of "memory" device — something that can remember the values and properties of objects or significant data. This type of memory device is referred to as a *variable*.

Variables are named storage places for changeable pieces of data (numbers and letters, for starters). One of the first obstacles for designers learning a scripting language is the concept that variable names in and of themselves have no meaning or value to the computer. Remember that the computer can't perform anything unless you tell it to. Even though any given scripting language has a certain set of built-in properties and functions, variables can simplify your scripting workload by creating shortcuts or aliases to other elements of the ActionScript language. One prime example of a "shortcut" variable is the path name to a deeply nested Movie Clip instance, such as:

```
root.birdAnim.birdHouse.birdNest.birdEgg
```

truncated to a variable named egg as:

```
var egg = root.birdAnim.birdHouse.birdNest.birdEgg;
```

If you wanted to declare egg in ActionScript 3.0 code, you would use the following syntax, which types the egg variable as a `MovieClip` object:

```
var egg:MovieClip = root.birdAnim.birdHouse.birdNest.birdEgg;
```

After egg is declared and given a value, you can reuse it without referring to the lengthy path name, as in:

```
with(egg){
    gotoAndPlay("start");
}
```

The important concept here is that you could just as easily have given egg a different name, such as myPath, or robPath, or whatever word(s) you want to use. As long as the syntax and formatting of the expression is correct, you have nothing to worry about.

Another example of a variable that stores path information is the URL to a Web resource, such as a server-side script. Oftentimes, you may have different server URLs for testing and deployment. Instead of changing the URL in every action of the Flash document, you can use a variable name. That way, you only need to change your variable's value once. In the following sample code, a variable named serverURL is set to the actual URL you want to access. You then refer to that serverURL name in other actions, such as getURL().

```
var serverURL = "http://www.flashsupport.com/";
navigateToURL(new URLRequest(serverURL));
```

NOTE Variables in ActionScript are "typed," meaning that their value is explicitly set to be either a string, number, boolean, or object. When working with variables, you must therefore know what data type the value is. We discuss data typing in Chapter 25, "Using Functions and Arrays."

Variables in ActionScript are attached to the timeline of the movie or MovieClip instance on which they are created. If you create a variable x on the Main Timeline, that variable is available for other scripting actions on that timeline. However, from other Movie Clip timelines, the variable is not directly accessible. To access the value of a variable on another timeline (such as a MovieClip instance), enter the target path to the clip instance in which the variable resides, a dot (.); then enter the variable name. For instance, this statement sets the variable foo to be equal to the value of the variable hitCount in the MovieClip instance named ball:

```
var foo = ball.hitCount;
```

This statement, on the other hand, sets the variable foo to be equal to the value of a variable named hitCount on the Main Timeline:

```
var foo = root.hitCount;
```

TIP Variables in ActionScript 1.0 are not case-sensitive and cannot start with a number. Variables in ActionScript 2.0 and 3.0 are case-sensitive.

String literals

In programmer-speak, a string is any combination of alphanumeric characters. By themselves, they have no meaning. It is up to you to assign something meaningful to them. For example, giving a variable the name `firstName` doesn't mean much. You need to assign a value to the variable `firstName` to make it meaningful, and you can do something with it. For example, if `firstName = "Susan"`, you could make something specific to "Susan" happen.

You can also use much simpler name/value pairs, such as `i = 0`, to keep track of counts. If you want a specific Movie Clip animation to loop only three times, you can increment the value of `i` by 1 (for example, `i = i + 1`, `i += 1`, and `i ++` all do the same thing) each time the animation loops back to the start. Then you can stop the animation when it reaches the value of 3.

Expressions

Flash uses the term *expression* to refer to two separate kinds of code fragments in ActionScript. An expression is either a phrase of code used to compare values in a conditional or a loop (these are known as *conditional expressions*), or a snippet of code that is interpreted at runtime (these are known as *numeric expressions* and *string expressions*). We discuss conditional expressions later in this chapter.

Numeric and string expressions are essentially just segments of ActionScript code that are dynamically converted to their calculated values when a movie runs. For example, suppose you have a variable, y, set to a value of 3. In the statement $x = y + 1$, the $y + 1$ on the right side of the equal sign is an expression. Hence, when the movie runs, the statement $x = y + 1$ actually becomes $x = 4$, because the value of y (which is 3) is retrieved (or "interpreted") and the calculation $3 + 1$ is performed. Numeric and string expressions are an extremely potent part of ActionScript because they permit most of the parameters used in actions to be based on mathematical calculations and external variables instead of requiring fixed information. Consider these two examples:

- The parameter of a `gotoAndPlay()` action could be set as an expression that returns a random number in a certain range, sending the movie to a random frame:

  ```
  this.gotoAndPlay(Math.round(Math.random()*100));
  ```

- The URL option in a `getURL()` action could be made up of a variable that indicates a server name and a literal string, which is the file path:

  ```
  var serverName = "http://localhost/";
  var filePath = "resources/showRecent.cfm";
  navigateToURL(new URLRequest(serverName + filePath));
  ```

As mentioned in an earlier section, to change all the URLs in your movie from a staging server to a live server, you just have to change the value of the server variable. So, to change the latter example's code for a live Web server, you simply change the `serverName` variable, as the following code demonstrates:

```
var serverName = "http://www.flashsupport.com/";
```

All the other lines of code stay the same because you only need to change the server location for the live Web site.

Anywhere that you see the word "expression" in any action options, you can use an interpreted ActionScript expression to specify the value of the option.

To use a string inside an expression, simply add quotation marks around it. Anything surrounded by quotation marks is taken as a literal string. For example, the conditional `if (status == ready)` wrongly checks whether the value of the variable `status` is the same as the value of the nonexistent variable `ready`. The correct conditional would check whether the value of `status` is the same as the string `"ready"` by quoting it, as in `if (status == "ready")`.

You can even have expressions that indirectly refer to previously established variables. In ActionScript, you can use the dot syntax (and array access operators) to indirectly refer to variables.

We like to use the phrase "setting and getting" to help beginners understand how equations and expressions work in ActionScript code. An equation is any line of code that sets an object or variable to a new value. The order of syntax terms can be confusing to designers and developers new to code writing. Do you specify a value first? How do you know where to insert the equal sign (=)? If you remember the phrase "setting and getting," you'll know how to write basic equations. The variable you want to set (or assign a new value) is always on the left side of the equation, and the new value is always on the right:

```
what you want to set = the value you want to get
```

For example, if you wanted to set a variable named `currentTime` to the amount of time that has elapsed since the Flash movie started playing in the Flash Player, you would place `currentTime` on the left side of the equation and place the actual value of the time on the right side:

```
current time in the movie = the number of milliseconds that have elapsed
```

Translated into actual code, this would be:

```
var currentTime = getTimer();
```

Again, another important aspect of variables to remember is that the name of a variable is quite arbitrary. What we called `currentTime` could just as well be named `myTime`, `movieTime`, `elapsedTime` — or whatever you want to call it. As long as you consistently refer to your variable's name in subsequent ActionScript code, everything will work as expected.

Array Access Operators

If you have a variable called `name_1` declared on the Main Timeline, you can write the expression `root["name_" + "1"]` to refer to the value of `name_1`. How is this useful? If you have more than one variable, but their prefixes are the same (for example, `name_1`, `name_2`, `name_3`, and so on), you can write an expression with two variables as a generic statement to refer to any one of the previously established variables: `root["name" + i]`, where `i` can be any predefined number. This type of expression is most commonly found in a code loop; you learn more about loops later in this chapter.

Variables as declarations

In most scripting languages, you usually don't have to declare a variable without its value; that is, you don't need to say variable `firstName` and then address it again with a value. In Flash ActionScript, you don't need to preestablish a variable in order to invoke it.

NOTE As you start to code more complex scripts in ActionScript 3.0, such as creating custom classes, you do need to predeclare variable names. As you're starting out with more basic scripts, you do not need to be so thorough with your code.

If you want to create a variable on-the-fly from a Movie Clip to the Main Timeline, you can. Most variables that you use in Flash are declared in a timeline's keyframes. We show you how to create a couple of simple variables in a Flash document:

1. **Open a new Flash file (File ⇨ New).** In the New Document dialog box, choose Flash File (ActionScript 3.0) and click OK.

2. **Rename Layer 1 to** actions.

3. **Select frame 1 of the actions layer in the Timeline window, and open the Actions panel by pressing the F9 key/Option+F9.**

4. **Type the following action in the Script pane (see Figure 23.2):**

```
var firstName = "Franklin";
trace(firstName);
```

FIGURE 23.2

A variable declaration in the Actions panel

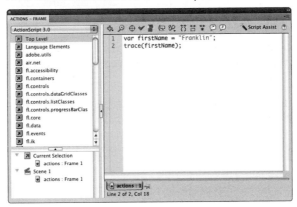

5. **Save your Flash document as** `variable_frame.fla`, **and test it (Ctrl+Enter/⌘+Enter).** In the Output panel, you see the following line of text:

```
Franklin
```

TIP By default, the Output panel is grouped with the Timeline and Motion Editor panels, and you may find it awkward to look for ActionScript messages in this small area. You can undock the Output panel into its own window by dragging its tab out of the default grouping.

As you can see in this example, the value of the `firstName` variable is shown in the Output panel. You can use `trace()` actions to help you track values and output in your Flash movie.

ON the CD-ROM You can find the sample file, `variable_frame.fla`, in the `ch23` folder of this book's CD-ROM.

Declaring Variables in ActionScript

There are several ways to establish, or declare, variables in a Flash movie. You can create them directly with ActionScript, load them from a text file or server-side script, or include them in HTML tags.

Using actions to define variables

The most common way to create a variable is to type the variable's name and value in the Script pane of the Actions panel, on a specific timeline's keyframe. Most basic variables have values that are string literals.

Loading variables from a predefined source

You can also establish variables by loading them from an external source, such as a text file located on your Web server or even through a database query or a server-side script. By using the `URLLoader` class, you can load variables in this fashion. There are four primary steps to implement the `URLLoader` class: Create an instance, specify the `dataFormat` type, listen for the "complete" event when the data has finished loading (and create a listener function), and initiate the loading of the external data source, and variables:

```
var myData:URLLoader = new URLLoader();
myData.dataFormat = URLLoaderDataFormat.VARIABLES;
myData.addEventListener(Event.COMPLETE, onDataLoaded);
myData.load(new URLRequest("variables.txt"));

function onDataLoaded(evt) {
   trace("variables loaded");
}
```

CROSS-REF There are several ways to load data into a Flash movie with ActionScript 3.0 code. The `URLLoader` class is discussed in Chapter 29, "Sending Data In and Out of Flash." You also learn more about URL-encoded text in that chapter.

Establishing variables with HTML

You can also send variables to Flash movies in the `<embed>` and `<object>` tags that call the Flash movie. Starting with Flash Player 6 and later, you can use the HTML attribute `flashvar`, which can specify name/value pairs that are declared in the Flash movie as soon as it loads into the Flash Player. With the `flashvars` attribute, you don't need to rely on the URL of the movie. Here's an example of declaring a few variables with the `flashvars` attribute:

```
<object ...>
<param name="movie" name="flash.swf" />
<param name="flashvars" name="firstName=Gregory&lastName=Smith&addres
    s=1234+Hollywood+Way" />
<embed src="flash.swf"
    flashvars="firstName=Greg&lastName=Smith&street=1234+Broadway" ... />
```

In practical use, you would not likely hard-code the name/value pairs directly into the HTML document. You can use client-side JavaScript or server-side scripting (such as PHP, ASP.NET, or ColdFusion) to dynamically "write" the name/value pairs into the HTML document before it is served to the user's Web browser.

 You can use the SWFObject JavaScript library to add variables and values to an embedded Flash object. Refer to the SWFObject site at `http://code.google.com/p/swfobject/wiki/documentation`.

Creating Expressions in ActionScript

You can write expressions either by manually typing in the primary option fields of ActionScript commands, or by dragging and dropping actions from action booklets in the Actions panel. There are no scripting wizards in Flash; Flash CS4 does not automatically script anything for you (not counting components, which already include many lines of code to perform specific tasks for you). However, Flash provides you with booklets of operators, objects, and functions available in the ActionScript language.

Operators

Operators perform combinations, mathematical equations, and value comparisons. See Table 23.1 for a list of common operators in the ActionScript language.

General and numeric operators

These operators are used for common mathematical operations of adding, subtracting, multiplying, and dividing. You can also use these operators to compare numeric values, such as > or <.

```
if (results > 1)
name = "Robert";
root["name_" + i] = "Ezra";
```

String operators

To join two string values to another in Flash Player 5 or later movies, use the + string operator, such as:

```
var fullName = firstName + " " + lastName;
```

Logical operators

These operators join several expressions to create conditions. We discuss these further in the "Checking conditions: if . . . else actions" section of this chapter.

```
// Flash Player 5 and later syntax below

if (results > 1 && newResults < 10){
    // do something...
}
```

Table 23.1 describes the ActionScript operators available in Flash Player 5 and later syntax.

TABLE 23.1

ActionScript Operators

Flash Player 5+	Description
+	Adds number values (all player versions) and joins, or *concatenates*, strings in Flash Player 5 and later.
−	Subtracts number values.
*	Multiplies number values.
/	Divides number values.
=	Equals; used for assignment of variables, properties, methods, and so on in Flash Player 4 or later.
==	Numeric operator: Is equal to; used for comparison in if/else . . . else if conditions.
!=	Numeric operator: Does not equal.
<	Less than.
>	Greater than.
<=	Less than or equal to.
>=	Greater than or equal to.
( )	Groups operations together, as in x = (x+y) * 3;.
" "	Indicates that the enclosed value should be interpreted as a string, not as an expression.
==	String operator: Is equal to; for example, if (name == "derek") or if (name eq "derek").

Flash Player 5+	Description
=== (FP6+)	Strict equality operator; both of the compared values must be the same data type and value. This operator is compatible only with Flash Player 6 or later.
!=	String operator: Is not equal to.
!== (FP6+)	Strict inequality operator; both of the compared values must have different values and data types. This operator is compatible only with Flash Player 6 or later.
<	Alphabetically before; if the strings compared have multiple characters, the first character determines the alphabetical position.
>	Alphabetically after.
<=	Alphabetically before or the same as.
>=	Alphabetically after or the same as.
+	Joins two strings together or adds a string to a variable.
&&	Logical comparison; requires that two or more conditions be met in a single comparison.
||	Logical comparison; requires that one of two or more conditions be met in a single comparison.
!	Logical comparison; requires that the opposite of a condition be met in a single comparison.

Checking conditions: if . . . else actions

Conditions lie at the heart of logic. To create an intelligent machine (or application), you need to create a testing mechanism. This mechanism (called a *conditional*) needs to operate on rather simple terms. Remember the true/false tests you took in grade school? if/else statements work on a similar principle: If the condition is true, execute a set of actions. If the condition is false, disregard the enclosed actions and continue to the next condition or action.

You can simply create isolated if statements that do not employ else (or else if) statements. Solitary if statements are simply ignored if the condition is false. else statements are used as a default measure in case the tested condition proves false. else if statements continue to test conditions if the previous if (or else if) was false. Refer to the following examples for more insight.

■ **Basic if statement:** The code between the curly braces is ignored if the condition is false.

```
if (condition is true){
    then execute this code
}
```

■ **Extended if. . .else if...else statement:** If the first condition is true, the code immediately after the first condition is executed and the remaining else if and else statements are disregarded. However, if the first condition is not true, the second condition is tested. If the second condition is true, its code executes and all other statements in the if group are ignored. If all conditions prove false, the code between the curly braces of the final else is executed:

```
if (first condition is true){
    then execute this code
} else if (second condition is true){
    then execute this code
} else {
    otherwise, execute this code
}
```

In production, you could have an `if`/`else` structure that assigned the value of one variable based on the value of another, such as:

```
if (x == 1){
    name = "Margaret";
} else if (x == 2){
    name = "Michael";
} else {
    name = "none";
}
```

> **CAUTION** Do not use a single = sign in a condition because this actually sets the variable's value. For example, if you wrote `if (x = 1) {}`, ActionScript actually sets `x = 1`, and does not check whether x's value is equal to 1. Moreover, the condition always evaluates to `true`. In our experience, many beginners make this common mistake in their ActionScript code. We can't emphasize enough the importance of making sure you use an `==` operator in `if` and `else if` expressions for "is equal to" comparisons.

You can add an `if` statement in ActionScript by choosing the `if` action from the plus (+) button in the toolbar of the Actions panel, or by selecting it from the Statements ➪ Conditions/Loops booklet. Between the parentheses of the `if()` statement, shown as the term *condition* in the code hint, enter the expression that identifies what circumstance must exist for the actions in your conditional to be executed. Remember that in your expression, literal strings must be quoted, and the `==` operator must be used for string or numeric comparisons. To add an `else` clause, position the text cursor after the closing curly brace (}) of the `if()` statement, and then double-click the `else` or `else if` action in the Statements ➪ Conditions/Loops booklet.

> **NOTE** There's nothing stopping you from just typing the actions directly in the Script pane as well. Use the booklets as a guide at first, to learn about the choices you have available.

> **TIP** If you find it confusing when to use parentheses or curly braces ({ }) with your code, use the shortcut keys to create code blocks such as `if` statements. With your cursor active in the Script pane, type Esc+i+f in sequence to create the `if` statement with the proper set of parentheses and curly braces.

You can join two conditions by using logical compound operators such as `and` (`&&`), `or` (`||`), or `not` (`!`), as in:

```
if (results > 1 && newResults < 10){
    gotoAndPlay ("end");
```

```
    } else if (results > 1 ! newResults < 10) {
        gotoAndPlay ("try_again");
    }
```

In this sample code, the first `if` statement has two expressions; both need to be true in order for the `gotoAndPlay("end");` code to execute. If both are not true, the `else if` condition executes. If the first condition is true *and* the second condition is not true, the `gotoAndPlay("try_again");` code executes. If neither the `if` nor the `else if` condition is true, then no code is executed.

We'll take a look at a step-by-step example of `if` statements in the exercise at the end of this chapter.

Branching conditions with switch() and case

In ActionScript, you can also use `switch()` and `case` statements. `switch()` and `case` can replace extended `if` and `else if` actions. Instead of declaring a true/false expression (as with `if` statements), `switch()` uses an expression that can return any value; you are not limited to true and false conditions with `switch()`. In pseudo-code, a `switch()` code structure looks like this:

```
test a value
    if the value equals this expression
        then execute this code
    if the value equals this expression
        then execute this code
    if none of the expressions match the value
        then execute this code
end test
```

In the previous code example, one or more `if` statements (called `case` clauses) can execute. Meaning, the tested value can execute more than one segment of code nested within the clauses. You could translate the previous pseudo-code into the following ActionScript code:

```
var currentFrame = this.currentFrame;
switch(currentFrame){
    case 10:
        helpBox.gotoAndStop("products");
    case 20:
        helpBox.gotoAndStop("services");
    case 30:
        helpBox.gotoAndStop("contact");
    default:
        helpBox.gotoAndStop("error");
}
```

In the previous code example, although it's only possible for `currentFrame` to equal one value, the `default` clause also executes, regardless of the value of `currentFrame`. However, you may not want to execute the `default` clause (or multiple `case` clauses). In this situation, you need to use the `break` action to "escape" the `switch()` action. The `break` action prevents subsequent clauses from being evaluated.

In the following code, only one clause can execute:

```
var currentFrame = this.currentFrame;
switch(currentFrame){
    case 10:
        helpBox.gotoAndStop("products");
        break;
    case 20:
        helpBox.gotoAndStop("services");
        break;
    case 30:
        helpBox.gotoAndStop("contact");
        break;
    default:
        helpBox.gotoAndStop("error");
}
```

You can use `switch()` actions for many other situations. If you wanted to make a card game in Flash, you could use a `switch()` expression to pick a card suit based on a random number:

```
1.  var suitNum = Math.round(Math.random()*3);
2.  switch(suitNum){
3.      case 0:
4.          suit = "diamonds";
5.          break;
6.      case 1:
7.          suit = "spades";
8.          break;
9.      case 2:
10.         suit = "hearts";
11.         break;
12.     case 3:
13.         suit = "clubs";
14.         break;
15. }
16. cardFace.gotoAndStop(suit);
```

In this code, a random number is picked (line 1) and used as an expression in the `switch()` action (line 2). The random number (represented as a variable named `suitNum`) is then matched to a `case` clause. The matching clause sets a variable named `suit` to equal a specific card suit and exit the `switch()` action (lines 3–15). A Movie Clip instance named `cardFace` will go to and stop on a frame named after one of the card suits (line 16).

> **TIP** In a working example of a card game, the `switch()` code for the suit matching would occur within a function. We discuss functions in Chapter 25, "Using Functions and Arrays."

Loops

A *loop* is a container for a statement or series of statements repeated as long as a specified condition exists. A basic loop has three parts: the condition, the list of statements to be repeated, and a counter update. There are four types of loops in ActionScript:

- `while`
- `do . . . while`
- `for`
- `for . . . in`

Each of these loop types has a specific use. Depending on the repetitive actions you want to loop, you need to decide how best to accommodate your code with loop actions.

CAUTION These types of code-based loops do not update the contents of the Stage with each pass of a loop execution. If you want to automate changes over time on the Stage through code, you'll need to use the `Event.ENTER_FRAME` event, the `Timer` class, or a `setInterval()` function. You learn more about these types of actions in Chapter 24, "Controlling Movie Clips," and Chapter 31, "Creating a Game in Flash."

while (condition) { actions }

In this loop type, the condition of the loop is evaluated first, and, if it is true, the actions within the curly braces are executed. The actions loop indefinitely (causing a script error) unless there is a way out of the loop — a counter update. A counter update increments (or decrements) the variable used in the `while` condition. Here you see a breakdown of a typical `while` loop. Note that a variable used in the condition is usually set just before the `while` action is executed.

```
var count = 1;  // Initial variable
while (count <= 10){  // Condition
  root["clip_" + count].scaleX = 100/count; // Statements to be
    repeated
  count = count + 1; // Counter update
}   // Termination of loop
```

In this example, a variable named `count` starts with a value of 1. The first time the `while` action executes, `count`'s value is less than (or equal to) 10. Therefore, the actions within the curly braces are executed. The first action in the loop uses the `count` value to form the name of a Movie Clip instance, `clip_1`, and alter its X scale property by a value of 100/1 (which is equal to 100). Then the `count` variable is incremented by 1, giving it a new value of 2. The `while` condition is then reevaluated.

The second time the `while` action is executed, `count`'s value, 2, is still less than (or equal to) 10. Therefore, the actions within the curly braces are executed again. This time, however, the first action in the loop addresses the `clip_2` instance's X scale property, and makes that property's value 50 (100/2 = 50). Then, `count` is incremented by 1, giving it a new value of 3. Again, the `while` condition is reevaluated.

The `while` condition continues to execute its nested actions until `count` exceeds a value of 10. Therefore, `clip_1` through `clip_10` shows a decrease in X Scale.

do { actions } while (condition);

This type of loop is very similar to the `while` loop we discussed previously, with one important exception: The actions in the `do{}` nesting are always executed at least once. In a `do . . . while` loop, the condition is evaluated after the actions in the loop are executed. If the `while` condition is `true`, the actions in the `do{}` nesting execute again. If the `while` condition is `false`, the loop no longer executes.

```
count = 1;  // Initial variable
do {  // do loop
  // Statements to be repeated
  root["clip_" + count].scaleX = 100/count;
  count = count + 1; // Counter update
} while (count <= 1); // Condition
```

In this example, the actions within the `do{}` nesting execute automatically without checking any condition. Therefore, the X Scale of `clip_1` is set to 100, and the `count` value increases by 1, giving it a new value of 2. After the actions execute once, the condition is checked. Because the value of `count` is not less than (or equal to) 1, the loop does not continue to execute.

for (initialize; condition; next) { actions }

The `for` loop is a supercondensed `while` loop. Instead of assigning, checking, and reassigning a variable action in three different actions, a `for` loop enables you to define, check, and reassign the value of a counter variable.

```
for(i = 1; i <= 10; i++){ // Initial variable value, condition, and
    update
  root["clip_" + i].scaleX = 100/i; // Statements to be repeated
}  // Termination of loop
```

This `for` loop does exactly the same thing as the `while` loop example we used earlier. When the loop is started, the variable `i` is given a starting value of 1. A condition for the loop is specified next, `i <= 10`. In this case, we want the loop to repeat the nested actions until the value of `i` exceeds 10. The third parameter of the `for` loop, `i++`, indicates that `i`'s value should be increased by 1 with each pass of the loop. Note that this parameter can use `++` (to increase by 1) or `--` (to decrease by 1) operators. You can also use expressions such as `i = i*2` for the update.

for (variable|Iterant in object) { actions }

Another type of loop, `for . . . in`, is one of the most complex looping mechanisms. A `for . . . in` loop does not need a condition statement. Rather, this loop works with a find-and-replace keyword mechanism. Basically, a *variableIterant* is declared, which is simply a placeholder for a property or position index within an object or array, respectively. For every occurrence of the variableIterant, the actions within the `for . . . in {}` nesting are executed. The `for . . . in` loop can be used only with objects and arrays, and even then, not all properties of this element can be enumerated.

```
// A generic book object
var book = new Object();
book.title = "Flash CS4 Bible";
book.author = "Robert Reinhardt & Snow Dowd";
for(var prop in book){
   // Show each property in the book object
   trace(prop + " = " + book[prop]);
} // Termination of loop
```

In the preceding code example, the term `prop` is used to designate a property of the `book` object. In this case, you see the name and value of each property in the `book` object in the Output panel, using a `trace()` action:

```
author = Robert Reinhardt & Snow Dowd
title = Flash CS4 Bible
```

for each (propertyValue in object) { actions }

In ActionScript 3.0, you can also use a `for each` loop, which is very similar to a `for...in` loop in that it can cycle through a collection of properties in an object. A `for each` loop, however, retrieves the property value rather than the property name for an object.

```
// A generic book object
var book = new Object();
book.title = "Flash CS4 Bible";
book.author = "Robert Reinhardt & Snow Dowd";
for each(var propVal in book){
   // Show each property in the book object
   trace("property value = " + propVal);
} // Termination of loop
```

In the preceding code example, the term `propVal` is used to designate each property value within the book object. If you test this code in a Flash movie, you see the value of each property value in the book object in the Output panel:

```
Property value: Robert Reinhardt & Snow Dowd
Property value: Flash CS4 Bible
```

 The `for each` loop is most useful for grabbing values from XML data. You learn more about XML data in Chapter 29, "Sending Data In and Out of Flash."

break

The break action is not a type of loop. It is an action that enables you to quickly exit a loop if a subordinate condition exists. Suppose you wanted to loop an action that hides, at most, clip_1 through clip_10 (out of a possible 20 Movie Clip instances), but you want to have a variable control the overall limit of the loop, as upperLimit does in the following code block. upper-Limit's value could change at different parts of the presentation, but at no point do you want to hide more than clip_1 through clip_10. You could use a break action in a nested if action to catch this:

```
var count = 1;
while(count <= upperLimit){
    if(count > 10){
        break;
    }
    root["clip_" + count].visible = false;
    count++;
}
```

continue

Like the break action, continue enables you to exit the execution of actions within a loop. However, a continue action won't exit the loop action. It simply restarts the loop (and continues evaluating the current condition). Usually, you place a continue action with an if nest; otherwise, it always interrupts the actions within the loop action. For example, if you wanted to omit a particular value from going through the loop actions, you could use the continue action to bypass that value. In the following code block, we hide clip_1 through clip_10, except for clip_5:

```
count = 1;
while(count <= 10){
    if(count == 5){
        count++;
        continue;
    }
    root["clip_" + count].visible = false;
    count++;
}
```

Adding a loop to your actions list

To create a loop, add one of the loop-type actions in the Actions panel, using the plus (+) button in the toolbar of the panel (or from the ActionScript 3.0 booklets on the top left pane of the panel) and choosing Language Elements ➪ Statements, Keywords & Directives ➪ statement. With code hints enabled, replace the *condition* code hint term with an expression that describes the conditions under which the loop should continue repeating. Before the end of the loop, be sure to update whatever the loop relies on in order to continue, usually a counter. If you forget to update a counter, you will be stuck forever in the loop, and Flash imperiously stops the script from continuing.

Loops in ActionScript are not appropriate for running background processes that listen for conditions to become true elsewhere in the movie. While a loop is in progress, the screen is not updated and no mouse events are captured, so most Flash actions are effectively not executable from within a loop. Loop actions are best suited to abstract operations such as string handling (for example, to check each letter of a word to see whether it contains an @ symbol) and dynamic variable assignment.

You should create frame-based loops to execute repetitive actions over time, which affect tangible objects in the movie. To create a permanently running process, make a Movie Clip symbol with two keyframes. On the first frame, call the subroutine or add the statements that you want to execute; on the second frame, use a `gotoAndPlay(1);` action to return to the first frame. Alternatively, you can use the `Timer` class or the `setInterval()` function to execute repetitive actions.

Properties

Properties are characteristics (such as width and height) of objects like Movie Clip instances that can be retrieved and set. You can use variables to store the current value of a given property, such as:

```
var xPos = root.mouseX;
```

which stores the current X position of the mouse pointer (relative to the Stage coordinates of the Main Timeline) in the variable xPos.

Built-in functions

ActionScript contains a number of native programming commands known as *functions*. Among others, these functions include `getTimer()`, `getVersion()`, `parseFloat()`, `parseInt()`, `escape()`, and `unescape()`. It's beyond the scope of this chapter (and this book) to discuss the practical use of every new function and ActionScript element in Flash CS4. We do, however, discuss many built-in functions throughout this part of the book.

CROSS-REF Because ActionScript has expanded so much over recent versions of the Flash authoring tool, Robert Reinhardt and Joey Lott created a companion book series on Flash ActionScript to specifically address all the terms of the ActionScript language. Refer to the *ActionScript Bible* series (Wiley) for more in-depth coverage of ActionScript.

Creating and calling subroutines

Whether they're called functions, subroutines, or methods, most programming languages provide a mechanism for programmers to create self-contained code modules that can be executed from anywhere in a program. ActionScript supports subroutines by using the ActionScript `function` constructor. You can create functions on any timeline, and, just like Movie Clip instances, functions have absolute or relative paths that must be used to invoke them. For example, if you have the following function on the Main Timeline:

```
function makeClip(target, limit){
    for(var i=1; i<=limit; i++){
```

```
        var mc = new MovieClip();
        mc.name = target + "_" + i;
        this.addChild(mc);
    }
}
```

to invoke it, you would execute it as follows:

```
makeClip("clip", 5);
```

Executing it creates five Movie Clip instances, naming the instances `clip_1`, `clip_2`, `clip_3`, `clip_4`, and `clip_5`.

Creating a Login Sequence with Variables

In this section, we show you how to use variables to create an interactive form in Flash that accepts or rejects user input. You create two input text fields into which Web visitors type a username and password. Using ActionScript, you check the values of the entered data with predefined name/value pairs.

CAUTION Do not use the following example for secure information over the Web. You could use a logon sequence like this in a Flash adventure game, or modify it to work in a Flash quiz. The logon information is not secure within the confines of a Flash movie file (.swf). This example is intended to demonstrate using conditional statements in a Flash movie.

1. **Open a new Flash file (ActionScript 3.0).**

2. **Create two text fields on one layer called** text fields. Make each text field long enough to accommodate a single first name and/or password. In the Text Type drop-down menu of the Properties panel, select the Input Text option for both fields. For demonstration purposes, make the text in the text fields large — around 24 points. Make sure that you use a non-white fill color for the text.

3. **Access the properties for each text field by selecting the text field (with the Selection tool) and opening the Properties panel, as shown in Figure 23.3.** For the top text field, assign the instance name `userField`. For the other text field, assign the instance name `passwordField` and choose the Password option in the Behavior menu of the Paragraph section.

4. **Create a new layer and name it** static text. Create text blocks that describe the two text fields, as shown in Figure 23.4. For example, make a text block with the word **Login:** and another one with the word **Password:**. Align these text blocks to the left of the text fields. Note that these text blocks do not need the Input text behavior; they should be Static text blocks.

5. Create a new Movie Clip symbol (Ctrl+F8/⌘+F8), called errorMessageClip, **that displays an error message, such as INVALID or LOGIN ERROR.** In this new Movie Clip timeline, rename Layer 1 to **actions**. Add a stop(); frame action to the first frame of this layer.

FIGURE 23.3

The passwordField instance will be an input text field with the password option enabled.

FIGURE 23.4

Here you have four text areas: two static text blocks on the left, and two input text fields on the right. ActionScript cannot alter and/or "read" the static text.

6. **Create another layer called** labels. On frame 5 of this layer, make a keyframe and assign it the label **start** in the Name field of the Label section of the Properties panel.

7. **Create a new layer called** artwork **and move it underneath the actions layer.** On this layer, create a tweening animation of your message fading in and out (or scaling up and down, and so on). Start the motion tween on frame 5 of the artwork layer, underneath the `start` label of the labels layer. You'll need to make the message a graphic symbol of its own in order to tween the alpha state. Add enough frames and keyframes to cycle this message animation twice. The very last frame of the animation should have a frame action (on the actions layer) `gotoAndStop(1);`. When you are finished with this step, your Movie Clip timeline should resemble the one shown in Figure 23.5.

FIGURE 23.5

The errorMessageClip symbol contains an empty first frame and an animation that begins on the start label. This animation plays only if the user enters an incorrect login.

8. **In the main movie timeline (Scene 1), create a new layer called** errorMessage. Drag the errorMessageClip symbol from the Library panel on to the Stage. Position it underneath the user and password text fields. Select the Movie Clip instance on the Stage and access its settings in the Properties panel. Assign the instance name of `errorMessage`.

TIP

In the Properties panel, you can temporarily change the symbol type of the `errorMessage` instance to a Graphic instance, and specify frame number 5 in the first field. This technique enables you to more accurately place a symbol that has an empty first frame. When you are finished positioning the instance, make sure that you switch the instance behavior back to Movie Clip and rename the instance. Do not change the behavior of the symbol in the Library panel; this method applies only to the symbol behavior on an instance level.

9. **Create another layer named** labels. Assign a frame label of **start** to frame 1 of the labels layer. Add a keyframe to frame 10 of the labels layer, and label it **success**. Make sure that all other layers on frame 10 have empty keyframes.

10. **Create an** actions **layer, and place it at the top of the layer order.** On the first frame, add a `stop();` frame action in the Actions panel.

11. **Extend all the layers to frame 20 by selecting frame 20 across all the layers and pressing F5.**

12. **Make a new layer called** success **and place a text block and/or other graphics suitable for a successful login entry.** It should appear only on frame 10, so if necessary, move its initial keyframe to that frame. When you're finished with the step, your Stage and Main Timeline should resemble Figure 23.6.

FIGURE 23.6

Your Main Timeline should have three key elements: a login frame, an error message Movie Clip instance, and a success frame.

13. **Create a new layer on the Main Timeline called** button, **and make a Button symbol on it.** You can make one of your own, or use one from Flash's Buttons library (Window ⇨ Common Libraries ⇨ Buttons). Place it to the right of or underneath the user and password fields. Select the Button symbol instance, and name the instance **submitButton** in the Properties panel.

14. **Select frame 1 of the actions layer, and add the following ActionScript code in the Script pane below the existing** `stop();` **action created in Step 10** (note that the ⤶ character indicates a continuation of the same line of code; do not type or insert this character into your actual code):

```
submitButton.addEventListener(MouseEvent.CLICK, ⤸
  onSubmitClick);

function onSubmitClick(evt){
  if (userField.text == "Sandra" && ⤸
    passwordField.text == "zebra24"){
      this.gotoAndStop("success");
  } else {
      this.errorMessage.gotoAndPlay("start");
  }
}
```

You can change the compared values for the `userField.text` and `passwordField.text` values to whatever string value you want.

15. **Add an empty keyframe (F7) on frame 10 of the button layer.**

16. **Save the Flash document as** `login_100.fla`. Test the movie's functionality with the Test Movie command (Control ➪ Test Movie).

Most login forms like this work with the Return or Enter key active to submit the information. However, this key press also has functionality in the Test Movie environment, so if you want to create additional ActionScript code to listen for a key press, do so only *after* you have tested the initial ActionScript code. You can also choose Control ➪ Disable Keyboard Shortcuts in Test Movie mode to avoid any key press conflicts.

ON the CD-ROM You can find the completed example, `login_100.fla`, in the `ch23` folder of this book's CD-ROM. You will also find other logon examples that use different methods to make the username and password comparisons.

WEB RESOURCE We want to know what you think about this chapter. Visit `www.flashsupport.com/feedback` to send us your comments.

Summary

- Before you begin to add complex interactivity to your Flash document, you need to break down the steps in the interactive process in a natural language that you can understand.

- After you know what you want your presentation to do, you can start to clarify the interactive steps and translate those steps into Flash-compatible actions.

- You can add ActionScript to your Flash document with the Actions panel. The Actions panel's Script pane is where you type or insert the actions that are invoked from elements in a Flash movie.

- Variables, a programming device, enable you to store property values, strings, paths, or expressions in order to reduce the redundancy of code and to simplify the process of computing information.

- Variables can be declared with actions, input, or dynamic text fields, or by loading them from an external data source, such as a server-side script, text document, or HTML-specified `flashvars` values.

- Expressions are equations that refer to a mathematical operation, a string concatenation, or an existing code object (another variable or object value).

- You can use `if`, `else if`, and `else` actions to add intelligence to your interactive actions. These actions test a condition and execute a certain set of actions if the condition is true.

- Loop actions execute a given set of actions repeatedly until a loop condition is no longer true.

Chapter 24

Controlling Movie Clips

I n Chapter 18, "Building Timelines and Interactions," we established the key role that Movie Clips have within the Flash movie structure. By having a timeline that plays separately from other timelines, Movie Clips enable multiple events to occur — independently or as part of an interaction with other Movie Clips. In this chapter, we explore how to manipulate Movie Clips beyond navigation actions such as `gotoAndPlay()` or `stop()`.

> **NOTE** In ActionScript 3.0, much of the functionality assigned to `MovieClip` instances in ActionScript 2.0 has shifted to other classes, like the `Sprite` class, for example. In AS3, the `MovieClip` class should be used for elements that specifically need a timeline, such as an animation. In AS1 or AS2, the `MovieClip` class still remains a central element of production.

IN THIS CHAPTER

Understanding the
`MovieClip` **class**

Working with properties of the
`MovieClip` **class**

Creating mouse drag behaviors

Event models explained

Making sliders that dynamically change properties

Movie Clips: The Object Overview

Since Flash Player 5, the implementation of ActionScript has resembled that of true object-oriented programming languages. Much like JavaScript, each element in a Flash movie has a data type. A data type is simply a category to which an element belongs. In ActionScript 3.0 (and ActionScript 2.0), there are several data types available — `boolean`, `number`, `string`, `object`, `function`, and `movieclip`, among others.

> **TIP** If you want to see a list of all data types in ActionScript, open the Actions panel (make sure that code hints are turned on), and type `var a:`. After you type the colon (`:`), you'll see a list of supported data types.

785

For our purposes, a Movie Clip instance *is* an object, and we refer to it as such throughout Part VII of this book. An object is any element in Flash that has changeable and accessible characteristics *through ActionScript*. Objects can be user defined (you create and name them) or predefined by the programming language. The `MovieClip` class is a predefined or *intrinsic* class, meaning that all of its characteristics are already described in the ActionScript language.

A `MovieClip` object is the same Movie Clip instance you've seen in previous chapters. Any instance of a Movie Clip symbol is a unique object in ActionScript. However, you haven't treated it like an object in your scripting. Before we can proceed with a discussion of Movie Clips as Flash movie assets, you need to understand what predefined characteristics are available in a `MovieClip` object. See Figure 24.1 for more information.

Movie Clip properties

Each Movie Clip instance has definable properties, or attributes, that control its appearance, size, and position. For example, you can move a Movie Clip instance to a new position by changing the value of its X or Y coordinate. This property in ActionScript 3.0 is denoted as `x` or `y`, respectively. Some properties have read-only values, meaning these values can't be altered. One read-only property is `mouseX`, the value of which indicates the X position of the mouse cursor relative to the registration point of the Movie Clip instance. Figure 24.2 is a summary of the properties of the `MovieClip` object. For more information on each property, see Table 24.1, "Flash Movie and Movie Clip Properties."

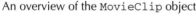

FIGURE 24.1

An overview of the `MovieClip` object

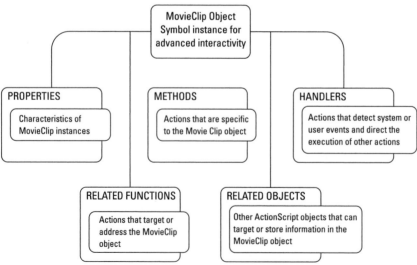

FIGURE 24.2

Properties of a `MovieClip` object

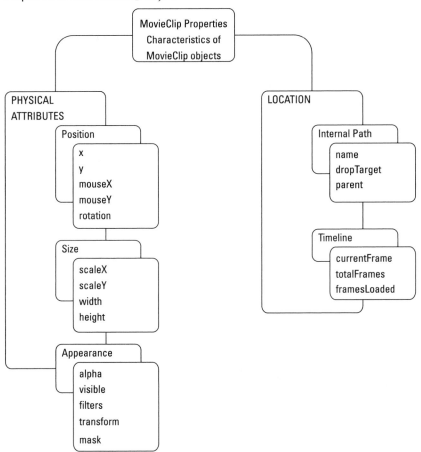

In Table 24.1, each property has an R (as in "read") and/or W (as in "write") designation. All properties can be read, which means that you can retrieve that property's current value. The values of some properties can also be changed through ActionScript. The table represents these properties with the W designation.

CROSS-REF We don't review the more advanced properties of the `MovieClip` object in this chapter. For the most comprehensive coverage, refer to the `MovieClip` class coverage in the *ActionScript Bible* series (Wiley).

NOTE Most of these properties are inherited from the `DisplayObject` class, which is a parent class of the `MovieClip` class. If you're looking up properties of the `MovieClip` class in the Help system of Flash CS4, be sure to view inherited properties if you want to see all properties available to the `MovieClip` class.

Flash Movie and Movie Clip Properties

TABLE 24.1

Category	Property	Timeline	Flash Player 9+	Definition
Position	x	MC	RW	The horizontal distance between a Movie Clip's center point and the top left corner of the Stage upon which it resides. It increases as the clip moves to the right, and is measured in pixels.
		Movie	RW	
	y	MC	RW	The vertical distance between a Movie Clip's center point and the top left corner of the Stage upon which it resides. It increases as the clip moves downward, and is measured in pixels.
		Movie	RW	
	mouseX	MC	R	The horizontal distance (in pixels) between the zero point of a Movie Clip (or the movie) and the current position of the mouse pointer.
		Movie	R	
	mouseY	MC	R	The vertical distance (in pixels) between the zero point of a Movie Clip (or the movie) and the current position of the mouse pointer.
		Movie	R	
	rotation	MC	RW	The amount (in degrees) that a Movie Clip is rotated off plumb. It returns values set both by the Transform panel (or Transform tool) and by ActionScript.
		Movie	RW	
Size	scaleX	MC	RW	The width of a Movie Clip instance (or movie) as a percentage of the parent symbol's actual size. The percentage is expressed as a decimal value, where 1 is equal to 100% of the original size.
		Movie	RW	
	scaleY	MC	RW	The height of a Movie Clip instance (or movie) as a percentage of the parent symbol's actual size. The percentage is expressed as a decimal value, where 1 is equal to 100% of the original size.
		Movie	RW	

Category	Property	Class	Access	Description
	width	MC	RW	The width (in pixels) of a Movie Clip or the main movie Stage. It is determined not by the width of the canvas but by the width of the space occupied by elements on the Stage (meaning it can be less than or greater than the canvas width set in the Movie Properties dialog box).
		Movie	R	
	height	MC	RW	The height (in pixels) of a Movie Clip or the main movie. It is determined not by the height of the canvas but by the height of the space occupied by elements on the Stage.
		Movie	R	
Appearance	alpha	MC	RW	The amount of transparency of a Movie Clip or movie. It is measured as a decimal: 1 is completely opaque; 0 is completely transparent.
		Movie	RW	
	visible	MC	RW	A Boolean value that indicates whether a Movie Clip instance is shown or hidden. It is set to true to show, false to hide. Buttons in "hidden" movies are not active.
		Movie	RW	
	filters	MC	RW	This property enables you to add visual effects to MovieClip objects. The filters property uses an array to describe which filters have been applied to the clip.
		Movie	RW	
	transform	MC	RW	This property enables you to control physical characteristics of a MovieClip object via a transformation object. In Chapter 26, "Interacting with Movie Clips," we discuss the ColorTransform class, which can control the color properties of a MovieClip object.
		Movie	RW	
	mask	MC	RW	This property can assign another MovieClip object (or DisplayObject instance) as a mask for the content of the MovieClip object.
		Movie	RW	

continued

TABLE 24.1 *(continued)*

Category	Property	Timeline	Flash Player 9+	Definition
Internal Path	name	MC	RW	This property returns or reassigns the Movie Clip instance's name (as listed in the Properties panel).
		Movie	R	
	dropTarget	MC	R	This property returns a reference to the last Movie Clip instance upon which a draggable Movie Clip instance was dropped. For usage, see "Creating Draggable Movie Clips" in this chapter.
		Movie	R	
	parent	MC	R	This property returns a reference to the parent timeline of the current MovieClip object. For example, if an instance named bird_1 exists within another instance named flock, then bird_1.parent refers to the flock instance.
		Movie	R	*_parent returns a valid reference from the Main Timeline only if the Flash movie is loaded into a MovieClip (or DisplayObjectContainer) instance of another Flash movie.
Timeline	currentFrame	MC	R	This property returns the number of the current frame (for example, the frame on which the playhead currently resides) of the movie or a Movie Clip instance.
		Movie	R	
	totalFrames	MC	R	This property returns the number of total frames in a movie or Movie Clip instance's timeline.
		Movie	R	
	framesLoaded	MC	R	This property returns the number of frames that have downloaded over the network.
		Movie	R	

MC = Movie Clip; R = Read property (cannot be modified); W = Write property (can be modified)

ON the CD-ROM Use the propInspector Movie Clip in the library of the `property_inspector.fla` file, located in the `ch24` folder of this book's CD-ROM, to see the values of Movie Clip or movie properties.

Movie Clip methods

Although the name might sound intimidating, don't be scared. Methods are simply actions that are attached to objects. As you now know, Movie Clips qualify as objects in ActionScript. A method looks like a regular action, except it doesn't (and, in most cases, can't) operate without a dot syntax reference to a target or an object:

Action: `gotoAndPlay("start");`

becomes

Method: `myMovieClip.gotoAndPlay("start");`

As actions, interactive commands are executed from the timeline on which they are written. As methods, interactive commands are tied to specific (or dynamic) targets. Figure 24.3 lists many of the methods and Table 24.2 reviews them in more detail. Some methods can be used with `MovieClip` instances and with the entire Flash movie (`root`), and others can be used only with `MovieClip` instances. Some commands need to be written in dot syntax, as a method (designated as M in the table) of a timeline or `MovieClip` object. Other commands can be used as actions (designated as A in the table), meaning that the `MovieClip` object name need not precede the command.

CROSS-REF Figure 24.3 and Table 24.2 do not contain all methods of the `MovieClip` class. For comprehensive descriptions and usage of the methods, refer to the *ActionScript Bible* series (Wiley).

FIGURE 24.3

Common methods of the `MovieClip` object

TABLE 24.2

Common Movie and Movie Clip Methods

Category	Method	Flash 4	Definition	Usage
Position	hitTest	No	Determines if a MovieClip object overlaps with the boundaries of another MovieClip object, or if an X-Y coordinate intersects with a MovieClip instance. For more information on this method, see Chapter 26, "Interacting with Movie Clips."	*timeline.hitTest(MovieClip object);* OR *timeline.hitTest(x coordinate, y coordinate, shapeFlag);*
M			Note: The hitTest() method applies to any DisplayObject instance, such as a Sprite instance.	myMC.hitTest(myOther_mc); myMC.hitTest(root.mouseX, root.mouseY, true);
	startDrag	Yes	Enables the user to move a Movie Clip instance on the Stage. The Movie Clip instance moves (or drags) in tandem with the movements of the mouse. You can optionally specify whether the mouse pointer locks to the center of the Movie Clip instance and if the drag area is constrained to a range of X and Y coordinates (in the parent symbol or timeline space). Constraining the drag area is useful for slider controls.	*timeline.startDrag(lock, rect);*
M, A				myMC.startDrag(false);
	stopDrag	Yes	Stops any startDrag action currently in progress. No target needs to be specified with this action.	*timeline.stopDrag();*
M, A				myMC.stopDrag();

Playback				
	play	Yes	Starts playback from the current position of the playhead on a specified timeline.	`timeline.play();`

	M, A			`root.play(); // plays the Main Timeline`
				`root.myMC.play(); // plays myMC`

	stop	Yes	Stops playback on a specified timeline.	`timeline.stop();`

	M, A			`root.stop(); // stops the Main Timeline`
				`root.myMC.stop(); // stops myMC`

	gotoAndPlay	Yes	Jumps the playhead of a specified timeline to a label, frame number, or expression, and starts playing from there.	`timeline.gotoAndPlay(position);`
	M, A			`myMC.gotoAndPlay("start");` `// plays from the "start" label of the myMC timeline`
	gotoAndStop	Yes	Jumps the playhead of a specified timeline to a label, frame number, or expression, and stops playback.	`timeline.gotoAndStop(position);`
	M, A			`myMC.gotoAndStop("mute");` `// stops playback on the "mute" label of myMC`
	nextFrame	Yes	Moves the playhead of the specified timeline to the next frame.	`timeline.nextFrame();`
	M, A			`myMC.nextFrame();`
	prevFrame	Yes	Moves the playhead of the specified timeline to the previous frame.	`timeline.prevFrame();`
	M, A			`myMC.prevFrame();`

M = Method; A = Action

Event listener methods: The flexible Movie Clip handler

In ActionScript 3.0, event handlers for `MovieClip` objects can be written and executed from any other event handler. Although this may not seem like a monumental leap forward, this event model enables you to create event handlers that are not directly attached to instances of a Movie Clip placed on the Stage in the authoring environment. For a summary of common event methods, see Table 24.3. The typical steps for event processing are

1. **Listen for a specific event, such as a mouse click with the** `MouseEvent.CLICK` **event, on a particular object, such as a** `MovieClip` **object, and specify a function to process the event:**

   ```
   object.addEventListener(eventName, functionToProcessEvent);
   ```

2. **Define the function that will process the event, passing the event object created by the event to the function:**

   ```
   function processEvent(eventObject){
      // Create actions to handle event
   }
   ```

3. **Optional: Remove an event listener by using the** `removeEventListener()` **method when you no longer need to listen for the event:**

   ```
   object.removeEventListener(eventName, functionToProcessEvent);
   ```

Most classes in ActionScript 3.0 can use the methods `addEventListener()` and `removeEventListener()` for events specific to each class.

CROSS-REF   For more information on functions, refer to Chapter 25, "Using Functions and Arrays." It is beyond the scope of this book to discuss all the event methods available in ActionScript 3.0. Refer to the *ActionScript 3.0 Bible* (Wiley, 2008) for more information. For ActionScript 1.0/2.0 coverage of the `MovieClip` class, refer to older editions of the *Flash Bible* (Wiley).

To get a better idea of how this event model works, create this simple example:

1. **Create a new Flash file (ActionScript 3.0).**

2. **Draw some artwork, and make it a Movie Clip symbol.**

3. **Select the new instance on the Stage.** Name the instance `tracker` in the Properties panel.

4. **Create a new layer on the Main Timeline (that is, Scene 1).** Name the layer **actions**.

5. **Select frame 1 of the actions layer, and open the Actions panel (F9/Option+F9).** Type the following code into the Script pane:

   ```
   //MovieClip tracker;
   tracker.addEventListener(MouseEvent.MOUSE_MOVE, updateTracker);

       function updateTracker (evt){
       tracker.x = root.mouseX;
   ```

```
        tracker.y = root.mouseY;
        evt.updateAfterEvent();
    }
```

This code adds an `MouseEvent.MOUSE_MOVE` listener to the `tracker` instance. Each time the user's mouse moves, the function added as the listener, `updateTracker`, executes. We discuss functions in the next chapter.

6. **Save your Flash document as** `tracker_eventmodel.fla`, **and test it (Ctrl+Enter/ ⌘+Enter).** The artwork follows your mouse pointer as you move it on the Stage.

ON the CD-ROM You can find the completed document, `tracker_eventmodel.fla`, in the ch24 folder of this book's CD-ROM. You will also find another document, `tracker_ eventmodel_adv.fla`, which uses multiple event handlers.

You can continue to add more event listeners to the `tracker` instance, in order for the instance to respond to mouse clicks, time elapsing, and so on.

CAUTION This event model for Flash movies works in Flash Player 9 or later, using ActionScript 3.0.

Other classes and functions that use the MovieClip object

You can use Movie Clip instances with other ActionScript classes to control appearances and sounds, and to manipulate data.

ColorTransform class

This class can control the color effects of the targeted Movie Clip instance.

TIP The `MovieClip` class features a powerful property, `transform`. The `transform` property controls color transformations applied to a `MovieClip` instance. For more information about this new feature, read Chapter 26, "Interacting with Movie Clips."

Mouse class

This class controls the appearance of the mouse pointer within the Flash movie. After the `Mouse` object is hidden, you can attach a `MovieClip` object (or any `DisplayObject` instance) to the X and Y coordinates of the mouse pointer.

PrintJob API

`PrintJob` objects enable you to send `MovieClip` artwork (or any `DisplayObject` instance) — as pages — to a user's printer. You learn more about the `PrintJob` API in Chapter 26, "Interacting with Movie Clips."

with() action

This action enables you to avoid needless replication of object references and paths. By specifying a target for the `with()` action, you can omit the path from nested actions. We demonstrate the `with()` action in the next section.

TABLE 24.3

Common ActionScript 3.0 Event Handlers for MovieClip Objects

Category	Event name	Definition
Playback	`"enterFrame"` `Event.ENTER_FRAME`	This event executes when each frame on a Movie Clip instance's timeline is played. Note that `enterFrame` events execute repeatedly (at the same rate as the movie's frame rate), regardless of whether any timelines within the movie are actually playing frames.
User Input	`"mouseMove"` `MouseEvent.MOUSE_MOVE`	This event is triggered each time the mouse moves within the boundaries of the `MovieClip` instance.
	`"mouseDown"` `MouseEvent.MOUSE_DOWN`	This event occurs each time the left mouse button is pressed (or "down") within the boundaries of the `MovieClip` instance.
	`"mouseUp"` `MouseEvent.MOUSE_UP`	This event is triggered each time the left mouse button is released (when the user lets up on the mouse button).

Working with Movie Clip Properties

Now that you have a sense of what a Movie Clip instance can do (or be told to do), it's time for you to get some practical experience with the Movie Clip properties. In this section, we show you how to access Movie Clip appearance properties that control position, scale, and rotation.

> **NOTE** The following exercises use Button symbols from the prebuilt libraries that ship with Flash CS4. To access buttons from these libraries, use Window ➪ Libraries ➪ Buttons to open the Flash library file, and drag an instance of any button into your Flash document. Our examples useButton symbols from the classic buttons folder of the Buttons library.

Positioning Movie Clips

You can change the location of MovieClip instances on-the-fly with position properties such as x and y. How is this useful? If you want to create multiple MovieClip instances that move randomly (or predictably) across the Stage, you can save yourself the trouble of manually tweening them by writing a few lines of ActionScript code on the object instance. Here are the steps to take:

1. **Create a new Flash file (ActionScript 3.0) by choosing File ➪ New (Ctrl+N/ ⌘+N).**

2. **Rename Layer 1 to** circle.

3. **On frame 1 of the circle layer, draw a simple shape such as a circle.** Select the shape and press F8 to convert it into a symbol. Choose the Movie Clip type in the Convert to Symbol dialog box, and give the new Movie Clip symbol a unique name such as **Circle**.

4. **Select the instance on the stage of the Main Timeline, and in the Properties panel, name the instance** circle.

5. **Create a new layer on the Main Timeline (that is, Scene 1), and name the layer** actions.

6. **Select frame 1 of the actions layer, and open the Actions panel (F9/Option+F9).** Type the following code into the Script pane:

    ```
    //MovieClip circle;

    circle.addEventListener(Event.ENTER_FRAME, moveCircle);

    function moveCircle(evt){
        var target = evt.currentTarget;
        target.x += 5;
    }
    ```

7. **Save your document as** movieclip_x.fla, **and test the movie (Ctrl+Enter/ ⌘+Enter).** The MovieClip instance moves across the Stage.

> **ON the CD-ROM** You can find the movieclip_x.fla in the ch24 folder of this book's CD-ROM.

How does this code work? In Step 6, you specified that the `Event.ENTER_FRAME` event should be processed by the `moveCircle()` function. Regardless of the number of frames on any playing timeline, the `"enterFrame"` event is triggered continuously. Therefore, any actions nested within the listener function execute repeatedly.

The `moveCircle()` function contains two actions. The first action determines which object is broadcasting the event being listened to. In this example, the circle instance is emitting the event. All event objects have a `currentTarget` property, which can be accessed to determine which object is broadcasting the event. As such, the `target` variable references the `circle` instance. The second action moves the `target` instance: `target.x += 5`. Immediately after the instance reference is the property for the X position, `x`. By adding the property `x` to the object, Flash knows that you want to change the value of this object's property.

On the right side of the action are the operators `+=` and the value 5. By combining the + and = operators, you've created a shortcut to adding the value of 5 to the current X position of the `circle` Movie Clip instance. Each time the `"enterFrame"` event occurs, the `circle` object moves 5 pixels to the right.

To show how quickly you can replicate this action on multiple Movie Clip instances, select the `circle` instance on the Stage, and duplicate it (Ctrl+D/⌘+D) as many times as you want. Name each new instance with a different name in the Properties panel, such as `circle_2`, `circle_3`, and so on. For each instance you create, you can duplicate the code on frame 1, specifying the same actions. For example, for the two objects `circle_2` and `circle_3`, you could write the following code on frame 1:

```
circle_2.addEventListener(Event.ENTER_FRAME, moveCircle);
circle_3.addEventListener(Event.ENTER_FRAME, moveCircle);
```

When you test your movie, each instance moves independently across the Stage. After a listener function has been defined for one object, you can reuse it with other objects' methods.

> **TIP** To move the instance diagonally across the Stage, add the action `target.y += 5` to the `moveCircle()` function. This moves the instance down 5 pixels each time the handler is processed. Also, we show you how to consolidate duplicated actions in Chapter 25, "Using Functions and Arrays."

Scaling Movie Clips

In the last example, you learned how to access the `x` and `y` properties of the `MovieClip` object. The next example shows you how to use a Button symbol to enlarge or reduce the size of a Movie Clip on the Stage:

1. **Create a new Flash file (ActionScript 3.0).**

2. **Draw a shape (or multiple shapes), select the shape(s), and press F8 to convert the artwork into a symbol.** Give the Movie Clip symbol a distinct name to identify it in the Library panel.

3. **Select the instance of the Movie Clip on the Stage, and open the Properties panel.** Give the Movie Clip instance a unique name. In this example, we've named the instance `circle`.

4. **From the Buttons library, drag an instance of a button onto the Stage.** Name the instance `incrButton` (short for increase button) in the Properties panel.

5. **Now create the ActionScript code that enlarges the `circle` instance.** Create a new layer named **actions**. Select frame 1 on this layer, and open the Actions panel. Type the following code into the Script pane:

```
//SimpleButton incrButton;
//MovieClip circle;

incrButton.addEventListener(MouseEvent.CLICK, increaseProp);

function increaseProp(evt){
  with (circle){
    scaleX += 0.1;
    scaleY += 0.1;
  }
}
```

This code uses the `with()` action to target the `circle` instance with a nested group of actions. In this case, you've increased the values of the `scaleX` and `scaleY` properties by 10 percent; scale properties in ActionScript 3.0 use decimal values, not percentage values. With each click event on the Button symbol instance, the scale properties of the `circle` instance are changed.

6. **Save your document as `movieclip_scale.fla`, and test the movie (Ctrl+Enter/ ⌘+Enter).** Each time you click the Button instance, your `circle` instance enlarges by 10 percent.

7. **Duplicate the Button instance (Ctrl+D/⌘+D).** With the new copy of the Button instance selected, rename the instance to `decrButton` (short for decrease button) in the Properties panel. Select frame 1 of the actions layer, and add the following code to the existing code in the Actions panel:

```
//SimpleButton decrButton;

decrButton.addEventListener(MouseEvent.CLICK, decreaseProp);

function decreaseProp(evt){
  with (circle){
    scaleX -= 0.1;
    scaleY -= 0.1;
  }
}
```

By changing the += operator to -=, each click on this Button instance reduces (shrinks) the `circle` instance by 10 percent.

8. **Resave your Flash file and test the movie again.** Make sure that each Button instance behaves appropriately. If one doesn't work (or works in an unexpected manner), go back to the Flash document and check the code on both Button instances.

ON the CD-ROM You can find the `movieclip_scale.fla` document in the `ch24` folder of this book's CD-ROM.

CAUTION In this simple exercise, we haven't placed any limits on how much the Movie Clip instance can be reduced or enlarged. If you click the reduce button enough times, the Movie Clip instance actually flips vertically and starts enlarging again. We look at creating conditions and logic for Movie Clips in Chapter 26, "Interacting with Movie Clips."

Rotating Movie Clip instances

Let's move along to the rotation property, `rotation`, which is used to control the angle at which your Movie Clip instance is shown. In this sample, you'll use the same Flash document that you created in the previous section.

NOTE If you drew a perfect circle in past exercises for the `MovieClip` object, then you will want to edit your Movie Clip symbol to include some additional artwork that provides an indication of orientation and rotation. If you try to rotate a perfect circle, you won't see any visual difference on the Stage. Because the value of the `rotation` property is determined from the center point of the Movie Clip symbol, you can also move the contents of the Movie Clip symbol (in Edit mode) off-center to see updates in the `rotation` value.

1. **Select frame 1 of the actions layer, and open the Actions panel.** Change the `increaseProp()` function code to:

```
function increaseProp(evt) {
   circle.rotation += 10;
};
```

2. **Now, change the `decreaseProp()` function code in the Actions panel to:**

```
function decreaseProp(evt){
   circle.rotation -= 10;
};
```

3. **Save your document as** `movieclip_rotation.fla`, **and test the movie.** Each button should rotate the `circle` instance accordingly.

ON the CD-ROM You can find the `movieclip_rotation.fla` document in the `ch24` folder of this book's CD-ROM.

At this point, you should have a general knowledge of how to access a Movie Clip instance's properties. Repeat these examples by using other properties that can be modified, such as `width` and `height`. Try combining all the properties into one function!

Creating Draggable Movie Clips

Drag-and-drop behavior in a Flash movie can be accomplished with Movie Clip instances. So, if you want a drawing of a triangle to be moveable by the user, you have to first put that triangle into a Movie Clip symbol, and then place a named instance of that symbol onto the Stage. Flash's drag-and-drop support is fairly broad, but more-complex drag-and-drop behaviors require some ActionScript knowledge.

Drag-and-drop basics

In mouse-based computer interfaces, the most common form of drag-and-drop goes like this: A user points to an element with the mouse pointer, clicks the element to begin moving it, and then releases the mouse button to stop moving it. One method of adding drag-and-drop functionality is the use of a button event handler with a `MovieClip` instance. A `startDrag()` action is added to a listener function for the mouse press event of that `MovieClip` instance. Let's try out this technique.

1. **Start a new Flash file (ActionScript 3.0).** Rename Layer 1 to **dragger**.

2. **Create a circle with the Oval tool.** Select the artwork and press F8. In the Convert to Symbol dialog box, select the Movie Clip type. Name the symbol **Dragger**. Make sure that the registration point is set to the center of the clip.

3. **With the new Movie Clip instance selected, open the Properties panel.** Give the instance the name `dragger`.

4. **On the Main Timeline (that is, Scene 1), create a new layer named** actions **and place this layer at the top of the layer stack.** Select the first frame of the actions layer, and open the Actions panel (F9/Option+F9). Type the following code into the Script pane:

   ```
   //MovieClip dragger;

   dragger.addEventListener(MouseEvent.MOUSE_DOWN, activateDrag);

   function activateDrag(evt) {
     dragger.startDrag();
   }
   ```

5. **At this point, your** `MovieClip` **instance button, when clicked, causes the instance to start following the mouse pointer.** Now you have to tell the Movie Clip to stop following the pointer when the mouse button is released. After the last curly brace (}) highlighted in the actions list of the Script pane, type the following code:

   ```
   dragger.addEventListener(MouseEvent.MOUSE_UP, deactivateDrag);

   function deactivateDrag(evt){
     dragger.stopDrag();
   }
   ```

6. **Save your Flash document as** `movieclip_button_drag.fla`. Test your movie with Control ⇨ Test Movie (Ctrl+Enter/⌘+Enter). Click the circle and drag it around the Stage. To stop dragging, release the mouse button.

ON the CD-ROM | You can find the `movieclip_button_drag.fla` document in the ch24 folder of this book's CD-ROM.

Did it work? Great! Now we can tell you about the other basic settings for the `startDrag()` action. Next, you'll look at additional features of the `startDrag()` action. You may want to select an existing `startDrag()` action in the Script pane of the Actions panel and click the Reference icon in the panel's toolbar to more clearly see these options.

Lock mouse to center

This setting, which is the first option specified in the parentheses of the `startDrag()` method, controls how the Movie Clip instance positions itself relative to the position of the mouse pointer. There are two values for this option: `true` or `false`. When set to `true`, this option makes the dragged Movie Clip instance center itself under the mouse pointer for the duration of the drag movement. If the dragged Movie Clip instance is not already under the mouse pointer when the `startDrag()` action occurs, the instance automatically moves under the pointer, providing that the pointer is not outside the region defined by a `Rectangle` parameter (discussed in the next section). The following code "snaps" the center of the Movie Clip instance `dragger` to the mouse pointer:

```
dragger.startDrag(true);
```

When this option is set to `false`, the instance moves with the mouse pointer from the point at which it was clicked. For example, if you click the draggable object on its left edge, then that's where the object "snaps" the mouse pointer:

```
dragger.startDrag(false);
```

Constrain dragging area to a rectangle

In order to specify the limits of the rectangular region within which a draggable Movie Clip instance can be dragged, you can add another parameter to the `startDrag()` method. First, determine the pixel locations of the four corners of the rectangle. The pixel coordinates are set relative to the top left corner of the Stage upon which the draggable Movie Clip instance resides. For example, the following code constrains the draggable Movie Clip instance named `dragger` to a 300-pixel square region in the top left corner of the Main Timeline's Stage:

```
var rect:Rectangle = new Rectangle(0, 0, 300, 300);
dragger.startDrag(false, rect);
```

NOTE | If the draggable instance is located outside of the defined drag region when the `startDrag()` action occurs, the instance is automatically moved into the closest portion of the drag region.

Detecting the drop position: Using dropTarget

In the "Drag-and-drop basics" section, we show you how to make Movie Clip instances that users can move around. But what if you want to force users to move an object into a certain location before you let them drop it? For example, consider a child's shape-matching game in which a small circle, square, and triangle should be dragged onto corresponding larger shapes. If the child drops the small circle onto the large square or large triangle, the circle returns to its original location. If, on the other hand, the child drops the small circle onto the large circle, the small circle should stay where it is dropped, and the child should receive a "Correct!" message. That kind of game is quite possible in Flash, but it requires some understanding of Movie Clip properties. Here's how it works — you'll use the circle as an example.

1. **Create a new Flash file (ActionScript 3.0), and save it as** `movieclip_droptarget.fla`.

2. **Rename Layer 1 to** circle.

3. **On frame 1 of the circle layer, use the Oval tool to draw a circle that is 100 x 100 pixels.** Convert the artwork to a Movie Clip symbol named **Circle**, and name the instance `circle`. Scale the artwork to 25 percent in the Transform panel. Position this instance along the bottom left of the Stage, as shown in Figure 24.4.

FIGURE 24.4

The `circle` instance

4. Copy the `circle` instance by selecting it on the Stage and choosing Edit ➪ Copy (Ctrl+C/⌘+C).

5. Create a new layer, and name the layer circleBig. Place the layer below the circle layer.

6. On frame 1 of the circleBig layer, choose Edit ➪ Paste (Ctrl+V/⌘+V). Place the new copy above the original instance, as shown in Figure 24.5. Scale the artwork to 125 percent in the Transform panel, and name the instance `circleBig` in the Properties panel.

FIGURE 24.5

The `circleBig` instance

7. Create a new Movie Clip symbol from scratch by choosing Insert ➪ New Symbol (Ctrl+F8/⌘+F8). Name the symbol StatusMessage. Inside of this symbol, create a short animation displaying the text "Correct!" Leave the first frame of the symbol empty, and create the text (and supporting tweens, if desired) on frame 2 and higher. Create a frame label named `correct` on frame 2 of a new layer named labels, as shown in Figure 24.6. Also, place a `stop()`; action on frame 1 of an actions layer in the timeline.

8. Go back to the Main Timeline (that is, Scene 1), and place an instance of `status Clip` along the bottom of the Stage, centered. With the instance selected, open the Properties panel and name the instance `statusMsg`. Now, you will make the `circle` instance draggable by adding some frame actions.

FIGURE 24.6

The StatusMessage symbol timeline with a Blur filter tween

9. **On the Main Timeline, create a new layer named** actions **and place this layer above the other layers.** Select frame 1 of the actions layer, and in the Actions panel type the following code into the Script pane:

```
//MovieClip circle;
//MovieClip circleBig;
//MovieClip statusMsg;

circle.addEventListener(MouseEvent.MOUSE_DOWN, activateDrag);

function activateDrag(evt){
     circle.startDrag();
}
```

Here, the MouseEvent.MOUSE_DOWN event is used with a function named activate Drag. In this code, you tell the circle instance to start dragging when it is clicked on the Stage.

Next, you need to tell the circle instance to stop dragging when the mouse button releases.

10. **Create a listener for the** MouseEvent.MOUSE_UP **event that tells the** circle **instance to stop the drag action:**

```
circle.addEventListener(MouseEvent.MOUSE_UP, deactivateDrag);

function deactivateDrag(evt){
```

```
      circle.stopDrag();
      if (circle.dropTarget.parent == circleBig) {
        statusMsg.gotoAndPlay ("correct");
      } else {
        circle.x = 112;
        circle.y = 316;
      }
    }
```

The code for the `deactivateDrag` function is executed when the mouse button is released after a mouse click on the `circle` instance. The instance is told to stop dragging, and then ActionScript evaluates if the `circle` instance is dropped on top of `circleBig`. When the user drops any Movie Clip instance, the instance's `dropTarget` property is updated. The `dropTarget` property specifies the bottom-most `DisplayObject` upon which a `MovieClip` instance was dropped. When you use a drawing tool in Flash CS4 to create a shape such as a filled circle, you're actually creating a new `Shape` instance, and that's what is inside of the Circle symbol. Therefore, if you want to determine if `circleBig` is the container object upon which `circle` was dropped, you must specify the `parent` property of the `dropTarget` value. If no instance is underneath the dragged instance, `dropTarget` returns `null`. If the `dropTarget` is the large circle, then the dragged instance stays where it was dropped and the `statusMsg` instance plays its "Correct!" animation. Otherwise, the dragged instance (`circle`) returns to the X and Y coordinates of its starting point (112, 316).

11. **Save your Flash document as** `movieclip_droptarget.fla`, **and test it (Ctrl+Enter/ ⌘+Enter).** Click and drag the `circle` instance on top of the `circleBig` instance. The dragged instance stays put on top of the larger circle, and the "Correct!" message animates. Click and drag the `circle` instance off the `circleBig` instance, and release the drag outside of the larger circle. The smaller circle snaps back to its original starting point.

You can continue this example with other shapes, using the same methodology. Create separate listeners for each new drag interaction.

ON the CD-ROM For further study, we've included this basic drag-and-drop game as a sample document called `movieclip_droptarget.fla` in the ch24 folder of this book's CD-ROM.

Making alpha, scale, and blur sliders

A compelling use of a draggable Movie Clip instance is a slider that can alter the properties of another object. By checking the position of a Movie Clip instance, you can use the position's x or y coordinate value to alter the value of another Movie Clip instance. In this section, we show you how to create two sliders (one for alpha and another for scale) that dynamically change the transparency and size of a Movie Clip instance on the Stage. Many thanks to Sandro Corsaro (http:// sandrocorsaro.com) for supplying the artwork of our dog Stella and the park sign.

ON the CD-ROM You need to copy the `slider_basic_starter.fla` file from the ch24 folder of this book's CD-ROM. You'll use premade artwork to understand the functionality of `startDrag` and `stopDrag`, and using linkages with the new constructor.

Assembling the parts

In this section, you set up the basic composition of the Stage, using elements from the `slider_basic_starter.fla` library. You will add artwork of a dog and a park sign to the movie. The dog artwork is duplicated by using the new constructor, and the duplicate instance is manipulated by the sliders that you create in the next section. The park sign is used to remove the duplicate instance by using the `dropTarget` property and the `removeChild()` method.

1. **Open your copy of the** `slider_basic_starter.fla`. Resave this document as `slider_basic_100.fla`.

2. **Rename Layer 1 to** `dog_1`.

3. **Access the document's Library panel by pressing Ctrl+L/⌘+L.** Open the dogElements folder, and drag the `dogClip` symbol onto the Stage. Place the instance in the upper left corner of the Stage.

4. **With the** `dogClip` **instance selected, open the Properties panel.** Name the instance `dog_1`, as shown in Figure 24.7.

FIGURE 24.7

The `dog_1` instance will be used as your reference `MovieClip` object. The scale and transparency of this dog instance will not be changed.

5. **Using the Text tool, add the words** Original Dog **under the** dog_1 **instance.** You don't need to make a new layer for this artwork.

6. **Create a new layer and name it** sign. Move this layer below the dog_1 layer. Drag the parkSignClip symbol, located in the `parkSignElements` folder in the Library panel, to the lower left corner of the Stage. In the Properties panel, assign the instance the name `sign`. In the Transform panel, reduce the size of the `sign` instance to 50%, as shown in Figure 24.8.

FIGURE 24.8

The `sign` instance will be used to remove duplicates of the dog_1 Movie Clip instance.

In order to create a new dogClip symbol instance in ActionScript 3.0, you need set the dogClip to export from the library when the Flash movie (.swf file) is published or tested.

7. **Open the Library panel, and right-click/Ctrl+click the dogClip symbol in the** dogElements **folder.** Choose Properties in the context menu. In the Symbol Properties dialog box, shown in Figure 24.9, select the Export for ActionScript check box. This option automatically enables the Export in frame 1 option as well. In the Class field, type the name **Dog**. The dogClip symbol can now be accessed with a class named Dog in ActionScript 3.0 code. Click OK.

You may see a warning dialog box appear, indicating that a definition for the class could not be found, as shown in Figure 24.10. This warning means that a Dog.as ActionScript file was not available and as such, Flash CS4 will create an empty class. Click OK to dismiss the warning.

FIGURE 24.9

The Symbol Properties dialog box for the dogClip symbol

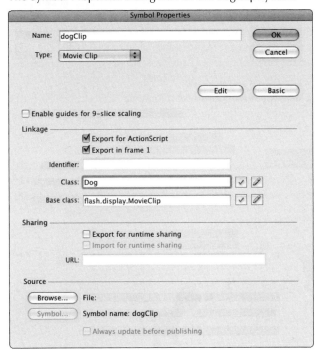

FIGURE 24.10

A warning dialog box appearing after you have assigned a new class name for the symbol

8. **Now, create a new layer called** actions, **and place it above all the other layers.** Select the first keyframe of this layer. In the Actions panel, add the following actions:

```
//MovieClip dog_1;
var dog_2 = new Dog();
dog_2.x = 350;
dog_2.y = 175;
addChild(dog_2);
```

This line of code creates a new instance of the dogClip symbol, referenced with the class named Dog created in Step 7. The new instance is named dog_2. The new constructor enables you to create a new instance of the Dog class. The next lines of code position the dog_2 instance at the x coordinate of 350 (350 pixels from the left corner of the Main Timeline Stage) and the y coordinate of 175 (175 pixels down from the left corner). The last line of code displays the new instance on the stage, using the addChild() method of the DisplayObjectContainer class. MovieClip instances are derived from this class, as well as the DisplayObject class.

9. **Save the Flash document, and test the movie (Ctrl+Enter/⌘+Enter).** You should see a new instance of the dogClip symbol appear on the right side of the Stage (see Figure 24.11).

FIGURE 24.11

The new constructor a class creates a new instance of the object. Unless you alter the new instance's X and Y positions, it will appear at the x-y coordinate of 0,0.

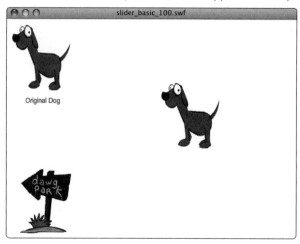

Now that you have some artwork on the Stage, you can manipulate the new Movie Clip instance with a pair of dynamic sliders.

Building the sliders

In this section, you'll create two sliders: one for scale, and one for transparency. You'll need to make only one slider Movie Clip symbol and use a new instance for each slider. The basic "problems" of a dynamic slider are to (a) retrieve the position value of an object on the slider (you'll call this the slider bar), and (b) set the value of another object equal to (or some factor of) the position value of the slider bar. Finding the position of a slider bar is relatively straightforward. The difficulty lies in creating the value range for the slider.

Because you have already determined the properties that will be altered (scale and transparency), you need to establish a range of values that each property can use. Luckily, both scale (as `scaleX` and `scaleY` in ActionScript 3.0) and transparency (as `alpha`) use decimal units. However, scale can be any value that's greater than 0 and less than 32, which is 3200%. Alpha has a range of 0 to 1. If you want to use the same parent slider for each property slider, you need to manipulate the position values of the slider bar differently for each property. Let's start with building the basic slider.

ON the CD-ROM Resume using the same file you finished in the previous section. Otherwise, you can open a copy of `slider_basic_100.fla`, located in the `ch24` folder of this book's CD-ROM.

1. Resave the `slider_basic_100.fla` file as `slider_basic_101.fla`.

2. Create a new Movie Clip symbol (Ctrl+F8/⌘+F8) and name it Slider. In Edit mode, rename the first layer **sliderRule**. On this layer, drag an instance of the sliderRule symbol (located in the `sliderBarElements` folder of the Library panel) onto the Movie Clip symbol's Stage.

3. With the sliderRule graphic selected, open the Properties panel and type the values –28 for the X coordinate and –12 for the Y coordinate.

4. Create another layer in the Slider symbol and name it pos. Drag an instance of the sliderBar symbol (located in the `sliderBarElements` folder of the Library panel) to the Stage.

5. With the `sliderBar` instance selected, open the Transform panel. Type 90 in the Rotate field and press Enter. In the Properties panel, enter 100 for the X coordinate and 0 for the Y coordinate.

   To control the position of the `sliderBar` instance with ActionScript, you must assign a unique instance name.

6. Select the `sliderBar` instance and type pos as the instance name in the Properties panel, as shown in Figure 24.12.

   Now you need to make the pos instance draggable. In this example, you're going to make a draggable Movie Clip instance, using the `MouseEvent.MOUSE_DOWN` and `MouseEvent.MOUSE_UP` events for `MovieClip` objects, just as you did in the earlier exercise.

7. Create a new layer in the sliderClip symbol, name it actions, and move it above the pos layer. Open the Actions panel (F9/Option+F9). Type the following code in the Script pane.

TIP To quickly set up the code for a blank function, type Esc+f+n with consecutive key presses. Do not press all three keys simultaneously.

```
//MovieClip pos;

pos.addEventListener(MouseEvent.MOUSE_DOWN, activateDrag); pos.
    addEventListener(MouseEvent.MOUSE_UP, deactivateDrag);

function activateDrag(evt){
```

```
    var rect = new Rectangle(0, 0, 200, 0);
    pos.startDrag(true, rect);
}

function deactivateDrag(evt){
    pos.stopDrag();
}
```

To make the pos instance draggable, you must detect a mouse-down event (MouseEvent.
MOUSE_DOWN) on the pos instance. When a mouse down event occurs on the instance,
the actions nested within the activateDrag function are executed.

The activateDrag function enables the dragging behavior of the pos instance by
using the startDrag() method. The arguments prescribed here lock the mouse to the
center of the object and constrain the draggable region to a bounding box defined by 0,0
and 200,0. In ActionScript 3.0, you use a Rectangle object to define the draggable
region. The region specified in this code effectively keeps the pos instance confined to
the line of the sliderRule graphic.

Next, you need to be able to stop dragging the pos object when the mouse button is
released. You'll use the deactivateDrag function to listen for the mouse-up event
(MouseEvent.MOUSE_UP). Once a mouse up event (the act of releasing the left mouse
button) is detected, you stop the dragging of the pos instance.

In the next step, you'll create two instances of the sliderClip symbol on the Main
Timeline Stage: one for scale, and one for alpha.

FIGURE 24.12

The starting X coordinate for the pos Movie Clip instance is set to 100. When the Flash
movie starts, this value is applied to the scale and alpha properties of the dog_2
instance on the Main Timeline.

8. **Exit Edit mode of the symbol timeline, and return to the Scene 1 timeline (the Main Timeline).** Create a new layer called **scaleSlider**. Open the Library panel and drag an instance of the Slider symbol to the Stage. Name this instance `scaleSlider` in the Properties panel.

9. **Move the `scaleSlider` instance to the lower right of the Stage.**

10. **Create another layer called** alphaSlider. Drag another instance of the Slider symbol onto the Stage, and name the instance `alphaSlider`. Rotate this instance –90 degrees. Place the instance just left of center of the Stage, as shown in Figure 24.13.

FIGURE 24.13

At this point, your Flash document's Stage should contain the dogClip and parkSignClip artwork, as well as two instances of the Slider symbol.

11. **Save your Flash document and test it.** You should be able to drag the position bars on both sliders.

NOTE In ActionScript 3.0, the finger icon does not appear by default when you enable button events and roll over `MovieClip` instances. To enable the finger icon, add the following code to the frame 1 actions of the Slider symbol:

```
pos.buttonMode = true;
```

The **slider_basic_101.fla** file in the **ch24** folder of this book's CD-ROM contains this code.

Checking the positions of the sliders

When you have a slider bar that is draggable, you need to access the new values of the `pos` instance and apply the values to the properties of the `dog_2` instance. To do this, you must have an event handler whose sole job is to check the X coordinate of the `pos` instance. In this section, you'll learn how to make an `"enterFrame"` event listener on the Main Timeline.

ON the CD-ROM Resume using the Flash document that you created in the last section. If you didn't complete that section, make a copy of the `slider_basic_101.fla` file located in the `ch24` folder of this book's CD-ROM.

1. Save the `slider_basic_101.fla` file as `slider_basic_102.fla`.

2. **Select frame 1 of the actions layer in the Main Timeline (that is, Scene 1).** Open the Actions panel. In the Script pane, type the bold code shown in Listing 24.1.

   The `updateDog` function executes continuously in your Flash movie. Why? The function is specified as the listener for the `"enterFrame"` event (designated by the `Event.ENTER_FRAME` constant). Any timeline will continuously enter a frame for playback, even if a `stop()` action is applied to all timelines. The speed at which the `"enterFrame"` event occurs is determined by the frame rate of the Flash movie (as defined by the Modify ⇨ Document dialog box). The frame rate of 24 fps was already set in the sample file before you opened it. Therefore, this block executes 24 times each second.

   What happens on each execution of the `updateDog` function? The first two lines in the function create variables that reference the X positions of the `pos` instances with your two sliders, and divide the values by 100 to return a fraction. (Remember, the `pos` instance slides from X values of 0 to 200.) The third line of code uses the `with()` action to target the `dog_2` object with the remaining nested actions. The fourth and fifth lines of code in the function set the X and Y scale properties of the `dog_2` instance to the values calculated earlier from the `pos` instance (relative to the coordinates within the Slider symbol) nested within the `scaleSlider` instance. The sixth line sets the `alpha` property of the `dog_2` instance equal to the value calculated on the second line.

3. **Save your Flash document and test it.** When you drag the bar on the bottom scale slider, notice how the *size* of the `dog_2` instance increases as you drag it to the right. When you drag the bar down on the left alpha slider, you'll see that the *opacity* of the `dog_2` instance decreases.

NOTE You may be wondering why the X coordinate of the `pos` instance is used for the `alphaSlider` instance, rather than the Y coordinate. Indeed, you do drag the bar on a vertical axis rather than a horizontal one. However, the `pos` instance exists within the space of the Slider symbol, which has a horizontal orientation in the Edit mode. The X coordinate is derived from the Stage of the Edit mode, regardless of the instance's orientation.

Okay, you have the sliders changing the size and opacity of the `dog_2` instance. However, nothing happens as you drag the bar on the `alphaSlider` instance toward its upper limit. Because the X coordinate of the `pos` instance starts at 100, you won't see any visual effect to the `alpha` property as it increases beyond a decimal value of 1. Therefore, it would be better to have the `alphaSlider` slider convert the X coordinate of the `pos` instance to a true 0–1 range of decimal values.

To do this, you need to develop an equation that does the work of automatically remapping values to a 0–1 range. We know that the lowest X coordinate of the `pos` instance is 10, and that the highest X coordinate is 200. If you want the highest position of the bar to provide a decimal value of 1 (which is 100 percent opacity), then you must divide 200 by a number that will give you a value of 1. Dividing 200 by 200 returns 1. How does that work for the low end? If the X coordinate returns the lowest value of 10, your lowest opacity value will be 1/20, or 0.05, which is 5% opacity. Because line 2 of the `update Dog` function already divides the X position value by 100, you only need to divide the existing value used for the `alpha` property by 2.

LISTING 24.1

The Listener Function for Event.ENTER_FRAME

```
//MovieClip dog_1;
//MovieClip scaleSlider;
//MovieClip alphaSlider;

var dog_2 = new Dog();
dog_2.x = 350;
dog_2.y = 175;
addChild(dog_2);

this.addEventListener(Event.ENTER_FRAME, updateDog);

function updateDog(evt) {
   var scaleVal = scaleSlider.pos.x/100;
   var alphaVal = alphaSlider.pos.x/100;
   with (dog_2) {
      scaleX = scaleVal;
      scaleY = scaleVal;
      alpha = alphaVal;
   }
}
```

4. With frame 1 of the actions layer of the Main Timeline selected, open the Actions panel (F9/Option+F9), and modify the sixth line of the `updateDog` function to read:

   `alpha = alphaVal/2;`

5. **Save your Flash document and test it.** Now, as you drag up with the bar for the `alphaSlider` instance, the opacity increases. As you drag down, it decreases.

So far, so good. However, it would be useful if the `alphaSlider`'s pos instance started with an X coordinate of 200. This would initialize the `dog_2` instance with an opacity of 100 percent. You could physically move the `pos` instance within the sliderClip symbol to an X coordinate of 200, but that would increase the scale of the `dog_2` instance to 200 percent at the start. To change only the `pos` instance of `alphaSlider` at the start of the movie, you'll add another line of code to frame 1 of the actions layer on the Main Timeline.

6. **Select frame 1 of the actions layer, and open the Actions panel.** Add the following code to the Script pane, before the start of the `updateDog` function declaration:

   ```
   alphaSlider.pos.x = 200;
   ```

   This block of code executes once, when the `pos` instance (a `MovieClip` object) first appears (or loads) on the Stage.

7. **Save the Flash document and test it.** This time, the `alphaSlider`'s bar (its pos instance) immediately starts at the upper limit. Now, let's take advantage of the filter effects available in the Flash Player.

8. **Create a new layer on your Main Timeline (that is, Scene 1), and name it** blurSlider. Make a copy of the `scaleSlider` instance and paste it on frame 1 of the blurSlider layer.

9. **Name the new copied instance** blurSlider **in the Properties panel, and position the instance near the top of the** `alphaSlider` **instance, parallel to the** `scaleSlider` **instance.**

   To enable a blur effect with this slider, you need to modify the code in the `updateDog` function on frame 1 of the actions layer.

10. **Select frame 1 and open the Actions panel.** Modify the function with the bold code shown in Listing 24.2.

    This code creates a new `BlurFilter` instance named `bf`. A similar calculation used for the `alpha` value is used for the blur quantities, `blurX` and `blurY`. The `bf` filter is applied to the `dog_2` instance's `filter` property at the end of the `with()` statement.

LISTING 24.2

The New BlurFilter Effect Applied to the dog_2 Instance

```
//MovieClip dog_1;
//MovieClip scaleSlider;
//MovieClip alphaSlider;
//MovieClip blurSlider;

var dog_2 = new Dog();
dog_2.x = 350;
dog_2.y = 175;
addChild(dog_2);

this.addEventListener(Event.ENTER_FRAME, updateDog);
```

```
alphaSlider.pos.x = 200;

function updateDog(evt) {
   var scaleVal = scaleSlider.pos.x/100;
   var alphaVal = alphaSlider.pos.x/100;
   var blurVal = blurSlider.pos.x;
   var bf = new BlurFilter();
   bf.blurX = blurVal/2;
   bf.blurY = blurVal/2;
   bf.quality = 3;
   with (dog_2) {
      scaleX = scaleVal;
      scaleY = scaleVal;
      alpha = alphaVal/2;
    filters = [bf];
   }
}
```

11. **Save the Flash document and test the movie.** The dog_2 instance should now initialize with a blurred look, as shown in Figure 24.14.

FIGURE 24.14

The new BlurFilter effect applied to the dog_2 instance

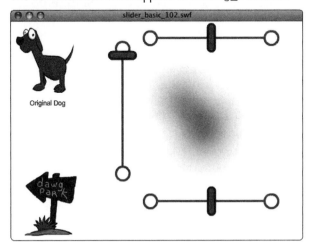

12. In order to keep a clear visual of the dog_2 instance when the movie first loads, add this line of code before the updateDog function declaration on frame 1 of the actions layer:

```
blurSlider.pos.x = 0;
```

13. **Save the Flash document and test it.** Now, the blurSlider instance initializes a blurX and blurY value of 0.

Removing Movie Clip instances

At this point in the chapter, you have three sliders that dynamically control the scale and alpha of the dog_2 Movie Clip instance on the Stage. What if you wanted to get rid of the dog_2 instance? How would you delete it? The only way to remove a new instance is to use the removeChild() method of the DisplayObjectContainer class (the MovieClip class belongs to this parent class). In this section, we show you how to use the dropTarget property and the removeChild() method.

ON the CD-ROM **Resume using the same document, slider_basic_102.fla, that you created in the last section. Alternatively, you can open the slider_basic_102.fla file located in the ch24 folder of this book's CD-ROM.**

1. **Select frame 1 of the actions layer on the Main Timeline, and open the Actions panel.** Type the bold code shown in Listing 24.3.

   Most of this code is already familiar to you. Here you want to make only your new dog instance (dog_2) draggable.

   When a mouse down event is detected on the dog_2 instance, the dragDog function declared as the listener function executes. The startDrag() method of the dog_2 instance is enabled and constrained to the dimensions of the Flash movie Stage.

   When a mouse up event is detected over the dog_2 instance, the dropDog function executes. The last if statement checks whether the parent object of dropTarget property is equal to the sign instance. If the dog_2 instance is over the sign instance on the Stage when the dragging stops, then the dog_2 instance is removed with the removeChild() method.

   Finally, if the dog_2 instance is removed, you must remove the Event.ENTER_FRAME listener assigned to the Main Timeline (this), the parent of the dog_2 instance; otherwise, the updateDog function generates errors in the Output window. By using the removeEventListener() method, the updateDog function earlier established as a listener is deleted.

2. **Save your Flash document as** slider_basic_103.fla **and test it.** When you drag the dog_2 instance over the sign instance, the dog_2 instance disappears.

LISTING 24.3

The Drag-and-Drop Code for the dog_2 Instance

```
//MovieClip dog_1;
//MovieClip scaleSlider;
//MovieClip alphaSlider;
//MovieClip blurSlider;

var dog_2 = new Dog();
dog_2.x = 350;
dog_2.y = 175;
addChild(dog_2);

this.addEventListener(Event.ENTER_FRAME, updateDog);
dog_2.addEventListener(MouseEvent.MOUSE_DOWN, dragDog); dog_2.
    addEventListener(MouseEvent.MOUSE_UP, dropDog);

alphaSlider.pos.x = 200;
blurSlider.pos.x = 0;

function updateDog(evt) {
    var scaleVal = scaleSlider.pos.x/100;
    var alphaVal = alphaSlider.pos.x/100;
    var blurVal = blurSlider.pos.x;
    var bf = new BlurFilter();
    bf.blurX = blurVal/2;
    bf.blurY = blurVal/2;
    bf.quality = 3;
    with (dog_2) {
        scaleX = scaleVal;
        scaleY = scaleVal;
        alpha = alphaVal/2;
      filters = [bf];
    }
}

function dragDog(evt){
    var rect = new Rectangle(0, 0, 550, 400);
    dog_2.startDrag (true, rect);
}

function dropDog(evt){
    dog_2.stopDrag ();
    if(dog_2.dropTarget.parent == sign){
        this.removeEventListener(Event.ENTER_FRAME, updateDog);
        removeChild(dog_2);
    }
}
```

ON the CD-ROM You can find a completed version of `slider_basic_103.fla` in the `ch24` folder of this book's CD-ROM. Another version, `slider_basic_104.fla`, has a button handler to reduplicate the `dog_2` instance and reorganize the actions within a function.

In the next chapter, you expand your knowledge of ActionScript code by using functions and arrays. These code devices enable you to organize code and data much more efficiently with ActionScript.

WEB RESOURCE We want to know what you think about this chapter. Visit `www.flashsupport.com/feedback` to send us your comments.

Summary

- The `MovieClip` class has unique properties, methods, and handlers. Using dot syntax, you can access these characteristics of a `MovieClip` object.

- You can change a Movie Clip instance's position, scale, and rotation by using ActionScript. Most physical attributes are accessed by specifying the Movie Clip instance's path followed by the property name, as in `instance.rotation`.

- You can create draggable Movie Clip instances in ActionScript without using any Button instances, by using the listeners for the `MouseEvent.MOUSE_DOWN` and `MouseEvent.MOUSE_UP` events.

- The `dropTarget` property of a Movie Clip instance (instance A) indicates the Movie Clip instance (instance B) upon which a Movie Clip instance (instance A) is dropped.

- As the sliders example demonstrated, you can use the values of one Movie Clip instance's properties to change the property values of another Movie Clip instance.

Chapter 25

Using Functions and Arrays

N ow that you've had some practice applying ActionScript to `MovieClip` objects, you can start to explore the programming concepts behind subroutines and arrays. In this chapter, we introduce you to data types, subroutines, arrays, and complex uses of functions.

In previous chapters, you may have found yourself repeating the same actions (or type of actions) in several event handlers within a movie. Functions enable you to group actions into code blocks, referred to by custom names. Arrays are a different kind of grouping mechanism — instead of grouping actions, an array is used to group multiple items of data. Before we can discuss functions and arrays, however, you need to understand the types of data that are available in ActionScript.

NOTE As discussed in past chapters, the event listener model of ActionScript 3.0 utilizes functions to process common events associated with interactive elements, such as button clicks and drag-and-drop behaviors.

What Are Data Types?

Simply put, ActionScript has several types of data that can be declared (or loaded) into the Flash movie. So far, you have worked primarily with three types of data in previous chapters: strings, numbers, and `MovieClip` objects. In this section, we define more data types available in ActionScript.

Understanding data types is rather straightforward. One of the difficult aspects of working with data types is knowing which data types work correctly with the operation you want to perform in ActionScript. We show you examples throughout this chapter to help you understand how data types are used.

String

You've seen String data types throughout this book already. Anytime you have a value in quotes, it is typed as a string. If you have an expression that refers to String data types, then its data type is a string as well. All the following examples have a String data type:

```
var firstName = "Frank";
var lastName = "Houston";
var fullName = firstName + lastName;
var pathSuffix = "1";
```

> **TIP**   All text contained within input and dynamic text fields have a data type of String. If you need to perform numeric operations with text field values, make sure that you convert the string data to number data by using the **Number()** or **parseInt()** function. We discuss the Number data type in the next section.

> **NOTE**   Feel free to try out the following code examples in new Flash files. Create a new file, and rename Layer 1 to actions. Using the Actions panel, add the code examples to frame 1 of the actions layer. After you type each code block, test the movie to see the output from the **trace()** actions appear in the Output panel.

If a variable has a String data type, any of the String object methods can be used with that data. For example, if you want to convert the case of all characters in the value of firstName to uppercase (turn "Frank" into "FRANK"), you can do the following operation:

```
var firstName = "Frank";
var firstName = firstName.toUpperCase();
trace("firstName = " + firstName);
```

Here, the String object method toUpperCase() converts any lowercase characters in a string value to uppercase characters. Likewise, you can extract specific information from a string. For example, if you wanted to find where a space occurs within a string, and return the value of the string from the point in the value to the end of the value, you could use the following code:

```
var myVersion = "Firefox 3.0";
var startChar = myVersion.indexOf(" ") + 1;
myVersion = myVersion.substr(startChar);
trace("myVersion = " + myVersion);
```

In the preceding code, the indexOf() method searches for the first occurrence of a space (" ") within the string value for myVersion. indexOf(" ") for myVersion returns the position (as a number, counting from left to right) of the space character. For this example, indexOf (" ") returns 7. Then, 1 is added to this value to determine the character position after the space. In this example, the ninth position of myVersion's value is a "3". Then, by using the slice() method, you can extract the rest of the string from the startChar value of 8. Note that in this example, the final value of myVersion is a string value of "3.0".

Number

A Number data type is any value (or expression value) that refers to a discrete numeric value in ActionScript. A value must be typed as a number in order for it to work properly in mathematical operations.

```
var myAge = "33";
var futureYears = "5";
myAge = myAge + futureYears;
trace("I will be " + myAge + " years old in " + futureYears + "
    years.");
```

If this code was added to frame 1 of your Flash document and tested, the following `trace()` information would appear in the Output panel:

```
I will be 335 years old in 5 years.
```

Obviously, this isn't the answer you were looking for. Because `myAge` and `futureYears` were specified as string values (with quotes), ActionScript simply concatenated (joined) the two string values as `"33"` + `"5"`, which is `"335"`. To see these values as numbers, you need to change the code to the following:

```
var myAge = 33;
var futureYears = 5;
myAge = myAge + futureYears;
trace("I will be " + myAge + " years old in " + futureYears + "
    years.");
```

Now, the values of `myAge` and `futureYears` appear as real numbers to ActionScript, and the mathematical operation adds the values of `myAge` and `futureYears` correctly. The `trace()` output now reads:

```
I will be 38 years old in 5 years.
```

You can convert string data values to number data values by using the `Number()` function. In the string example from the last section, you could convert the `myVersion` string value to a number value by adding this line of code:

```
myVersion = Number(myVersion);
```

So, you can now perform mathematical operations on the `"7.2"` value of `myVersion`, which is now simply 7.2.

> **NOTE** The process of converting one data type to another is sometimes referred to as *casting*.

> **TIP** In ActionScript 3.0, you have a wider range of numeric data types, including `int` and `uint`. The `int` data type is used for *int*egers, or whole numbers such as –1, 22, or 100. The `uint` data type is used for *unsigned int*egers, or non-negative numbers such as 1, 30, or 53.

Boolean

There will be times when you will designate a variable's value as either `true` or `false`. Variables that use `true` or `false` are said to have a Boolean value. Boolean values are useful for either/or situations, or when you need a toggle switch — just like a light switch, which is on or off. In the code that follows, a variable named `isLoading` is initialized with a `true` value, but later switched to a `false` value when loading is complete:

```
var isLoading = true;
trace("isLoading's type = " + typeof(isLoading));

this.addEventListener(Event.ENTER_FRAME, checkLoad);
stop();

function checkLoad(evt){
    if(this.framesLoaded >= this.totalFrames){
        isLoading = false;
    }
}
```

This code could be placed on the first frame of the Main Timeline of a Flash movie. When the movie initializes in Test Movie mode, the Output panel displays the following:

```
isLoading's type = boolean
```

You can check the data types of declared variables and objects with the `typeof` operator.

Object

This data type refers to most code-based objects you create with ActionScript. The following variable would be typed as Object:

```
var myObject = new Object();
```

Several ActionScript classes return a data type of `object` if tested with the `typeof` operator. We discuss the `typeof` operator later in this chapter.

Function

In ActionScript, you can define your own subroutines of ActionScript code. We discuss subroutines and constructor functions later in this chapter. The function data type will be assigned to any ActionScript code that begins with the `function` action, such as:

```
function myGoto(label){
        gotoAndStop(label);
}
```

You can also use the following syntax:

```
var myGoto = function(label){
    gotoAndStop(label);
};
```

CAUTION There is a difference between declaring a function with the first technique versus the second technique. If you declare a function with the former method, you can place the function anywhere within your code block, on any layer for a given frame — the function will be available to any other actions declared on that frame. If you use the latter method, the function will be available only to actions that occur below the function declaration and/or layers beneath the layer on which it was declared.

Undefined

If you check for the data type of a nonexistent code element, ActionScript returns a data type of undefined. For example, if you tried to create a variable that stored a reference to a MovieClip object that was not currently present on the Stage, a data type of undefined would be returned. Create a new Flash document with no elements on the Stage, in any frame. With the first frame of the document selected, type the following code into the Script pane of the Actions panel:

```
var myMovieClip = this["ballAnim"];
trace("the data type of myMovieClip is " + typeof(myMovieClip));
```

Test your Flash movie (Ctrl+Enter/⌘+Enter). The Output panel reports:

```
the data type of myMovieClip is undefined
```

Checking data types with typeof

Now that you know the various data types in ActionScript, you'll want to know how to check the data type of a given piece of information. Using the typeof operator, you can determine the data type of an ActionScript element. The typeof operator accepts only one option: the name of the ActionScript element that you want to test. For example, you can trace a variable (or object) type in the Output panel:

```
var firstName:String = "Robert";
trace("firstName has a data type of " + typeof(firstName));
```

When this movie is tested, the Output panel displays

```
firstName has a data type of string
```

ON the CD-ROM You can see the returned values of the typeof operator in the typeof_simple_AS3.fla file, located in the ch25 folder of this book's CD-ROM.

Strict Typing in ActionScript 3.0

In ActionScript 3.0 (as well as ActionScript 2), you can declare variables with a strict data type. The format for such declarations is

```
var variableName:datatype;
```

or

```
var variableName:datatype = value;
```

For example, if you create a new Flash file (ActionScript 3.0) and type the following code into the Actions panel, you declare a strictly typed string variable:

```
var myName:String = "Robert";
```

In this example, the variable myName can only use values that have a data type of String. If a different data type is assigned to the variable, the ActionScript compiler reports an error when you publish or test your Flash movie. Try the following code in a new Flash document, on the first frame:

```
var myName:String;
myName = 7.2;
```

After you have entered this code, choose Control ⇨ Test Movie. The Compiler Errors panel reports the following error:

```
1067: Implicit coercion of a value of type Number to an unrelated type
    String.
```

Interesting, eh? That's a pretty specific error message, letting you know that you declared a number where a string value was expected. If you change the second line of code to

```
myName = "Robert";
```

and retest the movie, you no longer see the error message. So, why is strict typing important, after all is said and done? For the most part, strict typing forces you to carefully plan and map out the goals of your Flash movie, and discourages you from "free-form" coding, or coding haphazardly. By using strict typing with your ActionScript code, you can more easily debug problems in your Flash movies. Throughout this book and for the remainder of this chapter, we put strict typing to use.

Checking class type in ActionScript 3.0

There's more than one way to determine the exact class to which an object belongs in ActionScript 3.0. In this section, you learn about two ways to pinpoint the class type of an object.

Using the is operator

With the is operator, you can check the class type of a specific object in ActionScript. A class is similar to a data type, but a little more detailed. As mentioned in the object data type discussion, some different objects returned object as their data type. However, these objects belong to different classes.

We show you an example that compares `typeof` to `is`. Create a new Flash file (ActionScript 3.0), and select frame 1 of the default layer. In the Actions panel, type the following code into the Script pane:

```
var today:Date = new Date();
trace("the data type of today is " + typeof(today));
```

After you've written this code, test the Flash movie (Ctrl+Enter/⌘+Enter). The Output panel displays the following text:

```
the data type of today is object
```

Now, use the `typeof` operator in an `if` statement. After the last line of code that you typed, enter the following code:

```
if(typeof(today) == "object"){
  trace("today has a data type of object");
}
```

When you save and test this movie, the last line of the Output panel will be

```
today has a data type of object
```

However, if you wanted to check what kind of object `today` was, the `typeof` operator would not be able to help you out. Enter the `instanceof` operator. Add the following code to the actions list for frame 1:

```
if(today is Date){
  trace("today is a Date object");
}
```

When you test the movie, you see the following text appear in the Output panel:

```
today is a Date object
```

Now, try an `if`/`else` statement that compares `today` to a different class, such as `Sound`. Add the following code into the Actions panel for frame 1:

```
if(today is Sound){
  trace("today is a Sound object");
} else {
  trace("today is not a Sound object");
}
```

When you test your movie, you see the following text appear in the Output panel:

```
today is not a Sound object
```

Although these are simple tests, you can start to see how `is` allows you to check the class types of your data.

What Is a Package?

A package is a collection of classes, functions, or constants in a programming language. Flash Player 9 or later and ActionScript 3.0 contain numerous packages that you can utilize in your own code. A package name defines where the code element is located. For example, the `flash` package contains all the classes that are built into the Flash Player. These classes are called *intrinsic* classes. The `MovieClip` class, for example, belongs to the `flash.display` package, and the `TextField` class belongs to the `flash.text` package. The `flash.display` package containsall the `DisplayObject` classes, such as `Sprite` and `SimpleButton`. The `Event` and `MouseEvent` classes belong to the `flash.events` package. You can use a package or a class within one by using the `import` keyword in your ActionScript code.

NOTE When you use the `is` operator, you do not wrap the compared value in quotes, as you do with `typeof`. For example, do not use `if(today is "Date")`. Simply refer to the class by name, without the quotes: `if(today is Date)`.

Using the getQualifiedClassName() method

ActionScript 3.0 includes a `getQualifiedClassName()` method in the `flash.utils` package. (To learn more about packages, see the sidebar, "What Is a Package?".) This method returns a string value representing the class name of the object passed to the method. For example, the following code displays the text `"today belongs to the Date class"` in the Output panel when the Flash movie is tested:

```
var today:Date = new Date();
trace("today belongs to the " + getQualifiedClassName(today) + "
    class");
```

TIP You can use the `getDefinitionByName()` method of the `flash.utils` package to access the constructor of a class. This method enables you to create new instances of a class whose name you may have retrieved with the `getQualifiedClassName()` method.

Overview of Functions as Procedures

A primary building block of any scripting or programming language is a procedure. A *procedure* is any set of code that you want to reserve for a specific task. A procedure is useful for code that you want to reuse in multiple event handlers (for example, Button instances and keyframes). In Flash ActionScript, procedures are called functions and are created with the `function` action.

What functions do

A function (or procedure) sets aside a block of code that can be executed with just one line of code. Functions can execute several actions, and pass options (called *arguments* or *parameters*) to those actions. All functions must have a unique name so that you know what to reference in later lines of code. In a way, functions are equivalent to your own custom additions to the Flash ActionScript language. In ActionScript, you can define a function on a specific timeline, and refer to its path and name to execute it.

When to create a function

For people new to scripting, perhaps the most confusing aspect of functions is knowing when to create them in a Flash movie. Use the following guidelines to help you determine when a function should be created:

- If you find yourself reusing the same lines of code with the listener functions for several Button instances, MovieClip objects, or keyframes, then you should consider moving the actions to a function.

- If you need to perform the same operation throughout a Flash movie, such as hiding specific Movie Clip instances on the Stage, you should consider defining a function to take care of the work for you.

- When you need to perform operations to determine a value (such as determining the current day of the week or calculating values in a mathematical formula), you should move the operations to a function.

How to define a function

When you add a function to a keyframe on the Main Timeline or a Movie Clip Timeline, you are defining the function. All functions have a target path, just like other objects in ActionScript. All functions need a name followed by opening and closing parentheses, but arguments (options to pass to the function) inside the parentheses are optional.

 Functions are usually defined at the very beginning of a Flash movie. In ActionScript 3.0, you can define functions only on timeline keyframes or within custom classes.

As a simple example, let's say you want to create a function that has one gotoAndStop() action. This function will have a shorter name than gotoAndStop(), and will be faster to type and use in your ActionScript code. Functions that you define should follow a naming convention of a verb followed by a noun, where the first word (or words) indicates a "to do" action and the second word indicates the target of such action. Place this code on the first keyframe of the Main Timeline.

```
function jumpFrame():void {
    this.gotoAndStop("start");
}
```

This function, when evoked, sends the current timeline playhead to the start label. You could further expand the functionality of jumpFrame() by adding an argument, which we'll call frameLabel:

```
function jumpFrame(frameLabel:String):void {
    this.gotoAndStop(frameLabel);
}
```

TIP

You can specify ActionScript 3.0 data typing on function arguments as well. Note that the void data type is used to indicate that no value is returned from this function. We talk about return values from functions next.

In this version of the jumpFrame() function, instead of hard-coding a frame label such as start into the actual gotoAndStop() action, you specify an argument with the name frameLabel. Just like variable names, the names of your function and its arguments are entirely up to you; the name frameLabel has no significance. ActionScript simply knows that if you pass an argument to the jumpFrame() function, that it should place that argument where the frameLabel term occurs in your actions. An argument acts as a placeholder for information that will be supplied to the function on a per-use basis; that is, you can specify a different value for frameLabel each time you evoke the jumpFrame() function. You can also use as many (or as few) arguments as you need. Insert a comma between each argument in the function declaration:

```
function calculateRange (min:Number, max:Number):Number{
    var diff:Number = Math.abs(max - min);
    return diff;
}
```

CAUTION

Beware of naming your functions (and arguments) after already existing ActionScript terms. If in doubt, you should probably choose a word that does not resemble any current ActionScript, JavaScript, or ECMAScript syntax (with later upgrades to ActionScript in mind). You'll see many examples in tutorials or books in which programmers always prefix names with my, as in myColor or myLabel, to avoid any potential naming conflicts.

How to execute a function

After you have defined a function on a timeline's keyframe, you can create actions that refer to the function's actions. The standard method for executing a function is

```
path_to_function.functionName(arguments);
```

At the end of the previous section, you defined a function named jumpFrame() on the Main Timeline. If you added a Button instance named homeButton to your movie, you could then execute the function from a keyframe containing the Button instance with the following code:

```
homeButton.addEventListener(MouseEvent.CLICK, onHomeClick);

function onHomeClick(evt:MouseEvent):void {
        this.jumpFrame("home");
}
```

When this Button instance is clicked, the function jumpFrame() on the current timeline (this) is executed, and passed the argument "home". In your function jumpFrame(), you defined frameLabel as an argument that occurs in the gotoAndStop() action. Therefore, the Main Timeline will go to and stop on the "home" frame label.

CAUTION A function cannot be executed unless it was previously defined in the movie and recognized by the Flash Player. The keyframe containing the function declaration needs to be "played" before the function is available for use. For example, if you define a function on frame 10 of a Movie Clip instance that has stopped on frame 1 (and never played to frame 10), the Flash Player will not have registered the function in memory. For this reason, it's usually a good idea to place your functions on the first frame of the Flash movie, or at a location where they are initialized before you need to use them.

Managing Related Data: The Array Class

Have you ever had a bunch of variables that have a lot in common? For example, do you have variables such as name_1, name_2, name_3, name_4, and so on? These variables look like lists of common information, such as:

```
var name_1:String = "Jeremy";
var name_2:String = "Django";
var name_3:String = "Maia";
var name_4:String = "Phillip";
```

In programming languages, an *array* is a list of values that can be addressed by their position in the list. An array is created by using the Array constructor:

```
var visitors:Array = new Array();
```

The preceding code object simply creates the array container for data. You create an array with information already specified, such as:

```
var visitors:Array = new Array("Jeremy","Django","Maia","Phillip");
```

or

```
var visitors:Array = ["Jeremy", "Django", "Maia", "Phillip"];
```

To access an item in visitors, you would use the array access operators with an array index number. To access the first position's data, you use the following code:

```
var message:String = "Hello " + visitors[0] + ", and welcome.";
```

Here, visitors[0] returns the value "Jeremy". If you traced the message variable, it would read:

```
Hello Jeremy, and welcome.
```

In most programming languages, the first index value (the starting position) is 0, not 1. In the following table, you see how the index number increases with the sample visitors array.

Index Position	0	1	2	3
Index Value	Jeremy	Django	Maia	Phillip

You can set and get the values within an array by using the array access operators. You can replace existing array values by setting the index position to a new value, and you can add values to the array by increasing the index number, as in:

```
var visitors:Array = new Array("Jeremy","Django","Maia","Phillip");
visitors[3] = "Nicole";
visitors[4] = "Candice";
```

In the example, "Nicole" replaces "Phillip", and "Candice" is added to the end of the array. You can also add elements to the array by using the push() method of the Array class, as in:

```
var visitors:Array = new Array("Jeremy","Django","Maia","Phillip");
var visitorsLength:Number = visitors.push("Nicole","Candice");
```

This code adds "Nicole" and "Candice" after "Phillip", and sets the variable visitors-Length equal to the length of the visitors array. length is an Array property that returns the number of elements in the array. In the preceding example, visitorsLength is equal to 6 because there are now six names in the array.

Creating a Dynamic Reusable Flash Menu

In this section, you use arrays to create a dynamic code-built menu that you can adjust for any Flash movie. You create a Main Timeline with six sections for a mock photographer's site and a menu that navigates to those six sections. Although that sounds simple enough, you create the menu entirely from ActionScript code. Figure 25.1 displays the menu and its items as it appears during runtime.

FIGURE 25.1

The completed Flash movie with the menu items

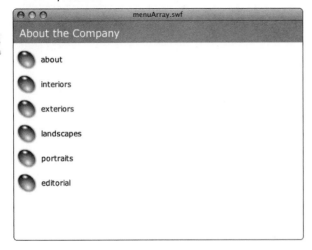

In the following steps, you build a Flash movie that uses this menu system.

1. **Create a new Flash file (ActionScript 3.0).**

2. **Rename Layer 1** labels. Create new keyframes (press F6) on frames 2, 10, 20, 30, 40, and 50. Select frame 60 and press F5.

3. **Starting on frame 2 of the labels layer, assign the following label names to the keyframes you created in Step 2:** about, interiors, exteriors, landscapes, portraits, **and** editorial.

4. **Add a new layer, and name it** actions. Add a keyframe on frame 2 of the actions layer. With that keyframe selected, open the Actions panel (F9/Option+F9) and add a stop(); action. In the Properties panel, type **//stop** in the Name field of the Label section. This creates a frame comment of stop. The stop(); action on frame 2 prevents the Main Timeline from playing past the about section when the movie first loads.

5. **Create another layer called** heading. Add keyframes on this layer, matching the keyframes in the labels layer. Insert some graphics in each keyframe for each section. As a starting point, you can simply add text headings to each section (for example, About the Company, Interior Photography, and so on). You need this heading layer so that you have some indication that the playhead on the Main Timeline actually moves when an item in the menu is clicked.

6. **Create another layer called** background. Place this layer at the bottom of the layer stack. Draw a filled rectangle that spans the top of the document, as shown in Figure 25.2.

Now you create an array that contains the names of each of your frame labels.

7. **Add a new layer to the Main Timeline, and name it** menu actions. Select the first keyframe on the menu actions layer. Open the Actions panel (F9/Option+F9/), and add the following code (note that the ⤶ indicates a continuation of the same line of code; do not insert this character into your actual code):

```
var sectionNames:Array = new Array("about", "interiors", ⤶
  "exteriors", "landscapes", "portraits", "editorial");
```

This line of ActionScript creates an Array object named sectionNames. You can now refer to each section of your timeline by using array syntax, such as sectionNames[0], sectionNames[1], and so on. You use this array to build the actual button text in our menu.

8. **In the same block of code, add the following line to the Script pane for frame 1 of the menu actions layer, after the existing code:**

```
var sectionCount:int = sectionNames.length;
```

This code creates a new variable named sectionCount. The length property of an array returns the current number of elements inside of the array. Therefore, because you put six elements into the array (in Step 7), sectionCount is equal to 6. You may be wondering why you just didn't manually insert the value 6 here. The reason for using an array is that you can change the elements of the array at any point, and the rest of your code updates automatically to reflect the changes. In this way, you are building a dynamic menu system.

9. **Save your Flash document as** `menuArray.fla`. At this point, your Flash document should resemble the document shown in Figure 25.2.

   Now you need to create the menu element that you can use to build a dynamic menu from ActionScript.

FIGURE 25.2

The Main Timeline has frame labels and artwork for each section of the presentation.

10. **Create a new Movie Clip symbol by pressing Ctrl+F8/⌘+F8.**Name this symbol **MenuItem**, and choose the Movie Clip type.

11. **Within the timeline of the MenuItem symbol, rename Layer 1 to** button. On this layer, create or add a Button symbol. In our example, we used the Oval buttons — the blue button from the classic buttons\Ovals folder of the Buttons library (Window ⇨ Libraries ⇨ Buttons). This will be the actual button that appears in the menu. Center your Button instance on the Stage, using the Align panel. In the Properties panel, name the Button instance `clickButton`.

12. **Add a new layer to the MenuItem symbol, and name it** labelField. On this layer, create a dynamic text field that can accommodate the longest name you specified in the `sectionNames` array. In the Properties panel, give this dynamic text field the instance name `labelField`. Use whatever font face you prefer. Place the text field to the right of the button, as shown in Figure 25.3.

FIGURE 25.3

The MenuItem symbol will be used to create each button in the dynamic menu. Using ActionScript, the labelField instance will be filled with the appropriate section name.

13. **Add another layer to the MenuItem symbol, and rename it** actions. Select frame 1 of this layer, and in the Actions panel add the following code:

```
//TextField labelField;
//SimpleButton clickButton;

var labelName:String;
var targetClip:MovieClip;

labelField.text = labelName;
clickButton.addEventListener(MouseEvent.CLICK, onClick);

function onClick(evt:MouseEvent):void   {
   targetClip.gotoAndStop(labelName);
}
```

This code puts the value of a variable named `labelName` into the `labelField` instance. You will see how `labelName` is declared in Step 17.

The `onClick()` handler created as the listener for the `clickButton` instance uses the value of a `labelName` variable as the frame label for the `gotoAndStop()` action. Notice that you will control the playhead of a dynamically assigned timeline, indicated by `targetClip`. This value is assigned to each menu item with ActionScript in a later step. You use the MenuItem symbol as a prototype for the real buttons in the menu. In the remaining steps of this exercise, you'll create a `Sprite` object in ActionScript to hold several instances of the MenuItem symbol.

14. Save your Flash file.

15. **Go back to the Main Timeline (that is, Scene 1) and open the Actions panel for frame 1 of the menu actions layer.** Add the following ActionScript to the Script pane, after the existing code:

```
var menu:Sprite = new Sprite();
menu.x = 25;
menu.y = 70;
this.addChild(menu);
```

This code makes a new `Sprite` instance, named menu. In the second and third lines, the x and y coordinates of the menu instance are set to a position just below the heading artwork on the left side of the Stage. The menu instance is added to the display list of the Main Timeline in the last line of code.

> **NOTE** In ActionScript 3.0, a `Sprite` instance is much like a `MovieClip` instance, except that a `Sprite` instance does not have multiple frames.

After you have created a `Sprite` object to contain instances of the MenuItem symbol, you're ready to prepare the MenuItem symbol for use in ActionScript.

16. **In the Library panel (Ctrl+L/⌘+L), right-click (Control+click on Mac) the MenuItem symbol and choose Properties in the contextual menu.** In the Properties dialog box, view the Advanced properties by clicking the Advanced button in the lower right corner of the dialog box. (If there's a button labeled Basic, then you're already viewing Advanced properties.) Select the Export for ActionScript check box, as shown in Figure 25.4. The Class field auto-fills with the symbol's name, MenuItem. You can now refer to this class name in ActionScript 3.0 to dynamically include the symbol in the Flash movie at runtime. Click OK to accept the new linkage parameters.

> **NOTE** If you see a warning dialog box appear after you close the Symbol Properties dialog box, click OK to dismiss the warning. Flash CS4's warning indicates that there is no custom ActionScript 3.0 class file found for the newly linked symbol asset and that a default class file will be automatically generated.

17. **Select frame 1 of the menu actions layer, and open the Actions panel.** Now, you're ready to add the ActionScript code that dynamically attaches several instances of the itemClip symbol to the menu instance created in Step 15.

```
buildMenu();

function buildMenu():void {
   for(var i:int=0; i < sectionCount ; i++){
      var item:MovieClip = new MenuItem();
      item.labelName = sectionNames[i];
      item.targetClip = this;
      item.y = i*45;
      menu.addChild(item);
   }
}
```

FIGURE 25.4

The Symbol Properties dialog box

This code invokes and defines a function named `buildMenu`. The `buildMenu` function uses a `for` loop that attaches the MenuClip symbol for each element in the `section Names` array. It also sets the value of `labelName` in each attached instance (`item`) to the name of the appropriate section name. Notice that you specify `i` for the index number of the `sectionNames` array because the position index of every array starts at 0 — your menu item numbering also starts at 0.

After an instance is attached for the section name, the `targetClip` variable (mentioned in Step 13) is set to the current timeline, `this`. All of your frame labels exist on the Main Timeline, where this code is being invoked.

You then position the `item` instance at multiples of 45. The first `item` is positioned at a Y coordinate of 0 ($0 \times 45 = 0$), the second `item` is positioned at 45 ($1 \times 45 = 45$), the third `item` is positioned at 90 ($2 \times 45 = 90$), and so on.

TIP Be sure to click the Check Syntax icon in the toolbar of the Actions panel to make sure you didn't make a typo in the code. As an alternative, you can press Ctrl+T/ ⌘+T while focus is in the Actions panel.

18. **Save your Flash document again and test it (Ctrl+Enter/⌘+Enter).** Unless you had a syntax error in your ActionScript, you see a dynamic menu, built by ActionScript. (Refer to Figure 25.1 in Chapter 25.) Each menu item has a unique `labelName` value, which is used in the `gotoAndStop()` action by each Button instance.

You can enhance this dynamic menu by adding animation to the MenuItem symbol timeline. You can also restructure the ActionScript to work with separate Movie Clip instances for each `sectionName`, rather than frame labels. If you use this properly, you may never need to script a menu again! Simply change the Button instance artwork and text styles for unique menu interfaces.

ON the CD-ROM You will find the completed `menuArray.fla` file in the `ch25` folder of this book's CD-ROM.

CROSS-REF In Chapter 31, "Creating a Game in Flash," you learn how to use functions as constructors of custom classes. In ActionScript 3.0, you can only use a function as a constructor within a custom class file.

WEB RESOURCE We'd like to know what you think about this chapter. Visit `www.flashsupport.com/feedback` to send us your comments.

Summary

- ActionScript has several data types, including Boolean, function, movieclip, number, object, and string.

- You should create a procedure when the same actions are repeated within a Flash movie, or when you want to avoid storing long action lists within Button instances.

- A function is defined with the `function` action, in the format `function name(arguments){actions}`.

- Arrays can manage related information, such as lists. An array is initiated with the `Array` constructor, as in `myArray = new Array();`.

- Array elements have an index number, indicating their position in the array. Array index numbers start with 0 and increment by 1 with each new element.

Chapter 26

Interacting with Movie Clips

This chapter continues your exploration of the `MovieClip` class in ActionScript 3.0. You explore the ins and outs of collision detection for `MovieClip` objects and learn how to control the visibility of the mouse pointer or to attach a custom cursor to the mouse pointer. You look at other ActionScript elements such as `ColorTransform` and `Sound` objects that work with `MovieClip` objects to create visual and audio effects, respectively.

You also learn how to print Flash content with the `PrintJob` class. The Flash Player creates high-quality output for hard copy artwork.

Movie Clip Collision Detection

Have you ever wanted to detect the intersection of two elements in a Flash movie? If two Movie Clip instances overlap on the Stage, how would you know? How would you tell ActionScript to look for an overlap? In ActionScript, there are two primary types of intersections (or collisions):

- **User-initiated collisions:** This type of intersection occurs when you click and drag an object (a `MovieClip` object) and overlap another `MovieClip` object as you drag or release. You can also consider the mouse pointer an "object" that can intersect with another object. For example, if you move the mouse pointer over a `MovieClip` object, you can detect when the mouse pointer enters the space of the `MovieClip` object.

- **Script- or time-based collisions:** This type of intersection between objects happens when randomly moving objects collide with one another, such as balls bouncing around the Stage, detecting the edges of the frame, and responding to other boundaries or objects.

In this section, you look at examples in each of these categories. Let's begin with a quick review of the dropTarget property of the MovieClip object.

Using dropTarget

A collision between two MovieClip objects can occur if the user drags one Movie Clip instance to the location of another Movie Clip instance. We first examine the startDrag() action and method in Chapter 24, "Controlling Movie Clips." In the dog movie, you used the dropTarget property of a MovieClip object to detect whether the area of one MovieClip object occupied the area of another MovieClip object. To recap, you can test the intersection of two Movie Clips with the following code:

```
//MovieClip mc_1;
//MovieClip mc_2;

mc_1.addEventListener(MouseEvent.MOUSE_DOWN, activateDrag);
mc_1.addEventListener(MouseEvent.MOUSE_UP, deactivateDrag);

function activateDrag(evt:MouseEvent):void {
   mc_1.startDrag();
}

function deactivateDrag(evt:MouseEvent):void {
   trace(mc_1.dropTarget.parent);
   if(mc_1.dropTarget.parent == mc_2){
      trace("mc_1 overlaps mc_2");
   } else {
      trace("mc_1 does NOT overlap mc_2");
   }
   mc_1.stopDrag();
}
```

This code could occur on a MovieClip object named mc_1. When the user clicks the MovieClip instance, the MovieClip.startDrag() method is invoked, and the user can drag the Movie Clip instance on the Stage. When the user releases the mouse, the dropTarget property returns the object reference of the artwork upon which the initiating MovieClip instance was dropped. If the parent object of dropTarget property returns a reference to another instance, the if condition sees whether the path matches mc_2. If the objects match, the trace() action indicating an overlap is executed. Otherwise, a separate trace() action notifies you that the instance is not on top of mc_2.

Collision detection with hitTestObject() and hitTestPoint()

You can also perform more advanced collision detection by using the hitTestObject() method of the MovieClip object. hitTestObject() does exactly what it says — it tests to see whether a "hit" occurred between two objects. hitTestObject() has the following format:

```
mc.hitTest(anotherInstance);
```

The `hitTestPoint()` method can determine whether the tested X and Y coordinates are within the space occupied by the Movie Clip instance.

```
mc.hitTest(x coordinate, y coordinate, shapeFlag);
```

NOTE The `hitTestObject()` and `hitTestPoint()` methods are also available with the closely related `Sprite` class in ActionScript 3.0. In fact, any `DisplayObject` class has these methods.

The shape flag attribute of the `hitTestPoint()` method defines the actual test area for the hit. If the shape flag is set to `true`, a hit occurs only if the X and Y coordinates occur within the actual artwork of the Movie Clip instance. If the shape flag is set to `false`, a hit occurs whenever the X and Y coordinates occur within the bounding box of the Movie Clip instance. In Figure 26.1, if the left circle uses a shape flag of `true`, a hit is reported whenever the X and Y coordinates occur within the shape of the circle (not within the bounding box). If the right circle uses a shape of `false`, a hit is reported when the X and Y coordinates occur within the bounding box.

FIGURE 26.1

The shape flag determines the boundary of the Movie Clip instance for the `hitTest()` method.

shape flag = true

shape flag = false

ON the CD-ROM You can see a working example of shape flags and the `hitTestPoint()` method in the `hitTestPoint_xy.fla` file, located in the `ch26` folder of this book's CD-ROM. Open this Flash document, and test the movie. As you move your mouse within the space of each object, you will notice that the hit area is different for each object. You create your own Flash movie that uses `hitTest()` in our coverage of the `Mouse` class in this chapter.

With the `hitTestObject()` method, you simply specify a target path to compare for a hit occurrence. With this syntax, you cannot use a shape flag option; if any area of the bounding box for a Movie Clip instance touches the bounding box of the tested instance, a hit occurs.

ON the CD-ROM You can see a working example of targets and the `hitTestObject()` method in the `hitTestObject_target.fla` file, located in the `ch26` folder of this book's CD-ROM. You will create a Flash movie that uses the `hitTestObject()` method in our coverage of the `Sound` class later in this chapter.

Using the Mouse Class

With ActionScript, you can emulate custom mouse pointers (that is, the graphic shown for the mouse pointer) by using the `startDrag()` behavior (with lock to center `true`) on Movie Clips containing icon graphics. However, this technique does not hide the original mouse pointer — it appears directly above the dragged Movie Clip instance. ActionScript features a static `Mouse` class, which has the following two simple methods:

- `show()`: This method reveals the mouse pointer. By default, the mouse pointer appears at the start of a movie.

- `hide()`: This method turns off the mouse pointer's visibility. To reveal the mouse pointer again, execute the `show()` method.

When the `Mouse` object (that is, the mouse pointer) is hidden, you can lock a `MovieClip` object containing a new icon graphic to the position of the mouse pointer. In this section, you create a Flash movie with a large circle `MovieClip` object. When the mouse pointer moves into the area of this object, you attach a smaller circle to the mouse pointer's position. The `hitTestPoint()` method is used to determine when the mouse pointer moves into the area of the large circle, and a new `MovieClip` object affixes the small circle to the mouse pointer's position.

1. **Create a new Flash file (ActionScript 3.0) (Ctrl+N/⌘+N).** Rename Layer 1 to **circleBig**.

2. **Select the Oval tool and draw a circle.** In the Properties panel, set the circle's size to 25 × 25.

3. **With the circle artwork selected, press the F8 key to convert the artwork into a Movie Clip symbol.** Name the symbol **Circle**.

4. **Name the instance on the Stage** circleBig **in the Properties panel.** Increase the size of this particular instance to 200 × 200, and apply a Tint effect to fill the instance with a different solid color. Center the instance on the Stage by using the Align panel.

   Now you have to link the Circle symbol in the Library panel to the exported Flash movie file (.swf).

5. **Right-click (Control+click on Mac) the circle symbol, and choose Properties.** If the extended properties shown in Figure 26.2 are not visible, click the Advanced button. Select the Export for ActionScript check box, and the Class field auto-fills with the text Circle, as shown in Figure 26.2. Click OK to accept these settings. Also, click OK to the class warning dialog box.

   After the Circle symbol is linked, you can dynamically insert the symbol into the Flash movie with ActionScript. Remember that you want to attach the circle to the mouse pointer when it enters the space of the `circleBig` instance.

6. **On the Main Timeline (that is, Scene 1), create a new layer and name it** actions. Select frame 1 of this layer, and open the Actions panel. Type the code shown in Listing 26.1 into the Script pane as follows. Do not type the ⤶ character, which indicates a continuation of the same line of code.

FIGURE 26.2

The Circle symbol is now linked to the Flash movie.

TIP **Any code listings, such as Listing 26.1, are available on this book's CD-ROM, in the respective chapter folder. Listing files are .as files, so you can even use the `include` directive to just add the listing's code to your .fla file.**

Here, you use the `MouseEvent.MOUSE_MOVE` event in line 5 to capture the movement of the mouse anywhere within the Flash movie. By assigning the event and `checkCircle` listener function (lines 7 to 24) to `this.stage`, any mouse movement is captured and processed. If the event listener were added to the `circleBig` instance, only mouse movement that occurred within the artwork of the `circleBig` instance would be captured. On line 3, a variable named `circleSmall` is created to store a reference to another circle that is created and added if the mouse cursor is within the artwork of the `circleBig` instance. Note that the `circleSmall` instance is not created on line 3 — that happens only when a hit has been detected with the mouse cursor and the `circleBig` instance.

If the X and Y positions of the mouse pointer intersect with the `circleBig` instance, the nested actions for the `if` condition in line 8 execute. Line 9 checks to see if the new graphic (that is, the `circleSmall` instance) exists in the movie. If it doesn't, a new instance of the Circle symbol is created (line 10) and added to the display list of the Main Timeline (line 11).

Lines 13 and 14 position the X and Y coordinates of the `circleSmall` instance by referencing the current position of the mouse pointer (`this.mouseX` and `this.mouseY`). Line 15 hides the mouse pointer icon, and line 16 uses the `updateAfterEvent()` function to force a video refresh of the Flash movie. This enables the `circleSmall` to move very smoothly across the Stage.

Lines 17–23 execute if the mouse pointer is not within the space of the `circleBig` instance. Line 18 checks to see if `circleSmall` exists in the movie — if it does, it is removed. The mouse pointer reappears when the mouse moves outside of the `circleBig` instance (line 22).

7. **Save your Flash document as** `mouse_hitTestPoint.fla`, **and test it (Ctrl+Enter/⌘+Enter).** In the Test Movie window, move the mouse pointer into the space of the large circle. When the mouse enters this area, the small circle from the library attaches itself to the position of the mouse cursor and hides the original pointer. When you move the mouse out of the large circle, the small circle disappears and the original mouse pointer returns. See Figure 26.3 for these comparisons.

FIGURE 26.3

The left image shows the mouse outside the large circle, whereas the right image shows the mouse inside the large circle with the small circle attached.

LISTING 26.1

The checkCircle Listener for the MouseEvent.MOUSE_MOVE Event

```
1.  //MovieClip circleBig;
2.
3.  var circleSmall:MovieClip;
4.
5.  this.stage.addEventListener(MouseEvent.MOUSE_MOVE, checkCircle);
6.
7.  function checkCircle(evt:MouseEvent):void {
8.      if(circleBig.hitTestPoint(this.mouseX, this.mouseY, true)){
```

```
9.        if(circleSmall == null){
10.           circleSmall = new Circle();
11.           this.addChild(circleSmall);
12.        }
13.        circleSmall.x = this.mouseX;
14.        circleSmall.y = this.mouseY;
15.        Mouse.hide();
16.        evt.updateAfterEvent();
17.    } else {
18.        if(circleSmall != null){
19.           this.removeChild(circleSmall);
20.           circleSmall = null;
21.        }
22.        Mouse.show();
23.    }
24. }
```

That might seem like a lot of work to hide a mouse pointer, but in the process, you have learned how to attach your own icons to the mouse pointer. You can use this same methodology to add any custom graphic to the mouse pointer. Simply add a different linked symbol to the Library panel, and change the new constructor name (line 10).

ON the CD-ROM You can find the completed example, `mouse_hitTestPoint.fla`, in the `ch26` folder of this book's CD-ROM.

Manipulating Color Attributes

The `ColorTransform` class in ActionScript gives you control of the color and appearance of your `MovieClip` objects. By controlling the color (and transparency) of your artwork with ActionScript's `ColorTransform` class, you can:

- Create on-the-fly color schemes or "skins" for Flash interfaces.
- Enable users to select and view color preferences for showcased products on an e-commerce site.
- Instantly change the color attributes of a Flash design-in-progress for a client.

Because color is controlled through the `ColorTransform` class, we quickly review the unique properties within this class. Refer to Table 26.1 for more information. Note that this table is organized by order of practical use.

TABLE 26.1

Properties for the ColorTransform Class

Property	Definition	Options
`color`	Retrieves or sets the RGB offset for the targeted Movie Clip. This property changes all colors in the targeted instance to one solid RGB color.	*ct.rgb = 0xRRGGBB;* where: *ct* is the name of the ColorTransform object. We discuss the creation of ColorTransform objects in this section. *RR, GG,* and *BB* are the offset values (in hexadecimal) for the Red, Green, and Blue channels, respectively.
[*Channel*]Multiplier	Retrieves or sets the multiplier used by a specific color channel in the targeted Movie Clip. Acceptable values are between (and including) –1 and 1. You can preview a channel's multiplier effect by using the left-hand column of values in the Advanced Effect dialog box of the Color mode, as accessed in the Properties panel settings for a Movie Clip instance.	*ct.redMultiplier = 0.2;* *ct.greenMultiplier = 0.65;* *ct.blueMultiplier = -1;* *ct.alphaMultiplier = 0.1;* where: *ct* is the name of a ColorTransform object. We discuss the intricacies of these properties in the following sections.
[*Channel*]Offset	Retrieves or sets the offset used by a specific color channel in the targeted Movie Clip. Acceptable values are between (and including) –255 and 255. You can preview a channel's offset effect by using the left-hand column of values in the Advanced Effect dialog box of the Color mode, as accessed in the Properties panel settings for a Movie Clip instance.	*ct.redOffset = 100;* *ct.greenOffset = 50;* *ct.blueOffset = 25;* *ct.alphaOffset = 0;* where: *ct* is the name of a ColorTransform object. You'll practice the use of offsets in an exercise within this section.

Creating a ColorTransform object

To manipulate the color attributes of a Movie Clip instance, you need to create a new ColorTransform object that is applied to transform.colorTransform property of the Movie Clip instance. In the following steps, you learn to use the constructor for the ColorTransform object. Let's work out the steps required to take control of color properties.

ON the CD-ROM For the exercises with the `ColorTransform` object, make a copy of the dog-Color_starter.fla document in the ch26 folder of this book's CD-ROM. Thank you, Sandro Corsaro, of www.sandrocorsaro.com, for supplying the dog artwork!

1. Save the starter file as `dogColor_100.fla`.

2. **Select the instance of the dog graphic on the Stage.** Open the Properties panel and name this Movie Clip instance `dog_1`.

3. **Create a new layer on the Main Timeline, and name the layer** buttons.

4. **Open the Components panel and drag an instance of the `Button` component onto the Stage.** Place the instance near the left corner of the Stage. We discuss components in more detail in Chapter 32, "Using Components." For now, we guide you through the use of this component for the purposes of this exercise.

5. **Name the new Button instance** `redButton` **in the Properties panel.**

6. **Select the `redButton` instance on the Stage, and open the Component Inspector panel (Window ⇨ Component Inspector).** Make sure that the Parameters tab is selected in the inspector. Type the text Red in the label field. Refer to the settings shown in Figure 26.4.

FIGURE 26.4

The parameters for this instance of the Button component

Now you need to create a `changeColor()` function in the movie. This function is executed by the `redButton` instance when the button is clicked.

7. **Create a new layer on the Main Timeline and name it** actions. Select frame 1 of the actions layer, and open the Actions panel (F9/Option+F9). Type the following code into the Script pane:

```
1.  //MovieClip dog_1;
2.  //Button redButton;
3.
```

```
4.   import flash.events.MouseEvent;
5.   import flash.geom.ColorTransform;
6.   import fl.controls.Button;
7.
8.   redButton.addEventListener(MouseEvent.CLICK,⊃
     changeColor);
9.
10.  function changeColor(evt:MouseEvent):void {
11.      var ct:ColorTransform = new ColorTransform();
12.      ct.color = 0xFF0000;
13.      dog_1.transform.colorTransform = ct;
14.  }
```

As we discuss in earlier chapters, lines 1 and 2 are code comments which enable code hints for authortime instances. These lines are not required, but ease the use of ActionScript code with the specified instances. Lines 4–6 use the `import` keyword to enable the ActionScript 3.0 classes used in this script. Past exercises in this book haven't explicitly imported classes such as `flash.events.MouseEvent`, but it's a good habit (and a standard convention) to import all classes you use in a script. The `ColorTransform` class is part of the `flash.geom` package, and the Button component belongs to the `fl.controls` package. (Note that packages starting with `fl.` are components or utility classes that are not intrinsic classes to the Flash Player.)

Line 8 tells the `redButton` instance to register the `changeColor()` function as a listener for click events. Whenever the `redButton` instance is clicked, the `changeColor()` function is invoked.

The `changeColor()` function is defined on lines 10–14. In this function, the `evt` argument represents the `MouseEvent` object that the `Button` instance passes to the function. Line 11 creates a new `ColorTransform` object called `ct`. After the `ct` object is initiated, you can access properties of the `ColorTransform` object, such as `color`. In line 12, you set the color to pure red, designated by `0xFF0000` in hexadecimal. In line 13, you apply the `ct` instance to the `colorTransform` property of the `MovieClip`. `transform` property of the `dog_1` instance.

8. **Save the Flash document and test the movie.** Click the `redButton` instance on the Stage. The color of the `dog_1` Movie Clip should change to bright red. Close the Flash movie and return to the Flash CS4 authoring environment.

   To see that `color` is both a property you can write and read, let's create some `trace()` messages for the Output panel.

9. **Go back to the `changeColor()` function on frame 1 and add the following line of code just before the closing curly brace (}) of the `changeColor()` function.** Type this as one line of code:

   ```
   trace("ct's RGB numeric value = " + ct.color);
   ```

10. **Save the document and test the movie.** When you click the `redButton` instance, the Output panel opens and displays the following text:

```
ct's RGB numeric value = 16711680
```

To change this value back to the hexadecimal value you entered in the `rgb` property, you need to convert the value to base 16.

11. **Add the following action after the last** `trace()` **action from Step 9:**

```
trace("ct's RGB hex value = " + ct.color.toString(16));
```

12. **Save the document and test the movie.** When you click the `redButton` instance, the Output panel should open and display the new value:

```
ct's RGB numeric value = 16711680
ct's RGB hex value = ff0000
```

However, you won't need to convert `color`'s native return value to set another `ColorTransform` object equal to a previous `color` value. In the following steps, you will create another dog and `ColorTransform` object team.

13. **Duplicate the dog_1 Movie Clip instance on the Stage (Edit ⇨ Duplicate), and name the new instance dog_2 in the Properties panel.** Position the `dog_2` instance to the right of `dog_1`.

14. **Duplicate the Button component instance on the Stage and position the new instance below the original one.** In the Properties panel, change its instance name to `passRedButton`. Change its `label` value to **Pass Red** in the Component Inspector panel.

15. **Select frame 1 of the actions layer and open the Actions panel.** Add the code shown in bold in Listing 26.2. With this new code, the same event listener for the `redButton` instance is used for the `passRedButton` instance and the `MouseEvent.CLICK` event. Now, when the `changeColor()` function is invoked, a `switch` statement carries out different actions based on which button is clicked. The local variable named button determines which button was clicked. If the `passRedButton` instance is clicked, the `colorTransform` value for the `dog_1` instance is passed to the `dog_2` instance.

> **TIP** For this example, we wanted to demonstrate the reading and writing of the `color` property. You can also simply pass the `transform` property, which includes the `MovieClip` instance's alpha value, to another `MovieClip` object:
>
> ```
> dog_2.transform.colorTransform = dog_1.transform.colorTransform;
> ```

16. **Save the Flash document and test the movie.** When you click the `redButton` instance, the `dog_1` Movie Clip instance turns red. When you click the `passRedButton` instance, the `dog_2` Movie Clip instance turns red.

LISTING 26.2

Checking for the Pass Red Label

```
//MovieClip dog_1;
//MovieClip dog_2;
//Button redButton;
//Button passRedButton;

import flash.events.MouseEvent;
import flash.geom.ColorTransform;
import fl.controls.Button;

redButton.addEventListener(MouseEvent.CLICK, changeColor);
passRedButton.addEventListener(MouseEvent.CLICK, changeColor);

function changeColor(evt:MouseEvent):void {
    var button:Button = evt.currentTarget as Button;
    var ct:ColorTransform = new ColorTransform();
    switch(button){
      case redButton:
          ct.color = 0xFF0000;
          dog_1.transform.colorTransform = ct;
          trace("ct's RGB numeric value = " + ct.color);
          trace("ct's RGB hex value = " + ct.color.toString(16));
          break;
      case passRedButton:
          ct.color = dog_1.transform.colorTransform.color;
          dog_2.transform.colorTransform = ct;
          break;
    }
}
```

> **NOTE**
> If you click the second `Button` instance first, the `dog_2` Movie Clip instance turns black. Why? Because the first button's actions were not executed, and there was no previous `color` property value for the new `rgb` property. Consequently, ActionScript returns a zero value. In hexadecimal color, zero is equivalent to black.

Now that you've had some experience with the `ColorTransform` object's `color` property, let's move on to a more complex use of `ColorTransform`. You'll use the Flash document from this exercise, so keep the dogs on the Stage!

> **ON the CD-ROM**
> You can find the completed Flash document, `dogColor_100.fla`, in the `ch26` folder of this book's CD-ROM.

Setting multiplier and offset values

The `ColorTransform` class also features multiplier and offset properties, which require a more thorough understanding of RGB color space.

The multiplier and offset properties of the `ColorTransform` class are

- `redMultiplier` — The Red channel percentage
- `redOffset` — The Red channel offset
- `greenMultiplier` — The Green channel percentage
- `greenOffset` — The Green channel offset
- `blueMultiplier` — The Blue channel percentage
- `blueOffset` — The Blue channel offset
- `alphaMultiplier` — The Alpha channel percentage
- `alphaOffset` — The Alpha channel offset

The *multiplier* properties are decimal values, ranging in value from –1 to 1. The *offset* properties are integer-based from –255 to 255 (derived from 24-bit RGB color space, in which each 8-bit color channel can have a range of 256 values).

These properties and values may seem complex, so refer to the Advanced options of the Style menu in the Color Effect section of the Properties panel for symbol instances for guidance. With the Advanced option chosen in the Style menu, you can edit the multiplier and offset values for an instance. The left-hand color controls are percentage-based (or multipliers), whereas the right-hand controls are offset-based. Admittedly, color is difficult to visualize from numbers. To accurately predict the color changes with `ColorTransform`, we use the Advanced settings in the Properties panel to help us out.

ON the CD-ROM Make a copy of the `dogColor_100.fla` file if you didn't complete the previous section's exercise. This document is located in the `ch26` folder of this book's CD-ROM.

1. **Resave the Flash document from the previous section as** `dogColor_200.fla`.

2. **Select the original** `dog_1` **Movie Clip instance on the Stage.** Open the Properties panel, and expand the Color Effect section. In the Style menu, choose the Advanced option. In those settings, enter the following value on the left-hand side: **–100%** Blue. On the right-hand side, enter these values: **37** G and **255** B. See Figure 26.5. With these values, the `dog_1` instance should be a monochrome blue with yellow eyes. Normally, you would want to write these values down so that you have them to use later. Because you have them printed here in this book, erase them by choosing None from the Color menu in the Properties panel. The `dog_1` instance should now appear in its original state.

FIGURE 26.5

These settings change the color of the dog_1 instance.

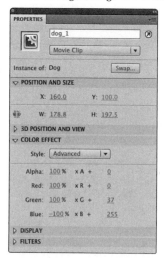

3. **Duplicate one of the existing** Button **component instances on the Stage.** Place the duplicated instance underneath the last Button component instance. Name the instance rabidButton. Change the label value to **Rabid**.

    With this new instance, you will create some code that initiates a new ColorTransform object. The new object will be given properties that have the same values as those determined in Step 2.

4. **Select frame 1 of the actions layer and open the Actions panel (F9/Option+F9).** Add the bold code shown in Listing 26.3.

    In addition to color, ColorTransform instances can have offset and multiplier values for each color (and alpha) channel. In Listing 26.3, you assigned the values you determined in Step 2. Offset values have a one-to-one relationship with the offset values displayed in the Advanced Effect dialog box, but multiplier values are divided by 100. So, if you have a multiplier value of –100% in the Advanced Effect dialog box, the equivalent ColorTransform multiplier value would be –1. After you have set the appropriate offset and/or multiplier values, you apply the ct instance to the colorTransform property of the transform property of the dog_1 instance.

NOTE The ColorTransform class is one of two types of alterations to Movie Clips that can be made with the Transform class. The transform property of the MovieClip class uses the Transform class and encompasses a wide range of characteristics that can be applied to the MovieClip class. For more detailed information of the Transform class, refer to the Flash Help panel (F1).

5. **Save the Flash document and test the movie.** Click the new `Button` instance that you added in Step 3. The colors of the `dog_1` Movie Clip instance should change to match those you saw in Step 2. Close the Test Movie window, and return to the Flash CS4 authoring environment.

   Now you will create a button that restores the original look of the `dog_1` Movie Clip instance.

6. **Duplicate one of the `Button` instances, and place the new instance underneath the last `Button` instance.** In the Properties panel, name this component instance `restoreButton`. Change the `label` value to **Restore**.

7. **Select frame 1 of the actions layer, and open the Actions panel (F9/Option+F9).** Add the bold code shown in Listing 26.4 to the Script pane.

   In Listing 26.4, you simply need to pass a new unaltered `ColorTransform` instance to the `colorTransform` property of the `MovieClip` instance, `dog_1`. A new `ColorTransform` instance has default multiplier and offset values. So, when it's passed to a `MovieClip` object, the color properties are set back to the original values.

8. **Save the Flash document again and test the movie.** Click the `rabidButton` instance you created in Step 3. After the `dog_1` Movie Clip instance changes color, click the `restoreButton` instance you created in Step 6. Voila! The `dog_1` Movie Clip instance reverts to its original color. Click the `redButton` instance that you created in the preceding section. This button changes the appearance of the `dog_1` Movie Clip instance to a solid red color. Now click the `restoreButton` instance — the `dog_1` Movie Clip instance reverts to its original look!

LISTING 26.3

Checking for the Rabid Button

```
//MovieClip dog_1;
//MovieClip dog_2;
//Button redButton;
//Button passRedButton;
//Button rabidButton;

import flash.events.MouseEvent;
import flash.geom.ColorTransform;
import fl.controls.Button;

redButton.addEventListener(MouseEvent.CLICK, changeColor);
passRedButton.addEventListener(MouseEvent.CLICK, changeColor);
rabidButton.addEventListener(MouseEvent.CLICK, changeColor);

function changeColor(evt:MouseEvent):void {
   var button:Button = evt.currentTarget as Button;
```

continued

LISTING 26.3   *(continued)*

```
    var ct:ColorTransform = new ColorTransform();
    switch(button){
        case redButton:
            ct.color = 0xFF0000;
            dog_1.transform.colorTransform = ct;
            trace("ct's RGB numeric value = " + ct.color);
            trace("ct's RGB hex value = " + ct.color.toString(16));
            break;
        case passRedButton:
            ct.color = dog_1.transform.colorTransform.color;
            dog_2.transform.colorTransform = ct;
            break;
        case rabidButton:
            ct.blueOffset = 255;
            ct.blueMultiplier = -1;
            ct.greenOffset = 37;
            dog_1.transform.colorTransform = ct;
            break;
    }
}
```

LISTING 26.4

Checking for the Restore Button

```
//MovieClip dog_1;
//MovieClip dog_2;
//Button redButton;
//Button passRedButton;
//Button rabidButton;
//Button restoreButton;

import flash.events.MouseEvent;
import flash.geom.ColorTransform;
import fl.controls.Button;

redButton.addEventListener(MouseEvent.CLICK, changeColor);
passRedButton.addEventListener(MouseEvent.CLICK, changeColor);
rabidButton.addEventListener(MouseEvent.CLICK, changeColor);
restoreButton.addEventListener(MouseEvent.CLICK, changeColor);

function changeColor(evt:MouseEvent):void {
    var button:Button = evt.currentTarget as Button;
    var ct:ColorTransform = new ColorTransform();
    switch(button){
        case redButton:
```

```
        ct.color = 0xFF0000;
        dog_1.transform.colorTransform = ct;
        trace("ct's RGB numeric value = " + ct.color);
        trace("ct's RGB hex value = " + ct.color.toString(16));
        break;
    case passRedButton:
        ct.color = dog_1.transform.colorTransform.color;
        dog_2.transform.colorTransform = ct;
        break;
    case rabidButton:
        ct.blueOffset = 255;
        ct.blueMultiplier = -1;
        ct.greenOffset = 37;
        dog_1.transform.colorTransform = ct;
        break;
    case restoreButton:
        dog_1.transform.colorTransform = ct;
        break;
    }
}
```

 You can find the completed document, `dogColor_200.fla`, in the `ch26` folder of this book's CD-ROM.

Although the `ColorTransform.color` property can alter basic color properties of `MovieClip` objects, the offset and multiplier properties are the color-control powerhouse. Any look that you can accomplish with the Advanced Effect dialog box, you can reproduce with the `ColorTransform` class.

Enabling Sound with ActionScript

ActionScript offers many classes, and one of the most exciting classes to use is the `Sound` class. As with most classes, the `Sound` class has predefined methods that you can use to control each new `Sound` class. Table 26.2 provides an overview of the `Sound` class and its common methods.

TIP Flash Player 8 and later can support up to 32 channels of audio (or 16 channels of stereo audio) simultaneously.

TABLE 26.2

Common Methods to Control Sound in ActionScript 3.0

Method	Definition	Options
Sound.load	Loads a separate MP3 audio source file (.mp3) into a Sound object. You can begin playback of the MP3 sound as soon as enough bytes have downloaded, or wait until the entire file has downloaded. We show you how to use this method in Chapter 28.	*soundObject.load (URLRequest, SoundLoaderContext);*
		where:
		URLRequest is the location of the MP3 file specified by a URLRequest instance. This location can be a relative or absolute path.
		SoundLoaderContext determines if the loading sound begins playback as soon as enough bytes have downloaded (true), or if the entire sound must download before playback can begin (false).
Sound.play	Plays the targeted Sound instance. A sound must be loaded into the Sound instance (or created with a linked sound asset) before it can play. The method returns an instance of the SoundChannel class which can be used to control further playback options of the sound.	*soundObject.play(inPoint, loop Factor, SoundTransform);*
		where:
		inPoint is the time (in seconds) in the sound where playback should begin.
		loopFactor is the number of times the sound should be repeated. *SoundTransform* is a SoundTransform instance specifying transformations for the volume and channel output.
		All these parameters are optional and can be omitted.

Method	Definition	Options
SoundChannel. stop	Stops playback of the targeted SoundChannel instance. Note that this is not equivalent to pausing a sound. If a stopped sound is played later, it starts at the beginning (or at the *inPoint*).	*soundObject.stop(libraryID);*
		where:
		libraryID is the name of the sound in the Linkage properties (available in the Library panel).
SoundTransform. volume	Sets or retrieves the overall volume of the specified Sound instance. A SoundTransform instance with this property must be assigned to the soundChannel property of the SoundChannel instance playing the sound. The volume property accepts values between 0 and 1 (in decimal units).	*soundTransform.volume = volumeLevel;*
		where:
		volumeLevel is a number between 0 and 1.
SoundTransform. pan	Sets or retrieves the offset of sound output from both the left and right channels.	*soundTransform.pan = panValue;*
		where:
		panValue is a value between –1 (full left-speaker output) and 1 (full right-speaker output). Use a value of 0 to balance sound output evenly.
SoundChannel. soundTransform	Sets or retrieves the sound characteristics for the targeted SoundChannel instance, accepting a SoundTransform instance as its value. This property also enables you to play the right channel in the left channel and vice versa.	*soundChannel.soundTransform = soundTransformInstance;*
		where:
		soundTransformInstance is the name of an object that has percentage properties for left and right output for the left channel, and left and right output for the right channel.

The following list of Sound class features offers reasons for using Sound instances over traditional keyframe sounds. You have:

- Dynamic event sounds that play in a random or user-defined order
- Precise control over volume and panning
- The ability to dump (or erase) a Sound object when the sound is no longer needed

NOTE All Sound objects are treated as event sounds. You cannot use Sound objects to control the playback or frame rate like stream sounds can. However, ActionScript does enable you to load MP3 files on-the-fly and "stream" their playback — these types of sounds, however, cannot control playback or frame-rate synchronization. For more information on Synch modes for sound, refer to Chapter 14, "Adding Sound." (The usage of the term "stream" in this context does not imply real-time streaming, but rather a progressive download for the MP3 file.)

The Sound class uses sounds directly from the movie's library or from an MP3 file loaded at runtime. You cannot use the Sound class to control sounds specified in the Properties panel for any given keyframes.

The next section shows you how to create Sound objects by using the object constructor with class names of linked assets in the Library panel.

Creating sounds with ActionScript

In this section, you learn how to export a sound asset from a Flash document's Library panel to use with ActionScript 3.0 code.

ON the CD-ROM Use the pianoKeys_sounds_starter.fla file found in the ch26 folder of this book's CD-ROM. This file contains seven imported piano key sounds in the key-Sounds folder of the Library panel.

1. **Open a copy of the** pianoKeys_sounds_starter.fla **file in Flash CS4.** This starter file already has seven buttons shaped to fit the seven piano keys shown in the imageSequence instance on the Stage. Each button has been assigned a name, using the prefix key_. The first key is named key_1, and the last key is named key_7. Resave this document as **pianoKeys_sounds.fla**.

   In order to use this document's sound files in ActionScript 3.0, you need to export the sounds from the library when the movie is published.

2. **Open the document's Library panel (Ctrl+L/⌘+L).** Open the keySounds folder, and select all the sound files by clicking the top sound file, Key1, and Shift+clicking the last sound file, Key7. Right-click (or Control+click on Mac) the selected items and choose Properties. In the Properties dialog box, select the Export for ActionScript check box and choose Yes in the drop-down menu, as shown in Figure 26.6. Choose Yes in the Export in frame 1 drop-down menu as well. Click OK when you have finished.

3. **Expand the Library panel horizontally to reveal the linkage names of the key sounds.** Each key sound is now being exported as a class name for ActionScript 3.0. The class for each sound is named after the sound's name in the Library panel, such as `Key1`, `Key2`, and so on. Close the `pianoKeys_sounds` Library panel, and save your Flash document.

FIGURE 26.6
_____

The imported sounds with their linkage identifiers displayed

4. **Now, add the ActionScript code that creates `Sound` objects from the exported sounds.** On the Main Timeline (that is, Scene 1), Alt+double-click/Option+double-click frame 1 of the actions layer. This opens the Actions panel. Type the following code into the Script pane, below the existing starter code which enables code hints for the key buttons on the Stage:

```
var key1:Sound = new Key1();
var key2:Sound = new Key2();
var key3:Sound = new Key3();
var key4:Sound = new Key4();
var key5:Sound = new Key5();
var key6:Sound = new Key6();
var key7:Sound = new Key7();
```

Because each key sound has been exported from the library, you can instantiate each sound with the new constructor, using the class name automatically created for the linked asset.

Now, you need to enable the seven Button instances on the Stage. When the user moves the mouse cursor over a Button instance, the key sound corresponding to that Button instance should play.

5. In the Actions panel, add the following ActionScript to the code from Step 4:

```
key_1.addEventListener(MouseEvent.MOUSE_OVER, onKeyOver);
key_2.addEventListener(MouseEvent.MOUSE_OVER, onKeyOver);
key_3.addEventListener(MouseEvent.MOUSE_OVER, onKeyOver);
key_4.addEventListener(MouseEvent.MOUSE_OVER, onKeyOver);
key_5.addEventListener(MouseEvent.MOUSE_OVER, onKeyOver);
key_6.addEventListener(MouseEvent.MOUSE_OVER, onKeyOver);
key_7.addEventListener(MouseEvent.MOUSE_OVER, onKeyOver);
```

> **TIP**   Type the first line of ActionScript code shown in Step 5 and simply copy and paste the line over and over again, renaming the Button instance name (key_2, key_3, and so on) until you reach key_7.

Each Button instance (key_1, key_2, and so on) passes the MouseEvent.MOUSE_OVER event to a custom function named onKeyOver. This custom function processes the event and plays the correct key sound for each Button instance rollover.

Now create a custom function named onKeyClick to process the events from the Button instances.

6. After the code you added in Step 5, type the following code:

```
function onKeyOver(evt:MouseEvent):void {
  var button:SimpleButton = evt.currentTarget as SimpleButton;
  var num:Number = Number(button.name.substr(-1));
  var snd:Sound = this["key" + num] as Sound;
  snd.play();
  imageSequence.gotoAndStop("key_" + num);
}
```

This function determines which Button instance is currently rolled over by the mouse cursor. The local variable button indicates this Button instance. After you've determined which Button instance has been rolled over, you can determine which key sound to play by looking at the Button instance's name. If the key_1 instance is rolled over, then the key1 instance should be played. The local variable num indicates the key number, by looking at the last character (-1) of the name property of the Button instance. This value is then glued to the string "key" to return a reference back to the Sound instance associated with the Button instance. The play() method of this Sound instance is invoked, enabling the sound to be heard. Finally, the key sound number is used to tell the imageSequence instance which frame to display with a gotoAndStop() action.

7. **Save the Flash document and test it (Ctrl+Enter/⌘+Enter).** When you roll over each Button instance on top of the piano keys image, you should hear the respective sound play. The imageSequence instance should also show the current key pressed by going to and stopping on the right frame.

ON the CD-ROM You can view the completed sound library movie, `pianoKeys_sounds.fla`, located in the `ch26` folder of this book's CD-ROM. We've also included a bonus file, `pianoKeys_sounds_advanced.fla`, that demonstrates a more efficient way to create the key sounds and event listeners.

Creating a SoundTransform object

When a `Sound` instance is played, a reference to a `SoundChannel` instance is returned. This instance can be further manipulated with the `SoundTransform` class. (You can also pass a `SoundTransform` instance to the new `Sound` constructor to control sound attributes.) The `SoundTransform` class can control volume distribution across channels.

Luckily, the `SoundTransform` class doesn't have as many properties as the `ColorTransform` class, and they're much simpler to predict with trial-and-error testing. The properties of the `SoundTransform` class are

- `leftToLeft` — The portion of left channel output in the left speaker

- `leftToRight` — The portion of left channel output in the right speaker

- `rightToRight` — The portion of right channel output in the right speaker

- `rightToLeft` — The portion of right channel output in the left speaker

The first word of each property determines which channel output is being affected. The third word determines which speaker is being targeted. Each property can have a decimal value between –1 and 1.

These channel output properties are not exactly routine manipulations, though, that you'll need to perform on sound output. The last two properties of the `SoundTransform` class enable you to control volume and balance of output more easily:

- `pan` — The balance of sound output between the left and right speakers, ranging from –1 (full pan left) to 1 (full pan right). A value of 0 indicates no panning, balanced center between left and right speakers.

- `volume` — The overall output on both speakers, ranging from 0 (silent) to 1 (full volume).

Creating volume and balance sliders for sounds

In this section, you learn how to control the volume and balance output from a `Sound` instance by using the slider mechanism from Chapter 24, "Controlling Movie Clips." The slider mechanism works by taking the X position value of the slider's bar and applying it to a property of another object. In Chapter 24, you applied the position value of the bar to Movie Clip properties such as `scaleX`, `scaleY`, and `alpha`. In this exercise, you apply the position values to the `volume` and `pan` properties of a `SoundTransform` object to control the volume and balance output, respectively.

ON the CD-ROM In this section, you need to use the `slider_basic_104.fla` file, located in the `ch24` folder of this book's CD-ROM. If you want to learn how this slider was built, read Chapter 24, "Controlling Movie Clips."

The first part of this exercise shows you how to add the slider to a new document, import a sound, and control the volume of the sound with the slider. In the last steps, you apply the same methodology to the balance slider.

1. Open your copy of the `slider_basic_104.fla` file via the File ⇨ Import ⇨ Open External Library command.

2. Create a new Flash file (ActionScript 3.0). Save this document as `soundSlider.fla`.

3. Rename Layer 1 to volumeSlider.

4. Drag the Slider symbol from the `slider_basic_104.fla` Library panel to the new document's Stage. When you finish, close the `slider_basic_104.fla` Library panel.

5. With the slider instance selected on the Stage, open the Properties panel. Name the instance `volumeSlider`. In the Transform panel, rotate the instance –90 degrees. (You can also use the Free Transform tool to rotate the instance.)

   Now you need to create a `Sound` object.

6. Import a sound file into the Flash document. Use a sound file that is at least 20 seconds long. You can import the `atmospheres_1.mp3` file located in the `resources` folder of this book's CD-ROM.

7. After you have imported a sound file, select the sound in the Library panel. Right-click (Control+click on Mac) the sound file and choose **Properties** in the contextual menu. In the Properties dialog box, click the Advanced button to display the extended properties. Select the **Export for ActionScript** check box and type `BackgroundSound` in the Class field. Click OK to close the dialog box, and click OK to the general warning dialog box about automatic class generation.

8. Create a new layer on the Main Timeline (that is, Scene 1) and name the layer actions.

9. Select frame 1 of the actions layer and open the Actions panel (F9/Option+F9). In the Script pane, type the following code:

```
//MovieClip volumeSlider;

var bgSound:Sound = new BackgroundSound();
var bgChannel:SoundChannel = bgSound.play(0, 999);
```

This code creates the `Sound` object that the `volumeSlider` instance will control. Line 1 uses the `new BackgroundSound()` constructor to establish a `Sound` object named `bgSound`. Line 2 plays the sound, starting at the beginning of the sound (0), and looping it 999 times for near-indefinite playback. The playback of the sound is controlled by the `SoundChannel` instance named `bgChannel`.

10. **Save your Flash document and test the movie (Ctrl+Enter/⌘+Enter).** You hear the sound attached to the bgSound object begin to play. However, if you click and drag the bar on the slider, you do not hear a volume change.

   To change the volume of the bgSound object, you need to take the position of the bar in the slider and apply its value to the volume property of a new SoundTransform instance applied to the bgChannel instance. You'll use ActionScript 3.0's MouseEvent.MOUSE_MOVE event to accomplish this.

11. **Select frame 1 of the actions layer on the Main Timeline.** Open the Actions panel, and insert the following code after the last action in the Script pane (do not type the ⤸ which indicates a continuation of the same line of code):

```
volumeSlider.addEventListener(MouseEvent.MOUSE_MOVE, ⤸
   updateSound);

function updateSound(evt:MouseEvent):void {
   var vol:Number = volumeSlider.pos.x/200;
   var trans:SoundTransform = new SoundTransform();
   trans.volume = vol;
   bgChannel.soundTransform = trans;
}
```

   This code creates an event listener named updateSound for the MouseEvent.MOUSE_ MOVE event of the volumeSlider instance. Each time a mouse move is detected, the function defined for this listener executes. The first line of the function retrieves the current x value of the pos instance inside of volumeSlider and divides it by 200. (See our coverage of the slider in Chapter 24, "Controlling Movie Clips," to learn more about this operation.) This value, declared as vol, is then applied to the volume property of a new SoundTransform instance named trans. This instance is then passed to the soundTransform property of the bgChannel instance established in Step 9.

12. **Save your Flash document again, and test it.** Click and drag the bar on the slider. As you move it up, the sound increases in volume. As you move it down, the volume decreases.

   Creating a slider that controls the balance output is almost identical to the process of creating the volumeSlider instance. You will make another instance of the Slider symbol, and add a new MouseEvent.MOUSE_MOVE listener for the new instance.

13. **Create a new layer on the Main Timeline and name it** balanceSlider.

14. **Drag an instance of the Slider symbol from the Library panel to the Stage.** Place the instance to the right of the volumeSlider instance. In the Properties panel, name the instance balanceSlider.

15. **Select frame 1 of the actions layer, and open the Actions panel.** Add the bold code shown in the following code:

```
//MovieClip volumeSlider;
//MovieClip balanceSlider;
```

```
var bgSound:Sound = new BackgroundSound();
var bgChannel:SoundChannel = bgSound.play(0, 999);

volumeSlider.addEventListener(MouseEvent.MOUSE_MOVE, ↩
   updateSound);
balanceSlider.addEventListener(MouseEvent.MOUSE_MOVE, ↩
   updateSound);

function updateSound(evt:MouseEvent):void {
   var vol:Number = volumeSlider.pos.x/200;
   var bal:Number = (balanceSlider.pos.x - 100)/100;
   var trans:SoundTransform = new SoundTransform();
   trans.volume = vol;
   trans.pan = bal;
   bgChannel.soundTransform = trans;
}
```

This code adds a MouseEvent.MOUSE_MOVE event listener for the balanceSlider
instance. When the mouse moves within the Flash movie, the updateSound function
executes. In this updated version of the function, though, we need to translate the x
property of the pos instance differently. Because pan values are within a range of –1 to 1,
we must map the 0 to 200 range of the slider accordingly. In order for the lowest value
(0) to equal –1 and the highest value (200) to equal 1, you simply subtract 100 from the
current x property value returned by the pos instance and then divide by 100. You then
apply this value to the pan property of the trans object.

16. **Save your Flash document and test it.** As you drag the bar on the balanceSlider
instance to the right, you should hear the sound play in the right speaker. As you drag
the bar to the left, you should hear the sound play in the left speaker.

ON the CD-ROM   You can find the completed soundSlider.fla file in the ch26 folder of this
book's CD-ROM.

Printing with ActionScript

Using the PrintJob class in ActionScript 3.0, you can enable your Flash movies to output Flash
artwork, text, and bitmaps. With these actions, you can do the following:

- **Create Flash ads that have printable specifications for e-commerce merchandise.**
  Imagine if the next car ad you saw on your favorite Web site automatically printed dealer
  locations and maps without having to go to the car manufacturer's Web site?

- **Make Flash coupons.** You can design printable coupons for e-tailers on the Web that
  can be printed and redeemed at their brick-and-mortar stores.

- **Automate dynamic Web-generated invoices and receipts at e-commerce sites.** With
  ActionScript, you can format ordered items and add dynamic data to printable sheets.

- **Print rich vector illustrations or photorealistic bitmaps from a Web site.** You can design Flash portfolio sites that print samples of stock images, or create personalized vector artwork that can print unique images for each visitor.

- **E-mail printable Flash artwork to clients.** The next time you have a proof of concepts or finished artwork that needs final approval, you can e-mail your clients the Flash artwork in a stand-alone projector or .swf file.

- **Design custom contact information pages.** Are you sick of HTML tables that won't print your nice row-and-column–formatted pages of information consistently from browser to browser? Printable Flash content prints beautifully each time. You can even add a visitor's contact information to a dynamic database and print it.

Although we can't describe how to do all these tasks in the space of this chapter, we show you how to get started with the last idea. The following exercise shows you how to use the `PrintJob` class to build pages that can be sent to a user's printer. You'll also practice ActionScript 3.0 coding conventions, using strict data types.

NOTE Because Flash natively uses vector artwork, it translates best when it is output to a PostScript printer. Nevertheless, the Flash Player produces high-quality output to both PostScript and non-PostScript printers.

1. **Open the** `printjob_starter.fla` **file in the** `ch26` **folder of this book's CD-ROM.** This document has sample artwork in the library that you can use to practice printing exercises. Resave this document as `printjob_noscale.fla`.

2. **Rename Layer 1 to** content.

3. **Create a new Movie Clip symbol (Insert ⇨ New Symbol) named** PageContent. Inside of this symbol (in Edit mode), rename Layer 1 to **page border**.

4. **Select frame 1 of the page border layer.** Using the Rectangle tool, draw a nonfilled rectangle with a black stroke. After you have drawn the rectangle, select the entire outline, and open the Properties panel. Choose a line style of Solid, at 1 px. In the width and height fields, enter values that are in the same aspect ratio as an 8.5-x-11-inch piece of paper. For example, as shown in Figure 26.7, the size 320 x 440 uses the same aspect ratio. Position the artwork's left corner at 0, 0.

5. **Add another layer in the PageContent timeline, and rename this layer** content.

6. **Open the Library panel (Ctrl+L/⌘+L) and drag an instance of the siteLogo symbol to frame 1 of the content layer.** Use the Free Transform tool to resize the artwork to fit within the frame artwork you created in Step 3. See Figure 26.8.

7. **Save your Flash document.**

8. **Go back to the Main Timeline (that is, Scene 1).** On frame 1 of the content layer, drag an instance of the PageContent symbol from the Library panel to the Stage. In the Properties panel, name this instance `pageContent`. Do not resize the instance. For now, just let the bottom edge of the instance run off the Stage.

FIGURE 26.7

The frame artwork

FIGURE 26.8

The siteLogo artwork

9. **On the Main Timeline, create another layer named** printButton. Place this layer above the content layer. The printButton layer will hold a `Button` component that the user can click to print the `pageContent` instance.

10. **On frame 1 of the printButton layer, drag an instance of the `Button` component from the Components panel (Window ⇨ Components) to the Stage.** In the Properties panel, name this instance `printButton`. In the Parameters tab of the Component Inspector panel (Window ⇨ Component Inspector), type `Print` into the `label` field. Refer to the settings shown in Figure 26.9.

FIGURE 26.9

The `printButton` instance

11. **Create another layer and name it** actions. Place this layer above the other layers.

    Now, you're ready to add the ActionScript that prints the `pageContent` instance.

12. **Select frame 1 of the actions layer and open the Actions panel (F9/ Option+F9).** In the Script pane, type the code shown in Listing 26.5.

    Lines 1 and 2 declare the class types of the `printButton` and `pageContent` instances on the Stage. By using these code comments, the Actions panel displays the code hints for that variable (or instance) whenever you type the name and follow it with a period.

    On line 4, a `printContent()` function is added as a `MouseEvent.CLICK` event listener for the `printButton` instance (line 16). Now, when the user clicks the `Button` component, the `printContent()` function is invoked.

Line 6 declares the `printContent()` function. Line 7 declares a local variable named `pj`, set to use the `PrintJob` data type, which invokes the constructor for the `PrintJob` class. Line 8 creates a local variable named `mc`, pointing to the `pageContent` instance.

Line 9 uses the `start()` method of the `PrintJob` class to initiate a print session on the user's machine. When the `start()` method is invoked, the system's standard Print dialog box appears. If the user clicks OK in this dialog box, lines 11–13 execute. If the user cancels the print request, lines 14–16 execute. If the user clicks OK, the local variable `init` is set to `true`. If the user cancels the dialog box, `init` is set to `false`.

Line 10 checks the result of the user's input in the Print dialog box. If `init` is `true`, lines 11–13 execute. In line 10, a `trace()` message is sent to the Output panel, indicating that a print job is being submitted. In line 11, the `addPage()` method of the `PrintJob` class is invoked, specifying the `pageContent` instance, represented by the variable `mc`, as the target instance to print. The `addPage()` method enables you to submit individual pages in a print job that is sent to the printer. When all the `addPage()` methods are finished, you must initiate a `send()` method to complete the print job, as demonstrated in line 13.

If the user cancels the Print dialog box, lines 14–16 execute. In line 15, a `trace()` message is sent to the Output panel, indicating that the print request was cancelled.

13. **Save your Flash document and test the movie.** When you click the `printButton` instance, you should see the Print dialog box. If you click OK, the Output panel displays the `"printing..."` message. The first frame of the `pageContent` instance prints at 100 percent on the outputted page. To accurately foretell what your printed dimensions will be in inches, divide the pixel width and height of your content clip by 72 — there are 72 pixels to an inch. So, 320 x 440 will print at a size of 4.4 x 6.1 inches. You can, however, scale the content clip to be printed so that it fills the entire page. In the next step, you learn how to do just that.

14. **Select frame 1 of the actions layer and open the Actions panel.** Add the bold code shown in Listing 26.6 to the `printContent()` function. Here, you use the `pageWidth` and `pageHeight` properties of the `PrintJob` object, `pj`, to calculate two variables, `xVal` and `yVal`. `pageWidth` and `pageHeight` return the size of the page output by the printer, in pixels. By dividing each value by the respective width and height of the `pageContent` instance (`mc`), you can determine how much you need to scale the `pageContent` instance to fill the entire page.

15. **Save your Flash document as `printjob_scale.fla` and test it.** When you click the `printButton` instance, the `pageContent` instance scales to a larger size. The printed output fills the entire page with the `pageContent` instance's artwork.

The last step is to scale the `pageContent` clip back to original size after the print output has been sent to the printer.

16. **Add the bold code shown in Listing 26.7 to the `printContent()` function.**

17. **Save your Flash document and test it.** When you click the `printButton` instance, the artwork no longer scales on the Stage, but the printed output is scaled.

LISTING 26.5

The printContent() Function

```
1.  //Button printButton;
2.  //MovieClip pageContent;
3.
4.  printButton.addEventListener(MouseEvent.CLICK, printContent);
5.
6.  function printContent(evt:MouseEvent):void {
7.    var pj:PrintJob = new PrintJob();
8.    var mc:MovieClip = pageContent;
9.    var init:Boolean = pj.start();
10.   if (init) {
11.     trace("printing...");
12.     pj.addPage(mc);
13.     pj.send();
14.   } else {
15.     trace("print aborted by user");
16.   }
17. }
```

LISTING 26.6

Scaling Content in the printContent() Function

```
//Button printButton;
//MovieClip pageContent;

printButton.addEventListener(MouseEvent.CLICK, printContent);

function printContent(evt:MouseEvent):void {
  var pj:PrintJob = new PrintJob();
  var mc:MovieClip = pageContent;
  var init:Boolean = pj.start();
  if (init) {
    trace("printing...");
    var pageW:Number = pj.pageWidth;
    var pageH:Number = pj.pageHeight;
    var xVal:Number = (pageW / mc.width);
    var yVal:Number = (pageH / mc.height);
    with (mc) {
      scaleX = xVal;
      scaleY = yVal;
```

continued

LISTING 26.6 *(continued)*

```
    }
    pj.addPage(mc);
    pj.send();
  } else {
    trace("print aborted by user");
  }
}
```

LISTING 26.7

Resetting the Scale of the Clip Instance

```
//Button printButton;
//MovieClip pageContent;

printButton.addEventListener(MouseEvent.CLICK, printContent);

function printContent(evt:MouseEvent):void {
  var pj:PrintJob = new PrintJob();
  var mc:MovieClip = pageContent;
  var init:Boolean = pj.start();
  if (init) {
    trace("printing...");
    var pageW:Number = pj.pageWidth;
    var pageH:Number = pj.pageHeight;
    var scaleX_orig:Number = mc.scaleX;
    var scaleY_orig:Number = mc.scaleY;
    var xVal:Number = (pageW / mc.width);
    var yVal:Number = (pageH / mc.height);
    with (mc) {
      scaleX = xVal;
      scaleY = yVal;
    }
    pj.addPage(mc);
    pj.send();
    with (mc) {
      scaleX = scaleX_orig;
      scaleY = scaleY_orig;
    }
  } else {
    trace("print aborted by user");
  }
}
```

ON the CD-ROM You can find the completed documents, `printjob_noscale.fla` and `print-job_scale.fla`, in the `ch26` folder of this book's CD-ROM.

WEB RESOURCE You can find additional `PrintJob` tutorials written by Robert Reinhardt at Community MX. You can find a list of Robert's content at `www.flashsupport.com/cmx`.

WEB RESOURCE We'd like to know what you think about this chapter. Visit `www.flashsupport.com/feedback` to send us your comments.

Summary

- Collisions occur when two or more elements in a Flash movie touch each other. Whenever the space occupied by one Movie Clip instance occupies the space of another, a collision, or "hit," has occurred.

- You can detect simple user-initiated collisions by using the `startDrag()` method and `dropTarget` property of the `MovieClip` object.

- Using the `hitTestPoint()` method of the `MovieClip` object, you can detect the intersection of X and Y coordinates with a specified Movie Clip instance. You can use the `hitTestObject()` method in a similar fashion to `dropTarget`, where the overlap of two specific Movie Clip instances is detected.

- You can use the `ColorTransform` class to create new color values and apply them to Movie Clip instances.

- You can create sound libraries in less time by using ActionScript and the `Sound` object. You create ActionScript 3.0 `Sound` objects by exporting sounds files and assigning class names in the movie's library.

- By using the `PrintJob` class, you can output high-quality artwork to a PostScript or non-PostScript printer.

Part VIII

Applying ActionScript

Tweens and motion presets are fun, but the real power of Flash animation happens when you put ActionScript to work for you instead. Learn how to animate without being tied to the timeline in Chapter 27. One of the other most powerful features of the Flash Player is the capability for dynamic data loading. Chapter 28 introduces you to MP3, JPEG/PNG/GIF, and FLV loading, and covers how to share and load assets between multiple .swf files. You will be surprised to find in Chapter 29 how easy it is to create a dynamic Flash movie that sends data with the URLLoader class and to integrate XML data with your Flash movies. Chapter 30 gives you the tools you need to take control of Flash text fields using HTML tags and the TextFormat class. This chapter also introduces the CSS features and text rendering options in Flash CS4.

Chapter 31 gives you an opportunity to apply your new ActionScript know-how to build an interactive game, using design patterns with your ActionScript code. Components are the secret weapon that Flash developers employ to quickly prototype data-enabled projects and to integrate media elements with ready-made interface controls. In Chapter 32, you learn how to add and modify the User Interface components that ship with Flash CS4. Chapter 33 takes you through the steps for creating an extensible Gallery component that makes use of the ScrollPane and UILoader components to support externally loaded JPEG thumbnails and full-size images with PHP scripts. The graphic polish is up to you, but the sample site provides a good foundation for building projects that reduce the need for manual updates and scale gracefully as new content is added.

Note: If you're hungry for more ActionScript, you can find everything you need for more advanced code in *ActionScript 3.0 Bible* (Wiley, 2008).

Chapter 27

Animating with ActionScript

This chapter teaches you how to use features of Flash animation capabilities with ActionScript 3.0. If you've ever wondered how dynamic random motion can be created in Flash content, look no farther. You can start learning about ActionScript-based motion by using good old-fashioned motion tweens that you learned how to create in earlier chapters of this book.

You can use the ActionScript 3.0 `Tween` class to help you move objects around on the Stage. The `Tween` class enables you to animate properties of any object, including `MovieClip` objects. In this section, you learn how to add motion to elements with the `Tween` class.

CROSS-REF We explore only some aspects of the `Tween` class in this chapter. For more information, refer to the Flash CS4 Help pages and search with the phrase "Tween class," where you can find several examples of other methods and properties of the `Tween` class.

NEW FEATURE We've updated this section to include coverage of 3D properties of `DisplayObject` instances, such as `rotationX`, `rotationY`, and `z`, now available in Flash Player 10.

Reviewing the Tween Parameters

To use the `Tween` class in ActionScript 3.0 code, you need to import the `fl.transitions.Tween` class at the top of your script, such as:

```
import fl.transitions.Tween;
```

This class is not an intrinsic class for the Flash Player, which means that the `Tween` class is created at runtime when the Flash movie loads into the Flash Player. The `Tween` class adds about 2K to your Flash movie (.swf) file size.

This size also includes an easing function, which is discussed later in this section.

After you import the class into your code, you can create a Tween instance by using the new Tween() constructor. The following sample code creates a Tween instance named tweenX, which controls the x property of a MovieClip instance named circle. The tweenX instance moves the circle instance from the X coordinate of 10 to the X coordinate of 200, over the span of 5 seconds.

```
import fl.transitions.Tween;
import fl.motion.easing.*;

//MovieClip circle;

var tweenX:Tween = new Tween(
                       circle,  // Target object
                       "x",  // Target property
                       Regular.easeInOut, // Easing function
                       10,  // Start value
                       200, // End value
                       5,  // Duration
                       true  // Use seconds
                   );
```

The constructor requires seven parameters, in the following order:

- **Target object** (Object): The first parameter indicates the object you want to control with the Tween instance. This object can be a MovieClip instance, or another object with controllable properties. For animated elements on the Stage, you will likely use MovieClip instances.

- **Target property** (String): The second parameter specifies a numeric property of the target object, as a string value. You can only tween properties that use a Number data type. An example of such a property is the x property of a MovieClip instance. This property is targeted as "x" when specified in the new Tween() constructor.

- **Easing function** (Function): The third parameter specifies an easing function that calculates the in-between values of the motion tween. You can use any of the easing functions available in the fl.transitions.easing classpath. Learn more about the easing functions in the sidebar, "Picking an Easing Function."

- **Start value** (Number): The fourth parameter indicates the initial value of the property being tweened. The object's tweened property is set to this value at the start of the tween.

- **End value** (Number): The fifth parameter defines the final value of the property being tweened.

- **Duration** (Number): The sixth parameter indicates the length of time to tween the values between the start and end value. The duration value can be specified in one of two units: frames or seconds.

- **Use seconds** (Boolean): The seventh and last parameter indicates which unit type is utilized for the duration value. A value of true indicates seconds as the measure of time, and a value of false indicates frames as the measure of time.

Now that you have an understanding of the Tween class, you're ready to animate a sample piece of artwork in ActionScript.

Picking an Easing Function

The Tween class requires an easing function as a parameter to control the rate and range of values calculated between the start and end values. You can find a list of available easing types by browsing to the following location on your system.

In the application folder storing the Adobe Flash CS4 program files, browse to this folder:

```
Common\Configuration\ActionScript 3.0\projects\Flash\src\fl\transitions\
    easing
```

In this folder, there are six easing classes you can use with the Tween class. You do **not** need to copy these ActionScript (.as) files for your project — you simply reference the classes with an import statement in your ActionScript 3.0 code:

```
import fl.transitions.easing.*;
```

This statement makes all the easing classes available to the ActionScript code you're writing. All these easing types offer easeIn, easeOut, and easeInOut functions, enabling you to modify the initial and final motion effect. Although we can do our best to describe each easing type, we recommend that you try each of the easing types and their easeIn, easeOut, and easeInOut functions with your own Tween instances:

- Back: This easing type creates a slingshot effect, pulling the property value below the starting value and then pulling it closer to the end value. This type also stretches beyond the end value and pulls back.

- Bounce: This easing type re-creates values that mimic a gravitational pull on the property, where the property fluctuates up and down after the end value has been reached. If you want to create a bouncing-ball effect, this easing type is for you.

- Elastic: This easing type feels like an overemphasized Back easing type, producing a reverberating elastic band effect.

continued

- **None:** This easing type removes any easing effect from the tween, effectively creating a normal motion tween without any ease in or ease out effect. Each of the easing functions creates the same effect — easeIn, easeOut, and easeInOut produce a normal motion tween *without* any easing.

- **Regular:** This easing type builds a motion tween with 50 percent easing. Using this easing type creates the same effect as a timeline motion tween with a 50 and/or -50 easing value applied in the Property inspector.

- **Strong:** This easing type builds a motion tween with 100 percent easing. Using this easing type creates the same effect as a timeline motion tween with a 100 and/or -100 easing value applied in the Property inspector.

You can apply only one easing type to each Tween instance you build, but you can create several Tween instances for an object, applying each to a property of the object you want to manipulate.

Making an Object Move Back and Forth

The best way to understand how the Tween class works is to experiment with the different easing types with a MovieClip instance. In the following steps, you learn how to control a circle graphic with the Tween class.

ON the CD-ROM If you want to skip the artwork creation process, open the `tween_as3_starter.fla` file from the `ch27` folder of this book's CD-ROM, save a copy, and jump to Step 6.

1. **Create a new Flash file (ActionScript 3.0).** Save the file as `tween_as3_back_and_forth.fla`.

2. **Rename Layer 1 to** circle.

3. **With the Oval tool, draw a perfect circle.** You can Alt+click/Option+click with the Oval tool to use a dialog box to specify an exact width and height of the circle. Use any fill color you prefer.

4. **Select the circle artwork and choose Modify ⇨ Convert to Symbol (F8).** In the Convert to Symbol dialog box, name the symbol **circle**, choose the Movie Clip type, and place the registration point in the center, as shown in Figure 27.1.

5. **Select the new instance on the Stage.** In the Properties panel, name the instance circle. Position the instance at X 40, and Y 80.

FIGURE 27.1

The Convert to Symbol dialog box

6. **Create a new layer named** actions. Select frame 1 of the actions layer, and open the Actions panel (F9,/Option+F9).

7. **Add the code shown in Listing 27.1.** This code creates a new `Tween` instance for the x property of the `circle` instance, animating the circle from the left edge of the Stage to the right edge within three seconds. This tween uses the `Strong.easeIn` function, easing the starting motion.

8. **Save the Flash file and test the movie by choosing Control ⇨ Test Movie (Ctrl/Cmd+Enter).** The `circle` instance should move from the left edge of the Stage to the right edge.

   To make the circle instance animate back and forth continuously, you can use the `Tween.yoyo()` method with the `TweenEvent.MOTION_FINISH` event. This event fires whenever a `Tween` instance reaches its end value. The `yoyo()` method reverses the start and end values of a `Tween` instance, switching the direction of the motion.

9. **After the existing code on frame 1 of the actions layer, add the following code.** Be sure to add the `import` statement at the top of the actions list, along with the other import statements:

```
import fl.transitions.TweenEvent;

twX.addEventListener(TweenEvent.MOTION_FINISH, ⤶
  onTweenFinish);

function onTweenFinish(evt:TweenEvent):void {
  twX.yoyo();
}
```

10. **Save the Flash file and then test the movie.** When the circle reaches the right edge of the Stage, the `Tween` instance restarts and sends the circle back to the left edge. Because the `TweenEvent.MOTION_FINISH` event fires each time the `Tween` instance reaches its end value, the motion never stops!

LISTING 27.1

Animating the Circle Across the Stage

```
import fl.transitions.Tween;
import fl.transitions.easing.*;

//MovieClip circle;

var twX:Tween = new Tween(
                    circle,
                    "x",
                    Strong.easeIn,
                    circle.x,
                    stage.stageWidth - (circle.width/2),
                    3,
                    true
              );
```

Continue to explore this example on your own, changing the values specified in the new Tween() constructor. Try out different easing classes, such as Bounce.easeInOut and Elastic.easeOut.

ON the CD-ROM You can find the finished example, **tween_as3_back_and_forth.fla**, in the **ch27 folder of this book's CD-ROM.**

Animating 3D Properties

With Flash Player 10 content, you can now control 3D properties of ActionScript 3.0 DisplayObject instances, which includes MovieClip and TextField instances. The basic principles of the Tween class apply exactly the same way to 3D properties as properties discussed in the last section. In this section, you learn how to use the Tween class with the rotationX and z properties of a TextField instance.

1. **Create a new Flash file (ActionScript 3.0) and save it as** tween_as3_3D.fla.

2. **Rename Layer 1 to** myText.

3. **On frame 1 of the myText layer, use the Text tool to create a dynamic text field with some sample text, such as the word "Hello."** Use the Properties panel to name the instance myText. Turn off the show border option in the Character section of the panel, and center-align the text within the Paragraph section.

4. **Select the text field with the Selection tool and open the Align panel (Ctrl+K/⌘+K).** Align the text field to the horizontal and vertical center of the Stage. The position of the text field on the Stage affects the look and feel of 3D transformations because the 3D camera's focal point is the middle of the Stage area.

5. **Create a new layer named** actions.

6. **Select frame 1 of the actions layer and add the code shown in Listing 27.2.** This code uses the same structure as the last exercise, and animates the rotationX and z properties of the myText instance. Because two Tween instances use the same listener function named onMotionFinish, the currentTarget property of the TweenEvent parameter (evt) is used to determine which Tween instance to yoyo.

7. **Save the Flash document and test the movie (Ctrl+Enter/⌘+Enter).** When the movie loads, the text field animates back and forth along the Z axis, swinging the text back and forth along its top edge.

LISTING 27.2
_____

Animating 3D Properties of a TextField Instance

```
import fl.transitions.Tween;
import fl.transitions.TweenEvent;
import fl.transitions.easing.Regular;

//TextField myText;

var twRotX:Tween = new Tween(myText, "rotationX", Regular.easeInOut, ⤵
  -100, 100, 1, true);
twRotX.addEventListener(TweenEvent.MOTION_FINISH, onMotionFinish);

var twZ:Tween = new Tween(myText, "z", Regular.easeInOut, 0, -200, ⤵
  2, true);
twZ.addEventListener(TweenEvent.MOTION_FINISH, onMotionFinish);

function onMotionFinish(evt:TweenEvent):void {
   var tw:Tween = evt.currentTarget as Tween;
   tw.yoyo();
}
```

_____

ON the CD-ROM You can find the finished example, tween_as3_3D.fla, in the ch27 folder of this book's CD-ROM.

Following the Mouse Cursor

You can also use the Tween class to create interactive effects, such as a graphic following the mouse cursor. In this section, you learn how to use the following aspects of the Tween class:

- **Multiple Tween instances:** You learn how to integrate two Tween instances, one for the x property of the animated element and one for the y property.

- **Tween.continueTo() method:** This method enables you to specify a new end value for the Tween instance, enabling you to update the direction of movement for an animated element.

- **Tween.position and Tween.finish properties:** These properties enable you to retrieve the current value and the end value, respectively, of a Tween instance. You use these values to determine the horizontal flip of the animated element.

 TIP To flip a MovieClip instance horizontally in ActionScript, simply use a negative scaleX value.

In the following steps, you learn how to make the hero artwork follow the mouse cursor.

1. Open the tween_as3_follow_mouse_starter.fla file from the ch27 folder of this book's CD-ROM.

2. **Resave the Flash file as** tween_as3_follow_mouse.fla. Notice that the Stage already contains an instance of the hero clip. The instance is named hero in the Properties panel.

3. **Examine the hero clip's timeline by double-clicking the symbol in the Library panel.** You can see that the timeline has two frame labels: defense and offense. When the hero instance is moving, the defense label is shown. If the hero instance catches up to the position of the mouse cursor, the offense label is shown.

4. **Go back to the Main Timeline (that is, Scene 1), and select frame 1 of the actions layer.** Open the Actions panel (F9/Option+F9), and add the code shown in Listing 27.3. Review the comments in the code to understand its functionality.

ON the CD-ROM You can find the code for Listing 27.3 in the Listing27-3.as file located in the ch27 folder of this book's CD-ROM.

5. **Save the Flash file and test the movie (Ctrl/⌘+Enter).** Move the mouse across the movie, and watch the hero instance follow the mouse! As you move the mouse, the hero instance flips horizontally to face the appropriate direction.

LISTING 27.3

Creating Tween Instances That Follow the Mouse Cursor

```
//Import the Tween, TweenEvent and easing classes
import fl.transitions.Tween;
import fl.transitions.TweenEvent;
import fl.transitions.easing.*;

// Declare the hero instance on the Stage
//MovieClip hero;

// Establish variables to store Tween instances,
// one for the X position of the hero and
// one for the Y position of the hero
var twX:Tween;
var twY:Tween;

// Add an event listener for mouse movement
// on the main stage
this.stage.addEventListener(MouseEvent.MOUSE_MOVE, updateHero);

// Create a listener function for mouse movement
function updateHero(evt:MouseEvent):void {

  // Retrieve the current position of the mouse
  var xPos:Number = this.mouseX;
  var yPos:Number = this.mouseY;

  // Establish the duration of a tween, in seconds
  var duration:Number = 1;

  // If a Tween instance has not been created yet
  if(twX == null){

    //  Create a new Tween for the X position
    twX = new Tween(
            hero,
            "x",
            Regular.easeOut,
            hero.x, // Start value: current hero X position
            xPos, // End value: current mouse X position
            duration,
            true
        );
```

continued

LISTING 27.3   (continued)

```
    // Create a new Tween for the Y position
    twY = new Tween(
            hero,
            "y",
            Regular.easeOut,
            hero.y, // Start value: current hero Y position
            yPos, // End value: current mouse Y position
            duration,
            true
        );

    // Whenever the X position Tween instance
    // starts (or restarts), show the defense frame
    twX.addEventListener(TweenEvent.MOTION_START, onMotionStarted);

    // Whenever the X position Tween instance
    // finishes its motion, show the offense frame
    twX.addEventListener(TweenEvent.MOTION_FINISH, onMotionFinished);

// If a Tween instance has already been initiated
} else {
    // Change the end value of the X position Tween instance
    // to the new X position of the mouse
    twX.continueTo(xPos, duration);

    // Change the end value of the Y position Tween instance
    // to the new Y position of the mouse
    twY.continueTo(yPos, duration);

    // Retrieve the current absolute scale of the hero
    var scale:Number = Math.abs(hero.scaleX);

    // If the end value of the X position Tween instance
    // is to the right of the mouse, use a positive X scale value.
    // Otherwise, if the end value is to the left of the mouse,
    // invert the X scale value to flip the graphic horizontally
    hero.scaleX = (twX.finish > twX.position) ? scale : -scale;
}
}
```

```
// Whenever the X position Tween instance
// starts (or restarts), show the defense frame
function onMotionStarted(evt:TweenEvent):void {
  hero.gotoAndStop("defense");
}

// Whenever the X position Tween instance
// finishes its motion, show the offense frame
function onMotionFinished(evt:TweenEvent):void {
  hero.gotoAndStop("offense");
}
```

ON the CD-ROM You can find the completed file, `tween_as3_follow_mouse.fla`, in the `ch27` folder of this book's CD-ROM.

WEB RESOURCE We'd like to know what you think about this chapter. Visit `www.flashsupport.com/feedback` to send us your comments.

Summary

- The ActionScript 3.0 Tween class enables you to manipulate any numeric property of an object. The Tween class is especially useful for animating properties of the MovieClip class.

- The Tween class can utilize six easing classes. Each class has easeIn, easeOut, and easeInOut functions.

- The Tween.yoyo() method reverses the start and end values of a Tween instance and restarts the cycle.

- You can detect Tween events by using TweenEvent.MOTION_START and TweenEvent.MOTION_FINISH event listeners with the Tween instance.

- You can update the end of a Tween instance by using the continueTo() method.

Chapter 28

Sharing and Loading Assets

ecause most Flash movies are downloaded and viewed over the Web, ActionScript 3.0 has a number of advanced actions that are dedicated solely to controlling the download and display of movies and library assets. Actions that check the loaded bytes of a Flash movie file (.swf) or media file let developers prevent a movie from playing before a specified portion of it has finished loading. The Loader class enables Flash content to be broken into small pieces or assets that are downloaded only when they are needed.

> **TIP** ActionScript 3.0 can load PNG, GIF, and progressive JPEG images into your Flash movies, in addition to MP3, .flv, and .swf files. We show you how to load these media files in this chapter.

> **NOTE** This chapter discusses ActionScript 3.0 implementations of asset loading and sharing. For legacy ActionScript 2.0 applications, refer to earlier editions of the *Flash Bible* series (Wiley).

Managing Smooth Movie Download and Display

When Flash movies are played back over the Internet, they *progressively download*, meaning that the Flash Player plug-in shows as much of the movie as it can during download, even if the whole file has not been transferred to the user's system or browser cache. The benefit of this feature is that users start seeing content without having to wait for the entire movie to finish downloading.

> **NOTE** Technically, a Flash movie file is not a streaming file format, but a progressive download file format. A progressive download can be viewed before the browser receives the entire file. Streaming file formats are never saved as actual files in the browser cache. You can't save a true streaming file, but you can typically save a shortcut or link to the file's location on the Web. Adobe Flash Media Server audio and video streams, for example, cannot be cached as a file on the user's system.

Nevertheless, progressive downloading has potential drawbacks. During download and playback, the movie may unexpectedly halt at arbitrary points on the timeline because a required portion of the movie has not yet downloaded. Worse yet, if you use several linked assets (that is, assets in the library that are set to export for ActionScript, such as components), by default the first frame of your Flash movie won't play until all those assets have downloaded.

Thankfully, there's a solution. You can regulate the playback of the movie by using ActionScript code to prevent the movie from playing until a specified portion of it has downloaded. This technique is often referred to as *preloading*. A common preload sequence, or *preloader,* involves displaying only a short message, such as "Loading . . . Please Wait," while the movie loads. After the appropriate amount of the movie has been retrieved, the movie is allowed to play. ActionScript provides basic and advanced methods of producing a preloader. There are two ways to check the download status of a Flash movie with ActionScript 3.0:

- `MovieClip.framesLoaded` **and** `MovieClip.totalFrames`: These properties can be checked on a Movie Clip timeline or the main movie timeline (Scene 1, Scene 2, and so on). `framesLoaded` returns the current number of frames that have downloaded into the plug-in, whereas `totalFrames` returns the number of frames that exist on the specified target timeline.

- `LoaderInfo.bytesLoaded` **and** `LoaderInfo.bytesTotal`: The most accurate way to check the progress of a Flash movie download is to use these methods with ActionScript code. You can use these methods to check the download progress of SWF, JPEG, progressive JPEG, PNG, and GIF files with the `Loader` class.

In this edition of the book, we show you how to use the latter method in ActionScript to check the download progress of movie assets.

> **CROSS-REF** You can find our coverage of Flash Player 3 and 4 movie preloaders in *Flash 5 Bible* (Wiley, 2001). Other ActionScript 2.0 methods can be found in *Flash CS3 Professional Bible* (Wiley, 2007).

Preloading a Flash Movie

In this section, you learn how to preload a Flash movie whose assets are all internal. You construct a movie timeline containing a preload section. This section contains two consecutive frames that loop until the entire movie has loaded into the Flash Player. While the movie is loading, a loader graphic updates to display the progress of the download. In the following steps, you learn how to build such a preloader.

> **NOTE** The method described in this exercise is compatible with Flash Player 5 and later. Later in this chapter, you learn how to adapt this method to a Flash Player 6 and later routine.

> **ON the CD-ROM** Make a copy of the `preloader_as3_starter.fla` file, located in the `ch28` folder of this book's CD-ROM.

1. With the starter file open in Flash CS4, resave the document as `preloader_as3_100.fla`.

> **NOTE** If you choose File ➪ Publish Settings and click the Flash tab, you'll notice that this movie is set to export as a Flash Player 10 movie. All code is written in the ActionScript 3.0 syntax.

2. Rename Layer 1 to content.

3. **Create an empty keyframe (F7) on frame 10 of the content layer.** Drag an instance of the pilonsImage symbol to the Stage on this keyframe. Center the instance on the Stage. Select frame 20 of the content layer and press F5 to extend the layer to this frame.

4. **Create a new layer and rename it** labels. Place this layer at the top of the layer stack.

5. **Add a keyframe on frame 2 of the labels layer.** In the Properties panel, assign this frame a label of **preload**.

6. **Add a keyframe on frame 10 of the labels layer and label this frame main in the Properties panel.** Your document should now resemble Figure 28.1.

7. **Create a new layer and name it** loaderDisplay. Place this layer underneath the labels layer.

8. **With frame 1 of the loader layer highlighted, select the Rectangle tool — do *not* use the Rectangle Primitive tool for this step.** Make sure that you have a stroke and fill color specified in the Tools panel. Draw a rectangle on the Stage. In the Properties panel, size both the stroke and fill of the rectangle to 300 x 10. This rectangle is the progress bar that grows as the movie's bytes load into the Flash Player.

> **TIP** If you select the Rectangle tool in the Tools panel and press Alt (or Option on Mac) when you first click the Stage, you'll get a Rectangle Settings dialog box that enables you to enter the width and height of the rectangle shape to draw.

FIGURE 28.1

The content of this movie starts on the main label.

9. **With the stroke and fill of the rectangle selected, press F8.** In the Convert to Symbol dialog box, choose the Movie Clip type. Name the symbol **LoaderDisplay** and click the top left registration point, as shown in Figure 28.2. Click OK.

FIGURE 28.2

The rectangle artwork will be part of the loader symbol.

10. **With the new instance selected on the Stage of the Main Timeline, name the instance** `loaderDisplay` **in the Properties panel.**

11. **Double-click the** `loaderDisplay` **instance on the Stage.** In Edit mode, rename Layer 1 of the loader symbol to **bar**. Create another layer and name it **frame**. Make sure that the frame layer is above the bar layer.

12. **Select the stroke of the rectangle and cut it (Ctrl+X/⌘+X).** Select frame 1 of the frame layer and paste the stroke in place (Edit ⇨ Paste in Place, or Ctrl+Shift+V/ ⌘+Shift+V).

13. **On the bar layer, select the fill of the rectangle.** Convert this fill to a Movie Clip symbol named **bar**. In the Convert to Symbol dialog box, choose the middle left registration point, as shown in Figure 28.3.

14. **With the new instance selected on the Stage of the LoaderDisplay symbol, name the instance `bar` in the Properties panel.** In the Transform panel, scale the width of the instance to 1.0%, as shown in Figure 28.4. Be sure that the X position for the bar instance is set to 0. When the movie first starts to load, you do not want the `bar` instance scaled at full size (100%) — as the bytes of the movie load into the Flash Player, the `scaleX` of the `bar` instance increases. (You will insert the code to do this later.)

FIGURE 28.3

The bar symbol settings

FIGURE 28.4

Decrease the X scale of the `bar` instance to 1.0% in the Transform panel.

15. **Create another layer and name it** text. Place this layer at the bottom of the layer stack.

16. **Select the Text tool and create a Dynamic Text field on frame 1 of the text layer.** Place the text field underneath the `bar` instance, as shown in Figure 28.5. In the Properties panel, assign an instance name of `labelField`. You will use this text field to display the current percent loaded of the Flash movie. You do not need to enable the Show Border option (or other options) for this text field.

17. Go back to the Main Timeline (that is, Scene 1). Select the `loaderDisplay` instance on the Stage and center it by using the Align panel. Select frame 4 of the loader layer and insert an empty keyframe (F7). You only need the `loaderDisplay` instance to appear as the movie is preloading.

18. Create a new layer and name it actions. Place this layer underneath the labels layer.

19. Select frame 1 of the actions layer and open the Actions panel (F9/Option+F9). In the Script pane, type the following code:

```
// Declare a count variable to pause at 100% load
var count:int = 0;
```

20. Select frame 3 of the actions layer and insert an empty keyframe (F7). With this frame selected, open the Actions panel (F9/Option+F9). In the Script pane, type the code shown in Listing 28.1. (Do not type the ⤶ character in your actual code. This symbol indicates a continuation of the same line of code.) Each line of code is explained in comments within the code.

FIGURE 28.5

The `labelField` instance displays the current percent loaded of the movie.

21. Save your Flash document and test it (Ctrl+Enter/⌘+Return). When you enter Test Movie mode, choose View ➪ Simulate Download or press Ctrl+Enter/ ⌘+Return again. As shown in Figure 28.6, you will see the movie's download progress reflected in the `scaleX` property of the `bar` instance as well as an updating percent value and total file size in the `labelField` instance. When the movie is fully loaded, the `loaderDisplay` instance pauses for about a second and goes to the `main` label.

FIGURE 28.6

The progress bar grows as the movie loads into the Flash Player.

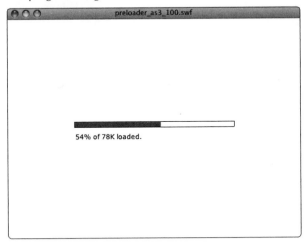

LISTING 28.1

The Preloading Script Routine

```
// lb stores the current bytes that have loaded

var lb:Number = this.loaderInfo.bytesLoaded;

// tb stores the total bytes of the movie

var tb:Number = this.loaderInfo.bytesTotal;

// pl calculates the portion (as a fraction) of the
// movie that has loaded into the Flash Player.

var pl:Number = lb/tb;

// Apply the pl value to the X scale of the bar
// instance within the loaderDisplay instance

loaderDisplay.bar.scaleX = pl;
```

continued

LISTING 28.1   *(continued)*

```
// Fill the labelField instance within the loaderDisplay
// instance with the pl value followed by the text
// "% of " and the total kilobytes of the movie. For
// example, when half of a 64K movie has loaded, the text
// field will display "50% of 64K loaded."

loaderDisplay.labelField.text = Math.floor(pl*100) + "% of " + ↵
  Math.floor(tb/1024) + "K loaded.";

// If the loaded bytes are greater than or equal to the
// total bytes of the movie and the total bytes are
// greater than 0

if (lb >= tb && tb > 0) {

  // Check to see if the count variable is greater than
  // or equal to 12. If it is, execute the nested code.
  // This if/else code pauses the movie once 100% of the
  // movie has loaded into the Flash Player.

  if (count >= 12) {

    // exit the loading sequence

    gotoAndStop("main");

  // otherwise, if the movie has completely loaded and
  // count is less than 12.

  } else {

    // add 1 to the count variable
    count++;

    // continue to loop the loading sequence
    gotoAndPlay("preload");
  }

// if the movie hasn't finished loading into the Flash
// Player then execute this code

} else {

  // loop back to the "preload" frame label
  gotoAndPlay("preload");
}
```

Preloading a Flash Movie Containing Components

If you've used any of the ActionScript 3.0 User Interface or Video components (including the FLVPlayback component), you may have noticed that the file size of your Flash movie jumps significantly. Adding a List component and a TextInput component to your Flash movie, for example, adds about 31KB to your final .swf file's size! More important, by default, these components export on frame 1 of the Flash movie, as do their respective ActionScript 3.0 (AS3) class files. Despite the fact that you can specify the export frame for AS3 class files in the Advanced ActionScript 3.0 Settings dialog box (File ⇨ Publish Settings, Flash tab, Settings button for ActionScript), Flash CS4 still exports most, if not all, AS3 class files on frame 1. Your best bet is to forgo the creation of an internal preloader for this type of Flash content, and load the SWF into another smaller SWF at runtime. You learn how to load an external SWF file in the next section.

ON the CD-ROM You can find the completed file, `preloader_as3_100.fla`, in the `ch28` folder of this book's CD-ROM.

CAUTION We recommend against using the `ProgressBar` (ActionScript 3.0) component for internal preloading. Because the component itself weighs nearly 16K, the first frame of the movie "pauses" on an empty screen until the component has fully loaded. The `ProgressBar` component is truly designed to work with external assets, as we discuss in Chapter 32, "Using Components."

Loading Flash Movies

A long sequence of Flash animation or any Flash movie that contains many internal assets naturally requires the preloading described in the previous section to guarantee smooth playback. But traditional information-based Web sites done in Flash require a different kind of download management. Suppose you're building a Web site with three sections: products, staff, and company history. Each section is roughly 100K in size. In a normal Flash movie, you'd place those sections in a sequential order on the Main Timeline or create a scene for each of them. The last section you place on the timeline would, of course, be the last section to download. Might sound fine so far, but here's the problem: What if the section that appears last on the timeline happens to be the first and only section the users want to see? They'd have to wait for the other two sections to download before they could view the one they want — but they don't even want to see the other two sections, so really they're waiting for nothing. The solution to this problem is the `Loader` class.

NOTE It's not just a matter of the user waiting for a Flash movie to load; it's also an issue of bandwidth. You can rack up unnecessary bandwidth usage fees with your Web hosting provider. You wouldn't want to download every page of an HTML site just to look at one page of it, and the same principle applies to Flash movies. Paying careful attention to your Flash movie architecture not only saves your users time, but it can also save you money.

The `Loader` class provides a means of inserting one or more external .swf files into a Flash movie (whether that movie resides in a browser or on its own in the stand-alone player). The `Loader` class can be used to display multiple movies simultaneously. It can also be used, as in our company Web site example, to enable a parent movie to retrieve and display content kept in independent .swf files on a need-to-retrieve basis (similar to the way a frame in an HTML frameset can call external pages into different frames).

 TIP You can use the `Loader` class to load JPEG images directly into your Flash movies. We show you how to load JPEG files later in this chapter.

TIP If you are concerned about getting accurate usage statistics in your Web server's access logs, you can use the `Loader` class to break up the content on your Flash-based site. If all of your content is stored in one Flash movie file (.swf), you will only see that the Web user has downloaded the site file; you have no idea which sections of the site the user has actually visited. By breaking up the Flash movie into several smaller files, your site's access logs will show which section of .swf files the user downloaded and viewed.

Basic overview of Flash site architecture

You can produce and distribute straight Flash content on the Web in the following two primary ways:

- Create several small .swf files, with each one living within a standard HTML page on a Web site.
- Create one HTML page that hosts one main .swf file that loads additional content through the Flash Player plug-in.

Figure 28.7 illustrates these alternatives.

FIGURE 28.7

The diagram on the left illustrates a Web site that uses multiple HTML pages, each with an individual .swf file. The diagram on the right shows a Web site that uses one HTML page (or frameset, or iframe) that has one primary .swf file, which loads other .swf files as needed.

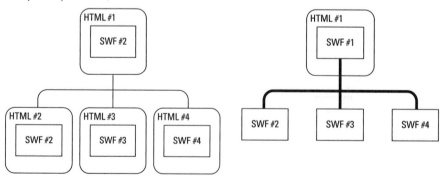

If you decide to break up your Flash movies across several HTML pages, your site visitors will experience the following:

- Short download times for each page
- Easy bookmarking of discrete sections of your Web site
- Abrupt transitions between each section of the Web site

However, if you use one primary Flash movie in one HTML page, your visitors benefit from:

- Short download times for each SWF file (download times vary with file size)
- Seamless integration of new Flash content
- Controllable transitions between SWF asset changes

Which method should you use for your Flash projects? The answer depends on the specifics of each Web project. You may decide to use a combination of both methods, especially for larger sites that use several technologies (Apple QuickTime, Adobe Flash, Real Networks RealPlayer, Microsoft Windows Media, and so on). In either scenario, you can use the `Loader` class to manage Flash content more easily.

TIP Because the Flash Player enables you to download JPEG, MP3, and video content, you may not need to rely on other plug-in technologies for the Web sites you design and develop. Each player version since Flash Player 6 has only expanded the options for runtime asset loading.

Loading an external .swf file into a movie

A new movie is imported into the Flash Player when the `Loader` class is utilized. In the following steps, you'll learn how to make a button click load an external movie named `bandwidth.swf`.

ON the CD-ROM Before you begin these steps, make a copy the `bandwidth.swf` file from the `ch28` folder of this book's CD-ROM. Copy the file to the location on your hard drive where you will save the new Flash document in the forthcoming exercise.

1. **Create a new Flash file (ActionScript 3.0).** Save this document as `loader_100.fla` in the same location as your copy of the `bandwidth.swf` file.

2. **Rename Layer 1 to** loadButton.

3. **Drag an instance of the** `Button` **component from the Component panel to your document's Stage.** Place the instance in the lower left corner of the stage. In the Properties panel, name the component `loadButton`. In the Parameters tab of the Component Inspector panel (Window ➪ Component Inspector), select the `label` field and type `load movie`. Refer to Figure 28.8 to see this setting.

4. **Create a new layer and rename it** actions.

CROSS-REF We discuss components more thoroughly in Chapter 32, "Using Components."

FIGURE 28.8

The parameters for the `loadButton` instance

5. **Select frame 1 of the actions layer and open the Actions panel (F9/Option+F9).** In the Script pane, type the code shown in Listing 28.2. This code creates a listener function for the `loadButton` instance. When the `loadButton` instance is clicked, the `band-width.swf` movie loads into a `Loader` instance.

6. **Save your Flash document and test it by choosing Control ⇨ Test Movie (Ctrl+Enter/⌘+Return).** When you click the `loadButton` instance, the `bandwidth.swf` movie's top left corner aligns with the top left corner of the hosting SWF's Stage (see Figure 28.9). You can reload the same .swf file by clicking the load movie button again.

FIGURE 28.9

The `bandwidth.swf` file loads into the top left corner of the Stage.

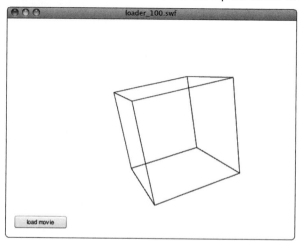

CAUTION Make sure that you copied the `bandwidth.swf` file from the book's CD-ROM to the same location as the `loader_100.fla` document. Otherwise, the `Loader` actions will fail.

NOTE The loaded .swf file inherits the frame rate of the base .swf file, regardless of the original frame rate assigned to the loaded SWF at authortime.

LISTING 28.2

The Listener Code for the loadButton Instance

```
//Button loadButton;

// Listen for the click event on the loadButton instance
loadButton.addEventListener(MouseEvent.CLICK, onLoadClick);

// Define the listener function
function onLoadClick(evt:MouseEvent):void {
  //Create a new Loader instance
  var loader:Loader = new Loader();
  // Load the SWF file into the instance
  loader.load(new URLRequest("bandwidth.swf"));
  // Add the instance to the main timeline's display list
  addChild(loader);
}
```

You can apply this technique to any .swf file that you want to load into another Flash movie. You can make a series of buttons, each one loading a different .swf file. You can modify the `onLoad-Click()` function to switch the URL of the loaded movie, depending on which button is pressed.

 You can find the completed example file, `loader_100.fla`, in the `ch28` folder of this book's CD-ROM.

When a movie is loaded above any other movie (including the main movie), the buttons and Movie Clips in the movies on lower depths continue to be active, even though they may not be visible. To prevent this undesired behavior, you need to send movies on lower depths to an idle or blank frame where no buttons are present. Do that by adding a `goto` action before your `Loader` actions that sends the current movie to the idle frame. This technique is known as "parking" the movie. If you have to park multiple movies, you'll need to know how to communicate between movies on different levels. We discuss this shortly.

How Flash handles loaded movies of differing dimensions

A loaded movie that is smaller in width and height than the base movie is positioned in the top left corner of the Stage. You may have noticed this phenomenon in the last section. In this situation, it is possible to have elements that are off-stage within the loaded .swf file. However, when you load a smaller .swf file Stage into a larger .swf file Stage, these off-stage elements appear on the Stage of the larger .swf file. To prevent objects from appearing, you would have to create a curtain layer or a mask layer above all the other layers in the loaded movie that covers up the *work area* (the space outside the movie's Stage).

Placing, scaling, and rotating externally loaded Flash movies

Especially when your movies have different width and height dimensions, it's not very convenient to have newly loaded movies dropped ingloriously in the top left corner of the Stage. To give you more flexibility with the placement, rotation, and scale of your loaded movies, ActionScript provides the capability to reposition the loaded Flash movie file (.swf) via the `Loader` instance. But, if you don't want to do every transformation in code, you can add the `Loader` instance to an authortime `MovieClip` instance. So far, this may not make a whole lot of sense. Adding a `Loader` instance to a `MovieClip` instance seems like a strange feature at first, until you find out what it can do — then it seems indispensable. The easiest way to understand what happens when you load a movie into a `MovieClip` instance is to think of this procedure as a "Convert Loaded Movie to MovieClip instance" action.

When a movie is added to a `MovieClip` instance, many attributes of the original `MovieClip` instance are applied to the newly loaded movie. The loaded movie assumes the following properties from the original `MovieClip` instance:

- Scale percentage
- Color effects, including alpha
- Rotation degree
- Placement (X and Y position)
- Visibility (with respect to the `visible` property)

We like to refer to `MovieClip` instances that are used to load other movies as `MovieClip` holders. Usually, you load movies into empty Movie Clips that don't have any artwork or actions.

However, because you may need a physical reference to the actual area that your loaded movie will occupy on the Stage, it's useful to create temporary guides or artwork that indicates this area.

The following steps show you how to create a `MovieClip` holder and how to load an external .swf file into it. You will use the same file you created in the previous section.

 If you didn't complete the example in the last section, make a copy of the `loader_100.fla` file located in the `ch28` folder of this book's CD-ROM. You will also need to copy the `bandwidth.swf` file from the folder.

1. Open the `loader_100.fla` document. Resave this document as `loader_101.fla`.

2. **Create a new layer on the Main Timeline and rename the layer to** holder. Place this layer at the bottom of the layer stack.

3. **Select the Rectangle tool and draw a rectangle on frame 1 of the holder layer.** The shape should have the same dimensions as the external Flash movie's Stage, as defined in its Document Properties dialog box. For our example, size the rectangle to 640 x 400 by using the Properties panel.

NOTE You do not need to include an outline (or stroke) with the rectangle artwork.

TIP In Flash CS4, you can select the Rectangle tool and Alt/Option+click the Stage to enter custom width and height settings for a new rectangle shape.

4. **With the rectangle selected, choose Modify** ⇨ **Convert to Symbol or press F8 to convert the artwork into a symbol.** In the Convert to Symbol dialog box, name the symbol Holder and choose the Movie Clip type. In the Registration grid, click the top left corner point, as shown in Figure 28.10. Movies loaded into Movie Clip instances load from the top left corner of the original target Movie Clip instance.

FIGURE 28.10

An instance of the Holder symbol will hold the loaded .swf file.

5. **With the new instance on the Stage selected, name the instance** `holder` **in the Properties panel.** Position the instance on the Stage, where you want the external SWF movie to appear. At this point, you can also tween, scale, or apply any color effect to the instance as well. For our example, apply an orange tint to the instance in the Properties panel, and reduce the size of the instance by 50% in the Transform panel.

6. **After you've manipulated the** `holder` **instance, edit the original Holder symbol by double-clicking the symbol in the Library panel.** Convert the layer within the symbol's timeline to a guide layer by right-clicking (Control+clicking on Mac) the layer icon and selecting Guide from the context menu. Guide layers do not export with the .swf file.

   Now, you need to modify the `onLoadClick` function called by the `loadButton` component instance (already on the document's Stage). This method needs to target the `holder` instance.

7. **Select frame 1 of the actions layer on the Main Timeline.** Open the Actions panel (F9 /Option+F9 on Mac) and change the script to the following lines shown in bold:

```
//Button loadButton;
//MovieClip holder;

// Listen for the click event on the loadButton instance
loadButton.addEventListener(MouseEvent.CLICK, onLoadClick);

// Define the listener function
function onLoadClick(evt:MouseEvent):void {
  //Create a new Loader instance
  var loader:Loader = new Loader();
  // Load the SWF file into the instance
  loader.load(new URLRequest("bandwidth.swf"));
  // Add the instance to the main timeline's display list
  holder.addChild(loader);
}
```

> **NOTE**   The instance must be present on Stage at the time the `addChild()` action occurs.

8. **Save the Flash document and test it (Ctrl+Enter/⌘+Enter).** When you click the load movie button, the `bandwidth.swf` file loads into the top left corner of the `holder` instance. The orange tint effect and transform values applied to the `holder` instance also apply to the loaded movie.

If you need to add functionality to the loaded movie, use ActionScript to control the new loaded movie instance. The next section shows you how to communicate with loaded movies.

> **ON the CD-ROM**   You can view the completed file, `loader_101.fla`, in the `ch28` folder of this book's CD-ROM.

Loading External Files through Proxy Servers

If you are creating Flash movies that will be loaded through proxy servers set up by internal company networks or large Internet service providers (ISPs) on the Internet, you may need to know how to trick them into loading "fresh" .swf files every time a user visits your site. What is a proxy server? With the growth of high-speed Internet connections, such as DSL and cable, many networks process all outgoing HTTP requests through a go-between computer that caches previous requests to the same URL. Anytime you type a Web site URL into a browser, you're making an HTTP request. If that computer, called a *proxy server*, sees a request that was made previously (within a certain time frame), it serves its cached content to the end user instead of downloading the actual content from the remote server.

Why do you need to be concerned about caching? If you or your client needs accurate usage statistics for a Web site, you will likely want to know which portions of the site your users are actively using (that is, downloading into their browsers). Your Web server does not log a request it never receives — if a proxy server delivers the content to the end user, you will not even know a user is looking at your content.

When a Flash movie makes an HTTP request with a URLRequest instance, a proxy server may serve the cached .swf file instead of the one that actually exists on your server. Why is this a problem? If you are updating that .swf file frequently or if you want precise Web usage statistics for your Flash movies and content, then you'll want users to download the actual .swf file on your server each time a request is made.

The question remains: How do you trick a proxy server into serving the real .swf file rather than its cached one? The proxy server knows what's in its cache by the URL for each cached item. So, if you change the name of the loaded Flash movie each time you make a request for it, the proxy server won't ever see an identical match with its cached content.

To change the name of a loaded Flash movie, simply add a random number to the end of the movie's name in the URLRequest wrapper. This random number won't actually be part of the movie's filename. Rather, it will appear as a query at the end of the filename. Place the following actions on the event handler that initiates a loadMovie() action:

```
var today:String = escape(new Date().toString());
loader.load(new URLRequest("external_1.swf?cacheBuster=" + today));
```

In the preceding example, a variable called today is established and given a value of the current date and time. Each time the event handler calling these actions is executed, a different date is appended to the filename of the loaded movie. The proxy server thinks that each request is different and routes the request to your Web server.

Not only does this method prevent a proxy server from serving a cached Flash movie file, it also prevents some browsers from caching the loaded movie in the user's local cache folder.

Loading Images into Flash Movies

Flash Player has the incredible capability to load all the popular Web image formats into a Flash movie at runtime — while the movie plays in a Web browser! In this section, you learn how to pull off this feat.

Some basic rules for using images that are loaded into Flash movies are as follows:

- Use only supported image formats, which include PNG (all bit depths), GIF, standard JPEG, and progressive JPEG image files. You cannot load JPEG 2000 images into Flash movies.

- Watch the file size of image files. Unless your image files are extremely small and/or within a reasonable limit of your target audience's data rate, you will likely want to build a preloader for your JPEG files.

- All images that are loaded dynamically will be smoothed in the Flash Player. Smoothed bitmaps may have an adverse effect on playback performance. You can control the global rendering of bitmaps and all artwork by using the `Stage.quality` property of any `DisplayObject` instance. For example, `this.stage.quality = StageQuality.LOW;` turns off smoothing for all artwork. Use this property with care: Most vector artwork and text looks unsightly with low-quality rendering.

- Control the physical characteristics of the image (X and Y coordinates, X and Y scale, rotation, and so on) by controlling those properties of the `Loader` (or parent) instance holding the image.

- Check the user's version of the Flash Player with ActionScript or JavaScript. The user must have Flash Player 9 or later to load all these image formats directly into Flash movies published with ActionScript 3.0. We discuss Flash Player detection in Chapter 20, "Publishing Flash Movies," and Chapter 21, "Integrating Flash Content with Web Pages."

CROSS-REF Keep in mind general issues for bitmap usage in Flash movies. Read our coverage of using bitmap images in Chapter 15, "Importing Artwork."

When in doubt, test the specific JPEG images with your Flash movies. If you encounter problems with loading the JPEG, check the following:

- **URL:** Make sure that you have the correct path and filename specified in the `URLRequest` wrapper.

- **Format:** Is the image a supported format? Or does it use an unsupported encoding such as JPEG 2000?

Without further ado, we'll show you how to create a Flash movie that dynamically loads a JPEG image. In this example, you load a JPEG file located in the same directory as the Flash movie file (.swf). In ActionScript, the `Loader` class is used to load JPEG images, using the following syntax:

```
instanceName.load(new URLRequest(URL));
```

where *instanceName* is the Loader object that holds the JPEG image and *URL* is the relative or absolute path to the JPEG file. In the following code, a JPEG file named cat.jpg is loaded into a Loader object named imageLoader:

```
imageLoader.load (new URLRequest("cat.jpg"));
```

or

```
imageLoader.load(new URLRequest("http://domain.com/cat.jpg"));
```

ON the CD-ROM **For this exercise, you will use the loader_101.fla document that we discussed earlier in this chapter. You can also make a copy of this completed file from the ch28 folder of this book before you begin this exercise. You need to copy the beach.jpg file in this location to your local folder as well.**

In the following steps, you create a Flash movie that can load an external image file:

1. **Open a copy of the loader_101.fla document.** Resave this file as loader_image_101.fla.

2. **In the Library panel, double-click the Holder symbol.** Right-click its only layer, and choose the checked Guide option to convert the layer back to a normal layer. Go back to editing the Main Timeline (that is, Scene 1) when you are done.

3. **Remove the tint effect from the holder instance.** Select the instance, and choose None in the Style menu of the Color Effect section of the Properties panel. Also, position the holder instance at the coordinate 18, 18 in the Properties panel.

4. **Create a new layer named** imageField. Place this layer anywhere above the holder layer.

5. **On Frame 1 of the imageField layer, select the Text tool and create an Input text field above the load movie button.** With the text field selected, open the Properties panel and name the instance imageField. Enable the Show Border option as well. In the Paragraph section of the Properties panel, choose Single line in the Behavior menu. When you are finished, your document's Stage should resemble Figure 28.11.

6. **Select the loadButton instance on the Stage.** In the Component Inspector panel, change the label value to **Load Image**.

7. **Select frame 1 of the actions layer and open the Actions panel.** In the Script pane, edit the code to reflect the bold changes shown in Listing 28.3.

    Here, you add a reference to the imageField instance as a code comment at the top of the script, to enable code hints for the instance name. You also add code to hide the initial artwork within the holder instance. In the onLoadClick() function, you retrieve the current text in the imageField instance and use it as the URL of the load() method. When the loadButton component instance is clicked, the onLoadClick function executes and loads the image file specified in the imageField instance into the holder instance.

FIGURE 28.11

The `imageField` instance specifies the path to the JPEG image.

8. **Save your Flash document and test it (Ctrl+Enter/⌘+Return).** In the Test Movie window, type `beach.jpg` in the text field. When you click the load button, the `beach.jpg` image loads into the `holder` instance.

LISTING 28.3

Modifying the onLoadClick Function

```
//Button loadButton;
//MovieClip holder;
//TextField imageField;

// Listen for the click event on the loadButton instance
loadButton.addEventListener(MouseEvent.CLICK, onLoadClick);

// Hide the artwork inside of the holder instance
var shape:Shape = holder.getChildAt(0) as Shape;
shape.visible = false;
```

```
// Define the listener function
function onLoadClick(evt:MouseEvent):void {
    // Create a new Loader instance
    var loader:Loader = new Loader();
    // Retrieve the text from the textfield
    var imgURL:String = imageField.text;
    // Load the new URL into the loader instance
    loader.load(new URLRequest(imgURL));
    // Add the instance to the main timeline's display list
    holder.addChild(loader);
}
```

Try typing other known image URL locations into the text field. For example, you can download the same image from the following location. Be sure to type the full URL, including the `http://` protocol:

        http://www.flashsupport.com/images/beach.jpg

You can also try some of these image URLs:

        http://www.flashsupport.com/images/waterfall.png
        http://www.flashsupport.com/images/logo.gif

You may want to go back to the Flash document and move the location of the `holder` instance to better accommodate the size of the image you are loading. Remember, the `holder` instance is transformed to 50% of its original size. You can reset the transform back to 100% in the Transform panel.

Also, if you specify one image URL, press the load button, and then specify another image URL and press the button again, the images stack on top of each other. Why? The `addChild()` method of the `DisplayObject` class does not remove previous children. If you want to overwrite an existing child, use the `addChildAt()` method, specifying a fixed index value, such as 1 or 2.

You can learn how to build a loading graphic for image files in Chapter 32, "Using Components."

 You can find the completed file, `loader_image_100.fla`, in the ch28 folder of this book's CD-ROM.

Loading MP3 Audio into Flash Movies

If you thought image loading was exciting, wait until you see the support for MP3 audio loading into Flash movies. You can load MP3 files directly into `Sound` objects that you create with ActionScript 3.0.

CROSS-REF If you don't know how to use Sound objects, read our coverage of Sound objects in Chapter 26, "Interacting with Movie Clips." You may also want to read Chapter 14, "Adding Sound," if you are unfamiliar with general sound use in Flash movies.

Here are a few tips for using MP3 files that will be loaded into Flash movies:

- Watch file size. MP3 files, especially those of full-length songs, can be very large in file size, easily exceeding 3MB. Make sure that your target audience's bandwidth can accommodate the file sizes you are loading.

- Test your specific MP3 encoding method(s) before you use the same encoding on several files that you intend to use with Flash movies. In our tests, we have not encountered problems with any MP3 files that we loaded into the Flash Player. However, there are several variations of CBR (Constant Bit Rate) and VBR (Variable Bit Rate) encoding methods available across audio applications.

- Depending on the Flash Player release version, MP3 files may not cache on the user's hard drive. All MP3 files loaded through the Sound object in ActionScript are stored in the computer's virtual memory. Be careful with the number of MP3 files downloaded and stored in memory simultaneously.

CROSS-REF Review the troubleshooting tips we listed for the Loader class and images in the previous section. The same principles apply to MP3 files.

The core method to the Sound object that can access external MP3 files is the load() method. With this method, you can specify a path to an MP3 file just like you did for JPEG images with the Loader.load() method. However, the load() method has an additional argument: SoundLoaderContext. We discuss this in a moment. The syntax for using the Sound.load() method is:

```
soundObject.load(URLRequest, SoundLoaderContext);
```

soundObject indicates the name of a Sound object created previously in ActionScript 3.0, and URLRequest is the relative or absolute path to the MP3 file. SoundLoaderContext is an instance of the SoundLoaderContext class that specifies the buffer time and security measures for the MP3 file. The SoundLoaderContext.bufferTime property is a Number value specifying the number of milliseconds of the MP3 file that must download before playback begins. The SoundLoaderContext.checkPolicyFile property is a Boolean value (true or false) that determines whether a cross-domain policy file should be downloaded before loading the MP3 file. A policy file is an XML file located on a remote server where the MP3 file resides. You only need to worry about a policy file if the Flash movie (.swf file) and the MP3 file don't reside on the same domain. For more information on this property, refer to the SoundLoaderContent class definition in the Flash CS4 Help pages.

ON the CD-ROM Before you begin the following exercise, make a copy of the `loader_image_100.fla` file located in the `ch28` folder of this book's CD-ROM. You will modify the existing structure of the document that you built in earlier sections of this chapter. You also need an MP3 file copied to the same location on your hard drive. You can use the `atmospheres_1.mp3` file located in the `resources` folder as well.

In the following steps, you learn how to load an MP3 file into a `Sound` object.

1. **Open the `loader_image_100.fla` document.** Resave this document as `sound_load_100.fla`.

2. **Select the load image Button component instance on the Stage.** In the Parameters tab of the Component Inspector panel, change the label value to **load mp3**.

3. **Select the Input text field on the Stage and change the instance's name to `soundField` in the Properties panel.**

   Now you need to change the ActionScript in the document to use the `Sound`, `SoundChannel`, and `SoundLoaderContext` classes.

4. **Select frame 1 of the actions layer and open the Actions panel (F9/ Option+F9).** Change the code in the Script pane to match the code shown in Listing 28.4.

   In line 3, you rename the code hint comment to indicate the new name of the TextField instance from Step 4. In lines 13 and 15, you declare the variable names that will be used throughout the script. Here, you add a `Sound` variable named `mp3Sound` which creates a new `Sound` instance in line 13, and a placeholder variable named `mp3Channel` to later store a `SoundChannel` instance.

   In lines 19–30, the `onLoadClick()` listener function is invoked by the `loadButton` instance. In line 21, the URL of the MP3 file is grabbed from the `soundField` instance. In lines 24 and 25, a new `SoundLoaderContext` instance is created to control the buffer time for the MP3 file. In line 27, the `load()` method of the `mp3Sound` instance is executed, using the URL specified in the `soundField` instance. The playback of the sound is controlled with the `mp3Channel` instance, set in line 29.

5. **Save your Flash document and test it (Ctrl+Enter/⌘+Return).** In the Test Movie window, type `atmospheres_1.mp3` into the `soundField` instance. Click the load mp3 button, and the MP3 begins to play.

LISTING 28.4

Using Sound.load() for External MP3 Files

```
1.   //Button loadButton;
2.   //MovieClip holder;
3.   //TextField soundField;
4.
5.   // Listen for the click event on the loadButton instance
6.   loadButton.addEventListener(MouseEvent.CLICK, onLoadClick);
7.
8.   // Hide the artwork inside of the holder instance
9.   var shape:Shape = holder.getChildAt(0) as Shape;
10.  shape.visible = false;
11.
12.  // Create a new Sound instance
13.  var mp3Sound:Sound = new Sound();
14.  // Declare a variable to store a new
15.  // SoundChannel instance to play the sound
16.  var mp3Channel:SoundChannel;
17.
18.  // Define the listener function
19.  function onLoadClick(evt:MouseEvent):void {
20.    // Retrieve the text from the textfield
21.    var mp3URL:String = soundField.text;
22.    // Create a SoundLoaderContext instance
23.    // to set a 5 second buffer time
24.    var slc:SoundLoaderContext = new SoundLoaderContext();
25.    slc.bufferTime = 5000;
26.    // Load the new URL into the Sound instance
27.    mp3Sound.load(new URLRequest(mp3URL), slc);
28.    // Play the sound as soon as 5 seconds has loaded
29.    mp3Channel = mp3Sound.play();
30.  }
```

Try using other URLs of MP3 files, either locally or remotely. You can specify the following URL to stream the same MP3 file from our Web server:

```
http://www.theMakers.com/sounds/atmospheres_1.mp3
```

NOTE   It may take a few moments for remote sound files to load into Flash Player.

You can continue modifying the Sound object into which the MP3 file loads. For example, you can apply the same volume and balance output control from the examples in Chapter 26, "Interacting with Movie Clips," to the Sound object in this Flash movie.

We show you how to monitor the download progress of an MP3 file (and other external files) later in this chapter.

ON the CD-ROM You can see the completed Flash document, `sound_load_100.fla`, in the `ch28` folder of this book's CD-ROM.

Loading a Flash Video into a Flash Movie

Since Flash Player 7, you have had the capability to load Flash Video files (.flv) directly into a Flash movie at runtime. With ActionScript 3.0, you can continue to load video content into Flash movies.

NEW FEATURE Flash Player 9.0.115 (or Update 3) added two new video codecs to the Flash Player: AVC/H.264 and On2 VP6-S. Be sure to use Flash Player detection scripts, as discussed in Chapter 21, "Integrating Flash Content with Web Pages," to make sure that the user has the appropriate version of the Flash Player for any given piece of video content.

CROSS-REF If you don't know what a Flash Video file (.flv) is, see Chapter 16, "Displaying Video."

TIP You could — and still can — stream Flash Video files (.flv files) with the aid of Adobe Flash Media Server. In fact, to get the best performance out of video content for the Flash Player, we still recommend that you consider Flash Media Server (or a Flash Video Streaming Service provider) as a solution for real-time audio/video streaming.

In this section, you learn how to progressively download a .flv file into a Flash movie at runtime.

ON the CD-ROM You need to make a copy of the `load_image_100.fla` document used earlier in this chapter, as well as the `stella_speak_keyed.flv` file found in the `resources` folder of this book's CD-ROM. This .flv file uses the On2 VP6 codec and features an 8-bit alpha channel.

1. **Open the `loader_image_100.fla` document, and save it as `netstream_100.fla`.**

2. **Delete the `holder` instance and layer in the document.** Delete the Holder symbol from the Library panel as well. Flash Video files are not loaded into `MovieClip` objects.

NOTE You can add a `Video` object to any `DisplayObjectContainer` instance, such as a `MovieClip` or `Sprite` instance. In this example, though, the `Video` instance that displays the video clip is added to the Main Timeline's display list.

3. **Select the** `loadButton` **instance on the Stage.** In the Parameters tab of the Component Inspector panel, change the label value to **load flv**.

4. **Select the** `imageField` **instance, and in the Properties panel, change its instance name to** `videoField`. Rename the imageField layer to **videoField** as well.

Now you're ready to add the ActionScript 3.0 code necessary to load an external .flv file, and display it in the `Video` instance.

5. **Select frame 1 of the actions layer, and open the Actions panel (F9/Option+F9).** Change the code to that shown in bold in Listing 28.5.

In line 2, you rename the `TextField` instance used on the Stage to enable code hints in the Actions panel.

In line 4, you import the `FocusManager` class, which is part of the `fl.managers` package. This class enables you to control the focus of interactive elements on the stage. In lines 9 through 12, you create a new FocusManager instance named `fm`, and set its `defaultButton` property to the `loadButton` instance. This action enables the Enter key for the `loadButton` instance. When you test the movie, make sure that you choose Control ➪ Disable Keyboard Shortcuts to remap the Enter key to the Flash movie.

> **NOTE** The `FocusManager` class is automatically available in your Flash movies whenever you add AS3 User Interface components to your Flash movie.

In lines 14 through 17, a new `NetConnection` instance named `nc` is created. This object is required as the sole parameter of the `NetStream` constructor (line 21). In line 17, the `nc` instance is connected to a `null` URL. If you were streaming content from an Adobe Flash Media Server application or Flash Video Streaming Service, you would specify an RTMP location here. For progressively downloaded .flv files from a standard Web server, though, you simply connect to a `null` location.

In line 21, a new `NetStream` instance named `ns` is created. A NetStream instance is required to play a .flv file.

In line 23, a listener function is added to the `NetStream` instance for the `NetStatusEvent.NET_STATUS` event. This listener is called whenever an event occurs on the stream. In this example, the `onNetStatus` function (lines 52 through 58) simply outputs `trace()` messages to the Output panel, letting you know what's happening with the stream.

> **NOTE** The `\t` backslash pairs shown in the `trace()` actions enable you to shift trace messages to the right, inserting tab characters. You'll see the effect of each `\t` when you test the movie.

In line 26, the `client` property of the `NetStream` instance is set to the Main Timeline, indicated by the keyword `this`. Any custom method calls from the loaded video file are directed to the `client` object. In this example, the only custom call from the FLV sample file is `onMetaData`. Therefore, a function named `onMetaData` is created on the `client` object (`this`), which is the current script.

On line 28, a buffer time is set for the stream. This value determines how many seconds of the video must download before playback begins.

Lines 33 through 40 create a new `Video` instance named `vid`. By default, new `Video` instances have a dimension of 320 x 240. The new instance is positioned at an X, Y coordinate of 20, 20 (lines 35 and 36). In line 38, the `attachNetStream()` method of the `Video` class is invoked on the `vid` instance. The parameter for the `attachNet-Stream()` method is the instance name of the `NetStream` object created in line 21. In line 40, the `vid` instance is added to the Main Timeline's display list so that the instance is visible on the Stage.

Like previous examples in this chapter, the behavior for the Button component is tied to statements within the `onLoadClick` listener function, defined in lines 43 through 48. In line 45, the URL of the video file is grabbed from the `videoField` instance. In line 47, the `play()` method of the `NetStream` class is invoked on the `ns` instance. For .flv files that are not accessed from a Flash Media Server application, the parameter for the `play()` method is the HTTP-based URL of the .flv file. You can use relative or absolute paths for this URL.

Lines 62 through 68 define the `onMetaData()` handler for the `NetStream` instance. This handler is invoked when the .flv file's metadata is received. The metadata is located at the front of the .flv file's byte order. As such, this handler invokes before the video begins to play. The file's metadata includes information describing the media file, including its `width`, `height`, and `duration`.

6. **Save your Flash document.** Make sure that you have copied the `stella_speak_keyed.flv` file from the `resources` folder of this book's CD-ROM to the location where you saved the Flash document for this exercise. Test the movie (Ctrl+Enter/ ⌘+Enter) and type the text `stella_speak_keyed.flv` into the `videoField` field. Click the load video button, and the video plays in the `vid` instance, as shown in Figure 28.12. You can now also press Enter instead of clicking the load button.

NOTE You might notice that the `stella_speak_keyed.flv` file appears distorted on playback. That particular .flv file has a frame size of 380 x 320, and the picture is being stretched on playback within the 320 x 240 dimensions of the `vid` object. In the next section, you learn how to adjust the size of the `Video` object based on the actual dimensions of the .flv file.

FIGURE 28.12

The video as it plays in the vid instance

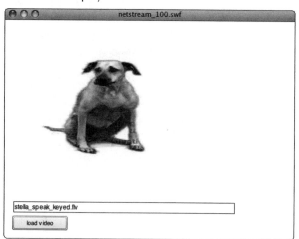

LISTING 28.5

Creating a NetStream Object to Access Flash Video Content

```
1.  //Button loadButton;
2.  //TextField videoField;
3.
4.  import fl.managers.FocusManager;
5.
6.  // Listen for the click event on the loadButton instance
7.  loadButton.addEventListener(MouseEvent.CLICK, onLoadClick);
8.
9.  // Create a new FocusManager to enable
10. // the Enter key for the loadButton instance
11. var fm:FocusManager = new FocusManager(this);
12. fm.defaultButton = loadButton;
13.
14. // Create a new NetConnection instance
15. // to use with the video file
16. var nc:NetConnection = new NetConnection();
17. nc.connect(null);
18.
19. // Create a new NetStream instance
20. // to play the video file
21. var ns:NetStream = new NetStream(nc);
```

```
22.  // Listen for status events on the NetStream
23.  ns.addEventListener(NetStatusEvent.NET_STATUS, onNetStatus);
24.  // Assign the current timeline as the client
25.  // to receive additional events
26.  ns.client = this;
27.  // Buffer 5 seconds of video before playback begins
28.  ns.bufferTime = 5;
29.
30.  // Create a Video instance to display
31.  // the video clip on stage
32.  // (default size: 320x240)
33.  var vid:Video = new Video();
34.  // Position the vid instance at 50, 50
35.  vid.x = 20;
36.  vid.y = 20;
37.  // Attach the NetStream to the vid instance
38.  vid.attachNetStream(ns);
39.  // Add the Video instance to the display list
40.  addChild(vid);
41.
42.  // Define the listener function
43.  function onLoadClick(evt:MouseEvent):void {
44.     // Retrieve the text from the textfield
45.     var vidURL:String = videoField.text;
46.     // Load and play the video
47.     ns.play(vidURL);
48.  }
49.
50.  // Define a listener function for NetStatus events
51.  // with the NetStream instance
52.  function onNetStatus(evt:NetStatusEvent):void  {
53.     trace("onNetStatus >>>");
54.     var info:Object = evt.info;
55.     // Display events related to the NetStream
56.     trace("\tlevel:\t"+info.level);
57.     trace("\tcode:\t"+info.code);
58.  }
59.
60.  // Define the onMetaData function
61.  // for the NetStream client
62.  function onMetaData(meta:Object):void  {
63.     trace("onMetaData >>>");
64.     // Display basic metadata for the video
65.     trace("\twidth: "+meta.width);
66.     trace("\theight: "+meta.height);
67.  trace("\tduration: "+meta.duration);
68.  }
```

ON the CD-ROM   You can find the completed file, `netstream_100.fla`, in the ch28 folder of this book's CD-ROM.

Try creating some of your own Flash Video files and using them with this Flash movie. Remember to go back to Chapter 16, "Displaying Video," for more information on Flash Video encoding.

Displaying a Flash Video at Its Native Size

There's the very likely possibility that when you're building a Flash user interface intended to display video, you won't be able to predict all the possible sizes of the video clips you want to play. In this section, you learn how to use the metadata encoded into .flv files in order to appropriately size the `Video` object in which the video plays.

CAUTION   Not all Flash Video encoding utilities add appropriate metadata to the .flv files they create. Most current encoding utilities, including the Adobe Media Encoder CS4 that ships with Flash CS4, add accurate metadata. If the `NetStream.onMetaData()` handler does not fire, or if it reports 0 values for the `width` and `height` properties of the clip, then it's likely that there's no metadata in the .flv file. Luckily, there are tools that can add metadata to your .flv files after you have created them. Check the "Flash Video Utilities" section of the `www.flashsupport.com/links` page for specific resources.

Before you proceed with the tutorial for this section, though, you must understand one important concept: The `Video` class has two sets of dimension properties: `videoWidth`/`videoHeight` and `width`/`height`. The `width` and `height` properties control the displayed size of the `Video` instance on the Stage, and the `videoWidth` and `videoHeight` properties report the actual dimensions of the video stream playing. You can set the `width` and `height` properties but not the `videoWidth` and `videoHeight` properties. As you'll see in the second part of this section, you can use the `videoWidth` and `videoHeight` properties to check the actual width and height of the .flv file even if there is no metadata in the .flv file.

NOTE   The `videoWidth` and `videoHeight` properties of the `Video` class do not necessarily report the width and height values that appear in the Properties panel when you select the `Video` instance on the Stage. To check the displayed width and height of an instance, use the `width` and `height` properties of the `Video` instance.

Adjusting video size with metadata

If your .flv file has metadata available, you can use the `NetStream.onMetaData()` handler to resize the `Video` instance displaying the .flv file. As described in the last exercise, the `onMetaData()` handler is invoked before the video begins to play.

ON the CD-ROM Make a copy of the `netstream_100.fla` file from the **ch28** folder of this book's CD-ROM. You'll use this file as the starter document for this section.

1. Open your copy of the `netstream_100.fla` document, and save it as `netstream_resize_100.fla`.

2. **Select frame 1 of the actions layer, and open the Actions panel (F9/Option+F9).** Add or modify the bold lines shown in Listing 28.6. In this updated code, you set the `width` and `height` properties of the `vid` instance (a `Video` object) to the same values as the returned `width` and `height` properties in the metadata object, `meta`. Note that the visibility (the `visible` property) of the `vid` instance is set to `true` as well. In the `onLoadClick` handler, the visibility of the `vid` instance is turned off. This step is taken so that you don't see the video properties snap and update when the video begins to play. The video is visible only after the transformations have been applied.

3. **Save your document and test it (Ctrl+Enter/⌘+Enter).** Type the name `stella_speak_keyed.flv` into the `videoField` text field, and press the load video button. The clip of Stella plays at the original size of the .flv file, 320 x 380. Compare the sizes of the clip from the last exercise with this new resized clip.

   You probably noticed that the video clip was playing on top of the text field and buttons on the Stage. You can also shrink or enlarge the video size by performing further mathematical operations on the width and height values.

4. **Select frame 1 of the actions layer, and open the Actions panel.** Change the w and h values in the `onMetaData()` handler, as shown in the following bold code. Here, you divide the width and height data by 2, reducing the size of the video display.

```
function onMetaData(meta:Object):void {
    trace("onMetaData >>>");
    var w:Number = meta.width/2;
    var h:Number = meta.height/2;
    trace("\twidth: " + w);
    trace("\theight: " + h);
    vid.width = w;
    vid.height = h;
    vid.visible = true;
};
```

5. **Save the document and test it (Ctrl+Enter/⌘+Enter).** Type the name `stella_speak_keyed.flv` in the `videoField` instance, and press the load video button. As shown in Figure 28.13, you should now see Stella's video at a quarter of the size.

NOTE Even though you divided the width and height values by 2, the new displayed pixel area is one fourth of the original pixel area of the clip.

FIGURE 28.13

The newly resized video clip

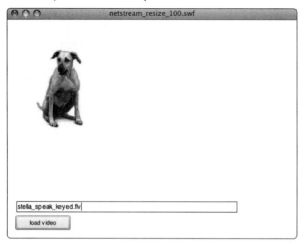

stella_speak_keyed.flv

load video

LISTING 28.6

The Updated onMetaData() Handler

```
//Button loadButton;
//TextField videoField;

import fl.managers.FocusManager;

// Listen for the click event on the loadButton instance
loadButton.addEventListener(MouseEvent.CLICK, onLoadClick);

// Create a new FocusManager to enable
// the Enter key for the loadButton instance
var fm:FocusManager = new FocusManager(this);
fm.defaultButton = loadButton;

// Create a new NetConnection instance
// to use with the video file
var nc:NetConnection = new NetConnection();
nc.connect(null);

// Create a new NetStream instance
// to play the video file
var ns:NetStream = new NetStream(nc);
```

```
// Listen for status events on the NetStream
ns.addEventListener(NetStatusEvent.NET_STATUS, onNetStatus);
// Assign the current timeline as the client
// to receive additional events
ns.client = this;
// Buffer 5 seconds of video before playback begins
ns.bufferTime = 5;

// Create a Video instance to display
// the video clip on stage
// (default size: 320x240)
var vid:Video = new Video();
// Position the vid instance at 50, 50
vid.x = 20;
vid.y = 20;
// Attach the NetStream to the vid instance
vid.attachNetStream(ns);
// Add the Video instance to the display list
addChild(vid);

// Define the listener function
function onLoadClick(evt:MouseEvent):void {
  // Retrieve the text from the textfield
  var vidURL:String = videoField.text;
  // Load and play the video
  ns.play(vidURL);
  // Hide the vid instance during loading
  vid.visible = false;
}

// Define a listener function for NetStatus events
// with the NetStream instance
function onNetStatus(evt:NetStatusEvent):void  {
  trace("onNetStatus >>>");
  var info:Object = evt.info;
  // Display events related to the NetStream
  trace("\tlevel:\t"+info.level);
  trace("\tcode:\t"+info.code);
}

// Define the onMetaData function
// for the NetStream client
function onMetaData(meta:Object):void  {
  trace("onMetaData >>>");
```

continued

LISTING 28.6   *(continued)*

```
// Retrieve the width and height
var w:Number = meta.width;
var h:Number = meta.height;
trace("\twidth: " + w);
trace("\theight: " + h);
// Update the size of the vid instance
// with the retrieved dimensions
vid.width = w;
vid.height = h;
// Show the vid instance
vid.visible = true;
}
```

ON the CD-ROM   You can find the completed file, `netstream_resize_100.fla`, in the `ch28` folder of this book's CD-ROM.

Setting the video size without metadata

You might not always have the luxury of loading .flv files that have metadata. Luckily, you can still resize the `Video` object by using the native width and height properties of the `Video` class. In this section, you learn how to alter the `onMetaData()` event handler to check for the existence of metadata and make the appropriate modifications to the video display area.

We intentionally included a clip without accurate metadata on this book's CD-ROM. Make a copy of the `stella_speak_no_meta.flv` file from the CD-ROM's `resources` folder to the same location as the `netstream_resize_100.fla` file you created in the last section. Test the Flash movie for that document, and type `stella_speak_no_meta.flv` into the text field and click the load video button. The .flv file loads, and if you have your speakers turned on, you'll hear the audio, but you won't see the video. Why? Because the clip has no metadata, the width and height properties are being set to 0. In order to fix this problem, you'll have to make some modifications to the `onMetaData()` event handler.

ON the CD-ROM   Continue using the `netstream_resize_100.fla` file from the last section, or make a copy of the file from the `ch28` folder of this book's CD-ROM. Make sure that you have made a copy of the `stella_speak_no_meta.flv` file as well.

1. Open the `netstream_resize_100.fla` file and resave it as `netstream_resize_no_meta_100.fla`.

2. **Select frame 1 of the actions layer, and open the Actions panel.** Modify the `onMetaData()` event handler, as shown in the following bold code. Here, you check to see if the w variable is equal to 0, an undefined value, or if it's not a number. If any of those conditions are true, you'll assume that there isn't valid metadata for both the width and

height of the .flv file. As such, check the width and height properties of the `vid` instance, which will return the FLV's native dimensions. As with our previous example, the values are divided in half to size Stella more appropriately for the movie's Stage.

```
function onMetaData(meta:Object):void  {
  trace("onMetaData >>>");
  // Retrieve the width and height
  var w:Number = meta.width/2;
  var h:Number = meta.height/2;
  trace("\twidth: " + w);
  trace("\theight: " + h);
  // Check if the width value is invalid
  if(w == 0 || isNaN(w)){
    trace("\tclip has empty metadata");
    // Set the dimensions to internal frame size
    w = vid.videoWidth/2;
    h = vid.videoHeight/2;
  }
  // Update the size of the vid instance
  // with the retrieved dimensions
  vid.width = w;
  vid.height = h;
  // Show the vid instance
  vid.visible = true;
}
```

3. **Save the document and test it (Ctrl+Enter/⌘+Enter).** Type `stella_speak_no_meta.flv` into the text field, and click the load video button. You should see the same size video as the clip you sized in the previous section.

ON the CD-ROM You can find the completed file, `netstream_resize_nometa_100.fla`, in the ch28 folder of this book's CD-ROM.

Accessing Items in Shared Libraries

Since Flash 5, Web designers and developers have had the good fortune of using an exciting feature to manage assets in Flash movies: the capability to link the symbols, sounds, bitmaps, and font symbols within external .swf files to other Flash movies that they use on their Web sites. These external .swf files, called *shared libraries*, are different than loaded .swf files. Flash CS4 enables you to easily use shared libraries and has an intuitive interface and dialog boxes to create shared items.

TIP Flash CS4 enables you to easily update shared assets in the Flash document files (.fla) that use them. Flash CS4 refers to shared assets as *runtime sharing*. We explain this feature later in this chapter. Authortime shared libraries are discussed in Chapter 6, "Symbols, Instances, and the Library."

The primary benefit of using a shared library .swf file is that it needs to be downloaded only once, even though several other Flash movies may need to access the same element. For example, if you want to use Blur Medium as an embedded font in several Flash movie files (.swf), you would need to embed the font into each movie. A font can easily consume more than 30K in each movie. Multiply that by 10 or 20 files in your Web site that use the font, and you may be eating up a lot of bytes just for the font usage. Instead, if you add a Font symbol to one Shared library .swf file and use that shared asset in all the Flash movies, you will need to download the font only once, even though it's used by several movies.

A shared library .swf file doesn't load into a Movie Clip instance location. Instead, you set up the Library panel of a Flash document file (.fla) with assets that you want to use in other Flash movies. This document is the basis of the shared library .swf file. After you assign an identifier to each asset in the Library, you save the Flash document, publish a Flash movie file (.swf) from it, and close the Flash document. Then you open another Flash document file (.fla) and, using File ➪ Import ➪ Open External Library, you open the shared library Flash document file (.fla). Its Library panel opens (in a dimmed, gray state), and you can drag and drop assets to your new Flash movie file.

> **NOTE** Even though the assets are linked to the external shared library .swf file, the Flash document file (.fla) actually stores copies of the assets. However, they do not export with the published Flash movie.

After you have established a shared library file, any changes to the actual contents of the shared library Flash document file (.fla) and movie file (.swf) propagate to any Flash movie that uses the shared assets. In the following sections, you learn how to create a shared library file and use it with other Flash movies.

> **CAUTION** It is recommended that you use only small (low byte size) elements in your shared libraries to ensure that they are downloaded and available for Flash movies that use them. As with any Web production, make sure that you test early and often before you complete an entire project.

Setting up a shared library file

To share assets among several Flash movies, you need to establish a shared library file (or files) available to other Flash movie files. To create a shared library file, follow these steps:

1. **Create a new Flash file (ActionScript 3.0).**

2. **To place Flash artwork into the Library panel, draw the shapes and other elements (text, lines, gradients, and so on).** Select the artwork and choose Modify ➪ Convert to Symbol (F8). In the Convert to Symbol dialog box, choose a symbol type (for example, Graphic, Button, or Movie Clip) that best suits the nature of your artwork.

   Flash CS4 also enables you to define export parameters directly in this dialog box. Click the Advanced button. In the extended options, check Export for runtime sharing. This action automatically selects the Export for ActionScript and Export in frame 1 check boxes. Specify a Class name, and type the relative or absolute URL for the shared .swf file in the URL field. This URL should simply be the path to this Flash movie on the Web server, such as `http://mydomain.com/files/sharedLib.swf`. Alternatively, if you know all of your Flash movies will be stored in the same directory on the Web server, you can simply type the name of the .swf file, as shown in Figure 28.14.

3. **To place bitmaps and sounds into the Library panel, import the source files as you normally would, using File ⇨ Import ⇨ Import to Library.**

NOTE For all ActionScript 3.0–enabled content, make sure that you enable the Export for ActionScript check box in the asset's Properties dialog box from the Library panel.

4. **Delete all artwork that you have placed on the Stage.** Every asset that you want to share should be in the Library panel.

5. **To place an entire font (or typeface) into the Library panel, open the Library panel and choose New Font from the options menu located at the top right corner of the Library panel.** In the Font Symbol Properties dialog box, type a reference name for the font, choose the font face from the Font menu, a font style from the Style menu, and select a faux font style (Bold or Italic) to be applied (optional). Enable the Export for runtime sharing check box as well. (See Figure 28.15.)

FIGURE 28.14

Add runtime-sharing information directly in the Convert to Symbol dialog box.

FIGURE 28.15

Give each embedded font face a descriptive name that indicates its functionality within the Flash movie.

> **NOTE** In Flash CS4, you can specify bitmap text and size settings in the Font Symbol Properties dialog box. However, in our tests, we could not see any visible difference in the way in which a shared font (or any Font symbol) was rendered.

Specifying the shared library's location

A required setting for each asset of the Shared library document is the relative or absolute path (as a URL) to the shared library SWF on your Web server. To change the URL for all the assets with the current Shared library document, follow these steps:

1. In the options menu in the Library panel, choose Shared Library Properties.

2. In the URL field, type the location of the Shared library .swf file (or where you intend to publish it on the Web). This location is prepended to each shared asset's identifier in the movies that use the assets.

> **CAUTION** Make sure that you specify this URL before you start using the Shared library document file (.fla) with other Flash document files (.fla). The URL location is stored within each document that uses the Shared library .swf file, and it will not update if you decide to change the URL later in the Shared library .fla file. Also, the URL applies to all items in the Shared library .fla and .swf file; you cannot set unique URLs for each item in a shared library.

Publishing the shared library movie file

After the assets of the Flash document have been assigned identifiers and the URL of the shared library has been set, you need to publish a .swf file of the Flash document.

1. **Save the Flash document file (.fla).** Use a descriptive name that notifies other members of your Web production team that this is a shared library file, such as `shared_lib.fla`.

2. **Publish the Flash movie as a .swf file.** No other publish formats are necessary. In the Publish Settings dialog box (File ➪ Publish Settings), select only the Flash format in the Format tab. Click OK. Choose File ➪ Publish to create an .swf file from your document.

3. **Close the Flash document.**

CAUTION Shared library documents that specify Flash Player 9 or 10 with ActionScript 3.0 in the Publish Settings dialog box cannot be shared with ActionScript 2.0 movies, regardless of Flash Player version.

Linking to assets from other movies

After the shared library .swf file is published, you can use the shared assets in other Flash movies.

1. **Create a new Flash file (ActionScript 3.0) or open an existing one.**

2. **Using the File ➪ Import ➪ Open External Library command, browse to the folder where your Shared library Flash document file (.fla) was saved.** For testing purposes, you should keep this document in the same folder as the other Flash documents that share it. Select the shared library .fla file and click Open. A separate grayed-out Library panel for the shared library .fla file opens in the Flash CS4 authoring environment.

3. **Drag the asset(s) that you want to use into the new Flash document's library or onto its Stage.** Even though Flash CS4 copies the contents of each shared asset, the asset loads from the separate Shared library .swf file at runtime.

4. **To see whether an asset is native to the Flash movie or from a shared library .swf file, right-click (or Control+click on Mac) the symbol or asset in the library.** Select Properties from the contextual menu. The Symbol Properties dialog box, shown in Figure 28.16, indicates whether the symbol (or asset) will be imported from an external Shared library .swf file.

TIP You can also expand the width of the Library panel to reveal the Linkage column, which indicates whether a library item is exported or imported.

When you are done dragging the assets from the Shared library file, close its Library panel. When you publish the new Flash movie(s) that use the Shared library .swf file, make sure that you put all the files on your Web server for live testing. If you used relative URL locations for the shared library .swf file(s), make sure that the files are stored in the proper directories on your Web server.

FIGURE 28.16

If a Shared library asset is used in another movie, the Symbol Properties indicate the name (and path) of the Shared library .swf file.

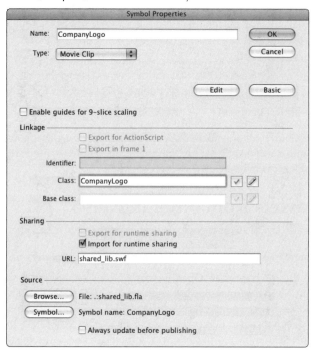

ON the CD-ROM You can find a shared library document and Flash document that uses the shared assets in the `ch28/sharedLib` folder of this book's CD-ROM.

Updating shared assets

Flash CS4 has an update feature for assets that have been imported from a Shared library document. To see which assets in your current document are imported, expand the width of the Library panel to view the Linkage column, as shown in Figure 28.17.

If you have changed the contents of an asset in a shared library document file (.fla) and published the new Flash movie file (.swf), you can choose to update the reference assets in other Flash documents that use the shared assets.

TIP Actually, you can use the update feature with any symbol that you have dragged, copied, or imported into one .fla file from another. Flash CS4 stores the name of the original .fla file with the copied symbol.

FIGURE 28.17

The Library panel enables you to quickly view the Linkage settings for each item.

Let's walk through the complete process of updating a shared library asset.

1. **Open the shared library document file (.fla).**

2. **Open the Library panel and edit the shared asset you want to update.** For example, if you need to change the artwork with a Movie Clip symbol, double-click the symbol and edit the symbol's content.

3. **When you're done editing the asset, save the Flash document and publish a Flash movie.** Close the Shared library document.

4. **Open a Flash document that uses an asset from the shared library.**

5. **Open the Library panel for the document.** Notice that any changed elements still appear as they did before the update occurred. Select the asset that was changed in the Shared library document and choose Update from the Library panel's options menu. Or right-click (Control+click on Mac) the asset and choose Update from the contextual menu. The Update Library Items dialog box appears, as shown in Figure 28.18. Select the check box next to the asset's name you want to update and then click the Update button.

You can also select multiple items in the Library panel and choose Update in the Options menu to update several items at once.

FIGURE 28.18

You can update shared assets in other Flash documents that use them.

WEB RESOURCE We'd like to know what you think about this chapter. Visit `www.flashsupport.` `com/feedback` to send us your comments.

Summary

- If you want to make sure that your larger Flash movies don't pause during playback over the Web, you may want to make a preloader for each Flash movie you make.

- Preloaders can use different ways to test the download progress of the Flash movie .swf file: `MovieClip.framesLoaded/MovieClip.totalFrames`, and `LoaderInfo.` `bytesLoaded/LoaderInfo.bytesTotal`. The most accurate mechanism uses the latter method.

- You can break up large Flash projects into several smaller Flash movie components that are loaded into a primary Flash movie when they're needed.

- The `Loader` class in ActionScript 3.0 enables you to download .swf files into a Flash movie.

- You can load most popular Web image formats, including JPEG, PNG, and GIF, with the `Loader` class in Flash Player 9 or later movies.

- You can download MP3 files directly into Flash movies, using the `Sound.load()` method.

- You can load video content into Flash movies, using the `NetStream` class. A `NetStream` instance is attached to a `Video` object to display the clip.

- You can share Flash assets with the shared library feature. Assets are stored in one or more Shared library .swf files and referenced by other Flash movies.

Chapter 29

Sending Data In and Out of Flash

A powerful feature of ActionScript is the extraordinary control of data acquisition and management it provides within a Flash movie. You can load external text data into Flash movies, making it possible to include fresh dynamic content every time a Flash movie is viewed over the Web. In this chapter, you learn how to access text data stored in a variety of formats that are separate from the actual Flash movie.

Many Flash-enabled Web sites use external data to display a wide range of information in a user interface. The home page of this book's support site, www.flashsupport.com, features a Flash movie that consumes and displays an RSS (Really Simple Syndication) feed of our recent articles and tutorials from Community MX. You can use dynamic data to display current news articles, catalog information, weather information, and more!

> **TIP** Flashloaded.com offers the rssReader component to easily consume and display RSS feeds in your own Flash movies. For more information, go to www.flashloaded.com/flash components.

> **NOTE** In this edition of the *Flash Bible*, all ActionScript code is presented in ActionScript 3.0. For legacy ActionScript 2.0 coverage, refer to *Flash CS3 Professional Bible* (Wiley, 2007) or earlier editions.

IN THIS CHAPTER

Understanding TextField objects

Using data in text fields

Managing data acquisition in Flash movies

Using ColdFusion with Flash movies

Loading XML data into Flash movies

Using Text Fields to Store and Display Data

Before we can discuss sending and receiving data with Flash movies, you need to know the basic mechanisms of input and output. You may find that, most of the time, your data in Flash will be text based, which means that you will gather information from the user and display new and updated information with text. In ActionScript, input text fields gather data from the user, and dynamic text fields display live and updated text to the user.

Input text fields

Input text fields can be created at authortime with the Text tool or at runtime with ActionScript. In the Properties panel, the topmost drop-down menu must be set to Input Text for the selected text field. A text field can be a scriptable object with an instance name. The text typed inside of an input text field is the value of the `text` property of the text field's instance name. For example, if you assigned an instance name of `visitorField` to the text field, you would access the contents of the text field with the `visitorField.text` property. To test this, let's create a simple input text field.

> **CAUTION** You can no longer use a variable name for a text field in ActionScript 3.0 Flash movies. If you are editing legacy ActionScript 2.0 content in Flash CS4, be sure to remove any assigned variable name in the Options section of the Properties panel. You need to switch the ActionScript version to ActionScript 1.0 or 2.0 in the Flash tab of the Publish Settings dialog box in order to edit the Variable field in the Properties panel.

1. **Using the Text tool, create a text field on the Main Timeline (that is, Scene 1) of a Flash document (ActionScript 3.0).** Make the box long enough to hold 20 characters. You can type a temporary word or phrase into the text field, but delete these characters before proceeding to the next step.

2. **In the Properties panel, select Input Text in the top menu.** In the <Instance Name> field, type **visitorField**. In the Character section of the panel, click the Show Border option, located just below the Anti-alias menu. See Figure 29.1 for these settings.

> **CAUTION** Remember that ActionScript 3.0 is case-sensitive. Make sure that you type `visitor Field` with a capital *F* so that the ActionScript code you add later in this section works properly.

3. **Save your Flash document as** `input_text.fla` **and test the movie (Ctrl+Enter/ ⌘+Return).** In the Test Movie window, click the text field and type your first name into the field.

4. **While you're still testing the movie, choose Debug ➪ List Objects, and the Output panel displays the** `visitorField` **object with the value you typed in Step 3.** The value will be wrapped with HTML tags specifying the text formatting you assigned in the Properties panel. In our example, we entered the name **Charlie**. Therefore, the Output panel displays (among other text):

```
Level #0: Frame=1
  Edit Text: Target="_level0.visitorField" Variable= Visible=true
    Text = <TEXTFORMAT LEADING=\"2\">
<P ALIGN=\"LEFT\"><FONT FACE=\"Verdana\" SIZE=\"24\"
COLOR=\"#000000\" LETTERSPACING=\"0\" KERNING=\"0\">
Charlie</FONT></P></TEXTFORMAT>"
```

FIGURE 29.1

The Properties panel controls the settings for text fields.

NOTE If you change the text in the `visitorField` text field, the value automatically updates for the `visitorField.text` value.

Input text fields not only accept input from the user, but they can also be set to an initial value or updated with a new value with ActionScript code. You can test this with the preceding Flash movie example.

5. **If you are viewing the** `input_text.swf` **file from Step 4, close the Test Movie window to return to the Flash CS4 authoring environment.** Create a new layer, and rename it **actions**. Select the first frame of the actions layer and press F9/Option+F9 to open the Actions panel. Add the following code to the Script pane. Here, you set the `text` property when the movie initializes, and you create a `MouseEvent.CLICK` event listener that displays the text property of the `visitorField` instance when the mouse is clicked on the movie's Stage.

931

```
//TextField visitorField;
visitorField.text = "enter your name here";

this.stage.addEventListener(MouseEvent.CLICK, outputText);

function outputText(evt:MouseEvent):void {
  trace("visitorField.text: " + visitorField.text);
}
```

TIP By inserting the comment code on line 1, you'll see code hints for that instance name whenever you use it in subsequent lines of code.

6. **Save your Flash document and test it (Control ⇨ Test Movie).** As soon as the movie loads, you should see the text "enter your name here" in the `visitorField` text field. Click anywhere on the movie's stage, and you should see that same text displayed in the Output panel. Now, replace the text in the field with your name, and click again anywhere on the movie's stage. The Output panel displays the new `text` value.

ON the CD-ROM You can find the `input_text.fla` document in the `ch29` folder of this book's CD-ROM.

As you can see, input text fields can accept text input from the user, just like an HTML form. Later in this chapter, you use input text fields to create a fully functional Flash form that can send and receive information with a server-side script.

Dynamic text fields

If you want to display text information in Flash movies, you have two options: (A) create static text blocks whose contents cannot be updated with ActionScript, or (B) create dynamic text fields that can be filled with internal Flash data or external text data.

CAUTION Do not use input or dynamic text fields unless you need to accept or display editable text data to the user. Static text is perfectly fine for text used for graphical purposes, where the text does not need to be changed during the presentation.

Dynamic text fields are also objects with instance names, just as input text fields. The only difference between input and dynamic text fields is that you can type into input text fields at runtime. Dynamic text fields are most useful for displaying text information that will be changed by the movie (via ActionScript), rather than by the user. Using dynamic text fields, you can display news articles that change on a daily (or hourly) basis, a player's score during a Flash game, and the system time and date, just to name a few.

TIP Both input and dynamic text fields can use HTML text formatting tags to change the display of text. We discuss HTML use within text fields in Chapter 30, "Applying HTML and Text Field Formatting."

In the following steps, you create a dynamic text field updated with an ActionScript variable action. You can also load external variables for use in dynamic text fields, which we discuss in the next section. To insert text into a dynamic text field:

1. **Create a new Flash file (ActionScript 3.0) and save the document as** `dynamic_text.fla`.

2. **Rename Layer 1 to** outputField.

3. **Using the Text tool, create a text field on the Main Timeline of a Flash document.** Make a field large enough to accommodate multiple lines of text, as shown in Figure 29.2. Choose a normal font size, such as 12.

4. **In the Properties panel, select Dynamic Text in the topmost menu.** In the <Instance Name> field, enter the text **outputField**. In the Character section of the panel, click the Selectable and Show Border options. In the Paragraph section, select Multiline from the Behavior menu. Refer to Figure 29.2 for these settings.

FIGURE 29.2

The dynamic text field settings in the Properties panel

5. **Add a new layer and name it** actions. Select the first keyframe of the actions layer and press F9/Option+F9 to open the Actions panel. Enter the second line of the following code on one single line in the Script pane. (You can enable word wrapping in the options menu of the Actions panel if you want.)

```
//TextField outputField;

outputField.text = "WANTED: Flash Input & Output\r\rA start-
up dotcom company is looking for a qualified web technology
that will present text input and output to web visitors in a
more compelling animated and visually stunning environment
than that possible with HTML. Please call:\r\r1-800-555-
CODE";
```

In this code, you specify string values (denoted with quotes) for the actual text you want to insert into the `outputField` dynamic text field instance. To insert a carriage return in the text, the `\r` character entity is inserted between string values.

6. **Save the Flash document as** `dynamic_text.fla`.

7. **Test the movie (Ctrl+Enter/⌘+Enter).** The `outputField` dynamic text field updates with the value assigned to the `text` property of the `outputField` instance in ActionScript.

ON the CD-ROM   You can find the `dynamic_text.fla` document in the `ch29` folder of this book's CD-ROM.

You can also load text data into input and dynamic text fields. This data can be returned from a simple text file (.txt file) or from an application that resides on your Web server. In the next section, you learn how to send and receive text from a Flash movie.

Defining a Data Process with States

When you manipulate text fields with ActionScript properties of the `TextField` object, the data for the text fields is available for use immediately. Meaning, if you declare a variable and a value for that variable, any text field can be given that value as well. When you want to load external data into a Flash movie, you need to create the appropriate steps, or *states,* in your movie to make sure that the data is available for use in the Flash movie. For example, suppose you want to retrieve a news article from a Web server, and the text for that article is contained within a variable named `article_1`. You can't use or assign the value of `article_1` to any other Flash element *unless* the article has fully downloaded to the Flash movie.

So, how do you know when data is available in a Flash movie? Any Flash movie that relies on data exchange between the Flash movie and the Web server should contain four separate states:

- An **input** state to gather the information from the user or the movie
- A **send** state in which a Flash action sends the data out of the movie
- A **wait** state during which the data downloads to the movie
- An **output** state in which the Flash movie can use the data in text fields and other ActionScript code

Input state

The first step for data exchange requires that you have something to send out of the Flash movie. The input can be a Flash form into which a user types text. The data could be environment variables, such as the time of the day, or the Flash Player version. There could be various substeps in the input state, such as multiple forms or the completion of a quiz to calculate a test score that will be sent to the server.

> **NOTE** Not all data transactions require input. For example, if you need to retrieve the latest stock quotes or news article from a server application, you may simply need to send a request for that data without providing any additional information to the server application.

Send state

After the input data has been set or retrieved in the Flash movie, you're ready to send the data to another host, such as an application or script on your server. You can use the following ActionScript 3.0 actions or object methods to send data out of the Flash movie:

- `navigateToURL()` function
- `URLLoader.load()` method
- `URLStream.load()` method
- `XMLSocket.send()` method
- `NetConnection.call()` method for Flash Remoting or Flash Media Server transactions

Of these actions, the `navigateToURL()` function is restricted to a one-way data path with the Flash movie. That is, you can only send data out with this action; you cannot receive external data with the function. The `navigateToURL()` function must target the sought URL to the current browser (or frame) or a new browser window. In many situations, you may only need to send data out of the Flash movie without needing to receive any further data. To send information with the user's e-mail client, you can use a simple `mailto:` URL in a `navigateToURL()` action assigned to a listener function for a Button instance. (Note that the ⏎ character indicates a continuation of the same line of code.)

```
//SimpleButton sendButton;

    sendButton.addEventListener(MouseEvent.CLICK, sendMail);

function sendMail(evt:MouseEvent):void {
  var email:String = "admin@server.com";
  var subject:String = escape("Visitor Feedback");
  var body:String = escape("Please let us know how you feel.");
  var request:URLRequest = new URLRequest();
  request.url = "mailto:" + email + "?subject=" + subject + ⏎
    "&body=" + body;
  navigateToURL(request);
}
```

In the preceding code block, the variables email, subject, and body are inserted into the navigateToURL() action with a URLRequest wrapper. Note that you can automatically set subject and body text for the e-mail message as well. To add specific variables to a URL string, you should use the escape() function in ActionScript, which converts illegal URL characters such as spaces and question marks into URL form-encoded text (for example, a space is converted into %20).

 Not all e-mail clients support the passing of subject and body variables. Be sure to test this code with your targeted e-mail clients.

Wait state

If you are sending data from the Flash movie, you likely need to know when the script or application running on your Web server receives the requested data. Usually, you build server-side scripts that return some data back to the Flash movie upon successful receipt of data. All transactions over the Internet take time to complete, and the wait state should include graphic elements indicating to the user that information is being sent and received. After the data is loaded, the Flash movie is directed to the appropriate output state.

All wait states should have a timeout condition: If the data fails to load within a certain timeframe, you will assume the server (or script) is not functioning correctly. If the timeout condition occurs, the Flash movie goes to the appropriate output state. You create a wait state for the Flash form in the next section.

Output state

The final step in a data exchange is the actual display of any received data in the Flash movie. However, as indicated in the last state, there are two separate output states: a success display or an error display. If the data was properly received during the wait state, the Flash movie displays the success output state. If the server failed to return any data to the Flash movie, the movie displays an error output state, indicating that there was a problem with the server.

Creating a User Comment Form

In this section, you create a Flash form that submits user-entered information to a server-side ColdFusion script that e-mails the data to an e-mail address that you specify in the script. By accessing a remote ColdFusion script, you make a Flash movie with five data exchange states: input, send, wait, output, and error. You learn how to submit name/value pairs from Flash to remote URLs and learn how to check the receipt of variables from the ColdFusion script by using the URLLoader class. The URLLoader class can detect the loading of the external variable data.

ON the CD-ROM You can find the ColdFusion script (`sendmail.cfm`) and supporting Flash documents for this section in the `ch29/form` folder of this book's CD-ROM. Note that you need a ColdFusion-enabled server to configure and use the `sendmail.cfm` script. We have also included the `sendmail.asp` script (Microsoft ASP version) and the `sendmail.pl` script (Perl 5) that we included with previous editions of the *Flash Bible*, as well as a `sendmail.php` script for PHP 4 or later. The ASP script requires the installation of the free w3JMail component, available at `http://tech.dimac.net`.

WEB RESOURCE You can download a trial version of ColdFusion at `www.adobe.com/products/ coldfusion`. You can also find installation instructions on the Web site. For a list of preferred ColdFusion hosting providers, check the "ColdFusion Hosting Providers" section of the `www.flashsupport.com/links` page.

Flash forms are user data entry forms (just like HTML forms) created in Flash CS4 by using Input text fields. When a user types information in these text fields, the information is stored as a property of the text field instance (`text`). The values of these properties are assigned to variable names and are then sent to a specified server by using standard GET or POST communication. These variables are available to the server and can be processed there by a server-side program or script. Server-side programs can be written to e-mail this information, manipulate it, store it in a database, or perform many other applications. The same server-side script can also return values to the Flash movie. These can then be displayed or used by the originating Flash movie.

In this exercise, the Flash form solicits feedback from visitors, giving them an opportunity to submit comments, report bugs, or make suggestions for improvement. As each form is submitted, it's e-mailed directly to the e-mail address that you specify in the ColdFusion script.

1. **Open a new Flash file (ActionScript 3.0), and save it as** `sendmail_cfm.fla`.

2. **Rename Layer 1 to** labels. Select frame 1 of this layer and assign a frame label of **input** in the Properties panel.

3. **On the labels layer, create keyframes (F6) on frames 10, 20, and 30.** Give these keyframes the labels **wait**, **output**, and **error**, respectively. Select frame 40 and press F5 to insert more empty frames at the end of the layer.

4. **Create a new layer and name it** actions. Select frame 1 of the actions layer, and open the Actions panel. In the Script pane, add a `stop();` action. In the Properties panel, add a comment of `//setup form` in the Name field of the Label section.

5. **Create a new layer, and name it** text fields. Insert keyframes on frames 10, 20, and 30.

6. **On frame 1 of the text fields layer, insert three separate input text fields.** From top to bottom, assign the following instance names to the input text fields (in the Properties panel): `fromNameField`, `fromEmailField`, and `commentField`. The `fromName Field` and `fromEmailField` text fields should accommodate one line of text, and the

`commentField` instance should be set to Multiline (in the Behavior menu of the Paragraph section of the Properties panel) in order to hold multiple lines of text. All the input text fields should have the Show Border option selected, unless you plan to create your own background graphics. Make each text field long enough to accommodate about 45 characters of text. The comments field should be able to show between five and ten lines of text (see Figure 29.3).

7. **Create a new layer, and name it** static text. Insert keyframes on frames 10, 20, and 30. On frame 1, add static text blocks to the left of the text fields, indicating the purpose of each field, as shown in Figure 29.3.

FIGURE 29.3

These text fields accept input from your site visitors.

 For our example, the Flash movie background color is black, and the static text is white. You can change the movie's background color by choosing Modify ⇨ Document.

8. On frame 10 of the static text layer (underneath the `wait` label), insert a static text block indicating that the information is being sent to the server and that the movie is waiting for confirmation. In our example, we used the text "Checking the server. . . ."

9. On frame 20 of the static text layer (underneath the `output` label), insert a static text block containing a successful receipt of the visitor's information. In our example, we used the text "Thank you. Your feedback was received at:".

10. You can see that you are setting up the output state to display the time that the server received the data (Figure 29.4). The ColdFusion script returns the time and date of the receipt to the Flash movie. On frame 20 of the text field's layer, create a dynamic text field with an instance name of `receiptField` and place it underneath the static text you just made.

FIGURE 29.4

The `receiptField` instance displays the time that the server received the Flash form data.

11. On frame 30 of the static text layer (underneath the `error` label), insert static text that indicates the data was not successfully received. In our example, we used the text "Sorry, there was an error processing your form."

12. Save your Flash document. Now you have all of your states defined with placeholder artwork. You can go back later and refine the text and graphics to suit your particular needs. Next, you need to add functions to transfer the data from the text fields to a `URLVariables` object and send the data to the server with `URLRequest` and `URLLoader` instances.

These actions need to put on the appropriate Flash event handlers. Start by defining a function named `sendComments` that creates a `URLVariables` object, a `URLRequest` object, and a `URLLoader` object. The form data is specified in the `URLVariables` object, inserted into a `URLRequest` object, and then sent out of the Flash movie with a `URLLoader` object. When the ColdFusion script receives the data, the server returns some confirmation data to the Flash movie, including the time and date the user's comments were received. When this data loads completely into the Flash movie, the movie then goes to and stops on the `output` frame label.

Before you define these functions, however, let's add a Button component to the Stage. This component button will initiate the `sendComments()` function.

13. Create a new layer and name it button. Insert an empty keyframe on frame 10 of this layer.

14. On frame 1 of the button layer, drag an instance of the Button component from the User Interface grouping of the Components panel to the document's Stage.

15. With the component selected, open the Properties panel. Name the instance `send-Button`. In the Parameters tab of the Component Inspector panel, type **send comments** in the `label` field. You may need to stretch the width of the `Button` instance to accommodate the label text.

16. Select frame 1 of the actions layer, and open the Actions panel F9/Option+F9). In the Script pane, add the code shown in Listing 29.1. This code defines the `sendComments` function used by the `sendButton` instance.

This script declares all the objects present on the stage as code comments to enable code hinting, in lines 1 through 4. Lines 6 through 9 create an instance of the `FocusManager` class to enable the `sendButton` instance as the default button; these actions enable you to use the Enter key to submit the form information instead of clicking the button.

In line 11, the URL of the ColdFusion script is defined, using a live server URL we specifically set up for this exercise. If you have installed the ColdFusion script on your local machine or server, change the path of this variable to reflect your custom location.

In line 12, a variable named `formLoader` is declared as a `URLLoader` data type. The instance is not created here; the variable is simply declared so that it can be used throughout the entire movie.

In line 14, the `sendComments()` function is added as a listener of the `sendButton` instance's `MouseEvent.CLICK` event. In line 16, the Main Timeline stops on the first frame.

Lines 18 through 39 define the `sendComments()` function. This function establishes all the data that the `sendmail.cfm` script requires for successful operation. Line 18 declares the function and its name, `sendComments`. The function starts by creating a `URLVariables` instance, which stores all the text information from the form fields in lines 20 through 24. In line 24, a `keyID` variable is added to the instance. This ID is used by the live FlashSupport.com version of the script to limit your testing to twenty attempts; otherwise, the script would be vulnerable to hackers for sending unlimited spam mail. Lines 26 through 29 create a `URLRequest` instance that references the URL of the ColdFusion script (line 27), sets the HTTP method for sending the data to the script as "POST" (line 28), and stores the `URLVariables` data (line 29). Lines 31 through 36 create the `URLLoader` instance named `formLoader`. In line 32, the format of the data is set to `URLLoaderDataFormat.VARIABLES`, because variables will be sent and loaded to and from the script. In line 33, a listener function named `onFormDataReceived` is added for the `Event.COMPLETE` event of the `formLoader` instance, which occurs when the Flash movie receives the server's response. Lines 34 and 35 create listener functions for the `IOErrorEvent.IO_ERROR` and `HTTPStatusEvent.HTTP_STATUS` events. Both of these listener functions, defined in lines 51 through 64, send the movie to the "error" frame label if an error has occurred with transmission to and from the server script. In line 36, the ColdFusion script is sent the variables from the Flash movie. In line 38, the movie goes to and stops on the `"wait"` frame label as the movie waits for a response from the server script.

Lines 41 through 49 define an `onFormDataReceived()` listener function for the `Event.COMPLETE` event of the `formLoader` instance. In this example, if the data is successfully received and the server-side script doesn't encounter any errors (lines 43 and 44), the movie goes to and stops on the `output` frame label. If the data is not received or there is an error in sending the data (line 46), the movie goes to and stops on the `error` frame label (line 47).

> **NOTE** You can change the values of the `Form.toEmail` and `Form.subject` variables in the `sendmail.cfm` script to change where the server sends the data from the Flash movie. If you use the live script located on the `www.flashsupport.com` site, Mr. Reinhardt will receive all of your test e-mails, so please be careful. For security measures, don't include private information such as your own e-mail address inside of an .swf file, including ActionScript code. SWF decompiler utilities can extract any data, including code, from .swf files delivered over the Web.

17. **Finally, add a keyframe to frame 20 of the actions layer.** With this keyframe selected, open the Actions panel and add the following actions:

```
//TextField receiptField;
receiptField.text = formLoader.data.timeDate;
```

This action takes the time and date returned by the server, and uses its value for the `text` property of the `receiptField` instance.

941

18. Save your Flash document again and test it (Ctrl+Enter/⌘+Return). Type some information into the text fields and click the send comments button. If the server script is available, you should see the output state display the time/date receipt from the server.

LISTING 29.1

The sendComments() Function

```
1.   //Button sendButton;
2.   //TextField fromEmailField;
3.   //TextField fromNameField;
4.   //TextField commentField;
5.
6.   import fl.managers.FocusManager;
7.
8.   var fm:FocusManager = new FocusManager(this);
9.   fm.defaultButton = sendButton;
10.
11.  var formURL:String = "http://www.flashsupport.com/sendfdmail.cfm";
12.  var formLoader:URLLoader;
13.
14.  sendButton.addEventListener(MouseEvent.CLICK, sendComments);
15.
16.  stop();
17.
18.  function sendComments(evt:MouseEvent):void  {
19.    trace("sendComments >>>");
20.    var formData:URLVariables = new URLVariables();
21.    formData.fromEmail = fromEmailField.text;
22.    formData.fromName = fromNameField.text;
23.    formData.body = commentField.text;
24.    formData.keyID = "FLASHSUPPORT-FLASHBIBLE";
25.
26.    var formRequest:URLRequest = new URLRequest();
27.    formRequest.url = formURL;
28.    formRequest.method = URLRequestMethod.POST;
29.    formRequest.data = formData;
30.
31.    formLoader = new URLLoader();
32.    formLoader.dataFormat = URLLoaderDataFormat.VARIABLES;
33.    formLoader.addEventListener(Event.COMPLETE, onFormDataReceived);
34.    formLoader.addEventListener(IOErrorEvent.IO_ERROR, onIOError);
35.    formLoader.addEventListener(HTTPStatusEvent.HTTP_STATUS, ↵
         onHttpStatus);
36.    formLoader.load(formRequest);
```

```
37.
38.   gotoAndStop("wait");
39. }
40.
41. function onFormDataReceived(evt:Event):void {
42.   trace("onFormDataReceived >>>");
43.   var success:Number = Number(formLoader.data.success);
44.   if (success) {
45.    gotoAndStop("output");
46.   } else {
47.     gotoAndStop("error");
48.   }
49. }
50.
51. function onIOError(evt:IOErrorEvent):void {
52.   trace("onIOError >>>");
53.   gotoAndStop("error");
54. }
55.
56. function onHttpStatus(evt:HTTPStatusEvent):void {
57.   trace("onHttpStatus >>> " + evt.status);
58.   switch(evt.status){
59.     case 0:
60.     case 404:
61.       gotoAndStop("error");
62.       break;
63.   }
64. }
```

The server script supports either GET or POST methods. Remember, every data exchange with a Flash movie should use input, wait, output, and error states.

ON the CD-ROM Use the `sendmail.cfm` script on `www.flashsupport.com` only for development and/or testing purposes. Remember that live Flash movies on a server can access only server-side scripts located on the same server unless special permissions are granted. Although you can use the `sendmail.cfm` script on `www.flashsupport.com` for local testing in the Flash CS4 authoring environment, it does not work after you upload your Flash movie to your own server — you'll have to install the `sendmail.cfm` script (or equivalent) on your own server. The same ColdFusion script is available on this book's CD-ROM, in the `ch29/form` folder. You can find the completed version of the Flash document, `sendmail_cfm.fla`, in the `ch29/form` folder. We have also created equivalents of the `sendmail.cfm` script in other popular middleware languages: `sendmail.asp` (Microsoft ASP.NET), `sendmail.php` (PHP 4 or later), and `sendmail.pl` (Perl 5 or later). Note that we do not have live versions of these alternative server-side scripts; you must install them on your own server to test and deploy them.

Using XML Data in Flash Movies

ActionScript 3.0 Flash movies can load (and send) XML data. This is a very powerful feature, because XML has become a standard data structure for e-commerce purposes and for news services, as well as for easier control over HTML formatting (and style sheets) in the browser. You can organize external data with simple XML formatting and use the XML data for text fields and ActionScript code in your Flash movies.

Understanding XML

XML is an acronym for *eXtensible Markup Language*. *Extensible*, in this case, means that you can create your own markup tag names and attributes. Although there are a few additional rules with XML, its structure very much resembles traditional HTML:

```
<tag name opener>Information here</tag name closer>
```

For basic XML-Flash usage, your XML document needs one "container" tag in which all other subordinate tags are nested. Each opener and closer tag set is called a *node*. In the following XML example, the <section> tag is the primary container tag, and the <article> tags are nodes of the <section> tag:

```
<section>
    <article>First article node</article>
    <article>Second article node</article>
</section>
```

NOTE   Technically, for XML to be to specification, you should have an XML declaration at the very top of your document. It's a good habit to add the declaration:

```
<?xml version="1.0" encoding="utf-8" ?>
```

You should make sure that you also save the document as Unicode (UTF-8). In Adobe Dreamweaver, look for this option under Modify ⇨ Page Properties. In other text editors, look for the Unicode UTF-8 option in the Save As dialog box.

You can create as many *child* nodes as you need. In the preceding example, the <section> tag has two child nodes: the first occurrence of <article> . . . </article> and the second occurrence of <article> . . . </article>. In the following example, the first <article> node has two child nodes:

```
<section>
    <article>
        <title>WANTED: New Computer</title>
        <description>Insert description here</description>
    </article>
    <article>Second article node</article>
</section>
```

`<title>` . . . `</title>` is the first child node of the first `<article>` . . . `</article>` node. The value of `<title>` is also considered a child of `<title>`. In the previous example, "WANTED: New Computer" is the child of `<title>`.

Loading an XML document into a Flash movie

After you have an XML document structured to use in a Flash movie, you can use the XML document tree in the Flash movie. When an XML document is loaded into a Flash movie, the structure and relationship of all nodes are retained within the Flash Player.

NOTE In ActionScript 3.0, the ActionScript 2.0 `XML` class becomes the `XMLDocument` class. The ActionScript 3.0 `XML` class uses E4X, a specific implementation of traversing XML data structures.

The XML object

Before you can load an XML document into Flash, you need to make an object that will hold the XML data. To do this, use the `XML` constructor function, as in:

```
var xmlData:XML = new XML();
```

Just as you created new objects for the `URLVariables` and `URLRequest` objects in earlier ActionScript, you can create as many new instances of the `XML` object as you need for your movie. You can also use an `XML` object to store Flash-created XML structures and send them to a server for further processing.

The URLLoader class revisited

One of the great benefits of learning ActionScript 3.0 is the standardization of operations, from event listening to data requests. Because loading an external file requires a transfer of data, you use the same techniques described earlier in this chapter. Create a `URLRequest` and `URLLoader` instance to specify the XML file you want to load, and continue processing the XML data in a listener function for the `Event.COMPLETE` event of the `URLLoader` instance. Here's a typical listener function that creates a new XML instance from loaded data:

```
var xmlData:XML;
var xmlLoader:URLLoader = new URLLoader()
xmlLoader.addEventListener(Event.COMPLETE, onXMLReceived);
xmlLoader.load(new URLRequest("articles.xml"));

function onXMLReceived(evt:Event):void {
  xmlData = new XML(xmlLoader.data);
}
```

ON the CD-ROM Check out the XML document load examples on this book's CD-ROM in the `ch29/ xml` folder. These examples demonstrate how XML node values can be manipulated with ActionScript 3.0. You may want to review Chapter 25's coverage of the `Array` object before looking at these examples.

CROSS-REF You learn more about loading XML at runtime with ActionScript 3.0 in Chapter 33, "Building an Image Gallery Component."

WEB RESOURCE We'd like to know what you think about this chapter. Visit www.flashsupport. com/feedback to send us your comments.

Summary

- Input text fields can accept text data from anyone viewing the Flash movie (.swf).

- Dynamic text fields can display any string values retrieved with ActionScript in the Flash movie.

- Any data exchange between Flash and a remote application or server-side script should use four steps, or states: input, send, wait, and output.

- You can use a Flash form to gather feedback from your site's visitors. The form's data can be sent to a properly configured server-side script for further data processing, such as sending the data in an e-mail to the site administrator.

- The URLLoader class can send and load text data to a server script or application.

- XML data structures have become a standard for data exchange over the Internet. Flash movies can use XML data structures to send and receive data from your server.

Chapter 30

Applying HTML and Text Field Formatting

I n this chapter, we show you how to control text field formatting and focus by using internal HTML tags and ActionScript 3.0. Flash gives you an incredible amount of control over text field formatting when you use the `TextFormat` class with `TextField` objects (that is, input and dynamic text fields). We also show you how to highlight text within text fields by using the `Selection` class.

> **TIP** Because the Flash Player supports PNG, GIF, and progressive JPEG image, you can load these file types into HTML-enabled Flash text fields as well. Flash movies can also use the FlashType text rendering engine, which improves the readability of text at small point sizes.

Exploring HTML Usage in Text Fields

As you use Flash CS4, you may notice the HTML button in the Character section of the Properties panel for text fields. Even though one of the primary advantages of using Flash movies is that you can avoid the fuss and often unpredictable nature of HTML page layout, you can use HTML formatting tags within input and dynamic text fields. You can use `<font>` tags to specify multiple typefaces, colors, styles, and sizes within one text field. You can also use `<a href>` tags to link to internal ActionScript functions or external URLs!

947

Supported HTML tags

You can use the following HTML tags to format your Flash text fields. You can insert these tags into string variables in ActionScript code, or you can apply them (without knowing or writing the syntax) by using the Properties panel. As you already know, text fields in ActionScript are real objects with instance names. As such, you need to address specific properties of the `TextField` object to insert HTML text. In previous chapters, you've used the following syntax to assign text to a text field instance:

```
//TextField lastNameField;
    lastNameField.text = "Enter your last name here";
```

You cannot assign HTML tags in the `text` property of a `TextField` object. You must use the `htmlText` property to assign HTML-formatted text, such as:

```
//TextField lastNameField;
    lastNameField.htmlText = "Enter your <b>last</b> name here.";
```

Here, the `<b>` tag is used to bold the text "last" in the text field instance. In a moment, you will create your own examples that use the `htmlText` property. Let's review the HTML tags that are available in ActionScript.

> **NOTE** In the ActionScript 2.0 version of the `TextField` class, you also need to set the `html` property of the `TextField` instance to `true`, to let the Flash Player know that it should parse the HTML text you specify for the `htmlText` property. In ActionScript 3.0, the `TextField` class does not have a property named `html`. You simply set the `htmlText` property of the instance to the HTML text you want to display.

Font and paragraph styles

The basic `<font>` and physical "faux" styles for text (bold, italic, and underline) can be applied to Flash text.

- `<b>`: Placing `<b></b>` tags around Flash text in string values for text field variables applies **bold** formatting to the enclosed text.

- `<i>`: Placing `<i></i>` tags around Flash string values *italicizes* the enclosed text.

- `<u>`: The `<u></u>` tags underline the enclosed text.

- `<p>`: The `<p>` tag inserts a paragraph break between lines of text. You can use the `align` attribute to specify `left`, `right`, `center`, or `justify`, applying the respective justifications to the Flash text.

- `<br/>`: The `<br/>` tag inserts a carriage return at the point of insertion. This is equivalent to the `newline` operator in ActionScript.

- `<font color='#hex code'>`: The `<font>` tag with the `color` attribute can change the color of your Flash text. This color is specified in hexadecimal values, just as with regular HTML. For example, `"<font color='#FF0000>This is red text.</font>"` uses full red for the text color.

- `<font face>`: The `<font>` tag with the `face` attribute enables you to specify a type-face for the enclosed text. You can specify Flash device fonts for the `face` value, such as `<font face='_sans'>` to use the Sans Serif device font.

- `<font size>`: The `size` attribute of the `<font>` tag enables you to specify the point size of Flash text. You can use absolute values (in point sizes), such as `<font size='18'>`, or relative values, such as `<font size='+1'>`, to change the size of text.

- `<font letterSpacing>`: The `letterSpacing` attribute of the `<font>` tag enables you to uniformly add horizontal space around each character. You can use positive or negative integers, such as `<font letterSpacing='18'>`. This attribute is supported only in Flash Player 8.

- `<font kerning>`: The `kerning` attribute of the `<font>` tag enables you to turn kerning on (1) or off (0). Kerning is the space between characters of a specific font, and is not available for some fonts such as Courier New.

- `<textformat>`: This tag is a Flash-specific formatting tag that you won't find in traditional HTML. `<textformat>` has four attributes, `indent`, `leading`, `leftmargin`, and `rightmargin`, that control the margin and line spacing of text within the text field. Each of these attributes uses pixels as the unit of measurement. To get a feel for how these attributes work, create a paragraph of static text, click the Format button in the Properties panel for the selected text field, and change the settings in the Format Options dialog box.

TIP You can only use the `<textformat>` tag within text fields for Flash movies.

- `<span>`: As with its real HTML counterpart, `<span>` enables you to apply a style from a style sheet to the encompassed range of text. This tag has only one supported attribute, `class`. This attribute can be set to the name of the style class declared in the style sheet. For example, `<span class="heading">` applies the style named `heading` to the enclosed text.

- `<img>`: A potentially exciting tag supported in Flash HTML is the `<img>` tag, short for image. As you may have guessed, this tag enables you to insert images inline with other text in a text field. This tag supports the following attributes: `src`, `id`, `width`, `height`, `align`, `hspace`, and `vspace`. The `src` attribute can be set to one of the following: the linkage identifier of a symbol in the library, the external URL to an .swf file, or the external URL to an image file. The JPEG, progressive JPEG, GIF, and PNG formats are supported in Flash movies.

URL and ActionScript linking

You can use the anchor, or `<a>`, tag with the `href` attribute to apply URL links within Flash text fields. For example, you can insert the following HTML into a string value for the `htmlText` property of a text field instance to link the text [*the* MAKERS] Web site to the appropriate URL:

```
<a href='http://www.theMakers.com'>the Makers Web site</a>
```

You can also specify a target attribute for the `<a>` tag. The target attribute determines which browser window or frame displays the URL link in the `href` attribute. As with regular HTML, you can use the default `_top`, `_parent`, `_self`, or `_blank` values, as described for the `getURL()` action. Later in this section, you also learn how to execute internal ActionScript functions from `<a href>` tags.

CAUTION   You cannot type HTML tags directly into any text block or field — the actual tags show up in the text field as the Flash movie runs in the Flash Player. The formatting tags are specified in ActionScript code or are "hidden" in static text. (The Properties panel applies the formatting.)

Formatting text with the Properties panel

You don't necessarily need to write out HTML tags to apply them to your Flash text. You can use the Properties panel to assign HTML formatting to all text types (that is, static, input, and dynamic). For input and dynamic text fields, you need to enable HTML formatting by pressing the Render text as HTML button in the Character section of the Properties panel. In this section, we demonstrate the use of HTML formatting within static and dynamic text fields.

1. **Create a new Flash file (ActionScript 3.0).** If the background color of your document is a non-white color, set the background color to white in the Document Properties dialog box (Ctrl+J/⌘+J). Save your Flash document as `htmlText_static.fla`.

2. **Select the Text tool and open the Properties panel.** Make sure that the Text type menu (in the top left corner of the inspector) is set to Static Text. Click once on the Stage and type the following text (with carriage returns) in the text block, using Verdana at 18 points:

   ```
   Flash CS4 Bible
   by Robert Reinhardt & Snow Dowd
   ```

3. **With the text block still active, select the Flash CS4 Bible text and, in the Character section of the Properties panel, change the point size to 24 and click the B (for bold) option, as shown in Figure 30.1.** Enter the following URL in the Link field of the Options section of the Properties panel and choose _blank in the Target menu:

   ```
   http://www.flashsupport.com
   ```

4. **With the text block still active, select the Robert Reinhardt text, and, in the Properties panel, enter the following text for the URL field in the Link field:**

   ```
   mailto:robert@theMakers.com
   ```

5. **Select the Snow Dowd text and enter the following text in the URL field of the Link field in the Properties panel:**

   ```
   mailto:snow@theMakers.com
   ```

   See Figure 30.2 for an example of how the URL-linked text will appear.

FIGURE 30.1

You can selectively change text within one text block or field.

FIGURE 30.2

URL-linked text appears with dashed underlines. You will not see this dashed underline in the actual Flash movie file (.swf).

6. **Save the Flash document, and test the Flash movie file (.swf) by choosing Control ➪ Test Movie.** When you click the Flash CS4 Bible text, a browser opens and loads the official support site for *Flash CS4 Professional Bible* in a new window. When you click either author's name, your e-mail client opens a new message window.

ON the CD-ROM You will find the completed `htmlText_static.fla` document in the `ch30` folder on this book's CD-ROM.

Try making another example with your own text and URL links. You can even add `javascript:` commands to URL links.

Inserting HTML tags into text fields with ActionScript

In this section, we continue with the example that you created in the last section. You convert the static text block into a dynamic text field and manipulate the formatting with ActionScript.

1. **Resave your Flash document from the preceding section as** `htmlText_dynamic. fla`. You will convert this static text into a dynamic text field, so you'll want to keep your original static text example for future reference.

2. **Select the text block and open the Properties panel.** Change the text type to Dynamic Text and make sure that the HTML option is enabled. In the `<Instance Name>` field, type the name `bookField`. This text field can be updated with ActionScript directed at the `bookField` instance. You can also disable the Show Border option if you don't want to see a bounding box around your text.

NOTE If switching the text type removes the formatting you applied in the previous section's exercise, reapply the formatting, including the `mailto:` links.

3. **Rename the static text layer to** dynamic text.

4. **Create a new layer named** actions. Select frame 1 of the actions layer, and open the Actions panel (F9/Option+F9). Add the following code to the Script pane. This code displays the `htmlText` value of the `bookField` field in the Output window when you test the movie.

```
//TextField bookField;
trace("htmlText: " + bookField.htmlText);
```

5. **Save the Flash document and test it (Ctrl+Enter/⌘+Return).** While the Flash movie is playing in the Test Movie window, you should see the HTML formatting tags displayed in the Output window. The `htmlText` property reads as one continuous line displaying the following markup:

```
htmlText: <TEXTFORMAT LEADING="2"><P ALIGN="LEFT"><FONT
FACE="Verdana Bold" SIZE="24" COLOR="#000000" LETTERSPACING="0"
   KERNING="0"><A
HREF="http://www.flashsupport.com" TARGET="_blank">Flash CS4
```

```
Bible</A></FONT></P></TEXTFORMAT><TEXTFORMAT LEADING="2">
<P ALIGN="LEFT"><FONT FACE="Verdana" SIZE="18"
COLOR="#000000" LETTERSPACING="0" KERNING="0">by
<A HREF="mailto:robert@theMakers.com" TARGET="">Robert
Reinhardt</A> &amp; <A HREF="mailto:snow@theMakers.com"
TARGET="">Snow Dowd</A></FONT></P></TEXTFORMAT>
```

You can observe the requisite ActionScript syntax for HTML formatting in the Output panel.

> **NOTE** HTML tag names are not case-sensitive in Flash. We prefer to use XHTML-compliant code; as such, you'll see our examples later in this chapter use all lowercase characters in HTML tag and attribute names. The values of attributes, such as file URLs in `href` or `src`, require attention to case-sensitivity.

6. **Close the Test Movie window and go back to the Main Timeline of your Flash document.** Create a new dynamic text field below the existing `bookField` instance, and in the Properties panel, enable the HTML option. In the `<Instance Name>` field, type the name `bookField2`.

7. **Select the first frame of the actions layer and open the Actions panel (F9/ Option+F9).** In the Script pane, specify an HTML-formatted string value for the `html-Text` property of the `bookField2` instance, such as the following code. Comment out the `trace()` action you inserted earlier as well. (Note that the \ character is required before additional quotes within a string value. The ⤵ character indicates a continuation of the same line of code.)

```
//TextField bookField;
//TextField bookField2;
//trace("htmlText: " + bookField.htmlText);
bookField2.htmlText = "<font face=\"Verdana\" ⤵
  size=\"24\" color=\"#0000FF\"><b><a ⤵
  href=\"http://www.communitymx.com\"> ⤵
  CommunityMX</a></b></font>";
```

> **NOTE** The last line of code should appear as one line number in the Script pane of the Actions panel.

8. **Save the Flash document and test it.** The `bookField2` text field displays the HTML-formatted value that you specified in the actions layer.

You can also use variables in expressions for HTML-formatted text fields, such as the following (note that the `bookURL` variable and value should appear on one line of code):

```
var bookURL:String = "http://www.flashsupport.com";
var bookTitle:String = "Flash CS4 Bible";
bookField.htmlText = "<a href=\"" + bookURL + "\">" + bookTitle + "</
  a>";
```

By using other ActionScript variables and methods, you can apply specific text formatting to external data sources that have been loaded into the Flash movie, such as database records or lists. In the next section, you learn how to format text within text fields by using the TextFormat object in ActionScript.

 You can find the completed htmlText_dynamic.fla document in the ch30 folder on this book's CD-ROM.

Formatting fields with the TextFormat object

ActionScript offers a wide range of options for the TextField object. Many properties of the MovieClip object, such as x and y, can be controlled with TextField objects, too. One interesting method of the TextField object is the setTextFormat() method. This method enables you to control the formatting of text within a TextField object without relying on HTML tags. The setTextFormat() method requires another object — a TextFormat object — that contains individual properties and values in order to adjust the targeted instance's text contents.

TIP　ActionScript 3.0 code can also create text fields on-the-fly, using the new TextField() constructor.

In this section, you create a Flash movie that makes a dynamic text field on-the-fly and applies formatting to the field with the TextFormat object. You also use the TextFormat object to determine the dimensions of the TextField instance.

1. **Create a new Flash file (ActionScript 3.0).** Save the document as textFormat_ 100.fla.

2. **Rename Layer 1 to** actions. ActionScript creates the entire contents of this movie. You will not use any tools from the Tools panel to create the text.

3. **Select frame 1 of the actions layer and open the Actions panel.** Type the following code into the Script pane:

```
var titleFormat:TextFormat = new TextFormat();
with(titleFormat){
    font = "Verdana";
    bold = true;
    color = 0x0000FF;
    url = "http://www.flashsupport.com/";
    target = "_blank";
}
```

This code creates a new TextFormat object named titleFormat (line 1). This formatting is used for site links displayed in the Flash movie. Within this object, properties of the site link text are specified. Lines 2 through 8 assign the font, bold, color, url, and target properties of the style. In later steps, you apply this style to a TextField instance.

4. **After the last line of code listed in Step 3, add the following code.**

```
var sitesField:TextField = new TextField();
with(sitesField){
  x = 10;
  y = 10;
  text = "FlashSupport.com";
  setTextFormat(titleFormat);
  autoSize = TextFieldAutoSize.LEFT;
}
addChild(sitesField);
```

The first line of code uses the new TextField() constructor of the TextField class to make a new dynamic text field named sitesField.

The second line begins a with() statement, to apply all the nested code to the new sitesField object.

The third and fourth lines position the field at the X and Y coordinates of 10, 10.

The fifth line fills the text field with the value of "FlashSupport.com".

Line 6 applies the titleFormat object to the entire contents of the sitesField instance.

The seventh line sets the autoSize property to the TextFieldAutoSize.LEFT constant, which automatically resizes the TextField instance to fit the contents specified by the text property.

Line 8 closes the with() statement, and line 9 adds the sitesField instance to the display list of the Main Timeline, making the field visible.

> **NOTE** In ActionScript 3.0, make sure that you use the setTextFormat() method if you want to apply formatting to existing text in a TextField instance. If you want to apply formatting before you populate a field with text, use the defaultTextFormat property.

5. **Save the Flash document as** textFormat_100.fla **and test it (Ctrl+Enter/ ⌘+Return).** The sitesField instance appears in the top left corner of the Stage. When you click the text, the default browser opens, displaying the URL for www.flashsupport.com.

> **ON the CD-ROM** You can find the completed textFormat_100.fla file in the ch30 folder on this book's CD-ROM.

Applying style sheets to text fields

In this section, you learn how to load an external style sheet, as a Cascading Style Sheet (CSS) file, and apply its styles to text in a Flash movie.

Making the style sheet

Before you can apply an external style sheet to Flash text, you need to create the CSS file describing the styles. In the following steps, use any text editor such as Notepad or TextEdit, or a full-featured CSS editor, such as Adobe Dreamweaver CS4.

CAUTION   If you use Dreamweaver to create a new CSS file, remove the `@charset "UTF-8";` line of code from the top of the CSS document. This line of code can interfere with the Flash Player's ability to parse the CSS file.

1. Create a new text document.

2. **Define two styles,** `h1` **and** `h2`. These styles should use bold 14- and 12-pixel type, respectively. The font face should be Verdana for both. (See Listing 30.1.)

3. **Define a** `p` **style.** This style is used for regular text in paragraphs. This style uses Arial at 10 px. The color of this text is dark gray, using the hexadecimal value `#666666`. (See Listing 30.1.)

4. **Save your text file as** `styles.css`.

LISTING 30.1

The h1, h2, and Body Styles

```
h1 {
    font-family: Verdana;
    font-weight: bold;
    font-size: 14px;
}

h2 {
    font-family: Verdana;
    font-weight: bold;
    font-size: 12px;
}

p {
    font-family: Arial;
    font-size: 10px;
    color: #666666;
}
```

Loading the style sheet into a Flash movie

After you have a CSS file ready, you can create the ActionScript 3.0 (AS3) code required to load the style sheet into a Flash movie. In the following steps, you'll do just that. In AS3, you load an external style sheet file in the same way you load any external data file — using a `URLLoader` instance. After the file is loaded, the data is parsed into a new `StyleSheet` instance and applied to the `styleSheet` property of a `TextField` instance.

1. Create a new Flash file (ActionScript 3.0).

2. Rename Layer 1 to actions.

3. **Select frame 1 of the actions layer, and open the Actions panel (F9 Option+F9).**
    Type the code shown in Listing 30.2 into the Script pane.

    In line 1 of this code, you create a new URLLoader instance named cssData to load
    the external CSS file. In line 2, you create a listener function named showText for the
    Event.COMPLETE event from the cssData instance. This event fires when the CSS file
    has fully loaded into the Flash movie. You define the showText function in lines 18
    through 30. In line 3, the styles.css file starts loading into the cssData instance.

    In line 5, you create a new StyleSheet instance named css. This instance parses the
    data received by the URLLoader instance you created in line 1.

    In lines 7 through 16, you create a new TextField instance named displayField.
    This large field (400 x 400 pixels) is positioned at an X, Y coordinate of 10,10. The mul-
    tiline and wordWrap properties of the field are set to true, to enable several lines of
    auto-wrapping text.

    In lines 18 through 30, you define the showText function. This function is invoked
    when the external CSS file has finished loading into the movie. Line 19 displays a
    trace() statement in the Output panel when you test the movie in Flash CS4. If you
    don't see this trace output when you test, you know there's a syntax error in your earlier
    lines of code. Line 20 uses the StyleSheet.parseCSS() method to parse the data
    from the styles.css file into the css instance you created in line 5. Line 21 sets the
    styleSheet property of the displayField instance to the css instance. Lines 23
    through 27 create a long string of text that is inserted into the displayField field.
    Here, you can see that each of the styles is used, defined in the class attributes of vari-
    ous <h1>, <h2>, and <p> tags. Because you defined a style for these tags in the style
    sheet, the styles are automatically applied to any text enclosed by the specified tags in
    HTML text. In line 29, the htmlText property of the displayField instance is set to
    the value of the fieldText variable.

4. **Save your Flash document as** css_styles_100.fla **in the same location where
    you saved your** styles.css **file from the previous section.**

5. **Test the movie (Control ⇨ Test Movie).** You should see nicely formatted text, speci-
    fied by the details of the style sheet and the HTML text, as shown in Figure 30.3.

FIGURE 30.3

The formatted text

Flash Player Style Support

You can use style sheets in your Flash Player 7 or higher movies.

Supported styles

More text here...

LISTING 30.2

Loading an External CSS File

```
1.   var cssData:URLLoader = new URLLoader();
2.   cssData.addEventListener(Event.COMPLETE, showText);
3.   cssData.load(new URLRequest("styles.css"));
4.
5.   var css:StyleSheet = new StyleSheet();
6.
7.   var displayField:TextField = new TextField();
8.   with(displayField){
9.     x = 10;
10.    y = 10;
11.    width = 400;
12.    height = 400;
13.    multiline = true;
14.    wordWrap = true;
15.  }
16.  addChild(displayField);
17.
18.  function showText(evt:Event):void {
19.    trace("showText >>>");
20.    css.parseCSS(cssData.data);
21.    displayField.styleSheet = css;
22.
23.    var fieldText:String = "<h1>Flash Player Style Support</h1><br/>";
24.    fieldText += "<p>You can use style sheets in your Flash ↝
         movies.</p><br/>";
25.    fieldText += "<h2>Supported styles</h2><br/>";
26.    fieldText += "<p>More text here...</p>";
27.
28.    displayField.htmlText = fieldText;
29.  }
```

ON the CD-ROM   You can find the completed files, `styles.css` and `css_styles_100.fla`, in the ch30 folder on this book's CD-ROM.

You can also use other nonsystem fonts in style sheets, but you'll need to make sure that you have created linked font symbols in your movie's library or that you have created empty authortime text fields that include the embedded fonts.

Inserting images into text fields

In this section, you learn how to load a JPEG image into a `TextField` object. Continue using the same Flash document you created in the last section.

ON the CD-ROM Open the `css_styles_100.fla` document from the `ch30` folder on this book's CD-ROM if you didn't complete the previous section.

1. **In the** `css_styles_100.fla` **document, select frame 1 of the actions layer, and open the Actions panel (F9/Option+F9).** Change the script to the code shown in Listing 30.3. Remember that you shouldn't include the ⊃ character in your actual code. This character denotes a continuation of the same line of code.

   This code uses the same structure of the `showText()` function from the last section. However, in line 1, you include the `bio.as` file, which you can find in the `ch30` folder of this book's CD-ROM. A copy of this file should exist in the same location as your .fla file. The `bio.as` file declares a string variable named `bioText`, containing a sample biography.

TIP For a final production version of this Flash movie, you may want to load the data stored in the `bio.as` into the Flash movie at runtime. For example, the biography text could be stored in an XML document and loaded with an `XML` object, or it could be loaded from a server-side script. For more information on data loading, read Chapter 29, "Sending Data In and Out of Flash."

   Within the `showText()` function, you use the `<img>` tag to include a JPEG image, `portrait.jpg`, in the `displayField` instance. You can find this JPEG file in the `ch30` folder of this book's CD-ROM, and it's also located at the URL shown in the function.

2. **Save your Flash document as** `img_insert_100.fla` **and test it.** When the movie loads, you should see the header and biography text wrap around the JPEG image, as shown in Figure 30.4.

FIGURE 30.4

The JPEG image with wrapping text

LISTING 30.3

The Modified showText() Function

```
include "bio.as";

var cssData:URLLoader = new URLLoader();
cssData.addEventListener(Event.COMPLETE, showText);
cssData.load(new URLRequest("styles.css"));

var css:StyleSheet = new StyleSheet();

var displayField:TextField = new TextField();
with(displayField){
  x = 10;
  y = 10;
  width = 400;
  height = 400;
  multiline = true;
  wordWrap = true;
}
addChild(displayField);

function showText(evt:Event):void {
  trace("showText >>>");
  css.parseCSS(cssData.data);
  displayField.styleSheet = css;

  var fieldText:String = "<img ⟳
    src='http://www.flashsupport.com/bio/portrait.jpg' id='portrait' ⟳
    width='200' height='200' vspace='4' hspace='8' align='left'>";
  fieldText += "<h1>Robert Reinhardt</h1><br/>";
  fieldText += bioText;

  displayField.htmlText = fieldText;
}
```

ON the CD-ROM You can find the completed document, `img_insert_100.fla`, in the ch30 folder on this book's CD-ROM.

You can also use class names of exported Movie Clip symbols as the value of the `src` attribute of the `<img>` tag. However, you may find that if you use several `<img>` tags in a text field, not all the images load and/or display. In some of our experiments, we noticed that text realigned itself when text with URLs was rolled over. Be sure to test your Flash movies with the latest Flash Player revisions, as Adobe releases them.

Using the TextEvent.LINK event with anchor tags

In ActionScript 3.0, not only can you use HTML formatting in Flash text, but you can also execute Flash actions from your text fields with the `<a>` tag and an `href` attribute value of `event:Your custom event string`. For example, if you wanted to link text to a function that loads a new Flash movie file (.swf) into a `Loader` instance, you can create a custom function that uses the `Loader.load()` action and reference that action from your `<a href>` tag for a text field. See the following code (note that the ⤵ indicates a continuation of the same line of code; do not insert this character into your actual code):

```
var loader:Loader = new Loader();
addChild(loader);

var displayField:TextField = new TextField();
displayField.addEventListener(TextEvent.LINK, getSWF);
displayField.htmlText = "<a href='event:movie.swf'> ⤵
  Click to load movie</a>";
addChild(displayField);

function getSWF(evt:TextEvent):void {
  var swfURL:String = evt.text;
  loader.load(new URLRequest(swfURL));
}
```

In this code example, the text within the `<a></a>` tags executes the `getSWF` listener function, passing the string `movie.swf` as the `text` property of the `evt` parameter. The `TextEvent.LINK` event is broadcast from a `TextField` instance when an HTML link within its text is clicked.

> **TIP** If you need to pass more than one argument, you will need to send all the values as one string separated by a comma (or preferred character). Then you would use the `String.split()` method on the `evt.text` value to separate the arguments.

> **ON the CD-ROM** You can see examples of HTML-formatted Flash text and the `TextEvent.LINK` event in the `ch30/textevent_link` folder on this book's CD-ROM.

Controlling Text Field Properties

Input and dynamic text fields have several properties that are accessible with ActionScript 3.0. In this section, you learn how to control the scrolling and font rendering properties of the `TextField` class.

Scroll properties

Four of the `TextField` class properties, `scrollH`, `scrollV`, `maxScrollH` and `maxScrollV`, control the viewable area of a text field that has more lines of text than the text field can show.

- scrollV: This property can retrieve the current line number (from the top of the field), and it can also move to a new line number in a text field. This property's unit is a line number, not a pixel value.

- scrollH: This property can retrieve the current horizontal position of text within a field. This value is specified as pixels, not lines. If a text field's width is not wide enough to accommodate the width of a line of text, you can manipulate this property to move the text from the right to left or vice versa.

- maxScrollV: This property returns the maximum value of the scrollV property for a given text field. You can only retrieve this value — you cannot set it.

- maxScrollH: This property returns the maximum value of the scrollH property for a given text field. You can only retrieve this value — you cannot set it.

NOTE   The scrollV property advances text line by line in the viewable area of the TextField instance. To learn more about pixel-level vertical scrolling, see the coverage later in this chapter.

To understand how the scrollV and maxScrollV properties work, you need to see how lines are enumerated in a text field. Suppose you had ten lines of text as a string value for a variable called myText. If you want to use this text in a dynamic text field named articleField, which only has a viewable area of five lines, then the remaining five lines of the myText variable will not be seen in the text field. To make the text field "scroll" to the next line of text by showing lines 2 to 6 (instead of lines 1 to 5), you can create a Button instance, such as a down-arrow button, with ActionScript to advance the lines:

```
//SimpleButton downButton;
//TextField articleField;

downButton.addEventListener(MouseEvent.CLICK, scrollText);

function scrollText(evt:MouseEvent):void {
  articleField.scroll++;
}
```

The maxScrollV property returns the maximum value for the top line number in a text field. In our previous 10-line text value example, the maxScrollV property would equal 6. If you had 20 lines of text in the articleField instance, the maxScrollV property would return a value of 16.

TIP   Flash CS4 has a TextArea component that automatically creates a text field and scroll bar. You can find more information on User Interface components in Chapter 32, "Using Components."

ON the CD-ROM   In the ch30/scroll folder on this book's CD-ROM, you will find a Flash document named scrollProp_simple.fla. This movie demonstrates the use of the scroll property to view the entire Gettysburg Address within a text field. A more advanced scrolling mechanism can be found in the scrollProp_advanced.fla file, which features a draggable scroll bar.

Text rendering properties

The Flash Player offers incredible text rendering to your Flash text. The anti-aliasing engine for text is dubbed FlashType, and collectively refers to the properties of text fields that enable you to control the readability of text. In this section, you learn about the following `TextField` properties:

- `antiAliasType:String`: This property controls whether or not the `TextField` instance uses the new FlashType rendering engine. If you set a `TextField` instance's `antiAliasType` property to `"normal"` (or the constant, `AntiAliasType.NORMAL`), the instance renders text just as it did in Flash Player 7 or earlier. If you set the property to `"advanced"` (or the constant, `AntiAliasType.ADVANCED`), the text in the field is displayed with the FlashType engine.

- `thickness:Number`: This property controls the thickness of the glyph edges in the `TextField` instance and is applied only if the `antiAliasType` mode is set to `"advanced"`. The value for this property can be in the range of –200 (less thick) to 200 (more thick).

NOTE A *glyph* refers to any individual character in the font face. The letter *a*, for example, is a glyph.

- `sharpness:Number`: This property controls the sharpness (or softness) of glyph edges in the `TextField` instance. Acceptable values are in the range of -400 (softer) to 400 (sharp). This property affects only text rendered with the `"advanced"` value of the `antiAliasType` property.

TIP In general, we have found that you don't need to tweak thickness and sharpness values of `TextField` instances. However, you may find a particular font that requires some finessing to get the level of readability you desire.

- `gridFitType:String`: This property controls how the pixels of text are rendered when the `antiAliasType` property is set to `"advanced"`. There are three acceptable values:

  - `"none"`: This value specifies that there is no special grid fitting applied to the text rendering. You can also use the constant, `GridFitType.NONE`.

  - `"pixel"`: This value forces the text to be rendered against actual pixels of the computer monitor, rather than across multiple pixels (which would blur the text). If the `TextField` instance is set to use `"advanced"` for `antiAliasType`, the `"pixel"` value is the default value of `gridFitType`. This value is best used for left-aligned text fields. You can also use the constant, `GridFitType.PIXEL`.

  - `"subpixel"`: This value forces the text to be rendered on a subpixel grid, which is best for right-aligned or justified text fields. This value can only be used with `TextField` instances that have the `antiAliasType` property set to `"advanced"`. You can also use the constant, `GridFitType.SUBPIXEL`.

CAUTION These settings apply only to text that uses embedded fonts. If you are using device fonts with text, then you will not see any changes applied to your text.

Working with authortime TextField instances

In this section, you learn how to apply the new anti-aliasing features to `TextField` instances that you place on the Stage at authortime.

1. **Create a new Flash file (ActionScript 3.0) and save it as** `flashtype_100.fla`.

2. **Rename Layer 1 to** fields.

3. **Using the Text tool, add a dynamic text field on the Stage.** In the Properties panel, name the instance `displayField_1`. Make sure you choose Anti-alias for animation and Multiline (see Figure 30.5). You can use any font face you prefer, but use a small text size such as 10 point.

FIGURE 30.5

The settings for the displayField_1 field

NOTE Choosing the Anti-alias for animation setting in the Properties panel is the equivalent of setting the `antiAliasType` property to `"normal"` (or `AntiAliasType.NORMAL`) in ActionScript 3.0.

4. **In the Properties panel, click the Character Embedding button and select the ranges shown in Figure 30.6.** Remember, you can't use the new anti-aliasing features unless you have embedded the font used by the `TextField` instance.

FIGURE 30.6

The Character Embedding options

5. **Duplicate the `displayField_1` field by selecting the instance on the Stage and choosing Edit ➪ Duplicate (Ctrl+D/⌘+D).** Place the new instance to the right of the original instance, and in the Properties panel, rename the instance `displayField_2`. Also, in the Character section of the Properties panel, change the aliasing setting to Anti-alias for readability, as shown in Figure 30.7.

 Choosing the Anti-alias for readability setting is the same as setting the `antiAlias Type` property to `"advanced"` (or `AntiAliasType.ADVANCED`) in ActionScript 3.0.

To add some text to the fields, you will set the text property of the fields in ActionScript.

6. **Create a new layer named** actions. Select frame 1 of the actions layer, and open the Actions panel. Add the following code to the Script pane:

```
//TextField displayField_1;
//TextField displayField_2;
var bodyText:String = "The quick brown fox jumps over ↩
  the lazy dog.";
displayField_1.text = displayField_2.text = bodyText;
```

FIGURE 30.7

The settings for the displayField_2 field

> **TIP** You can use more than one assignment operator (=) in an ActionScript expression. In this example, you first set the `text` property of the `displayField_2` to the value of `bodyText`. Then the text property of the `displayField_1` is set from the same value.

7. **Save the document and test it (Ctrl+Enter/⌘+Enter).** The left field should show the regular anti-aliasing quality of the text, which is difficult to read at 10 point. As shown in Figure 30.8, though, the right field uses the new FlashType engine, which greatly improves its legibility.

FIGURE 30.8

The two primary settings for anti-aliasing in Flash movies

> **ON the CD-ROM** You can find the completed file, `flashtype_100.fla`, in the `ch30` folder on this book's CD-ROM.

Controlling anti-aliasing with runtime TextField instances

In this section, you learn how to use ActionScript to create `TextField` instances and set their anti-aliasing properties.

1. **Continue using the `flashtype_100.fla` file you created in the last section, or make a copy of the same file from this book's CD-ROM.** Resave this file as `flashtype_101.fla`.

2. **Delete the fields layer.** You will re-create these fields in ActionScript. Even though you will use ActionScript to create TextField instances at runtime, you still need to embed the font you want to use with your TextField instances.

3. **Create a new layer named** embedded fonts.

4. **Using the Text tool, add a dynamic text field to the document, preferably offstage above the Stage area, as shown in Figure 30.9.** Type the text abc into this field. In the Properties panel, make sure that the text field type is Dynamic Text, and name this instance `embedField_1`. Choose your preferred font face for the field; for this example, we used Verdana. In the Character section of the Properties panel, enable the HTML button (< >) for this instance as well. Click the Character Embedding button and select the same ranges shown earlier in Figure 30.6.

FIGURE 30.9

The settings for the embedField_1 field

NOTE Some Flash designers and developers prefer to embed fonts by creating font symbols in the document's Library panel. Font symbols are useful if you need every character (including a wide range of foreign language characters and ASCII art symbols) in your Flash movie, but they greatly increase your .swf file size. Adding the entire Verdana font face as a Font symbol, for example, adds 20K to your Flash movie file (.swf) size! But if you only need the character ranges shown in Figure 30.6, using a dynamic text instance on the Stage adds only 12K to your Flash movie file (.swf) size.

Because the HTML option is enabled on the `embedField_1` instance, you can control the formatting of the abc characters you typed into the field.

5. **Select the b character, and bold it in the Character section of the Properties panel.** Select the c character and italicize it in the Character section of the Properties panel. When you are finished, your field should resemble the one shown in Figure 30.10.

FIGURE 30.10

The abc text with styles applied to the b and c characters

TIP By adding the bold and italic styles to the `embedField_1` field, you are effectively embedding Verdana Bold and Verdana Italic font faces in the .swf file for this example. As such, you can use bold and italic formatting in `TextField` instances, with applied `TextFormat` instances or HTML text. You'll use HTML text later in this exercise. However, embedding these additional styles adds more weight to the SWF's file size. If you prefer to use font symbols, you can add a new font symbol for each font face style you want to embed.

Now you're ready to modify the ActionScript on frame 1 of the actions layer. The new script, shown in Listing 30.4, creates two `TextField` instances by using the same instance names used in the previous section's example. Near the end of the `init()` function, notice that `displayField_1` uses the `AntiAliasType.NORMAL` value for the `antiAliasType` property, and `displayField_2` uses the `AntiAliasType.ADVANCED` value. (Note that the ⤸ character indicates a continuation of the same line of code — do not include this character in your actual code.)

> **TIP** This script also creates an inline style sheet, `movieStyles`. The local variable `styles` in the `init()` function shows the inline style, which is exactly the same text you would insert into a CSS file. You can use the `parseCSS()` method of the `StyleSheet` class to convert a `String` value into a full-fledged style sheet.

6. **Save the Flash document and test it (Ctrl+Enter/⌘+Enter).** As shown in Figure 30.11, you should see similar anti-aliasing results as you saw in the last section.

FIGURE 30.11

The two text fields with `"normal"` anti-aliasing (left) and `"advanced"` anti-aliasing (right)

LISTING 30.4

Applying Anti-Aliasing to TextField Instances

```
var displayField_1:TextField;
var displayField_2:TextField;
var movieStyles:StyleSheet;
var fieldText:String = "<h1>Typing Lessons 101</h1><p>The <i>quick</i> brown
    fox jumps over the lazy dog.</p>";

init();

function init():void {
  movieStyles = new StyleSheet();
  var styles:String = "p { font-family: Verdana; font-size: 10; }";
```

continued

LISTING 30.4   *(continued)*

```
styles += "h1 { font-family: Verdana Bold; font-size: 14; }";
movieStyles.parseCSS(styles);

displayField_1 = new TextField();
displayField_1.x = 25;
addChild(displayField_1);
displayField_2 = new TextField();
displayField_2.x = 250;
addChild(displayField_2);

var fields:Array = [displayField_1, displayField_2];
for(var i:int = 0; i < fields.length; i++){
  var t:TextField = fields[i];
  with(t){
    y = 25;
    width = 200;
    height = 100;
    border = true;
    multiline = true;
    wordWrap = true;
    selectable = true;
    embedFonts = true;
    styleSheet = movieStyles;
  }
}
displayField_1.antiAliasType = AntiAliasType.NORMAL;
displayField_2.antiAliasType = AntiAliasType.ADVANCED;
displayField_1.htmlText = displayField_2.htmlText = fieldText;
}
```

ON the CD-ROM You can find the completed file, `flashtype_101.fla`, in the `ch30` folder on this book's CD-ROM.

Comparing anti-aliasing effects

To help demonstrate the new sharpness and thickness properties of the `TextField` class, open the `flashtype_200.fla` file located in the `ch30` folder of this book's CD-ROM. On the Stage of this document, you'll see an instance of the displayClip symbol, named `display`. If you test the Flash movie (Ctrl+Enter/⌘+Enter), you can type text into the input text field, and change the anti-aliasing mode of the field. You can also change the alignment of the field, the grid fitting value (`gridFitType`), as well as the `thickness` and `sharpness` values of the `"advanced"` anti-aliasing mode.

ON the CD-ROM You can run the `flashtype_200.swf` file directly in the stand-alone Flash Player or in a browser window. You can find this file in the `ch30` folder on this book's CD-ROM. You can add more instances of the displayClip symbol on to the Stage of the Flash document (`flashtype_200.fla`) to have side-by-side comparisons of text and anti-aliasing values.

Pixel-based Text Scrolling with Movie Clips

The `MovieClip.scrollRect` property controls the viewable area of a `MovieClip` instance on the Stage and can only be set with ActionScript (that is, you won't find a `scrollRect` setting in the Properties panel for Movie Clip symbols). You can think of the `scrollRect` property as a built-in mask that selectively shows content within the `MovieClip` object.

TIP In ActionScript 3.0, you need to use the `Rectangle` class to create the rectangle shape that will be used by a `MovieClip` object's `scrollRect` property. You learn how to create a `Rectangle` object in this section's example.

You can use the `scrollRect` property to show and hide any type of content within a `MovieClip` object. In this section, you learn how to use the `scrollRect` property to create a scrollable area with text content within a `MovieClip` object. You learn how to control the y property of a `TextField` instance with the UIScrollBar component. Typically, the UIScrollBar component is used to update the `scroll` property of a `TextField` instance, not the `TextField` instance's y property.

ON the CD-ROM To get a sense of these two different types of scrolling, open the `scroll_comparison.html` document in the `ch30/scroll` folder on this book's CD-ROM. This page shows a Flash movie comparing text scrolling with the `scroll` property versus the y property of a `TextField` instance.

In the following steps, you learn how to build a Flash movie that pixel-scrolls a `TextField` instance with the UIScrollBar component.

1. **Make a copy of the** `as3_pixelscroll_starter.fla` **file from the** `ch30/scroll` **folder on this book's CD-ROM.** Open the file in Flash CS4, and resave it as `as3_pixelscroll_100.fla`. This starter file has a `TextField` instance named `displayField` on the Stage. This field is set to embed the same range of Verdana font characters just like the previous examples in this chapter and already contains the text from the Gettysburg Address.

2. **Nest the** `displayField` **instance into a new Movie Clip symbol by selecting the** `displayField` **instance on the Stage, and choose Modify ⇨ Convert to Symbol.** Name the symbol Holder, and set the registration to the top left corner, as shown in Figure 30.12. Click OK to finish creating the symbol.

FIGURE 30.12

The Convert to Symbol dialog box

3. **Select the new Holder symbol instance on the Main Timeline (that is, Scene 1) Stage.** In the Properties panel, name this instance `holder`. Also, rename the displayField layer to **holder**.

   Now you're ready to create a `Rectangle` object to use as the `scrollRect` value for the `holder` instance. As you can see, the `displayField` instance nested within the `holder` instance continues offstage. The `scrollRect` for the `holder` will be 300 x 300 pixels.

4. **Create a new layer named** actions. Select frame 1 of the actions layer, and open the Actions panel (F9/Option+F9). Add the code shown in Listing 30.5.

   The first line after the code comment imports the `Rectangle` class, which is part of the `flash.geom` class. The next two lines of code create variables for the `Rectangle` and `TextField` instances that will be used within the `init()` function.

   The `init()` function creates the `Rectangle` instance and uses the instance for the `scrollRect` property of the `holder` instance. The w and h variables establish the width and height, respectively, of the viewable area of the `MovieClip` instance. The `Rectangle` constructor uses four arguments: the starting X position, the starting Y position, the width, and the height of the rectangle shape. After the shape is created, it is set to be the value of the `scrollRect` property of the `holder` instance. The `display-Field` variable is also set to equal the `displayField` instance inside of the `holder` instance, to create a shorter reference name for the `TextField` instance.

   Before the `init()` function is defined, the function is invoked so that the `Rectangle` instance is bound to the `holder` instance when the Flash movie starts.

   NOTE   Due to rendering oddities of the FlashType engine, you buffer the width of the `Rectangle` instance (`win`) by 5 pixels. This buffer makes sure that any text bleeding outside of the `TextField` instance is still viewable.

5. **Save the document and test it (Ctrl+Enter/⌘+Enter).** You should see that the new `Rectangle` instance now masks the text, as shown in Figure 30.13.

FIGURE 30.13

The `scrollRect` property masks the lower half of the `TextField` instance.

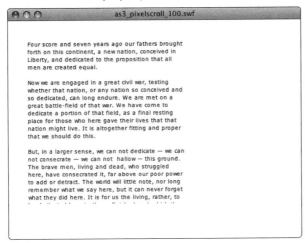

After the field is masked, you can add a scroll bar to enable the user to view the entirety of the text.

6. **Open the Components panel (Ctrl+F7/⌘+F7), expand the User Interface grouping, and drag a copy of the `UIScrollBar` instance to the document's Stage.** After you've added the component to the Stage, select the instance and delete it. You simply need a copy of the UIScrollBar component in the movie's Library panel. In the next step, you attach the component to the movie's Stage via ActionScript.

7. **Select frame 1 of the actions layer, and open the Actions panel.** Add the bold code shown in Listing 30.6 to the existing script. In this modified script, you import two new classes: `UIScrollBar` and `ScrollEvent`.

   The `init()` function adds four new lines of code, which create a new instance of the UIScrollBar component. The new instance is named `sb` and is positioned to the right of the `holder` instance. More important, the minimum and maximum values that the scroll bar should return for its `scrollPosition` property are defined. The height of the Rectangle object is subtracted from the total height of the `displayField` instance because you don't want to scroll the `TextField` instance off the Stage. The size of the UIScrollBar instance is also sized to the height of the `Rectangle` instance. The `init` function also adds the new handler, `onScroll`, as a listener to the `"scroll"` event (represented by the constant, `ScrollEvent.SCROLL`) broadcasted from the UIScrollBar component.

973

The last block of code defines the onScroll() function, which is invoked whenever the user interacts with the UIScrollBar instance, sb. The scrollPosition property returned by the sb is used to set the y position of the displayField instance. Note that the value is inverted so that the top of the TextField instance moves up. (You can come back to this code and remove the – sign to see what happens if it's not there.)

8. **Save the document and test it (Ctrl+Enter/⌘+Enter).** You should now see an instance of the UIScrollBar component attached to the right of the holder instance displaying the text, as shown in Figure 30.14. If you click and drag the scroll box, you can smoothly scroll the text.

FIGURE 30.14

The scroll bar attached to the right of the text display

LISTING 30.5

Creating a Rectangle Object

```
//MovieClip holder;

import flash.geom.Rectangle;

var win:Rectangle;
var displayField:TextField;

init();
```

```
function init():void {
  var w:Number = 300;
  var h:Number = 300;
  win = new Rectangle(0, 0, w+5, h);
  holder.scrollRect = win;
  displayField = holder.displayField;
}
```

LISTING 30.6

Attaching a UIScrollBar Component

```
//MovieClip holder;

import flash.geom.Rectangle;
import fl.controls.UIScrollBar;
import fl.events.ScrollEvent;

var win:Rectangle;
var displayField:TextField;
var sb:UIScrollBar;

init();

function init():void {
  var w:Number = 300;
  var h:Number = 300;
  win = new Rectangle(0, 0, w+5, h);
  holder.scrollRect = win;
  displayField = holder.displayField;

  sb = new UIScrollBar();
  with(sb){
    x = holder.x + holder.width + 5;
    y = holder.y;
    setScrollProperties(h, 0, displayField.height - h);
    setSize(sb.width, h);
    addEventListener(ScrollEvent.SCROLL, onScroll);
  }
  addChild(sb);
}

function onScroll(evt:ScrollEvent):void {
  displayField.y = -sb.scrollPosition;
}
```

ON the CD-ROM You can find the completed file, `as3_pixelscroll_100.fla`, in the ch30/ `scroll` folder on this book's CD-ROM.

WEB RESOURCE We'd like to know what you think about this chapter. Visit `www.flashsupport.com/feedback` to send us your comments.

Summary

- You can use HTML text formatting within Flash text fields. Only basic HTML text formatting is allowed.

- You can insert HTML tags into the values of ActionScript variables that refer to input or dynamic text fields. Any quotes used with HTML attributes should be preceded by a backward slash, \.

- You can now apply style sheets to text within Flash movies. The `TextField` class can also display inline artwork with the HTML `<img>` tag.

- The `event:` parameter for the `HREF` attribute of the `<a>` tag enables you to execute ActionScript functions from text fields. You can pass a string value to the specified function.

- The `scrollV` property of input and dynamic text fields enables you to control the portion of a text field value that appears within the text field. `maxScrollV` returns the highest line number for a given set of text in a text field.

- The FlashType rendering engine of the Flash Player enables you to create Flash movies with small text that is more legible than in older versions of the Flash Player.

Chapter 31

Creating a Game in Flash

Creating a game requires much more than programming. It is a combination of many skills — game design, interaction design, visual and sound design, and scripting — that brings it all together. These skills also represent the different phases of game design and are covered in this chapter. You must devote your attention to all these aspects of design to produce a successful game.

To illustrate the different aspects of game design, we deconstruct a simple game, the universally known Hangman.

ON the CD-ROM Before reading through this chapter, copy the `ch31` folder on the CD-ROM onto your hard drive. Double-click the `hangman.html` file located inside of the copied folder to play the game in a browser and become acquainted with our project. The functionality of the game is broken down into three custom classes: `GameModel`, `GameView`, and `GameController`. You learn about the purpose of each class file as you proceed with this chapter.

The Game Plan: Four Phases of Game Design

Game development includes the four phases we introduced earlier: game design, interaction design, visual and sound design, and scripting. The following sections discuss those phases in detail.

NOTE   Many thanks to Jonathan Brzyski for contributing his illustrations to the Flash movie used in this chapter. You can learn more about Jonathan at `www.humanface.com/brzyski`. This edition of the *Flash Bible* uses a modified version of the original `hangman.fla` file created by Veronique Brossier, discussed in *Macromedia Flash MX Bible* (Wiley, 2002). We've updated this version to use an object-oriented programming model with ActionScript 3.0.

Game design

Designing a game is creating a fantasy world, a story, and characters with defined roles and goals. It establishes a structure with a clearly defined set of rules and a scoring system. In a single-player computer game, such as the one we created for this chapter, the computer acts both as the opponent and the referee.

This traditional Hangman game presents the user with a number of empty slots corresponding to the letters of a word. The player must guess the word, entering one letter at a time. When a player guesses correctly, the letter appears in the appropriate slot. A wrong guess and the hangman is revealed, one body part at a time. It is clearly understood that the hangman is a representation of the state of the user in the game. Being hanged represents defeat, but no harm is done. If the user guesses the word before the body is complete, he or she wins the round; otherwise, the man is hanged, and the user has lost the round.

Interaction design

Interaction design is creating the visual representation of the mechanisms of a game: It determines how to play the game and communicates the rules to the user.

The interaction of our game is very simple, and the design should be just as simple. To keep the interface to a minimum, the alphabet both represents the choices and displays the user's selection. The character's physical state is a character representation of the user as well as an indication of the score within one round.

For the Hangman interface, you need the following:

- Text fields to display the empty slots for the letters of the word to guess.
- A listing of the alphabet that indicates letters already selected as well as ones that remain. This listing is also the device by which the user can select a letter.
- A field for feedback from the computer referee.
- An area to display the score.
- The hangman character.

Visual and sound design

The visual design is essential because it is the first and longest-lasting impression. It communicates the mood of the game. Ours is fun, colorful, and somewhat humorous.

This particular game is fairly limited, with not much of a narrative. Nonetheless, the character drawing and animation should keep the user entertained: The hangman is now an alien character going back to the mother ship. Each round was designed with a different set of colors to give some visual diversity. The alien choice is meant to be humorous, both as a homage to the old computer games that used such characters and as a spoof of the multitude of computer demonstrations and illustrations using aliens.

The alien character and the background, including the selection of color schemes, were created by Jonathan Brzyski, a talented artist with a sense of humor (see Figure 31.1).

Of course, good sound effects are an important complement to the visual. They translate a mood and are helpful to indicate a win or a loss. They also are crucial in supporting and reinforcing animation.

FIGURE 31.1

Our version of the hangman is a tribute to aliens and old computer games.

Scripting

Scripting (or programming) a game is the task of asking a series of questions and making decisions, including asking new questions based on the answers, in a language and syntax that the computer can understand. Writing short and task-specific functions is helpful to break down the logic of the game into discrete elements.

The programmer must deconstruct the game in terms of a dialogue between the computer and the player. It must address every detail, no matter how obvious it seems. By thinking of the flow of events ahead of time, you can write code that can handle several aspects of a problem at different times of your game cycle.

Finally, with every new update, Flash provides new functions to simplify our scripting task. Becoming acquainted with them streamlines this process and makes your code easier to write and more elegant.

In the ActionScript 3.0 version of the game in this book, we've rebuilt the code base for the Hangman game. The three class files associated with the project, `GameModel.as`, `GameView.as`, and `GameController.as`, use a loose interpretation of the Model-View-Controller (MVC) design pattern. There are whole books dedicated to the topic of design patterns in computer programming, and it's beyond the scope of our chapter coverage to describe this pattern in intricate detail.

For starters, though, let's define a design pattern. A design pattern, when discussed with respect to computer programming, is simply a standard solution to a common programming problem. Because ActionScript 3.0 is object oriented, the Flash developer community has implemented several design patterns from other computer languages in its ActionScript coding practices. Many of our examples in this book simply use a collection of function calls to build interactivity into the Flash movie's user interface. However, as you start to build more complex Flash movies, you will find that you have to designate roles for each piece of your code — if you just add one function after another on frame 1 of your Main Timeline, pretty soon, you'll have 600 lines of code with little or no organizing principle. So, a design pattern can help you organize your code because the pattern provides a framework for your code. Of course, you still have to write your own code, but the pattern establishes rules for how operations within the code can be conducted.

Let's break down the design pattern used by this version of the Hangman game. The overarching design pattern is called the Observer pattern. The Observer pattern's "rule" is fairly simple: An object in your code can facilitate changes to other objects. In ActionScript, you've likely practiced this concept a few times when you've used the User Interface components in previous examples shown in this book. For example, you can have a button component's `"click"` (or `Mouse Event.CLICK`) event observed by several other components within the movie. With respect to the Hangman game, the Observer pattern enables a core object (called the *model*) to broadcast changes in the game's state to other objects, such as a `MovieClip` instance responsible for displaying the current challenge word and the `MovieClip` instance responsible for displaying what letter(s) have been selected by the user. The MVC design pattern used by the game consists of three discrete pieces:

- **Model:** The model for the Hangman game is a class named `GameModel`. This model has the following responsibilities:
  - Maintain a list of chosen words used within the game.

■ Track the current displayed state of the game, from loading the challenge words from a text (.txt) file to the active/inactive states of the hangman alien pieces.

■ Check letters selected by the user for matches to the current challenge word.

■ **View:** The view for the Hangman game is defined with a class named `GameView`. GameView is also a Movie Clip symbol in the `hangman.fla` document's library. The view contains the necessary graphical elements to display the current game state to the user. For this game, the view consists of the hangman body parts, the artwork behind the hangman, the text fields to display the state of the challenge word, and the text to display the number of wins and losses during the current game. Some of these items, such as the background artwork and the hangman artwork, are created at authortime and placed on the GameView symbol timeline. The text fields, however, are all generated in ActionScript.

■ **Controller:** The controller for the game is defined with a class named `GameController`. The controller is responsible for communicating changes to the game state back to the model. In this game, the controller is fairly simple: a collection of buttons displaying the letters of the alphabet. When the user clicks a letter button, the model is informed of the new letter selection and processes that input accordingly.

You learn more about each of these classes as we deconstruct the Hangman game in the rest of the chapter.

Building the Project

This section discusses the creation of the art and assets for the interface and then talks about assembling the game's mechanics.

In the tradition of character animation, the alien puppet is constructed of independent Movie Clip symbols for each body part for maximum flexibility. (Figure 31.2 shows the timeline of the head-Clip symbol in the View Assets ➪ hangMan ➪ hangMan elements folder of the document's Library panel.) Each Movie Clip in the hangMan elements folder is made of nine frames used for the nine rounds of the game. Each frame displays the same Movie Clip symbol with different advanced color effects. You can view the color settings by selecting the Movie Clip symbol, opening the Properties panel, and clicking the Settings button to the right of the Color menu. Note that by using the color effects, you can use the same symbols over and over, keep your file small, and still develop a very large visual vocabulary.

When the game is a loss and the alien is complete, an animation is triggered. This animation uses the beamClip symbol and the BlurFader component. Both of these symbols are attached dynamically in ActionScript, which you'll see later in this chapter.

FIGURE 31.2

The headClip symbol uses the head symbol and displays it with different color schemes. This timeline is shown with the Preview in Context option enabled in the timeline window.

Scripting the Game

The Hangman game consists of a series of rounds, corresponding to the number of available words to guess. In each round, the computer randomly chooses a word and generates slots as placeholders for the letters. The user attempts to guess the word one letter at a time. For each right guess, the letter appears. For each wrong guess, a piece of the alien character appears. After six wrong guesses, the alien character is completed, does a little animation for us, and the round is over. The score for each round appears on the screen.

The three primary states to the game are the setup, user input, and interpretation of the user input. Most of the code for this aspect of the game is located in the class files located in the `ch31/src` folder on this book's CD-ROM.

The game has an additional feature: The user name and his or her score are saved on the local machine, and the data is available the next time the user plays the game. Most of the code for this feature is located in the `GameModel` class. However, we cover this feature last.

TIP   The `SharedObject` class enables you to save data locally, similar to the way a JavaScript cookie saves data in a browser.

Initializing the Game

Before examining the code structure the game uses, you learn about a few of the variables that are vital to structure of the game.

Main Timeline and Document Class overview

Open the `hangman.fla` file in the `src` folder of the `ch31` folder you copied earlier in this chapter. Amazingly, you won't find any ActionScript code on a keyframe of the Main Timeline. In ActionScript 3.0 and Flash CS4, you can create a document class file that binds to the Flash document upon publishing or testing a movie. The only two layers on the Main Timeline are an embedded font layer and a temporary position reference instance of the `GameView` class. We talk about the document class and each of these layers in this section.

The Hangman.as document class

With the `hangman.fla` file open, view the Properties panel and make sure nothing is selected on the Stage — you can press the Esc key to deselect active elements. As shown in Figure 31.3, the Properties panel for the Flash file features a Class field, which allows you to link an ActionScript 3.0 class file to the entire Flash document. The `hangman.fla` file is already linked to a custom class named `Hangman`, which is part of the `com.flashsupport.games` package. You do not type the .as file extension for a class file specified in the Class field of the Properties panel.

> **TIP** You can also specify the document class in the Publish Settings dialog box. Choose File ⇨ Publish Settings, and in the Flash tab, click the Settings button next to the Script version menu. In the Advanced ActionScript 3.0 Settings dialog box, you can edit the document class name.

In the `src/com/flashsupport/games` folder of `ch31` folder you copied from the book's CD-ROM, open the `Hangman.as` file. The actions of this class file, shown in Listing 31.1, establish the following structure, common among any custom class file you might create:

- **Package name:** In ActionScript 3.0, a class file must begin with the package keyword (excluding comments). A package name refers to the path of the class, where it can be found for compiling into the published .swf file. In this example, the package name, `com.flashsupport.games`, means that this class is stored in the `com/flashsupport/games` folder. Simply replace directory separators (`/`) with a period (`.`) and you have a package name! When you build your own classes, it's a good idea to create a unique package name. Most developers use their domain names as a unique identifier, with a reverse order. So, a domain name such as `flashsupport.com` (which is the domain for this book) becomes `com.flashsupport` as a package name and folder structure.

- **Import statements:** After the package name, the class file lists any class dependencies. For example, if you reference the `MovieClip` class as a data type in the class, you must specify the class path to the `MovieClip` class. Unlike actions on the Main Timeline of a Flash document (.fla file), every data type used in a class file requires an `import` statement. The only exceptions to this rule are data types such as `XML`, `Array`, `Boolean`, `Number`, `String`, `int`, `uint`, or `void`. A class path that begins with the name `flash.` is an intrinsic class of the Flash Player and does not add any additional file size to your published Flash movie. In this example, though, every class inside of the `com.flash-support.games.hangman` package is imported, using the wild card character, `*`. Note that the `import` statement itself only makes the specified class path(s) available for the ActionScript compiler. If a class file is imported but not used in the actual code, it does not get added to the final Flash movie.

- **Class name:** After necessary class files are imported into the class, you define the class name with the `class` keyword. In this example, the class name is `Hangman`. The `public` keyword enables this class to be accessed by other Flash content, such as a separate movie that loads the `hangman.swf` file. In general, a document class is declared as a `public` class.

> **NOTE** The `private` keyword has the opposite behavior of the `public` keyword. If a class member is defined as `private`, only the class itself has the ability to access that element. Other classes cannot access a `private` member.

- **Property declarations:** After the class name is declared, public and private variables that can act as properties for the class are listed. For the `Hangman` class, three variable names — `gm`, `gv`, and `gc` — are reserved for `GameModel`, `GameView`, and `GameController` instances, respectively. The actual instances for these classes are created later in the `Hangman` class. The one authortime `TextField` instance named `embed_1` is declared as a public variable.

- **Constructor function:** The constructor function is a function with the same name as the class. The `Hangman` function is automatically invoked when the Flash movie loads. In addition to the `trace()` output, the constructor function calls the private `init` method to set up the game.

> **NOTE** It is not necessary for an ActionScript 3.0 class to have a constructor function — if nothing needs to automatically occur when a new instance of a class is created, you can omit the constructor function.

- **Methods:** The only method in this class is named `init`, which is automatically invoked by the constructor function. The procedures within this private function are discussed next.

The first two sections of code within the `init` method create an instance of the `GameView` and `GameController` classes, `gv` and `gc`, respectively. The `GameView` and `GameController` classes are found in the com.flashsupport.games.hangman package. Note that the data types of the gv and gc instances are the names of these classes. After you cast a data type for a variable, the ActionScript compiler can more thoroughly check your code for errors, letting you know if you're trying to set a nonexistent property or set a property to an invalid value. We discuss these instances a bit later in this chapter.

TIP The GameView instance placed on the gvTemp layer of the Main Timeline is there as a placeholder, to determine where the instance should be placed, in terms of X and Y position, for the new GameView() constructor. This layer is turned into a guide layer to prevent it from exporting in the published (or tested) .swf file.

The third section of code within the init method creates the model for the game. The model is the central "brain" of the game. The model keeps track of the game state, and determines if the user has correctly selected a letter contained in the challenge phrase. The model does not belong to a DisplayObjectContainer class like the Sprite or MovieClip class as our GameView and GameController instances do. An instance of the GameModel needs to be created at the beginning of the movie in ActionScript code. After an instance is created, there's only one thing to do with the model: Supply it with the URL (or path) to the data provider for the game.

NOTE When the new instance of GameModel is created, all the actions in the init() function of the GameModel class are executed. The actions in the init() function set up all the game's status messages displayed to the user during game play. These messages are stored in the labels property of the GameModel class. You can follow along with the deconstruction of the GameModel class by opening the GameModel.as file in the com/flashsupport/games/hangman folder.

In our game, the data provider is a simple text document named words.txt. If you open the words.txt file in a text editor, you can see that the structure is simple: a pipe character (|) separates each TV show title in the document.

The url property of the GameModel class is known as a getter/setter property, which enables you to process further actions when a new value is set to the property. After a URL is supplied to the GameModel, a chain of events is automatically put into motion within the class:

1. The loadWords() function is invoked. This function creates a new URLLoader instance, and loads the text file into the model.

2. The onWordsLoaded() function is called when the text finishes loading, which converts each line into a separate element in the wordList array property of the GameModel class.

3. The wordList property of the GameModel class is an array containing the words (or more appropriately, challenge phrases) to guess. For our game, the user must guess the names of popular TV shows.

NOTE Some of the challenge phrases contain a space; if a challenge phrase comprises several words, each word is placed on a separate line in the `GameView` class as defined by the `displayWord()` function of that class. This additional feature makes the challenge phrase easier to guess, as well as creates a more attractive layout.

4. After the `wordList` property is set, the `checkLocalData()` function within the `GameModel` class is invoked. Here, a `SharedObject` instance named `so`, which was created in the `init()` function of the `GameModel` class, is checked to see if the user previously played the game. If the user's name, win score, or loss score is found in the `SharedObject`'s data storage, the game's state (controlled by the `gameState` property) is set to `GameState.SHOW_STATS`. The `gameState` getter/setter property then broadcasts a new event to any listener of the model. If the user is playing the game for the first time, the `gameState` property is set to `GameState.INIT` and the model broadcasts the change to any listener as well.

Going back out to the `Hangman` document class, the remaining lines of code set up the `GameController` and `GameView` instances as listeners of the `GameModel` instance, `gm`:

```
gc.model = gm;
gc.view = gv;
gv.model = gm;
```

If you go inside of the `GameController` and `GameView` class files and search for the `model` getter/setter properties, you'll see that the classes register themselves as listeners for specific events from the `GameModel` class. For example, in the `GameController` class, the `model` setter property contains the following code:

```
public function set model(m:GameModel):void {
  _model = m;
  m.addEventListener(GameModel.LETTER_PICKED, onLetterPicked);
  m.addEventListener(GameModel.GAME_STATE, onGameState);
}
```

Here, there are two events that the `GameController` class needs to listen for: `GameModel.LETTER_PICKED` and `GameModel.GAME_STATE`. When the user picks a letter, the `GameModel` class broadcasts a `GameModel.LETTER_PICKED` event. When the `GameController` class hears this event, the `onLetterPicked()` function within the `GameController` class is invoked.

The `GameController` class also has a `view` property, which designates which `MovieClip` instance is responsible for displaying the game state to the user. In the `Hangman` document class, you set the `view` property to the `gv` instance (an instance of the `GameView` class). Finally, we also assign the `GameModel` instance, `gm`, to the `GameView` instance, `gv`. If you open the `GameView` class file (`GameView.as`) and find the `model` setter property, you see which events the `GameView` class listens for:

```
public function set model(m:GameModel):void {
  trace("GameView.model > " + m);
  _model = m;
  m.addEventListener(GameModel.WORD_UPDATE, onWordUpdate);
  m.addEventListener(GameModel.HANGMAN_UPDATE, ⤵
    onHangManUpdate);
  m.addEventListener(GameModel.GAME_STATUS, onGameStatus);
  m.addEventListener(GameModel.HIT_STATUS, onHitStatus);
  m.addEventListener(GameModel.GAME_STATE, onGameState);
  m.addEventListener(GameModel.SCORE_UPDATE, onScoreUpdate);
}
```

The GameModel class broadcasts several events that the GameView class listens to. Each event is assigned to a unique handler within the GameView class.

The shared font layer

This layer contains a text field that uses the LabelFont symbol in the Library panel. This font symbol imports the Futura Medium font face from the shared_fonts.swf file located in the ch31/ deploy folder. The shared_fonts.swf file must accompany the hangman.swf file on the Web server or other runtime location. The Futura font face is specified as "Futura Medium" in the TextFormat objects initialized in the createStyles() function of the GameView class. All the TextField instances created by the GameView class use the shared Futura Medium font.

An Overview of Events and the EventDispatcher Class

If you write your ActionScript 3.0 class files according to Adobe's specifications, you should add Event metadata at the top of each class file. If you open the class files associated with this game, you find the events each class broadcasts at the top of the script, just below the import declarations. The syntax for declaring an event is

```
Event[("eventName")]
```

where *eventName* is the String value used in the dispatchEvent() function calls you make in the class. In ActionScript 3.0, most classes — including DisplayObjectContainer classes — are descendants of the EventDispatcher class, automatically enabling them to use an event listener framework. Because the GameModel class does not inherit from a DisplayObjectContainer class like the GameController and GameView classes do, the GameModel class is the only class in the game that explicitly extends the EventDispatcher class.

The placeholder GameView instance

This instance is created from the GameView symbol. The instance is named `gvTemp` and is not included in the published movie. If you look at the properties for the GameView symbol in the Library panel, you can see that the symbol is linked to the `GameView.as` class file. Open the Library panel, and right-click (or Ctrl+click on Mac) the GameView symbol and choose Properties in the context menu. The advanced view of the Symbol Properties dialog box, shown in Figure 31.3, specifies the `com.flashsupport.games.hangman.GameView` class path in the Class field.

> **NOTE**   You don't need to include the .as file extension when you specify a class file.

FIGURE 31.3

The Symbol Properties dialog box

Symbol Properties	
Name: GameView	OK
Type: Movie Clip	Cancel
	Edit Basic
☐ Enable guides for 9-slice scaling	
Linkage	
☑ Export for ActionScript	
☑ Export in frame 1	
Identifier:	
Class: m.flashsupport.games.hangman.GameView ✓ ✎	
Base class: ✓ ✎	
Sharing	
☐ Export for runtime sharing	
☐ Import for runtime sharing	
URL:	
Source	
Browse... File:	
Symbol... Symbol name: Symbol 1	
☐ Always update before publishing	

988

LISTING 31.1

The Hangman Document Class

```
package com.flashsupport.games {

  import flash.display.MovieClip;
  import flash.text.TextField;
  import com.flashsupport.games.hangman.*;

  public class Hangman extends MovieClip {

    private var gv:GameView;
    private var gc:GameController;
    private var gm:GameModel;

    public var embed_1:TextField;

    public function Hangman(){
      trace("Hangman >");
      init();
    }

    private function init():void {
      trace("Hangman.init >");

      gv = new GameView( -7, -7);
      addChild(gv);

      gc = new GameController();
      gc.x = 6;
      gc.y = 220;
      addChild(gc);

      gm = new GameModel();
      //gm.clearSaved();
      gm.url = "words.txt";

      gc.model = gm;
      gc.view = gv;
      gv.model = gm;

    }
  }
}
```

Building the Interface

As you've seen in earlier chapters of this book, ActionScript can create a wide variety of runtime assets, such as text fields and sounds. We take advantage of this feature to create the rest of our assets.

Creating text fields

The new TextField() constructor method creates a new empty text field instance. Note that after a TextField instance is created, several of its properties are set, such as x position, y position, width, and height. Most important, any newly created asset that needs to be visible on the Stage must be added to the display list with the addChild() method.

One of the core functions of the game is the onGameState() function, found in the GameView class. This function controls much of the layout for each state of the game, as shown in the following code:

```
private function onGameState(evt:Object):Void {
    trace("GameView.onGameState >");
    var stateVal:String = evt.target.gameState;
    switch(stateVal){
        case GameState.INIT:
            cleanStage();
            onFirstPlay();
            break;
        case GameState.SHOW_STATS:
            cleanStage();
            onNextPlay();
            break;
        case GameState.START:
            cleanStage();
            onFirstRound();
            break;
        case GameState.NEW_ROUND:
            onNextRound();
            break;
        case GameState.LOST:
            onLost();
    }
}
```

Whenever the GameModel's gameState property changes, the onGameState() function is invoked. The first thing this function does is retrieve the current state of the game, expressed in the gameState property value of the GameModel (evt.target). For each value of the gameState property, the switch() statement directs the appropriate course of action. For example, when the game player runs the game for the very first time, the gameState property is equal to GameState.INIT. As such, the onFirstPlay() function within the GameView class is invoked, and creates two TextField instances: one to create some descriptive text and another to accept the input from the user's keyboard. In the following code, the nameField field displays the text "Please Enter Your Name:" (as retrieved from the labels property in the GameView class), and the nameEntryField instance is displayed as an input text field. The btn instance is a button that broadcasts a GameView.START_CLICKED event via the onClick() function within the GameView class. Because the GameController instance, gc (created in the Hangman document class), is listening for this event, the gc instance controls the model, telling it to advance to the next game state.

NOTE All items created with game state changes are added to the displayedItems property of the GameView class so that the cleanStage() function in the GameView class knows what items to remove between game states.

```
private function onFirstPlay():void {
  trace("GameView.onFirstPlay >");
  nameField = new TextField();

  with(nameField){
    x = 46;
    y = 232;
    width = 200;
    height = 20;
    autoSize = TextFieldAutoSize.LEFT;
    embedFonts = true;
    antiAliasType = AntiAliasType.ADVANCED;
    selectable = false;
    text = labels["name"];
    setTextFormat(tfOpening);
  }
  addChild(nameField);

  // add nameField instance to displayed items
  displayedItems.push(nameField);

  nameEntryField = new TextField();
```

```
with (nameEntryField) {
  x = 50;
  y = 250;
  width = 150;
  height = 18;
  background = true;
  type = TextFieldType.INPUT;
  defaultTextFormat = tfInput;
}
addChild(nameEntryField);

// add nameEntryField to displayed items
displayedItems.push(nameEntryField);

btn = new ButtonClip();

with(btn){
  x = nameEntryField.x + nameEntryField.width + 5;
  y = nameEntryField.y - 2;
  buttonMode = true;
  addEventListener(MouseEvent.CLICK, onClick);
}

addChild(btn);

// add btn instance to displayed items
displayedItems.push(btn);

// direct focus to the input field
stage.focus = nameEntryField;
}
```

A `TextFormat` object also can be created and applied to each of these text fields. In the `createStyles()` function of the `GameView` class, you'll see several `TextFormat` objects created, which are used by the various `TextField` instances created by other functions in the class.

NOTE   The `createStyles()` function is invoked in the `init()` function of the `GameView` class, as soon as the `gv` instance appears in the Flash movie at runtime.

When the `onFirstRound()` function is invoked from the `onGameState()` function of the `GameView` class, three `TextField` instances are created, as shown in Figure 31.4.

FIGURE 31.4

The `statusField` instance displays status messages initiated from the `GameModel` class throughout the game. The `lostField` and the `wonField` instances display the score.

Creating the alphabet

Sprites can be created dynamically with the new `Sprite()` constructor method. Furthermore, with ActionScript 3.0's event framework, both `Sprite` and `MovieClip` instances can be used as buttons, as described in earlier chapters.

We use the alphabet as both visual feedback of the user selection and an input device for the user to make a selection. To take care of both aspects, we are going to create `Sprite` instances and then create text fields as their children.

> **TIP**
>
> The `Sprite` and `MovieClip` classes are very similar to each other. If you don't need a multiframe timeline associated with a `MovieClip` instance, use the `Sprite` class instead.

Because the functionality of each letter button in the alphabet controller is identical, we created a dedicated ActionScript 3.0 class named `GameLetter` (as defined in the `GameLetter.as` file found in the `com/flashsupport/games/ui` folder). This class is utilized in the `createAlphabet()` function of the `GameController` class, as shown in the following code:

```
private function createAlphabet():void {
  trace("GameController.createAlphabet >");
  alphabet = new Sprite();
  addChild(alphabet);
  var nXPos:Number = 0;
  for (var i:int = 65; i <= 90; i++) {
    var letter:String = String.fromCharCode(i);
    var gl:GameLetter = new GameLetter(letter);
    gl.name = "gl_" + letter;
    gl.x = nXPos;
    gl.addEventListener(GameLetter.CLICK, onLetterClicked);
    alphabet.addChild(gl);
    nXPos += 14;
  }
}
```

The `for()` loop of this function cycles through the entire alphabet, creating a new instance of `GameLetter` for each letter. You can create ASCII characters by using the `String.fromChar-Code()` method, which uses the number corresponding to a letter and returns its corresponding string (A=65, B=66, and so on). Each letter of the alphabet is displayed in the `GameLetter` instance, as shown in Figure 31.4. The `GameController` is registered as the event listener for the `GameLetter.CLICK` event for each `GameLetter` instance created.

`GameLetter`'s sole purpose is to create a clickable `TextField` instance. When the user clicks an instance of `GameLetter`, its `GameLetter.CLICK` event is broadcast to any listeners. The only listener for each `GameLetter` instance is the `GameController` class. When the `GameController` detects this event, the `onLetterClicked()` function is invoked:

```
private function onLetterClicked(e:Object):Void {
  trace("GameController.onLetterClicked >");
  var gl:GameLetter = GameLetter(evt.target);
  if (controlsEnabled) model.checkLetter(gl.letter);
}
```

If the game is not between rounds, the `controlsEnabled` property of the `GameController` is set to `true`, allowing the `checkLetter()` function of the `GameModel` class to be invoked. The letter property of the clicked `GameLetter` instance is retrieved and passed to the `checkLetter()` function. This function determines whether or not the clicked letter occurs in any of the character positions of the current challenge phrase. If one or more occurrences are found, the `GameView` class resets the `displayedWord` property to a new value, which, in turn, fires a `GameModel.WORD_UPDATE` event to the `GameView` class. There the new `displayedWord` property value is retrieved and rebuilt in the `word` instance.

Starting the Game

The functions that we cover next are built with the framework of the game in a circular fashion: All the functions are used within one game cycle and again within the next game cycle. This kind of flow is specific to games, and you must keep it in mind when writing code. In particular, game states need to be reset properly at the beginning of a new cycle.

At the beginning of each round, some of our assets need to be edited and some variables initialized. The createNewRound() function, defined in the GameModel class, takes care of establishing initial settings for each round in the game:

```
public function createNewRound():void {
  trace("GameModel.createNewRound >");
  roundNumber++;
  hangManStates = [
          {id: HangmanState.HEAD, active: false},
          {id: HangmanState.BODY,  active: false},
          {id: HangmanState.LEFT_ARM, active: false},
          {id: HangmanState.RIGHT_ARM, active: false},
          {id: HangmanState.LEFT_LEG, active: false},
          {id: HangmanState.RIGHT_LEG, active: false}
          ];
  var avail:Array = new Array();
  for(var i:int = 0; i < wordList.length; i++){
    var item:Object = wordList[i];
    if(item.active) avail.push(i);
  }
  var idx:int = Math.floor(Math.random() * avail.length);
  selectedIndex = avail[idx];
  wordList[selectedIndex].active = false;
  createChoices();
  createDisplayedWord();
  gameState = GameState.NEW_ROUND;
  gameStatus = GameStatus.BEGIN_PLAY;
}
```

createNewRound() also prepares the states of the hangman character. The hangManStates property is an array created to store the state of each body part. Because the model is simply tracking states of the game, the model doesn't need to know which MovieClip objects are actually representing those body parts — that job is the responsibility of the GameView class. If you look at the hangmanStates getter/setter property of the GameModel class, you can see that an event is dispatched every time new values are set:

```
public function set hangmanStates(val:Array):void {
    _states = val;
    dispatchEvent(new Event(GameModel.HANGMAN_UPDATE));
}
```

Whenever the GameModel.HANGMAN_UPDATE event is dispatched from the GameModel, the onHangmanUpdate() function is invoked within the GameView class:

```
private function onHangmanUpdate(evt:Event):void {
    trace("GameView.onHangmanUpdate >");
    var m:GameModel = evt.target as GameModel;
    var states:Array = m.hangmanStates;
    var count:int = states.length;
    for (var i:int = 0; i < count; i++) {
        var hangmanState:Object = states[i];
        var mc:MovieClip = matchStateToClip(hangmanState.id);
        mc.visible = hangmanState.active;
        mc.gotoAndStop(m.roundNumber);
    }
}
```

Here, a for() loop cycles through the states stored within the hangmanStates property of GameModel. The matchStateToClip() function within the GameView class matches the id value shown earlier in the createNewRound() function of the GameModel class to each MovieClip object responsible for displaying that body part. Each body part also jumps to the frame number corresponding to the GameModel's roundNumber to display a new color scheme.

The hangmanStates property is set in two places within the GameModel class: the create NewRound() function (as previously discussed) and the lookForMatch() function. This function sequentially sets the active flag within each object of the hangmanStates array. Initially, at the start of each round,all the hangman's body parts have their active property set to false. However, if the lookForMatch() function determines that a selected letter is not found within the challenge phrase, the active property of the "next in line" object within the hangman-States array is set to true. The hangmanStates property is then reset to itself, forcing a GameModel.HANGMAN_UPDATE event broadcast. As such, the onHangmanUpdate() function within the GameView class is called again, setting the visibility of the "next in line" hangman body part to true.

Display the letters of the alphabet

The createNewRound() function of the GameModel also sets the gameState property to a value of GameState.NEW_ROUND, which is broadcasted to any listener of this event. The Game Controller class listens for these changes and invokes its positionAlphabet() function.

This function moves the vertical position of the GameLetter components displaying the clickable letters of the GameController class. This function also sets the text color of each GameLetter instance to black. (Whenever a GameLetter instance is clicked, the text color of the instance is set to gray in the onLetterPicked() function of the GameView class.)

```
private function positionAlphabet():void {
  trace("GameController.positionAlphabet >");
  for (var i:int = 0; i < alphabet.numChildren; i++) {
    if(alphabet.getChildAt(i) is GameLetter){
      var gl:GameLetter = GameLetter(alphabet.getChildAt(i));
      gl.y = 0;
      gl.letterColor = 0x000000;
    }
  }
}
```

Choose a random word

The selection of words (or challenge phrases) is stored in an array called wordList, which is defined at the beginning of the game in the GameModel class. In the createNewRound() function, a challenge phrase is randomly picked from the wordList array:

```
var avail:Array = new Array();
for(var i:int = 0; i < wordList.length; i++){
  var item:Object = wordList[i];
  if(item.active) avail.push(i);
}
var idx:int = Math.floor(Math.random() * avail.length);
selectedIndex = avail[idx];
wordList[selectedIndex].active = false;
```

The avail array is used to store any challenge phrase that has yet to be played in the game. The for() loop cycles through each object stored in the wordList property and checks its active property. If it hasn't been played (that is, its active value is true), the object is added to the avail array. After the available challenge phrases have been gathered, a random index number is selected for the avail array. This value is then used to set the selectedIndex property of the GameModel class. The selectedIndex property is used to determine which word is active during the round. In the last line of the previous code block, the active property for that word is set to false so that it can't be picked again in future rounds.

NOTE In this version of the game, a word is randomly selected from a pool for each round. As such, the difficulty of each word (number of characters, number of words, and so on) is not ranked. You can modify the game to create a series of word arrays, each one varying in level of difficulty. As the player progresses to the next round, a word from another array can be chosen.

Create the letters of the displayed word

The `createDisplayedWord()` function, invoked from the `createNewRound()` function of the `GameModel` class mentioned in the previous section, builds the current state of the displayed word to the game player.

At the beginning of the `createDisplayedWord()` function, we create a `String` variable named `word` to hold the individual letters of the displayed word (or challenge phrase). Because the `createNewRound()` function already set a new `selectedIndex` value, the `selectedItem.label` value will be set to the new challenge phrase. In this `for()` loop, the `word` variable is built into a series of question marks (`"?"`) or empty spaces (`" "`). So, if the challenge phrase (that is, `selectedItem.label`) was set to "Lost," the `word` variable would equal `"????"`. Or, if the challenge phrase was "The Office," the `word` variable would equal `"??? ??????"`. After the `word` string has been generated, the `displayedWord` property of the `GameModel` is set to the value of `word`.

```
private function createDisplayedWord():void {
   var word:String = "";
   var count:int = selectedItem.label.length;
   for(var i:int = 0; i < count; i++){
      word += (selectedItem.label.substr(i, 1) != " ") ? "?" :
   " ";
   }
   displayedWord = word;
}
```

Because the `displayedWord` property's setter function dispatches the event `GameModel.WORD_UPDATE`, the `GameView` class's `displayWord()` function is invoked, fetching the new `displayedWord` property from the `GameModel` class:

```
private function displayWord():void {
   trace("GameView.displayWord>");
   if(word is Sprite) removeChild(word);

   word = new Sprite();

   with(word){
     x = 35;
     y = 25;
   }

   addChild(word);

   var displayedWord:String = model.displayedWord;
   var nX:Number = 0;
   var nY:Number = 0;
```

```
for (var i:int = 0; i < displayedWord.length; i++) {
  var chr:String = displayedWord.substr(i, 1);
  if (displayedWord.substr(i, 1) == " ") {
    nX = 0;
    nY += 30;
    continue;
  }

  var t:TextField = new TextField();

  with (t) {
    x = nX;
    y = nY;
    width = 20;
    height = 20;
    border = true;
    embedFonts = true;
    background = true;
    selectable = false;
    antiAntiAliasType = AntiAliasType.ADVANCED;
    gridFitType = GridFitType.SUBPIXEL;
    backgroundColor = (chr == "?") ? 0x99CCFF : 0x9999FF;
    text = chr;
    setTextFormat(tfCentered);
  }

  word.addChild(t);

  nX += 25;
  }
}
```

The displayWord() function completes one primary task: to generate a series of TextField instances displaying each of the characters in the displayedWord value of the GameModel class. A Sprite instance named word is created, and a for() loop cycles over each character of the displayedWord value (represented as the local variable, displayedWord). In each for() loop cycle, a TextField instance is created to display an individual character. If an empty space (" ") is found in the displayedWord variable, the Y position of the subsequent TextField instance is shifted down 30 pixels. This procedure places each word in a multiword challenge phrase on its own line. You can see this effect in Figure 31.1, where the second line of the word instance is below the first line.

CROSS-REF The TextField instances of this function use the FlashType rendering engine. Because the centeredFormat instance (a TextFormat instance) uses center alignment, the gridFitType property of the TextField instance is set to GridFitType. SUBPIXEL, to render the text more sharply. For more information about FlashType, read Chapter 30, "Applying HTML and Text Field Formatting."

The User Input

The user enters his or her selection by clicking one of the GameLetter instances in the GameController class, represented in the Flash movie as an instance named gameController on the Main Timeline. When a GameLetter instance is clicked, the onLetterClicked() function of the GameController class is invoked. This function, as discussed earlier in this chapter, submits the letter property of the clicked GameLetter instance to the GameModel's checkLetter() function.

Interpreting the User Input

This process is the bigger part of our project. A series of questions are asked, and their answers determine the next step in the process. You can find the checkLetter() function in the GameModel.as file:

```
public function checkLetter(ltr:String):void {
    trace("GameModel.checkLetter >" + ltr );
    if (isLeft(ltr)) {
        lookForMatch(ltr);
    } else {
        gameStatus = GameStatus.ALREADY_PICKED;
    }
}
```

The isLeft() function looks to see if the selected letter was already chosen, and the lookForMatch() function checks the letter against the word to guess.

Was the letter selected before?

Using a for() loop, the isLeft() function compares the lettersLeft array to the chosen letter (char), one element at a time. If the letter is contained in the array, the letter is deleted from the array, the selectedLetter property is set to the chosen letter, and the function returns true.

```
private function isLeft(char:String):Boolean {
    for (var i:int = 0; i < lettersLeft.length; i++) {
        if (lettersLeft[i].toLowerCase() == char.toLowerCase())
        {
            lettersLeft.splice(i, 1);
            selectedLetter = char;
            return true;
        }
    }
    return false;
}
```

NOTE In ActionScript 3.0, you can specify the data type of the value returned from the function. The data type is declared after the parentheses of the arguments, separated by a colon (:). In the `isLeft()` function, the data type of the return value is `Boolean`.

After the `selectedLetter` property is set, the `GameModel.LETTER_PICKED` event is broadcasted from the `GameModel` to any listeners:

```
public function set selectedLetter(val:String):void {
    _letter = val;
    dispatchEvent(new Event(GameModel.LETTER_PICKED));
}
```

In our code framework, the `GameController` class is listening for this event, and invokes the `onLetterPicked()` function, which sets the Y position of the appropriate `GameLetter` instance 10 pixels below the other `GameLetter` instances, and changes the color of the text within the `GameLetter` instance:

```
private function onLetterPicked(evt:Event):void {
    trace("GameController.onLetterPicked >");
    var ltr:String = evt.target.selectedLetter;
    trace("\tltr: " + ltr);
    var gl:GameLetter = alphabet.getChildByName("gl_" + ltr) ⤵
        as GameLetter;
    gl.y = 10;
    gl.letterColor = 0x666666;
}
```

Is the letter part of the word?

The `lookForMatch()` function of the GameModel class compares the selected letter to the value of the `selectedItem.label` property, one character at a time, and determines the course of action from the result:

```
private function lookForMatch(char:String):void {
    trace("GameModel.lookForMatch > " + char );
    var word:String = selectedItem.label;
    var display:String = "";
    var match:Boolean = false;
    for (var i:int = 0; i < word.length; i++) {
        if (word.substr(i, 1).toLowerCase() == char.toLowerCase()) {
            display += word.substr(i, 1);
            match = true;
        } else {
            display += displayedWord.substr(i, 1);
        }
    }
    displayedWord = display;
```

```
        if (match) {
          trace("\tfound match");
          hitStatus = HitState.HIT;
          gameStatus =  GameStatus.MATCH_HIT;
        } else {
          trace("\tdidn't find match...");
          for(var j:int = 0; J < hangmanStates.length; j++){
            var item:Object = hangmanStates[j];
            if(!item.active){
                item.active = true;
                break;
            }
          }
          hangmanStates = hangmanStates;
          hitStatus = HitState.MISS;
          gameStatus = GameStatus.MATCH_MISS;
        }
        checkStatus();
    }
```

The `toLowerCase()` method converts the character to lowercase so that the two compared elements match if they are the same letter, regardless of their case.

If the letter is found in the `selectedItem.label` value (represented as the `word` variable), the corresponding letter is concatenated (or added) to the value of the `display` variable, which is set to an empty string just prior to the `for()` loop. If there isn't a match, the current letter in the displayed state of the word (`displayedWord`) is retrieved and added to the `display` variable. If a match is found, the variable `match` is assigned the value of `true`.

Regardless of the matched letters, the `displayedWord` property is set to the value of the `display` variable. The `GameView` class intercepts the `GameModel.WORD_UPDATE` event broadcasted by the `displayedWord` getter property, and redraws the challenge phrase for the user.

The rest of the `lookForMatch()` function changes the values of the `hitStatus` and `gameStatus` properties of the `GameModel` class, depending on the value of `match`. If a match was found, the `hitStatus` property is set to `HitState.HIT`. The `GameView` class is listening for changes to the `hitStatus` property, and plays a sound clip of applause (`clap.mp3` in the movie's library). The `statusField` field of the `GameView` class also displays a success message to the player.

However, if the choice doesn't match, a `for()` loop cycles through the objects stored within the `hangmanStates` property. If the loop finds an object whose `active` property is `false`, the `active` property is set to `true` and the `break` action exits the loop. When the `hangmanStates` property is reset to itself, a `GameModel.HANGMAN_UPDATE` event is broadcasted from the `GameModel`. This event is received by the `GameView` class, which then updates the visibility of the hangman's body parts. The `hitStatus` property is also set to `HitState.MISS`. This value broadcasts the GameModel.HIT_STATUS event to the GameView class, which, in turn, plays the loss.mp3 sound in the movie's library.

After the proper states have been set in the model, the checkStatus() function of the GameModel class is invoked to determine the next state of the game. The next section discusses this function.

Checking the Status of the Game

The last step in our process is to check the status of the game. More specifically, is the word complete, is the hangman completely drawn, and/or is the game complete? The checkStatus() function is defined in the GameModel class and asks all these questions. In the following sections, we discuss questions and conditions that exist in the game and the programming logic behind their answers and actions.

Is the word complete?

To check whether the word is complete, we check for any remaining ? characters in the letter text fields. We use a for() loop (with the value of the displayedWord.length as the condition to exit the loop). Note how the Boolean variable allMatched is assigned the value of true if the word is complete and false if the word is not complete.

```
var allMatched:Boolean = true;
for (var i:Number = 0; i <= displayedWord.length; i++) {
    if (displayedWord.substr(i, 1) == "?") {
        allMatched = false;
        break;
    }
}
```

Is the hangman complete?

We also need to check the status of the hangman: If all of its parts are visible (that is, active), the round is lost. The alive variable determines whether or not the player is still "alive" during the current round:

```
var alive:Boolean = false;
var item:Object;
for(var j:Number = 0; i < hangmanStates.length; j++){
    var item:Object = hangmanStates[j];
    if(!item.active){
        alive = true;
        break;
    }
}
```

If one of the `hangmanState` objects has an `active` value of `false`, the Hangman still has remaining parts to display, and the player is still in the round. As such, the `alive` variable is set to `true`. Otherwise, the `alive` variables remains `false`.

Are there more words to guess?

After the `hangmanStates` property has been checked, we need to do the same type of check for active words in the game. In others, is it the end of a round, or the end of the game? Has the player played the game long enough to exhaust all the challenge phrases?

```
var wordsAvailable:Boolean = false;
for(var k:int = 0; k < wordList.length; k++){
   var item:Object = wordList[k];
   if(item.active){
      wordsAvailable = true;
      break;
   }
}
```

How do you end the round?

If the player successfully matches all the characters, the `gameStatus` property is set to `GameStatus.WON_ROUND`. All `gameStatus` properties are `String` constants (see the `GameStatus` class file) that are looked up in another `GameModel` property named `labels`. Therefore, if the `gameStatus` property is set to `GameStatus.WON_ROUND`, that index value is looked up in the `labels` property, which returns the value "You won this round!" Whenever the `gameStatus` property is updated, the `GameView` class (as a listener) sets the `statusField` field to that value, displaying the text to the player.

> **NOTE** All status messages are declared in the `init()` handler of the `GameModel` class. Also, the `labels` property is actually an *associative* array, which enables you to use a `String` value as the key to each element in the array. So, instead of using `labels[0]` to look up a value in the array, you pass a `String` value as the key, such as `labels["wonRound"]`. Note that the `GameStatus.WON_ROUND` constant returns the string value `"wonRound"`.

As we continue to break down the `GameModel` class's `checkStatus()` function, you can see that `gameStatus` is set to `GameStatus.WON_ROUND` if `allMatched` is set to `true`:

```
var reset:Boolean = false;
if (allMatched) {
   gameStatus = GameStatus.WON_ROUND;
   win++;
   reset = true;
   gameState = GameState.WIN;
} else if (!alive) {
   gameStatus = GameStatus.LOST_ROUND;
```

```
            loss++;
            reset = true;
            gameState = GameState.LOST;
            displayedWord = selectedItem.label;
        }
```

The win property of the GameModel class is also incremented if the player successfully matched
all the characters in the challenge phrase, and the reset value is set to true. When the win
property is updated, the wonField instance in the GameView class updates the current win
score.

 If reset remains false, the GameModel knows that there are remaining words —
thus game rounds — to play.

When the gameState property is set to GameState.WIN, the GameView and GameController
classes do not respond with any particular action — you could further enhance this game by having the hangman character animate when the player wins the round (that is, provide a bigger
payoff to the player for winning the round). If allMatched and alive are false, the player
has lost the current round. The gameStatus property is set to GameStatus.LOST_ROUND,
the loss value is incremented, reset is set to true, and the gameState property is set to
GameState.LOST. The "lost" value tells the GameView class to run the onLost() function,
which is described in the next section.

Removing the hangman

The onLost() function of the GameView class is executed when the gameState property
change is broadcasted from the GameModel class to the GameView class.

```
    private function onLost():void {
        bc = new BeamClip();
        bc.x = 245;
        bc.y = 0;
        bc.targetClip = hangman;
        bc.addEventListener(BeamClip.END, removeBeam);
        addChild(bc);
    }
```

This function creates a new instance of the BeamClip class, which is attached to the BeamClip
symbol from the library. A variable on the bc instance named targetClip is set equal to the
hangman instance. This variable is used by yet another class, BlurFader, found inside of the
BeamClip class.

In the com/flashsupport/games/hangman folder, open the BeamClip.as file, which is the
BeamClip class. This class has a public method named fadeBlur:

```
public function fadeBlur():void {
  fader = new BlurFader(targetClip, "out", 0.5);
  fader.addEventListener(BlurFader.COMPLETE, removeFader);
  addChild(fader);
}
```

Here, the BlurFader symbol, linked in the Library panel, is dynamically attached to the GameView instance (which is the parent timeline of the BeamClip instance added earlier). The BlurFader component, which we used in Chapter 19, "Making Your First Flash CS4 Project," uses three parameters: target, dir, and duration. In the new BlurFader() constructor method, we pass these parameters and their values. The fader instance is then set up to make the alien hangman (hangman, as set by the targetClip parameter) fade and blur out from the movie.

Reset the game or just the round?

Go back to the GameModel class to resume the deconstruction of the checkStatus function. If all the challenge phrases have been played (that is, wordsAvailable is false) and it's the end of the current round, the game is over.

```
if (!wordsAvailable && reset) {
  gameStatus = GameStatus.GAME_OVER;
  gameState = GameState.GAME_OVER;
} else if (reset) {
  gameState = GameState.ROUND_OVER;
}
```

As such, the gameStatus property of the GameModel class is set to GameStatus.GAME_OVER, which leads to the display of the text "Thanks for playing!" in the statusField instance of the GameView class. The gameState is also set to GameState.GAME_OVER. In this version of the game, nothing happens to the GameView or GameController classes when the game is over — the player simply sees the message and is prohibited from playing further rounds.

If there are still challenge phrases left to play and the round is over, the gameState property is set to GameState.ROUND_OVER, which is detected by the GameController class. There, the moveToNextRound() function is invoked three seconds after the event is received from the GameModel. (You can see the Timer class used within the onGameState() function of the GameController class.) The moveToNextRound() function calls the createNewRound() function on the GameModel:

```
private function moveToNextRound(evt:TimerEvent):void {
  model.createNewRound();
}
```

The moveToNextRound() function is delayed by three seconds so that the previous gameStatus property change has time to display the current game status to the player in the statusField instance. If the moveToNextRound() function was not delayed, the user would jump right into the next round, missing any updated display of text.

Added Feature: Storing User and Game Information

Being able to save information opens exciting dimensions to game development. For example, users particularly enjoy playing a multilevel game if they know the next time they visit the site, they can pick up where they left off because the computer remembers which level they last completed and their current score.

For our Hangman game, the following section demonstrates a very simple application of saving data onto the user's local hard drive and recalling it when the player returns to the game at a later time.

Flash Player 6 introduced the `SharedObject` class, which enables you to save data locally, similar to a Web browser cookie. The next time the user runs the game, it displays the saved information. The information can be saved in two ways: when the movie ends or as soon as the information is entered. For our game, the information is saved right away, in the `init()` function of the `GameModel` class. The `SharedObject.getLocal()` method creates a new object named `so`.

```
so = SharedObject.getLocal("hangMan");
```

To store data in a `SharedObject` instance, you access the `data` property of the instance, followed by a variable name. For example, to store a variable named `firstName` in a `SharedObject` instance named `so`, you could use the following code:

```
so.data.firstName = "Scott";
```

For the purposes of this game, we check that the data was saved for the username and the win and loss scores. If any of this information is unavailable, the `GameModel` class dispatches the event `GameState.INIT` when the `gameState` property is set to `GameState.INIT` in the `checkLocalData()` function of the `GameModel` class.

When the game is played for the very first time, the player enters his/her name. Every time after that, the name and score are remembered and displayed.

After the user enters his/her name and clicks the orange button (`btn` instance of the `GameView` class) on the screen, the data is saved by calling the `saveName()` function of the `GameModel` class:

```
public function saveName(val:String):void {
  trace("GameModel.saveName > " + val);
  so.data.user = val;
  so.flush();
}
```

 The `flush()` method of the `SharedObject` class forces the data to be written to the local data file.

The saveScore() function of the GameModel class is called from within the game at the end of each round and stores the win and loss scores.

```
private function saveScore():void {
  trace("GameModel.saveScore >");
  trace("\twin: " + win);
  trace("\tloss: " + loss);
  if(!isNaN(win)) so.data.winScore = win;
  if(!isNaN(loss)) so.data.lossScore = loss;
  var flushResult:Object = so.flush();
  trace("\tflushResult: " + flushResult);
}
```

And that ends our deconstruction of the Hangman game! We encourage you to modify the elements in the View Assets folder to suit your own particular tastes for the game's look and feel.

WEB RESOURCE We'd like to know what you think about this chapter. Visit www.flashsupport. com/feedback to send us your comments.

Summary

- Creating a game is much more than programming. It involves other talents, such as game design, interaction design, and visual and sound design.

- Scripting a game is asking a series of questions and responding to them appropriately, depending on the user input.

- Functions are essential to intelligent programming. Writing small, task-focused functions allows for greater flexibility, particularly for complex games.

- Movie Clip instances and text fields can be created dynamically. Additionally, text fields' properties can be manipulated via ActionScript. In addition to adding flexibility, the creation of runtime instances (versus authortime instances) reduces the file size of your movie.

- The Timer class can call a function after a delay period. Here, we are using it to create a delay between rounds.

- Using the SharedObject class is a great way to save data on the local drive. We are using it to store the user's name as well as the game's score.

Chapter 32

Using Components

A major revolution in past versions of the Flash authoring tool was the addition of a whole new set of components, known as V2 components, and the architecture that they use. Flash CS4 continues to offer the same variety of components, with some modifications to solve minor bugs present in the previous versions. Flash CS4 also offers an entire set of components written in ActionScript 3.0. Components offer an easy way to reuse complicated elements within your movie without having to build them on your own. Although it's beyond the scope of this chapter, you can also build your own custom components. In this chapter, we take a look at what components are, their parameters, and how to work with many of the components included with Flash CS4.

Flash CS4 ships with 22 User Interface components (ActionScript 2.0), 6 Data components (ActionScript 2.0), and several components related to Flash Video playback and control. Flash CS4 has 17 User Interface components written in ActionScript 3.0, as well as updated versions of the FLVPlayback components.

TIP

The updated FLVPlayback components enable you to play Flash Video files (.flv) with extreme ease. We discuss these components at length in Chapter 16, "Displaying Video."

CAUTION

This chapter discusses User Interface (UI) components for ActionScript 3.0. Most of the ActionScript 2.0 UI components use similar, if not identical, operations as those discussed in this chapter.

What Are Components?

Components are complex Movie Clips with parameters that you define during the authoring process. They are essentially containers, holding many assets that work together to add enhanced interactivity, productivity, or effects to your movies. You can use components to control your movie, such as moving from one frame to another, or to perform more complex tasks, such as sending data to and from a server.

We look at many of the components found in the User Interface components set in this chapter. You can download additional components from Adobe and third-party developers to add to those already bundled with Flash CS4, although many of the most useful and regularly used elements, such as buttons, combo boxes, and lists, are already included with the program.

Why Use Components?

Components make it easy for you to rapidly create proof-of concepts or prototypes for larger Rich Internet Application (RIA) frameworks, to share your work with other Flash developers who work in your production team, or to share your innovations with other developers in the Flash community.

Although this chapter focuses on the components bundled with the release of Flash CS4, the way in which these components are used will also help you understand how other components work — from Adobe or a third party. Components you download sometimes come in *sets,* which may include many similar small applications. You may need the Adobe Extension Manager to install them into Flash CS4.

CROSS-REF For more information on exchanging and downloading components, see the section "Exchanging and acquiring components" at the end of this chapter.

One of the arguments against using components is the file size they add to your productions. Even though this may be the case, there are several reasons to use components apart from the ease of dragging them to your Stage and modifying the parameters.

CAUTION Many of the ActionScript 3.0 components in Flash CS4 are substantially large in file size. For example, including a Button component adds 15K to the Flash movie file (.swf) size. Adding a List component contributes 29K to the Flash movie size. However, adding both List and Button components to your movie puts only 31KB into your Flash movie size, not 44K. Why is this the case? Because the List component uses the Button component class, the Button component is already included in the class packages exported to the Flash movie. Flash intelligently includes class files only once, not multiple times.

First of all, usability is an integral part of effective interface design. Components are an extremely effective way of ensuring that your end user understands how to use certain elements of your Flash movie. A predictable interface does not have to be boring or cliché. Furthermore, because components can be skinned, they can have a unique look from one site to the next. The components shipped with Flash CS4, for the most part, are also reliable, given they were built, developed, and tested by professionals. This is not to say that the same level of construction cannot be achieved by thousands of others, but the time and effort spent in complicated coding and testing has already been done for you. And because components are a quick solution to common interface requirements, you will have more time to spend on more complicated and interesting creative tasks instead of repetitive authoring.

CAUTION   Exercise care with third-party components — even those that you can download from the Adobe Exchange. Not all components have been thoroughly tested, and some are specifically developed for one particular use in mind. Be sure to test your implementation of a component throughout the development process.

Compiled Clips: A Specific Component Format

A component is made up of one or more internal assets. One of the changes introduced with Flash MX 2004's component architecture (and continued in Flash CS4), though, is that components can be compiled. This means that when you add a compiled component to the Flash document and open your Library panel, you see only one symbol for the component (see Figure 32.1). In Flash CS4, ActionScript 2.0 components are compiled — as such, you cannot easily edit the component skin symbols that comprise a component's look and feel.

TIP   The ActionScript 3.0 UI components in Flash CS4 offer the best of both worlds. Although the core component functionality is precompiled, you can easily change the skin symbols used by the component, directly in the Library panel (Figure 32.2).

FIGURE 32.1

The ComboBox component (ActionScript 2.0) in Flash CS4

FIGURE 32.2

The ComboBox component (ActionScript 3.0) in Flash CS4

The symbol type for prepackaged components is called *compiled clip*. There are a couple of major differences with this component format and architecture:

- You can no longer edit the symbols of a component that has been compiled. As such, you need to use ActionScript code to change the appearance of a component. You can also overwrite the linked symbols embedded with a compiled clip with your own new linked assets.

- Developers can now create and distribute components without the user being able to easily see the code used to create the component. This is a big "win" for developers who are concerned about their intellectual property rights.

If you were familiar with components in older versions of Flash, we highlight other differences between V1 and V2 components throughout this chapter.

How to Add a Component

You can add a component to your Stage in the following ways:

1. **Open the Components panel by going to Window ➪ Components or by pressing Ctrl+F7/⌘+F7.**

2. **Add a component to the Stage by:**

   - **Double-clicking:** You can double-click a component and it will be added to the center of your Document window's workspace.

   - **Dragging:** You can add an instance by clicking the component icon and dragging it onto the Stage.

After your component is on the Stage, you can modify its parameters and properties manually in various panels or by using ActionScript code on objects or keyframes in a timeline.

> **NOTE** You can add additional instances of your component to your document by dragging it from your Library panel onto the Stage instead of from the Components panel.

You can also add an ActionScript 3.0 component to your movie by using the new constructor method in ActionScript after the component is added to your library. An example of adding a Button component to the Stage at runtime and setting a few properties by using ActionScript is as follows. (This code uses standard ActionScript 3.0 syntax.)

```
import fl.controls.Button;

var button:Button = new Button();
button.label = "music";
addChild(button);
```

This creates an instance of a push button, labeled "music," on the Stage.

Where to Find Components, Assets, and Parameters

You can find, control, and edit your components in many areas of the Flash interface. Understanding each of these areas will help you add custom features to your Flash movies that use components.

Components panel

You can find this panel, shown in Figure 32.3, by going to Window ➪ Components or by using the Ctrl+F7/⌘+F7 shortcut. This panel includes all the components that ship with Flash CS4.

If you add components that you have downloaded from other sites, such as the Adobe Exchange, you can access the sets from this panel as well. Each set appears as a new nesting.

NOTE   The Components panel uses a tree structure, in which every set is shown in the panel. The components of each set are nested with each node. The contents of the panel vary based on the ActionScript version of the Flash file. You can change the ActionScript version in the Script menu of the Flash tab of the Publish Settings dialog box (File ➪ Publish Settings).

FIGURE 32.3

The Components panel for ActionScript 2.0 (left) and ActionScript 3.0 (right)

Component Inspector panel

The Component Inspector panel is the central control area for component parameters and bindings. You can find this panel by choosing Window ➪ Component Inspector or by using the Shift+F7 shortcut. In the Parameters tab (Figure 32.4), you can set values for each parameter of a component instance. This tab can also be used to display custom user interface movie files (.swf) for components.

The Component Inspector features two additional tabs: Bindings and Schema (see Figure 32.6 later in this chapter). These tabs can be used only with legacy ActionScript 2.0 components. ActionScript 3.0 components cannot use these additional tabs.

FIGURE 32.4

The Component Inspector panel

Library panel

After dragging a UI component to the Stage, you will notice a new Component symbol for the component added to your Library panel. If you want to remove a component from your Flash document, be sure to delete it and its assets from the Library panel as well as from the Stage.

Actions panel and ActionScript

Not only is there ActionScript hidden within the compiled components that ship with Flash CS4, but you can also write ActionScript to control components or modify their appearance. The built-in components that ship with Flash CS4 have several methods and properties that you can use to customize their functionality. Later in this chapter, you learn how to tap some of these scripted resources.

Modifying Component Color Properties and Parameters

There are several ways you can easily modify the appearance and functionality of your components. With the Flash CS4 User Interface components, you can customize the face color of each instance with little effort. Let's look at how you accomplish this.

First of all, open the Properties panel. As you have already seen, the Properties panel contains information on the color attributes of your component. This is possibly the easiest and quickest way to change the appearance of your component. Simply by expanding the Color Effect section, you can alter the Brightness, Tint, Alpha, or a combination of these elements by choosing Advanced. You can see the changes made to the face of your component after publishing or previewing your movie.

The Parameters tab of the Component Inspector enables you to change the built-in component parameters to ones better matching your site or the usage of your component. For example, on a `ScrollPane` instance, you can change the horizontalScrollPolicy and verticalScrollPolicy attributes (visibility of horizontal and vertical scrollbars, respectively) in this area by clicking the value area and selecting an option from the list.

CROSS-REF For more information on changing the look of components, refer to the section later in this chapter called "Modifying Components."

Removing Components from Your Movie

It is important to understand how to properly remove components from your movie. Removing compiled ActionScript 2.0 components is usually very straightforward: Select the compiled clip in the Library panel, and delete it.

ActionScript 3.0 components, on the other hand, can often be linked to many other assets spread across several folders in the Library panel. Some components share assets, such as the scrollbar skins. Therefore, care must be taken when removing assets from the library. You should have a solid understanding of component structure and asset usage if you attempt to manually remove items from folders in the library.

Components in Flash CS4

Flash CS4 includes several User Interface (or UI) components, which provide user interface elements and functionality frequently used by developers. You should be able to find a use for some or all of these components at one time or another. Let's take a look at what each of the core UI components does and how to use them in your movies. After dragging any component instance to your Stage, open up the Properties panel and select the Parameters tab to view the parameters discussed in this section.

The parameters for each component discussed in the following sections are also the respective names of each component's properties. Note that not all of a component's properties may be exposed in the Component Inspector panel. Also, only the ActionScript 3.0 versions of the components and their respective parameters are discussed.

Button component

This component is essentially a standard button with built-in up, over, and down states. The button is designed to resemble an HTML form button (such as a submit button). The Button component, shown in Figure 32.5, is very easy to use and can aid in quick development of mockups or be modified to suit more aesthetically inclined productions.

CAUTION Do not confuse a Button component with a Button symbol. In this chapter, any reference to `Button` instance implies a `Button` component, not a Button symbol. In ActionScript 3.0, traditional Button instances belong to the `flash.display.SimpleButton` class, whereas Button components belong to the `fl.controls.Button` class.

FIGURE 32.5

The ActionScript 3.0 `Button` component

Parameters

The `Button` parameters are perhaps some of the easiest to manage. As with other components, you can enter text for the button's label and add one or more listener functions to execute when the button is pressed.

- `emphasized`: This Boolean parameter determines if a border is drawn on the face of the button in its up state. The default value is `false`.
- `enabled`: This Boolean parameter determines if the button can be clicked or not. When set to `false`, the face of the button is dimmed. The default value is `true`.
- `label`: This is the text appearing on the button face. The default text is simply "Label."
- `labelPlacement`: This optional parameter is a menu with left, right, top, or bottom options. This setting determines how the label text is aligned to the button's icon symbol. The default value is `right`. If you do not use an icon symbol for the instance, this setting has no effect.

> **TIP** The `icon` parameter available in the ActionScript 2.0 version of the Button component is now a style property of the ActionScript 3.0 version. Use `myButton.setStyle("icon", exported_symbol_name);` to assign a custom icon that appears next to the label of the button, where `myButton` is the instance name of the Button instance, and `exported_symbol_name` is the class name of the exported symbol asset in the library.

- `selected` and `toggle`: These two parameters work together to enable a Button component instance to act as an on/off button. As a toggle button, the rim of the instance displays an "on" color (dark gray is the default shade color) if `selected` is set to `true`. The `selected` property has no effect if `toggle` is not set to `true`. The default value for both the `selected` and `toggle` parameters is `false`.

- `visible`: This parameter determines if the instance can be seen on the Stage when the instance loads. The default value is `true`.

How it works

An instance of a Button component can have regular, disabled, or active states, which can be customized graphically. It is a very quick way to add interactivity to your movie. For additional functionality of the button, you need to write ActionScript by using the `Button` methods.

> **TIP** The `MouseEvent.CLICK` event is sent to any listeners when a `Button` component instance is clicked.

> **CROSS-REF** You can find several examples of the `Button` component throughout many chapters of this book. You can also search for "button component" in the Flash CS4 Help pages to find more information on the Button component.

CheckBox component

The CheckBox component, as the name implies, is a user interface element that has a selection box next to text. As with HTML form check boxes, the CheckBox component enables you to easily add form options to a Flash movie. The CheckBox component returns a `true` or `false` value. If the box is checked, it returns a `true` value; if not, it returns `false`. These states are shown in Figure 32.6.

FIGURE 32.6

The on and off states of the ActionScript 3.0 CheckBox component

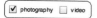

Parameters

CheckBox parameters can be changed to customize the default label text and its placement in relation to the check box graphic. You can also set the initial state and have the option of setting a function, executing as soon as the button state changes.

- `enabled`: This Boolean parameter determines if the check box can be selected or not. When set to `false`, the check box graphic and label text are dimmed.

- `label`: This is the name appearing next to the check box. The default value is set to `Label`.

- `labelPlacement`: This parameter sets the label to the left, right (default), top, or bottom of the check box.

 Make sure to set the height of the instance appropriately to accommodate top and bottom alignment.

- `selected`: Assigning a `true` value checks the box initially, although the default value for this is set to `false` (unchecked).

- `visible`: This parameter determines if the instance can be seen on the Stage when the instance loads. The default value is `true`.

How it works

The CheckBox component has a hit area that encompasses the check box itself, as well as the label next to it. The width of a CheckBox instance can be transformed to accommodate more text. Added functionality using ActionScript is possible by using the methods, events, and properties of the `fl.controls.CheckBox` class.

ComboBox component

The ComboBox component is similar to any standard HTML form drop-down list. When you click the component instance, a list of options appears below the default value in the list. You can also navigate the list by using the Up Arrow, Down Arrow, Page Up, Page Down, Home, and End keys. This component is very useful and essentially has the following two different functionalities:

- As a regular combo box, the component can display a list of choices from which the user can select an option. If the combo box has focus, the user can type a letter to jump to a label starting with the same letter (see Figure 32.7). Note that the ActionScript 3.0 version is not shown.

FIGURE 32.7

A standard ComboBox instance, shown closed (left) and open (right)

- As an editable combo box, a user can enter text into the top field to specify a value that is not displayed in the list. The typed value is the active value for the ComboBox instance. Figure 32.8 shows a value being entered into the ComboBox instance at runtime.

FIGURE 32.8

An editable ComboBox instance, shown with default display (left) and entered text (right)

Parameters

ComboBox parameters can be changed to set labels and data for each item in the drop-down box, set the top of the pull-down to be a text input box (an editable combo box), and customize how many items are viewable when the arrow is selected.

- `dataProvider`: This array is composed of values that correspond to each `label` and `data` pair added as an item to the ComboBox instance. For example, if you had a `label` value of "Red," you may want a `data` value of "0xFF0000." Similarly, if you have a catalog of items, the product's name may be the `label` value and its catalog number may be the data value. The user does not see the `data` value(s).

 When you set values for the `dataProvider` array in the Component Inspector panel, the values are typed as strings. You need to set the `data` values in ActionScript if you want to type the values differently.

- `editable`: This parameter is set to define whether the `ComboBox` instance can have text entered into the top of the list to specify a value not listed in the menu. This typed value can be passed as data to the movie by using the `value` property of the `ComboBox` class.

- `enabled`: This Boolean parameter determines if the combo box can be opened or not. When set to `false`, the check box graphic and label text are dimmed.

- `prompt`: This parameter sets the text value displayed in the text area of the ComboBox instance when the instance's `selectedIndex` property has a value of –1. For example, you could use a text value such as "-- select an option --" to instruct the user to pick a value in the combo box. The default value is an empty string.

- `restrict`: This parameter enables you to restrict the characters that a user can type into a combo box that is editable. You can use a hyphen to specify ranges, such as "A-Z" to allow only the letters A through Z to be typed into the combo box. For more information on how to specify restriction ranges, refer to the Flash CS4 help content for the `TextField.restrict` property.

- `rowCount`: The number entered here represents how many labels are seen on the drop-down box before a scroll bar appears. The default value is set to 5.

- ■ `visible`: This parameter determines if the instance can be seen in the movie when the instance loads. The default value is `true`.

How it works

When you click the `dataProvider` field in the Component Inspector panel, you will notice a magnifying glass icon next to the drop-down area. This button, when clicked, opens a Values panel where you can enter the array of values by using the + or – buttons.

When a user clicks the ComboBox instance and selects an item, the `Event.CHANGE` event is broadcast from the instance to its event listeners.

Functionality can be added with ActionScript, and the `fl.controls.ComboBox` class's methods, properties, and event handlers can be used with each instance of this component.

List component

The `List` component also enables you to create lists just as the `ComboBox` does, but the list menu is always visible (see Figure 32.9). If there are more items than the height of the instance allows, a scroll bar is automatically added to the list. This component enables selection of one or more items. As with the `ComboBox` component, keyboard navigation is allowed, and a `dataProvider` array populates the `label` and `data` parameters.

FIGURE 32.9

The ActionScript 3.0 `List` component at runtime

Parameters

The `List` component (ActionScript 3.0) parameters include an additional option to select multiple values. Other settings in this tab are similar in function to components mentioned earlier.

- ■ `allowMultipleSelection`: This parameter is set to either `true` or `false`. A `true` value enables end users to select multiple values at once when holding down the Ctrl or ⌘ key. The default value of `false` allows only one selection to be active at any time.

- ■ `dataProvider`: This array is composed of values that correspond to each `label` and `data` pair added as an item to the List instance.

- enabled: This Boolean parameter determines if the list items can be selected or not. When set to false, the list and its contents are dimmed.

- horizontalLineScrollSize: This parameter determines how much of the horizontal area of the list's content, in pixels, is scrolled with each click of an arrow button on the horizontal scroll bar of the list. The default value is 4.

- horizontalPageScrollSize: This parameter controls how much of the horizontal area of the list's content, in pixels, is scrolled when the user clicks the scroll track on the horizontal scroll bar of the list. The default value is 0, which indicates the width of the list.

- horizontalScrollPolicy: This parameter controls how the horizontal scroll bar for the list is displayed. The default setting of "auto" means a horizontal scroll bar appears only if necessary. A value of "on" ensures that it is always visible, and an "off" value turns it off.

- verticalLineScrollSize, verticalPageScrollSize, and verticalScrollPolicy: These parameters behave the same as the corresponding horizontal scroll parameters, except that they control the vertical scroll bar of the list.

- visible: This parameter determines if the instance can be seen on the Stage when the instance loads. The default value is true.

How it works

This component's functionality is very similar to that of the ComboBox component. The main difference in a List component is the visibility of the labels and the ability to select multiple values.

When a user clicks an item within the List instance, the Event.CHANGE event is broadcast from the instance to its event listeners.

If you want to add functionality by using ActionScript, the methods, property, and events of the fl.controls.List class are used.

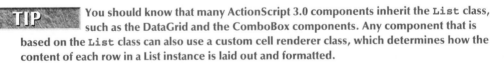

TIP   You should know that many ActionScript 3.0 components inherit the List class, such as the DataGrid and the ComboBox components. Any component that is based on the List class can also use a custom cell renderer class, which determines how the content of each row in a List instance is laid out and formatted.

RadioButton component

The RadioButton component looks and feels similar to those found in HTML forms. Based on the design of radio button functionality, only one radio button can be selected within a group of buttons. Figure 32.10 shows a group of RadioButton instances in a Flash movie.

FIGURE 32.10

A group of ActionScript 3.0 RadioButton instances

Parameters

The RadioButton component has the unique attribute for setting a Group name, which associates the instance with others on the Stage. Other parameters resemble those of components discussed earlier.

- ■ enabled: This Boolean parameter determines if the radio box can be selected or not. When set to false, the radio box graphic and label text are dimmed.

- ■ groupName: The value of this parameter specifies which group of RadioButton instances on the Stage the particular instance is associated with. Therefore, only one radio dot appears in this group at one time. You can have several groups, each with its own set of associated RadioButton instances. The default value is RadioButtonGroup.

- ■ label: This is the text you see alongside the RadioButton instance.

- ■ labelPlacement: By default, the label placement is set to the right of the radio button. The options include left, right, top, and bottom.

- ■ selected: This parameter sets the initial state of the button to be true or false (default). A false selection is clear. All buttons having the same group name allow only one radio button to be selected at one time. If you set more than one RadioButton instance in the same group to initially have a true value, the last instance is selected when you publish your movie.

- ■ value: The value entered here is the data associated with the RadioButton instance.

- ■ visible: This parameter determines if the instance can be seen on the Stage when the instance loads. The default value is true.

How it works

The groupName parameter is important to understand. Groups of buttons can be added to your document, and in each group, only one button can be selected at a time. Both the RadioButtonGroup and RadioButton classes in ActionScript 3.0 broadcast Event.CHANGE and MouseEvent.CLICK events — you'll most likely want to create event listeners for the RadioButtonGroup instance, though, rather than for the individual RadioButton instances within the group.

You can resize the width and height of an instance with the Free Transform tool, the Properties panel, or the Transform panel to accommodate your label alignment parameter. The hit area of the RadioButton instance surrounds both the button and the label area. Added functionality can be controlled by using the RadioButton class's methods, properties, and events in ActionScript.

NOTE It is important to consider the interactive design of your movie when you add radio buttons or check boxes to your movies. Your decision should not be based on the "look" of a radio button versus a check box. Radio buttons should be used only when you need *one* selection to be made from several choices, and a radio button should never exist outside of a group (that is, you shouldn't have a single radio button appearing on its own). Check boxes should be used when you need to allow *one or more* selections to be made from several choices. You can also use a check box for a single option (for example, a form may have a check box asking if you want to receive promotional e-mails for a product). We recommend that you carefully consider how these elements are designed for use in applications because this enhances the usability of your production.

ScrollPane component

The ScrollPane component is potentially a very powerful and diverse tool. It adds a window with vertical and horizontal scroll bars on either side and is used to display linked symbols from the Library panel on to the Stage. Because the component features scroll bars, you are able to accommodate more content within a smaller footprint on the Stage. Figure 32.11 shows an ActionScript 3.0 ScrollPane instance displaying a linked Movie Clip symbol.

FIGURE 32.11

The ScrollPane component at runtime

Parameters

Parameters for the ScrollPane component link it to a Library asset or an external image or SWF file and also control how your end user manipulates the ScrollPane content. You can also control scroll bar positioning and visibility with these parameters:

- enabled: This Boolean parameter determines if the check box can be selected or not. When set to false, the check box graphic and label text are dimmed.

- horizontalLineScrollSize, horizontalPageScrollSize, and horizontalScrollPolicy: These parameters behave the same way as those for the List component discussed earlier in this chapter. Refer to that coverage for more details.

- scrollDrag: Setting this parameter to true enables your users to drag the area within the instance window in order to view the content. A setting of false (default) requires scroll bars to be used instead.

- source: Enter a text string set to the class name of a Movie Clip symbol (set to export in the Library panel) or of an external image file (JPEG, PNG, or GIF) or a Flash SWF file that you want to appear in the ScrollPane instance.

- verticalLineScrollSize, verticalPageScrollSize, and verticalScrollPolicy: These parameters behave the same way as those for the List component discussed earlier in this chapter. Refer to that coverage for more details.

- visible: This parameter determines if the instance can be seen in the movie when the instance loads. The default value is true.

How it works

The ScrollPane component can display DisplayObject classes or load external bitmap images or SWF files. If you want to use an internal asset, the Movie Clip (or bitmap image) simply has to be in the Library panel and have the Export for ActionScript setting checked in the Properties dialog box.

If you want to further extend the capabilities of the ScrollPane component, refer to the Flash CS4 help pages for the fl.containers.ScrollPane class.

TextArea component

The TextArea component (ActionScript 3.0), shown in Figure 32.12, can be thought of as a ScrollPane component for text. The purpose of the TextArea component is to display text or HTML-formatted text within a display window, complete with vertical and/or horizontal scroll bars.

FIGURE 32.12

The TextArea component displaying HTML-formatted text

Parameters

The settings for the TextArea component in the Parameters tab of the Component Inspector panel control the text that is displayed in the instance.

- condenseWhite: This parameter determines if extra white space in HTML text assigned to the htmlText parameter of the component is ignored or not. If set to true, line breaks and extra spaces between words or characters in HTML text are removed, and tags such as <br/> and <p> need to be included in the HTML text to indicate line breaks. If the component does not have any value for the htmlText parameter defined, the condenseWhite parameter is ignored. The default value for this parameter is false.

- editable: This parameter controls whether or not the user can change the text in the instance at runtime. The default value is true. If it is set to false, the user cannot change the text.

- enabled: This Boolean parameter determines if the user can interact with the controls of a TextArea instance, such as scrolling text with its scroll bars. When set to false, the text and controls of the instance are dimmed.

CAUTION We strongly recommend that you get in the habit of setting the editable parameter to **false**. You usually won't want users to change the contents of your **TextArea** component.

- horizontalScrollPolicy: For more details, refer to our coverage of the List component parameter of the same name.

- htmlText: This parameter enables you to specify text by using HTML tags in the instance.

- maxChars: If the editable parameter is set to true, use this parameter to restrict the amount of text a user can type into the instance.

- restrict: Use this parameter to restrict which characters the user can type into the instance. Refer to our coverage of the ComboBox parameter with the same name.

- text: The value of this parameter is the actual text displayed in the instance's text field.

TIP For larger blocks of text, draft the text in a separate text editor and copy and paste the text into the text parameter field of the Properties panel. Alternatively, you can set the **text** property via ActionScript.

- verticalScrollPolicy: For more information about this parameter, refer to our coverage of the List component parameter with the same name.

- visible: This parameter determines if the instance can be seen on the Stage when the instance loads. The default value is true.

- wordWrap: This parameter controls how the text wraps in the instance. If the parameter is set to true (default), the text wraps at the visible horizontal boundary of the display area. If the parameter is set to false, the text wraps only when a carriage return or line break is specifically embedded in the text value, or with a <br/> or <p> tag in the htmlText value.

Horizontal scroll bars are added only to TextArea instances if `wordWrap` is set to `false` and the text width for a line extends beyond the visible display area.

How it works

The TextArea component takes the `text` or `htmlText` parameter value and displays it within the visible area of the instance. The `TextArea` component can be further enhanced or controlled with ActionScript, by utilizing the methods, properties, and event handlers of the `fl.controls.TextArea` class.

CROSS-REF You can see the TextArea component in Chapter 19, "Making Your First Flash CS4 Project."

UIScrollBar component

The `UIScrollBar` component, shown in Figure 32.13, can scroll text within your own `TextField` instances, and you can scroll other `MovieClip`-based content. (In fact, you can use the `UIScrollBar` component to control the properties of any object.) The `UIScrollBar` component can snap to objects on the Stage, and auto-resize its height to match the height of the snapped-to `TextField` instance.

CROSS-REF Read our coverage of the `scrollRect` property of the `MovieClip` class in Chapter 30, "Applying HTML and Text Field Formatting," to learn more about using the UIScrollBar component to scroll `MovieClip` object content.

FIGURE 32.13

The `UIScrollBar` component beside a TextField instance

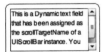

Parameters

The settings for the UIScrollBar component in the Properties panel control the target to which the scroll bar is linked and whether the scroll bar is scrolling horizontal content or vertical content.

- `direction`: This parameter controls the orientation of the scroll bar. By default, the value is `"vertical"` to scroll content up and down. You can change this value to `"horizontal"` to scroll content from left to right.

- `scrollTargetName`: This parameter sets which `TextField` instance is linked to the UIScrollBar instance. This value is automatically filled in if you snap the UIScrollBar instance to a named `TextField` instance on the Stage at authortime. The `TextField` instance must be on the same parent timeline as the UIScrollBar instance in order for `scrollTargetName` to work properly.

- `visible`: This parameter determines if the instance can be seen on the Stage when the instance loads. The default value is `true`.

> **TIP** You can also use the `scrollTarget` property of the UIScrollBar class in ActionScript 3.0 to set the `TextField` instance target. It's also not a requirement to set a scroll target for a UIScrollBar instance — you can use the `setScrollProperties()` method of the UIScrollBar class to determine the scroll range of an instance, and use the `ScrollEvent.SCROLL` event of the component with listeners to enable scrolling movement. This technique is used with the `scrollRect` property of the `MovieClip` class in Chapter 30, "Applying HTML and Text Field Formatting."

How it works

When you set the `scrollTargetName` property to the name of a `TextField` instance, the UIScrollBar component controls the `scrollV` or `scrollH` property of that `TextField` instance. It can determine the range of the scroll bar movement by looking at the `TextField` instance's `maxScrollV` or `maxScrollV` property.

> **CROSS-REF** To learn more about the `scrollV`, `scrollH`, `maxScrollV`, and `maxScrollH` properties of the `TextField` class, read Chapter 30, "Applying HTML and Text Field Formatting."

> **NOTE** Flash CS4 also includes other UI components written in ActionScript 3.0, including the Label, UILoader, NumericStepper, and ProgressBar components. We discuss the UILoader and ProgressBar components later in this chapter, and an example of the `NumericStepper` component is available in the CD-ROM files for Chapter 30, "Applying HTML and Text Field Formatting."

Understanding the Listener Event Model for Components

Although it's rather simple to drag and drop components into your Flash document and use the Component Inspector panel to set up initial values for them, the result of any component behavior needs to be described *by you*, in your own ActionScript code. When the user interacts with a component, a specific event — tailored for the component — is sent out to the Flash movie. Just as you can yell when you're alone in a forest, the Flash movie just ignores these broadcasted events unless you create something to listen to the events. Such functions are called *listeners* because their purpose is to intercept broadcasted messages from other objects that generate events — such as components.

What a typical listener looks like

Just about anything in a Flash movie can be a listener. You can add custom methods to your own classes for example, or you can just create a simple function. To create a basic listener function, use the following syntax:

```
function hearEvent(evt):void {
  trace("heard an event!");
}
```

After you have created a function that behaves as a listener, you can use the function as a listener to a specific component instance.

Letting the component know who its listeners are

After a listener function is created, you need to assign the listener function to the component that will be broadcasting events. For our previous example, you could assign the listener to a Button component instance named `formButton` by using the following code:

```
formButton.addEventListener(MouseEvent.CLICK, hearEvent);
```

The `addEventListener()` method requires a minimum of two parameters: the event being broadcast and the listener function. Each component has its own set of event names. The `Button` component, used in this example, has a click event (represented by the constant `MouseEvent.CLICK`), which is broadcast to all listeners when the user clicks the Button component instance.

All components also broadcast additional information to the listeners, passed as a parameter to the listener's method. All the UI components pass an event information object to their listeners. The exact properties of this object vary from one component to the next, but some are consistent. In the following listener method, the `evt` parameter from the `Button` instance contains several properties, including `evt.currentTtarget`, which is a reference to the `Button` instance.

```
function hearEvent(evt:MouseEvent):void {
  trace(evt.currentTarget + " was clicked");
  trace("The broadcasted event was " + evt.type );
}
```

NOTE You can change the parameter name to any term you want. In our example, the parameter is referred to as `evt`, but you can use a term such as `event`. Just be sure to use the term consistently throughout your listener function.

The `type` property, as you can see in the example code, can tell the listener what type of event was broadcast to it. In this way, you can create one method for a listener and have it handle different event types with specific code.

We'll show you how to create a simple example that demonstrates how a listener works:

1. Create a new Flash file (ActionScript 3.0), and save it as `button_listener.fla`.

2. Rename Layer 1 to submitButton. This layer will hold an instance of the `Button` component.

3. Open the Components panel (Ctrl+F7/⌘+F7) and drag an instance of the Button component from the User Interface set to the Stage.

4. Select the new instance, and in the Properties panel, name the instance `submit Button`.

5. Open the Component Inspector panel (Shift+F7), and click the Parameters tab. Assign a new label to the button, such as **submit**.

6. Create a new layer named actions and place it at the top of the layer stack.

7. Select frame 1 of the actions layer and open the Actions panel (F9/Option+F9). Add the following code to the Script pane:

```
//Button submitButton;

submitButton.addEventListener(MouseEvent.CLICK, showEvent);

function showEvent(evt:MouseEvent):void {
  trace("evt.currentTarget: " + evt.currentTarget);
  trace("evt.type: " + evt.type);
}
```

8. Save your document and test it (Ctrl+Enter/⌘+Enter). When you click the `submit Button` instance, you should see the following text in the Output panel:

```
evt.currentTarget = [object Button]
evt.type = click
```

This output illustrates the two properties of the `evt` object the `Button` component broadcasts. The event's name is `"click"` and the `currentTarget` property is a reference to the object broadcasting the event, `submitButton` (`[object Button]`).

> **NOTE**   If you're wondering why the `trace()` action for the `evt.type` property returns `"click"` instead of `MouseEvent.CLICK`, the reason lies behind the constants already defined in ActionScript 3.0. Technically, you could use the following code to add an event listener for this example:
>
> ```
> submitButton.addEventListener("click", showEvent);
> ```
>
> However, with this syntax, the ActionScript 3.0 compiler has no way of knowing if `"click"` is a real event — the event name is simply a string value. For example, if you mistyped the event name as `"clic"`, you would not receive an error when you test the movie — the Button component instance would register the event listener for a nonexistent event. By using a constant such as `MouseEvent.CLICK`, the compiler has a predefined value it can reference. So, if you mistype the constant, such as `MouseEvent.CLIC` and test your movie, the compiler issues a warning. Go ahead and try it! Although you do need to type a bit more text for the code, it saves you a headache or two when you're debugging your code, especially when you're feeling fatigued.

You can find the completed example file, `button_listener.fla`, in the ch32 folder of this book's CD-ROM.

Using Components in Your Movie

In the following exercise, you use various ActionScript 3.0 components in a movie to activate and deactivate a series of elements. In the process, you learn how you can use components to build interactivity.

 The source file for this exercise called `components_starter_as3.fla` is located in the ch32 folder on this book's CD-ROM. You will notice several components have been added to the Stage and have been given instance names. You'll also need to copy the `component.txt` file from this folder as well.

1. **Open the** `components_starter_as3.fla` **file and resave it as** `components_100.fla`.

2. **Locate the** `TextArea` **instance on the first frame.** This instance is already named `infoArea`. You will write the ActionScript code to dynamically load a text file named `component.txt` into the movie at runtime. If you open the `component.txt` file in a text editor, you'll see that this file declares a variable named `intro_text`, whose value is used by the `TextArea` component. Add the code shown in Listing 32.1 to frame 1 of the actions layer.

   Here, a `URLLoader` object named `textData` loads the `component.txt` file, and sets the `text` property of the `infoArea` component instance to the `intro_text` variable declared in the `component.txt` file.

   CROSS-REF For more information on the `URLLoader` class, refer to Chapter 29, "Sending Data In and Out of Flash."

3. **Save the Flash document and test it (Ctrl+Enter/⌘+Enter).** When the movie loads, you should see a `trace()` message appear in the Output panel indicating whether or not the text file loaded successfully. If it did load, the `TextArea` component should have filled with the text described in the component.txt file.

   Now that text is loading into the `TextArea` component, you will assign a group name to the two `RadioButton` instances on the Stage so that they cannot be selected at the same time.

4. **On frame 1 of the Main Timeline, select each instance of the** `RadioButton` **components.** In the Component Inspector panel, enter the same text string into the `groupName` parameter for each instance. Let's give the radio buttons a group name of `newsGroup`, which best describes their purpose in the movie. This identifier places both buttons in the same group.

5. **Give each instance a different value in the** `value` **field in the Properties panel's Parameters tab.** This data is what is returned to the movie indicating the selection. Give the first `RadioButton` instance, `digestButton`, a value of `digest`. For the `normalButton` instance, assign a `data` value of `normal`.

6. **It is also a good practice to have one radio button already selected by default. In the Parameters tab for the** `digestButton` **instance, set the** `selected` **value to** `true`.

    Now you are ready to have the "sign me up" button (the `signupButton` instance) send the movie to the right location, based upon which `RadioButton` instance is selected.

7. **Add the bold code shown in Listing 32.2.**

    The first line of code adds a code comment to enable code hints for the `signupButton` instance, and the second new line of code imports the `RadioButtonGroup` class that was discussed earlier in the chapter.

    Next, a new listener function, `onSignUpClick`, is added for the `MouseEvent.CLICK` event from the `signupButton` instance.

    In the `onSignUpClick` function, the current value of the `newsGroup` group is assigned to a local variable named `val`. Notice that the way in which you can retrieve the value of a radio button group is through the `selectedData` property. If `val` is equal to `"digest"` (the `value` property for the `digestButton` instance), the movie goes to the `digest` frame label. If `val` is equal to `"normal"` (the `value` property for the `normalButton` instance), the movie goes to the `normal` frame label.

8. **Save your Flash document and test it (Ctrl+Enter/⌘+Enter).** When you click the "sign me up" button, the movie should jump to the `digest` frame label. Close the Test Movie window and retest the movie. Now, choose the Normal radio button, and click the "sign me up" button. The movie jumps to the `normal` frame label.

    Let's activate the `ComboBox` instance, `sectionsBox`, so that users who select an item from the menu are automatically taken to a certain area of your movie. This is very similar to what you have accomplished with the `RadioButton` instances, although you use a different method this time. The instance name of the `ComboBox` component has already been set to `sectionsBox`. The values for the combo box's labels and data have also already been entered for you into the `label` and `data` fields, respectively. To make your drop-down box automatically take your user to a different area of the movie, you create a listener function for the `sectionsBox` instance.

9. **Add the bold code shown in Listing 32.3 to the code on frame 1 from Step 7.** Here, a function named `onSectionChange` is created. The function retrieves the currently selected value from the `sectionsBox` instance (`evt.currentTarget.value`) and sets that as the value of a frame label used for a `gotoAndStop()` action.

10. **Save your Flash document and test it.** Click the `ComboBox` instance, and choose a section name. When you make a choice, the movie goes to the appropriate frame of the Flash movie.

11. **Now add a `ScrollPane` instance to the movie.** The `ScrollPane` component enables you to add an exported symbol or external image asset to a scrollable window. On frame 15 of the pages layer, drag an instance of the `ScrollPane` component onto the Stage from the Components panel. Size and position the new instance however you prefer.

12. **Open the Library panel.** Select the file named `beach.jpg`, and drag it to the Stage. Convert it to a Movie Clip symbol by pressing the F8 key. In the Convert to Symbol dialog box, name the symbol **Picture**. Assign a registration point in the top left corner. Click the Advanced button in the dialog box. Select the Export for ActionScript check box (which also selects the Export in first frame check box). The Class value should also automatically be set to `Picture`. See Figure 32.14 for these details.

> **NOTE** If you receive a warning dialog box after clicking OK in the Convert to Symbol dialog box, just click OK and proceed. Flash CS4 is letting you know that an empty class is automatically being generated for the new Picture symbol.

FIGURE 32.14

The settings for the `Picture` symbol

13. **Delete the Picture instance from the Stage.** An instance of the image is automatically added to the `ScrollPane` instance at runtime.

14. **Select the instance of the `ScrollPane` component on your Stage.** Open the Properties panel, and name the instance `imgPane`.

15. **Open the Component Inspector panel and select the Parameters tab.** For the `source` parameter, enter the string `Picture` that you set as your symbol's class name.

16. **Save your Flash document and test the movie.** Choose new from the `ComboBox` instance, and, on the new frame, you will see the image within the `ScrollPane` window. If you want to be able to drag the picture with the mouse, go back to the Parameters tab in the Component Inspector panel and change `scrollDrag` to `true`.

LISTING 32.1

The textData Instance

```
//TextArea infoArea;

var textData:URLLoader = new URLLoader();
textData.dataFormat = URLLoaderDataFormat.VARIABLES;
textData.addEventListener(Event.COMPLETE, showText);
textData.load(new URLRequest("component.txt"));

stop();

function showText(evt:Event):void {
  trace("---text file loaded successfully");
  infoArea.text = textData.data.intro_text;
}
```

LISTING 32.2

The onSignUpClick() Handler for the Button Component

```
//Button signupButton;
//TextArea infoArea;

import fl.controls.RadioButtonGroup;

var textData:URLLoader = new URLLoader();
textData.dataFormat = URLLoaderDataFormat.VARIABLES;
textData.addEventListener(Event.COMPLETE, showText);
```

```
textData.load(new URLRequest("component.txt"));

signupButton.addEventListener(MouseEvent.CLICK, onSignUpClick);

stop();

function showText(evt:Event):void {
  trace("---text file loaded successfully");
  infoArea.text = textData.data.intro_text;
}

function onSignUpClick(evt:MouseEvent):void {
  trace(evt.currentTarget.name + " clicked");
  var group:RadioButtonGroup =  RadioButtonGroup.getGroup("newsGroup");
  var val:String = group.selectedData as String;
  trace("\tval: " + val);
  if (val == "digest") {
    this.gotoAndStop("digest");
  } else if (val == "normal") {
    this.gotoAndStop("normal");
  }
}
```

LISTING 32.3

The onSectionChange() Handler for the ComboBox Component

```
//Button signupButton;
//ComboBox sectionsBox;
//TextArea infoArea;

import fl.controls.RadioButtonGroup;

var textData:URLLoader = new URLLoader();
textData.dataFormat = URLLoaderDataFormat.VARIABLES;
textData.addEventListener(Event.COMPLETE, showText);
textData.load(new URLRequest("component.txt"));

signupButton.addEventListener(MouseEvent.CLICK, onSignUpClick);
sectionsBox.addEventListener(Event.CHANGE, onSectionChange);

stop();
```

continued

1035

LISTING 32.3   (continued)

```
function showText(evt:Event):void {
  trace("---text file loaded successfully");
  infoArea.text = textData.data.intro_text;
}

function onSignUpClick(evt:MouseEvent):void {
  trace(evt.currentTarget.name + " clicked");
  var group:RadioButtonGroup = RadioButtonGroup.getGroup("newsGroup");
  var val:String = group.selectedData as String;
  trace("\tval: " + val);
  if (val == "digest") {
    this.gotoAndStop("digest");
  } else if (val == "normal") {
    this.gotoAndStop("normal");
  }
}

function onSectionChange(evt:Event):void {
  var val:String = evt.currentTarget.value as String;
  this.gotoAndStop(val);
}
```

ON the CD-ROM   You can find the finished file, `components_100.fla`, in the `ch32` folder of this book's CD-ROM.

Modifying Components

We have already discussed how to alter the color, alpha, or brightness of your component, allowing you to match it to the content on your production. It is a bit more complicated, but not difficult, to change more than just the symbol's effects in the Properties panel. There are two ways in which you can change the look and feel of Flash CS4 ActionScript 3.0 components:

- Use the StylesManager API.

- Modify or replace a component's skins.

For the purposes of this introduction to components, you'll learn how to change the look of components by using styles in ActionScript 3.0.

Global style formats

You can use ActionScript to change the look of your components. Using ActionScript to change properties is often much easier than doing so manually or making your own graphics. Luckily, you can change attributes of components on an instance or global level — with the help of ActionScript. Most of these changes will be limited to colors, alignment, and text.

In Flash CS4, you can control the look and feel of all ActionScript 3.0 UI components in your Flash movie by using the `fl.managers.StyleManager` class.

ON the CD-ROM Open the `components_100.fla` document from the `ch32` folder of this book's CD-ROM to test this new feature.

1. **Create a new layer, and rename it** global styles. Place this layer above the existing actions layer.

2. **On frame 1 of the global styles layer, open the Actions panel (F9/Option+F9), and add the code shown in Listing 32.4.**

   Here, the `setStyle()` method is used to apply a new color and font face to all component instances on the Stage.

3. **Save the Flash document as** `components_101.fla` **and test it**. All the components change to the new style settings.

LISTING 32.4

An Example of Using the StyleManager Class

```
import fl.managers.StyleManager;

var fontStyle:TextFormat = new TextFormat();
with(fontStyle){
  font = "Impact";
  color = 0x333333;
}

StyleManager.setStyle("textFormat", fontStyle);_
```

ON the CD-ROM You can find the `components_101.fla` document in the `ch32` folder of this book's CD-ROM.

Changing styles for a component class

You can also create a custom style for each type of component in your Flash movie. For example, if you want all RadioButton components to use a specific font, you can write ActionScript code to do just that, without having to set a global style or change the style on each individual instance.

1. **Open the** components_101.fla **file created in the previous section.** Resave this document as components_102.fla.

2. **Select frame 1 of the global styles layer and open the Actions panel.** Add the code shown in Listing 32.5 to the existing code. Be sure to add the import fl.controls. RadioButton; line of code to the top of your script along with the other import statements.

    This code creates a new TextFormat object named rbStyle. This object uses a different font and color for the text formatting to be applied to all RadioButton instances in the movie. To apply a new TextFormat object for any particular class of component, use this syntax format: StyleManager.setComponentStyle(ComponentClass, styleName, value);, where *ComponentClass* is the class name of the component you're controlling with the style.

LISTING 32.5

Changing the Style of a Specific Component Class

```
import fl.controls.RadioButton;

var rbStyle:TextFormat = new TextFormat();
with(rbStyle){
  font = "Arial Black";
  color = 0x3333FF;
}

StyleManager.setComponentStyle(RadioButton, "textFormat", rbStyle);
```

Changing styles for individual instances

It is relatively easy to change the font color and face on individual component instances now that you understand style formats. You can accomplish this task by using single lines of ActionScript. Because this code uses fonts in the system, it is important to remember that a default system font is displayed if your end user does not have the particular font installed on his or her system.

CROSS-REF Using custom font faces and embedded fonts with buttons is covered in the next section, "Using Embedded Fonts with Components."

1. **Create a new Flash file (ActionScript 3.0), and save it as** `component_style.fla`.

2. **Rename Layer 1 to** sampleButton. On frame 1 of this layer, add an instance of the `Button` component from the Components panel. In the Properties panel, name this instance `sampleButton`.

3. **Make a new layer and name it** actions. On frame 1 of this layer, add the following lines of code in the Actions panel:

```
//Button sampleButton;

var buttonStyle:TextFormat = new TextFormat();
with(buttonStyle){
   font = "Verdana";
   color = 0x333333;
}

sampleButton.setStyle("textFormat", buttonStyle);
```

This sets your button font face as Verdana, with a dark gray color.

4. **Save the Flash document and test it.** The `Button` component instance should now have a different appearance.

ON the CD-ROM In the ch32 folder of this book's CD-ROM, you can find the completed file, `component_style.fla`.

Using Embedded Fonts with Components

This section explores how to use a custom font for a `Button` component. There are two ways to accomplish this: Use a dummy text field that embeds the font you want to use in the component, or add a Font symbol set to export from the Library panel. Both involve some ActionScript. First, let's look at the easier of the two methods.

1. **Open the** `component_style.fla` **document from the preceding section, and resave the document as** `component_embedded_font.fla`.

2. **Select frame 1 of the actions layer and add the following line of code to the existing code:**

```
sampleButton.setStyle("embedFonts", true);
```

This new line of code tells the component instance that it should display only embedded fonts. If you tested your movie at this point, the label text for the component would be empty because the Verdana font is not embedded in the movie.

3. **Create a new layer and name it** embedField. On frame 1 of this layer, select the Text tool and make a dynamic text field off-stage. Give the field an instance name of `embed-Field` in the Properties panel. In the Family menu of the Character section of the

Properties panel, choose Verdana. Next, click the Character Embedding button in the Character section of the Properties panel. In the Character Embedding dialog box (shown in Figure 32.15), click the Basic Latin option. Click OK to accept this setting. You have now embedded the Verdana font in the Flash movie.

FIGURE 32.15

The Character Embedding dialog box

4. **Save your Flash document and test it.** The Verdana font (or your substituted font, if applicable) is the font the `sampleButton` instance uses.

ON the CD-ROM You can find the completed document, `component_embedded_font.fla`, in the ch32 folder of this book's CD-ROM.

If you don't want to use a dummy text field as this example illustrated, there is another way you can use an embedded font with a component. You can add a Font symbol to the Library panel, and set the font to export with the Flash movie. This method, however, significantly adds more weight (in bytes) to the movie's file size because all characters in the font are exported with the movie. We highly recommend that you use an empty `TextField` instance with specific character ranges to minimize the size of your Flash movies.

CROSS-REF We show you how to embed specific styles of a font in Chapter 30, "Applying HTML and Text Field Formatting."

Modifying AS3 Component Skins

You can also edit the skin symbols of ActionScript 3.0 UI components in your Flash movie's Library panel. For example, if you don't like the check mark graphic for a CheckBox component, you can add your own background symbol(s) for the CheckBox component to use in place of the default skins.

Let's try this process with the CheckBox component. In the following steps, you learn how to change the check mark graphic of the CheckBox component.

1. **Create a new Flash file (ActionScript 3.0) and save it as** component_skin.fla.

2. **Rename Layer 1 to** sampleBox.

3. **On frame 1 of the sampleBox layer, drag the** CheckBox **component from the Components panel to the Stage.** In the Properties panel, name the new instance sampleBox.

4. **Open the Library panel (Ctrl+L/⌘+L) to view the folders containing the assets for the** CheckBox **component.** Expand the Component Assets folder, and then expand the CheckBoxSkins folder. You'll find that the check mark graphic is contained within a symbol called CheckBox_selectedIcon, as shown in Figure 32.16. Although this Movie Clip symbol is not set to export, it is included in the other check box symbols set to export. Double-click the CheckBox_selectedIcon symbol to edit the check mark graphic.

5. **On the CheckBox_selectedIcon symbol timeline, turn the existing layer (icon) into a Guide layer, and lock and hide the layer.** By doing this, you're preserving the original graphic, just in case you want to go back to it. Create and name a new layer, and draw a new check mark graphic. For our example, we drew an X shape with the Brush tool, as shown in Figure 32.17.

> **TIP** To more easily create a new properly sized graphic, use the Zoom tool to magnify the view of the symbol's Stage. You want to match the original graphic's size as closely as possible. You can unhide the original Icon layer and turn on the outline mode of the layer to see the original icon shape while drawing your new artwork.

6. **Save the** component_skin.fla **document and test it (Ctrl+Enter/⌘+Enter).** When you click the CheckBox instance in the movie, you should see the new check mark graphic you created in Step 5. You may need to go back and adjust the position and size of your new artwork within the CheckBox_selectedIcon symbol to fit the default background box of the CheckBox component.

> **ON the CD-ROM** You can find the completed file, component_skin.fla, in the ch32 folder of this book's CD-ROM.

FIGURE 32.16

The CheckBox_selectedIcon symbol in the Library panel

FIGURE 32.17

The new check mark graphic

Using the UILoader and ProgressBar Components

If you're thinking it takes too much effort to create your own ActionScript code for preloaders in ActionScript, you may be in luck. Flash CS4 includes two User Interface components, `UILoader` and `ProgressBar`, which make the task of loading external files into Flash movies at runtime very simple.

> **CAUTION** Flash CS4 has two sets of User Interface (UI) components: ActionScript 2.0, and ActionScript 3.0. This section discusses the ActionScript 3.0 version. The ActionScript 2.0 UI components are compatible with Flash Player 7 and later, whereas the ActionScript 3.0 UI components are compatible with Flash Player 9 or later.

You might be wondering why we even bothered to have you get your hands dirty, per se, with our earlier coverage of preloading assets in Chapter 28, "Sharing and Loading Assets." It's extremely important for you to be able to build your own functionality into your projects. Chances are, you'll come across situations where components won't do exactly what you need them to do. As such, you'll need to know how to build interactivity into your movie on your own.

Adding a UILoader component to your Flash movie

The UILoader component can automatically load an external image or .swf file into your Flash movie, and it's incredibly simple to use. One of the nice features of the UILoader component is that it can scale the image to fit within the boundaries of the component. This example shows you how to use the UILoader component:

1. Create a new Flash file (ActionScript 3.0) and save it as `uiloader.fla`.

2. Rename Layer 1 to imgLoader.

3. **Open the Components panel, and expand the User Interface grouping.** Drag the UILoader component to the Stage. Place the instance near the top left corner of the Stage.

4. **Select the new instance and name it `imgLoader` in the Properties panel.**

5. **Open the Component Inspector panel, and select the Parameters tab.** Leave the `autoLoad` setting at its default value (`true`). In the `source` field, type **http://www. flashsupport.com/images/beach.jpg**. Make sure that the `scaleContent` setting is `true` (see Figure 32.18).

6. **Save the document and test it.** You can watch the asset load into the Flash movie.

> **NOTE** Understand that the image is being loaded into the Flash movie at runtime, not at authortime. Even though the component displays a live preview of the image in the component on the Stage, it still needs to load the image dynamically when the Flash movie file (.swf) loads into a browser. In other words, the JPEG image is not being imported into the .fla file and exported with the .swf file.

FIGURE 32.18

The parameters of the UILoader component

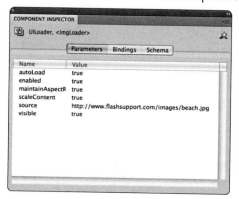

ON the CD-ROM You can find the `uiloader.fla` document in the `ch32` folder of this book's CD-ROM.

You can use this procedure to load "fixed" content into your Flash movie, meaning, if you don't need to change the URL of the loaded asset for a given presentation, using the component with hard-coded values in the Component Inspector panel can take care of your needs. However, if you want to be able to change or display several images in the same instance over the course of your presentation, you must know how to change the parameters of the UILoader component instance in ActionScript. In the next section, you learn how to do just that.

Applying the ProgressBar component

Now you'll learn how to use the ProgressBar component with the example you created in the previous section. The ProgressBar component displays the download progress of a loading asset and can be used with the UILoader component.

1. **Open the `uiloader.fla` from the last section.** Save this file as `uiloader_progressbar.fla`.

2. **Open the Components panel and drag an instance of the ProgressBar component from the User Interface grouping to the Stage.**

3. **Delete the new instance of the ProgressBar component from the Stage.** You need to have only the ProgressBar component in the Library panel for use in this exercise.

4. **Create a new layer and name it** actions. Place this layer at the top of the layer stack.

5. **Select frame 1 of the actions layer and open the Actions panel.** Add the code shown in Listing 32.6.

   This code creates a new instance of the ProgressBar component, places it below the UILoader instance, sizes the width of the instance to match that of the UILoader instance, and, most important, sets the source property of the ProgressBar instance to the UILoader instance. The source property tells the ProgressBar instance which asset to monitor. The removeBar function is added as an event listener for the Event.COMPLETE event, which the ProgressBar instance broadcasts when the asset is finished loading. The removeBar function removes the ProgressBar instance from the Stage.

6. **Save the Flash document and test the movie (Ctrl+Enter/⌘+Enter).** When the UILoader instance begins to load its image asset, the ProgressBar instance displays the percent loaded. When the asset is done loading, the ProgressBar instance disappears.

LISTING 32.6

Adding the ProgressBar Component with ActionScript

```
import fl.controls.ProgressBar;

var imgBar:ProgressBar = new ProgressBar();
imgBar.x = imgLoader.x;
imgBar.y = imgLoader.y + imgLoader.height + 10;
imgBar.width = imgLoader.width;
imgBar.source = imgLoader;
imgBar.addEventListener(Event.COMPLETE, removeBar);
addChild(imgBar);

function removeBar(evt:Event):void {
    removeChild(imgBar);
}
```

Custom Components

One of the most exciting aspects of components in Flash CS4 is being able to make your own creations for distribution or reuse. Custom components usually require a significant amount of ActionScript or at least a solid understanding of the language in order to modify an established component. If you learn how to make your own components to suit common requirements, you will inevitably save a lot of valuable development time. Components were created to be easily reused among projects, and they also allow for simple modifications without having to alter the ActionScript code in the component. Given the robust nature of components, you should be able to develop complex applications, detailed right down to custom icons for the library. Although we will not go into detail on how to create custom components in this chapter due to their complexity, we do explore more custom component creation in Chapter 33, "Building an Image Gallery Component."

TIP   As discussed earlier in this chapter, components can be compiled clips. Flash CS4 enables you to compile your own custom components so that you can distribute the components without giving away your source code.

Live preview

If you are creating custom components, a Live Preview can be extremely useful. This feature enables you to create an updated view of your component in the authoring environment, so you do not have to publish your movie to view the current state of your component. Creating a Live Preview requires a number of steps to set up your movie structure properly and also to activate ActionScript. It is definitely worth it if you are spending a lot of time creating your own components.

TIP   If you create a component, a live preview layer is automatically generated for your component. Usually, anything within the component that uses a getter/setter property is automatically included in the automatic live preview in the compiled clip.

Exchanging and acquiring components

After you have made your own components, you may be interested in distributing them. Or you may also be looking for a place to find new prebuilt elements for your Web site. Luckily, there are many extensive resources online where you can find components for download or for submission. A good place to start searching is at Adobe:

    www.adobe.com/exchange/flash

To install components, you need to download the latest version of the free Extension Manager. There is also a specific method for making your components ready for exchange. You need to package it into a .mxi file, which this Manager can read. The file tells the Manager information regarding the file and the creator. Information about making your components ready for the Extension Manager is available from the same section of the Web site, which includes help and FAQ links.

WEB RESOURCE   We'd like to know what you think about this chapter. Visit www.flashsupport.com/feedback to send us your comments.

Summary

- Components are a fast and easy way to add interactivity to a movie. They save time and increase usability through consistency, intuitiveness, and solid ActionScript.

- Both ActionScript 2.0 and ActionScript 3.0 User Interface components ship with Flash CS4. You cannot edit an ActionScript 2.0 component's assets in its compiled version. The visual elements of an ActionScript 3.0 component are directly editable in the Library panel.

- Some of the most useful UI elements are already built into Flash CS4, including radio buttons, click buttons, combo boxes, lists, and scrolling panes. Using these facilitates user friendliness with your Flash projects because they emulate the user-interface elements commonly used across the Internet and on many desktop applications.

- You can change the look and feel of the ActionScript 3.0 components by using the `setStyle()` method of the individual component or of the `StyleManager` class.

- If you are changing the fonts on your components, you probably want to embed them to avoid problems if your end user does not have the font you are calling for.

- Advanced users of Flash may want to create their own custom components. Custom components can be reused from movie to movie, exchanged, or sold on the Internet. You can download additional components to add to your own movie from online resources, such as the Adobe Exchange.

Chapter 33

Building an Image Gallery Component

In Chapter 32, you learned how to use many of the user interface and data components of Flash CS4. Now that you're familiar with common production tasks associated with components, you can start to learn how to create your own custom components. In this chapter, you learn how to build a Gallery component. By the end, you will know the steps and procedures required to build a fully functional component.

Also in this chapter you learn how to build a Flash movie that can dynamically load a list of JPEG files that the user can browse as a series of thumbnails. When the user clicks one of the thumbnails, a larger version of the image loads into the Flash movie. To see the final project, open your browser and go to www.flashsupport.com/fb/as3/gallery.

NOTE   Make sure that you have Flash Player 10 installed to view the completed project.

At this location, you see the interface shown in Figure 33.1. When you click an image thumbnail, the original JPEG loads into the area below the thumbnail bar. The active selection within the bar is highlighted with a bevel filter. When you click another thumbnail, the previously selected thumbnail transitions to a muted grayscale version.

FIGURE 33.1

The completed project

Scrolled root at dusk, San Fernando Valley, CA

Creating a Plan

Before you can start to build the Gallery component, you need to plan the scope of the project. Just what will the component do? We distill the planning process by telling you the component's features, but in the real world, you will need to brainstorm your ideas and formulate directives for a workable production schedule, accountable to your client's budget and your time.

CROSS-REF Read Chapter 3, "Planning Flash Projects," for more information on production guidelines for Flash projects.

Describing the feature set

It might sound too simple to state, but you have to have a plan before you can build anything — even a Flash movie. And more often than not, the lack of proper planning before you start to build a Flash project only results in bigger problems later — the kind that keep you up late at night days before the final delivery date. One of the most common problems that arises early in a Flash project is the desire to overbuild, or add more features to a project than are necessary to satisfy the goals of the project.

The goals we're aiming to fulfill with the Gallery component include:

- **Quick updates to images on the server:** Many of your business clients love the capability to just upload some images to a server, and voilà — the images are automatically loading into a Flash user interface you designed for them. One of the goals of this project, therefore, is to use server-side scripting (in this case, using PHP as the server-side language) to dynamically read the filenames in a given server folder and deliver that data to the Flash movie. Whenever a new JPEG file is uploaded to that server folder, the PHP script automatically includes the file in the XML feed it sends to the Flash movie.

- **Unique yet useable interface for browsing images:** At the end of the day, if your Flash movie's user interface is too confusing for a site visitor to understand, the project has lost the potential that Flash offers over standard HTML-based sites. The Gallery component should indicate the state of image browsing clearly, with rollover and rollout states for thumbnail buttons. The thumbnails should also remember if they've been clicked previously or not.

- **Downloadable images:** If a user likes an image, he or she should be able to download the image to the desktop. In this component, you learn how to use the new `FileReference` API to download files directly from the Flash movie. You use this feature with the `ContextMenu` class to enable the user to right-click the large image area to download the JPEG file currently displayed.

> **TIP** In ActionScript 3.0, you can also use the `FileReference` API to upload files from the user's computer to your server. Such functionality requires a server-side application or script to receive file uploads.

- **Utilizing JPEG metadata:** If you've used a digital camera, you know that JPEG images can store a lot of useful data related to the exposure, camera model, flash settings, and so on. You can also use an application like Adobe Photoshop to add more metadata, such as a caption and an author byline. If the JPEG image displayed in the Gallery component has a caption, the component should display the caption below the image.

- **Dynamic resizing of original JPEG files for thumbnails:** With the power of server-side scripting, you can create dynamically resized JPEG images on-the-fly — without ever having to manually create a thumbnail version yourself in a program like Adobe Photoshop. The Gallery component features a property that specifies the URL to a resizing script.

Determining the server-side scripting requirements

As mentioned in the previous section, our Gallery component requires the power of server-side scripting to work its magic. We picked PHP as the server-side language to use for this project, although you could adapt the same functionality with any server-side language, including Adobe ColdFusion, Microsoft .NET/ASP, Perl, and so on. One of the reasons we use PHP for this project is that PHP is available on practically every Web-hosting account that you purchase from an Internet Service Provider (ISP) or Internet Presence Provider (IPP). The following list provides the server-side requirements for this project.

ON the CD-ROM You can upload the info.php document to your Web server account to discover more details about your server's PHP installation. You can find this file in the ch33/ finished files/prod/wwwroot folder of this book's CD-ROM.

- **PHP5:** We recommend that you use PHP5 for this project, but you should be able to use PHP4 as well.

- **GD library:** This library enables your PHP scripts to manipulate image data, including the capability to resize JPEG images. Without this library, you won't be able to create the thumbnail images for the Gallery component. If you run the info.php script on your server, search for the term "gd" to see if the GD library is installed, as shown in Figure 33.2.

FIGURE 33.2

The GD library information as displayed by the info.php script

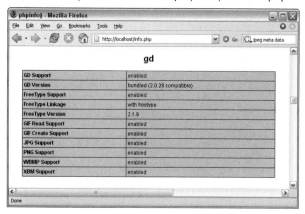

After you've determined that your server has met the core requirements, you're ready to use the three PHP scripts we've included in the ch33/finished files/prod/wwwroot folder on this book's CD-ROM.

TIP You can quickly determine if your server has PHP installed and enabled. Upload the info.php script to an HTTP-accessible folder on your server, and access the info. php script in a browser. If the browser asks you to download the info.php file, your server most likely does not have PHP enabled.

NOTE It's beyond the scope of this chapter to discuss the PHP scripting used in each script file. We provide a basic overview of the each file's functionality in the following sections. We encourage you to open the PHP files in your preferred text editor to review the syntax. For the PHP experts out there, note that the $doc_root variable (found in both the files.php and resize.php scripts) uses a nonstandard way — for portability reasons — to determine the document root of the server. The syntax we use enables the scripts to function properly in both Windows IIS server and Apache Web server environments. Feel free to modify any of the scripts to suit your particular needs.

files.php

This script dynamically reads a specified server folder to search for JPEG files and displays the found JPEG files in an XML document. You must pass a directory name, either relative or from the server root, as a variable named dir. For example, if you specify

```
files.php?dir=images/
```

the script looks for a folder named images in the same folder where the files.php script resides. You can also specify a directory with the syntax:

```
files.php?dir=/gallery/images/
```

which tells the script to look for a folder named gallery at the server root, and then looks for a folder named images within that gallery folder.

To see a sample XML document created by this script, type the following URL into a Web browser:

```
www.flashsupport.com/fb/as3/gallery/files.php?dir=images/
```

When this page loads, you should see the XML data shown in Listing 33.1. (Note that the ⊃ character indicates a continuation of the same line of code.) The schema for this XML file uses a parent node named <gallery>, which contains several child nodes named <img>. Each <img> tag represents a JPEG file found in the images folder. The files.php script retrieves all the information listed for each JPEG file, including the image's width and height (in pixels), the path to the image on the server (src), the caption stored within the JPEG's metadata (if a caption exists), and the name of the file (filename) without the directory path.

NOTE In order for the files.php script to function properly, the JPEG-Meta.php script must be located in the same server folder as the files.php file. We discuss the JPEG-Meta.php script later in this section.

The XML data provided by the files.php script is loaded into the Flash movie, which turns the XML data into an array to pass as a data provider to the Gallery component.

LISTING 33.1

The XML Data for the JPEG Files

```xml
<?xml version="1.0" encoding="utf-8"?>
<gallery>
    <img width="500" height="200" src="images/darkPine.jpg"
        caption="Dark pine and setting sun, Griffith Park, CA"
        filename="darkPine.jpg" />
    <img width="500" height="200" src="images/dustHalo.jpg"
        caption="Dust halo on small tree, Griffith Park, CA"
        filename="dustHalo.jpg" />
    <img width="500" height="200" src="images/dustyClearing.jpg"
        caption="Dusty clearing with slanting sun, Runyon Canyon Park,
        CA" filename="dustyClearing.jpg" />
    <img width="500" height="200" src="images/japaneseTree.jpg"
        caption="Japanese tree in fog, Runyon Canyon Park, CA"
        filename="japaneseTree.jpg" />
    <img width="500" height="200" src="images/rainbowTower.jpg"
        caption="Rainbow sky and metal tower, Hollywood Hills, CA"
        filename="rainbowTower.jpg" />
    <img width="500" height="200" src="images/roadNorth.jpg"
        caption="Road north to Mulholland Drive, Runyon Canyon, CA"
        filename="roadNorth.jpg" />
    <img width="500" height="200" src="images/scrolledRoot.jpg"
        caption="Scrolled root at dusk, San Fernando Valley, CA"
        filename="scrolledRoot.jpg" />
    <img width="500" height="200" src="images/skyPools.jpg"
        caption="Rain pools under cloudy sky, Runyon Canyon Park, CA"
        filename="skyPools.jpg" />
    <img width="500" height="200" src="images/valleyOverlook.jpg"
        caption="Overlook, San Fernando Valley, CA"
        filename="valleyOverlook.jpg" />
    <img width="500" height="200" src="images/weepingTree.jpg"
        caption="Weeping  dark tree, Mulholland Drive, CA"
        filename="weepingTree.jpg" />
    <img width="500" height="200" src="images/wiredCity.jpg"
        caption="Phone poles and palms, Hollywood, CA" filename="wiredCity.
    jpg" />
    <img width="500" height="200" src="images/wiredHill.jpg"
        caption="Dark hills and paths under wires, Los Angeles, CA"
        filename="wiredHill.jpg" />
</gallery>
```

resize.php

This PHP script performs the task of resizing a copy of the original JPEG image to fit a specific height. In this project, the Gallery component's thumbnails should be 50 pixels tall. The `resize.php` script requires two parameters: `height` and `img`. The `height` parameter should be an integer value, while the `img` parameter specifies the path and name of the JPEG file to resize. For example, if you type the following URL into a browser, you should see a picture of a beach on Prince Edward Island, Canada, resized to a height of 50 pixels:

> www.flashsupport.com/fb/as3/gallery/resize.php?height=50&img=/images/
> beach.jpg

With the Gallery component, you can specify the `resize.php` script as the value of the `thumbScript` property.

TIP You can quickly determine if you have the GD library installed (and/or enabled) on your server by uploading the `resize.php` script to a publicly accessible folder and accessing the script in the browser as we demonstrated with the beach picture. Specify an `img` path that points to a JPEG you've uploaded to another folder on the server.

JPEG-Meta.php

This amazing script, provided to us by Rob Williams at CommunityMX.com, enables the `files.php` script to retrieve the metadata, if any exists, of each JPEG file in the specified folder. This script must be uploaded to the same folder as the `files.php` script. Without this file, the `files.php` script does not function.

WEB RESOURCE For more information about using Rob William's PHP script, read his tutorial at CommunityMX.com. You can find a link to this tutorial in the PHP Utilities section of the www.flashsupport.com/links page.

NOTE You also need to upload the JPEG images to your server, into a folder whose path you specify with the `files.php` script from the Flash movie.

Phase 1: Setting Up the Gallery Class

On this book's CD-ROM, in the ch33 folder, you can find two folders: `starter files` and `finished files`. Each folder has the same structure, featuring `src` and `deploy` folders. The `src` folder contains all the source files, such as .fla files and ActionScript files, and the `deploy` folder contains all the production-ready files that should be uploaded to the server for final deployment.

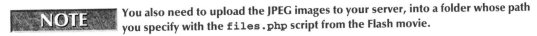 **CROSS-REF** You can learn more about our `src` and `deploy` folder structures in Chapter 3, "Planning Flash Projects."

Reviewing the starter files

Let's review the files that have already been built in the `starter files` folder. You can access each of these files from the `gallery.flp` file in the Project panel.

EasyFilter.as

This class file, which can be found in the `src/flash/com/themakers/effects` folder, contains one method named `saturate`. This method can create a `ColorMatrixFilter` instance. This filter is the ActionScript class responsible for enabling the Adjust Color filter available for `MovieClip` and `TextField` instances in the Filters section of the Properties panel. For the Gallery component, you use the `EasyFilter.saturate()` method to easily control the saturation color values of thumbnail images. The `saturate()` method accepts values from −100 to 100, just like the Saturation slider in the Adjust Color filter of the Filters tab of the Properties panel. The following code sample illustrates a typical use of the method:

```
import com.themakers.effects.EasyFilter;

var myLogo:MovieClip;
myLogo.filters = [EasyFilter.saturate(-50)];
```

NOTE   Many thanks to Joey Lott and Guy Watson for their help with creating the ActionScript code within the `saturate()` method. It's beyond the scope of this book to discuss the intricacies of using matrix values with the `ColorMatrixFilter` class — look to *ActionScript 3.0 Bible* (Wiley, 2008) for more information.

main_starter.fla

This Flash document contains the basic layout for the Gallery component and can be found in the `ch33/starter files/dev/flash/main_starter.fla` folder. If you open this file, you can see that the Main Timeline of the movie has three layers:

- **_captionField:** This layer has a `TextField` instance of the same name. The instance is located near the bottom of the Stage. This field displays the caption text for the JPEG image. This field also embeds most of the Basic Latin characters for the Arial font, and the field uses the new Anti-alias for readability setting in the Properties panel. Note that not all JPEG images have caption metadata — we specifically added caption data to each sample JPEG image in the project, using Adobe Photoshop's File ➪ File Info command.

- **_scrollPane:** This layer has a ScrollPane component of the same name. The instance is located at the top of the Stage. The ScrollPane instance stores `Sprite` holders for each of the loaded JPEG thumbnail images.

- **_loader:** This layer has a UILoader component of the same name. The instance is located below the ScrollPane instance. When a user clicks a thumbnail image in the ScrollPane instance, the full-size JPEG image loads and scales within the width and height of the UILoader instance.

The publish settings for the `main_starter.fla` file have already been set up to publish the .swf and .html files for the document to the `deploy` folder. The .swf file is named `main.swf`, and the .html file is named `main.html`.

Constructing the Gallery component

Before you start to modify the starter files, create a copy of the starter files folder on your computer. In the following steps, you learn how to create a `Gallery` class file for the Gallery component. Then you associate the class with a new Gallery clip in the Library panel.

ON the CD-ROM Make a copy of the `c33/starter files` folder on your computer.

1. **Browse to the** `src/flash/com/themakers` **folder in the** `starter files` **folder you copied.**

2. **Create a new folder named** portfolio. This folder is used to store the `Gallery.as` file you create in the next steps. This folder could also be used to store other class files related to a portfolio set of components, such as a gallery chooser.

3. **Create a new ActionScript document by choosing File ⇨ New and selecting ActionScript File in the New Document dialog box.** Save the new ActionScript file as `Gallery.as` in the `src/flash/com/themakers/portfolio` folder you created in Step 2.

4. **In the** `Gallery.as` **script file, add the code shown in Listing 33.2.** This code declares the package name, imports all the necessary ActionScript 3.0 (AS3) classes that the `Gallery` class requires, and creates the constructor for the class. We discuss many of the imported classes as we add further portions of code to the class. For now, you declare three variables representing the three elements currently on the Stage of the `main_starter.fla` document. The class constructor invokes the `init()` function, which contains a `trace()` action to indicate that the class has instantiated.

5. **Save the** `Gallery.as` **file.**

6. **In Flash CS4, open the** `main_starter.fla` **file located in the** `src/flash` **folder.**

7. **In the Timeline window, select all the frames, from top to bottom, across the three layers.** Right-click (or Control+click on Mac) the frame selection, and choose Copy Frames from the contextual menu.

8. **Choose Insert ⇨ New Symbol.** In the Create New Symbol dialog box, type **Gallery** in the Name field. Make sure that the advanced settings are displayed — if not, click the Advanced button in the lower right corner of the dialog box. In the Linkage section, select the Export for ActionScript check box. The Class field should automatically fill with the name Gallery. Replace this name with the text **com.themakers.portfolio. Gallery**. This path points to the `Gallery.as` file you saved in Step 5. Note that the path is relative to the `main_starter.fla` document and does not include the .as file extension. As Listing 33.2 shows, the `Gallery` class extends the `Sprite` class. As such, the Base class field in this dialog box should contain the path for the `Sprite` class, which is `flash.display.Sprite`. (See Figure 33.3.) Click OK.

> **TIP**   You can assign global class paths in the Flash tab of the Publish Settings dialog box — click the Settings button next to the Script menu.

9. **In the new timeline of the Gallery symbol, select frame 1 of Layer 1.** Right-click (or Control+click on Mac) the frame, and choose Paste Frames. The elements from the Main Timeline should now be pasted into the Gallery symbol timeline. Note that the layer names are automatically copied as well.

10. **With all the elements selected on the Stage, open the Properties panel.** The elements are not aligned to the top left corner of the symbol's registration point. In general, it's considered best practice to align elements within components to the top left corner. In the Properties panel, change the X position to 0 and the Y position to 0. When you deselect the elements on the Stage, the registration point should be at the top left corner of the ScrollPane component.

    Believe it or not, that's all you need to do on the timeline of the Gallery symbol. Everything else happens within the `Gallery.as` file. Remember, because you attached the `Gallery` class in the Class field for the Gallery clip, all the code within the class file is automatically associated with the symbol.

> **TIP**   If you want to change the embedded font used for caption text, select the `_captionField` instance on the Stage of the Gallery clip and change the font name in the Properties panel.

11. **Go back to the Main Timeline (Edit ⇨ Edit Document).** Create a new layer named **gallery**, and delete the other layers.

12. **Open the Library panel (Ctrl+L/⌘+L), and drag an instance of the Gallery symbol on to the Stage.** Place the instance near the top left corner of the Stage. In the Properties panel, name the instance `gallery`.

13. **To make sure that the `Gallery.as` class file is attaching correctly to the Gallery symbol, save the Flash document and test it (Ctrl+Enter/⌘+Enter).** When the movie loads, you should see the `Gallery.init >` statement appear in the Output panel. If this message does not appear, right-click (or Control+click on Mac) the Gallery clip in the Library panel, choose Properties, and check the Class path value.

FIGURE 33.3

The Create New Symbol dialog box

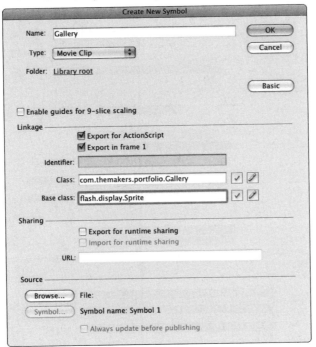

LISTING 33.2

The Gallery Class Constructor

```
package com.themakers.portfolio {

    import flash.display.Bitmap;
    import flash.display.BitmapData;
    import flash.display.Sprite;
    import flash.text.TextField;
    import flash.events.ContextMenuEvent;
    import flash.events.Event;
    import flash.events.MouseEvent;
    import flash.filters.BevelFilter;
    import flash.filters.BlurFilter;
    import flash.net.FileReference;
    import flash.net.URLRequest;
```

continued

LISTING 33.2   *(continued)*

```
import flash.ui.ContextMenu;
import flash.ui.ContextMenuItem;
import fl.containers.ScrollPane;
import fl.containers.UILoader;
import flash.events.ProgressEvent;
import com.themakers.portfolio.Thumbnail;

public class Gallery extends Sprite {

  public var _scrollPane:ScrollPane;
  public var _loader:UILoader;
  public var _captionField:TextField;

  function Gallery(){
    init();
  }

  private function init():void {
    trace("Gallery.init >");
  }
 }
}
```

ON the CD-ROM   You can find this version of the `main_starter.fla` file as `main_100.fla` in the `ch33/in_process` folder. The `Listing33-1.as` file located in the `ch33` folder can be renamed to `Gallery.as` and inserted into your `portfolio` folder.

Phase 2: Loading Thumbnails into the ScrollPane

In this section, you learn how to modify the `Gallery.as` and `main_starter.fla` files to load JPEG thumbnails from your PHP-enabled server.

Uploading scripts and images to your Web server

Before you can continue to modify the Flash documents for this project, you need to upload the files in the `starter files/deploy` folder to a publicly accessible location on your PHP-enabled server. If possible, try uploading the files to the HTTP document root of the server. For example, if your site's domain is `www.mydomain.com`, try putting the PHP script files at the document root where you can load them by typing the following URL into a browser:

```
http://www.mydomain.com/info.php
```

Also, if you have directory browsing enabled on your server, you should be able to access the images folder (and browse the image files within) by typing:

```
http://www.mydomain.com/images
```

After you've completed the project, you can move your script files and images to other folders and modify the script parameters in the Flash movie as needed.

> **TIP** You can also configure a local HTTP server on your computer for testing purposes. During the writing of this chapter, we used PHP5 with Microsoft IIS on Windows XP. If you test locally, make sure that `http://localhost/info.php` loads properly before continuing.

Building data properties for the Gallery class

After you have uploaded the `wwwroot` files to your own server, you're ready to go back to Flash production tasks. In this section, you add several data properties to the component, enabling the component to access the `resize.php` script and to store the JPEG file information for the Gallery.

1. **Go back to the `Gallery.as` file you created in Phase 1 and add the bold code shown in Listing 33.3.** This new code creates the following properties. Each property has an associated private variable listed at the top of the class.

   - `items`: This property saves an array of JPEG filenames in the `_data` private variable. The `items` property is accessed later in this chapter when the thumbnails are built. Whenever information related to the active thumbnail or JPEG image displayed in the UILoader component is needed, the `items` property can be utilized.

   - `rootURL`: This property stores a root path to the server with the PHP scripts and images. This value is appended to image URLs used throughout the class. The private variable `_rootURL` stores the String data associated with this property.

   - `thumbHeight`: This property stores the height, in pixels, that should be passed to the `resize.php` script for the creation of the thumbnail images. The private variable `_thumbHeight` stores the value for this property.

   - `thumbScript`: This property stores the name of the script file to call for dynamic resizing of the JPEG images as thumbnails. The default value is set to `resize.php`, the script file you've already put on your server.

   - `thumbURL`: This read-only property formats the `thumbScript` value with the `rootURL` value, the `thumbHeight` value for the `height=` variable for the `resize.php` script, and the `img=` variable required by the `resize.php` script. The actual image name is appended to `thumbURL` in a later function. The String value for this property is stored in the private variable `_thumbScript`.

2. **Save the `Gallery.as` file.**

> **NOTE** Any property that is preceded by an `[Inspectable]` tag is available in the
> Parameters tab of the Component Inspector panel for the Gallery component. You
> won't see such properties appear unless you specify the AS3 class name in the Component
> Definition dialog box, which we discuss later in this chapter.
>
> Also, while the use of the underscore (_) for private variable names used within a class is a com-
> mon practice, you can name your private variables with your own custom naming convention.

LISTING 33.3

The Data Properties of the Gallery Class

```
package com.themakers.portfolio {

  import flash.display.Bitmap;
  import flash.display.BitmapData;
  import flash.display.Sprite;
  import flash.text.TextField;
  import flash.events.ContextMenuEvent;
  import flash.events.Event;
  import flash.events.MouseEvent;
  import flash.filters.BevelFilter;
  import flash.filters.BlurFilter;
  import flash.net.FileReference;
  import flash.net.URLRequest;
  import flash.ui.ContextMenu;
  import flash.ui.ContextMenuItem;
  import fl.containers.ScrollPane;
  import fl.containers.UILoader;
  import flash.events.ProgressEvent;

  public class Gallery extends Sprite {

    public var _scrollPane:ScrollPane;
    public var _loader:UILoader;
    public var _captionField:TextField;

    private var _data:Array;
    private var _rootURL:String;
    private var _thumbHeight:Number;
    private var _thumbScript:String;

    function Gallery(){
      init();
    }
```

```
public function set items(val:Array):void {
  _data = val;
}

public function get items():Array {
  return _data;
}

[Inspectable(defaultValue="",name="Server Host")]
public function set rootURL(path:String):void {
  _rootURL = path;
}

public function get rootURL():String {
  return _rootURL != null ? _rootURL : "";
}

[Inspectable(defaultValue=50)]
public function set thumbHeight(val:Number):void {
  _thumbHeight = val;
}

public function get thumbHeight():Number {
  return _thumbHeight;
}

[Inspectable(defaultValue="resize.php")]
public function set thumbScript(path:String):void {
  _thumbScript = path;
}

public function get thumbScript():String {
  return _thumbScript;
}

public function get thumbURL():String {
  return rootURL +thumbScript + "?height=" + thumbHeight + "&img=";
}

private function init():void {
  trace("Gallery.init >");
  }
 }
}
```

Architecting the Thumbnail class

Just as the UILoader and ScrollPane components contain their own classes to perform their tasks, the `Gallery` class shouldn't do all the work needed to load images, display them as thumbnails, and display an enlarged view of a clicked image. You could create a `Gallery` class that handled all the necessary tasks, but a more efficient (and comprehensible) approach would be to leave core functionality to the `Gallery` class and delegate other tasks to related classes. One such feature is the thumbnail functionality. Don't misunderstand this point — the `Gallery` class *could* create and manage all the properties, methods, and events of each thumbnail. However, we can keep our `Gallery` class more compact and manageable if we create a separate class to handle thumbnail features. In this section, you create a class named `Thumbnail`, which has the following responsibilities:

- Load a thumbnail image.
- Track whether the thumbnail is the current thumbnail selected or clicked by the user.
- Display rollover, rollout, and clicked states for each thumbnail.

You add more features that enhance these core responsibilities later in this chapter. For now, let's get the core responsibility accomplished. To load a thumbnail image:

1. **In Flash CS4, create a new ActionScript file.** Save this file in the `src/com/themakers/portfolio` folder as `Thumbnail.as`.

2. **Type the code shown in Listing 33.4, or copy and paste the code from the `Listing33-4.as` file from the `ch33` folder of this book's CD-ROM.** This code creates a class named `Thumbnail` which extends the `Sprite` class.

   The constructor function creates a new instance of the `Loader` class assigned to the `loader` property of the `Thumbnail` class. The `onThumbInit` function is added as a listener of the `Event.INIT` on the `contentLoaderInfo` property of the `Loader` instance. This event is broadcast whenever an asset is finished loading and initialized within a `Loader` instance. The `buttonMode` property of the `Sprite` class is set to `true`, enabling the hand cursor for button-related events. (You add these events later in the chapter.) Because the `Thumbnail` class inherits — or extends — the `Sprite` class, any property of the `Sprite` class can be set within the `Thumbnail` class.

CROSS-REF   To learn more about the `Loader` class, review Chapter 28, "Sharing and Loading Assets." The `Loader` class is an intrinsic class of ActionScript 3.0. Don't confuse the `Loader` class with the UILoader component. The UILoader component is part of the `fl.containers` package, which adds several kilobytes to the final .swf file.

A public method named `load` is created, which accepts a `URLRequest` instance as its parameter. The request is passed on to the `load()` method of the `Loader` instance created in the constructor function.

A private method named onThumbInit is also defined, which is invoked by the Event.INIT event of the Loader instance when a thumbnail finishes loading. Here, something incredibly special occurs with ActionScript 3.0 event handling — event bubbling! The dispatchEvent() method of the EventDispatcher class, which is the base class for many intrinsic classes including the Sprite class, creates a new Event instance by using the same Event.INIT constant as the Loader class. The event bubbling functionality is enabled by adding the true parameter as the second parameter of the new Event constructor. So what does event bubbling do? Put simply, an event that is "bubbled" is passed on to the parent DisplayObject of the child emitting the event. Ok, so what does *that* mean? It means that we can listen for the Event.INIT event from the outer container, such as the ScrollPane's content instance, instead of adding event listeners on each and every Thumbnail instance. Later in this chapter, you'll see where this feature comes into play.

3. Save the Thumbnail.as file. You're now ready to create Thumbnail instances in the Gallery class!

> **TIP** You might be wondering why you don't need to bind the Thumbnail class to a MovieClip symbol back in the main_starter.fla Flash file. Because no author-time assets are needed for the Thumbnail class — everything happens in code — you don't need to create a symbol in the Flash authoring document.

LISTING 33.4

The First Draft of the Thumbnail Class

```
package com.themakers.portfolio {

  import flash.display.Loader;
  import flash.display.Sprite;
  import flash.events.Event;
  import flash.net.URLRequest;

  public class Thumbnail extends Sprite {

    public var id:int;

    private var loader:Loader;

    function Thumbnail(){
      super();

      loader = new Loader();
```

continued

LISTING 33.4   *(continued)*

```
        loader.contentLoaderInfo.addEventListener(Event.INIT, onThumbInit);
        addChild(loader);

        buttonMode = true;
    }

    public function load(request:URLRequest):void {
        loader.load(request);
    }

    private function onThumbInit(evt:Event):void {
        dispatchEvent(new Event(Event.INIT, true));
    }
  }
}
```

Creating thumbnail holders in the Gallery class

After you create the data properties for the `Gallery` class and set up the beginnings of the
`Thumbnail` class, you're ready to add the code that makes new `Sprite` holders within the nested
`ScrollPane` instance, `_scrollPane`, of the Gallery symbol.

1. **In the** `Gallery.as` **file, add the bold code shown in Listing 33.5.** (Note that the ⤸
   character denotes a continuation of the same line of code.) The modifications and additions are as follows. The functions are described in the order that they are invoked in the class.

   - `init`: The init function now sets a private variable named `_thumbSpacing`. This
     variable stores the number of pixels to insert between thumbnail images. You can
     change this number to increase or decrease the horizontal gap between thumbnails. As
     you see in the `buildHolders` function, you need to create new `Sprite` instances
     within the `ScrollPane` instance — you can't add content within the `ScrollPane`
     instance without first setting the source property of the `ScrollPane` instance. In the
     `init` function, a new `Sprite` instance is created and set to the `source` property of
     the instance.

   - `buildHolders`: This function goes through the `items` property (which contains a
     list of all the JPEG file information) and builds nested `Thumbnail` instances within
     the `ScrollPane` instance's `content` child. Each object in the `items` array contains
     a `src` property (mapped from the XML generated by the `files.php` script), which
     is used as the `path` variable value to format the URL for the `resize.php` script.
     Note that the `Thumbnail` class is now added to the import list at the top of the class
     (`import com.themakers.portfolio.Thumbnail;`).

- calcThumbW: This function is used within the buildHolders() function to determine how wide a thumbnail image should be based on the aspect ratio of the original image. The width and height properties of the JPEG file are retrieved from nested objects within the items array.

NOTE You haven't actually loaded any data into the Gallery instance back in the main_starter.fla file. In the next few steps, you learn how to load the XML data and format it as a data provider for the items property.

- load: This public function initiates the thumbnail creation and loading process. This is the only method that needs to be called outside of the class.

NOTE The properties added to the Gallery class in Listing 33.3 are not displayed in the printed listing of Listing 33.5, but the complete code is available in the Listing33-5.as file in the ch33 folder of this book's CD-ROM.

2. Save the Gallery.as file.

3. **Switch over to the** main_starter.fla **document.** Now you're ready to load XML data from the files.php script on your server.

4. **Create a new layer named** actions, **and place it at the top of the layer stack.** Select frame 1 of the actions layer, and open the Actions panel (F9/Option+F9). Add the code shown in Listing 33.6.

   This code reserves two variables names, imageData and imageXML, to load the external XML data for the gallery images. The host variable should be set to the domain name of your server. Do not use the localhost value unless you are testing against a server running on your computer.

NOTE When you're ready to deploy the final version of the Flash movie, you can set host to an empty string or to the folder path leading to the PHP script files. Also, if you have difficulties testing against your own PHP server, you can use http://www.flashsupport.com/fb/as3/gallery/ as the value for the host variable to test your Flash movie.

The init() function uses the URLLoader.addEventListener() method to delegate the Event.COMPLETE event of the imageData instance to the onFileData() function. When the XML data has loaded from the PHP script, the onFileData() function is invoked. The host value is appended to the files.php?dir=images/ string in the load() method of the imageData instance.

The onFileData() function cycles through the returned XML data, which resembles that shown earlier in Listing 33.1. The for each() loop goes through each <img> node (imageXML.img) and maps each attribute to a property of the same name on an object (item) that is passed to the items array. After each <img> node has been processed, the items array is used for the items property of the Gallery instance, gallery. (Remember, earlier in this chapter, you placed an instance of the Gallery symbol on the Stage and named it gallery.)

The rootURL, thumbScript, and thumbHeight properties of the Gallery instance are also set in the onFileData() function. After these properties have been set, the load() function is invoked, starting the process of loading the thumbnail images.

5. **Save the** main_starter.fla **document and test the movie (Ctrl+Enter/⌘+Enter).** If the PHP script files are uploaded and correctly specified in the frame 1 script, the thumbnail images load into the ScrollPane instance of the Gallery component, as shown in Figure 33.4. Note that the scroll bar for the ScrollPane instance does not automatically appear — you fix that in a later section.

FIGURE 33.4

The basic thumbnails loading into the Gallery component

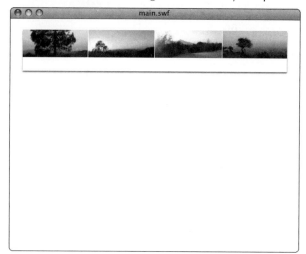

LISTING 33.5

The Thumbnail Creation Process

```
package com.themakers.portfolio{

    import flash.display.Bitmap;
    import flash.display.BitmapData;
    import flash.display.Sprite;
    import flash.text.TextField;
    import flash.events.ContextMenuEvent;
    import flash.events.Event;
    import flash.events.MouseEvent;
```

```
import flash.filters.BevelFilter;
import flash.filters.BlurFilter;
import flash.net.FileReference;
import flash.net.URLRequest;
import flash.ui.ContextMenu;
import flash.ui.ContextMenuItem;
import fl.containers.ScrollPane;
import fl.containers.UILoader;
import flash.events.ProgressEvent;
import com.themakers.portfolio.Thumbnail;

public class Gallery extends Sprite {

  public var _scrollPane:ScrollPane;
  public var _loader:UILoader;
  public var _captionField:TextField;

  private var _data:Array;
  private var _rootURL:String;
  private var _thumbHeight:Number;
  private var _thumbScript:String;
  private var _thumbSpacing:Number;

  function Gallery() {
    init();
  }

  [Public properties omitted from this listing...]

  public function load():void {
    buildHolders();
  }

  private function buildHolders():void {
    var holder:Sprite = _scrollPane.content as Sprite;
    var files:Array = items;
    var w:Number = 0;

    for(var i:int = 0; i < files.length; i++){
      var item:Object = files[i];
      var th:Thumbnail =  new Thumbnail();
      th.id = i;
      th.x = (i == 0) ? 0 : (holder.getChildAt(i-1) ↩
        as Thumbnail).x + calcThumbW(files[i-1]) + _thumbSpacing;
      var path:String = thumbURL + escape(item.src);
```

continued

LISTING 33.5 *(continued)*

```
        th.load(new URLRequest(path));
        holder.addChild(th);
      }
    }

    private function calcThumbW(file:Object):Number {
      var w:Number = file.width;
      var h:Number = file.height;
      var factor:Number = thumbHeight/h;
      return w*factor;
    }

    private function init():void {
      trace("Gallery.init >");
      _thumbSpacing = 1;

      var holder:Sprite = new Sprite();
      _scrollPane.source = holder;
    }
  }
}
```

LISTING 33.6

Loading the XML Data

```
var imageData:URLLoader;
var imageXML:XML;

var host:String = "http://localhost/";

init();

function init():void {
  imageData = new URLLoader();
  imageData.addEventListener(Event.COMPLETE, onFileData);
  var url:String = host + "files.php?dir=images/";
  imageData.load(new URLRequest(url));
}

function onFileData(evt:Event):void {
  imageXML = new XML(evt.currentTarget.data);
  var items:Array = new Array();
```

```
for each(var prop:XML in imageXML.img){
  var item:Object = {
    src: prop.@src,
    width: Number(prop.@width),
    height: Number(prop.@height),
    caption: prop.@caption,
    filename: prop.@filename
  };
  items.push(item);
}
gallery.items = items;
gallery.rootURL = host;
gallery.thumbScript = "resize.php";
gallery.thumbHeight = 50;
gallery.load();
}
```

ON the CD-ROM You can find this version of the `main_starter.fla` file as `main_101.fla` in the `ch33/in_process` folder on this book's CD-ROM.

Phase 3: Displaying the Full-Size JPEG Image

Because the XML data provided by the `files.php` script completely describes each JPEG image in the chosen server folder, your work with the `main_starter.fla` document is finished. You complete the remaining changes within the `Gallery` class file.

Loading the full-size image

After you have the thumbnail JPEG images loading from the `resize.php` script, you're ready to add more functionality to each `Thumbnail` instance containing a JPEG thumbnail. The `th` instance created in the `for()` loop of the `buildHolders()` function is the primary instance to target for adding button behaviors.

You also need to track which thumbnail is currently selected. Just as the List and ComboBox components have a `selectedIndex` property indicating which entry in the list is active, the Gallery component needs a `selectedIndex` property to indicate which thumbnail the user has clicked.

1. Go back to the `Gallery.as` file and add the bold code shown in Listing 33.7. This code has the following changes:

- buildHolders: This function now invokes the addEventListener() method for each th instance holding a JPEG thumbnail image. The MouseEvent.CLICK event is broadcast to the onThumbClick() function of the Gallery class.

- onThumbClick: This function is invoked whenever the user clicks a thumbnail image in the ScrollPane instance. When a thumbnail is clicked, the selected Index property is set to that Thumbnail instance's id value. Remember, the for() loop of the buildHolder() function assigns an id value to each th instance. The id value matches the index of the corresponding JPEG data in the items array.

- loadImage: This function does the work of changing the source property of the UILoader instance, _loader, to the full-size JPEG image URL. The selected Index value is used to look up the JPEG file data from the items array. The src property, as built by the script in Listing 33.7, contains the URL to the JPEG image. This value is appended to the rootURL value and then set as the new source property value. The loadImage() function, by design, is invoked only by the selected Index setter function.

- selectedIndex: This pair of setter/getter functions creates a new property named selectedIndex. This property tracks which index of the items array is currently selected. Whenever the user clicks a thumbnail button, the selectedIndex value is updated and the loadImage() function is invoked.

2. Save the Gallery.as file.

3. Go back to the main_starter.fla document and test it (Ctrl+Enter/⌘+Enter). After the thumbnails load, click the first thumbnail image. The full-size JPEG then loads into the UILoader component of the Gallery component, as shown in Figure 33.5.

FIGURE 33.5

The full-size JPEG image for the first thumbnail

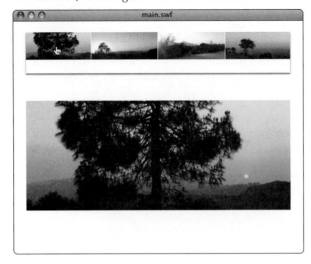

LISTING 33.7

Loading the Large Image from a Clicked Thumbnail

```
package com.themakers.portfolio{

  import flash.display.Bitmap;
  import flash.display.BitmapData;
  import flash.display.Sprite;
  import flash.text.TextField;
  import flash.events.ContextMenuEvent;
  import flash.events.Event;
  import flash.events.MouseEvent;
  import flash.filters.BevelFilter;
  import flash.filters.BlurFilter;
  import flash.net.FileReference;
  import flash.net.URLRequest;
  import flash.ui.ContextMenu;
  import flash.ui.ContextMenuItem;
  import fl.containers.ScrollPane;
  import fl.containers.UILoader;
  import flash.events.ProgressEvent;
  import com.themakers.portfolio.Thumbnail;

  public class Gallery extends Sprite {

    public var _scrollPane:ScrollPane;
    public var _loader:UILoader;
    public var _captionField:TextField;

    private var _data:Array;
    private var _rootURL:String;
    private var _selectedIndex:int;
    private var _thumbHeight:Number;
    private var _thumbScript:String;
    private var _thumbSpacing:Number;

    function Gallery() {
      init();
    }

    [Other public properties omitted from this listing...]

    public function set selectedIndex(idx:int):void {
      _selectedIndex = idx;
      loadImage();
    }
```

continued

LISTING 33.7   (continued)

```
public function get selectedIndex():int {
  return _selectedIndex;
}

public function load():void {
  buildHolders();
}

private function buildHolders():void {
  var holder:Sprite = _scrollPane.content as Sprite;
  var files:Array = items;
  var w:Number = 0;

  for(var i:int = 0; i < files.length; i++){
    var item:Object = files[i];
    var th:Thumbnail =  new Thumbnail();
    th.id = i;
    th.x = (i == 0) ? 0 : (holder.getChildAt(i-1) ⤴
      as Thumbnail).x + calcThumbW(files[i-1]) + _thumbSpacing;
    th.addEventListener(MouseEvent.CLICK, onThumbClick);
    var path:String = thumbURL + escape(item.src);
    th.load(new URLRequest(path));
    holder.addChild(th);
  }
}

private function calcThumbW(file:Object):Number {
  [No changes to this function]
}

private function init():void {
  [No changes to this function]
}

private function loadImage():void {
  var idx:int = selectedIndex;
  var item:Object = items[idx];
  _loader.source = rootURL + item.src;
}

private function onThumbClick(evt:MouseEvent):void {
  var clickedThumb:Thumbnail = evt.currentTarget as Thumbnail;
  selectedIndex = clickedThumb.id;
}
  }
}
```

Updating the scroll bar and auto-loading the first image

As Figures 33.4 and 33.5 illustrate, the scroll bar of the nested `ScrollPane` instance (`_scroll-Pane`) is not visible as more thumbnails load into the instance. The `ScrollPane` instance needs to be told when to redraw its UI elements — the ScrollPane component does not automatically detect when more content has been added beyond its visible frame.

1. **Go to the** `Gallery.as` **file and add the functions shown in Listing 33.8.** Place these functions alphabetically within the list of existing private functions in the class. This listing contains updated code for the `buildHolders` function and two new functions:

   - `onThumbInit`: This function is an event listener for the `Event.INIT` event now added in the `buildHolders()` function. Whenever a thumbnail image has finished loading, the `onThumbInit()` function is automatically invoked by the `content` instance within the `ScrollPane` instance. If you recall from our past work in the `Thumbnail` class, the `Event.INIT` event is allowed to bubble to any parent container of a `Thumbnail` instance. A reference to the `Thumbnail` instance is passed to the function, where the `id` value assigned to the `Thumbnail` instance is accessed. When the first thumbnail in the series of images within the `ScrollPane` instance loads, the `selectedIndex` property is set to 0, which invokes all the code in the `public function set selectedIndex()` area of the class file. This process sets the loading of the first full-size JPEG image into action. Whenever a thumbnail is loaded into the `ScrollPane` instance, the `updateScroller()` function is invoked.

   - `updateScroller`: This function fires one action: `_scrollPane.refreshPane();`. This action forces the `ScrollPane` instance to reexamine its contents and determine if a vertical and/or horizontal scroll bar is necessary.

 The `Listing33-8.as` file in the `ch33` folder of this book's CD-ROM shows the new code within the entire `Gallery` class file.

2. Save the `Gallery.as` file.

3. Go back to the `main_starter.fla` document and test it (Ctrl+Enter/⌘+Enter). When all the thumbnails have loaded, the horizontal scroll bar for the `ScrollPane` instance should appear, enabling you to scroll to more thumbnail images. See Figure 33.6.

FIGURE 33.6

The updated ScrollPane instance

LISTING 33.8

The buildHolders, onThumbInit, and updateScroller Functions

```
private function buildHolders():void {
  var holder:Sprite =  _scrollPane.content as Sprite;
  var files:Array = items;
  var w:Number = 0;
  holder.addEventListener(Event.INIT, onThumbInit);

  for(var i:int = 0; i < files.length; i++){
    var item:Object = files[i];
    var th:Thumbnail =  new Thumbnail();
    th.id = i;
    th.x = (i == 0) ? 0 : (holder.getChildAt(i-1) as ⊃
      Thumbnail).x + calcThumbW(files[i-1]) + _thumbSpacing;
    th.addEventListener(MouseEvent.CLICK, onThumbClick);
    var path:String = thumbURL + escape(item.src);
    th.load(new URLRequest(path));
    holder.addChild(th);
  }
```

```
}

private function onThumbInit(evt:Event):void {
  var th:Thumbnail = evt.target as Thumbnail;
  var id:int = th.id;
  if(id == 0)  selectedIndex = 0;
  updateScroller();
}

private function updateScroller():void {
   _scrollPane.refreshPane();
}
```

Phase 4: Enhancing the Thumbnail and Image States

Right now, you have a Gallery component that can load clickable thumbnails that load full-size JPEG images. Although this functionality is critical to the success of the Gallery component, the same functionality could be accomplished with less effort in a regular HTML page. Let's add some features that are truly within the domain of Flash technology.

Tracking the selected thumbnail

In this section, you learn how to keep track of a selected thumbnail image. To enable such functionality, you need to modify the `Gallery` and `Thumbnail` classes. The `Thumbnail` class needs a property that can determine whether it was the last thumbnail clicked. We name this property `active`. When a thumbnail is clicked, it should know that it has been clicked and its `active` property should be set to `true`. Similarly, the `Gallery` class should know which `Thumbnail` instance is active so that when a new `Thumbnail` instance is clicked, the former `Thumbnail` instance's `active` property can be set to `false` before setting the newly clicked instance's `active` property to `true`. In the following steps, you add the `active` property to the `Thumbnail` class and track it in the `Gallery` class. Note that there are no visible changes to the images or user interface just yet — you'll see new visual states in the next section.

1. **Go back to the** `Thumbnail.as` **file and add the bold code shown in Listing 33.9.** This code adds new getter/setter functions to add a new property named `active`, whose value is stored in a private variable named `_active`.

2. **Save the** `Thumbnail.as` **file.**

3. Switch over to the `Gallery.as` file and add the bold code shown in Listing 33.10. This code adds new getter/setter functions to add a new property named `thumbnail`, whose value is stored in a private variable named `_thumb`. When a new `Thumbnail` instance is set as the value of the `thumbnail` property, any previous `Thumbnail` instance's `active` property is set to `false` and the new instance's `active` property is set to `true`.

4. Save the `Gallery.as` file.

LISTING 33.9

The Active Property of the Thumbnail Class

```
package com.themakers.portfolio {

  import flash.display.Loader;
  import flash.display.Sprite;
  import flash.events.Event;
  import flash.net.URLRequest;

  public class Thumbnail extends Sprite {

    public var id:int;

    private var _active:Boolean;
    private var loader:Loader;

    function Thumbnail(){
      [No changes to this function]
    }

    public function set active(val:Boolean):void {
      _active = val;
    }

    public function get active():Boolean {
      return _active;
    }

    public function load(request:URLRequest):void {
      loader.load(request);
    }

    private function onThumbInit(evt:Event):void {
      dispatchEvent(new Event(Event.INIT, true));
    }
  }
}
```

LISTING 33.10

The Thumbnail Property and Updated Gallery Class

```
package com.themakers.portfolio{

  import flash.display.Bitmap;
  import flash.display.BitmapData;
  import flash.display.Sprite;
  import flash.text.TextField;
  import flash.events.ContextMenuEvent;
  import flash.events.Event;
  import flash.events.MouseEvent;
  import flash.filters.BevelFilter;
  import flash.filters.BlurFilter;
  import flash.net.FileReference;
  import flash.net.URLRequest;
  import flash.ui.ContextMenu;
  import flash.ui.ContextMenuItem;
  import fl.containers.ScrollPane;
  import fl.containers.UILoader;
  import flash.events.ProgressEvent;
  import com.themakers.portfolio.Thumbnail;

  public class Gallery extends Sprite {

    public var _scrollPane:ScrollPane;
    public var _loader:UILoader;
    public var _captionField:TextField;

    private var _data:Array;
    private var _rootURL:String;
    private var _selectedIndex:int;
    private var _thumb:Thumbnail;
    private var _thumbHeight:Number;
    private var _thumbScript:String;
    private var _thumbSpacing:Number;

    function Gallery() {
      init();
    }

    [Other public properties omitted from this listing...]

    public function set thumbnail(val:Thumbnail):void {
      if(_thumb != null)  _thumb.active = false;
      _thumb = val;
```

continued

LISTING 33.10   *(continued)*

```
    _thumb.active = true;
  }

  public function get thumbnail():Thumbnail {
    return _thumb;
  }

  public function load():void {
    buildHolders();
  }

  private function buildHolders():void {
    var holder:Sprite = _scrollPane.content as Sprite;
    var files:Array = items;
    var w:Number = 0;
    holder.addEventListener(Event.INIT, onThumbInit);

    for(var i:int = 0; i < files.length; i++){
      var item:Object = files[i];
      var th:Thumbnail =  new Thumbnail();
      th.id = i;
      th.x = (i == 0) ? 0 : (holder.getChildAt(i-1) as ⤵
        Thumbnail).x + calcThumbW(files[i-1]) + _thumbSpacing;
      th.addEventListener(MouseEvent.CLICK, onThumbClick);
      if(i == 0) thumbnail = th;
      var path:String = thumbURL + escape(item.src);
      th.load(new URLRequest(path));
      holder.addChild(th);
    }
  }

  private function calcThumbW(file:Object):Number {
    [No changes to this function]
  }

  private function init():void {
    [No changes to this function]
  }

  private function loadImage():void {
    [No changes to this function]
  }

  private function onThumbClick(evt:MouseEvent):void {
    var clickedThumb:Thumbnail = evt.currentTarget as Thumbnail;
    thumbnail = clickedThumb;
```

```
      selectedIndex = clickedThumb.id;
   }

   private function onThumbInit(evt:Event):void {
      [No changes to this function]
   }

   private function updateScroller():void {
      _scrollPane.refreshPane();
   }
 }
}
```

Framing the selected thumbnail with the BevelFilter class

In this section, you learn how to add a bevel filter to the selected thumbnail image. The BevelFilter class is just one of several graphics filters that can be applied at runtime to MovieClip, TextField, and Sprite instances in Flash movies.

1. Go back to the Thumbnail.as file and add the code shown in Listing 33.11. This code adds two new functions, and an updated active setter function:

   ■ active **setter function:** When the active property of a Thumbnail instance is set, the Boolean value (true or false) determines how the Thumbnail instance displays itself. When set to true, the frame() method of the class is called. When set to false, the dim() method of the class is invoked.

   ■ frame: This function creates a new BevelFilter instance named bf. The bf instance is assigned to the filters array of the instance, and the alpha of the clip is set to 100% (1.0).

> **TIP** We use the default values of the BevelFilter class. If you search the Flash CS4 Help pages for "BevelFilter class," you can find more information on changing the look and feel of the filter with the thumbnail images, using BevelFilter properties such as distance and angle.

   ■ dim: This function removes any filters applied to the instance, and sets the alpha of the thumbnail to 75% (0.75).

2. Save the Thumbnail.as file.

3. Go back to the main_starter.fla document and test it (Ctrl+Enter/⌘+Enter). When the movie loads, the first thumbnail appears with a bevel border. If you click another thumbnail, the previously selected thumbnail's bevel is removed and the alpha is reduced, as shown in Figure 33.7.

FIGURE 33.7

The `BevelFilter` instance applied to the thumbnail image

LISTING 33.11

Framing the Selected Thumbnail

```
package com.themakers.portfolio {

  import flash.display.Loader;
  import flash.display.Sprite;
  import flash.events.Event;
  import flash.filters.BevelFilter;
  import flash.net.URLRequest;

  public class Thumbnail extends Sprite {

    public var id:int;

    private var _active:Boolean;
    private var loader:Loader;

    function Thumbnail(){
      [No changes to this function]
    }

    public function set active(val:Boolean):void {
      if(val)  frame();
```

```
    else dim();
    _active = val;
}

public function get active():Boolean {
    return _active;
}

public function load(request:URLRequest):void {
    loader.load(request);
}

private function dim():void {
    this.filters = [];
    this.alpha = 0.75;
}

private function frame():void {
    var bf:BevelFilter = new BevelFilter();
    this.filters = [bf];
    this.alpha = 1.0;
}

private function onThumbInit(evt:Event):void {
    dispatchEvent(new Event(Event.INIT, true));
}
}
}
```

Creating a loading transition with the BitmapData and BlurFilter classes

Let's continue the fun with Flash filters! In this section, you learn how to use the `BitmapData` and `Bitmap` classes to make a copy of the thumbnail image over the UILoader component area. The thumbnail, of course, is not as large as the full-size JPEG image. As such, the thumbnail image is stretched and pixilated when it's set to the same width and height of the full-size image. You use the `BlurFilter` class to smooth the thumbnail's pixilation. The filter's strength is inversely proportional to the loaded percent of the full-size JPEG image. As the full-size JPEG image loads into the UILoader component, the intensity of the `BlurFilter` instance is gradually diminished.

Before you can alter the `Gallery` class to make a copy of the JPEG thumbnail image, you need to add a property to the `Thumbnail` class to retrieve an unaltered version of the thumbnail image. Remember, the active thumbnail has a bevel filter applied. For the blur transition effect, the bevel filter should not be included.

1. **Open the** `Thumbnail.as` **file and add the bold code shown in Listing 33.12.** The new `imageData` property is declared with a getter function, retrieving the `content` property of the internal `Loader` instance within the `Thumbnail` instance. Because the `Loader` instance is being used to load bitmap graphic files, the `content` property is of the `Bitmap` type. To retrieve the actual pixel data of this `Bitmap` instance, the `bit-mapData` property is used and returned whenever the `Thumbnail.imageData` property is retrieved. Note that the `Bitmap` and `BitmapData` classes are added to the import list at the top of the class.

> **TIP** You don't always need to declare a setter function for class properties. If you only need to retrieve — and not set — data from a class, then declare only a getter function.

Now you're ready to copy and blur enlarged copies of the `Thumbnail` instances.

2. **Go back to the** `Gallery.as` **file and add the bold code shown in Listing 33.13.** This code modifies existing functions and adds a few new ones:

   - `init`: This function uses a new private variable, `_blurStrength`, which indicates the maximum blur applied to the copied thumbnail when the copy is made. This function is also modified to add two event listeners to the UILoader component, `_loader`. The `ProgressEvent.PROGRESS` event is broadcasted from the UILoader component as new bytes of a loaded full-size JPEG image arrive into the Flash movie. This event is captured by the `onImgProgress` function. The `Event.COMPLETE` event is broadcasted by the UILoader component when the full-size JPEG image has fully loaded into the Flash movie. This event is captured by the `onImgComplete` function.

   - `overlayThumb`: This function creates a bitmap copy of the selected thumbnail, scales the copy to fit within the dimensions of the UILoader component, and sets the initial blur of the scaled copy to a maximum intensity. The `selectedIndex` property invokes the `overlayThumb` function when a new thumbnail is clicked. Here, the `BitmapData` and `Bitmap` classes create the copy of the loaded thumbnail JPEG image. The new bitmap is attached to a new `Sprite` holder, used as the value of a new `_overlay` property of the `Gallery` class. The `_overlay` instance is then resized, using the same procedure that the UILoader component uses to fit loaded images within its display area. (A new private variable named `_overlay` is declared at the top of the `Gallery` class to store the `Sprite` instance.)

   - `blurOverlay`: This function creates the `BlurFilter` instance responsible for blurring the copied thumbnail image. The function requires one parameter: the percent loaded of the full-size JPEG image. If the loading process has just started, the percent loaded is equal to 0. This value is remapped to a blur intensity value (`blurVal`), as indicated by the `_blurStrength` variable set in the `init()` function. As more bytes of the JPEG image load into the movie, the `blurVal` amount is reduced. The `BlurFilter` instance is applied to the `filters` array of the `_overlay` instance.

- `onImgProgress`: This handler is invoked whenever the UILoader component broadcasts a `ProgressEvent.PROGRESS` event. When this event occurs, the loaded percent of the JPEG is retrieved with the `percentLoaded` property of the UILoader component and passed to the `blurOverlay` function.

- `onImgComplete`: When the UILoader component broadcasts the `Event.COMPLETE` event, the `onImgComplete` function is invoked. This event signals that the full-size JPEG image has loaded completely into the Flash movie. At this point, the `_overlay` instance can be removed to reveal the full-size JPEG below it.

- `selectedIndex`: The `overlayThumb` function is added to the setter function for the `selectedIndex` property. Whenever the user clicks a new thumbnail image, the process of copying, scaling, and blurring the thumbnail starts.

3. Save the `Gallery.as` file.

4. Go back to the `main_starter.fla` document and test it (Ctrl+Enter/⌘+Enter). When you click a thumbnail image, a copy of the thumbnail is created, scaled, blurred, and positioned above the UILoader component. The blur intensity is minimized as the full-size JPEG loads into the movie. Figure 33.8 shows a snapshot of this animated transition.

FIGURE 33.8

The blurred copy of the thumbnail image

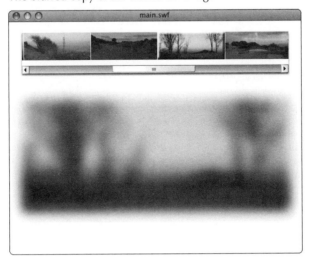

LISTING 33.12

Declaring an imageData Property for the Thumbnail Class

```
package com.themakers.portfolio {

  import flash.display.Bitmap;
  import flash.display.BitmapData;
  import flash.display.Loader;
  import flash.display.Sprite;
  import flash.events.Event;
  import flash.filters.BevelFilter;
  import flash.net.URLRequest;

  public class Thumbnail extends Sprite {

    public var id:int;

    private var _active:Boolean;
    private var loader:Loader;

    function Thumbnail(){
      [No changes to this function]
    }

    public function set active(val:Boolean):void {
      [No changes to this function]
    }

    public function get active():Boolean {
      return _active;
    }

    public function get imageData():BitmapData {
      if(loader.content != null){
        var content:Bitmap = loader.content as Bitmap;
        var bd:BitmapData = content.bitmapData;
        return bd;
      }
      return null;
    }

    public function load(request:URLRequest):void {
      loader.load(request);
    }
```

```
      private function dim():void {
           [No changes to this function]
      }

      private function frame():void {
        [No changes to this function]
      }

      private function onThumbInit(evt:Event):void {
        dispatchEvent(new Event(Event.INIT, true));
      }
    }
}
```

LISTING 33.13

Enabling the Blur Effect on an Enlarged Thumbnail Copy

```
package com.themakers.portfolio{

  import flash.display.Bitmap;
  import flash.display.BitmapData;
  import flash.display.Sprite;
  import flash.text.TextField;
  import flash.events.ContextMenuEvent;
  import flash.events.Event;
  import flash.events.MouseEvent;
  import flash.filters.BevelFilter;
  import flash.filters.BlurFilter;
  import flash.net.FileReference;
  import flash.net.URLRequest;
  import flash.ui.ContextMenu;
  import flash.ui.ContextMenuItem;
  import fl.containers.ScrollPane;
  import fl.containers.UILoader;
  import flash.events.ProgressEvent;
  import com.themakers.portfolio.Thumbnail;

  public class Gallery extends Sprite {

    public var _scrollPane:ScrollPane;
    public var _loader:UILoader;
```

continued

LISTING 33.13   *(continued)*

```
public var _captionField:TextField;

private var _blurStrength:Number;
private var _data:Array;
private var _overlay:Sprite;
private var _rootURL:String;
private var _selectedIndex:int;
private var _thumb:Thumbnail;
private var _thumbHeight:Number;
private var _thumbScript:String;
private var _thumbSpacing:Number;

function Gallery() {
  init();
}

[Other public properties omitted from this listing...]

public function set selectedIndex(idx:int):void {
  _selectedIndex = idx;
  overlayThumb();
  loadImage();
}

public function load():void {
  buildHolders();
}

private function blurOverlay(pl:Number):void {
  var n:Number = (pl*(_blurStrength/10))/10;
  var blurVal:Number = _blurStrength - n;
  var bf:BlurFilter = new BlurFilter(blurVal, blurVal, 3);
  _overlay.filters = [bf];
}

private function buildHolders():void {
  var holder:Sprite = _scrollPane.content as Sprite;
  var files:Array = items;
  var w:Number = 0;
  holder.addEventListener(Event.INIT, onThumbInit);

  for(var i:int = 0; i < files.length; i++){
    var item:Object = files[i];
    var th:Thumbnail =  new Thumbnail();
    th.id = i;
    th.x = (i == 0) ? 0 : (holder.getChildAt(i-1) as ⏎
      Thumbnail).x + calcThumbW(files[i-1]) + _thumbSpacing;
```

```
      th.addEventListener(MouseEvent.CLICK, onThumbClick);
      if(i == 0) thumbnail = th;
      var path:String = thumbURL + escape(item.src);
      th.load(new URLRequest(path));
      holder.addChild(th);
   }
}

private function calcThumbW(file:Object):Number {
   [No changes to this function]
}

private function init():void {
   trace("Gallery.init >");
   _thumbSpacing = 1;
   _blurStrength = 20;

   _loader.addEventListener(ProgressEvent.PROGRESS, onImgProgress);
   _loader.addEventListener(Event.COMPLETE, onImgComplete);

   var holder:Sprite = new Sprite();
   _scrollPane.source = holder;
}

private function loadImage():void {
   [No changes to this function]
}

private function onImgComplete(evt:Event):void {
   removeChild(_overlay);
}

private function onImgProgress(evt:ProgressEvent):void {
   var loader:UILoader = evt.currentTarget as UILoader;
   blurOverlay(loader.percentLoaded);
}

private function onThumbClick(evt:MouseEvent):void {
   [No changes to this function]
}

private function onThumbInit(evt:Event):void {
   [No changes to this function]
}

private function overlayThumb():void {
   var th:Thumbnail = thumbnail;
   var thW:Number = th.width;
```

continued

LISTING 33.13 *(continued)*

```
    var thH:Number = th.height;

    var bm:Bitmap = new Bitmap(th.imageData);

    _overlay = new Sprite();
    _overlay.addChild(bm);

    var lW:Number = _loader.width;
    var lH:Number = _loader.height;
    var factor:Number = thH >= thW ? lH/thH : lW/thW;
    _overlay.scaleX = _overlay.scaleY = factor;
    _overlay.x = _loader.x + ((lW - _overlay.width)/2);
    _overlay.y = _loader.y + ((lH - _overlay.height)/2);

    addChild(_overlay);

    blurOverlay(0);
  }

  private function updateScroller():void {
    _scrollPane.refreshPane();
  }
 }
}
```

Transitioning thumbnail states with the Tween and ColorMatrixFilter classes

The thumbnails in the ScrollPane component can also use a scripted tween to fade to a desaturated state as the user changes the active thumbnail. In this section, you see how the Tween class can programmatically update the thumbnail images. You can create a Tween instance by using the following syntax:

```
import fl.transitions.Tween;
import fl.transitions.easing.*;
var sprite:Sprite = new Sprite();
addChild(sprite);
var tw:Tween = new Tween(
                  sprite,  // Target of the tween
                  "x", // Property to change
                  Regular.easeOut, // Type of easing motion
                  sprite.x, // Start value
                  sprite.x + 100, // End value
                  5, // Duration of tween, in seconds
                  true // Use seconds instead of frames
              );
```

CROSS-REF Refer to Chapter 27, "Animating with ActionScript," for more information on the ActionScript 3.0 `Tween` class and its properties.

1. Go back to the `Thumbnail.as` file and add the code shown in Listing 33.14. This code replaces the existing `dim` function with a new set of actions to utilize the `Tween` class.

   ■ `dim`: This function is invoked from the `active` property, just as it was in earlier sections of this project. Two new `Tween` instances are created for the thumbnail instance. The first `Tween` instance named `twSaturation` is responsible for modifying the saturation value of the thumbnail instance. The `Regular.easeOut` static class is specified as the easing class for both `Tween` instances. The starting value for the saturation tween is 0 (no change) and the ending value is –100 (color removed, desaturated). The duration of both tweens is two seconds. The `twAlpha` instance animates the current alpha of the thumbnail instance to the muted 75% used earlier. The new `onTweenFinish` function is added as a listener of the `TweenEvent.MOTION_FINISH` event to both `Tween` instances; therefore, the `onTweenFinish` handler of the `Thumbnail` class is fired when the tweens finish. Because the saturation value is not a native property of the `Sprite` class (upon which the `Thumbnail` class is based), a new getter/setter property named `saturation` is created for the `Thumbnail` class. The `Tween` instances are added and stored as an array in a new `tweens` property of the `Thumbnail` class. This array is used to determine which tweens have finished or are still in progress.

   ■ `saturation` **getter/setter functions**: The `saturation` setter function is invoked whenever the saturation tween (`twSaturation`) updates the `saturation` property of the `Thumbnail` instance. Here, the new value created by the tween is passed to the `EasyFilter.saturate()` method to create a new `ColorMatrixFilter` instance. We discuss the `EasyFilter.saturate()` method in greater detail at the start of this chapter.

   ■ `onTweenFinish`: This handler is invoked by each `Tween` instance when the respective tween has completed. Each tween is removed from a `tweens` array stored within each `Thumbnail` instance.

   ■ `controlTweens, clearTweens`: These functions manage the playback of the `Tween` instances. You add more functions later in this chapter that take advantage of these functions.

2. Save the `Thumbnail.as` file.

3. Go back to the `main_starter.fla` document and test it (Ctrl+Enter/⌘+Enter). After the thumbnail images load, click a new thumbnail in the ScrollPane component. The previously selected thumbnail desaturates and fades to 75 percent opacity.

LISTING 33.14

Tweening the Thumbnail States

```
package com.themakers.portfolio {

  import flash.display.Bitmap;
  import flash.display.BitmapData;
  import flash.display.Loader;
  import flash.display.Sprite;
  import flash.events.Event;
  import flash.filters.BevelFilter;
  import flash.net.URLRequest;
  import fl.transitions.Tween;
  import fl.transitions.TweenEvent;
  import fl.transitions.easing.Regular;
  import com.themakers.effects.EasyFilter;

  public class Thumbnail extends Sprite {

    public var id:int;

    private var _active:Boolean;
    private var loader:Loader;
    private var saturationValue:Number;
    private var tweens:Array;

    function Thumbnail(){
      super();

      loader = new Loader();
      loader.contentLoaderInfo.addEventListener(Event.INIT, onThumbInit);
      addChild(loader);

      tweens = new Array();

      buttonMode = true;
    }

    public function set active(val:Boolean):void {
      [No changes to this function]
    }

    public function get active():Boolean {
      return _active;
    }
```

```
public function get imageData():BitmapData {
  [No changes to this function]
}

public function set saturation(val:Number):void {
  filters = [EasyFilter.saturate(val)];
  saturationValue = val;
}

public function get saturation():Number {
  return saturationValue;
}

public function load(request:URLRequest):void {
  loader.load(request);
}

private function clearTweens():void {
  controlTweens("stop");
  tweens = new Array();
}

private function controlTweens(action:String):void {
  for(var i:int = 0; i < tweens.length; i++){
    tweens[i][action]();
  }
}

private function dim():void {
  if(tweens.length > 0) clearTweens();
  var twSaturation:Tween = new Tween(this, "saturation", ⤶
    Regular.easeOut, 0, -100, 2, true);
  var twAlpha:Tween = new Tween(this, "alpha", Regular.easeIn, ⤶
    this.alpha, 0.75, 2, true);
  twSaturation.addEventListener(TweenEvent.MOTION_FINISH, ⤶
    onTweenFinish);
  twAlpha.addEventListener(TweenEvent.MOTION_FINISH, onTweenFinish);
  tweens = [twSaturation, twAlpha];
}

private function frame():void {
  [No changes to this function]
}

private function onThumbInit(evt:Event):void {
  dispatchEvent(new Event(Event.INIT, true));
}
```

continued

1093

LISTING 33.14   *(continued)*

```
    private function onTweenFinish(evt:TweenEvent):void {
      var tw:Tween = evt.currentTarget as Tween;
      for(var i:int = 0; i < tweens.length; i++){
        if(tweens[i] == tw) tweens.splice(i, 1);
      }
      if(tweens.length < 1) tweens = new Array();
    }
  }
}
```

Setting the image caption

After you have the full-size JPEG image loading into the UILoader component, you're ready to populate the _captionField TextField instance, which you copied into the Gallery symbol earlier in this chapter. The JPEG files provided in the starter files and finished files folders have had metadata added to them. The caption metadata is read by the JPEG-Meta.php script on the server and inserted into the XML data sent to the Flash movie with the files.php script.

1. **Go back to the** Gallery.as **file and add the bold code shown in Listing 33.15.** Add the new private variable _captionSpacing to the list of existing private variables at the top of the class file, modify the existing init() and loadImage() functions, and add the new displayCaption() function below the last private function in the class file.

   ■ init: The new _captionSpacing variable stores the gap, in pixels, that should buffer the top of the _captionField instance and the bottom of the full-size JPEG image.

   ■ loadImage: After the full-size JPEG image starts to load into the UILoader component, the displayCaption() function is invoked to show the image's caption. The caption text is stored in the caption property of the current object within the items array, as described by the XML document delivered by the files.php script.

   ■ displayCaption: This function populates the _captionField instance with the new caption text and positions the field below the lower left corner of the image.

2. **Save the** Gallery.as **file.**

3. **Return to the** main_starter.fla **document and test it (Ctrl+Enter/⌘+Enter).** When a new full-size JPEG image is loaded, its caption text (if available) appears below the image, as shown in Figure 33.9.

FIGURE 33.9

The caption text below the JPEG image

Dust halo on small tree, Griffith Park, CA

LISTING 33.15

The displayCaption() Function

```
private var _captionSpacing:Number;

private function init():void {
  trace("Gallery.init >");
  _thumbSpacing = 1;
  _blurStrength = 20;
  _captionSpacing = 5;

  _loader.addEventListener(ProgressEvent.PROGRESS, onImgProgress);
  _loader.addEventListener(Event.COMPLETE, onImgComplete);

  var holder:Sprite = new Sprite();
  _scrollPane.source = holder;
}

private function loadImage():void {
  var idx:int = selectedIndex;
```

continued

LISTING 33.15 *(continued)*

```
    var item:Object = items[idx];
    _loader.source = rootURL + item.src;
    displayCaption(item.caption);
}

private function displayCaption(val:String):void {
    _captionField.text = val;
    _captionField._x = _overlay.x;
    _captionField._y = _overlay.y + _overlay.height + _captionSpacing;
}
```

Completing the thumbnail button handlers

The thumbnail functionality is nearly complete. In its current state, the thumbnail images, when clicked, remain muted — even when the user rolls over a previously selected thumbnail. In this section, you add `MouseEvent.ROLL_OVER` and `MouseEvent.ROLL_OUT` event listeners to each thumbnail instance.

1. Go back to the `Thumbnail.as` file and add the bold code shown in Listing 33.16. This code contains the following changes:

   ■ `Thumbnail` **constructor function:** This function, which creates the thumbnail, is modified to assign `MouseEvent.ROLL_OVER` and `MouseEvent.ROLL_OUT` event listeners. The `addEventListener()` method delegates these events to the `onThumbOver` and `onThumbOut` functions of the `Thumbnail` class.

   ■ `onThumbOver`: This handler checks to see if any tweens are active on the thumbnail when the rollover event occurs. If there are any active tweens, they are paused. Any active filters applied to the instance are stored in a new property named `existingProps`. This property is used in `onThumbOut` to restore the last state of the button. Any filters on the thumbnail instance are removed, and the alpha is set to 100%. Note that these actions are applied to a thumbnail instance only if it is not the active thumbnail.

   ■ `onThumbOut`: This handler resumes any active tweens that may have been in progress when the user rolled over the thumbnail instance. Any filters that were applied to the instance before the rollover event occurred are also reapplied to the clip.

   ■ `storeProps`: When a thumbnail's active property is set to `true`, the `storeProps` function initializes a new `existingProps` property with the filters that are applied to the selected thumbnail.

2. Save the `Gallery.as` file.

3. **Return to the** `main_starter.fla` **file and test it (Ctrl+Enter/⌘+Enter)**. After the thumbnail images load, start clicking each one. After the previously selected thumbnail fades out, roll back over the thumbnail. The original saturation and alpha of the thumbnail should appear; when you roll off the thumbnail, the desaturated view of the thumbnail returns.

That's it with the `Thumbnail` class! In the remaining sections, you add extended functionality to the `Gallery` class.

LISTING 33.16

Enabling Mouse Events within the Thumbnail Class

```
package com.themakers.portfolio {

  import flash.display.Bitmap;
  import flash.display.BitmapData;
  import flash.display.Loader;
  import flash.display.Sprite;
  import flash.events.Event;
  import flash.events.MouseEvent;
  import flash.filters.BevelFilter;
  import flash.net.URLRequest;
  import fl.transitions.Tween;
  import fl.transitions.TweenEvent;
  import fl.transitions.easing.Regular;
  import com.themakers.effects.EasyFilter;

  public class Thumbnail extends Sprite {

    public var id:int;

    private var _active:Boolean;
    private var existingProps:Object;
    private var loader:Loader;
    private var saturationValue:Number;
    private var tweens:Array;

    function Thumbnail(){
      super();

      loader = new Loader();
      loader.contentLoaderInfo.addEventListener(Event.INIT, onThumbInit);
```

continued

LISTING 33.16   *(continued)*

```
    addChild(loader);

    tweens = new Array();

    addEventListener(MouseEvent.ROLL_OVER, onThumbOver);
    addEventListener(MouseEvent.ROLL_OUT, onThumbOut);

    buttonMode = true;
}

public function set active(val:Boolean):void {
    if(val)  frame();
    else dim();
    storeProps();
    _active = val;
}

[Other public properties omitted from this listing...]

public function load(request:URLRequest):void {
    loader.load(request);
}

private function clearTweens():void {
    [No changes to this function]
}

private function controlTweens(action:String):void {
    [No changes to this function]
}

private function dim():void {
    [No changes to this function]
}

private function frame():void {
    [No changes to this function]
}

private function onThumbInit(evt:Event):void {
    dispatchEvent(new Event(Event.INIT, true));
}

private function onThumbOver(evt:MouseEvent):void {
```

```
    if(!active){
      if(tweens.length > 0) controlTweens("stop");
      storeProps();
      this.filters = new Array();
      this.alpha = 1.0;
    }
  }

  private function onThumbOut(evt:MouseEvent):void {
    if(tweens.length > 0 && !active){
      controlTweens("resume");
    } else if(existingProps != null) {
      filters = existingProps.filters;
      alpha = existingProps.alpha;
    }
  }

  private function onTweenFinish(evt:TweenEvent):void {
    [No changes to this function]
  }

  private function storeProps():void {
    var existingFilters:Array = new Array();
    for(var i:int = 0; i < filters.length; i++){
      existingFilters.push(filters[i]);
    }
    existingProps = { filters: existingFilters, alpha: alpha};
  }
 }
}
```

Building a right-click download menu item for the full-size JPEG

To enable the user to download the full-size JPEG image, you use the `ContextMenu` class to add a new custom menu item to the Flash Player's context menu that appears when the user right-clicks (or Control+clicks on Mac) the UILoader component display area.

1. Go back to the `Gallery.as` file and add the bold code shown in Listing 33.17. This code creates or modifies the following functions:

   ■ `init` function: This handler, which is invoked automatically when the Gallery instance loads in the Flash movie, now invokes the `addContextMenu()` function.

- addContextMenu: This function creates a new instance of the ContextMenu class. The built-in items of the Flash Player contextual menu (such as Zoom In, Zoom Out, and so on) are disabled for this new menu. A new custom menu item is created, named "Download this image," retrieved from a new constant in the class, CONTEXT_ MENU_CAPTION. When the user selects this menu item, the downloadImage() function is invoked. The new menu is then assigned to the UILoader component, _loader.

- downloadImage: This function uses the FileReference API to enable the user to download a file from the server. The current JPEG file URL and JPEG filename values are retrieved from the items array, and passed to the download() method of the fileRef instance.

2. Save the Gallery.as file.

3. Go back to the main_starter.fla document and test it (Ctrl+Enter/⌘+Enter). When a full-size JPEG image loads into the Flash movie, right-click (or Control+click on Mac) the JPEG image. The contextual menu displays the "Download this image" option, as shown in Figure 33.10. If you select this menu item, a Save dialog box appears, enabling you to save the JPEG file to your computer.

FIGURE 33.10

The new right-click menu item

LISTING 33.17

Utilizing the FileReference API

```
public static const CONTEXT_MENU_CAPTION:String = "Download this image";

private function addContextMenu():void {
    var cm:ContextMenu = new ContextMenu();
    cm.hideBuiltInItems();
    var mi:ContextMenuItem = new ContextMenuItem(CONTEXT_MENU_CAPTION);
    mi.enabled = true;
    mi.addEventListener(ContextMenuEvent.MENU_ITEM_SELECT, downloadImage);
    cm.customItems.push(mi);
    _loader.contextMenu = cm;
}

private function downloadImage(evt:ContextMenuEvent):void {
    var fileRef:FileReference = new FileReference();
    var item:Object = items[selectedIndex];
    var path:String = rootURL + item.src;
    fileRef.download(new URLRequest(path), item.filename);
}

private function init():void {
    trace("Gallery.init >");
    _thumbSpacing = 1;
    _blurStrength = 20;
    _captionSpacing = 5;

    _loader.addEventListener(ProgressEvent.PROGRESS, onImgProgress);
    _loader.addEventListener(Event.COMPLETE, onImgComplete);

    var holder:Sprite = new Sprite();
    _scrollPane.source = holder;

    addContextMenu();
}
```

Phase 5: Finalizing the Component

You've completed all the scripting for the Gallery component — Congratulations! You can now deploy Flash movies with the Gallery component. In this last section, you learn how to enable inspectable properties of the Gallery class to display in the Parameters tab of the Component Inspector panel.

Copying existing component class files

In order for the complete the component process for the Gallery symbol, you need to copy the ActionScript 3.0 class files for the User Interface (UI) components placed within the Gallery symbol. In this example, we use the ScrollPane and UILoader components. To keep things simple, you copy the entire fl package into your src/flash folder.

> **NOTE**   You must complete this task in order to build component parameters for the Gallery component as discussed in the next section.

1. Browse to the following location in the `C:\Program Files\Adobe` **folder** (Windows) or `[Boot disk]\Applications` **folder (Mac):**

   ```
   Adobe Flash CS4\Common\Configuration\Component Source\ ⊃
   ActionScript 3.0\User Interface
   ```

2. At this location, right-click (or Control+click on Mac) the `fl` folder and choose Copy in the context menu.

3. Browse to the `src/flash` folder you created at the beginning of this chapter. Right-click (or Control+click on Mac) an empty area in the folder window, and choose Paste. The class files for the UI components are now available to the Flash documents (.fla files) in your `src/flash` folder.

Adding the component definition

If you open the Library panel of the `main_starter.fla` document, you can see that the symbol type of the Gallery symbol is a Sprite. In order to convert the component to a full-fledged component (complete with component icon!), you need to specify the `Gallery` class in the Component Definition dialog box.

1. With the `main_starter.fla` document active, open the Library panel (Ctrl+L/ ⌘+L).

2. Right-click (or Control+click on Mac) the Gallery clip and choose Component Definition.

3. **In the Component Definition dialog box, type** com.themakers.portfolio.Gallery **in the Class field, as shown in Figure 33.11.** Select the Require minimum player version check box, and choose Flash Player 9. Select the Require minimum ActionScript version, and choose ActionScript 3.0. If you want to choose a custom icon for your component, click the icon button below the "Description" label. Click OK.

FIGURE 33.11

The Component Definition dialog box

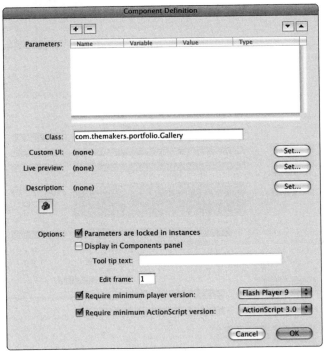

4. **To see the inspectable parameters, repeat Step 2 to see the parameters automatically created for you by Flash CS4, as shown in Figure 33.12.**

5. **To see the new parameters, select the** gallery **instance of the Gallery component on the Stage and open the Component Inspector panel.** When you select the Parameters tab, you should see the new inspectable parameters, as shown in Figure 33.13.

FIGURE 33.12

The updated Component Definition dialog box

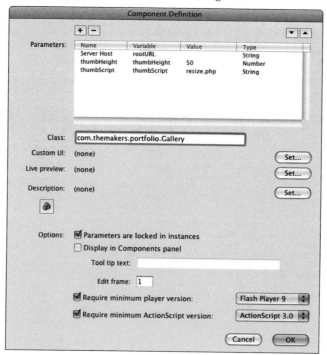

FIGURE 33.13

The Parameters tab for the `gallery` instance

Now, you can change the thumbnail height, server host, and thumbnail script values directly in the Properties panel.

You still need to specify an `items` value for the `Gallery` instance in ActionScript code, and invoke the `load()` handler to initiate the thumbnail loading process.

Changing script paths for final deployment

When you're ready to deploy a Flash movie featuring the Gallery component, keep in mind that you may very likely need to change to the values used in the frame 1 script to initiate loading of the XML data from the `files.php` script. Make sure that you specify a valid server folder name (or path) as the `dir` value appended to the `files.php` filename in the `URLLoader.load()` handler. You may also need to update the name and path to the `resize.php` script in the `onFileData()` handler written within the frame 1 script.

WEB RESOURCE We'd like to know what you think about this chapter. Visit `www.flashsupport.com/feedback` to send us your comments.

Summary

- The process for planning a Flash component can require ample time to properly spec the functionality you want to build.
- The Gallery component can load thumbnail versions of JPEG images on your Web server and display the full-size JPEG image when the thumbnail is clicked.
- Server-side scripting can enable a wide range of functionality within your Flash movies. For the Gallery component, the PHP script files provide XML data and dynamically resized JPEG images to the Flash movie.
- The `JPEG-Meta.php` script written by Rob Williams can retrieve JPEG metadata within your own PHP scripts.
- The `BitmapData` class can create a copy of a bitmap image such as a loaded JPEG file. You can use this class to replicate graphics within your Flash movies.
- The Flash Player filters can add more visual effects to interactive button states.
- You can use the `FileReference` API to download and upload files, without relying on the browser to intervene.

Part IX

Appendixes

If you're wondering what the CD-ROM included with this book is for and how to make the most of it, refer to Appendix A. To learn more about the Flash talent that provided expert tutorials for this edition of the book, browse their bios and visit their URLs listed in Appendix B. The experts who have provided e-mail addresses would be glad to hear from you, but we cannot guarantee that they will reply right away — they are all kind people but they are busy, too.

Audio and video are both complex topics to which many other books are dedicated. We have done our best to include key information in Appendix C and Appendix D. This material will get you off on the right foot when you start creating and editing audio and video to enhance your Flash projects. Hopefully, this will help you to avoid common pitfalls and keep your media assets looking and sounding as good as your Flash content.

Whether you have reached this last section by carefully reading each and every page of the book or just by flipping randomly through it, we hope that you have enjoyed it and learned something along the way. Please let us know what you thought of specific parts of the book or of the book as a whole by visiting www.flashsupport.com/feedback to fill out an online form with your comments. We appreciate your input and we always love to hear how you are using the book now and how you think it could help you in the future.

Appendix A

Using the CD-ROM

This appendix provides information on the contents of the CD-ROM that accompanies this book, and the system requirements for using the sample files and trial applications that enhance the text content of the book.

> **NOTE** For the latest version of this appendix, including any late-breaking updates, refer to the ReadMe file located in the root directory of the CD-ROM.

> **CAUTION** If your CD-ROM is missing from the book when you purchase it, return it to the store where you bought it and get a copy of the book that has a CD-ROM included. If you lose or damage your CD or it gets stolen, your best option is to contact the publisher (Wiley) and tell them your story — they may be able to help you, but there are no guarantees that you'll get a free replacement. The phone and e-mail contact info for Wiley Publishing is provided at the end of this appendix. You can also find more info on what to do about missing CD-ROMs online at www.flashsupport.com/lostcd.

Here is what you will find on the CD-ROM:

- System requirements
- Source .swf and .fla files for step-by-step exercises
- Reusable ActionScript

Before loading the CD-ROM, make sure that your computer meets the minimum system requirements listed in this section. If your computer doesn't match up to most of these requirements, you may have a problem using the contents of the CD-ROM.

For Windows 2000/XP/Vista:

- PC with a Pentium 4 or faster processor, including Intel Centrino, Intel Xeon, or Intel Core Duo (or compatible) processor

- Windows XP with Service Pack 3 or Windows Vista with Service Pack 1 (certified for 32-bit editions)

- At least 1GB of total RAM installed on your computer (note that you need additional RAM to open other programs with Flash)

- 2.5GB available hard-disk space (additional required during CS4 installation)

- 16-bit color monitor capable of 1024 x 768 display recommended

- A CD-ROM drive (DVD-ROM drive required for Creative Suite installer discs)

For Macs:

- PowerPC G5 or later running OS X 10.4.9 and later, running at 1 GHz or faster

- 1GB of RAM

- 2.5GB available hard-disk space required during installation

- 1,024 x 768 monitor resolution

- A CD-ROM drive (DVD-ROM drive required for Creative Suite installer discs)

CS4 applications also require an Internet or phone connection for product activation.

> **NOTE** Some features of Flash CS4 require the latest version of QuickTime. During the installation of QuickTime, select the "Recommended" installation type to install the components Flash requires. To download a trial or purchase the latest version of QuickTime, go to www.apple.com/quicktimewww.quicktime.com.

Reviewing Example .swf and .fla Files

Many of the examples we discuss in the text and in step-by-step tutorials are included in the relevant chapter folder on the CD-ROM. Opening the Flash movie (.swf) is the quickest way to see how the finished example is supposed to look. The fonts should display correctly, and as long as you haven't moved the file to a new location, any loaded assets should also work.

When you open a Flash document (.fla), you may get a warning about missing fonts. This warning simply means that you do not have the same fonts installed on your machine as the original author of the file. Select a default font and you will be able to review and edit the Flash document on your machine. However, without the proper fonts installed, the layout may not appear as it was originally designed.

Installing and Using Plug-Ins and Applications

To download the Mac and Windows trial versions of Flash CS4, go to www.adobe.com/ downloads. Additional plug-ins and trial versions of applications discussed in this book can also be found online, in most cases.

Source Files and Applications

The CD-ROM included with this book aids you with many examples and tutorials by providing relevant files, including the following:

- Custom components for image loading and effects, scripted by Robert Reinhardt and integrated with project examples in Chapters 19, "Making Your First Flash CS4 Project," and 33, "Building an Image Gallery Component."

- Just about every .fla and .swf file that is discussed in the book, including many shown in examples from guest experts.

Shareware programs are fully functional, trial versions of copyrighted programs. If you like particular programs, register with their authors for a nominal fee and receive licenses, enhanced versions, and technical support. *Freeware programs* are copyrighted games, applications, and utilities that are free for personal use. Unlike shareware, these programs do not require a fee or provide technical support. *GNU software* is governed by its own license, which is included inside the folder of the GNU product. See the GNU license for more details.

Trial, demo, or *evaluation versions* are usually limited either by time or functionality (such as being unable to save projects). Some trial versions are very sensitive to system date changes. If you alter your computer's date, the programs "time out" and are no longer functional.

Troubleshooting

If you have difficulty installing or using any of the materials on the companion CD-ROM, try the following:

- **Turn off any antivirus software that you may have running.** Installers sometimes mimic virus activity and can make your computer incorrectly believe that it is being infected by a virus. (Be sure to turn the antivirus software back on later.)

- **Close all running programs.** The more programs you're running, the less memory is available to other programs. Installers also typically update files and programs; if you keep other programs running, installation may not work properly.

- **Reference the ReadMe:** Please refer to the `ReadMe` file located at the root of the CD-ROM for the latest product information at the time of publication.

Customer Care

If you have trouble with the CD-ROM, call the Wiley Product Technical Support phone number at 800-762-2974. Outside the United States, call 1-317-572-3994. You can also contact Wiley Product Technical Support at `http://support.wiley.com`. John Wiley & Sons provides technical support only for installation and other general quality-control items. For technical support on the applications themselves, consult the program's vendor or author.

To place additional orders or to request information about other Wiley products, call 877-762-2974.

Appendix B

Guest Experts' Information

Bazley, Richard
Bazley Films
Corsham, England, UK
richard@bazleyfilms.com
www.bazleyfilms.com
* Animation examples from *The Journal of Edwin Carp* in Part III

Brown, Scott
Los Angeles, California, USA
sbrown@artcenter.edu
www.spicybrown.com
* Tutorial: "Designing for Usability" in Chapter 3

Corsaro, Sandro
sandro corsaro animation
Los Angeles, California, USA
info@sandrocorsaro.com
www.sandrocorsaro.com
* Tutorial: "Flash Character Design Strategies" in Chapter 13

Lott, Joey
Valley Village, California, USA
joey@person13.com
* Tutorial: "Adding New Tools to Flash," in Chapter 4, and sendmail.pl
script on the CD-ROM: Cross-Reference in ch29

Stumpf, Felix
Stuttgart, Germany
info@felixstumpf.de
www.felixstumpf.de
* Tutorial: "Using Video As a Basis for Fluid, Hand-Drawn Animation" in Chapter 13

Turner, Bill
Turnertoons Productions, Inc.
Melbourne, Florida, USA
* Animation examples and tutorial: "Lip-Syncing Cartoons" in Chapter 13

Winkler, Tom
doodie.com
Hollywood, California, USA
tomwink@earthlink.net
www.doodie.com
* Animation examples in Chapter 10

Appendix C

Digital Audio Basics

I f you plan carefully and pay attention to technical detail, sound can add dimension to your Flash projects. That's because sound introduces another mode of sensory perception. Coordinated with visual form and motion, sound deepens the impact and can even enhance the ease of use of your Flash creation.

CROSS-REF For detailed information on adding sound to your Flash productions, refer to Chapter 14, "Adding Sound." Chapter 14 explains how to work with imported sound in Flash CS4, covering topics from codecs and compression to syncing to behaviors.

IN THIS APPENDIX

Audio sampling and quality basics

Production tips

Understanding the Basics of Sampling and Quality

Before you begin integrating sound with your Flash project, it's important to understand the basics of digital audio. To help you with this, this appendix is dedicated to sampling, bit resolution, and file size.

What is sound?

Hearing is one of our five senses; it's the sense that's produced when vibrations in the air strike the aural receptors located within your ears. When you hear a sound, the volume of the sound is determined by the intensity of the vibrations, or sound waves.

The *pitch* that you hear — meaning how high (treble) or low (bass) — is determined by the frequency of those vibrations (waves). The frequency of sound is measured in hertz (abbreviated as Hz). Theoretically, most humans have the ability to hear frequencies that range from 20 to 20,000 Hz. The frequency of the sound is a measure of the range of the sound — from the highest high to the lowest low. It's important to note here that, when starting to work with sound, the most common error is confusing the frequency of the sound with the recording sample.

What affects the quality and size of sound files?

When you add sound to a Flash movie, a number of factors affect the final quality of the sound and the size of the sound file. The quality of the sound is important because it determines the aesthetic experience of the sound. The file size is important because it determines how quickly (or slowly) the sound arrives at the end user's computer. The primary factors that determine the quality and size of a sound file are sample rate and bit resolution.

Sample rate

The sample rate, measured in hertz (Hz), describes the number of times an audio signal is sampled when it is recorded digitally. In the late 1940s, Harry Nyquist and Claude Shannon developed a theorem, which said that, for optimal sound quality, a sampling rate must be twice the value of the highest frequency of a signal. Thus, the higher the sample rate, the better the audio range. Generally, higher sample rates result in a richer, more complete sound. According to Nyquist and Shannon, in order for the audible range of 20 to 20,000 Hz to be sampled correctly, the audio source needs to be sampled at a frequency no lower than 40,000 Hz, or 40 kHz. This explains why CD audio, which closely resembles the source sound, is sampled at 44.1 kHz.

 A sound *sample* refers to one "analysis" of a recorded sound, whereas a sound *file* refers to the entire collection of samples recorded, which compose a digital recording.

The less a sound is sampled, the further the recording will deviate from the original sound. However, this tendency toward loss of the original quality of the sound yields one advantage: When the sample rate of a sound file is decreased, the file size drops proportionately. For example, a 300KB, 44.1 kHz sound file would be 150KB when saved as a 22.05 kHz file. See Table C.1 for more details on how sample rates affect quality.

Because the native playback rate of most common audio cards is 44.1 kHz, sound that is destined for playback on any computer should be a multiple of 11.025. Thus, we recommend sample rates of 44.1 kHz, 22.05 kHz, and 11.025 kHz for *any* use on computers. (Although sample rates that deviate from the rule of 44.1 may sound fine on your development platform, and may sound fine on many other computers, some may have problems. This simple rule goes a long way toward reducing complaints of popping and distorted sound.) These standard rates become more important with Flash. When Flash imports sounds that are not multiples of 11.025, the sound file is resampled, which causes the sound to play at a lower or higher pitch than the original recording. This same logic applies to sound export, which we discuss in Chapter 14. Finally, although Flash menus list sample rates as 11, 22, and 44, these are abbreviations for the truly precise sample rates of 11.025, 22.05, and 44.1 kHz.

TABLE C.1

Audio Sample Rates and Quality

Sample Rate	Quality Level	Possible Uses
48 kHz	Studio quality	Sound or music recorded to a digital medium such as miniDV, DAT, DVCam, and so on
44.1 kHz	CD quality	High-fidelity sound and music
32 kHz	Near-CD quality	Professional/consumer digital camcorders
22.050 kHz	FM radio quality	Short, high-quality music clips
11.025 kHz	Acceptable for music	Longer music clips; high-quality voice; sound effects
5 kHz	Acceptable for speech	"Flat" speech; simple button sounds

> **NOTE** Although the Flash Player can play a wide range of sampling rates with runtime assets, the Flash Player resamples all audio to 44.1 kHz during playback. You may want to make sure that all external assets that you intend to play at runtime use 44.1 kHz for consistency.

Bit resolution

The second key factor that influences audio quality is bit resolution (or bit depth). *Bit resolution* describes the number of bits used to record each audio sample. Bit resolution is increased exponentially, meaning that an 8-bit sound sample has a range of 28, or 256, levels, whereas a 16-bit sound sample has a range of 216, or 65,536, levels. Thus, a 16-bit sound is recorded with far more information than an 8-bit sound of equal length. The result of this additional information in a 16-bit sound is that background hiss is minimized, while the sound itself is clearer. The same sound recorded at 8-bits will be noisy and washed out.

A 16-bit sound file is twice the size of the same file saved at 8-bit quality. This is due to the increase in the amount of information taken to record the higher-quality file. So, if your sound is too big, what can you do? Well, a sound that's been recorded at a higher bit resolution can be converted to a lower bit resolution, and a sound with a high sample rate can be converted to a lower sample rate. Although a professional studio might perform such conversions with hardware, you can do either of these conversions with software.

> **TIP** If you're having difficulty understanding the significance of bit depths, yet are familiar with the intricacies of scanning photographic images, consider the difference between an 8-bit grayscale image and a 24-bit color image of equivalent dimensions. The file size for the 8-bit grayscale image (such as a black-and-white photograph) is much smaller than the 24-bit color image (such as a color photograph). The grayscale image doesn't have as much tonal information — only 256 levels of gray — yet the 24-bit color image records a range of 16.7 million colors. Unlike photographs, sound samples don't require anything close to a range of 16.7 million values. Also, 16-bit sound samples deliver a dynamic range of over 64,000 values, which is more than the human ear can detect.

Table C.2 lists the various bit depths of sound along with their quality levels and possible uses.

TABLE C.2

Audio Bit Resolution and Quality

Bit Depth	Quality Level	Possible Uses
16-bit	CD quality	High-fidelity sound and music
12-bit	Near-CD quality	Professional/consumer digital camcorder audio
8-bit	FM radio quality	Short, high-quality music clips
4-bit	Acceptable for music	Longer music clips; high-quality voice; sound effects

> **NOTE** As hardware technology improves, we're seeing even better audio bit resolution beyond the 16-bit and 44 kHz range. The DVD-Audio format, for example, offers audio bit resolutions of 16, 20, or 24, and sampling rates of 48, 96, or 192 kHz. Obviously, these extraordinarily high-fidelity recordings are appreciated by extreme audiophiles who have superior playback devices and speakers. Don't worry if your multimedia presentations don't use such extremes — trust us when we say that 16-bit 44 kHz audio is more than enough quality for average computer-audio devices and speakers.

See Figures C.1 and C.2 for a comparison of the differences between sounds at different sample rates and bit depths. Both figures show a waveform derived from the same original sound file, differing only in their sample rates and bit depths. The waveform of the 16-bit 44.1 kHz sound has twice as many *points* — or samples of information — as the 8-bit 11.025 kHz sound. Because the 16-bit 44.1 kHz sound has more samples, the gap between each sample isn't as large as the gaps of the 8-bit 11.025 kHz sound. More samples result in a much smoother, cleaner sound.

> **TIP** A common mistake novices make with sound is the assumption that 8-bit audio is acceptable, especially because it ought to result in a much smaller file than 16-bit sound. This is wrong for at least two reasons. First, 8-bit is unacceptable because it sounds far worse than 16-bit sound. Second, the horrible sound does not pay for itself in diminished file size because most audio compression codecs (especially those used by Flash) won't work with 8-bit sound.

FIGURE C.1

A waveform of a sound sampled at 44.100 kHz with a 16-bit resolution, as displayed in a high-end sound application

Channels

Audio files are either mono (single channel) or stereo (dual channel: left and right). Stereo files are twice the size of mono files because they have twice the information. Most audio-editing applications offer the option to mix the two stereo channels together and either save or export a stereo sound to a one-channel mono sound. Most audio applications also have the capability to save the right or left channel of a stereo sound separately as a .wav or .aif file.

With the more robust, multitrack-editing applications such as Deck, ProTools, Sound Forge, or Cool Edit Pro, it's not unusual to work with eight or more audio tracks — limited only by your system configuration. As you may imagine, these applications give the sound artist greater control over the final sound mix. For use in Flash, these multitrack audio project files need to be "bounced" or mixed down to a stereo or mono file in order to be saved as .wav or .aif files.

FIGURE C.2

The same sound that is shown in Figure C.1, but it's down-sampled to 11.025 kHz with an 8-bit resolution

Getting Tips on Production

The primary goal of sound optimization for limited delivery networks (such as the Internet) is to deliver an acceptable quality without a large file-size "cost." You should be concerned about the file size of your audio clips for several reasons:

- Sound files require a large amount of drive space.
- Managing large sound files and importing them into Flash can be cumbersome and slow.

■ Download times for large, elaborate sound clips (even when heavily compressed upon export from Flash) can be detrimental to the appreciation of your Flash project (even if your target audience has what may be considered a high-speed Internet connection).

When you're working with audio clips, it's important to create the shortest audio clips possible. That means trimming off any excess sound that you don't need, especially any blank lead-in or lead-out *handles* (also called in and out points) at either the beginning or the end of a clip.

CROSS-REF We discuss trimming excess sound briefly in Chapter 14, "Adding Sound," with reference to Flash's sound tools.

If you plan to have a background music track in your Flash project, it's a good idea to use a small audio clip that can be looped.

CROSS-REF We describe looping audio clips in Chapter 14, "Adding Sound."

Here is a simple formula to determine the file size, in bytes, of a given audio clip:

Seconds of audio × sample rate × # of channels × (bit depth ÷ 8) = file size

NOTE In the preceding formula, the sample rate is expressed in Hz (hertz), not kHz (kilohertz). The bit depth is divided by 8 because there are 8-bits per byte.

Thus, a 20-second stereo audio loop at 8-bits, 11 kHz would be calculated like this:

20 sec × 11,025 Hz × 2 channels × (8-bits ÷ 8-bits/byte) = 441,000 bytes = 430KB

There are two schools of thought regarding the ideal quality of sound files for import into Flash. These schools are pretty much divided into those who have high-end sound-editing tools and those who don't. In an effort to delineate the best path for each group, we've noted the following:

■ If you don't have high-end sound tools available, you may be among those who always prefer to start with audio source files of the highest possible quality (16-bit, 44.1 kHz is ideal), and then use the Flash sound settings to obtain optimal compression upon export.

CROSS-REF See Chapter 14, "Adding Sound," for detailed information on the sound export settings for Flash movies.

■ If you do have high-end sound tools available, you may prefer to compose most of your clients' music from scratch and may very rarely work with the MP3 format before importing into Flash. You may also disagree with those who advise you to bring sound into Flash at the highest quality before optimizing. This workflow difference may be attributable to the plethora of options available to those with high-end sound tools. We know of one sound engineer who converts all of his audio to 16-bit, 22.1 kHz mono files, "with major bass reduction," before importing into Flash.

You should always keep in mind that Flash can retain imported MP3 compression settings only with those MP3 files that will be used for non-Stream sync options. Anytime you set a sound to use Stream sync on a timeline, Flash needs to recompress the file with the Stream export settings found in the Publish Settings dialog box.

Finally, all linked sounds, or those set to export from the Library and played back via ActionScript, are treated as non-Stream sounds. If you use linked sounds, you may find it useful to import pre-compressed MP3 files at your preferred bit rate. Flash does not recompress the MP3 file upon export to an .swf file.

Appendix D

Digital Video Basics

A

s you begin to create more complex Flash presentations that include digital video, you need to know how to achieve the highest-quality image and playback. In this appendix, you learn how to prepare a digital video file for use in a Flash CS4 document.

CROSS-REF After you have successfully created a digital video file, you can learn how to import and use digital video files within a Flash CS4 document by reading Chapter 16, "Displaying Video."

Before you consider importing digital video footage into Flash CS4 or exporting your video with Adobe Media Encoder CS4, you need to plan how the video will be used within the Flash movie (or Web site). Will you be using several video clips for product demonstrations, interviews, or prerecorded events? Will you be using video for special effects such as a time-lapse effect of moving clouds or the sun setting? The more footage you plan to use, the more important it is to make sure that you're acquiring the footage properly — you wouldn't want to redo all your footage after you've seen the results in the Flash movie! This appendix provides tips for making sure that you have the best possible video quality for your Flash presentations.

IN THIS APPENDIX

An overview of videotape formats

Video production tips

File formats for digital video

1123

Garbage In, Garbage Out: Controlling Video Quality

You may have heard this phrase before, which means that you can't get something from nothing. Ever tried making a soup with bad ingredients, thinking it would still taste good? The same principle holds true for video production. Four primary factors influence the quality of your video footage: source format, image quality, sound quality, and subject matter.

Source format

The source format is the container in which the video is stored, whether it's a digital recording encoded on miniDV or DVCAM tape, an analog recording on VHS or Hi8 tape, or a file recorded on your digital camera. Each recording medium has inherent resolution limitations — some formats can store more information than others. The more information the medium stores, the higher the quality of the recording.

The following list outlines the resolution capacities of common recording mediums. For the purposes of our discussion, this list is restricted to video formats and excludes film formats, such as 35mm or 16mm motion picture film. The video formats are compared by *line resolution,* which is the number of horizontal scan lines the format can capture. Line resolution is not the definitive attribute for video quality, but it does measure the capacity of potential visual information captured by the camera or recording device. The most important factor to remember when comparing line resolutions is that video is primarily targeted at television screens that, in North America, display 525 lines of resolution.

NOTE Practically speaking, standard definition (SD) television sets display a maximum of 483 lines of visible resolution — the remaining lines convey other information such as the sync pulse. High-Definition TV (HDTV) is capable of displaying up to 1,080 lines of resolution, and many multimedia producers are using HD cameras to record video.

- **VHS, VHS-C, or 8mm videotape:** These tape formats, especially VHS, are common video formats in use by consumers today. The average household VCR records video in VHS format. These tape formats can record about 240 lines of resolution. This resolution is less than half of the potential scan lines that can be shown on a TV screen, which is why the VHS recordings of your favorite TV shows don't exactly match the live broadcasts. These tape formats are analog in nature — the signal they record is not digital and can deteriorate from copy to copy. To translate this tape format into digital video for use in a multimedia production, you need to capture the footage with an analog video capture card.

- **S-VHS or Hi8 videotape:** S-VHS and Hi8 video use the same tape sizes as their VHS and 8mm equivalents, but they capture up to 400 lines of resolution. This resolution capacity comes very close to the 525 lines of resolution that a television can display. You probably won't encounter many S-VHS camcorders anymore, but Hi8 video camcorders are still popular and in use today. Although the video quality is a noticeable improvement, the video signal is still analog, so as with VHS, you must capture it with an analog video capture card.

- **miniDV, Digital8, or DVCAM tape:** A popular breed of video recording devices for consumer, prosumer, and professional use is the DV (Digital Video) format. DV formats use the DV codec to digitally record video, while storing audio at near-CD or CD-quality sampling rates. The native resolution for the DV format is 525 lines, but the actual resolution a DV camcorder records varies from model to model. Most high-end DV camcorders are considered broadcast quality, meaning the video image is good enough to use on a television show such as the evening news. Many computer systems today ship with an IEEE 1394 (also known as FireWire or iLink) port to capture digital video from DV recording devices. When video is transferred digitally from a camera to a computer over an IEEE 1394 connection, there is no loss of quality.

- **HDV tape:** One of the newer video recording formats is HDV, or High-Definition Video. HDV content is recorded on the same tape cassette used by miniDV cameras. HDV content uses the same bit rates as miniDV content, but uses MPEG-2 compression to store a much larger frame size — usually 1920 x 1080. Most HDV camcorders record content at 1440 x 1080, but on playback, the content is stretched to 1920 x 1080 with the proper 16:9 aspect ratio. Host HDV camcorders can also record or down-convert HD content to regular standard definition (SD) video, on the fly. Video is transferred from an HDV camcorder or player to a computer by using an IEEE 1394 (also known as FireWire or iLink) cable. Newer HDV camcorders can record directly to an internal hard drive on the camera, enabling videographers to more easily transfer recorded content over USB or FireWire.

- **Betacam SP, Digital Betacam:** These tape formats are for serious video professionals who work in the television industry. Betacam SP has been the industry standard for network television for more than 30 years. Although Betacam SP is an analog format, Digital Betacam (also known as DigiBeta) records video with a proprietary Sony codec. Both formats capture 550 or more lines of resolution.

- **MPEG file recording:** Many digital cameras and camcorders can record MPEG video at various sizes and resolutions. Most digital still cameras use an MPEG codec. Many MPEG recording devices can only capture at line resolutions equal to or less than VHS quality. The popular AVC/H.264 codec, part of the MPEG-4 family of codecs, is becoming more widely used in consumer and professional camcorders. This codec can be used to record incredibly high-quality video with much less bit rate than other codecs, and is commonly used with HD frame sizes such as 1280 x 720 or 1920 x 1080.

As a general guideline, we recommend using the highest-quality camcorder available with your resources to record video that you intend to use for multimedia presentations within a Flash movie. Several factors beyond the recording format affect the quality of any recording. In the next two sections, we discuss variables that influence the visual and audio portions of a recording.

WEB RESOURCE If you're a beginner videographer and want to know more about video resolution, check out the following links:

    www.bealecorner.com/trv900/respat
    hometown.aol.com/ajaynejr/vidres.htm

Image quality

Regardless of the source format that you use for your video recording, the recording device may have other limitations. The recorded resolution of your camera may be significantly lower than the upper limit of your recording format's line resolution. For example, the DV format is capable of storing 525 lines of resolution. However, your specific DV camcorder may have an effective resolution of 490 lines. The following variables can affect the quality of the picture recorded by the camera. Note that this list is by no means exhaustive for the professional videographer — we chose these topics as a general summary to guide you in your video production.

- **Optics:** The characteristics of the lens (or lens system) that your camera uses are known as the optics. The optical quality of video camcorders varies wildly. Many camcorders boast Carl Zeiss lenses, which are known for their precision and accuracy. Some lenses are constructed of plastic, whereas others are glass. Neither lens type is necessarily better than the other, but the only way to accurately judge the optical system of your camera is to conduct extensive testing with a resolution target.

- **CCD or CMOS:** The CCD, or charged-coupled device, is the electronic plate that captures the image that the camera's lens renders. Newer video cameras are offering a CMOS () chip rather than a CCD, for longer battery life and better color sampling. You can think of the CCD or CMOS as the digital film that's being exposed to the light coming through the lens. Imaging chips come in a variety of sizes, ranging from $1/4$ inch to 1 inch. Although these sizes may sound incredibly small, even $1/4$-inch chips can capture amazing detail. The larger a chip is, however, the more information it can capture. Most cameras only have one chip, but some cameras have three chips — one for each color of the RGB (red, green, and blue) spectrum. These are known as three-chip cameras, and they have better color fidelity than single-chip cameras. Color fidelity, simply put, is the measure of how closely the recorded color of an image matches the original colors of the subject.

- **Tape quality:** The quality of the tape on which you record the video can also affect the quality of the overall image. Each tape brand has unique characteristics, such as the type of metal particles that are magnetized onto the tape. Some brands (or stocks) are more durable and can withstand the rigors of repeated recordings. In general, you should always record on a fresh tape — and preferably one listed as premium or high quality.

TIP Make sure that you use the same brand and model of tape consistently throughout a shoot. There are slight color variations and differences in quality in each brand and tape type. Preferably, all the tapes used for a shoot should be manufactured from the same batch, and as such, you should buy bulk boxes of your preferred tape brands and formats.

- **Shutter mechanism:** The shutter mechanism is the device that controls how quickly the imaging chip samples the image rendered by the lens. Most camcorders have shutters that record interlaced video, which records two interwoven fields (or separate halves of a picture) to create one frame of video. Have you ever noticed how the image on your TV flickers when you pause a VHS recording? You're seeing the two fields of the frame alternating. Computer monitors do not display interlaced video. Rather, they use progressive scanning to minimize a flicker effect. Some higher-end camcorders have progressive scan shutters that record the image with higher apparent resolution. We discuss de-interlacing video later in this appendix.

- **Exposure:** You should make every effort to shoot your video footage with the correct exposure. Exposure refers to the amount of light captured by the imaging chip and the shutter mechanism. Some camcorders do not allow you to control the exposure — it's all automatic. The biggest pitfall for most videographers is underexposing video footage or shooting in low light. When you try to record a poorly lit subject, you tend to get noise in the darkest areas of the image. Video noise is a random pattern of dots that shows up on the image. Finally, make every effort to properly white-balance your shot to suit the color temperature of the dominant light source — some camcorders enable you to control the color temperature. You'll notice the effects of color temperature in the video samples on the CD-ROM. You learn more about white balance later in this appendix.

So what do all these variables boil down to? In a nutshell, we recommend that whenever possible, you should shoot video with a camcorder that has a superior optical system with three imaging chips, use high-quality tapes, and properly control your exposure. Avoid shooting in low light, unless you are shooting with a particular effect in mind, such as infrared lighting.

Sound quality

Every videographer should consider how audio is recorded during production. Most video camcorders have a decent built-in stereo microphone, but professional videographers equip themselves with accessories beyond those that ship with the camera. Review the following guidelines for capturing sound with your video recording:

- **External microphones:** To achieve the best audio recording, put an external microphone as close as possible to the source of the sound. If you want to record a person talking, an external microphone, such as a wireless Lavaliere mic that's pinned to the person's shirt, collar, or tie, produces a much cleaner recording than the microphone on the camera.

- **Balanced vs. unbalanced audio:** Most microphones you find at electronics stores use a stereo or mono 3.5mm mini-adapter that plugs into the microphone jack on your camcorder. These microphones are considered "unbalanced" audio sources, due to the nature of their internal wiring. For many video shoots, this may not pose a problem. However, professional audio engineers use balanced audio for all sound sources. The cabling for balanced audio tends to be a heavier gauge than that of the consumer variety. Many balanced microphones have a three-pin XLR connector, and most camcorders require an XLR adapter to connect these sources to the mini microphone jack. Many professional video cameras have built-in XLR jacks.

■ **Sampling rate and bit depth:** Unless you're using a DV format camcorder, you likely have little or no control over the specific sampling rate and bit depth used to record audio on the camera. DV camcorders enable you to record with either 32 kHz or 48 kHz. 32 kHz audio is recorded at 12-bit, which is suitable for recording dialog and live action. 48 kHz is recorded at 16-bit, which is suitable for recording live musical performances or any other scene requiring high fidelity.

■ **Audio levels:** One of the most overlooked aspects of video production is monitoring the audio levels of your source while recording. Most camcorders record audio only with AGC, or Automatic Gain Control. This "feature" allows the camcorder to determine how much an audio signal should be boosted or minimized during recording. Professional audio engineers prefer to manually monitor and adjust sound levels while the recording is taking place. Undesirable side effects of using AGC include amplified background noise during silent periods, audio distortion, and sudden jumps or drops in audio levels. Whenever possible, listen to your audio source through headphones connected to the camera.

■ **Unwanted noise:** Do your best to minimize any background noise when you are recording. The microphone(s) connected to your camera pick up more noise than you may realize. Each microphone has a different "pick-up" pattern, determining the range and direction of sound that it receives.

In summary, you should record audio as close as possible to the source, using balanced microphones and monitoring the audio feed with headphones connected to the camera. For most video recording, either the 32 kHz or 48 kHz sampling rates yield superior audio reproduction.

Subject matter

Last, but by no means least, the type of subject matter you are shooting can influence the results of video compression in video deployed to the Flash platform. When it comes to video compression, the most important factor to remember is variability from frame to frame. That is, how much and how often does your subject matter change? Are you recording the Indy 500, panning race cars accelerating at incredibly fast speeds? Or, are you recording a time lapse of a flower slowly blooming? In general, you will achieve the best results with video compression if the subject matter does not move randomly or quickly.

Here are some general guidelines when choosing and shooting your subject matter:

- **Use a tripod:** One of the most common mistakes amateur videographers make is to handhold the video camcorder. Unless you need to freely move with your camera or intentionally want to introduce shakiness to your video image, always mount your camera on a tripod.

- **Avoid quick and jerky movements:** If you need to follow your subject matter by panning the head on the tripod, practice the movement a few times before recording. Try to be as slow and fluid as possible. The more quickly you pan a video camera while recording, the more likely you'll see compression artifacts show up in your final video in the Flash movie.

- **Avoid zooming:** Although it may be tempting, do not zoom the lens while recording your subject matter. It's better to use the zoom to frame the shot before you record. Of course, you may intentionally want to use wild zooming effects to re-create the next *Blair Witch* mockumentary, but be aware that any rapid movement from zooming the lens will likely compress very poorly in the Flash movie.

- **Lock focus:** All camcorders can auto-focus the lens. If you plan to record a stationary object, you may want to switch to manual focus. If your subject matter moves away from the camera's focus "spot," the camera may refocus on areas behind the subject matter. This type of focus drifting may yield very unpleasant compression artifacts in the Flash video.

- **Watch white balance:** White balance refers to how the camera interprets color. You might notice that your skin looks much less appealing under fluorescent light than it does under an incandescent or soft white indoor light bulb. The human eye can "correct" the perception of a light source's color (or color temperature) with greater ease than an automatic setting on your camera. Be sure to match the white-balance setting on your camcorder to the predominant light source in your video composition. Most cameras have at least two white-balance settings: indoor (for tungsten light) and outdoor (for daylight). Some cameras enable you to perform a custom white balance. To set a custom white balance, focus the entire viewing area on a solid field of white and engage the white-balance lock on your camera.

Another factor to consider is the area of the video composition that changes from frame to frame. In a previous example, we mention panning a racecar. In that example, the entire picture changes in every frame. Compression works best on video footage with the least amount of movement per pixel in the frame. For example, if you mount your camera on a tripod and keep the camera motionless, you can record the motion of a single subject, such as the flight of a bee between flowers. In such an example, the video compression with the Sorenson Spark codec is much more effective than it would be in the example of the racecar.

TIP
Although we mention these general rules for better-looking video shoots, it is also crucial to develop a look and feel for whatever you are shooting. Establish a set of rules that apply to everything in the shoot. For example, perhaps you *want* to shoot everything handheld, rack the focus regularly, underexpose the image slightly, dutch the angle on all wide shots, and so on. With today's cutting-edge video and film effects, it is more important to develop a style and operate to achieve a consistent look than to worry excessively over conventional dos and don'ts.

Comparing Video Sources

On the CD-ROM in the back of this book, you will find three video samples in the `resources` folder. You can use these examples to test compression settings in Flash CS4, the Flash Video Encoder, or a third-party utility such as Sorenson Squeeze or On2 Flix. Each sample was recorded with a different camera.

- `sample_low.mpg`: This video file was recorded with a Sony DSC-S70 Cybershot camera. Although this camera is designed to shoot stills, it can also record MPEG-1 video files. This file was recorded in high-quality mode at 320 x 240, 15 frames per second. The microphone on this camera is mono (single-channel).

- `sample_mid.avi`: This video file was recorded with a Sony DCR-PC100 miniDV camcorder. This camcorder has a stereo built-in microphone and a single CCD. The quality captured by this camera is average for most DV camcorders. Compare the color temperature of this recording to that of `sample_low.mpg` and `sample_high.avi` files.

- `sample_high.avi`: This video file was recorded with a Sony DSR-PD150 mini-DVCAM camcorder. This professional camera has superior exposure and color temperature control. Among other differences with the previous samples, the audio was recorded with a wireless Shure microphone and a UP4 receiver, which uses a three-pin XLR output. The PD150 can accept this XLR output.

When you open these files in some video viewers, the .avi files recorded by the DV camcorders might appear stretched horizontally. The DV format uses non-square pixels, whereas most display devices, such as computer monitors, use square pixels. Unless the video display or video player application compensates for non-square pixels, the video image will appear stretched. Flash CS4's video import process may not automatically compensate for non-square pixel footage, so make sure you resize the video in the Advanced properties, which we discuss in more detail in Chapter 16, "Displaying Video."

We provided these samples so that you may experiment with them in Flash CS4. You will find that cleaner video (such as that shot with the high-end video camcorder) exhibits less video noise in the compressed version within the Flash document.

Editing Footage

After you have recorded the video with your camcorder, it's time to start editing the footage in a digital video editor such as Adobe Premiere or Apple Final Cut Pro.

It's beyond the scope of this book to fully explain the process of editing video footage, but we offer the following pointers to maximize the compression benefits of the video codecs that the Flash Player uses:

- **Watch transitions and filter effects:** Keep the general rule in mind that we mention previously — refrain from global changes to the entire frame. Some effects and transitions, such as cross-fades and slow dissolves, introduce rapid changes to successive frames of video. These changes require more keyframes to retain quality, and these keyframes add significant weight to the file size of the compressed video. Otherwise, if you don't want the extra weight, you'll have to accept less quality in the overall image.

- **Minimize duration:** The shorter you make your finished video clip, the smaller the file size of your Flash movie (.swf). Although you can stream video content just like any Flash content, you should keep in mind the data rate of your target audience.

When you finish editing your video, make a master version that can serve other purposes beyond your Flash movie presentation. You may even want to output a final version of the edited footage to DV tape. In the next section, we discuss what output format to use for your edited footage. Later, this output format will be compressed and embedded in the Flash document.

Choosing an Import Format

After you complete the editing phase for your video footage, you're ready to output a final version of your video project that you can use with your Flash document. The following checklist should help you determine how to get the most effective use out of the Flash Player's video codecs, Sorenson Spark, On2 VP6, or AVC/H.264. Just as you don't want to re-JPEG a JPEG (that is, save a JPEG file again with more JPEG compression), you will find that it's best to retain as much original quality from the video as possible before you bring it into Flash.

- **Frame size:** Most video sources are captured and edited at full frame NTSC sizes, such as 640 x 480 and 720 x 480. It's unlikely that you'll want to expend the bandwidth required to display this full-frame size. A starting frame size should be 320 x 240; work your way up or down from there. If you are targeting Web users with dial-up connection speeds such as 28.8 or 56 Kbps, you may want to consider a frame size of 160 x 120. Remember, when you scale down a bitmap-based element in the Flash authoring environment, you don't actually throw away any pixels — the full size of the graphic is retained in the final Flash movie file (.swf).

- **Frame rate:** When you capture video from your camcorder to your desktop video-editing application, the video has a frame rate of 29.97 fps (NTSC) or 25 fps (PAL). This frame rate, as with regular video frame sizes, requires more bit rate to play with equivalent quality than a lower frame rate. As a general rule, keep your video frame rate as close as possible to (or lower than) the frame rate of your Flash movie, as defined in the Document Properties dialog box (Modify ⇨ Document). Most video on the Internet has a frame rate of 15, 24, or 30 fps.

NOTE   As fast broadband Internet connections become more predominant, you'll find more and more sites featuring Flash Video that uses video clips with 24, 29.97, or 30 fps. If you plan to load .flv files at runtime into Flash movies with Flash Player 7 or later, the video content's frame rate can differ from the host Flash movie without any conflict. Slower processors, such as Pentium III or older PowerBook G3 computers, however, may have a more difficult time decoding Flash Video that uses high frame rates such as 24, 29.97, or 30 fps.

- **Video compression:** Use a lossless video codec for your final video file that you export from your video editing software. If you're outputting a QuickTime file, use the Animation codec set to Best (100%) quality. You can also use the Uncompressed option (available in Apple QuickTime Player Pro or any video-editing application such as Adobe Premiere or Apple Final Cut Pro) when you save your final video file.

- **Audio compression:** Follow the same guidelines for video compression. DV-formatted video stores audio uncompressed.

- **De-interlacing:** We mention earlier in this chapter that video recorded by camcorders is interlaced. However, computer monitors (and the graphics appearing on them) are progressively scanned and do not require interlacing. (You may notice how "soft" your DV footage appears in most desktop video-editing applications; this is due to the even and odd "interlaces" being multiplied to accommodate the progressive scanning of computer video.) The general rule of thumb is to use a de-interlace filter (or export option) on any video footage that you intend to use for computer playback. However, if you resize your video to 320 x 240 or smaller and decrease the frame rate from its original rate, you effectively de-interlace the video footage. Usually, you do not see any difference enabling a de-interlace filter on top of these reductions.

After you have gone through this checklist for your video footage, export a final video file that you can compress with Adobe Media Encoder. Most video applications (including Apple QuickTime Player Pro) can resave a finished video file with a new frame size, frame rate, video and audio compressions, and other options such as de-interlacing. Adobe Media Encoder can import a variety of video file formats, listed in Table D.1.

Video Import Formats for Adobe Media Encoder

Format	Platform	Required Drivers	Description
AVI (.avi) Audio Video Interleaved	Windows Mac	DirectX 7 or later, or QuickTime 4 or later	Standard Windows video format; usually the format in which video is captured on Windows; can use any combination of video and audio codecs
DV (.dv) Digital Video stream	Windows Mac	QuickTime 4 or later	Format saved from applications such as Adobe Premiere or Apple QuickTime Player Pro; uses the DV codec for video and uncompressed audio
MPEG (.mpg, .mpeg) Motion Picture Experts Group	Windows Mac	DirectX 7 or later, or QuickTime 4 or later	Precompressed video in the MPEG-1, MPEG-2, or MPEG-4 codec; a format used by many digital cameras that save to media formats such as Compact Flash (CF) and Memory Stick
QT (.mov) Apple QuickTime	Windows Mac	QuickTime 4 or later	Standard video format on the Mac; usually the format in which video is captured on the Mac; can use any combination of video and audio codecs
WMV (.wmv, .asf) Windows Media files	Windows	DirectX 7 or later	Precompressed video in a modified MPEG-4 codec developed by Microsoft to use with the Windows Media Player

Of the formats listed in Table D.1, we recommend that you import formats that don't apply any recompression to the original source format of your video. If you can avoid using compressed video such as Windows Media and MPEG files, you can prevent the video codecs available in the Flash Player from introducing further artifacts into the video. *Compression artifacts* are areas in the video frame where detail is lost. The process of compressing a file already using compression is known as *recompression*.

CAUTION If you try to import MPEG files into the Mac version of Adobe Media Encoder, you may not be able to convert the audio track in the final output file. Only Windows' DirectX driver successfully converts both the video and audio tracks in most MPEG files to a format useable in the final video file. To import an MPEG via QuickTime on the Mac, you may need to use an application such as MPEG Streamclip (www.squared5.com) to convert the MPEG to a QuickTime movie that uses another codec.

Index

Symbols and Numerics

&& (ampersand) as logical comparison operator, 769

{ } curly braces, 609

= (equals sign)
    as assignment operator, 768
    as comparison operator (==), 768
    as equality operator (===), 768

! (exclamation mark)
    as inequality operator (!==), 769
    as not operator, 768, 769

> (greater than symbol)
    as alphabetically after operator, 769
    as comparison operator, 768

< (less than symbol)
    as alphabetically before operator, 769
    as comparison operator, 768

- (minus sign) as subtraction operator, 768

( ) parentheses
    in code, 607
    as grouping operator, 768

+ (plus sign)
    as addition operator, 768
    as concatenation operator, 769

" (quotation marks) as string operator, 768

; semicolons, 609

/ (slash) as division operator, 768

|| (vertical bars) as logical comparison operator, 769

8-bit color, 206

8-bit lossless source files, 536

8-bit resolution sound, 1118

8mm videotape, 1124

4-bit sound resolution, 1118

32-bit lossless source files, 535–536

3D Rotation tool
    described, 286
    symbols transformed with, 288–292

3D space
    overview, 286–287
    perspective in, 287–288
    vanishing point in, 287–288

3D Translation tool
    described, 286
    symbols moved with, 292

`3D_rotationFlip.fla` file, 370

`3D_rotationReverse.fla` file, 369

12-bit sound resolution, 1118

24-bit color, 206

24-bit lossless source files, 535–536

A

`<a>` anchor tag, 949–950

absolute color control, 403–404

absolute path, 632, 634

acceleration in animation, 325

Accessibility panel, 666–669

accessibility support, 665–669

accessing items in shared libraries
    linking to assets from other movies, 925–926
    location for shared library, specifying, 924
    overview, 921–922
    publishing shared library movie file, 925
    setting up a shared library file, 922–924
    updating shared assets, 926–928

action/reaction force pairs in animation, 326–327

actions. *See also specific actions*
    deleting, 606
    deprecated, 608
    described, 601
    event handlers for, 601–602
    `gotoAndPlay()`, 609–610
    `gotoAndStop()`, 609–610
    incompatible, 608
    keyframe, adding action to, 619
    list of common, 615
    `navigateToURL()`, 613–615

P

Wiley Publishing, Inc.
End-User License Agreement

READ THIS. You should carefully read these terms and conditions before opening the software packet(s) included with this book "Book". This is a license agreement "Agreement" between you and Wiley Publishing, Inc. "WPI". By opening the accompanying software packet(s), you acknowledge that you have read and accept the following terms and conditions. If you do not agree and do not want to be bound by such terms and conditions, promptly return the Book and the unopened software packet(s) to the place you obtained them for a full refund.

1. **License Grant.** WPI grants to you (either an individual or entity) a nonexclusive license to use one copy of the enclosed software program(s) (collectively, the "Software") solely for your own personal or business purposes on a single computer (whether a standard computer or a workstation component of a multi-user network). The Software is in use on a computer when it is loaded into temporary memory (RAM) or installed into permanent memory (hard disk, CD-ROM, or other storage device). WPI reserves all rights not expressly granted herein.

2. **Ownership.** WPI is the owner of all right, title, and interest, including copyright, in and to the compilation of the Software recorded on the physical packet included with this Book "Software Media". Copyright to the individual programs recorded on the Software Media is owned by the author or other authorized copyright owner of each program. Ownership of the Software and all proprietary rights relating thereto remain with WPI and its licensers.

3. **Restrictions on Use and Transfer.**

   (a) You may only (i) make one copy of the Software for backup or archival purposes, or (ii) transfer the Software to a single hard disk, provided that you keep the original for backup or archival purposes. You may not (i) rent or lease the Software, (ii) copy or reproduce the Software through a LAN or other network system or through any computer subscriber system or bulletin-board system, or (iii) modify, adapt, or create derivative works based on the Software.

   (b) You may not reverse engineer, decompile, or disassemble the Software. You may transfer the Software and user documentation on a permanent basis, provided that the transferee agrees to accept the terms and conditions of this Agreement and you retain no copies. If the Software is an update or has been updated, any transfer must include the most recent update and all prior versions.

4. **Restrictions on Use of Individual Programs.** You must follow the individual requirements and restrictions detailed for each individual program in the "Using the CD-ROM" appendix of this Book or on the Software Media. These limitations are also contained in the individual license agreements recorded on the Software Media. These limitations may include a requirement that after using the program for a specified period of time, the user must pay a registration fee or discontinue use. By opening the Software packet(s), you agree to abide by the licenses and restrictions for these individual programs that are detailed in the "Using the CD-ROM" appendix and/or on the Software Media. None of the material on this Software Media or listed in this Book may ever be redistributed, in original or modified form, for commercial purposes.

5. Limited Warranty.

  (a) WPI warrants that the Software and Software Media are free from defects in materials and workmanship under normal use for a period of sixty (60) days from the date of purchase of this Book. If WPI receives notification within the warranty period of defects in materials or workmanship, WPI will replace the defective Software Media.

  (b) WPI AND THE AUTHOR(S) OF THE BOOK DISCLAIM ALL OTHER WARRANTIES, EXPRESS OR IMPLIED, INCLUDING WITHOUT LIMITATION IMPLIED WARRANTIES OF MERCHANTABILITY AND FITNESS FOR A PARTICULAR PURPOSE, WITH RESPECT TO THE SOFTWARE, THE PROGRAMS, THE SOURCE CODE CONTAINED THEREIN, AND/OR THE TECHNIQUES DESCRIBED IN THIS BOOK. WPI DOES NOT WARRANT THAT THE FUNCTIONS CONTAINED IN THE SOFTWARE WILL MEET YOUR REQUIREMENTS OR THAT THE OPERATION OF THE SOFTWARE WILL BE ERROR FREE.

  (c) This limited warranty gives you specific legal rights, and you may have other rights that vary from jurisdiction to jurisdiction.

6. Remedies.

  (a) WPI's entire liability and your exclusive remedy for defects in materials and workmanship shall be limited to replacement of the Software Media, which may be returned to WPI with a copy of your receipt at the following address: Software Media Fulfillment Department, Attn.: *Flash CS4 Professional Bible*, Wiley Publishing, Inc., 10475 Crosspoint Blvd., Indianapolis, IN 46256, or call 1-800-762-2974. Please allow four to six weeks for delivery. This Limited Warranty is void if failure of the Software Media has resulted from accident, abuse, or misapplication. Any replacement Software Media will be warranted for the remainder of the original warranty period or thirty (30) days, whichever is longer.

  (b) In no event shall WPI or the author be liable for any damages whatsoever (including without limitation damages for loss of business profits, business interruption, loss of business information, or any other pecuniary loss) arising from the use of or inability to use the Book or the Software, even if WPI has been advised of the possibility of such damages.

  (c) Because some jurisdictions do not allow the exclusion or limitation of liability for consequential or incidental damages, the above limitation or exclusion may not apply to you.

7. U.S. Government Restricted Rights. Use, duplication, or disclosure of the Software for or on behalf of the United States of America, its agencies and/or instrumentalities "U.S. Government" is subject to restrictions as stated in paragraph (c)(1)(ii) of the Rights in Technical Data and Computer Software clause of DFARS 252.227-7013, or subparagraphs (c) (1) and (2) of the Commercial Computer Software - Restricted Rights clause at FAR 52.227-19, and in similar clauses in the NASA FAR supplement, as applicable.

8. General. This Agreement constitutes the entire understanding of the parties and revokes and supersedes all prior agreements, oral or written, between them and may not be modified or amended except in a writing signed by both parties hereto that specifically refers to this Agreement. This Agreement shall take precedence over any other documents that may be in conflict herewith. If any one or more provisions contained in this Agreement are held by any court or tribunal to be invalid, illegal, or otherwise unenforceable, each and every other provision shall remain in full force and effect.